GEORGETOWN LAW SCHOOL

31-140.

8	253- 346.	Chp. 5
9-10	347-404.	chp. 6.
11	409- 460	Chp. 7
12-13	461-522	Chp. 8
14	523- 602	Chp. 9.

PROBLEMS IN
PROFESSIONAL RESPONSIBILITY

PROBLEMS IN PROFESSIONAL RESPONSIBILITY

Third Edition

Andrew L. Kaufman

Charles Stebbins Fairchild Professor of Law
Harvard University

Little, Brown and Company
Boston   Toronto   London

Library of Congress Catalog Card No. 88-083076
ISBN 0-316-48385-0
Third Edition

MV NY

Published simultaneously in Canada
by Little, Brown & Company (Canada) Limited

Printed in the United States of America

To Anne, David and Carol, Elizabeth, and Daniel
For the joy they have added to my life

SUMMARY OF CONTENTS

CONTENTS

Chapter 10. Who May Practice Law   603

Chapter 11.   Competence, Malpractice, and Discipline   639

Chapter 12.   Professional Responsibility and the Judicial System   689

PREFACE

Students often tell me they don't get around to reading the preface to a casebook until they are reviewing for an examination, if then. I think that it is as important for students as it is for teachers to have some sense of what this book is about; I have therefore written an introduction discussing the approach of the book to the teaching of professional responsibility. This introduction follows and should be part of the first day's assignment.

The purpose of this preface is only to explain a few matters of form and to express a few words of thanks.

Omissions of textual material in excerpted cases, articles, books, or other works is always indicated by ellipses. Footnotes and references to records, however, have been omitted freely in cases and in some of the other written material. I have also corrected, without notation, a variety of minor typographical errors in quoted materials.

I am grateful to the many authors and publishers who gave me permission to reprint copyrighted material. They are acknowledged in the following pages.

Finally, there is one more pleasant task, and that is to acknowledge all the help I have received in the preparation of this book. In 1969 Derek Bok, now President of Harvard University but then Dean of the Harvard Law School, started me off by asking me to put together some materials for a first-year course on professional responsibility. James Vorenberg, one of the early users of those materials and later Dean of Harvard Law School, encouraged me in my resolve to follow a problem-oriented approach. Livingston Hall, Richard Field, Charles Ares, and Justice Robert Braucher used different versions of these materials when they were in mimeographed form and contributed to them in a variety of ways. Judge John Cratsley participated in the development of the materials that have now become Chapter 9 and also in some class sessions dealing with them. He aided considerably in my thinking about the problems of the availability of legal services. Finally, Gary Bellow used a large part of a near final version in the fall of 1975 and made numerous valuable and stimulating suggestions about particular matters, the general approach of the book, and the teaching of professional responsibility.

Three lawyers and teachers made important contributions to the second edition. My law school classmate and friend, Laurence Fordham of Fordham & Starrett, Boston, who formerly taught professional responsibility at Harvard Law School, read and criticized the materials of Chapter 2 more carefully, more thoughtfully, and more incisively than anyone has read anything I have written since I graduated from college and law school. His expert knowledge has improved that chapter greatly. Another practitioner, Daniel Coquillette, who formerly taught professional responsibility at Harvard Law School and is now Dean at Boston College Law School, was a consistent user of these materials and has given me a stream of helpful comments, suggestions, and above all, encouragement in their preparation. I only regret that I have not had the space to insert the chapter on comparative professional responsibility that he has urged on me. A third practitioner, Alan Morrison, of the Public Citizen Litigation Group, Washington, D.C., also a current colleague at the Harvard Law School on a part-time basis, has been a constant source of discussion about current professional responsibility matters and for information and advice that is reflected throughout these materials.

There is one other teacher, with whom I have never spoken about this book and whom I do not know well, whose assistance should also be acknowledged. Anyone who teaches professional responsibility, and especially anyone who teaches it by the problem method, is indebted to Robert Mathews. His Problems Illustrative of the Responsibilities of Members of the Legal Profession (6th Printing 1974) was the pioneering effort in the field, and for long years he was one of the premier teachers and thinkers about professional problems.

This book has also profited greatly from the reactions and criticism of the numerous students who have used it and from the help of several research assistants. One of them in particular deserves special mention. Margaret Porter, my research assistant in the summer of 1975, contributed enormously to making a first edition out of what was largely a mere mass of materials. Although I cannot adequately describe in a sentence all her contributions to this book, I know them when I see them — and they were very valuable. I am also grateful to three student research assistants who worked on the second edition. Donald Board, now Assistant Professor of Law at Boston Unviersity Law School, carried over from his work on my Commercial Law book to do very useful work at the beginning of this version. His contributions are also reflected specifically in the materials of Chapter 2. See p. 39 note *. Jonathan Strauss made very helpful contributions during the two months he was able to devote to the work. Susan Skelley Price then worked long and hard on many projects and her valuable assistance made it possible for the manuscript to be completed in time.

Finally, I must thank those people who have worked with me longest on these materials. My secretary from the day I began teaching, the late Sally Littleton, prepared many early versions of what became the first edition, and I wish to acknowledge my appreciation of her and of her assistance. Betsey Glaser, my next secretary, helped turn multilithed, skeleton chapters into a manuscript in six months. I trust that she knows how grateful I am. Virginia Severn shared in the final operations by which the manuscript became a book. She has earned my everlasting gratitude for having read the Code of Professional Responsibility more carefully than most lawyers ever will. Completion of the manuscript of the second edition on time and in "perfect" condition was the work of my long-time secretary, Kathleen Harrison. She became a veteran in manuscript preparation and I appreciate greatly not only her work but the good humor that always accompanied it. She also helped convince me to obtain a computer, then helped teach me to use it, and so contributed enormously to the editing of this third edition. A second piece of technology that was useful to this edition was provided by Mead Data Central. They made their LEXIS service available to me on a full-time basis so I had new material at my desk whenever I wanted it. My secretary, Nancy McHose, helped with various aspects of preparation of this edition and after she left, Mary De Bever put the finishing touches on the volume. I am grateful to them both.

A.L.K.

January 1989

ACKNOWLEDGMENTS

I gratefully acknowledge the permissions granted to reproduce the following materials.

American Bar Association, Formal Opinion 87-353, copyright © by the ABA. All rights reserved.

American Bar Association, Formal Opinion 334, copyright © by the ABA. All rights reserved.

American Bar Association, Informal Opinion 1203 (1972), copyright © by the ABA. All rights reserved.

American Bar Association, Note, 60 A.B.J. 1045 (1974). Reprinted with permission from the American Bar Journal.

ABA Special Committee on Evaluation of Disciplinary Enforcement, Problems, and Recommendations in Disciplinary Enforcement (1970). Copyright © by, and reprinted with the permission of, the American Bar Association.

Association of the Bar of the City of New York, Committee on Professional and Judicial Ethics, Inquiry Reference 80-23.

Roger Cramton, Crisis in Legal Services for the Poor, 26 Villanova L. Rev. 521-556. Reprinted with permission from Roger Cramton and Villanova Law Review. Copyright © 1981 by Villanova University.

Richard Crouch, The Dark Side Is Still Unexplored, 4 The Family Advocate 327 (No. 3 Winter 1982). Copyright © 1982 Family Advocate, American Bar Association and reprinted with its permission and that of the author.

John M. Ferren, The Corporate Lawyer's Obligation to the Public Interest, 33 Bus. Law. 1253-1254 (Special Issue March 1978). Copyright © by the American Bar Association. All rights reserved. Reprinted with the permission of Judge Ferren and the American Bar Association and its Section of Corporate, Banking and Business Law.

Charles Frankel, Book Review, The Code of Professional Responsibility, 43 U. Chi. L. Rev. (1976). Copyright © 1976 by the University of Chicago and reprinted with its permission and that of Professor Frankel.

Marvin E. Frankel, The Search for Truth: An Umpireal View, 123 Pa. L. Rev. (1975). Copyright © by the author and reprinted with permission. This article also appears, in slightly different form, in 30 The Record of the Association of the Bar of the City of New York 14 (1975).

Monroe Freedman, Professional Responsibility of the Criminal Defense Lawyer: The Three Hardest Questions, 64 Mich. L. Rev. 1469 (1966). Copyright © 1966 and reprinted with permission of Professor Freedman and the Michigan Law Review.

Alan H. Goldman, The Moral Foundations of Professional Ethics 133-138 (Rowman and Littlefield, 1980). Reprinted with permission of the author and publisher.

Joel B. Grossman, A Political View of Judicial Ethics, 9 San Diegᵣ L. Rev. 803 (1972). Copyright © 1972 San Diego Law Review Association and reprinted with its permission and that of the author.

Charles Halpern and John Cunningham, Reflections on the New Public Interest Law, 59 Geo. L.J. 1095 (1971). Reprinted with permission of the authors and the Georgetown Law Journal Association.

Kenny Hegland, Beyond Enthusiasm and Commitment, 13 Ariz. L. Rev. 805 (1971). Copyright © by the Arizona Board of Regents. Reprinted with their permission and that of Professor Hegland.

Andrew L. Kaufman, A Commentary on Pepper, 1986 Am. B. Found. Res. J. 651. Reprinted with permission of the author and the American Bar Foundation.

Robert Keeton, Trial Tactics and Methods, 4-5, 104-105, 326-327 (2d ed. 1973). Reprinted with permission of the author and Little, Brown & Company.

Abe Krash, Professional Responsibility to Clients and the Public Interest, 55 Chicago Bar Record 31 (1974). This article originally appeared in the Chicago Bar Record. It is reproduced here with the permission of Mr. Krash, the Chicago Bar Record, and the Chicago Bar Association.

Robert P. Lawry, Who Is the Client of the Federal Government? An Analysis of the Wrong Question, 37 Fed. Bar J. 61. Reprinted with permission of the author and the Federal Bar Journal.

David Luban, The Lysistratian Prerogative: A Response to Stephen Pepper, 1986 Am. B. Found. Res. J. 637-651. Reprinted with permission of the author and the American Bar Foundation.

Neil Mickenberg, The Silent Clients: Legal and Ethical Considerations in Representing Profoundly Retarded Individuals, 31 Stanford Law Rev. 625 (1979). Copyright © 1979 by the Board of Trustees, Leland Stanford Junior University and reprinted with the permission of the Stanford Law Review and Mr. Mickenberg.

Bryce Nelson, Ethical Dilemma: Should Lawyers Turn in Clients? Los Angeles Times, July 2, 1974, p. 1, col. 1, Copyright © 1974, Los Angeles Times. Reprinted by permission.

Stephen Pepper, The Lawyer's Amoral Ethical Role, 1986 Am. B. Found. Res. J. 613-635. Reprinted with permission of the author and the American Bar Foundation.

Project, An Assessment of Alternative Strategies for Increasing Access to Legal Services, 90 Yale L.J. 128-138, 146-154 (1980). Reprinted with permission of the Yale Law Journal Company and Fred B. Rothman & Company.

Deborah L. Rhode, Why the ABA Bothers: A Functional Perspective on Professional Codes, 59 Texas L. Rev. 689 (1981). Copyright © 1981 by the Texas Law Review and reprinted with its permission and that of the author.

Alvin B. Rubin, A Causerie on Lawyers' Ethics in Negotiation, 35 La. L. Rev. 578 (1975). Reprinted with permission of the author and the Louisiana Law Review.

A.A. Sommer, The Emerging Responsibilities of the Securities Lawyer, ¶79,631 of the Federal Securities Law Reports. Reprinted with permission of the author and Federal Securities Law Reports, published and copyrighted by Commerce Clearing House, Inc., Chicago, Illinois 60646.

Eric Steele and Raymond Nimmer, Lawyers, Clients, and Professional Regulations, 1976 Am. B. Found. Res. J. 919, 1014-1016. Reprinted with permission of the authors and the American Bar Foundation.

M.B.E. Smith, Should Lawyers Listen to Philosophers About Legal Ethics?, unpublished paper. Reprinted with permission of the author.

Alan A. Stone, M.D., The Myth of Advocacy, 30 Hospital and Community Psychiatry 819-822 (December 1979). Reprinted with permission of Dr. Stone and Hospital and Community Psychiatry.

E. Wayne Thode, The Development of the Code of Judicial Conduct, 9 San Diego L. Rev. 793 (1972). Copyright © 1972, San Diego Law Review Association and reprinted with its permission and that of the author.

E. Wayne Thode, Summary of the Reply to Suggestions of Professor Grossman, 9 San Diego L. Rev. 816 (1972). Copyright © 1972, San Diego Law Review Association and reprinted with its permission and that of the author.

Richard Uviller, The Virtuous Prosecutor in Quest of an Ethical Standard: Guidance from the ABA, 71 Mich. L. Rev. 1155-1159 (1973). Reprinted with permission of the author and the Michigan Law Review.

Richard Wasserstrom, Lawyers as Professionals: Some Moral Issues, 5 Human Rights 1 (1975). Permission to reprint granted by Richard Wasserstrom, the ABA Section of Individual Rights and Responsibilities, and the Southern Methodist University School of Law.

James J. White, Machiavelli and the Bar, 1980 Am. B. Found. Res. J. 926. Reprinted with permission of the author and the American Bar Foundation.

INTRODUCTION

A commonplace remark of students, teachers, and practitioners of law is that the practice of professional responsibility is very different from the precepts of the profession in that practice includes a great deal of "unethical" conduct condemned by the precepts. My own view is that whatever the magnitude of "unethical" conduct in the profession, and it is very difficult to measure, even assuming agreement on the meaning of that phrase, there is widespread insensitivity to issues of professional responsibility. A great deal of this insensitivity derives, I believe, from the fact that the typical lawyer has not devoted enough thought to those issues before they arise in practice. The problems then are often ignored because they are not recognized as such. Or if they are recognized, they are dealt with inadequately because the lawyer has not developed a philosophy of, or at least a general attitude toward, practice and a sense of the kind of lawyer he or she wants to be. How and why the profession is in that situation is an interesting question. There are many institutions that can share the blame, for there is more than enough to go around. That is a subject, however, that is largely, but not wholly, beyond the scope of this book.

One impetus for the development of these materials was the desire to expose students to issues of professional responsibility by discussion of the difficult problems that lawyers face in their daily practice. While students are in law school, they are able to examine difficult professional issues without the heavy weight that self-interest exerts on the practitioner to reach a particular result that is financially rewarding. If students see the issues and competing considerations involved in typical problem situations and begin to develop their own reactions and philosophies before the issues arise in their own professional lives, then they will be better equipped to recognize and respond to them in practice. Obviously, subsequent experience may modify views, but students will have some background with which to face their experiences.

A second impetus to development of these materials was the desire to familiarize students with issues of professional responsibility that are facing the profession as a whole — questions of the quantity and quality of the provision of legal services to the public, admission and discipline, specialization, and the like. The textual materials presented in these particular chapters are somewhat more adapted to discussion in themselves, but even here many of the issues are developed in problem form. The organization of this book reflects its dual purpose: problems illustrating issues encountered in individual practice are presented first, followed by materials presenting issues facing the profession as a whole. Succeeding editions, however, have differed from the first in that they present considerably more text analysis of current developments and more theoretical materials to complement the Problems.

Professional responsibility is a course in which students can and should be engaged deeply in the materials. In addition to providing exposure to pervasive ethical issues, the problem method has proved, at least for me, to be the best way to achieve student involvement. It has also made classes a great deal more fun. Either we discuss what the lawyer should do, or I take the role of the client, and the "lawyer" conducts an interview with me based on the fact situation set out in the Problem. Other students then try their hand as lawyer or evaluate the first lawyer's performance, or sometimes we simply discuss the issues. Occasionally, I will take the lawyer's role.

Students sometimes ask whether the Problems are "real." They are. They have either been related to me or have happened to me or have been adapted from reported cases. The Problems have been designed to force students to think through some difficult areas in the practice of law. None are easy or have solutions that are noncontroversial. The Problems therefore cannot be answered by following the old bar examination cliche of advising the lawyer to do what is "most ethical." Usually a clash of values is involved. In focusing on difficult problem situations, the book omits large areas of the "dos" and "don'ts" of law practice. To make sure that students have familiarity with these matters, I make use of computer exercises entitled "Drill on the Code of Professional Responsibility," and "Drill on the Rules of Professional Conduct" prepared by Professors Roger Park of the University of Minnesota Law School and Kenneth Kirwin of William Mitchell College of Law. These are compilations of problems developed to encourage familiarity with the myriad requirements of the Model Code and Model Rules. Each calls for approximately an hour's study beforehand and two hours of computer time, and, especially when undertaken by two or more students together, provides good basic instruction. I tell students to do the Drill corresponding to the jurisdiction where they are likely to begin practice.

While the Problems are the heart of the course and can be used in a variety of ways, supporting materials are provided to present background information and insight. I have tried to provide enough materials to illuminate the issues in the Problems without overwhelming the

Problems (or the students). These supporting materials have been designed for the most part so that if time pressure develops — and that often seems to occur in this course — very little class time needs to be spent explicitly on them, unless, of course, one would rather focus on the supporting materials than on the Problems. Sometimes I do just that.

One characteristic of this approach to teaching professional responsibility is that it is essentially inductive. No structural approach to the profession is presented of which these Problems and their solutions are illustrative. The idea is for students to face situations, see what guidelines the law of professional responsibility offers or fails to offer, and decide for themselves what the appropriate solution or solutions should be. After developing "solutions" to a number of Problems, which is perhaps analogous to the developing of practical experience, the student is then invited to see whether these "solutions" fit together into some coherent professional attitude. Obviously, since the materials are designed to provide exposure to professional responsibility problems encountered in actual practice, they presume a legal system that resembles our present one. However, their purpose is not to invite automatic acceptance of our system's premises. The premises should first be understood and then evaluated. There are a number of places in this book, beginning most explicitly with the selections on pages 153 and 246 that are designed to provide some insight into the present system and to stimulate consideration of specific and general alternatives to it. I should also mention the fact that, while these materials are designed to present problems of professional responsibility, they do so in the context of a given factual setting. Often, therefore, an appropriate question is whether a problem of professional responsibility is in fact raised, or whether the problem of professional responsibility may and should be dealt with by avoiding it.

This book is designed to be used in a course of approximately 30 classroom hours. Some years I cover nearly the whole book. Some years I do not. When I do not, I cover Chapters 1, 2, 3, 4 and 9 and then pick different topics from the remainder.

PROBLEMS IN
PROFESSIONAL RESPONSIBILITY

CHAPTER 1

THE PROFESSION — AN INTRODUCTION

This chapter introduces issues of professional responsibility by presenting two different types of materials. The first selection is an excerpt from an article by Richard Wasserstrom, a lawyer-philosopher. He raises some serious and disturbing questions about the lawyer's role that should be of concern to every lawyer. Other perspectives on this issue are presented throughout the book and it may be preferable to defer detailed discussion of Professor Wasserstrom's article until later, perhaps in connection with the materials on confidentiality in Chapter 4. But the issues he raises should be in every student's mind right from the beginning of the course.

The remaining materials of this chapter discuss the nature of the substantive law of professional responsibility. A text Note introduces us to the Model Code of Professional Responsibility and the Model Rules of Professional Conduct, two of the major sources of that law. They are followed by a "book review" of the former document by a philosopher, Charles Frankel, which seeks to place the Model Code into a broader framework of thought about approaches to "legislating ethics."

A word about bibliography. Selected materials are referred to at various places. A comprehensive historical treatment would be useful, but I am not able to recommend any one work that does the job. See James Willard Hurst, The Growth of American Law (1950) for pre-1950 coverage and Martin Mayer, The Lawyers (1967) for a balanced, albeit somewhat dated factually, picture of what lawyers do. This book successfully conveys the lawyer's world to a mass audience. The best historical work dealing with a bar is the well-written book by lawyer, opera critic, and public-minded citizen George Martin, entitled Causes and Conflict — The Centennial History of the Association of the Bar of the City of New York, 1870-1970 (1970). A very valuable and comprehen-

1

sive study of the provision of legal services in Great Britain is contained in the two-volume Final Report of the Royal Commission on Legal Services (1979). A useful collection of excerpted materials that complement the coverage of this course is Hazard and Rhode, The Legal Profession (2d ed. 1988). A different kind of book that also complements this book is Philip Heymann and Lance Liebman, The Social Responsibilities of Lawyers — Case Studies (1988). This is a soft-cover collection of quite lengthy case studies of specific problems of professional responsibility that enable students to analyze the issues in the real-world setting of facts and documents that they will work in when they practice law. A collection of essays on the lawyer's role in our adversary system, many of them by philosophers, is David Luban ed., The Good Lawyer (1984). See also Luban, Lawyers and Justice (1988). A detailed sociological analysis of the structure of the legal profession in one city is Heinz and Laumann, Chicago Lawyers (1982).

Recently, some useful new books have appeared on the substantive law of professional responsibility. The most comprehensive is a hornbook, Charles Wolfram, Modern Legal Ethics (1986). A similar effort is L. Ray Patterson, Legal Ethics: The Law of Professional Responsibility (1982). Yet another, focusing on the Model Rules of Professional Conduct, is Hazard and Hodes, The Law of Lawyering (1986). Two helpful books that discuss lawyers' problems in litigation are Keeton, Trial Tactics and Methods (2d ed. 1973) and Underwood and Fortune, Trial Ethics (1988). A comprehensive compilation of statistical information about lawyers in the United States is contained in Barbara Curran ed., The Lawyer Statistical Report: A Statistical Profile of the U.S. Legal Profession in the 1980s (1985). Different teachers using these materials will doubtless have their own recommendations among the myriad other books and articles that touch various aspects of the life of the legal profession in this country and elsewhere.

WASSERSTROM,* LAWYERS AS PROFESSIONALS: SOME MORAL ISSUES
5 Human Rights 1 (Fall 1975)

In this paper I examine two moral criticisms of laywers which, if well-founded, are fundamental. Neither is new but each appears to apply with particular force today. Both tend to be made by those not in the

*B.A. 1957, Amherst College; M.A. 1958, Ph.D. 1960, University of Michigan; LL.B. 1960, Stanford. Professor of Law and Professor of Philosophy, University of California School of Law, Los Angeles. [Now Professor, Kresge College, University of California-Santa Cruz.] This article is a revised version of a lecture given at Amherst College in 1974 as a part of the Copeland Colloquium series on morality and the professions.

mainstream of the legal profession and to be rejected by those who are in it. Both in some sense concern the lawyer-client relationship.

The first criticism centers around the lawyer's stance toward the world at large. The accusation is that the lawyer-client relationship renders the lawyer at best systematically amoral and at worst more than occasionally immoral in his or her dealings with the rest of mankind.

The second criticism focuses upon the relationship between the lawyer and the client. Here the charge is that it is the lawyer-client relationship which is morally objectionable because it is a relationship in which the lawyer dominates and in which the lawyer typically, and perhaps inevitably, treats the client in both an impersonal and a paternalistic fashion.

To a considerable degree these two criticisms of lawyers derive, I believe, from the fact that the lawyer is a professional. And to the extent to which this is the case, the more generic problems I will be exploring are those of professionalism generally. But in some respects, the lawyer's situation is different from that of other professionals. The lawyer is vulnerable to some moral criticism that does not as readily or as easily attach to any other professional. And this, too, is an issue that I shall be examining.[1]

1. Because of the significance for my analysis of the closely related concepts of a profession and a professional, it will be helpful to indicate at the outset what I take to be the central features of a profession.

But first there is an ambiguity that must be noted so that it can be dismissed. There is one sense of "professional" and hence of "profession" with which I am not concerned. That is the sense in which there are in our culture, professional athletes, professional actors, and professional beauticians. In this sense, a person who possesses sufficient skill to engage in an activity for money and who elects to do so is a professional rather than, say, an amateur or a volunteer. This is, as I have said, not the sense of "profession" in which I am interested.

I am interested, instead, in the characteristics of professions such as law, or medicine. There are, I think, at least six that are worth noting.

(1) The professions require a substantial period of formal education — at least as much if not more than that required by any other occupation.

(2) The professions require the comprehension of a substantial amount of theoretical knowledge and the utilization of a substantial amount of intellectual ability. Neither manual nor creative ability is typically demanded. This is one thing that distinguishes the professions both from highly skilled crafts — like glassblowing — and from the arts.

(3) The professions are both an economic monopoly and largely self-regulating. Not only is the practice of the profession restricted to those who are certified as possessing the requisite competencies, but the questions of what competencies are required and who possesses them are questions that are left to the members of the profession to decide for themselves.

(4) The professions are clearly among the occupations that possess the greatest social prestige in the society. They also typically provide a degree of material affluence substantially greater than that enjoyed by most working persons.

(5) The professions are almost always involved with matters which from time to time are among the greatest personal concerns that humans have: physical health, psychic well-being, liberty, and the like. As a result, persons who seek the services of a professional are often in a state of appreciable concern, if not vulnerability, when they do so.

(6) The professions almost always involve at their core a significant interpersonal relationship between the professional, on the one hand, and the person who is thought to require the professional's services: the patient or the client.

Although I am undecided about the ultimate merits of either criticism, I am convinced that each is deserving of careful articulation and assessment, and that each contains insights that deserve more acknowledgment than they often receive. My ambition is, therefore, more to exhibit the relevant considerations and to stimulate additional reflection, than it is to provide any very definite conclusions.

I

As I have indicated, the first issue I propose to examine concerns the ways the professional-client relationship affects the professional's stance toward the world at large. The primary question that is presented is whether there is adequate justification for the kind of moral universe that comes to be inhabited by the lawyer as he or she goes through professional life. For at best the lawyer's world is a simplified moral world; often it is an amoral one; and more than occasionally, perhaps, an overtly immoral one.

To many persons, Watergate was simply a recent and dramatic illustration of this fact. When John Dean testified before the Select Senate Committee inquiring into the Watergate affair in the Spring of 1973, he was asked about one of the documents that he had provided to the Committee. The document was a piece of paper which contained a list of a number of the persons who had been involved in the cover-up. Next to a number of the names an asterisk appeared. What, Dean was asked, was the meaning of the asterisk? Did it signify membership in some further conspiracy? Did it mark off those who were decision makers from those who were not? There did not seem to be any obvious pattern: Ehrlichman was starred, but Haldeman was not; Mitchell was starred, but Magruder was not. Oh, Dean answered, the asterisk really didn't mean anything. One day when he had been looking at the list of participants, he had been struck by the fact that so many of them were lawyers. So, he marked the name of each lawyer with an asterisk to see just how many there were. He had wondered, he told the Committee, when he saw that so many were attorneys, whether that had had anything to do with it; whether there was some reason why lawyers might have been more inclined than other persons to have been so willing to do the things that were done in respect to Watergate and the cover-up. But he had not pursued the matter; he had merely mused about it one afternoon.

It is, I think, at least a plausible hypothesis that the predominance of lawyers was not accidental — that the fact that they were lawyers made it easier rather than harder for them both to look at things the way they did and to do the things that were done. The theory that I want to examine in support of this hypothesis connects this activity with a feature of the lawyer's professionalism.

As I have already noted, one central feature of the professions in general and of law in particular is that there is a special, complicated relationship between the professional, and the client or patient. For each of the parties in this relationship, but especially for the professional, the behavior that is involved is, to a very significant degree, what I call role-differentiated behavior. And this is significant because it is the nature of role-differentiated behavior that it often makes it both appropriate and desirable for the person in a particular role to put to one side considerations of various sorts — and especially various moral considerations — that would otherwise be relevant if not decisive. Some illustrations will help to make clear what I mean both by role-differentiated behavior and by the way role-differentiated behavior often alters, if not eliminates, the significance of those moral considerations that would obtain, were it not for the presence of the role.

Being a parent is, in probably every human culture, to be involved in role-differentiated behavior. In our own culture, and once again in most, if not all, human cultures, as a parent one is entitled, if not obligated, to prefer the interests of one's own children over those of children generally. That is to say, it is regarded as appropriate for a parent to allocate excessive goods to his or her own children, even though other children may have substantially more pressing and genuine needs for these same items. If one were trying to decide what the right way was to distribute assets among a group of children all of whom were strangers to oneself, the relevant moral considerations would be very different from those that would be thought to obtain once one's own children were in the picture. In the role of a parent, the claims of other children vis-à-vis one's own are, if not rendered morally irrelevant, certainly rendered less morally significant. In short, the role-differentiated character of the situation alters the relevant moral point of view enormously.

A similar situation is presented by the case of the scientist. For a number of years there has been debate and controversy within the scientific community over the question of whether scientists should participate in the development and elaboration of atomic theory, especially as those theoretical advances could then be translated into development of atomic weapons that would become a part of the arsenal of existing nation states. The dominant view, although it was not the unanimous one, in the scientific community was that the role of the scientist was to expand the limits of human knowledge. Atomic power was a force which had previously not been utilizable by human beings. The job of the scientist was, among other things, to develop ways and means by which that could now be done. And it was simply no part of one's role as a scientist to forego inquiry, or divert one's scientific explorations because of the fact that the fruits of the investigation could be or would be put to improper, immoral, or even catastrophic uses. The moral issues concerning whether and when to develop and use nuclear weapons were to be decided by others; by citizens and statesmen; they were not the concern of the scientist qua scientist.

In both of these cases it is, of course, conceivable that plausible and even thoroughly convincing arguments exist for the desirability of the role-differentiated behavior and its attendant neglect of what would otherwise be morally relevant considerations. Nonetheless, it is, I believe, also the case that the burden of proof, so to speak, is always upon the proponent of the desirability of this kind of role-differentiated behavior. For in the absence of special reasons why parents ought to prefer the interests of their children over those of children in general, the moral point of view surely requires that the claims and needs of all children receive equal consideration. But we take the rightness of parental preference so for granted, that we often neglect, I think, the fact that it is anything but self-evidently morally appropriate. My own view, for example, is that careful reflection shows that the *degree* of parental preference systematically encouraged in our own culture is far too extensive to be morally justified.

All of this is significant just because to be a professional is to be enmeshed in role-differentiated behavior of precisely this sort. One's role as a doctor, psychiatrist, or lawyer, alters one's moral universe in a fashion analogous to that described above. Of special significance here is the fact that the professional qua professional has a client or patient whose interests must be represented, attended to, or looked after by the professional. And that means that the role of the professional (like that of the parent) is to prefer in a variety of ways the interests of the client or patient over those of individuals generally.

Consider, more specifically, the role-differentiated behavior of the lawyer. Conventional wisdom has it that where the attorney-client relationship exists, the point of view of the attorney is properly different — and appreciably so — from that which would be appropriate in the absence of the attorney-client relationship. For where the attorney-client relationship exists, it is often appropriate and many times even obligatory for the attorney to do things that, all other things being equal, an ordinary person need not, and should not do. What is characteristic of this role of a lawyer is the lawyer's required indifference to a wide variety of ends and consequences that in other contexts would be of undeniable moral significance. Once a lawyer represents a client, the lawyer has a duty to make his or her expertise fully available in the realization of the end sought by the client, irrespective, for the most part, of the moral worth to which the end will be put or the character of the client who seeks to utilize it. Provided that the end sought is not illegal, the lawyer is, in essence, an amoral technician whose peculiar skills and knowledge in respect to the law are available to those with whom the relationship of client is established. The question, as I have indicated, is whether this particular and pervasive feature of professionalism is itself justifiable. At a minimum, I do not think any of the typical, simple answers will suffice.

One such answer focuses upon and generalizes from the criminal defense lawyer. For what is probably the most familiar aspect of this role-differentiated character of the lawyer's activity is that of the defense of a client charged with a crime. The received view within the profession (and to a lesser degree within the society at large) is that having once agreed to represent the client, the lawyer is under an obligation to do his or her best to defend that person at trial, irrespective, for instance, even of the lawyer's belief in the client's innocence. There are limits, of course, to what constitutes a defense: a lawyer cannot bribe or intimidate witnesses to increase the likelihood of securing an acquittal. And there are legitimate questions, in close cases, about how those limits are to be delineated. But, however these matters get resolved, it is at least clear that it is thought both appropriate and obligatory for the attorney to put on as vigorous and persuasive a defense of a client believed to be guilty as would have been mounted by the lawyer thoroughly convinced of the client's innocence. I suspect that many persons find this an attractive and admirable feature of the life of a legal professional. I know that often I do. The justifications are varied and, as I shall argue below, probably convincing.

But part of the difficulty is that the irrelevance of the guilt or innocence of an accused client by no means exhausts the altered perspective of the lawyer's conscience, even in criminal cases. For in the course of defending an accused, an attorney may have, as a part of his or her duty of representation, the obligation to invoke procedures and practices which are themselves morally objectionable and of which the lawyer in other contexts might thoroughly disapprove. And these situations, I think, are somewhat less comfortable to confront. For example, in California, the case law permits a defendant in a rape case to secure in some circumstances an order from the court requiring the complaining witness, that is the rape victim, to submit to a psychiatric examination before trial.[2] For no other crime is such a pretrial remedy available. In no other case can the victim of a crime be required to undergo psychiatric examination at the request of the defendant on the ground that the results of the examination may help the defendant prove that the offense did not take place. I think such a rule is wrong and is reflective of the sexist bias of the law in respect to rape. I certainly do not think it right that rape victims should be singled out by the law for this kind of special pretrial treatment, and I am skeptical about the morality of any involuntary psychiatric examination of witnesses. Nonetheless, it appears to

---

2. Ballard v. Superior Court, 64 Cal. 2d 159, 410 P.2d 838, 49 Cal. Rptr. 302 (1966). [Such orders are now prohibited by California Penal Code §1112. — Ed.]

be part of the role-differentiated obligation of a lawyer for a defendant charged with rape to seek to take advantage of this particular rule of law — irrespective of the independent moral view he or she may have of the rightness or wrongness of such a rule.

Nor, it is important to point out, is this peculiar, strikingly amoral behavior limited to the lawyer involved with the workings of the criminal law. Most clients come to lawyers to get the lawyers to help them do things that they could not easily do without the assistance provided by the lawyer's special competence. They wish, for instance, to dispose of their property in a certain way at death. They wish to contract for the purchase or sale of a house or a business. They wish to set up a corporation which will manufacture and market a new product. They wish to minimize their income taxes. And so on. In each case, they need the assistance of the professional, the lawyer, for he or she alone has the special skill which will make it possible for the client to achieve the desired result.

And in each case, the role-differentiated character of the lawyer's way of being tends to render irrelevant what would otherwise be morally relevant considerations. Suppose that a client desires to make a will disinheriting her children because they opposed the war in Vietnam. Should the lawyer refuse to draft the will because the lawyer thinks this is a bad reason to disinherit one's children? Suppose a client can avoid the payment of taxes through a loophole only available to a few wealthy taxpayers. Should the lawyer refuse to tell the client of a loophole because the lawyer thinks it an unfair advantage for the rich? Suppose a client wants to start a corporation that will manufacture, distribute and promote a harmful but not illegal substance, e.g., cigarettes. Should the lawyer refuse to prepare the articles of incorporation for the corporation? In each case, the accepted view within the profession is that these matters are just of no concern to the lawyer qua lawyer. The lawyer need not of course agree to represent the client (and that is equally true for the unpopular client accused of a heinous crime), but there is nothing wrong with representing a client whose aims and purposes are quite immoral. And having agreed to do so, the lawyer is required to provide the best possible assistance, without regard to his or her disapproval of the objective that is sought.

The lesson, on this view, is clear. The job of the lawyer, so the argument typically concludes, is not to approve or disapprove of the character of his or her client, the cause for which the client seeks the lawyer's assistance, or the avenues provided by the law to achieve that which the client wants to accomplish. The lawyer's task is, instead, to provide that competence which the client lacks and the lawyer, as professional, possesses. In this way, the lawyer as professional comes to inhabit a simplified universe which is strikingly amoral — which regards as morally irrelevant any number of factors which nonprofessional citizens might take to be important, if not decisive, in their everyday lives. And the difficulty I have with all of this is that the arguments for such a way of life seem to be not quite so convincing to me as they do to many lawyers. I am, that is, at best uncertain that it is a good thing for lawyers to be so professional — for them to embrace so completely this role-differentiated way of approaching matters.

More specifically, if it is correct that this is the perspective of lawyers in particular and professionals in general, is it right that this should be their perspective? Is it right that the lawyer should be able so easily to put to one side otherwise difficult problems with the answer: but these are not and cannot be my concern as a lawyer? What do we gain and what do we lose from having a social universe in which there are professionals such as lawyers, who, as such, inhabit a universe of the sort I have been trying to describe?

One difficulty in even thinking about all of this is that lawyers may not be very objective or detached in their attempts to work the problem through. For one feature of this simplified, intellectual world is that it is often a very comfortable one to inhabit.

To be sure, on occasion, a lawyer may find it uncomfortable to represent an extremely unpopular client. On occasion, too, a lawyer may feel ill at ease invoking a rule of law or practice which he or she thinks to be an unfair or undesirable one. Nonetheless, for most lawyers, most of the time, pursuing the interests of one's clients is an attractive and satisfying way to live in part just because the moral world of the lawyer is a simpler, less complicated, and less ambiguous world than the moral world of ordinary life. There is, I think, something quite seductive about being able to turn aside so many ostensibly difficult moral dilemmas and decisions with the reply: but that is not my concern; my job as a lawyer is not to judge the rights and wrongs of the client or the cause; it is to defend as best I can my client's interests. For the ethical problems that can arise within this constricted point of view are, to say the least, typically neither momentous nor terribly vexing. Role-differentiated behavior is enticing and reassuring precisely because it does constrain and delimit an otherwise often intractable and confusing moral world.

But there is, of course, also an argument which seeks to demonstrate that it is good and not merely comfortable for lawyers to behave this way.

It is good, so the argument goes, that the lawyer's behavior and concomitant point of view are role-differentiated because the lawyer qua lawyer participates in a complex institution which functions well only if the individuals adhere to their institutional roles.

For example, when there is a conflict between individuals, or between the state and an individual, there is a well-established institutional mechanism by which to get that dispute resolved. That mechanism is the trial in which each side is represented by a lawyer whose job it is both to present his or her client's case in the most attractive, forceful light and to seek to expose the weaknesses and defects in the case of the opponent.

When an individual is charged with having committed a crime, the trial is the mechanism by which we determine in our society whether or not the person is in fact guilty. Just imagine what would happen if lawyers were to refuse, for instance, to represent persons whom they thought to be guilty. In a case where the guilt of a person seemed clear, it might turn out that some individuals would be deprived completely of the opportunity to have the system determine whether or not they are in fact guilty. The private judgment of individual lawyers would in effect be substituted for the public, institutional judgment of the judge and jury. The amorality of lawyers helps to guarantee that every criminal defendant will have his or her day in court.

In addition, of course, appearances can be deceiving. Persons who appear before trial to be clearly guilty do sometimes turn out to be innocent. Even persons who confess their guilt to their attorney occasionally turn out to have lied or to have been mistaken. The adversary system, so this argument continues, is simply a better method than any other that has been established by which to determine the legally relevant facts in any given case. It is certainly a better method than the exercise of private judgment by any particular individual. And the adversary system only works if each party to the controversy has a lawyer, a person whose institutional role it is to argue, plead and present the merits of his or her case and the demerits of the opponent's. Thus if the adversary system is to work, it is necessary that there be lawyers who will play their appropriate, professional, institutional role of representative of the client's cause.

Nor is the amorality of the institutional role of the lawyer restricted to the defense of those accused of crimes. As was indicated earlier, when the lawyer functions in his most usual role, he or she functions as a counselor, as a professional whose task it is to help people realize those objectives and ends that the law permits them to obtain and which cannot be obtained without the attorney's special competence in the law. The attorney may think it wrong to disinherit one's children because of their views about the Vietnam war, but here the attorney's complaint is really with the laws of inheritance and not with his or her client. The attorney may think the tax provision an unfair, unjustifiable loophole, but once more the complaint is really with the Internal Revenue Code and not with the client who seeks to take advantage of it. And these matters, too, lie beyond the ambit of the lawyer's moral point of view as institutional counselor and facilitator. If lawyers were to substitute their own private views of what ought to be legally permissible and impermissible for those of the legislature, this would constitute a surreptitious and undesirable shift from a democracy to an oligarchy of lawyers. For given the fact that lawyers are needed to effectuate the wishes of clients, the lawyer ought to make his or her skills available to those who seek them without regard for the particular objectives of the client.

Now, all of this certainly makes some sense. These arguments are neither specious nor without force. Nonetheless, it seems to me that one dilemma which emerges is that if this line of argument is sound, it also appears to follow that the behavior of the lawyers involved in Watergate was simply another less happy illustration of lawyers playing their accustomed institutional role. If we are to approve on institutional grounds of the lawyer's zealous defense of the apparently guilty client and the lawyer's effective assistance of the immoral cheat, does it not follow that we must also approve of the Watergate lawyer's zealous defense of the interests of Richard Nixon?

As I have indicated, I do not think there is any easy answer to this question. For I am not, let me hasten to make clear, talking about the easy cases — about the behavior of the lawyers that was manifestly illegal. For someone quite properly might reply that it was no more appropriate for the lawyer who worked in the White House to obtruct justice or otherwise violate the criminal law than it would be for a criminal defense lawyer to shoot the prosecution witness to prevent adverse testimony or bribe a defense witness in order to procure favorable testimony. What I am interested in is all of the Watergate behavior engaged in by the Watergate lawyers that was not illegal, but that was, nonetheless, behavior of which we quite properly disapprove. I mean lying to the public; dissembling; stonewalling; tape-recording conversations; playing dirty tricks. Were not these just effective lawyer-like activities pursued by lawyers who viewed Richard Nixon as they would a client and who sought, therefore, the advancement and protection of his interests — personal and political?

It might immediately be responded that the analogy is not apt. For the lawyers who were involved in Watergate were hardly participants in an adversary proceeding. They were certainly not participants in that institutional setting, litigation, in which the amorality of the lawyer makes the most sense. It might even be objected that the amorality of the lawyer qua counselor is clearly distinguishable from the behavior of the Watergate lawyers. Nixon as President was not a client; they, as officials in the executive branch, were functioning as governmental officials and not as lawyers at all.

While not wholly convinced by a response such as the above, I am prepared to accept it because the issue at hand seems to me to be a deeper one. Even if the involvement of so many lawyers in Watergate was adventitious (or, if not adventitious, explicable in terms of some more benign explanation) there still seems to me to be costs, if not problems, with the amorality of the lawyer that derives from his or her role-differentiated professionalism.

As I indicated earlier, I do believe that the amoral behavior of the *criminal* defense lawyer is justifiable. But I think that jurisdiction depends at least as much upon the special needs of an accused as upon any more general defense of a lawyer's role-differentiated behavior. As a matter of fact I think it likely that many persons such as myself have

been misled by the special features of the criminal case. Because a deprivation of liberty is so serious, because the prosecutorial resources of
the state are so vast, and because, perhaps, of a serious skepticism about
the rightness of punishment even where wrongdoing has occurred, it is
easy to accept the view that it makes sense to charge the defense counsel
with the job of making the best possible case for the accused — without
regard, so to speak, for the merits. This coupled with the fact that it is
an adversarial proceeding succeeds, I think, in justifying the amorality
of the criminal defense counsel. But this does not, however, justify a
comparable perspective on the part of lawyers generally. Once we leave
the peculiar situation of the criminal defense lawyer, I think it quite likely that the role-differentiated amorality of the lawyer is almost certainly
excessive and at times inappropriate. That is to say, this special case to
one side, I am inclined to think that we might all be better served if
lawyers were to see themselves less as subject to role-differentiated behavior and more as subject to the demands of the moral point of view.
In this sense it may be that we need a good deal less rather than more
professionalism in our society generally and among lawyers in particular.

Moreover, even if I am wrong about all this, four things do seem to
me to be true and important.

First, all of the arguments that support the role-differentiated amorality of the lawyer on institutional grounds can succeed only if the enormous degree of trust and confidence in the institutions themselves is
itself justified. If the institutions work well and fairly, there may be good
sense to deferring important moral concerns and criticisms to another
time and place, to the level of institutional criticism and assessment. But
the less certain we are entitled to be of either the rightness or the self-
corrective nature of the larger institutions of which the professional is a
part, the less apparent it is that we should encourage the professional to
avoid direct engagement with the moral issues as they arise. And we are,
today, I believe, certainly entitled to be quite skeptical both of the fairness and of the capacity for self-correction of our larger institutional
mechanisms, including the legal system. To the degree to which the institutional rules and practices are unjust, unwise or undesirable, to that
same degree is the case for the role-differentiated behavior of the lawyer
weakened if not destroyed.

Second, it is clear that there are definite character traits that the
professional such as the lawyer must take on if the system is to work.
What is less clear is that they are admirable ones. Even if the role-differentiated amorality of the professional lawyer is justified by the virtues
of the adversary system, this also means that the lawyer qua lawyer will
be encouraged to be competitive rather than cooperative; aggressive
rather than accommodating; ruthless rather than compassionate; and
pragmatic rather than principled. This is, I think, part of the logic of

the role-differentiated behavior of lawyers in particular, and to a lesser degree of professionals in general. It is surely neither accidental nor unimportant that these are the same character traits that are emphasized and valued by the capitalist ethic — and on precisely analogous grounds. Because the ideals of professionalism and capitalism are the dominant ones within our culture, it is harder than most of us suspect even to take seriously the suggestion that radically different styles of living, kinds of occupational outlooks, and types of social institutions might be possible, let alone preferable.

Third, there is a special feature of the role-differentiated behavior of the lawyer that distinguishes it from the comparable behavior of other professionals. What I have in mind can be brought out through the following question: Why is it that it seems far less plausible to talk critically about the amorality of the doctor, for instance, who treats all patients irrespective of their moral character than it does to talk critically about the comparable amorality of the lawyer? Why is it that it seems so obviously sensible, simple and right for the doctor's behavior to be narrowly and rigidly role-differentiated, i.e., just to try to cure those who are ill? And why is it that at the very least it seems so complicated, uncertain, and troublesome to decide whether it is right for the lawyer's behavior to be similarly role-differentiated?

The answer, I think, is twofold. To begin with (and this I think is the less interesting point) it is, so to speak, intrinsically good to try to cure disease, but in no comparable way is it intrinsically good to try to win every lawsuit or help every client realize his or her objective. In addition (and this I take to be the truly interesting point), the lawyer's behavior is different in kind from the doctor's. The lawyer — and especially the lawyer as advocate — directly says and affirms things. The lawyer makes the case for the client. He or she tries to explain, persuade and convince others that the client's cause should prevail. The lawyer lives with and within a dilemma that is not shared by other professionals. If the lawyer actually believes everything that he or she asserts on behalf of the client, then it appears to be proper to regard the lawyer as in fact embracing and endorsing the points of view that he or she articulates. If the lawyer does not in fact believe what is urged by way of argument, if the lawyer is only playing a role, then it appears to be proper to tax the lawyer with hypocrisy and insincerity. To be sure, actors in a play take on roles and say things that the characters, not the actors, believe. But we know it is a play and that they are actors. The law courts are not, however, theaters, and the lawyers both talk about justice and they genuinely seek to persuade. The fact that the lawyer's words, thoughts, and convictions are, apparently, for sale and at the service of the client helps us, I think, to understand the peculiar hostility which is more than occasionally uniquely directed by lay persons toward lawyers. The verbal, role-differentiated behavior of the lawyer qua advocate puts the lawyer's integrity into question in a way that distinguishes the lawyer from the other professionals.[3]

Fourth, and related closely to the three points just discussed, even if on balance the role-differentiated character of the lawyer's way of thinking and acting is ultimately deemed to be justifiable within the system on systemic instrumental grounds, it still remains the case that we do pay a social price for that way of thought and action. For to become and to be a professional, such as a lawyer, is to incorporate within oneself ways of behaving and ways of thinking that shape the whole person. It is especially hard, if not impossible, because of the nature of the professions, for one's professional way of thinking not to dominate one's entire adult life. Thus, even if the lawyers who were involved in Watergate were not, strictly speaking, then and there functioning as lawyers, their behavior was, I believe, the likely if not inevitable consequence of their legal acculturation. Having been taught to embrace and practice the lawyer's institutional role, it was natural, if not unavoidable, that they would continue to play that role even when they were somewhat removed from the specific institutional milieu in which that way of thinking and acting is arguably fitting and appropriate. The nature of the professions — the lengthy educational preparation, the prestige and economic rewards, and the concomitant enhanced sense of self — makes the role of professional a difficult one to shed even in those obvious situations in which that role is neither required nor appropriate. In important respects, one's professional role becomes and is one's dominant role, so that for many persons at least they become their professional being. This is at a minimum a heavy price to pay for the professions as we know them in our culture, and especially so for lawyers. Whether it is an inevitable price is, I think, an open question, largely because the problem has not begun to be fully perceived as such by the professionals in general, the legal profession in particular, or by the educational institutions that train professionals. . . .

[The second part of the article takes a critical look at the personal relationship between the lawyer and client.]

NOTES

1. Professor Wasserstrom's piece was deliberately chosen for its critical approach, for it is representative of a whole body of modern literature about the norms of the legal profession. We should remember, however, as we consider the materials of professional responsibility, that it is not enough to resolve each professional problem for ourselves, i.e., to an-

3. I owe this insight, which I think is an important and seldom appreciated one, to my colleague, Leon Letwin.

swer the question "What would (will) I do in this particular situation?" We must then go on to answer the question, "Would I impose my solution on other professionals or would I give them some discretion?" The question regarding discretion then requires us to consider whether lawyers with discretion in certain circumstances should attempt to let clients and would-be clients know how they will exercise that discretion so as to provide relevant information, to assist in the lawyer selection process, and to assist in client decision-making about what to tell (and not to tell) the lawyer. As we shall see throughout these materials, these questions are consistently troublesome.

2. Professor Wasserstrom returned to the subject many years later in "Roles and Morality," an essay that appears in David Luban ed., The Good Lawyer 25 (1984). He advances a number of arguments that he reports as going "some appreciable distance in reducing or dissolving the initial worry" about the consequences of role-differentiated behavior. The arguments he mentions are that role-differentiated behavior will yield better overall moral outcomes than ad hoc judgments; that the expectations of those to be benefited by such behavior ought to count in arriving at judgment; and that the benefits conferred by role-differentiated behavior often are the trade-off for certain requirements imposed on the beneficiaries of that behavior. Nevertheless, Professor Wasserstrom concludes that he still has "certain nagging dissatisfactions" about efforts to put his worries to rest. Id. at 34.

NOTE: *The Model Code of Professional Responsibility and the Model Rules of Professional Conduct*

The subject of the professional responsibility of lawyers has been receiving increasing attention during the past two decades, from the general public as well as within the profession, and a good deal of substantive law has developed to deal with its problems. That substantive law has been growing increasingly more complex and sophisticated as lawyers, courts, and commentators have begun to analyze the ramifications of the various general principles in the context of many different situations in which lawyers find themselves.

Most jurisdictions now have formal statements of the rules governing the conduct of their members. As of August 1983, every state and the District of Columbia, in one form or another, had adopted, at least in part, the Model Code of Professional Responsibility as substantive law to govern the conduct of lawyers. In most states the adoption was by formal act of the highest court of the state. In some states, there was a combination of action by either court or legislature, and state bar association. California has had a unique combination of court rules and statutes that govern lawyers' conduct.

The Model Code of Professional Responsibility was drafted for the profession and adopted by the American Bar Association in 1969. It replaced the former Canons of Ethics, which had been promulgated by the ABA in 1908 and amended several times subsequently. In many states the Canons of Ethics had been formally adopted, either by statute or by pronouncement of the highest state court, sometimes with local modifications, as stating the principles governing the practice of law in that jurisdiction. In most of the other states the Canons were recognized as a source of guidance to practitioner and court, although not formally adopted.

The Canons of Ethics themselves were based on a code of ethics, the first of its kind in the United States, that was promulgated by the Alabama State Bar Association in 1887. Before that, principles of professional responsibility were part of the common law of the profession or the common law or even the statutory law of a particular jurisdiction and enforced as such in the courts. There was a moderate amount of literature devoted to matters of professional responsibility in the nineteenth century. See William B. Moore, Dark Ages or Enlightenment? A Survey of Legal Ethics in Theory and Practice in the United States Between the Years 1825 and 1905 (unpublished manuscript in the Harvard Law School Library 1975) and Brian Shaw, A Survey of Legal Ethics in the Nineteenth Century (unpublished manuscript in the Harvard Law School Library 1980). The best-known discussions of principles of legal ethics were David Hoffman's Professional Deportment, published in his book, A Course of Legal Study (1817), and George Sharswood's lectures to the Law Class of the University of Pennsylvania published in 1854 under the title of Professional Ethics. Sharswood was a well-known lawyer and teacher and later a justice of the Pennsylvania Supreme Court. See Dickson, "George Sharswood," in 6 Great American Lawyers 121 (William Draper Lewis ed. 1909). His book was widely regarded as authoritative throughout the nineteenth century, and the Alabama Code of Ethics drew heavily on both the Sharswood and Hoffman works. It is interesting to reflect upon the changes in the profession and in the society it serves that engendered the reduction of the general "common law" principles of professional responsibility first to a written statement of principles in the Canons of Ethics and then to the much more detailed statement of rules of conduct in the Model Code of Professional Responsibility. See the brief discussion of the development of the Canons of Ethics in Henry S. Drinker, Legal Ethics 23-26 (1953).

The old Canons of Ethics were quite brief — 47 Canons that could be printed on four and a half pages and could be read, if not completely understood in all their ramifications, in a few minutes. With brevity goes generality, and a constant complaint about the Canons was that they were not much help to the lawyer who needed guidance in a particular case. Some guidance had been given in the form of case law and the written opinions of the Committee on Professional Ethics of the American Bar Association and similar committees at the state and local levels.

It was thought by many, however, that the Canons themselves needed to be rewritten. In 1964, at the request of its president, later Justice Lewis F. Powell, the American Bar Association appointed a committee to undertake the task. In 1969, the committee produced a new Model Code of Professional Responsibility, which was adopted by the House of Delegates, the decision-making body of the American Bar Association. The ABA thereafter amended the Model Code several times.

Shortly after the Model Code was promulgated, the involvement of so many lawyers in Watergate focused the attention of the public and the profession on lawyers' conduct. In addition, a number of substantive problems, especially conflict of interest and confidentiality, became part of the staple of lawyers' daily routine. Moreover, decisions of the Supreme Court held a number of the profession's rules relating to the provision of legal services unconstitutional. All these factors combined with a variety of particular criticisms to lead many people to conclude that the Model Code of Professional Responsibility was inadequate for the needs of the profession. Therefore, in 1977 the ABA appointed a Commission on Evaluation of Professional Standards "to undertake a comprehensive rethinking of the ethical premises and problems" of the legal profession.

This commission, which became known as the Kutak Commission, concluded that a new code was needed. Unlike the effort that produced the Model Code, the Kutak Commission's work was involved in controversy from the start. The controversy reflected the change in thinking in the profession and in the general public about problems of professional responsibility. The drafters of the Model Code worked largely in secret and their product was adopted by the ABA and in the states largely without controversy. Most lawyers still believed then that "legal ethics" was a matter of knowing right from wrong, and they further believed that the rules of professional conduct didn't affect their practices very much at all. Watergate, disqualification motions for conflict of interest, the debate over whistle blowing and presentation of perjured testimony, and Supreme Court decisions on advertising, solicitation, minimum fee schedules, and group legal services have ended that perception.

Thus the work of the Kutak Commission was involved in substantial debate among lawyers and in the press from the moment it issued its first tentative discussion draft in 1980. Indeed, the Kutak Commission encouraged debate about the issues it was dealing with. The debate and the criticism were fierce, and in response the Commission modified many of its positions, especially those with respect to mandatory pro bono service by lawyers and the confidentiality obligation. Indeed, its final recommendations with respect to the latter were rejected in substantial part by the House of Delegates and new provisions were substituted. Finally, in August 1983, the ABA adopted the Model Rules of Professional Conduct and recommended their adoption by state and federal courts. Throughout this book, the term Model Code will indicate the 1969 document, as amended, and Model Rules the 1983 document.

As noted previously, action of the ABA by itself has no effect on lawyers' obligations. It is only governmental adoption or at least formal declaration by a court that the provisions of the Model Code or Model Rules are to be looked to for guidance that gives either proposal any authority. A great many states have adopted the Model Rules, although most of the adopting states have amended them in some respects because, as we shall see later in this book, some provisions of the Model Rules continue to be quite controversial. The Model Code has been retained in a great many states, including some of the larger jurisdictions, and it remains to be seen whether the Model Rules will eventually displace the Model Code as the basic guidelines of professional conduct.

Special note should be taken of the situation in the federal courts. Some federal courts have explicitly adopted the governing rules of professional responsibility of the jurisdiction in which they sit. In those courts adoption of the Model Code or Model Rules automatically follows the local practice. Other jurisdictions have not formally adopted a body of professional responsibility law but typically state, when an issue arises, that they look to the Model Code or Model Rules for guidance. See, for example, p. 44 n.2.

A word about format. The drafters of the Model Code and the Model Rules sought to modernize the professional rules and to be more helpful to practitioners by providing much more specific and detailed rules than the drafters of the former Canons of Ethics had done. In attempting to remedy the perceived defects of the Canons, the drafters of the Model Code and Model Rules have transformed a brief document into a book that cannot be read in a few minutes. In fact, it cannot be read consecutively from beginning to end unless one has extraordinary powers of concentration. In concept, the Model Code and Model Rules are both more like textbooks designed to be used by a lawyer with a problem than a statement to be read at once in its entirety.

The drafters of the Model Code and Model Rules chose different drafting techniques. The Model Code is divided into three parts, Canons, Ethical Considerations, and Disciplinary Rules. The drafters' Preliminary Statement sets forth the purpose of this division:

> The Canons are statements of axiomatic norms, expressing in general terms the standards of professional conduct expected of lawyers in their relationships with the public, with the legal system, and with the legal profession. They embody the general concepts from which the Ethical Considerations and the Disciplinary Rules are derived.
>
> The Ethical Considerations are aspirational in character and represent

the objectives toward which every member of the profession should strive. They constitute a body of principles upon which the lawyer can rely for guidance in many specific situations.

The Disciplinary Rules, unlike the Ethical Considerations, are mandatory in character. The Disciplinary Rules state the minimum level of conduct below which no lawyer can fall without being subject to disciplinary action.

In the design of the Code, the nine general statements of principle called Canons were cast in such general language that while they may be useful as statements of ideals, they are not likely to be much help to the lawyer with a problem. One might quarrel with the notion that they are "statements of axiomatic norms." Some of them may be self-evident or universally accepted principles, but some are not. "A Lawyer Should Avoid Even the Appearance of Professional Impropriety" (Canon 9) is a statement that cannot be made without so many qualifications that the principle is in danger of being swallowed by them. The same problem exists with other Canons.

The crucial division in the Model Code is between the Disciplinary Rules, the mandatory minimum standards of conduct, and the Ethical Considerations, the aspirational objectives of the profession. The fact is, however, that there is no such clear-cut division in the content and function of these two parts of the Model Code. Sometimes the Ethical Considerations are phrased as if they are aspirational, sometimes as if they are interpretive, and sometimes one simply cannot tell. What one can tell, however, is that it is the Disciplinary Rules and not the Ethical Considerations that are the substantive law in those jurisdictions that have adopted the Model Code and that we should not make the mistake of treating them as equivalents.

The format of the Model Rules is quite different. The drafters dropped the distinction between mandatory and aspirational conduct that characterized the Model Code in favor of a Restatement, or Uniform Commercial Code, format of black-letter law and interpretive Comments. This format should avoid some of the confusion created by the Model Code's format but will bring problems where the Comments strike out on their own, as they frequently do. It does not seem enough to say, as the Scope note does, that the "Comments are intended as guides to interpretation, but the text of each Rule is authoritative." A prime example of a troublesome Comment is discussed in the confidentiality materials at pp. 211–213.

One other matter should be mentioned. Before the Model Code, courts adopted a rather relaxed attitude toward the wording of the Canons of Ethics. Commonly they would say, if circumstances seemed to warrant it, that the Canons stated general principles, did not envisage all possible fact situations, and were not intended to be read like statutes.

The elaborateness of the Model Code and the Model Rules and the formats chosen (Disciplinary Rule and Ethical Consideration or Rule and Comment) make them look more like statutes. When necessary courts have occasionally, but not always, interpreted the model Code quite freely. See p. 119. It remains to be seen whether courts and disciplinary bodies will regard themselves as free to interpret the provisions of Model Code and Model Rules as creatively as they interpreted the old Canons of Ethics. See J. P. Foley & Co. v. Vanderbilt, 523 F.2d 1357, 1359 (2d Cir. 1975) (Gurfein, J. concurring).

CHARLES FRANKEL,† BOOK REVIEW, THE CODE OF PROFESSIONAL RESPONSIBILITY

43 U. Chi. L. Rev. 874 (1976)

I

It is a convention of the public dialogue today that Watergate and attendant scandals have created a crisis of public confidence in the moral integrity of lawyers. Probably this is so. But why should Watergate have had such an effect? Many lawyers did honor to themselves as the affair unfolded, and its eventual outcome revealed the powers of self-correction latent in American legal institutions. More to the point, Watergate was not the American public's first introduction to the duplicities of lawyers; these are among the oldest themes of American humor and folk wisdom. Watergate has a certain uniqueness, of course, because in this affair lawyers at the very top of the federal government engaged in forms of misconduct not merely crude and careless of the law but hostile to the fundamental spirit of constitutional processes. But it can hardly be said that Watergate revealed facts of life about the legal profession of which either lawyers or the American public had been unaware.

Why, then, its shock effect? The reason, I suspect, lies not in the new knowledge Watergate brought but in the old knowledge it made impossible any longer to suppress from consciousness. Watergate brought to the surface a condition of ethical malaise and confusion within the legal profession of such long standing that it can well be called chronic — a condition of which many have been cognizant, and not least the leaders of the legal profession itself. Doubts about the ethics of lawyers, indeed, have gone far deeper than doubts that individual practitioners live up to the rules which the legal profession has accepted as guides for professional conduct. The doubts have focused on the very significance, the

†Old Dominion Professor of Philosophy and Public Affairs, Columbia University School of Law.

practicality, the meaning and coherence of these rules, and, indeed, of any rules that might be substituted in their place.

The history of the adoption of codes of legal ethics in the United States suggests the caution with which lawyers have approached the business of formulating such rules.[1] In 1854 Judge George Sharswood published a series of lectures for lawyers under the title An Essay on Professional Ethics. In 1887, thirty-three years later, the Alabama State Bar Association officially adopted a Code of Ethics based in part on Judge Sharswood's lectures. In 1908 the American Bar Association, taking its lead from the Alabama Code, officially adopted thirty-two Canons of Legal Ethics. Twenty years later, in 1928, and then again in 1933 and in 1937, special committees of the ABA ventured the opinion that these Canons needed revision. Seventeen years later, in 1954, a committee created by the American Bar Foundation at the request of the ABA reiterated that judgment. But it was not until 1964 that the ABA, at the request of its President, Lewis Powell, created the Special Committee on Evaluation of Ethical Standards, which carried the task of revision through to completion and recommended a new Code of Professional Responsibility. . . .

This is not a record of unseemly haste. . . . Why this reluctance of the professions to deal formally with problems of professional ethics? Is it simply the desire to enjoy professional privileges and ignore professional responsibilities? Perhaps, but I suspect there is more. The cause lies not only in bad will but in puzzled intelligence. For there are difficult questions which haunt any effort to frame an ethical code. Is an ethical code something which is better left informal and unwritten? Are the problems that professionals encounter too subtle for fixed rules? Can such rules be formulated if there is no agreement on the basic functions of the profession? Can there be such agreement if the members of the profession disagree, as they have a right to do, on underlying political, social and philosophic issues? It is with questions like these that the formulators of a code of professional ethics must ultimately grapple, and it is not surprising that they have repeatedly found their task more formidable than they had expected.

This, certainly, is what the Special Committee on Evaluation of Ethical Standards, which produced the new Code of Professional Responsibility, discovered. It worked for five years before it reached agreement, and it completed its task with a quite different conception of its mission than that with which it began. In the words of its chairman:

> A completely changed document was not envisioned by either those who gave the Committee its task or the Committee members themselves. . . .

1. See generally H. Drinker, Legal Ethics (1953).

The initial efforts of the Committee were directed toward reorganizing the concepts included in the Canons. . . . The Committee encountered many doubts as to what much of the language meant, which in turn led to detailed analysis of what in fact the duties of a lawyer are and should be. And so our original efforts merely to reorganize and reword the Canons became an extended search for the full meaning of professional responsibility in the context of modern-day society, a search that culminated in the formulation of the Code.[11]

The new Code of Professional Responsibility was produced by a committee that understood the magnitude and difficulty of the task to which it had been assigned. It produced a Code that represents a considerable improvement on the older Canons.

But has it succeeded in spelling out "the full meaning of professional responsibility in the context of modern-day society"? It is impossible in the scope of a brief article to review each of the specific rules and recommendations which compose the Code of Professional Responsibility. I propose instead to focus more broadly on the fundamental intellectual distinction on which the Code is based — the distinction between "ethical considerations" and "disciplinary rules" — and to scrutinize the adequacy of its rationale.

II

The most obvious difference between the new Code and the older Canons of Legal Ethics is that the new Code has a tighter and more logical structure. The thirty-two old Canons have been reduced to nine. These "are statements of axiomatic norms, expressing in general terms the standards of professional conduct expected of lawyers in their relationship with the public, with the legal system, and with the legal profession."

The actual impact of these nine canons, however, is spelled out in the "ethical considerations" and "disciplinary rules" which ae attached to each of them, and it is this apparatus of "considerations" and "rules" which represents the significant departure in the Code's mode of attack on the problems of legal ethics. The "ethical considerations" are described as "aspirational in character." They express "objectives" towards which every lawyer should strive, and enunciate principles by which he should be guided when he has moral choices to make. In contrast, the "disciplinary rules" are mandatory. They state "the minimum level of

---

11. Wright, The Code of Professional Responsibility: Its History and Objectives, 24 Ark. L. Rev. 1, 5-6 (1970).

conduct below which no lawyer can fall without being subject to discpli-nary action."

As Lon Fuller[17] and Samuel Stumpf[18] have argued, this distinction between standards of excellence and standards of minimal performance is in many contexts an indispensable one. Among the values which so-ciety has an interest in promoting are some which cannot be made the objects of direct command. To order people to be heroes, for example, or to command them to be charitable or forgiving or dispassionate, is to impose obligations which most people cannot realistically be expected to meet and which can expose them, if a serious effort to enforce such norms is undertaken, to punishing surveillance and tyranny. The law, in concert with other social institutions like the family, school, and church, can provide assistance and encouragement to such values, for example, by giving tax incentives favoring charity. But it can attach direct sanc-tions to them only at excessive cost. They must be seen as "aspirations," not legal duties. The new Code of Professional Responsibility is based on belief that a similar distinction between aspirations and minimal du-ties is useful for the governance of the legal profession itself. . . .

Is it [also] possible that . . . the authors of the Code had in mind not a distinction between a morality of aspiration and a morality of duty but something rather different — a distinction between an ethic of broad guidelines as against an ethic of rigid imperatives? In making their dis-tinction between "ethical considerations" and "disciplinary rules," the authors of the Code have touched upon the classic jurisprudential prob-lem of determining the proper line between "law" and "morality." On what basis do we distinguish between those areas of human conduct fit for regulation by an apparatus of determinate rules and punitive sanc-tions and those areas which should be regulated by less rigid and more informal methods? This large issue is buried, unless I am mistaken, in the Code's distinction between "ethical considerations" and "disciplinary rules."

There are at least three reasons for distinguishing between "law" and "morals." One is the reason the Code makes explicit: some values can only be projected as "aspirational." We cannot, for example, look to the comparatively precise rules and attached sanctions of the law to enforce such standards of high morality as "Love thy neighbor" without risking excessive regimentation and invasions of individual autonomy. If we dis-tinguish between "law" and "morality" on this basis, we look to the law — or, within a professional code, to "disciplinary rules" — only to en-

---

17. L. Fuller, The Morality of Law (1964) (distinguishing between the morality of duty and morality of aspiration).
18. S. Stumpf, Morality and the Law (1966) (distinguishing between "legal order" and "moral order").

force minimal obligations. As regards the "aspirational," the law — or a professional code — can try to give encouragement, but no more.

A second and independent distinction is also often embedded in the comparison between "law" and "morality." There are domains of conduct — e.g., the use of violence — with regard to which it is relatively easy to formulate rules free from undue vagueness and to expect that there will be few conditions excusing departures from them. At the other extreme, there are domains of conduct — e.g., relations between friends, between parents and children, between professional colleagues — where circumstances vary widely, where qualities like affection, integrity, imagination, sympathy, and judgment are the primary desiderata, and where hard-and-fast rules are likely to be encumbrances. To distinguish between "law" and "morals," or between "disciplinary rules" and "ethical considerations," with this contrast in mind carries implications different from a distinction resting on the contrast between ideal aspirations and minimally decent conduct. It is not because "ethical considerations" aim higher than "disciplinary rules," but because they deal with questions less easily codified, that they are to be treated as different. Lawyers face many issues of a subtle or highly exceptional character which call not for simple "dos" and "don'ts," but for an enlarged and more sensitive consciousness of the variety of values at stake.

The decision of the authors of the Code to place many rules that might otherwise seem minimal in the more fluid category of "ethical considerations" can be explained, I believe, only on these grounds. But the failure of the Code to articulate its rationale here leads to a generic ambiguity, for the distinction between rules that are more fluid and rules that are less so is not a categorical one; even more than the distinction between aspirations and minimal obligations, it is a matter of degree. The point at which we draw the line between an informal and hortatory "morality" on the one side and a system of formal rules and coercive sanctions on the other depends on a pragmatic judgment as to where the weight of the unforeseen and the exceptional is likely to be so heavy as to make formal rules inefficacious. All rules, not only moral rules, have a penumbra of indeterminacy around them. To take the standard illustration, does an ordinance prohibiting vehicles in a public park apply to baby carriages? Further, there are always excusing conditions in which it is patently unfair to apply a given rule, and the list of these excusing conditions cannot be fully set out in advance.

Yet just as these considerations do not justify turning homicide laws or speeding laws into mere statements of aspiration, they do not adequately rationalize in all instances the merely "aspirational" character ascribed to the Code's ethical considerations. Ethical Consideration 7-16, for example, states that when a lawyer appears before a legislative body, either in connection with legislation or in an investigatory or impeachment proceeding, "he should identify himself and his client, if identity of his client is not privileged." Ethical Consideration 4-6 states that "a lawyer should not attempt to sell a law practice as a going business because, among other reasons, to do so would involve the disclosure of confidences and secrets." I presume that such rules are not made "disciplinary rules" because exceptions and excuses can be imagined which limit their applicability. But if they were treated as disciplinary rules, it would be possible over time to build up an analogue to case law which would gradually fill out and make more precise the obligations they do and do not impose.

Why was this alternative not chosen? So far as I can guess, it is because still a third reason for distinguishing between "law" and "morality" is implicit in the Code. We sometimes distinguish between the two not on the ground either of the higher aspirations or greater fluidity of "morality" but on the ground of its comparative insusceptibility to reasonable or just modes of firm enforcement. Accordingly, the sanctions we wish to use to enforce morality must depend more on the hortatory and persuasive than on threats to life, liberty, or property. The problem of censorship is an example. The case against censorship can hardly be that it is unrealistic to try to prohibit the publication of subversive or pornographic materials. These have been suppressed fairly effectively in many societies. Nor does the case rest only on the vagueness of the criteria defining the subversive or the pornographic. If a lawmaker is willing to paint with a big enough brush and doesn't particularly care about the good that is sacrificed with the bad, he can be reasonably clear about what he means to forbid. But the case against censorship lies precisely in this tyranny of the big brush. To trust in censorship you have to be blind or indifferent to the probable stupidities, malice, and inflexibility with which the censorship laws will be enforced. In brief, a major reason for leaving certain matters to moral suasion is that we think they can be regulated by the blunt instruments of the law only at great risk to liberty, fairness, and other values.

The formulators of the new Code of Professional Responsibility did not explicitly make this point. But they were influenced, I suspect, by a feeling that the disciplinary procedures available to the bar are not sufficiently trustworthy and do not possess the necessary general credibility and legitimacy to bear a heavy burden of enforcement duties. In consequence, they leaned hard on their category of "ethical considerations." They may well have made the prudent choice. The ideological and political differences in the nation at large have grown more acute, and the currents of distrust affecting all authority-laden institutions are considerable. The legal profession has not been, and cannot be, insulated from its larger environment. Under the circumstances, a decision to adopt only a minimum baggage of "disciplinary rules" is intelligible.

Nevertheless, the logic of the decision needs to be spelled out. To opt for exhortation as against definite sanctions requires a judgment in which the harm done by potentially increased violation of norms is weighed against the dangers implicit in close regulation and the use of an organized enforcement machinery. And this judgment depends, in turn, not only on an estimate of the probabilities of given risks but on a judgment of the relative importance of the social values involved in one alternative as against the other. It was once considered better, for example, to be on the good will of employers and the benefits of free individual enterprise than to bet on closer regulation of the conditions of labor. The social judgment as to the wisdom of this bet has changed. In relation to the behavior of lawyers, the Code of Professional Responsibility makes its bet on lawyers' judgment and good will. Is this bet the wise one? Many in and out of the legal profession will disagree. If it is to be adequately defended, the Code requires a general discussion of the function of lawyers in society and of the relative weight to be ascribed to different social values. In the absence of such a discussion, many of the specific judgments made in the Code may seem, if not arbitrary, at least suspect.

III

In 1934, Justice Harlan Fiske Stone, in his address on The Public Influence of the Bar, said that the legal profession's "canons of ethics for the most part are generalizations designed for an earlier era." The need, he said, was to "pass beyond the petty details of form and manners which have been so largely the subject of our Codes of Ethics, to more fundamental considerations of the way in which our professional activities affect the welfare of society as a whole."[24] "The welfare of society as a whole" is a sweeping term. Can a profession composed of people who hold radically different political and moral outlooks come to an agreement about its meaning? Probably not, if what is sought is an official doctrine to which all must swear fealty. But the function of a professional code, as the authors of the new Code recognized implicitly, is not to provide practioners with textbook maxims. It is to sensitize them to the scope, depth and complexity of the commitments they have undertaken in entering the profession.

The value of a code, therefore, lies less in its specific "oughts" and "musts" than in its utility as a catalyst for a continuing discourse on the profession's *raison d'etre*. From this point of view the most conspicuous shortcoming of the new Code is its lack of a catalytic general discussion of the relation of the practice of law to "the welfare of society as a whole." Its authors have quoted Justice Stone's words approvingly, but they have not taken the cue. The new Code, although it is more sensitive to moral dilemmas and more ambitious in its expectations than the old Canons,

24. Quoted in Preface, ABA Code of Professional Responsibility (1975).

is offered to the legal profession and the public in a form detached from an explicit consideration of the law's major functions in contemporary society and of the general context in which ethical problems arise for modern lawyers. If there had been such a discussion, to what problems might it have been addressed? I can merely suggest a few.

(1) Lawyers are professionals, and share with other professionals modes of conduct that clash with normal rules of everyday morality. One of the reasons for the widely-held view that morality is in a peculiar state of decline today and that a dangerous "relativism" has taken over is simply the proliferation in our society of specialized professions, like the law, which have distinctive functions and therefore distinctive ethical norms. What is seen as the "decline" of ethics is in part the emergence of multiple ethical systems, attuned to the performance of tasks more intricate and impersonal than those to which the great sweeping principles of traditional ethical codes apply. But when the specialized codes depart too frequently and radically from commonplace notions of acceptable behavior, demoralizing tensions are created within individuals and in society at large. A consequence is a disposition to look upon both professional and general moral codes with indifference or contempt.

Is there a remedy? An essential element in any remedy, though of course not a sufficient one, is a process of continuing philosophic criticism and interpretation conducted within the legal profession and between it and the outside world. The purpose of such a process, on one side, would be to explain the legitimate differences that exist between professional and popular codes, and, on the other, to correct professional or popular codes when the clash between them is indefensible. What I describe, of course, is simply moral philosophy in one of its classic forms — reflection on moral norms and the critical reconstruction of them to restore their coherence. The present Code of Professional Responsibility, because it is not embedded in an explicit examination of the issues raised by the differences between professional and general ethical codes, seems incomplete; and it leaves untouched one major cause for the public distrust of lawyers and for lawyers' distrust of themselves.

(2) Over and above the specialized roles played by members of the professions, another circumstance also invites public suspicion. In the United States the professions have been surrounded by a democratic and egalitarian ethos. During the nineteenth century many states in the Union refused to license doctors and lawyers. The rationale was simple enough: by what right did lawyers or doctors claim to know something that other people did not know? Was their claim to special knowledge not simply a way of shutting off competition and exercising monopolistic control of the market? In fact, when the American Medical Association was formed in 1847, it adopted a code of ethics as part of its campaign for greater public respect for trained physicians.

Much of the new Code for lawyers can be understood in a similar

·

context. Of its nine canons, five are directly related to the defense of the
profession against competitors and detractors and to the establishment
of its claim to be accorded special rights and powers.[26] Indeed, so much
of the Code is devoted to matters of this sort that a malicious critic might
question whether Code is not really more concerned with the protection
of a guild's privileges than with the advancement of the public interest.
The indictment, I believe, is unjustified. But the indictment is invited
because the Code says little or nothing, except by implication, about two
basic issues: one, the special ways in which values like liberty and impartial justice require distinctive institutions manned by people with distinctive professional obligations; two, the dangers of converting this special
role into a kind of professional imperialism.

An overhanging problem for lawyers today is whether their methods
of dealing with human problems are invariably the appropriate ones.
We have become a litigious society, attempting to settle more and more
of our problems in the courts, and using adversary methods even in
settings like universities where collegiality has traditionally been thought
to be a primary desideratum. But surely it is a professional conceit, if
not a kind of magical thinking, to suppose that all, or most, social problems can be compressed into the forms of an adversary system in which
there are only two sides, one of which has to be right. What services can
lawyers perform as negotiators, arbitrators, bargainers, compromisers?
What services can they perform by stepping aside and allowing the better informed to make the fundamental decisions? For example, why is
fault in malpractice decided by judges and juries, and not by doctors?
Beyond this, do lawyers have an obligation to explore more systematically the social problems that might better be solved by leaving them to
the political process? Further, what materials and questions ought to be
introduced into law schools to sensitize future lawyers to the limits as
well as the strengths of the law as a system of social control? So long as
such issues are not conspicuous in the legal profession's examination of
itself, its ethical preoccupations are likely to seem distorted and somewhat provincial.

(3) Systematic examination is needed as well of the implications for
legal ethics of the greatly altered setting in which lawyers now practice
their profession. The preoccupations of the old Canons still lie heavy in
the new Code, and they are the preoccupations of a profession composed overwhelmingly of individual practitioners serving individual
clients. Only about a third of all lawyers today, however, are individual

26. Canon 1: "A Lawyer Should Assist in Maintaining the Integrity and Competence
of the Legal Profession." Canon 2: "A Lawyer Should Assist the Legal Profession in
Fulfilling Its Duty to Make Legal Counsel Available." Canon 3: "A Lawyer Should Assist
in Preventing the Unauthorized Practice of Law." Canon 8: "A Lawyer Should Assist in
Improving the Legal System." Canon 9: "A Lawyer Should Avoid Even the Appearance
of Professional Impropriety."

practitioners; about twenty-five percent work for government or for private corporations; and the remainder, for the most part, practice law in collective settings, working for large firms and serving clients who are not individuals but legally created entities.[28] What are the responsibilities of individuals in such settings? What are the ethical issues, for example, when lawyers serve not as counselors to a corporation but as involved participants in its daily activities? What view of their responsibilities should lawyers hold, to take another example, when more and more of their work is devoted not to guiding individuals through a network of essentially settled rules but to changing the law to fit their client's or employing organization's needs? These are the kinds of issues, I suspect, that bear heavily on the consciences of young lawyers today and lead to their disaffection from their chosen profession. The obligations of the lawyer have become elusive in an environment in which rules from a simpler time still dominate ethical reflection.

This is a mere checklist of important problems, and an incomplete one, but it will suggest what I venture to think is a necessary supplement to the promulgation of a detailed Code. It is the emergence of a body of critical discourse on basic problems affecting the sense of purpose of the legal profession. The Code of Professional Responsibility is a useful point of departure for such a discussion, but its principal potential utility will be lost if the discussion remains at the starting line it has defined. For in the legal profession, as in most other domains of life, the elevation of standards comes in the main from neither exhortation nor codification. It comes from renewed attention to first principles, from a freshened awareness of the changed problems people confront, and from a sustained debate about the best ways to deal with them.

NOTE

Professor Frankel's review of the Model Code is a balanced, sympathetic look at the work of its drafters that attempts to set it in a larger context of the world of law, ethics, and morality. He raises a number of issues that are major themes in a course on professional responsibility and therefore deserve to be introduced early. The first is one that philosophers discuss under the label of role-differentiated morality: What is the justification for exempting lawyers from the ordinary moral rules that apply to everyone else in particular situations? Professor Wasserstrom addressed the same issue with a different point of view, and this book returns to the issue in several other places.

A second matter touched on by Professor Frankel is that of the special privileges enjoyed by the profession, its "monopoly" status. That also is

28. American Bar Foundation, The 1971 Lawyer Statistical Report 10-12 (1972).

an issue that infuses much of the following materials. A thoroughgoing attack on the former Canons of Ethics based on such a perception, which appeared in the first edition of this book but whose factual underpinning is now a little out of date, is Shuchman, Ethics and Legal Ethics: The Propriety of the Canons as a Group Moral Code, 37 Geo. Wash. L. Rev. 244 (1968). A modern version, but without the sociological examination of the profession, is Morgan, The Evolving Concept of Professional Responsibility, 90 Harv. L. Rev. 702 (1977). See also p. 745.

CHAPTER 2

REPRESENTATION OF CONFLICTING INTERESTS

Once a lawyer or law firm has more than one client, it must consider whether its present or past representations preclude it from taking on a new matter. Obviously, lawyers could not serve their function in anything like our present system of justice if they were to represent both the prosecution and the defense in a criminal case, or the buyer and the seller of goods in the trial of a breach of contract matter. But the issues are not so clear when the issue is whether different members of a firm may be on opposite sides of the same matter or whether a lawyer may oppose a former client when the matter involved in the new representation is not the same as that involved in the former representation.

Conflict of interest problems did not used to be regarded as presenting difficult problems for law firms. Now, however, the mounting use of the motion to disqualify opposing counsel in litigation, the growth in size of law firms, and the increasing amount and sophistication of the substantive law of conflict of interest have made the subject of paramount interest for anyone who practices law. Indeed, many law firms are now turning to complex computer programs to help them keep track of their cases and clients in order to be able to identify conflict problems more readily.

The following materials present a variety of situations in which conflict of interest problems occur. All involve to some extent considerations of the fiduciary principle, the loyalty owed to clients and would-be clients. But we should note that the fiduciary consideration is often a two-edged sword. Loyalty toward one client may suggest or even require rejection of another. But the rejected client may also have had demands of loyalty on the client, having spent much time, effort, and money on educating the lawyer about the complexities of the client's life or business only to be told that he or she must seek a new lawyer because of the law of professional responsibility. Conflict of interest problems also implicate other principles besides the fiduciary principle, such as the freedom of individuals to select their own lawyers and of lawyers to make their own assessment of what constitutes a conflict, or the principle of promoting economic efficiency by not increasing the costs of representation through rules that require hiring of new, uneducated counsel.

One problem for those charged with formulating the law of professional responsibility has been whether rules relating to conflict of interest should be codified, and if so, whether they should be codified at a fairly abstract level, leaving considerable leeway to lawyers as they decide how to resolve particular problems, or whether they should be stated as specifically as possible to guide and constrain lawyers' decisions.

Not considered in this chapter are conflict of interest problems in the context of group legal services. Those are considered separately in Chapter 9, which presents a variety of materials and specialized problems on that subject.

The organization of the materials of this chapter presents some difficulties, for it would be useful in discussing the earlier subsections to have some knowledge about the concluding subsections. Nevertheless, experience suggests that it is preferable to examine first the situations when a lawyer or law firm seeks to represent either simultaneously or successively clients with actual or potentially conflicting interests. That is where the substantive law developed first. In the last 15 years or so, consideration has been given to the possibility that the disqualification of a member of a law firm might not necessarily require the disqualification of the whole firm if the disqualified member were "screened off" from participation in the matter. That argument was first accepted, for policy reasons relating to maintaining the attractiveness of public service, in a number of cases involving former government employees joining private law firms. More recently, the argument has been increasingly made that policy reasons justify a similar result not only in cases of successive representation but also in cases involving simultaneous representation in the totally private law firm context. Considerations of these developments is postponed to the end of the chapter because of the difficulty of presenting the necessary materials earlier. The possibility of a "screening" defense, however, should be kept in mind as we proceed through the materials that develop the justifications for the substantive law of disqualification for conflict of interest.

A. SIMULTANEOUS REPRESENTATION — OPPOSING A CURRENT CLIENT

PROBLEM 1

Lawyer practices in a small town, which has three active practitioners. She is handling a title closing for Buyer when Grocer, a regular client, requests her to take action, including suit if necessary, against Buyer, who has run up a $400 bill. Lawyer is currently handling two small matters for Grocer and the other two lawyers in town are engaged on the opposite side of those matters. The nearest town in which there is another lawyer is 25 miles away, and Grocer states that it is not worth the amount of the claim for him to seek assistance there. What response does Lawyer make to Grocer's request?

PROBLEM 2

O, a partner in X, Y, and Z, is a specialist in oil and gas leases. Petroleum Co. comes to her to work out a complication that has arisen with one of its leases. While she is working on the matter, Oil Co. comes to X, who has always done its antitrust work, to start an antitrust action against Petroleum Co. The oil leases on which O is working have nothing to do with the antitrust action. The secretary to the executive committee, which is responsible for keeping track of new matters, puts the fact of the representation of, and against, Petroleum on the committee's agenda. What course of action should it follow? In the future should O be told to tell clients who bring specialized one-shot matters to her that the firm reserves the right to take matters against their interests or even against them on behalf of regular firm clients?

PROBLEM 3

D-1 and D-2 have been charged with housebreaking and grand larceny and wish you to represent them. They are partners in a gas station and long-time clients. Each insists that he is innocent, that at the time the crime was committed he was with another person, and that the case must be one of mistaken identity. Would you represent both? If you could obtain separate trials for D-1 and D-2, what effect would that have on your decision? Is your ability to represent both a proper factor to consider in making a decision whether to seek separate trials? In what capacity do you participate in that decision? Suppose that after you have undertaken the representation, you discover that the prosecution has a modest amount of evidence linking D-1 to the crime but very little linking D-2 to it. Does that change the situation? What do you do? Compare Campbell v. United States, 352 F.2d 359 (D.C. Cir. 1965) and People v. Keesee, 250 Cal. App. 2d 794, 58 Cal. Rptr. 780 (1967) with Holloway v. State, 32 Wis. 2d 559, 146 N.W.2d 441 (1966). See Starrs, Professional Responsibility, 5 Am. Crim. L.Q. 17, 18 (1966): "A frequent occasion for . . . antagonistic claims upon the lawyer arises in a conspiracy trial where two of the conspirators are represented by the same lawyer, who argues on behalf of one that which will convict the other. That the lawyer is representing conflicting interests is evident. That he may do so under the command of Canon 6 is not so clear. Yet, there is enough strongly worded dictum in enough cases [People v. Rocco, 209 Cal. 68, 285 P. 704 (1930); People v. Friedrich, 20 Ill. 2d 240, 169 N.E.2d 752 (1960); People v. Walsh, 28 Ill. 2d 405, 192 N.E.2d 843 (1963); In re Shuttle, 214 A.2d 48 (Vt. 1965)] for us to say that the constitutional right of an accused to counsel of his own choice supersedes and, indeed, overrides the ethical standard of Canon 6." A recent illustration of joint representation interfering with the constitutional guarantee of effective assistance of counsel is Holloway v. Arkansas, 435 U.S. 475 (1978). See also Cuyler v. Sullivan, 446 U.S. 335, 350 (1980), which held that a defendant who raised no objection at trial must demonstrate that a conflict of interest in a multiple representation case "adversely affected his lawyer's performance," and Wheat v. United States, 108 S. Ct. 1692 (1988), which upheld against a Sixth Amendment attack a district court's refusal to allow a defendant to substitute a co-defendant's counsel for his own when there was a conflict of interest, even though defendant was willing to waive it. But see Commonwealth v. Hodge, p. 51 n. 11, for a different conclusion from *Cuyler* under state law. If you decide that you should not represent both defendants in Problem 3, and D-2 says that he will get another lawyer, would you represent D-1? In that event, do you need D-2's consent to do so?

There has been a great deal of writing on the subject of multiple representation of criminal defendants in recent years, especially as prosecutors faced with the difficulty of bargaining with several defendants who have the same lawyer have pushed for more restrictive conflict rules in this situation. See Geer, Representation of Multiple Criminal Defendants, 62 Minn. L. Rev. 119 (1978); Lowenthal, Joint Representation in Criminal Cases, 64 Va. L. Rev. 939 (1978); see also Moore, Disqualification of an Attorney Representing Multiple Witnesses Before a Grand Jury, 27 UCLA L. Rev. 1 (1979) for discussion of a somewhat related problem.

PROBLEM 4

Parts Corporation and Auto Corporation are regular clients of X, Y, and Z. They are interested in negotiating a supply contract. It is expected that the negotiations will be lengthy and complicated. For many years Partner Q of the New York office has handled contracts work for Parts and Partner Z of the Washington office has done the same for Auto. Q has never worked on an Auto matter and Z has never worked on a Parts matter. Both Parts and Auto ask Q and Z to represent them in the negotiations. May Q and Z do so? Is there any kind of disclosure, other than the fact of representation of the other side by a partner, that Q and Z should make?

PROBLEM 5

The legislature in your state has passed a statute permitting silent prayer in public school classrooms at the start of each school day. You discover that different branches of your law firm have filed declaratory judgment suits in different county courts attacking and defending the constitutionality of the statute under the federal Constitution. May the firm handle both suits? Assume first that both sides consent and then that they do not. Would it make a difference if the two branches of the firm were located in Denver and Seattle but the Colorado and Washington statutes were identically worded? Is paragraph 8 of the Comment to Model Rule 1.7 sufficiently responsive to this issue? Would it make a difference if the issue on which the branches of the firm were on opposite sides involved an evidentiary matter in otherwise unrelated litigation, such as the reach of the attorney-client privilege to a low-level corporate employee?

1. The General Rule

At war in all of these Problems are the notion that effective representation means whole-hearted devotion to the interests of the client (and that may not be possible if the interests of two clients are in actual or potential conflict), and the notion that in many situations of potential or even actual conflict of interests independent representation of each party merely means added legal expense without commensurate benefit to the parties.

Canon 6 of the old Canons of Ethics dealt with the problem explicitly by stating that it was "unprofessional to represent conflicting interests, except by express consent of all concerned given after a full disclosure of the facts." Literally read, this seemed to mean that a lawyer could always represent conflicting interests if only he or she had disclosed the conflict or possibility of conflict to the clients and had received their consent. Courts and committees on ethics, however, frequently stated that Canon 6 was not meant to cover the whole problem and should not be read as if it were a statute. Such statements were made in the context of rulings that a particular conflict was so severe that a lawyer could not represent the parties even with consent after full disclosure. The former Canon also gave little theoretical content to the concept of "conflicting interest" except for the statement that "a lawyer represents conflicting interests when, in behalf of one client, it is his duty to contend for that which duty to another client requires him to oppose."

The Model Code of Professional Responsibility attempts to provide a more comprehensive treatment of conflict of interest in DR 5-105 and ECs 5-14–5-20 than was provided in the Canons. As originally promulgated and widely adopted, the prohibition contained in the Disciplinary Rules was not phrased in terms of "conflicting" or "differing" interests. Paragraphs (A) and (B) of DR 5-105 were worded solely in terms of the lawyer's independent professional judgment. The focus of the former Canons on the relationship of the clients to one another was introduced by the 1974 amendments, which added the test of likelihood of involvement in representing differing interests. The emphasis on clients' interests provides a more familiar and a more objective standard for lawyers. Note, however, that the prohibition has been broadened from that contained in the former Canons by use of the word "differing" instead of "conflicting" interests. Note also that the words "differing interests" are defined following DR 9 of the Model Code in a way that fuses the emphasis on the lawyer's judgment with the emphasis on the clients' interests, thus indicating that both are subcategories, or perhaps definitions, of the more abstract term "loyalty," which also appears in that definition. We should remember, however, that the 1974 amendment did not replace the Model Code's original test of preservation of independent judgment. It has merely added a new test to the original version, and both must now be met in any case of multiple employment.

In any situation where multiple employment occurs that falls within the prohibitions of DR 5-105(A) or (B), the multiple employment may still be undertaken if it meets the conditions of DR 5-105(C). That crucial section sets forth three conditions: (1) full disclosure of the possible effects of the multiple representation to all the clients, (2) consent by all the clients, and (3) it must be "obvious" that the lawyers can "adequately" represent the interests of each client.

Each of these conditions presents problems. What constitutes "full disclosure"? Must every remote possibility be mentioned? Must lawyers reveal all the details of their relationships with the other client, with other lawyers in the matter, and indeed must they psychoanalyze themselves for the benefit of their client if the information revealed might have some bearing on consent? As for consent itself, how does the lawyer know when consent is truly informed, uncoerced consent? Does the client ever need independent advice from another lawyer on the issue of consent? Is the consent coerced if the client consents in order to keep on the good side of the lawyer? And on the other hand, is the representation proper if the lawyer perceives a forbidden conflict but accepts multiple representation on the urgent pleading of all the clients, that is, if the "coercion" is by the client?

A purpose of the third condition is to deal with this latter situation. The premise of the provision is that the profession and society have a stake in representation of conflicting interests beyond the desires of the parties themselves, that there are situations where consent after full disclosure is insufficient to permit the representation. The wording of the provision has caused some difficulty. The first question is: "obvious" to whom, the particular lawyer or the "reasonable" lawyer? Most have assumed that the words impose the objective test of the reasonable lawyer. More problematic is the combination of the words "obvious" and "adequately represent." "Obvious" seems to tilt rather heavily against multiple representation in case of doubt. "Adequately represent," however, with its suggestion that something like "sufficiently," but less than "whole-heartedly" zealous (see Canon 7) representation may be possible in multiple representation cases, appears to tilt in the opposite direction. Not surprisingly, perhaps, many courts and ethics committees dealing with problems under DR 5-105(C) have preferred to find solutions by strict interpretation of the disclosure and consent requirements instead of by elaboration of the objective test required by the third condition. Sometimes, however, the latter issue cannot be avoided. See Unified Sewerage Authority v. Jelco, Inc., p. 52.

The general conflict of interest rule of the Model Rules, Rule 1.7, follows the conceptual framework of the Model Code but the drafters sought a formulation to reduce the ambiguities of the Model Code's wording. The same three tests are present although the word "consultation," which is a defined term, replaces the Model Code's "disclosure." The most important change is the explicit adoption of the "reasonable" lawyer test as the sole statement of the objective condition that must be met. It remains to be seen whether the elimination of the words "obvious" and "adequately represents" is seen as effecting some relaxation of the rule to permit more multiple representation or whether it is seen simply as the sensible codification of the former, relatively strict rule.

A major difficulty for lawyers attempting to deal with problems of representation of multiple parties is the abstract quality of DR 5-105 and Model Rule 1.7. The text is not much help in resolving particular difficult cases or even in identifying the particular problems with which they are designed to deal. The Ethical Considerations of the Model Code and the Comment to the Model Rule give some insights but not in any connected way and, if anything, emphasize the essentially ad hoc nature of the resolution of each situation. The concerns of both rules are with the lawyer's obligation not to reveal or misuse confidential information and with the lawyer's obligation of loyalty to clients, looked at from the perspective both of the clients' situations and the lawyer's independent judgment. The Model Code (in Canon 4) and the Model Rules (in Rule 1.6) speak directly to confidentiality but take loyalty rather for granted, perhaps assuming familiarity with the general principles of fiduciary duty owed by an agent to a principal. What we mean when we say a lawyer owes a "duty of loyalty" to a client is at the core of our notion of what kind of adversary system we have. There is no obvious answer. The British system, from which ours is derived, has a very different view of the issue insofar as client representation is concerned. See Mellinkoff, The Conscience of a Lawyer (1973).

At all events, it is important in resolving questions of conflict of interest to keep in mind what interests are being served by the particular principles being advocated. It is not enough to invoke the biblical injunction from Matthew 6:24, as so many courts are fond of doing, that "No man can serve two masters." Of course a lawyer can serve two masters, i.e., two clients. They do it all the time. The question is to identify the problem with such representation in a particular case with specificity and to make an estimate of the likelihood and seriousness of harm to one or more of the relevant interests from proposed concurrent representation.

For example, consider the situation when a lawyer (L) is asked to represent a client, C-2, in connection with a matter in which he is already representing C-1, and the proposed representation is adverse. Taking on C-2 would affect L's representation of C-1 in three ways. First, there is the potentiality that advancing C-2's interests would harm C-1's interests in the very matter in which L was hired by C-1. That would be disloyal. Second, there is the possibility that representing C-2 would cause L to diminish his efforts on behalf of C-1. That would also be disloyal, although one could characterize the action as a threat to L's competence. Third, there is the substantial possibility that confidential information of C-1 would be abused in the service of C-2. That would violate the specific aspect of the duty of loyalty that the professional rules deal with under the heading of confidentiality (DR 4 and Model Rule 1.6).

However, let us change the example so that there are two completely unrelated matters. L represents only C-1 in matter one and only C-2 in matter two. C-1's interests in matter two, which are adverse to C-2, are represented by someone else. Then the analysis is different. Since the matters are different, there will probably not be any problem of abuse of confidential information. Likewise there is no problem of disloyalty from harming C-1's interests in matter number one. By definition, success for C-2 in matter two has nothing to do with matter one. Diminishment of L's efforts on behalf of C-1 in matter one by reason of being adverse to C-1 in matter two is still a possibility but somewhat less obvious than it was in the first example.

But there is another aspect to the loyalty problem here. L has put himself in a position where he can do real harm to C-1 in matter two. Indeed, if the matter is litigated, he may even personally subject C-1 to unpleasant cross-examination. The effect of such action, especially in litigation, is likely to disrupt the attorney-client relation between L and C-1 in matter one. Hence the action of L in taking on C-2 in matter two in such a case can be analyzed in terms of breach of duty of loyalty, both from the "differing interests" client-oriented perspective ("my lawyer is attacking me") and from the likely effect on the lawyer's independent professional judgment and zealousness on behalf of the client.*

These examples and analyses of problems of representation of conflicting interests could be multiplied indefinitely. They are offered here as illustrations of the need to analyze each specific fact situation to understand why the prohibitions should or should not be applied in a particular case.

Aside from the duty of loyalty and the issue of confidential communications, courts also occasionally refer to one other factor in deciding conflict of interest questions, what Canon 9 of the Model Code refers to as the "appearance of impropriety." The expression is meant to evoke the potential erosion of confidence in the profession that may occur if its members are seen in situations that carry potential for improper conduct even if in particular cases there is no actual misconduct. The drafters of Canon 9 offer three examples of the "appearance of impropriety" that warrant disciplinary sanction. Two relate to conflict of interest matters with respect to former public employees. See DR 9-101. It is important to be very precise when offering this expression as a reason for prohibiting or requiring action because it is so broad that many traditional professional activities, such as defending a guilty person, could be proscribed by resort to it. See EC 9-2. Often the term is used as a substitute for analysis, and what is really meant is that in a particular situation a client has reasonable grounds to fear that the lawyer might misuse confidential information or act disloyally. Where public employment is involved, however, courts sometimes use the phrase as meaning that

---

*The analysis in the last three paragraphs owes a great deal to the work of Donald P. Board, Harvard Law School '83, then my research assistant, now Assistant Professor of Law, Boston University School of Law, as it appears in Developments in the Law — Conflicts of Interest in the Legal Profession, 94 Harv. L. Rev. 1244, 1292-1303 (1981), of which section he was the principal author, and in A Unified Analysis of Forbidden Representations (unpublished manuscript on file in Harvard Law School Library). He will understand, albeit he may not agree with, my failure to accept all the categories he uses in his lengthy analysis.

even if such reasonable fears do not exist, it is important to bar the particular representation to safeguard the reputation of the public service. A little later we shall examine specifically these issues in the context of public employment. See pp. 117-133.

There has been interaction between increasing interest in the subject of professional responsibility since the early 1970s and the discovery of tactical advantages to be gained by successful motions for disqualification of opposing counsel who are discovered to be involved in a forbidden conflict of interest. Indeed, there has been unfavorable reaction in some courts to the increase in the number of disqualification motions because many are believed to be made for purposes of harassment or delay. The reaction has taken two forms. In the first place, although originally the majority of federal courts of appeals had permitted appeals from denials of motions to disqualify counsel, many reversed themselves and the Supreme Court finally ruled that courts of appeals had no jurisdiction to entertain appeals from such nonfinal orders. Mandamus is still available as a remedy, but only in exceptional circumstances. Firestone Tire & Rubber Co. v. Risjord, 449 U.S. 368 (1981).

Following *Firestone*, the Supreme Court held in Flanagan v. United States, 465 U.S. 259 (1984), and then in Richardson-Merrell, Inc. v. Koller, 472 U.S. 424 (1985), that orders disqualifying counsel in criminal and in civil cases are not immediately appealable under the "collateral order" exception to the final judgment requirement of 28 U.S.C. §1291. The Court did leave open the possibility of mandamus, certification of the question for interlocutory review under 28 U.S.C. §1292(b), or even eventual reversal of the judgment on the merits in a particular case as methods of correcting erroneous disqualifications. It seems unlikely that the latter event will occur very often. One state court that does not permit an appeal from an order granting disqualification has suggested that the way around that rule is for the disqualified lawyer to submit to a contempt order for refusal to withdraw and then to appeal the contempt order. See Index Futures Group v. Street, 163 Ill. App. 3d 654, 516 N.E.2d 890 (1st Dist. 1987). Adoption of that suggestion, however, would cut the heart out of the "final judgment" rule.

In addition, some state and federal courts began to clamp down on disqualification motions in other ways. Invoking a doctrine akin to "standing," some courts began to ask whether the party raising the issue was the party harmed or whether a prohibited conflict was likely to disadvantage a party in the proceeding before it. The courts did not reject the traditional notion that they had power, on their own motion, to raise questions of the violation of their own disciplinary rules and hence could act when a party brought the matter to their attention, but rather they asserted that a disciplinary matter ought to be handled as such by the regular disciplinary process unless the representation interfered with the trial itself. See, e.g., Board of Education v. Nyquist, 590 F.2d 1241 (2d Cir. 1979), discussed in Armstrong v. McAlpin, p. 119, at 123, 127.

There was also a reaction on the part of many lawyers who were disqualified against this use of the conflict of interest rules. Although an argument has been made that some of the conflict rules represent the profession's effort to make more work for lawyers and spread it around, see Morgan, The Evolving Concept of Professional Responsibility, 90 Harv. L. Rev. 702, 727-728 (1977), lawyers individually do not like to lose clients and the spate of successful disqualification decisions in the 1970s produced a great deal of discontent throughout the profession, especially in large law firms and in small firms in small communities, both of which have substantial conflict of interest problems. The combination of those views of courts and firms may account for the language in the Comment to Model Rule 1.7 that an objection by opposing counsel raising the issue of conflict of interest "should be viewed with caution, however, for it can be misused as a technique of harassment."

There is, however, another side to the issue. The fact that many disqualification motions have been granted suggests that there is a problem of obedience to the disciplinary rules. In addition, these rules are the courts' own rules and they are as appropriate a body to enforce their own rules in the first instance as the regular disciplinary bodies. The disciplinary machinery is so uncertain in many states (see Chapter 11) that the threat of prompt disqualification is likely to be a more effective enforcement mechanism than a disciplinary sanction. Moreover, many conflict problems do not have obvious solutions and disqualification in such difficult cases will usually be a much more appropriate remedy than disciplinary punishment. If these arguments are sound, one can only hope that courts will not overreact to whatever abuses may have occurred by abdicating the field to the much slower, overworked, and perhaps inappropriate disciplinary process.

For a survey and overview of the whole field of conflict of interest law, see Developments in the Law — Conflicts of Interest in the Legal Profession, 94 Harv. L. Rev. 1244 (1981).

2. *Simultaneously Representing and Opposing a Client in Litigation*

It remains now to consider some typical problems of simultaneous representation of multiple clients. Most of the cases involve the problem of simultaneous representation in the litigation context. The following case, which resembles Problem 2, p. 33, is a good example of how a conflict may arise in the ordinary course of a busy law firm's practice and how failure to pay enough attention to the problem when it arises may lead to difficulties. The court's resolution of the problem is typical.

INTERNATIONAL BUSINESS MACHINES CORP. v. LEVIN

579 F.2d 271 (3d Cir. 1978)

MARIS, Circuit Judge.

This petition for a writ of mandamus and these appeals and cross-appeals seek our review of an interlocutory order of the United States District Court for the District of New Jersey entered in this private anti-trust suit directing Carpenter, Bennett & Morrissey (herein "CBM"), counsel for the plaintiffs, Howard S. Levin (herein "Levin") and Levin Computer Corporation (herein "LCC"), to withdraw from the case and allowing CBM to turn over its past work on the case to substitute counsel for the plaintiffs with consultation with such counsel to effect the turn-over permitted for a period of sixty days.

The plaintiffs' lawsuit against the International Business Machines Corporation (herein "IBM"), alleging violations of sections 1 and 2 of the Sherman Act, 15 U.S.C.A. §§1 and 2, and of the laws of the State of New Jersey, was filed about ten months after Levin caused LCC to be incorporated under the laws of New Jersey for the purpose, stated in the complaint, of engaging in the business of purchasing for lease certain data processing equipment manufactured by IBM, known as the 370 series or IBM fourth generation computer equipment. When IBM refused to extend installment credit to Levin and LCC on other than terms which the latter considered to be unfair and unreasonable, this action was filed. . . .

[Motions and discovery occupied the period from 1973 to 1977 when the disqualification motion was filed.]

We turn then to outline the facts out of which this controversy arose. It appears that CBM had represented both Levin and the corporation with which he was then associated, Levin Townsend Computer Corporation (herein "LTC"), a computer leasing corporation, from 1965 to 1969. From 1966 to 1969 CBM performed considerable work for LTC including representing the corporation in several disputes with IBM in connection with IBM's installment sale to LTC of IBM computer equipment. In January 1970 when Levin terminated his association with LTC, CBM withdrew as attorneys for LTC but continued to represent Levin sporadically in matters unrelated to LTC. In the latter part of 1971 CBM resumed an active attorney-client relationship with Levin. At that time CBM arranged for the incorporation of LCC on behalf of Levin. One of the firm's partners, Stanley Weiss, became a director of LCC and another, David M. McCann, assumed the office of secretary of the corporation.

LCC's effort in late 1971 and 1972 to secure installment credit on terms acceptable to it for the purchase of IBM equipment was handled by McCann dealing with Joseph W. S. Davis, Jr., counsel for IBM's Data Processing Division located in White Plains, New York. As LCC's prospects for a satisfactory credit arrangement with IBM diminished with IBM's successive rejections of LCC's applications for installment credit, Levin's determination to take legal action against IBM grew. In February 1972 McCann advised Davis of the plaintiffs' intention to file suit to enjoin IBM from imposing more stringent credit requirements on LCC than were applied to prospective lessees of the equipment LCC desired to purchase. . . . On June 23, 1972, CBM filed the present suit on behalf of the plaintiffs and has prosecuted it until the present time.

In April 1970 a member of IBM's legal staff in the general counsel's office at Armonk, Robert Troup, contacted Edward F. Ryan, a CBM partner and one of five members of the firm specializing in labor matters, for the purpose of retaining CBM's services in the preparation of an opinion letter for IBM regarding a jurisdictional dispute with an electrical workers' union. The CBM partners considered and rejected the possibility that acceptance of the IBM assignment in the labor matter might create a conflict of interest in the light of CBM's former representation of LTC. Ryan prepared an opinion on the jurisdictional dispute question and accepted a second assignment from Troup in July 1970 dealing with a union's right to picket IBM in the event IBM cancelled a subcontracting arrangement and a third assignment in May 1971 relating to the availability of injunctive relief against certain union picketing.

In April 1972 Ryan accepted Troup's telephoned request for another opinion letter in a labor matter concerning the right of temporary employees to form a separate bargaining unit. At this point Ryan's account of the facts diverges from that of Troup. Ryan's sworn statement is that his acceptance of IBM's fourth assignment caused him some concern since he was aware of CBM's current representation of LCC and LCC's difficulty in procuring credit from IBM. Consequently, a few days after Troup's call, Ryan consulted with McCann and Weiss about a possible conflict of interest in CBM's representation of both IBM and LCC simultaneously. Weiss informed Ryan of the contemplated antitrust suit against IBM and advised him to obtain IBM's consent to the firm's representation of both IBM and the plaintiffs. Ryan stated that shortly thereafter he called Troup at his Armonk office and in a conversation lasting about three minutes brought to Troup's attention the contemplated antitrust suit against IBM by CBM's client, Levin. Troup's response, according to Ryan's testimony, was that the matter was not significant from IBM's point of view and he directed Ryan to proceed with the assignment given him. Various members of the CBM firm testified to their understanding at the time that Ryan had obtained IBM's consent to the dual representation. Troup, however, by affidavit and deposition, denied ever having been informed by Ryan of the proposed Levin lawsuit or that CBM might represent another client in a suit against IBM. CBM obtained Levin's consent to CBM's representation of IBM in labor matters and the antitrust suit was filed by Weiss acting for the firm June 23, 1972, one week after the completion of CBM's fourth opinion letter for IBM.

Weiss testified, also, in connection with IBM's knowledge of CBM's possible conflict of interest involving IBM, that in July 1973 while he and Charles Danzig, a partner of Ricker, Danzig, Scherer & Debevoise, IBM's counsel in the antitrust suit, rode together in a train from Philadelphia to Newark, Weiss mentioned that CBM performed occasional work for IBM in labor matters. Danzig denied that such a statement was made to him by Weiss.

It is undisputed that during CBM's prosecution of the antitrust suit, Ryan accepted four additional labor relations assignments from Troup without further discussing with Troup CBM's concurrent representation of Levin and LCC. . . .

Subsequently, at a law school alumni luncheon in New York City on January 28, 1977, John Lynch, a partner of CBM, met Richard McDonough, then a member of IBM's legal staff, and Lynch mentioned to McDonough his role in prosecuting the plaintiffs' antitrust suit against IBM. McDonough indicated surprise in the CBM was, to his knowledge, representing IBM in labor matters. In April 1977, at a dinner attended by McDonough and counsel for IBM in the antitrust suit, McDonough expressed to the latter an interest in knowing how CBM's conflict of interest had been reconciled to permit CBM's representation of Levin and LCC in the suit against IBM. McDonough's remarks caused IBM to investigate the matter further and led to the filing in June 1977 of the motion to disqualify CBM. . . .

We turn then to consider the order under review. . . .

CBM's principal contention is that under a proper interpretation of the disciplinary rules . . . an attorney who has asserted a claim against a client pursuant to his representation of a second client may continue to represent the first client with respect to matters unrelated to the lawsuit without disclosing fully the facts of the dual representation to the client being sued and without obtaining his consent.

The pertinent rule of the Code of Professional Responsibility, which Code the district court adopted in 1970 under its Local Rule 6 as the controlling standard of conduct for the members of the bar practicing before it,[2] provides as follows: [the court quoted DR 5-105 in its 1969

2. It seems clear that the conduct of practitioners before the federal courts must be governed by the rules of those courts rather than those of the state courts. . . .

version, which does not have the "differing interests" language. (See p. 36)].

CBM argues that clauses (A) and (B) of DR 5-105 are not applicable since no effect adverse to IBM resulted from CBM's concurrent representation of both IBM and the plaintiffs and no adverse effect on CBM's exercise of its independent professional judgment on behalf of IBM was likely to result from CBM's representation of these clients in two entirely unrelated areas. Since clauses (A) and (B) do not apply, CBM argues, the consent requirement of clause (C) of DR 5-105 also is not applicable.

We think that CBM takes too narrow a view of the meaning of the phrase "adversely affected" in clauses (A) and (B), and that a somewhat more generous interpretation is called for. The rule does not define the nature or extent of the adverse effect contemplated on the attorney's exercise of independent judgment. However, DR 5-105(C) makes clear that situations entailing the likelihood of an adverse effect include circumstances in which such an effect may be minor permitting the performance of adequate services in spite of it. In those cases the multiple representation may take place if the attorney believes in good faith that he can adequately represent both clients and if the consent of the clients is obtained.

We think, however, that it is likely that some "adverse effect" on an attorney's exercise of his independent judgment on behalf of a client may result from the attorney's adversary posture toward the client in another legal matter. See Cinema 5, Ltd. v. Cinerama, Inc., 528 F.2d 1384, 1386-1387 (2d Cir. 1976); Grievance Committee of the Bar of Hartford County v. Rottner, 152 Conn. 59, 65, 203 A.2d 82, 84 (1964). . . . For example, a possible effect on the quality of the attorney's services on behalf of the client being sued may be a diminution in the vigor of his representation of the client in the other matter. See Cinema 5, Ltd. v. Cinerama, Inc., supra, at 1387. A serious effect on the attorney-client relationship may follow if the client discovers from a source other than the attorney that he is being sued in a different matter by the attorney. The fact that a deleterious result cannot be identified subsequently as having actually occurred does not refute the existence of a likelihood of its occurrence, depending upon the facts and circumstances, at the time the decision was made to represent the client without having obtained his consent. . . .

An attorney must be cautious in this area and, if he is to adhere to the high standards of professional responsibility, he must resolve all doubts in favor of full disclosure to a client of the facts of the attorney's concurrent representation of another client in a lawsuit against him. As the Second Circuit Court of Appeals has stated, "Putting it as mildly as we can, we think it would be questionable conduct for an attorney to participate in any lawsuit against his own client without the knowledge and consent of all concerned." Cinema 5, Ltd. v. Cinerama, Inc., 528

F.2d 1384, 1386 (1976). Indeed, in the present case the record indicates that the members of CBM themselves apparently took the same view of the applicability of the disciplinary rules to their situation both during the course of the dual representation and, it appears, in their arguments and admissions in the district court.

During the course of CBM's representation of the plaintiffs and IBM, the firm twice considered the possibility of the existence of a conflict of interest which might require some responsive action by CBM, once in 1970 and again in 1972. . . . Thus, at the time they were faced with the question of the propriety of their continuing representation of a client about to be sued or being sued by them, the involved members of the firm apparently considered that the better course was to obtain consent. Moreover, at the hearing on IBM's motion to disqualify CBM, held August 31, 1977, CBM's counsel twice indicated to the court his understanding that a law firm could not, with impunity, sue a client with whom it had a currently ongoing relationship.

Having, in spite of CBM's concession in the district court, nonetheless considered the legal point it raises here and having decided that the continued representation of a client being sued in an unrelated matter without the client's consent may be violative of the Code, in particular DR 5-105, we turn to the question of whether the district court erred in disqualifying CBM and, if not, whether the court abused its discretion in permitting CBM to turn over its work product to plaintiff's new counsel during a period of sixty days.

The district court concluded that its rule applying the Code required that CBM obtain IBM's consent to the firm's representation of it after full disclosure of the facts of CBM's representation of the plaintiffs. In support of this conclusion the court made several findings. The court found as a fact that at all relevant times CBM had an ongoing attorney-client relationship with both IBM and the plaintiffs. This assessment of the relationship seems entirely reasonable to us. Although CBM had no specific assignment from IBM on hand on the day the antitrust complaint was filed and even though CBM performed services for IBM on a fee for service basis rather than pursuant to a retainer arrangement, the pattern of repeated retainers, both before and after the filing of the complaint, supports the finding of a continuous relationship.

The court also found that although the services required of CBM by IBM dealt consistently exclusively with labor matters, this was not the result of any special arrangement between them and that at any time IBM, unaware of CBM's participation in the plaintiffs' action, might have sought CBM's assistance in legal matters more closely related to the lawsuit. Thus, it was perhaps fortuitous that CBM, as the court found, never acquired any confidential information from IBM useful in the prosecution of the antitrust suit.

These findings, with which we agree, support the district court's conclusion, which seems to us reasonable and just, that CBM was obligated in these circumstances at the very least to disclose fully to IBM the facts of its representation of the plaintiffs and obtain its consent.

The district court determined that CBM did not meet its burden of proving that such a full disclosure was made and that consent by IBM to CBM's dual representation was obtained thereafter. CBM asserts that disclosure and consent were not necessary in that IBM had constructive knowledge of the pertinent facts since its labor lawyers knew of CBM's representation of IBM in that area and its lawyers handling the defense of IBM in the antitrust action knew of CBM's participation in that matter. This assertion is without merit. Clause (C) of DR 5-105 specifically imposes upon an attorney the burden of affirmatively providing disclosure and obtaining consent. Clearly, full and effective disclosure of all the relevant facts must be made and .brought home to the prospective client. The facts required to be disclosed are peculiarly within the knowledge of the attorney bearing the burden of making the disclosure. To accept CBM's position would be to engraft an unwarranted exception on the requirement of DR 5-105 that disclosure must be sufficient to enable the prospective client himself to make an informed decision as to whether in the circumstances counsel will be retained. . . .

CBM alternatively argues that IBM's consent was in fact obtained. . . .

The district court did not deem it necessary to resolve these issues of credibility between Ryan and Troup and between Weiss and Danzig since it determined that even accepting CBM's version of this disputed testimony a full and adequate disclosure as required by DR 5-105 had not been made to IBM and that the IBM antitrust attorneys did not in fact know during the relevant period that CBM was representing IBM in labor matters. We conclude that the district court did not err in so determining and in concluding that since IBM's informed consent to the concurrent representation by CBM of it and the plaintiffs had not been obtained, CBM had violated DR 5-105. While we accept the district court's finding that the antitrust lawyers in IBM's legal department did not know that its labor lawyer in the same department was repeatedly retaining the services of CBM in labor matters, we cannot refrain from expressing our belief that such a situation could not have existed for over five years if the activities of the IBM legal department had been properly coordinated and controlled. . . .

CBM and the plaintiffs urge that even if CBM is held to have violated DR 5-105, the district court's disqualification of CBM from the case is too harsh a sanction and penalizes the plaintiffs unnecessarily in view of the termination of CBM's relationship with IBM and the district court's finding that, in the course of its representation of IBM, CBM did not obtain any information which would aid it in the prosecution of the antitrust suit against IBM.

In considering this contention, we bear in mind the proposition that the plaintiffs do not have an absolute right to retain particular counsel. Kramer v. Scientific Control Corp., 534 F.2d 1085, 1093 (3d Cir. 1976).

The plaintiffs' interest in retaining counsel of its choice and the lack of prejudice to IBM resulting from CBM's violation of professional ethics are not the only factors to be considered in this disqualification proceeding. An attorney who fails to observe his obligation of undivided loyalty to his client injures his profession and demeans it in the eyes of the public. The maintenance of the integrity of the legal profession and its high standing in the community are important additional factors to be considered in determining the appropriate sanction for a Code violation. See Hull v. Celanese Corp., 513 F.2d 568, 572 (2d Cir. 1975). The maintenance of public confidence in the propriety of the conduct of those associated with the administration of justice is so important a consideration that we have held that a court may disqualify an attorney for failing to avoid even the appearance of impropriety. . . . Indeed, the courts have gone so far as to suggest that doubts as to the existence of an asserted conflict of interest should be resolved in favor of disqualification. . . . Mindful of these considerations, we cannot say that the district court erred in ordering the disqualification of CBM.

It is true that the plaintiffs will be injured by the disqualification of CBM, their counsel for a number of years. Here the district court ameliorated the harsh effect upon the plaintiffs of its sanction against CBM by permitting the turnover to substitute counsel for the plaintiffs within sixty days of the past work product of CBM on the case. IBM contends that the allowance of a turnover of work product with consultation, particularly work product prepared after the filing of IBM's motion, was an abuse of discretion.

In support of its contention IBM cites First Wisconsin Mortgage Trust v. First Wisconsin Corp., 571 F.2d 390 (7th Cir. 1978), and Fund of Funds, Ltd. v. Arthur Andersen & Co., 567 F.2d 225 (2d Cir. 1977). To the extent that the Seventh Circuit Court of Appeals lays down a legal tenet in *First Wisconsin Mortgage Trust* against permitting the turnover of a disqualified attorney's work product, we disagree, but we note that the court in that case expressly limited its holding to the facts of the case. 571 F.2d 390, 399. . . .

As we have already indicated, disqualification in circumstances such as these where specific injury to the moving party has not been shown is primarily justified as a vindication of the integrity of the bar. We think the turnover provisions of the district court's order of disqualification are sufficient for that purpose and a proper exercise of the court's discretion. . . .

NOTES

1. The court notes that the federal district court had adopted the Model Code as the controlling standard of conduct for lawyers practicing before it. That is not the universal practice and where that has not

occurred, one finds statements in federal court opinions that the standards of the Model Code should be looked to for guidance. See, e.g., p. 52 n. 1. Footnote 2 in IBM suggests the possibility of conflict between state and federal rules of professional conduct. That conflict and interstate conflict present potentially enormous problems for lawyers that shall be noted from time to time in this book.

2. The court treated both the general loyalty and the specific confidentiality problems presented by CBM's representation of, and against, IBM. Under the former topic, it discussed the possible effect on the quality of the lawyer's services and also the effect on the lawyer-client relationship. It might also have mentioned the financial aspect of the representation — IBM's financial support of a firm that was suing it without consent. Note that the court viewed the case as one of simultaneous representation because CBM was *representing* IBM at the same time it was *suing* IBM, even though it ceased to represent IBM after the disqualification motion was filed. That seems appropriate since otherwise the purposes of the rule could be easily evaded by carrying on dual representation until challenged. See p. 54 n. 4.

As a simultaneous representation case, what are the disqualifying factors here? Lack of independent judgment in representing Levin because of representing IBM? How is that affected by Levin's consent? Lack of independent judgment in representing IBM in the labor matters because the firm is suing IBM in an antitrust matter? Is that likely? Or is it obvious that CBM could not adequately represent the interests of Levin and IBM in their respective matters? Or is it that in representing Levin vis à vis IBM without IBM's consent, the firm has impaired IBM's confidence in its ability to represent IBM zealously? Is that a reasonable reaction by IBM? Is our judgment on this issue clouded by the fact that the client is IBM? If the firm had sued Levin on behalf of IBM while it was representing Levin on another matter, would we feel differently? Does this explain the need for a prophylactic rule because it is so difficult to measure both the effect on the independent professional judgment of the lawyer and the reasonableness of the client's perception?

3. The trial court also found a pattern of continuous representation of IBM by CBM triggering operation of DR 5-105 when the antitrust complaint was filed even though CBM was not handling any matter for IBM at that precise moment. The court appears to be saying that DR 5-105 would have been applicable even if no matters had come to CBM from IBM after the antitrust complaint was filed. That decision of the court not to rely on a mechanical rule of actual current representation is an important one for lawyers for it adds an element of significant uncertainty to a firm's attempt to keep track of its "current" clients for purposes of DR 5-105.

However, does the court really mean that if CBM had properly sought IBM's consent and been turned down, it could not have severed its connection with IBM at that time and, assuming it had no relevant confidential information, brought the suit by Levinin against IBM? That would seem harsh in view of the fact that CBM was not handling any matter for IBM at that moment and was not in any sense its general outside counsel. Note that if CBM would have been permitted to represent Levin in that circumstance, the result of its failure to seek IBM's consent in the actual case was that CBM ended up representing neither party.

4. The court's holding on what constitutes consent after full and adequate disclosure should also be noted. The court apparently holds that brief mention to the client's lawyers followed by a direction to continue representation is not enough (p. 47).

5. In allowing CBM to consult with, and to turn over its work product to, successor counsel, the court was impressed with the harsh consequences for plaintiff of a contrary rule, especially since the case had progressed so far. The opinion in First Wisconsin Mortgage Trust v. First Wisconsin Corp., which it distinguished and with which it disagreed, was withdrawn after rehearing en banc, the court holding that denial of access to the work product was not warranted in the circumstances of that case. 584 F.2d 201 (7th Cir. 1978). See also E. F. Hutton & Co. v. Brown, 305 F. Supp. 371 (S.D. Tex. 1969) for another case where the court refused to enter an order limiting access to work product of disqualified counsel, and Fund of Funds, Ltd. v. Arthur Andersen & Co., p. 135, for a case where the court refused to grant the even more severe sanction of dismissal of the complaint with prejudice or suppression of all information gathered by the disqualified firms.

6. The Third Circuit relied heavily in its opinion on the prior opinion of the Second Circuit in Cinema 5, Ltd. v. Cinerama, Inc., 538 F.2d 1384 (2d Cir. 1976). That much-cited case reached the same result as IBM v. Levin in a case where the firm in the position of CBM was really two firms in different cities linked by one common partner who had participated minimally in one of the lawsuits. Yet the court treated the firms as one for purposes of disqualification.

7. The rule of *IBM* and *Cinerama* was followed in The McCourt Co., Inc. v. FPC Properties, Inc., 386 Mass. 145 (1982), a case where the court rejected an argument by insurance company counsel that an exception should be created that would allow simultaneous representation of, and opposition to, a client when the subsequent representation of the client it was already suing came about by virtue of the request of the insurance company for which the firm did substantial assigned defense work.

8. A case disposed of largely on the ground that no attorney-client relationship existed was Fred Weber, Inc. v. Shell Oil Co., 566 F.2d 602 (8th Cir. 1977), cert. denied, 436 U.S. 905 (1978). The law firm for A, co-defendant with B in a criminal antitrust case, represented C in a subsequent civil antitrust suit against B. The court found no actual receipt

of confidences by the law firm, and thus no appearance of impropriety under Canon 9, and refused to apply the presumption of Canon 4 in the absence of an attorney-client relationship. The court stressed that the law firm's prior representation of A had not gone beyond the initial stages of defense, and reserved the question whether a full substantive defense by the law firm for A would either trigger Canon 9 so that B could disqualify the law firm or shift the burden of proof with respect to "impropriety" from B, as in this case, to the law firm.

9. For a case where different branches of a large law firm represented a client in a judicial forum, and opposed the same client on essentially the same matter in a legislative forum, see Westinghouse Elec. Corp. v. Kerr-McGee Corp., 580 F.2d 1311 (7th Cir. 1978), cert. denied, 439 U.S. 955 (1978). The court held that members of a trade association who, on request, transmitted information to Washington counsel for the association reasonably believed they did so in the context of a fiduciary relationship, even though no attorney-client relationship may have been formed. In that situation, it was a violation of Canons 4, 5, and 9 for counsel's Chicago office to represent a client suing these members with respect to the same matter on which the Washington office was representing the trade association. In framing a remedy, the court presented the client with the choice of either dismissing the law firm as counsel in the lawsuit or dismissing those defendants who had conveyed confidential data to the Washington office.

10. Insurance litigation provokes a variety of conflict of interest problems, especially because of the common provision giving control over litigation involving an insured to the insurance company. In representing the insured, the company's lawyer is faced with very diffcult problems of professional responsibility. See, e.g., Parsons v. Continental National American Group, 535 P.2d 17 (Ariz. Ct. App. 1975), holding that an attorney could not obtain information from the insured by reason of the attorney-client relationship and then use it as the basis for establishing lack of coverage by his company's policy of the claim being made against insured. For extensive discussions of the many conflicts of interest that can arise in the liability insurance context, see Keeton, Basic Text on Insurance Law 490-534, especially 493-499 (1971), and Mallen, Insurance Counsel: The Fine Line Between Professional Responsibility and Malpractice, 45 Ins. Counsel J. 244 (1978).

11. IBM v. Levin was a civil case in which a court had to decide what to do after the fact of improper multiple representation. The issue arises in criminal cases as well. In Commonwealth v. Hodge, 386 Mass. 165 (1982), the court held that where the partner of defense counsel currently represented the prosecution's rebuttal witness in an unrelated civil matter, the possibility of conflict involved in deciding whether and how to conduct a vigorous cross-examination of the witness-client required a new trial even though defendant had been informed of that represen-

tation before trial began. The court held that unlike the Sixth Amendment requirement of demonstration of adverse effect on the lawyer's performance, Cuyler v. Sullivan, p. 34, the Massachusetts constitutional requirement of effective assistance of counsel did not require such a showing. No waiver by defendant could be found when the record did not reveal any disclosure by counsel of the implications of his firm's representation of the prosecution witness.

Cases like *IBM, Cinerama,* and *McCourt* raise the issue of whether there should be a per se rule against simultaneous representation of, and suit against, a client. Courts have generally refused to impose such a ban on the theory that fact situations might arise where the policy considerations looking toward permitting such representation would outweigh those forbidding it. The opinion in *McCourt* referred to one such situation although it was not involved in that case, viz., the client that spread its work around among many law firms to insulate itself from suit. (But see ABA Informal Opinion 1495 (1982) concluding that simultaneous representation is not permissible even in such a case.) The following opinion and Notes and the opinion in the next section suggest other situations where the rule may not apply.

UNIFIED SEWERAGE AUTHORITY v. JELCO, INC.
646 F.2d 1339 (9th Cir. 1981)

Goodwin, Circuit Judge.

Jelco moved to disqualify the plaintiff's law firm on the theory that the attorneys were suing their own client in violation of Canons 4, 5 and 9 of the Code of Professional Responsibility of the State of Oregon (1980).[1] The trial judge denied the disqualification motion and Jelco appealed.

---

1. Cord v. Smith, 338 F.2d 516 (9th Cir. 1964), clarified, 370 F.2d 418 (1966), involved an appeal from the denial of a motion to disqualify plaintiff's attorney. The court rejected the plaintiff's argument that state law applied. It said: "[W]e do not think that the rule of Erie Railroad Co. v. Tompkins, 1938, 304 U.S. 64, 58 S. Ct. 817, 82 L. Ed. 1188, compels the federal courts to permit, in proceedings before those courts, whatever action by an attorney-at-law may be sanctioned by the courts of the state. When an attorney appears before a federal court, he is acting as an officer of that court, and it is that court which must judge his conduct." 388 F.2d at 524. In this case, the United States District Court for the District of Oregon has adopted as its rules the disciplinary rules of the State Bar of Oregon. See Local Rule 3(d) of the District Court for the District of Oregon. Therefore, in deciding whether the district court properly denied Jelco's motion to disqualify the plaintiff's law firm, we must decide whether the district court properly applied the Code of Professional Responsibility adopted by the State Bar of Oregon. . . .

We express no opinion on the law to apply where the district court has not designated the applicable rules of professional responsibility (e.g., state law, the Model Code

We treat the appeal as a petition for mandamus.

Jelco, based in Salt Lake City, was the prime contractor on a sewer plant project in Oregon. Teeples & Thatcher was the subcontractor for concrete work, and Ace Electric Co. was an electrical subcontractor. Kobin & Meyer is a Portland law firm experienced in representing construction companies. Kobin & Meyer had represented Teeples & Thatcher for ten years prior to this litigation.

In 1975, a dispute arose between Ace Electric and Jelco over Ace's claim for additional compensation under its subcontract. Ace contended that a change Jelco made in suppliers constituted a change in the terms of the subcontract. Jelco's Salt Lake City counsel, one Beesley, and another Jelco agent contacted Paul Meyer of Kobin & Meyer in mid-1975, and asked that firm to join in Jelco's representation in the Ace Electric controversy.

Meyer told Beesley that Kobin & Meyer represented Teeples & Thatcher in what was then an embryonic dispute between Teeples & Thatcher and Jelco. Teeples & Thatcher's expressions of dissatisfaction with Jelco's scheduling and sequence of concrete work had reached the stage of lawyer discussions. Beesley nonetheless recommended to Jelco management that Kobin & Meyer be retained to assist in the Ace Electric litigation. Jelco's management, with full knowledge of Jelco's potential conflict with Teeples & Thatcher on the same project, and with full knowledge of Kobin & Meyer's long-standing relationship with Teeples & Thatcher, retained Kobin & Meyer.

In mid-1976, after a proposed settlement of the Teeples-Jelco dispute collapsed, Meyer told Beesley that the Teeples-Jelco dispute could ripen into a lawsuit. Meyer asked Beesley, and through him, Jelco's management, to re-evaluate whether Jelco wished Kobin & Meyer to continue to represent Jelco in the Ace Electric litigation. Meyer made it clear that if it came to a choice, Kobin & Meyer preferred to keep Teeples as a client. Jelco, through Beesley, replied unequivocally that it desired Kobin & Meyer to continue as counsel in the Ace litigation regardless of what happened in the Jelco dispute with Teeples & Thatcher.

The liability issues in the Ace litigation were tried in July 1976, and were determined adversely to Jelco. In December 1976, Kobin & Meyer filed an action for Teeples & Thatcher against Jelco.

---

of Professional Responsibility, or a federal common law of professional responsibility). . . .

The reporter for the ABA Committee that drafted the Code of Professional Responsibility recently noted that the Code's Disciplinary Rules were drafted for use in disciplinary proceedings and were not intended to be used as rules governing disqualification motions. Sutton, How Vulnerable is the Code of Professional Responsibility?, 57 N.C.L. Rev. 497, 514-516 (1979). Nevertheless, the Code will continue to provide guidance to the courts in determining whether a case would be tainted by the participation of an attorney or firm as shown by the District of Oregon's Local Rule 3(d).

In March 1977, with the damages issue in the Ace litigation still to be tried, Meyer again asked Beesley and Jelco's house counsel if Jelco desired to have Kobin & Meyer continue to represent Jelco against Ace. Meyer repeated his firm's expressed desire to avoid prejudicing Kobin & Meyer's representation of Teeples. Jelco again decided to continue with Kobin & Meyer in the Ace litigation.

In May 1977, Jelco discharged Beesley, obtained new Salt Lake City counsel, and discharged Kobin & Meyer from the Ace Electric litigation as soon as a substitute attorney could take over that case. In December 1977, Jelco filed this motion to disqualify Kobin & Meyer from further representation of Teeples & Thatcher in the action against Jelco. . . .

The trial court viewed the case as one involving an attorney's acceptance of employment adverse to a *former* client, and therefore tested Kobin & Meyer's actions against the standards set forth in Canon 4. In general Canon 4 prohibits an attorney from divulging confidences and secrets of a client. Under Canon 4 an attorney may not represent interests adverse to a former client if the factual context of the later representation is similar or related to that of the former representation. Trone v. Smith, 621 F.2d 994, 998 (9th Cir. 1980). See generally, Pennwalt Corp. v. Plough, Inc., [p. 65].

The case, however, is one in which the attorney undertook representation adverse to a *present* client. The questions thus raised are more appropriately treated under Canon 5.[4] In contrast to representation undertaken adverse to a *former* client, representation adverse to a *present* client must be measured not so much against the similarities in litigation, as against the duty of undivided loyalty which an attorney owes to each of his clients. See . . . Cinema 5, Ltd. v. Cinerama, Inc., [p. 50, Note 6]. See also, Pennwalt Corp. v. Plough, Inc., [p. 65]. [The court quoted DR 5-105(B).] In International Business Machines Corp. v. Levin, [p. 42], the Third Circuit did not require that "adverse effect" be specifically demonstrated. It presumed that adverse effect resulted when an attorney took an adverse position to a present client. We agree that a specific adverse effect need not be demonstrated to trigger DR 5-105 (B) if an attorney undertakes to represent a client whose position is adverse to that of a present client. . . . Accordingly, Kobin & Meyer's dual representation of Teeples & Thatcher and Jelco triggers DR 5-105(B) because

---

4. Teeples & Thatcher argue that the "present-client approach" is inapplicable here because Jelco has dismissed Kobin & Meyer from its employ. Jelco correctly cites Fund of Funds, Ltd. v. Arthur Andersen & Co. 435 F.Supp. 84, 95 (S.D.N.Y.), aff'd in part, rev'd in part on other grounds, 567 F.2d 225 (2nd Cir. 1977), for the proposition that the present-client standard applies if the attorney simultaneously represents clients with differing interests. This standard continues even though the representation ceases prior to filing of the motion to disqualify. If this were not the case, the challenged attorney could always convert a present client into a "former client" by choosing when to cease to represent the disfavored client.

the representation is presumed to affect adversely Kobin & Meyer's representation of each.

Teeples & Thatcher argues, however, that Kobin & Meyer should not be disqualified under DR 5-105(B) because of the exception set forth in DR 5-105(C). To avoid disqualification under DR 5-105(B), an attorney must satisfy DR 5-105(C)'s two conditions. First, each client must consent to the multiple representation after full disclosure of the risks. Second, it must be "obvious" that the attorney can adequately represent the interests of each client.

CONSENT

The leading case on the meaning of "consent" in Canon 5 of the disciplinary rules of the State Bar of Oregon is In re Boivin, 271 Or. 419, 533 P.2d 171 (1975). The court stated that the consent must be an "informed consent" made after full disclosure of all of the material facts. 533 P.2d at 174. The court further said:

> To satisfy the requirement of full disclosure by a lawyer before undertaking to represent two conflicting interests, it is not sufficient that both parties be informed of the fact that the lawyer is undertaking to represent both of them, but he must explain to them the nature of the conflict of interest in such detail so that they can understand the reasons why it may be desirable for each to have independent counsel, with undivided loyalty to the interests of each of them. Id.

Jelco asserts that it did not give "informed consent" because Kobin & Meyer merely "informed" it of the conflict, rather than explained to it the "implications" of the conflict. The district court, on the other hand, found that "there was an informed and knowing waiver by Jelco of any conflict or apparent conflict. . . ." This finding does not offend Fed. R. Civ. P. 52(a).

The record shows that Jelco knew from the beginning that Kobin & Meyer represented Teeples & Thatcher in a long-standing client relationship and that Teeples & Thatcher was involved in an embryonic dispute with Jelco. Jelco also knew that Kobin & Meyer would accept Jelco as a client only if that relationship would not inhibit Kobin & Meyer in continuing to act as Teeples & Thatcher's counsel.

As the dispute between Teeples & Thatcher and Jelco developed, Kobin & Meyer twice alerted Jelco's counsel to the potential conflict and asked whether Jelco wished to continue Kobin & Meyer's retainer. After consulting with Jelco's management, Jelco's counsel assured Kobin & Meyer that Jelco wished Kobin & Meyer to continue representing Jelco. We have no doubt that Jelco consented to the representation after full

disclosure was made to Jelco and its own attorney.[6] The record shows
that after Kobin & Meyer's disclosure, Jelco discussed the two actions
and the possible conflict which would result with its own attorney, and
then agreed to Kobin & Meyer's multiple representation. Consent was
expressed not just on one occasion, but on two occasions.

Thus, the "consent" prong of DR 5-105(C) is satisfied.

"ADEQUATE REPRESENTATION"

The requirements of DR 5-105(C) are not satisfied, however, by a
mere showing of consent after full disclosure. The rule also requires that
it be "obvious that [the lawyer] can adequately represent the interest of
each [client]. . . ." As the Oregon Supreme Court said in In re Porter,
283 Or. 517, 584 P.2d 744, 749 n.5 (1978), "[t]his is troubling language."
The *Porter* court acknowledged, but did not resolve, the very issue confronting the court in this case — the meaning of the "adequate representation" part of DR 5-105(C). The court said:

> Because we have found that the full disclosure requirement of DR 5-
> 105(C) was not met, we need not address the apparent further require-
> ment of DR 5-105(C) that it be "obvious that he [the lawyer] can adequately
> represent the interest of each."
>
> This is troubling language. The Bar contends that DR 5-105(C) states
> a two-part test. The issue of consent after full disclosure is not even
> reached until the initial requirement that "it is obvious that he [the lawyer]
> can adequately represent the interest of each" is satisfied. The Bar argues
> that this requirement embodies the policy that differing interests may be
> represented only in rare cases. The following ethics opinions provide sup-
> port [for] the Bar's position by treating the requirement that adequate rep-
> resentation be obvious as a separate standard: Opinions of the Committee
> on Legal Ethics of the Oregon State Bar numbers 218 and 376; ABA For-
> mal Opinion number 331 (12/15/72); ABA Informal Opinions numbers
> 1235 (8/24/72) and 1282 (11/21/73). To read the language of DR 5-105(C)
> literally, however, would make the representation of conflicting interests
> nearly impossible. The difficulty lies in the word "obvious." Once it is
> shown that the exercise of the lawyer's independent professional judgment
> would be or would likely be adversely affected (DR 5-105(A)), how could

6. Jelco obviously no longer consents to Kobin & Meyer's representation of Teeples
& Thatcher. Our analysis nonetheless turns on the effectiveness of Jelco's consent, however, because Jelco would be estopped from revoking its consent by everyone's reliance
on its long-standing position.

Jelco has also argued that it was unaware of the conflict and that its counsel could
not bind Jelco on the question of dual representation. We are not prepared to so hold.
The district court apparently treated the agency question as settled by general principles of agency, and counsel have cited to us no law that calls for a re-examination of
this issue on the present record.

a nothing a obvious in law school

it ever be *"obvious"* that he could adequately represent the interest of each party? 584 P.2d 749, n.5.

Our analysis of the history of DR 5-105(C), the structure of the Code, and the relevant policy considerations convinces us that the latter approach mentioned by the *Porter* court (i.e., that if adverse affect is shown, it is never *obvious* that an attorney can adequately represent both) is not the correct approach to DR 5-105(C).

1.   Legislative History of DR 5-105(C)

The history of the consent provision in the Code of Professional Responsibility's conflict of interest section indicates that consent was never intended to be meaningless or ineffective. Canon 6 of the 1908 Code of Professional Responsibility,[7] provided that:

> It is unprofessional to represent conflicting interests, except by express consent of all concerned given after a full disclosure of the facts. Within the meaning of this canon, a lawyer represents conflicting interests when, in behalf of one client, it is his duty to contend for that which duty to another client required him to oppose.[8]

Although Canon 6 seemingly allowed multiple representation whenever the clients consented, the courts have interpreted it in a more restrictive manner.[9] . . .

Indeed, Henry Drinker, one of the leading authorities on the old Code, argued that "[Canon 6] does not sanction representation of conflicting interests in every case where such consent is given, but merely forbids it except in such cases." H. Drinker, Legal Ethics 120 (1953). . . .

Thus, Canon 6 of the old Code of Professional Responsibility contemplated that consent would be available to authorize multiple representation which would otherwise be inappropriate.

In 1969, a new Model Code of Professional Responsibility was enacted. Disciplinary Rule 5-105(C), which differed from old Canon 6 in sev-

---

7. For a brief history of the development of the 1908 Code of Professional Responsibility — the first of the ABA — see H. Drinker, Legal Ethics 23-25 (1953).

8. See *Drinker*, supra, note 7, at 311.

9. See, e.g., Jedwabny v. Philadelphia Transp. Co., 390 Pa. 231, 135 A.2d 252, 254 (1957), cert. denied, 355 U.S. 966, 78 S. Ct. 557, 2 L. Ed. 2d 541 (1958) (held, no abuse of discretion to grant a new trial because the litigant did not have full knowledge of the conflict, but stating that some conflicts are so critically adverse that representation is not allowed); ABA Comm. on Professional Ethics, Formal Opinions No. 132 (1935); ABA Comm. on Professional Ethics, Informal Opinions No. 1157 (1970); Opinions of the Comm. on Legal Ethics of the Oregon State Bar, No. 135 (1964) (and opinions cited therein).

eral respects, provided that: [the court then quoted DR 5-105(C)]. DR 5-105(C) has a broader scope than Canon 6. Canon 6 only applied to "conflicting interests" which arose when the lawyer had a "duty to contend for that which duty to another client required him to oppose." DR 5-105(C), in contrast to Canon 6 applies whenever the attorney's representation of one client is likely to be adversely affected by his representation of another client, or when it would involve him in representing "differing interests." Moreover, whereas Canon 6 on its face would have allowed representation of conflicting interests if there were "consent after full disclosure," DR 5-105(C) requires that it also be "obvious"[12] that an attorney can "adequately represent" the clients with differing interests. The changes in the new Code appear to be changes in substance, not merely form.

The case law and bar association opinions have continued, however, under DR 5-105(C), to allow multiple representation in certain situations if there has been consent after full disclosure. . . .

2.   Structure of the Code

Giving effect to both elements of DR 5-105(C) is not inconsistent with the remainder of the Code of Professional Responsibility. We note that although an attorney's actions are generally governed by the Code, with the attorney deciding the propriety of his actions, a few limited situations exist under the Code in which client consent justifies certain actions. See DR 5-104(A) (business transactions with a client); DR 5-101(A), DR 5-105(A) and (B) (declining or discontinuing employment when judgment on behalf of a client is likely to be affected); DR 4-101(B) (revealing confidences of a client); DR 5-105 (settling similar claim of clients). DR 5-105(C) is one of those few cases when consent can justify otherwise improper actions. This section has remained in the Code despite objections.

3.   Policy Grounds

Policy reasons support our decision not to interpret DR 5-105(C)'s "adequate representation" language in such a way as to abolish consent.

---

12. DR 5-105(C) underwent one significant change during the drafting process. In the Tentative Draft, the rule read "a lawyer may represent multiple clients if a lawyer of ordinary prudence would believe that he could adequately represent the interest of each. . . ." In the Preliminary Draft, the words "a lawyer of ordinary prudence would believe he could" were replaced by the current wording, "it is obvious that he can." See American Bar Foundation, Annotated Code of Professional Responsibility, Textual & Historical Notes p. 242 (1979). The Annotation notes that some confusion over the meaning of "obvious" has occurred. Id. at 243. Without belaboring the point, we think "obvious" must refer to an objective standard under which the ability of the attorney adequately to represent each client is free from substantial doubt.

It is true that from its representation of Jelco in the *Ace* matter, Kobin & Meyer was likely to gain information and insights from Jelco about such things as Jelco's institutional attitudes towards negotiation and settlement and Jelco's method of doing business. Such information undoubtedly could prove useful to an opponent. Nevertheless, while the practice of suing a client can be neither condoned nor encouraged,[14] we are not prepared to enunciate a per se rule that a client must forego in all circumstances his choice of a particular attorney merely because there is the foreseeability of a future conflict with one of the attorney's existing clients.

It is true that the court has an obligation to safeguard the integrity of the judicial process in the eyes of the public. See Pennwalt Corp v. Plough, Inc., [p. 65]; see also, Silver Chrysler Plymouth, Inc. v. Chrysler Motor Corp., 518 F.2d 751, 754, 759 (2nd Cir. 1975), and at p. 759 (Adams, J., concurring). . . . But the impact upon the public's respect for lawyers may be too speculative to justify overriding the client's right to take a calculated risk and, with full knowledge, engage the attorney of his choice. We do not find it necessary to create a paternalistic rule that would prevent the client in every circumstance from hiring a particular attorney if the client knows that some detriment may result from that choice in a later suit. Clients who are fully advised should be able to make choices of this kind if they wish to do so. Our responsibility is to preserve a balance, delicate though it may be, between an individual's right to his own freely chosen counsel and the avoidance of representations where undivided loyalty is impossible. See Trone v. Smith, 621 F.2d 994, 1001 (9th Cir. 1980); *Silver Chrysler*, supra, 518 F.2d at 753. We think the Code strikes a balance on the side of an individual's right to choose his own counsel and against a per se rule forbidding multiple representation. See also, In re Taylor, 567 F.2d 1183, 1191 (2nd Cir. 1977) (stating that once the court decides that client consent was given, the court is without power to unilaterally obstruct the choice of counsel).[15]

---

14. The Code, the cases and the commentators agree that if there is any doubt as to whether multiple representation would be appropriate, the attorney should decline the representation. See, e.g., Complaint of Hershberger, 288 Or. 559, 606 P.2d 623, 624 (Or. 1980) (and cases and authorities cited therein); International Business Machines Corp. v. Levin, [p. 59]; EC 5-15.

15. We do not express any view about whether such conduct could serve as a basis for disciplinary proceedings. The Code's purpose is to guide lawyers in ethical conduct and to serve as a disciplinary code. Some of the same considerations are present in the litigation context, but the court is in addition concerned with the balancing of hardships to the litigants. We think it possible that, in unusual circumstances, counsel might properly be subjected to discipline and yet be allowed to continue representing the client in ongoing litigation.

4.   Defining "Adequate Representation"

Of course, saying that there will be situations in which it is appropriate for an attorney to represent a client who is suing another client is much easier than defining when the representation will meet DR 5-105(C)'s "adequacy" requirements. Under both Canon 6 and DR 5-105(C), the courts have consistently said that representation is unavailable where the public interest is impaired or where there is a great likelihood that one party will be prejudiced. Examples of such cases include a government attorney's representation of a client who is suing the government, and an attorney's representation of both the plaintiff and the defendant in a particular suit. We believe the "public interest" and "prejudice" language used on occasion by the courts is merely another way of saying that "adequate representation" could not be provided in those cases.

None of the cases, however, sets forth the specific factors to use in determining when the representation is adequate. In determining whether it is obvious that an attorney can represent adverse parties, the court should look at factors such as: the nature of the litigation; the type of information to which the lawyer may have had access; whether the client is in a position to protect his interests or know whether he will be vulnerable to disadvantage as a result of the multiple representation; the questions in dispute (e.g., statutory construction versus disputes over facts) and whether a government body is involved.

Thus, the court will undoubtedly look at some of the factors which are considered in deciding whether representation against a former client is appropriate. . . .

5.   The Merits of This Case

We now consider whether it was "obvious" that Kobin & Meyer could adequately represent each of its clients in this instance. As a preliminary matter, we must decide whether the findings of fact made by the district court may be relied upon in deciding whether it was obvious that Kobin & Meyer could provide adequate representation. The district court found that there was "no substantial or close relationship between the subject matter of the Ace litigation and the subject matter of the Teeples & Thatcher litigation," and "no evidence to justify a finding that Kobin & Meyer [had] any special insight or advantage arising on account of its representation of Jelco in the Ace case which would give to Teeples & Thatcher any unfair advantage over Jelco." These findings of fact are consistent with Fed. R. Civ. P. 52(a).

Although the two actions arose out of the same construction contract between Jelco and Unified Sewerage, the nature of the cases is quite different. The action which Kobin & Meyer handled for Jelco involved only a narrow issue of contract interpretation. The issue was whether the use of a certain aeration equipment manufacturer constituted a change in Jelco's subcontract with Ace because Ace allegedly had to provide different and additional equipment than originally planned. The facts were virtually undisputed.

The action which Kobin & Meyer handled for Teeples & Thatcher and against Jelco involved the scheduling and sequencing of concrete work which was to be performed by Teeples & Thatcher for Jelco. Each party claimed that the other party delayed and interfered with its work. The only information furnished by Jelco to Kobin & Meyer in connection with the first action concerned the pre-bid proposals on aeration equipment and electrical work, project specifications for aeration work, the subcontract negotiations between Jelco and Ace, the shop drawings and submittals prepared by Ace and expert testimony relative to costs differentiations for electrical installations. We conclude that the district court's findings of fact are not clearly erroneous.

The next question this court must address is whether the district court abused its discretion in denying the motion to disqualify, given the above findings of fact. . . .

We find that the district court did not abuse its discretion. It is sufficiently obvious, for the purposes of the canon, that Kobin & Meyer could adequately represent both Jelco and Teeples & Thatcher in the several actions. The litigation in the two cases was quite different; one involved a question of contract interpretation and the other was a highly disputed factual claim concerning each party's performance. Although one umbrella contract covered each case, the individual contracts involved were quite different. As the findings of fact indicate, Kobin & Meyer did not have access to any specific information that would help Teeples & Thatcher prevail against Jelco (other than general information concerning the personality of a client, which is always helpful in later suits against the client). Jelco, fully advised by its regular counsel, was in a position to know all the risks it was taking in employing Kobin & Meyer.

We find no facts that suggest that Kobin & Meyer would be tempted to "soft pedal" the rights of one client in these cases so as not to jeopardize the position of another client. Nothing suggests that Kobin & Meyer had an incentive *not* to represent zealously the interests of each client in their respective cases. Accordingly, we find that it was as "obvious" as necessary that Kobin & Meyer could adequately represent Jelco and Teeples & Thatcher within the meaning of the canon.

III. CANON 9 AND THE APPEARANCE OF IMPROPRIETY

Jelco has argued that Kobin & Meyer should be disqualified because the challenged multiple representation carries the appearance of impropriety. The point does, of course, raise questions. But, to paraphrase the *Silver Chrysler* court, we do not believe Canon 9 was intended to override the delicate balance created by Canon 5 and the decisions thereunder. *Silver Chrysler,* supra, 518 F.2d at 757. Having decided that Canon 5 was written to allow multiple representation in exceptional cases if all clients consented after full disclosure and if the attorney could adequately represent both parties, we do not read Canon 9 as an implied repeal of the multiple representation language in Canon 5 because it has "the appearance of impropriety."

The district court's failure to disqualify Kobin & Meyer was not an abuse of discretion on the facts of this case. Jelco consented after full disclosure and the court found that Kobin & Meyer could adequately represent both parties.

Accordingly, the ruling of the district court will not be disturbed.

Affirmed.

NOTES

1. The court noted in footnote 1 the view of Dean Sutton, Reporter for the Committee that drafted the Model Code, that the standards embodied in the disciplinary rules were not intended to be used as governing rules in disqualification cases. That view reflects the efforts, noted earlier, to reduce the numbers of disqualification motions in litigation. The Model Rules, in their Scope provisions, also caution that the "fact that a Rule is a just basis for a lawyer's self-assessment, or for sanctioning a lawyer under the administration of a disciplinary authority, does not imply that an antagonist in a collateral proceeding or transaction has standing to seek enforcement of the Rule." Whatever that general remark is meant to imply in conflict of interest litigation, it seems natural to expect that courts will, and should, use the standards of conduct they have adopted as disciplinary rules to guide them in disqualification motions, especially since disqualification is such an appropriate enforcement tool. Of course, as the court noted in footnote 15, there may be cases where other considerations will affect the court's judgment about remedy for violation of these standards.

2. The court nowhere mentions that the firm's long-standing client, Teeples, had consented to its representation of Jelco against Ace Electric. If it did not do so, should it not have been asked? And would not full disclosure have made it seem apparent that the firm should not represent Jelco? But should the firm's failure to seek Teeples' consent be available to Jelco in its motion to disqualify the firm from representing Teeples?

3. On the merits of *Jelco* it is instructive to compare the facts of *Jelco* with those of IBM v. Levin [see p. 42]. In the former, the court found

that Jelco knew enough to give informed consent; in the latter, the court found that the client's lawyers (i.e., house counsel for IBM) did not know enough to give informed consent.

The issue of "informed consent" arose in a somewhat different setting in Aetna Cas. & Sur. Co. v. United States, 438 F. Supp. 886 (S.D.N.C. 1977), rev'd, 570 F.2d 1197 (4th Cir. 1978), cert. denied, 439 U.S. 821 (1978). The district court disqualified the Department of Justice from representing both individual air traffic controllers and the United States in a lawsuit arising out of an airplane crash. The court reviewed the possible positions that counsel for each defendant might take in conflict with that of the United States and held that the individual defendants' consent "can not be presumed to be fully informed when it is procured without the advice of a lawyer who has no conflict of interest" and further that DR 5-105 was not complied with because it was not "'obvious that [the attorney] can adequately represent the interest' of each individual defendant." On appeal, the order was reversed. The court rejected the theory that independent advice was necessary before there could be valid consent. It held that multiple representation was permissible after disclosure and consent because of the representations that there was no conflict in testimony among the defendants, because the government conceded that the individual defendants were acting within the scope of their employment, and because under the Tort Claims Act there was little possibility of individual liability in the case.

The district court's rule would probably result in separate lawyers in many litigation situations where DR 5 would not require it. Calling a lawyer in to consult on the conflict problem would doubtless often lead to hiring that person in the main cause just to avoid any possible problem. The court of appeals' rule, however, may well result in multiple representation where DR 5 should preclude it. Although the court did not advert to practical risks of its rule, one large risk is that individual defendants, such as the air traffic controllers in that case, may well decide not to tell everything to a lawyer whose joint representative role requires that he or she must tell the employer everything the employee says, especially if the lawyer tells the employee that — as the lawyer should. The lawyer therefore may not learn that a conflict does exist.

4. An important technique for avoiding disqualification is illustrated by Kennecott Copper Corp. v. Curtiss-Wright Corp., 78 Civ. 1295 (S.D.N.Y. 1978) (unpublished opinion). A law firm, specializing in corporate takeover matters, was asked by Curtiss-Wright to represent it on a one-shot basis. It sought to protect itself against subsequent disqualification problems by discussing potential conflicts with the lawyer-president and the general counsel of the company and then entering into the following agreement: "Should your corporation or any person affiliated with it seek to acquire or invest in any company which is a client of

our office we will be free to represent that client and the same shall not result in a reduction of the retainer." Was that agreement sufficient to accomplish the law firm's purpose? Later, at a time when the takeover attempt had failed but the law firm was still representing Curtiss-Wright in litigation arising out of the takeover, the firm represented Kennecott in a divestiture and an acquisition matter. Curtiss-Wright then attempted to take over Kennecott, and the firm advised the Kennecott management of its rights in the ensuing proxy fight waged by Curtiss-Wright. Litigation developed and regular counsel represented Kennecott. Curtiss-Wright's effort to disqualify regular counsel and the firm from any representation of Kennecott failed because of the quoted waiver provision. Kennecott Copper Corp. v. Curtiss-Wright Corp., 78 Civ. 1295 (S.D.N.Y. 1978).

How would you draft a consent clause after the Kennecott case? Would you make it as broad as possible? Is there anything you would exclude? Future clients? Simultaneous representation? Substantially related matters? Use of confidential information? Use of some confidential information? Would you agree to screen off some employees in any situations? Would you preserve a right to withdraw in a situation of actual conflict?

5. The growing tendency of law firms to merge with one another presents great danger that the merged firm may find itself representing conflicting interests simultaneously. Such a situation occurred in Harte Biltmore Ltd. v. First Nat'l Penn. Bank, 655 F. Supp. 419 (S.D. Fla. 1987). The firm sought to resolve the problem of representing and suing a client at the same time by withdrawing from its representation. It was nevertheless disqualified in the second suit. Accord, Picker International, Inc. v. Varian Associates, 670 F. Supp. 1363 (N.D. Ohio 1987).

6. A fascinating analysis of the charges of unethical conduct made against Louis Brandeis at the time of his appointment by President Wilson to the Supreme Court is contained in John P. Frank, The Legal Ethics of Louis D. Brandeis, 17 Stan. L. Rev. 683 (1965), reprinted almost in its entirety and followed by author's Notes at pp. 93-109 of the first edition of this book. Most of the charges involved conflict of interest matters.

3.   Simultaneously Representing and Opposing Affiliated Companies

Another kind of situation that is bound to cause difficulty in this day of acquisitions and mergers is the applicability of conflict rules when it is not the same client, but affiliated clients, that are involved. The following is one of the few opinions to deal with that issue.

PENNWALT CORP. v. PLOUGH, INC.
85 F.R.D. 264 (D. Del. 1980)

MURRAY M. SCHWARTZ, District Judge.

The issue presented is whether plaintiff's counsel should be disqualified from further participation in this Lanham Act, 15 U.S.C. §1125(a), action by reason of its representation of defendant's sister corporation, Scholl, Inc. ("Scholl"), in an anti-trust suit. A chronological statement of largely uncontested facts is essential to an understanding of the conclusion that defendant's motion to disqualiffy should be denied.

The Philadelphia law firm of Dechert, Price & Rhoads ("DP&R") has been plaintiff Pennwalt Corporation's ("Pennwalt") primary and lead outside litigation counsel continuously since 1956. In 1977, Pennwalt, a manufacturer of an athlete's foot remedy, DESENEX, became unhappy with the comparative advertising claims made by defendant Plough, Inc. ("Plough") with respect to its athlete's foot remedy, "AFTATE." The parties, with in-house and outside legal counsel including DP&R attorneys Matthew Broderick and Aaron Finkbiner, met on June 16, 1977. At that meeting, Pennwalt reiterated its intention first stated on May 13, 1977 to institute suit against Plough if the challenged advertisements were not stopped. Michael Pietrangelo, house counsel and Vice-President of Plough and Associate General Counsel of Schering-Plough Corporation ("Schering-Plough"), also attended the June 16, 1977 meeting. By letter dated July 5, 1977, over the signature of Pietrangelo, Plough, after stating its advertising claims were proper, undertook to terminate certain offending commercials, reserving the right to engage in comparative advertising in the future.

Plough did not run the offending advertisements in 1978. Instead, it took the offensive by filing challenges with the three national television networks to Pennwalt's "nothing is better than DESENEX" advertisement. Pennwalt did not use the services of DP&R, instead opting to retain a specialist in network television advertising challenge procedures in defending against Plough's network challenge to Pennwalt's advertising.

A then unrelated event, but nonetheless one of considerable portent to the present motion, took place in 1978. In June of that year, DP&R undertook in the Eastern District of Pennsylvania to defend Scholl, along with four other shoe manufacturers and an employee of one of them, in a matter styled The Shoe Barn Ltd. v. Acme Boot Co., Inc., et al., C.A. No. 78-1666. *Shoe Barn* is an anti-trust case filed by a plaintiff who alleges a conspiracy to refuse to deal and to fix resale prices of shoes by roughly 100 named defendants. At that time Scholl was headquartered in Chicago operating two divisions, footwear and footcare, with one legal department servicing both divisions. But for follow-up billing reminders by the accounting department of DP&R, all DP&R communications with Scholl have been by two attorneys of DP&R, Henry Kolowrat and Jean Weyman Burns. All of the Kolowrat and Burns communications with Scholl until their withdrawal as counsel for Scholl in the *Shoe Barn* case have been limited to the operating personnel of Scholl's footwear division, Scholl's accountants, Scholl's inside counsel still located in Chicago, and Scholl's outside referral counsel, Henry L. Mason of the Chicago law firm of Sidley & Austin. Mr. Kolowrat and Ms. Burns during the course of their representation of Scholl never obtained any information concerning Schering-Plough or Plough or any of their activities and in fact never had any communications of any kind with either Schering-Plough or Plough.

On April 2, 1979, Schering-Plough acquired Scholl as a wholly owned subsidiary. Since Plough was already a wholly-owned subsidiary of Schering-Plough, Scholl and Plough became sister corporations as of that date with some overlap of boards of directors and officers. On May 11, 1979, DP&R filed this lawsuit on behalf of Pennwalt against Plough charging it with false, misleading and deceptive advertising claims with respect to its athlete's foot remedy AFTATE vis-à-vis Pennwalt's DESE-NEX, all in violation of §43(a) of the Lanham Act, 15 U.S.C. §1125(a), as well as pendant state-law violations. While DP&R did not know Scholl, the corporation it had been defending in the anti-trust litigation since June 1978, and Plough, the corporation it sued on May 11, 1979, were sister corporations on that date, it became aware that Scholl had been purchased by Schering-Plough around the end of May, 1979.

DP&R never informed either Scholl or Pennwalt that it was acting on behalf of one sister corporation and against the other. Instead, Pietrangelo, who undoubtedly knew of DP&R's representation of Pennwalt against Plough in the instant litigation in May 1979, learned of DP&R's representation of Scholl in October 1979 when a statement for legal services from DP&R to Scholl came to his attention as the individual having principal legal responsibility for Schering-Plough's U.S. Consumer Operations Division. Scholl was placed in that division on the date of its acquisition by Schering-Plough. Plough was already a member of that division.

Pietrangelo's late acquisition of knowledge of DP&R's representation of Scholl is explained by the fact that in June 1979 he began preliminary steps to consolidate the Scholl legal services and staff into the legal department of the division in Memphis, Tennessee, which included among other things institution of a new reporting system requiring all Scholl legal matters to be reported directly to him. . . .

Pietrangelo's discovery of DP&R's representation of Scholl was brought to the attention of Donald Green, of the Washington, D.C. law firm of Wald, Harkrader & Ross, who in turn raised the matter directly with DP&R. Thereafter, there followed an increasingly acrimonious exchange of correspondence, highlighted by the following: DP&R took the position there was no ethical conflict; defendant Plough unilaterally terminated all discovery without benefit of court order; DP&R offered to withdraw as counsel for Scholl if requested; Schering-Plough (a nonparty to the litigation involving its wholly-owned subsidiaries, Plough and Scholl) requested in writing that DP&R withdraw from its representation of Pennwalt in the instant litigation against Plough and specifically did not request that DP&R withdraw in the Scholl litigation; DP&R responded to Schering-Plough, advising it no longer desired to represent Scholl; Schering-Plough took the position DP&R had violated the American Bar Association Code of Ethics, which could only be cured by withdrawal from representation of Pennwalt in the matter sub judice, and refused to permit DP&R to withdraw from the *Shoe Barn* litigation.

The above deterioration of relationships culminated with DP&R's filing a motion to withdraw from its Scholl representation in the Eastern District of Pennsylvania. During oral argument on the disqualification motion in this district, DP&R, while disputing it was currently in a conflict position, candidly acknowledged it would inevitably be in a conflict situation in the future if it were not permitted to withdraw in the Scholl litigation. Subsequently, Scholl's response to the DP&R motion to withdraw in the Eastern District of Pennsylvania was to request deferral of a ruling on DP&R's withdrawal request until this Court ruled on Plough's disqualification motion. On December 28, 1979, DP&R's motion to withdraw in the Scholl litigation was granted.

Resolution of charges of unethical conduct arising from concurrent representation of sister corporations is necessarily approached with caution. The proliferation of national or multi-national public corporations owning or partially owning subsidiaries which may also be national or multi-national, the spawning of varied types of corporate affiliates, and the creation of joint ventures yield an infinite variety of potential disqualification problems. The potential for inadvertent unethical conduct is exacerbated by the pronounced trend toward national and international law firms. . . .

Plough and Pennwalt urge diametrically opposed positions. Plough, citing International Business Machines Corp. v. Levin, [p. 42], urges a rule of per se disqualification absent DP&R having obtained consent from Pennwalt and Scholl. It argues "Dechert Price & Rhoads, by representing Scholl, also has a duty of loyalty to Scholl's affiliates. When two corporations are subject to common ownership and control, any injury or risk of injury to one will necessarily cause injury or risk to the other. The duty of undivided loyalty thus requires an attorney to refrain from taking an adversary posture toward one corporation while simultaneously representing its affiliate unless, at a minimum, the attorney has first obtained informed client consent." At oral argument Plough succinctly summarized its position by graphically stating: ". . . if you scratch

Plough, Scholl bleeds." In response, Pennwalt urges the filing of the disqualification motion accompanied by Plough's refusal to engage in further discovery was nothing more than a litigation ploy designed to frustrate a December 31, 1979 termination of discovery date. It points out that before any duty can be owed to any entity, DP&R must have at least represented that entity. Having never represented the parent, Schering-Plough, or the sister corporation, Plough, DP&R concludes it has violated no ethical duty. Further, it asserts Schering-Plough purchased a conflict when it bought Scholl for which its client Pennwalt should not have to pay by suffering disqualification of its counsel in the matter sub judice. . . .

The basic positions espoused by Plough and Pennwalt are rejected. The urged prophylactic rule for disqualification where there is concurrent dual representation of sister corporations cannot be accepted for the simple factual reason that DP&R has never represented Plough or Schering-Plough. Vigorous advocacy cannot change the fact that Scholl is a corporate entity distinct from Plough and Schering-Plough. Similarly, Pennwalt's claim that the ethicality of its position is unassailable because it never represented the "client," Plough or Schering-Plough is overly broad. Representation under the Code has been prohibited in varied circumstances even though the attorney-client relationship never existed. See Fund of Funds, Ltd. v. Arthur Andersen & Co., [p 135]; Whiting Corp. v. White Machinery Corp., 567 F.2d 713 (7th Cir. 1977) (motion to disqualify plaintiff's law firm denied but law firm's representation of non-party touching upon the subject matter of litigation ordered curtailed where non-party corporation owned 20% of the stock and appointed 40% of the Board of Directors of defendant); Wilson P. Abraham Const. v. Armco Steel Corp., 559 F.2d 250 (5th Cir. 1977) (remand required to ascertain whether past and present actions were substantially related and whether confidential information had been divulged between counsel in prior action where plaintiff's counsel in civil anti-trust action was proceeding against a codefendant of a former client in a concluded criminal anti-trust action); but see Fred Weber, Inc. v. Shell Oil Co. [p. 50, Note 8]. . . .

In my view, striving to determine whether to affix the label of "client" obscures what must be the basic inquiry where a question of the ethicality of the representation of an attorney or his law firm has arisen: Does or will the complained of conduct violate the ultimate objective of each of the Canons considered separately, and of the Code considered in its entirety? The Canons, Ethical Considerations and Disciplinary Rules serve as a comprehensive guide providing the Bar with standards of conduct expressed as axiomatic norms, aspirational objectives and mandatory minimum levels of conduct respectively. Obviously, no Code could be drafted which would address all of the problems and possible permutations and combinations of relationships between lawyers and their clients, colleagues, and the public in a changing society. Instead, it establishes general guidelines against which proposed and actual conduct can be evaluated. . . . Application of Canon 4 most often occurs in "prior representation" cases. While the case sub judice is not a "prior representation" case, there would be no hesitation to find DP&R disqualified if that firm could not pass the widely adopted "substantial relationship" test analogized to concurrent representation of sister corporations. . . .

Analogizing to the substantial relationship test, it is found that the subject matter of the *Shoe Barn* litigation is not related to the instant litigation. It is realistic to infer that the Scholl staff and Scholl attorneys still based in Chicago and with whom DP&R communicated have provided confidential information with respect to Scholl and its footwear products in defense of the anti-trust litigation. However, it is unrealistic to conclude that any of the confidential information provided by Scholl is relevant to any issue in this Lanham Act litigation involving the relative merits of athlete's foot remedies. DP&R having received no confidential information from Scholl relevant to the instant litigation, it is found there has been no violation of Canon 4 prior to December 28, 1979, the date of DP&R's withdrawal as counsel for Scholl.

One can persuasively argue that DP&R's defense of Scholl until permitted to withdraw and representation of Pennwalt against Plough must be viewed as concurrent, in that both were occurring at the same time. . . .

The refusal in International Business Machines Corp. v. Levin and Cinema 5, Ltd. v. Cinerama, Inc. [p. 50, Note 6], to consider the subject matter of each representation teaches that the underlying purpose of Canon 5 is to ensure the absolute and unfettered loyalty of an attorney to a particular client. All the responsibilities and decisions entrusted to the attorney, such as the force with which an argument is pressed or the recommendation to the client with regard to an offer of settlement, cannot and must not be influenced in even the slightest measure by considerations of the attorney's future relations with his client's adversary. Conscious calculation by the attorney is not alone prohibited; the very threat of divided loyalty is a basis for disqualification under Canon 5.

In assessing whether this threat exists in circumstances such as those presented here, the Court properly may examine the relationship between the sister corporations. The object of this inquiry is not to determine whether Plough can be affixed with the label "client." Rather, it is to gauge the degree, if any, to which DP&R's representation of either Pennwalt or Scholl may be influenced by a regard for the alternate client's welfare.

Until it moved to withdraw as Scholl's counsel, the record conclusively demonstrates that DP&R provided both Pennwalt and Scholl with nothing less than undivided and undiluted loyalty with no "actual or apparent conflict in loyalties or diminution in vigor . . . of representation."

Unlike the situation in International Business Machines Corp. v. Levin where an attorney was suing the same corporate defendant, Scholl and Plough did not become sister corporations until May 1979, ten months after DP&R undertook the defense of Scholl. Further, the merger of Scholl headquarters, personnel and legal departments is ongoing, with the major move and realignment of staff to be accomplished in 1980. Under these circumstances, it is highly unlikely that as of the date of DP&R's withdrawal of representation of Scholl there was any adverse effect on DP&R's exercise of its independent judgment on behalf of either Pennwalt or Scholl by reason of DP&R's adversary posture toward Scholl's sister corporation, Plough.

If DP&R were not permitted to timely withdraw as counsel for Scholl, it volunteered at oral argument that it would eventually find itself in a conflict position. The DP&R conflict would be caused by the changing circumstances of Scholl, viz., Scholl and Plough were placed in the same division, with the Chief Executive Officer of the division sitting on both boards of directors, and more importantly the upcoming headquarters consolidation with the personnel of one legal department under what will be the active supervision of the same attorney. Having met its burden with respect to the absence of an actual conflict and the withdrawal from the Scholl litigation precluding a conflict certain to occur in the future, DP&R has satisfied its burden that it has not violated Canon 5 under the peculiar facts and circumstances of this case. In arriving at the holding that Canon 5 has not been violated, the Court does not suggest that counsel may eliminate an *existing* conflict merely by choosing to represent the more favored client and withdrawing its representation of the other. Such conduct is expressly disfavored. Here, no conflict yet existed. DP&R's withdrawal from *Shoe Barn* simply obviated the occurrence of a conflict certain to arise in the future by virtue of the evolving assimilation of Scholl into the Schering-Plough division which contains Plough.

It is emphasized, however, that there could be many situations where withdrawal might not be permitted, cf., Cinema 5, Ltd. v. Cinerama, Inc., supra, at 1387, or where even though withdrawal occurs, the concern with protecting the integrity of the Bar might nonetheless dictate disqualification. The precise facts and circumstances, as well as the timing involved, would be factors to be assessed in determining whether an ethical violation has or will occur and the appropriate remedial measures for the same.

Canon 9 states "A Lawyer Should Avoid Even the Appearance of Impropriety." Canon 9, unlike Canons 4 and 5, does not reference a client. The articulated tests gaining circuit court approval for disqualification by reason of violation of Canon 9 are:

> [A]n attorney should be disqualified under Canon 9 only when "there is a
> reasonable possibility of improper professional conduct" and "the likeli-

hood of public suspicion or obloquy outweighs the social interests which will be served by a lawyer's continued participation in a particular case." Westinghouse Elec. Corp. v. Kerr-McGee Corp., 580 F.2d 1311, 1321 (7th Cir.), cert. denied, 439 U.S. 955, 99 S. Ct. 353, 58 L. Ed. 2d 346 (1978) (approving district court formulation, 448 F. Supp. 1304).

and

[U]nder this canon there must be a showing of a reasonable possibility that some specifically identifiable impropriety in fact occurred and that the likelihood of public suspicion must be weighed against the interest in retaining counsel of one's choice. Brennan's, Inc. v. Brennan's Restaurants, Inc., supra, 590 F.2d at 172.

Disqualification of DP&R is not required under either test [that has been used for interpreting Canon 9.] On this record there is no "reasonable possibility of improper professional conduct" as articulated in *Westinghouse*, [p. 51, Note 9] supra, much less a showing of any "specifically identifiable impropriety" as set forth in *Brennan's, Inc.* [p. 101] supra. Further, there is nothing in the record to warrant any public suspicion. It is found DP&R has not violated Canon 9.

In arriving at the conclusion that DP&R has not violated Canons 4, 5 and 9, each was analyzed separately. As stated earlier, due regard must be had for the policies embraced within the Code in its entirety. For example, there is no reason why breach of the duty of undivided loyalty under Canon 5 could not also contravene the prohibition or policies against disclosure of confidential information proscribed by Canon 4. It is difficult to perceive how there could be free, unfettered communications between DP&R and Scholl after the merger of headquarters is completed in 1980, and a small staff of in-house attorneys located at the same physical site and under the active supervision of one attorney are handling both Plough and Scholl matters. Similarly, there would be reasonable grounds to believe there would or could be an "adverse effect" proscribed by DR 5-105(A) and (B). In the case at bar, however, DP&R's conduct has not run afoul of these policies.

The interface between Canon 4 and Canon 5 nevertheless suggests that counsel in concurrent dual representation cases should proceed with the utmost caution. For, while obtaining the consent of both clients under DR 5-105(C) may make multiple representations permissible under Canon 5, it would not permit the use of confidential information by an attorney against his own client. In fact, a close reading of EC 4-5 would suggest an attorney can never "use information acquired in the course of the representation of the client to the disadvantage of the client" although he can use such information for his own purposes after full disclosure and with consent. See, Westinghouse Elec. Corp. v. Gulf Oil Corp., supra, 588 F.2d at 228. Thus, it follows that Plough's proposed prophylactic rule could not work even if it did not have to hurdle the problem of sister or affiliated corporations.

While DP&R has been absolved of any ethical infraction, the facts in this case amply illustrate the need for law offices to use the utmost vigilance and, to the extent feasible, make maximum use of current technology as an aid in avoiding potential conflict. Further, it illustrates how projected changes in mode of internal operation of the client unknown to the attorney can cause a potential for conflict. Given that the duty is upon the attorney to ferret out such conflicts, and not upon the client to divulge them,[10] Westinghouse Elec. Corp. v. Kerr-McGee Corp., supra, 580 F.2d at 1321, I have no hesitance in suggesting that a law firm would be well advised to inform both clients in writing as soon as it finds it is, or will be, in an adversarial position as between parent and subsidiary corporations, wholly owned or otherwise, sister corporations, affiliated corporations or joint venturers. Only in that manner can the potential for ethical impropriety be evaluated, if not amicably resolved, at the earliest practicable time. Failure to obtain consent, assuming a consent to be effective, would not necessarily mean a firm is or should be disqualified. It would, however, alert the litigants and their attorneys to the problem.

NOTES

1. The court refers to, but ignores, the fact that DP&R discovered the potential conflict five months before Plough discovered it but did not inform Plough or Scholl or take any action to resolve the problem. Should that have made any difference in the court's decision?

2. The court notes that the decision to put Plough and Scholl in the same division and to consolidate the legal activities of the conglomerate indicated the imminence of actual conflict. Is it suggesting that DP&R might have been able to continue its representation of Pennwalt and Scholl, even without consent of both parties, if those decisions had not been made? See the *McCourt* case, p. 50, Note 7, for a contrary suggestion.

3. An unusual case involving representation in an "affiliates" situation was presented in FTC v. Exxon Corporation, 636 F.2d 1336 (D.C. Cir.

10. The Court notes that most, if not all, large corporations likely to be involved in the problem here employ house counsel. Like their outside counterparts, house counsels' conduct is governed by the Code. While this case, in which house counsel acted promptly, was not an appropriate vehicle to address the issue, one can reasonably expect that conduct of house counsel will become another factor to be considered in determining whether an ethical impropriety has occurred. More specifically, it may become necessary to examine whether due diligence by house counsel could have prevented an existing conflict, and if so, whether outside counsel alone must shoulder the responsibility in eliminating the conflict.

1980). Exxon proposed to acquire Reliance Electric Co. The FTC sought to prevent the acquisition on a potential competitor theory of antitrust liability. The trial court permitted the acquisition but required Exxon to hold separate the Drives Group portion of Reliance during the pendency of the FTC proceeding, which looked to divestiture. Thereafter the court entered an order forbidding both inside and outside Exxon counsel from having an attorney-client relationship with the Drives Group or its personnel in connection with the FTC litigation. The Court of Appeals affirmed, holding that there was a conflict between the interests of Exxon and those of the Drives Group. Insofar as there was a possibility of divestiture, the interests of a potentially separate Drives Group were very different from those of Exxon and therefore should not be represented by Exxon counsel.

4. *Joint Representation of an Entity and Its Employees*

PROBLEM 6

Lawyer is retained to represent Towing Service Inc. against prospective claims of large property damage as a result of an accident between one of Towing's wreckers and a gasoline truck. Lawyer is about to interview Towing's driver. What, if anything, should she say to Towing Service about the matter of representing Driver? Should Towing Service offer Lawyer's representation to Driver? Should it tell Driver to get his own counsel? See E. F. Hutton & Co. v. Brown, 305 F. Supp. 371 (S.D. Tex. 1969).

───────────────

The following group of materials presents one of the more difficult conflict of interest problems that a lawyer may face: simultaneous representation by an attorney of an entity and some of its employees. The question may come up as an evidentiary matter in the context of litigation against the company. Discovery may be sought of relevant communications between company counsel and company employees. In that setting, attention is focused on the reach of the attorney-client privilege via the attorney's representation of the company and not on whether the employee has also become a client. The question asked is: How does the general rule that communications received by the attorney from the client during the course of representation are privileged from inquiry during litigation apply to employees of a corporation or other business entity? Obviously, such an entity can act only through agents. Are all communications between the corporation counsel and corporation employees covered by the attorney-client privilege? Or are there circumstances in which the position of the corporate employee is more analogous to that of a witness? Some divergence of views exists among the courts that have considered the issue. See the discussion in Note, Attorney-Client Privilege for Corporate Clients: The Control Group Test, 84 Harv. L. Rev. 424 (1970), contrasting the "traditional view," allowing the corporation to claim privilege so long as the employees were acting as agents of the corporation in making the communication; the "dominant" state court view, allowing the corporation to claim privilege if the communication was made by the employee at the direction of the employer for the purpose of obtaining legal advice; the test of Harper & Row Publishers, Inc. v. Decker, 423 F.2d 487, 491-492 (7th Cir. 1970), aff'd by an equally divided court, 400 U.S. 348 (1971), allowing the corporation to claim privilege "where the employee makes the communication at the direction of his superiors in the corporation and where the subject matter upon which the attorney's advice is sought by the corporation and dealt with in the communication is the performance by the employee of the duties of his employment"; and the "control group" test, enunciated first in City of Philadelphia v. Westinghouse Elec. Corp., 210 F. Supp. 483, 485 (E.D. Pa. 1962), which would allow the corporation to claim the privilege only if the employee "is in a position to control or even to take a substantial part in a decision about any action which the corporation may take upon the advice of the attorney, or if he is an authorized member of a body or group which has that authority."

A substantial amount of confusion in the federal courts was cleared away by the Supreme Court's decision in Upjohn Co. v. United States, 449 U.S. 383 (1981). Although the Court refused to lay down a general rule, it also refused to adopt the control group test, and its holding protected communication of information from lower-level employees that was needed to provide a basis for legal advice. While the reach of the attorney-client privilege is now clearer in federal courts, there still exists the possibility of different rules in federal and state courts in a given jurisdiction as well as different rules in different states. Since lawyers are likely to be unable to predict the forum of future litigation when they discuss business with corporate or other entity employees, any conflict in potentially applicable law makes the process of communication with lower-level employees very difficult.

Sometimes, however, the issue is not whether the corporate attorney's relationship with the corporate employee is such that communications between them are privileged, but whether the attorney may undertake representation of one or more entity employees at the same time that he or she is representing the entity with respect to the same subject matter. The issue arose in that context in the following case, which should be read not only from the perspective of passing judgment after the fact but also in terms of the choice that was made by the attorney when asked to act. There is further discussion of related aspects of this issue in Chapter 5, especially at pp. 366 ff.

In re MERRILL LYNCH, PIERCE, FENNER & SMITH, INC.

Securities and Exchange Commission, File No. 3-4329
(Unpublished opinion, December 6, 1973)

SIDNEY ULLMAN, Administrative Law Judge.

These proceedings were instituted by Commission order dated June 22, 1973 (Order) to determine whether respondents have violated certain provisions of the Securities Exchange Act of 1934 (Exchange Act) and of the Securities Act of 1933 (Securities Act), and if so, what remedial action is appropriate. The Order names as respondents Merrill Lynch, Pierce, Fenner and Smith (Merrill Lynch or Registrant), two men employed in its Research Division during the relevant period of approximately 21 months from March 1968 to November 1969, Philip E. Albrecht (Albrecht) and Willard Pierce (Pierce), and 47 persons then employed as registered representatives in Merrill Lynch offices throughout the nation.

The Order asserts charges by the Division of Enforcement (Division) that the Research Division employees, Albrecht and Pierce, violated the anti-fraud provisions of the securities laws[1] by preparing and disseminating to 250 branch offices and to Merrill Lynch registered representatives a series of false and misleading opinions and recommendations with respect to Scientific Control Corporation (Scientific), a company then in the business of manufacturing computers and components thereof. The Order alleges, and the answer of Merrill Lynch admits, that during the relevant period "a minimum of 4,000 public customers of Registrant purchased a minimum of 400,000 shares of the common stock of Scientific." It alleges also that these opinions and recommendations for the purchase and holding of Scientific shares were transmitted in both oral and written form to customers of Merrill Lynch.

Also transmitted to purchasers and prospective purchasers of Scientific, in violation of the anti-fraud provisions by the 47 registered representatives named as respondents, were untrue statements of material facts relating to Scientific, and statements made untrue by omissions of material facts, according to the allegations of the Order.

In addition, Albrecht and Pierce are alleged to have violated and aided and abetted violations of Section 10(b) of the Exchange Act and Rule

---

1. Section 17(a) of the Securities Act, Section 10(b) of the Exchange Act and Rule 10b-5 thereunder.

10b-5 thereunder in connection with the purchase and sale of securities of Scientific by making "recommendations concerning transactions in the said securities and [inducing] the purchase thereof by said customers and prospective customers . . . in part on the basis of material information . . . received from Scientific and not . . . disclosed or disseminated to the investing public, including those persons on the other side of said securities transactions."

Merrill Lynch is charged with failure to supervise the persons subject to its supervision who committed the violations charged in the Order, and Albrecht, similarly, is charged with failure to supervise "a person who was subject to his supervision and who committed such violations." Merrill Lynch is charged with responsibility for all of the violations allegedly committed by each of the 49 other respondents.

The law firm Brown, Wood, Fuller, Caldwell and Ivey ("Brown Wood") filed answers on behalf of all [but two] respondents. . . .

As a result of a letter dated August 20, 1973 from the Division to the undersigned, raising an issue of an alleged conflict of interest in Brown Wood's representation of Merrill Lynch, the employer, and some 47 registered representative employees or former employees, a pre-hearing conference for the purpose of hearing argument on that issue was held in New York City on September 26, 1973. . . .

Brown Wood's documents . . . included a written opinion dated September 24, 1973 from the law firm Simpson Thatcher & Bartlett ("Simpson Thatcher") to the effect that on the basis of the facts then known to that firm and stated in its opinion letter, Brown Wood's representation of Merrill Lynch and the . . . other respondents in these proceedings presented "no legal or ethical impediments.". . .

The conclusion reached in this order is that if the decisions of the individual respondents to retain Brown Wood as their counsel are *informed* decisions, such representation may be continued. Accordingly, this order is being directed to each individual respondent to assure that he is substantially apprised of the arguments on both sides of the issue, and that his decision with regard to the selection of counsel, whether now re-affirmed or changed, is made with such knowledge. . . .

The basic contentions of the Division are that Brown Wood, having served for years as counsel to Merrill Lynch, and serving at present as its counsel in a host of legal proceedings including class actions deriving from the sale of Scientific shares, is unable to give to the defense of individual respondents its undivided loyalty and to defend their positions with the zeal required in an attorney-client relationship.[2] Apart from the Division's contentions with regard to professional ethics inher-

---

2. The Division also asserts that potential pressure exists on individual respondents currently serving as account executives because their salaries and bonuses are subject to flexible subjective standards of management. [Footnote moved from omitted portion of opinion.]

ent in requirements and proscriptions of the pertinent codes of ethics applicable to attorneys, it disputes the adequacy of representation by Brown Wood, and maintains that during the proceeding conflicts will arise which will make it impossible for Brown Wood to serve with equal diligence two masters, one of which is a substantial source of business for the firm. Without in any way questioning the integrity of the firm, the Division contends that Brown Wood has an indomitable desire to protect the Registrant, and that it is not sufficiently mindful of the needs of the individuals in anticipating their respective defenses. It seems to suggest, also, that the ability of a competent attorney to develop arguments in his client's favor cannot be minimized, and that the direction and emphasis of the attorney's thinking are important factors in developing such arguments and positions: that wholehearted attention and zeal cannot be given to such effort when presented with divergent positions of two clients.

As an example, the Division cites a recent case in which the Commission reduced a sanction imposed by the National Association of Securities Dealers Inc. on a registered representative because it found that, among other factors, "the pervasiveness of the misconduct in [his] office, led by his manager, may have misled a man of his limited experience in the securities business." The Division argues, assuming certain investor-witnesses testify credibly in these proceedings, that counsel representing Merrill Lynch could not urge that an atmosphere of over-optimism for Scientific shares existed within certain Merrill Lynch offices, "spawned by a barrage of over-optimistic (and fraudulent) recommendations issued by Merrill," with encouragement to sell, and with failure of adequate supervision as an added factor that might suggest mitigation of an offense by an account executive.

Similarly, the Division contends that the exploration of the many charges during the hearing will be extensive and complex, and that differing approaches will be required for the defenses of individual respondents and for that of Merrill Lynch during the examination or cross-examination of witnesses and perhaps of individual respondents, whether account executives or research analysts. It also argues that because of the several pending class actions against Merrill Lynch arising out of the sale of Scientific, Brown Wood would be unable to fairly evaluate and recommend a settlement favorable to an individual respondent in the event Merrill Lynch believed that a settlement or settlements generally might compromise its own defense either in the instant proceedings or in other litigation.

The Division recognizes that a respondent in administrative proceedings normally has the right to be represented by counsel of his choice, and that an unfair denial of that right might constitute a denial of due process under the Constitution. It was pointed out and agreed at the oral argument, for example, that the Commission has no obligation to appoint counsel for a respondent who is unable to pay counsel fees. And in its reply brief the Division seems to concede that where it is not clear that a conflict of interests will occur between two or more clients of an attorney, the informed consent of the client or clients whose interests more likely would suffer in the event a conflict should develop can provide justification for the continuation of multiple representation, as here. This is the position reached in this order.

Brown Wood points out that it has represented each of the individual respondents during and prior to their respective depositions by the Division; that in each of the interviews the individual respondent was advised of Brown Wood's long-standing representation of Merrill Lynch, and was told that representation of the individual would be feasible "only if he was sure in his own mind that he had done nothing wrong"; that if a conflict of interest appeared to develop, Brown Wood would have to withdraw as his counsel and that, in turn, if a respondent felt that there was divergence of interest "he need only advise us and we would withdraw." Brown Wood points out that each individual respondent whom the firm represents has independently decided to retain it, that at the taking of depositions the Division advised each deposed witness of his right to choose other counsel; that in questionnaires sent by the Division to other registered representatives they were advised of their right to confer with and choose counsel other than Merrill Lynch's counsel; and that each registered representative chose to adhere to his original decision. They point out, further, that a copy of a letter of August 20, 1973 to the undersigned from William D. Moran, Regional Administrator of the Commission's New York Regional Office (representing the Division) was sent by Brown Wood "to each individual respondent whom we represent," and that no negative response was made to the suggestion that "if any respondent wished to engage different counsel he should so advise us."

The conclusion reached here is consistent with the requirements of due process, with the decisions of the courts insofar as the factual situations of related cases approximate those before us, and at this stage of the proceedings it has not been shown to be inconsistent with the applicable codes of ethics. The opinion of Simpson Thatcher reaches a similar conclusion but expresses a caveat clearly recognized by Brown Wood — that it is Brown Wood's continuing duty to be on the alert for new information that may change what now appears to it to be proper representation into representation that is improper for counsel and precarious for the client.

This is a basis for the Division argument that Brown Wood is accepting and crediting assertions of innocence by all of the individual respondents it represents, while failing to recognize, for example, that investor-witnesses may give credible testimony as to false and improper representations regarding Scientific by any or all of such respondents.

A Merrill Lynch employee, says the Division, does not tell Merrill Lynch attorneys that he violated the law.

Brown Wood argues that this argument is based on only a slight and a hypothetical possibility of any conflict of interest arising, and it maintains that it can adequately represent all of its clients in this proceeding. The firm recognizes its professional responsibility and values highly its reputation: it is entirely familiar with the ethical considerations involved here, and its decision on this issue has not been made lightly. Its counsel quotes one sentence from EC 5-17: "Whether a lawyer can fairly and adequately protect the interests of multiple clients in these and similar situations depends upon analysis of each case." Of course Brown Wood agrees with the caveat in the Simpson Thatcher opinion, that it must be continually alert for information which might indicate a conflict of interest; and that if such information is received it must apprise its client or clients thereof and re-evaluate its position. This is a part of the risk taken by individual respondents who retain Brown Wood as counsel — that at some stage of the proceedings it is possible that new counsel, unfamiliar with the case, may have to be substituted.

The decision reached here also is consistent with the precept that a litigant's choice of counsel is an extremely important right which should not be denied him, absent considerations compelling a contrary conclusion: and it is consistent with a practical approach of permitting the clients to choose as their counsel, if they wish to do so on an informed basis, the attorneys who are most familiar with the case and with the potential vulnerability of those charged with the offenses. Apparently, it also may obviate problems that could arise with regard to some of the respondents — the matter of the cost of retaining counsel for their defense, even though reasonable efforts will be made to limit the introduction of evidence against individual respondents to particular sessions of hearing. . . .

While the courts have stated that "The obligation to search out and disclose potential conflicts is placed on the attorney in order to put the client in a position to protect himself by retaining substitute counsel if he so desires,"[4] the client is not thereby freed from responsibility for his own informed decision. It is understood that the individual respondents are educated, experienced business-men. . . .

NOTES

1. The issue of the *Merrill Lynch* case may come up in contexts other than a corporation and its employees, and the reservation of the right

4. E. F. Hutton & Company v. Brown . . . [305 F. Supp. 372 (S.D. Tex. 1969)]

to represent the entity if a conflict develops with its employees is not always successful. Yablonski v. United Mine Workers, 448 F.2d 1175 (D.C. Cir. 1971) is an example of both those propositions. It involved a suit by a dissident member of the UMW against the union, its president, and two other officers under the Labor-Management Reporting and Disclosure Act. The suit alleged misappropriation of union funds by the individual defendants. The court concluded that regular UMW outside counsel who had appeared on behalf of both the union and the individual defendants and then withdrew from representation of the individual defendants was disqualified from continuing its representation of the union in this case. The court held that the ability of counsel to advise the union with respect to its true interests was undermined by the fact that counsel was concurrently representing the union's president in many other lawsuits in which his activities as a union official were being examined. Although it noted that any successor union counsel would be chosen by the union president, it stated that at least successor counsel would have only the union as its client.

In view of that result, counsel probably withdrew from representation of the wrong clients. Its past representation of the union would not seem to have precluded it from continuing to represent the individual defendants in this suit if it had withdrawn from representing the union.

After remand, the firm withdrew from representation of UMWA and UMWA general counsel and all four members of his staff entered appearances for UMWA. The district court refused to disqualify them but a petition for mandamus to compel compliance with its earlier order was granted by the court of appeals on the ground that house counsel were disqualified for the same reasons that had disqualified original counsel. 454 F.2d 1036 (1971), cert. denied, 406 U.S. 906 (1972).

2. What is the importance of the last sentence of the *Merrill Lynch* case to the holding? How does it relate to footnote 2 and the other arguments of the Division? In other cases, we have seen courts stressing the importance of prophylactic rules. Here we see the "court" engaging in a weighing test measuring the experience of the individual respondents and their desire to choose their own counsel against the pressures to maintain a common front that are inherent in the employer-employee relationship. Would a prophylactic rule barring joint representation be a wiser policy? Even if it meant that some of the individual respondents had no counsel?

3. What is the difference between an argument by Brown Wood's counsel in *Merrill Lynch* that its conduct was proper and an "expert opinion" from Simpson Thatcher to the same effect?

4. During a strike against the Washington Post and at a time when a large number of pressmen were in the pressroom, damage estimated to be in excess of one million dollars was inflicted on the machinery at the Post and a foreman was beaten. The pressmen's union hired Mr. Sol

Rosen to represent its members in connection with a grand jury investigation arising out of that incident. Recognizing the professional difficulties involved in representing all the potential witnesses, Mr. Rosen advised them as a group and gave them Xerox copies of instructions regarding the invocation of the privilege against self-incrimination. He did not interview the witnesses personally so that he did not advise with respect to each witness's potential criminal liability or chances for a grant of immunity. He did, however, advert to the possibility of each individual's potential liability as a conspirator regardless of actual participation in the destruction.

The grand jury subpoenaed 21 union members who were working in the pressroom at the critical time. Except for two who testified that they had seen nothing, the remainder invoked the privilege against self-incrimination, many quite indiscriminately. On motion of the government, Judge Jones disqualified Mr. Rosen from representing more than one individual at the grand jury hearing and required pressmen who wanted counsel to hire counsel who did not represent any other subpoenaed pressman. Balancing the interests of the witnesses to counsel of their choice against the harm to the public interest in effective functioning of the grand jury, although not including cost of separate counsel in the balance, he found only slight impairment to the interests of the former but substantial impairment to those of the latter. He noted the inability of Mr. Rosen to advise each client of his best interest because of potential harm to his other clients and the consequent unnecessary and uninformed invocation of the privilege by each pressman. Furthermore, he pointed out that the multiple representation would lead to breach of the secrecy of grand jury proceedings. Finally, he stressed that the consequences of the multiple representation made it impossible for the government to determine to whom immunity should be granted to further the investigation. In re Grand Jury Investigation, 403 F. Supp. 1176 (D.D.C. 1975).

On appeal, the Court of Appeals reversed. 531 F.2d 600 (D.C. Cir. 1976). The court noted that:

what is strikingly absent from the record is any indication of the views of the individual witnesses with respect to their legal representation. . . . It may well be . . . that the subpoenaed witnesses do not view Mr. Rosen as their legal representative, but rather as a legal consultant retained *by the union* both to instruct them with respect to the protection afforded by the Fifth Amendment and to be on hand outside the grand jury room in the event they have any general questions on that matter; and the individual subpoenaed witnesses may also have no intention of retaining personal legal representatives to investigate the particulars of their involvement, to offer qualified legal advice with respect to their assertion of the privilege and their available options, or to negotiate on their behalf with the United States Attorney.

The court also stated that the district court's invocation of grand jury secrecy was erroneous since federal grand jury witnesses could discuss their testimony with anyone. It concluded that the government should proceed in the traditional way to bring each witness before the district court for a ruling with respect to proper assertion of the privilege against self-incrimination and that if the privilege had been properly invoked, the government could then decide whether to grant immunity. Until those procedures had been pursued and demonstrated to be not feasible or not in the public interest, the court held that it was "premature to seek it through disqualification of counsel whose advice to his clients the Government does not like."

For a similar case of counsel representing multiple defendants before a grand jury, see Pirillo v. Takiff, 462 Pa. 511, 466 Pa. 187 (1975), appeal dismissed and cert. denied, 423 U.S. 1083 (1976). That case reached Judge Jones's conclusion but is complicated by the presence of an unusual fee arrangement that was a factor in disqualification of counsel. However, in United States v. RMI Co., 467 F. Supp. 915 (W.D. Pa. 1979), the court refused to allow joint representation of a company indicted for antitrust violations and employees who had testified before a grand jury following a grant of immunity after they had asserted their privilege against self-incrimination. The court concluded that there was an actual conflict of interest notwithstanding affidavits from the employees asserting their desire for joint representation and waiving their right to effective assistance of counsel and notwithstanding the representation of the company that it conceded the truth of the employees' grand jury testimony. The court noted that nevertheless their testimony could be an important part of the government's case, that further discussions with counsel might reveal adverse information, and that tactical judgments to be made with respect to their testimony should not be left to counsel with obligations both to government witnesses and to defendant.

5. In a shareholders' derivative suit against four officer-directors and two corporations charging the individual defendants with misappropriation of corporate funds and violation of federal and state securities laws, Judge Prentice Marshall reviewed the whole range of disqualification cases in this field and held that the law firm that sought to represent both the corporation and the individual defendants was disqualified from representing the corporation because of the conflict inherent in the dual representation. Cannon v. U.S. Acoustics Corp., 398 F. Supp. 209 (N.D. Ill. 1975), affirmed in this regard, 532 F.2d 1118 (7th Cir. 1976). Accord, In re Kinsey, 660 P.2d 660 (Or. 1983) (imposing a public reprimand on an attorney for such conduct).

6. A common situation in which joint representation of an entity and its employees raises conflict of interest problems involves suits under 42 U.S.C. §1983 against a municipality and some of its officials and employees, for example, the mayor, the police chief, police officers, and

individual police on account of actions taken by the latter. The conflict of interest questions are intertwined with the potential liability of each of the defendants as a matter of federal constitutional and statutory law and state law, including state indemnity law. Courts have divided in their attitude toward allowing joint representation of defendants, although sometimes the result has appeared to depend very much on the particular factual and legal situation. Compare Dunton v. County of Suffolk, 729 F.2d 903 (2d Cir. 1984) and Shadid v. Jackson, 521 F. Supp. 87 (E.D. Tex. 1983) (holding joint representation improper) with In re Petition for Review of Opinion 552, 102 N.J. 194, 507 A.2d 233 (1986) (rejecting an ethics committee opinion adopting a per se rule against joint representation of a governmental entity and its employees in a civil rights action) and Sherrod v. Barry, 589 F. Supp. 433 (N.D. Ill. 1984) (holding joint representation proper).

7. The danger posed by the disqualification rules to lawyers representing more than one client in litigation was dramatically presented by In re Corn Derivatives, 748 F.2d 157 (3d Cir. 1984). A law firm represented three named plaintiffs, but not the entire class, in class action litigation. When a settlement was negotiated, two of the firm's clients accepted it while one was opposed. After the law firm filed an appeal on behalf of the dissenter from the district court's order approving the settlement, it withdrew from representation of the two clients who had accepted the settlement. One of them moved in the Court of Appeals to disqualify it from representing the dissenter. The court, finding guidance in both the Model Rules and the Model Code, granted the motion, finding that considerations of loyalty, the keeping of confidences relating to strengths and weaknesses of the case, and the maintenance of public confidence in the integrity of the bar warranted application of the general rule forbidding the law firm from taking a position adverse to its clients in the very same case. The majority opinion, and especially the concurring opinion, noted that the situation would have been quite different if counsel had been class counsel. See p. 550–882, infra. As noted in the *Merrill Lynch* opinion, the situation might also have been different if the law firm had explained at the outset of the litigation that its principal client was the dissenting client and that in the event of a difference of opinion over strategy, it would withdraw from representation of the other two.

5. *The Advocate-Witness Rule in Simultaneous Representation*

DR 5-101(B) and DR 5-102 of the Model Code and Rule 3.7 of the Model Rules require withdrawal from, or refusal of, employment by lawyers in most situations where they are or ought to be called as witnesses. Both documents state exceptions where the testimony relates to uncontested issues or the value of the lawyer's services, and each contains a somewhat differently worded hardship on the client exception. The Model Code is considerably more strict in imposing vicarious disqualification on the firm in all cases. The Model Rules impose such disqualification only where a prohibited conflict of interest is involved, for example, when the lawyer's testimony would be adverse to the client.

The purposes of the rule, to avoid prejudicing the client or the opposing party and to avoid confusion of role, are set forth in EC 5-9 and 5-10 of the Model Code and the Comments to Model Rule 3.7. Although there has been general recognition of the harsh effect that the rule often has on the client, most courts have applied it rather strictly and have refused to read the exceptions broadly for fear that they would then swallow the whole rule. Courts have generally not permitted waiver and even when they suspect that invocation of the rule by the opposing party has been largely for strategic reasons, have stated that the remedy for abuse is not to refuse to apply the rule, but to refer an abuser to disciplinary authorities. Indeed, courts have noted that like other conflict of interest matters, they may raise the issue sua sponte. A good illustration of a thoughtful and thoroughgoing application of the advocate-witness rule is contained in Judge Sofaer's opinion in MacArthur v. Bank of New York, 524 F. Supp. 1205 (S.D.N.Y. 1981). For some interesting diverse applications of the rule, compare United States ex rel. Sheldon Elec. Co. v. Blackhawk Heating & Plumbing Co., 423 F. Supp. 486 (S.D.N.Y. 1976) with Greenebaum-Mountain Mortgage Co. v. Pioneer Nat'l. Title Ins. Co., 421 F. Supp. 1348 (D. Colo. 1976) and Freeman v. Kulicke & Soffa Industries, Inc., 449 F. Supp. 974 (E.D. Pa. 1978).

More recently, there has perhaps been a little movement in the direction of permitting somewhat more generous use of the substantial hardship exception to avoid the great difficulty that changing counsel may impose on a client, especially when there is suspicion that a disqualification motion may be a delaying tactic. See Lumbard v. Maglia, Inc., 621 F. Supp. 1529 (S.D.N.Y. 1985) and Council v. American Home Improvement Society, 632 F. Supp. 144 (D.D.C. 1985). Responding to the perceived harshness of the rule, as applied, New Hampshire amended Model Rule 3.7 by changing the words "substantial hardship" to "unreasonable hardship" in order to give its courts more flexibility in balancing the interests of the testifying lawyer's client and those of the opposing party. McElroy v. Gaffney, 129 N.H. 382, 529 A.2d 889 (N.H. 1987). Several courts have also refused even under the Model Code to disqualify the whole prosecutor's office when one member testifies against a defendant. E.g., Clausell v. State, 474 So.2d 1189 (Fla. 1985) (citing cases from other jurisdictions) and State v. Johnson, 702 S.W.2d 65 (Mo. 1985). Finally, the rule has been inapplicable to a testifying lawyer appearing pro se as one of the litigants. Gorovitz v. Planning Board, 394 Mass. 246, 474 N.E.2d 377 (1985).

6. *Simultaneously Representing and Opposing a Client in Nonlitigation*

PROBLEM 7

Seller and Buyer have agreed on the terms for the sale of Seller's house — the price, the items of personal property that will be sold with the house, and the date of the closing of title — and have signed a memorandum of agreement on a broker's standard form. Lawyer handled Seller's original purchase of the property and is familiar with the chain of title and its problems. Buyer wants to avoid the additional expense required for another attorney to familiarize himself with the title and wishes Lawyer to represent him in closing the title. There are currently no matters in dispute between the parties. May Lawyer undertake to represent Buyer while also representing Seller in the same transaction?

(a) Does it make a difference that it is common practice in the community for the same attorney to represent buyer and seller in this type of transaction?

(b) Does it make a difference that usually this type of transaction is consummated without any major problem?

(c) Suppose Lawyer undertakes the representation and, because of some problem, the closing date must be extended. Buyer, however, wishes to move in and is willing to pay rent. Can Lawyer satisfy his obligation by getting the parties together, explaining the advantages and dangers of this procedure to the parties, and then saying, "You decide what you wish you to do"?

It remains now to examine problems of simultaneous representation of multiple clients in situations that do not involve litigation. Formally, the same words of the disciplinary rules of the Model Code and the Model Rules apply to conflict problems whether litigation is involved or not. The so-called Ethical Considerations of the Model Code are quite explicit in stating that there are many more situations when a lawyer may represent multiple clients with potentially conflicting interests in nonlitigation than in litigation situations. See EC 5-15. The Comments to the Model Rules are rather less clear on this point. See Comments to MR 1.7, ¶ 10.

The courts have dealt with the problem much less often in nonlitigation matters, but one can perceive a rather more permissive attitude even in situations where one might have expected the court to lay down a prophylactic rule of nonrepresentation because of the inherently antagonistic positions of the parties. One recurrent, troublesome situation involves the purchase and sale of real estate. The Supreme Court of New Jersey has considered the situation involved in Problem 7 twice in recent years. It laid down the following rules in In re Kamp, 40 N.J. 588, 595-596, 194 A.2d 236, 240-241 (1963):

> A conflict of interest is inherent in the relationship of buyer and seller; and Canon 6 [of the former Canons of Ethics] is applicable to every occasion in which an attorney undertakes to represent both the seller and the buyer under a sales contract. . . .
>
> Full disclosure requires the attorney not only to inform the prospective client of the attorney's relationship to the seller, but also to explain in detail the pitfalls that may arise in the course of the transaction which would make it desirable that the buyer have independent counsel. The full significance of the representation of conflicting interests should be disclosed to the client so that he may make an intelligent decision before giving his consent. If the attorney cannot properly represent the buyer in all aspects of the transaction because of his relationship to the seller, full disclosure requires that he inform the buyer of the limited scope of his intended representation of the buyer's interests and point out the advantages of the buyer's retaining independent counsel. A similar situation may occur, for example, when the buyer of real estate utilizes the services of the attorney who represents a party financing the transaction. To the extent that both parties seek a marketable title, there would appear to be no conflict between their interests. Nevertheless, a possible conflict may arise concerning the terms of the financing, and therefore at the time of the retainer the attorney should make clear to the buyer the potential area of conflict. In addition, if the buyer's interests are protected only to the extent that they coincide with those of the party financing the transaction, the attorney should explain the limited scope of this protection so that the buyer may act intelligently with full knowledge of the facts.

The New Jersey Supreme Court treated the problem as one of disclosure. It pointed out, however, that a "conflict of interest is inherent in the relationship of buyer and seller." Would it have been preferable for the court to lay down a rule that an attorney may never represent both the buyer and the seller of property? Even if one believed in a prophylactic rule of that sort, are there exceptions that ought to be considered?

The court went on to deal with a situation where it believed that a lawyer might represent two parties (the buyer and the lender) to a transaction to the limited extent that their interests were not in conflict. Is it healthy for a buyer to be relying on an attorney and to enter a confidential relation with him or her with respect to part of a transaction but to be at arm's length for another part of the transaction? Does it make a difference whether the buyer has an independent attorney with regard to the other part of the transaction? Is the reluctance to enforce rigid prohibitions on representation conceivably a reflection of the idea that in some situations it is unsound as a practical matter, and even a poor use of the pool of lawyers' talents, to require multiple lawyers? If that is so, should the prohibition be stated solely in terms of the loss of independence of judgment or representation of differing interests, or should the practical economic and societal interests be introduced frankly into the balance? How should individual lawyers be instructed to strike the balance in particular cases?

The New Jersey Supreme Court reconsidered the *Kamp* decision in In re Dolan, 76 N.J. 1, 384 A.2d 1076 (1978) and while elaborating on the nature of the disclosure and consent that were required, it essentially retained a rule that required consideration of the facts of each case before deciding whether dual representation was permissible. The majority and a concurring judge debated the propriety of a per se disqualification. The majority stated:

> While tenable arguments have been made in favor of a complete bar to any dual representation of buyer and seller in a real estate transaction . . . on balance we decline to adopt an inflexible per se rule. Confining ourselves to the type of situation before us (assuredly there are others, entirely unrelated to financial pressures), the stark economic realities are such that were an unyielding requirement of individual representation to be declared, many prospective purchasers in marginal financial circumstances would be left without representation. That being so, the legal profession must be frank to recognize any element of economic compulsion attendant upon a client's consent to dual representation in a real estate purchase and to be circumspect in avoiding any penalization or victimization of those who, by force of these economic facts of life, give such consent.

Judge Pashman, however, viewed the matter differently:

> . . . The result herein continues the Court's acceptance of dual representation in circumstances where, notwithstanding full disclosure and knowing consent by the derivative client, the intrinsic degree of divided allegiance is so intolerable that the proscribed adverse effect on the exercise of the attorney's independent professional judgment on behalf of that client must ipso facto be conclusively presumed. See DR 5-105(B). In so doing, the Court relies on the fiction that a lay client can effectively consent to dual representation and perpetuates the cruel myth that adequate representation can be provided in such cases by an attorney who supposedly can simultaneously protect the inevitably adverse interests of his two masters. The reality, of course, is that it is well-nigh impossible for the derivative client to be so well attuned to the numerous legal nuances of the transaction that his consent can be said to have been truly informed. The propriety of according dispositive effect to consent so obtained is fur-

ther undermined when it is frankly acknowledged that the consent is induced by the derivative client's reliance on a promise by the attorney which cannot be fulfilled — the promise of adequate representation of each of his two clients.

Surely the Court is not so naive as to the economic realities of such transactions as its utopian stance would indicate. Any conflicting interests which are potentially disruptive of the ultimate goal — the expeditious consummation of the sales transaction — must inevitably be resolved in favor of the primary client and for that same reason will probably not even be brought to the attention of the derivative client. This problem is even more aggravated in circumstances such as those of the instant case where the primary client of the attorney is a developer with whom the attorney has a potentially long-term and profitable relationship. Consequently, the attorney has a substantial economic stake in maintaining the continued goodwill of this primary client.

In re Kamp and In re Dolan are typical cases for testing the propriety of representation of multiple parties to a contract in that they came up in the context of disciplinary action against a lawyer. That context may exert subtle pressure on a court to avoid finding a violation when it wishes to avoid imposing discipline in what it regards as a close case. See also Beal v. Mars Larsen Ranch Corp., Inc., 586 P.2d 1378 (Idaho 1978) (not misconduct for attorney to draft contract as "scrivener" for buyer and seller, with their consent, after they have agreed on its basic terms). A dramatic illustration of the conclusion that the pressure of discipline need not lead to such results is afforded by the Oregon experience. The Oregon Supreme Court imposed discipline in the nonlitigation context in 12 instances between 1974 and 1985 for improper simultaneous representation of multiple interests and in one instance of improper successive representation. In re Barrett, 269 Or. 264, 524 P.2d 1208 (1974); In re Boivin, 271 Or. 419, 533 P.2d 171 (1975); In re Banks, 283 Or. 459, 584 P.2d 284 (1978); In re Galton, 289 Or. 565, 615 P.2d 317 (1980); In re Robertson, 290 Or. 639, 624 P.2d 603 (1981); In re Kinsey, 294 Or. 544, 660 P.2d 660 (1983); In re Jayne, 295 Or. 16, 663 P.2d 405 (1983); In re Hill, 295 Or. 71, 663 P.2d 764 (1983); In re Jans, 295 Or. 289, 666 P.2d 830 (1983); In re Boyer, 295 Or. 624, 669 P.2d 326 (1983); In re Baer, 298 Or. 29, 688 P.2d 1324 (1984); and In re Vaile, 300 Or. 91, 707 P.2d 52 (1985). See also In re Brandsness, 299 Or. 420, 702 P.2d 1098 (1985) (successive representation). It may be that in some jurisdictions the courts are less likely to find a violation of the rules in the nonlitigation context as compared to the litigation context, but Oregon demonstrates that the rules are capable of being applied equally strictly in both cases. The facts and the reasoning of the 13 cited Oregon cases provide a comprehensive statement of approach to the practice, or rather to the forbidden practice, of law in that jurisdiction.

7. Simultaneous Representation of a Client and the Lawyer's Own Interest

Model Code DR 5-101(A) and Model Rule 1.7(b) preclude representation of a client when the lawyer's personal interests might interfere with the representation. The considerations that must be taken into account in assessing the seriousness of the conflict or potential conflict of interests are quite similar to those that must be assessed when it is the interests of another client that are involved. A major difference between the language of the Model Code and the Model Rules is that the former allows the representation if the client consents but the latter prescribes the same objective test in addition to consent that is required in multiple representation of two clients with conflicting interests. If an objective test is desirable in the situation where the conflicting interest involves representation of another client, it is difficult to see why the Model Code did not impose the same requirement where the conflicting interest is the lawyer's self-interest. Although it has not often been done, it is possible, in an egregious case, to interpret the Model Code as not permitting a lawyer, even with client consent, to represent a client when the lawyer's own interests are in conflict by finding such representation to be in conflict with some other provision of the Model Code, such as DR 6-101, DR 7-101(A), or DR 1-102(A) (5). See Massachusetts Committee on Professional Ethics, Opinion 86-1.

Model Rule 1.8 goes beyond the more general language of Model Rule 1.7 to prohibit or regulate a number of specific transactions between lawyers and clients. Note that client consent after consultation removes some of the prohibitions but not others. Note also that the disqualification enforced by Model Rule 1.8(i) when a specified relative is representing an adverse party is personal and is not imputed to other members of the firm.

B. SUCCESSIVE REPRESENTATION — OPPOSING A FORMER CLIENT

PROBLEM 8

In the situations involved in Problems 1 and 2, would it make any difference if the second client had come to the office shortly after the work for the first client had been completed?

PROBLEM 9

In the *Jelco* case, p. 52, if the dispute between Teeples & Thatcher and Jelco had occurred after the suit between Ace Electric and Jelco had been concluded, would it have been permissible for Kobin & Meyer to have represented Teeples against Jelco without Jelco's consent?

Analysis of problems of conflict of interest with respect to simultaneous representation required us to pay attention to both confidential communications and broader aspects of the duty of loyalty to clients. In dealing with problems of successive representation, we deal with duties that, by hypothesis, arise only by reason of a former relationship. In that setting, the focus of analysis has been primarily on the duty to the client that arises out of the past receipt of confidential information. Those are not the only issues, however, for problems may arise if a lawyer's current employment is perceived as involving an attack on a result achieved for a former client.

Surprisingly, the Model Code, which addresses the problem of simultaneous representation in Canon 5 and its accompanying Disciplinary Rules, does not address the problem of successive representation explicitly, except for DR 9-101(A) and (B), which deal with the particular problem of the government lawyer who contemplates private employment. Some courts have inferred a rule from Canon 4's requirements as to confidentiality, but that overlooks the fact that loyalty more broadly defined has also been viewed as part of the underlying rationale for the rules regarding successive representation. Other courts have by brute force read the rules of Canon 5 to refer to successive as well as simultaneous representation. See, for example, In re Brandsness, 299 Or. 420, 702 P.2d 1098 (1985); E.F. Hutton & Co. v. Brown, 305 F. Supp. 371, 394 n. 63 (S.D. Tex. 1969). Still other courts, especially in the early period of substantial conflict of interest litigation in the 1970s, used Canon 9's appearance of impropriety language, occasionally by itself, although more often in conjunction with Canon 4. "Under the ABA Code, there was no express prohibition against representation of interests adverse to former clients, although this court has used Canon 9, 'the appearance of impropriety,' to imply such a duty." In re Corn Derivative Antitrust Litigation, 748 F.2d 157 (3d Cir. 1984). Most of the rules governing successive representation cases, however, have developed in common law fashion and a codification of the general principles has been adopted in Model Rule 1.9. The most often cited statement of the common law rule is that of Judge Weinfeld in T. C. & Theatre Corp. v. Warner Bros. Pictures, 113 F. Supp. 265, 268-269 (S.D.N.Y. 1953) (one footnote omitted), applying Canon 6 of the former Canons of Ethics. Judge Weinfeld stated the rule to be that:

. . . the former client need show no more than that the matters embraced within the pending suit wherein his former attorney appears on behalf of his adversary are substantially related to the matters or cause of action wherein the attorney previously represented him, the former client. The Court will assume that during the course of the former representation confidences were disclosed to the attorney bearing on the subject matter of the representation. It will not inquire into their nature and extent. Only in this manner can the lawyer's duty of absolute fidelity be enforced and the spirit of the rule relating to privileged communications be maintained.

To compel the client to show, in addition to establishing that the subject of the present adverse representation is related to the former, the actual confidential matters previously entrusted to the attorney and their possible value to the present client would tear aside the protective cloak drawn about the lawyer-client relationship. For the Court to probe further and sift the confidences in fact revealed would require the disclosure of the very matters intended to be protected by the rule. It would defeat an important purpose of the rule of secrecy — to encourage clients fully and freely to make known to their attorneys all facts pertinent to their cause. Considerations of public policy, no less than the client's private interest, require rigid enforcement of the rule against disclosure. . . . Were he permitted to represent a client whose cause is related and adverse to that of his former client he would be called upon to decide what is confidential and what is not, and, perhaps, unintentionally to make use of confidential information received from the former client while espousing his cause. . . .

The following case presents an interesting discussion of successive representation rules. The court did not even pause to state whether it was applying the Model Code, the Model Rules, or simply a common law of professional responsibility. It doubtless regarded them as fungible for purposes of this problem. The case is a good example of how a lawyer may be found to have undertaken, by design or inadvertence, a secondary representation that later precludes representation of a regular client. The case also discusses the increasingly important issue of how lawyers may assume at least some of the obligations of an attorney-client relation with a party even though no formal relation has been undertaken.

ANALYTICA, INC. v. NPD RESEARCH, INC.
708 F.2d 1263 (7th Cir. 1983)

Posner, Circuit Judge.

Two law firms, Schwartz & Freeman and Pressman and Hartunian, appeal from orders disqualifying them from representing Analytica, Inc. in an antitrust suit against NPD, Inc. Schwartz & Freeman also appeals from an order directing it to pay NPD some $25,000 in fees and expenses incurred in prosecuting the disqualification motion; and NPD cross-appeals from this order, contending it should have got more.

John Malec went to work for NPD, a closely held corporation engaged in market research, in 1972. His employment agreement allowed him to, and he did, buy two shares of NPD stock, which made him a 10 percent owner. It also gave him an option to buy two more shares. He allowed the option to expire in 1975, but his two co-owners, in recognition of Malec's substantial contributions to the firm (as executive vice-president and manager of the firm's Chicago office), decided to give him the two additional shares — another 10 percent of the company — anyway and they told Malec to find a lawyer who would structure the transaction in the least costly way. He turned to Richard Fine, a partner in Schwartz & Freeman. Fine devised a plan where by the other co-owners would each transfer one share of stock back to the corporation, which would then issue the stock to Malec together with a cash bonus. Because the stock and the cash bonus were to be deemed compensation for Malec's services to the corporation, the value of the stock, plus the cash, would be taxable income to Malec (the purpose of the cash bonus was to help him pay the income tax that would be due on the value of the stock), and a deductible business expense to the corporation. A value had therefore to be put on the stock. NPD gave Fine the information he needed to estimate that value — information on NPD's financial condition, sales trends, and management — and Fine fixed a value which the corporation adopted. Fine billed NPD for his services and NPD paid the bill, which came to about $850, for 113 hours of Fine's time plus minor expenses.

While the negotiations over the stock transfer were proceeding, relations between Malec and his co-owners were deteriorating, and in May 1977 he left the company and sold his stock to them. His wife, who also had been working for NPD since 1972, left NPD at the same time and within a month had incorporated Analytica to compete with NPD in the market-research business. She has since left Analytica; Mr. Malec apparently never had a position with it.

In October 1977, several months after the Malecs had left NPD and Analytica had been formed, Analytica retained Schwartz & Freeman as its counsel. Schwartz & Freeman forthwith complained on Analytica's behalf to the Federal Trade Commission, charging that NPD was engaged in anticompetitive behavior that was preventing Analytica from establishing itself in the market. When the FTC would do nothing, Analytica decided to bring its own suit against NPD, and it authorized Schwartz & Freeman to engage Pressman and Hartunian as trial counsel. The suit was filed in June 1979 and charges NPD with various antitrust offenses, including abuse of a monopoly position that NPD is alleged to have obtained before June 1977. . . . In June 1981 the judge disqualified both firms and ordered Schwartz & Freeman to pay NPD's fees and expenses. Analytica has not appealed the orders of disqualification, having retained substitute counsel to prosecute its suit against NPD. . . .

For rather obvious reasons a lawyer is prohibited from using confidential information that he has obtained from a client against that client on behalf of another one. But this prohibition has not seemed enough by itself to make clients feel secure about reposing confidences in lawyers, so a further prohibition has evolved: a lawyer may not represent an adversary of his former client if the subject matter of the two representations is "substantially related," which means: if the lawyer could have obtained confidential information in the first representation that would have been relevant in the second. It is irrelevant whether he actually obtained such information and used it against his former client, or whether — if the lawyer is a firm rather than an individual practitioner — different people in the firm handled the two matters and scrupulously avoided discussing them. . . .

There is an exception for the case where a member or associate of a law firm (or government legal department) changes jobs, and later he or his new firm is retained by an adversary of a client of his former firm. In such a case, even if there is a substantial relationship between the two matters, the lawyer can avoid disqualification by showing that effective measures were taken to prevent confidences from being received by whichever lawyers in the new firm are handling the new matter. See Novo Terapeutisk Laboratorium A/S v. Baxter Travenol Laboratories, Inc., 607 F2d 186, 197 (7th Cir. 1979) (en banc); Freeman v. Chicago Musical Instrument Co., supra, 689 F.2d at 722-23; LaSalle Nat'l Bank v. County of Lake, 703 F.2d 252 (7th Cir. 1983). The exception is inapplicable here; the firm itself changed sides.

Schwartz & Freeman's Mr. Fine not only had access to but received confidential financial and operating data of NPD in 1976 and early 1977 when he was putting together the deal to transfer stock to Mr. Malec. Within a few months, Schwartz & Freeman popped up as counsel to an adversary of NPD's before the FTC, and in that proceeding and later in the antitrust lawsuit advanced contentions to which the data Fine received might have been relevant. Those data concerned NPD's profitability, sales prospects, and general market strength — all matters potentially germane to both the liability and damage phases of an antitrust suit charging NPD with monopolization. The two representations are thus substantially related, even though we do not know whether any of the information Fine received would be useful in Analytica's lawsuit (it might just duplicate information in Malec's possession, but we do not know his role in Analytica's suit), or if so whether he conveyed any of it to his partners and associates who were actually handling the suit. If the "substantial relationship" test applies, however, "it is not appropriate for the court to inquire into whether actual confidences were disclosed," Westinghouse Elec. Corp. v. Gulf Oil Corp., 588 F.2d at 224, unless the exception noted above for cases where the law firm itself did not switch sides is applicable, as it is not here. . . .

Schwartz & Freeman argues . . . that Malec rather than NPD retained it to structure the stock transfer, but this is both erroneous and irrelevant. NPD's three co-owners retained Schwartz & Freeman to work out a deal beneficial to all of them. All agreed that Mr. Malec should be given two more shares of the stock; the only question was the cheapest way of doing it; the right answer would benefit them all. Cf. Coase, The Problem of Social Cost, 3 J. Law & Econ. 1 (1960). The principals saw no need to be represented by separate lawyers, each pushing for a bigger slice of a fixed pie and a fee for getting it. Not only did NPD rather than Malec pay Schwartz & Freeman's bills (and there is no proof that it had a practice of paying its officers' legal expenses), but neither NPD nor the co-owners were represented by counsel other than Schwartz & Freeman. Though Millman, an accountant for NPD, did have a law degree and did do some work on the stock-transfer plan, he was not acting as the co-owners' or NPD's lawyer in a negotiation in which Fine was acting as Malec's lawyer. As is common in closely held corporations, Fine was counsel to the firm, as well as to all of its principals, for the transaction. If the postion taken by Schwartz & Freeman prevailed a corporation that used only one lawyer to counsel it on matters of shareholder compensation would run the risk of the lawyer's later being deemed to have represented a single shareholder rather than the whole firm, and the corporation would lose the protection of the lawyer-client relationship. Schwartz & Freeman's position thus could force up the legal expenses of owners of closely held corporations.

But it does not even matter whether NPD or Malec was the client. In Westinghouse's antitrust suit against Kerr-McGee and other uranium producers, Kerr-McGee moved to disqualify Westinghouse's counsel, Kirkland & Ellis, because of a project that the law firm had done for the American Petroleum Institute, of which Kerr-McGee was a member, on competition in the energy industries. Kirkland & Ellis's client had been the Institute rather than Kerr-McGee but we held that this did not matter; what mattered was that Kerr-McGee had furnished confidential information to Kirkland & Ellis in connection with the law firm's work for the Institute. Westinghouse Elec. Corp. v. Kerr-McGee Corp. As in this case, it was not shown that the information had actually been used in the anti-trust litigation. The work for the Institute had been done almost entirely by Kirkland & Ellis's Washington office, the antitrust litigation was being handled in the Chicago office, and Kirkland & Ellis is a big firm. The connection between the representation of a trade association of which Kerr-McGee happened to be a member and the representation of its adversary thus was rather tenuous; one may doubt whether Kerr-McGee really thought its confidences had been abused by Kirkland & Ellis. If there is any aspect of the *Kerr-McGee* decision that is subject to criticism, it is this. The present case is a much stronger one for disqual-ification. If NPD did not retain Schwartz & Freeman — though we think it did — still it supplied Schwartz & Freeman with just the kind of con-fidential data that it would have furnished a lawyer that it had retained; and it had a right not to see Schwartz & Freeman reappear within months on the opposite side of a litigation to which that data might be highly pertinent.

We acknowledge the growing dissatisfaction, illustrated by Lindgren, Toward a New Standard of Attorney Disqualification, 1982 Am. Bar Foundation Research J. 419, with the use of disqualification as a remedy for unethical conduct by lawyers. The dissatisfaction is based partly on the effect of disqualification proceedings in delaying the underlying lit-igation and partly on a sense that current conflict of interest standards, in legal representation as in government employment, are too stringent, particularly as applied to large law firms — though there is no indication that Schwartz & Freeman is a large firm. But we cannot find any au-thority for withholding the remedy in a case like this, even if we assume contrary to fact that Schwartz & Freeman is as large as Kirkland & Ellis. NPD thought Schwartz & Freeman was its counsel and supplied it with-out reserve with the sort of data — data about profits and sales and marketing plans — that play a key role in a monopolization suit — and lo and behold, within months Schwartz & Freeman had been hired by a competitor of NPD's to try to get the Federal Trade Commission to sue NPD; and later that competitor, still represented by Schwartz & Free-man, brought its own suit against NPD. We doubt that anyone would argue that Schwartz & Freeman could resist disqualification if it were still representing NPD, even if no confidences were revealed, and we do not think that an interval of a few months ought to make a critical dif-ference.

The "substantial relationship" test has its problems, but conducting a factual inquiry in every case into whether confidences had actually been revealed would not be a satisfactory alternative, particularly in a case such as this where the issue is not just whether they have been revealed but also whether they will be revealed during a pending litigation. Apart from the difficulty of taking evidence on the question without compro-mising the confidences themselves, the only witnesses would be the very lawyers whose firm was sought to be disqualified (unlike a case where the issue is what confidences a lawyer received while at a former law firm), and their interest not only in retaining a client but in denying a serious breach of professional ethics might outweigh any felt obligation to "come clean." While "appearance of impropriety" as a principle of professional ethics invites and maybe has undergone uncritical expan-sion because of its vague and open-ended character, in this case it has meaning and weight. For a law firm to represent one client today, and the client's adversary tomorrow in a closely related matter, creates an unsavory appearance of conflict of interest that is difficult to dispel in the eyes of the lay public — or for that matter the bench and bar — by the filing of affidavits, difficult to verify objectively, denying that improper communication has taken place or will take place between the lawyers in the firm handling the two sides. Clients will not repose confidences in lawyers whom they distrust and will not trust firms that switch sides as nimbly as Schwartz & Freeman. . . .

The order assessing fees and expenses against Schwartz & Freeman is affirmed. No costs will be awarded in this court.

[Judge Coffey agreed that the substantial relationship test applied to disqualify Richard Fine, the "ostensible" counsel for NPD because of his access to confidential financial and operating data that would be vital in the monopolization suit. He strongly dissented, however, from the holding that his firm should be automatically disqualified because of an irrebuttable presumption that the confidences were shared with the entire firm. The matter of vicarious disqualification is the subject of the next section of materials.]

NOTES

1. We have already seen in the *Westinghouse* case, p. 51, Note 9, how a law firm can find itself in a fiduciary, if not an actual attorney-client, relationship with a party who never formally retained it. Judge Posner relied on that case to find that Schwartz & Freeman, which was hired by Malec, occupied a fiduciary relationship towards NPD by reason of the transmission of confidential information and also occupied an actual attorney status to NPD on the facts of the case. The *Westinghouse* opinion awakened the profession to that issue, and it has now been litigated in a number of cases.

A recent case in the securities field discussed the problem at length, holding that in the circumstances of that case, counsel for an investment banker became counsel for the corporate client of the investment banker, notwithstanding the fact that that corporation also had its own counsel. Jack Eckerd Corp. v. Dart Group Corp., 621 F. Supp. 725 (D. Del. 1985). The court reached its conclusion both under the *Westinghouse* reasoning and under the more restrictive dictum of Committee on Professional Ethics & Griev. v. Johnson, 447 F.2d 169, 174 (3d Cir. 1971), which stated that "an attorney-client relationship is one of agency and arises only when the parties have given their consent, either express or implied, to its formation." The court distinguished In re John Doe Corp., 675 F.2d 482 (2d Cir. 1982), a case where an underwriter's attorney was held not to be the attorney for a company whose stock was being underwritten by reason of its demand for, and receipt of, an internal report that had been prepared by the company. In that case, however, the company was being investigated by a grand jury and the report had been demanded so that the underwriter could decide whether to go ahead with the offering.

Even a government lawyer has been held to have become an attorney for a private entity by virtue of his responsibilities to the government agency in which he was employed. Production Credit Assn. v. Buckentin, 410 N.W.2d 820 (Minn. S.C. 1987) involved the responsibilities of an attorney for one of the 12 Federal Intermediate Credit Banks (FICB), federal agencies set up regionally under the Farm Credit System to lend money to independent cooperative associations called Production Credit Associations (PCAs), which exist to lend money to farmers. The district FICBs have supervisory authority over the local PCAs and can even remove their officers and directors and set officers' salaries. As part of their duties, federal lawyers conducted seminars for the local PCAs that discussed, among other things, the kinds of legal issues likely to arise between the PCAs and their farmer-borrowers. In *Buckentin,* a former general counsel to a FICB was disqualified from representing two farmer-debtors against two different PCAs in proceedings arising out of PCA loans. The trial judges each rejected the former government lawyer's argument that his federal responsibility was adverse to PCAs and indeed that part of his job was to see that PCAs had their own independent attorneys, finding instead that an attorney-client relationship had been created. The Minnesota Supreme Court, although noting that it might have found differently as an original matter, affirmed the finding as not clearly erroneous.

These cases point out the importance to lawyers of being aware of the possibility that their dealings with other parties may involve the creation of an unexpected, and even undesired, fiduciary relationship.

2. Judge Posner argued that if the Schwartz & Freeman position were accepted, there was a risk to the corporation that used only one lawyer to advise it on matters of shareholder compensation, namely, that the lawyer might be held to have represented a shareholder and hence the corporation would lose the attorney-client privilege. Is that argument applicable to these facts? Fine had never been NPD's lawyer and indeed was selected by Malec. His relationship to NPD was ambiguous, especially in view of the deteriorating relations among the stockholders of the close corporations. The *Westinghouse* reasoning helps the court's conclusion considerably.

Judge Posner, however, casts some doubt on the correctness of the application of the *Westinghouse* "rule" to the actual facts in that case. He doubts whether Kerr-McGee, which transmitted confidential information to counsel for the trade association of which it was a member, really thought that its confidences "had been" (might be?) abused. But Judge Posner really doesn't know what Kerr-McGee thought, and we may wonder whether he really would want to substitute that subjective test for the objective test of "substantial relationship" that he made the basis for his conclusion that Schwartz & Freeman ought to be disqualified.

3. Judge Posner also argued that acceptance of the Schwartz & Freeman position could force up the legal expenses of owners of closely held corporations. That argument sounds rather strange in the context of the facts of this case. Mr. Fine charged only $850 for the work that he did. That sounds like something of a bargain for work done for three individuals and their closely-held corporation. Given the deteriorating relationships among the parties, it ought to have been obvious if in fact Schwartz & Freeman had thought it was representing everyone that there was considerable exposure to the firm in that representation. If it was responsible for looking out for everyone's interests in that situation, it was entitled to have its bill reflect that exposure. Indeed, the low charge is some evidence of its contention that it was not representing everyone. Moreover, with respect to Judge Posner's larger argument, it will not always be the case that the charge of one lawyer representing all the parties in a touchy situation will be less than the combined charges of, say, two lawyers where one does the work for one of the parties clearly seen as the only client and the other simply reviews that work. The exposure factor may cause the bill of one lawyer to be higher than the bill of two lawyers.

Another point to note is Judge Posner's use of the fact of NPD's payment of Schwartz & Freeman's bill to support his conclusion that the firm represented NPD. But other courts have quite properly pointed out that that circumstance is not of itself conclusive. See DCA Food Industries, Inc. v. Tasty Foods, Inc., 626 F. Supp. 54 (W.D. Wis. 1985), distinguishing *Analytica* and citing other cases.

4. In In re Boone, 83 F. 944 (C.C.N.D. Cal. 1897), a lawyer sought to interpret a release from a client as permitting him to be employed by an adversary with respect to the very matter in which he had represented his client. The court refused to interpret the release in that fashion, but went on to state emphatically that a "client may waive a privilege which the relation of attorney and client confers upon him, but he cannot enter into an agreement whereby he consents that the attorney may be released from all the duties, burdens, obligations and privileges pertaining to the duty of attorney and client. . . . The inevitable result of such a doctrine would be to degrade the profession and bring the courts themselves into disrepute. . . . Courts owe a duty to themselves, to the public, and to the profession which the temerity or improvidence of clients cannot supersede." Id. at 957.

A modern case relying on In re Boone is Westinghouse Elec. Corp. v. Gulf Oil Corp., 588 F.2d 221 (7th Cir. 1978), another piece of the same litigation discussed in Note 1. In disqualifying a law firm notwithstanding client A's alleged consent that the firm would not be precluded from representing client B in the event of conflict, the court held that such an agreement would not be read as including consent to possible use of A's confidential information against it.

5. For a case that on its face appeared to allow a form of side-switching and was described by the court as probably bringing it "as close to the outer limits as we shall want to go," see Mailer v. Mailer, 390 Mass. 371, 375 (1982). Mrs. Mailer consulted a lawyer in 1973 about the possibility of bringing a divorce action against her husband, the author Norman Mailer. After discussing the matter for about an hour with the lawyer, Mrs. Mailer left and decided not to file suit. Five years later, represented by another attorney, she filed a suit for divorce. Mr. Mailer was represented by the original lawyer whom she consulted. The trial court refused to disqualify the attorney and eventually the Supreme Judicial Court concluded that the original lawyer's representation of Mr. Mailer "does not require reversal of the judgment of divorce." It relied on the combination of the weakness of the relationship between Mrs. Mailer and the original lawyer, the length of time since her discussions with him, and the evidence, which permitted a finding that most of the information she supplied was known to the defendant and that no confidential information was used by the original attorney against her. It did not mention the rule that confidential information is presumed to have been transmitted in a successive representation case, perhaps because a formal attorney-client relationship was never formed.

6. Similar concerns may arise when a nonlawyer employee of a law firm leaves one firm and joins another that is representing an adverse interest. One court dealt with the problem of a secretary with confidential information switching sides by applying the Seventh Circuit's rebuttable presumption doctrine. It held that the presumption had been rebutted in that case, even in the absence of formal screening mechanisms. Kapco Mfg. Co. v. C. & O. Enterprises, Inc., 637 F. Supp. 1231 (N.D. Ill. 1985). Other courts have applied different tests. One Florida court held that when a side-switching secretary had been privy to confidences in her former firm, it nevertheless had to be shown that the result of her employment by her new firm was that its client had "obtained an advantage over the other [client] that can only be alleviated by removal of the lawyer." Esquire Care Inc. v. Maguire, 1988 Fla. App. Lexis 4316 (2d Dist. 1988). Another Florida court, however, has held that the fact that the side-switching secretary had been privy to confidences in her old firm is enough to disqualify the new firm. Lackow v. Walter E. Heller & Co., 466 So.2d 1120 (Fla. Dist. Ct. App. 1985).

PROBLEM 10

A, B, and C, represented by L, form a corporation to develop a new business. A supplies the scientific know-how, B, the necessary capital and financial and management ability, and C, the promotional and sales ability. They are the only stockholders and each owns one-third of the stock. Initially the business is small, the stock is worthless, and the owners do not want to bother with a stockholders' agreement or employment contracts. L becomes the corporation's lawyer, attending board meetings and drafting its minutes, negotiating and drawing contracts, and handling its few small litigation matters. When the business becomes profitable, L suggests that the time has come for the stockholders to "bother" with their personal arrangements with one another. All agree but close investigation by them into operation of the business leads A and C to become very unhappy with B's past management. They decide to sue him for misappropriation of corporate opportunities. A and C ask L to represent them in the lawsuit. B objects. L says that there is no problem in such representation: his representation of A and C is not substantially related to the work he did for B in organizing the corporation; moreover, to the extent that he has any confidential information from B, he learned it in the context of joint representation of A, B, and C and for that reason it is not confidential among them. Therefore, he does not need B's consent and there is no impediment to his representation of A and C and indeed the corporation against B. Is he correct?

The following case illustrates the problems that may arise for a lawyer who has represented several clients jointly in a common enterprise when the clients' relationship ruptures. It also illustrates the tie between the rules governing conflicts of interest and the rules, which we shall examine in the next chapter, governing confidential information. There is a general rule of evidence, often called the coclient or joint attorney rule, that no attorney-client privilege exists in litigation between two parties jointly represented by a lawyer in a common enterprise with respect to testimony relating to that enterprise, although the privilege does exist with respect to the outside world. See 8 Wigmore on Evidence §2312 (McNaughton rev. ed. 1961). There is less substantive law with respect to whether the same policy considerations that gave rise to the rule of evidence should also produce the same result with respect to the lawyer's obligations as a matter of the rules of ethics. The issue may arise in two contexts: representation of one joint client against another (the subject of the case that follows) and the decision whether to transmit relevant information from one joint client to another over the objection of the confiding client (treated in the next chapter). See pp. 234–244.

What the use of the coclient evidence rule as a rule of ethics means in a case like Problem 10 or the following case is that a joint client sued by one of the group that was jointly represented may not be able to use the general rule regarding transmission of confidential information in order to disqualify the common attorney. But, as *Brennan's* indicates, that observation only begins the analysis. There are other considerations that may lead to disqualification.

BRENNAN'S, INC. v. BRENNAN'S RESTAURANTS, INC.
590 F.2d 168 (5th Cir. 1979)

TJOFLAT, Circuit Judge:

This is an action for trademark infringement and unfair competition. This appeal, however, concerns the disqualification of attorneys. The district court barred the appellants' attorneys from further representing them on grounds of conflict of interest. The correctness of this order is the only issue before us.

The underlying dispute in this case arises out of the business affairs of the Brennan family of New Orleans, Louisiana, who have been in the restaurant business for many years. All of the corporate parties are owned and closely held by various members of the Brennan family. Appellee Brennan's, Inc., the plaintiff below, owns and operates Brennan's restaurant at 417 Royal Street in New Orleans. The corporate appellants own and operate other restaurants in Louisiana, Texas, and Georgia. There has been no trial as yet, but a review of the facts leading to the present suit, as disclosed by the pleadings and affidavits, is necessary to a decision of this appeal. For convenience, the parties will be referred to in the capacities in which they appear in the court below.

Prior to 1974, all the members of the Brennan family were stockholders and directors of plaintiff, and some of them were stockholders and directors of the corporate defendants. All the corporations were independent legal entities in the sense that none held any of the stock of another, but they were all owned by members of the Brennan family and had interlocking boards of directors. In 1971, Edward F. Wegmann became general counsel for the family businesses, and his retainer was paid pro rata by all the corporations. He continued this joint representation until November 1973.

As part of his services, Mr. Wegmann, in close cooperation with trademark counsel in Washington, D.C., prosecuted applications for the federal registration of three service marks: "Brennan's," "Breakfast at Brennan's," and a distinctive rooster design. A registration for the rooster design was issued in February 1972, but the applications for the other two marks were initially denied on the ground that they were primarily a surname. On the advice of Washington trademark counsel, Mr. Wegmann collected data supporting a demonstration that the marks had acquired a secondary meaning, and the applications were amended to include this material. Registrations were subsequently issued in plaintiff's name in March 1973. These registered service marks are the subject of this lawsuit.

Later in 1973 a dispute developed within the Brennan family over the operation and management of the family businesses. This dispute was resolved in November 1974 by dividing the corporations' stock between the two opposing family groups. Plaintiff became 100% owned by one group and the corporate defendants became 100% owned by the second group, composed of the individual defendants. Mr. Wegmann elected to continue to represent defendants and severed his connections with plaintiff and its shareholders.

At no time during the negotiations which culminated in the November 1974 settlement was there any discussion of who would have the right to use the registered service marks. Both sides claimed ownership of the marks and continued to use them after the settlement. Attempts to negotiate a license or concurrent registration were unsuccessful. Plaintiff filed this suit for trademark infringement and unfair competition on May 21, 1976. In their answer and counterclaim defendants alleged that the marks were registered in plaintiff's name for convenience only, and, "in truth and actuality, the applications were filed and the registrations issued for the benefit and ownership of all of the Brennan family restaurants, including the corporate defendants." . . . Defendants also alleged that the marks and registrations are invalid.

Upon the filing of this suit, Mr. Wegmann, on behalf of the defendants, retained the services of Arnold Sprung, a New York patent and trademark attorney, to assist him in the defense of the case. On October 22, 1976, plaintiff moved for the disqualification of both attorneys: Mr. Wegmann on the ground that his present representation was at odds with the interests of plaintiff, his former client, and Mr. Sprung by imputation of Mr. Wegmann's conflict. After a hearing, the district court granted the motion. It found that the subject matter of the present suit is substantially related to matters in which Mr. Wegmann formerly represented plaintiff, and to allow him now to represent an interest adverse to his former client creates the appearance of impropriety. It also found that "the close working relationship which has been shown to exist between Mr. Wegmann and Mr. Sprung creates a significant likelihood that Mr. Sprung would have had access to or been informed of confidential disclosures made to Mr. Wegmann by his former client." . . .

We have not addressed this precise question before. In Wilson P. Abraham Construction Corp. v. Armco Steel Corp., we reaffirmed the standard that "a former client seeking to disqualify an attorney who appears on behalf of his adversary, need only to show that the matters embraced within the pending suit are *substantially related* to the matters or cause of action wherein the attorney previously represented him," 559 F.2d at 252 (emphasis in original), but we acknowledged that "[t]his rule rests upon the presumption that confidences potentially damaging to the client have been disclosed to the attorney during the former period of representation," id. Defendants contend that this presumption cannot apply in this case. This argument, in our view, interprets too narrowly an attorney's duty to "preserve the confidences and secrets of a client." ABA Code of Professional Responsibility, Canon 4 (1970). The fundamental flaw in defendants' position is a confusion of the attorney-client evidentiary privilege with the ethical duty to preserve a client's confidences. Assuming the prior representation was joint, defendants are quite correct that neither of the parties to this suit can assert the attorney-client privilege against the other as to matters comprehended by that joint representation. Garner v. Wolfinbarger, 430 F.2d 1093, 1103 (5th Cir. 1970), cert. denied, 401 U.S. 974, 91 S. Ct. 1191, 28 L. Ed. 2d 323 (1971). But the ethical duty is broader than the evidentiary privilege: "This ethical precept, unlike the evidentiary privilege, exists without regard to the nature or source of information or the fact that others share the knowledge." ABA Code of Professional Responsibility, EC 4-4 (1970). "A lawyer should not use information acquired in the course of the representation of a client to the disadvantage of the client. . . ." Id. EC 4-5. The use of the word "information" in these Ethical Considerations as opposed to "confidence" or "secret" is particularly revealing of the drafters' intent to protect all knowledge acquired from a client, since the latter two are defined terms. See id., DR 4-101(A). Information so acquired is sheltered from use by the attorney-client relationship. This is true without regard to whether someone else may be privy to it. NCK Organization v. Bregman, 542 F.2d 128, 133 (2d Cir. 1976). The obligation of an attorney not to misuse information acquired in the course of representation serves to vindicate the trust and reliance that clients place in their attorneys. A client would feel wronged if an opponent prevailed against him with the aid of an attorney who formerly represented the client in the same matter. As the court recognized in E. F. Hutton & Co. v. Brown, 305 F. Supp. 371, 395 (S.D. Tex. 1969), this would undermine public confidence in the legal system as a means for adjudicating disputes. We recognize that this concern implicates the principle embodied in Canon 9 that attorneys "should avoid even the appearance of professional impropriety." ABA Code of Professional Responsibility, Canon 9 (1970). We have said that under this canon there must be a showing of a reasonable possibility that some specifically identifiable impropriety in fact occurred and that the likelihood of public suspicion must be weighed against the interest in retaining counsel of one's choice. Woods v. Covington County Bank, 537 F.2d 804, 812-813 (5th Cir. 1976). The conflict of interest is readily apparent here, however, and we think that the balance weighs in favor of disqualification. . . . The need to safeguard the attorney-client relationship is not diminished by the fact that the prior representation was joint with the attorney's present client. Accordingly, we find the rule of Wilson P. Abraham Construction Corp. v. Armco Steel Corp. fully applicable to this case. Since the district court's findings of prior representation and substantial relationship are not disputed, we affirm the disqualification of Mr. Wegmann.

Whether Mr. Sprung should be disqualified presents a more difficult case. He has never had an attorney-client relationship with plaintiff; the district court disqualified him by imputation of Mr. Wegmann's conflict. Up to this point we have accepted, for the sake of argument, defendants' assertion that they were formerly joint clients with plaintiff of Mr. Wegmann. There is no dispute that plaintiff and defendants were previously represented by Mr. Wegmann simultaneously, but plaintiff maintains that, at least with respect to the registration of the service marks, Mr. Wegmann was representing plaintiff alone. The district court made no findings on the issue. Because we think that the disqualification of Mr. Sprung may turn on this fact and others not found by the court below, we vacate that part of the court's order relating to Mr. Sprung and remand the cause for further proceedings. For the guidance of the court on remand, we set forth our view of the applicable ethical standards.

If the court finds that Mr. Wegmann previously represented plaintiff and defendants jointly, we can see no reason why Mr. Sprung should be disqualified. As between joint clients there can be no "confidences" or "secrets" unless one client manifests a contrary intent. . . . Thus, Mr. Sprung could not have learned anything from Mr. Wegmann that defendants did not already know or have a right to know. Plaintiff argues that this permits the defendants indirectly to gain the benefit of Mr. Wegmann's services when they could not do so directly. If the representation was joint, however, defendants possess no information as to which plaintiff could have had any expectation of privacy in relation to the defendants. The only remaining ground for disqualification then would be an appearance of impropriety. In Part II of this opinion, we decided there is such an appearance when an attorney represents an interest adverse to that of a former client in a matter substantially related to the subject of the prior representation. Mr Sprung has never been plaintiff's counsel, however; he is only the cocounsel of one who was. We are enjoined not to give Canon 9 an overly broad application and to maintain "a reasonable balance between the need to ensure ethical conduct on the part of lawyers . . . and other social interests, which include the litigant's right to freely chosen counsel." Woods v. Covington County Bank, 537 F.2d 804, 810, (5th Cir. 1976). In the case of Mr. Sprung, we think the balance weighs against disqualification. Assuming that Mr. Wegmann's prior retainer was joint, plaintiff has suffered no actual prejudice from communications between Mr. Wegmann and Mr. Sprung. There is a possibility that Mr. Sprung has obtained informally information that he would otherwise have had to seek through discovery.[7] The Second Circuit has indicated that circumvention of the discovery rules is grounds for automatic disqualification. See NCK Organization v. Bregman, 542 F.2d 128, 131-132, 134 (2d Cir. 1976). This seems to us an overly rigid approach. In a disqualification case, it is well to remember that "in deciding questions of professional ethics men of good will often differ in their conclusions." Fund of Funds, Ltd. v. Arthur Andersen & Co., 567 F.2d 225, 227 (2d Cir. 1977). . . . Under the peculiar facts of this case, we do not think there would be such an appearance of impropriety in Mr. Sprung's continued representation of defendants as to warrant his disqualification.

If the district court finds that Mr. Wegmann did not previously represent these parties jointly, it does not necessarily follow that Mr. Sprung should be disqualified. The courts have abjured a per se approach to the disqualification of cocounsel of disqualified counsel. Akerly v. Red Barn System, Inc., 551 F.2d 539 (3d Cir. 1977); American Can Co. v. Citrus Feed Co., 436 F.2d 1125 (5th Cir. 1971). In the absence of an attorney-client relationship between Mr. Sprung and plaintiff, a presumption of disclosure of confidences is inappropriate. Wilson P. Abraham Construction Corp. v. Armco Steel Corp., 559 F.2d 250, 253 (5th Cir. 1977). Mr. Sprung should not be disqualified unless he has learned from Mr. Wegmann information the plaintiff had intended not be disclosed to the defendants. See id. . . .

NOTES

1. The court bases its holding on EC 4-5. It would have been preferable had it used DR 4-101(B)(2), which covers the same subject matter and is not open to attack on the ground of being merely "aspirational." The term "secret" is sufficiently broad that the court did not have to worry about needing to use the term "information" in EC 4-5. Perhaps the court's reliance on the Ethical Considerations was an attempt to meet the argument that since there are no confidences or secrets between joint clients, this suit is just like the ordinary suit against a former client, which is permitted when there is no danger of revelation of confidences. It may

---

7. It is very likely that Mr. Wegmann will be a witness in this case. He handled the registrations for the service marks which are the subject of this suit. Moreover, he prepared and notarized two affidavits that were executed at the time the registrations were issued. Defendants rely on these affidavits in support of their claim of ownership of the marks. The circumstances of their execution and the facts to which these affidavits purport to attest will undoubtedly be a subject of dispute at trial and Mr. Wegmann's knowledge may be relevant. If he represented all the family corporations at the time, however, none of his knowledge is privileged and his testimony could freely be sought by either side.

have thought there the use of the term "information" in EC 4-5 evaded that argument since the lawyer would certainly be using "information" against his former client. It could have pointed out that the successive representation rule is based not only on fear of transmission of confidences but also on notions of loyalty. At least absent some understanding to the contrary, it would certainly seem to be contrary to general understandings about loyalty for a lawyer to switch sides in a particular matter by bringing suit against a former client with respect to a matter that was substantially related to the former representation.

2. The court uses Canon 9 to buttress its confidentiality analysis but, unlike so many opinions, it does so in a way that attempts to give more precise and more restricted meaning to the vague, open-ended language of Canon 9. An analysis of judicial use of the "appearance of impropriety" doctrine is contained in Victor Kramer, The Appearance of Impropriety Under Canon 9, 65 Minn. L. Rev. 243 (1981).

3. On the issue of disqualification of cocounsel, who had never represented any of the parties previously, compare Fund of Funds, Ltd. v. Arthur Andersen & Co., p. 135.

4. Rosman v. Shapiro, 653 F. Supp. 1441 (S.D.N.Y. 1987) is a recent case following *Brennan's* in the situation of an attorney representing a close corporation with two 50-50 shareholders who then sought to represent the corporation and one shareholder against the other. The court held that it was reasonable for the shareholders to believe that the attorney was representing them individually. Although the court held that DR 4 of the Model Code was not applicable because neither shareholder could have had an expectation of confidentiality with respect to the other when there was joint representation, the court used DR 9 to hold that the loyalty obligation required the lawyer's disqualification in the litigation.

5. There is a line of cases, discussed in Kempner v. Oppenheimer & Co., 662 F. Supp. 1271 (S.D.N.Y. 1987), that reaches a conclusion opposite to *Brennan's* by stopping in the middle of the reasoning used by the *Brennan's* court. *Kempner* and the cases it cites conclude that since there was no confidentiality between the joint clients, a suit brought by the attorney for joint clients against one of them did not threaten any confidentiality interest of the defendant and hence disqualification was not required. *Kempner* and most if not all of the cases it cites may perhaps be explained on the basis that it was understood that one of the joint clients was the primary client of the attorney and that in the event of dispute the attorney was free to continue representing its primary client. See also *Merrill Lynch*, p. 75. The *Kempner* court does refer briefly to that factor. Moreover, it points out that in the particular case it was the joint client, there an employee of the primary client, who switched sides in the midst of the litigation, and not the attorney. However, while the expectations of the joint clients may be important in differentiating these

two cases, the differentiation is not so sharp as the court's language makes it appear. In some cases, at least, the joint subsidiary client will have imparted very damaging confidential information to the attorney and the threat that such information will be used to his or her detriment by a former lawyer raises a strong loyalty issue that looks toward disqualification. (On the issue of the advance consent by a client to such adverse representation, see p. 63, Note 4 and p. 198, Note 4).

Another issue of successive representation has been a hotly debated issue of professional responsibility — the situation of the government lawyer who goes into private practice. But before discussing that issue, we should turn to the matter of vicarious disqualification because that concept relates quite specifically to the former government lawyer problem.

C. VICARIOUS DISQUALIFICATION

1.   The General Rule

PROBLEM 11

(a) In the situation involved in Problem 1, may Lawyer's partner, Smith, handle Grocer's suit against Buyer?

(b) Suppose that after Lawyer represented Buyer but before Grocer arrived at her office with respect to this particular problem, Smith and Lawyer had dissolved their partnership. When Lawyer declines to represent Grocer in his suit against Buyer, may Smith represent him?

(c) Suppose that Lawyer had agreed to represent Grocer against Buyer and thereafter Lawyer and Smith dissolved their partnership. Buyer's lawyer then filed a disqualification motion against Lawyer, who withdrew from the case. May Smith represent Grocer against Buyer?

The common law of vicarious disqualification, codified in DR 5-105(D) of the Model Code and Rule 1.10(a) of the Model Rules, imputes disqualification of one member of a firm to the rest of the firm. As the common law of disqualification has developed, it has worked out a series of presumptions to avoid the necessity for a party seeking to disqualify a present or former lawyer from having to reveal the very confidences the rules are designed to protect. The first is that a client who consults a lawyer is presumed to have transmitted confidences about the matter. The second is that the lawyer is presumed to have transmitted those confidences to all partners and associates at the firm. The current debate is over the circumstances in which those presumptions ought to be able to be rebutted.

The Model Code, as originally drafted, limited the vicarious disqualification principle to disqualification for conflict of interest under DR 5. After it was realized that that formulation did not cover other relevant situations, such as disqualification under DR 4, the Model Code was revised to cover all disqualifications under the Code. The revision, however, was soon realized to be so broad that it could not be read literally, for it covered disqualification by reason of illness or incompetence to handle a specific area of law. Other pressures were exerted against the rule because of its far-reaching effect on the mobility of lawyers and on the private and public practice of law in general. Thus, when the Model Rules were drafted, the vicarious disqualification principle was enunciated much more carefully and precisely in Model Rules 1.10 and 1.11. Of course the specific codification may tend to freeze the common law development of the principle, and that is an issue for drafters and for the courts, both in their legislative (i.e., shall this particular Model Rule be adopted?) and judicial capacities.

A major issue with respect to vicarious disqualification relates to the question whether lawyers vicariously disqualified in Firm A carry that disqualification with them when they move to Firm B so that not only they but all members of Firm B are disqualified. The following case and Notes discuss that issue. The principal case also discusses the extent to which a lawyer in Firm A needs to work on a client's affairs to warrant personal, as opposed to vicarious, disqualification.

SILVER CHRYSLER PLYMOUTH, INC. v. CHRYSLER MOTORS CORPORATION
518 F.2d 751 (2d Cir. 1975)

MOORE, Circuit Judge.

An action is pending before Judge Weinstein in the Eastern District of New York entitled Silver Chrysler Plymouth, Inc. v. Chrysler Motors Corporation and Chrysler Realty Corporation. It awaits trial. The controversy alleged therein essentially is whether Silver Chrysler's dealership agreement with Chrysler was for five years (the term specified in a written lease executed between the parties in 1968) as asserted by Chrysler or for twenty-five years as alleged by Silver Chrysler on the basis of a 1967 agreement. This seemingly simple breach of contract complaint also contains a cause of action under the so-called Dealers' Day in Court Act, 15 U.S.C. §§1221 et seq. The claim alleges threats amounting to coercion or intimidation which forced Silver Chrysler under threat of eviction to sign a new agreement at a higher rental in May 1973 (the expiration date of the five-year term). This brief recital of the nature of the action is required only as a background to the issue on this appeal, which is disqualification of counsel.

Chrysler for many years has been represented by the law firm of Kelley Drye Warren Clark Carr & Ellis (Kelley Drye) and its predecessors, which also represents Chrysler in this action. Although many other law firms represent Chrysler on various matters throughout the country, only Kelley Drye is listed on Chrysler's annual reports as "Counsel." Silver Chrysler is represented by the firm of Hammond & Schreiber, P.C. Dale Schreiber of that firm had been employed as an associate by Kelley Drye, and while there worked on certain Chrysler matters. Because of this fact Kelley Drye by motion sought to disqualify both Schreiber and his firm from representing Silver Chrysler in this action. In support of, and in opposition to, the motion respectively, the parties submitted voluminous affidavits, copies of pleadings in cases in which Schreiber had allegedly worked, and extensive memoranda of law.

With this material before him and after oral argument, the Judge proceeded to analyze the motion on the theory that "[d]ecision turns on whether, in the course of the former 'representation,' the associate acquired information reasonably related to the particular subject matter of the subsequent representation." The Judge reviewed the subject matter of the cases on which Schreiber was claimed to have worked and the law as it appears in this Circuit from decided cases and in a comprehensive opinion . . . concluded that "[d]isqualification of plaintiff's counsel is not warranted." From this decision Chrysler appeals. . . .

Upon graduation from law school in 1965, Dale Schreiber was hired by Kelley Drye to commence work in September 1965. He worked at the firm briefly before accepting a position as a law clerk to a federal judge. His work at Kelley Drye began again in September 1966 and continued to February 1969.

Kelley Drye is one of New York's larger law firms, having had at the time some 30 partners and 50 associates. Several of New York's firms have well over 100 associates and over 50 partners. Many firms hire a dozen or more law graduates each year and it has now become the practice to hire for summer work (usually between their second and third years at law school) a substantial number of law students. These "summer associates" most frequently perform tasks assigned to them by supervising associates or partners. Many of the summer students do not return to the same firms with which they have been associated or even remain in New York City. Even after an initial association with a firm upon graduation, it is not uncommon for young lawyers to change their affiliation once or even several times. It is equally well known that the larger firms in the metropolitan areas have hundreds (collectively thousands) of clients. It is unquestionably true that in the course of their work at large law firms, associates are entrusted with the confidences of some of their clients. But it would be absurd to conclude that immediately upon their entry on duty they become the recipients of knowledge as to the names of all the firm's clients, the contents of all files relating to such clients, and all confidential disclosures by client officers or employees to any lawyer in the firm. Obviously such legal osmosis does not occur. The mere recital of such a proposition should be self-refuting. And a rational interpretation of the Code of Professional Responsibility does not call for disqualification on the basis of such an unrealistic perception of the practice of law in large firms.

Fulfilling the purpose of the disqualification remedy, "namely the need to enforce the lawyer's duty of absolute fidelity and to guard against the danger of inadvertent use of confidential information," Ceramco, Inc. v. Lee Pharmaceuticals, supra, 510 F.2d at 271, does not require such a blanket approach. Nor are such broad measures required to maintain "in the public mind, a high regard for the legal profession." General Motors Corp. v. City of New York, supra, [p. 131]. Thus, while this Circuit has recognized that an inference may arise that an attorney formerly associated with a firm himself received confidential information transmitted by a client to the firm, that inference is a rebuttable one. Laskey Bros. . . . v. Warner Bros. Pictures, 224 F.2d 824 (2d Cir. 1955), cert. denied, 350 U.S. 932 (1956); United States v. Standard Oil Co., 136 F. Supp. 345, 364 (S.D.N.Y. 1955). And in Laskey, the court cautioned that: "It will not do to make the presumption of confidential information rebuttable and then to make the standard of proof for rebuttal unattainably high. This is particularly true where, as here, the attorney must prove a negative, which is always a difficult burden to meet." The importance of not unnecessarily constricting the careers of lawyers who started their practice of law at large firms simply on the basis of their former association underscores the significance of this language. . . .

Over the intervening years the cases in which disqualification has been granted have also fallen into, or have come close to, the "patently clear" category. . . .

[The court then discussed Hull (p. 113, Note 2), General Motors (p. 131), and conflict of interest cases in other federal courts, including a group of cases decided differently by different courts apparently on nearly identical facts.]

In contrast to the foregoing decisions, quite a different situation is presented here. Schreiber was not counsel for Chrysler in the sense that the disqualified attorneys were in those cases. Although Kelley Drye had pervasive contacts with Chrysler, Schreiber's relationship cannot be considered co-extensive with that of his firm. The evidence submitted to Judge Weinstein on the motion was admittedly somewhat conflicting. By affidavits submitted by the head of the litigation department at Kelley Drye, Chrysler sought to show not only the purportedly "substantially related" cases upon which Schreiber worked but also the extensive amount of Chrysler-dealer litigation in the office and in which Schreiber was concededly not involved. Schreiber responded by affidavit, detailing his responsibilities in Chrysler matters upon which he recalled working. Schreiber also obtained, amongst other things, supporting affidavits of Clark J. Gurney (the associate who handled the bulk of Chrysler dealer matters) and Hugh M. Baum, two former colleagues at Kelley Drye (presently employed elsewhere).

As we recently recognized in Hull v. Celanese Corp., supra: "The district court bears the responsibility for the supervision of the members of its bar. . . . The dispatch of this duty is discretionary in nature and the finding of the district court will be upset only upon a showing that an abuse of discretion has taken place." 513 F.2d at 571. . . . Judge Weinstein was well aware of the tests to be applied. He examined (370 F. Supp. at 585-586) Checker v. Chrysler, an antitrust action and Schreiber's principal Chrysler case while at Kelley Drye, and concluded that the case was not substantially related to this litigation. As to other matters that Schreiber recalled working on, the judge was entitled to conclude that they also were not substantially related. . . . With respect to still others . . . there was ample basis for crediting Schreiber's denial of having worked on them and concluding that Schreiber's involvement was, at most, limited to brief, informal discussions on a procedural matter or research on a specific point of law. The affidavits of Gurney and Baum provided support for such a conclusion. In this respect we do not believe that there is any basis for distinguishing between partners and associates on the basis of title alone — both are members of the bar and are bound by the same Code of Professional Responsibility. See Consolidated Theatres v. Warner Bros. Circuit Management Corp., 216 F.2d 920, 927 (2d Cir. 1954). But there is reason to differentiate for disqualification purposes between lawyers who become heavily involved in the facts of a particular matter and those who enter briefly on the periphery for a limited and specific purpose relating solely to legal questions. In large firms at least, the former are normally the more seasoned lawyers and the latter the more junior. This is not to say that young attorneys in large firms never become important figures in certain matters but merely to recognize that some of their work is often of a far more limited variety. Under the latter circumstances the attorney's role cannot be considered "representation" . . . so as to require disqualification. Those cases and the Canons on which they are based are intended to protect the confidences of former clients when an attorney has been in a position to learn them. To apply the remedy when there is no realistic chance that confidences were disclosed would go far beyond the purpose of those decisions. Chrysler was in a position here conclusively to refute Schreiber's position that his role in these cases had been non-existent or fleeting. Through affidavits of those who supervised Schreiber on particular matters or perhaps through time records, the issue was capable of proof.

Chrysler instead chose to approach the matter in largely conclusory terms.[8] We cannot realistically subscribe to the contention that proof submitted for this limited purpose, by time records or otherwise, would have necessitated disclosure of any confidences entrusted to Kelley Drye.

Judge Weinstein also concluded that Schreiber had rebutted any inference, arising merely from his former association with Kelley Drye, that he possessed confidences that can be used against Chrysler in this lawsuit. We think the district judge was plainly correct. There may have been matters within the firm which, had Schreiber worked on them, would have compelled disqualification here. But Schreiber denied having been entrusted with any such confidences. He was supported in this respect by the affidavits of Gurney and Baum. This was sufficient. . . .

Finally, in view of the conclusion that Schreiber's work at Kelley Drye does not necessitate disqualification, we agree with the district court that refusal to disqualify Schreiber and his firm will not create an appearance of impropriety. Neither Chrysler nor any other client of a law firm can reasonably expect to foreclose either all lawyers formerly at the firm or even those who have represented it on unrelated matters from subsequently representing an opposing party. Although Canon 9 dictates that doubts should be resolved in favor of disqualification, Hull v. Celanese Corp., supra, 513 F.2d at 571, it is not intended completely to override the delicate balance created by Canon 4 and the decisions thereunder. . . .

[In a concurring opinion, Judge Arlin Adams concluded by remarking that: "candor requires that I express misgivings respecting the wisdom of attorneys accepting representations when former clients are involved. Although it was not established that the representation here warrants disqualification, my concurrence should not be understood as an approval of the practice, a practice which ofttimes necessitates an examination of the obligation due a former law firm and client, and imposes on the court the duty to probe the outer reaches of the Canons of Ethics."]

NOTES

1. Judge Weinstein's opinion notes that Schreiber had worked extensively on a treble damage suit under the Sherman Act in which a taxicab manufacturer alleged that Chrysler was conducting a predatory campaign to put it out of business. 370 F. Supp. at 585-586. Suppose Schrei-

---

8. Example from a Kelly Drye (Chrysler) affidavit: "[Schreiber] obtained unmeasurable confidential information regarding the practices, procedures, methods of operation, activities, contemplated conduct, legal problems, and litigations of [Chrysler]." . . .

ber in defending that suit became familiar with the operations of management so as to know who called the shots on pricing policy and therefore whom to notice for depositions, and that he had also learned what the basic policy was about destruction of memoranda and hence knew what kinds of memoranda ought to be kept and where and also knew to ask about the destruction policy. If Schreiber had that kind of sense of client's business, should that be sufficient to disqualify him?

2. Hull v. Celanese Corporation, discussed by the court, p. 110, involved a woman lawyer who was employed by defendant as part of its house counsel staff and was working on a sex-based discrimination case instituted by other employees of defendant. After some time she decided that she had a cause of action for discrimination and hired plaintiffs' counsel to intervene in plaintiffs' suit on her behalf. They cautioned her against revealing any confidential information. A motion to disqualify plaintiffs' counsel from any further participation in the case was granted, the court viewing it as sufficient that confidential information might be transmitted and not requiring any proof that it had been. The court was careful to state that it was not holding that she could not sue her employer at all, although it must have been clear that the same danger of transmittal existed if she hired other counsel. Presumably, if the court were to distinguish the two situations, it would be on the basis that the danger to the system was greatest when the possibility of transmittal of confidential information would accrue to the benefit of a third party. Many persons believe that increased ethical sensitivity always results in a loss of business for the particular lawyers involved. *Hull* is a case where an appreciation of the Second Circuit's views of professional responsibility would have saved the plaintiffs' law firm some business. For a similar case where former house counsel was disqualified from serving as class representative, but not from pursuing his personal claim, against his former employer, see Doe v. A Corp., 709 F.2d 1043 (5th Cir. 1983). On the other hand, *Hull* was distinguished in a case where a law firm was representing former counsel for plaintiffs in a malpractice suit against them by plaintiffs arising out of the very suit in which the law firm was presently representing the defendants. The court applied a rebuttable presumption rule to this unique case and held that the lawyer handling the malpractice suit had rebutted the presumption of transfer of confidential information and that the plaintiffs were estopped anyway from raising the issue because they sat on the information for so long. Warpar Mfg. Corp. v. Ashland Oil, Inc., 606 F. Supp. 852 (N.D. Ohio 1984).

3. *Silver Chrysler Plymouth* involved the effect on the departing associate of the usual rule imputing the firm's knowledge to him and held that the usual rule did not apply once he had left the firm. Novo-Terapeutisk Laboratorium A/S v. Baxter Travenol Laboratories, Inc., 607 F.2d 186, 194 (7th Cir. 1979) (en banc) involved the reverse situation. In that case,

the partner who had Baxter's confidential information regarding a potential suit by Novo left the firm and continued representing Baxter. Subsequently the firm undertook to represent Novo against Baxter with respect to that very suit. The court refused to disqualify the law firm from representing Novo against Baxter in the absence of any allegation that the departing partner shared confidences with his firm and in the face of denials from the firm that he had.

4. The result in *Baxter Laboratories* has been codified in Model Rule 1.10(c) and the result in *Silver Chrysler Plymouth* would appear to be codified in Model Rule 1.10(b), especially as explained in the Comment to that Rule.

PROBLEM 12

Isacson was an employee of Sargoy & Stein and participated in numerous lawsuits involving motion picture theater clients of that firm. Some time after leaving that firm, Isacson joined Malkan and that firm began to receive plaintiff antitrust business in the motion picture field. Malkan and Isacson then broke up their firm and Malkan formed a new firm, Malkan & Ellner. That firm filed complaints in two plaintiff antitrust actions that included former clients of Sargoy & Stein as defendants. They moved to disqualify Malkan & Ellner as plaintiffs' counsel. One of the antitrust actions, the Laskey suit, came initially to the firm of Malkan & Isacson. The second, the Austin case, came to the new firm of Malkan & Ellner. It is apparent that Isacson had confidential information relating to the Sargoy & Stein clients by reason of his prior employment with that firm. With the departure of Isacson, may Malkan & Ellner resist the disqualification motion by rebutting the presumption that it received any confidential information from Isacson?

Those are the facts of a very well known and much cited vicarious disqualification case that was decided before the Model Rules and Model Code were adopted. Laskey Bros. v. Warner Bros. Pictures, 224 F.2d 824 (2d Cir. 1955), cert. denied, 350 U.S. 932 (1956). A divided court held that the presumption of transmission of confidences was irrebuttable with respect to the *Laskey* case, which came to Malkan & Isacson, but that the presumption was rebuttable with respect to the *Austin* case, which came to the new firm after the departure of Isacson. Moreover, the court held that the new firm had successfully rebutted the presumption. The dissenting judge would have disqualified the firm in the *Austin* case as well. Moreover, he would not have limited the order of disqualification against Ellner to the time when he continued his association with Malkan.

With those facts and that holding in mind, how should the disqualification motions be decided under the Model Rules?

This fact situation, which was known to the drafters of the Model Rules, puts great strain on the seemingly straightforward language of MR 1.10. To answer the question how a court should decide the *Laskey* and *Austin* cases under Model Rule 1.10 requires close study of the language and policies of the Rule. The precise issue to be addressed is whether Malkan should be permitted to prove that he has no material information protected by Rule 1.6 and 1.9(b) and hence ought to be allowed to continue to represent the plaintiffs in both the *Laskey* and *Austin* cases once Isacson has left his firm. Four interpretations suggest themselves.

(1) The argument may be made that when Isacson joined Malkan and they took on the *Laskey* case, that was improper because Isacson was disqualified under Rule 1.9. His disqualification was imputed to Malkan under Rule 1.10(a) and under the traditional law of vicarious disqualification codified in 1.10(a), the disqualification remains when Isacson leaves. The remainder of Rule 1.10 states some rules for removing disqualifications in peripheral situations, but they do not apply. Rule 1.10(c) makes an exception for the side-switching firm but that is not involved in this case. Malkan stays with Laskey. Since there is no exception with respect to remaining on the same side when one was formerly disqualified, the original disqualification against Malkan remains. The policy justification is that the same reason that forbade Malkan from showing he had no confidential information from Isacson in order to represent Laskey while Isacson was his partner still exists. The defendants will have a reasonable fear that Isacson revealed information while he was Malkan's partner because the *Laskey* case against them was in the office then.

As to the *Austin* case, however, Rule 1.10(a) never comes into play because that case came to Malkan after Isacson left. Therefore, under Rule 1.10, Malkan may represent Austin. No imputed disqualification occurs and indeed any requirement that Malkan show he did not receive relevant confidential information from Isacson about defendants will have to be teased out of some other Rule (or out of some common law principle). Under this argument then, unless resort is made to supplementary common law principles, a court might reach the same bizarre contradictory result in *Laskey* and *Austin* that the court reached in the actual cases.

(2) The argument may be made that the above presentation misreads Model Rule 1.10(a). That rule only prescribes principles for the period "[w]hile lawyers are associated in a firm." Therefore, although Malkan was disqualified from representing Laskey while he was a partner with Isacson under Rule 1.10(a), his disqualification thereafter is governed by 1.10(c). The purpose of that Rule is to state the situation when a firm continues to be disqualified. It continues to be disqualified only when it fails to meet conditions (1) and (2) in a situation where it seeks to rep-

resent "interest materially adverse to those of a client represented by the formerly associated lawyer." It is possible that those quoted words contemplate only the Baxter Laboratories (p. 114 Note 4) situation: i.e. whether to permit a firm to represent the other side when a lawyer leaves the firm and a client goes along, and no one left in the firm has any confidential information relating to the client of the departing lawyer. If that is the proper interpretation of Rule 1.10(c), then it does not cover the *Laskey* or *Austin* cases. Since Rule 1.10(a) doesn't apply after Isacson leaves, Malkan is not disqualified in either case (unless again some supplementary common law principle is invoked). The policy argument for this result is that once Isacson leaves, the danger of revelation of confidences is gone, and Malkan should be allowed to prove he received no such information while Isacson was in the office.

(3) It is possible, however, that the above interpretation of Rule 1.10(c) is too narrow. Literally the words "representing a person with interests materially adverse to those of a client represented by the formerly associated lawyer" may be read to mean that the firm is not prohibited from "representing a person (Laskey) with interests materially adverse to those of a client (the defendants) represented by the formerly associated lawyer (Isacson)." It reads the representation by a formerly associated lawyer to cover Isacson's representations before he joined Malkan and is not limited to representations while he was Malkan's partner. Under that interpretation, Malkan is permitted to prove that he has no relevant confidential information and would therefore be permitted to represent both Laskey and Austin. This interpretation and interpretation 2 both reverse the result in the actual *Laskey*, but not the actual *Austin*, case.

(4) A final series of interpretations would proceed from the premise that Model Rule 1.10 does not cover the whole field and that supplemental common law rules are still needed. Building on any of the above interpretations, a court might properly hold that the Model Rules simply do not deal with the situation where a firm's initial representation of a client was improper, as the *Laskey* representation was for Malkan & Isacson. Therefore, whatever is the proper interpretation had the initial representation been proper, Malkan may not profit from the original improper representation of Laskey. A court might go further to say that Malkan's handling of *Austin* is tainted by his handling of *Laskey* and his new firm should be disqualified from handling both cases.

Which of these arguments do you prefer?

The drafting history of Model Rule 1.10 (and Rule 1.11 too) discloses that these sections were completely redrafted at the last minute. The problematic results of *Laskey* and *Austin* under the Model Rules suggest the dangers of last minute drafting. On the other hand, the enormous problems created by the previous versions of Model Rules 1.10 and 1.11 suggest also the dangers of not engaging in last minute drafting.

2. *Former Government Lawyers and Vicarious Disqualification*

PROBLEM 13

Hall, a leading practitioner in the criminal law field, was elected district attorney of his county eight years ago. After two terms, he was recently defeated for reelection. He has been approached with attractive offers of partnership by several firms in his county that have extensive criminal practices. The new district attorney has stated publicly that he will move to disqualify any firm that his predecessor joins in every criminal case in which his office is involved that was pending during his predecessor's term of office even if his predecessor is "screened off" from all participation in such cases. Should such motions be granted?

In *Silver Chrysler Plymouth* the court decided that although the departing attorney had been vicariously disqualified while at Kelly, Drye, he was not personally disqualified because he was not in possession of relevant confidential information. The court cited and followed the earlier *Laskey* decision in refusing to pile vicarious disqualification on vicarious disqualification. When Mr. Schreiber moved to a new firm, he therefore shed the vicarious disqualification. The more debated question, however, has been the effect on a new firm that hires a lawyer who is personally disqualified from representing an interest adverse to a former client. Should the general rule that the whole firm is disqualified when one lawyer is disqualified by reason of conflict of interest be rigorously applied in that circumstance?

The first cases in which the issue was debated involved the former government lawyer who joins a private firm upon leaving government service, although it should be pointed out that the issue of the application of the disqualification rules, especially the vicarious disqualification rules, to former government lawyers went largely unnoticed in the profession for a long time. The cases that did arise involved personal disqualification of former government lawyers because of their previous involvement in substantially related matters. The issue suddenly became a major one in the late 1970s, perhaps because the increasing frequency of disqualification motions brought greater awareness of the problem, perhaps because of greater movement of high-level government lawyers to large law firms. At all events, the issue first surfaced when the Ethics Committees of the American Bar Association and of the District of Columbia Bar, in a draft opinion, offered different advice on the issue. The importance of the latter committee's view was heightened by the fact that it potentially affected so many lawyers who practiced for the federal government and then moved to private practice in Washington.

At issue was the proper interpretation of DR 5-105(D), which in its original form required vicarious disqualification of a firm only if a firm lawyer were disqualified "under DR 5-105." The 1974 amendments changed the quoted words to "under a Disciplinary Rule." Whether or not the pre-1974 language, which was drafted to codify the common law rule of vicarious disqualification, should be applied to the former government attorney whose conduct is specifically covered by DR 9, it is clear that the revised language literally reaches that situation.

In giving its advice about the proper interpretation of DR 5-105(D), the ABA Committee considered both the situation of the private practitioner who joined the government and the government lawyer who joined a private firm. It concluded in its Opinion 342 (Nov. 24, 1975) that given the different mission of the salaried government lawyer to seek just results and given the inhibition on government's ability to recruit if a too strict application of DR 5-105(D) is adopted, the vicarious disqualification rules should be different in this context. The government ought to be able to waive disqualification if the former government attorney now in a firm representing an adverse interest is sufficiently screened off, physically and financially, from any participation in the matter.

The Ethics Committee of the District of Columbia Bar took a dramatically different tack in its draft opinion. It identified a whole series of concerns addressed by the application of the disqualification rules to former government attorneys: unfair advantage to one private party over others; favoritism to former colleagues; side switching; buying the opposition's best people; ingratiating oneself with a potential employer; using governmental action to obtain future employment or to obtain an advantage over a potential opponent in future private litigation. It considered and rejected screening as meeting the concerns suggested by these objections and concluded that the traditional rule of vicarious disqualified should be applied to the case of a former government attorney.

Although a majority of the District of Columbia Ethics Committee favored adoption of the tentative opinion, it fell one vote short of the ten votes needed to issue an opinion. In addition, the proposed opinion caused a storm of protest from lawyers. Eventually, with somewhat changed membership, the committee came to believe that it should deal with the subject by proposing a rule for adoption by the District of Columbia Court of Appeals. That court finally adopted new disciplinary rules under Canon 9 providing generally for a screening procedure similar to that suggested by ABA Opinion 342. It also provided mechanics for giving notice to the appropriate government agency and filing documents attesting to the compliance procedures proposed to be followed in the matter. But it did not adopt the requirement of consent by the government advocated by ABA Opinion 342. ("Revolving Door"), No. M-81-88, 445 A.2d 615 (1982). Various agencies of the federal government have also adopted rules that authorize screening devices to avoid the effects of DR 5-105(D)'s vicarious disqualification rules. See, e.g., 46 C.F.R. §502.32(c) (1978) (Federal Maritime Commission); 31 C.F.R. §10.26(c) (IRS); 17 C.F.R. §200.735-8(e) (SEC); and 16 C.F.R. §4.1(b)(8) (FTC).

The so-called revolving door problem has also become a subject for litigation. The subject was well canvassed in the following case.

ARMSTRONG v. McALPIN
625 F.2d 433 (2d Cir. 1980) (en banc)

FEINBERG, Circuit Judge

. . . Clovis McAlpin and Capital Growth Real Estate Fund, Inc., two of numerous defendants in a suit seeking over $24 million for violation of federal securities laws, appeal from an order of the United States District Court for the Southern District of New York, Henry F. Werker, J., denying their motion to disqualify the law firm representing plaintiffs. The appeal was first heard by a panel of this court, which concluded that the trial judge had erred in denying defendants' disqualification motion. 606 F.2d 28 (2d Cir. 1979). A majority of this court voted to grant en banc reconsideration of the appeal. . . . After full consideration, we affirm the order of the district court and vacate the earlier decision of the panel. . . .

Appellants' motion to disqualify is based on the prior participation of Theodore Altman, now a partner in the law firm representing plaintiffs-appellees, in an investigation of and litigation against appellants conducted when he was an Assistant Director of the Division of Enforcement of the Securities and Exchange Commission (the SEC). In September 1974, after a nine-month investigation, the SEC commenced an action in the United States District Court for the Southern District of New York against Clovis McAlpin and various other individual and institutional defendants. The complaint alleged that McAlpin and the other defendants had looted millions of dollars from a group of related investment companies, referred to here collectively as the Capital Growth companies; McAlpin was the top executive officer of these companies. The SEC suit sought, among other things, the appointment of a receiver to protect the interests of shareholders in the Capital Growth companies. When McAlpin fled to Costa Rica and certain other defendants failed to appear, the SEC obtained a default judgment; in September 1974, Judge Charles E. Stewart appointed Michael F. Armstrong, the principal appellee in this appeal, as receiver of the Capital Growth companies. See SEC v. Capital Growth Company, S.A. (Costa Rica) et al., 391 F. Supp. 593 (S.D.N.Y. 1974).

One of Armstrong's principal tasks as receiver for the Capital Growth companies is to recover all moneys and property misappropriated by defendants; to further this task, Armstrong was authorized to initiate litigation in the United States and abroad. In October 1974, Judge Stewart granted Armstrong's request to retain as his counsel the New York firm of Barrett Smith Schapiro & Simon.[1]. . .

In early 1976, however, the receiver and Barrett Smith became aware of a potential conflict of interest involving an institutional client of Barrett Smith that might become a defendant in litigation brought by the receiver. Thus, despite Barrett Smith's substantial investment of time, the receiver concluded that it was necessary to substitute litigation counsel. The task, however, was not an easy one; McAlpin had fled to Costa Rica with most of the assets of the Capital Growth companies and hence the funds available to Armstrong to secure new counsel were quite limited. It was therefore necessary to find a firm that could not only handle difficult litigation in Costa Rica and in the United States, but would also commit itself to conclude the task, even if little or no interim compensation was available. Moreover, it was important to retain a law firm large enough to cope with the immense paper work soon to be generated by the firms that would probably represent the institutional defendants.

Because of these considerations, appellees assert, the receiver focused on firms already involved in litigation against Robert L. Vesco, who, like McAlpin, had fled to Costa Rica rather than face possible prosecution for numerous alleged securities fraud violations. After abortive negotiations with two such firms, the receiver in April 1976 retained the law firm of Gordon Hurwitz Butowsky Baker Weitzen & Shalov, the firm that is the target of appellants' disqualification motion. According to Armstrong, the Gordon firm was chosen in part because one partner, David M. Butowsky, was then Special Counsel to International Controls Corporation and was involved in legal work in Costa Rica relating to the alleged Vesco defalcations, while another partner had specialized experience in prosecuting complex fraud cases. In accepting the representation, the Gordon firm agreed to "conduct all Capital Growth litigation through to a conclusion" even if the receiver could not compensate the firm as the litigation progressed.

In October 1975, some seven months before the receiver obtained substitute counsel for Barrett Smith, Theodore Altman ended his nine-year tenure with the SEC to become an associate with the Gordon firm. At the time of his resignation, Altman had been an Assistant Director of the Division of Enforcement for three years, and had about twenty-five staff attorneys working under him. As a high-ranking enforcement officer of the SEC, Altman had supervisory responsibility over numerous cases, including the Capital Growth investigation and litigation. Although he was not involved on a daily basis, he was generally aware of the facts of the case and the status of the litigation. The SEC's complaint

---

1. Armstrong was a partner of that firm, which is now Barrett Smith Schapiro Simon & Armstrong.

was prepared and filed by the staff of the New York Regional Administrator, and the litigation was handled by the New York office. Altman's name appeared on the SEC complaint, although he did not sign it.

At the time that Altman joined the Gordon firm, the receiver had no reason to know that Altman had left the SEC or to be aware of his new affiliation. Subsequently, during the initial meetings with the Gordon firm, Armstrong first learned that Altman had recently become associated with the firm. Both the Gordon firm and Barrett Smith researched the question of the effect of Altman's prior supervisory role in the SEC suit. The two firms concluded that under applicable ethical standards discussed in Part IV of this opinion, Altman should not participate in the Gordon firm's representation of the receiver, but that the firm would not be disqualified if Altman was properly screened from the case. The matter was brought to the attention of Judge Stewart, who nonetheless authorized the receiver to retain the Gordon firm. Shortly thereafter, the firm asked the SEC if it had any objection to the retention, and was advised in writing that it did not, so long as Altman was screened from participation. Barrett Smith then turned over its litigation files to the Gordon firm, including those received from the SEC; in September 1976, the receiver filed the action by plaintiffs-appellees against defendants-appellants that gave rise to this appeal.

In June 1978, almost two years after the commencement of this action, appellants filed their motion to disqualify the Gordon firm because of Altman's prior activities at the SEC. In December 1978, Judge Werker, to whom the case had been reassigned, denied the motion. In his opinion, the judge concluded that the Gordon firm had carried out the letter and spirit of the relevant bar association ethical rulings, that the firm's representation of the receiver was not unethical and did not threaten the integrity of the trial, and that appellants had suffered no prejudice as a result of the representation. 461 F. Supp. 622 (S.D.N.Y. 1978). As already indicated, in September 1979 a panel of this court reversed the decision of the district court; in December 1979, this en banc proceeding was ordered. . . .

[The court first concluded that henceforth denials of motions to disqualify counsel would not be appealable. It nevertheless decided to reach the merits in this case.]

In his thorough opinion refusing to disqualify the Gordon firm, Judge Werker reviewed the facts set forth in . . . this opinion and carefully analyzed the ethical problem defendants had raised. He noted that Altman was concededly disqualified from participating in the litigation under Disciplinary Rule 9-101(B) of the American Bar Association Code of Professional Responsibility. That Rule prohibits an attorney's private employment in any matter in which he has had substantial responsibility during prior public employment. The judge then considered the effect of Disciplinary Rule 5-105(D), which deals with disqualification of an entire law firm if one lawyer in the firm is disqualified. . . .

Judge Werker then carefully examined the screening of Altman by the Gordon firm, noting that:

Altman is excluded from participation in the action, has no access to relevant files and derives no remuneration from funds obtained by the firm from prosecuting this action. No one at the firm is permitted to discuss the matter in his presence or allow him to view any document related to this litigation, and Altman has not imparted any information concerning Growth Fund to the firm. . . .

[N]othing before this court indicates that Altman, while employed by the SEC, formed an intent to prosecute a later action involving Growth Fund. Indeed, sworn affidavits reveal that he has never participated in any fashion whatever in the Gordon firm's representation of the Receiver, nor has he shared in the firm's income derived from prosecution of this action. And . . . Altman and his two partners Velie and Butowsky have attested under penalty of perjury that Altman has never discussed the action with other firm members. These statements are uncontradicted by defendants and provide a basis for *not* imputing Altman's knowledge to other members of the firm.

461 F. Supp. at 624-625 (emphasis in original). Under all the circumstances, the district judge concluded that "the proper screening of Altman rather than disqualification of the Gordon firm is the solution to the present dispute." Id. at 626. Accordingly, the motion to disqualify was denied. On appeal, as already indicated, a panel of this court reversed the order of the district court, apparently on the ground that disqualification was required "as a prophylactic measure to guard against misuse of authority by government lawyers." 606 F.2d at 34.

On this rehearing en banc, we are favored with briefs not only from the parties but also from the United States,[18] the Securities and Exchange Commission, the Interstate Commerce Commission, the Federal Maritime Commission, the Commodities Futures Trading Commission and twenty-six distinguished former government lawyers now employed as practicing attorneys, corporate officers, or law professors, all attesting to the importance of the issues raised on appeal. Thus, the United States asserts that a "decision to reject screening procedures is certain to have a serious, adverse effect on the ability of Government legal offices to recruit and retain well-qualified attorneys"; this view is seconded by the other government amici. And the former government lawyers, including two former Attorneys General of the United States and two former Solicitors General of the United States, state that they are all "affected at

18. The brief of the United States also states that it presents the views of the Federal Trade Commission, the Civil Aeronautics Board, the Federal Energy Regulatory Commission, and the Federal Legal Council, a committee consisting of the General Counsels of fifteen executive branch agencies and chaired by the Attorney General of the United States.

least indirectly, by the panel opinion's underlying assumption that government lawyers cannot be trusted — trusted to discharge their public responsibilities faithfully while in office, or to abide fully by screening procedures afterwards." While the tone of these assertions may be overly apocalyptic, it is true that a decision rejecting the efficacy of screening procedures in this context may have significant adverse consequences. Thus, such disapproval may hamper the government's efforts to hire qualified attorneys; the latter may fear that government service will transform them into legal "Typhoid Marys,"[19] shunned by prospective private employers because hiring them may result in the disqualification of an entire firm in a possibly wide range of cases. The amici also contend that those already employed by the government may be unwilling to assume positions of greater responsibility within the government that might serve to heighten their undesirability to future private employers. Certainly such trends, if carried to an extreme, may ultimately affect adversely the quality of the services of government attorneys.

Not only is the panel decision possibly of great practical importance, the ethical issues it addresses are also complex and are currently being hotly contested by various groups. . . .

We do not believe that it is necessary or appropriate for this court to enter fully into the fray, as the panel opinion did.[22] Indeed, the current uncertainty over what is "ethical" underscores for us the wisdom, when considering such issues, of adopting a restrained approach that focuses primarily on preserving the integrity of the trial process. We expressed this view in Board of Education v. Nyquist, [p. 123], in which we reviewed at length our precedents on attorney disqualification and pointed out:

> Our reading of the cases in this circuit suggests that we have utilized the power of trial judges to disqualify counsel where necessary to preserve the integrity of the adversary process in actions before them. In other words, with rare exceptions disqualification has been ordered only in essentially two kinds of cases: (1) where an attorney's conflict of interests in violation of Canons 5 and 9 of the Code of Professional Responsibility undermines the court's confidence in the vigor of the attorney's representation of his client, . . . or more commonly (2) where the attorney is at least potentially in a position to use privileged information concerning the other side through prior representation, for example, in violation of Canons 4 and 9, thus giving his present client an unfair advantage. . . . But in other kinds of cases, we have shown considerable reluctance to disqualify attorneys

---

19. Kesselhaut v. United States, 555 F.2d 791, 793 (Ct. Cl. 1977) (per curiam).

22. Judge Newman, dissenting from this portion of the en banc opinion, asserts that the present provisions of the Code of Professional Responsibility should be "appl[ied] as written." At 454. We regard this "plain meaning" approach to disqualification motions to be particularly ill-advised in light of the continuing uncertainty and disagreement over the meaning and application of the Code's provisions.

despite misgivings about the attorney's conduct. . . . This reluctance probably derives from the fact that disqualification has an immediate adverse
effect on the client by separating him from counsel of his choice, and that
disqualification motions are often interposed for tactical reasons. . . . And
even when made in the best of faith, such motions inevitably cause delay.

Id. at 1246 (citations and footnotes omitted). Judge Mansfield, concurring in *Nyquist,* pointed out that a trial could also be tainted because:

. . . the former Government attorney might in the later private action use
information with respect to the matter in issue which was gained in confidence as a public employee and was unavailable to the other side.

Id. at 1246 n.1. We ended our review in *Nyquist* by adopting a restrained
approach to disqualification.

Weighing the needs of efficient judicial administration against the potential advantage of immediate preventive measures, we believe that unless an attorney's conduct tends to "taint the underlying trial" . . . by
disturbing the balance of the presentations in one of the two ways indicated above, courts should be quite hesitant to disqualify an attorney.
Given the availability of both federal and state comprehensive disciplinary machinery, see, e.g., Local Rules of the United States Court of Appeals for the Second Circuit §46(h) (1978), there is usually no need to
deal with all other kinds of ethical violations in the very litigation in
which they surface. . . .

We believe that this approach is dispositive here and requires our affirmance of the ruling of the district court. It is apparent from a close
reading of Judge Werker's opinion that he saw no threat of taint of the
trial by the Gordon firm's continued representation of the receiver. Nor
did the panel opinion in this case challenge that view. Although appellants assert that the trial will be tainted by the use of information from
Altman, we see no basis on the record before us for overruling the district court's rejection of that claim. Using the *Nyquist* analysis, there is
certainly no reason to fear any lack of "vigor" by the Gordon firm in
representing the receiver; this is not a case where a law firm, by use of
a "Chinese wall," is attempting to justify representation of conflicting
interests at the same time. Cf. Fund of Funds, Ltd. v. Arthur Andersen
& Co., [p 135]; Cinema 5 Ltd. v. Cinerama, Inc., [p. 50, Note 6]. Nor is
the Gordon firm "potentially in a position to use privileged information"
obtained through prior representation of the other side. And finally, the
receiver will not be making unfair use of information obtained by Altman as a government official, since the SEC files were turned over to
the receiver long before he retained the Gordon firm and Altman has
jeen entirely screened from all participation in the case, to the satis-

faction of the district court and the SEC.[24] Nor is there any reason to believe that the receiver retained the Gordon firm because Altman was connected with it or that Altman had anything to do with the retention. If anything, the presence of Altman as an associate at that time was a problem, not a benefit, for the Gordon firm, as the district court, the receiver and the Gordon firm all apparently recognized.

Thus, because the district court justifiably held that the Gordon firm's representation of the receiver posed no threat to the integrity of the trial process, disqualification of the firm can only be based on the possible appearance of impropriety stemming from Altman's association with the firm. However, as previously noted, reasonable minds may and do differ on the ethical propriety of screening in this context. But there can be no doubt that disqualification of the Gordon firm will have serious consequences for this litigation; separating the receiver from his counsel at this late date will seriously delay and impede, and perhaps altogether thwart, his attempt to obtain redress for defendants' alleged frauds. Under the circumstances, the possible "appearance of impropriety is simply too slender a reed on which to rest a disqualification order . . . particularly . . . where . . . the appearance of impropriety is not very clear." *Nyquist*, supra, 590 F.2d at 1247. Thus, we need not resolve the ethical propriety of the screening procedure used here at this time as long as the district court justifiably regarded it as effective in isolating Altman from the litigation.

We recognize that a rule that concentrates on the threat of taint fails to correct all possible ethical conflicts. In adopting this approach, we do not denigrate the importance of ethical conduct by attorneys practicing in this courthouse or elsewhere, and we applaud the efforts of the organized bar to educate its members as to their ethical obligations. However, absent a threat of taint to the trial, we continue to believe that possible ethical conflicts surfacing during a litigation are generally better addressed by the "comprehensive disciplinary machinery" of the state and federal bar, see *Nyquist*, supra, 590 F.2d at 1246, or possibly by legislation.[27] While there may be unusual situations where the "appearance of impropriety" alone is sufficient to warrant disqualification, we are satisfied that this is not such a case. Nor do we believe, as Judge Newman asserts, that a failure to disqualify the Gordon firm based on the possible appearance of impropriety will contribute to the "public skepticism

---

24. The case therefore is entirely distinguishable from General Motors Corp. v. City of New York, [p. 131], where an attorney who had substantial responsibility over an antitrust litigation against General Motors Corporation while he was employed by the Antitrust Division of the Justice Department later accepted employment as plaintiff's attorney in a private antitrust action against the same defendant for substantially the same conduct.

27. Cf. 18 U.S.C. §207.

about lawyers," While sensitive to the integrity of the bar, the public is also rightly concerned about the fairness and efficiency of the judicial process. We believe those concerns would be disserved by an order of disqualification in a case such as this, where no threat of taint exists and where appellants' motion to disqualify opposing counsel has successfully crippled the efforts of a receiver, appointed at the request of a public agency, to obtain redress for alleged serious frauds on the investing public. Thus, rather than heightening public skepticism, we believe that the restrained approach this court had adopted towards attempts to disqualify opposing counsel on ethical grounds avoids unnecessary and unseemly delay and reinforces public confidence in the fairness of the judicial process.

Accordingly, we vacate the panel opinion in this case and affirm the judgment of the district court.

NEWMAN, Circuit Judge, concurring in part and dissenting in part:

. . . The majority's opinion does not deal with the ultimate issue on the merits: whether a law firm's representation violates Disciplinary Rule 5-105(D) when one of its partners is disqualified under Disciplinary Rule 9-101(B). Instead the majority concludes that, whether or not the firm's representation violates the Code of Professional Responsibility, a trial court should not disqualify the firm unless (a) the firm's representation would taint the trial or (b) the case is one of those "unusual situations where the 'appearance of impropriety' alone is sufficient to warrant disqualification." 625 F.2d at 446. In this case the majority finds neither a threat of taint nor a sufficient basis to disqualify to avoid the appearance of impropriety. I disagree with both this standard for disqualification and its application to this case.

As expressed by the majority, this standard makes trial taint the primary and nearly exclusive basis for disqualification, relegating "appearance of impropriety" to a remote and uncertain role at best.[2] In my view, the judiciary should be much more willing to use the sanction of disqualification to make sure that the canons of ethics are not violated in the courtroom. I can agree that not every violation of the Code should result in disqualification. Especially when a violation occurs after litigation has begun, it will sometimes be fairer to the interests of both the public and the client to permit the trial to continue to conclusion and then use the grievance procedures for appropriate discipline. But when the alleged violation concerns the propriety of undertaking representa-

---

2. Limiting disqualification to instances of trial taint may have been somewhat more justified prior to today's decision, when denials of disqualification were subject to interlocutory appeal. It may be that fear of dilatory interlocutory appeals played some part in the emergence of the "trial taint" standard, limiting the grounds for court-enforced disqualification. It is somewhat ironic that a "trial taint" standard should now become virtually absolute at the very time that interlocutory appeals from denial of disqualification are being prohibited.

tion at the outset, a court should inquire into whether a lawyer and his firm are violating the Code by appearing in the litigation, whether or not such representation will taint the trial.[3]

The appropriateness of such inquiry is especially high when the Code provision at issue regulates the ethical conduct of government attorneys. DR 9-101(B) is not concerned solely with the trial taint that may occur if an attorney handles a matter for which he previously had substantial responsibility as a government lawyer. It also seeks to avoid "the manifest possibility that . . . [a former Government lawyer's] action as a public legal officer might be influenced (or open to the charge that it had been influenced) by the hope of later being employed privately to uphold or upset what he had done." General Motors Corp. v. City of New York, 501 F.2d 639, 648-649 (2d Cir. 1974). Courts traditionally have been most sensitive to the enforcement of standards designed to limit governmental power. They should be at least as sensitive to the enforcement of standards specifically designed to protect against the misuse of such power. The purposes of DR 9-101(B) cannot be fully achieved unless there is no possibility that the government attorney can be (or seem to be) influenced by the prospect of later private employment. To remove that possibility requires disqualification not only of the attorney, when handling a related matter, but also of his firm.

Even under the majority's limited standard for disqualification, Altman's firm should be disqualified in this case. First, if threat of taint is accepted as the primary ground for disqualification, such threat is present here. In Board of Education v. Nyquist, 590 F.2d 1241 (2d Cir. 1979), it was recognized that a former Government attorney's possession of confidential information unavailable to the other side would risk trial taint sufficiently to warrant his disqualification. Id. at 1247-1248 n.1 (Mansfield, J., concurring). That risk is not eliminated by screening the lawyer from his firm. In Fund of Funds, Ltd. v. Arthur Andersen & Co., 567 F.2d 225, 229 n.10 (2d Cir. 1977), a Chinese Wall within a law firm was thought to be inadequate protection against the risk that information from one of the firm's clients, with interests adverse to another of

---

3. It is clear that trial courts could appropriately enforce, at the outset of litigation, disqualification rules that are not concerned only with trial taint. However, such an approach would pose different issues for an appellate court considering a trial court's denial of disqualification on appeal from a final judgment after trial. At that point reversal of the judgment might sometimes be an excessive penalty for violation of the canons, too costly to both the litigants and the public. Perhaps the penalty for representation in violation of the canons, where trial taint has not occurred should be simply forfeiture of attorney's fees. Even if reversal of a judgment were inappropriate, appellate rulings on whether the representation was proper would increase observance of the canons and provide useful guidance for trial courts. Whatever sanctions might be appropriate for an appellate court to impose when, after judgment, denial of disqualification is held to have been erroneous, the disqualification sanction, not limited to instances of trial taint, should be available for use by trial courts when the canons are violated at the outset of litigation.

the firm's clients, would be transmitted from one partner to another. If in this litigation it should become crucial to the outcome for the lawyers representing the plaintiff to know some confidential information learned by Altman while in government employ, I do not see why a Chinese Wall should be thought more impervious to information that originated from a government investigation than to information learned from a client with adverse interests.[5]

Second, this case should be deemed to meet the majority's exception to the taint standard for an unusual situation where the appearance of impropriety warrants disqualification. In addition to the need to disqualify the firm to avoid all risk that a government attorney might misuse his authority in hope of later private gain, appearance of impropriety exists here because of the further risk that the screening procedure will not be effective. It may well be that no matter how this litigation develops, Altman will in fact not disclose to his partners anything he learned while exercising substantial government responsibilities for related matters. But the public will not believe it. Of course, the rules of law, including the rules of disqualification, cannot cater to all the often unfounded apprehensions of the public. But we do not deal here with just a generalized public skepticism about lawyers. The policymaking body of the legal profession's largest and most influential membership organization has adopted a Code of Professional Responsibility that bars Altman from representing the plaintiff in this case (DR 9-101(B)) and bars his partners as well (DR 5-101(D)). The public understandably will see an appearance of impropriety when, despite the clarity of these prohibitions, Altman's law firm is allowed to continue its representation because of the assurance that Altman and his partners will not discuss this case. The public will also justifiably perceive impropriety when, despite the prohibition of the canons, a government lawyer handles a matter and the law firm he subsequently joins is not disqualified from representation in a substantially related matter.[6] To allow such representation

5. The majority opinion suggests that the absence of risk of taint is a factual finding of the District Court, not shown to be clearly erroneous. I would agree that whether a Chinese Wall within a law firm has been breached would be an issue of fact. However, whether such a device is prospectively a sufficient safeguard to justify a representation forbidden by the Code is an issue of law. That issue was not considered in the panel opinion because disqualification of the firm was thought to be required by the Code and the principle of the *General Motors* case, regardless of whether a Chinese Wall could adequately prevent taint.

6. The majority opinion suggests that countervailing considerations are to be found in the public expectation of efficiency in the judicial process, and that further delay resulting from disqualification of the Gordon firm should not be tolerated. I do not think efficiency, even in the pursuit of alleged wrongdoing, justifies a failure to enforce a rule of ethics that is specifically designed to remove the temptation and opportunity for misuse of governmental authority. Moreover, I cannot agree that the delay to date and subsequently, if disqualification were ordered, is chargeable to appellants. The onus quite properly rests with the Gordon firm, which undertook a representation in the face of the Code's clear prohibition.

leaves the government lawyer open to the charge that his action as a public legal officer might have been influenced by the hope of later being employed to uphold what he had done, as this Court warned in *General Motors,* supra. The appearance of impropriety should be avoided by disqualification of Altman's firm.

Whether the Code of Professional Responsibility should maintain its present rule requiring the disqualification of the former government attorney's firm is a matter on which reasonable minds may differ. Serious concerns have been expressed that the Code, as now written, may unduly restrict private employment opportunities of government lawyers and thereby impair the government's ability to attract competent attorneys. That issue is now receiving attention by those charged with responsibility for reviewing and perhaps revising the content of the Code. But until some concrete evidence of adverse consequences supplies grounds for changing the Code's present provisions, I would apply them as written, find Altman's firm to be in violation of the Code by its representation in this case, and grant the motion to disqualify to maintain the important ethical principles on which the Code is based.

[Other opinions, directed to the issue of appealability, are omitted.]

NOTES

1. After the Supreme Court decided Firestone Tire & Rubber Co. v. Risjord, p. 40, holding denial of disqualification motions nonappealable, it vacated the judgment in *Armstrong* and remanded with instructions to dismiss the appeal. 449 U.S. 1106 (1981). Nevertheless, the Second Circuit's opinion on the merits continues to be cited frequently.

2. The materials in this chapter have already discussed one of the issues that divide the court, viz., the use of disqualification to enforce the standards of the Disciplinary Rule. In reading Judge Newman's dissent, it is important to keep his views on that issue distinct from his views on the merits of "screening." One can agree with his views on the former without necessarily agreeing with his views on the latter.

3. The *Armstrong* court referred to the federal conflict of interest statute (p. 125, n.27). Former government counsel must pay close attention to these and to similar state statutes, which are common, in connection with subsequent private representation. The federal conflict of interest statutes are contained in 18 U.S.C. §207. In general, they make criminal (1) representation of a party other than the United States by a former government employee in connection with any matter in which *the employee participated personally and substantially* as an employee; (2) personal appearance by a former employee (or aiding someone else's personal appearance) within two years after cessation of employment before any department, court, or agency of the United States on behalf of anyone

other than the United States in a matter in which the United States is interested and *that was under the employee's official responsibility* at any time within one year prior to the termination of such responsibility; and (3) *personal appearance* within a year after leaving government employment by a former employee, except a special employee serving less than 60 days in a given year, on behalf of a party other than the United States *before a department in which the employee served* in connection with any proceeding before it or in which it has a substantial interest.

The federal Ethics in Government Act of 1978, in addition to revising §207, also established an Office of Government Ethics, one of whose jobs, under the supervision of the Office of Personnel Management, is, in consultation with the Attorney General, to coordinate conflict of interest policies in the executive branch. Its advisory opinions may be found in the Ethics in Government Reporter.

4. An interesting case involved refusal by a court, notwithstanding the government's consent, to permit screening of a former government lawyer in order to permit his firm to continue to handle a group of 260 asbestos cases in which it was co-counsel. The court noted the danger of inadvertent disclosure of confidential information by reason of the small size of the firm (six people), the potential length of the litigation, and the participation of the former government employee in over 1,000 other asbestos cases in which the firm was involved. In re Asbestos Cases, 514 F. Supp. 914 (E.D. Va. 1981). On appeal, the disqualification order was reversed, 2-1, by a panel of the Court of Appeals for the Fourth Circuit. (The opinion is summarized in 50 U.S. Law Week 2533 (Mar. 16, 1982) and printed in full in Lexis.) A hearing en banc was granted, the panel opinion withdrawn, and an order of affirmance of the district court order entered without opinion. (The Lexis report and a note on the face of the opinion in the Clerk's Office of the Court of Appeals state that the affirmance was by an equally divided court.) Could the court reach the same result under Model Rule 1.11?

5. The disqualification issue arises not only when the government lawyer enters private practice but also when the private lawyer enters government service. In Arkansas v. Dean Foods Prods. Inc., 605 F.2d 380 (8th Cir. 1979), when a private practitioner became head of the Arkansas state antitrust division, not only he but the whole division he supervised was disqualified from prosecuting an antitrust action for price-fixing against a former client even though the trial court found that he personally had received no relevant confidences relating to this matter while in private practice. The implications for the state of the vicarious disqualification of staff seem considerable since it removes the making of policy from the responsible department. Those considerations led another court of appeals not to disqualify the entire United States Attorney's Office from prosecuting a defendant when one of his lawyers joined the Office. United States v. Caggiano, 660 F.2d 184 (6th Cir. 1981), cert.

denied, 455 U.S. 945 (1982). The Model Rules also adopt the policy of not disqualifying the entire office of a public agency when one lawyer is disqualified by virtue of his former or prospective private practice activities. Model Rule 1.11(c) and Comment.

6. A similar kind of problem has arisen with respect to a different kind of government employee, the public defender. In United States v. Judge, 625 F. Supp. 901 (D. Hawaii 1986), the court permitted such an office to represent a defendant when it had also previously represented a crucial government witness against the defendant. The government sought disqualification because of its fear that defendant's counsel would use confidential information to attack the witness's credibility. The court held that the defendant's choice of counsel was entitled to great deference and that the screening procedures adopted were sufficient to prevent such misuse of confidential information.

7. The Model Rules address the screening issue with respect to former government lawyers in Model Rule 1.11 and permit it in both the situation where the former government lawyer had participated substantially in a matter and also where the former government lawyer has confidential information about a person acquired in government service that could be used in a particular matter adversely to that person. Interestingly, insofar as the personal disqualification of the former government lawyer is concerned, it can be removed by government consent in the former situation, where the government's interests are involved, but not in the latter situation, where they are not. In addition, the screening that avoids vicarious disqualification requires notification to the government, but not its consent, in the former situation. No notification is required to make the screening effective in the latter situation.

NOTE: Other Problems of Government Employees and Vicarious Disqualification

An important issue relating to former government lawyers was raised in General Motors Corp. v. City of New York, 501 F.2d 639 (2d Cir. 1974). George Reycraft, an attorney in the Antitrust Division, participated in the investigation of alleged monopolization of the bus business by GM and signed the government's complaint against GM that charged violation of the Sherman Act. Subsequently, after he had left the government and with the consent of the Justice Department, Reycraft agreed to represent New York City in a private antitrust action against GM that the court found sufficiently similar to the United States' action to constitute the "same matter" under DR 9-101(B). The court, noting that "there lurks great potential for lucrative returns in following into private practice the course already charted with the aid of government resources," id. at 650, held that Reycraft should be disqualified because of the appearance of impropriety. It is clear that if Reycraft had moved from one private firm to another and were representing a different, but nonadverse, private interest in the same matter with the consent of the former client, there would be no problem. Government employment, however, is one area where the admonition of Canon 9 supplies independent justification for disqualification on the theory that since the client of the government is, in some sense, "the public interest," see pp. 303 ff., there is more reason to take steps to avert public suspicion, where feasible, than with the ordinary private employment case. On the other hand, given the consent of the government, it would appear that *General Motors* would have come out the other way under the Model Rules. See MR 1.11(a). The issue of course is whether "consent" sufficiently meets the concerns that prompted the decision of the Second Circuit.

The *General Motors* result has not always been followed, however, to an inexorable conclusion. In Woods v. Covington County Bank, 537 F.2d 804 (5th Cir. 1976), the court refused to disqualify a lawyer from representing an ex-serviceman whom he had first represented in the same matter while he was engaged in his annual two-week tour of duty as a reserve officer in the Judge Advocate General's Corps. The court first held that by statute the lawyer had not been a federal employee while in training. The court distinguished the *General Motors* case because there could be no suspicion of misuse of public position inasmuch as the lawyer acted under orders from his superior when he was in service and also because as a legal assistance officer, his duty had been owed to the individual client and not to the government. There had thus been no exercise of any official governmental authority by the lawyer.

Another issue that must often be faced in cases in which former government lawyers or their firms are sought to be disqualified is whether the "matter" in which the firm is seeking to participate is the same "matter" in which the former government lawyer participated when a government employee. A good example of the difficulties of defining what is the same matter for purposes of DR 9-101(B) and Model Rule 1.11 is Brown v. Board of Adjustment, 486 A.2d 37 (D.C. Ct. App. 1984) (en banc).

A developer was seeking approval for a residential and commercial complex known as the Westbridge. There were negotiations with the Corporation Counsel's office over building height restrictions, the legality of a proposed air rights condominium, and an application for a special exception permitting increased off-street parking spaces. After the first two problems had been disposed of, the Corporation Counsel and his assistant joined the law firm representing the developer with respect to the parking problem.

The Board of Zoning Adjustment made factual findings that the underlying facts and issues of each of the three transactions were not related. The Court of Appeals relied on those findings to hold that the former government employees were not disqualified from representing the developer with respect to the parking problem. The dissenters would have disqualified them and required "screening" partly because parking spaces were necessarily involved in the first two negotiations and partly because the same economic unit was involved. They were also willing, where the majority was not, to rely heavily on the appearance of impropriety where former government lawyers were involved.

Brown presents an important problem for the future and it offers two different approaches: the majority's factually oriented approach focusing on the precise issues and the precise conduct of government lawyers, and the dissent's more broad ranging view of what constitutes a single piece of litigation or a single project and its perception that a prophylactic rule is better than trying to judge the zealousness of performance by government counsel on a case-by-case basis. The majority does not quite address the argument that its approach looks at the "trees" of particular issues instead of the "forest" of a single case or project and that sideswitching with respect to a project presents such a significant danger of impropriety, or public perception thereof, that actual proof ought not be required where government attorneys are involved.

Not all the problems of vicarious disqualification involve the "former" government employee. An issue may arise for current government employees as well. For example, in some places in the country it is common for prosecutors to hold those positions part-time and to have a private practice in addition. Indeed, without private income they could not survive. The question will then arise whether members of their law firms may represent criminal defendants. A recent opinion of the Georgia Supreme Court declined to follow a host of ethics opinions from other jurisdictions to hold that so long as the state continued to use part-time prosecutors, necessity required relaxation of the usual rules of vicarious disqualification so that no disqualification would be ordered without a finding of actual conflict of interest. Thompson v. State, 254 Ga. 393, 330 S.E.2d 348 (1985).

3. Vicarious Disqualification — Recent Developments in the Private Context

Once an exception to the vicarious disqualification rules had been made for the former government employee on the basis of public policy considerations, it was natural for parties in other situations to seek like exemptions by urging other kinds of public policy considerations. Lawyers who formerly worked in legal services organizations have urged that the need of those public service organizations to attract lawyers to these relatively low-paying jobs justifies the same kind of exceptions as are enjoyed by former government employees. The specific issue has arisen in only a few cases and the argument has not been accepted. See, for example, Cheng v. GAF Corp., 631 F.2d 1052 (2d Cir. 1980), vacated on jurisdictional grounds, 450 U.S. 903 (1981), where the court disqualified the firm to which a former legal services employee had moved because it doubted the efficacy of the screening procedures that had been adopted and because it viewed the public policy considerations as weaker than in *Armstrong*. One may assume, however, that former legal services employees moving to private firms will not be worse off than lawyers moving from one private law firm to another, and that to the extent that there is any relaxation of the vicarious disqualification rules in the latter situation, it will apply to the former situation as well. And indeed, there are opinions holding that because of public policy considerations the traditional vicarious disqualification rules themselves will not be applied to large public-defense entities so that they may represent adverse interests even simultaneously as long as there are no actual conflicts of interests through sharing of confidential information or the like. See People v. Wilkins, 28 N.Y.2d 53, 268 N.E.2d 756 (1971) and People v. Chambers, 508 N.Y.S.2d 378 (Sup. Ct. 1986) (citing other cases throughout the country).

There has been increasing pressure on the vicarious disqualification rules from large law firms as they have grown larger and opened more and more branches throughout the country. They have urged that many instances of vicarious disqualification ought to be dealt with by screening-off procedures so as to rebut the presumption that confidences have been shared by the disqualified lawyer with his or her partners. Screening off a lawyer with confidential information of an adverse party has been permitted by a few courts in the situation of a lawyer moving from one firm to another. See Analytica v. NPD Research, p. 91, at 93, and NFC, Inc. v. General Nutrition, Inc., 562 F. Supp. 332 (D. Mass. 1983). Indeed, some courts have indicated that while screening mechanisms are the best evidence to rebut the presumption that confidential information is shared among members of a firm, other evidence will suffice. United States for the benefit of Lord Elec. Co. v. Titan Pacific Construction Corp., 637 F. Supp. 1556 (W.D. Wash. 1986) (citing many private firm cases permitting rebuttal of the presumption). While rebuttal of the presumption of shared confidences has been permitted in some cases, that breach in the vicarious disqualification rule is still controversial. Indeed, although the Model Rules specifically provide for screening in the case of the former government attorney in MR 1.11, they do not so provide in MR 1.10, the general rule governing movement from one private law firm to another, although some find ambiguity in the Comment to that Rule. See Hammermesh, In Defense of a Double Standard, 20 Mich. J.L. Ref. 245 (1986).

By and large, however, the presumption of shared confidences among members of a firm has not been considered rebuttable in private law firm situations other than when a lawyer moves from one firm to another. For example, in Fund of Funds, Ltd. v. Arthur Andersen & Co., 567 F.2d 225 (2d Cir. 1977), Firm ML represented, with other lawyers, a group of clients whose interests were adverse to the interests of AA, another current client. The group began a series of lawsuits that ML perceived would likely lead to the naming of AA as a defendant. ML nonetheless sought to continue to represent the group and devised a set of techniques to allay the conflict of interest problem. First, ML instructed its lawyers to avoid making a case against AA and to turn over all adverse material to the group's other counsel. Second, it erected a "Chinese Wall" to screen off the ML lawyers working for AA from those working for the group. Third, whenever AA's potential liability was discussed by the group and its counsel, ML lawyers excused themselves from the discussion. Fourth, ML tried unsuccessfully to obtain AA's consent to the representation of group. Fifth, when one of the group sought to join AA as a defendant, ML suggested a cross-ratification agreement, by which the rest of the group did not join AA, but agreed to share in any recovery from AA. Finally, ML called in MT, another law firm that had worked together with ML on group matters, to handle a separate suit against AA. The Second Circuit disqualified MT from representing the group against AA because its close relationship to ML in the total litigation resulted in violation of Canons 4, 5, and 9. In the course of its opinion, the court also stated that it inclined to the view that a "Chinese Wall" screening off procedure could not operate within a single firm. Id. at 229, n.10.

Moreover, in Westinghouse Electric Corp. v. Kerr-McGee Corp., p. 51 Note 9, the court also discussed whether a "Chinese Wall" procedure would have allowed different branches of the same firm to represent, and oppose, the same client on the same general matter, one in a judicial and one in a legislative forum. The court found that no "Chinese Wall" procedure existed and stated that it would not have made any difference. One judge thought it might. 580 F.2d at 1321 n.28.

Nevertheless, there have been instances when the presumption of shared confidences has been permitted to be rebutted in situations not involving movement of a lawyer from one private firm to another. In Hughes v. Paine, Webber, Jackson and Curtis, Inc., 565 F. Supp. 663 (N.D. Ill. 1983), a law firm was representing plaintiffs in a dispute with defendants. An individual defendant consulted another partner in that firm about the possibility of representation regarding an SEC investigation of the matter although he eventually went elsewhere. When that firm brought suit against defendants with respect to plaintiffs' claim, defendants sought to disqualify it. Relying on the *Westinghouse* case, p. 51, Note 9, the court found that an attorney-client relationship had existed between the firm and the individual defendant. Reviewing the somewhat muddled state of the law of successive representation in the

Seventh Circuit, the court concluded that it would not permit the presumption that the individual defendant imparted confidential information to the firm about the matter in issue to be rebutted. The court then held that the second presumption, that the information was communicated by the particular lawyer who had it to other members of the firm, should not be irrebuttable in the circumstances of this case. Since the individual defendant did not become a firm client and since a long-established relationship between the firm and plaintiffs would be destroyed by the brief conversation between the partner and the individual defendant, the court permitted the defendant to rebut that presumption. Moreover, it did not regard the fact that the firm did not undertake a screening procedure until the matter was brought to their attention by the defendant as requiring disqualification.

Some would carry the relaxation of the vicarious disqualification rule considerably further. The most thoroughgoing and thoughtful argument for that result, which has not yet won support in case law, was pressed quite forcefully by Judge Coffey, dissenting in *Analytica*, p. 91.

ANALYTICA, INC. v. NPD RESEARCH, INC.
708 F.2d 1263 (7th Cir. 1983)

COFFEY, Circuit Judge, dissenting.

[The first part of the dissent argued that *LaSalle National Bank, Freeman*, and *Novo*, the three Seventh Circuit opinions cited by Judge Posner in *Analytica*, at p. 93, stood for the proposition that the presumption of intrafirm sharing of confidences was rebuttable in all successive representation cases and not just in cases where a lawyer moved from one firm to another. He therefore argued that although Attorney Fine was individually disqualified, his law firm should have been permitted to attempt to rebut the presumption that he shared confidences with others in the firm.]

The irrebuttable presumption that all information is shared among every attorney in a firm ignores the practical realities of modern day legal practice. The practice of law has changed dramatically in recent years, with many lawyers working in firms consisting of 20, 30, 60, 100 or even 300 or more attorneys, and with some firms having offices located throughout the country or even throughout the world. Additionally, the trend within law firms has been toward greater specialization and departmentalization. Surely, it defies logical and common sense to establish a presumption, with no opportunity for rebuttal, that every individual lawyer in such a multi-member and multi-specialized firm has *substantial knowledge* of the confidences of each of the firm's clients. Recognizing these realities of the modern practice of law, we must continue to take a more realistic view toward the law of attorney disqualification by allowing the presumption that confidences have been shared throughout a firm to be rebuttable, as we have held in *Freeman* and *Novo*. The district court's decision to automatically disqualify the entire law firm based on an irrebuttable presumption is unreasonable and unrealistic and is directly contrary to our holdings in *LaSalle National Bank, Freeman* and *Novo*.

Recognizing that the district court's decision directly contradicts the mandates of the *LaSalle National Bank, Freeman* and *Novo* holdings, the majority feebly attempts to distinguish those cases and states that they do not apply when the firm itself opposes a prior client and, in effect, "changes sides", but apply only to situations where an individual member of a law firm changes employment. This is "poppycock," a distinction without a difference and one which defies both logic and the practical realities of our modern legal system. First, reason tells us that a law firm is indeed nothing more than a group of individual attorneys who have formed an association to further the practice of law. A clear understanding of *LaSalle National Bank, Novo* and *Freeman* establishes that once the appearance of impropriety has arisen, the law firm, as well as an individual attorney, must be given the opportunity to demonstrate an absence of professional impropriety or misconduct. The point the majority overlooks is that it is irrelevant when analyzing the allegations of impropriety whether the potential conflict emanates from one new associate or from several partners or even, for that matter, the entire law firm. The governing legal principle must be the same regardless of whether the alleged conflict arises from the firm itself changing sides or from an individual attorney changing employment; a lawyer or law firm must be given an opportunity to rebut the inference of professional impropriety by demonstrating that the former client's confidences have not been shared with the individuals involved in the current litigation. Why must a lawyer or law firm be disqualified if in fact, they have no substantial knowledge of the former client's confidences because of the out-dated irrebuttable presumption? The mere existence of a possible conflict of interest is of such serious magnitude that the trial judge must afford the litigants (law firms) a hearing and explore the ethical questions in their entirety, unless there are unrebutted facts in the pleadings on file supporting disqualification.

More importantly, however, the majority's analysis ignores a basic principle of law, fairness to all litigants. I believe that fairness requires that any law firm and/or individual lawyer accused of professional impropriety, questionable ethics, or misconduct be given the opportunity to rebut any and all adverse inferences which may have arisen by virtue of a prior representation, and this court so held in *LaSalle National Bank* and *Freeman*. A law firm should not be disqualified with only a summary proceeding conducted by a judge on a sparse factual record such as in this case. To disqualify a lawyer or law firm, and besmirch their professional reputation, based on a sparse and inadequate factual record and an antiquated irrebuttable presumption is to trip lightly through the valley of due process since due process guarantees, at the very least, fundamental fairness to litigants. . . .

The right to rebut allegations of impropriety is necessary because of the immediate and often irreparable ramifications as to both client and counsel alike that a disqualification order carries with it. I believe counsel and, in this instance, the law firm should not only be allowed to protect their relationship with their present client but also their good name and reputation for high ethical standards. After all, an attorney's and/or a law firm's most valuable asset is their professional reputation for competence, and above all honesty and integrity, which should not be jeopardized in a summary type of disqualification proceeding of this nature. As court proceedings are matters of public record, a news media report concerning a summary disqualification order, based on a scant record of this type, can do irreparable harm to an attorney's or law firm's professional reputation. We must recognize that the great majority of lawyers, as officers of the court, do conduct themselves well within the bounds of the Code of Professional Responsibility.

Moreover, as we recognized in *Freeman,* disqualification of an attorney may also adversely affect the client as disqualification deprives the individual of the representation of the attorney of his choice and "it may also be difficult, if not impossible, for an attorney to master 'the nuances of the legal and factual matters' late in the litigation of a complex case." 689 F.2d at 720. However, the majority dismisses this important consideration again citing a supposed "fact" which is nothing more than a bald assumption, without any basis in the record, that "Analytica appears content with whatever substitute counsel it has procured. . . ." A court should order a lawyer or law firm disqualified only after a factual inquiry allowing for subsequent appellate review, if necessary, in the absence of a clear and unrebutted factual basis supporting disqualification. . . .

The majority attempts to justify the irrebuttable presumption by stating "clients will not . . . trust firms that switch sides as nimbly as Schwartz & Freeman." If we accept this as true, the "test of the market" and the law of economics will prevail. A fair and just result will be obtained since the concerned client will select other counsel if he does not trust the present firm. Cf. Merritt v. Faulkner, 697 F.2d 761 at 769-770 (7th Cir. 1983) (Posner, J., concurring in part and dissenting in part); McKeever v. Israel, 689 F.2d 1315, 1325 (7th Cir. 1982) (Posner, J., dissenting).

The majority makes a second attempt to justify the irrebuttable presumption of intra-firm sharing of confidences by stating that a law firm's "interest not only in retaining a client but in denying a serious breach of professional ethics might outweigh any felt obligation to 'come clean'". Evidently, the majority believes that lawyers generally are not to be trusted to honor their ethical obligations. I, on the other hand, believe that the great majority of attorneys, as officers of the court, will and do live up to their ethical duties and "come clean" *if given an opportunity to do so.* See generally, Hazard, The Lawyer's Obligation to be Trustworthy when Dealing with Opposing Parties, 33 S.C.L. Rev. 181 (1981). As for those attorneys who chose not to "come clean," the district court distinguishes between the meritorious and the frivolous on a regular basis in other types of cases, and I see no reason why the courts cannot perform that task equally well in the context of attorney disqualification, without relying on an ancient out-dated irrebuttable presumption.

I wish to emphasize there are indeed situations where orders of disqualification are both legitimate, necessary and proper. The attorney-client relationship has been most properly described as sacrosanct and "[i]t is part of a court's duty to safeguard the sacrosanct privacy of the attorney-client relationship." *Freeman*, 689 F.2d at 721. However, the majority's irrebuttable presumption that all confidences are shared among every lawyer in a law firm, even a large multi-office firm, ignores the fact that in many firms, particularly large firms, there is little exchange of confidences between, for example, the antitrust, personal injury, tax, patent, securities or corporate sections of a firm because of the work load and the varied nature of the different department's practices. The majority's analysis fails to give Schwartz & Freeman, or even contemplate in the future giving other law firms, large or small, the opportunity to demonstrate to the court the absence of impropriety. . . .

The time has come to abandon this "irrebuttable" presumption, since the principles of *LaSalle National Bank, Freeman* and *Novo* are equally applicable in this situation. Fairness requires that a law firm, as well as any partner or associate, must be given the opportunity to rebut this presumption. A rebuttal may be accomplished by demonstrating that the presence of a "Chinese Wall" or some other method will *effectively* insulate against any flow of confidences and/or secrets from the tainted attorney to any other member of the firm. This rebuttal requires a case-by-case factual determination, but in any event, the fairness doctrine mandates that the opportunity to rebut the presumption must exist.

I wish to stress that the fact finding process of the trial court can indeed be based on objective and verifiable factors. In determining whether a devised plan can effectively prevent disclosures, the trial court should consider a wide variety of factors. For example, the court should consider the size of the law firm, its structural divisions, the likelihood of contact between a "screened" attorney and one handling an adverse representation, and the existence of a rule prohibiting the "tainted" attorney from sharing in the fees derived from the representation in question. The effectiveness of a plan also depends on what type of routine internal safeguards have been developed in the firm for handling confidential information, such as curtailing access to files by keeping files in a locked file cabinet, with the keys controlled by two partners and issued to others only on a "need to know" basis. *LaSalle National Bank,* at 258-259. The court should also look at the steps the firm has taken to make all members of the firm aware of the ban on exchange of information as well as any steps taken to enforce this ban. *LaSalle National Bank,* at 258-259. Finally, the court must keep in mind what should be the lawyer's and the law firm's most valuable assets, their reputations for honesty and integrity, along with competence. While some may argue that this final factor is more subjective than objective in nature, it merely requires an evaluation which district court judges are qualified to make, especially in light of the fact that they make credibility determinations in other cases daily. Only after considering the above factors can a district court make a determination as to whether a devised plan can *effectively* shield a tainted attorney. Reliance upon antiquated notions of disqualification such as irrebuttable presumptions simply will no longer suffice in today's specialized practice of law.

My concern in this area lies in the effect a disqualification motion has on both a law firm as well as a newly hired individual in a firm. . . . If prior representation of a particular client will irrebuttably disqualify an entire firm from handling certain cases, the result could easily be whole law firms of "Typhoid Marys." This would have a drastic impact on the careers of attorneys in entire firms, would impede clients' rights to be represented by attorneys of their choice and would discourage attorneys with expertise in a particular field of law from handling cases in their respective specialties. Just as in cases of individual attorneys changing employment, such a result must be avoided by allowing the presumption of shared confidences to be rebutted. Fairness demands that we now do no less for the law firm itself. . . .

Judge Coffey's dissent sets out the current agenda with respect to proposed reform of vicarious disqualification law. Do the policies justifying the modest inroads that have been made in the general rule mandating disqualification of the entire firm when one member possesses confidential information from an adverse party justify even further inroads? We may confidently expect that developments in the organization of the legal profession will keep these issues before the courts and force them to reassess the competing policies.

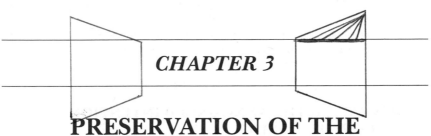

CHAPTER 3

PRESERVATION OF THE CONFIDENCES AND SECRETS OF A CLIENT

The problem of representation of conflicting interests has dimensions of its own but it is also related to the problem of preserving the "confidences" and "secrets" of a client. As we have seen, a reason often given for a broad interpretation of the prohibitions in the conflict of interest rules is the desirability of preserving the client's confidences to the fullest extent. In fact, the rules relating to confidentiality are at the heart of the adversary system. The breadth of the confidentiality principle is seen by some to be too much of an obstacle to the truth-seeking function of judge or jury and by others to conflict with the normal rules of morality. The exceptions that are recognized determine to a great degree what we mean when we say that we have an adversary system.

Canon 4 of the Model Code and Rules 1.6, 3.3, and 4.1 of the Model Rules should be read in their entirety at this point. Note that the Model Code creates two categories of confidentiality — the narrower "confidences," which are matters covered by the attorney-client privilege, and the broader "secrets," which consist of information gained in the professional relationship that "the client has requested be held inviolate or the disclosure of which would be embarrassing or would be likely to be detrimental to the client." With one possible exception, see p. 174, the Model Code does not draw any distinction between confidences and secrets in the obligations it places on lawyers. The Model Rules state the basic rule of confidentiality in one sweeping generalization embracing all "information relating to representation of a client," thus making it clear that the rule applies "to all information relating to the representation, whatever its source." Comment to Model Rule 1.6.

Problems of the reach of the confidentiality obligation will be examined by looking at particular categories of situations in which issues arise.

141

More theoretical material relating to the confidentiality obligation and the adversary system is grouped together in Chapter 4. Whether that material is considered after or with this chapter, it is highly relevant to the issues presented in this chapter.

A.   REVEALING THE ANNOUNCED INTENTION TO COMMIT A CRIME

PROBLEM 14

While Client is at an appointment in Lawyer's office, he excuses himself for a moment, telling Lawyer that he is about to put a second quarter in the meter at which he is parked. This is a misdemeanor. Lawyer tells him so, and, with a light touch, suggests that he not do it. Client laughs and leaves to feed the meter. Lawyer looks out the window and sees a police officer approaching. May Lawyer advise the officer of his client's intention to commit a crime? Should he do so?

PROBLEM 15

Client leaves Lawyer's office for an important appointment in a city 70 miles away with only an hour to spare. The speed limit on the interstate highway between the two cities is 55 mph but Client says that he will make the appointment on time by driving at 80 mph all the way, as he usually does. Client also seems to have been drinking rather heavily. Lawyer tries unsuccessfully to stop Client from undertaking the trip. May Lawyer warn the State Police? Should she do so?

PROBLEM 16

An anti-discrimination law guaranteeing women equal access to places of public accommodation has recently been passed in Lawyer's city. Client has for the past 25 years operated a "men only" bar in the business district. Fearing a loss of distinctiveness with a consequent loss of business, he tells Lawyer that he is going to take active steps to discourage patronage by women. He is going to encourage his regular customers to help him, but states that he will not condone violence of any sort. His activities violate the statute and clearly constitute criminal conduct. Client says that he is going to take his chances and disregard Lawyer's advice to obey the law. May Lawyer call the police or the district attorney and report Client's intentions to them? Should he do so?

PROBLEM 17

In discussing a federal tax return about to be filed, Lawyer advises a waiter that it is clear that he must report all tips as income. The client replies that it isn't fair to tax such receipts, that none of his friends report such items, that none has ever been caught, and that he will not report the receipts as income. If the client asks what the audit rate is and what his chances of being caught are, how should Lawyer respond? Information about the percentage of audit returns in various categories is in the public domain. In any event, may Lawyer warn the IRS that client is not reporting income? Should Lawyer do so?

PROBLEM 18

Client has been involved in bitter litigation with a former partner who has wound up not only taking control of the whole business but also marrying Client's wife. Client has said several times that if the law doesn't give justice, he will do his own justice. After the judge has rendered his decision against Client, Client and Lawyer have an angry session in discussing appeal. Client storms out of the office, stating that he has brought his gun and is going to go looking for the other party. Lawyer tries to stop him, but Client breaks away and rushes out of the building. May and should Lawyer warn the opposing party?

PROBLEM 19

With respect to the problems already considered, if the lawyer is about to exercise her discretion under DR 4-101(C)(3) or Model Rule 1.6 to reveal a confidence, should she tell the client in advance? At that point, if the client says, "If you are going to do that, I'll change my mind," what should the lawyer then do?

One of the great problems with Canon 4 of the Model Code is that despite the drafters' criticism of the former Canons as not being "an effective teaching instrument" and failing "to give guidance to young lawyers beyond the language of the Canons themselves" (see the preface to the Model Code), Canon 4 gives very little guidance to lawyers, young or old, about the very difficult problems relating to the lawyer's obligation to preserve the confidences and secrets of his or her client. In fact, in some ways Canon 4 creates problems. An example is contained in the language of DR 4-101(C). It states the exceptions to the general rule of confidentiality. "A lawyer *may* reveal . . . [c]onfidences or secrets when permitted under Disciplinary Rules or required by law or court order." DR 4-101(C)(2). (Emphasis added.) The word "may" is a confusing guide for lawyers. It is joined with "permitted," which seems to give an option, and "required," which seems mandatory. If "may" means "may," what then of the exception relating to the "intention of the client to commit a crime" in DR 4-101(C)(3)? Does "may" always mean "may" with respect to that exception? May it ever be interpreted as meaning "must"? See footnotes 15 and 16 to DR 4-101(C), citing ABA Opinions advising that a lawyer is obligated to break a confidence in particular situations, and footnote 1 to the Preamble to the Code, minimizing the value of the footnotes. Before Florida adopted the Model Rules, it had replaced the "may" with "shall" in DR 4-101(C)(3). Was that an improvement?

The purpose of the exception in DR 4-101(C)(3) may simply be to indicate a situation in which a lawyer will not be disciplined for revealing a confidence, and the word "may" might therefore be understood as intended only to accomplish that limited end. If that is the case, the drafters certainly performed their task inartistically. Moreover, they should not have footnoted the Disciplinary Rule with an opinion that sets out a situation in which the Committee on Professional Ethics believed that the lawyer "must" break the client's confidence. Finally, if the Disciplinary Rule is designed only to state when a lawyer is not subject to discipline for breaking a confidence, one would expect the Ethical Considerations to advert to the use of the word "may," pointing out the wide discretion given to lawyers and giving some guidelines on how that discretion should be exercised, or at least listing some factors for lawyers to take into consideration in deciding whether or not to reveal a confidence. The Ethical Considerations, however, do not address the matter at all.

Lawyers in a Model Code jurisdiction are thus left to deal with the issue as best they can. The drafters of the Model Rules sought to be more precise. Their earliest public draft included a provision *requiring* disclosure "to the extent it appears necessary to prevent the client from committing an act that would result in death or serious bodily harm to another person, and to the extent required by law or the rules of professional conduct." That draft also conferred substantial discretion on a lawyer to reveal confidential information "to the extent it appears necessary to prevent . . . a deliberately wrongful act by the client." (See then Model Rule 1.7 in Discussion Draft of Jan. 30, 1980.) This provision extended the area of discretion to reveal confidential information beyond the area of crime at least into the area of intentional tort.

These proposals, as well as other applications of the confidentiality rules, created a storm of controversy within the profession. They were widely attacked as destructive of the confidentiality principle, and hence of the adversary system. It was also argued that if the wide variety of situations in which lawyers were granted discretion to break confidences included violations of the myriad administrative regulations to which business is subject, state and federal agencies would then have license to make the discretion mandatory since the confidentiality obligation would already have been declared not to exist. In the face of the uproar, the drafters eliminated the mandatory disclosure requirement with respect to prevention of harm and replaced the wide-ranging discretionary provision with a more narrowly focused provision allowing revelation of information "to the extent the lawyer reasonably believes necessary: (1) to prevent the client from committing a criminal or fraudulent act that the lawyer reasonably believes is likely to result in death or substantial bodily harm, or in substantial injury to the financial interests or property of another. . . ." The drafters thus yielded to the arguments that the Model Code conferred too much discretion on lawyers to reveal a client's intention to commit less serious crimes and rejected the contention that some crimes have such serious consequences that the lawyer's obligation to forestall them should be mandatory. See ABA Commission on Evaluation of Professional Standards (Kutak Commission), Final Draft, Rule 1.6 and Comment thereto (June 30, 1982).

The ABA House of delegates at its February 1983 meeting in New Orleans rejected this solution. It tightened up the "bodily harm" provision to reduce the lawyer's discretion in that situation and removed entirely any discretion to reveal in the case of financial or property damage. The American College of Trial Lawyers, which drafted the prevailing language, urged that the Kutak Commission's solution would make it very difficult for many clients to get adequate legal counsel if lawyers had discretion, based on reasonable belief, to reveal their confidences. The Kutak Commission's final draft had represented its best effort to identify the situations of serious harm where lawyers ought to have discretion to reveal, whatever effect such discretion might have on a client's willingness to impart information to his or her lawyer. The states that have adopted the Model Rules have looked quite critically at Model Rule 1.6, and a substantial majority have altered it. Some have adopted the final Kutak Commission recommendation; even more have retained the Model Code provision permitting disclosure of the intention to commit any crime; and a few have adopted their own idiosyncratic accommodations of the various interests.

One idiosyncratic amendment is that of Florida whose Rule 1.6 now reads as follows:

> (a) A lawyer shall not reveal information relating to representation of a client except as stated in paragraphs (b), (c), and (d) unless the client consents after disclosure to the client.

(b) A lawyer shall reveal such information to the extent the lawyer believes necessary:

(1) To prevent a client from committing a crime; or

(2) To prevent a death or substantial bodily harm to another.

(c) A lawyer may reveal such information to the extent the lawyer believes necessary:

(1) To serve the client's interest unless it is information the client specifically requires not to be disclosed;

(2) To establish a claim or defense on behalf of the lawyer in a controversy between the lawyer and client;

(3) To establish a defense to a criminal charge or civil claim against the lawyer based upon conduct in which the client was involved;

(4) To respond to allegations in any proceeding concerning the lawyer's representation of the client; or

(5) To comply with the Rules of Professional Conduct.

(d) When required by a tribunal to reveal such information, a lawyer may first exhaust all appellate remedies.

As you peruse the materials of Chapters 3 and 4 you should consider whether you think that the Florida version is preferable to the Model Rules or Model Code version, and why?

Problems 14-19 examine some of the particulars of the confidentiality rule. Later problems invite discussion focusing more on the theory underlying it. In each situation ask yourself whether the lawyer has discretion to disclose confidential information under the Model Code or Model Rules; if the answer is yes, what relevant considerations should guide its exercise and how would you answer the question; and finally, are you satisfied with the rules' prescription or lack thereof in each case and as a totality?

In considering Problem 17, one should be aware of the major and much-cited ethics opinion in the tax field, Opinion 314 of the ABA's Committee on Professional Ethics, issued in 1965 under the pre-1969 Canons of Ethics. This is one of the opinions already referred to as having been cited in footnote 16 to DR 4-101(C)(3) of the Model Code. In the course of a general discussion of the lawyer's responsibilities in dealing with the IRS, the opinion states that "the absolute duty not to make false assertions of fact" does not "require the disclosure of [the client's] confidences, unless the facts in the attorney's possession indicate beyond reasonable doubt that a crime will be committed." Nothing in the Model Code or Model Rules justifies such a statement of a mandatory requirement, and one might therefore conclude that that opinion has been rendered obsolete, notwithstanding the fact that the words just quoted from that opinion are quoted in the Model Code's footnote reference to DR 4-101(C)(3). However, Canon 37 of the pre-1969 Code also contained only discretionary language, and Opinion 314 interpreted that language to require disclosure in some circumstances. In 1987, the ABA Committee on Ethics and Professional Responsibility, noting the passage of the Model Code and the Model Rules since the publication of Opinion 314, returned in Opinion 87-352 to the issues of Opinion 314. But it specifically reconsidered and revised "only that part of Opinion 314 that relates to the lawyer's duty in advising a client of positions that can be taken on a tax return." It did not mention any need to correct the disclosure of confidences language just quoted and therefore missed the opportunity to inform lawyers that the Model Code and Model Rules both indicated that that language was no longer applicable.

In considering Problem 18, one should be aware of the possibility that a lawyer's duty may arise from law other than the law of professional responsibility, specifically tort law in such a situation. See Tarasoff v. Regents of University of California, 17 Cal. 3d 425, 551 P.2d 334 (1976) (allegation that failure of psychotherapist, who learned of danger to victim from patient through patient's confidential communication, to warn victim states a cause of action for damages as a result of subsequent murder of victim by patient; police, who learned of danger and failed to warn victim, would not be liable for lack of special relation to victim). Accord, McIntosh v. Milano, 168 N.J. Super. 466, 403 A.2d 500 (L. Div. 1979). At the very end of the drafting process, the attempt to defend a "may" instead of a "must" provision in the Model Rules for a case like Problem 18 was eliminated from the Comment to Rule 1.6.

In considering Problems 14-19 and the following Problems 20 and 21, note that they are all intended to depict situations where the lawyer's advice or work product has not been involved in the perpetration of the crime or fraud. If it has, a different situation arises and mandatory disclosure may be involved. See DR 7-102(A)(7) and DR 7-102(B)(1) of the Model Code, and Rules 1.2(d) and 3.3(a)(2) of the Model Rules, and the discussion at pp. 207-213. Nor are we discussing the problem of a lawyer's advance or subsequent knowledge of a client's perjury. That issue is dealt with separately. See pp. 171-207. We are simply dealing with the variety of situations in which the lawyer learns, with more or less certainty, that the client is intending to commit a crime. In discussions about the appropriate rule and about the appropriate exercise of discretion where a lawyer is given discretion, much of the focus is on a calculation of the costs and benefits of confidentiality as against disclosure. Advocates of more disclosure argue that lawyers are in a position to prevent great harm in specific situations to specific people. Advocates of more confidentiality argue that lawyers prevent harm by dissuading clients from pursuing proposed harmful conduct that they learn of only because the client, assured by the confidentiality principle, confides in them. They contend that they prevent more harm in that fashion than they would prevent were disclosure required because no one would reveal damaging information if the confidentiality principle were diluted. It is not easy to perceive how reliable information can be obtained to test this hypothesis and so the argument rages on the basis of the different perceptions of the disputants.

PROBLEM 20*

Trireme Aluminum Co., a closely held corporation manufacturing alloys primarily used by the aircraft industry, has developed a new, higher strength aluminum alloy especially for use in light planes. Largely because of significant demand for this one product, Trireme has turned around a three-year earnings deficit and is well into a second profitable year.

One evening over dinner, the company's chief engineer confided to Trireme's outside counsel, who was an old college friend, that he feared the worst. The engineer said that although the new alloy had met all applicable safety standards and design requirements when officially tested, the company lab's recent tests had convinced him that the alloy would crack at extremely cold temperatures; that the potential danger to the public had increased as Trireme marketed the alloy for use in larger planes flying at higher altitudes; and that he had kept the company president informed of this research but had been told not to discuss it with anyone else. He added that his conscience had bothered him for not telling anyone, but that for a number of reasons he was unwilling to "surface" with this information. Primarily, it appeared, he was afraid of losing his job. He told counsel to use this information as needed, but not to mention his name. He reasoned that his identity would be safe because the entire ten-member engineering staff was aware of the problem and most of them agreed with him; no one would immediately think that he was the source.

Counsel preserved his informant's anonymity, but mentioned what he had heard to the company president the next day. The president insisted that despite a majority view of the engineering staff that there was, in fact, a danger, a substantial minority of the more experienced members of that staff believed that the tests showed no danger or at worst were inconclusive. More important, he said, was the fact that the alloy unquestionably met established minimum design requirements and safety standards. He added, finally, that adjustments in the alloy formula were in the process of being tested, so that in due course any problem — which he believed not to exist anyway — would undoubtedly be resolved.

---

*This hypothetical was created by Judge John Ferren of the District of Columbia Court of Appeals for use at a conference on ethical responsibilities of corporate lawyers. A paper by Judge Ferren discussing this hypothetical, The Corporate Lawyer's Obligation to the Public Interest, appears in 33 Bus. Law. 1253 (1978). It is followed by further remarks by Judge Ferren and a panel discussion of the underlying issues.

Counsel raised the possibilities of informing Trireme's customers and of suggesting the recall of planes. He also suggested that Trireme consider repurchase of all inventory in the field. The president sharply rebuked him with references not only to the conflicting opinions about the tests themselves but also to the recent turnaround in company fortunes because of the alloy, the fact that 25 percent of company sales were now dependent on the alloy, and that employment in the local community, which had been depressed for years, would suffer severely if there were any break in production.

Counsel informed the board of directors about these conversations at the next regular meeting, but the board unanimously agreed with the president and informed counsel that the matter should be considered closed.

A month later a medium-range, higher altitude plane made of the alloy, the Roton S-12, crashed during a charter flight, killing everyone aboard. The investigation did not conclusively determine the cause; it stated that pilot error appeared to be the principal factor. A portion of the report, however, referred to unusual fractures in the aileron and elevator spars. One investigator questioned the ductility of the basic metal; another surmised that the particular assembly was defective — essentially human error rather than a deficiency in design.

No investigator had contacted Trireme. Without further evidence, however, the National Transportation Safety Board made a most unusual recommendation with respect to such ambiguous facts: that the FAA summarily issue an "Airworthiness Directive" (AD) suspending use of the new alloy until further investigation could take place, and grounding all Roton S-12s and other aircraft made of the alloy. The FAA did so. Trireme's president asked company counsel to join Roton Corp.'s counsel in a challenge to the suspension by going first to the FAA and, if necessary, to court.

Counsel agreed. Trireme and Roton prevailed in court, which ordered revocation of the AD solely on the basis of the government's scanty, ambiguous documentation. Trireme's counsel had successfully moved to quash government subpoenas of company records and employees on the ground of irrelevance, arguing that the FAA's summary issuance of the AD must be judged solely by reference to its prima facie case. The court held that, given the investigative report's emphasis on human error, the AD had been issued arbitrarily on purely speculative grounds. The government filed a notice of appeal and sought a stay of the trial court's action. Without waiting for completion of the judicial process, a Congressional subcommittee, upset by this rebuff to the FAA's authority when the public safety was involved, immediately announced an investigation, issuing subpoenas to company officials and to the engineering staff. The Trireme board of directors has asked to meet with outside counsel.

At this point in the materials consider only the lawyer's responsibility to make disclosure just before, and just after, the crash of the Roton S-12. Does he have any obligation or discretion to reveal the danger he believes to exist? Does the answer turn on whether a crime or fraudulent act has been committed? Why should disclosure of danger to life be forbidden when the danger arises from reckless or negligent, instead of from fraudulent or criminal, conduct? Note that although the problem deals with the dramatic danger posed by a "defective" airplane, similar issues would be posed by "defective" drugs or food or unnoticeable but "dangerous" pollution or the like. Besides the lawyer's obligation vis à vis the public, the problem also raises the question of the lawyer's responsibility to, and within, the corporation. These are the subject of Chapter 5.

PROBLEM 21

Housing Project, operated by the City Housing Authority, had become the object of a tenants' rent strike to protest intolerable living conditions in the Project. A Tenants' Association was formed, and rents withheld from the Housing Authority were turned over to representatives of the Tenants' Association. The Housing Authority filed suit for the rent money and sought a court order that the Association turn the rent money over to a custodial receiver. The Association opposed the application by giving assurances in affidavit form that the funds were intact and secure in a safe deposit box.

After oral argument by counsel for the Housing Authority and the Tenants' Association, the court denied the motion of the Housing Authority. It ordered the Association to account for all monies received, and directed that the funds not be removed from the safe deposit box except by order of the court, pending further determination as to the rights of the Housing Authority and the tenants to the funds. Subsequently, the trial judge determined that the tenants were not entitled to rent-free occupancy in the Project because of the living conditions, and that at the most they would be entitled to an abatement of rent. All tenants who had paid rent money into the fund were ordered to show cause on November 17 why the fund should not be turned over to the Housing Authority, subject to the tenants establishing the basis for any claimed refund.

A meeting of the Executive Committee of the Tenants' Association was held on November 13. Possible refund of the rent money was discussed. Lawyers for the Association counseled strongly against the disbursement of the funds, stating that it would be a violation of the court order and would subject those responsible to charges of contempt. The Executive Committee then decided to hold a meeting of all the contributing tenants the next day to decide what to do with the money. What should Lawyers do? Suppose that there had been discussion at the November 13 meeting of the possibility of having the rent money available at the November 14 meeting. Should that make any difference with respect to Lawyers' course of action?

The facts in this problem are based on In re Callan, 66 N.J. 401, 331 A.2d 612 (1975), which arose on contempt charges and did not pass on the issue whether there was any violation of the Disciplinary Rules of the Code of Professional Responsibility. The local grievance committee later dismissed charges against the three lawyers who were involved. The majority of the Supreme Court of New Jersey stated that if the lawyers in *Callan* knew that the Tenants' Association was going to distribute the escrowed funds "they would have been required to inform the court that its order as to the security of the funds was about to be violated. The attorney-client relationship would not require or justify silence in a situation where the integrity of the rule of law was at stake." 66 N.J. at 407. The court does not say where that rule of law comes from. It did not cite DR 4-101(C)(3) with its "may" language. Perhaps it was announcing a supplementary common law rule, one that applied only to court orders and not to statutory law because otherwise DR 4-101(C)(3) would have no function. Does the relationship of the lawyer to the court justify a different rule? Does the more specific focus of a court order justify a different rule?

PROBLEM 22

A new client has just come into Lawyer's office. At the outset of their conversations what, if anything, should Lawyer say about the lawyer-client relation as it pertains to the confidentiality principle? If Lawyer should say something, formulate the "set speech" or "speeches" that Lawyer should include in the opening interview. How do you define the principle? What do you say about the exceptions? Do you say anything about your view of the way you should exercise your discretion? Is it permissible to commit yourself in advance? Would you?

B. PERJURY AND MANDATORY DISCLOSURE OF CLIENT CONFIDENCES

PROBLEM 23

Client is a defendant in a murder case. From your very first interview when he blurted out his guilt, he has taken the position that, if necessary, he intends to lie about his whereabouts at the crucial time because he knows that identification of him by one witness for the state will be crucial. As the trial date approaches, it is clear that his chances of acquittal are small if he doesn't take the stand. He wants to take the stand and make the most persuasive statement he can that he was not, and has never been, at the place where the victim was killed. What alternatives are available to you? Which will you select?

One fact situation that has been especially troublesome for lawyers is that of client perjury. What is the lawyer to do when the client, a party, says that he or she is going to lie on the stand? Does it make a difference whether the case is civil or criminal? Although the situation might logically be thought to be simply another illustration of the problem of lawyers' obligations when they know of a client's intention to commit a crime, the particular problem of perjury, lying in court, has always been thought to be special. Resolution of this question and the stance it imposes on lawyers has been at the center of much of the debate about the confidentiality principle and the nature of, and justification for, the adversary system.

The debate is not new. A particularly bitter dispute over the confidentiality privilege took place in mid-nineteenth century England, see Mellinkoff, The Conscience of a Lawyer (1973), and there have been sporadic disputes in this country too. One was provoked by a speech and article prepared by Charles Curtis, an eminent Boston attorney, in 1951. The Ethics of Advocacy, 4 Stan. L. Rev. 3. The theme of his piece was that the devotion that a lawyer owes to the client is so great that it often requires lawyers to do many things for clients that they would not do for themselves.

> And why not? The relation between a lawyer and his client is one of the intimate relations. You would lie for your wife. You would lie for your child. There are others with whom you are intimate enough, close enough, to lie for them when you would not lie for yourself. At what point do you stop lying for them? I don't know and you are not sure. [Id. at 8.]

Curtis does draw the line at lying to the court since a "lawyer's duty to his client cannot rise higher than its source, which is the court." Id. at 7. He goes on to indicate, however, that occasionally a lawyer may have a duty "not to speak" to the court, id. at 9, giving as an illustration the story from Professor Williston's biography discussed by Dean Freedman at p. 155, infra.

Mr. Curtis's article provoked angry replies, the principal one from Mr. Henry Drinker, author of the leading work on professional ethics, Legal Ethics (1953), and chairman of the ABA Committee on Professional Ethics from 1944-1953 and 1955-1958. "Mr. Curtis to the contrary notwithstanding, no man can be either too honest, too truthful, or too upright to be a thoroughly good lawyer, and an eminently successful one. . . . A lawyer need never lie for his client. . . . Of course no one could say that an occasion might not possibly arise when there was no alternative except the truth or a lie and when the consequences of the truth were such that the lawyer might be tempted to lie. This, however, would not make it right for him to do so." Drinker, Some Remarks on Mr. Curtis' "The Ethics of Advocacy," 4 Stan. L. Rev. 349, 350 (1952). Mr. Drinker did go on to state, however, that there are occasions when a lawyer's duty to keep his client's confidences may require him to refuse to disclose information.

In 1953, shortly after the appearance of these articles, the ABA Committee on Professional Ethics was forced to deal with a situation rather similar to that envisaged by Mr. Curtis. In the best known and most influential opinion it ever wrote, Opinion 287, it responded to two inquiries relating to client fraud under the pre-1969 Canons of Ethics. The inquiry relevant to the present discussion involved a convicted client obtaining only a sentence of probation because of misinformation received by the judge at the sentencing hearing. The most difficult part of the inquiry related to the lawyer's duty when he knew from confidential information that the client lied to the judge in response to an inquiry about his prior record. The majority of a divided Committee, in an opinion by Mr. Drinker, concluded that the lawyer should "endeavor to persuade the client to tell the court the truth and if he refuses to do so should sever his relations with the client, but should not violate the client's confidence." The Committee advised that in that case the principles embodied in the confidentiality Canons 6 and 37 prevailed over the principles embodied in Canon 41, requiring disclosure of fraud on an injured party, and Canon 29, requiring lawyers to disclose perjury to the prosecuting authorities. Finding the conflict irreconcilable, the Committee viewed the requirement of confidentiality as the stronger.

Some years later Monroe Freedman delivered a talk and wrote an article that sought to give theoretical substance to the conclusions that had been reached by Mr. Curtis and the ABA Committee. He wrote in 1966, against the background of the pre-Model Code Canons of Ethics.

MONROE FREEDMAN, PROFESSIONAL RESPONSIBILITY OF THE CRIMINAL DEFENSE LAWYER: THE THREE HARDEST QUESTIONS*

64 Mich. L. Rev. 1469 (1966)

In almost any area of legal counseling and advocacy, the lawyer may be faced with the dilemma of either betraying the confidential commu-

*The substance of this paper was recently presented to a Criminal Trial Institute attended by forty-five members of the District of Columbia Bar. As a consequence,

nications of his client or participating to some extent in the purposeful deception of the court. This problem is nowhere more acute than in the practice of criminal law, particularly in the representation of the indigent accused. The purpose of this article is to analyze and attempt to resolve three of the most difficult issues in this general area:

1. Is it proper to cross-examine for the purpose of discrediting the reliability or credibility of an adverse witness whom you know to be telling the truth? [The portion of the article addressing this question is omitted.]

2. Is it proper to put a witness on the stand when you know he will commit perjury?

3. Is it proper to give your client legal advice when you have reason to believe that the knowledge you give him will tempt him to commit perjury? [The portion of the article addressing this question is printed at pp. 203-206.] . . .

I.   THE ADVERSARY SYSTEM AND THE NECESSITY
FOR CONFIDENTIALITY

At the outset, we should dispose of some common question-begging responses. The attorney is indeed an officer of the court, and he does participate in a search for truth. These two propositions, however, merely serve to state the problem in different words: As an officer of the court, participating in a search for truth, what is the attorney's special responsibility, and how does that responsibility affect his resolution of the questions posed above?

The attorney functions in an adversary system based upon the presupposition that the most effective means of determining truth is to present to a judge and jury a clash between proponents of conflicting views. It is essential to the effective functioning of this system that each adversary have, in the words of Canon 15, "entire devotion to the interest of the client, warm zeal in the maintenance and defense of his rights and the exertion of his utmost learning and ability." It is also essential to maintain the fullest uninhibited communication between the client and his attorney, so that the attorney can most effectively counsel his client and advocate the latter's cause. This policy is safeguarded by the requirement that the lawyer must, in the words of Canon 37, "preserve his client's confidences." Canon 15 does, of course, qualify these obligations

---

several judges (none of whom had either heard the lecture or read it) complained to the Committee on Admissions and Grievances of the District Court for the District of Columbia, urging the author's disbarment or suspension. Only after four months of proceedings, including a hearing, two meetings, and a de novo review by eleven federal district court judges, did the Committee announce its decision to "proceed no further in the matter."

by stating that "the office of attorney does not permit, much less does it demand of him for any client, violations of law or any manner of fraud or chicane." In addition, Canon 22 requires candor toward the court.

The problem presented by these salutary generalities of the Canons in the context of particular litigation is illustrated by the personal experience of Samuel Williston, which was related in his autobiography.[3] Because of his examination of a client's correspondence file, Williston learned of a fact extremely damaging to his client's case. When the judge announced his decision, it was apparent that a critical factor in the favorable judgment for Williston's client was the judge's ignorance of this fact. Williston remained silent and did not thereafter inform the judge of what he knew. He was convinced, and Charles Curtis[4] agrees with him, that it was his duty to remain silent.

In an opinion by the American Bar Association Committee on Professional Ethics and Grievances, an eminent panel headed by Henry Drinker held that a lawyer should remain silent when his client lies to the judge by saying that he has no prior record, despite the attorney's knowledge to the contrary.[5] . . . If these two cases do not constitute "fraud or chicane" or lack of candor within the meaning of the Canons (and I agree with the authorities cited that they do not), it is clear that the meaning of the Canons is ambiguous.

The adversary system has further ramifications in a criminal case. The defendant is presumed to be innocent. The burden is on the prosecution to prove beyond a reasonable doubt that the defendant is guilty. The plea of not guilty does not necessarily mean "not guilty in fact," for the defendant may mean "not legally guilty." Even the accused who knows that he committed the crime is entitled to put the government to its proof. Indeed, the accused who knows that he is guilty has an absolute constitutional right to remain silent. The moralist might quite reasonably understand this to mean that, under these circumstances, the defendant and his lawyer are privileged to "lie" to the court in pleading not guilty. In my judgment, the moralist is right. However, our adversary system and related notions of the proper administration of criminal justice sanction the lie.

Some derive solace from the sophistry of calling the lie a "legal fiction," but this is hardly an adequate answer to the moralist. Moreover, this answer has no particular appeal for the practicing attorney, who knows that the plea of not guilty commits him to the most effective ad-

---

3. Williston, Life and Law 271 (1940).

4. Curtis, It's Your Law 17-21 (1954). See also Curtis, The Ethics of Advocacy, 4 Stan. L. Rev. 3, 9-10 (1951); Drinker, Some Remarks on Mr. Curtis' "The Ethics of Advocacy," 4 Stan. L. Rev. 349, 350-351 (1952).

5. Opinion 287, Committee on Professional Ethics and Grievances of the American Bar Association (1953).

vocacy of which he is capable. Criminal defense lawyers do not win their cases by arguing reasonable doubt. Effective trial advocacy requires that the attorney's every word, action, and attitude be consistent with the conclusion that his client is innocent. As every trial lawyer knows, the jury is certain that the defense attorney knows whether his client is guilty. The jury is therefore alert to, and will be enormously affected by, any indication by the attorney that he believes the defendant to be guilty. Thus, the plea of not guilty commits the advocate to a trial, including a closing argument, in which he must argue that "not guilty" means "not guilty in fact."

There is, of course, a simple way to evade the dilemma raised by the not guilty plea. Some attorneys rationalize the problem by insisting that a lawyer never knows for sure whether his client is guilty. The client who insists upon his guilt may in fact be protecting his wife, or may know that he pulled the trigger and that the victim was killed, but not that his gun was loaded with blanks and that the fatal shot was fired from across the street. For anyone who finds this reasoning satisfactory, there is, of course, no need to think further about the issue.

It is also argued that a defense attorney can remain selectively ignorant. He can insist in his first interview with his client that, if his client is guilty, he simply does not want to know. It is inconceivable, however, that an attorney could give adequate counsel under such circumstances. How is the client to know, for example, precisely which relevant circumstances his lawyer does not want to be told? The lawyer might ask whether his client has a prior record. The client, assuming that this is the kind of knowledge that might present ethical problems for his lawyer, might respond that he has no record. The lawyer would then put the defendant on the stand and, on cross-examination, be appalled to learn that his client has two prior convictions for offenses identical to that for which he is being tried.

Of course, an attorney can guard against this specific problem by telling his client that he must know about the client's past record. However, a lawyer can never anticipate all of the innumerable and potentially critical factors that his client, once cautioned, may decide not to reveal. In one instance, for example, the defendant assumed that his lawyer would prefer to be ignorant of the fact that the client had been having sexual relations with the chief defense witness. The client was innocent of the robbery with which he was charged, but was found guilty by the jury — probably because he was guilty of fornication, a far less serious offense for which he had not been charged.

The problem is compounded by the practice of plea bargaining. It is considered improper for a defendant to plead guilty to a lesser offense unless he is in fact guilty. Nevertheless, it is common knowledge that plea bargaining frequently results in improper guilty pleas by innocent people. For example, a defendant falsely accused of robbery may plead guilty to simple assault, rather than risk a robbery conviction and a substantial prison term. If an attorney is to be scrupulous in bargaining pleas, however, he must know in advance that his client is guilty, since the guilty plea is improper if the defendant is innocent. Of course, if the attempt to bargain for a lesser offense should fail, the lawyer would know the truth and thereafter be unable to rationalize that he was uncertain of his client's guilt.

If one recognizes that professional responsibility requires that an advocate have full knowledge of every pertinent fact, it follows that he must seek the truth from his client, not shun it. This means that he will have to dig and pry and cajole, and, even then, he will not be successful unless he can convince the client that full and confidential disclosure to his lawyer will never result in prejudice to the client by any word or action of the lawyer. This is, perhaps, particularly true in the case of the indigent defendant, who meets his lawyer for the first time in the cell block or the rotunda. He did not choose the lawyer, nor does he know him. The lawyer has been sent by the judge and is part of the system that is attempting to punish the defendant. It is no easy task to persuade this client that he can talk freely without fear of prejudice. However, the inclination to mislead one's lawyer is not restricted to the indigent or even to the criminal defendant. Randolph Paul has observed a similar phenomenon among a wealthier class in a far more congenial atmosphere:

> The tax adviser will sometimes have to dynamite the facts of his case out of the unwilling witnesses on his own side — witnesses who are nervous, witnesses who are confused about their own interest, witnesses who try to be too smart for their own good, and witnesses who subconsciously do not want to understand what has happened despite the fact that they must if they are to testify coherently.[9]

Paul goes on to explain that the truth can be obtained only by persuading the client that it would be a violation of a sacred obligation for the lawyer ever to reveal a client's confidence. Beyond any question, once a lawyer has persuaded his client of the obligation of confidentiality, he must respect that obligation scrupulously.

II.   The Specific Questions . . .

The second question is generally considered to be the hardest of all: Is it proper to put a witness on the stand when you know he will commit perjury? Assume, for example, that the witness in question is the accused himself, and that he has admitted to you, in response to your assurances

---

9. Paul, The Responsibilities of the Tax Adviser, 63 Harv. L. Rev. 377, 383 (1950).

of confidentiality, that he is guilty. However, he insists upon taking the stand to protest his innocence. There is a clear consensus among prosecutors and defense attorneys that the likelihood of conviction is increased enormously when the defendant does not take the stand. Consequently, the attorney who prevents his client from testifying only because the client has confided his guilt to him is violating that confidence by acting upon the information in a way that will seriously prejudice his client's interests.

Perhaps the most common method for avoiding the ethical problem just posed is for the lawyer to withdraw from the case, at least if there is sufficient time before trial for the client to retain another attorney. The client will then go to the nearest law office, realizing that the obligation of confidentiality is not what it has been represented to be, and withhold incriminating information or the fact of his guilt from his new attorney. On ethical grounds, the practice of withdrawing from a case under such circumstances is indefensible, since the identical perjured testimony will ultimately be presented. More important, perhaps, is the practical consideration that the new attorney will be ignorant of the perjury and therefore will be in no position to attempt to discourage the client from presenting it. Only the original attorney, who knows the truth, has that opportunity, but he loses it in the very act of evading the ethical problem.

The problem is all the more difficult when the client is indigent. He cannot retain other counsel, and in many jurisdictions, including the District of Columbia, it is impossible for appointed counsel to withdraw from a case except for extraordinary reasons. Thus, appointed counsel, unless he lies to the judge, can successfully withdraw only by revealing to the judge that the attorney has received knowledge of his client's guilt. Such a revelation in itself would seem to be a sufficiently serious violation of the obligation of confidentiality to merit severe condemnation. In fact, however, the situation is far worse, since it is entirely possible that the same judge who permits the attorney to withdraw will subsequently hear the case and sentence the defendant. When he does so, of course, he will have had personal knowledge of the defendant's guilt before the trial began. Moreover, this will be knowledge of which the newly appointed counsel for the defendant will probably be ignorant.

The difficulty is further aggravated when the client informs the lawyer for the first time during trial that he intends to take the stand and commit perjury. . . .

If a lawyer has discovered his client's intent to perjure himself, one possible solution to this problem is for the lawyer to approach the bench, explain his ethical difficulty to the judge, and ask to be relieved, thereby causing a mistrial. This request is certain to be denied, if only because it would empower the defendant to cause a series of mistrials in the same fashion. At this point, some feel that the lawyer has avoided the ethical problem and can put the defendant on the stand. However, one objection to this solution, apart from the violation of confidentiality, is that the lawyer's ethical problem has not been solved, but has only been transferred to the judge. Moreover, the client in such a case might well have grounds for appeal on the basis of deprivation of due process and denial of the right to counsel, since he will have been tried before, and sentenced by, a judge who has been informed of the client's guilt by his own attorney.

A solution even less satisfactory than informing the judge of the defendant's guilt would be to let the client take the stand without the attorney's participation and to omit reference to the client's testimony in closing argument. The latter solution, of course, would be as damaging as to fail entirely to argue the case to the jury, and failing to argue the case is "as improper as though the attorney had told the jury that his client had uttered a falsehood in making the statement."[17]

Therefore, the obligation of confidentiality, in the context of our adversary system, apparently allows the attorney no alternative to putting a perjurious witness on the stand without explicit or implicit disclosure of the attorney's knowledge to either the judge or the jury. Canon 37 does not proscribe this conclusion; the Canon recognizes only two exceptions to the obligation of confidentiality. The first relates to the lawyer who is accused by his client and may disclose the truth to defend himself. The other exception relates to the "announced intention of a client to commit a crime." On the basis of the ethical and practical considerations discussed above, the Canon's exception to the obligation of confidentiality cannot logically be understood to include the crime of perjury committed during the specific case in which the lawyer is serving. Moreover, even when the intention is to commit a crime in the future, Canon 37 does not require disclosure, but only permits it. Furthermore, Canon 15, which does proscribe "violation of law" by the attorney for his client, does not apply to the lawyer who unwillingly puts a perjurious client on the stand after having made every effort to dissuade him from committing perjury. Such an act by the attorney cannot properly be found to be subornation — corrupt inducement — of perjury. Canon 29 requires counsel to inform the prosecuting authorities of perjury committed in a case in which he has been involved, but this can only refer to perjury by opposing witnesses. For an attorney to disclose his client's perjury "would involve a direct violation of Canon 37."[18] Despite Canon 29, therefore, the attorney should not reveal his client's perjury "to the court or to the authorities."[19]

Of course, before the client testifies perjuriously, the lawyer has a

17. [Johns v. Smyth, 176 F. Supp. 949, 953 (E.D. Va. 1959).]
18. Opinion 287, Committee on Professional Ethics and Grievances of the American Bar Association (1953).
19. Ibid.

duty to attempt to dissuade him on grounds of both law and morality. In addition, the client should be impressed with the fact that his untruthful alibi is tactically dangerous. There is always a strong possibility that the prosecutor will expose the perjury on cross-examination. However, for the reasons already given, the final decision must necessarily be the client's. The lawyer's best course thereafter would be to avoid any further professional relationship with a client whom he knew to have perjured himself. . . .

Comment on Dean Freedman's article is postponed to pp. 171-177 following Judge Frankel's article. It should be noted, however, that the Freedman article, like its predecessors, the Curtis articles, provoked a good deal of controversy besides that referred to in footnote *, p. 153. Specific disagreement with his answers is contained in Bress, Professional Ethics in Criminal Trials: A View of Defense Counsel's Responsibility, 64 Mich. L. Rev. 1493 (1966). Disagreement with his underlying premises and a focus on counsel's obligation to the search for truth is contained in Noonan, The Purposes of Advocacy and the Limits of Confidentiality, 64 Mich. L. Rev. 1485 (1966) and Professional Ethics and Personal Responsibility, 29 Stan. L. Rev. 363 (1977).

The role of truth-seeking in the adversary system was elaborated by Judge Frankel when he turned to the subject nine years later in the appropriate setting of the Benjamin N. Cardozo Lecture. A few years after delivering this talk Judge Frankel resigned from the bench, returned to the practice of law, and was one of the members of the Kutak Commission, which drafted the Model Rules.

MARVIN FRANKEL, THE SEARCH FOR TRUTH: AN UMPIREAL VIEW*
123 U. Pa. L. Rev. 1031 (1975)

What I have written for the thirty-first Benjamin N. Cardozo Lecture makes no pretense to be polished or finished wisdom. In the words of an imposingly great predecessor, Judge Charles E. Clark, beginning the fifth of these lectures in 1945, I propose "to suggest problems and raise doubts, rather than to resolve confusion; to disturb thought, rather than to dispense legal or moral truth."[1] Probably more rash than Judge Clark, I do not experience "trepidation"[2] for offering more questions rather

---

* This article also appears, in slightly different form, in 30 The Record of the Association of the Bar of the City of New York 14 (1975).

1. Clark, State Law in the Federal Courts: The Brooding Omnipresence of Erie v. Tompkins, 55 Yale L.J. 267, 268-269 (1946).

2. Id. 268.

than answers; honest exploration in any province of the law is surely no dishonor to the questing spirit of Judge Cardozo.

My questions, briefly stated, have to do with some imperfections in our adversary system. My purposes are to recall some perennial problems, to touch upon one or two familiar ideas for improvement, and to sketch some tentative lines along which efforts to reform our law might proceed. . . .

THE JUDICIAL PERSPECTIVE

My theme, to be elaborated at some length, is that our adversary system rates truth too low among the values that institutions of justice are meant to serve. Having worked for nine years at judging, and having evolved in that job the doubts and questions to be shared with you, I find it convenient to move into the subject with some initial reminders about our judges: who they are, how they come to be, and how their arena looks to them. . . . Trials occur because there are questions of fact. In principle, the paramount objective is the truth. Nevertheless, for the advocate turned judge this objective marks a sharp break with settled habits of partisanship. The novelty is quickly accepted because it has been seen for so long from the other side. But the novelty is palpable, and the change of role may be unsettling. Many judges, withdrawn from the fray, watch it with benign and detached affection, chuckling nostalgically now and then as the truth suffers injury or death in the process.[9] The shop talk in judges' lunchrooms includes tales, often told with pleasure, of wily advocates who bested the facts and prevailed. For many other judges, however, probably a majority at one time or another, the habit of adversariness tends to be rechanneled, at least in some measure, into a combative yearning for truth. With perhaps a touch of the convert's zeal, they may suffer righteously when the truth is being blocked or mutilated, turn against former comrades in the arena, feel (and sometimes yield to) the urge to spring into the contest with brilliant questions that light the way.

However the trial judge reacts, in general or from time to time, the bench affords a changed and broadened view of the adversary process. "Many things look different from the bench. Being a judge is a different profession from being a lawyer."[10] In the strictest sense I can speak only for myself, but I believe many other trial judges would affirm that the

___

9. As in the sentence just ended, this essay will be laced with general statements about matters of fact that are neither quantified nor tightly documented. These rest variously upon introspection, observation, reading, and conversations with fellow judges. They are believed to be accurate, but they are undoubtedly debatable in many instances.

10. H. Lummus, The Trial Judge 39 (1937). See also Medina, Some Reflections on the Judicial Function: A Personal Viewpoint, 38 A.B.A. J. 107 (1952).

different perspective helps to arouse doubts about a process that there had been neither time nor impetus to question in the years at the bar. It becomes evident that the search for truth fails too much of the time. The rules and devices accounting for the failures come to seem less agreeable and less clearly worthy than they once did. The skills of the advocate seem less noble, and the place of the judge, which once looked so high, is lowered in consequence. There is, despite the years of professional weathering that went before the assumption of the judicial office, a measure of disillusionment. . . .

THE ADVERSARIAL POSTURE

The preceding comments on the transition from bar to bench have touched explicitly upon the role of the advocate. That role is not, however, a matter of sharp and universally agreed definition. The conception from which this paper proceeds must now be outlined.

Presiding Justice David W. Peck [has] said:

> The object of a lawsuit is to get at the truth and arrive at the right result. That is the sole objective of the judge, and counsel should never lose sight of that objective in thinking that the end purpose is to win for his side. Counsel exclusively bent on winning may find that he and the umpire are not in the same game.[11]

Earlier, stating his theme that court and counsel "complement" each other, Justice Peck said:

> Unfortunately, true understanding of the judicial process is not shared by all lawyers or judges. Instead of regarding themselves as occupying a reciprocal relationship in a common purpose, they are apt to think of themselves as representing opposite poles and exercising divergent functions. The lawyer is active, the judge passive. The lawyer partisan, the judge neutral. The lawyer imaginative, the judge reflective.[12]

Perhaps unfortunately, and certainly with deference, I find myself leaning toward the camp the Justice criticized. The plainest thing about the advocate is that he is indeed partisan, and thus exercises a function sharply divergent from that of the judge. Whether or not the judge generally achieves or maintains neutrality, it is his assigned task to be nonpartisan and to promote through the trial an objective search for the truth. The advocate in the trial courtroom is not engaged much more than half the time — and then only coincidentally — in the search for

---

11. D. Peck, The Complement of Court and Counsel 9 (1954) (13th Annual Benjamin N. Cardozo Lecture).
    12. Id. 7.

truth. The advocate's prime loyalty is to his client, not to truth as such. All of us remember some stirring and defiant declarations by advocates of their heroic, selfless devotion to The Client — leaving the nation, all other men, and truth to fend for themselves. Recall Lord Brougham's familiar words:

> [A]n advocate, in the discharge of his duty, knows but one person in all the world, and that person is his client. To save that client by all means and expedients, and at all hazards and costs to other persons, and, among them, to himself, is his first and only duty; and in performing this duty he must not regard the alarm, the torments, the destruction which he may bring upon others. Separating the duty of a patriot from that of an advocate, he must go on reckless of consequences, though it should be his unhappy fate to involve his country in confusion.[13]

Neither the sentiment nor even the words sound archaic after a century and a half. They were invoked not longer than a few months ago by a thoughtful and humane scholar answering criticisms that efforts of counsel for President Nixon might "involve his country in confusion."[14] There are, I think, no comparable lyrics by lawyers to The Truth.

This is a topic on which our profession has practiced some self-deception. We proclaim to each other and to the world that the clash of adversaries is a powerful means for hammering out the truth. Sometimes, less guardedly, we say it is "best calculated to getting out all the facts. . . ."[15] That the adversary technique is useful within limits none will doubt. That it is "best" we should all doubt if we were able to be objective about the question. Despite our untested statements of self-congratulation, we know that others searching after facts — in history, geography, medicine, whatever — do not emulate our adversary system. We know that most countries of the world seek justice by different routes. What is much more to the point, we know that many of the rules and devices of adversary litigation as we conduct it are not geared for, but are often aptly suited to defeat, the development of the truth.

We are unlikely ever to know how effectively the adversary technique would work toward truth if that were the objective of the contestants. Employed by interested parties, the process often achieves truth only as a convenience, a byproduct, or an accidental approximation. The business of the advocate, simply stated, is to win if possible without violating the law. (The phrase "if possible" is meant to modify what precedes it,

---

13. 2 Trial of Queen Caroline 8 (J. Nightingale ed. 1821).

14. Freedman, The President's Advocate and the Public Interest, N.Y.L.J., Mar. 27, 1974, at 1, col. 1. Dean Freedman went on to explain that the system contemplates an equally single-minded "advocate on the other side, and an impartial judge over both." Id. 7, col. 2.

15. D. Peck, supra note [11], at 9.

but the danger of slippage is well known.) His is not the search for truth as such. To put that thought more exactly, the truth and victory are mutually incompatible for some considerable percentage of the attorneys trying cases at any given time.

Certainly, if one may speak the unspeakable, most defendants who go to trial in criminal cases are not desirous that the whole truth about the matters in controversy be exposed to scrutiny. This is not to question the presumption of innocence or the prosecution's burden of proof beyond a reasonable doubt. In any particular case, because we are unwilling to incur more than a minimal risk of convicting the innocent, these bedrock principles must prevail. The statistical fact remains that the preponderant majority of those brought to trial did substantially what they are charged with. While we undoubtedly convict some innocent people, a truth horrifying to confront, we also acquit a far larger number who are guilty, a fact we bear with much more equanimity.

One reason we bear it so well is our awareness that in the last analysis truth is not the only goal. An exceedingly able criminal defense lawyer who regularly serves in our court makes a special point of this. I have heard him at once defy and cajole juries with the reminder that the question is not at all "guilt or innocence," but only whether guilt has been shown beyond a reasonable doubt. Whether that is always an astute tactic may be debated. Its doctrinal soundness is clear.

Whatever doctrine teaches, it is a fact of interest here that most criminal defense counsel are not at all bent upon full disclosure of the truth. To a lesser degree, but stemming from the same ethos, we know how fiercely prosecutors have resisted disclosure, how often they have winked at police lapses, how mixed has been their enthusiasm for the principle that they must seek justice, not merely convictions. While the patterns of civil cases are different, and variable, we may say that it is the rare case in which either side yearns to have the witnesses, or anyone, give *the whole truth*. And our techniques for developing evidence feature devices for blocking and limiting such unqualified revelations.

The devices are too familiar to warrant more than a fleeting reminder. To begin with, we leave most of the investigatory work to paid partisans, which is scarcely a guarantee of thorough and detached exploration. Our courts wait passively for what the parties will present, almost never knowing — often not suspecting — what the parties have chosen not to present. The ethical standards governing counsel command loyalty and zeal for the client, but no positive obligation at all to the truth. Counsel must not knowingly break the law or commit or countenance fraud. Within these unconfining limits, advocates freely employ time-honored tricks and stratagems to block or distort the truth.

As a matter of strict logic, in the run of cases where there are flatly contradictory assertions about matters of fact, one side must be correct, the other wrong. Where the question is "Did the defendant pass a red light?" or "Does the plaintiff have a scarred retina?" or "Was the accused warned of the reasons why anyone of sound mind would keep quiet and did he then proceed nevertheless like a suicidal idiot to destroy himself by talking?" the "facts" are, or were, one way or the other. To be sure, honest people may honestly differ, and we mere lawyers cannot — actually, must not — set ourselves up as judges of the facts. That is the great release from effective ethical inhibitions. We are not to pass judgment, but only to marshall our skills to present and test the witnesses and other evidence — the skills being to make the most of these for our side and the least for the opposition. What will out, we sometimes tell ourselves and often tell others, is the truth. And, if worse comes to worst, in the end who really knows what is truth?

There is much in this of cant, hypocrisy, and convenient overlooking. As people, we know or powerfully suspect a good deal more than we are prepared as lawyers to admit or explore further. The clearest cases are those in which the advocate has been informed directly by a competent client, or has learned from evidence too clear to admit of genuine doubt, that the client's position rests upon falsehood. It is not possible to be certain, but I believe from recollection and conversation such cases are far from rare. Much more numerous are the cases in which we manage at counsel to avoid too much knowledge. The sharp eye of the cynical lawyer becomes at strategic moments a demurely averted and filmy gaze. It may be agreeable not to listen to the client's tape recordings of vital conversations that may contain embarrassments for the ultimate goal of vindicating the client. Unfettered by the clear prohibitions actual "knowledge" of the truth might impose, lawyers may be effective and exuberant in employing the familiar skills: techniques that make a witness look unreliable although the look stems only from counsel's artifice, cunning questions that stop short of discomfiting revelations, complaisant experts for whom some shopping may have been necessary. The credo that frees counsel for such arts is not a doctrine of truth-seeking.

The litigator's devices, let us be clear, have utility in testing dishonest witnesses, ferreting out falsehoods, and thus exposing the truth. But to a considerable degree these devices are like other potent weapons, equally lethal for heroes and villains. It is worth stressing, therefore, that the gladiator using the weapons in the courtroom is not primarily crusading after truth, but seeking to win. If this is banal, it is also overlooked too much and, in any event, basic to my thesis. . . .

I am among those who believe the laity have ground to question our service in the quest for truth. The ranks of lawyers and judges joining in this rueful stance are vast. Many have sought over the years to raise our standards and our functioning, not merely our image. There has been success. Liberalized discovery has helped, though the struggles over that, including the well-founded fears of tampering with the evidence, highlight the hardy evils of adversary management. We have, on the whole, seemed to become better over time, occasional lapses notwithstanding. At any rate, the main object of this talk is not merely to bewail, but to participate in the ongoing effort to improve. Modest thoughts on that subject . . . follow. . . .

SOME PROPOSALS

Having argued that we are too much committed to contentiousness as a good in itself and too little devoted to truth, I proceed to some prescriptions of a general nature for remedying these flaws. Simply stated, these prescriptions are that we should:

(1) modify (not abandon) the adversary ideal,
(2) make truth a paramount objective, and
(3) impose upon the contestants a duty to pursue that objective.

A.   MODIFYING THE ADVERSARY IDEAL

We should begin, as a concerted professional task, to question the premise that adversariness is ultimately and invariably good. For most of us trained in American law, the superiority of the adversary process over any other is too plain to doubt or examine. The certainty is shared by people who are in other respects widely separated on the ideological spectrum. The august Code of Professional Responsibility, as has been mentioned, proclaims, in order, the "Duty of the Lawyer to a Client,"[55] then the "Duty of the Lawyer to the Adversary System of Justice."[56] There is no announced "Duty to the Truth" or "Duty to the Community." Public interest lawyers, while they otherwise test the law's bounds, profess a basic commitment "to the adversary system itself" as the means of giving "everyone affected by corporate and bureaucratic decisions . . . a voice in those decisions. . . ."[57] We may note similarly the earnest and idealistic scholar who brought the fury of the (not necessarily consistent) establishment upon himself when he wrote, reflecting upon experience as devoted defense counsel for poor people, that as an advocate you must (a) try to destroy a witness "whom you know to be telling the truth," (b) "put a witness on the stand when you know he will commit perjury," and (c) "give your client legal advice when you have reason to believe that the knowledge you give him will tempt him to commit perjury."[58] The "policies" he found to justify these views, included, as the first and

55. [ABA Code of Professional Responsibility] (heading preceding EC 7-4).
56. Id. (heading preceding EC 7-19).
57. Halpern & Cunningham, Reflections on the New Public Interest Law. [p. 552, at 555.]
58. Freedman, Professional Responsibility of the Criminal Defense Lawyer: The Three Hardest Questions, 64 Mich. L. Rev. 1469 (1966).

most fundamental, the maintenance of "an adversary system based upon the presupposition that the most effective means of determining truth is to present to a judge and jury a clash between proponents of conflicting views."[59]

Our commitment to the adversary or "accusatorial" mode is buttressed by a corollary certainly that other, alien systems are inferior. We contrast our form of criminal procedure with the "inquisitorial" system, conjuring up visions of torture, secrecy, and dictatorial government. Confident of our superiority, we do not bother to find out how others work. It is not common knowledge among us, that purely inquisitorial systems exist scarcely anywhere; that elements of our adversary approach exist probably everywhere; and that the evolving procedures of criminal justice, in Europe and elsewhere, are better described as "mixed" than as strictly accusatorial or strictly inquisitorial.[60]

In considering the possibility of change, we must open our minds to the variants and alternatives employed by other communities that also aspire to civilization. Without voting firmly, I raise the question whether the virginally ignorant judge is always to be preferred to one with an investigative file. We should be prepared to inquire whether our arts of examining and cross-examining, often geared to preventing excessive outpourings of facts, are inescapably preferable to safeguarded interrogation by an informed judicial officer. It is permissible to keep asking, because nobody has satisfactorily answered, why our present system of confessions in the police station versus no confessions at all is better than an open and orderly procedure of having a judicial official question suspects.

If the mention of such a question has not exhausted your tolerance, consider whether our study of foreign alternatives might suggest means for easing the unending tension surrounding the privilege against self-incrimination as it frequently operates in criminal trials. It would be prudent at least to study closely whether our criminal defendant, privileged to stay suspiciously absent from the stand or to testify subject to a perjury prosecution or "impeachment" by prior crimes, is surely better off than the European defendant who cannot escape questioning both before and at trial, though he may refuse to answer, but is free to tell his story without either the oath or the impeachment pretext for using his criminal record against him. Whether or not the defendant is better off, the question remains open whether the balance we have struck is the best possible.

To propose only one other topic for illustration, we need to study

---

59. Id. 1470. See also id. 1471, 1477-1478, 1482.
60. W. Schaefer, The Suspect and Society 71 (1967); Damaska, Evidentiary Barriers to Conviction and Two Models of Criminal Procedure: A Comparative Study, 121 U. Pa. L. Rev. 506, 557-561, 569-570 (1973).

whether our elaborate struggles over discovery, especially in criminal
cases, may be incurable symptoms of pathology inherent in our rigid
insistence that the parties control the evidence until it is all "prepared"
and packaged for competitive manipulation at the eventual continuous
trial. Central in the debates on discovery is the concern of the ungener-
ous that the evidence may be tainted or alchemized between the time it
is discovered and the time it is produced or countered at the trial. The
concern, though the debaters report it in differing degrees, is well
founded. It is significant enough to warrant our exploring alternative
arrangements abroad where investigation "freezes" the evidence (that is,
preserves usable depositions and other forms of relatively contempo-
raneous evidence) for use at trial, thus serving both to inhibit spoilage
and to avoid pitfalls and surprises that may defeat justice. . . .

B. MAKING TRUTH THE PARAMOUNT OBJECTIVE

We should consider whether the paramount commitment of counsel
concerning matters of fact should be to the discovery of truth rather
than to the advancement of the client's interest. This topic heading contains for me the most debatable and the least thoroughly considered of
the thoughts offered here. It is a brief suggestion for a revolution, but
with no apparatus of doctrine or program.

We should face the fact that the quality of "hired gun" is close to the
heart and substance of the litigating lawyer's role. As is true always of
the mercenary warrior, the litigator has not won the highest esteem for
his scars and his service. Apart from our image, we have had to reckon
for ourselves in the dark hours with the knowledge that "selling" our
stories rather than striving for the truth cannot always seem, because it
is not, such noble work as befits the practitioner of a learned profession.
The struggle to win, with its powerful pressures to subordinate the love
of truth, is often only incidentally, or coincidentally, if at all, a service to
the public interest.

We have been bemused through the ages by the hardy (and somewhat
appealing) notion that we are to serve rather than judge the client.
Among the implications of this theme is the idea that lawyers are not to
place themselves above others and that the client must be equipped to
decide for himself whether or not he will follow the path of truth and
justice. This means quite specifically, whether in Anatomy of a Murder[66]
or in Dean Freedman's altruistic sense of commitment, that the client
must be armed for effective perjury as well as he would be if he were

---

66. R. Traver, Anatomy of a Murder (1958). For those who did not read or have
forgotten it, the novel, by a state supreme court justice, involved an eventually successful homicide defense of impaired mental capacity with the defendant supplying the
requisite "facts" after having been told in advance by counsel what type of facts would
constitute the defense.

himself legally trained. To offer anything less is arrogant, elitist, and undemocratic.

It is impossible to guess closely how prevalent this view may be as a practical matter. Nor am I clear to what degree, if any, received canons of legal ethics give it sanction. My submission is in any case that it is a crass and pernicious idea, unworthy of a public profession. It is true that legal training is a source of power, for evil as well as good, and that a wicked lawyer is capable of specially skilled wrongdoing. It is likewise true that a physician or pharmacist knows homicidal devices hidden from the rest of us. Our goals must include means for limiting the numbers of crooked and malevolent people trained in the vital professions. We may be certain, notwithstanding our best efforts, that some lawyers and judges will abuse their trust. But this is no reason to encourage or facilitate wrongdoing by everyone.

Professional standards that placed truth above the client's interests would raise more perplexing questions. The privilege for client's confidences might come in for reexamination and possible modification. We have all been trained to know without question that the privilege is indispensable for effective representation. The client must know his confidences are safe so that he can tell all and thus have fully knowledgeable advice. We may want to ask, nevertheless, whether it would be an excessive price for the client to be stuck with the truth rather than having counsel allied with him for concealment and distortion. The full development of this thought is beyond my studies to date. Its implications may be unacceptable. I urge only that it is among the premises in need of examination.

If the lawyer is to be more truth-seeker than combatant, troublesome questions of economics and professional organization may demand early confrontation. How and why should the client pay for loyalties divided between himself and the truth? Will we not stultify the energies and resources of the advocate by demanding that he judge the honesty of his cause along the way? Can we preserve the heroic lawyer shielding his client against all the world — and not least against the State — while demanding that he honor a paramount commitment to the elusive and ambiguous truth? It is strongly arguable, in short, that a simplistic preference for the truth may not comport with more fundamental ideals — including notably the ideal that generally values individual freedom and dignity above order and efficiency in government. Having stated such issues too broadly, I leave them in the hope that their refinement and study may seem worthy endeavors for the future.

C.   A DUTY TO PURSUE THE TRUTH

The rules of professional responsibility should compel disclosures of material facts and forbid material omissions rather than merely proscribe positive frauds. This final suggestion is meant to implement the broad and general proposition that precedes it. In an effort to be still more specific, I submit a draft of a new disciplinary rule that would supplement or in large measure displace existing Disciplinary Rule 7-102 of the Code of Professional Responsibility. The draft says:

> (1) In his representation of a client, unless prevented from doing so by a privilege reasonably believed to apply, a lawyer shall:
> (a) Report to the court and opposing counsel the existence of relevant evidence or witnesses where the lawyer does not intend to offer such evidence or witnesses.
> (b) Prevent, or when prevention has proved unsuccessful, report to the court and opposing counsel the making of any untrue statement by client or witness or any omission to state a material fact necessary in order to make statements made, in the light of the circumstances under which they were made, not misleading.
> (c) Question witnesses with a purpose and design to elicit the whole truth, including particularly supplementary and qualifying matters that render evidence already given more accurate, intelligible, or fair than it otherwise would be.
> (2) In the construction and application of the rules in subdivision (1), a lawyer will be held to possess knowledge he actually has or, in the exercise of reasonable diligence, should have.

Key words in the draft, namely, in (1)(b), have been plagiarized, of course, from the Securities and Exchange Commission's Rule 10b-5. That should serve not only for respectability; it should also answer, at least to some extent, the complaint that the draft would impose impossibly stringent standards. The morals we have evolved for business clients cannot be deemed unattainable by the legal profession.

Harder questions suggest themselves. The draft provision for wholesale disclosure of evidence in litigation may be visionary or outrageous, or both. It certainly stretches out of existing shape our conception of the advocate retained to be partisan. As against the yielding up of everything, we are accustomed to strenuous debates about giving a supposedly laggard or less energetic party a share in his adversary's litigation property safeguarded as "work product." A lawyer must now surmount partisan loyalty and disclose "information clearly establishing" frauds by his client or others.[72] But that is a far remove from any duty to turn over all the fruits of factual investigation, as the draft proffered here would direct. It has lately come to be required that some approach to helpful disclosures be made by prosecutors in criminal cases; "the suppression by the prosecution of evidence favorable to an accused upon request violates due process where the evidence is material either to guilt or to

---

72. ABA Code of Professional Responsibility, DR 7-102(B).

punishment, irrespective of the good faith or bad faith of the prosecution."[74] One may be permitted as a respectful subordinate to note the awkward placement in the quoted passage of the words "upon request," and to imagine their careful insertion to keep the duty of disclosure within narrow bounds. But even that restricted rule is for the *public* lawyer. Can we, should we, adopt a far broader rule as a command to the bar generally?

That question touches once again the most sensitive nerve of all. A bar too tightly regulated, too conformist, too "governmental," is not acceptable to any of us. We speak often of lawyers as "officers of the court" and as "public" people. Yet our basic conception of the office is of one essentially private — private in political, economic, and ideological terms — congruent with a system of private ownership, enterprise, and competition, however modified the system has come to be. It is not necessary to recount here the contributions of a legal profession thus conceived to the creation and maintenance of a relatively free society. It *is* necessary to acknowledge these contributions and to consider squarely whether, or how much, they are endangered by proposed reforms.

If we must choose between truth and liberty, the decision is not in doubt. If the choice seemed to me that clear and that stark, this essay would never have reached even the tentative form of its present submission. But I think the picture is quite unclear. I lean to the view that we can hope to preserve the benefits of a free, skeptical, contentious bar while paying a lesser price in trickery and obfuscation.

NOTE: Some Recent Developments

Predictably, there has been critical response to Judge Frankel's views, which also form a main theme of his book Partisan Justice. See Freedman, Judge Frankel's Search for the Truth, 123 U. Pa. L. Rev. 1060 (1975); Uviller, The Advocate, The Truth, and Judicial Hackles, 123 U. Pa. L. Rev. 1067 (1975); Alschuler, The Preservation of a Client's Confidences, 52 U. Colo. L. Rev. 349 (1981); and Pizzi, Judge Frankel and the Adversary System, 52 U. Colo. L. Rev. 357 (1981). An attitude similar to that of Judge Frankel is expressed in Dean Norman Redlich's Lawyers, the Temple and the Market Place, 30 Bus. Law. 65 (1975). One way to test Judge Frankel's general views about the undervaluation of truth as an objective in our adversary system is by his own specific proposal for amendment of DR 7-102 at p. 170. Assuming for a moment that the proposal is desirable, is it practicable? Under proposed (1)(a), would a lawyer be obligated to report to court and counsel every relevant

---

74. Brady v. Maryland, 373 U.S. 83, 87 (1963).

and material variation in a story told by a witness in successive interviews? Under proposed (1)(b), what would be the standard to guide a lawyer in deciding whether a witness had made an untrue or a misleading statement? Under (1) (c), would a lawyer be required when a client testified to a particular series of events to cross-examine that client before the court and jury with respect to every relevant and material variation in that story? Is the combined subjective-objective nature of Judge Frankel's "reasonably believed" test in subsection (1) a helpful guide to lawyers? What would be the consequence of the adoption of, and full compliance with, Judge Frankel's proposed rule? In answering this question, assume that the "unless" clause in paragraph 1 is not meant to nullify with respect to "clients" what seems to be required in subparagraphs (a) and (b), and perhaps (c), although in (b) he seems to exclude "clients" from the category of "witnesses." Are any disadvantages that you perceive worth incurring in order to achieve the goal? Could one modify the disadvantages without sacrificing the objectives of the proposal? Assuming that the proposal is practicable, is it desirable, as compared with the present disciplinary rule or some other alternative that you favor? Some of the earlier drafts of the Model Rules, which would have permitted or required greater breaches in confidentiality and greater openness by lawyers with other persons affected by a client's actions, may have reflected views similar to those expressed by Judge Frankel in this article, for he was a member of the Kutak Commission. Indeed, his presence on the Commission caused its work to be regarded with much suspicion by many proponents of a rule of strong confidentiality and may well have acted as a catalyst to the strong opposition to some of its initial proposals.

Consider yet another view of the lawyer's obligation regarding the perjurious client, that of Chief Justice (then Judge) Warren Burger in a paper entitled Standards of Conduct for Prosecution and Defense Personnel, 5 Am. Crim. L.Q. 11, 12-13 (1966):

> It is perfectly clear, not only in the legal profession in the United States, but in all common-law countries where witnesses are called and examined under the adversary system, that the lawyer must tell his client that he will not be proffered as a witness once the lawyer knows that he will testify falsely. But it has happened that, even after he has agreed on this before the trial, the defendant, in the midst of trial, insists upon taking the stand. Obviously the lawyer cannot physically or otherwise prevent him from walking to the witness chair and taking the oath. If in those circumstances the lawyer's immediate withdrawal from the case is either not feasible, or if the judge refuses to permit withdrawal, the lawyer's course is clear: *He may not engage in direct examination of his client to facilitate known perjury.* He should confine himself to asking the witness to identify himself and to make a statement, but he cannot participate in the fraud by conventional direct examination. Since this informal procedure is not uncommon with

witnesses, there is no basis for saying that this tells the jury the witness is lying. A judge may infer that such is the case but lay jurors will not.

Courts, commentators, and drafters of codes have continued to struggle with the perjury problem. In resolving the dilemma (or as Professor Freedman now calls it, the trilemma of being "required to know everything, to keep it in confidence and to reveal it to the court," Freedman, Lawyers' Ethics in an Adversary System 28 (1975)), Freedman's arguments based upon the practicalities of the situation, pp. 157-160, cannot be ignored. One must deal with the likelihood that in many circumstances at least, the lawyer may simply not be permitted to withdraw and with the danger that anything other than proceeding with examination in the ordinary course may telegraph to judge or jury the lawyer's disbelief of his or her client's story. Freedman demonstrates the extreme difficulty with Chief Justice Burger's solution in his discussion in the paragraph on page 159 beginning with "A solution." That solution was embodied in the first edition of the ABA's Standards Relating to the Defense Function, §7.7 (1st ed. 1971). (See Commentary thereto for further exposition of the position.) A similar standard was also approved by the ABA Standing Committee on Association Standards for Criminal Justice when the Standards were revised in 1979. The standard was withdrawn, however, before final submission to the ABA House of Delegates to await the final report of the Kutak Commission on the perjury question. 1 ABA, Standards for Criminal Justice, 4.94-4.95 (2d ed. 1980) (Editorial Note to deleted Standard 4-7.7). Freedman also notes that another way out of the trilemma, again at the expense of a major purpose of Canon 4, is to adopt the proposal of the Canadian Bar Association that would put the client on notice at the beginning of the relationship that the lawyer will follow a course like that set forth in the Standards if the client proposes to commit perjury. See Freedman, Lawyers' Ethics in any Adversary System 37-38 (1975). Is such notice required whatever solution is adopted? See Problem 22, p. 151.

The drafters of the Model Code did not resolve cleanly the problem of intention to commit perjury. DR 4-101(B) states a general rule of confidentiality. DR 4-101(C)(3) gives discretion to break a client's confidence when the client intends to commit a crime, and DR 4-101(C)(2) permits revealing a confidence or secret when permitted under the Disciplinary Rules or required by law or court order. DR 7-102(A)(4) forbids the knowing use of perjured testimony. Finally, there is the puzzling DR 7-102(B)(1), which in its original version required a lawyer as a last resort to reveal fraud perpetrated by his client during the course of his representation to the affected person or tribunal. While stated in terms of completed fraud, it has an effect on current perjury in the situation of the lawyer who knows that a client has committed perjury the instant the client has testified. While the perjury is past, the effect is yet to come and more perjury is likely to come on further examination or on cross-examination. Thus we shall have to take a preliminary look at the history and interpretation of DR 7-102(B)(1) although we shall also have to reconsider its provisions in subsections D and E, which deal with completed fraud.

That complex of provisions in the Model Code presents an unclear answer for the lawyer faced with a client about to commit perjury or who has just committed perjury. Opinion 341 (1975) of the ABA Committee on Ethics and Professional Responsibility took the position that the last-minute insertion of DR 7-102(B)(1) into the Model Code had inadvertently changed the result from the conclusions reached in the Committee's former Opinion 287. That view was not the only possible interpretation of the Model Code, although among the footnotes to DR 7-102(B)(1) is an ambiguous "but see ABA Opinion 287." Except for a brief reference in footnote 44 to Canon 7, that is the only reference in the footnotes of the Model Code to Opinion 287, although ABA Opinions 155 and 156, which espouse a philosophy contrary to that of Opinion 287, are quoted and cited in several places. On the other hand, given the unclear wording of Canon 4 and the lack of any stated purpose to overturn Opinion 287, it is also possible that the drafters of the Model Code set up the same conflict of principle that appeared in the former Canons of Ethics, thus leaving lawyers, ethics committees, and courts the problem of accommodating the conflicting principles differently in different factual situations. It seems fair to state, however, that the structure of the Model Code makes that argument more difficult because the permission to reveal is stated as an exception to the general confidentiality rule of DR 4-101(B) and not as a separate, and therefore conflicting, principle.

The contention by some commentators, courts, and especially federal agencies attempting to impose a greater disclosure obligation on lawyers that the reasoning of Opinion 287 had been undermined by the original version of DR 7-102(B)(1) led the ABA to propose the amending language at the end of DR 7-102(B) that now appears in its final clause. An exception to the obligation to disclose fraud was created for information "protected as a privileged communication." In their haste to draft the amendment, the drafters forgot the twofold division of protected information into the narrow category of "confidences" (information protected by the attorney-client privilege) and the broader category of "secrets." Nevertheless, even though it might have been more logical to have interpreted the words "privileged communication" in the amendment as relating only to confidences, the ABA Committee advised in Opinion 341 that the amendment covered secrets as well. Under that interpretation the amendment to DR 7-102(B)(1) may have swallowed up a great portion of the mandatory obligation embodied in the Rule.

In the perjury context, however, the Committee was more cautious. Although it concluded that the amendment reinstated "the essence of Opinion 287," it did so only in the context of the fact situation in which the perjury had taken place in a matter that had been concluded when the lawyer learned of the perjury. It studiously ignored the other fact situation in Opinion 287, in which the lawyer learned of client perjury while the matter was ongoing. In its Informal Opinion 1314, issued six months before its Opinion 341, however, the Committee had advised, without specifically justifying the distinction by the provisions of the Model Code, that a lawyer surprised by client perjury must not disclose but that if the lawyer knew of the intention beforehand he must either withdraw or report the falsity of the testimony to the court if the client so testified. The relation between this view and the actual wording of the relevant provisions of the Model Code was later discussed by the Committee in Opinion 87-353. See p. 195.

One other possibility for reading DR 4-101(C)(3) and DR 7-102(B)(1) together has, surprisingly, not been much considered. It is possible to read those two sections as providing a rather more straightforward approach to the problems of the lawyer's responsibility when a client-party tells the lawyer that he or she has just committed perjury during the course of a civil trial. The argument is as follows: Let us assume that Lawyer discovers that Client has committed perjury during a deposition a month ago but that the trial is still some time away. The past crime of perjury is clearly involved. However, Lawyer may be aware of Client's intention to commit any of several possible future crimes. One of those possibilities is a repetition of the perjury at the trial stage. Another possibility arises because Client appears to intend to secure a favorable judgment or settlement based on false testimony. That raises a question of substantive criminal law: since there is no general common law crime of fraud, will one of the state's criminal statutes relating to wrongful obtaining of the property of another (either by obtaining a money judgment to which the client is not entitled or by defeating a rightful claim) or the federal mail or wire fraud statutes, 18 U.S.C. §§1341, 1343, be construed to be applicable to this fact situation? Finally, many states include a course of obfuscation by a party within the notion of criminal contempt.

The most likely situation to arise is the one in which Lawyer is aware of Client's intention to repeat the perjury before the proceeding is concluded. This will often happen when the perjury occurred at depositions. It may also happen when the perjury occurred during the trial, especially in a long-lasting trial. In the event Lawyer is aware of Client's intention to commit perjury in the future course of the litigation or if Lawyer concludes that there are other criminal statutes that Client is intending to violate, then Lawyer has discretion under DR 4-101(C)(3) to reveal the intention to repeat the perjury at the trial and the information necessary to prevent it. In any of those situations, it will probably be necessary for Lawyer to "reveal" the past deposition perjury as part of "the information necessary to prevent the crime" of future perjury at trial. Although Lawyer, when exercising discretion under DR

4-101(C)(3), should reveal the minimum amount of confidential information necessary to prevent the future crime, it is difficult to see how Lawyer can prevent future specific perjury (or future criminal contempt or a future criminally obtained verdict if those exist in the particular jurisdiction) without being explicit about the proposed perjury (or other future crime). That seems bound to reveal the past perjury.

Lawyer's discretion under DR 4-101(C)(3) is not removed by virtue of the fact that revelation of the intention to commit future perjury is likely to reveal the commission of past perjury. The situation is much the same as when a pharmacist-client, seeking legal advice, reveals that he is putting cyanide in the cough medicine bottles in his drugstore and no one has yet purchased any of them. The fact that the insertion of the poison may constitute a crime in itself does not prevent the lawyer from revealing the insertion under DR 4-101(C)(3) to prevent the murder of future purchasers of the medicine. Indeed, it has long been held in the substantive evidence law of attorney-client privilege that the intention to commit crime or fraud is not "privileged."

Resolution of the problem does not stop with DR 4-101(C)(3). DR 7-102(B)(1) requires a lawyer to disclose fraud committed during the course of representation — which we have here — except when a "privileged communication" is involved. Let us assume first that this is a situation where Lawyer has discretion to reveal the confidential information under DR 4-101(C)(3). The issue then is whether DR 7-102(B)(1) makes that discretion mandatory, as prima facie it does, or whether the exception for "privileged communications" applies. It does not seem a sensible interpretation of "privileged communications" to read that phrase as removing the mandatory duty to disclose in those situations where the lawyer has already been granted discretion to disclose by the Rules. Communications that the Lawyer may disclose hardly seem "privileged" in that context. "Privileged communications" are more sensibly defined as those controlled by the client, that is, situations where the attorney-client privilege would apply. Therefore where perjured testimony is concerned, in those situations where future crime of the sort described above is in prospect, Lawyer must reveal it if Client refuses to correct the perjured testimony. Such an interpretation does not render the proviso in DR 7-102(B)(1) meaningless, even in the case of client perjury, for the exception will still apply to perjured testimony in cases that have been completed and to cases where no future crime is in prospect.

ABA Opinion 341 itself appears to support this line of argument. It contains the following response to the contention that the "privileged communication" exception wiped out the whole rule. "DR 4-101(C) sets out several circumstances under which revelation of a secret or confidence is permissible, and thus in cases where these exceptions apply, DR 7-102(B) may make the optional disclosure of information under DR 4-101 a mandatory one. For example, when disclosure is required by a law, the 'privileged communication' exception of DR 7-102(B) is not applicable and disclosure may be required." Another such example, although not mentioned by Opinion 341 would be DR 4-101(C)(3). The reason why the line of argument proposed in the last five paragraphs may not have gained immediate favor is that at least some of the proponents of the 1974 amendment to DR 7-102(B)(1) would like the same result in the case of perjury in ongoing litigation as in the completed perjury case. But the amendment does not seem to me to be adequate to such a goal.

It may be, however, that Lawyer will conclude that he is not aware of any intent on the part of Client to commit a future crime. That does not mean that Lawyer may proceed with the litigation in normal fashion. Lawyer knows that Client's past perjury about a material issue is aimed at reaching a result that constitutes fraud. DR 7-102(A)(7) explicitly forbids Lawyer from counselling or assisting Client in "conduct that the lawyer knows to be illegal or fraudulent." Pursuing litigation with knowledge that Client has knowingly and falsely authenticated a document that is material to the case would violate that Rule. In such a circumstance, Lawyer must at least withdraw.

If one transfers this problem to criminal cases, it looks different. For one thing, there are no depositions in criminal cases, and courts would probably be much less willing to find the criminal violations in addition to perjury of the sort mentioned above. For another it is possible to argue, even after Nix v. Whiteside, p. 179 infra, that there are constitutional issues still to be decided under both federal and state constitutions. It is also possible to argue that "fraud" in DR 7-102(B)(1) was not meant to include perjury in criminal cases. Nevertheless the argument, if persuasive with respect to civil cases, may also be persuasive with respect to criminal cases. If it is, it will make the result with respect to lawyers' obligations when they discover client perjury while a case is ongoing quite similar under the Model Code and the Model Rules.

In any event, it should be mentioned at this point that only a minority of the states that had adopted the Model Code thereafter adopted the amendment to DR 7-102(B)(1). A jurisdiction with either version of DR 7-102(B)(1), however, has the formidable task of reconciling that provision with DR 4-101. Of course the real problem in Model Code jurisdictions is that the Disciplinary Rules deal with the problem of the perjurious client only as a subset of more general rules dealing with "the intention to commit a crime" or with past commission of fraud. What is needed is a rule that deals explicitly with perjury.

A Note on the Model Rules

While the Model Code is subject to different interpretations with respect to the lawyer's obligation to report perjury by a client, the Model Rules in Rule 3.3(a)(2) take a clear stance mandating disclosure of the perjury, if the lawyer cannot get the client to correct the testimony, if the lawyer is unable to withdraw, or if withdrawal will not remedy the situation. The only caveat noted by the drafters is the possibility that Rule 3.3(a)(2)'s definition of a lawyer's ethical duty "may be qualified by constitutional provisions for due process and the right to counsel in criminal cases." Nix v. Whiteside, which follows, p. 179, addressed this caveat in substantial part.

A major argument in the analysis supporting the "disclosure when necessary" requirement is avoidance by the lawyer of implication in commission of perjury. As such, the requirement is seen as simply a special application of the general prohibition in Rule 1.2(d) that the lawyer avoid counseling or assisting a client in conduct known to be criminal or fraudulent. See Comment to Rule 3.3, ¶11. On the other hand, the obligation may arise under circumstances where the lawyer has not knowingly been implicated in its presentation. A clear case would be where the lawyer learns of perjury while the jury is considering its verdict, that is, after the testimony has been given and argued to the jury.

Other mandatory disclosure requirements are contained in Model Rule 3.3(a)(4), which requires a lawyer in some circumstances to disclose to a tribunal the falsity of material evidence introduced by the lawyer without knowledge of its falsity; Model Rule 4.1, which requires a lawyer in some circumstances to disclose information to a third party when necessary to avoid assisting a criminal or fraudulent act by a client; and Model Rule 3.3(d), which requires a lawyer proceeding ex parte to inform the tribunal of all relevant facts known to the lawyer, adverse or not, to permit the tribunal to make "an informed decision." This latter mandatory disclosure rule may be quite far-reaching for it rests on a different conceptual foundation from the other mandatory disclosure rules. As stated by the Comment, "The judge has an affirmative responsibility to accord the absent party just consideration. The lawyer for the represented party has the correlative duty to make relevant disclosures." The judge has the same duty in non ex parte proceedings. The difference is that all parties are "present." But when, because of chance or a breakdown in the process, one lawyer knows that important relevant information has not reached the tribunal, then that lawyer and the tribunal are in the same position vis à vis one another as in the situation when the lawyer proceeding ex parte possesses important adverse relevant facts. It is possible to draw a line where the Rules have drawn it, but that requires more justification than the Comment gives it. It remains to be seen whether Rule 3.3(d) represents a small step away from the prior situation and its further extension to all cases, as desired by Judge Frankel, represents a large step or whether Rule 3.3(d) represents a large step that if successfully taken will lead to the further small step of making it applicable in all cases. Resolution of that question will in part turn on the eventual interpretation of Rule 3.3(d). It could be interpreted to cover only situations like In re Greene, 290 Or. 291, 620 P.2d 1379 (1980), where a lawyer was disciplined for failure to disclose in ex parte proceedings designed to permit trust funds held by his wife for the benefit of her minor children to be used for real estate investment and improvements, that what was involved were paying off a mortgage and making improvements on a home owned by her. The Rule might also be interpreted, however, to cover the full panoply of situations envisioned by Judge Frankel. See pp. 169-171.

It is interesting that these mandatory disclosure provisions were not altered by the House of Delegates of the ABA when the discretionary disclosure provisions of Rule 1.6 were substantially reduced. The American College of Trial Lawyers fought hard to eliminate mandatory disclosure of perjured testimony but it lost that battle. The differing results can be explained in many ways. It may be that the public outcry after the changes in Rule 1.6 had an effect on the subsequent vote concerning Rule 3.3. It may be that harm to the judicial process involved in perjury was regarded more seriously than the harm to what were essentially private financial interests that were at stake in the changes in Rule 1.6. Or it may be that the change in Rule 1.6 reflected the power of the corporate bar, whose interests were heavily involved in that debate, while the failure to change Rule 3.3 reflected a relative lack of sufficient power in the criminal defense bar and, to a lesser extent, other litigators.

The issue of client perjury finally reached the Supreme Court in the context of a claim of ineffective assistance of counsel in the following case.

NIX v. WHITESIDE
475 U.S. 157 (1986)

Chief Justice BURGER delivered the opinion of the Court.

We granted certiorari to decide whether the Sixth Amendment right of a criminal defendant to assistance of counsel is violated when an attorney refuses to cooperate with the defendant in presenting perjured testimony at his trial.

I

A

Whiteside was convicted of second degree murder by a jury verdict which was affirmed by the Iowa courts. The killing took place on February 8, 1977 in Cedar Rapids, Iowa. Whiteside and two others went to one Calvin Love's apartment late that night, seeking marihuana. Love was in bed when Whiteside and his companions arrived; an argument between Whiteside and Love over the marihuana ensued. At one point, Love directed his girlfriend to get his "piece," and at another point got up, then returned to his bed. According to Whiteside's testimony, Love then started to reach under his pillow and moved toward Whiteside. Whiteside stabbed Love in the chest, inflicting a fatal wound.

Whiteside was charged with murder. . . . Robinson was . . . appointed and immediately began investigation. Whiteside gave him a statement that he had stabbed Love as the latter "was pulling a pistol from underneath the pillow on the bed." Upon questioning by Robinson, however, Whiteside indicated that he had not actually seen a gun, but that he was convinced that Love had a gun. No pistol was found on the premises; shortly after the police search following the stabbing, which had revealed no weapon, the victim's family had removed all of the victim's possessions from the apartment. Robinson interviewed Whiteside's companions who were present during the stabbing and none had seen a gun during the incident. Robinson advised Whiteside that the existence of a gun was not necessary to establish the claim of self defense, and that only a reasonable belief that the victim had a gun nearby was necessary even though no gun was actually present.

Until shortly before trial, Whiteside consistently stated to Robinson that he had not actually seen a gun, but that he was convinced that Love had a gun in his hand. About a week before trial, during preparation for direct examination, Whiteside for the first time told Robinson and his associate Donna Paulsen that he had seen something "metallic" in Love's hand. When asked about this, Whiteside responded that "in Howard Cook's case there was a gun. If I don't say I saw a gun I'm dead." Robinson told Whiteside that such testimony would be perjury and repeated that it was not necessary to prove that a gun was available but only that Whiteside reasonably believed that he was in danger. On Whiteside's insisting that he would testify that he saw "something metallic" Robinson told him, according to Robinson's testimony,

> we could not allow him to [testify falsely] because that would be perjury, and as officers of the court we would be suborning perjury if we allowed him to do it; . . . I advised him that if he did do that it would be my duty to advise the Court of what he was doing and that I felt he was committing perjury; also, that I probably would be allowed to attempt to impeach that particular testimony.

Robinson also indicated he would seek to withdraw from the representation if Whiteside insisted on committing perjury.

Whiteside testified in his own defense at trial and stated that he "knew" that Love had a gun and that he believed Love was reaching for a gun and he had acted swiftly in self defense. On cross examination, he admitted that he had not actually seen a gun in Love's hand. Robinson presented evidence that Love had been seen with a sawed-off shotgun on other occasions, that the police search of the apartment may have been careless, and that the victim's family had removed everything from the apartment shortly after the crime. Robinson presented this evidence to show a basis for Whiteside's asserted fear that Love had a gun.

The jury returned a verdict of second-degree murder and Whiteside moved for a new trial, claiming that he had been deprived of a fair trial by Robinson's admonitions not to state that he saw a gun or "something metallic." The trial court held a hearing, heard testimony by Whiteside and Robinson, and denied the motion. The trial court made specific findings that the facts were as related by Robinson.

The Supreme Court of Iowa affirmed respondent's conviction. State v. Whiteside, 272 N. W. 2d 468 (1978). That court held that the right to have counsel present all appropriate defenses does not extend to using perjury, and that an attorney's duty to a client does not extend to assisting a client in committing perjury. Relying on DR 7-102(A)(4) of the Iowa Code of Professional Responsibility for Lawyers, which expressly prohibits an attorney from using perjured testimony, and Iowa Code § 721.2 (now Iowa Code § 720.3 (1985)), which criminalizes subornation of perjury, the Iowa court concluded that not only were Robinson's actions permissible, but were required. The court commended "both Mr. Robinson and Ms. Paulsen for the high ethical manner in which this matter was handled."

B

Whiteside then petitioned for a writ of habeas corpus in the United States District Court for the Southern District of Iowa. In that petition Whiteside alleged that he had been denied effective assistance of counsel and of his right to present a defense by Robinson's refusal to allow him to testify as he had proposed. The District Court denied the writ. Accepting the State trial court's factual finding that Whiteside's intended testimony would have been perjurious, it concluded that there could be no grounds for habeas relief since there is no constitutional right to present a perjured defense.

The United States Court of Appeals for the Eighth Circuit reversed and directed that the writ of habeas corpus be granted. Whiteside v. Scurr, 744 F. 2d 1323 (CA8 1984). The Court of Appeals accepted the findings of the trial judge, affirmed by the Iowa Supreme Court, that trial counsel believed with good cause that Whiteside would testify falsely and acknowledged that under Harris v. New York, 401 U.S. 222 (1971), a criminal defendant's privilege to testify in his own behalf does not include a right to commit perjury. Nevertheless, the court reasoned that an intent to commit perjury, communicated to counsel, does not alter a defendant's right to effective assistance of counsel and that Robinson's admonition to Whiteside that he would inform the court of Whiteside's perjury constituted a threat to violate the attorney's duty to preserve client confidences. According to the Court of Appeals, this threatened violation of client confidences breached the standards of effective representation set down in Strickland v. Washington, 466 U.S. 668 (1984). The court also concluded that *Strickland*'s prejudice requirement was satisfied by an implication of prejudice from the conflict between Robinson's duty of loyalty to his client and his ethical duties. A petition for rehearing en banc was denied, with Judges Gibson, Ross, Fagg, and Bowman dissenting. We granted certiorari, 471 U.S. 1014 (1985), and we reverse.

II

A

The right of an accused to testify in his defense is of relatively recent origin. Until the latter part of the preceding century, criminal defendants in this country, as at common law, were considered to be disqualified from giving sworn testimony at their own trial by reason of their interest as a party to the case. . . .

By the end of the nineteenth century, however, the disqualification was finally abolished by statute in most states and in the federal courts. . . . Although this Court has never explicitly held that a criminal defendant has a due process right to testify in his own behalf, cases in several Circuits have so held and the right has long been assumed. . . . We have also suggested that such a right exists as a corollary to the Fifth Amendment privilege against compelled testimony. . . .

B

In Strickland v. Washington, we held that to obtain relief by way of federal habeas corpus on a claim of a deprivation of effective assistance of counsel under the Sixth Amendment, the movant must establish both serious attorney error and prejudice. To show such error, it must be established that the assistance rendered by counsel was constitutionally deficient in that "counsel made errors so serious that counsel was not functioning as 'counsel' guaranteed the defendant by the Sixth Amendment." To show prejudice, it must be established that the claimed lapses in counsel's performance rendered the trial unfair so as to "undermine confidence in the outcome" of the trial. [466 U.S.] at 694.

In *Strickland*, we acknowledged that the Sixth Amendment does not require any particular response by counsel to a problem that may arise. Rather, the Sixth Amendment inquiry is into whether the attorney's conduct was "reasonably effective." To counteract the natural tendency to fault an unsuccessful defense, a court reviewing a claim of ineffective assistance must "indulge a strong presumption that counsel's conduct falls within the wide range of reasonable professional assistance." Id., at 689. In giving shape to the perimeters of this range of reasonable professional assistance, *Strickland* mandates that

> Prevailing norms of practice as reflected in American Bar Association Standards and the like, . . . are guides to determining what is reasonable, but they are only guides. Id., at 688.

Under the *Strickland* standard, breach of an ethical standard does not necessarily make out a denial of the Sixth Amendment guarantee of assistance of counsel. When examining attorney conduct, a court must be careful not to narrow the wide range of conduct acceptable under the Sixth Amendment so restrictively as to constitutionalize particular standards of professional conduct and thereby intrude into the State's proper authority to define and apply the standards of professional conduct applicable to those it admits to practice in its courts. In some future case challenging attorney conduct in the course of a state court trial, we may need to define with greater precision the weight to be given to recognized canons of ethics, the standards established by the State in statutes or professional codes, and the Sixth Amendment, in defining the proper scope and limits on that conduct. Here we need not face that question, since virtually all of the sources speak with one voice.

C

We turn next to the question presented: the definition of the range of "reasonable professional" responses to a criminal defendant client who informs counsel that he will perjure himself on the stand. We must determine whether, in this setting, Robinson's conduct fell within the wide range of professional responses to threatened client perjury acceptable under the Sixth Amendment.

In *Strickland*, we recognized counsel's duty of loyalty and his "overarching duty to advocate the defendant's cause," Ibid. Plainly, that duty is limited to legitimate, lawful conduct compatible with the very nature of a trial as a search for truth. Although counsel must take all reasonable lawful means to attain the objectives of the client, counsel is precluded from taking steps or in any way assisting the client in presenting false evidence or otherwise violating the law. This principle has consistently been recognized in most unequivocal terms by expositors of the norms of professional conduct since the first Canons of Professional Ethics were adopted by the American Bar Association in 1908. . . . 1908 Canon 32. . . . Similarly, Canon 37, adopted in 1928, explicitly acknowledges as an exception to the attorney's duty of confidentiality a client's announced attention to commit a crime:

The announced intention of a client to commit a crime is not included within the confidences which [the attorney] is bound to respect.

These principles have been carried through to contemporary codifications of an attorney's professional responsibility. . . . Indeed, both the Model Code and the Model Rules do not merely *authorize* disclosure by counsel of client perjury; they *require* such disclosure. See Rule 3.3(a)(4); DR 7-102(B)(1). . . .

These standards confirm that the legal profession has accepted that an attorney's ethical duty to advance the interests of his client is limited by an equally solemn duty to comply with the law and standards of professional conduct; it specifically ensures that the client may not use false evidence. This special duty of an attorney to prevent and disclose frauds upon the court derives from the recognition that perjury is as much a crime as tampering with witnesses or jurors by way of promises and threats, and undermines the administration of justice. . . . An attorney who aids false testimony by questioning a witness when perjurious responses can be anticipated, risks prosecution for subornation of perjury under Iowa Code § 720.3 (1985).

It is universally agreed that at a minimum the attorney's first duty when confronted with a proposal for perjurious testimony is to attempt to dissuade the client from the unlawful course of conduct. Model Rules of Professional Conduct, Rule 3.3, Comment; . . . Similarly, the Model Rules and the commentary, as well as the Code of Professional Responsibility adopted in Iowa expressly permit withdrawal from representation as an appropriate response of an attorney when the client threatens to commit perjury. Model Rules of Professional Conduct, Rule 1.16(a)(1), Rule 1.6, Comment (1983); Code of Professional Responsibility, DR 2-110(B), (C) (1980). Withdrawal of counsel when this situation arises at trial gives rise to many difficult questions including possible mistrial and claims of double jeopardy.[6]

---

6. In the evolution of the contemporary standards promulgated by the American Bar Association, an early draft reflects a compromise suggesting that when the disclosure of intended perjury is made during the course of trial, when withdrawal of counsel would raise difficult questions of a mistrial holding, counsel had the option to let the defendant take the stand but decline to affirmatively assist the presentation of perjury by traditional direct examination. Instead, counsel would stand mute while the defendant undertook to present the false version in narrative form in his own words unaided by any direct examination. This conduct was thought to be a signal at least to the presiding judge that the attorney considered the testimony to be false and was seeking to disassociate himself from that course. Additionally, counsel would not be permitted to discuss the known false testimony in closing arguments. See ABA Standards for Criminal Justice, 4-7.7 (2d ed. 1980). Most courts treating the subject rejected this approach and insisted on a more rigorous standard, see, e.g., United States v. Curtis, 742 F. 2d 1070 (CA7 1984); McKissick v. United States, 379 F. 2d 754 (CA5 1967), aff'd after remand, 398 F. 2d 342 (CA5 1968); Dodd v. Florida Bar, 118 So. 2d 17, 19 (Fla. 1960). The Eighth Circuit in this case and the Ninth Circuit have expressed approval of the "free narrative" standards. Whiteside v. Scurr, 744 F. 2d 1323, 1331 (CA8 1984); Lowery v. Cardwell, 575 F. 2d 727 (CA9 1978).

The essence of the brief *amicus* of the American Bar Association reviewing practices long accepted by ethical lawyers, is that under no circumstance may a lawyer either advocate or passively tolerate a client's giving false testimony. This, of course, is consistent with the governance of trial conduct in what we have long called "a search for truth." The suggestion sometimes made that "a lawyer must believe his client not judge him" in no sense means a lawyer can honorably be a party to or in any way give aid to presenting known perjury.

D

Considering Robinson's representation of respondent in light of these accepted norms of professional conduct, we discern no failure to adhere to reasonable professional standards that would in any sense make out a deprivation of the Sixth Amendment right to counsel. Whether Robinson's conduct is seen as a successful attempt to dissuade his client from committing the crime of perjury, or whether seen as a "threat" to withdraw from representation and disclose the illegal scheme, Robinson's representation of Whiteside falls well within accepted standards of professional conduct and the range of reasonable professional conduct acceptable under *Strickland*.

The Court of Appeals assumed for the purpose of the decision that Whiteside would have given false testimony had counsel not intervened; its opinion states,

> [W]e presume that appellant would have testified falsely. . . . Counsel's actions prevented [Whiteside] from testifying falsely. We hold that counsel's action deprived appellant of due process and effective assistance of counsel. . . .
>
> Counsel's actions also impermissibly compromised appellant's right to testify in his own defense by conditioning continued representation by counsel and confidentiality upon appellant's restricted testimony. Whiteside v. Scurr, 750 F. 2d. 713, 714-715 (CA8 1984).

While purporting to follow the Iowa's highest court "on all questions of state law," 744 F. 2d., at 1330, the Court of Appeals reached its conclusions on the basis of federal constitutional due process and right to counsel.

The Court of Appeals' holding that Robinson's "action deprived [Whiteside] of due process and effective assistance of counsel" is not supported by the record since Robinson's action, at most, deprived White-

---

The Rule finally promulgated in the current Model Rules of Professional Conduct rejects any participation or passive role whatever by counsel in allowing perjury to be presented without challenge.

side of his contemplated perjury. Nothing counsel did in any way undermined Whiteside's claim that he believed the victim was reaching for a gun. Similarly, the record gives no support for holding that Robinson's action "also impermissibly compromised [Whiteside's] right to testify in his own defense by conditioning continued representation . . . and confidentiality upon [Whiteside's] *restricted* testimony." The record in fact shows the contrary: (a) that Whiteside did testify, and (b) he was "restricted" or restrained only from testifying falsely and was aided by Robinson in developing the basis for the fear that Love was reaching for a gun. Robinson divulged no client communications until he was compelled to do so in response to Whiteside's post-trial challenge to the quality of his performance. We see this as a case in which the attorney successfully dissuaded the client from committing the crime of perjury.

Paradoxically, even while accepting the conclusion of the Iowa trial court that Whiteside's proposed testimony would have been a criminal act, the Court of Appeals held that Robinson's efforts to persuade Whiteside not to commit that crime were improper, *first*, as forcing an impermissible choice between the right to counsel and the right to testify; and *second*, as compromising client confidences because of Robinson's threat to disclose the contemplated perjury.

Whatever the scope of a constitutional right to testify, it is elementary that such a right does not extend to testifying *falsely*. . . . The paucity of authority on the subject of any such "right" may be explained by the fact that such a notion has never been responsibly advanced; the right to counsel includes no right to have a lawyer who will cooperate with planned perjury. A lawyer who would so cooperate would be at risk of prosecution for suborning perjury, and disciplinary proceedings, including suspension or disbarment.

Robinson's admonitions to his client can in no sense be said to have forced respondent into an *impermissible* choice between his right to counsel and his right to testify as he proposed for there was no *permissible* choice to testify falsely. For defense counsel to take steps to persuade a criminal defendant to testify truthfully, or to withdraw, deprives the defendant of neither his right to counsel nor the right to testify truthfully. . . . When an accused proposes to resort to perjury or to produce false evidence, one consequence is the risk of withdrawal of counsel.

On this record, the accused enjoyed continued representation within the bounds of reasonable professional conduct and did in fact exercise his right to testify; at most he was denied the right to have the assistance of counsel in the presentation of false testimony. Similarly, we can discern no breach of professional duty in Robinson's admonition to respondent that he would disclose respondent's perjury to the court. The crime of perjury in this setting is indistinguishable in substance from the crime of threatening or tampering with a witness or a juror. A defendant who informed his counsel that he was arranging to bribe or threaten witnesses or members of the jury would have no "right" to insist on counsel's assistance or silence. Counsel would not be limited to advising against that conduct. An attorney's duty of confidentiality, which totally covers the client's admission of guilt, does not extend to a client's announced plans to engage in future criminal conduct. See United States v. Clark, 289 U.S. 1, 15 (1933). In short, the responsibility of an ethical lawyer, as an officer of the court and a key component of a system of justice, dedicated to a search for truth, is essentially the same whether the client announces an intention to bribe or threaten witnesses or jurors or to commit or procure perjury. No system of justice worthy of the name can tolerate a lesser standard.

The rule adopted by the Court of Appeals, which seemingly would require an attorney to remain silent while his client committed perjury, is wholly incompatible with the established standards of ethical conduct and the laws of Iowa and contrary to professional standards promulgated by that State. The position advocated by petitioner, on the contrary, is wholly consistent with the Iowa standards of professional conduct and law, with the overwhelming majority of courts, and with codes of professional ethics. Since there has been no breach of any recognized professional duty, it follows that there can be no deprivation of the right to assistance of counsel under the *Strickland* standard. . . .

E

We hold that, as a matter of law, counsel's conduct complained of here cannot establish the prejudice required for relief under the second strand of the *Strickland* inquiry. . . .

Whether he was persuaded or compelled to desist from perjury, Whiteside has no valid claim that confidence in the result of his trial has been diminished by his desisting from the contemplated perjury. Even if we were to assume that the jury might have believed his perjury, it does not follow that Whiteside was prejudiced.

In his attempt to evade the prejudice requirement of *Strickland*, Whiteside relies on cases involving conflicting loyalties of counsel. In Cuyler v. Sullivan, 446 U.S. 335 (1980), we held that a defendant could obtain relief without pointing to a specific prejudicial default on the part of his counsel, provided it is established that the attorney was "actively represent[ing] conflicting interests." Id., at 350.

Here, there was indeed a "conflict," but of a quite different kind; it was one imposed on the attorney by the client's proposal to commit the crime of fabricating testimony without which, as he put it, "I'm dead." This is not remotely the kind of conflict of interests dealt with in Cuyler v. Sullivan. Even in that case we did not suggest that all multiple representations necessarily resulted in an active conflict rendering the representation constitutionally infirm. If a "conflict" between a client's proposal and counsel's ethical obligation gives rise to a presumption that counsel's assistance was prejudicially ineffective, every guilty criminal's conviction would be suspect if the defendant had sought to obtain an acquittal by illegal means. Can anyone doubt what practices and problems would be spawned by such a rule and what volumes of litigation it would generate?

Whiteside's attorney treated Whiteside's proposed perjury in accord with professional standards, and since Whiteside's truthful testimony could not have prejudiced the result of his trial, the Court of Appeals was in error to direct the issuance of a writ of habeas corpus and must be reversed.

Justice BRENNAN, concurring in the judgment.

This Court has no constitutional authority to establish rules of ethical conduct for lawyers practicing in the state courts. Nor does the Court enjoy any statutory grant of jurisdiction over legal ethics. . . .

Unfortunately, the Court seems unable to resist the temptation of sharing with the legal community its vision of ethical conduct. But let there be no mistake: the Court's essay regarding what constitutes the correct response to a criminal client's suggestion that he will perjure himself is pure discourse without force of law. As Justice Blackmun observes, *that* issue is a thorny one, . . . but it is not an issue presented by this case. Lawyers, judges, bar associations, students and others should understand that the problem has not now been "decided." . . .

Justice BLACKMUN, with whom Justice BRENNAN, Justice MARSHALL, and Justice STEVENS join, concurring in the judgment.

How a defense attorney ought to act when faced with a client who intends to commit perjury at trial has long been a controversial issue. But I do not believe that a federal habeas corpus case challenging a state criminal conviction is an appropriate vehicle for attempting to resolve this thorny problem. When a defendant argues that he was denied effective assistance of counsel because his lawyer dissuaded him from committing perjury, the only question properly presented to this Court is whether the lawyer's actions deprived the defendant of the fair trial which the Sixth Amendment is meant to guarantee. Since I believe that the respondent in this case suffered no injury justifying federal habeas relief, I concur in the Court's judgment. . . .

In this case, respondent has failed to show any legally cognizable prejudice. Nor, as is discussed below, is this a case in which prejudice should be presumed.

The touchstone of a claim of prejudice is an allegation that counsel's behavior did something "to deprive the defendant of a fair trial, a trial whose result is reliable." Strickland v. Washington, 466 U.S., at 687. The only effect Robinson's threat had on Whiteside's trial is that Whiteside did not testify, falsely, that he saw a gun in Love's hand. Thus, this Court must ask whether its confidence in the outcome of Whiteside's trial is in any way undermined by the knowledge that he refrained from presenting false testimony. . . .

This Court long ago noted: "All perjured relevant testimony is at war with justice, since it may produce a judgment not resting on truth. Therefore it cannot be denied that it tends to defeat the sole ultimate objective of a trial." In re Michael, 326 U.S. 224, 227 (1945). When the Court has been faced with a claim by a defendant concerning prosecutorial use of such evidence, it has "consistently held that a conviction obtained by the knowing use of perjured testimony is fundamentally unfair, and must be set aside if there is any reasonable likelihood that the false testimony could have affected the judgment of the jury" (footnote omitted). United States v. Agurs, 427 U.S. 97, 103 (1976). . . .

To the extent that Whiteside's claim rests on the assertion that he would have been acquitted had he been able to testify falsely, Whiteside claims a right the law simply does not recognize. "A defendant has no entitlement to the luck of a lawless decisionmaker, even if a lawless decision cannot be reviewed." Strickland v. Washington, 466 U.S., at 695. Since Whiteside was deprived of neither a fair trial nor any of the specific constitutional rights designed to guarantee a fair trial, he has suffered no prejudice.

The Court of Appeals erred in concluding that prejudice should have been presumed. Strickland v. Washington found such a presumption appropriate in a case where an attorney labored under "'an actual conflict of interest [that] adversely affected his . . . performance,'" id., at 692, quoting Cuyler v. Sullivan, 446 U.S., at 348. In this case, however, no actual conflict existed. I have already discussed why Whiteside had no right to Robinson's help in presenting perjured testimony. Moreover, Whiteside has identified no right to insist that Robinson keep confidential a plan to commit perjury. . . . The prior cases where this Court has reversed convictions involved conflicts that infringed a defendant's legitimate interest in vigorous protection of his constitutional rights. See, e.g., Wood v. Georgia, 450 U.S. 261, 268-271 (1981) (defense attorney paid by defendants' employer might have pursued employer's interest in litigating a test case rather than obtaining leniency for his clients by cooperating with prosecution); Glasser v. United States, 315 U.S. 60, 72-75 (1942) (defense attorney who simultaneously represented two defendants failed to object to certain potentially inadmissible evidence or to cross-examine a prosecution witness in an apparent attempt to minimize one codefendant's guilt). Here, Whiteside had no legitimate interest that conflicted with Robinson's obligations not to suborn perjury and to adhere to the Iowa Code of Professional Responsibility.

In addition, the lawyer's interest in not presenting perjured testimony was entirely consistent with Whiteside's best interest. If Whiteside had lied on the stand, he would have risked a future perjury prosecution. Moreover, his testimony would have been contradicted by the testimony of other eyewitnesses and by the fact that no gun was ever found. In light of that impeachment, the jury might have concluded that Whiteside lied as well about his lack of premeditation and thus might have convicted him of first-degree murder. And if the judge believed that Whiteside had lied, he could have taken Whiteside's perjury into account in setting the sentence. United States v. Grayson, 438 U.S. 41, 52-54 (1978). In the face of these dangers, an attorney could reasonably conclude that dissuading his client from committing perjury was in the client's best interest and comported with standards of professional responsibility. In short, Whiteside failed to show the kind of conflict that poses a danger to the values of zealous and loyal representation embodied in the Sixth Amendment. A presumption of prejudice is therefore unwarranted.

In light of respondent's failure to show any cognizable prejudice, I see no need to "grade counsel's performance." Strickland v. Washington, 466 U.S., at 697. The only federal issue in this case is whether Robinson's behavior deprived Whiteside of the effective assistance of counsel; it is not whether Robinson's behavior conformed to any particular code of legal ethics.

Whether an attorney's response to what he sees as a client's plan to commit perjury violates a defendant's Sixth Amendment rights may depend on many factors: how certain the attorney is that the proposed testimony is false, the stage of the proceedings at which the attorney discovers the plan, or the ways in which the attorney may be able to dissuade his client, to name just three. The complex interaction of factors, which is likely to vary from case to case, makes inappropriate a blanket rule that defense attorneys must reveal, or threaten to reveal, a client's anticipated perjury to the court. Except in the rarest of cases, attorneys who adopt "the role of the judge or jury to determine the facts," United States ex rel. Wilcox v. Johnson, 555 F. 2d 115, 122 (CA3 1977), pose a danger of depriving their clients of the zealous and loyal advocacy required by the Sixth Amendment.

I therefore am troubled by the Court's implicit adoption of a set of standards of professional responsibility for attorneys in state criminal proceedings. See ante, at 9-12. The States, of course, do have a compelling interest in the integrity of their criminal trials that can justify regulating the length to which an attorney may go in seeking his client's acquittal. But the American Bar Association's implicit suggestion in its brief *amicus curiae* that the Court find that the Association's Model Rules of Professional Conduct should govern an attorney's responsibilities is addressed to the wrong audience. It is for the States to decide how attorneys should conduct themselves in state criminal proceedings, and this Court's responsibility extends only to ensuring that the restrictions a State enacts do not infringe a defendant's federal constitutional rights. Thus, I would follow the suggestion made in the joint brief *amicus curiae* filed by 37 States at the certiorari stage that we allow the States to maintain their "differing approaches" to a complex ethical question. . . . The signal merit of asking first whether a defendant has shown any adverse prejudicial effect before inquiring into his attorney's performance is that it avoids unnecessary federal interference in a State's regulation of its bar. Because I conclude that the respondent in this case failed to show such an effect, I join the Court's judgment that he is not entitled to federal habeas relief.

Justice STEVENS, concurring in the judgment.

. . . [B]eneath the surface of this case there are areas of uncertainty that cannot be resolved today. A lawyer's certainty that a change in his client's recollection is a harbinger of intended perjury — as well as judicial review of such apparent certainty — should be tempered by the realization that, after reflection, the most honest witness may recall (or sincerely believe he recalls) details that he previously overlooked. Similarly, the post-trial review of a lawyer's pre-trial threat to expose perjury that had not yet been committed — and, indeed, may have been prevented by the threat — is by no means the same as review of the way in which such a threat may actually have been carried out. Thus, one can be convinced — as I am — that this lawyer's actions were a proper way to provide his client with effective representation without confronting the much more difficult questions of what a lawyer must, should, or may do after his client has given testimony that the lawyer does not believe. The answer to such questions may well be colored by the particular circumstances attending the actual event and its aftermath.

Because Justice BLACKMUN has preserved such questions for another day, and because I do not understand him to imply any adverse criticism of this lawyer's representation of his client, I join his opinion concurring in the judgment.

NOTES

1. The majority opinion in *Nix* does not formally adopt a substantive rule establishing the conditions under which lawyers practicing in federal courts are required to disclose perjury. It is, however, strongly suggestive and it remains to be seen what federal district courts will do. The situation is complicated by the fact that many district courts have local rules adopting the professional responsibility rules of the state in which they sit as their own. In a state with Model Code 7-102(B)(1) in its amended form, lawyers practicing in a federal district court that has such a local rule surely face great uncertainty after Nix v. Whiteside if

the district court has not given further guidance. Not only is there uncertainty as to the lawyer's responsibility in federal court but there is also the potentiality of diametrically opposite obligations in the state and federal court systems should the client's conduct give rise to lawsuits in both jurisdictions.

2. Model Rule 3.3(a)(4) speaks in terms of evidence "known" by the lawyer to be false. The Comment does not illuminate that term and many different definitions are possible that would expand or contract the number of situations when a lawyer is required to make a disclosure. For example, does a lawyer ever "know" about a client's false testimony for purposes of this Rule if the source of the purported knowledge is other than the client, that is, the client has not admitted perjury and has not suddenly changed the story under circumstances when the only realistic explanation is that perjury is involved? Should the standard for the lawyer's knowledge be "reasonable doubt," or something else? Note that under DR 7-102(B)(1) of the Model Code, the standard is that the lawyer receive information "clearly establishing" that fraud was committed.

3. What would have happened in *Nix* if Robinson had withdrawn when his client stated that he intended to give false testimony and a new lawyer had been appointed who did not realize that Robinson's testimony was false? Would Robinson be required or even permitted to reveal the perjury under the Model Code or Model Rules? If the answer is no, is there a reason for the dramatically different result in the actual *Nix* factual situation?

4. Note 3 raises a question discussed by Professor Freedman at p. 158. He argued that withdrawal in a situation like *Nix* is ethically "indefensible, since the identical perjured testimony will ultimately be presented," albeit via different attorneys? The commission of perjury will be the same, and it will be criminal. But isn't the ethical question "What is the role of the attorney to be in its presentation"? Or perhaps, to put it another way, do we want to create a system that invites the client to tell the lawyer the truth and then forces the lawyer to continue to represent the client who announces that he or she is going to commit perjury? However one answers the question, can it really be maintained that it is ethically "indefensible" to consider allowing an attorney to withdraw in that situation? What about DR 2-110(C)(1)(b) or even DR 4-101(C)(3)? ABA Formal Opinion 90 (1932) dealt with withdrawal by a lawyer when the defendant made admissions inconsistent with innocence. The Committee stated that since the lawyer had not disclosed to the client his intent to withdraw if he became convinced of his client's guilt, it would be improper for him to do so. One committee member expressed the view that the lawyer should decide at the outset whether to appear or not and should not reserve any right of withdrawal.

5. The issue discussed in Notes 3 and 4 was considered by the ABA

Committee on Ethics and Professional Responsibility in its Formal Opinion 268. In that Opinion, which was also referred to in Opinion 287, p. 153, the Committee dealt with the situation where X, seeking a divorce, went to Lawyer A and learned that he had not yet resided in the state long enough to be able to file a suit. Lawyer A later learned that Lawyer B had filed a suit for divorce for X in which the residence had been backdated to meet the statutory requirement. The Committee stated that Lawyer A was precluded from disclosing X's confidences to the court or to Lawyer B. This is one case where the Committee read the language of the former Canons of Ethics, which also permitted a lawyer to reveal the intention to commit a crime, as not permitting revelation of the intention to commit perjury. It is conceivable that the Committee might have regarded the case as involving knowledge of past crime, but that is doubtful because of the forthcoming perjured testimony at the hearing to come. If the Committee did mean to preclude revelation of a client's intention to commit perjury, why should a distinction be made between perjury and other crimes?

The conclusion reached by the Committee is regarded as obviously right — although the ABA opinion is not mentioned — in Dean Thomas Shaffer's, Christian Theories of Professional Responsibility, 48 S. Cal. L. Rev. 721 (1975), a piece that deserves reading for two reasons: first, it honors Louis M. Brown, a lawyer and teacher who has long been concerned with the study and teaching of preventive law; second, it attempts to deal with the larger issues of the values that are important to law and lawyers — although one might ask whether his religious value base is uniquely Christian and indeed whether his value base does not owe as much to the perceptions of social psychology as to religion.

The British have also struggled with some of the same problems. For example, the Council of the Law Society was asked to express its opinion regarding a matter in which a client requested a solicitor to suppress the fact of marriage of a decedent in order to prevent the decedent's widow from inheriting an estate and, upon his refusal, had gone to other solicitors. The Council's Professional Purposes Committee stated that the first solicitor ought to communicate the facts revealed to the client's new solicitors. The Law Society, A Guide to the Professional Conduct of Solicitors ¶9.3(3), p. 51, citing P. P. Comm. 16.5, 1969 (7350).

6. The same problem arose in a well-publicized recent fraud case involving a computer leasing company known as OPM Leasing Services Inc. The company defrauded banks of more than $210 million by obtaining loans on forged computer leases. At some point, its lawyers learned about the fraudulent loans and realized that its services had been used to obtain them. When the company assured them that those practices had ceased, it continued to represent the company, which accounted for 60% of its billings. It finally withdrew when it learned that loans it had closed following the company's disclosure were also fraud-

ulent. When asked by a lawyer at OPM's new law firm why they had withdrawn, the senior partner at the old firm, a close friend of the inquirer, stated only that termination was by mutual agreement but that the circumstances could not be discussed because of the attorney-client privilege. Before the fraud was discovered, OPM used its new law firm to close $15 million in additional fraudulent loans. See Wall Street Journal, Dec. 31, 1982, p. 1, col. 6; New York Times, Jan. 9, 1983, Magazine Section, p. 31; and Comment, 34 UCLA L. Rev. 925 (1987).

Even assuming that a confidentiality obligation existed in the first lawyer not to make public disclosure of OPM's past fraud, would not the same obligation exist in OPM's new lawyers? If that is so, is any purpose served by the result in ABA Opinion 268 other than to allow a client like OPM to deceive its new lawyers into assisting it to commit further frauds? The Comment to Rule 1.6 of the Model Rules sharpens the lawyer's dilemma. See pp. 211-213.

7. Rubin v. Florida, 490 So.2d 1001 (Fla. Ct. App. 3d Dist. 1986), petition for review denied, 501 So.2d 1283 (Fla.), cert. denied, 107 S.Ct. 3228 (1987), upheld an order of contempt imposed on a lawyer who refused to represent a defendant whom he believed was about to commit perjury. The court, noting that he was the defendant's fourth attorney in the case, had refused to allow him to withdraw and had stated that he could permit the defendant to testify in the narrative form about the matters as to which the lawyer believed he would perjure himself. The lawyer, believing that the court's solution required him to violate the applicable ethical rules, refused. In upholding the order of contempt, the court stated that the lawyer had not exhausted review of its initial order and, in any event, was adequately protected from potential discipline if he followed its order even if that order was erroneous.

8. Despite the problems with the so-called "narrative testimony" solution to the dilemma posed by the client intending to commit perjury, see p. 172, it continues to retain some appeal. The District of Columbia Court of Appeals has accepted it in proposing a much amended version of the Model Rules for adoption. See Legal Times, Sept. 12, 1988 (Special Supplement).

9. Nix v. Whiteside dealt with one constitutional issue that has been much discussed in dealing with the problem of the perjurious client, but there are others it has not resolved. Professor Freedman argues that the Fifth Amendment problem is serious and still unresolved. Client Confidences and Client Perjury: Some Unanswered Questions, 136 U. Pa. L. Rev. 1939 (1988).

Following the promulgation of the Model Rules and the Supreme Court's decision in Nix v. Whiteside, the ABA's Committee on Ethics and Professional Responsibility reconsidered its former Opinions 287 and

341 and the relevant Informal Opinion 1341 in light of those developments. Only the portion of the Opinion relating to current perjury is
printed here. The portion dealing with a lawyer's obligation upon discovering past fraud is printed in the next subsection of materials, at p.
208. We should remember, however, that the former Opinions that were
reconsidered may be relevant in a jurisdiction that has not adopted the
Model Rules if it finds their reasoning persuasive. That is to say that we
should always remember that the Opinions of the ABA committee represent only the views of the eight people who comprise that body and
are only advisory and not "law."

ABA FORMAL OPINION 87-353
(April 20, 1987)

The professional obligations of a lawyer relating to client perjury as
now defined by the Model Rules of Professional Conduct (1983), particularly in Model Rule 3.3(a) and (b), require a reconsideration of Formal
Opinion 287 (1953), which was based upon an interpretation of the earlier Canons of Professional Ethics (1908), and Informal Opinion 1314
(1975), which interpreted the predecessor Model Code of Professional
Responsibility (1969, revised 1980). Formal Opinion 287 discussed in
part the lawyer's responsibility with regard to false statements the lawyer
knows that the client has made to the tribunal. Informal Opinion 1314
dealt with the lawyer's duty when the lawyer knows of the client's intention to commit perjury.

Formal Opinion 287 . . .

In the criminal fact setting, Formal Opinion 287 is directly contrary to
the Model Rules with regard to one part of its guidance to lawyers. Briefly, the criminal defense lawyer is presented with the following three situations prior to the sentencing of the lawyer's client: (1) the judge is told
by the custodian of criminal records that the defendant has no criminal
record and the lawyer knows this information is incorrect based on his
own investigation or from his client's disclosure to him; (2) the judge
asks the defendant whether he has a criminal record and he falsely answers that he has none; (3) the judge asks the defendant's lawyer
whether his client has a criminal record.

Formal Opinion 287 concluded that in none of the above situations is
the lawyer permitted to disclose to the court the information he has concerning the client's actual criminal record. The opinion stated that such
a disclosure would be prohibited by Canon 37, which imposed a paramount duty on the lawyer to preserve the client's confidences. In situations (1) and (3) Opinion 287 is still valid under the Model Rules, since

there has been no client fraud or perjury, and, therefore, the lawyer is prohibited, under Rule 1.6, from disclosing information relating to the representation.[5] However, in situation (2) where the client has lied to the court about the client's criminal record, the conclusion of Opinion 287 that the lawyer is prohibited from disclosing the client's false statement to the court is contrary to the requirement of Model Rule 3.3. This rule imposes a duty on the lawyer, when the lawyer cannot persuade the client to rectify the perjury, to disclose the client's false statement to the tribunal for the reasons stated in the discussion of Rule 3.3 below.[7]

CHANGE IN POLICY IN MODEL RULE 3.3

Model Rule 3.3(a) and (b) represent a major policy change with regard to the lawyer's duty as stated in Formal Opinions 287 and 341 when the client testifies falsely. It is now mandatory, under these Model Rule provisions, for a lawyer, who knows the client has committed perjury, to disclose this knowledge to the tribunal if the lawyer cannot persuade the client to rectify the perjury.

The relevant provisions of Rule 3.3(a) are:

> (a) A lawyer shall not knowingly; . . .
>
> (2) fail to disclose a material fact to a tribunal when disclosure is necessary to avoid assisting a criminal or fraudulent act by the client; . . .
>
> (4) offer evidence that the lawyer knows to be false. If a lawyer has offered material evidence and comes to know of its falsity, the lawyer shall take reasonable remedial measures.

Rule 3.3(a)(2) and (4) complement each other. While (a)(4), itself does not expressly require disclosure by the lawyer to the tribunal of the client's false testimony after the lawyer has offered it and learns of its falsity, such disclosure will be the only "reasonable remedial [measure]" the lawyer will be able to take if the client is unwilling to rectify the perjury. The Comment to Rule 3.3 states that disclosure of the client's perjury to the tribunal would be required of the lawyer by (a)(4) in this situation.

---

5. Although in situation (3), where the court puts a direct question to the lawyer, the lawyer may not reveal the client's confidences, the lawyer, also, must not make any false statements of fact to the court. Formal Opinion 287 advised lawyers facing this dilemma to ask the court to excuse the lawyer from answering the question. The Committee can offer no better guidance under the Model Rules, despite the fact that such a request by the lawyer most likely will put the court on further inquiry, as Opinion 287 recognized.

7. The Comment to Rule 3.3 suggests that the lawyer may be able to avoid disclosure to the court if the lawyer can effectively withdraw. But the Committee concludes that withdrawal can rarely serve as a remedy for the client's perjury.

Although Rule 3.3(a)(2), unlike 3.3(a)(4), does not specifically refer to perjury or false evidence, it would require an irrational reading of the language: "a criminal or fraudulent act by the client," to exclude false testimony by the client. While broadly written to cover all crimes or frauds a client may commit during the course of the proceeding, Rule 3.3(a)(2), in the context of the whole of Rule 3.3, certainly includes perjury.

Since 3.3(a)(2) requires disclosure to the tribunal only when it is necessary to "avoid assisting" client perjury, the important question is what conduct of the lawyer would constitute such assistance. Certainly, the conduct proscribed in Rule 3.3(a)(4) — offering evidence the lawyer knows to be false — is included. Also, a lawyer's failure to take remedial measures, including disclosure to the court, when the lawyer knows the client has given false testimony, is included. It is apparent to the Committee that as used in Rule 3.3(a)(2), the language "assisting a criminal or fraudulent act by the client" is not limited to the criminal law concepts of aiding and abetting or subornation. Rather, it seems clear that this language is intended to guide the conduct of the lawyer as an officer of the court as a prophylactic measure to protect against client perjury contaminating the judicial process. Thus, when the lawyer knows the client has committed perjury, disclosure to the tribunal is necessary under Rule 3.3(a)(2) to avoid assisting the client's criminal act.

Furthermore, as previously indicated, contrary to Formal Opinions 287 and 341 and the exception provided in DR 7-102(B)(1) of the Model Code, the disclosure requirement of Model Rule 3.3(a)(2) and (4) is not excused because of client confidences. Rule 3.3(b) provides in pertinent part: "The duties stated in paragraph (a) . . . apply even if compliance requires disclosure of information otherwise protected by Rule 1.6." Thus, the lawyer's responsibility to disclose client perjury to the tribunal under Rule 3.3(a)(2) and (4) supersedes the lawyer's responsibility to the client under Rule 1.6.

APPLICATION TO CRIMINAL CASES — EFFECT OF
NIX V. WHITESIDE

The Comment to Rule 3.3 makes it clear that this disclosure requirement applies in both civil and criminal cases. However, the Comment states that if such disclosure by a lawyer would constitute a violation of a criminal defendant's constitutional rights to due process and effective assistance of counsel, "[t]he obligation of the advocate under these Rules is subordinate to such a constitutional requirement." Subsequent to the publishing of this Comment, however, the Supreme Court of the United States held in Nix v. Whiteside, 475 U.S. 157, (1986) that a criminal defendant is not entitled to the assistance of counsel in giving false testimony and that a lawyer who refuses such assistance, and who even threatens the client with disclosure of the perjury to the court if the client does testify falsely, has not deprived the client of effective assistance of counsel. Some states, nevertheless, may rely on their own applicable constitutional provisions and may interpret them to prohibit such a disclosure to the tribunal by defense counsel. In a jurisdiction where this kind of ruling is made, the lawyer is obligated, of course, to comply with the constitutional requirement rather than the ethical one.

As stated earlier, the obligation of a lawyer to disclose to the tribunal client perjury committed during the proceeding, which the lawyer learns about prior to the conclusion of the proceeding, represents a reversal of prior opinions of this Committee given under earlier rules of professional conduct. However, the Committee has done nothing more in this opinion than apply the ethical rule approved by the American Bar Association when it adopted Rule 3.3(a) and (b) of the Model Rules of Professional Conduct. Even so, a question may be raised whether this application is incompatible with the adversary system and the development of effective attorney-client relationships.[8]

The Committee believes it is not. Without doubt, the vitality of the adversary system, certainly in criminal cases, depends upon the ability of the lawyer to give loyal and zealous service to the client. And this, in turn, requires that the lawyer have the complete confidence of the client and be able to assure the client that the confidence will be protected and honored. However, the ethical rules of the bar which have supported these basic requirements of the adversary system have emphasized from the time they were first reduced to written form that the lawyer's duties to the client in this regard must be performed within the bounds of law.

For example, these ethical rules clearly recognize that a lawyer representing a client who admits guilt in fact, but wants to plead not guilty and put the state to its proof, may assist the client in entering such a plea and vigorously challenge the state's case at trial through cross-examination, legal motions and argument to the jury. However, neither the adversary system nor the ethical rules permit the lawyer to participate in the corruption of the judicial process by assisting the client in the introduction of evidence the lawyer knows is false. A defendant does not have the right, as part of the right to a fair trial and zealous representation by counsel, to commit perjury. And the lawyer owes no duty to the client, in providing the representation to which the client is entitled, to assist the client's perjury.

On the contrary, the lawyer, as an officer of the court, has a duty to prevent the perjury, and if the perjury has already been committed, to prevent its playing any part in the judgment of the court. This duty the lawyer owes the court is not inconsistent with any duty owed to the client.

---

8. *See* Freedman, Professional Responsibility of the Criminal Defense Lawyer: The Three Hardest Questions, 64 Mich. L. Rev. 1469 (1966).

More particularly, it is not inconsistent with the lawyer's duty to preserve the client's confidences. For that duty is based on the lawyer's need for information from the client to obtain for the client all that the law and lawful process provide. Implicit in the promise of confidentiality is its nonapplicability where the client seeks the unlawful end of corrupting the judicial process by false evidence.

It must be emphasized that this opinion does not change the professional relationship the lawyer has with the client and require the lawyer now to judge, rather than represent, the client. The lawyer's obligation to disclose client perjury to the tribunal, discussed in this opinion, is strictly limited by Rule 3.3 to the situation where the lawyer *knows* that the client has committed perjury, ordinarily based on admissions the client has made to the lawyer.[9] The lawyer's suspicions are not enough. U.S. ex rel. Wilcox v. Johnson, 555 F.2d 115, 122 (3d Cir. 1977).

INFORMAL OPINION 1314

So far, this opinion has discussed the duty of the lawyer when the lawyer learns that the client has committed perjury. The lawyer is presented with a different dilemma when, prior to trial, the client states an intention to commit perjury at trial. This was the situation addressed in Informal Opinion 1314 (1975). The Committee, in that opinion, stated that the lawyer in that situation must advise the client that the lawyer must take one of two courses of action: withdraw prior to the submission of the false testimony, or, if the client insists on testifying falsely, report to the tribunal the falsity of the testimony.

The Committee distinguished, in Informal Opinion 1314, the situation where the lawyer does not know in advance that the client intends to commit perjury. In that case, the Committee stated that when the client does commit perjury, and the lawyer later learns of it, the lawyer may not disclose the perjury to the tribunal because of the lawyer's primary duty to protect the client's confidential communications. As stated earlier in this opinion, the Committee believes that Model Rule 3.3 calls for a different course of action by the lawyer.

The duty imposed on the lawyer by Informal Opinion 1314 — when the lawyer knows in advance that the client intends to commit perjury, to advise the client that if the client insists on testifying falsely, the lawyer must disclose the client's intended perjury to the tribunal — was based on the Committee's reading of DR 7-102(A)(4), (6) and (7). These pro-

---

9. The Committee notes that some trial lawyers report that they have avoided the ethical dilemma posed by Rule 3.3 because they follow a practice of not questioning the client about the facts in the case and, therefore, never "know" that a client has given false testimony. Lawyers who engage in such practice may be violating their duties under Rule 3.3 and their obligation to provide competent representation under Rule 1.1. ABA Defense Function Standards 4-3.2(a) and (b)(1979) are also applicable.

visions prohibit a lawyer from: (1) knowingly using perjured testimony or false evidence; (2) participating in the creation or preservation of evidence the lawyer knows to be false; and (3) counseling or assisting the client in conduct the lawyer knows to be illegal or fraudulent. However, none of these prohibitions *requires* disclosure to the tribunal of any information otherwise protected by DR 4-101. Although DR 4-101(C)(3) permits a lawyer to reveal a client's stated intention to commit perjury, this exception to the lawyer's duty to preserve the client's confidences and secrets is only discretionary on the part of the lawyer.

Informal Opinion 1314 in this regard is more consistent with Model Rule 3.3(a)(2) than with any provision of the Model Code, upon which the opinion was based. However, the Committee does not believe that the mandatory disclosure requirement of this Model Rule provision is necessarily triggered when a client states an intention to testify falsely, but has not yet done so. Ordinarily, after warning the client of the consequences of the client's perjury, including the lawyer's duty to disclose it to the court, the lawyer can reasonably believe that the client will be persuaded not to testify falsely at trial. That is exactly what happened in Nix v. Whiteside. Under these circumstances, the lawyer may permit the client to testify and may examine the client in the normal manner. If the client does in fact testify falsely, the lawyer's obligation to make disclosure to the court is covered by Rule 3.3(a)(2) and (4).

In the unusual case where the lawyer does know, on the basis of the client's clearly stated intention, that the client will testify falsely at trial, and the lawyer is unable to effectively withdraw from the representation, the lawyer cannot examine the client in the usual manner. Under these circumstances, when the client has not yet committed perjury, the Committee believes that the lawyer's conduct should be guided in a way that is consistent, as much as possible, with the confidentiality protections provided in Rule 1.6, and yet not violative of Rule 3.3. This may be accomplished by the lawyer's refraining from calling the client as a witness when the lawyer knows that the only testimony the client would offer is false; or, where there is some testimony, other than the false testimony, the client can offer in the client's defense, by the lawyer's examining the client on only those matters and not on the subject matter which would produce the false testimony. Such conduct on the part of the lawyer would serve as a way for the lawyer to avoid assisting the fraudulent or criminal act of the client without having to disclose the client's confidences to the court. However, if the lawyer does not offer the client's testimony, and, on inquiry by the court into whether the client has been fully advised as to the client's right to testify, the client states a desire to testify, but is being prevented by the lawyer from testifying, the lawyer may have no other choice than to disclose to the court the client's intention to testify falsely.

This approach must be distinguished from the solution offered in the initially ABA-approved Defense Function Standard 7.7 (1971). This proposal, no longer applicable, permitted a lawyer, who could not dissuade the client from committing perjury and who could not withdraw, to call the client solely to give the client's own statement, without being questioned by the lawyer and without the lawyer's arguing to the jury any false testimony presented by the client. This "narrative" solution was offered as a model by the ABA and supported by a number of courts[11] on the assumption that a defense lawyer constitutionally could not prevent the client from testifying falsely on the client's own behalf and, therefore, would not be assisting the perjury if the lawyer did not directly elicit the false testimony and did not use it in argument to the jury.

The Committee believes that under Model Rule 3.3(a)(2) and the recent Supreme Court decision of Nix v. Whiteside, [p. 179], the lawyer can no longer rely on the narrative approach to insulate the lawyer from a charge of assisting the client's perjury. Despite differences on other issues in Nix v. Whiteside, the Justices were unanimous in concluding that a criminal defendant does not have the constitutional right to testify falsely. More recently, this ruling was made the basis of the holding by the Seventh Circuit in United States v. Henkel, 799 F.2d 369 (7th Cir. 1986) that the defendant "had no right to lie" and, therefore, was not deprived of the right to counsel when the defense lawyer refused to present the defendant's testimony which he knew was false.

C.   OTHER ASPECTS OF PERJURY AND CONFIDENTIALITY

1.   *Preparing Testimony or Inducing a Client to Commit Perjury*

PROBLEM 24

You represent plaintiff, Paul Smith, a 55-year-old grocer who is bringing suit against his insurance company to recover for damage to his store resulting from a fire. The evidence is quite clear that the fire was set. Plaintiff's theory is that the store had become a hangout for jobless teenagers who were giving it a bad name, and that plaintiff's recent efforts

---

11. See, e.g., United States v. Campbell, 616 F.2d 1151, 1152 (9th Cir.), cert. denied, 447 U.S. 910 (1980); State v. Lowery, 111 Ariz. 26, 28-29, 523 P.2d 54, 56-57 (1974).

to bar the teenagers had led one or more of them to set the fire. Defendant's theory is that plaintiff set the fire to salvage something from a failing business. The defendant has conducted lengthy depositions which have developed a modest amount of circumstantial evidence in support of its theory, but you think that, based on the evidence to date, your client is highly likely to prevail.

One problem, however, is that five years ago, a printing business in which plaintiff owned one-quarter of the stock was destroyed by fire. The rest of the stock was owned by plaintiff's father-in-law, who ran the business. The plaintiff was secretary of the corporation, but his role was largely formal and he did no other work for the corporation. There was a grand jury investigation of the fire and plaintiff was called to testify. The grand jury, however, did not return any indictments, and subsequently the corporation's insurance company paid the claim. The corporation was then liquidated, and plaintiff received in excess of $25,000 as his share of the distribution, most of that money coming from the insurance company's proceeds.

You are concerned that defendants may try to make something out of that incident if they find out about it. No relevant questions, however, were asked during discovery. You and Mr. Smith have agreed that if questions are asked at trial, you will try to have them excluded on evidentiary grounds but that if you fail, he will tell the truth. You have also advised that given the strength of Smith's case and the outcome of the grand jury investigation, the early incident should not be very harmful.

Plaintiff's case did not go well at trial. Some of his witnesses did badly and he had not done well on his own examination. On cross-examination, defense counsel suddenly started to refer to earlier events. After argument the judge overruled your objections and agreed to let the testimony in conditionally. The following dialogue then occurred on defense counsel's questioning of your client.

> *Q:* Have you ever made a claim against an insurance company or any third party on account of destruction of property by reason of fire?
>
> *A:* No.
>
> *Q:* Have you ever been a partner in a business that made such a claim?
>
> *A:* No.
>
> *Q:* Have you ever been a stockholder in a company, other than a publicly owned company whose stock is traded on a stock exchange, that made such a claim?
>
> *A:* No.

What alternatives are available to you? Which will you select?

MONROE FREEDMAN, PROFESSIONAL RESPONSIBILITY OF THE CRIMINAL DEFENSE LAWYER: THE THREE HARDEST QUESTIONS

64 Mich. L. Rev. 1469 (1966)

. . . The third question is whether it is proper to give your client legal advice when you have reason to believe that the knowledge you give him will tempt him to commit perjury. This may indeed be the most difficult problem of all, because giving such advice creates the appearance that the attorney is encouraging and condoning perjury.

If the lawyer is not certain what the facts are when he gives the advice, the problem is substantially minimized, if not eliminated. It is not the lawyer's function to prejudge his client as a perjurer. He cannot presume that the client will make unlawful use of his advice. Apart from this, there is a natural predisposition in most people to recollect facts, entirely honestly, in a way most favorable to their own interest. As Randolph Paul has observed, some witnesses are nervous, some are confused about their own interests, some try to be too smart for their own good, and some subconsciously do not want to understand what has happened to them.[20] Before he begins to remember essential facts, the client is entitled to know what his own interests are.

The above argument does not apply merely to factual questions such as whether a particular event occurred at 10:15 or at 10:45.[21] One of the most critical problems in a criminal case, as in many others, is intention. A German writer, considering the question of intention as a test of legal consequences, suggests the following situation.[22] A young man and a young woman decide to get married. Each has a thousand dollars. They decide to begin a business with these funds, and the young lady gives her money to the young man for this purpose. Was the intention to form a joint venture or a partnership? Did they intend that the young man be an agent or a trustee? Was the transaction a gift or a loan? If the couple should subsequently visit a tax attorney and discover that it is in their interest that the transaction be viewed as a gift, it is submitted that they could, with complete honesty, so remember it. On the other hand, should their engagement be broken and the young woman consult an attorney for the purpose of recovering her money, she could with equal honesty remember that her intention was to make a loan.

Assume that your client, on trial for his life in a first-degree murder

20. See Paul, supra note 9, [p. 157].
21. Even this kind of "objective fact" is subject to honest error.
22. Wurzel, Das Juristische Denken 82 (1904), translated in Fuller, Basic Contract Law 67 (1964).

case, has killed another man with a penknife but insists that the killing was in self-defense. You ask him, "Do you customarily carry the penknife in your pocket, do you carry it frequently or infrequently, or did you take it with you only on this occasion?" He replies, "Why do you ask me a question like that?" It is entirely appropriate to inform him that his carrying the knife only on this occasion, or infrequently, supports an inference of premeditation, while if he carried the knife constantly, or frequently, the inference of premeditation would be negated. Thus, your client's life may depend upon his recollection as to whether he carried the knife frequently or infrequently. Despite the possibility that the client or a third party might infer that the lawyer was prompting the client to lie, the lawyer must apprise the defendant of the significance of his answer. There is no conceivable ethical requirement that the lawyer trap his client into a hasty and ill-considered answer before telling him the significance of the question.

A similar problem is created if the client has given the lawyer incriminating information before being fully aware of its significance. For example, assume that a man consults a tax lawyer and says, "I am fifty years old. Nobody in my immediate family has lived past fifty. Therefore, I would like to put my affairs in order. Specifically, I understand that I can avoid substantial estate taxes by setting up a trust. Can I do it?" The lawyer informs the client that he can successfully avoid the estate taxes only if he lives at least three years after establishing the trust or, should he die within three years, if the trust is found not to have been created in contemplation of death. The client then might ask who decides whether the trust is in contemplation of death. After learning that the determination is made by the court, the client might inquire about the factors on which such a decision would be based.

At this point, the lawyer can do one of two things. He can refuse to answer the question, or he can inform the client that the court will consider the wording of the trust instrument and will hear evidence about any conversations which he may have or any letters he may write expressing motives other than avoidance of estate taxes. It is likely that virtually every tax attorney in the country would answer the client's question, and that no one would consider the answer unethical. However, the lawyer might well appear to have prompted his client to deceive the Internal Revenue Service and the courts, and this appearance would remain regardless of the lawyer's explicit disclaimer to the client of any intent so to prompt him. Nevertheless, it should not be unethical for the lawyer to give the advice.

In a criminal case, a lawyer may be representing a client who protests his innocence, and whom the lawyer believes to be innocent. Assume, for example, that the charge is assault with intent to kill, that the prosecution has erroneous but credible eyewitness testimony against the defendant, and that the defendant's truthful alibi witness is impeachable on the basis of several felony convictions. The prosecutor, perhaps having doubts about the case, offers to permit the defendant to plead guilty to simple assault. If the defendant should go to trial and be convicted, he might well be sent to jail for fifteen years; on a plea of simple assault, the maximum penalty would be one year, and sentence might well be suspended.

The common practice of conveying the prosecutor's offer to the defendant should not be considered unethical, even if the defense lawyer is convinced of his client's innocence. Yet the lawyer is clearly in the position of prompting his client to lie, since the defendant cannot make the plea without saying to the judge that he is pleading guilty because he is guilty. Furthermore, if the client does decide to plead guilty, it would be improper for the lawyer to inform the court that his client is innocent, thereby compelling the defendant to stand trial and take the substantial risk of fifteen years' imprisonment.

Essentially no different from the problem discussed above, but apparently more difficult, is the so-called Anatomy of a Murder situation.[24] The lawyer, who has received from his client an incriminating story of murder in the first degree, says, "If the facts are as you have stated them so far, you have no defense, and you will probably be electrocuted. On the other hand, if you acted in a blind rage, there is a possibility of saving your life. Think it over, and we will talk about it tomorrow." As in the tax case, and as in the case of the plea of guilty to a lesser offense, the lawyer has given his client a legal opinion that might induce the client to lie. This is information which the lawyer himself would have, without advice, were he in the client's position. It is submitted that the client is entitled to have this information about the law and to make his own decision as to whether to act upon it. To decide otherwise would not only penalize the less well-educated defendant, but would also prejudice the client because of his initial truthfulness in telling his story in confidence to the attorney.

III. CONCLUSION

The lawyer is an officer of the court, participating in a search for truth. Yet no lawyer would consider that he had acted unethically in pleading the statute of frauds or the statute of limitations as a bar to a just claim. Similarly, no lawyer would consider it unethical to prevent the introduction of evidence such as a murder weapon seized in violation of the fourth amendment or a truthful but involuntary confession, or to defend a guilty man on grounds of denial of a speedy trial. Such actions are permissible because there are policy considerations that at times justify frustrating the search for truth and the prosecution of a just claim.

24. See Traver, Anatomy of a Murder (1958).

Similarly, there are policies that justify an affirmative answer to the three questions that have been posed in this article. These policies include the maintenance of an adversary system, the presumption of innocence, the prosecution's burden to prove guilt beyond a reasonable doubt, the right to counsel, and the obligation of confidentiality between lawyer and client.

NOTES

1. Both Professor Freedman and Judge Frankel refer to the situation portrayed in the novel Anatomy of a Murder as illustrative. (Pp. 168 and 205). There Judge John Voelker (under the pseudonym of Robert Traver) of the Michigan Supreme Court put the following thoughts into the mind of the sympathetically portrayed defense lawyer who was the "hero" of the book at the crucial moment in the interview of his client (Traver, Anatomy of a Murder 32, 35 (1958)):

> I paused and lit a cigar. I took my time. I had reached a point where a few wrong answers to a few right questions would leave me with a client — if I took his case — whose cause was legally defenseless. Either I stopped now and begged off and let some other lawyer worry over it or I asked him the few fatal questions and let him hang himself. Or else, like any smart lawyer, I went into the Lecture. . . .
> And what is the Lecture?
> The Lecture is an ancient device that lawyers use to coach their clients so that the client won't quite know he has been coached and his lawyer can still preserve the face-saving illusion that he hasn't done any coaching. For coaching clients, like robbing them is not only frowned upon, it is downright unethical and bad, very bad. Hence the Lecture, an artful device as old as the law itself, and one used constantly by some of the nicest and most ethical lawyers in the land. "Who, me? I didn't tell him what to say," the lawyer can later comfort himself. "I merely explained the law, see." It is a good practice to scowl and shrug here and add virtuously: "That's my duty, isn't it?"
> Verily, the question, like expert lecturing, is unchallengeable.

Is the question unchallengeable?

2. Since writing the quoted article, Professor Freedman has reconsidered his response to "the third question," p. 203. He has now changed his mind with respect to two of the examples he gave — the tax case, p. 203, and the Anatomy of a Murder case, p. 205. In both examples, he now believes that the lawyer has crossed the line, into active participation in fraud in the tax case and into active participation, indeed initiation, of a perjurious defense in the Anatomy of a Murder situation. However, he does not view the lawyer's role in supplying legal information in the

penknife (p. 203) or in the gift-loan situations (p. 203) as crossing that line. Freedman, Lawyers' Ethics in an Adversary System 70-72 (1975). How do lawyers in these cases avoid treating clients as if they believed the clients were likely to commit perjury and at the same time avoid leaving their clients with the impression that they are suggesting, even though they vociferously deny it, that clients ought to remember facts in a certain way.

3. With respect to Professor Freedman's hypothetical of the man with the penknife, p. 203, note that all he claims is that it is "entirely appropriate" to inform him of the reason for asking whether he customarily carries a penknife in his pocket. Is it also "entirely appropriate" not to inform him of the reason before ascertaining the answer to the question, which, after all, is not very complicated? If so, which course would you choose, and why?

D.   PAST CRIME OR FRAUD

PROBLEM 25

a) As house counsel for a corporation, you have recently obtained a final judgment for your company in a civil matter. In connection with other business an employee shows you a document that was called for in the litigation but, it now turns out, was deliberately concealed from you and therefore not produced. The document makes it quite clear that your client should not have prevailed. The board of directors fires the employee for not following instructions about producing all relevant documents but directs you not to reveal the failure to produce. What are your alternatives and which one would you choose?

b) Suppose that the litigation had been handled exclusively by outside counsel and that you had had nothing to do with it at all. The subsequent disclosure of the document, however, is made to you. What are your alternatives when the board of directors fires the employee but directs you not to tell anyone about the failure to produce, not even outside counsel? Which one would you choose?

PROBLEM 26

In the OPM Leasing case, p. 193, Note 6, a company had obtained loans from banks using forged computer leases as collateral. Let us assume that there was only one transaction and that some months after the transaction had been completed, the law firm that had handled the transaction for the borrower discovered that its client had obtained the much needed loan with forged collateral. What should the firm do?

The lawyer's obligation with respect to disclosure of crime or fraud that has been completed also has controversial elements. We should keep in mind that there are two situations that are involved — those where the crime or fraud activity is completed in the sense that although the consequences may be continuing, there are no new ones in the offing and those where there are new consequences in the offing. Problems 25 and 26 are examples of the former situation, which is the subject matter of this subsection. The client who tells you that someone else is to be executed tomorrow for the murder he, the client, committed (Problem 30, p. 214) is an example of the latter and will be dealt with in the next subsection.

A paradigm case for observing confidentiality in our adversary system involves a client who has hired or is assigned a lawyer to defend against a charge of crime or fraud and the lawyer comes to "know," as well as a lawyer ever "knows," that the client is in fact guilty. Our adversary system is built on the premise that we want (some?) lawyers to carry on the defense, although much has been written on the difficult situation in which that puts them. See John Kaplan, Defending Guilty People, 7 U. Bridgeport L. Rev. 223 (1986) for a recent analysis. This subsection, however, does not address that problem. It addresses the rather different situation in which a lawyer discovers that a client has committed some crime of fraud in connection with a matter the lawyer handled. In the last subsection we talked about a similar situation, perjury in the course of the litigation, where the lawyer is in a position to prevent the consequences of the fraud, there perjury. In this subsection, we address the question of whether the lawyer should break a confidence in order to undo the consequences. The situation may involve either completed litigation (Problem 25) or a completed transaction (Problem 26).

The discussion of the history and proper interpretation of DR 7-102(B)(1) in the last subsection, pp. 173-177, is also highly relevant here. Indeed, the same influential ABA Opinion 287 in addition to answering an inquiry about surprise perjury also responded to an inquiry about perjury discovered after completion of the litigation. It was summarized and reconsidered in Opinion 87-353, part of which has already been excerpted at p. 195.

ABA FORMAL OPINION 87-353
April 20, 1987

Formal Opinion 287 addressed two situations: one, a civil divorce case; the other, the sentencing procedure in a criminal case. In the civil matter, the client informs his lawyer three months after the court has entered a decree for divorce in his favor that he had testified falsely about the date of his wife's desertion. A truthful statement of the date would not have established under local law any ground for divorce and would have resulted in the dismissal of the action as prematurely brought. Formal Opinion 287 states that under these circumstances, the lawyer must advise the client to inform the court of his false testimony, and that if the client refuses to do so, the lawyer must cease representing the client.[2] However, Formal Opinion 287 concluded that Canon 37 of the Canons of Professional Ethics (dealing with the lawyer's duty to not reveal the client's confidences) prohibits the lawyer from disclosing the client's perjury to the court.

In this factual situation, Model Rule 3.3 also does not permit the lawyer to disclose the client's perjury to the court, but for a significantly different reason. Contrary to Formal Opinion 287, Rule 3.3(a) and (b) require a lawyer to disclose the client's perjury to the court if other remedial measures are ineffective, even if the information is otherwise protected under Rule 1.6, which prohibits a lawyer from revealing information relating to representation of a client. However, under Rule 3.3(b), the duty to disclose continues only "to the conclusion of the proceeding. . . ." From the Comment to Rule 3.3, it would appear that the Rule's disclosure requirement was meant to apply only in those situations where the lawyer's knowledge of the client's fraud or perjury occurs prior to final judgment and disclosure is necessary to prevent the judgment from being corrupted by the client's unlawful conduct.[3] Therefore, on the facts considered by Formal Opinion 287, where the lawyer learns of the perjury after the conclusion of the proceedings — three months after the entry of the divorce decree[4] — the mandatory disclosure requirement of Rule 3.3 does not apply and Rule 1.6, therefore, precludes disclosure.

NOTE

1. The Committee does not mention one interesting feature of Opinion 287. In dealing with the conflict between confidentiality and disclosure, it addressed the wording of Canon 41, the quite similarly worded

---

2. This requirement of withdrawal from the representation stated in Formal Opinion 287 is inconsistent with Model Rule 1.16, which, under the facts posited in the Opinion, provides only for discretionary withdrawal.

3. This explanation, at least, is consistent with the distinction between information relating to continuing crime, which is not protected by the attorney-client privilege, and information relating to past crime, which is protected. See, e.g., In re Grand Jury Proceedings, 680 F.2d 1026 (5th Cir. 1982) (discussing crime/fraud exception to attorney-client privilege).

4. The Committee assumes that there were no further proceedings and that this was a final decree. This is not to say, however, that the judgment could not be set aside by the court if the court subsequently learns of the fraudulent representations of the client.

predecessor of DR 7-102(B)(1). Canon 41 provided: "When a lawyer discovers that some fraud or deception has been practiced, which has unjustly imposed upon the court or a party, he should endeavor to rectify it; at first by advising his client, and if his client refuses to forego the advantage thus unjustly gained, he should promptly inform the injured person or his counsel, so that they may take appropriate steps." Opinion 287 advised that Canon 41 did not apply in the following language. "We do not believe that Canon 41 was directed at a case such as that here presented but rather at one in which, in a civil suit, the lawyer's client has secured an improper advantage over the other through fraud or deception." That suggests the possibility that that Committee might have advised revelation of the fraud at least in Problem 25 and perhaps in Problem 26.

We have already referred to the view of Opinion 341 that the amendment of Model Code DR 7-102(B)(1) reinstated "the essence of Opinion 287." See p. 171. Given the Committee's very broad view of the effect of the amendment, it is hardly possible that that Committee thought that the possibility of disclosure in Problems 25 and 26 was part of "the essence of Opinion 287" that was being reinstated.

PROBLEM 27

The ABC Co. has been obtaining loans from Bank by using forged computer leases as collateral. The three principals of the company, who comprise the board of directors, have all participated in the fraud. The company has used an outside law firm (LF #1) to do the paperwork on these loans. Believing that its assistant general counsel and its law firm are about to discover its fraud, it transferred the assistant general counsel to its subsidiary truck leasing division, fired LF #1, and hired a new firm (LF #2) to do the continuing legal work servicing these loans and obtaining new loans. The company instructs LF #1 to return its papers and states its expectation that LF #1 is not to discuss the company's affairs with anyone, including LF #2.

a) Assume that as a consequence of the firing, LF #1's suspicions crystallize and it discovers the fraud from documents in its possession. What conversation or action may it undertake with respect to LF #2, the assistant general counsel, and the Bank to apprise them of ABC's fraudulent activities?

b) Assume that the assistant general counsel, who had not done any work concerning the loan transactions other than to engage LF #1, found out about the fraud just before she was transferred. What conversation or action may she undertake with respect to LF #1, LF #2, and the Bank to apprise them of ABC's fraudulent activities?

c) Assume that LF #2 finds out on its own about ABC's fraudulent activities in its preparatory work before even getting in touch with the Bank. What conversation or action may it undertake with LF #1, the assistant general counsel, or the Bank to apprise them of ABC's fraudulent activities?

PROBLEM 28

A friend tells Lawyer that she is about to hire Lawyer's client, Jones. Lawyer knows, because of confidential information received from Jones, that Jones is completely unsuited for that particular job. Is it a violation of Rule 1.6(a) or 1.8(b) for Lawyer to respond "I wouldn't hire Jones if I were you"?

Problems 27 and 28 are designed to illustrate the enormous difficulty in interpreting the confidentiality provisions of the Model Rules that was created by the drafting process. The Kutak Commission's final draft Model Rules specifically addressed the problem of past crime or fraud in Rule 1.6(b)(2). It reduced the mandatory requirement of the Model Code's DR 7-102(B)(1) to discretion and retained the use of the lawyer's services to further the crime or fraud as the trigger of discretionary revelation. The Comment drew the distinction between this Rule and the prohibition of Rule 1.2(d) against assisting or counseling crime or fraud by noting that the lawyer's conduct in this situation is innocent. Hence, it argued, although there should be a professional right to correct the abuse of his or her services, there should not be a professional duty. See Kutak Commission, Final Draft, Rule 1.6 and Comment thereto (June 30, 1982). The ABA House of Delegates at its February 1983 meeting in New Orleans also rejected this provision, see pp. 144-145, and simply eliminated the discretion to break a confidence in the case where a lawyer's services had been used to commit a crime or fraud. The perjury problem continued to be treated separately, see p. 179, and the Delegates retained the provision that permitted lawyers to reveal confidences to defend themselves or collect a fee. See Model Rule 1.6(b)(2) and pp. 226ff.

That solution together with its revision of Rule 1.6(b)(1), both of which had been urged by the American College of Trial Lawyers, created a storm of protest in the press and among substantial portions of the bar. In the face of very bad publicity, proponents of the revised rule urged that they had been misunderstood and that there were many avenues open to the lawyer that could lead to protection of the public against crime or fraud, including the crime and fraud that had occurred in the OPM situation, p. 193, Note 6, which was being publicized in the press at that time. In the general revision of the Comment to Rule 1.6 that was necessitated by the House of Delegates amendments in New

Orleans, the following sentence was inserted to represent these views of the American College of Trial Lawyers' representatives. Referring to the lawyer's ability to withdraw, the Comment states: "Neither this rule nor Rule 1.8(b) nor Rule 1.16(c) prevents the lawyer from giving notice of the fact of withdrawal and the lawyer may also withdraw or disaffirm any opinion, document, affirmation, or the like." This is a stunning and potentially troublemaking Comment. It was obviously inserted to take some sting out of accusations that redrafted Rule 1.6 left lawyers whose services had been used to perpetrate a crime or fraud helpless to protect themselves or the public against misuse of their services. But instead of facing the substantive problem outright and stating in the Rules that certain kinds of revelations are permissible, the revisers adopted a bizarre course. First they revised Rule 1.6 to withdraw the discretion to reveal confidential information in this situation, and then they interpreted the nearly "absolute" Rule 1.6(a) as not preventing the lawyer from broadcasting a notice of withdrawal or disaffirming representations of fact or documents or legal opinions in a way that trumpets the lawyer's suspicion of the client. On what basis is that sentence in the Comment a possible interpretation of Rule 1.6? Only on the basis, I suggest, that such notice does not violate confidentiality.

That conclusion, when it finally sinks in, will certainly come as a great surprise to many members of the bar. Indeed, as we have seen from discussion of the perjury issue, p. 151ff., most people have assumed that a similar attempt by a lawyer to withdraw from representation after client perjury during a trial often does break a confidence; the argument for many years has been whether such a breach should be permitted. If the Model Rules are to be understood as stating that public withdrawals and disaffirmations are permitted, not as exceptions to the confidentiality obligation but because they do not involve confidential information at all, then the revisers may have ended up hurting the very principle of confidentiality that they were bent on protecting.

The question to be asked is how the revisers could possibly believe that public withdrawal or disaffirmation, which must almost always be based on information relating to representation of a client, does not violate the confidentiality obligation of Rule 1.6(a). The Comment, perhaps wisely, does not address that question. The revisers probably believed that public withdrawal or disaffirmation is permissible only when the lawyer's services have been used to perpetrate a fraud or crime. But why is that so? If a public withdrawal or disaffirmation does not constitute a violation of Rule 1.6(a), even when based on information relating to the representation, why does it make any difference what the purpose of the notice was? According to the Comment, giving notice of withdrawal or disaffirmation of an opinion or fact does not violate confidentiality of information. If that is so, why does it even make a difference whose legal opinion or statement of fact is disaffirmed if the act of giving such notice doesn't violate a secret or confidence? Furthermore, the Comment permits not only disaffirming of affirmations or legal opinions or documents but also "or the like." What does that mean?

The problem, of course, is that the revisers were adamant about the form of Model Rule 1.6 but sought to modify its effect by legislating in the Comment. Thus, what should have been a straightforward exception to the confidentiality obligation in the Rule itself turns out to be an interpretation in the Comment that appears to contradict it. If the revision is taken at face value, then the above questions must be faced, and if the notices referred to in the Comment are understood as not involving breaches of confidentiality, then other kinds of notices may also not involve breaches of confidentiality either, with a consequential narrowing of the whole concept. The alternative is to do some violence to the scheme of Rules and Comments by reading the interpretive Comment as if it were an exception to the Rule. A third alternative is to reject the Comment completely as a misinterpretation of the Rule. Such a rejection would be more difficult in this case than in the usual case because so much attention was paid to the Comment and because it was sponsored by the same persons who sponsored the change in Rule 1.6. None of these solutions is particularly satisfying. The Reporter for the Kutak Commission agrees with these comments about the enormous potentiality for mischief contained in the Comment to Model Rule 1.6. See Hazard and Hodes, The Law of Lawyering 106ff (1986 Supp.). Many jurisdictions adopting the Model Rules have retained the original Kutak Commission version that would have permitted lawyers to rectify harm caused by crime or fraud in which their services were used.

E.   PAST ACTS WITH FUTURE HARMFUL CONSEQUENCES: "CONTINUING" CRIME OR FRAUD

This is yet another area that has posed great difficulties in delineating the boundaries of the confidentiality principle. In recent years, the issue has been hotly debated in both the criminal and civil context. The largest issues in the civil context have involved corporate matters, which are discussed in Chapter 5. We have already seen the issue with respect to the special situation of perjury committed by a client and discovered by his or her lawyer while the trial is still ongoing. See pp. 151ff. That discussion of the relation between DR 7-102(B)(1) and DR 4-101(C)(3) is relevant to some of the problems that follow, but the factual situation of others is quite different from that of perjury in an ongoing lawsuit. The issue also arises in other circumstances in the criminal context. Consider the following problems.

PROBLEM 29

You represent Peter Jones, who has been charged with breaking and entering and grand larceny in connection with a housebreaking and is being held on $5000 bond. Ten days ago, just before his case was scheduled to be tried, Jones disappeared. You appeared in court and reported the disappearance, stating that you had not seen or heard from him since he was released on bail and had been unable to locate him. Several times since that date, on seeing the prosecutor in court, she has asked you whether you have heard from Jones. You have replied "No."

This evening, you receive a call from Jones, whose opening statement after identifying himself is that he is in a different state (not identified), has just gotten into some further trouble, and needs a recommendation to a lawyer. How would you conduct the telephone interview with Jones? How will you respond to the prosecutor tomorrow when she asks whether you have heard from Jones?

PROBLEM 30

An elderly client has consulted you for years about the continuing harassment he has encountered from children in his neighborhood. There have been discussions with police and social workers, but the harassment has continued sporadically and your client has constantly sought your advice. One day he comes to your office and says, "Well, I finally had my turn at bat. I put a laxative in the Halloween candy I gave some of those kids last night." You know that that is a criminal offense. From another matter, you also know that there are some people who have a violent allergic reaction to that laxative. You are also aware that it is highly likely that some of the recipients have not yet eaten the candy. Assuming that your client refuses to take any remedial action, what will you do? Does it make any difference whether you are in a Model Code or a Model Rules jurisdiction?

Suppose that your client had confessed to putting cyanide in painkilling tablets in the local drugstore? What would you do?

Suppose that an employee for whom you were handling a discriminatory discharge case told you that upon leaving she had inserted a "virus" into her employer's computer program that would destroy a major part of its files in two months. What would you do?

PROBLEM 31

A sensational murder case in your home town resulted in the conviction of the defendant for murder after a trial that turned solely on a question of identification. The conviction was affirmed and efforts at collateral attack have failed. A client of yours, while seeking legal advice, has told you certain facts that have led you to conclude that he, not the defendant, was the murderer. Your conclusion has been verified by the client and some independent checking has led you to be as positive as you can be that he is telling the truth. Efforts to persuade your client to turn himself in have failed. What do you do next? Are you influenced by any of the following factors:

(a) The nature and length of the defendant's sentence — a short or long term of years; life imprisonment; death.

(b) The circumstances of the defendant's situation — i.e., whether he has a wife and children; whether he has a long criminal record, including crimes of violence.

(c) The circumstances of your client's situation — whether he has a wife and children; whether he has a long criminal record, including crimes of violence; whether he has a possible defense, such as self-defense; whether mitigating circumstances exist, such as justification.

Would your views be any different if the crime was the negligent commission of bodily harm and the sentence was 30 days in jail? Would it make a difference if the sentence were suspended?

PROBLEM 32

Late one night you receive a telephone call from a client who tells you that he is calling from his house (which is 40 miles away), that he has just had an argument with, and then killed, a friend, and that he was going to commit suicide. If you do not succeed in talking him out of his asserted intention, what should you do? (This situation was presented to an attorney in People v. Fentress, 103 Misc. 2d 179, 425 N.Y.S.2d 485 (Cty. Ct. 1980) where the court avoided resolving the confidentiality question by finding waiver. For another case with a different bizarre twist, see Colman v. Heidenreich, 269 Ind. 419, 381 N.E. 2d 866 (1978).)

Problems 31 and 32, which probably rarely occur in practice, are designed to test the limits of our belief in the principle of confidentiality. Yet Judge Arthur Powell tells us that he experienced Problem 31 in the context of a celebrated case, the trial of Leo Frank. See Frank v. Magnum, 237 U.S. 309 (1915). After the conviction of Frank had been affirmed, a client informed Powell, then a practicing attorney, that he, not Frank, had committed the murder. Powell reports that his decision not to reveal the confidential communication was eased by the commutation of Frank's sentence to life imprisonment. Shortly thereafter, Frank was lynched by a mob. See Powell, I Can Go Home Again 287-292 (2d printing 1943) and Powell, Privilege of Counsel and Confidential Communications, 6 Ga. Bar J. 333 (1944). The case returned to the newspapers years later. An eyewitness to the crime broke 69 years of silence to state he had seen the state's chief witness carrying the unconscious or dead body of the victim. Obeying threats from the "murderer" and the injunction of his mother, he had kept quiet. New York Times, Mar. 8, 1982, p. A12, col. 1. The Georgia Board of Pardons, however, at first denied a posthumous pardon to Mr. Frank because it was not possible "to decide conclusively" his guilt or innocence," id., Dec. 10, 1983, p. A10, col. 1, but later reversed itself "because the state failed to protect him and because officials failed to bring his killers to justice." Id., Mar. 12, 1986, p. A16, col. 1.

For an instance where one lawyer, knowing of his client's guilt, successfully pressed a campaign to obtain a pardon by thrusting blame on the client's wife and her mother, and another lawyer eventually thwarted the scheme by revealing what the first lawyer had told him in confidence, see Carleton Allen, R. v. Dean, 225 L.Q. Rev. 85 (1941). See also Fred Heather, Attorney-Client Confidentiality: A New Approach, 4 Hofstra L. Rev. 685 (1976) for an attempt to solve Problem 31 by providing use immunity for the information derived from the broken confidence. Will the promise of a grant of use immunity be likely to induce a guilty party to come forward?

Professor Freedman responded orally in my class to the Problem 31 hypothetical by stating that in that situation, but not in the event of life imprisonment or any lesser penalty, he would break the confidence. He has asked me to add that he supports that position with reference to the book by Professor Charles Black, Capital Punishment (1974), in which Black argues that both culturally and legally we are committed to a recognition of the "uniqueness" of death. Pp. 21-36. It should also be noted that in dealing with the similar confidence provisions of Canon 37, Henry Drinker stated: "Although Canon 37 contains no specific exception covering communications where disclosure to the authorities is essential to the public safety, such is necessarily implied." Drinker, Legal Ethics 137 (1953). The references are to bar opinions dealing with information from a foreign government with whom the United States is at war and with subversive activities committed by a client. Do you think that the Model Code and Model Rules should be construed in similar fashion?

1.   A Note on the Model Code and the Fugitive

The question of disclosure of a fugitive client's whereabouts has been discussed in several opinions of the ABA's Committee on Professional Ethics. Opinion 23 (1930) says flatly that the information should not be disclosed to the authorities even if the source of information is the client's relatives and not the client because protection of the client's interest requires that the lawyer be able to obtain this knowledge. Indeed, in this particular case, the fugitive eventually surrendered. Subsequently, in Opinion 155 (1936), the Committee, which was composed of completely different personnel from the earlier Committee, stated that the attorney was bound to disclose the whereabouts of a fugitive since the latter was guilty of a continuing wrong. "One who is actually engaged in committing a wrong can have no privileged witnesses, and public policy forbids that an attorney should assist in the commission thereof. . . . In failing to disclose his client's whereabouts as a fugitive under these circumstances the attorney would not only be aiding his client to escape trial on the charge for which he was indicted, but would likewise be aiding him in evading prosecution for the additional offense of escape." The Committee asserted that Opinion 23 was not in conflict, although both were bail-jumping (and therefore continuing-crime) cases. At the same time, in Opinion 156, the Committee stated that an attorney who learns that a client has violated the terms of his parole must try to prevent continuance of the violation and failing that, must advise the proper authorities of the client's conduct.

In its subsequent Opinion 287 (1953), the Committee stated that "[a]ny inconsistency in this connection between our decisions in Opinions 155 and 156 and that in Opinion 23 we would resolve in favor of Opinion 23." It seems clear that the Committee that wrote Opinions 155 and 156 entertained a fundamentally different view of the requirements of confidentiality from the Committees that wrote Opinions 23 and 287. Which of the policy arguments that favor each position seems stronger? Is the fugitive situation one in which lawyers and the profession are better off with a flat rule one way or the other? Or does it make a difference what kind of person the fugitive appears to be and what the crime is with which he or she has been charged? Are there other considerations to be taken into account?

The Model Code of Professional Responsibility contains a fleeting reference to the problem. DR 4-101(C) states: "A lawyer may reveal . . . (2) Confidences or secrets when permitted under Disciplinary Rules or required by law or court order." The drafters, however, have added a footnote to this subparagraph, which consists only of four quoted paragraphs from Opinions 155 and 156, giving the holdings of the Committee in those opinions. There is no further word of explanation, no reference to Opinions 23 and 287 and the apparent conflict between them and the cited opinions, and no statement that the cryptic reference is intended to undercut Opinion 287 and reestablish the position taken in Opinions 155 and 156. Footnote 1 of the Preamble and Preliminary Statement of the Model Code, by the way, states that the footnotes are intended merely to enable the reader to relate the provisions of the Model Code to the former Canons of Ethics, the opinions of the ABA Committee on Professional Ethics, and a limited number of other sources.

The ABA's Committee on Ethics and Professional Responsibility (this is the current name of that committee) made a further attempt to clarify the situation in its Informal Opinion 1141 (1970), which was decided under the provisions of the Model Code. The Committee was asked whether a lawyer who is consulted by a deserter from the armed forces has any duty to reveal the client's whereabouts. It made its response turn on the purpose of consultation and concluded that "if the fugitive comes to see a lawyer concerning his rights, the information given to the lawyer would be privileged." If, however, the visit was to secure advice as to how best to remain a fugitive, "then the lawyer is obliged:

"(a) To advise him to turn himself in; and

"(b) To refuse to represent him if he declines to do so; and

"(c) To advise him that the lawyer will reveal his whereabouts to the authorities if he persists in his illegal conduct and the matter is brought to his attention again by the client."

The Committee saw no conflict among Opinions 23, 155, and 156. "The difference between the facts dealt with in Opinion 23 on the one hand and Opinions 155 and 156 on the other, is that in the latter situation the client is under the immediate jurisdiction of the court, being out on bail." But in fact the client was out on bail in the former case too.

The Committee did not talk about "continuing crime" in Informal Opinion 1141. That exception to Canon 4 may be viewed in terms of DR 4-101(C), seeing the client's actions as the announced intention to commit the future crime of remaining a "bail jumper." The thrust of Informal Opinion 1141, however, while referring to "the continuing nature of the offense of desertion," seems almost to treat the subject as not involving that aspect of Canon 4 at all. Otherwise, whether the lawyer turns the fugitive in ought not to turn on whether the client gets in touch with the lawyer a second time. Moreover, the line drawn by the Committee between advice on legal rights and advice on remaining a fugitive suggests that its counsel to the lawyer is directed at preventing the lawyer's involvement in the crime itself, and indeed the Committee does refer to the legal rules involving aiding and abetting criminal acts, conspiracy, and becoming an accessory. Advice by the lawyer that helps the deserter remain a fugitive might well make the lawyer an accessory to the crime after, or even before, the fact and hence, in terms of the Disciplinary Rule, involve a violation of DR 1-102(A)(3). If that is the case, the advice to the lawyer to desist from such involvement is sound.

But if the lawyer follows the Committee's advice and the client nevertheless "persists in his illegal conduct" and brings the matter to the lawyer's attention again, what is the basis for the Committee's conclusion that the lawyer must turn the client in? If DR 4-101(C)(3) is not seen as the basis, does any other provision permit or require it? Must there be a statute or specific court decision in the jurisdiction before DR 4-101(C)(2) applies? Or may the lawyer or ethics committee look for, and rely on, general professional principles such as those that used to guide the lawyer exclusively before there were written canons of ethics? The Committee's solution gives the lawyer one meeting or telephone call to persuade the client to surrender, but no more. One might argue that DR 7-102(B)(1) was relevant, especially in its original version, but it is interesting to note that the Committees that considered Opinions 23, 155, 156, and Informal Opinion 1141 did not think that DR 7-102(B) or its predecessor Canon 41 was relevant to the facts presented in those cases. See also Dike v. Dike, 75 Wash. 2d 1, 448 P.2d 490 (1968), holding that the attorney-client privilege did not immunize a lawyer from responding in court to inquiries about his client's whereabouts, which he had learned through a confidential communication when his client had removed her child from its custodian in contempt of a court order; but see Brennan v. Brennan, 281 Pa. Super. 362, 422 A.2d 510 (1980), reaching the contrary conclusion in a child custody case where the trial court had not yet passed on the defendant's motion challenging its jurisdiction.

2.   The Model Rules and Past Acts with Future Harmful Consequences

Although the problem of so-called continuing crime or fraud was well known to the drafters of the Model Rules and although the Comments in an early draft equated these situations to those of wholly future conduct (see Comment to then Rule 1.5, March 28, 1979 draft), the wording of the operative Rule 1.6(b)(1) is not quite so clear. That section, which with the elimination of Section 1.6(b)(2)'s reference to crime or fraud, see p. 211, is now the only section directed to "future harm," speaks in terms of preventing the client "from committing a criminal act. . . ." In many "continuing" crime cases, the criminal act has already been committed; its consequences continue. In order for the lawyer to have discretion to reveal the confidence and prevent the harm, one must construe "committing a criminal act" to include situations where the act, although physically performed in the past, still generates future criminal bodily harms. That is certainly a possible construction and, given the close relationship between the wholly future crime and the continuing crime with future consequences, there are strong arguments for giving the words that construction. Indeed, the "committing" a criminal act language was in the earlier draft when the Comment to the section explicitly stated that "continuing" and future crime cases should be treated alike. We should, however, note one significant difference between the two situations. In the continuing crime case, revelation of the confidence is likely to reveal past wrongdoing as well, a situation not present in the wholly future crime case. If there is discretion, a lawyer may wish to take that into account in an appropriate case. But the first question to be decided is whether there is. It may be that the politics of conciliating the opposition explains the drafters' decision to remove the relevant language of the Comment, but the lawyer seeking guidance may be pardoned for expressing exasperation at the obscurity of the Model Rules in the face of a known issue. The Model Rules are even less clear than the Model Code on this point.

Since the drafting of the Model Rules, the ABA's Committee on Ethics and Professional Responsibility has sought to cast some light on Problem 29 by withdrawing Opinions 155 and 156 as being inconsistent with both the Model Code and the Model Rules. But it did no more. It did not say in what way they were inconsistent. It did not replace them. It did not make any reference to Opinion 1141.

A recent case from Pennsylvania that deals with a Problem 29 situation illustrates the difference between the attorney-client privilege and the confidentiality obligation. In Commonwealth v. Maguigan, 511 Pa. 112, 511 A.2d 1327 (1986), a contempt conviction of a lawyer for refusal to reveal the whereabouts of a fugitive in a criminal case who had jumped bail was affirmed. The court reasoned that the attorney-client privilege did not apply because the fugitive had a continuing duty to the court to notify it of his whereabouts and therefore could not be said to have a legitimate expectation of confidentiality.

The court did not address the question whether the same reasoning would apply to, say, an admission by a client that it had not filed a required tax return or other obligatory report to some state or federal agency if an investigator were to ask the lawyer an open-ended question about the filing of all required returns or reports. This may be an instance where at least some courts will perceive the lawyer as owing a different obligation to the court's law than to the legislature's law. See p. 150 for another instance where that issue was raised. It is worth noting that *Maguigan* did not involve, and the court did not address, whether the lawyer was obliged, or had discretion, voluntarily to break the obligation of confidentiality under the Disciplinary Rules if she had not been asked the question in open court.

It is also worth noting that the lawyer ordered by a court to break a confidence will not find specific permission in the Model Rules to obey the court order. The Model Rules do not replicate the exception in DR 4-101(C)(2) of the Model Code for situations when the lawyer is "required by law or court order" to reveal a confidence. Surely, any court would read such an exception into the Model Rules, especially when the court is the source of both the court order and the law of professional responsibility.

The fact situation in Problem 31 certainly will not arise, at least not in that stark fashion, very often. Yet the answer that professional rules provide for such a situation does help set the public image of those rules. Is it not stunning that although the Model Rules provide for mandatory or discretionary disclosure of confidential information in some situations, they appear to mandate silence in the situation set forth in Problem 31? It is not as if the drafters never thought of the issue. In several early drafts, there was a mandatory disclosure provision, requiring disclosure of information necessary "to prevent the client from committing an act that would seriously endanger the life or safety of a person, result in wrongful detention or incarceration of a person. . . ." (Unofficial Drafts of Aug. 20, 1979 and Sept. 21, 1979, Rule 1.5(b)(1)). Presumably the failure to mention "execution" in the second clause is explained by the fact that the drafters must have believed that that most serious consequence was covered by the first clause (although the first clause is certainly not well drafted to accomplish that result). Subsequently, however, the second clause was removed entirely and the word "criminal" was inserted before the word "act" in the first clause. However reprehensible it may be for a murderer to let an innocent person be executed for his or her crime, keeping silent (or exercising one's Fifth Amendment privilege against incrimination if called to testify) would not appear to be "murder." Would you violate the Model Rules if presented with a Problem 31 situation? Don't you believe most lawyers would believe that their own moral codes would lead them to violate the Rule, at least where an innocent person is to be executed? If so, what is the justification for presenting the profession with such a Rule?

With this background in the relationship of past wrongdoing and future harm to the confidentiality principle, consider the following dilemma in which two attorneys found themselves.

BRYCE NELSON,* ETHICAL DILEMMA: SHOULD LAWYERS TURN IN CLIENTS?

Los Angeles Times, July 2, 1974, p. 1, col. 1

PAIR FACE DISBARMENT THREAT AFTER KEEPING
TWO SLAYINGS SECRET

. . . The issue of client-attorney confidentiality received wide attention in recent days after it was disclosed that two Syracuse, N.Y., lawyers, Frank Armani and Francis Belge, had known for six months the location of the bodies of two young women who had been killed but felt legally obligated to keep silent — because they got the information from their client.

Although many legal authorities say Armani and Belge acted properly in keeping their client's information secret, the two court-appointed lawyers have found themselves battered by protests and investigations that could lead to disbarment or criminal prosecution.

*Staff writer, Los Angeles Times

"Very rarely are lawyers put to these kinds of tests," Armani commented in an interview.

The case brings into sharp focus the ethical quandary of lawyers trying to protect the confidences of a client — a problem that faces doctors, psychiatrists, accountants, ministers, social workers and journalists also.

According to legal experts, the case promises to become one of the most studied examples of the confidentiality privilege.

"Any lawyer with any guts who knew what he was doing would have done the same thing," Armani said, "but the law profession is composed of many different kinds of lawyers."

Confidentiality is a privilege more easily defended in the tranquility of a law school than in the outside world. . . .

William Hauck, father of one of the murdered girls, has filed a complaint against the lawyers with the Onondaga County Bar Assn., which has referred it to the appellate division of the State Supreme Court, which has, in turn, asked for an investigation by the State Bar Assn.

The two lawyers may well be in a fight for their professional lives, and not all their fellow lawyers support the stand they have taken.

"It's outrageous," said a leading Minneapolis attorney. "They should both be put in jail. You have to report a crime if you know about it."

But the Syracuse lawyers have their supporters too.

"The only way this New York case is different," said George P. Lynch, a leading Chicago criminal lawyer, "is that the evidence is composed of human bodies. I recognize the unappealing position the lawyers were in, but the lawyer is duty-bound to remain silent about information from his client. If you reveal such information, you should be disbarred."

The client who put Armani and Belge on this spot is Robert Garrow, a 38-year-old Syracuse mechanic who has admitted that he killed four persons in upstate New York last summer.

Garrow was arrested Aug. 9 and indicted on charges of murdering 18-year-old Philip Domblewski. The court appointed Belge and Armani as Garrow's attorneys. In his conversations with the lawyers, Garrow told of the other murders he had committed.

One was that of Alicia Hauck, 16, a Syracuse high school student who had disappeared in July; the lawyers later found her body in a Syracuse cemetery. The other murders were those of Daniel Porter, a 22-year-old Harvard student, whose body had been found on July 20, and of Susan Petz, 21, of Skokie, Ill., a Boston University journalism student who had been Porter's camping companion in the Adirondack Mountains.

Following Garrow's directions, the two lawyers found and photographed the bodies of Miss Petz and Miss Hauck — but they said nothing to authorities.

Miss Hauck's family thought she might have run away from home.

The Petz family — knowing that their daughter's companion had been killed — feared the worst.

With the knowledge that the two Syracuse lawyers represented a client charged with a killing in the Adirondacks, Earl Petz, Susan's father, went to Syracuse to talk to Belge. The lawyer has since said he felt obligated not to tell Petz anything — and didn't — adding that his silence caused him "many, many sleepless nights."

The bodies of both girls were found accidentally last winter by students.

When Garrow testified at his trial about the other three killings he said he committed, the lawyers felt they had been released from their obligation of secrecy and disclosed they had known the locations of the bodies.

Garrow was convicted of Domblewski's murder Thursday. He was sentenced Monday to the maximum penalty of 25 years to life.

Roberta Petz, mother of Susan, angrily asked for the prosecution of the two attorneys.

She said, as have several lawyers, that she could not understand why the attorneys could not have given the information to the police anonymously, so that the parents could have been spared their troubled and seemingly interminable wait for information on their daughters.

One answer, say legal scholars, is that even an anonymous disclosure, if given without the client's permission, would be a breach of lawyer-client confidentiality. In addition, evidence obtained from or near the bodies, such as fingernail scrapings or footprints, might incriminate the client.

Armani and Belge understand from personal experience the anxieties caused by a death in a family. Belge suffered the death of a 12-year-old son. And Armani's brother was lost during an Air Force reconnaissance mission over the North Sea. The body was never recovered.

"We feel for these parents," Armani said. "I know what torment my mother went through in never having my brother's body returned. We know what hell these parents were going through.

"We both have daughters the same age as the girls who were killed. . . . We just couldn't figure any other way to do it.

"You have your duty to your state, to your law and order, but my primary duty is to my client — so long as I don't jeopardize anybody's life or property. If the girl had been alive, then we would have had the duty to save her life, because life is primary. A body is a sacred thing but I couldn't give it life, and I figured somebody is going to find it."

After their client had told them about the killing last summer, it took a while for the two attorneys to find the abandoned mineshaft in which Susan Petz's body had been left.

The bodies of Miss Petz and of Miss Hauck, which were back in the woods of the Syracuse cemetery, were found months after they had been located by the lawyers but well before Garrow's disclosures in court.

One aspect of the case that has raised questions is the lawyers' attempt to plea bargain with the Hamilton County district attorney and police investigators of four other upstate New York counties.

In September, after the two lawyers had found Miss Petz's body, they offered to help the district attorney and the police solve the Petz and Hauck murders if their client, Garrow, were placed in a mental institution. The district attorney rejected the offer and went ahead with the prosecution of Garrow for the murder of Domblewski. . . .

Several leading prosecutors interviewed, however, said that the New York lawyers had acted properly both in their refusal to divulge information about the bodies and in their attempt to bargain with the prosecutor.

"I'm in complete agreement with these lawyers," said Samuel Skinner, head of the criminal division of the U.S. attorney's office in Chicago. "They operated in accordance with the highest traditions of the legal profession at a time when the profession is in great trouble." . . .

But the lawyer-client confidentiality relationship is not clear-cut, and judges and official investigating bodies sometimes have a different view from that of a defense lawyer. . . .

NOTES

1. Was it proper for the lawyers to have gone to the mineshaft where the murder victims were alleged to have been left?

2. Having found the victims, what should they have done next?

3. Did they make the issue any different by taking photographs of the victims and keeping them secret?

4. Suppose as they were leaving the mine, one lawyer noted that they had left distinctive footprints in the mud and had not replaced the boulder that blocked the entrance to the mine. Should they smooth over the footprints and replace the boulder?

5. Suppose the lawyers had learned that the authorities had received a tip that the missing victims were murdered, that their bodies had been left in a mine, and, further, that the authorities were sending a team of spelunkers on a very dangerous descent to examine a different mine. Should they say anything? Suppose they learn from the doctor of Mr. and Mrs. Petz that their lives were seriously threatened by the anxiety of not knowing what had happened? Does that make a difference? Does it make a difference whether the Model Code or the Model Rules are in effect in the jurisdiction?

6. What about the efforts of the lawyers to bargain on the basis of their knowledge? Did they need the consent of their client to do that? If

they had questions about his mental capacity, how should they have proceeded? If they had client consent and there was no incapacity, was it proper to use the knowledge of where other victims' bodies were to obtain more favorable treatment? If you were one of those lawyers, how would you attempt to bargain? What would you say? As prosecutor, how would you respond?

7. A grand jury that investigated the conduct of one of the lawyers involved in this matter declined to take any action. Boston Globe, Feb. 9, 1975, at 17, col. 1. The second lawyer was indicted by the same grand jury, not for obstruction of justice but for violation of two statutes — one requiring a decent burial to be accorded to the dead and the other requiring a report of the death of any person without medical attendance. A motion to dismiss, based on the lawyer-client privilege, was granted. People v. Belge, Index No. 75/123, New York County Court, Onondaga County (August 1, 1975). On appeal, the Appellate Division, in a brief opinion, affirmed on the basis that the attorney-client privilege "effectively shielded the defendant-attorney from his actions which would otherwise have violated the Public Health Law." The court, however, went on to observe:

> In view of the fact that the claim of absolute privilege was proffered, we note that the privilege is not all-encompassing and that in a given case there may be conflicting considerations. We believe that an attorney must protect his client's interests, but also must observe basic human standards of decency, having due regard to the need that the legal system accord justice to the interests of society and its individual members.
>
> We write to emphasize our serious concern regarding the consequences which emanate from a claim of an absolute attorney-client privilege. Because the only question presented, briefed and argued on this appeal was a legal one with respect to the sufficiency of the indictments, we limit our determination to that issue and do not reach the ethical questions underlying this case.

People v. Belge, 50 A.D.2d 1088, 376 N.Y.S.2d 771, 772 (4th Dept. 1975), aff'd, 41 N.Y.2d 60, 359 N.E.2d 377 (1976) (under the relevant jurisdictional statute court was confined to deciding whether or not the dismissal of the indictment was an abuse of discretion as a matter of law; it held that the dismissal was not).

After the Court of Appeals handed down its opinion in this case, the Committee on Professional Ethics of the New York State Bar Assn. released its opinion No. 479, which it had prepared in 1974 but withheld until the proceedings had been terminated. Aside from stating that a lawyer ought not to move a corpse even for photographic purposes, the committee upheld the ethical propriety of the lawyers' entire conduct. Indeed, the committee stated that the course of conduct was required. See New York Law Journal, March 7, 1978, p. 1, col. 4 and p. 24, col. 1.

The case is discussed in Chamberlain, Legal Ethics, 25 Buffalo L. Rev. 211 (1975). The whole story of the case, including the differences between the two lawyers for Mr. Garrow, the pressures brought to bear on them by popular disapproval of their professional conduct, and the effect of those pressures on their health and professional careers is told in Alibrandi (with Armani), Privileged Information (1984).

While we have been discussing the issue of "continuing" crime in the criminal context, the issue arises in the civil context as well, and we shall meet some of those problems in Chapter 5. For the moment consider the issue in the following context.

PROBLEM 33

Ms. Smith is a single-parent mother of three small children; she has been on welfare for several years and lives in public housing. You have been assigned to represent her in connection with a criminal assault charge arising out of an altercation at the housing project after the judge found her to be "indigent." At the initial interview, you discover that Ms. Smith has been threatened that if convicted, she will be evicted from the housing project. You also discover that she has enough part-time earnings to take her out of the indigency category, to require reduction of her welfare payments, and conceivably even to affect her entitlement to public housing. On the other hand, she seems more moved by simply trying to make ends meet than to cheat and you want to help her. She is willing to talk about straightening things out with the welfare department but not until the criminal charges that threaten her freedom and her housing have been disposed of.

May you represent her on the criminal charges? Does it depend upon whether you are being paid with public funds as assigned private counsel? Suppose you were an assigned public defender. May you begin to straighten out her housing problems? May you talk with her about her welfare problems? Could you draw a will for her?

F. DISCLOSURE OF CONFIDENCES TO COLLECT A FEE OR IN SELF-DEFENSE

One final piece in the confidentiality puzzle needs to be put in place — the exception in DR 4-101(C)(4) of the Model Code and in 1.6(b)(2) of the Model Rules that permits lawyers to reveal confidences in order to collect their fees or defend themselves against accusations based on conduct in the client's cause. Many have characterized the exception as a blatant expression of the self-protective exercise of rule-making authority by the profession. See Levine, Self-Interest or Self-Defense: Lawyer Disregard of the Attorney-Client Privilege for Profit and Protection, 5 Hofstra L. Rev. 783 (1977), for a lengthy review of DR 4-101(C)(4) and its antecedents; see also Professor Goldman's pointed and sarcastic reference to this exception as "the cardinal sin of not paying a lawyer's fee" (p. 279). The existence of the exception raises both normative and practical questions for the profession and for individual lawyers.

PROBLEM 34

You are the house counsel in Problem 25, p. 207 once again. Assume that you concluded either that you were absolutely precluded by the rules relating to fraud on a third party from disclosing the information relating to the concealed document or that you had discretion under those rules but ought not to exercise it. You are concerned, however, about your own personal liability in the event that the information should be revealed. You have no evidence that you never knew about the document at the time it should have been disclosed other than your own word and the willingness of the employee who concealed it to tell the truth. That employee is unwilling to execute an affidavit exonerating you. What action, if any, may you take under Model Code 4-101(C)(4) or Model Rule 1.6(b)(2) to protect your own interests?

MEYERHOFER v. EMPIRE FIRE & MARINE INS. CO.
497 F.2d 1190 (2d Cir. 1974), cert. denied, 419 U.S. 998 (1974)

MOORE, Circuit Judge

. . . Empire Fire and Marine Insurance Company on May 31, 1972, made a public offering of 500,000 shares of its stock, pursuant to a registration statement filed with the Securities and Exchange Commission (SEC) on March 28, 1972. The stock was offered at $16 a share. Empire's attorney on the issue was the firm of Sitomer, Sitomer & Porges. Stuart Charles Goldberg was an attorney in the firm and had done some work on the issue.

Plaintiff Meyerhofer, on or about January 11, 1973, purchased 100 shares of Empire stock at $17 a share. He alleges that as of June 5, 1973, the market price of his stock was only $7 a share — hence, he has sustained an unrealized loss of $1,000. Amd. Compl. ¶9a. Plaintiff Federman, on or about May 31, 1972, purchased 200 shares at $16 a share, 100 of which he sold for $1,363, sustaining a loss of some $237 on the stock sold and an unrealized loss of $900 on the stock retained.

On May 2, 1973, plaintiffs represented by the firm of Bernson, Hoeniger, Freitag & Abbey (the Bernson firm), on behalf of themselves and all other purchasers of Empire common stock, brought this action alleging that the registration statement and the prospectus under which the Empire stock had been issued were materially false and misleading. Thereafter, an amended complaint, dated June 5, 1973, was served. The legal theories in both were identical, namely, violations of various sections of the Securities Act of 1933, the Securities Exchange Act of 1934, Rule 10b-5, and common law negligence, fraud and deceit. Damages for all members of the class or rescission were alternatively sought.

The lawsuit was apparently inspired by a Form 10-K which Empire filed with the SEC on or about April 12, 1973. This Form revealed that "The Registration Statement under the Securities Act of 1933 with respect to the public offering of the 500,000 shares of Common Stock did not disclose the proposed $200,000 payment to the law firm as well as certain other features of the compensation arrangements between the Company [Empire] and such law firm [defendant Sitomer, Sitomer and Porges]." Later that month Empire disseminated to its shareholders a proxy statement and annual report making similar disclosures.

The defendants named were Empire, officers and directors of Empire, the Sitomer firm and its three partners, A. L. Sitomer, S. J. Sitomer and R. E. Porges, Faulkner, Dawkins & Sullivan Securities Corp., the managing underwriter, Stuart Charles Goldberg, originally alleged to have been a partner of the Sitomer firm, and certain selling stockholders of Empire shares.

On May 2, 1973, the complaint was served on the Sitomer defendants and Faulkner. No service was made on Goldberg who was then no longer associated with the Sitomer firm. However, he was advised by telephone that he had been made a defendant. Goldberg inquired of the Bernson firm as to the nature of the charges against him and was informed generally as to the substance of the complaint and in particular the lack of disclosure of the finder's fee arrangement. Thus informed, Goldberg requested an opportunity to prove his non-involvement in any such arrangement and his lack of knowledge thereof. At this stage there was unfolded the series of events which ultimately resulted in the motion and order thereon now before us on appeal.

Goldberg, after his graduation from Law School in 1966, had rather specialized experience in the securities field and had published various books and treatises on related subjects. He became associated with the Sitomer firm in November 1971. While there Goldberg worked on phases of various registration statements including Empire, although another associate was responsible for the Empire registration statement and prospectus. However, Goldberg expressed concern over what he regarded as excessive fees, the nondisclosure or inadequate disclosure thereof, and the extent to which they might include a "finder's fee," both as to Empire and other issues.

The Empire registration became effective on May 31, 1972. The excessive fee question had not been put to rest in Goldberg's mind because in middle January 1973 it arose in connection with another registration (referred to as "Glacier"). Goldberg had worked on Glacier. Little purpose will be served by detailing the events during the critical period January 18 to 22, 1973, in which Goldberg and the Sitomer partners were debating the fee disclosure problem. In summary Goldberg insisted on a full and complete disclosure of fees in the Empire and Glacier offerings. The Sitomer partners apparently disagreed and Goldberg resigned from the firm on January 22, 1973.

On January 22, 1973, Goldberg appeared before the SEC and placed before it information subsequently embodied in his affidavit dated January 26, 1973, which becomes crucial to the issues now to be considered.

Some three months later, upon being informed that he was to be included as a defendant in the impending action, Goldberg asked the Bernson firm for an opportunity to demonstrate that he had been unaware of the finder's fee arrangement which, he said, Empire and the Sitomer firm had concealed from him all along. Goldberg met with members of the Bernson firm on at least two occasions. After consulting his own attorney, as well as William P. Sullivan, Special Counsel with the Securities and Exchange Commission, Division of Enforcement, Goldberg gave plaintiffs' counsel a copy of the January 26th affidavit which he had authored more than three months earlier. He hoped that it would verify his nonparticipation in the finder's fee omission and convince the Bernson firm that he should not be a defendant. The Bernson firm was satisfied with Goldberg's explanations and, upon their motion, granted by the court, he was dropped as a defendant. After receiving Goldberg's affidavit, the Bernson firm amended plaintiffs' complaint. The amendments added more specific facts but did not change the theory or substance of the original complaint.

By motion dated June 7, 1973, the remaining defendants moved "pursuant to Canons 4 and 9 of the Code of Professional Responsibility, the Disciplinary Rules and Ethical Considerations applicable thereto, and the supervisory power of this Court" for the order of disqualification now on appeal.

By memorandum decision and order, the District Court ordered that the Bernson firm and Goldberg be barred from acting as counsel or participating with counsel for plaintiffs in this or any future action against Empire involving the transactions placed in issue in this lawsuit and from disclosing confidential information to others.

The complaint was dismissed without prejudice. The basis for the

Court's decision is the premise that Goldberg had obtained confidential information from his client Empire which, in breach of relevant ethical canons, he revealed to plaintiffs' attorneys in their suit against Empire. The Court said its decision was compelled by "the broader obligations of Canons 4 and 9."

There is no proof — not even a suggestion — that Goldberg had revealed any information, confidential or otherwise, that might have caused the instigation of the suit. To the contrary, it was not until after the suit was commenced that Goldberg learned that he was in jeopardy. The District Court recognized that the complaint had been based on Empire's — not Goldberg's — disclosures, but concluded because of this that Goldberg was under no further obligation "to reveal the information or to discuss the matter with plaintiffs' counsel."

Despite the breadth of paragraphs EC 4-4 and DR 4-101(B), DR 4-101(C) recognizes that a lawyer may reveal confidences or secrets necessary to defend himself against "an accusation of wrongful conduct." This is exactly what Goldberg had to face when, in their original complaint, plaintiffs named him as a defendant who wilfully violated the securities laws.

The charge, of knowing participation in the filing of a false and misleading registration statement, was a serious one. The complaint alleged violation of criminal statutes and civil liability computable at over four million dollars. The cost in money of simply defending such an action might be very substantial. The damage to his professional reputation which might be occasioned by the mere pendency of such a charge was an even greater cause for concern.

Under these circumstances Goldberg had the right to make an appropriate disclosure with respect to his role in the public offering. Concomitantly, he had the right to support his version of the facts with suitable evidence.

The problem arises from the fact that the method Goldberg used to accomplish this was to deliver to Mr. Abbey, a member of the Bernson firm, the thirty page affidavit, accompanied by sixteen exhibits, which he had submitted to the SEC. This document not only went into extensive detail concerning Goldberg's efforts to cause the Sitomer firm to rectify the nondisclosure with respect to Empire but even more extensive detail concerning how these efforts had been precipitated by counsel for the underwriters having come upon evidence showing that a similar nondisclosure was contemplated with respect to Glacier and their insistence that full corrective measures should be taken. Although Goldberg's description reflected seriously on his employer, the Sitomer firm and, also, in at least some degree, on Glacier, he was clearly in a situation of some urgency. Moreover, before he turned over the affidavit, he consulted both his own attorney and a distinguished practitioner of securities law, and he and Abbey made a joint telephone call to Mr. Sullivan of the SEC. Moreover, it is not clear that, in the context of this case, Canon 4 applies to anything except information gained from Empire. Finally, because of Goldberg's apparent intimacy with the offering, the most effective way for him to substantiate his story was for him to disclose the SEC affidavit. It was the fact that he had written such an affidavit at an earlier date which demonstrated that his story was not simply fabricated in response to plaintiffs' complaint.

The District Court held: "All that need be shown . . . is that during the attorney-client relationship Goldberg had access to his client's information relevant to the issues here." See Emle Industries, Inc. v. Patentex, Inc., 478 F.2d 562 (2d Cir. 1973). However, the irrebuttable presumption of *Emle* has no application to the instant circumstances because Goldberg never sought to "prosecute litigation," either as a party, compare Richardson v. Hamilton International Corp., 62 F.R.D. 413 (E.D. Pa. 1974), or as counsel for a plaintiff party. Compare T. C. Theatre Corporation v. Warner Brothers Pictures, 113 F. Supp. 265 (S.D.N.Y. 1953). At most the record discloses that Goldberg might be called as a witness for the plaintiffs but that role does not invest him with the intimacy with the prosecution of the litigation which must exist for the *Emle* presumption to attach.

In addition to finding that Goldberg had violated Canon 4, the District Court found that the relationship between Goldberg and the Bernson firm violated Canon 9 of the Code of Professional Responsibility which provides that: "EC 9-6. Every lawyer [must] strive to avoid not only professional impropriety but also the appearance of impropriety." The District Court reasoned that even though there was no evidence of bad faith on the part of either Goldberg or the Bernson firm, a shallow reading of the facts might lead a casual observer to conclude that there was an aura of complicity about their relationship. However, this provision should not be read so broadly as to eviscerate the right of self-defense conferred by DR 4-101(C)(4).

Nevertheless, Emle Industries, Inc. v. Patentex, Inc., supra, requires that a strict prophylactic rule be applied in these cases to ensure that a lawyer avoids representation of a party in a suit against a former client where there may be the appearance of a possible violation of confidence. To the extent that the District Court's order prohibits Goldberg from *representing* the interests of these or any other plaintiffs in this or similar actions, we affirm that order. We also affirm so much of the District Court's order as enjoins Goldberg from disclosing material information except on discovery or at trial.

The burden of the District Court's order did not fall most harshly on Goldberg; rather its greatest impact has been felt by Bernson, Hoeniger, Freitag & Abbey, plaintiffs' counsel, which was disqualified from participation in the case. The District Court based its holding, not on the fact that the Bernson firm showed bad faith when it received Goldberg's affidavit, but rather on the fact that it was involved in a tainted association with Goldberg because his disclosures to them inadvertently violated Canons 4 and 9 of the Code of Professional Responsibility. Because there are no violations of either of these Canons in this case, we can find no basis to hold that the relationship between Goldberg and the Bernson firm was tainted. The District Court was apparently unpersuaded by appellees' salvo of innuendo to the effect that Goldberg "struck a deal" with the Bernson firm or tried to do more than prove his innocence to them. Since its relationship with Goldberg was not tainted by violations of the Code of Professional Responsibility, there appears to be no warrant for its disqualification from participation in either this or similar actions. A fortiori there was no sound basis for disqualifying plaintiffs or dismissing the complaint. . . .

NOTES

1. Later we shall discuss more specifically the efforts by the SEC to impose rather strict disclosure requirements on attorneys in connection with matters under its jurisdiction. See pp. 287-303. At this point, consider whether Goldberg's original disclosure to the SEC was justified by DR 4-101(C)(4) or would have been justified by Model Rule 1.6(b)(2). The court did not, because it did not have to, decide that issue. Is the reasonable likelihood of future accusation of wrongful conduct sufficient to permit the revelation of confidential communications by clients? If so, was there any other method of self-protection that would have been sufficiently effective besides disclosure to the SEC? Or should an attorney be permitted to make the form of disclosure that will be most self-protective?

2. *Meyerhofer* involved revelation of confidences because of accusations of wrongful conduct by third parties over whom the client had no control. If part of our concern in Problems 14-22 and the Bodies Case involves the effect of disclosure on free communication between clients and attorneys, how is our response affected by the rather open-ended exception in DR 4-101(C)(4) as interpreted in *Meyerhofer*? How do you assess the necessity for an exception in this case as compared to the necessity in Problems 29-32?

3. The Reporter for the Model Rules, Professor Hazard, suggests that the solution sought by the "notice of withdrawal" sentence in the Comment to Model Rule Rule 1.6 may sometimes be reached through use of the self-defense exception of Rule 1.6(b)(2). His suggested reading of that section would permit it to be used in situations like Problem 34 and at the time in *Meyerhofer* when Goldberg went to the SEC. Hazard's view requires an expansive reading of the exception, but he would permit it

to be used "as a matter of self-defense, in anticipation of otherwise being charged in civil, criminal or disciplinary proceedings." Hazard and Hodes, The Law of Lawyering 119 (1987 Supplement).

4. A dramatic illustration of the use of DR 4-101(C)(4) occurred in the Watergate hearings before the Ervin Committee when Gerald Alch, former attorney for James McCord, one of the Watergate burglars, asked for and received permission to make a televised response to statements contained in his client's televised testimony that imputed highly unprofessional conduct to him. Mr. Alch's lengthy rebuttal reviewed the entire history of his relationship with Mr. McCord, including the details of the various legal defenses that were considered and those that were made — although Mr. McCord's conviction was still appealable and was in fact subsequently appealed. Mr. Alch's testimony also implied that his successor attorney engaged in unprofessional conduct in connection with his representation of Mr. McCord. See 1 Hearings before the Senate Committee on Presidential Campaign Activities, 93d Cong., 1st Sess. 294 (1973).

NOTE: Lawyers and the "Obligation" to Commit Contempt

After the Watergate break-in in 1972, G. Gordon Liddy, its mastermind, went to discuss the break-in and its consequences with Robert Mardian, who had been an Assistant Attorney General in the Internal Security Division of the Justice Department. Mardian had become campaign coordinator for the Committee for the Re-election of the President but had undertaken to act as counsel for the Committee with respect to Watergate matters. When Mr. Mardian was called to testify before the Senate's Select Committee on Presidential Campaign Activities headed by Senator Ervin, his attorney, Mr. Bress, related the circumstances under which Mr. Mardian came to testify about that conversation with Mr. Liddy before the grand jury and why he was willing to testify before the Ervin Committee notwithstanding his belief that the conversation was protected by the attorney-client privilege.

> Mr. Bress. . . . Mr. Chairman, Mr. Mardian has conferred on two occasions with the United States Attorney's office in May 1973 before his appearance before the grand jury on May 7th. In those conferences and grand jury appearance, Mr. Mardian at no time asserted any constitutional privilege he might have, and he asserts none today.
>
> He did, however, on my advice, assert the attorney-client privilege insofar as questions related to conversations he had with Mr. Liddy on June 21, 1972. But as to all other attorney-client communications with other

persons no privilege was asserted because we were satisfied that such other persons had waived the privilege. Accordingly, by prearrangement with the United States Attorney's Office, when questions were propounded before the grand jury relating to his communications with Mr. Liddy, all counsel proceeded to Judge Sirica's court on the same day and argued the matter. After taking it under advisement the court ordered the questions to be answered and this was done.

Later, Mr. Mardian spent two days conferring with the staff of this Committee on June 1 and July 14, 1973. All questions were fully answered, and he now stands ready to answer any further questions. . . .

6 Hearings before the Senate Select Committee on Presidential Campaign Activities, 93d Cong., 1st Sess. 2345 (1973).

NOTES

1. Mr. Mardian apparently instituted the proceeding before Judge Sirica that resulted in the ruling that the lawyer-client privilege did not apply, and Mr. Liddy seems not to have been a party to that proceeding. Although Judge Sirica's order may not have been appealable, it could have been tested through refusal to testify and a contempt proceeding. Was it Mardian's obligation to proceed in that fashion if his "client" Liddy requested it? Indeed, since Liddy refused to testify, was it not fairly clear that he wished Mardian to proceed in that fashion?

2. If the result of such a proceeding were a jail sentence, and no stay were forthcoming, would Mardian have an obligation to go to jail to allow Liddy's rights to be tested? For an opinion that he has such an obligation, see People v. Kor, 277 P.2d 94, 101 (Cal. Dist. Ct. App. 1954), hearing in Cal. Sup. Ct. denied, 277 P.2d 101 (1955). For an instance where a lawyer, there the Attorney General of the United States, accepted a contempt citation to preserve his client's argument, see In re Attorney General, 596 F.2d 58 (2d Cir. 1979). See also In re Klein, 776 F.2d 628, 631 n.1 (7th Cir. 1985).

G.   CONFIDENCES AMONG COCLIENTS

It would be a mistake to think that conflict of interest or confidentiality problems arise neatly packaged as such. What follows is a review problem combining elements of both the last chapter and the current chapter. It raises issues that many, if not most, law firms with multiple clients in a single matter have failed to face carefully.

PROBLEM 35

You are a new associate in a law firm. The senior partner has left you the following memorandum.

"The following sticky situation confronts me. Two years ago, H, a long-standing client of mine, asked me to review his financial situation and to prepare an estate plan for him and his wife, W. They had been married for some years; both had worked; their assets had been largely commingled; and some were being held in joint name. I interviewed H and W and together we worked out an estate plan, making use of the marital deduction, that basically left property to one another, part outright and part in trust, with remainder to their children. H has just called me and asked me to revise his will and trust, substantially reducing W's interests. H said that he has not discussed the matter with W. He asked me not to inform W of the request or of the action he proposes to take.

"Is there any problem with my complying with H's wishes? If so, what is it? What are the various alternatives that are open to me? What are the pros and cons of each alternative and which alternative do you recommend? Do you have any views as to how we should handle situations like this to avoid this kind of problem in the future?"

How do you respond to this memorandum?

There is relatively little "law" on the disclosure problem involved in Problem 35, but there are two major points of view. Both are expressed in the following Opinion.

COMMITTEE ON PROFESSIONAL ETHICS NEW YORK STATE BAR ASSOCIATION OPINION NO. 555

(Jan. 17, 1984)

QUESTION

Where a lawyer is jointly representing two clients in a matter and receives from one a confidential communication relating to the subject of the representation that, if disclosed to the other, would be disadvantageous to the first in his relationship with the second, is the lawyer required or permitted to disclose the communication to the other client?

OPINION

A and B formed a partnership and employed Lawyer L to represent them in connection with the partnership affairs. Subsequently, B, in a conversation with Lawyer L, advised Lawyer L that he was actively breaching the partnership agreement. B preceded this statement to Lawyer L with the statement that he proposed to tell Lawyer L something "in confidence." Lawyer L did not respond to that statement and did not understand that B intended to make a statement that would be of importance to A but was to be kept confidential from A. Lawyer L had not, prior thereto, advised A or B that he could not receive from one communications regarding the subject of the joint representation that would be confidential from the other. B has subsequently declined to tell A what he has told Lawyer L. Lawyer L now asks what course he may or must take with respect to disclosure to A of what B has told him and with respect to continued representation of the partners.

It is the opinion of the Committee that (i) Lawyer L may not disclose to A what B has told him, and (ii) Lawyer L must withdraw from further representation of the partners with respect to the partnership affairs.

While a partnership may be of sufficient size and character to be deemed an entity of itself, in which case the partnership rather than the partners may be deemed to be the client, the Committee views the particular situation here presented as one where the partners are joint clients of the lawyer.

The situation here presented involves two basic, and here perhaps inconsistent, duties of a lawyer. One is the duty of loyalty and the other the duty to maintain client confidences. One generally recognized aspect of the duty of loyalty is the duty of a lawyer, as a fiduciary, to impart to the client information which the lawyer possesses that is relevant to the affairs as to which the lawyer is employed and that might reasonably affect the client's conduct with respect to such affairs. Spector v. Mermelstein, 361 F. Supp. 30 (S.D.N.Y. 1972). Indeed, this is a duty owed by any agent acting in a fiduciary capacity. Restatement (Second) Agency, Section 381 (1957). But a recognized agency exception is that the duty does not extend to matters the disclosure of which would violate a duty to a third person. Id., Comment e (which states this exception expressly as applying to lawyers). Thus, generally, the lawyer has no duty (and, indeed, no right) to disclose to one client confidential information learned from, or in the course of representing, another client, at least where the information does not relate to a subject matter as to which the clients are joint clients. The Restatement (Second) Agency in Section 392 deals with the situation where the agent is jointly employed by both parties to a transaction. It states in Comment b:

> The agent, however, is under no duty to disclose, and has a duty not to disclose to one principal, confidential information given to him by the other, such as the price he is willing to pay. If the information is of such a nature that he cannot fairly give advice to one without disclosing it, he cannot properly continue to act as adviser.

Of course, a lawyer is frequently held to higher standards of ethical conduct, both as to loyalty and as to confidentiality, than other fiduciaries. Still, the Committee believes that the foregoing comment suggests the appropriate result when the two ethical duties come into direct conflict.

The duty of confidentiality is stated clearly in Canon 4, "A Lawyer Shall Preserve the Confidences and Secrets of a Client." There is, however, a widely accepted exception to this that must be examined. It is generally accepted that, when an attorney acts for two or more clients jointly, communications to the attorney from one of the clients on the subject of the joint representation are not privileged as between the clients in subsequent litigation between them. 8 Wigmore, Evidence, §2312 (McNaughton rev. 1961); Annot. 4 ALR 4th 765 (1981); Wallace v. Wallace, 216 N.Y. 28, 36 (1915).

This exception, by its very terms, applies only to the evidentiary privilege and applies only in subsequent litigation between the clients. Without any examination of the question, it has occasionally been assumed that it is applicable as well at any time during the course of the representation and even absent any controversy or litigation between the clients. See, ABA Inf. 1476, n.2 (1981); Allegaert v. Perot, 434 F. Supp. 790, 799, n.12 (S.D.N.Y. 1977); Spector v. Mermelstein, supra (semble). ABA Committee opinions in the insurer-insured situation seem implicitly so to assume since, in order to prohibit disclosure to the insurer of matters learned from the insured by the attorney hired by the insurer to defend the insured, these opinions conclude that the insured is the client. See, ABA Inf. 1476 (1981); ABA Inf. 949 (1966). Indeed, as if to underscore the significance of identifying the client, earlier opinions of the ABA Committee which were premised on the assumption that the insurer and insured were joint clients had authorized disclosure to the insurer of facts supporting non-coverage learned while representing the insured. ABA Inf. 822 (1965).

On the other hand, there are also some authorities pointing in the opposite direction. In the Comment to Rule 2.2 of the Model Rules of Professional Conduct recently approved by the American Bar Association, it is stated:

> In a common representation, the lawyer is still required both to keep each client adequately informed and to maintain confidentiality of information relating to the representation. See Rules 1.4 and 1.6. Complying with both requirements while acting as intermediary requires a delicate balance. If the balance cannot be maintained, the common representation is improper. With regard to the attorney-client privilege, the prevailing rule is that as between commonly represented clients the privilege does not attach. Hence, it must be assumed that if litigation eventuates between the clients, the privilege will not protect any such communications, and the clients should be so advised.

This Comment certainly suggests a view that, notwithstanding the lack of privilege in later litigation between joint clients, there may still be communications from one of the clients relating to the representation that must or may be kept confidential from the other during the representation. This seems also to be the assumption upon which N.Y. County 646 (1975) is grounded. In these instances, however, it is recognized that if the communication discloses a conflict between the clients with respect to the subject of the representation, or if keeping of the confidence hinders the representation, full withdrawal is mandated.

While, as noted, the Committee has found indications in both directions on the question, the committee has not found any reasoned consideration of whether, although communications on the subject of the representation from one joint client are conceded not to be privileged from the other in subsequent litigation between them, the attorney is nevertheless bound or entitled to maintain such communication from one in confidence from the other during (or even following) the representation and prior to any litigation between them. While the answer might be suggested by reviewing the underlying reasons for the litigation rule, it appears that the rare statements of those underlying reasons are themselves conflicting. Wigmore, §2312 supra, says of communications from a joint client, "Yet they are not privileged in a controversy between the two original parties, inasmuch as the common interest and employment forbade concealment from the other." This brief rationale would suggest that the confidences from each other, even during the representation, should be forbidden. On the other hand, in Valente v. Pepsico, Inc., 68 F.R.D. 361, 368 (D. Del. 1975), the court stated as respects the litigation rule:

> The source of the rule is not clear, whether based on an assumption that where an attorney serves two different clients in relation to the same matter, neither anticipates that communications will have the same degree of confidence; or, as is more likely, the court will not allow the attorney to protect the interest of one client by refusing to disclose information received from that client, to the detriment of another client or former client. The fiduciary obligations of an attorney are not served by his later selection of the interests of one client over another.

If we accept the second of these posited rationales, the general rule should be limited to subsequent litigation and not extended to preclude communications from one joint client being kept confidential from the other during the representation. If we accept the first of these posited rationales, the matter is one of reasonable anticipation of the clients, which is another way of saying that, by virtue of the relationship, a consent to disclosure as between the clients may be implied.

While the Code of Professional Responsibility fails to afford a direct answer to the issue, it does make clear that the evidentiary privilege is more limited than the ethical obligation of the lawyer to guard confidences and secrets. EC 4-4. And there certainly are times when matters as to which the lawyer may be required to testify (i.e., that are non-privileged in litigation) still probably must be kept in confidence by the lawyer *until* he is required to testify (see DR 7-102(B)).

The Committee believes that the question ultimately is whether each of the clients, by virtue of jointly employing the lawyer, impliedly agrees or consents to the lawyer's disclosing to the other all communications of each on the subject of the representation. It is the opinion of the Committee that, at least in dealing with communications to the lawyer directly from one of the joint clients, the mere joint employment is not sufficient, without more, to justify implying such consent where disclosure of the communication to the other joint client would obviously be detrimental to the communicating client.* This is not to say that such consent is never to be found. The lawyer may, at the outset of the joint representation or even perhaps at some later stage if otherwise appropriate, condition his acceptance or continuation of the joint representation upon the clients' agreement that all communications from one on the subject of the joint representation shall or may be disclosed to the other. Where one joint client is a long-time client and the other is introduced to the lawyer to be represented solely in the one joint matter, it may be appropriate for the lawyer to obtain clear consent from the new client to disclosure to the long-time client. Cf. Allegaert v. Perot, 434 F. Supp. 790 (1977). Whatever is done, the critical point is that the circumstances must clearly demonstrate that it is fair to conclude that the clients have knowingly consented to the limited non-confidentiality. Both EC 5-16 and Rule 2.2 of the Model Rules emphasize that, before undertaking a joint representation, the lawyer should explain fully to each the implications of the joint representation. Absent circumstances that indicate consent in fact, consent should not be implied.

Of course, the instant fact situation is a fortiori. Here, the client specifically in advance designated his communication as confidential, and the lawyer did not demur. Under the circumstances, the confidence must be kept.

For the reasons stated, the question posed is answered in the negative.

DISSENT

A minority of the Committee respectfully dissents. This case involves issues of far-reaching importance concerning the ethical responsibilities

---

*The fact situation presented to the Committee does not involve communications to the lawyer (or knowledge gained by the lawyer) from third parties, and this opinion does not attempt to deal with that situation. It might be that in those circumstances, different relative weighting might be given to the duty of loyalty, and implied consent more readily found.

of an attorney representing joint clients, such as a partnership, and the rights of those joint clients to their attorney's undivided loyalty and disclosure of pertinent information.

On the fact pattern described in the first paragraph of its Opinion, the majority reaches two conclusions. The first, with which we disagree, is that notwithstanding partner B's refusal to inform partner A about the matter, the attorney for the partnership, Lawyer L, may not disclose to A what he was told "in confidence" by B concerning his continuing conduct in breach of the partnership agreement. The majority's second conclusion, with which we agree, is that Lawyer L must withdraw from further representation of the partners with respect to the partnership's affairs.

In consequence, as the majority sees it, partner A is not entitled to disclosure from Lawyer L concerning the facts and reasons requiring him to withdraw as the attorney for the partnership. Indeed, Lawyer L may not tell A in general terms that a conflict of interest has arisen, because even that would amount to a disclosure based on facts imparted to him by partner B. Nor may Lawyer L disclose any of these matters to a prospective or new attorney for the partnership or for A individually. Thus as the result of B's ongoing violation of his fiduciary duty as a partner to disclose the facts to A, compounded by Lawyer L's compelled silence, partner A is left to fend for himself in a defenseless state. Without explanation, he has been deprived of the advice and experience of the partnership's attorney. He is ignorant of B's continuing breach of the partnership agreement. He and any new attorney are without the requisite knowledge to obtain and provide effective representation for himself or the partnership.

Although the majority concedes that the attorney-client privilege does not protect B's disclosure to Lawyer L, it nevertheless concludes that his lips must remain sealed until such time, if ever, he is called to testify about his conversation with B in a subsequent litigation between the parties. Testimony by L as a witness assumes A sues B after learning about B's breach from another source at some later time. But by that time it may be too late to avert irreparable harm to the partnership or to A. In any event, the passage of time may cause serious monetary damage that might have otherwise been avoided by prompt disclosure. In fact, A may never find out about B's wrongs or about B's conversation with Lawyer L.

What emerges is that partner A is the innocent and injured victim of the ethical rule announced today by the Committee, imposing silence on Lawyer L at the time of his withdrawal as attorney for the partnership. B, the wrong-doing partner, is that rule's sole beneficiary.

We do not believe that such results can be justified on the basis of the ethical responsibilities of an attorney. Rather, it is our view that proper analysis leads to the conclusion that the attorney must at least have the discretion, if not the duty in the circumstances presented, to disclose to one partner the facts imparted to him by the other partner, that gave rise to the conflict of interest necessitating the lawyer's withdrawal as attorney for the partnership.

1. We begin with the general rule of law and professional ethics that an attorney, as a fiduciary to his client, must disclose to that client all material facts known by the attorney from any source concerning the subject of the representation. In Spector v. Mermelstein, 361 F. Supp. 30 (S.D.N.Y. 1972), an attorney was held liable for his failure to disclose material information to his client. Speaking of the client's right to such disclosure, Judge Lumbard set forth the applicable principles:

> A client is entitled to all the information helpful to his cause within his attorney's command. If an attorney negligently or willfully withholds from his client information material to the client's decision to pursue a given course of action, or to abstain therefrom, then the attorney is liable for the client's losses suffered as a result of action taken without benefit of the undisclosed material facts. Material facts are those which, if known to the client, might well have caused him, acting as a reasonable man, to alter his proposed course of conduct. (361 F. Supp. at 39-40)

True, an exception to this rule exists when an attorney is not engaged in the common representation of multiple clients, but instead represents them separately. If he learns facts from one client detrimental to that client's interest and advantageous to the other client's interest, he may not disclose those facts to the other client. N.Y. State 525 (1980); N.Y. State 512 (1979); ABA 341 (1975); ABA Inf. 1476 (1981).[1] But in the absence of compelling reasons, this or any other exception to the general rule requiring disclosure to clients, should not be broadened or implied to preclude disclosure by the attorney to all his joint clients of material information he learned from one of them.

We do not find any compelling reasons here for deviating from that general rule of disclosure. To the contrary, the attorney should not be permitted to be relieved of his primary and preexisting duty of disclosure because of his subsequent agreement or unwitting acquiescence (as here) to hold information from one joint client in confidence from the other. We would do violence to the underpinnings of ethical concepts if an attorney's duty and his clients' rights could be nullified by the attor-

---

1. But see, N.Y. County 270 (1929), cited approvingly in Drinker, Legal Ethics at 95 and n.10; 134 and n.35 (1953). In that case, a client introduced a woman to his lawyer for legal advice and service, who later indicated her intention to marry that client. It was decided the lawyer was bound to advise her of prior sexual offenses by the client which were a matter of public record in earlier judicial proceedings; and that he should withdraw as her attorney.

This decision typifies an unwillingness to impose silence on the attorney (as an exception to the general duty of disclosure), beyond the needs of justifiable policy.

ney's own acts of commission or omission, however well-intentioned or inadvertent.

Given the alternative of violating the lawyer's professional obligations of disclosure or violating his consensual agreement with one of his joint clients, the choice favoring disclosure to the other joint client seems clear. Certainly this is true in the partnership context.

2. The attorney's primary and overriding duty is to the partnership and not to any individual partner. Correlatively, the partnership entity has a right to its attorney's undivided loyalty. Such rights and duties are no different than those that exist in a corporate or similar setting. As EC 5-18 provides:

> A lawyer employed or retained by a corporation or similar entity owes his allegiance to the entity and not to a stockholder, director, officer, employee, representative, or other person connected with the entity. In advising the entity, a lawyer should keep paramount its interests and his professional judgment should not be influenced by the personal desires of any person or organization.

These principles of an attorney's duty of undivided loyalty to the entity that employs him and of his duty to advise that entity uninfluenced by the desires of any person, were applied in ABA 202 (1940). In that case, it was decided that a lawyer for a trust company should disclose to its board of directors the information he learned from the executive officers of the company concerning their wrongdoing. The Committee reasoned that the trust company's board of directors was its governing body and that disclosure to them should be made "in order that they may take such action as they deem necessary to protect the trust company from the wrongful acts of its executive officers." That disclosure, the Committee added, "would be to the client itself and not to a third person."

Here, the partnership's governing body consists of both partners, and there is no basis for differentiating the duty of an attorney for a partnership from the duty of an attorney for a corporation or other business entity.[2] Whatever the form of the entity, its governing body is entitled to disclosure so that action may be taken to protect that entity's interests.

However, it may be argued that ABA 202, and the partnership analogy, are not dispositive because nothing in that opinion suggests any agreement or tacit acquiescence by the corporate attorney that he would keep any information received from the corporate officers in confidence from the board. Again we confront the issue whether the attorney's in-

---

2. In this case, we are dealing with a partnership consisting of only general partners. We leave aside questions that may arise concerning an attorney's discretion or conduct to make disclosure to limited partners in a limited partnership setting or to stockholders in a corporate setting.

tentional or unwitting conduct in receiving information confidentially, can nullify his primary and preexisting duties of undivided loyalty and disclosure to the persons or entity employing him. Again, we conclude, for the same reasons previously discussed, that the attorney cannot be relieved or excused from fulfilling those duties by his own acts of commission or omission that are inconsistent with those duties, even if that results in his breach of an express or implied agreement with one of the partners to maintain confidentiality.

In addition, EC 5-16 cautions that "before a lawyer may represent multiple clients he should explain fully to each client the implications of a common representation and should accept or continue employment only if the clients consent." One of the implications of a common representation of a partnership is the attorney's discretion and duty to disclose to all partners, material facts concerning partnership affairs which he may learn from any one of the partners. Otherwise, he may find himself in a position of conflict such as the one arising here.

Whatever may be said retrospectively concerning Lawyer L's failure to advise and obtain the consent of the partners concerning this implication of the common representation and his later inadvertent receipt of B's communication in confidence, we believe that the Committee should be prospectively announcing a firm rule favoring disclosure by an attorney to all his joint clients. In this way, attorneys undertaking common representation of multiple clients shall be warned to advise their joint clients properly during all stages of that representation, and the rights of those clients shall be protected.

3. Unquestionably, as the majority opinion concedes, when an attorney acts for joint clients, communications to him from one of the clients on the subject of the common representation are not privileged as between the clients in subsequent litigation between them. Wallace v. Wallace, 216 N.Y. 28, 36 (1915); Matter of Friedman, 64 A.D.2d 70, 84 (2d Dep't 1978); Schaeffer v. Utica Mutual Insurance Co., 248 A.D. 279, 289 (4th Dep't 1936); Liberty Mutual Insurance Company v. Engels, 41 M.2d 49, 51 (Sup. Ct. Kings Cty. 1963); Richard, Evidence §413 (10th rev. ed., 1973); 8 Wigmore, Evidence §2312 (McNaughton rev. 1961); Annot. 4 A.L.R. 4th 765 (1981).

The majority opinion goes on to label this as an "exception" to the evidentiary attorney-client privilege, contending that this exception, by its very terms, applies only in subsequent litigation between the clients. From this, it is concluded that, in the circumstances here, disclosure by the attorney is forbidden at any time before the attorney is called, if ever, to testify about the conversation in a subsequent litigation.

This anomalous result is based on the erroneous premise that the attorney's testimony is an exception to the attorney-client privilege which forbids the attorney's disclosure *to third parties* of confidential communications received from the client unless the client consents. Rather, as among joint clients, the attorney-client privilege simply does not exist with respect to communications from one of them to their common attorney. As Wigmore has explained the rationale of this rule, the common interest of the joint clients and their employment of a single attorney to represent them, "'forbade concealment by either from the other'" of any communication either of them made to the joint attorney. Hence, the attorney is free to testify. Wallace v. Wallace, 216 N.Y. 28, 36 (1915), quoting Wigmore with approval.

On the same rationale, the attorney should be free to disclose the information to all his joint clients as soon as he receives it from one of them. To conclude otherwise, that the attorney must maintain silence until such time as he is called upon to testify, is to require him, as a matter of professional ethics, to participate in a forbidden concealment from one of his joint clients for some indeterminate period of time.

Thus, in permitting disclosure by the attorney to all his joint clients, the attorney-client privilege and the attorney's ethical obligation to preserve the secrets and confidences of his clients are not being undermined in any way. Instead, a rule permitting disclosure to all joint clients reaffirms the rights of those clients to such disclosure and to their attorney's undivided loyalty.

CONCLUSION

For the reasons stated, while it is agreed that Lawyer L must withdraw from further representation of the partners with respect to the partnership affairs, it is the opinion of a minority of the Committee that Lawyer L has a duty, or at least the discretion, to disclose to partner A what partner B has told him.

NOTES

1. The majority's conclusion in Opinion 555 turned on an assessment of client expectations. It is certainly possible that in different circumstances the majority might find that the expectations looked in the direction of disclosure.

2. The fact that the majority believed that the lawyer should not reveal one coclient's confidence to the other does not necessarily mean that the lawyer who followed such advice was exempt from a malpractice action or was even exempt from a finding of ethical impropriety. The issue still remains whether the lawyer was responsible for the situation in which he found himself by reason of his failure to have an appropriate discussion about the problem of disclosure of confidences at the beginning of his relationship with his coclients.

CHAPTER 4

THE LITERATURE OF CONFIDENTIALITY AND THE ADVERSARY SYSTEM

The last 20 years have seen a vast outpouring of writing on the confidentiality obligation and the adversary system. Much of the best of this writing is cited in the footnotes of the following excerpt. Not only lawyers but philosophers have interested themselves in the obligations of lawyers to clients, the profession, and society. A focus of this writing has been whether and when, on the one hand, lawyers should be permitted or indeed required to perform what they regard as antisocial activities for their clients, and on the other hand, whether and when lawyers should be required to perform pro bono activities of the "whistleblowing" variety on their clients, and indeed on other lawyers, when ordinary citizens would not be required to do so.

At this point in the book it seems advisable to put some of the issues we have been discussing into a larger context. Some of the materials of this book, the excerpts from Wasserstrom (p. 2), Freedman (p. 153), and Frankel (p. 160) have already addressed themselves to various aspects of these issues and should be considered in connection with the materials of this chapter. The following article by Professor Pepper does not focus specifically on the confidentiality obligation. It attempts to provide a moral justification for an amoral stance by lawyers in all their roles in our system. As such, it is relevant not only to the materials we have been considering up to now but also to those that we shall consider in succeeding chapters. The article is followed by commentary on it.

STEPHEN PEPPER,* THE LAWYER'S AMORAL ETHICAL ROLE: A DEFENSE, A PROBLEM, AND SOME POSSIBILITIES†

1986 Am. B. Found. Res. J. 613

Eleven years ago Richard Wasserstrom published a provocative paper focusing attention on the moral dimension of the lawyer-client relationship.[1] In the intervening decade the topic has received a great deal of attention both in the profession and in the academy.[3] Much of Wasserstrom's exposition concerned the role-differentiated morality of the lawyer-client relationship, what he referred to as the amoral professional role. Wasserstrom was critical, but "undecided," about the value of that role. This essay is a defense of the lawyer's amoral role.

The role of all professionals, observed Wasserstrom, "is to prefer . . . the interests of client or patient" over those of other individuals. "[W]here the attorney-client relationship exists, it is often appropriate and many times even obligatory for the attorney to do things that, all other things being equal, an ordinary person need not, and should not do."[4] This remains the generally accepted understanding within the profession of a lawyer's proper function. Once a lawyer has entered into the professional relationship with a client, the notion is that conduct by the lawyer in service to the client is judged by a different moral standard than the same conduct by a layperson. Through cross-examination, a lawyer may suggest to a jury that a witness is lying when the lawyer knows the witness is telling the truth. A lawyer may draft contracts or create a corporation for a client to enable the distribution and sale of cigarettes, Saturday Night Specials, or pornography. A lawyer may draft a will for a client disinheriting children should they marry outside the faith. The traditional view is that if such conduct by the lawyer is lawful, then it is morally justifiable, even if the same conduct by a layperson is

---

*Stephen L. Pepper is professor of law at the College of Law, University of Denver, and during the 1987-88 academic year [was] visiting professor of law at the Cornell Law School. A.B. 1969, Stanford University; J.D. 1973, Yale Law School.

†This essay was the winning submission in the Association of American Law Schools 1985 "Call for Scholarly Papers" competition, and was presented at the 1986 annual meeting, where it was commented upon by Professors Andrew Kaufman and David Luban. Those comments follow . . . along with a rejoinder by Professor Pepper.

1. Wasserstrom, Lawyers as Professionals: Some Moral Issues, 5 Hum. Rts. 1 (1975).

3. E.G., G. Bellow & B. Moulton, The Lawyering Process — Ethics and Professional Responsibility (1981); M. Freedman, Lawyers' Ethics in an Adversary System (1975); G. Hazard, Ethics in the Practice of Law (1978); Schneyer, Moral Philosophy's Standard Misconception of Legal Ethics, 1984 Wis. L. Rev. 1529; Dauer & Leff, Correspondence, The Lawyer as Friend, 86 Yale L.J. 573 (1977); Fried, The Lawyer as Friend: The Moral Foundations of the Lawyer-Client Relation, 85 Yale L.J. 1060 (1976). See also sources cited *infra* note 7.

4. Wasserstrom, *supra* note 1, at 5.

morally unacceptable and even if the client's goals or means are morally unacceptable. As long as what lawyer and client do is lawful, it is the client who is morally accountable, not the lawyer.

Although this amoral role is the accepted standard within the profession, no generally accepted moral justification for it has been articulated.[5] This remains true despite heated academic discourse on the subject during the ten years following Wasserstrom's article, discourse symbolized by the question: Can a good person be a good lawyer?[6] The criticism of the amoral role has been extraordinarily diverse, ranging from economics through jurisprudence to religion.[7] The most common justification for the role is framed in the language of the "adversary system," focusing on the justifiably different roles of the advocate and the judge.[8] Part I of this essay will suggest a far broader moral justification for the amoral professional role of the lawyer, the "first-class citizenship model." Part II will address two of the most common criticisms of the amoral role. Part III poses the serious difficulty for the model created when the amoral professional role is combined with the dominant legal realist view of the law. Part IV canvasses some possibilities for ameliorating the legal realism difficulty.

I. THE FIRST-CLASS CITIZENSHIP MODEL

As an introduction to the first-class citizenship model, I would like to begin with a brief explanation of the concept of professional obligation. The very idea of a profession connotes the function of service, the notion that to some degree the professional is to subordinate his interests to the interests of those in need of his services.[9] This orientation is sug-

---

5. Prominent descriptions and justifications are found in Curtis, The Ethics of Advocacy, 4 Stan. L. Rev. 3 (1951); Fried, *supra* note 3; and Freedman, Personal Responsibility in a Professional System, 27 Catholic U.L. Rev. 191 (1978). In some respects, the justification provided here is an elaboration and modification of those presented by Freedman and Fried.

6. The question, phrased slightly differently, is the first line of Charles Fried's article, *supra* note 3, at 1060.

7. See, e.g., Luban, The Adversary System Excuse, *in* D. Luban, ed., The Good Lawyer 83 (1984) (moral philosophy); M. Frankel, Partisan Justice (1980); T. Shaffer, On Being a Christian and a Lawyer (1981) (religion); Abel, Why Does the ABA Promulgate Ethical Rules? 59 Tex. L. Rev. 639 (1981) (socioeconomic analysis); D'Amato & Eberle, Three Models of Legal Ethics, 27 St. Louis U.L.J. 761 (1983) (moral philosophy); Rhode, Why the ABA Bothers: A Functional Perspective on Professional Codes, 59 Tex. L. Rev. 689 (1981) (socioeconomic analysis); Schwartz, The Zeal of the Civil Advocate, 1983 A.B.F. Res. J. 543 (legal analysis); Simon, The Ideology of Advocacy: Procedural Justice and Professional Ethics, 1978 Wis. L. Rev. 30 (jurisprudence); Wasserstrom, *supra* note 1 (moral philosophy).

8. See, e.g., Freedman, *supra* note 3; Fuller & Randall, Professional Responsibility: Report of the Joint Conference, 44 A.B.A.J. 1159 (1958); Curtis, *supra* note 5.

9. B. Bledstein, The Culture of Professionalism 87 (1976); M. S. Larson, The Rise of Professionalism 56-63 (1977); W. E. Moore, The Professions: Roles and Rules 13-15 (1970).

gested by the following seven characteristics that define the concept of a profession.[10]

1. A profession is a means of making a living.
2. A profession is based on specialized knowledge, training, and ability, often requiring intellectual labor and many years of higher education.
3. The services rendered by the professional, based upon this foundation of knowledge and ability, are necessary to individuals at various points in their lives and are frequently of the utmost personal concern (for example, services relating to physical health, liberty, religious salvation, or psychological well-being).
4. Because of the specialized knowledge involved, the quality of the services rendered by the professional is untestable from the perspective of the layman. The individual *needs* the service but is unable to evaluate it, and therefore the individual is *vulnerable* in relation to the professional.
5. The profession holds a monopoly on a service frequently needed by individuals, and as a result wields significant economic power.
6. The profession is largely self-regulated in determining and administering the qualifications for membership and in policing professional activities.
7. Part of the self-regulation usually includes ethical prescriptions that articulate a service orientation.

The sixth and seventh characteristics are the quid pro quo for the fact that the profession has a monopoly on and is making a living from a service the public needs but cannot evaluate.

The seven characteristics add up to an inherent advantage for the professional over those in need of his services and to a pervasive economic conflict of interest between the professional and those who need (and pay for) his services. As a remedy for this unbalanced conflict, there is a primary underlying professional obligation: When the client's interest and the professional's interest conflict, the professional is to forgo his interest in favor of the client's.

The legal profession's ethical code reflects the factors and the conflict listed above. Much of the ABA's Model Code of Professional Responsibility (the governing document in over three quarters of the states) appears to be designed to enhance the economic well-being of the profession. But much of it also appears designed to put the client's interest above that of the lawyer, to protect the client from the lawyer's self-interest. It

10. These characteristics are derived from a similar definition provided by Wasserstrom, *supra* note 1, at 2 n.1. See also Bledstein, *supra* note 9, at 87; Larson, *supra* note 9, at x; Moore, *supra* note 9, at 4-22.

is this second aspect of the legal profession's ethics with which this essay is concerned. Leaving aside the "guild" provisions, the role of the professional is to serve the client ahead of himself or herself. If anything justifies the asymmetrical power and opportunity sketched in the seven definitional elements listed above, it is this underlying ethic of professionalism. This ethic alone suggests that if a moral conflict between lawyer and client develops, the lawyer should honor the client's view. But this is not the argument to be presented here. This view of the theoretical service orientation of the professions only sets the stage.

The premise with which we begin is that law is a public good available to all. Society, through its "lawmakers" — legislatures, courts, administrative agencies, and so forth — has created various mechanisms to ease and enable the private attainment of individual or group goals. The corporate form of enterprise, the contract, the trust, the will, and access to civil court to gain the use of public force for the settlement of private grievance are all vehicles of empowerment for the individual or group; all are "law" created by the collectivity to be generally available for private use. In addition to these structuring mechanisms are vast amounts of law, knowledge of which is intended to be generally available and is empowering: landlord/tenant law, labor law, OSHA, Social Security — the list can be vastly extended. Access to both forms of law increases one's ability to successfully attain goals.

The second premise is a societal commitment to the principle of individual autonomy. This premise is founded on the belief that liberty and autonomy are a moral good, that free choice is better than constraint, that each of us wishes, to the extent possible, to make our own choices rather than to have them made for us. This belief is incorporated into our legal system, which accommodates individual autonomy by leaving as much room as possible for liberty and diversity. Leaving regulatory law aside for the moment (and granting that it has grown immensely, contributing to the legalization to be mentioned below), our law is designed (1) to allow the private structuring of affairs (contracts, corporations, wills, trusts, etc.) and (2) to define conduct that is intolerable. The latter sets a floor below which one cannot go, but leaves as much room as possible above that floor for individual decision making. It may be morally wrong to manufacture or distribute cigarettes or alcohol, or to disinherit one's children for marrying outside the faith, but the generality of such decisions are left in the private realm. Diversity and autonomy are preferred over "right" or "good" conduct. The theory of our law is to leave as much room as possible for private, individual decisions concerning what is right and wrong, as opposed to public, collective decisions.

Our first premise is that law is intended to be a public good which increases autonomy. The second premise is that increasing individual autonomy is morally good. The third step is that in a highly legalized society such as ours, autonomy is often dependent upon access to the law. Put simply, first-class citizenship is dependent on access to the law. And while access to law — to the creation and use of a corporation, to knowledge of how much overtime one has to pay or is entitled to receive — is formally available to all, in reality it is available only through a lawyer. Our law is usually not simple, usually not self-executing. For most people most of the time, meaningful access to the law requires the assistance of a lawyer. Thus the resulting conclusion: First-class citizenship is frequently dependent upon the assistance of a lawyer. If the conduct which the lawyer facilitates is above the floor of the intolerable — is not unlawful — then this line of thought suggests that what the lawyer does is a social good. The lawyer is the means to first-class citizenship, to meaningful autonomy, for the client.

For the lawyer to have moral responsibility for each act he or she facilitates, for the lawyer to have a moral obligation to refuse to facilitate that which the lawyer believes to be immoral, is to substitute lawyers' beliefs for individual autonomy and diversity. Such a screening submits each to the prior restraint of the judge/facilitator and to rule by an oligarchy of lawyers. (If, in the alternative, the suggestion is that the lawyer's screening should be based not on the lawyer's personal morality, but on the lawyer's assessment of society's moral views or on guidelines spelled out in a professional code of ethics, then one has substituted collective moral decision making for individual moral decision making, contrary to the principle of autonomy. Less room has been left for private decision making through a sub rosa form of lawmaking.) If the conduct is sufficiently "bad," it would seem that it ought to be made explicitly unlawful. If it is not that bad, why subject the citizenry to the happenstance of the moral judgment of the particular lawyer to whom each has access? If making the conduct unlawful is too onerous because the law would be too vague, or it is too difficult to identify the conduct in advance, or there is not sufficient social or political concern, do we intend to delegate to the individual lawyer the authority for case-by-case legislation and policing?

An example may help. Professor Wasserstrom implies that a lawyer ought to refuse to draft a will disinheriting a child because of the child's views concerning the war in Nicaragua. "But," asks Professor Freedman, "is the lawyer's paternalism toward the client preferable — morally or otherwise — to the client's paternalism toward her children?" And, he asks further, is there any reason to substitute the diversity of lawyers' opinions on the issue of disinheritance based on political belief for the diversity of clients' opinions? Ought we to have a law on the issue? If not, why screen use of the legal device of testacy either through the diverse consciences of lawyers or through the collective conscience of the profession? And if the law is clear but contrary to the lawyer's moral beliefs, such as a tax loophole for the rich or impeachment-oriented cross-examination of the truthful witness, why allow (let alone require) that the lawyer legislate for this particular person or situation?

It is apparent that a final significant value supporting the first-class citizenship model is that of equality. If law is a public good, access to which increases autonomy, then equality of access is important. For access to the law to be filtered unequally through the disparate moral views of each individual's lawyer does not appear to be justifiable. Even given the current and perhaps permanent fact of unequal access to the law, it does not make sense to compound that inequality with another. If access to a lawyer is achieved (through private allocation of one's means, public provision, or the lawyer's — or profession's — choice to provide it), should the extent of that access depend upon individual lawyer conscience? The values of autonomy and equality suggest that it should not; the client's conscience should be superior to the lawyer's. One of the unpleasant concomitants of the view that a lawyer should be morally responsible for all that she does is the resulting inequality: unfiltered access to the law is then available only to those who are legally sophisticated or to those able to educate themselves sufficiently for access to the law, while those less sophisticated — usually those less educated — are left with no access or with access that subjects their use of the law to the moral judgment and veto of the lawyer.

II. The Critique and a Response

A. THE ECONOMIC INEQUALITY CRITICISM

The foregoing quickly leads to the observation that law is a public good in theory but not in fact, and that one of the key premises justifying the first-class citizenship model is therefore false. Like almost everything else in our society, access to law is rationed through the market — in this case, the market for lawyers' services. Thus, the rich have disproportionate access over the poor, and this is particularly unacceptable given the public nature of law and its implementing relationship to individual autonomy and first-class citizenship. This is the focus of the first criticism of the amoral role: it would be justified if everyone had access to "first-class citizenship" through a lawyer, but everyone does not. The drastic and fundamental inequality of means in America vitiates the moral justification for an amoral professional ethic for lawyers.

Granting the truth of economic inequality does not, however, mean that the amoral role is a bad role, or that the lawyer currently fulfilling the role cannot be a good person. An analogous criticism might be made of the grocer and the housing contractor. Although food and shelter are (in our system) not public goods, they are more fundamentally enabling to autonomy than is law. Yet there is much less disquiet over the moral role of the grocer, housing contractor, or landlord than that of the lawyer. We live in a primarily market system, not a primarily socialist system, and the contemporary problem in defining lawyers' ethics is likely to have to be answered in this market context. Lawyers cannot magically socialize the economy or legal services.

Another way of saying this, perhaps more to the point, is that there are two issues here: the distribution of legal services and the content of what is distributed. The moral content of what is distributed — the ethical nature of the lawyer-client relationship once established — is the subject of this essay. The distribution of access to the law (legal services) is a different subject. While the effort to make law a more truly public good is under way (or assuming it fails and we are left with the status quo), the other issue remains: what is to be the moral content of the legal services that are available? To suggest that transforming the amoral facilitator role of the lawyer into the judge/facilitator role follows from the insufficient availability of legal services is a non sequitur. Such a transformation would compound inequality upon inequality — first the inequality of access to a lawyer, then the inequality of what law that particular lawyer will allow the client access to.

One can argue that the judge/facilitator role will not compound inequality but, to the contrary, will balance power because the advantage accruing to those with access to the law over those without will be balanced by the restraint of the lawyer's moral screening of access to the law. There are at least two reasons to react with skepticism to this argument. First, the inequality of distribution is neither complete nor uniform. At least some of the "outs" have had significant access to the law through lawyers. Labor unions, criminal defendants, and civil rights organizations are three prominent examples. Lawyers have played key roles in areas where many perceive gains to have been made in social justice. Second, there is little likelihood of a large difference in moral perception between lawyers and their "in" clients. Perhaps we need more (historical? empirical?) data: Looking back, would there have been more social justice, equality, or general welfare if lawyers had altered or withheld services on the basis of their own (largely middle- or upper-class) values? How would a moralistic as opposed to an amoral role for lawyers have affected 20th-century American social history? However one is inclined to answer such questions, to the extent that the first-class citizenship argument is otherwise valid, expansion and equalization of access to lawyers is a goal which is both consistent with and suggested by that argument. Transforming lawyers into moral screens for client access to the law, to the contrary, is a project quite problematic in its relation to equality of access to law.

Before moving on, one caveat related to the economic inequality criticism should be entered. The first-class citizenship model suggests that lawyers are a necessary item in a highly legalized society and that they should have an amoral role in relation to facilitating clients' wishes. It does not suggest how access to lawyers should be organized. The nature and extent of the legal profession's monopoly — for example, whether paraprofessionals should be allowed to practice independently, or whether unauthorized practice rules should be enforced against banker, realtors, or accountants — is a separate question from that examined in this paper.[32] The term "deprofessionalization" can refer to either (1) the market-limiting nature of professional rules or (2) the amoral professional role. The argument up to this point in this essay is that deprofessionalization in the second sense is a bad idea, but no position has been taken on deprofessionalization in the first sense.

B.   THE ADVERSARY SYSTEM CRITICISM

Much writing on the amoral role of the lawyer has dealt with the layperson's common conception of what lawyers do: criminal defense. The amoral role is justified by the need of the "man in trouble" for a champion familiar with the law to aid him in facing the vast resources of the state bearing down on him, attempting to seize his most basic liberties and put him in jail. In this context, however, there is another champion, the prosecutor, with greater resources, opposing and balancing the lawyer's amorality. More important, there are a neutral judge and a jury whose roles are significantly less amoral than the advocate's. Critics of the lawyer's role have had a field day distinguishing this situation from civil litigation and from nonlitigation (what most lawyers are working on most of the time). The critics suggest that a role justified by the rather unusual context of the criminal justice system simply is not justified in the far more common lawyer roles. Where there is no judge responsible for applying the law from a neutral stance, where there is no lawyer protecting those who may be victimized or exploited by another person's use of "the law" — in these situations the critics of the amoral role argue that the lawyer must take on the neutral judge's role and screen access to and use of the law. Their point is that a role modeled on Perry Mason does not fit the lawyer working for Sears drafting form consumer contracts.

It is therefore significant that the justification for the lawyer's amoral role sketched above has not once mentioned the adversary system, has not been based on any premise involving an opposing lawyer or a neutral judge or jury. In the usual justification of the lawyer's amoral role, the model is adjudication, and there is a difficult stretch adapting and

32. The literature is vast. See, e.g., Rhode, Policing the Professional Monopoly: A Constitutional and Empirical Analysis of Unauthorized Practice Prohibitions, 34 Stan. L. Rev. 1 (1981); Morgan, *supra* note 11; Ehrlich & Schwartz, Reducing the Costs of Legal Services: Possible Approaches by the Federal Government, *reprinted in* A. Kaufman, Problems in Professional Responsibility at 582 (1st ed. 1976).

applying this to the lawyer's office. In this essay, the model is the office lawyer advising about the law and implementing client goals through legally available devices, and one need not stretch to apply that model to litigation. Litigation is simply one of the available devices for implementing goals, like a trust or a corporation. When one focuses on a defendant, either civil or criminal, the moral validity of the autonomy and equality arguments is more apparent because the legal mechanism is being imposed on the individual rather than freely chosen, but the moral validity is not dependent on the defendant role. Thus, the arguments for the amoral role premised on the adversary system supplement the first-class citizenship model in the litigation setting, and the critique based on the limited scope of the adversary system is largely beside the point under the first-class citizenship model.

Two further observations concerning the relationship between the first-class citizenship model and the adversary system model are apposite. First, as noted above, the criminal defendant is only a special instance of the first-class citizenship model. In the criminal context the moral value of full access to all that the law allows is simply clearer and more dramatic. However, because of what is at stake and the procedural safeguards of the adversary system (an opponent lawyer, neutral decision makers), the law may allow more in the criminal context. For example, the criminal defendant has the right to not incriminate himself and he suffers no legal liability for exercising that right. (The jury is told *not* to base convictions on the exercise of that right.) Outside the context of litigation, however, civil liability may be based on nondisclosure of incriminating facts in certain contexts, such as sales of securities under federal regulatory laws or the sale of a house under the common law tort doctrine of misrepresentation. Similarly, to take an example with which we began, the litigant through her lawyer may mislead the court with a cross-examination that intentionally and incorrectly implies the witness was not telling the truth on direct examination, and there will be no liability under the law for the client or the lawyer. In the nonlitigation context of selling a termite-ridden house, however, utilizing similar implications and half-truths to communicate the absence of termites may generate tort liability on the part of the client for misrepresentation and an ethical violation on the part of the lawyer if she "assisted" the client in "fraudulent conduct."

Second, the lines between criminal and civil litigation and between litigation and nonlitigation are not as clear as the critics suggest. The criminal system pits "the state," with all its power, against an individual. But the very point of civil litigation is to allow the private plaintiff to gain the power of "the state" to enforce her claim against the defendant, thus removing the need for, or utility of, acquiring private police or armies to enforce claims. Civil litigation is a contest over which side is to have the vast power of "the state" on its side in a dispute.

Certainly the distinction between litigation and nonlitigation is clearer, but even that line is not as bright as one might at first assume. When the consumer and Sears differ over the validity of a form contract or the misleading nature of advertising or displays, the disparity in power and means is huge. Moving across the line into litigation does equalize the power in both form and substance. But a good deal of that equalization is due to the presence of a lawyer. "Having a lawyer on your side" is a lot of what litigation implies. (To what extent would the filing of a complaint by a *pro se* consumer plaintiff against Sears change the balance of power?) Thus, the more significant transaction — the brighter line — may be between having and not having a lawyer. For the consumer to have access to the law through a lawyer *prior* to litigation would seem to be a more realistic possibility for equalizing power (or actualizing autonomy) than would an obligation on the part of Sears's in-house lawyer to function as a moral screen and filter for Sears's use of the law. This observation circles us back to both the first-class citizenship justification for the amoral role and to the economic inequality critique.

Before moving on from the adversary system criticism, it is appropriate to note that the adversary system image of the lawyer as the champion against a hostile world — the hired gun — is not the proper image for the general role of the lawyer presented here (although it may be the proper image for the criminal defense lawyer). Rather, the image more concordant with the first-class citizenship model is that of the individual facing and needing to use a very large and very complicated machine (with lots of whirring gears and spinning data tapes) that he can't get to work. This is "the law" that confronts the individual in our society. It is theoretically there for his use, but he can't use it for his purposes without the aid of someone who has the correct wrenches, meters, and more esoteric tools, and knows how and where to use them. Or the image is that of someone who stands frustrated before a photocopier that won't copy (or someone whose car won't go) and needs a technician (or mechanic) to make it go. It is ordinarily not the technician's or mechanic's moral concern whether the content of what is about to be copied is morally good or bad, or for what purpose the customer intends to use the car.

III. The Problem of Legal Realism

This paper began with a moral justification for the lawyer's amoral ethical role. It then addressed, and for the most part rejected, two of the most common criticisms of that role. We turn now to a third, rarely articulated problem presented by the first-class citizenship justification for the amoral role. Up to this point in the discussion, access to the law as the primary justification for the amoral professional role has been presented with relatively little focus on what "the law" refers to. Three different facets of law have been recognized: (1) structuring mechanisms (trusts, corporations, civil litigation), (2) definitions of intolerable conduct (criminal law and litigation), and (3) regulatory law. The implication has been that the law is existent and determinable, that there is "something there" for the lawyer to find (or know) and communicate to the client. The "thereness" of the law is also the assumption underlying the commonly understood limit on the amoral role: the lawyer can only assist the client "within the bounds of the law."[41] This accords with the usual understanding of the law from the lay or client point of view, but not from the lawyer's point of view. The dominant view of law inculcated in the law schools, which will be identified here as "legal realism"[42] approaches law without conceiving of it as objectively "out there" to be discovered and applied. A relatively little explored problem is the dynamic between the amoral professional role and a skeptical attitude toward law.

By "legal realism" I mean a view of law which stresses its open-textured, vague nature over its precision; its manipulability over its certainty; and its instrumental possibilities over its normative content. From "positivism" modern legal education takes the notion of the separation of law and morality: in advising the client, the lawyer is concerned with the law as an "is," a fact of power and limitation, more than as an "ought." From "legal realism" it takes the notion of law as a prediction of what human officials will do, more than as an existent, objective, determinable limit or boundary on client behavior. From "process jurisprudence" it takes an emphasis on client goals and private structuring, an instrumental use of law that deemphasizes the determination of law through adjudication or the prediction of the outcome of adjudication. These three views of "the law" are mutually reinforcing rather than conflicting. To the extent that legal education inculcates these views, "the law" becomes a rather amorphous thing, dependent upon the client's situation, goals, and risk preferences. What is the interaction between this view of the law and the view of the lawyer as an amoral servant of the client whose assistance is limited only by "the law"?

The apt image is that of Holmes's "bad man." The modern lawyer is

41. ABA Code of Professional Responsibility, Ethical Considerations 7-1 and 7-19. This approach pervades the Code. See, e.g., Disciplinary Rules 4-101(C)(2) and (3), 7-101(A)(1), 7-102.

42. Although perhaps misleading the choice of the phrase "legal realism" derives from a perception that it will have the highest recognition level as descriptive of "the dominant view of law inculcated in the law schools." "We are all realists now" is a comment often heard from contemporary law professors. See, e.g., Kaufman, A Commentary on Pepper's "The Lawyer's Amoral Ethical Role," 1986 A.B.F. Res. J, at 654. Unfortunately, "legal realism" connotes rather different things to different persons. Robert Summers's usage, "pragmatic instrumentalism," is probably a better descriptive term. R. Summers, Instrumentalism and American Legal Theory (1982). My use of "legal realism" is intended to be more inclusive than Summers's use of "pragmatic instrumentalism," as the following paragraph elaborates.

taught to look at the law as the "bad man" would, "who cares only for the material consequences." The lawyer discovers and conveys "the law" to his client from this perspective and then is told to limit his own assistance to the client based upon this same view of "the law." The modern view of contract law, for example, deemphasizes the normative obligation of promises and views breach of contract as a "right" that is subject to the "cost" of damages. Breach of contract is not criminal and, normally, fulfillment of a contractual obligation is not forced on a party (not "specifically enforced," in contract law terminology). The client who comes in with a more normative view of the obligation of contracts (whether wishing the lawyer to assist in structuring a transaction through a prospective contract or in coping with the unwelcome constraints of a past contract) will be educated by the competent lawyer as to the "breach as cost" view of "the law." Similarly, modern tort law has emphasized allocation of the "costs" of accidents, as opposed to the more normative view of 19th- and early 20th-century negligence law. Thus, negligence law can be characterized as establishing a right to a nonconsensual taking from the injured party on the part of the tort-feasor, subject once again to the "cost" of damages. An industrial concern assessing and planning conduct which poses risks of personal injury or death to third parties will be guided by a lawyer following this view away from perceiving the imposition of unreasonable risk as a "wrong" and toward perceiving it as a potential cost.

There are, of course, variations in the extent to which legal realism will be encountered in a lawyer's office. One is more likely to find the cost-predictive view presented in relation to a contract problem than a tort problem, and it is more likely to come from a lawyer advising a large corporate enterprise than one advising an individual. But it is valid as a general suggestive model that most clients, most of the time, (1) will enter the lawyer's office thinking of law as more normative and more certain than does the lawyer, and (2) will go out having been influenced toward thinking of the law in terms of possible or probable costs more than they would have had they not consulted a lawyer.

From the perspective of fully informed access to the law, this modification of the client's view is good because it accords with the generally accepted understanding of the law among those who are closest to its use and administration — lawyers and judges. It is accurate; it is useful to the client. From the perspective of the ethical relationship between lawyer and client, it is far more problematic. First, the lawyer is to be an amoral technician who serves rather than judges the client. The lawyer is not the repository of moral limits on the client's behavior. Second, the law itself, as presented by the lawyer, also is not a source of moral limits. Rather, it is presented from the lawyer's technical, manipulative stance as a potential constraint, as a problem, or as data to be factored into decisions as to future conduct. Finally, in determining how far he or she can go in helping the client, the lawyer is instructed to look to that same uncertain, manipulable source: "the law." "Within the bounds of the law" sounds like an objective, knowable moral guide. Any second-year law student knows that as to any but the most obvious (and therefore uninteresting) questions, there will probably be no clear line, no boundary, but only a series of possibilities. Thus, if one combines the dominant "legal realism" understanding of law with the traditional amoral role of the lawyer, *there is no moral input or constraint in the present model of the lawyer-client relationship.*

Again, from the premises of the first-class citizenship model, this is as it should be. The client's autonomy should be limited by the law, not by the lawyer's morality. And if "the law" is manipulable and without clear limits on client conduct, that aspect of the law should be available to the client. If moral limits are not provided by the law and are not imposed by the lawyer, their source will be where it ought to be: the client. Morality is not to be inserted in the lawyer's office, its source either the lawyer or the law. Morality comes through the door as part of the client.

This shifts our focus from the lawyer and the law to the client. It should come as no surprise that many clients will come through the door without much internal moral guidance. Common sources of moral guidance are on the decline: religion, community, family. In a secularized society such as ours, religion no longer functions as the authoritative moral guide it once was. Geographic mobility and divorce have robbed many of the multigenerational moral guidance that families can provide. Small, supportive, usually continuous and homogenous moral communities are the experience of fewer and fewer people. The rural town, the ethnic neighborhood, the church attended for several generations, the local business or trade community (the chamber of commerce or the grocers' trade association) — all are the experience of a far smaller segment of the population than before. Even the role of the public school in inculcating values may have declined. For many, law has replaced alternative sources of moral guidance.

Our problem now posits: (1) a client seeking access to the law who frequently has only weak internal or external sources of morality; (2) a lawyer whose professional role mandates that he or she not impose moral restraint on the client's access to the law; (3) a lawyer whose understanding of the law deemphasizes its moral content and certainty, and perceives it instead as instrumental and manipulable; and (4) law designed as (*a*) neutral structuring mechanisms to increase individual power (contracts, the corporate form, civil litigation), (*b*) a floor delineating minimum tolerable behavior rather than moral guidance, and (*c*) morally neutral regulation. From this perspective, access to the law through a lawyer appears to systematically screen out or deemphasize moral considerations and moral limits. The client who consults a lawyer will be guided to maximize his autonomy through the tools of the law — tools designed and used to maximize freedom, not to provide a guide to good behavior. If one cannot rely on the client or an alternative social institution to provide that guide, to suggest a moral restraint on that which is legally available, then what the lawyer does may be evil: lawyers in the aggregate may consistently guide clients away from moral conduct and restraint.

Assume client consults lawyer concerning discharge of polluted water from a rural plant. Client wants to know what the law requires, respects "the law," and intends to comply. Removing ammonia from the plant's effluent is very expensive. The EPA limit is .050 grams of ammonia per liter of effluent, and the EPA has widely publicized this standard to relevant industries. In addition to this information, however, lawyer informs client that inspection in rural areas of the state is rare and that enforcement officials always issue a warning (give a second chance) prior to applying sanctions unless the violation is extreme. Moreover, lawyer also informs client that it is known informally that violations of .075 grams per liter or less are ignored because of a limited enforcement budget. In such a situation, lay ignorance of legal technicalities and the realities of enforcement would seem to lead toward more obedience of "the law" (the .050-gram limit). Access to an amoral, "legal realist" lawyer leads toward violation of "the law." Given the model elaborated above, unless the client comes equipped with strong moral guidance, there will be no pressure to obey the law as written. (Worse, if the client is a corporate manager, she may be bound by her own amoral professional role which perceives shareholder profit as its primary guide.)

IV. POTENTIAL ANSWERS TO THE PROBLEM OF LEGAL REALISM

What follows is a brief canvassing of the major responses that might ameliorate the dilemma sketched above. The first two possibilities are societal responses that do not focus on the ethic of the lawyer-client relation, while the last three explore various approaches to lawyers' ethics.

A. INCREASED SOCIETAL RESOURCES APPLIED TO LAW ENFORCEMENT

The first alternative is to accept the situation described above as either proper or unavoidable. To the extent that the pure "legal realist" view is the basis for conduct, law without enforcement is rendered meaningless. This in turn suggests the need for vast increases in resources devoted to law enforcement. Such a prospect is rather daunting in an era of insufficient government means. More important, the societal atmosphere likely to accompany such an emphasis on law enforcement is not pleasant to contemplate.

. B.   REBUILDING (OR CREATING ANEW) SOURCES OF MORAL
       AUTHORITY AND GUIDANCE OTHER THAN LAW

From right-wing fundamentalism through "values clarification" in the public schools to the renaissance in academic moral philosophy, the perceived need to revive or create sources of moral authority and guidance has become a pervasive societal concern. Commencing with the Enlightenment, secularization has progressively and thoroughly removed religion as the central source of moral authority in Western thought. Science and rationalism, whether taking the forms of logical positivism, anthropology, psychology, or scientism, are increasingly perceived as unable to answer moral and ethical questions. It is safe to say that the search for values and alternative methodologies to elucidate, compare, and validate values is and will remain one of the predominant intellectual (and perhaps political) themes of the last third of the 20th century. "Watergate" is often cited as the cause of the current academic interest in lawyers' professional ethics. Both that scandal and our intellectual endeavors, however, are part of a larger and more important historical process. To the extent that values and sources of moral authority are rebuilt external to the law, the moral vacuum of the "amoral lawyer/legal realism" combination will be ameliorated.

As elaborated above, law itself as it is currently conceived is not a primary source of moral authority or guidance. It is possible that the dominant practical philosophy conveyed in the law schools will change, and lawyers' understanding of and approach to the law will change also, but this seems less likely than does a change in the understanding of the lawyer-client ethic. We therefore turn now to some of the possible changes in lawyers' professional ethics.

C.   THE LAWYER AS POLICEMAN, JUDGE, AND/OR DECEIVER

The lawyer-client ethic analogous to the first possibility above, that of enhanced resources devoted to law enforcement, would alter the traditional balance of lawyer allegiance away from the client and toward society. In the 1970s the SEC took such a position toward the securities bar. In essence it asserted that the lawyer in our hypothetical above would have had to report to the government consistent discharges above .050 grams per liter, regardless of the likelihood or nature of enforcement and regardless of whether his knowledge was based upon client confidences. This is indeed to give policing responsibilities to the lawyer and, depending upon the client's understanding of the confidential nature of communications to a lawyer, perhaps makes the lawyer a deceiver.

If the lawyer does not become a policeman, but instead injects morality by refusing to communicate the legal realism view of law to the client, there is still a significant problem. For the lawyer to communicate to the client a "thereness" and a normative obligation to a written law that is contrary to the lawyer's legal realist view of that particular law is to practice deception, deception in service to obedience of the law. Imagine, for example, a lawyer advising a couple for whom there are significant tax and economic advantages in living together unmarried, in a jurisdiction where fornication remains a crime on the books but is never prosecuted. Is it not deception to fail to inform them of the benefits, or to inform them, but to add that the benefits are not available because the conduct would be criminal, but then to say nothing further?

To replace the amoral role with a moral responsibility role also transmutes the lawyer into an enforcement mechanism, although now it is not the written law but the lawyer's ethics which are being enforced on the client. The lawyer has become the judge of the client. This approach does ameliorate the dilemma by an injection of ethical constraint, but it does so at the expense of the moral values that inhere in the premises of the first-class citizenship justification elaborated above. That elaboration suggests that this would be a considerable price to pay because the values of individual autonomy, diversity, and equality are relatively fundamental to the traditional understanding of our society. Perhaps the expense is merited if one perceives the synergism of the lawyer's amoral role and the legal realist view of law as sufficiently destructive.

D. THE LAWYER AND CLIENT IN MORAL DIALOGUE

The fourth possibility emphasizes the utility of wide-ranging communication between lawyer and client. Instead of defining the client's goals in narrow material terms and approaching the law solely as means to or constraint on such goals, this view opens the relationship to moral input in two ways.

First, the lawyer's full understanding of the situation, including the lawyer's moral understanding, can be communicated to the client. The professional role remains amoral in that the lawyer is still required to provide full access to the law for the client, but the dilemma sketched above is ameliorated by moral input from the lawyer which supplements access to the law. The autonomy of the client remains in that she is given access to all that the law allows, but the client's decisions are informed by the lawyer's moral judgment. Just as the lawyer/policeman role is the analogue in ethics to the alternative of enhanced resource investment in law enforcement, the dialogue role is one possible source for rebuilding moral authority aside from the law. While the lawyer still may not judge or police the client in the sense of screening access to the law, this view of the professional role does allow the lawyer the moral role of moral educator.

The second way the dialogue model infuses a moral element into the lawyer-client relationship is from the side of the client. The current situation minimizes the client's moral input as well as the lawyer's. The client comes in with a human problem (family, business, corporate, etc.); the lawyer defines it in legal terms, usually including a legal goal and legal means to that goal, all perceived from the amoral legal realist stance. Both goal and means may well be defined by the client's interests as presumed by the lawyer: usually maximization of wealth or avoidance of incarceration. More communication drawn from the client by an open lawyer may substantially qualify those presumed goals as well as limit means. To the extent that the lawyer makes room in the professional relationship for a moral dialogue, the client's moral and ethical perceptions can affect decisions. Part of the dilemma sketched above was based on the limited extent of moral guidance with which many clients now come equipped; the dialogue model aims to draw out and actualize that which is there.

This paper began with the example of the lawyer cross-examining a witness known to be truthful in such a way as to suggest to the jury that the witness might be lying. Dialogue with the client may educate the lawyer to the fact that the client does not want to win that way, that the lawyer is wrong in assuming that winning by all lawfully available means is the task the client intended for the lawyer. To the contrary, the client may want to have "the facts" judged by "the law" and may have no desire to win if the truth does not lead to that conclusion. Or the client may believe that exposing the truthful witness to the implied accusation of dishonesty is a moral wrong of sufficient import to prevent its use even to gain that to which he believes justice entitles him. The client may simply not want to win by immoral means. Or, looking at the dialogue with the moral input coming from the lawyer, if the lawyer is the one morally troubled by such a cross-examination and the client is not, the lawyer's perception may engage or educate the client, or the client's overall regard for the lawyer may be sufficient for the client to agree that the tactic should not be used.

Two limits on the "moral dialogue" approach must be recognized. First, it is expensive. Such a dialogue requires time, and time is the lawyer's stock in trade. Either the client must be willing and able to pay for the expanded conversation at the lawyer's regular hourly rate, or the lawyer must be willing to accept a lower income. With traditional forms of legal services perceived as too expensive for the middle and lower classes, and a consequent shift occurring toward less expensive, more efficient structures for providing legal services, the dialogue model may be difficult (perhaps impossible) to incorporate as an integral part of the lawyers' professional ethic. It may be more likely to occur at the level of complex corporate practice because more time is devoted to analysis of legal alternatives. But even in this area of practice, efforts to limit the costs of legal services have been rapidly expanding.

Second, client receptivity to the approach will vary with the context.

The criminal defendant facing years in prison and represented by a public defender will be less open to the dialogue than will the corporate officer dealing with in-house counsel. Lawyers in some contexts may be simply unable to engage in dialogue with their clients; the larger the cultural and economic gap between lawyer and client, the less likely is meaningful moral dialogue. Thus, both limits suggest there will be a spectrum of the kinds of legal practice for which the moral dialogue ethnic is suitable or possible.

E. CONSCIENTIOUS OBJECTION

Part I of this essay suggests a moral justification for the amoral role of the lawyer. That there is such a moral justification does not tell us how that justification will balance with competing moral values which may be present in any given situation. Assuming a lawyer feels bound (either morally or under legally enforced professional ethics) to the amoral ethic, he or she may perceive in a particular situation a higher value that supports conduct contrary to the lawyer role. Conscientious objection always remains an alternative in such a situation: one can recognize the moral and legal validity of the amoral role, but choose not to follow it. This possibility ameliorates the dilemma sketched above by injecting the moral perception of the lawyer into certain cases. In such cases, the lawyer's moral perception will screen the client's access to all that the law allows.

If such conscientious objection is not limited to extreme cases, however, it is little different from the lawyer as policeman, judge, and/or deceiver. To the extent the lawyer allows moral considerations to trump professional obligation, his role is no longer amoral. David Luban appears to have reached this point in his conclusion that the amoral role is supported only by very weak moral values. He argues that in the absence of any countervailing moral value, the lawyer should follow the role. But if there is any valid moral objection to conduct mandated by the amoral role, he concludes that the role provides no justification. Part I above suggests, to the contrary, that the lawyer's amoral professional role has strong justification in several moral values. If this is true, conscientious objection should be rarely exercised by the lawyer.

The well-known "hidden bodies" case provides an example. A criminal defendant revealed to his lawyers the location of the hidden bodies of two murder victims, and the lawyers visited the location to determine the accuracy of the information. The lawyers did not reveal this information for six months, even when it was personally sought from them by the parents of one of the victims. Normal morality would condemn such callous behavior. The amoral role demanded such behavior, for the lawyers were not legally obligated to disclose the information and they perceived it to be in the client's legal interest to delay divulging the information. Professor Luban's approach implies that normal morality should have been applied by the lawyers. The first-class citizenship model suggests the contrary, particularly in the context of criminal defense. Assume for a moment, however, that upon investigation by the lawyers, one of the victims was observed to be alive. Assume further that there was no legal or professional obligation to assist or reveal the existence and location of the live victim to others who would assist (which is quite possibly an accurate statement of the law). Here one has the kind of extreme case for which conscientious objection to the amoral role seems appropriate. Even if the client will be hurt by the lawyers' revealing the plight of the living victim, normal morality in this instance must outweigh the generally strong moral values underlying the amoral role.

V. Conclusion: On the Moral Autonomy of the Lawyer

This paper began by presenting a moral justification for the lawyer's amoral professional role. It then turned briefly to two of the criticisms aimed at the amoral role: the economic one that focuses on the unequal distribution of legal service, and the "adversary system" one that focuses on the usual absence of a judge and the frequent absence of a second, counterbalancing advocate from the situations in which most lawyers function. The difficulty presented by the combination of the amoral professional role and the lawyer's "legal realism" was then elaborated. Last, some possible remedies for this problem were presented.

Where are we left? I would suggest that the moral values of autonomy and equality are imperative in relation to access to the law. Genuine autonomy is so dependent on access to the law, and inequality of access bears so directly on autonomy, that we are indeed dealing with a question of first- and second-class citizenship. This imperative is sufficient, in my view, to outweigh the problems presented by the amoral professional role.

Given this essay's stress on autonomy, it is fair to ask: Where in the amoral role is there a place for the lawyer's moral autonomy? Lawyers are far more intimately involved with and identified with their clients than grocers or landlords are with their customers and tenants. This causes much of the disquiet with the amoral role both within and without the profession. If the client chooses to be the "bad man," to do that which is lawful but morally wrong, does not the lawyer become a bad person, compelled by the amoral role to assist, yet intimately connected to and identified with the client's wrongdoing?

Part of the answer lies in the principle of professionalism sketched at the beginning of part I. Because of the large advantages over the client built into the lawyer's professional role, and because of the disadvantages and vulnerability built into the client's role, the professional must subordinate his interest to the client's when there is a conflict. That the conflict may be a moral one ought not change this precept. The lawyer is a good person in that he provides access to the law; in providing such access without moral screening, he serves the moral values of individual autonomy and equality. This ought to be enough, for the underlying professional ethic cautions that when there is a conflict between lawyer and client, the professional must remember that the raison d'être for his role is service to the client.

The rest of the answer can be found in those limited areas in which the moral autonomy of the lawyer can function compatibly with the amoral professional ethic. Initially, the lawyer has the choice of whether or not to be a lawyer. It should be clear that this choice involves important moral consequences. Second, the lawyer has the choice of whether or not to accept a person as a client. This choice also involves the exercise of moral autonomy. In light of the first-class citizenship model, exercise of the choice of client aspect of the moral autonomy of the lawyer is troubling if it leads to foreclosure of a person's access to the law. In that situation, the lawyer's autonomy results in second-class citizenship status for the denied individual. Third, a large degree of moral autonomy can be exercised through the lawyer-client moral dialogue. While there is a wide range of financial feasibility and client receptivity which will set limits on the extent of such dialogue, all lawyers have some opportunity in this area; and to a significant extent, each lawyer can take part in defining those limits. Fourth, conscientious objection is an ever present option within the realm of the lawyer's moral autonomy. These four areas combined create a meaningful field for the exercise of the lawyer's moral autonomy.

More important, if one adds together (1) the conscientious objection possibility, (2) the wide scope for moral dialogue, and (3) the inherent moral value of facilitating access to the law, the result, I believe is that the good lawyer can be a good person; not comfortable, but good.

DAVID LUBAN,* THE LYSISTRATIAN PREROGATIVE; A RESPONSE TO STEPHEN PEPPER

1986 Am. B. Found. Res. J. 637

My overall assessment of Stephen Pepper's interesting and complex argument may be summed up as follows:

I. Regarding his defense of the lawyer's amoral role: I disagree.

II. Regarding his claim that the existence of economic inequality does

*David Luban is research associate at the Center for Philosophy and Public Policy at the University of Maryland and associate professor of law at the Maryland Law School. B.A. 1970, Ph.D. 1974.

not vitiate the defense because to abdicate the amoral role "would compound inequality upon inequality — first the inequality of access to a lawyer, then the inequality of what law that particular lawyer will allow the client access to": I disagree.

III. Regarding his argument that the adversary system need not figure large in the justification of the amoral role: I partially agree.

IV. Regarding the "problem of realism": I completely agree, and indeed I view this as the major contribution of Pepper's essay.

V. Regarding his canvassing of possible solutions to the problem: I agree, with a few minor qualifications.

These are the five sections of my response.

I

. . . The argument for the amoral role goes as follows: *First premise:* "law is intended to be a public good which increases autonomy." *Second premise:* "autonomy [is] preferred over 'right' or 'good' conduct"; "increasing individual autonomy is morally good." *Third premise:* "in a highly legalized society such as ours, . . . access to the law . . . in reality . . . is available only through a lawyer." *Conclusion:* "what the lawyer does is a social good." "The lawyer is a good person in that he provides access to the law."

I deny the second premise, that individual autonomy is preferred over right or good conduct: it is the point at which the rabbit gets into the hat. Pepper appears to have blurred the crucial distinction between *the desirability of people acting autonomously* and *the desirability of their autonomous act.* It is good, desirable, for me to make my own decisions about whether to lie to you; it is bad, undesirable, for me to lie to you. It is good that people act autonomously, that they make their own choices about what to do; what they choose to do, however, need not be good.[13] Pepper's second premise is plausible only when we focus exclusively on the first of each of these pairs of propositions; it loses its plausibility when we turn our attention to the second. *Other things being equal,* Pepper is right that "increasing individual autonomy is morally good," but when the exercise of autonomy results in an immoral action, other things aren't equal. You must remember that some things autonomously done are not morally right.

Pepper's subsequent argument is that since exercising autonomy is

13. I'm not sure what force Pepper intends by calling it a "*social*" good. To be a social good is not quite the same as to be a moral good, since social goods — things that are good for a society — can be morally unacceptable. (Example: It was good for Spanish society that the conquistadores plundered the Inca Empire, but it was also immoral. "What the conquistadores did was socially good" is true, but so is "what the conquistadores did was immoral.") I shall assume that Pepper means "moral good," not "social good."

good, helping people exercise autonomy is good. Though this is true, it too is only half the story. The other half is that since doing bad things is bad, helping people do bad things is bad. The two factors must be weighed against each other, and this Pepper does not do.

Compare this case: The automobile, by making it easier to get around, increases human autonomy; hence, other things being equal, it is morally good to repair the car of someone who is unable by himself to get it to run. But such considerations can hardly be invoked to defend the morality of fixing the getaway car of an armed robber, assuming that you know in advance what the purpose of the car is. The moral wrong of assisting the robber outweighs the abstract moral goodness of augmenting the robber's autonomy.

Pepper admits that it "may be morally wrong to manufacture or distribute cigarettes or alcohol, or to disinherit one's children for marrying outside the faith, but the generality of such decisions are left in the private realm." That is true, but that doesn't imply that such exercises of autonomy are morally acceptable. On the contrary, it concedes that they are immoral. And this is simply to return to the distinction between the desirability of exercising autonomy and the undesirability of exercising it wrongly.

Pepper sees this. To make his argument work, he distinguishes between (merely) *immoral* conduct and *intolerable* conduct, and says that intolerable conduct "ought to be made explicitly unlawful"; at one point, indeed, he equates "not unlawful" conduct with conduct "above the floor of the intolerable." Using this distinction, he argues in effect that unlawful conduct *is* conduct the immorality of which does not outweigh the value of autonomous decision making. If we didn't want people to make up their own minds about such conduct, we would make it illegal, and thus the fact that we haven't shows that we do not disapprove of it sufficiently to take the decision out of people's own hands.

The conclusion does not follow, however. There are many reasons for not prohibiting conduct besides the reason that we don't think it's bad enough to take it out of people's hands. We should not put into effect prohibitions that are unenforceable, or that are enforceable only at enormous cost, or through unacceptably or disproportionately invasive means. We should not prohibit immoral conduct if it would be too difficult to specify the conduct, or if the laws would of necessity be vague or either over- or underinclusive, or if enforcement would destroy our liberties.

All these are familiar and good reasons for refraining from prohibiting conduct that have nothing whatever to do with the intensity of our disapprobation of the conduct. It is illegal to smuggle a bottle of non-duty-free Scotch into the country. It is not illegal to seduce someone through honey-tongued romancing, maliciously intending to break the lover's heart afterward (as in Kierkegaard's *Diary of a Seducer*). Surely this discrepancy does not show that we judge the smuggling (but not the seduction) "intolerable," or even that we judge the smuggling to be morally worse than the seduction. On the contrary, we judge the seduction to be worse conduct, perhaps even intolerable conduct, but we realize that prohibiting seductions would have obvious enormous social costs. The distinction between legal and illegal conduct simply does not correspond to the distinction between conduct that we think on moral grounds people should be free to engage in and conduct we find morally intolerable.

Pepper acknowledges this too, but resists its implication by posing this rhetorical question: "If making the conduct unlawful is too onerous because the law would be too vague, or it is too difficult to identify the conduct in advance, or there is not sufficient social or political concern, do we intend to delegate to the individual lawyer the authority for case-by-case legislation and policing?"

I do not treat this question as rhetorical; I answer it "yes." The reason goes, I think, to the heart of my disagreement with Pepper. What bothers Pepper the most, I believe, is the idea that lawyers should interpose themselves and their moral concerns as "filters" of what legally permissible projects clients should be able to undertake. His concern, in turn, appears to have two aspects to it, one specific to lawyers, the other more general: "Such a screening submits each to . . . rule by oligarchy of lawyers." More generally, it appears to me that Pepper objects to *anyone,* lawyer or not, interposing his or her scruples to filter the legally permissible projects of autonomous agents. He objects, that is, to informal obstacles to autonomy, allowing only the formal obstacles raised by the law itself. (That seems to be the force of his argument that any conduct which is not illegal is up to "individual decision making.") I suspect that part of Pepper's worry here is that to allow informal obstacles to autonomy is to take away people's first-class citizenship as granted by the law and thus to threaten the rule of law itself.

The first of these worries is illusory, for there is no oligarchy of lawyers, actual or potential, to worry about. An oligarchy is a group of people ruling *in concert,* whereas lawyers who refuse to execute projects to which they object on moral grounds will do so as individuals, without deliberating collectively with other lawyers. The worry about a hidden Central Committee of lawyers evaporates when we realize that the committee will never hold a meeting, and that its members don't even know they are on it. An analogy will clarify this. No doubt throughout history people have often been dissuaded from undertaking immoral projects by the anger, threats, and uncooperativeness of their spouses. It would scarcely make sense, however, to worry that this amounts to subjecting autonomous action "to rule by an oligarchy of spouses." There *is* no oligarchy of spouses.

The second worry is more interesting. Unlike Pepper, I am not troubled by the existence of informal filters of people's legally permissible projects. Far from seeing these as a threat to the rule of law, I regard them as essential to its very existence.

We — people, that is — are tempted to a vast array of reprehensible conduct. Some of it can be and is tolerated; some of it we do not engage in because of our scruples; and some of it the law proscribes. But the law cannot proscribe all intolerable conduct, for human society would then be crushed flat by a monstrous, incomprehensible mass of law. And scruples — conscience, morality — will not take up all the slack.

Instead, we rely to a vast extent on informal social pressure to keep us in check. Why do people break into the line at the cafeteria so seldom? Why do they bus their own trays? Why do they keep malicious, gossiping tongues in (relative!) check at the office? Why are they civil to subordinate employees? Why do they keep their word? Why are Kierkegaardian seducers few and far between? For many people the answer is scruples, morality; but for many people it is not. When conscience is too faint, I submit, the answer to all these questions is that people worry about what other people will say, think, and do, and guide their behavior accordingly.

Imagine now what would happen if we could no longer count on this sort of motivation, so that we would have to enforce desirable behavior legally — imprison or fine line-skippers or tray-nonbussers, gossips and rude deans and heartbreakers. Imagine policing these offenses! When we begin to reflect on the sheer magnitude of altruistic behavior we take for granted in day-to-day life, we realize that society could not exist without the dense network of informal filters provided by other people.

Among those filters is noncooperation. Many nefarious schemes are aborted because an agent's associates or partners or friends or family or financial backers or employees will have nothing to do with them. My argument is that far from this being an objectionable state of affairs, neither society nor law could survive without such filters.

And, to conclude the argument, I do not see why a lawyer's decision not to assist a client in a scheme that the lawyer finds nefarious is any different from these other instances of social control through private noncooperation. It is no more an affront to the client's autonomy for the lawyer to refuse to assist in the scheme than it is for the client's wife to threaten to move out if he goes ahead with it. Indeed, the lawyer's autonomy allows him to exercise the "Lysistratian prerogative" — to withhold services from those of whose projects he disapproves, to decide not to go to bed with clients who want to "set a whole neighborhood at loggerheads."

Pepper wants to allow the lawyer's autonomy a narrower scope: to refrain from being a lawyer, to engage in moral dialogue with clients, to decline to represent a client, and in extreme cases to engage in conscientious objection against odious professional obligations. The last two of these together add up to the Lysistratian prerogative, except for Pepper's limitation of conscientious objection to extreme cases. He includes this limitation because he thinks that only extremely objectionable actions outweigh the value of enhancing client autonomy. I believe, however, that in almost every case of significant client immorality the good of helping the client realize his autonomy will be outweighed by the bad of the immoral action the client proposes. The argument for this point will complete my response to Pepper's defense of the amoral role.

Autonomous decision making is valuable for two complementary reasons: metaphysically and axiologically, the exercise of freedom is one of the most important (if not the most important) components of human well-being; and psychologically, the exercise of freedom is developed in tandem with prized traits of character: rationality and prudence, adult commitment, self-actualization, and responsibility.

It is crucial to realize, however, that none of these values require *unlimited* autonomy in order to be satisfactorily realized — if they did, of course, then human autonomy would be incompatible with the very existence of law. This fact in turn implies that occasional or limited impositions pose no threat to the values underlying my autonomy, provided that my life contains plenty of other opportunities for developing and exercising the capacities associated with autonomous decision making — provided, in other words, that my life is by and large autonomous. A parent's autonomy is not jeopardized because her lawyer refuses to draft a will disinheriting her child because of the child's opposition to the war in Nicaragua: the parent still has plenty of other opportunities for free decision making (indeed, the parent probably even has plenty of other opportunities to make her child miserable). Her life is by and large autonomous.

And, since lawyers' interactions with clients are mostly occasional, lawyers' refusal to execute immoral designs of clients will not threaten the values underlying autonomy if the clients' lives are by and large autonomous in their other interactions. For this reason, in cases of conflict the threat to autonomy posed by Lincoln-like lawyers will typically be outweighed by the immorality of helping the clients.

In effect, Pepper has argued for a strong and a weak thesis. The strong thesis is that helping clients, even when they are doing bad, is good. The weak thesis is that withholding help from clients is bad. But both arguments fall: the rabbits came out of the hat only because they were waiting there to begin with.

II

What about the "economic inequality criticism"? Pepper puts his reply to it nicely when he distinguishes two issues: "the distribution of legal services and the content of what is distributed." He agrees that our current distribution of legal services is far from desirable but denies that this alters the moral standing of the content of what is distributed. I disagree.

The problem is that the content of what is distributed is *on Pepper's own account of the matter* partly a comparative good: first-class citizenship. It is comparative because its value is partly defined relative to other people's holdings of it — first class is first class only relative to second class. In this respect it is like a number at a "take-a-number" deli counter, the value of which is determined solely by how many people have lower numbers. Moreover, to give first-class citizenship selectively to some people is tantamount to bumping everyone else down one class: those who were first-class citizens are now second-class citizens, those who were second-class citizens — if such there were — are now third-class, and so on.

These facts are relevant because they undercut the case for saying that giving first-class citizenship to some but not all people is good — not as good as giving it to all but better than giving it to none, or to fewer. That case, I take it, is simply that Pareto improvements — distributional moves in which some people are helped and no one is hurt — are good. The comparative character of first-class citizenship, however, means that those who don't have it *are* hurt by others having it, as I am hurt if the deli manager gives his friends tickets with lower numbers than mine.

This becomes apparent when we look at the components of first-class citizenship that Pepper inventories. First-class citizenship makes available, among many other benefits, the "corporate form of enterprise, the contract, the trust, the will, and access to civil court to gain the use of public force for the settlement of private grievance." As he notes, all are "vehicles of empowerment for the individual or group." That is, the components of first-class citizenship allow you to leverage yourself into a better position (economic or otherwise) than those who don't have them. The resulting competitive advantage in turn give you further leverage to augment your position still more. And, insofar as the socioeconomic game is zero-sum — it isn't always, but it is often — the more the rich get richer, the more the poor get poorer. Finally, your augmented position will get you the influence and power to push for rule changes that further enhance the packet of perks accruing to first-class citizens.

In this way, the differential granting of first-class citizens yields a self-producing vicious spiral of social inequality and outright damage to those who don't have it. The problem is that when first-class citizenship is not universally available, its components are not mere *benefits*; they are *advantages*. Conferring benefits selectively can be a Pareto improvement, but conferring advantages is not, and I don't believe that it is good.

Am I arguing, then, that if everyone can't have first-class citizenship no one should? I believe I am. Lest this seem outrageous, let me present an analogous case. Let our society be as it is now, with second-class citizens — those who, because they can't afford lawyers, have no access to the law — and first-class citizens. Suppose the administration (in a fit of supply-side enthusiasm) proposes a bill to create a new, exclusive, very special kind of citizenship — "executive class citizenship." It contains all the perks of first-class citizenship plus a few others: dandy new tax shelters, first-refusal mineral rights in the national wilderness, no-wait federal courts unavailable to anyone else, diplomatic passports. Executive class citizenship is awarded to all and only those Americans in the top 1% of individual income.

Would you support the bill? Or would you say, as I would, that *if everyone can't have executive-class citizenship no one should?*

III

I agree with Pepper that his first-class citizenship theory of lawyers' ethics, which models the activity of the office lawyer rather well, is better than an adversary-system-based theory, which models the activity of the trial lawyer rather well. This is for the obvious reason that there are many more office lawyers than trial lawyers. I nevertheless believe that the adversary system must still figure prominently in the debate, because so many of the morally disturbing behaviors in legal practice grew up in the shadow of the courtroom and thus in the shadow of the adversary system. This affects even office law practice, in at least three ways.

1. Because of the adversary system, American lawyers are socialized into a "hardball culture" that necessarily affects even office practice. Lawyers are accustomed to discount the interests of nonclients to an extent that I believe is inexplicable without referring to the adversary system.

2. Deal making and document drafting, the paradigmatic office lawyering activities, must be done with the worst-case scenarios in mind, and these are scenarios of breakdown and litigation. The more adversarial the litigation practices are in a legal culture, the more cautious and complicated and fail-safe their anticipatory moves must be. This is true even of counseling: Consider how much a tax lawyer's advice on recordkeeping and creative accounting is colored by the level of adversariality adopted by the IRS.

3. Ethical rules that are unusual from the point of view of ordinary morality, such as the rules governing disclosures of confidential information to prevent clients from wrongdoing, are fashioned according to arguments based on the adversary systems. It was, after all, the trial law-

yers, using arguments of Professor Freedman, who succeeded in weakening the disclosure provisions in the Model Rules of Professional Conduct. The arguments invoked had to do with the exigencies of the adversary system, and thus they apply preeminently to courtroom lawyers, but the disclosure rules finally adopted govern office lawyers as well. The point is that the adversary system shapes the rules, and the rules shape even nonadversarial law practice. . . .

[Section 4 of Professor Luban's response, which deals with "legal realism" has been omitted. Professor Pepper's response to both commentaries, which includes a response to Professor Luban on this point, has also been omitted. They are in substantial agreement on the effects of "legal realism" on lawyers' conceptions of their obligations. They disagree, however, on where Professor Pepper's views fit in this debate.]

V

My comments on section IV of Pepper's essay are quite brief.[38] The responses to the problem he canvasses do seem to me to be the right ones. I myself sympathize most with the "moral dialogue" approach, which can be used in tandem with any of the others and should always constitute a lawyer's first step. That is, before a lawyer should consider conscientious objection, say, by blowing the whistle on a client, the lawyer should engage in moral dialogue with the client in order to change his or her purposes. My main criticism of this section is that I think that the difference between Pepper's section IV.C, the lawyer as judge — which Pepper rejects — and section IV.E, conscientious objection — which Pepper accepts — is more a matter of degree than kind. And, for reasons that I detailed at the end of section I, I see the difference in degree as being much slighter than Pepper does, so that in the end I assimilate C to E. Since (in my view) his reasons for accepting E are good ones, I think he should accept C as well.

---

38. One small point: on page [264], Pepper says (discussing the hidden bodies case), "Professor Luban's approach implies that normal morality should have been applied by the lawyers" (i.e., they should have revealed where the bodies were hidden). I have it on the best of authority that Luban thinks the opposite. He distinguishes the hidden bodies case from the fact situation of Spaulding v. Zimmerman, 116 N.W.2d 704 (1962) (in which a personal injury defense lawyer kept confidential the fact — known to him through a physician's report but not known to the plaintiff — that the plaintiff had a potentially fatal aortic aneurism). Luban says that, unlike the hidden bodies case, here there is no strong reason for the lawyer to keep the confidence, thereby implying (if I read him aright) that there *is* strong reason to keep confidential the knowledge of where the bodies are hidden. Luban, The Adversary System Excuse, in Luban, supra note 5, at 114-115 (1983).

ANDREW L. KAUFMAN, A COMMENTARY ON PEPPER*

1986 Am. B. Found. Res. J. 651

. . . I would like to make my comments from the perspective of practitioners, for after all it is lawyers who have to make decisions daily with respect to the issues that are the subject of today's essay. Ever since Charles Curtis gave a provocative talk on the topic of the lawyer's ethical role some 35 years ago, the subject has received increasing attention, first from lawyers and more recently from philosophers. With the notable exceptions of the contributions of Monroe Freedman and Charles Fried, however, most of the writings have been critical of the position that argues for an amoral ethical role. Moreover, the more completely argued presentations have tended to be those of the critics. Now, drawing on the insights of Freedman and Fried but advancing beyond them, Professor Pepper had produced a first-rate paper presenting a complete theory that seeks to justify, at least presumptively, an amoral role for lawyers.

As I survey the field of professional responsibility today, I must confess to a feeling of nakedness. Everyone who is anyone has either created or adopted a model. We have "the lawyer as moral force in a non-differentiated or weakly-differentiated role"; "the lawyer as friend"; and now "the lawyer as facilitator of first-class citizenship."

To start with a conclusion, my sense after practicing law for 10 years and teaching professional responsibility for nearly 20 years is that both sides of the argument over the moral accountability of lawyers have a good deal to teach practitioners — but that neither has the full answer, for there is more paradox in the lawyer's role than either theory provides for. In holding high the importance of autonomy, diversity, and equality, Professor Pepper links those goals with the notion that if proposed conduct has not been made unlawful, then at least generally the lawyer should help the client achieve his or her objective. Note that Professor Pepper does not make the lesser point that it is *permissible* for the lawyer to aid the client. He seems to be making the larger point that it is *wrong* for lawyers, except perhaps in exceptional cases, *to refuse to help their clients to achieve lawful ends.*

The comparison is to the technician fixing a car. Such a person, we are told, is normally held to have no responsibility for the use to which the car is to be put. But that judgment, I suggest, stems from the fact

---

*This comment was prepared for delivery in oral form on January 5, 1986, at the special session of the Association of American Law School's annual meeting held to honor Professor Pepper's prize-winning essay. The author has not attempted to redraft his remarks into a more formal presentation and they are being published in virtually the exact text that he prepared for the AALS session.

that the technician normally has no dilemma. Suppose that a technician fixes and delivers a car to a husband who tells the technician that he is leaving his wife and taking their jointly owned car with him at the time when the technician knows that the wife is expecting a child and needs the car to get to the hospital? Do we then all agree that the technician has no moral problem? The real difference between the lawyer's situation and that of the technician is simply one of opportunity: the opportunity to learn of other people's troubles creates moral dilemmas.

Professor Pepper's presentation on this point shares the same problem as Professor Fried's piece, since he finds it necessary to argue that it is always, or almost always, morally good to help the client achieve an end that is not unlawful. It is one thing, however, to *play up* the autonomy and equality points in urging an amoral role for lawyers. It is quite another to *play down* the moral aspect of the reality that sometimes — for a variety of reasons having nothing to do with morality — conduct generally agreed to be immoral is not made unlawful.

For example, to take a homely situation, it is not unlawful for a wife to cut her husband out of her will without telling him, even though she knows that his will favors her, but I think that most of us would agree that there are many situations in which it would be immoral for her to do so. As a lawyer drafting the will, I would not be assuaged by the argument that I am facilitating the wife's first-class citizenship in doing so. Moral dialogue may not be enough in that kind of case. And if that example does not grab you, how about doing the legal work that sets the seller of Saturday Night Specials up in business and helps him to continue. Professor Pepper is not bothered by that one, at least not in the abstract. Is it unfair of me to ask how many dead people shot by guns sold by his client would begin to make him worry? Note that I am not even arguing for the proposition that the lawyer ought to refuse to form the corporation for the client. I am only arguing for the proposition that the professional rules ought not to prevent him from declining to do so.

I realize that there is the problem of "the last lawyer in town" and that that situation sometimes does occur, but Professor Pepper is not dealing with that very special problem. His is a much more across-the-board view. Professor Pepper does leave the "out" of conscientious objection for extreme cases — but I don't think he would regard either of the ones I have put as extreme cases. In making that judgment I rely on his use of the "hidden bodies" case to make his point about extreme cases. He would find an extreme case if the lawyer were to discover that the body he had found were still alive. In choosing that example, I assume that he rejected the one that was much closer at hand, namely, that the lawyer is told by the doctor of the parent of the murder victim that the strain for the parent of not knowing whether her child was dead or alive was highly likely to kill her because she had a bad heart. We can change the adjectives describing the certainty of harm as much as we want, but moral dialogue is not going to work in this situation. The killer is not likely to allow the lawyer to let the parent know by any means that her daughter is dead. I believe that the case I have put, which is disturbingly close to the real case, is one that at least ought to be regarded as raising a hard question as to whether the amoral role is justified in that situation.

And so I have two problems with where Professor Pepper comes out on this point. For me and for many lawyers, I suspect that there are enough situations where the moral constraints are such that they outweigh what Professor Pepper calls the first-class citizenship considerations that they cannot be called truly exceptional. Moreover, I wonder about a system of law that compels lawyers to be conscientious objectors, that is, that makes the law such that lawyers must break it in order to achieve what are conceded to be highly desirable moral ends. It is an insufficient answer to say that it enables us to put a satisfactory label — "amorality" — on the role of the lawyer. And so I think that the ethic of professional responsibility should and does recognize that it is entirely appropriate for the lawyer to refuse the amoral role in a significant number of situations — not just in the matter of choice of client, but also in the performance of the actual tasks the client wishes the lawyer to do.

However, having said all that, I think I should also say that I part company with Professor Luban on the general thrust of his position as I have understood it. I believe that there is a great deal more scope for role-differentiated behavior than his position allows and that lawyers have to be very careful about overriding clients' wishes in the name of morality.

The issues we like to discuss under the heading of morality often turn out to be considerably less clear-cut in reality than we portray them in the classroom. It may not be so much that, as Professor Pepper suggests, our value sources have disappeared in the 20th century. (Indeed, it seems to me that as to some things — at least, for example, care about have-nots — there is more moral awareness in this century than there was in most recent ones.) But moral issues are often cloudy in the lawyer's office because in many, if not most, situations when people come to lawyers, it is very difficult for lawyers to get a strong sense of moral right and wrong because of one-sided, incomplete information about facts and especially about the consequences of particular actions.

And so the occasions on which lawyers may have a real moral choice to make in the advice they give — aside from the important initial choice they make about the kind of practice to which they aspire — may not be so numerous as the protagonists on this issue would have us believe. Likewise, there are other situations where it is perfectly appropriate for a lawyer with a strong moral position to recognize that there are other reasonable solutions to the moral dilemma and thus to defer to the client's differing moral judgment. That kind of deferring has a moral quality to it too. Thus, I believe that in a great many situations it is proper to separate Professor Pepper's view of the lawyer's role as "amoral" into two words. The role should in fact be regarded as "a moral" role.

Finally, there is the relationship stressed by Professor Pepper between legal realism and an amoral ethic for lawyers — the notion that the lawyer's role requires education of clients in the indeterminacy and manipulability of law. As law teachers, we are all realists who recognize the fictional nature of the common view that there is, in Professor Pepper's words, "'something there' for the lawyer to find (or know) and communicate to the client." He tells us that all second-year students know that where setting forth "the law" is concerned, except for obvious and therefore uninteresting questions, there are no lines, only possibilities. While that is all true, I think most practicing lawyers know that there is a great deal of law — statutes, doctrine — that does to inform our judgment about possibilities. We teachers are so caught up in the frontier questions that we sometimes see more chaos and manipulability than there really is. The lawyer who tells the client, "Do what you want; it is all indeterminate and manipulable," does the client no favor.

And while I am at it, I might add that I am a little puzzled by Professor Pepper's tendency to make his point that lawyers should not be screeners of moral conduct by treating as equivalent those situations in which lawyers are pictured as concealing the uncertainty of legal doctrine or enforcement of law from clients and those situations in which lawyers decline to undertake certain lawful means or ends for clients. For me, those two types of cases present very different moral issues in that the former involves a lawyer in deceiving a client whereas the latter does not.

Professor Pepper concludes his paper by saying that there is enough latitude for lawyers' exercise of their own moral autonomy in his picture of the generally amoral role he envisages, that "the good lawyer can be a good person, not comfortable, but good." It is a nice, ironic turn of phrase, but I can hear his critics saying that he has got it backwards, that the prescription is one for making lawyers comfortable at a time when they are not being good.

I do not know how Professor Luban comes out on the issue of comfort, but I am fairly certain that he believes that his own formulation comes closer to making the lawyer a good person than does Professor Pepper's. For myself, I hold eclectic views on the theoretical issue that divides Professors Pepper and Luban — and indeed, the whole community of professional commentators.

On those occasions when the issue of the appropriate professional role arises, it seems to me that there is no need to make the choice for all cases, even for all ordinary cases, between the views expressed by Professors Pepper and Luban. Here is where it is a good thing not to have a model that justifies, at least presumptively, an amoral or a moral role. In my opinion, it has been a good thing and not a bad thing that the rules of professional responsibility have recognized that there are strong principles supporting both views and that they have not opted for a mandatory rule one way or the other in a great many situations, and especially not at the metalevel of theory.

I do not think it all bad that the kind of advice clients get depends to some extent on the chance of whom they choose or have chosen for them as lawyers. That kind of chance happens all through life with the chance of whom we wind up with as parents, children, priests, ministers, or rabbis, teachers, friends, and leaders. In some cases there are costs of leaving things to chance. But so are there costs in trying to force very different lawyers with very different sensibilities into one attitudinal mold for nearly all situations.

In any event, when the issue of role arises in a particular situation that does not fit into an area where there is a rule, I think that it is good that we lawyers are not always given a prepackaged answer. There is something to be said for our being forced to figure out for ourselves what action is called for by the facts of a particular situation, being, in Professor Pepper's words, as good as we can, or perhaps, to put it another way, doing the least bad that we must — even if it is uncomfortable to have to work it out for ourselves.

Another counterweight to Professor Pepper's views is contained in the chapter on lawyers in Professor Alan Goldman's The Moral Foundations of Professional Responsibility (1980). The central question posed by Professor Goldman, a philosopher, is whether lawyers (and political officials, judges, doctors, and business people) should be governed in their decision-making by the moral rules that govern decision-making in everyday life or whether their roles require or permit the use of special moral rules justifying conduct that would otherwise be viewed as immoral. The latter role is denominated "strongly differentiated."

Professor Goldman begins by setting forth his understanding of the legal profession's existing ethical dogma and finds it unacceptable. His description relies on the Model Code of Professional Responsibility and on opinions of the American Bar Association's Committee on Professional Ethics, and his perception is a self-proclaimed, strongly differentiated role that he calls "full advocacy." This role is regarded as requiring or permitting a lawyer to pursue any objective of the client by any tactic as long as neither the objective nor the tactic is illegal, without any obligation to take account of the moral rights of others who may be affected (pp. 90-96). He construes the Model Code's explicit limitations on zealous advocacy as unimportant either because they have been watered down or because they merely prohibit what is otherwise illegal (p. 94). He then considers and rejects the major justifications that have been advanced for the model of full advocacy: advancement of the truth-seeking function of the adversary system (pp. 106-107), the autonomy of clients (pp. 107-109), the duty of confidentiality (pp. 110-111), and the preservation of democratic values by not permitting lawyers to control exercise of legal choice through refusal to urge legal interests of clients (pp. 108, 111-112). Only in the defense of those accused of crime does Professor Goldman see substantial justification for strong role differentiation and then only in situations of defendants not known to be guilty and in those cases involving important procedural rights where the crime alleged is "not serious."

Later in the materials, p. 774, I shall have more to say about Professor Goldman's view of "full advocacy" and his proposed alternative. More relevant at the moment is what Professor Goldman has to say about confidentiality:

> There remains . . . the argument regarding confidentiality. This argument condemned the failure to be as zealous as possible in pursuit of a client's objectives as a betrayal of trust or breach of confidence. The two wrongs claimed here are the frustration of the client's expectation for full advocacy, and, in some cases, the use of information supplied by the client under an assumption of confidentiality to his detriment. These wrongs are both intrinsic and instrumental, the latter in that clients will receive adequate representation only if they can trust their lawyers not to hold knowledge of incriminating facts against them, and in that lawyers can exert positive moral influence upon their clients only if they can learn of their intentions. In reply it may be noted first that, while breaking a promise or trust is wrong, it is not an absolute wrong, but must be weighed against the possible violation of other more important rights than the right to have a promise kept.
>
> Even the Code's fanatic defense of confidentiality recognizes this limitation in relation to revelations of intentions to commit future crimes (and in relation to the cardinal sin of not paying a lawyer's fee). The distinction in regard to the duty of confidentiality between past and future acts is not as sharp as the Code would have us believe. Maintenance of confidence regarding knowledge of future intentions would equally encourage disclosure and give lawyers more opportunity for moral influence. That the Code does not accept this argument here is not because it applies less well to revelation of future intention, but because serious harm can sometimes be prevented by such revelation. This can hold true of revelation of past acts too, as is illustrated [by the hypothetical case] in which another man is serving time in prison for a client's past crime. The distinction therefore does not justify the hard and fast rule implicit in the Code. The main point here, however, lies in the recognition that the wrong in any breach of confidence or trust must sometimes be weighed against more serious wrongs.
>
> The second point on this matter, is that an expectation to be aided in an immoral objective carries less weight. If I have promised a friend to aid him in some immoral end, say to murder his enemy, or less extremely to cheat an adversary out of something he deserves, then the fact that I later

refuse the aid does not entail that I have wronged my friend. I should never have made the promise in the first place, knowing that the fulfillment of it would have morally objectionable results; and, having made it, I should not now fulfill it. My friend or a third party might reasonably complain at my having made the promise, but not at my having failed to keep it. In the legal context, by analogy, if clients have any legitimate complaints when their lawyers refuse to use immoral means to their immoral ends, the complaints can be only that they should not have been led to believe that a principle of full advocacy applied in the first place, not that the lawyers refused to act on that principle. The principle must be antecedently fair, or at least not grossly unfair in application, in order for an expectation that it be honored to carry moral weight in favor of honoring it. It cannot be right to help achieve or acquire for a client what he does not deserve at the expense of moral rights of others solely on the ground that he has expected and trusted you to do so. Even if the refusal is based upon knowledge learned from a client under an understanding that it would not be held against him, the lawyer cannot be blamed for refusing to harm others in his client's behalf. If you tell me that an action I was to perform for you will seriously harm another person, trusting fully that your revelation will not affect my loyalty to your objective, I cannot be faulted for then refusing to act in your behalf.

Third, there is a breach of trust only if the client is led to believe that the lawyer is willing to violate the moral rights of others in pursuit of his interests. Refusal to fully advocate immoral objectives or utilize objectionable tactics is a breach of trust only if the client reveals the objectionable aspects of his intentions with the understanding that this will not negatively affect his lawyer's zealousness. A simple disclaimer at the beginning could avoid completely the intrinsic wrong of a breach of trust later. It can be replied to this point that such a disclaimer would discourage clients from being open with their lawyers. Fear of consequences might prevent innocent criminal suspects from revealing incriminating facts of which the lawyer must be informed to defend adequately. In the noncriminal context the lawyer might be prevented from exerting a positive moral influence if he does not learn of client intentions.

Thus the most plausible argument here in favor of the contested principle appeals to the goal of adequate representation and the necessity of willingness on the part of clients to reveal all. If the client knows that certain revelations will result in reduced advocacy in his behalf, he will choose to remain silent. His silence may be damaging to his legitimate interests or to those of others, if it is a question of a future act from which he might be dissuaded. In the criminal context a lawyer's allowing knowledge gained from the client to operate against him by weakening his defense appears to be in violation of principles of due process and the right against self-incrimination. This violation too can be mitigated by the lawyer's informing the client in advance that knowledge of guilt may cause him to refrain from using certain tactics to secure acquittal that he might have otherwise used.

Would such disclaimers have morally disastrous effects? They might cause guilty clients to try to hide their guilt or to omit certain incriminating facts in their accounts to their lawyers. But if a client is guilty, then it is not so troubling that he might want to hide this from his lawyer. If he is innocent, the lawyer should still be able to convince him that it is best for his lawyer to know all incriminating facts in advance in order to defend him effectively. Part of the convincing can consist in the lawyer's assurance that he will assume innocence in the absence of indubitable knowledge of guilt. As for the argument that in non-criminal contexts lawyers will be unable to exert positive moral influence upon clients without knowledge of their intentions and objectives, it seems to me that this influence is rather minimized when clients know that their attorneys are committed to aid in their morally objectionable aims. Refusal to aid can itself be a far stronger influence and show of disapproval. It is true that the lawyer can exert this influence only if he learns of his client's intentions. But the client might reveal them if he requires the lawyer's aid even without any guarantee of obtaining it. In any case a promise of complicity is too high a price to pay for knowledge of wrongdoing. (Pp. 133-137).

Finally, it also seems appropriate to outline briefly the alternative to "full advocacy" that Professor Goldman advocates. Initially, he outlines the possibilities:

> First, the lawyer could be required to advance his client's cause only through means compatible with settlement of the conflict on the legal merits. He would then forego those tactics that are not strictly illegal, but that function in the circumstances to delay, impose prohibitive expenses on adversaries, or force settlement based upon ignorance of law or fact. . . .
>
> A second possible principle would require a lawyer to aid his clients in achieving all and only that to which they have moral rights. This would call upon lawyers to exercise independent judgment in refusing to violate moral rights of others even in the pursuit of that to which clients might be legally entitled. It also might call upon them to exceed legal bounds in order to realize moral rights of their clients.
>
> A third principle, one that grants lawyers yet more moral authority, would have them aid clients only in doing what is moral to do. (Pp. 137-138).[21]

Professor Goldman recommends adoption of the second alternative as the one most morally appropriate for lawyers.

He considers these alternatives in the context of three hypothetical cases, but two seem most important: (1) A childless couple that wants to fabricate evidence for an amicable divorce in a jurisdiction that does not grant divorces by mutual consent; and (2) A welfare mother who has failed to report income to the welfare bureau and wants the lawyer to ignore this in filing required reports in a divorce proceeding, lest she

---

21. Under the third principle, the lawyer would refuse to help a client exercise a moral right if it were "morally wrong" to exercise the right in a particular way.

lose her benefits and face a possible jail term. Professor Goldman finds his chosen alternative preferable in case (1) because it would permit (why not require?) the lawyer to advise them so as to achieve their aim. "Faced with such an archaic and objectionable law, it seems to me that only a fanatic on the subject of obedience to law would find either the lawyer's or the couple's action objectionable if they pursued their moral right" (p. 139). Likewise in case (2), "the strict application of law would again have an unjust result, a jail sentence for the struggling mother and failure to provide for the basic needs of her children" (pp. 139-140). Therefore, while a lawyer who did not want to risk his career might be excused, the "morally praiseworthy act" is to submit the false documents to the court.

The justification for these decisions is that "moral rights form too fine a grid to be captured by general rules" and that law, as a "blunt social instrument," cannot be "a substitute for good moral sense of citizens, lawyers included" (p. 140). The realization of a client's moral autonomy depends upon the lawyer's "overlooking the precise bounds of law," although of course "he would have to risk the penalty for doing so" (pp. 141, 146).

NOTE

Other philosophers have also looked closely at the morality of the legal profession's rules in recent years. Postema, Moral Responsibility in Professional Ethics, 55 N.Y.U.L. Rev. 63 (1980) is a thoughtful view from a different perspective from that presented by Goldman. Luban, The Adversary System Excuse, in Luban ed., The Good Lawyer (1984) takes a position similar to the Goldman view, which he elaborates substantially in his later book, Lawyers and Justice (1988). See also Simon, The Ideology of Advocacy: Procedural Justice and Professional Ethics, 1978 Wis. L. Rev. 29. For the views of a philosopher who takes a contrary position, see Kipnis, Professional Responsibility and the Responsibility of Professions, in W. Robison, M. Pritchard, and J. Ellin eds., Profits and Professions (1983) and his later small volume, Legal Ethics (1986). An interesting attempt by two lawyers at a nonutilitarian, or deontological, view of the duties of lawyers is D'Amato and Eberle, Three Models of Legal Ethics, 27 St. Louis L.J. 761 (1983).

CHAPTER 5

THE LAWYER'S RESPONSIBILITY TO SOME SPECIAL CLIENTS

The previous chapters have discussed issues of lawyers' responsibilities in the context of situations where it was generally quite clear who the clients were to whom the lawyers had fiduciary relationships. There are, however, situations where that is a problem. This chapter deals with four of them — the lawyer for a corporation, for the government, for an individual who is or may be "incompetent," and the lawyer in a mediation setting.

A. THE LAWYER FOR THE CORPORATION

PROBLEM 36

Corporation, which is about to file a registration statement with the SEC, has its main operations on a piece of real estate that has been discovered by Lawyer to contain a defect in title. Lawyer has advised Corporation that since the defect has existed for 20 years, Corporation will own the piece of property free and clear of any claim if no suit is filed within the next year. If the defect is discovered by the adjoining landowner, however, it would at the very least cause a great deal of expense to the Corporation and, at the very worst, it could be disastrous. What advice does Lawyer give with respect to the registration statement? (This problem has been used by many as illustrative of the difficulty of this field. See William T. Coleman, The Different Duties of Lawyers and Accountants, 30 Bus. Law. 91, 92 (Special Issue March 1975). See also Loss, Fundamentals of Securities Regulation 1269 (1983), who points out that it is a crime willfully to fail to file a required report or to file it late and it is also a crime willfully and knowingly to make any statement in a required report that is "false or misleading as to any material fact.")

Suppose that it was not a registration statement that was involved but rather that Lawyer had received a request from Corporation's accountants to list "all contingent liabilities of the Corporation of which you have knowledge." How should Lawyer respond? Suppose that the discovery that Lawyer had made involved (a) payment of bribes to government officials, either in the United States or abroad, or (b) payment of an apparently exorbitant salary to the agent in charge of a foreign subsidiary, when Lawyer's suspicion is that the salary includes a bribe fund. What should Lawyer do in such cases when an annual report is to be filed with the SEC, assuming that the payments were made with the knowledge of the board of directors?

(An interesting review of various models when corporate counsel are chosen to investigate possible violations of law, either by voluntary or involuntary request of the corporation, is contained in Grunebaum and Oppenheimer, Special Investigative Counsel: Conflicts and Roles, 33 Rutgers L. Rev. 865 (Summer 1981).)

PROBLEM 37

Lawyer is a member of the corporate legal staff of Steel Corporation, which is under a court order obtained at the instigation of Agency to reduce smoke emissions to a designated level at its Springfield plant. It has spent $5 million on new equipment to comply with the order. Lawyer's major corporate responsibility is to give legal advice to the Springfield plant manager. Lawyer inquires about the status of the plant's compliance. Plant Manager replies happily, "Our new equipment is working wonderfully. Except on the 'worst' days of summer and a few days in winter, we are well within the requirements of the order. But that's only about 5% of the time and while the technology exists to achieve 100% compliance, it would cost an astronomical amount to buy that equipment." What does Lawyer do next? She knows, but has never told Plant Manager, that Agency monitors compliance on one of the first three business days of the month. Compare your view in this case with the advice you decided to give in Problem 20 (p. 148). In the Problem 20 situation, at what point would you have communicated your fears about flaws in the company's alloy to the board of directors?

PROBLEM 38

Assume the same situation as Problem 37 except that what is involved is a decision by the board of directors of a small corporation not to report a spill of toxic waste on the corporation's own land. This is a violation of the state agency's rules requiring all spills to be reported by a landowner upon discovery, even if the material was not spilled by the landowner and even if the spill occurred years ago. The agency's position is based on the tendency of all spilled materials to leach through the ground to other property and especially to underground water. The agency has also taken the position that a statute requiring all persons to report spills applies to all corporate agents, including lawyers, and furthermore that the Model Code and Model Rules also support its position in this very special situation. What arguments can be made to support the agency's position? What are the contrary arguments? Which ones seem most persuasive to you?

If your jurisdiction were now trying to decide whether to adopt the Model Rules and you were advising whether the Model Code, Model Rules, or some other provision would best answer this case, what advice would you give?

(There is a large volume of literature on these problems. In addition to the other articles cited in part A of this chapter, see Maupin, Environmental Law, The Corporate Lawyer, and The Model Rules of Professional Conduct, 36 Bus. Lawyer 431 (1981); Lorne, The Corporate Securities Adviser, The Public Interest, and Professional Ethics, 76 Mich. L. Rev. 423 (1978); see also the brief but useful dialogue on many of the issues contained in the responses of Paul Freehling and Warren Grienenberger to a particular factual situation, Legal Ethics Forum, 62 A.B.A.J. 1049 (Aug. 1976) and the Report by the Special Committee of the Association of the Bar of the City of New York on Lawyers' Role in Securities Transactions, in 32 Bus. Law. 1879 (July 1977). On the related matter of opinion giving by lawyers, see Vagts, Legal Opinions in Quantitative Terms, 34 Bus. Lawyer 421 (1979) and James J. Fuld, Rendering Opinions, 33 Bus. Law. 1295 (Spec. Issue March 1978). That special issue also contains a large number of articles and transcripts of panel discussions relating to the topic of the "Ethical Responsibilities of Corporate Lawyers.")

Whenever problems arise in the corporate context so that it appears to the lawyers involved that there is a possibility that crimes or fraud may have been, or may be about to be, committed, they have two immediate matters to consider. With whom in the corporate hierarchy should they pursue the issue? What is their obligation or discretion to disclose the information outside the corporate hierarchy?

The Model Code does not concern itself very much with problems of corporate, or other organization, lawyers. The only language it provides to aid lawyers in situations like Problems 36-38 is EC 5-18, which states the proposition that a lawyer for an entity, including a corporation, "owes his allegiance to the entity and not to a stockholder, director, officer, employee, representative, or other person connected with the entity." That does not provide much guidance to a lawyer with a specific problem although it has been generally understood that ultimately the board of directors speaks for the entity and may and sometimes at least should be consulted by lawyers in such a situation. See ABA Formal Opinion 202 (1940), which is often cited for that proposition.

Identification of the client became very important with the emergence in the courts and especially in the Securities and Exchange Commission of "new" theories of the attorney's responsibility. Garner v. Wolfinbarger, 430 F.2d 1093 (5th Cir. 1970), cert. denied, 401 U.S. 974 (1971), involved a stockholders' derivative suit based on alleged violations of the securities acts in connection with sale of stock by the corporation to them. The plaintiffs sought discovery of the advice given by the corporate attorney to the corporation. The court did not hold that the would-be stockholders were "clients" of the corporation's attorney in connection with advice he gave to the corporation regarding the sale, although it did refer to the joint client exception to the attorney-client privilege as "instructive." But without supplying any logical connection between the joint client exception and the situation in *Garner,* the court did hold that the corporation would be precluded from asserting the attorney-client privilege in this stockholders' derivative suit arising out of their transaction with the corporation if they showed good cause for obtaining the information. The logical connection must be some notion of responsibility of the corporation toward would-be purchasers of its stock. If the corporation has that responsibility, can the responsibility of the attorney be far behind?

The Kutak Commission took as one of its major charges the task of defining the responsibilities of lawyers for organizations. Its answer, Rule 1.13, was one of the most discussed provisions of the Model Rules and it was redrafted many times in response to severe criticism that its original version of that provision encouraged corporate lawyers to seek the advice of the board of directors much too often and to make disclosures of confidences outside the corporation much too often. The Rule in its final form seeks to limit the instances of recourse to the highest corporate authority to extreme cases. The version of the Model Rules recommended to the House of Delegates of the ABA by the Kutak Commission limited possible disclosure of confidential information outside the corporation to instances where the lawyer believed that the highest authority had acted contrary to the organization's interest to further its members' own personal or financial interests and that revelation of such information was in the organization's best interest. The House of Delegates struck out the disclosure provision entirely.

Professor Monroe Freedman has argued that the Kutak Commission version of Rule 1.13 provided considerably less discretion for a lawyer to disclose confidential information in the corporate or other organization setting than in the individual client setting. Professor Freedman desired less discretion and argued for moving what he called the "individual" confidentiality rules of Rules 1.6, 3.3, and 4.1 more in the direction of Rule 1.13. At the same time, he viewed the provisions as actually drafted to be highly discriminatory. While it is theoretically possible to construe Model Rule 1.13 as preemptive of Model Rules 1.6, 3.3., and 4.1 in the corporate setting, there is a much more reasonable interpretation of those Rules: namely, that Model Rule 1.13 deals only with revelation of confidential information where an organization agent is acting to harm the organization, while Model Rules 1.6, 3.3, and 4.1 provide the rules in both the individual and the organization setting where harm to a third party is involved. That is the interpretation that has been given by Professor Hazard, the Reporter for the Kutak Commission. See Freedman, Lawyer-Client Confidences: The Model Rules' Radical Assault on Tradition, 68 A.B.A.J. 428, 432 (1982). Although the House of Delegates revised all the confidentiality rules, the difference in discretion to disclose confidences in Model Rule 1.13 and in the other Model Rules means that the problem raised by Professor Freedman remains to be resolved. See Comment to Rule 1.13, ¶6, for the drafters' effort to make sure that Professor Freedman's interpretation is not accepted.

The issue of a corporate lawyer's obligations within the corporate hierarchy was the subject of recent litigation pursued by the SEC in a proceeding to discipline two partners of a well-known Wall Street law firm. In re Carter and Johnson was a proceeding instituted by the SEC pursuant to Rule 2(e) of its Rules of Practice, 17 C.F.R. §201(e)(1), which provides:

> The Commission may deny, temporarily or permanently, the privilege of appearing or practicing before it in any way to any person who is found by the Commission after notice of and opportunity for hearing in the matter (i) not to possess the requisite qualifications to represent others, or (ii) to be lacking in character or integrity or to have engaged in unethical or improper professional conduct, or (iii) to have willfully violated, or willfully aided and abetted the violation of any provision of the Federal securities laws.

In re CARTER AND JOHNSON
1981 Fed. Sec. L. Rep. ¶82,847 (SEC 1981)

[This was a Rule 2(e) proceeding in which administrative law judge found that two lawyers, William Carter and Charles Johnson, Jr., had willfully violated, and aided and abetted violations of, various provisions of the Securities and Exchange Act of 1934 and of Rules enacted thereunder and had engaged in unethical and improper professional conduct. The judge therefore suspended them from appearing or practicing before the Commission for a period of time. The Commission first upheld the validity of its disciplinary authority by rejecting an attack on its authority to promulgate Rule 2(e). See Comment, SEC Disciplinary Proceedings Against Attorneys under Rule 2(e), 79 Mich. L. Rev. 1270 (1981). It then reversed the findings of statutory violation. It also stated that since the Commission had not adopted applicable standards of professional conduct and since there were no unambiguous professional norms of conduct in the situation presented, it would reverse the findings of unethical and improper professional conduct.

Carter and Johnson (and Socha, a third lawyer not involved in this proceeding) were partners in the New York firm of Brown, Wood, Ivey, Mitchell & Perry, which represented National Telephone Company, a lessor of sophisticated telephone equipment systems. National's business required enormous amounts of capital to finance purchases of equipment whose rental would cover the cost only over an extended period of time. The principal shareholder, president, treasurer, and chairman of the board of National at the relevant time was Sheldon Hart. For the year prior to the filing of National's bankruptcy, the company was faced with enormous financial pressure. Hart and his in-house counsel, Lurie, were consistently uncooperative in following the advice of Carter and Johnson concerning the disclosure requirements of federal securities laws. The lawyers were aware that National's press releases and letters and reports to stockholders contained insufficient disclosures of its financial troubles and they knew that their recommendations regarding disclosures in the Annual Report and letters to stockholders had been ignored. Later when National was required to implement the so-called LMP, a plan to curtail activity because certain conditions outlined in its loan agreements with its lenders had occurred, Hart refused for a month to follow the lawyers' advice that disclosure of those occurrences was required. Only after Hart's resignation was disclosure made.

The SEC reviewed the evidence relating to all these events in great detail and concluded that although it was a "close judgment," the evidence was "insufficient to establish that either respondent acted with sufficient knowledge and awareness or recklessness to satisfy the test for willful aiding and abetting liability."

The Commission then turned to professional responsibility matters.]

Ethical and Professional Responsibilities

A. THE FINDINGS OF THE ADMINISTRATIVE LAW JUDGE

The Administrative Law Judge found that both respondents "failed to carry out their professional responsibilities with respect to appropriate disclosure to all concerned, including stockholders, directors and the investing public . . . and thus knowingly engaged in unethical and improper professional conduct, as charged in the Order." In particular, he held that respondents' failure to advise National's board of directors of Hart's refusal to disclose adequately the company's perilous financial condition was itself a violation of ethical and professional standards referred to in Rule 2(e)(1)(ii).

Respondents argue that the Commission has never promulgated standards of professional conduct for lawyers and that the Commission's application in hindsight of new standards would be fundamentally unfair. Moreover, even if it is permissible for the Commission to apply — without specific adoption or notice — generally recognized professional standards, they argue that no such standards applicable to respondents' conduct existed in 1974-75, nor do they exist today.

We agree that, in general, elemental notions of fairness dictate that the Commission should not establish new rules of conduct and impose them retroactively upon professionals who acted at the time without reason to believe that their conduct was unethical or improper. At the same time, however, we perceive no unfairness whatsoever in holding those professionals who practice before us to generally recognized norms of professional conduct, whether or not such norms had previously been explicitly adopted or endorsed by the Commission. To do so upsets no justifiable expectations, since the professional is already subject to those norms.[64]

The ethical and professional responsibilities of lawyers who become aware that their client is engaging in violations of the securities laws have not been so firmly and unambiguously established that we believe all practicing lawyers can be held to an awareness of generally recognized norms.[65] We also recognize that the Commission has never articulated

---

64. For example, the universally recognized requirement that a lawyer refrain from acting in an area where he does not have an adequate level of preparation or care, e.g., ABA Code of Professional Responsibility, Disciplinary Rule ("ABA D.R.") 6-101.

65. We are aware that ABA D.R. 1-102(A)(4) provides that "a lawyer shall not . . . engage in conduct involving dishonesty, fraud, deceit or misrepresentation" and that ABA D.R. 7-102(A)(7) provides that a lawyer may not, in the course of his representation, "counsel or assist his client in conduct that the lawyer knows to be illegal or fraudulent." Although we believe the prohibitions embodied in ABA D.R. 1-102(A)(4) and 7-102(A)(7) to be of such a fundamental nature that we would not hesitate to hold that their coverage plainly falls within the area of conduct prohibited by Rule 2(e)(1)(ii), two factors convince us not to apply them in this case. First, it is unclear whether the operative terms used in these Disciplinary Rules are coextensive with the use of such terms

or endorsed any such standards. That being the case, we reverse the Administrative Law Judge's findings under subparagraph (ii) of Rule 2(e)(1) with respect to both respondents. Nevertheless, we believe that respondents' conduct raises serious questions about the obligations of securities lawyers, and the Commission is hereby giving notice of its interpretation of "unethical or improper professional conduct" as that term is used in Rule 2(e)(1)(ii). The Commission intends to issue a release soliciting comment from the public as to whether this interpretation should be expanded or modified.

B.   INTERPRETIVE BACKGROUND

Our concern focuses on the professional obligations of the lawyer who gives essentially correct disclosure advice to a client that does not follow that advice and as a result violates the federal securities laws. The subject of our inquiry is not a new one by any means and has received extensive scholarly treatment[66] as well as consideration by a number of local bar ethics committees and disciplinary bodies. Similar issues are also presently under consideration by the ABA's Commission on Evaluation of Professional Standards in connection with the review and proposed revision of the ABA's Code of Professional Responsibility.

While precise standards have not yet emerged, it is fair to say that there exists considerable acceptance of the proposition that a lawyer must, in order to discharge his professional responsibilities, make all efforts within reason to persuade his client to avoid or terminate proposed illegal action. Such efforts could include, where appropriate, notification to the board of directors of a corporate client. . . .

We are mindful that, when a lawyer represents a corporate client, the client — and the entity to which he owes his allegiance — is the corporation itself and not management or any other individual connected with

---

in the statutory prohibitions of Section 10(b) of the Exchange Act. Second, it is not apparent that the reach of ABA D.R. 1-102(A)(4) or 7-102(A)(7) is greater or any different from the reach of Rule 2(e)(1)(ii) in the case of a lawyer who willfully aids and abets a violation of Section 10(b). Accordingly, in this opinion, we have elected to analyze respondents' actions in the context of the provisions of subparagraph (iii), as discussed above, rather than under subparagraph (ii) of Rule 2(e)(1).

66. E.G., Hoffman, On Learning of a Corporate Client's Crime or Fraud — The Lawyer's Dilemma, 33 Bus. Lawyer 1389 (1978); Association of the Bar of The City of New York, Report By Special Committee on The Lawyers' Role in Securities Transactions, 32 Bus. Lawyer 1879 (1977); Cooney, The Registration Process: The Role of the Lawyer in Disclosure, 33 Bus. Lawyer 1329 (1978); Cutler, The Role of the Private Law Firm, 33 Bus. Lawyer 1549 (1978); Sonde, The Responsibility of Professionals under the Federal Securities Laws — Some Observations, 68 Nw. U.L. Rev. 1 (1973); New York Law Journal, "Expanding Responsibilities under the Securities Laws" (1972), 29 (remarks of Manuel F. Cohen, Esq.).

the corporation.[73] Moreover, the lawyer should try to "insure that decisions of his client are made only after the client has been informed of relevant considerations."[74] These unexceptionable principles take on a special coloration when a lawyer becomes aware that one or more specific members of a corporate client's management is deciding not to follow his disclosure advice, especially if he knows that those in control, such as the board of directors, may not have participated in or been aware of that decision. Moreover, it is well established that no lawyer, even in the most zealous pursuit of his client's interests, is privileged to assist his client in conduct the lawyer knows to be illegal.[75] The application of these recognized principles to the special role of the securities lawyer giving disclosure advice, however, is not a simple task.

The securities lawyer who is an active participant in a company's on-going disclosure program will ordinarily draft and revise disclosure documents, comment on them and file them with the Commission. He is often involved on an intimate, day-to-day basis in the judgments that determine what will be disclosed and what will be withheld from the public markets. When a lawyer serving in such a capacity concludes that his client's disclosures are not adequate to comply with the law, and so advises his client, he is "aware," in a literal sense, of a continuing violation of the securities laws. On the other hand, the lawyer is only an adviser, and the final judgment — and, indeed, responsibility — as to what course of conduct is to be taken must lie with the client. Moreover, disclosure issues often present difficult choices between multiple shades of gray, and while a lawyer's judgment may be to draw the disclosure obligation more broadly than his client, both parties recognize the degree of uncertainty involved.

The problems of professional conduct that arise in this relationship are well-illustrated by the facts of this case. In rejecting Brown, Wood's advice to include the assumptions underlying its projections in its 1974 Annual Report, in declining to issue two draft stockholders letters offered by respondents and in ignoring the numerous more informal urgings by both respondents and Socha to make disclosure, Hart and Lurie indicated that they were inclined to resist any public pronouncements that were at odds with the rapid growth which had been projected and reported for the company.

If the record ended there, we would be hesitant to suggest that any unprofessional conduct might be involved. Hart and Lurie were, in effect, pressing the company's lawyers hard for the minimum disclosure required by law. That fact alone is not an appropriate basis for a finding

73. See ABA Code of Professional Responsibility, Ethical Consideration ("ABA E.C.") 5-18.
74. ABA E.C. 7-8.
75. ABA D.R. 7-102(A)(7).

that a lawyer must resign or take some extraordinary action. Such a finding would inevitably drive a wedge between reporting companies and their outside lawyers; the more sophisticated members of management would soon realize that there is nothing to gain in consulting outside lawyers.

However, much more was involved in this case. In sending out a patently misleading letter to stockholders on December 23 in contravention of Socha's plain and express advice to clear all such disclosure with Brown, Wood, in deceiving respondents about Johnson's approval of the company's quarterly report to its stockholders in early December and in dissembling in response to respondents' questions about the implementation of the LMP, the company's management erected a wall between National and its outside lawyers — a wall apparently designed to keep out good legal advice in conflict with management's improper disclosure plans.

Any ambiguity in the situation plainly evaporated in late April and early May of 1975 when Hart first asked Johnson for a legal opinion flatly contrary to the express disclosure advice Johnson had given Hart only five days earlier, and when Lurie soon thereafter prohibited Kay from delivering a copy of the company's April 1975 Form 8-K to Brown, Wood.

These actions reveal a conscious drive on the part of National's management no longer to look to Brown, Wood for independent disclosure advice, but rather to embrace the firm within Hart's fraud and use it as a shield to avoid the pressures exerted by the banks toward disclosure. Such a role is a perversion of the normal lawyer-client relationship, and no lawyer may claim that, in these circumstances, he need do no more than stubbornly continue to suggest disclosure when he knows his suggestions are falling on deaf ears.

c. "UNETHICAL OR IMPROPER PROFESSIONAL CONDUCT"

The Commission is of the view that a lawyer engages in "unethical or improper professional conduct" under the following circumstances: When a lawyer with significant responsibilities in the effectuation of a company's compliance with the disclosure requirements of the federal securities laws becomes aware that his client is engaged in a substantial and continuing failure to satisfy those disclosure requirements, his continued participation violates professional standards unless he takes prompt steps to end the client's noncompliance. The Commission has determined that this interpretation will be applicable only to conduct occurring after the date of this opinion.

We do not imply that a lawyer is obliged, at the risk of being held to have violated Rule 2(e), to seek to correct every isolated disclosure action or inaction which he believes to be at variance with applicable disclosure standards, although there may be isolated disclosure failures that are so serious that their correction becomes a matter of primary professional concern. It is also clear, however, that a lawyer is not privileged to unthinkingly permit himself to be co-opted into an ongoing fraud and cast as a dupe or a shield for a wrongdoing client.

Initially, counselling accurate disclosure is sufficient, even if his advice is not accepted. But there comes a point at which a reasonable lawyer must conclude that his advice is not being followed, or even sought in good faith, and that his client is involved in a continuing course of violating the securities laws. At this crucial juncture, the lawyer must take further, more affirmative steps in order to avoid the inference that he has been co-opted, willingly or unwillingly, into the scheme of nondisclosure.

The lawyer is in the best position to choose his next step. Resignation is one option, although we recognize that other considerations, including the protection of the client against foreseeable prejudice, must be taken into account in the case of withdrawal. A direct approach to the board of directors or one or more individual directors or officers may be appropriate; or he may choose to try to enlist the aid of other members of the firm's management. What is required, in short, is some prompt action[77] that leads to the conclusion that the lawyer is engaged in efforts to correct the underlying problem, rather than having capitulated to the desires of a strongwilled, but misguided client.

Some have argued that resignation is the only permissible course when a client chooses not to comply with disclosure advice. We do not agree. Premature resignation serves neither the end of an effective lawyer-client relationship nor, in most cases, the effective administration of the securities laws. The lawyer's continued interaction with his client will ordinarily hold the greatest promise of corrective action. So long as a lawyer is acting in good faith and exerting reasonable efforts to prevent violations of the law by his client, his professional obligations have been met. In general, the best result is that which promotes the continued, strongminded and independent participation by the lawyer.

We recognize, however, that the "best result" is not always obtainable, and that there may occur situations where the lawyer must conclude that the misconduct is so extreme or irretrievable, or the involvement of his client's management and board of directors in the misconduct is so thor-

---

77. In those cases where resignation is not the only alternative, should a lawyer choose not to resign, we do not believe the action taken *must be successful* to avoid the inference that the lawyer had improperly participated in his client's fraud. Rather, the acceptability of the action must be considered in the light of all relevant surrounding circumstances. Similarly, what is "prompt" in any one case depends on the situation then facing the lawyer.

oughgoing and pervasive that any action short of resignation would be futile. We would anticipate that cases where a lawyer has no choice but to resign would be rare and of an egregious nature.[78]

D.   CONCLUSION

As noted above, because the Commission has never adopted or endorsed standards of professional conduct which would have applied to respondents' activities during the period here in question, and since generally accepted norms of professional conduct which existed outside the scope of Rule 2(e) did not, during the relevant time period, unambiguously cover the situation in which respondents found themselves in 1974-75, no finding of unethical or unprofessional conduct would be appropriate. That being the case, we reverse the findings of the Administrative Law Judge under Rule 2(e)(1)(ii). In future proceedings of this nature, however, the Commission will apply the interpretation of subparagraph (ii) of Rule 2(e)(1) set forth in this opinion.

[One of the four participating Commissioners would have affirmed the finding that Carter had aided and abetted National's securities laws violations.]

NOTES

1. While much of the discussion about this case concerned possible violation of the rules of professional conduct, note that that was not the lawyers' only concern. The Commission indicated that the lawyers had come quite close to aiding and abetting criminal violations. See the *National Student Marketing* litigation, p. 299, where such violations were found.

2. In re Carter and Johnson is very relevant to the debate that occurred during the drafting of the Model Rules concerning the provisions of Rule 1.13. The Commission followed up its opinion by soliciting public comments about adoption of the following "Standard of Conduct Constituting Unethical or Improper Professional Practice Before the Commission":

---

78. This case does not involve, nor do we here deal with, the additional question of when a lawyer, aware of his client's intention to commit fraud or an illegal act, has a professional duty to disclose that fact either publicly or to an affected third party. Our interpretation today does not require such action at any point, although other existing standards of professional conduct might be so interpreted. See, e.g., ABA D.R. 7-102 (B).

> When a lawyer with significant responsibilities in the effectuation of a company's compliance with the disclosure requirements of the federal securities laws becomes aware that his client is engaged in a substantial and continuing failure to satisfy those disclosure requirements, his continued participation violates professional standards unless he takes prompt steps to end the client's uncompliance. 23 SEC Docket 821 (1981).

However, the Commission has taken no further formal action with respect to its proposal.

Defining the nature of the lawyer's obligation within the organizational, hierarchy is one problem that has recently become a pressing matter. Knowing one's responsibility toward third parties has been an even more pressing problem for the corporate lawyer. During the 1970s a number of governmental agencies, especially the Securities and Exchange Commission, indicated in a variety of ways that they expected lawyers to be forthcoming to protect the public from their clients' illegal activities. A flood of commentary was let loose by a series of cases, the best known of which is SEC v. National Student Marketing Corp., 457 F. Supp. 682 (D.D.C. 1978), see p. 299, in which lawyers have been named as defendants in either civil or criminal proceedings as a result of actions taken in the course of corporate representation. (A symposium in 30 Bus. Law. (Special Issue, March 1975) explored a variety of aspects of the responsibilities of lawyers and accountants as advisers to management. See especially id. at 110-155 for a list of the voluminous literature and cases to date. See also Freedman, Lawyers' Ethics in an Adversary System 20-24 (1975).) Much of the initial focus of concern related to the civil or criminal liability of lawyers at the suit of the United States or private parties. But the focus has broadened to include the meaning of the initial retainer and the question whether an agreement to perform particular services for the corporation, such as the furnishing of an opinion letter, involves the undertaking of responsibilities to, and even of a lawyer-client relationship with, a variety of parties other than the corporation that is the primary client.

The thrust of the series of complaints issued by the SEC was to emphasize its view that the attorney in these situations has responsibilities to the public at large, or at least to certain segments of it, as well as to the party paying the fee and that whether the source of that responsibility is statute, common law, or the lawyers' disciplinary rules, liability will follow from its breach. Aside from the proceedings it instituted, various SEC commissioners and lawyers traveled around the country during the 1970s to address gatherings of lawyers and to set forth their "personal" views of the professional responsibility of lawyers with respect to matters that are the concern of the SEC. One of the most active of these speakers was Commissioner Sommer, and an excerpt from one of his most publicized speeches follows:

A. A. SOMMER, THE EMERGING
RESPONSIBILITIES OF THE
SECURITIES LAWYER*

(1974) Fed. Sec. L. Rep. ¶79,631

. . . Attorneys have since the earliest days of the federal securities laws been at the heart of the scheme that developed in response to those laws. While their formal participation mandated by the '33 and '34 Acts was limited — the only reference to counsel was in Item (23) of Schedule A to the 1933 Act which required the inclusion in registration statements of "the names and addresses of counsel who have passed on the legality of the issue . . ." — nonetheless, the registration statement has always been a lawyer's document and with very, very rare exceptions the attorney has been the field marshal who coordinated the activities of others engaged in the registration process, wrote (or at least rewrote) most of the statement, made the judgments with regard to the inclusion or exclusion of information on the grounds of materiality, compliance with registration form requirements, necessities of avoiding omission of disclosure necessary to make those matters stated not misleading. The auditors have been able to point to clearly identifiable parts of the registration statements as their responsibility and they have successfully warded off efforts to extend their responsibility beyond the financial statements with respect to which they opine. With the exception of the financial statements, virtually everything else in the registration statement bears the imprint of counsel.

Counsel have been involved in many other ways with the federal securities laws. They are frequently called upon to give opinions with respect, principally, to the availability of exemptions from the requirements for registration and use of a statutory prospectus. None would deny the importance of these opinions: millions upon millions of dollars of securities have been put into the channels of commerce — not just sold once, but permanently into the trading markets — in reliance upon little more than the professional judgment of an attorney. In many, perhaps most, instances these opinions have been confined to questions concerning the technical availability of the exemption and have not been concerned with questions of disclosure, compliance with the somewhat amorphous mandates of Rule 10b-5 and other anti-fraud provisions of the federal securities laws.

Attorneys' opinions have played other roles as well. They are customarily rendered in connection with the closing of registered public offer-

---

*The Securities and Exchange Commission, as a matter of policy, disclaims responsibility for any private publication or speech by any of its members or employees. The views expressed here are [Commissioner Sommer's] own and do not necessarily reflect the views of the Commission or of [Commissioner Sommer's] fellow Commissioners.

ings, both by issuer and underwriter counsel, and in those opinions conclusions with respect to disclosure begin to emerge. In opining that a registration statement complies as to "form" with the requirements of the Securities Act of 1933, often counsel may be saying more about the contents of the statement than he realizes and if his opinion goes to the question of the legality of the offering as distinguished from the securities, certainly clear questions concerning the adequacy of disclosure are raised.

Of course, the attorney appears in many other contexts: often he appears in court or before the Commission as an advocate in formal proceedings; his advocacy may also be discerned in various discussions with the staff. For the moment I would put those matters aside and suggest that the resolution of the responsibilities of the advocate, as distinguished from the counselor, registration statement writer and opinion giver, are somewhat more amenable to resolution with traditional notions.

In a word, and the word is Professor Morgan Shipman's, the professional judgment of the attorney is often the "passkey" to securities transactions. If he gives an opinion that an exemption is available, securities get sold; if he doesn't give the opinion, they don't get sold. If he judges that certain information must be included in a registration statement, it gets included (unless the client seeks other counsel or the attorney crumbles under the weight of client pressure); if he concludes it need not be included, it doesn't get included. . . .

We are consistently reminded that historically the attorney has been an advocate, that his professional ethics have over the years defined his function in those terms, that such a role includes unremitting loyalty to the interests of his client (short of engaging in or countenancing fraud). . . .

I would suggest that the security bar's *conception* of its role too sharply contrasts with the *reality* of its role in the securities process to escape notice and attention — and in such situations the reality eventually prevails. Lawyers are not paid in the amounts they are to put the representations of their clients in good English, or give opinions which assume a pure state of facts upon which any third year law student could confidently express an opinion.

I would suggest that in securities matters (other than those where advocacy is clearly proper) the attorney will have to function in a manner more akin to that of the auditor than to that of the advocate. This means several things. It means he will have to exercise a measure of independence that is perhaps uncomfortable if he is also the close counselor of management in other matters, often including business decisions. It means he will have to be acutely cognizant of his responsibility to the public who engage in securities transactions that would never have come about were it not for his professional presence. It means he will have to adopt the healthy skepticism toward the representations of management which a good auditor must adopt. It means he will have to do the same thing the auditor does when confronted with an intransigent client — resign. . . .

I would suggest that the bar will make a serious error if it seeks to defend itself against the emerging trends by reliance upon old shibboleths and axioms. Society will not stand for it, any more than it will stand for the accounting profession saying that all it does is determine whether financial statements are prepared in accordance with generally accepted accounting principles and that it has no professional concern with their overall fairness or the adequacy of their portrayal of economic reality. Everyone has been shocked by the massive betrayal of public investors in recent years and inevitably the focus is upon the people and the process through which these debacles came about. This spotlight will, I predict, increasingly focus upon the role of attorney who is invariably a keeper of the stop and go signal.

I would not have you understand that I believe the attorney must become the guarantor of his client's probity any more than I would suggest that the auditor is the guarantor of the accuracy of his client's financial statements. Attorneys and auditors can be the victims of unprincipled clients as can the public and even regulatory agencies. And I would not suggest that whenever there is a financial collapse there is necessarily or invariably involved derelictions on the part of the attorney or auditor. But I do suggest that the role of the attorney, the conduct of the attorney, the competence of the attorney, the integrity of the attorney, and yes, in some measure, the independence of the attorney will be increasingly scrutinized. . . .

However, the Commission and its staff must be cautious in the steps it takes in realizing this enhancement of responsibility. All of us know of the dramatic and unfortunate impact any litigation questioning the conduct of a professional can have on his career, as well as his finances. Corporations can withstand legal attacks and go forward to thrive and not infrequently corporate executives can do the same. However, it is far more difficult for a professional to retain his community standing, his self-respect, and his financial security after questions have been raised publicly concerning his integrity or his competence. The Commission and its staff must be extremely cautious when it is confronted with a seeming involvement of counsel in securities misconduct. It is too easy, too tempting to believe that an attorney always has knowledge or awareness sufficient to rouse inquiry into the misshapen schemes of his client. It is too facile to conclude that the presence of counsel is a necessary ingredient of every witch's brew. It is too easy to confuse vigorous, even commendable, representation of a client with countenancing misconduct. Before the Commission files a complaint, institutes a Rule 2(e) proceeding or makes a criminal reference, it must be as certain as it can be that it is not confusing counsel diligence for counsel coverup, that it does not demand a standard of conduct beyond that which can reasonably be expected of professionals. . . .

I realize that caution on the part of the Commission may not be sufficient; there still exists the possibility of civil suits for damages. Very frequently, these are the consequence of initiatives of the Commission; consequently, if the Commission does not take action in a given situation, the possibility of other civil litigation is substantially reduced. There is little the Commission can do to mitigate the rigors of such suits for attorneys and I recognize that it is difficult for counsel to accept with any complacency the possibility of ruinous damages. We would all hope that counsel for would-be civil litigants would exercise a degree of responsibility which I believe the Commission does, but that may be too sanguine an expectation. It is also scant consolation to the legal profession to suggest that the fear of civil liability and the imposition of money damages has throughout the history of our legal system been a deterrent against misconduct and has generally had the effect of raising professional and other standards of conduct. And, yet, that is so, and I am sure that it will have the same effect with respect to those who practice that variety of law called securities law. . . .

I would argue that as lawyers we not be hesitant in representing our clients, but let us not be hesitant, either, in protecting those who rely, sometimes rather blindly, upon the protections of professional judgment. Corporate law lawyers are paid well, ultimately by society, for doing a professional job and assuming professional responsibility. Let us not, I urge, appear to society fearful and hesitant as we adapt to the emerging responsibilities of this age where consumer is king.

Commissioner Sommer focused on lawyers' professional responsibility. But lawyers must also pay close attention to the requirements of statutory law. In the famous *National Student Marketing* case, the court scrutinized the obligations of lawyers for both the acquiring, and the acquired, publicly-owned company in a merger when on the day of closing information was transmitted by accountants that indicated that interim financial statements of the acquiring company were erroneous. The executives of the acquired company made a business decision to close the deal anyway. The SEC filed complaints against both sets of lawyers, charging various violations of the securities acts. The lawyers for the acquiring company entered into a consent decree. The case against the lawyers for the acquired company proceeded to trial. The District Court for the District of Columbia stated that the lawyers should have refused to proceed with the merger absent disclosure to, and re-solicitation of, the shareholders of their client because of the materiality of the adjustments required to be made in the interim financial statements. It held that their actions constituted an aiding and abetting of the violations of the antifraud provisions of §17a of the Securities Act of 1933 and §10b and Rule 10b-5 of the Securities Exchange Act of 1934 by the defendant executives of their client. The court, however, refused to enter the injunction sought by the SEC because of the unlikelihood of repetition of the conduct. 457 F. Supp. 682 (D.D.C. 1978).

In considering the *National Student Marketing* litigation, it should be emphasized that although the case provoked several years of discussion about the corporate lawyer's obligation to disclose confidence in order to protect what were at least arguably "third parties," namely the stockholders of their client, the case was decided not on the basis of violation of rules of professional conduct but rather on the basis of lawyers' violation of criminal statutes.

The new theory of lawyer obligation that surfaced in the 1970s in SEC complaints and in some court opinions had a variety of effects. Some lawyers were made quite cautious, causing loud complaints that the unprofessionalism being exhibited was the exact opposite of what Commissioner Sommer was complaining about: lawyers were in fact breaking their obligations of zealous representation and confidentiality by caving in to SEC pressure. See Freedman, Lawyers' Ethics in an Adversary System 20-24 (1975). The ABA's House of Delegates took the extraordinary step of adopting a Statement of Policy setting forth a view of the lawyer's confidentiality obligation that implicitly rejected the "auditor" notion advanced by Commissioner Sommer. (The Statement is published in full in 31 Bus. Law. 543 (Nov. 1975).)

The ABA also addressed another problem involving the same area of confidential and potentially detrimental information possessed by lawyers. This problem was the bounds of appropriate questioning by accountants and appropriate responses by a lawyer with respect to loss contingencies, potential liabilities of a client, about which the lawyer had confidential information. In December 1975 the ABA Board of Governors approved a Statement of Policy on this matter. A coordinated Statement on Auditing Standards (known as Financial Accounting Standards 5) was approved by the American Institute of Certified Public Accountants' Auditing Standards Executive Committee in January 1976. The crucial part was Paragraph 5, which provides as follows:

> 5. *Loss Contingencies.* When properly requested by the client, it is appropriate for the lawyer to furnish to the auditor information concerning the following matters if the lawyer has been engaged by the client to represent or advise the client professionally with respect thereto and he has devoted substantive attention to them in the form of legal representation or consultation:

(a) *overtly threatened or pending litigation*, whether or not specified by the client;

(b) *a contractually assumed obligation* which the client has specifically identified and upon which the client has specifically requested, in the inquiry letter or a supplement thereto, comment to the auditor;

(c) *an unasserted possible claim or assessment* which the client has specifically identified and upon which the client has specifically requested, in the inquiry letter or a supplement thereto, comment to the auditor.

With respect to clause (a), overtly threatened litigation means that a potential claimant has manifested to the client an awareness of and present intention to assert a possible claim or assessment unless the likelihood of litigation (or of settlement when litigation would normally be avoided) is considered remote. With respect to clause (c), where there has been no manifestation by a potential claimant of an awareness of and present intention to assert a possible claim or assessment, consistent with the considerations and concerns outlined in the Preamble and Paragraph 1 hereof, the client should request the lawyer to furnish information to the auditor only if the client has determined that it is probable that a possible claim will be asserted, that there is a reasonable possibility that the outcome (assuming such assertion) will be unfavorable, and that the resulting liability would be material to the financial condition of the client. Examples of such situations might (depending in each case upon the particular circumstances) include the following: (i) a catastrophe, accident or other similar physical occurrence in which the client's involvement is open and notorious, or (ii) an investigation by a government agency where enforcement proceedings have been instituted or where the likelihood that they will not be instituted is remote, under circumstances where assertion of one or more private claims for redress would be normally expected, or (iii) a public disclosure by the client acknowledging (and thus focusing attention upon) the existence of one or more probable claims arising out of an event or circumstance. In assessing whether or not the assertion of a possible claim is probable, it is expected that the client would normally employ, by reason of the inherent uncertainties involved and insufficiency of available data, concepts parallel to those used by the lawyer (discussed below) in assessing whether or not an unfavorable outcome is probable; thus, assertion of a possible claim would be considered probable only when the prospects of its being asserted seem reasonably certain (i.e., supported by extrinsic evidence strong enough to establish a presumption that it will happen) and the prospects of non-assertion seem slight.

It would not be appropriate, however, for the lawyer to be requested to furnish information in response to an inquiry letter or supplement thereto if it appears that (a) the client has been required to specify unasserted possible claims without regard to the standard suggested in the preceding paragraph, or (b) the client has been required to specify all or substantially all unasserted possible claims as to which legal advice may have been obtained, since, in either case, such a request would be in substance a general inquiry and would be inconsistent with the intent of this Statement of Policy.

The information that lawyers may properly give to the auditor con-

cerning the foregoing matters would include (to the extent appropriate)
an identification of the proceedings or matter, the stage of proceedings,
the claim(s) asserted, and the position taken by the client.

In view of the inherent uncertainties, the lawyer should normally refrain from expressing judgments as to outcome except in those relatively
few clear cases where it appears to the lawyer that an unfavorable outcome
is either "probable" or "remote"; for purposes of any such judgment it is
appropriate to use the following meanings:

(i) *probable* — an unfavorable outcome for the client is probable if the
prospects of the claimant not succeeding are judged to be extremely
doubtful and the prospects for success by the client in its defense are
judged to be slight.

(ii) *remote* — an unfavorable outcome is remote if the prospects for the
client not succeeding in its defense are judged to be extremely doubtful
and the prospects of success by the claimant are judged to be slight.

If, in the opinion of the lawyer, considerations within the province of
his professional judgment bear on a particular loss contingency to the degree necessary to make an informed judgment, he may in appropriate
circumstances communicate to the auditor his view that an unfavorable
outcome is "probable" or "remote," applying the above meanings. No inference should be drawn, from the absence of such a judgment, that the
client will not prevail.

The lawyer also may be asked to estimate, in dollar terms, the potential
amount of loss or range of loss in the event that an unfavorable outcome
is not viewed to be "remote." In such a case, the amount or range of potential loss will normally be as inherently impossible to ascertain, with any
degree of certainty, as the outcome of the litigation. Therefore, it is appropriate for the lawyer to provide an estimate of the amount or range of
potential loss (if the outcome should be unfavorable) only if he believes
that the probability of inaccuracy of the estimate of the amount or range
of potential loss is slight.

The considerations bearing upon the difficulty in estimating loss (or
range of loss) where pending litigation is concerned are obviously even
more compelling in the case of unasserted possible claims. In most cases,
the lawyer will not be able to provide any such estimate to the auditor. . . .

The Statement on Auditing Standards is an important effort to set
forth a professional view of the extent of desirable disclosure by clients,
via lawyers, of their contingent liabilities. In particular, the Statement
suggests an answer to Problem 36. Lawyers who accept and attempt to
follow the ABA recommendations, however, should be aware that the
Statement is not "law" and that its particular accommodation is not necessarily the one that the SEC will, or will always, accept. See, however,
Tew v. Arky, Freed, Stearns et al., 655 F. Supp. 1571, 1573 (S.D. Fla.
1987), both aff'd without published opinion, 846 F.2d 753 (11th Cir.
1988) — the court relied in part on the ABA Statement in dismissing a
malpractice complaint against a lawyer for failure to disclose his alleged
knowledge of a company's financial difficulties to its auditors when the

lawyer and his firm were not retained with respect to the company's financial problems and the company did not identify its financial problems in the auditors' inquiry letters or request the firm to comment on them.

There has not been a showdown between the profession and the SEC because, with a change in the composition of the SEC in the 1980s, the SEC has backed away from treating the lawyer as an "auditor," a position towards which it seemed to be edging in the 1970s. That does not mean, however, that lawyers on the firing line need not be concerned about the issue or that students of professional responsibility should conclude that the problem of the appropriate obligation to be imposed on lawyers has been resolved. For one thing, a change in emphasis that comes from a change in political administration may change once again when the political administration changes. For another, a view of lawyer obligation so powerfully focused on protection of the consumer public, once loosened, is not likely to be suppressed so easily. Also, there are other agencies beside the SEC with power to affect, if not to control, the conduct of lawyers. An example is the position taken with respect to situations like that presented in Problem 38 by the Department of Environmental Quality Engineering of the Commonwealth of Massachusetts. In a letter dated January 6, 1988, it expressed the view that both the governing statute and the rules of professional responsibility require lawyers to notify the DEQE of toxic waste spills when their clients do not.

The legal profession has also been made increasingly aware, from within, of lawyers' exposure to liability by reason of their clients' exposure. There has been a large increase in litigation against lawyers. That litigation has resulted not only in judgments against lawyers but also in settlements entered into by insurance companies fearful of new opinions finding liability that would only highlight the new vulnerability of lawyers. The consequence has been an enormous increase in the cost of malpractice insurance, especially for lawyers practicing in the securities field. A consequence of that increase has been the growing decision of many lawyers to "go bare," that is, to practice without the protection of any malpractice insurance at all. The consequences of those decisions, both for lawyers and for parties injured by the misconduct of lawyers, is bound to be quite serious.

B.   THE GOVERNMENT LAWYER

PROBLEM 39

Under Title IV of the Civil Rights Act of 1964, the Attorney General is authorized to bring suit if a complaint is made by parents that their schoolchildren as members of a class are being denied equal protection and if the Attorney General determines that the signers of the complaint are unable to initiate and maintain a suit on their own. §407(a), 78 Stat., at 248. Suppose that the Attorney General begins a lawsuit pursuant to that statute and the court finds de jure segregation in a particular town. When the time comes to decide what remedy should be sought, how does the Attorney General decide whose interests to consider and what weight to give them? Does the Attorney General in a sense represent all citizens' interests, including those who prefer racial separation? Does the Attorney General represent only the interests of the children on behalf of whom the Department of Justice originally brought suit? If the latter group is not regarded as the client, or as the only client, who will represent their interests before the court? Cf. United States v. Allegheny-Ludlum Industries, Inc., 517 F.2d 826 (5th Cir. 1975).

If there is a change of administration and the Attorney General concludes that the metropolitan remedy being advocated by the United States is unwise, may the Attorney General cause the United States to switch sides? Must there be consultation with the plaintiffs first? Cf. Washington v. Seattle School District No. 1, 102 S. Ct. 3817, 3196 (1982). See Note, Professional Ethics in Government Side-Switching, 96 Harv. L. Rev. 1914 (1983).

PROBLEM 40

City Solicitor, under the city's charter, is the attorney for the Mayor. While discussing a contract that the city had just awarded, after negotiations in which the Mayor took an important part, the Mayor mentioned to the City Solicitor that he owned a small amount of stock in the winning bidder. The participation of the Mayor in that award violated the state's conflict of interest statute and the City Solicitor has so advised the Mayor. The Mayor professed ignorance of the statute, expressed concern for his political future, promised never to violate the statute again and to sell his stock, but refused to take any action to undo what he had done because that would make the conflict public. What should City Solicitor do?

PROBLEM 41

Under state law the Attorney General of the State is the chief law officer, with responsibility to advise various state agencies. The State Personnel Board was considering holding a closed meeting in a controversial disciplinary matter involving a member of the State Police. At the direction of the Attorney General, an Assistant Attorney General attended a board meeting at which the matter was discussed. The discussion necessarily included the matters uncovered by the Board's investigation. The Assistant Attorney General reported the Attorney General's opinion that there should be an open meeting and advised it most strongly to follow that advice. When the Board held a closed meeting, the Attorney General brought suit to invalidate its decision because it had been rendered after an illegal closed meeting. The Board then hired private lawyers to file a complaint with the State Bar charging that the Attorney General's actions violated his duties under the Code of Professional Responsibility with respect to maintaining his client's confidences and avoiding conflicts of interest. The Attorney General then brought suit in state court to enjoin the proceedings on the ground that the primary obligation of the Attorney General was owed to the public as his client and that he was not bound by all the professional rules that apply to private attorneys. How should that case be decided? Compare People ex rel. Deukmajian v. Brown, 29 Cal.3d 150, 624 P.2d 1206 (1981) with State Bar Rule 4-102, Standard 69 (1988), as promulgated by the Georgia Supreme Court after an attempt by the State Bar's Disciplinary Board to proceed with disciplinary action against the state Attorney General. The latter took legal action against a state agency that acted contrary to advice given by his office after it had been consulted by the agency. The Supreme Court adopted retroactively a Standard that first set forth the general rule that a lawyer may not represent a client against a former client in a substantially related matter without the former client's consent. It then excepted from the definition of "client" a public agency, officer or employee represented by a lawyer who is a full-time public official.

The issue for government lawyers suggested by Problems 39, 40, and 41 is one to which government lawyers must constantly be sensitive, for it is important for them not only to have a sense of the nature of their relations among one another and with non-lawyer government personnel but also to have some sense of what the attorney-client relationship means in the government context. To attempt to provide some guidance in this area to the approximately 16,000 federal government lawyers, the National Council of the Federal Bar Association in 1973, after consultation with the general counsel of the executive agencies and the judge advocate generals of the military departments, adopted federal ethical considerations to the Code of Professional Responsibility. See Poirier, The Federal Government Lawyer and Professional Ethics, 60 A.B.A.J. 1541 (1974), reprinting the text of the Federal Ethical Considerations at 1542-1544. Of special interest with respect to Problems 39-41 are the following ethical considerations:

Canon 4. A Lawyer Should Preserve the Confidence and Secrets of a Client.

F.E.C.-4-1. If, in the conduct of official business of his department or agency, it appears that a fellow employee of the department or agency is revealing or about to reveal information concerning his own illegal or unethical conduct to a federal lawyer acting in his official capacity the lawyer should inform the employee that a federal lawyer is responsible to the department or agency concerned and not the individual employee and, therefore, the information being discussed is not privileged.

F.E.C.-4-2. If a fellow employee volunteers information concerning himself which appears to involve illegal or unethical conduct or is violative of department or agency rules and regulations which would be pertinent to that department's or agency's consideration of disciplinary action, the federal lawyer should inform the individual that the lawyer is responsible to the department or agency concerned and not the individual employee.

F.E.C.-4-3. The federal lawyer has the ethical responsibility to disclose to his supervisor or other appropriate departmental or agency official any unprivileged information of the type discussed above in F.E.C.-4-1 and 2.

F.E.C.-4-4. The federal lawyer who has been duly designated to act as an attorney for a fellow employee who is the subject of disciplinary, loyalty, or other personnel administration proceedings or as defense counsel for court-martial matters or for civil legal assistance to military personnel and their dependents is for those purposes acting as an attorney for a client and communications between them shall be secret and privileged. In respects not applicable to the private practitioner the federal lawyer is under obligation to the public to assist his department or agency in complying with the Freedom of Information Act, 5 U.S.C. §552 (1970), and regulations and authoritative decisions thereunder.

Canon 5. A Lawyer Should Exercise Independent Professional Judgment on Behalf of a Client.

F.E.C.-5-1. The immediate professional responsibility of the federal lawyer is to the department or agency in which he is employed, to be performed in light of the particular public interest function of the department or agency. He is required to exercise independent professional judgment which transcends his personal interests, giving consideration, however, to the reasoned views of others engaged with him in the conduct of the business of the government.

Canon 8. A Lawyer Should Assist in Improving the Legal System.

F.E.C.-8-1. The general obligation to assist in improving the legal system applies to federal lawyers. In such situations he may have a higher obligation than lawyers generally. Since his duties include responsibility for the application of law to the resolution of problems incident to his employment there is a continuing obligation to seek improvement. This may be accomplished by the application of legal considerations to the day to day decisional process. Moreover, it may eventuate that a federal lawyer by reason of his particular tasks may have insight which enhances his ability to initiate reforms, thus giving rise to a special obligation under Canon 8. In all these matters paramount consideration is due the public interest.

F.E.C.-8-2. The situation of the federal lawyer which may give rise to special considerations, not applicable to lawyers generally, includes certain limitations on complete freedom of action in matters relating to Canon 8.

For example, a lawyer in the office of the Chief Counsel of the Internal Revenue Service may reasonably be expected to abide, without public criticism, with certain policies or rulings closely allied to his sphere of responsibility even if he disagrees with the position taken by the agency. But even if involved personally in the process of formulating policy or ruling there may be rare occasions when his conscience compels him publicly to attack a decision which is contrary to his professional, ethical or moral judgment. In that event, however, he should be prepared to resign before doing so, and he is not free to abuse professional confidences reposed in him in the process leading to the decision.

F.E.C.-8-3. The method of discharging the obligations imposed by Canon 8 may vary depending upon the circumstances. The federal lawyer is free to seek reform through the processes of his agency even if the agency has no formal procedure for receiving and acting upon suggestions from lawyers employed by it. Such intra-agency activities may be the only appropriate course for him to follow if he is not prepared to leave the agency's employment. However, there may be situations in which he could appropriately bring intra-agency problems to the attention of other federal officials (such as those in the Office of Management and Budget or the Department of Justice) with responsibility and authority to correct the allegedly improper activities of the employing agency. Furthermore, it may be possible for the lawyer to participate in bar association or other activities designed to improve the legal system within his agency without being involved in a public attack on the agency's practices, so long as the requirement to protect confidences is observed.

Sound policy favors encouraging government officials to invite and consider the views of counsel. This tends to prevent the adoption of illegal policies. Even where there are choices between legal alternatives, the lawyer's viewpoint may be valuable in affecting the choice. Lawyers in federal service accordingly should conduct themselves so as to encourage utilization of their advice within the agencies, retaining at all times an obligation to exercise independent professional judgment, even though their conclusions may not always be warmly embraced. The failure of lawyers to respect official and proper confidences discourages this desirable resort to them.

NOTES

1. How does a government lawyer to whom information about illegal conduct is revealed by a fellow employee decide whether the revelation is made to him or her in an official capacity, that being a requirement of F.E.C. 4-1 for imposing responsibility on the lawyer to act?

2. F.E.C. 4-3 implies that there is privileged information of the type discussed in F.E.C. 4-1 and 4-2. In what sort of situation would the information given to a government lawyer be privileged?

3. Is the agency head, the agency, the government, or the public the government lawyer's client?

4. Note the provisions of F.E.C. 8-2. Why should the government lawyer be prepared to resign before denouncing unethical or immoral conduct in his or her agency?

ROBERT P. LAWRY,* WHO IS THE CLIENT OF THE FEDERAL GOVERNMENT LAWYER? AN ANALYSIS OF THE WRONG QUESTION

37 Fed. Bar J. 61 (Issue No. 3 1979)

In a speech given at the National Conference on Teaching Professional Responsibility, held in Detroit in the fall of 1977, William R. Robie, a government lawyer deeply immersed in teaching professional responsibility to other government lawyers, stated that the problem of teaching the subject "is compounded by the lack of definitive and binding guidance on the question of who the client is that most federal government attorneys are supposed to represent."[1] Thus, one authority is quoted as saying that "The ultimate client, if not the only client of the government attorney, is the advancement of the common good;"[2] while another maintains that . . . "The administrator whom the lawyer advises . . . is the real client."[3]

The lack of binding guidelines on the question might be attributed to the fact that federal attorneys are bound by the Code of Professional Responsibility adopted in the jurisdictions where each is admitted to practice rather than to a federal code; however, since the American Bar Association Code has been adopted with minor variations in all American jurisdictions, this problem would not seem significant except that "The Code has not provided definitive guidelines in areas of considerable concern to federal attorneys."[6] On the question who is the client of the government lawyer, for example, the Code is silent.[7] Therefore, guidance for the federal attorney is normally sought in the special Federal Ethical Considerations, adopted by the National Council of the Federal Bar Association, on November 17, 1973, and in Opinion 73-1 of the Committee on Professional Ethics of the Federal Bar Association. Both

---

*Professor of Law, Case Western Reserve University. B.A., 1963, Fordham University; J.D., 1966, University of Pennsylvania; Diploma in Law, 1967, Oxford University.

1. Robie, "The Teaching of Professional Responsibility to Federal Government Attorneys: The Uneasy Perceptions" (unpublished), p. 1. Mr. Robie is the Associate Director, Legal Education Institute, U.S. Civil Service Commission.

2. "Risher Speaks on Legal Ethics, Calls for Decisions of Conscience," 15 The Forum, No. 2 (January-February, 1977), at 1, quoted in Robie, id.

3. "Debate on Legal Ethics Continues," 15 The Forum, No. 4 (April-May, 1977) at 3, quoted in Robie, id.

6. Robie, supra, note 1.

7. The provision closest in point is EC 5-18, which talks of "entity" representation. See discussion infra at notes 40 and 41 and accompanying text.

of these documents speak to the question of who is the client. . . . However, the Federal Ethical Considerations seem internally contradictory;[11] and while it has been said that Opinion 73-1 "comes down . . . squarely on the side of the agency and its administrators as the clients of the government attorney,"[12] the ambiguities within the Opinion itself allow both sides to find support for contradictory positions. Thus, the debate continues, generating more heat than light.

This article examines the question "Who is the client for the government attorney?" in order to demonstrate that it is the kind of question that masks several more practical and important questions, and it is these other questions that need far more attention than they are presently receiving. To answer the question "Who is the client?" resolves none of the more important questions. Consequently, it is the thesis of this article that "Who is the client?" is the wrong question to ask. It is less than useless as a pathway leading to any clarification of the unique nature of a government lawyer's professional responsibilities.

I

The primary reason why the question "Who is the client?" is the wrong question for the government lawyer to ask is that there is an unstated assumption that many specific questions concerning ethical conduct will be answered as soon as client identification is achieved. But this is not true. The assumption, based primarily on the traditional ethical rules of the profession, posits that there are two kinds of people in the lawyer's world: clients and non-clients. From that premise, as Geoffrey Hazard has put it, the rules of ethics ". . . tell the lawyer that whomever he considers his client should be embraced and whomever he considers his non-client should be placed at arm's length."[14]

However, despite what the Code says, representing a client independently,[15] competently[16] and zealously within the bounds of the law[17] and preserving a client's confidences and secrets[18] are not statements of axiomatic norms[19] embodying general concepts from which specific rules

---

11. Compare FEC 5-1 ("The immediate professional responsibility of the federal lawyer is to the department or agency in which he is employed. . ."). . . . with FEC 7-2 ("The federal lawyer is under the professional obligation faithfully to apply his professional talents to the promotion under law and applicable regulations of the public interest. . ."). . . .

12. Robie, supra, note 1.

14. G. Hazard, Ethics in the Practice of Law, 45 (1978).

15. See Code, Canon 5.

16. See Code, Canon 6.

17. See Code, Canon 7.

18. See Code, Canon 4.

19. The Preliminary Statement to the Code calls the 9 Canons "statements of axiomatic norms, expressing in general terms the standards of professional conduct expected of lawyers. . . ."

for specific contexts can be derived[20] — at least not for the government lawyer.[21] For the questions for the government lawyer are:

(1) Whose directions shall I take? On what subjects?
(2) Whose confidences shall I respect? With whom may I further discuss "confidences"?
(3) What role does my own judgment play in determining what I ought to do?

These are the questions that count. And no amount of definitiveness concerning the answer to the question "Who is the client?" is going to resolve these questions. This is so because the government lawyer has obligations to a multitude of people, entities, institutions, ideas, etc., that require special analysis depending on context. Often the private lawyer has similar antagonistic obligations and responsibilities. It is only that they are less apparent in the private world.

II

To demonstrate the thesis that "Who is the client?" is the wrong question today, we need look no further than Federal Bar Association Opinion 73-1, . . .

Opinion 73-1 addressed itself to the following three questions:

(1) Under what circumstances may a federally employed lawyer disclose information concerning a Government official of any rank which would reveal corrupt, illegal or grossly negligent conduct?
(2) If disclosure is properly made, to whom may it be made?
(3) Who is the client of a government attorney in the Executive or Legislative branches of Government?

After defining some terms, the Opinion states that "answers to the three questions can be more clearly developed by considering first the question posed as to who is the client. . . ." It goes on: "Problems of disclosure involved in the other questions should be considered in light of the answer to the client question." This approach would be acceptable in the more typical private attorney-private client case, but is merely confusing

20. The Preliminary Statement goes on to say: "They [the Canons] embody the general concepts from which the Ethical Considerations and the Disciplinary Rules are derived."

21. Professor Hazard at least is not sanguine about the deductive possibilities for private lawyers either. See Hazard, supra, note 14, at 43-57.

in the case of the government lawyer. The Opinion itself shows why this is so.

In answering the question "Who is the client?" Opinion 73-1 properly differentiates between the usual case of the federally employed lawyer who works for a department, agency or other organizational entity of the government and the government lawyer who is designated to represent another individual in disciplinary matters, courts-martial, etc. Clearly in the latter cases, the individual represented is the client and the usual attorney-client relationship exists. In the former case, however, according to Opinion 73-1 the lawyer "assumes a public trust, for the government, overall and in each of its parts." The lawyer, therefore "is responsible to the people in our democracy with its representative form of government." But, Opinion 73-1 concludes, the public is not "the client as the client concept is usually understood." Rather, the way this responsibility is discharged is by observing the public interest to be served by the governmental organization (the agency) of which the lawyer is a part. Thus, the lawyer's client, "using the term in the sense of where lies his immediate professional obligation and responsibility, is the agency where he is employed." The agency concept includes agency officials "insofar as they are engaged in the conduct of the public business." Moreover, "the relationship is a confidential one."

Despite the alleged matter-of-factness of this answer, ambiguity remains. For the answer to the question as to who is the client seems to come to this for the draftsmen of Opinion 73-1: the client is the public interest. But since "public interest" is so ambiguous a term, the client is only one aspect of the public interest as that aspect is identified with an agency; and since "agency" is so ambiguous a term, the client is really the agency officials in so far as they are conducting the public business. Logically, this means that as soon as the official behaves in a manner which is either illegal or perhaps merely inconsistent with the public interest as entrusted to his agency, then the government lawyer is free to disregard the confidential lawyer-client relationship with that official. If this is the case, then surely, as with the "public," the agency is not "the client as the client concept is usually understood." The closest analogy to this approach is to the famous constitutional case, Ex parte Young.[32]

In *Young*, the Supreme Court held that a citizen of another state could sue the Attorney General of Minnesota, despite the 11th Amendment:

---

32. 209 U.S. 123 (1908). The analogy to Ex parte Young has also been used to argue that the agency has no Sixth Amendment "right to unlimited free representation by counsel with the prestige and resources of an attorney general's . . . office." Schnapper, Legal Ethics and the Government Lawyer, 32 The Record of the Association of the Bar of the City of New York 649, at 649-50 (1977).

> If the act which the state attorney general seeks to enforce be a violation of the Federal Constitution, the officer, in proceeding under such enactment, comes into conflict with the superior authority of that Constitution, and he is in that case stripped of his official or representative character and is subjected in his person to the consequences of his individual conduct.[33]

Analogously, the agency official is stripped of his protection of confidentiality as soon as he acts inconsistently with the "public interest" with which his agency is entrusted.

Opinion 73-1 does not follow the Ex parte Young analogy in so many words. Instead, it halts abruptly at the twin conclusions that the "agency" is the client and that the relationship is a "confidential" one; then it proceeds to try to answer the first two questions presented. However, the answers given show the Ex parte Young analogy to be apt. The first question asked: Under what circumstances may a federally employed lawyer disclose information concerning a government official of any rank which would reveal corrupt, illegal or grossly negligent conduct? The second question asked: if disclosure is proper, then to whom? The word "corrupt" was construed in 73-1 to mean "venal conduct in violation of law and duty, engaged in for personal gain of another, the gain ordinarily being of a pecuniary or other valuable nature which is measurable." The Opinion then divided the concept of "illegal" conduct into two categories. The first category consisted of the "willful or knowing disregard of or breach of law." The second category of "illegality" consisted of conduct about which the lawyer may hold a firm position as to its illegality, but which he nevertheless recognizes is in an area subject to reasonable differences of professional opinion as to its legality. "Grossly negligent" conduct was not further defined. Questions 1 and 2 were then answered as follows:

(1) "Corrupt" and the "first category of illegal conduct" may always be disclosed to the head of the agency, who must report it to the Attorney General. If the agency head is involved, then the disclosure may be made to the Attorney General directly or another appropriate official of the Justice Department.[35]

(2) The "second category of illegality" and "grossly negligent" conduct should not be disclosed "beyond the immediate persons involved, including if need be, other members of the agency."

---

33. 209 U.S. at 159-160.

35. This result was obtained by a reading of section 535 of Title 28 of the United States Code, of House Concurrent Resolution No. 175 (Code of Ethics for Government Service) and of the Regulations of the Civil Service Commission (5 C.F.R. §735.10), rather than by an analysis of lawyer's ethics as embodied in the Code of Professional Responsibility.

However, the Opinion goes on to say that, for "some very good reason" the lawyer may disclose to unspecified others, so long as the agency has the first crack at handling the matter.

What distinguishes answer (2) from answer (1) is nothing that can be stated in the form of a rule or principle. The difference is simply prudential. In the second conduct group, a government lawyer should be less sanguine that he or she is doing "the right thing" by moving beyond the agency level to tell a tale of improper conduct.

Thus, the analysis contained in Opinion 73-1 is not even tied to the "agency-as-client" idea. This is confirmed by a statement placed near the end of the Opinion, which declares that the government lawyer may even disclose improper conduct beyond "the agency or other law enforcing or disciplinary authorities of the Government." Such a disclosure may be made if the lawyer, acting as a reasonably prudent professional, "concludes that these authorities have without good cause failed in the performance of their own obligation to take remedial measures required in the public interest." Presumably the lawyer himself is to determine whether the remedial measures taken are sufficient. Thus, the traditional client concept, at least in its relationship to "confidentiality," has been swallowed whole by Opinion 73-1, though no one seems to have noticed.

III

What Opinion 73-1 strains to say is: the government and each department or agency contained therein needs to have legal advice and assistance like individuals and other groups. Therefore, there ought to be a confidential relationship between the government, its departments, its officials and the lawyers who advise them and work for them. If lawyers could (or did) breach confidences whenever they thought a government official acted improperly (illegally, unwisely), the officials would not be frank and open in consultations[39] with their lawyers, and the government would be hampered seriously in its functioning. On the other hand, government lawyers cannot be used by the wicked or dishonorable to hide their crimes and follies. But we cannot draw lines to say when silence must be maintained and when disclosures are permissible.

The conclusion is inescapable: Opinion 73-1 does not stand for the proposition that the agency is the client, nor even that the federal government is the client — at least not in any traditional sense. It stands for the proposition that the public (or the public interest) is to be served, and that the government lawyer may disclose improper conduct to the

---

39. FEC 8-3 states the position directly: "Sound policy favors encouraging government officials to invite and consider the view of counsel. . . . The failure of lawyers to respect official and proper confidences discourages this desirable resort to them."

public presumably, for example, if the authorities fail to take appropriate remedial measures. The appropriateness is to be judged by the lawyer as a prudent and responsible professional — though this will be translated by most to mean, "the dictates of conscience."

Given the complexities of the matter, this conclusion may be, and probably is, the best that can be drawn. However, the question addressed in Opinion 73-1 can be reexamined using the concept of the "client" in ways that are more closely tied to its traditional use in the Code. Doing so may demonstrate how useless and confusing is the attempt to solve the unique problems of the government lawyer by focusing on such questions as "Who is the client?" Either the concept must be redefined or it must be abandoned.

Under a traditional approach, the answer to the question is obvious: the client of the federal government lawyer is the federal government. If we can analogize to the corporate world, we find how unusual and disconcerting it is to suggest that the agency or agency officials can ever be considered the client. Under EC 5-18, the lawyer employed or retained by a corporation or similar entity is said to owe his allegiance to the "entity" and not to directors, officers, stockholders, or other persons connected with the entity. "The counterpart rule for government says it is the government that is the client."[40] The need for confidentiality is as great in one lawyer-client relationship as in any other; yet it has not been suggested that a confidential attorney-client relationship exists between individuals working for the corporation and the corporation itself.[41] Surely someone must make decisions for the corporation, but a chain of command approach is entirely appropriate. A line attorney may perhaps speak to the general counsel first, and eventually work his way up to the board of directors, which presumably has the ultimate authority to act for the entity. This approach was recognized explicitly by the ABA Ethics Committee in Formal Opinion 202. There, house counsel for a trust company learned that company officials had purchased the beneficial interest in a trust without making disclosures concerning embezzlements by the manager of the trust and of the trust company's liability to the beneficiaries as a result of those embezzlements. The lawyer had advised the trust company officials of the legal necessity of making such disclosures, but the officials disregarded the advice. After learning of the purchase without the disclosures, the attorney went to the general counsel with the information. Rebuffed at that level, he went to an officer and director of the company. In approving this action, Opinion 202 stated:

40. Hazard, supra, note 14, at 26.
41. EC 5-18. . . .

Since, however, the board of directors of the trust company is its governing body, we think A [the attorney], with propriety, may and should make disclosures to the board of directors in order that they may take such action as they deem necessary to protect the trust company from the wrongful acts of executive officers. Such a disclosure would be to the client itself and not to a third person.

Surely the draftsmen of Opinion 73-1 wanted to accomplish a similar end. They desired an orderly progression of disclosure to take place within the "entity," hoping that each agency can and will keep its own house in order, thereby minimizing the need for wider disclosures. This is the most efficient way of operating; and, in terms of both accountability and fairness, it seems the most sensible procedure. Calling the agency the "client" only confuses this sound policy, for it is never the case that the matter cannot be pursued by the individual lawyer at least to the Attorney General or Justice Department level. If the lawyer is working in the Executive Branch, the process may not stop until it reaches the President himself.

All of this can be accomplished through a traditional analysis of "client" if we understand the client to be the large entity, the federal government, and analogize to similar large corporate entities like General Motors. The lawyer who works for General Motors works neither for the president of the company nor for the marketing or sales departments. He works for General Motors.

Now what can be disclosed? Presumably, anything that seems problematic to the lawyer. What use is there in distinguishing "corrupt" from "grossly negligent" or even "stupid" behavior? Prudence, in large doses, may be called for here, but with the knowledge that people — even lawyers — are normally fearful about losing their jobs or displeasing their superiors, and are also not unreasonable (usually) about their own infallibility in judging complex matters, normal prudential cautions seem to be sufficient to forestall large-scale disruptions in the way government agencies function. The fact that agency life is often marked by interagency rivalries (Agriculture may be warring with the EPA on land use) is no argument for maintaining that a lawyer should be responsible to the agency in its role as part-protector of the public interest. Although there are specific jobs to be done, often under specific legislative mandates, that is no reason to think of a government agency as responsible only to one or another aspect of the public interest. Such thinking allows the internecine warfare to continue instead of fostering a spirit of cooperation among multitudinous government groups.

Continuing with the more traditional approach we must determine when disclosures may be permitted beyond the level of the Attorney General or of the President. Here is where the traditional approach goes awry. Canon 4 forbids the lawyer to reveal a "confidence" or "secret" of a client except in four cases. The first case is with "consent." Thus, if the Attorney General or the President, acting for the government, permits disclosures to the press or elsewhere, the lawyer may reveal. A second case is when permitted under Disciplinary Rules or when required by court order. . . . A third case would be when it was necessary to collect the lawyer's fee (probably not applicable to the federal government lawyers) or for the lawyer to defend himself against an accusation of wrongful conduct. If the government charged the lawyer with a crime while in office, presumably disclosures could be forthcoming to allow an adequate defense. The final case is the crucial one. Under the Code, a lawyer may reveal the intention of his client to commit a crime and the information necessary to prevent the crime. Although the federal government cannot technically commit a crime, this provision could be construed to apply to future criminal acts by any government employees or to any "continuing crimes,"[49] without seriously harming the policy behind the provision, i.e., to prevent clients from using their lawyers as a shield to hide continuing criminal wrongs.[50]

Any traditional analysis would have to conclude at this point, leaving the lawyer bound to silence regarding past crimes and all other illegalities, immoralities and stupidities. Of course, here is the crux of the entire matter. Most writers do not want any lawyer (or any government official) to be able to hide any illegal conduct of any other government official or employee.[51] This includes "past" illegal conduct as well as "ongoing" or "future" conduct. And the confidentiality rules are deliberately designed to allow the "client" to be able to disclose certain "bad acts" to his lawyer without fear of further disclosures. Why? So the lawyer can help the client to "cut his losses"; or make the best out of past mistakes. But government lawyers are said to be in the "justice business."[52] We do not

---

49. The "continuing crime" concept has been applied to cases involving "fugitives" like parole violators (ABA Formal Opinions, Nos. 23, 155, 156) and deserters (ABA Informal Opinions, No. 1141). See Kaufman, [1st ed. of this book], at 115-118.

50. The future crime or fraud exception to the attorney-client privilege has deep historical roots. 8 Wigmore §2298 (McNaughton Rev. 1961).

51. E.g. "If there is wrongdoing in government, it must be exposed. The law officer has a special obligation not to permit a cover-up of illegal activity on the ground that exposure may hurt his party. His duty to the people, the law, and his own conscience requires disclosure and prosecution." Weinstein, Some Ethical and Political Problems of a Government Attorney, 18 Maine L. Rev. 155, 160 (1966). See also Schnapper, supra, note 32 at 655. (". . . if an agency official is in fact violating the law, the state or city would have no interest in obscuring that fact.") If the "client" were the officials themselves, this statement would be both false and naive.

52. See EC 7-13 ("The responsibility of a public prosecutor differs from that of the usual advocate; his duty is to seek justice, not merely to convict;") and EC 7-14 ("A government lawyer who has discretionary power relative to litigation should refrain from instituting or continuing litigation that is obviously unfair. . . . A government law-

want the government "cutting its losses." If mistakes have been made in the past, we want those mistakes rectified so that "justice" can be done. Rectification may only be possible after disclosures are made.

Of course these platitudes are too simply stated. What they say may be entirely unacceptable to the vast majority of those who are actually on the firing line. Lawyers are placed in positions of trust and confidentiality, but with no guarantees to those consulting the lawyers that the trust reposed or the confidentialities enjoyed will be respected. We do not want that situation either. The draftsmen of Opinion 73-1 apparently did not want it. That is why they chose to call the government lawyer's client, the "agency." It seems to keep matters at a more intimate level of trust. However, they wanted it both ways: they wanted a typical lawyer-client confidential relationship, but a relationship that could not ever be used or abused for improper ends. But calling the client the "agency" or the "federal government" or even the "people" is not helpful to this desired end, because the notions of loyalty and confidentiality that are normally associated with a lawyer-client relationship simply do not exist in the government context, unless, of course, a truly traditional approach were tried. Such an approach has had eloquent defenders in the past. Writing in 1963, after more than 20 years of work as a federal attorney, but obviously before Watergate, John Carlock said:

A few years ago I sat with a panel of lawyers, discussing the role of the lawyer in government. At the meeting the thesis was postulated that an agency lawyer had some inherent and compelling responsibility, superior even to that of the agency head, to determine whether various courses of action can or cannot be undertaken. The theory seemed to be that the lawyer, by virtue of having taken the oath as a member of the bar, had acquired some duty — divine, sovereign, or constitutional, I am not quite sure which — to be the final arbiter of right and wrong. I cannot quite agree with this philosophy, though I have found it widely and earnestly held. Certainly it is the agency lawyer's duty to make his views felt by the agency head; for without that, his counseling becomes a cipher. Certainly he must have ideals, for technique without ideals is dangerous. But I do not believe that the ritual of becoming a member of the bar invests a government lawyer with a power of life and death over the agency he serves. The agency head takes his own oath of office, and he is also subject to the inscrutable forces of public opinion. In carrying out his responsibility to decide policy, the agency head looks to his lawyer's counseling as one of his strongest supports; but the lawyer's counsel can never usurp the decision which must be made by the responsible head of the agency.[53]

---

yer in a civil action or administrative proceeding has the responsibility to seek justice. . . .")

53. Carlock, The Lawyer in Government, in Listen to Leaders in Law, 255, 268-269 (1963).

For Carlock, the only option to silence was resignation, and then, presumably, without disclosures being made. He continues on this subject:

> If an agency lawyer feels strongly enough that he does not want to be associated with a given program, he can, of course, always resign . . . No lawyer is wise enough to decide that his concept of legal principle can never give way to the course of action which a responsible administrator, charged with a legal duty and clothed with a Constitutional responsibility, thinks is wise. If the lawyer's skills as a counselor cannot convince the administrator that he is heading down a dangerous course, then how can he be sure that his judgment as a lawyer is infallible? . . . Let the agency lawyer who stakes his reputation on disagreeing beware: time and history have a way of vindicating the rightness of actions responsible officers have found necessary.[54]

These words may sound hollow in 1978. Behind them, however, lies the good sense of an experienced federal lawyer. They cannot be heeded as they stand, for we have suffered too much in the interim; nevertheless, the concern that great damage may be done by the self-righteous is real and serious. At this juncture, with the focus on questions like "Who is the client?" the dilemma can be particularly paralyzing for the federal lawyer seeking to serve both government and his conscience.

The final conclusion concerning whether to disclose or not rests with the government lawyer. This is the pattern that the Code of Professional Responsibility has adopted concerning breaches of confidentiality: all the exceptions to strict confidentiality are permissive, not mandatory in nature. Until we have a more thorough airing of the problem and some consensus concerning it, it can be argued that the federal government lawyer need never reveal any past illegality or stupidity unless, of course, such silence amounts to a breach of law. He should not be disciplined by the bar for being a traditionalist. However, he should not be disciplined by the bar for being forthright about an injustice or other wrong, whether he resigns or not. . . .

NOTE

Professor Lawry underlines the differences between the situations of the government lawyer and the private lawyer. He also notes that the treatment of confidentiality in the Model Code by and large leaves all lawyers with discretion to disclose client confidences in a substantial number of troublesome situations. The drafters of the Model Rules cut

---

54. Id. at 269.

down greatly the area of discretion. However, they also took note of the special position of the government attorney, mentioning in both the Scope note and in the Comment to Rule 1.13 that the government attorney may have special authority both to make decisions normally made by clients and to make disclosures in situations where disclosure would not be appropriate for a private attorney. The drafters, however, did not attempt to give any specific guidance, possibly because they concluded that one rule was not appropriate for all government attorneys and possibly also because they concluded that substantive law apart from the Model Rules might affect the solution.

A Piece of History — Watergate

In connection with the proceedings looking toward the impeachment of President Nixon, Mr. James St. Clair was hired to represent the President and was paid with public funds. He was quoted as saying that he represented "the office of the Presidency," not the occupant of that office "individually." (New York Times, March 13, 1974, p. 1 at col. 7.) What does that concept mean? If Mr. Nixon had wished to follow a particular line of defense that would hurt the Presidency, could Mr. St. Clair have declined to pursue that defense on the ground that the Presidency and not Mr. Nixon was his client? If Mr. St. Clair represented the Presidency, what was the relation between his duties and those of the Attorney General? In the case of a public official, is it a beneficent or dangerous notion that a lawyer who represents the official as far as official actions are concerned has a duty to the public that may transcend the duty to the official? Who could hire a lawyer to fulfill such a role? Who could give him or her instructions?

Compare the views of Dean Freedman attacking New York Times columnist Anthony Lewis' criticism of Mr. St. Clair for making the statement quoted above. "Was Mr. St. Clair representing 'the Office of the Presidency'? Obviously, Mr. Lewis did not think so, nor did I. But there are people who, in good faith, did think so (apparently they included Professor Charles A. Wright). For those who believe in the need for a strong presidency, at any cost, Mr. St. Clair's assertion was certainly not frivolous. Nor was Mr. St. Clair's contention even an uncommon one. A lawyer seeking to exclude unlawfully seized evidence against a client in a narcotics prosecution, for example, would similarly stress that the true issue is not the guilt or innocence of the defendant, but the integrity of the law enforcement under the Constitution — in short, that the lawyer is not representing a heinous criminal, but the Fourth Amendment." Freedman, Lawyers' Ethics in an Adversary System 13 (1975). Is there a difference between claiming to represent the Fourth Amendment and Mr. Nixon's lawyer claiming to represent the office of the Presidency?

C. THE CLIENT UNDER A MENTAL DISABILITY

PROBLEM 42*

A district court judge who knows your interest in mental health matters has appointed you counsel for the respondent in an involuntary commitment proceeding to be held before him in fourteen days. Your client is fifty-seven years of age and has a history of mental illness. He is presently an inmate in a locked ward in a state institution where he was brought on an emergency commitment after his brothers reported to his doctor that he was beginning to hear voices and get into trouble again as a result, apparently, of not taking his medication. When you visit the institution to see your client, the nurses tell you that he is having an anxiety attack, but that you are welcome to see him if you like. When you go into his room, he is startled by your entry, backs into a corner, and makes it clear that he is not interested in talking. The nurse with you attempts an introduction, but your client starts chanting "No, I don't want to see this man. He's not a lawyer. No, I don't want to see him." You decide to leave for the moment and take the time to check your client's records.

The records reveal several previous commitments at the same institution starting at the age of 16. All of the previous institutionalizations have been voluntary, but he has refused consent this time. Each time, he has been released after the proper balance of medication has been found for him and he has been sent back to live with his brothers where he occupies himself in assisting one brother in his work as a plumber. So long as he stays on medication, he seems to function well. However, he has a tendency to develop side effects if the medication is not closely monitored. Each time he has been committed it has been because he has stopped taking medication, and he is released ultimately after he has "recompensated" on a new regimen of medication. However, on two occasions he has spent as long as two years in the institution.

After another vain attempt to communicate with the client, you return to your office to pursue other lines in the case. Telephone discussions with the brothers reveal evidence which is likely to provide the judge with a sufficient basis for an involuntary commitment. However, the brothers would prefer that an involuntary commitment not be on their brother's "record," and they believe that he would prefer that too. A discussion with the lawyer for the Department of Public Health indi-

---

*This problem was prepared largely by Professor Charles H. Baron, Boston College Law School, with some assistance from the author, in connection with their participation in a conference held at Boston College Law School, February 21, 1980, under the auspices of the Mental Health Legal Advisors Committee of The Supreme Judicial Court of Massachusetts. It is reproduced here with the permission of Professor Baron.

cates that he believes that he has an open-and-shut case, but would prefer a voluntary commitment, and is willing to agree to extended continuances until the respondent gets to the point where he is willing to consent or is released to a less restrictive alternative.

The next day you return to the institution to review records, speak to the medical personnel, and make another attempt to communicate with your client. You discover that he is still highly delusional but less anxious. You also discover that the hospital is understaffed with doctors and lacks the medical personnel to make sure that his medication is as closely monitored as it needs to be to get him recompensated as quickly as possible. It seems to you that the best course might be to have the client put under the guardianship of one of the brothers. This would provide him with a competent and caring person who might force the medical staff to discuss and justify plans for a medical regimen in a way which would get him the attention he needs. It would also provide you with someone who could advise you as to whether you should agree to a continuance. However, the irony of suggesting a guardianship for your own client does not escape you. In hopes of avoiding this problem, you make an effort to speak to the client again. This time he is quiet but looks suspicious. You explain that you are his lawyer and try to explain what is going on. When you are finished he says, "Who says you're my lawyer, anyway? You're not my lawyer. You're trying to commit me. I'm represented by Richard Nixon. Go away. I don't want to see you." You leave.

The following day you receive a call from the hospital telling you that your client has signed a voluntary commitment.

1. Do you still represent the client?

2. Suppose that you had not been appointed counsel by the district court but that you were regular counsel for that patient. After the conversation reported above, would you still regard yourself as representing the client?

3. Assuming that you are still counsel, do you challenge a voluntary commitment on the ground that your client was not competent to consent? Do you challenge the giving of medication on that ground?

4. If there is to be a hearing on the petition for involuntary commitment, do you ask for the appointment of a guardian ad litem who can give you direction as to whether you can seek an indefinite continuance?

5. Do you seek to initiate or have initiated a proceeding for the appointment of one of the brothers as guardian for the purpose of consenting to medical care?

6. If a guardian ad item is appointed and wishes to approve a particular course of medication that your "client" rejects, do you still regard yourself as representing your "client"?

7. Suppose that the situation was just at the point where a brother of your client reported that your client had ceased taking medication and was beginning to act peculiarly, in much the same fashion as had occurred before prior commitments. You talk to your client who says that

he does not want your help or counsel. His brother seeks your advice about getting help for your client. What do you do?

8. If there is to be a hearing on the petition for involuntary commitment and an attorney for the hospital says that she proposes to call you as a witness to testify about your observation of the client's conduct — but not any communications — may you continue as attorney in the matter?

———————————

The lawyer faced with a situation like that depicted in Problem 42 must deal with the combination of new developments in the substantive law about clients' choice with regard to their own medical needs — refusal to undertake medical treatment, whether it is psychiatric care or blood transfusions, or the so-called right to die — and the uncertain professional duties of lawyers. The Model Code does not provide much assistance. The short paragraph in EC 7-12 highlighted a few issues but hardly gave any conclusive solutions. The importance of the problem for lawyers is recognized in Model Rule 1.14 and its Comment. The drafters have recognized the complexity of the issues and have highlighted the difficulty of the lawyers' situation. They are advised that they should maintain as much of a lawyer-client relation as possible, even if there is a guardian, that they may (and therefore need not) seek the appointment of a guardian when the client appears unable to act in his or her own interest, that they should be concerned about disclosure of a client's disability, and that "ordinarily" (but not always) they should look to an appointed guardian for instructions. Much is therefore left to the lawyer's discretion, including an overall choice of theory: whether the lawyer is to be guided by the "best interests" of the client or whether the lawyer should whenever possible and as soon as possible look to someone else, a guardian or the court, for instructions whenever there is doubt about the appropriate course of action. The selections that follow address that issue. See also Perlin and Sadoff, Ethical Issues in the Representation of Individuals in the Commitment Process, 45 Law & Contemp. Prob. 161 (No. 3 1982).

MICKENBERG,* THE SILENT CLIENTS: LEGAL AND ETHICAL CONSIDERATIONS IN REPRESENTING SEVERELY AND PROFOUNDLY RETARDED INDIVIDUALS
31 Stan. L. Rev. 625 (1979)

A basic tenet of legal ethics requires lawyers to zealously represent their clients' interests. Ordinarily, of course, the client determines the

———————————

*B.S. 1966, Cornell University; J.D. 1969, Fordham University Law School. Partner,

nature and scope of his or her interest, and the lawyer merely uses special skills and training to achieve the goals defined by the client. Yet this principle, so rarely a problem in attorney-client relationships, presents great difficulties when the client is severely or profoundly retarded and lacks the mental capacity and skills in communication to provide the necessary guidance to the attorney. This article identifies some of these difficulties and suggests ways of ensuring effective legal representation of severely and profoundly retarded persons. . . .

THE ROLE OF THE ATTORNEY REPRESENTING A SEVERELY OR PROFOUNDLY RETARDED PERSON

Reports on the quality of legal representation provided to retarded clients, even within the past decade, tell of inadequate effort, unjustified compromise of clients' rights, and distorted perceptions of legal ethics.[39] Although a "new breed" of mental health and mental retardation lawyers is emerging,[40] advocates in this area are inevitably exposed to influences which discourage aggressive advocacy: In bringing litigation, the attorney must, for example, maintain good relationships with adverse government officials whose cooperation will be needed later to secure legislative reform, and with service agencies with whom the attorney will be dealing in informal negotiations in later cases.[41]

Another barrier to effective representation is the apparently widespread belief that courts have failed to define the role of the attorney in representing mentally retarded clients.[42] In fact, the courts repeatedly

---

Mickenberg, Dunn, Sirotkin & Kupersmith, Burlington, Vt.; former Deputy Director, Vermont Legal Aid; former director, Vermont Developmental Disabilities Advocacy Project; former managing attorney, Minnesota Developmental Disabilities Advocacy Project.

39. See, e.g., Lessard v. Schmidt, 349 F. Supp. 1078, 1097-1099 (E.D. Wis. 1972) [vacated and remanded on other grounds, 414 U.S. 473, on remand, 379 F. Supp. 1376 (E.D. Wis. 1974), vacated and remanded on other grounds, 421 U.S. 957 (1975), reinstated, 413 F. Supp. 1318 (E.D. Wis. 1976)]; Hultquist v. People, 77 Colo. 310, 236 P. 995 (1925); In re Wretlind, 225 Minn. 554, 32 N.W.2d 161 (1948); In re Quesnell, 83 Wash. 2d 224, 517 P.2d 568 (1973); State ex rel. Hawks v. Lazaro, 202 S.E.2d 109, 126 (W. Va. 1974). See also Cohen, Advocacy, in [President's Committee on Mental Retardation, The Mentally Retarded Citizen and the Law, 597-609 (M. Kindred ed. 1976)] at 597-609; . . . Dix. Hospitalization of the Mentally Ill in Wisconsin: A Need for a Reexamination, 51 Marq. L. Rev. 1, 33-34 (1967).

40. See Herr, Advocacy: The Missing Link to Fundamental Rights and Services in Protection and Advocacy Systems for the Developmentally Disabled 5-11 (G. Clark & J. Stearns eds. 1977).

41. Other factors include the attorney's likely ignorance of a field pervaded with medical and psychological experts, the complexity and ambiguity in this evolving area of the law, the inability of clients to guide counsel or to protest unreasonable accommodations by counsel, and the close professional and personal ties that often exist among advocates, service agencies, and state officials in this narrow field. See Bellow, [Turning Solutions into Problems: The Legal Aid Experience, 34 Nat'l Legal Aid & Defender A. Briefcase 108 (1977).]

42. See Lessard v. Schmidt, 349 F. Supp. 1078, 1097-1099 (E.D. Wis. 1972); In re

have made clear that the attorney with a mentally disabled client must not only act as an adversary counsel, but must "represent his client as zealously as the bounds of ethics permit."[43] The American Bar Association's Code of Professional Responsibility also makes clear that the attorney with a severely or profoundly retarded client must raise every possible claim or defense, just as he would for any other client.[44] The attorney cannot waive any substantial rights of an incompetent client, or take any action that is prejudicial to the client's interests.[45]

The requirement of zealous advocacy of course requires that the attorney advance the interests and goals of the "client" — the mentally retarded person — and not those of the parent, guardian, or other third-party representative. When an attorney is first contacted by a third-party representative, the attorney should carefully explain that it is the handicapped person who is the "client" and whose interests will govern the course of litigation. As long as the attorney is satisfied that the third-party representative — whether a legal or natural guardian, close relative, or friend — is guided by the best interests of the retarded person, the attorney can expect the third-party representative to protect and help define the goals of the retarded person. Legal and ethical principles require that the attorney obtain a guardian ad litem whenever a severely or profoundly retarded person lacks a third-party representative or has a representative whose interests conflict with his own. But what is the responsibility of counsel when he or she disagrees with the course designated by the guardian ad litem? Even the most concerned representative may project his own views and prejudices into the "best interests" of a mentally disabled person, and the possibility for disagreement will be great as both guardian and counsel attempt to define and pursue those interests.

The Code of Professional Responsibility leaves little doubt that the lawyer must look to the client-representative for those decisions that are normally the prerogative of the client to make.[46] However, the Code also

---

Quesnell, 83 Wash. 2d 224, 517 P.2d 568 (1973); . . . Dix, supra note 39, at 33.

43. State ex rel. Hawks v. Lazaro, 202 S.E.2d 109, 126 (W. Va. 1974). See also Heryford v. Parker, 396 F.2d 393, 396 (10th Cir. 1968); Stamus v. Leonhardt, 414 F. Supp. 439, 448 (S.D. Iowa 1976); Bell v. Wayne County Gen. Hosp., 384 F. Supp. 1085, 1092-1094 (E.D. Mich. 1974); In re Quesnell, 83 Wash. 2d 224, 517 P.2d 568 (1973).

44. See ABA Code of Professional Responsibility EC 7-3, 7-4, 7-19, 7-20; id. DR 7-101(A)(1). See also McCartney v. United States, 343 F.2d 471, 472 (9th Cir. 1965). Practical application of these ethical standards would, for example, compel an attorney appointed to represent a severely retarded client in a civil commitment hearing to look beyond the state commitment law. The lawyer should consider the constitutional arguments which might be raised at a commitment hearing: that the procedures employed fail to comport with due process, that the standards for commitment are unconstitutionally vague, or that the statute improperly fails to provide for less drastic alternatives to commitment.

45. See Pettengill v. Gillman, 126 Vt. 387, 232 A.2d 773 (1967); In re Quesnell, 83 Wash. 2d 224, 235-240, 517 P.2d 568, 577-579 (1973).

46. ABA Code of Professional Responsibility EC 7-12.

requires attorneys to act in their clients' best interests,[47] and to advise clients regarding alternative courses of action and their possible consequences.[48] Thus, while the guardian ad litem or other representative will have the ultimate responsibility for defining the goals of representation, the lawyer is not required to meekly succumb to any course of action suggested by the client-representative.

Occasionally, disagreements may arise between the attorney and the guardian ad litem. In Vermont, for example, the courts in civil commitment proceedings for mentally retarded and mentally ill persons appoint a guardian ad litem whenever the client cannot communicate with counsel. Typically, the guardian will meet with the client, review the client's records, and thereafter discuss the case with counsel. In most cases, the attorney suggests an approach which he or she perceives as best for the client, and the guardian concurs. Occasionally, however, the attorney and guardian disagree over such things as community placement. These disagreements are usually resolved without referring to the court, but that option is available to either representative. Case law in other jurisdictions makes clear that whenever an attorney feels that a guardian ad litem is advancing goals that are not in the best interest of the client, he can seek judicial removal of the present guardian and appointment of a new guardian ad litem.[49] If the guardian ad litem is acting generally in the interests of the retarded person but insists upon a particular course of action that the attorney feels is unwise, then the attorney can seek judicial resolution of the disagreement with the guardian,[50] or can withdraw from the case.[51]

A relationship between a client-representative and lawyer in which neither side dominates will most closely achieve the goals the client would have sought, had he or she been able to communicate directly with counsel. . . .

ALAN A. STONE, M.D.,* THE MYTH OF ADVOCACY

30 Hospital & Community Psychiatry 819 (No. 12 Dec. 1979)

Several years ago, a congressman wrote to me asking if I would testify on behalf of a bill he had filed. His staff, with the assistance of the Department of Health, Education, and Welfare and the Library of Con-

47. Id. EC 7-9.
48. Id. EC 7-8.
49. See Fong Sik Leung v. Dulles, 226 F.2d 74, 82 (9th Cir. 1955) (Boldt, J., concurring); Parks v. Barnes, 173 Ky. 589, 191 S.W. 447 (1917).
50. See Metropolitan Life Ins. Co. v. Carr, 169 F. Supp. 377, 378 (D. Md. 1959).
51. ABA Code of Professional Responsibility EC 7-8.
*Dr. Stone, 108th president of APA, is professor of law and psychiatry at Harvard University in Cambridge, Massachusetts. This paper is the address he gave at the 31st

gress, had determined that it would cost $60 million a year to provide every psychiatric inpatient in the United States with a lawyer. In his letter, he claimed that he had read my book, Mental Health and Law: A System in Transition [1975], and he was confident that I would support his bill on behalf of patient advocates. I responded by return mail that I would be delighted to testify if he would amend his bill to ask for $120 million so that there would be good legal representation on both sides. I never heard from the congressman again. But recently legislation providing for federally funded advocates for patients has surfaced again in Congress, with no recognition of the need for legal representation on the other side.

This is the era of advocacy. We have consumer advocates, child advocates, and patient advocates. The American Psychiatric Association has even amended its constitution and bylaws so that psychiatry too has an advocacy mission. Like the Congress, we want to climb on the bandwagon; we want the public to know we are for advocacy. Advocacy is by no means a new idea. One of the eponyms for Jesus Christ was "the Advocate," but surely his version of salvation was different than the one the lawyers have recently proposed for our patients and for us. It is time to unpack this buzzword, this slogan of advocacy.

The APA's notion of advocacy is that we will champion the medical needs of our patients. The lawyers' notion of advocacy is that they will champion the legal rights of their clients. Where we want the best treatment setting for our patients, they want the least restrictive alternative. Where we want careful treatment planning and continuity of care, they want immediate deinstitutionalization and maximum liberty. Where we are concerned about access to treatment, they are concerned about stigma and the right to refuse treatment. Where we are trying to salvage what is salvageable in the state hospital system, they are trying to close down the state hospital system. Where we want to advocate the medical model, they want to advocate the legal model. Our advocacy and theirs conflict more often than not, but for those who know little about the mental health system, the buzzword "advocacy" suggests both kinds with no conflict.

The root problem of the conflict is only understood when the last difference I mentioned, the legal model versus the medical model, is examined not in terms of goals but of procedures. The lawyers' notion of advocacy comes naturally; it is part of the Anglo-American adversarial system of justice. Each side is meant to have a zealous advocate. The work of the court advances as these advocates joust with each other.

The lawyers' canons of ethics give great importance to this duty to be a zealous advocate. Indeed, it would be fair to say that the basic credo

Institute on Hospital & Community Psychiatry, held September 3–6, 1979, in New Orleans.

of legal ethics is that the lawyer should feel free to proceed almost un-restrained as an advocate because there is a zealous advocate on the other side. This is the very basis of our adversarial system of justice. It is not a search for truth. Rather, each side struggles for an advantage, and out of the struggle the judge and jury pluck the just resolution.

The lawyers, then, have a long tradition of advocacy. It combines a notion of rights and a professional way of doing things. When their form of advocacy is applied in the political arena, it can become a formidable tool for achieving change. During the past decade, such advocacy has been the means for giving power to the powerless. Consumer advocates have given consumers who as individuals had no power the ability to assert their common demands. Civil rights advocates have done the same for minority groups. Advocates for welfare recipients and the aged have been able to have an impact on the entrenched federal bureaucracies. These advocates use the courts, the class-action suit, the media, and the political process to advance the needs and interests of the group they represent. They do so by presenting the needs and interests of their group as legal rights.

Given the success of this kind of advocacy, one can easily understand how advocacy has become a buzzword and a slogan appealing to liberals and populists alike. But it is crucial to recognize that where advocacy has really worked, it has worked because, first, the group's needs and interests could be readily defined; second, the interests could be formulated as some legal right; and third, paradoxically to us but basic to the system of law, the legal adversary had a powerful opponent, an adversary who had something to lose. Without an adversarial struggle, the judge has no real ability to find a resolution that is balanced.

None of these crucial elements have been present in most of the litigation in the field of mental health over the past decade. Legal advocates for the mentally ill have not been willing to consider seriously the needs of the mentally ill and to formulate those needs as legal rights. Instead they have done the reverse. They have treated rights as if they constituted the needs of the mentally ill.

And who is the powerful adversary for the mental health advocate to attack? There is none. Instead, mental health advocates, with the assistance of the radical antipsychiatrists, had to invent a powerful adversary — the psychiatric establishment. But the last decade has made it clear that psychiatrists are anything but a powerful adversary. Wherever the mental health advocate pressed, the psychiatric profession gave way. In the court rooms, there was almost never a zealous legal advocate to oppose the self-appointed patient advocate.

Consider the kind of case in which Congress wants to provide legal advocates, for the patient who may be involuntarily confined. Take for example, a prototypical patient, named Mr. Jones. He has, for the past month, been increasingly agitated. For some time he has been convinced that people at work were conspiring against him. Last week he decided people were reading his mind, and he began to hear voices accusing him of sexual perversity. Since then, he has been unable to sleep and has stopped going to work. He now refuses to communicate with his wife or children. He paces up and down with a pained expression on his face; he is obviously suffering. He is now either crazy, or, as his legal advocate might argue, exercising his right to be different.

Mrs. Jones begs and cajoles her husband to come with her to the emergency room of the nearby community hospital. He reluctantly agrees. There he sees a psychiatrist who, after interviewing Mr. Jones and getting a history from Mrs. Jones, makes a diagnosis of acute paranoid schizophrenia and recommends hospitalization. Mr. Jones adamantly refuses any treatment at all. Mrs. Jones begs the doctor to do something: she is afraid her husband will lose his job, and she worries about the effect of this strange behavior on the children.

The question is, What does Mr. Jones need? What should happen now? The following is what the legal advocates believe should happen before Mr. Jones' psychiatric needs can even be considered.

First, Mr. Jones must be provided with his own lawyer, presumably paid for by the federal government, whose duty is to advocate Mr. Jones' freedom. Second, he must have a hearing before a judge within 48 hours and, no matter how disturbed he may get, the doctors are not to begin treatment until that hearing. At that hearing, his lawyer will argue that he should not be further confined and that, if confined, he has a right to refuse treatment. Third, the lawyer will insist that the psychiatrist must inform Mr. Jones of his right to remain silent and his fifth-amendment privilege against self-incrimination.

Fourth, Mr. Jones and his lawyer must be given timely notice of the charges justifying his confinement so that they can prepare a defense. Fifth, he must have notice of the right to a jury trial. Sixth, he is entitled to a full hearing, a trial with the right to cross-examine Mrs. Jones and his doctors, who must testify about the details of his illness and his dangerous behavior. Seventh, it must be proved by clear and convincing evidence that Mr. Jones is mentally ill and dangerous. And, finally, there must be inquiry into whether some less restrictive alternative can be found for Mr. Jones before involuntary inpatient care is ordered. "Less restrictive" for the lawyer will mean least loss of freedom and not "best treatment setting."

I have already mentioned that the estimated cost of these legal procedures was $60 million several years ago; it is undoubtedly much more today. That covers only the cost of lawyers for all of the Joneses; it does not include the court costs, the time of the hospital staff who must testify, and the lawyers, if any, for the other side.

The total costs will far exceed $60 million, and if the federal government doesn't pay it, who will? Why should any state or prosecutor want to go to all that trouble and expense? The state is being asked to use all that money and all those legal resources to justify putting Mr. Jones in a hospital so that the state can spend still more to treat him. What is in it for the state? Prosecutors have all sorts of incentives for putting away criminals, but what is their incentive for putting away Mr. Jones? And what about the incentives of the psychiatrist? Experience demonstrates that psychiatrists have always disliked being involved in civil commitment; with these new procedures, that dislike has become abhorrence.

In sum, legal advocacy is proposed to advance the interests of the patients against a powerful adversary, but it turns out that no one but Mrs. Jones really has an incentive to confine Mr. Jones. The powerful adversary of the mental patient turns out to be a paper tiger, and the psychiatrist is soft as a grape. Nor is it clear that the advocate is concerned or will care about Mr. Jones' needs in all this rhetoric of rights.

There are two important points I want to make here. The first is that the legal adversary system doesn't work well unless there are adversaries on both sides. But you won't have adversaries on both sides unless both sides have an incentive. In the ordinary psychiatric case, the state and the prosecutor have no real incentive, and the psychiatrist doesn't either. Thus in most states today, given the existing statutes and the lack of any real adversary, a conscientious legal advocate should be able to prevent all involuntary confinement. Many lawyers who work as members of the mental health bar candidly admit this to be the case, and some acknowledge that even they sometimes question the value of what they do.

Let me briefly mention another striking example of how the adversary legal model goes astray in our field. During the Supreme Court's deliberation of the need for legal advocates for children who are to be admitted to treatment facilities, a startling case was presented as an example of a violation of rights indicating the need for a lawyer. A child with Down's syndrome was being reared at home with the assistance of various professional programs. His parents, under a respite program, were to take the other children on a one-week vacation while the retarded child was placed temporarily in a facility. This kind of respite program is thought to be one good way to support families of retarded children and to encourage them to keep their children at home rather than abandon them. The legal advocates insisted that the child should be provided with a lawyer whose obligation it would be to resist this one-week respite program, using most of the procedures I described for Mr. Jones.

Once again, the question arises about what incentive the state has to use its lawyers to resist such advocacy. In the end, the kind of legal advocacy the Congress wants to provide every patient would destroy the respite program in the name of children's rights, ignoring the fact that the child needs a family and the family needs the support they get from the respite program.

Some lawyers may insist that I am drawing a caricature of legal advocacy rather than a true picture. One distinguished lawyer, for example, sees the advocacy role as one that tries to place the retarded child in the best facility available during the respite. He sees the lawyer's role as getting Mr. Jones into the best treatment setting with the least loss of freedom. His kind of advocacy is my kind of advocacy, and I can find it nowhere in the lawyers' canons of ethics. He would have the legal advocate take on the duties of the expert in access to mental health facilities. His kind of advocacy looks to needs, as well as rights.

But when I describe this kind of advocacy to the lawyers who are increasingly being recruited to the mental health bar, they generally resist it. In the first place, they don't want to be social workers, and they don't want to be responsible for taking care of clients' nonlegal problems. Their vision of advocacy is the lawyer as adversary, providing a limited legal service: Mr. Jones and the retarded child have a right to be free; it is their job to see to that freedom, and what happens afterward is not their business.

When legal advocates listen to my arguments and hear them, and admit that a system of legal advocates on one side won't work, they usually come to the conclusion that it is up to psychiatrists to see that the hospitals and the state supply lawyers for the other side. Theoretically they are right, and that is why I was willing to write the congressman to ask for $120 million. That would restore the integrity of the adversarial system; the two sides of the argument could be heard.

But no one has ever said that providing lawyers for alleged criminals would reduce the problem of crime in the streets or assist in the rehabilitation of criminals. At best, it ensures that alleged criminals obtain justice from the courts. Similarly, no one can claim that providing individual legal advocates for psychiatric patients will reduce mental illness or assist in the treatment of mental patients. The best it can do is to see that alleged patients get justice in the courts. But it is not at all clear what justice is in this context.

When the Congress supports legal advocacy for mental patients, it ignores the distinction and the conflict between advocacy of rights and advocacy of needs. But that distinction is crucial to the future of effective mental health care in this country. How can we make that distinction clear to the courts, to the legislatures, and to the public? How can we make them realize that legal advocacy will mean that lawyers and courts will be telling us how to practice our profession?

Here we confront a paradox that many psychiatrists do not appreciate. If the American Psychiatric Association is to become an advocate for patients, then to be at all effective, we too have to hire lawyers and learn to work with them, for better or worse. There is no alternative; we will have to do it their way. We have no tradition of advocacy of our own, and without legal advocacy we are helpless. The central task of working with lawyers is to create new laws that will reverse the trend of making rights into needs. We have begun to do that in the last few years and with growing success, as illustrated by the following comment about recent Supreme Court decisions[1] in the Mental Disability Law Reporter, a publication that has frequently been a critic of the psychiatric establishment:

> The Supreme Court's decisions seem to be signaling de-emphasis of procedural due process and a new awareness of the right to treatment in a broad medical as well as legal sense. The Supreme Court has also discussed the tragic implications of denying proper care to those who actually need that care, saying a person who "is suffering from a debilitating mental illness, and in need of treatment is neither wholly at liberty nor free of stigma." Now one sees a new emphasis that promotes the need to allow psychiatrists to practice their profession unhindered by time-wasting legal procedures. There can be little doubt that the American Psychiatric Association through its amicus briefs has made a significant impact upon the legal profession.

Perhaps the author goes too far in saying that we have made an impact on the legal profession, but we have made a significant impact on the future of our own profession and our capacity to treat our patients. With the help of our lawyers, we have taken our professional destiny into our own hands, and surely that is a good thing.[2]

D. THE LAWYER IN A MEDIATION SETTING

PROBLEM 43

(A) You have represented a married couple, George and Nancy, for many years. You have drawn their wills, handled their purchases and sales of several family homes and a number of small business and personal problems. In the process, you and your spouse have become personal friends of theirs and see them relatively frequently on a social basis. George teaches at the local high school and has a modest income from an inheritance from his parents. He is not well versed in financial matters and a friend manages his money for him. Nancy is a partner in a management consulting business that she began with a friend after

---

1. Addington v. Texas, 439 U.S. 908 (1979); Parham v. J.R. et al., 442 U.S. 584 (1979).
2. "Historic Supreme Court Decision on the Voluntary Admission of Minors Issued," Mental Disability Law Reporter, Vol. 3, July-August 1979, pp. 231-234.

their youngest child went to college. Nancy has turned out to have an excellent head for business and the consulting firm seems ready for financial success. George and Nancy have just come to tell you that after 27 years of marriage, they have decided to get a divorce. After discussion, you discover, to your surprise, that they have been having difficulties for at least five years, have sought marital counselling on several occasions, and have reached what appears to be a final decision. There does not seem to be any particular "cause," or bitterness; they have just decided that their lives together have finished.

They want you to handle the details of their divorce. They trust you and fear that if another lawyer gets into the picture, that will only cause trouble. You learn that while they have talked through some of the financial details, they have not reached a complete agreement. Indeed, there are some sticky items, like a vacation cabin and the current home, which both want, and an aged family dog that both love. They are willing to have you serve either as lawyer for both, mediator, arbitrator, or intermediary — they don't really care about the capacity in which you see yourself — but they are desperate to have you see them through this difficult time in their lives so that the divorce is accomplished as painlessly as possible. What will you do for them?

(B) Suppose that you agree to act as intermediary pursuant to Model Rule 2.2, after having explained all your obligations in that capacity. At some point in discussions you become quite suspicious from George's attitude that he may have some assets that he has not disclosed. Do you mention your suspicion to Nancy? Do you continue as intermediary? Would your answers be different if you were acting as a mediator?

(C) Suppose that after many sessions in which you are helping them to bargain, George and Nancy come in and announce that they have reached an agreement. Nancy will receive the vacation home and may reside in the family home rent free as long as she likes. When and if the house is sold, they will divide the proceeds. George will receive the dog. Nothing has been said about whether Nancy will have "visitation rights" with respect to the dog. Do you raise the question?

Given their family circumstances, you regard the whole agreement as very unfair to George. As intermediary, do you say this? Would your answer be different as a mediator? Are your answers affected by whether your suspicions about George's undisclosed assets have been allayed?

(D) Suppose that finally an agreement has been reached that the parties (and you) regard as "fair." The parties ask you to draft the document. Will you do so? Would your answer be the same if you had been acting as mediator? If not, what does that say about the difference between acting as intermediary and acting as mediator?

Alternative, less adversarial, methods of resolving disputes have become increasingly attractive in recent years, not only for their potential for saving time and money, but also for their potential for resolving disputes with a smaller residue of rancor between the parties. Arbitration was an early procedure, but it retained many of the traditional adversary forms, especially insofar as the lawyer's role was concerned. The current experiments in mediation have implicated new roles for lawyers, and it is important in assessing whether lawyers may undertake them to differentiate the many different roles and tasks open to lawyers under the broad heading of mediation. Opinions of courts and ethics committees often do not do so.

Traditionally, courts and ethics committees have emphasized the inherently adversarial nature of a divorce proceeding and have discouraged joint representation in any setting, although that has not invariably been their attitude. More recently, there has been at least a partial shift in attitude. See, e.g., Levine v. Levine, 56 N.Y.2d 42 (1982), 436 N.E.2d 476 (upholding a separation agreement drafted by an attorney on behalf of both parties in a non-mediation setting); Mass. Bar Assn. Committee on Professional Ethics Opinion No. 85-3; Assn. of the Bar of the City of New York, Committee on Professional Ethics Opinion 80-23 and materials cited in those opinions; and Klemm v. Superior Court of Fresno County, 75 Cal. App. 3d 893, 142 Cal. Rptr. 509 (1977).

This trend is discussed sympathetically in Linda Silberman, Professional Responsibility Problems of Divorce Mediation, 16 Family Law Q. 107 (1982). Her article discusses current attitudes toward the major problems of conflict, unauthorized practice, lay intermediaries, and solicitation that arise in many of these different mediation models. A more critical approach, one that is much more concerned about the ability of lawyers to function appropriately in these mediation models, is presented in the article by Richard Crouch, which follows the excerpt from Opinion 80-23.

COMMITTEE ON PROFESSIONAL AND JUDICIAL ETHICS, ASSOCIATION OF THE BAR OF THE CITY OF NEW YORK

Inquiry Reference No. 80-23

We have been asked whether lawyers may ethically participate in a divorce mediation program organized by a non-profit organization. The organization has a staff of licensed mental health professionals who provide marital and family therapy. It now proposes to offer what is known as "structured mediation" in marital cases. Such mediation involves a trained therapist consulting with separating or divorcing couples to aid them in working out various aspects of the separation or divorce, including issues of property division, and child custody, visitation and support. We have been asked whether a lawyer could (a) become part of the mediating team, (b) give impartial legal advice to the parties, such as advice on the tax consequences of proposed separation or divorce agreements, or (c) draft a divorce or settlement agreement after the terms of such agreement have been approved by the parties. We have also been asked whether a participating lawyer could be paid, either by the parties to the mediation or by the organization.

This inquiry raises important and difficult questions concerning the participation of lawyers in non-adversarial roles in dispute resolution. The Code of Professional Responsibility provides comparatively detailed guides for the lawyer representing clients in the adversarial role of zealous advocate or confidential adviser. The Code also recognizes that lawyers may serve as "impartial arbitrators or mediators" (EC 5-20). However, the Code nowhere defines these latter roles and their responsibilities or expressly considers the role of lawyers asked to provide impartial legal assistance to parties with differing interests, in an effort to compose their differences without resort to adversary negotiation or litigation. The Committee nevertheless believes that the principles of the Code permit the extrapolation of certain guidelines for lawyers asked to participate in such non-adversarial activities.

We conclude, first, that the Code does not impose a per se bar to lawyer participation in divorce mediation activities, or to the provision of impartial legal assistance to parties engaged in divorce mediation. At the same time, we believe that particularly in the sensitive area of divorce, the application of labels such as "mediation" or "impartial" advice does not satisfy the Code's concerns for the administration of justice, the dangers inherent in the reliance of laymen with differing interests on the legal advice of a single lawyer, and the appearance of impropriety attendant on such situations. Rather, we conclude that a lawyer asked to participate in divorce mediation and to provide impartial legal advice or assistance in drawing up an agreement must take certain precautions, specified hereafter, to assure that the parties fully understand the lawyer's limited role and all of the risks involved and to minimize the dangers of subsequent charges that the lawyer favored the interests of one party to the detriment of the other. We also conclude that there are some situations, also discussed below, where these dangers and the potential harm to the interests of the parties are so great that it is entirely inappropriate for a lawyer to participate in mediation or to attempt to give impartial legal assistance. . . .

I

The issues raised here require the harmonization of differing policies reflected in the Code of Professional Responsibility. On the one hand, the Code provides that a lawyer may represent multiple clients only "if it is *obvious* that he can adequately represent the interest of each and if each consents to the representation after full disclosure of the possible effect of such representation on the exercise of his independent professional judgment on behalf of each." DR 5-105 (C). (Emphasis supplied) Applying this principle, it has been repeatedly held that the conflicts inherent in a matrimonial proceeding are such, that it is never appropriate to represent both spouses. . . . Such representation is improper even if the parties consent and merely are seeking to have the lawyer reduce to writing an agreement that the parties independently arrived at.

On the other hand, EC 5-20 states that a lawyer may serve in the capacity of an "impartial arbitrator or mediator" even for present or former clients provided the lawyer makes appropriate disclosures and thereafter declines to represent any of the parties in the dispute. . . .

The difficulty arises because the Code nowhere explains what activities constitute "mediation," what responsibilities a lawyer has when acting as a mediator, when a lawyer is "representing" parties or whether it is possible for a lawyer to give legal guidance to all parties to a dispute — to "represent the situation" — without representing any of them or being involved in the conflicts which representing them would involve. See Hazard, Ethics in the Practice of Law 58-68 (1978).

Mediation, particularly in the context of divorce disputes, could have a number of meanings. It could mean acting as an intermediary between the parties to find common ground between them on such matters as who gets what piece of property or who gets custody of a child. Such activity may or may not involve the exercise of professional legal judgments.*

On the other hand, mediation could mean attempting to resolve matters that involve complicated tax or other legal ramifications. As Professor Hazard has pointed out, the word "mediator" can:

> imply that the lawyer is a spokesman for the position of each of the parties, as well as one who listens to the parties express their positions for themselves. It can imply that the lawyer is actively involved, indeed aggressively involved, in exploring alternative arrangements by which the positions of the parties can be accommodated in a comprehensive resolution of the matter at hand. Hazard, supra at 63.

Two other Bar Associations, to our knowledge, have rendered opinions in circumstances similar to those involved here. They have conclud-

---

*The American Arbitration Association has a program for divorce mediation in which the family mediator is not permitted to give legal advice; once the mediator produces a resolution, the parties are referred to their own attorneys. See generally, Spencer and Zammit, Mediation-Arbitration: A Proposal for Private Resolution of Disputes Between Divorced or Separated Parents, 1976 Duke L.J. 911, notes 34-42 and accompanying text.

ed that lawyer participation in divorce mediation — including the rendering of impartial legal advice and the preparation of a written agreement — is permissible because the Code permits mediation and because the lawyer is not "representing" either party and hence does not come within the strictures of DR 5-105 on the representation of clients with differing interests. Oregon State Bar Proposed Opinion 79-46 (1980); Boston Bar Opinion 78-1 (1978). Both opinions recognize the dangers in such situations of inequalities in the bargaining power of the parties and the potential for misunderstandings and later recrimination against the lawyer. They nevertheless conclude, with considerable reluctance, that the lawyer may undertake divorce mediation activities including the provision of impartial legal assistance, provided the lawyer makes it clear that the lawyer represents neither party, and obtains the parties' consent. . . .

II

This Committee recognizes that there are circumstances where it is desirable that parties to a matrimonial dispute be afforded an alternative to the adversarial process, with its legal and emotional costs. The Code's recognition that lawyers may serve as mediators (EC 5-20), as well as ethical aspirations which recognize a lawyer's duty to assist the public in recognizing legal problems and aiding those who cannot afford the usual costs of legal assistance (EC 2-1; EC 2-25), make it inconceivable to us that the Code would deny the public the availability of non-adversary legal assistance in the resolution of divorce disputes.

At the same time, the Committee also recognizes that in some circumstances, the complex and conflicting interests involved in a particular matrimonial dispute, the difficult legal issues involved, the subtle legal ramifications of particular resolutions, and the inequality in bargaining power resulting from differences in the personalities or sophistication of the parties make it virtually impossible to achieve a just result free from later recriminations of bias or malpractice, unless both parties are represented by separate counsel. In the latter circumstances, informing the parties that the lawyer "represents" neither party and obtaining their consent, even after a full explanation of the risks, may not be meaningful; the distinction between representing both parties and not representing either, in such circumstances, may be illusory. Whether characterized as a mediator or impartial advisor, the lawyer asked to exercise his or her professional judgment will be relied upon by parties who may lack sophistication to recognize the significance of the legal issues involved and the impact they have on their individual interests. Further, the "impartial" lawyer may in fact be making difficult choices between the interests of the parties in giving legal advice or in drafting provisions of a written agreement which purports merely to embody the parties' prior agreement. Although the parties may consent to the procedure, one or both may not be capable of giving truly informed consent due to the difficulty of the issues involved. In such circumstances, a party who is later advised that its interests were prejudiced in mediation or that the impartial advice offered or written agreement drawn, by the lawyer-mediator, favored the other spouse is likely to believe that it was misled into reliance on the impartiality of the lawyer-mediator. In short, we believe there are some activities and some circumstances in which a lawyer cannot undertake to compose the differences of parties to a divorce proceeding, without running afoul of the strictures and policies of DR 5-105 — even if the lawyer disclaims representing the interests of any party, purports to be acting impartially and obtains the consent of the parties to the arrangement.

On the other hand, there are clearly circumstances where these difficulties are not involved and where the parties can truly understand, and the lawyer can plainly carry out, a representation that the lawyer represents neither party.

This seems likely, for example, where the lawyer is not being asked to exercise any professional legal judgment — for example where the lawyer is seeking to bring about a compromise or find a common ground for the division of articles of personal property. Such typical mediation activities can be performed by non-lawyers and we cannot conclude that the Code (which permits lawyers to serve as mediators) intended to bar lawyers from performing the same activities.

It also seems true that the lawyer can meaningfully state that he or she represents neither of the parties where the parties simply ask the lawyer to describe the legal consequences of a particular agreement they have reached. Performing such activities would not involve the lawyer in making choices between the interests of the parties.

Nevertheless, even with regard to such activities, there are likely to be situations of such complexity and difficulty that the lawyer must make the judgment that one or both of the parties' consent cannot be considered fully informed. This may be true even where the lawyer merely is asked to provide services that lay mediators may perform or where the legal question he is asked does not require him to choose between the parties' interests. . . .

Accordingly, to harmonize these various considerations, we have concluded that lawyers may participate in the divorce mediation procedure proposed in the inquiry here, only on the following conditions.

To begin with, the lawyer may *not* participate in the divorce mediation process where it appears that the issues between the parties are of such complexity or difficulty that the parties cannot prudently reach a resolution without the advice of separate and independent legal counsel.

If the lawyer is satisfied that the situation is one in which the parties can intelligently and prudently consent to mediation and the use of an impartial legal adviser, then the lawyer may undertake these roles provided the lawyer observes the following rules:

First, the lawyer must clearly and fully advise the parties of the limitations on his or her role and specifically, of the fact that the lawyer represents neither party and that accordingly, they should not look to the lawyer to protect their individual interests or to keep confidences of one party from the other.

Second, the lawyer must fully and clearly explain the risks of proceeding without separate legal counsel and thereafter proceed only with the consent of the parties and only if the lawyer is satisfied that the parties understand the risks and understand the significance of the fact that the lawyer represents neither party.

Third, a lawyer may participate with mental health professionals in those aspects of mediation which do not require the exercise of professional legal judgment and involve the same kind of mediation activities permissible to lay mediators.

Fourth, lawyers may provide impartial legal advice and assist in reducing the parties' agreement to writing only where the lawyer fully explains all pertinent considerations and alternatives and the consequences to each party of choosing the resolution agreed upon.

Fifth, the lawyer may give legal advice only to both parties in the presence of the other.

Sixth, the lawyer must advise the parties of the advantages of seeking independent legal counsel before executing any agreement drafted by the lawyer.

Seventh, the lawyer may not represent either of the parties in any subsequent legal proceedings relating to the divorce.

Underlying these guidelines is the requirement that the lawyers' participation in the mediation process be conditioned on *informed* consent by the parties. . . . [The Opinion goes on to conclude that the divorce mediation program does not violate DR 2-103(D)(4).]

NOTES

1. The advisory opinion's remark that it "has been repeatedly held that the conflicts inherent in a matrimonial proceeding are such, that it is never appropriate to represent both spouses" (p. 335) was written before the contrary holding of the New York Court of Appeals in Levine v. Levine, p. 333.

2. The Ethics Committee never really differentiates the variety of roles that lawyers may be asked to fulfil in a mediation setting. But it is quite clear that when dealing with two parties in a mediation setting, they may participate only by representing neither and not by representing both. Why? Just whom is the lawyer representing? Is it, as the advi-

sory opinion suggests by quoting Professor Hazard, "the situation"? Is
that a good "client" to have in the case? To whom is the lawyer giving
legal advice? Who will pay the lawyer's fee? See pp. 99-103 of the first
edition of this book, where John Frank discusses Louis Brandeis's representation of "the situation." Mr. Frank's article is cited at p. 64, Note
6.

From the client's point of view, is it better that the lawyer represents
no one or both parties? If we look at all the interests involved, is it preferable to structure the situation so that the lawyer has no clients or two
clients? Does having no clients mean that the lawyer has no fiduciary
duties?

3. The advisory opinion envisages a variety of situations of unequal
bargaining power or of complex issues where the lawyer ought not to
act. It does not discuss the method by which the lawyer is to arrive at the
judgment that this is such a case. The conversation with both clients that
elicits the relevant facts often will not be easy. In other cases, where the
lawyer may proceed with consent, the necessary disclosures that precede
consent may also prove very difficult.

4. The advice that the lawyer will not keep the confidences of one
party from the other would also have to be given if the lawyer were
viewed as representing both parties. See pp. 235-244.

CROUCH, THE DARK SIDE
IS STILL UNEXPLORED*

4 The Family Advocate 327 (No. 3 Winter 1982)

It is as difficult today to be against mediation as it once was to be
against motherhood. This dispute-resolution process is riding the crest
of an immense wave of fad appeal, within both the professions and the
media.

Because mediation is peddled as a proconsumer, antilawyer movement, lawyers and judges who may have reservations are afraid to speak
up lest they be tarred with the brush of institutional greed. Any efforts
to criticize the new practice or restrict it by rules can be condemned as
a selfish profession's attempt to protect its turf and maintain high fees.
While the legal world tries to debate some of the questions raised, it is
assaulted by literature that glorifies mediation as the surefire remedy.
The literature rolls blithely on as if there were no other side to the story.

But there is another side; one which has not yet been explored. I see

*An expanded version of this article appears at 16 Fam. L.Q. 219 (1982). When this
article was written, Mr. Crouch was Consulting Editor, The Family Law Reporter, and
Chairman, Ethical Practices and Procedures Committee, Family Law Section, American
Bar Association.

glaring ethical problems to which no one has provided solutions that stand up under logical analysis. There is danger of ethics code violations and malpractice liability for lawyers, as well as a great potential for exploiting unsuspecting clients. I have asked the questions sincerely and politely, and I am still waiting for the answers.

I am talking here about lawyers who are involved in mediation — as mediators or postmediation advisors, draftsmen, or advisor-draftsmen — not about the psychologists and social workers who are trying their hands at it. I also leave aside court-run mediation programs, which have their own ethical problems but are generally more palatable.

The response from authorities thus far has been a curious sideways movement that avoids coming to grips with the tough ethical issues. Although some state and local bar groups have expressed opinions on mediation and dual representation, if they don't reject mediation schemes entirely, they tend to point out the ethical dangers and conclude nevertheless that something so good just couldn't be unethical. The result is a grudging and unexplained approval, bracketed by warnings that lawyers must carefully restrict the alternatives to the few cases in which mediation will be ethically safe. (See generally Silberman, Professional Responsibility Problems of Divorce Mediation, 7 F.L.R. 4001 (1981). See also N.Y. City Bar Ass'n. Committee on Prof. & Jud. Ethics Op. 80-23 (1981), 7 F.L.R. 3097.)

Each new opinion then cites previous ones as being approvals of mediation and dual representation, even if the theoretical class of permissible cases is so thin that it isn't likely to exist in real life. Scholarly articles, built on these ambiguous bar opinions, give reluctant recognition to this fact and argue that things ought to be better. These articles are then cited as promediation authority.

Mediation is being heralded as a financial rescue, but does it really save money? I have seen fairly expensive mediation services added as an extra layer to the already long and costly process of negotiating a separation agreement. In some cases, I think two adversary lawyers would hash out an agreement by means of traditional divorce negotiation — with the ever-present threat of litigation as a backdrop — in a fairly short time.

The parties may not feel the same personal identification with the agreement that supposedly keeps them more loyal to it in the future. But sometimes the traditional method, which keeps the parties apart, is not only quicker and cheaper, but less stressful. Sometimes I suspect that the people who want to continue intense hostile involvement and personal stress, and who aren't interested in saving money or time, are just the ones that mediation gets. And those who go into it seeking reduced costs and less stress and end up with neither will feel that lawyers have swindled them once again.

EXPLOITATION

I also wonder about the mediators who unwittingly facilitate the exploitation of one party. In trying to preserve the mediation climate, a lawyer has to make some very subtle judgments about when to alert the other party to overreaching. The new ideas of client self-determination and autonomy are consistent with letting one party freely choose to be a victim of exploitation. However, the degree to which a person's choice is free is questionable. For one thing, the facts of long-standing marriages can be so subtle that the dominant party is actually the one who appears as the weaker, fooling even experienced observers.

The lawyer may go to unwarranted lengths to keep the tenuous mediation agreement from breaking down. Whether the lawyer lets mediation go on or solves the problem by cutting mediation off, he or she is probably acting for one party and against the other. In most exploitation situations, continuing the mediation means that one party benefits while the other loses.

In addition, ignorance of what a court would do with the particular case usually benefits one party. If the lawyer sounds the alarm of overreaching and stops mediation, it had better be sufficiently exploitative to warrant this remedy. Scuttling the mediation effort not only hurts the party who was dominant at that moment, but wastes the time, money, and effort of both parties.

Both lawyers and mediation centers have an interest in seeing "successful" mediation proceed. Publicity from two satisfied clients who serve as "living advertisements" is a tempting inducement in mediation. In fact, it is just what you don't get in law practice. Therefore, producing a compromise that is not entirely fair may appear the preferable alternative in some close cases.

The mediation movement's strong bias against anything morally "judgmental" has led to an ideological belief that you can compromise anything. This means meeting halfway some propositions that may be not only unspeakable, but plainly irrational.

IS ANYONE REPRESENTED?

Next, what is this nonsense about "representation"? Representation, as conceived by the legal profession as well as the English language, is something far removed from what goes on in mediation. The lawyer who plays mediator is more like an impartial umpire and discussion leader, and is certainly not "representing the interests" of one person against the other as an advocate.

Yet this confused idea of simultaneously representing the two opponents is found throughout much of the rhetoric. It is particularly evident when you ask for an explanation of a separation agreement paragraph saying "each party acknowledges he or she has had independent legal representation," and the response is, "Oh, the mediator was the independent legal representation for us both."

The Kutak Commission's suggested new ethics rule on conflict of interest embodies an even more confused concept. It starts out talking about a single lawyer representing codefendants or coplaintiffs to the court, and then applies this concept to the vastly different notion of representing opposing parties to each other and to the courts. Because of the pressures for legitimizing a lawyer-mediation industry, this plainly inapplicable language will most certainly be used to justify dual representation in divorce.

Some lawyers grasping for rationalizations say that they are really representing the family unit or, if custody is involved, the children. But if the family unit could be a lawyer's client, its interests would differ from those of some of the individuals. Any lawyer who doesn't think so has not explored all the ramifications. (See Pelham v. Griesheimer, 417 N.E.2d 882, 7 F.L.R. 2403 (Ill. App. 1981); Md. State Bar Ass'n. Eth. Committee Op. 80-55A (1980), Informal Ethics Opinion, Md. Bar J., Jan. 1981, at 8.) The kids do not pay the bills, and it has to be presumed that the person who does is usually the one who receives the lawyer's loyalty.

The best mediators and postmediation lawyers say as clearly as possible that they are not representing anybody in this business. But these disavowals, which are required by some of the ethics opinions, may not be effective when offset by other seductive and confusing generalities. (See Or. State Bar Legal Eth. Committee Op. 70-46 (1980); N.Y. op., supra.)

It is not enough to disavow "representation" in just those words. Clients should be told clearly that an attorney-client relationship has not been formed and that the "service" they are receiving is not the kind lawyers traditionally provide. The contract and waiver which the clients sign should indicate that this is a new, experimental product designed to save them money.

We assume that clients knowingly agree to do without all those good things expected of an advisor-advocate. But we are being fooled along with our clients. What most of them really seek, and at first think they are getting, is the modern alternative plus the traditional lawyer-client relationship.

RATIONALIZATIONS

Many lawyers rationalize their divided loyalties by saying they serve as a "mere scrivener," which would mean that they simply "put into legal language" what the parties have already agreed to without lawyers. While this sounds nice, it doesn't hold up and has been rejected by legal ethics opinions. Since legal language is just plain English, the clients themselves could put a separation agreement into writing. The only thing a drafting lawyer can add is what will protect or advance a contracting party's interests.

This is why the best lawyers ask, "How can you draft anything impartially?" Every slight variation in wording, every comma and period, makes one side's potential future court position better. The most scrupulous practitioners say they will "draft for both" only if each party also has an independent private lawyer. This three-lawyer scheme is ideal for many reasons, but how great a device is it for saving money?

This is where it begins to get sticky. The various schemes might include:

- "impartial legal advice" by one lawyer after lay mediation;
- "impartial legal advice" by a second lawyer after lawyer mediation;
- mediation and post mediation advice or drafting, or both, by the same lawyer;
- "representation" to the court for divorce-procurement purposes by the mediator-lawyer;
- the same thing by the postmediation advice and drafting lawyer; or
- divorce procurement by yet another postmediation, postadvice, and postdrafting lawyer.

The most influential ethics opinions so far have said that a lawyer can get involved in the mediation scheme in some way as long as he or she does not represent either of the parties afterwards in court. (See N.Y. op., supra; and Md. op., supra; Or. State Bar proposed op. 79-46 (1980); Boston Bar Ass'n. op. 78-1 (1979).)

It is agreed that there should be no postmediation representation by involved lawyer if the agreement breaks down resulting in a contested divorce case. As to an uncontested case, opinion is divided. But the New York City bar opinion, the Oregon bar opinion, and the Boston bar opinion said "no."

Lawyer conflict-of-interest questions have long been resolved by resorting to the legal principle that no wrong is done to one who consents. But consent to a waiver this complicated and this far reaching is something else again. Considering the number of lawyers who fail to appreciate the amount of conflict of interest being consented to or protections forfeited, it is unlikely that clients appreciate how much protection they are giving up. While truly informed consent in this situation may be impossible, it certainly would require a full explanation of what, in terms of legal ethics, is going on.

The recent ethics opinions that carve out a niche for mediation try to cure this problem by saying that, after taking all the other precautions required, a lawyer must stop trying to be "impartial" when the conflict seems so severe that the effort should not persist. Earlier ethics codes, however, made it easier. They just said that we can assume divorce is one area where the conflict of interest will always be so severe that you can't serve opposing masters, no matter how much they consent. Now the idea is that a new rule will let the individual lawyer — a mass of ethically sensitive nerve endings — be the judge of that.

THE LAWYER'S PERILOUS CHOICE

Of course, making the lawyer the judge of his or her own cause in ethics matters is an old idea. The lawyer, erring on the side of caution and avoiding the very appearance of evil, is supposed to perceive and avoid conflicts of interest. But the old code gave the lawyer better guidelines to do that with. Perceiving when a divorce matter is too conflict ridden to go on with is a very difficult concept. It can be downright ridiculous when you consider the background against which this decision will be made.

The lawyer who cuts off mediation at any point will have many people to answer to. In addition to losing some anticipated fees, if not some earned ones, the lawyer isn't likely to get much new business by word-of-mouth advertising from clients who have wasted their time and money. If this happens often enough, the lawyer won't get any more referrals from that mediation center either.

As a result, sensitive lawyers worry about another point of conflict between modern mediation plans and the ethics rules as we have known them. A lawyer is not supposed to sacrifice his or her independence by becoming subject to the control of lay agencies. Yet the desire to stay on a mediation referral panel can put great pressure on a lawyer. The mediation shops do not want a vast number of mediations to be terminated.

Controls can be tight. In one of the most aggressively merchandised mediation variants being pushed today, the couple has a lawyer picked for them if they can't agree on one from the acceptable group, and they promise at the outset not to seek any independent legal advice. (See Cooggler, supra, at 123.)

The current ABA ethics code forbids referral-panel schemes that will mean lay-organization control over the content of a lawyer's advice. Some commentators suggest the freedom-of-association exception for First Amendment organizations and their causes as an answer to this, but ethics opinions have held that mediation shops don't come within that exception. (See Va. State Bar. op. of June 10, 1980.) Rather, it looks like the kind of organizational influence on professional advice that could easily happen in a mediation shop is exactly what the code provision was written to avoid.

For these reasons, some analysts wonder whether it is ever possible to secure a truly ironclad waiver from parties who consent to the ethical shortcuts. Whenever the lawyer comes into the mediation process, he or she will be asking two opponents to waive legal rights they don't fully understand, without consulting an independent advisor who doesn't also "represent" the other side.

PROCEEDING WITH CAUTION

The most careful lawyers in the mediation business avoid many of these problems by being very stingy with themselves. These lawyers will provide the mediation, the drafting, or the "joint independent advice" only if there are two other lawyers outside the process to provide individual counsel. They often announce at the outset that some other lawyer will have to go to court for one or both of the parties. They don't try to combine mediation with drafting, drafting with advice, or any of these with court representation, but instead are content to be paid for only one phase.

Thus, they deny themselves any of the shortcuts to which greed, laziness, or excess zeal may otherwise lead. This doesn't help much to reduce expenses, but many of these mediators say they never promised it would. They conduct their practices in accordance with the Maryland and New York City bar opinions, which I think represent the best thinking so far on the subject. While their practices don't meet all of the ethical objections, they do meet many of them.

I recently asked another lawyer, who has for years preached antiadversary divorce and whose judgment I respect highly, how he answers some of these grave mediation problems. His reply was quite frank: "If you mean could I ever draft a waiver that would insulate me from malpractice liability when I'm counseling both parties in a mediation case, the answer is no. But I think the search for an alternative is important enough that I must take the risk. Somebody's got to do it."

Maybe that is the answer; it is the best one I have heard so far. Maybe it is impossible to do any more for clients than we are doing now and still insulate ourselves.

But maybe the real villain of the piece is "defensive practice." It is the cruel law to which attorneys interested in survival have to conform their practices, and yet it runs up the costs of divorce in a way clients will hardly understand. Lately, it has run to illogical, indefensible extremes. . . .

Ultimately, I think either mediation or extreme defensive practice has to go. If we phrase our new ethics rules to endorse any of the various mediation experiments popular today, then we are really rejecting some of the important defensive-practice assumptions, and we should say so. This would be a tremendous service to the bar and to our clients. In its current form, defensive practice exerts a baneful influence on traditional family law practice and a crippling influence on the honest effort to find alternatives.

Conclusion

I am not against mediation. In fact, I can list several reasons why divorcing couples need an alternative to the dismal spectacle of unnecessarily destructive litigation. I also know that there are some cases in which the parties can legitimately say that the divorce settlement was going smoothly until the lawyers got into it.

Mediation is not the cure-all that the hucksters, the cultists, and the happy zealots among the learned professions would have us believe, but it is a worthwhile idea. If mediation lowers the cost of divorce by replacing expensive lawyer hours with less expensive mediator hours, and gives people settlements they are more willing to live with because they can't blame the mistakes on their lawyers, then it will be a noble achievement.

This is why I would like to see the questions answered. The answers provided by the movement so far have been mere conclusory assertions — or no answers at all. To call them replies is to insult the intelligence of an entire profession. I keep hearing that the real answers are just around the corner. I am not hostile toward mediation, but I am still waiting.

CHAPTER 6

SOME SPECIAL OFFICE AND COURT ISSUES

This chapter continues our discussion of specific problems that may come up in handling contested matters in our adversary system, either in the office or in court. The Model Code and Model Rules contain a good deal of general language, but also some specific prohibitions, in connection with many of these situations. See DR 7-101 through DR 7-110 and EC 7-19 through EC 7-39 and Rules 3.1-3.4, 3.8, 4.1, and 4.4.

ABA Standards Relating to The Prosecution Function and The Defense Function

Many of the problems that follow relate to criminal matters, and in fact one way to consider the materials in the chapter is to treat the criminal and civil matters as separate groups. A special note, however, should be added about the former. There has been a wealth of writing in recent years about the professional responsibility of prosecutors and defense counsel. A compilation appears in ABA Standards Relating To The Prosecution Function and The Defense Function 322-327 (1st ed. 1971). The Model Code and the Model Rules address criminal matters directly in a number of places, but their coverage of specific problems that arise in the criminal context is spotty.

However, at the same time that the ABA's Special Committee on Evaluation of Ethical Standards was preparing the Model Code for submission to the appropriate state and federal authorities for adoption, its Special Committee on Standards for the Administration of Criminal Justice was sponsoring a study whose aim was the preparation of "standards" relating to "the entire spectrum of the administration of criminal justice, including the functions performed by law enforcement officers, by prosecutors and by defense counsel, and the procedures to be followed in the pretrial, trial, sentencing and review stages." Id. at vi. In preparing standards for that part of the project relating to the prosecution and defense function, the drafters noted the paucity of authority: "The former ABA Canons of Ethics and advisory opinions under them and the new ABA Code of Professional Responsibility are cited where pertinent, and the opinions of writers are noted in some instances, but these too are not comprehensive and their weight may be open to question in some cases on the ground that their authors had limited personal experience in the field." Id. at 7. The drafters continued, rather sententiously, "The true authority in the areas dealt with in these two reports resides in tradition and sound practices; relatively little is to be found in holdings of courts or the general literature." Id. In any event, the drafters proceeded to draw up standards of conduct for prosecutors and defense counsel in order to provide education and guidance and also to serve as the basis for imposition of discipline. The Standards were revised in 1979 but the changes were "for the most part relatively minor." 1 ABA, Standards for Criminal Justice 3.5 (2d ed. 1981). Paralleling the distinction in the Model Code between Disciplinary Rules and Ethical Considerations, the Standards characterize certain types of conduct as "unprofessional conduct," and hence subject to disciplinary action, but in other places where conduct is not so characterized, the standard "is intended to serve as a guide to honorable professional conduct and performance." Ibid. The Standards were not designed to be adopted by a process similar to that envisaged for the Model Code. The drafters suggested that adoption as a code, or as rules of court, or simply by encouraging that they be looked to as authority to be used in deciding cases, were all appropriate, and various jurisdictions have followed these different methods although the last has been by far the most common utilization of the Standards. Id. at xix, xxvii.

A. THE PROSECUTOR'S CHARGING FUNCTION

PROBLEM 44

You are a prosecutor and as a practical matter your office has for many years treated as misdemeanors certain kinds of cases that could have been prosecuted as felonies whenever there is a short, or no, prior criminal record. However, your office also charges a felony in all cases where a felony charge is possible because there is insufficient time to make a thorough enough investigation to be sure that discretion should be exercised to treat the case as a misdemeanor. When, at plea bargaining time in a particular case, you conclude that the case should be so treated, should you disclose that fact to defense counsel immediately, or should you use the presence of the felony charge to help conclude a misdemeanor plea more readily?

PROBLEM 45

You are a prosecutor, and your first assistant has just reported that she is about to file criminal charges in the following circumstances. The defendant has been arrested many times in connection with a variety of theft and assault situations but never convicted. The police have been working on a very large robbery and have discovered some evidence linking defendant to it but not enough, in her opinion, to make out a case of probable cause. The statute of limitations is about to run and the detective in charge of the case has just been given a tip that he believes will provide the needed evidence. Do you authorize the filing of charges? Is DR 7-103(A) or Rule 3.8(a) conclusive? Suppose there is enough evidence to support a finding of probable cause but not enough to convict. Do you authorize the filing of charges then? Suppose that there is enough to convict but you are doubtful whether you would convict if you were a juror. Do you authorize the filing of charges then?

The ABA Standards for the Prosecution Function (2d ed. 1980) provide the following guidance with respect to this problem:

Standard 3-3.9.   Discretion in the Charging Decision

(a) It is unprofessional conduct for a prosecutor to institute, or cause to be instituted, or to permit the continued pendency of criminal charges when it is known that the charges are not supported by probable cause. A prosecutor should not institute, cause to be instituted, or permit the continued pendency of criminal charges in the absence of sufficient admissible evidence to support a conviction.

(b) The prosecutor is not obliged to present all charges which the evidence might support. The prosecutor may in some circumstances and for good cause consistent with the public interest decline to prosecute, notwithstanding that sufficient evidence may exist which would support a conviction. Illustrative of the factors which the prosecutor may properly consider in exercising his or her discretion are:

(i) the prosecutor's reasonable doubt that the accused is in fact guilty;

(ii) the extent of the harm caused by the offense;

(iii) the disproportion of the authorized punishment in relation to the particular offense or the offender;

(iv) possible improper motives of a complainant;

(v) reluctance of the victim to testify;

(vi) cooperation of the accused in the apprehension or conviction of others; and

(vii) availability and likelihood of prosecution by another jurisdiction.

(c) In making the decision to prosecute, the prosecutor should give no weight to the personal or political advantages or disadvantages which might be involved or to a desire to enhance his or her record of convictions.

(d) In cases which involve a serious threat to the community, the prosecutor should not be deterred from prosecution by the fact that in the jurisdiction juries have tended to acquit persons accused of the particular kind of criminal act in question.

(e) The prosecutor should not bring or seek charges greater in number or degree than can reasonably be supported with evidence at trial.

The Commentary to the Standard notes with respect to the second sentence of paragraph (a) that violation is not characterized as unprofessional conduct "[b]ecause of the frequent difficulty of assessing the existence of 'sufficient admissible evidence.'"

Professor H. Richard Uviller, for many years Assistant District Attorney for New York County, has analyzed that Standard (in its first edition form which, for purposes of the issues discussed, is virtually the same as the second edition form) and set forth personal views in the following excerpt, based on his own experience.

UVILLER, THE VIRTUOUS PROSECUTOR IN QUEST OF AN ETHICAL STANDARD: GUIDANCE FROM THE ABA
71 Mich. L. Rev. 1145, 1155-1159 (1973)

While ABA standard 3.9(a) condemns in its strongest terms the prosecutor who institutes or causes to be instituted criminal charges when he knows them to be unsupported by "probable cause," paragraph (b)(i) of the same standard suggests that the prosecutor may decline to prosecute a case when he himself entertains "a reasonable doubt that the accused is in fact guilty."

The matter is somewhat complicated by paragraph (e), which injects, subcutaneously, a third standard of certitude in the charging decision. On its surface, paragraph (e) instructs the prosecutor not to "bring or seek" charges greater in number or degree than he can "reasonably support with evidence at the trial." The term "reasonably support" may occasion some mystification, which the commentary seeks to explain. The paragraph, we are informed, is addressed exclusively to permissible multiplicity and gravity of charges at the point of accusation, providing the prosecutor's ethical escape from an imputation of harassment or the un-toward acquisition of leverage for future plea negotiation. In this con-text, the commentary paraphrases the provision: "hence, he [the prosecutor] may charge in accordance with what he then believes he can establish as a prima facie case." With this enlightenment, the rather awk-wardly expressed phrase "can reasonably support with evidence at trial" may be read: "can reasonably expect that at the time of trial — despite evaporation, suppression, or other misfortune — he will be able to sup-port with legally sufficient evidence."

The standard of probable cause does not require exacting judgment from the prosecutor, for it does not entail great certainty concerning the underlying truth of the matter; "probable cause" may be predicated on hearsay, and, indeed, does not even import a substantial likelihood of guilt. Like probable cause, the prima facie standard takes little account of credibility questions, but it is a significantly more demanding crite-rion, satisfied only by (1) "legal" (i.e., admissible) evidence (2) sufficiently complete to establish every element of the crime in question, credence aside. So the standard countenances accusation on no greater certitude than the belief warranting arrest (probable cause), but the prosecutor should not "overcharge," that is, he should not accuse of more than he reasonably anticipates he will be able to support with legally sufficient evidence. Read together, then, the trio of provisions sounds like this: The prosecutor *must* abjure prosecution without probable cause, *should* refuse to charge without a durable prima facie case, and *may* decline to proceed if the evidence fails to satisfy him beyond a reasonable doubt.

The interesting part of the standard is the suggestion that if the pros-ecutor, imagining himself in the seat of a juror, would not vote for a verdict of guilty, he may decline to present the matter to the system's designated fact finder. I have heard prosecutors, as a matter of personal conscience, take this notion as an ethical imperative. "I never try a de-fendant," so runs the credo, "unless I am personally convinced of his guilt beyond a reasonable doubt." Or, for some: "beyond any doubt." Realistically, the prosecutor figures that, inflamed by the brutal facts of the crime or for some other reason, the jury may overlook the basis for the doubt which nags his own judgment. And he could not sleep at night having contributed to the conviction of a man who might just possibly be innocent. Of course, in reaching this extra-judicial judgment, the prosecutor will allow himself to consider relevant items which might be excluded from trial evidence. Nor would his refusal to prosecute the case necessarily mean he would decline to recommend the acceptance of a guilty plea, for the confession which normally accompanies the plea may remove the prosecutor's doubt.

Yet withal, the prosecutor's conscientious stand represents a notable modification of our system of determining truth and adjudicating guilt. At the least it creates a new subtrial, informal and often ex parte, interposed between the determinations of the accusing and judging authorities.

Can there be any objection to the prosecutor's transformation of the standard's "may" into a personal "must"? A defendant, of course, can only benefit from this additional safety procedure, and its adoption may move the prosecutor to more diligent and painstaking pretrial investigation, including an open-minded search for persuasive defense evidence. This latter effort comports nicely with the familiar injunction duly intoned by standard 1.1(c): "The duty of the prosecutor is to seek justice, not merely to convict." From these features it may appear that the standards should have placed this burden of internal persuasion on the prosecutor in every case. I think not.

A concrete, commonplace example may illustrate the operation of the precept and flesh out our appraisal of its wisdom. Practitioners know too well a sticky item: the one-eye-witness-identification case. For instance, an elderly white person is suddenly grabbed from behind in a dimly lit vestibule by a black youth who shows a knife and takes the victim's wallet. The entire incident occupies thirty seconds. Some days later, the victim spots the defendant in the neighborhood and has him arrested by the nearest policeman. Although the prosecutor presses him hard, the victim swears he has picked the right man. There is nothing unusual about the defendant's appearance, the victim never saw him before the crime, and he admits he does not know many Negroes personally, but his certainty cannot be shaken. He insists that in those few moments of terror his attacker's face was "indelibly engraved on his memory." The defendant may have an alibi: his mother will testify that at the time of the crime he was home watching television with her (not evidence readily credited). And that is the entire case.

Many prosecutors, I think, would concede that as jurors they would hesitate to vote "guilty" on this evidence. His sincerity unmistakable, the victim might well be correct in his identification of the defendant; perhaps it is more likely than not that the defendant is the perpetrator. And juries regularly convict in such cases. But since he knows the fallibility of identification under such circumstances, the basis for reasonable doubt is clear to the prosecutor.

Should the ethical prosecutor refuse to put this sort of evidence before the jury, withhold from the regular fact-finding process the opportunity to decide the issue? Indeed, should the conscientious prosecutor set himself the arduous task of deciding whether in this instance the complainant is right? If it is his duty to do so, how does he rationally reach a conclusion? For this purpose, are his mental processes superior to the jurors' or the judge's? Or may he — should he — abstain from prejudging the case and simply pass the responsibility to those who cannot escape it? . . .

I confess I have no clear release from the prosecutor's predicament.

I recognize as laudable the taking of one more precaution to avert the horror of convicting an innocent person. Yet, on balance, I do not believe the prosecutor must — or should — decide to proceed only in those cases where he, as a fact finder, would resolve the issue for the prosecution.

Where the prosecutor, from all he knows of the case, believes that there is a substantial likelihood that the defendant is innocent of the charge, he should, of course, not prosecute. Similarly, if he has good reason to believe that a witness is lying about a material fact, he should not put the witness on the stand, and if his case falls without the witness' testimony he should dismiss it regardless of whether inadmissible evidence persuades him of the culpability of the defendant. Short of these grounds for declining prosecution on the merits, I deem the ethical obligations of the prosecutor satisfied if he makes known to the court, or the defense, discovered adverse evidence and defects of credibility in witnesses. . . . Although the prosecutor's discretionary powers may be important, and his detached and honorable presence vital, he is not, after all, the sole repository of justice. Thus, I do not believe that the system is served by canons which overplay the prosecutor's "quasi-judicial" role. He is, let us remember, an advocate as well as a minister of public justice, and the due discharge of his many obligations of fair and detached judgment should not inhibit his participation in what is, for better or worse, essentially a dialectic process. In our well-guided efforts to imbue the system with flexibility and personal qualities of sympathy, we need not sacrifice the values which may yet inhere in the design of controlled contention. . . .

[For the view that the prosecutor should not prosecute in this situation, see Freedman, Lawyers' Ethics in an Adversary System 84-88 (1975).]

B.   INVESTIGATION: POSSESSION OF TANGIBLE EVIDENCE BY A LAWYER

PROBLEM 46

Your client, Paula Bryce, has been questioned repeatedly about stealing $500,000 in a bank robbery. One day she hurries into your office and hands a parcel to you. You ask what's going on and she replies that she believes that the police are about to arrest her, that the parcel contains money from the robbery, that she wants you to return the money anonymously by dumping it down the night depository box, and that if you will not, she will go to the ladies' room and destroy the money. What do you do? Would it make any difference if the money had been stolen not from a bank but from a mattress of an aged couple and represented their life savings? Would it make any difference if it was the Mona Lisa and not money that had been stolen?

What lawyers should do with physical evidence that comes into their possession has become a subject of considerable interest in recent years. See Note, Ethics, Law and Loyalty: The Lawyer's Duty to Turn Over Incriminating Physical Evidence, 32 Stan. L. Rev. 977 (1980). The issue may have constitutional dimensions, raising questions of the privilege against self-incrimination, as when a client gives written information to a lawyer. The Supreme Court dealt in part with the problem in Fisher v. United States, 425 U.S. 391 (1976), where it held that compelled production of documents from an attorney did not "implicate whatever Fifth Amendment privilege the [client] might have enjoyed from being compelled to produce them himself," id. at 402, but that the attorney-client privilege would apply to documents possessed by an attorney that would have been privileged under the Fifth Amendment in the hands of the client. *Fisher,* however, did not address the lawyer's more general obligation apart from the evidentiary issue of the scope of the attorney-client issue. Does the obligation to maintain a client's confidences and secrets, which we discussed earlier, see pp. 141-244 and the obligation to represent a client zealously permit or require lawyers to refrain from transmitting evidence that has come into their possession to the police? Is there a difference between possession of a letter from a client containing a confession and possession of a letter containing a map of the bank's premises detailing the planned holdup? Is there a difference between possession of a parcel containing the stolen goods and possession of a parcel containing a murder weapon? Does the source of evidence, the client or a third party, make a difference?

Some of the issues discussed in the preceding paragraph are suggested by the following case, especially as one considers variations of its facts.

MORRELL v. STATE
575 P. 2d 1200 (Alaska 1978)

[Cline, a lawyer representing Morrell, who was charged with kidnapping and rape, was given a pad containing a written kidnapping plan by Wagner, a friend of Morrell. Wagner had found it in one of Morrell's vehicles after Morrell had asked him to clean it out. Cline arranged to have Wagner turn the pad over to the police. On appeal from his conviction, Morrell claimed that the admission of the pad into evidence denied him the effective assistance of counsel because the pad was obtained through improper behavior by Cline.]

RABINOWITZ, Justice.

. . . As Morrell notes, authority in this area is surprisingly sparse. The existing authority seems to indicate, however, that a criminal defense attorney has an obligation to turn over to the prosecution physical evidence which comes into his possession, especially where the evidence comes into the attorney's possession through the acts of a third party who is neither a client of the attorney nor an agent of a client. After turning over such evidence, an attorney may have either a right or a duty to remain silent as to the circumstances under which he obtained such evidence, but Morrell presents no authority which establishes that a criminal defendant whose attorney chooses to testify regarding to these matters is defined effective assistance of counsel.

Most of the decisions which discuss the situation in question involve bar disciplinary proceedings or contempt proceedings against the attorney for refusing to answer questions or to turn over evidence. In State v. Olwell, 64 Wash. 2d 828, 394 P.2d 681 (1964), an order holding an attorney in contempt was reversed. The attorney had refused to comply with a subpoena duces tecum or answer questions at a coroner's inquest concerning a knife owned by a client. The Washington Supreme Court assumed for purposes of its decision that the attorney had obtained the knife in question as a result of a confidential communication with his client. The court stated that if the evidence had been obtained from a third party with whom no attorney-client relationship existed, communications concerning the knife would not be privileged.

The court in *Olwell* held that incriminating objects delivered to a criminal defense attorney by his client may be withheld by the attorney for a reasonable time to help the attorney prepare his case, and then they must be given to the prosecution. In addition, the court held that in order to protect the attorney-client relationship, the prosecution must not reveal the source of such evidence in the presence of the jury when it is introduced at trial. In discussing the scope of this limited privilege, the court stated that to be protected as a privileged communication at all, the objects obtained by the attorney must have been delivered to the attorney by the client or have been acquired as a direct result of information communicated by the client and not merely have been obtained by the attorney while acting in that capacity for the client. In short, the *Olwell* rule requires a criminal defense attorney to turn over to the prosecution physical evidence that the attorney obtains from his client. This rule requires the defense attorney to avoid giving to investigating or prosecuting authorities any information concerning the source of the evidence or the manner in which it was obtained. Finally, if the evidence is obtained from a non-client third party who is not acting as the client's agent, even the privilege to refuse to testify concerning the manner in which the evidence was obtained is inapplicable.

In People v. Lee, 3 Cal. App. 3d 514, 83 Cal. Rptr. 715 (1970), a district attorney obtained a search warrant for a pair of blood-stained shoes held by a judge pursuant to an agreement between the district attorney and the public defender. The judge and the two attorneys had agreed that the judge would hold the shoes pending a judicial determination of the proper disposition of the shoes. The public defender later testified at his client's trial that he had received the shoes from his client's wife and that he had delivered the shoes to the judge.

In both the *Lee* case and the case at bar a criminal defendant sought suppression of evidence delivered by his attorney to the authorities. The attorney obtained the evidence not from his client, but from a person with whom his client had a close personal relationship. Further, the attorney testified at the defendant's trial concerning the circumstances under which he obtained the evidence.

The court in *Lee* held that the attorney-client privilege does not give an attorney the right to withhold evidence. The court stated that it would be an abuse of a lawyer's duty of professional responsibility to knowingly take possession of and secrete instrumentalities of a crime. (The shoes were an instrumentality because the defendant had allegedly kicked the victim in the head.) In dicta, the court noted that although a client's delivery of evidence to the attorney may be privileged, the object itself does not become privileged. Thus, the California court held that seizure of the shoes by warrant was proper and that the objection to introduction of the shoes as evidence was properly overruled.

Further, the *Lee* court held that the attorney-client privilege did not cover the trial testimony of the attorney concerning the circumstances under which he obtained the shoes because he received the shoes from his client's wife rather than from his client. The court stated that the attorney-client privilege does not protect information which comes to an attorney unless the third party is acting as the client's agent. Although the attorney in *Lee* had obtained the shoes from his client's wife, the court found that she was not acting as the client's agent in turning the shoes over to the attorney.

Also of significance is In re Ryder, 263 F. Supp. 360 (E.D. Va. 1967), aff'd 381 F.2d 713 (4th Cir. 1967). *Ryder* involved a proceeding to determine whether an attorney should be suspended or disbarred. The attorney had taken possession from his client of stolen money and a sawed-off shotgun, knowing that the money was stolen and that the gun had been used in an armed robbery. The attorney intended to retain the property until after his client's trial and then to return the money to its rightful owner.

The client in *Ryder* had put the money and the gun in his safe deposit box. The attorney, knowing that the money in the box was marked and disbelieving his client's story about how the client had acquired the money, went to the bank to transfer the money to his own safe deposit box. Upon opening the client's box, the attorney discovered the shotgun and transferred both the money and the gun to his own box. The court stated in dicta that the attorney's state of mind when he transferred the evidence demonstrated sufficient knowledge to fall within the statute prohibiting knowing concealment of stolen property.

The court in *Ryder* suspended the attorney, holding that his actions did not fall within the protection of the attorney-client privilege. The court noted, however, that neither the client nor his attorney could be compelled to produce merely evidentiary articles, as opposed to fruits or instrumentalities of the crime. This dictum was based on the notion that such merely evidentiary articles could not even be seized in a legal search; and, therefore, their production could not be compelled. In re Ryder, supra at 366, citing Hayden v. Warden, 363 F.2d 647 (4th Cir. 1966), rev'd 387 U.S. 294, 87 S. Ct. 1642, 18 L. Ed.2d 782 (1967). The rule that mere evidence may not be seized in a lawful search has since been disapproved. Warden v. Hayden, 387 U.S. 294, 306-307, 87 S. Ct. 1642, 1649-1650, 18 L. Ed. 2d 782, 791-92 (1967). Therefore, we think that no distinction should be drawn in the privilege context between physical evidence obtained by a criminal defense attorney which is "mere evidence" of a client's crime and that which may be said to be either a fruit or an instrumentality of the crime. . . .

From the foregoing cases emerges the rule that a criminal defense attorney must turn over to the prosecution real evidence that the attorney obtains from his client. Further, if the evidence is obtained from a non-client third party who is not acting for the client, then the privilege to refuse to testify concerning the manner in which the evidence was obtained is inapplicable. We think the foregoing rules are sound, and we apply them in reaching our resolution of the effective assistance-of-counsel issue in the case at bar.

Morrell correctly cites cases which establish that misprision statutes are generally interpreted to require an affirmative act of concealment in addition to a failure to disclose a crime to the authorities. See United States v. Daddano, 432 F.2d 1119 (7th Cir. 1970), cert. denied, 402 U.S. 905, 91 S. Ct. 1366, 28 L. Ed. 2d 645 (1971). However, the cases disciplining attorneys for failing to turn over evidence or upholding denials of motions to suppress evidence turned over by attorneys do not rest alone on the notion that an attorney who does not turn over such evidence may be guilty of a crime. The cases cited are also based on the proposition that it would constitute unethical conduct for an attorney — an officer of the court — to knowingly fail to reveal relevant evidence in a criminal case.

We believe that Cline would have been obligated to see that the evidence reached the prosecutor in this case even if he had obtained the evidence from Morrell. His obligation was even clearer because he acquired the evidence from Wagner, who made the decision to turn the evidence over to Cline without consulting Morrell and therefore was not acting as Morrell's agent.

Since Cline was obligated to see that the evidence reached the prosecutor, Morrell cannot have been deprived of effective assistance of counsel by Cline's decision to return the evidence to Wagner. Further, Cline's efforts to aid Wagner's transfer of the evidence to the police appear to have been within the scope of Cline's obligation. Cline could have properly turned the evidence over to the police himself and would have been obliged to do so if Wagner had refused to accept the return of the evidence.[17]

One additional aspect of this issue remains for discussion. As was noted earlier, the Ethics Committee of the Alaska Bar Association gave Cline an advisory opinion as to what to do with the questioned legal pad. The opinion advised Cline to return the subject papers to Wagner, to explain to Wagner the law on concealment of evidence,[18] and to withdraw from the case if it later became obvious to Cline that a violation of ethical rules would result from his continued representation of Morrell. On June 6, 1977, the Board of Governors of the Alaska Bar Association adopted Ethics Opinion 76-7 which embodied the advice the Ethics Committee had earlier given Cline. The opinion also stated, however, that Cline would be ethically obligated not to reveal the existence of the physical evidence "unless required to do so by statute." The Bar Association declined to render an opinion as to the applicability of AS 11.30.-315 or other state law.

We think Cline followed the advice of the Bar Association in relation to his dealings with Wagner. It also appears to us that Cline could have reasonably concluded that AS 11.30.315 required him to reveal the existence of the physical evidence; and thus, although he affirmatively involved himself in the revelation of the evidence's existence, he did follow the advice of the Bar Association as it dealt with his obligation to preserve his client's secrets.

Assuming Ethics Opinion 76-7 is a correct statement of the law,

---

17. The only remaining question is whether Cline's testimony concerning the Wagner incident was within the attorney-client privilege and, if it was, whether the testimony deprived Morrell of his rights to effective assistance of counsel and to a fair trial. While the *Olwell* rule might have imposed a duty on Cline to remain silent as to these matters if Cline had obtained the evidence from Morrell, the acquisition of incriminating evidence from a nonclient third party who is not acting as a client's agent falls outside the attorney-client privilege. Cline could not have claimed that the attorney-client privilege precluded him from testifying as to his acquisition of the evidence from Wagner. Therefore, Morrell cannot have been deprived of effective assistance of counsel by Cline's testimony.

18. AS 11.30.315 provides:

Destroying, altering or concealing evidence. A person who wilfully destroys, alters or conceals evidence concerning the commission of a crime or evidence which is being sought for production during an investigation, inquiry or trial, with the intent to prevent the evidence from being discovered or produced, is guilty of a misdemeanor and upon conviction is punishable by imprisonment for not more than one year, or by a fine of not more than $1,000, or by both.

whether Cline rendered effective counsel then turns on whether he could reasonably have concluded that AS 11.30.315 required him to reveal the existence of the evidence. Otherwise, the opinion states that he had an ethical obligation not to reveal the evidence. AS 11.30.315 makes it a crime to willfully destroy, alter or conceal evidence concerning the commission of a crime or evidence which is being sought for production during an investigation, inquiry or trial, with the intent to prevent the evidence from being discovered or produced. While statutes which address the concealing of evidence are generally construed to require an affirmative act of concealment in addition to the failure to disclose information to the authorities, taking possession of evidence from a nonclient third party and holding the evidence in a place not accessible to investigating authorities would seem to fall within the statute's ambit. Thus, we have concluded that Cline breached no ethical obligation to his client which may have rendered his legal services to Morrell ineffective. . . .

NOTES

1. The court in *Morrell* discusses most of the major cases that have considered the issue of lawyers' obligations when physical evidence comes into their possession. Some of these cases involved receipt of the evidence from a third party and some receipt from the defendant. *Morrell* and the cases it discusses hold that lawyers have an obligation to turn over physical evidence in both situations. The only situation in which it might make a difference is the evidentiary issue of testimony by lawyers as to how they obtained the evidence. See footnote 17.

2. Note that it has not seemed to the courts to make a difference whether the physical evidence possessed by the lawyer was the instrumentality of the crime (the knife with which a homicide was committed), the fruits of the crime (the stolen money) or evidence that would link the defendant with the crime (bloodstained shoes or a kidnapping plan). But suppose that Morrell had shown up in Cline's office bringing with him a statement of how he had committed the crime so that his lawyer should know everything? Would Cline be obligated to turn that statement over to the police? Suppose Morrell said that he didn't have to prepare a statement because he had already written out in his diary how the crime occurred and had brought the diary with him. The diary even contained a map. Does Cline have an obligation to turn the diary over to the police?

3. How should the lawyer in *Ryder*, p. 356, have behaved if his client, Cook, had appeared in his office, dumped the shotgun on his desk, and headed for the door saying that he was getting out while he still had a chance?

4. If Cook had mailed the money to Ryder, saying that he was fleeing and leaving no return address, what should Ryder have done with the money?

5. Suppose that Cook had written to Ryder saying that he was about to flee and directing Ryder to a rural area where he would meet Ryder. Ryder went and found not Cook but several sacks of money in Bank of Virginia wrappers. What should he do with them? If snow was beginning to cover the sacks and it seemed likely that the money would be destroyed in the coming winter, what should he do with it? If it was not money that Ryder found but a distinctive sawed-off shotgun that fit the description of the one carried by the robber, what should Ryder do? Does DR 7-109(a) help answer the question?

6. An interesting debate on the lawyer's obligation with respect to physical evidence occurred in Hitch v. Pima County Superior Court, 708 P.2d 72 (Ariz. 1985). The majority held that a lawyer may return physical evidence to the source (in this case the woman companion of the client) instead of turning it over to the police, if and only if the lawyer reasonably believes that it will not be destroyed and if the lawyer explains the law on concealment and destruction of evidence. That possibility adds yet another element of risk to the lawyer's decision, the element of retroactive second-guessing of the reasonableness of his or her belief. The dissenters, however, in an opinion by Justice Feldman (author of the opinion on p. 617), would have permitted the item to be returned if the lawyer's purpose in having accepted it had been legitimate, as it was in that case because it was important for the lawyer to examine the item. The only exception would be for items that were contraband or dangerous. The dissenters, however, also advised against seeking to obtain inculpating physical evidence except in special circumstances. See Commonwealth v. Stenhach, 356 Pa. Super. 5, 514 A.2d 114 (1986), petition for allowance of appeal denied, 534 A.2d 769 (1987), for a prosecution of two lawyers for a variety of crimes relating to tampering with evidence and hindering prosecution. Counsel, believing that the attorney-client privilege applied, had been led by defendant to a broken rifle stock used in the homicide but did not turn it over to the prosecution. The court held that the stock should have been turned over but reversed their conviction because the statutes under which they were prosecuted were vague and overbroad as applied to defense attorneys.

A different kind of issue with respect to lawyers' possession of evidence has been presented by the growing use, by state and federal prosecutors, of the subpoena power to seize and examine lawyers' files and to force lawyers to testify before grand juries in connection with matters in which they are currently representing clients. See Suni, Subpoenas to Criminal Defense Lawyers, 65 Or. L. Rev. 215 (1986). Responding to the complaint that such actions and the threat of such actions seriously impinged upon the ability of lawyers to defend those accused of crime, the Supreme Judicial Court of Massachusetts has sought to deal with part of the problem by promulgating Rule PF 15 stating that it is unprofessional conduct for a prosecutor to subpoena an attorney before a grand jury without prior judicial approval where the prosecutor is seeking to compel the attorney to testify concerning a matter in which the lawyer is representing a client.

That Rule has provoked litigation by federal prosecutors seeking to enjoin the state disciplinary authorities from enforcing the rule against them. The Rule was upheld by the district court, 639 F. Supp. 117 (D. Mass. 1986), which thereupon specifically adopted PF 15 as a local district court rule. The district court was affirmed by a panel of the Court of Appeals, 832 F.2d 449, but on rehearing, that opinion was withdrawn and the district court's judgment was affirmed by an equally divided court. The court produced a "majority" opinion and two dissents, one on substantive grounds and one largely on procedural grounds. United States v. Klubock, 832 F.2d 664 (1987).

C. DESTRUCTION OF EVIDENCE: FILES OF THE LAWYER AND THE CLIENT

PROBLEM 47

Client has consulted Lawyer about possible antitrust liability in connection with certain business practices. No suits, either public or private, have been brought or threatened. In reviewing the files, Lawyer points out certain internal memoranda that are likely to be damaging if litigation ever ensues. Does Lawyer have any obligation if without any further advice Client picks up the offending memoranda, and saying that they are the only copies, starts to destroy them? May Lawyer advise that they be destroyed? May Lawyer advise the establishment of a policy of destruction of all memoranda older than a certain date (which includes the damaging memoranda)?

TESTIMONY OF GORDON STRACHAN
6 Hearings before the Senate Select Committee on Presidential
Campaign Activities, 93d Cong., 1st Sess. 2457 (1973)

[The following testimony relating to destruction of files was given during the Ervin Committee's Watergate hearings by Gordon Strachan, a lawyer and assistant to H. R. Haldeman, White House Chief of Staff to President Nixon.]

Mr. Strachan: The next day [June 19, 1972, just after the Watergate break-in], . . . I began going through my files, Mr. Haldeman's files, to see if there were any indications of any information that would be in any way related to this act.

Mr. Dash: Well, did you come to any conclusion as to whether there was anything in the files that would be in any way related?

Mr. Strachan: Yes. I pulled out several documents, most particularly the political matters memorandum No. 18.

Mr. Dash: And that was the one that referred to the sophisticated intelligence plan?

Mr. Strachan: That is correct.

Mr. Dash: Did you also pull out that memorandum or these little notes that you had taken concerning the communication that you had from Mr. Haldeman to contact Mr. Liddy about his capabilities being switched from Muskie to McGovern?

Mr. Strachan: Well, I pulled that document out but I did not take that up to Mr. Haldeman.

Mr. Dash: Now, what did you believe at that time when you took the document out? Did you believe that a break-in at the Democratic National Committee Headquarters was in fact related to this plan?

Mr. Strachan: I didn't know for sure but I had pretty strong suspicions.

Mr. Dash: Did you meet with Mr. Haldeman shortly after you did that, after you pulled that file out?

Mr. Strachan: Yes, I did.

Mr. Dash: Could you tell us when?

Mr. Strachan: I believe it was the morning of June 20. He had returned from Florida. I had given a note to Mr. Higby that I thought I should see Mr. Haldeman. Mr. Haldeman summoned me to his office, and I walked in with the political matters memorandum.

Mr. Dash: I think you had indicated that you were somewhat concerned about Mr. Haldeman's reaction to you about not being informed. Were you still concerned when you met with Mr. Haldeman on June 20th?

Mr. Strachan: Yes, I was scared to death. I thought I would be fired at that point for not having figured that out.

Mr. Dash: Were you fired or did he berate you?

Mr. Strachan:	No, he did not berate me. He said almost jokingly, "Well, what do we know about the events over the weekend?" And I was quite nervous and retreated to sort of legal protective terms and I said, "Well, sir, this is what can be imputed to you through me, your agent," and opened the political matters memorandum to the paragraph on intelligence, showed it to him. He acknowledged his check and that he had read that, and said that he had not read the tab, which had been attached, turned, began reading it, said, maybe I should have been reading these, these are quite interesting, and read the tab.
Mr. Dash:	What tab was that?
Mr. Strachan:	That was Sedan Chair II [the designation given to a political intelligence report on Senator Humphrey's campaign activities prepared by the Committee for the Reelection of the President].
Mr. Dash:	Then what, if anything, did you tell him or did he tell you after he had gone through this memorandum again?
Mr. Strachan:	He told me, "Well, make sure our files are clean."
Mr. Dash:	What did that mean to you?
Mr. Strachan:	Well, I went down and shredded that document and others related.
Mr. Dash:	Now, did you do that on your own initiative as such, or did you feel that you were making sure that you were following Mr. Haldeman's instruction that you should make sure the files are clean?
Mr. Strachan:	No, I believed I was following his orders.
Mr. Dash:	And you shredded all of . . . the political matters Memorandum No. 18?
Mr. Strachan:	That is correct.
Mr. Dash:	What about the memorandum that you had made on the communication with regard to Mr. Liddy?
Mr. Strachan:	Yes, I shredded that also.
Mr. Dash:	Were there any other documents that you shredded?
Mr. Strachan:	Yes, I did go through and make sure our files were clean. I shredded the talking paper between Mr. Haldeman and Mr. Mitchell on April 4. I shredded a reference to Mr. Segretti. I shredded Mr. Segretti's telephone number.
Mr. Dash:	What reference was that to Mr. Segretti?
Mr. Strachan:	Well, there had been a dispute between whether or not Mr. Segretti should continue out in the field functioning somewhat independent. Mr. Magruder wrote a

memorandum to Mr. Mitchell entitled "Matter of Potential Embarrassment" in which he described this individual in the field and how that individual should be
under the direction of Mr. Liddy. Mr. Mitchell had a
copy of that and Mr. Haldeman had a copy of that.
And Mr. Haldeman had told me to call up Mr. Segretti
and to tell him to expect a call and his directions from
Mr. Liddy. I shredded that memorandum also. . . .

NOTES

1. Was there any impropriety at all in what Mr. Strachan did? If so,
what, specifically, was its nature?

2. Suppose the instruction to "keep the files clean" had been given to
Strachan when he took his job. Would the shredding of the same files as
soon as they had been read have been improper? Does the answer dependent on Strachan's state of mind each time he shredded a document,
regardless of whether or not the particular document related to an illegal action?

In United States v. IBM Corp., 58 F.R.D. 556 (S.D.N.Y. 1973), the
court dealt with an unusual question of destruction of records. During
lengthy proceedings in a private antitrust action against IBM, a lawyer
for Control Data Corporation prepared a computerized "database" that
was an essential feature of CDC's ability to locate documents in the vast
IBM files. At the same time the United States was pursuing an antitrust
action against IBM based on the same events that give rise to the private
action. An order was entered in that suit requiring both parties to preserve "all documents, writings, recordings or other records of any kind
whatsoever which relate in any way to electronic data processing. . . ."
Id. at 557 n.1. IBM settled its lawsuit with Control Data, and as part of
the settlement the parties agreed to destroy "work product generated in
support of the litigation." Id. at 558. As a result of that agreement, the
computerized database was destroyed. The government claimed that the
database, or one like it, was indispensable to its preparation for trial and
sought to force IBM to pay for the cost of reconstructing a database.

While the court did not grant that particular relief because it regarded its order as preserving documents and not as adjudicating whether
any particular documents were discoverable, it condemned the "unseemly behavior" of "respected members of the bar" for the action they took
without informing the court. Id. at 559. The court rejected as irrelevant
"affidavits from many distinguished lawyers which affirm the ethical
propriety of destroying work product prepared during the course of
litigation at the time of settlement of the suit" because the affidavits did
not deal with a situation where there was a document preservation order.

Would the position taken in the affidavits be sound if there were no such order? Does it depend upon whether it is clear that the documents destroyed are not discoverable because they are work product? Does it depend on whether the parties seeking destruction know that the documents might be discoverable and will, or are likely to, be sought by another party?

3. A comprehensive description and analysis of the various civil and criminal liabilities for intentional destruction of evidence by clients and lawyers is contained in Solum and Marzen, Truth and Uncertainty: Legal Control of the Destruction of Evidence, 36 Emory L.J. 1085 (1987). The authors discuss the general provisions of the Model Code and the general and specific provisions of the Model Rules, especially Rule 3.4(a), that relate to destruction of evidence by attorneys and their obligation to reveal destruction of evidence by clients. See id., at 1125-1137.

4. Several jurisdictions have recognized a new tort for "spoilation of evidence," which imposes liability for intentional or negligent destruction of evidence. The leading case is Smith v. Superior Court, 151 Cal. App. 3d 491, 198 Cal. Rptr. 829 (1984). See Solum and Marzen, supra note 3, at 1100-1106.

5. Another line of attack in destruction, or nonproduction, of documents cases is suggested by Cresswell v. Sullivan & Cromwell, 668 F. Supp. 166 (S.D.N.Y. 1987), leave to appeal denied, 1988 U.S. Dist. Lexis 1435 (1988). Claiming that they were induced to settle earlier litigation against Prudential-Bache Securities because that company and its lawyers intentionally failed to produce a document called for by a document request, plaintiffs chose not to attempt to reopen the former settlement under Fed. R. Civ. P. 60(b) but instead brought an action in fraud against that company and its lawyers. In the cited opinion, the court denied a motion to dismiss on the ground that Rule 60(b) provided the exclusive remedy and permitted the action to proceed.

6. An interesting twist on the destruction of documents problem is presented by Herbster v. North American Company, 150 Ill. App. 3d 21, 501 N.E.2d 343 (1986). The court refused to extend the tort of retaliatory discharge to a company's chief legal officer, who was employed under a contract at will and who alleged that he was discharged because he refused to destroy or remove from company files documents requested by plaintiffs in a pending lawsuit. The court believed that extension of the tort would have too severe an impact on the special attributes of the attorney-client relationship. Accord, Willy v. The Coastal Corporation, 647 F. Supp. 116 (S.D. Tex. 1986). A bill to reverse the result in *Herbster* by permitting a suit by an attorney fired for refusing to violate a law or ethical rule has passed the Illinois Senate and is pending before the House. The bill also would free the fired attorney from the attorney-client privilege in order to establish the cause of action. The American

Corporate Counsel Association, however, has been quoted as opposing the bill on the ground that in-house counsel should not be treated differently from other lawyers and that the client's right to determine its counsel should override the lawyer-employee's rights in this setting. National Law Journal, May 30, 1988, p. 3, col. 2.

D. INVESTIGATION: TALKING WITH A "PARTY"

PROBLEM 48

Your firm represents the insurance carrier of a surgeon sued by a patient for malpractice. The hospital in which the malpractice is alleged to have occurred was joined as a co-defendant and cross claims have been filed by the surgeon and the hospital against one another. You have been told to interview the head nurse of the hospital to get her version of what happened in the operating room. What problems of professional responsibility do you want to consider before you go to see her? Would it make any difference if the interview was about to take place at a time when the suit had not yet been brought?

PROBLEM 49

Your firm is representing a plaintiff in a class action gender discrimination suit attacking an employer's hiring and promotion policies. The former assistant personnel manager of the defendant has said to a friend who is a member of the class that he is willing to talk with plaintiff's counsel about defendant's informal hiring and promotion policies and has indicated that he knows "where the bodies are buried." He says, however, that he will not talk in the presence of defendant's counsel. May the lawyer have such a discussion without permission of defendant's counsel? May the lawyer avoid any problem by telling the member of the class who brought him the information that she should get the relevant information from her friend and then tell the firm?

There are a variety of issues to be considered in the typical fact situations involved in these problems. In considering the applicable Code provision, DR 7-104(A), the first question is whether the head nurse is to be regarded as "a party" for purposes of application of the rule as opposed to being viewed as a witness, as she would be if an accident had happened in a doctor's office and she were simply an employee who saw, but had no other involvement in, the incident. That question conceals several subquestions. Does use of the term "party" mean that suit must actually have been filed for the rule to be operative? If not, when does the rule become operative? When suit has been decided upon? When suit is likely? When suit is possible, however remotely? Furthermore, is any employee or member of an entity a "party" under the rule if only the entity is in fact a "party"? If "any" employee or member is not a party, what class of employees or members is? What is the relation of this issue to the question, previously noted at pp. 73-75, of the reach of the attorney-client privilege to lower level employees in the organization context? Many of these issues, as well as some others, were discussed in the following advisory ethics opinion. (I should disclose at this point that I was chairman of the committee that produced this opinion.)

COMMITTEE ON PROFESSIONAL ETHICS, MASSACHUSETTS BAR ASSOCIATION
Formal Opinion No. 82-7

FACTS

A lawyer represents a woman in an employment discrimination case in federal court against a major corporation. At a social occasion, lawyer inquired of a friend who works at defendant corporation, but not in a management or policy-making situation, whether she knew of others who may have experienced similar discrimination at the hands of the defendant. Lawyer's friend responded affirmatively and gave lawyer the names of several persons to contact. Lawyer inquires whether he may inquire of such employees about such discriminatory incidents without violating DR 7-104(A)(1) and further asks whether the answer turns on whether those employees occupy management or policy-making positions.

DISCUSSION

We assume that plaintiff's counsel is only seeking evidence relating to the claim sought to be established on behalf of his present client. Other considerations may apply if he is seeking information with respect to potential formation of a class of defendant's employees for purposes of a suit against defendant.

A crucial fact to note is that the inquiry concerns conduct relating to a case pending in the federal court. The jurisdiction of this Committee pursuant to its rules is to interpret the rules of professional conduct promulgated by the Supreme Judicial Court. However, the federal district court has in effect adopted as its rules of professional conduct the rules adopted by the Supreme Judicial Court [see Rule 5(4)(B) of the District Court Rules] and we therefore believe that the inquiry falls within our jurisdiction.

DR 7-104(A)(1) provides that "During the course of his representation of a client a lawyer shall not: Communicate. . . . on the subject of a representation with a *party* he knows to be represented by a lawyer in that matter unless he has the prior consent of the lawyer representing such other party or is authorized by law to do so." (emphasis added) Since a corporation or other organization can speak only through its agents, the issue is the circumstances under which an employee who is not personally a party to the litigation ought to be treated as a "party" by reason of his or her employment.

Interpretations of the reach of DR 7-104(A)(1) when a corporate party is involved, have varied in the relatively few opinions of courts and ethics committees that have considered the matter. All have recognized that a corporation may speak only through its agents and that DR 7-104(A)(1) should be interpreted to forbid a lawyer for another party from communicating with some corporate employees without consent in the situation covered by that Rule. Many have limited the prohibition narrowly to include only employees in the "control group," the senior management with power to commit the corporation. See Sobol v. Yeshiva University, 28 EPD 32,479 (S.D.N.Y. 1981); ABA Informal Opinion 1410 (Feb. 14, 1978); and Los Angeles Bar Opinion 234 (1956) and Los Angeles Bar Informal Opinion 1966-6. A few have extended the group more widely, see New York County Opinion 528 (1965), but until recently there has been little extensive consideration of the rationale for DR 7-104(A)(1) in the opinions.

Recently, however, the Committee on Professional Ethics of the Association of the Bar of the City of New York has canvassed the whole subject in an exhaustive opinion. See Inquiry Reference No. 80-46. Overruling a prior opinion, the opinion concluded that "the principal interest reflected in DR 7-104(A)(1) is the party's right to effective representation of counsel" and "that the corporation's right to effective representation can be guarded adequately only by viewing all present employees of a corporation as 'parties' for purposes of DR 7-104 where the proposed interview concerns matters within the scope of the employee's employment."

The Committee noted that while an attorney might not "alter or shade the facts under the guise of zealous representation," effective representation involved the control, to some extent, of the flow of information to an adversary; "it is an acknowledged aspect of effective representation that the attorney aid his client both to avoid procedural pitfalls and to present truthful statements in the most effective manner."

We agree with the conclusion and reasoning of the New York City committee. We further agree with its views that although there are countervailing interests in the desire of the adversary party to obtain evidence, these considerations have already been weighed in the formulation of the rule, which specifically subordinates this need to the need to protect a lay party from unsupervised communications with its opponent's counsel.

Support for the notion that effective representation of counsel is the touchstone for interpreting DR 7-104(A)(1) is derived from the fact that all who have considered the matter appear to agree that the prohibition of the Rule applies only to present, not former, employees of the corporation. The reason is that former employees enjoy no present agency relationship that is being served by the representation of corporate counsel. Even more important, the position we are adopting is also in accord with the law of evidence as exemplified in Federal Rule 801(d)(2)(D), which recognizes an exception to the hearsay rule as to "a statement by his agent or servant concerning the matter within the scope of his agency or employment, made during the existence of the relationship." This rule binds the corporation with respect to admissions by employees far beyond the "control group" of the corporation. Thus for example, in litigation arising out of motor vehicle accidents it is not uncommon that the corporate defendant has only one agent involved, the driver, who will usually not be a management employee. Rule 801(d)(2)(D) permits the driver's admission about the accident to be introduced against the defendant corporation, and it seems quite in line with the consequences to the corporation to include the driver within the group to be covered by the prohibitions of DR 7-104(A)(1).

It should be noted that we are not attempting to assert that in reality the broader test being adopted by this opinion is the same as the control group test because the law of evidence gives employees the power to "commit" the corporation by reason of their statements, because made with respect to matters within the scope of their employment. Those who advocate the "control group" test and refer to management employees who have power to commit the corporation are referring to management employees with power to commit the corporation more generally, those with power to commit the corporation to policy decisions in the course of litigation and to settlement decisions. Loose use of language concerning employees "with power to commit the corporation" often makes it difficult to be certain whether a particular opinion is advocating the pure control group formulation or the one being advocated in this opinion. See ABA Informal Opinions 1377 and 1410.

The rule adopted by this opinion does not preclude a lawyer from interviewing employees of an adversary corporation without its lawyer's consent in all situations. Where employees have information that does not relate to matters within the scope of their employment, that is, where they are not in a position to bind the corporation by their statements, then their situation seems more analogous to that of the ordinary witness and not an agent and the prohibition of DR 7-104(A)(1) ought not to apply. The familiar example is that of the employee who merely witnesses a traffic accident involving a corporate vehicle.

This discussion now permits us to address the facts of the particular inquiry and to advise the lawyer that in our opinion he may discuss incidents relating to discrimination at a particular corporation without seeking the consent of the corporation's lawyer so long as the subject matter of the inquiry is not part of the particular employee's corporation responsibilities. We do not have sufficient facts to be able to answer the question with greater specificity and indeed in some situations it will not be easy for the lawyer to be certain whether the prohibitions of DR 7-104(A)(1) apply. That, however, would be a problem with any standard that draws a line among corporate employees.

Since this is the first opinion of the Committee discussing DR 7-104(A)(1), we should make explicit what we have chosen not to cover in this opinion. We have not covered the applicability of the Rule to criminal proceedings or to situations where the entity involved is the government or is a non-corporate entity. It has been argued that different considerations may apply to those situations, but we are expressing no point of view. We should add, however, that one argument made for a "control group" interpretation of DR 7-104(A)(1) is that if the entity were a sole proprietorship, an adversary attorney would not be prohibited from seeking information from its employees without its lawyer's consent. While that issue is not before us, we would advise that the premise of the argument seems doubtful. If the employee of a corporation may be a "party" for purposes of DR 7-104(A)(1), there seems to be no special reason why an employee of a sole proprietorship who has power to commit the sole proprietorship ought not be able to be considered as a "party" as well.

One final, important problem should be noted. The Committee on Professional Ethics of the Association of the Bar of the City of New York in its Inquiry Reference 80-46 found support for its rejection of the control group interpretation of DR 7-104(A)(1) in the recent rejection by the United States Supreme Court of the argument for a control group limitation to the reach of the attorney-client privilege in the corporate context. Upjohn Co. v. United States, 449 U.S. 383 (1981). We do not believe that the attorney-client privilege and DR 7-104(A)(1) necessarily require the same coverage of employees within the corporate context. For example, a policy to encourage conversations by lower level employees with corporate counsel through an expansive reading of the attorney-client privilege does not necessarily require the adoption of a reading of DR 7-104(A)(1) to discourage conversations with counsel for an opposing party. However, once we read the policy behind DR 7-104(A)(1) as assuring effective representation of counsel and hence rejecting the "control group" test for DR 7-104(A)(1), it would strike us as somewhat unusual if the same jurisdiction were to have a lesser coverage of corporate employees in the attorney-client situation than in the DR 7-104(A)(1) situation.

The situation in Massachusetts with respect to that problem is very unclear at the moment. Although the Advisory Committee Notes to Rule 502 of the Proposed Massachusetts Rules of Evidence quite rightly point out that there has been no definitive pronouncement of the coverage of the attorney-client privilege in the corporate context in Massachusetts, an unreported Superior Court opinion by Judge Young follows the recommendation of the Advisory Committee and adopts the control group test. In the Matter of a Civil Investigative Demand Addressed to Yankee Milk, Inc. (Superior Court No. 9175 1979). We would hope that when this matter is finally resolved, the Supreme Judicial Court would follow the reasoning of the United States Supreme Court in the *Upjohn* case. In the first place, that would avoid inconsistency between DR 4, the confidentiality rule, which adopts the law of attorney-client privilege as its test, and what we believe is the proper interpretation of DR 7-104(A)(1). In the second place, that would obviate the possibility of different interpretations of both DR 4 and DR 7-104(A)(1) in the federal and state courts in Massachusetts. Different interpretations would create enormous uncertainty among lawyers as to their obligations under those rules, especially since it is often impossible to tell in advance whether one is operating under the federal or state rules and one may in fact be operating under both. Indeed, although we began this opinion by noting that the federal district court had in effect adopted the rules of professional conduct as promulgated by the Supreme Judicial Court, we close by noting that if Massachusetts rejects the *Upjohn* reasoning, we will end up with divergent interpretations of DR 4, and possibly of DR 7-104(A)(1) as well, in the state and federal courts. If the Supreme Judicial Court rejects *Upjohn,* we would then wish to reconsider the interpretation of DR 7-104(A)(1) adopted in this opinion.

NOTES

1. In contrasting the reach of DR 7-104(A)(1) and of the attorney-client privilege to lower-level employees, the Committee notes the different purposes embodied in those rules. Yet it went on to note the relevance of an argument for a control group reading of DR 7-104(A)(1) if a jurisdiction adopted such a test for its attorney-client privilege. More importantly, the Committee was concerned about the possibility of differing interpretations of both those rules by the federal and state courts in a given jurisdiction. That worry is of course compounded, as the Committee notes, by the fact that when lawyers want to converse with employees, they often do not know whether the potential controlling law

will be federal or state. Of course a similar problem exists on an inter-state level as well.

2. As Opinion 82-7 noted, many courts adopt a much more limited reading of DR 7-104(A)(1) and its successor Model Rule 4.2. One such opinion is Wright v. Group Health Hospital, 103 Wash. 2d 192, 691 P.2d 564 (1984), which dealt with a fact situation similar to Problem 48. The court reviewed the various approaches to definition of the term "party" when a corporation is involved. It refused to draw a distinction between employees who merely witness an event and those whose act or omission have caused the event giving rise to the lawsuit. It therefore defined the term "party" as including only those employees who have "speaking authority" for the corporation.

3. A far-reaching attack on DR 7-104(A)(1) as overly protective of lawyers' interests is contained in Leubsdorf, Communicating with Another Lawyer's Client: The Lawyer's Veto and the Client's Interests, 127 U. Pa. L. Rev. 683 (1979). Another critical piece urging a restrictive interpretation of DR 7-104(A)(1) when a "government party" is involved is contained in Note, DR 7-104 of the Code of Professional Responsibility Applied to the Government Party, 61 Minn. L. Rev. 1007 (1977).

4. Rule 4.2 of the Model Rules adopts the substance of DR 7-104(A)(1) in quite similar language. The Comment to that section originally interpreted it to adopt a "control group" definition of the word "party." At the last minute, without changing a word of the Rule, the Comment was rewritten to interpret "party" along the lines suggested by the New York and Massachusetts opinions. Remember that in the Scope note, the drafters of the Model Rules stated: "The Comments are intended as guides to interpretation, but the text of each Rule is authoritative." As far as Rule 4.2 is concerned, the text is hardly authoritative and the Comments are an uncertain guide if they can be written in opposing ways under the same text. The history of this particular Comment also provides a good example of an attempt to use the Comment instead of the Rule to effect policy change.

5. The policy change that was made in the Comment turned out to be controversial. Frank Rosiny, a representative of the New York State Bar Association, was quoted as stating that this provision "caved in to the parochial interests of the corporate bar" by making it more difficult in a suit against a corporation to obtain information from lower-level employees. New York Times, Aug. 3, 1983, p. B9, col. 3.

6. DR 7-104(A)(1) also applies in criminal cases. The Michigan Supreme Court was sharply divided in fashioning a remedy when a defendant while in custody voluntarily made a statement to investigating officers accompanied by an assistant prosecutor who had not obtained prior consent to the interview from defense counsel. All agreed that DR 7-104(A)(1) had been violated. Four judges refused to apply a prophylactic exclusionary rule suppressing the statement, holding that the

Model Code represented simply self-imposed internal regulations that did not govern rules of evidence. They found no constitutional violation and held that bar disciplinary action was the appropriate remedy. Three judges would have suppressed the evidence. Two focused heavily on that remedy as the appropriate remedy for violation of the court's own rules of practice. People v. Green, 405 Mich. 273, 274 N.W.2d 448 (1979). That view of the issue is quite similar to the view of the purposes of the rules of professional responsibility expressed by Judge Newman in a different context, see p. 126, and indeed Justice Levin's dissenting opinion relied heavily on cases disqualifying lawyers in conflict of interest situations.

In United States v. Hammad, 846 F.2d 854, petition for reh'g denied with opinion, 855 F.2d 36, opinion revised, 858 F.2d 834 (1988), the Court of Appeals for the Second Circuit dealt with the applicability of DR 7-104(A)(1) in the context of a case in which a prosecutor had supplied an informant with a fictitious subpoena and had then "wired" him and recorded his conversation with the defendant, knowing that the defendant was represented by counsel. The Court agreed with the district court that the Disciplinary Rule was not coextensive with the Sixth Amendment and hence applied at the investigation stage. However, it rejected the district court's limitation of the Rule to situations where the defendant "had retained counsel specifically for representation in conjunction with the criminal matter in which he is held suspect." The Court reasoned such a limitation might restrict the government's ability to conduct criminal investigations "in that small but persistent number of cases where a career criminal has engaged 'house counsel' to represent him in connection with an ongoing fraud or criminal enterprise." Id. at 839. The Court then stated that it regarded legitimate use of informants as falling within the "authorized by law" exception to DR 7-104(A)(1). In the present case, however, the Court regarded the use of a counterfeit grand jury subpoena with a false signature of the clerk of the court as egregious misconduct making the informant the alter ego of the prosecutor so that a violation of DR 7-104(A)(1) followed. It also held that suppression of the evidence would be an appropriate remedy, although it reversed the suppression in the instant case because the law had previously been so unsettled. For our purposes, however, the bottom line is that the Court did not craft a rule to deal just with the "house counsel" problem. It stated a broad rule that absent egregious misconduct, the use of informants in pre-indictment, noncustodial situations will generally not constitute a violation of DR 7-104(A)(1).

7. In recent years, some courts have suggested the possibility that ex parte communication with former employees may also be within the reach of Model Rule 4.2 and even DR 7-104(A)(1). E.g., Porter v. Arco Metals Co., 642 F. Supp. 1116 (D. Mont. 1986); and Chancellor v. Boeing Co., 678 F. Supp. 250 (D. Kan. 1988). The suggestion that Model

Rule 4.2 reaches former employees relies heavily on the language of the Comment to that section stating that it prohibits communications with those with managerial responsibility and "any other person" whose act or omission may be imputed to the organization of whose statement may constitute an admission by the organization. The contrary view of the Massachusetts committee, p. 369, has been reaffirmed, rejecting the cases cited in this Note. Opinion 88-5.

E.   LITIGATION TACTICS

PROBLEM 50

Lawyer is representing a man charged with passing a forged check. The only substantial issue at trial is identification. The bank teller to whom the check was passed identified the defendant, who was sitting at counsel table, as the person who deposited the forged check. During a recess in the trial, the lawyer had his client switch clothes with another man who bore a superficial resemblance to the defendant. That person then replaced the defendant at the counsel table. On cross-examination, the lawyer specifically directed the witness' attention to the man sitting at the counsel table and asked if he was sure that this was the person who deposited the forged check. The witness answered that he was. Was that a proper tactic?

Consider the words of Robert Keeton, experienced practitioner, thoughtful teacher of litigation skills, and now judge of the federal District Court for the District of Massachusetts.

KEETON, TRIAL TACTICS AND METHODS
4-5, 104-105, 326-327 (2d ed. 1973)

From a long range point of view, as distinguished from concern with the immediate case only, you have an interest in avoiding customary use of methods designed to win cases on grounds that may be regarded as unfair, though legal. A reputation for this type of practice becomes a handicap to you in representing your clients in future cases, since even your more substantial contentions come to be viewed with suspicion by judges familiar with your reputation. The duty of supporting the client's cause is sometimes so forcefully stated as to support the argument that as a trial lawyer you are obliged to assert every legal claim or defense available, except those you reject on tactical grounds relating to the immediate case.[4] But the aim of the trial system to achieve justice, the interests of future clients, and your legitimate interest in your own reputation and future effectiveness at the bar compel moderation of that extreme view.

Consider the use of surprise tactics as an illustration of this problem. The Code of Professional Responsibility does not refer to the use in general of surprise tactics,[5] but clearly the use of such tactics to defeat an admittedly just claim or defense is not supportable. On the other hand, the use of surprise to expose falsification is clearly justifiable. The intermediate ground presents the timeless controversy of "means versus ends." Is it proper to use surprise tactics to defeat on a technical ground a claim or defense that you consider unjust upon grounds that you may not be able to establish? Does it make a difference whether the grounds that you consider meritorious but difficult to prove are factual or legal? It is in some such "intermediate" form that the problem of professional responsibility usually arises. Most cases are settled; in the smaller percentage going to trial, each lawyer generally thinks that the other party is at least seeking more than is justly due, if not making a wholly unjustified claim or defense. Probably the answer implicit in prevailing practice is that it is permissible to use any legally supportable ground of claim or defense, though it is a surprise move, to uphold a position you believe just, whatever the basis of your belief may be. Nevertheless, many individual lawyers practice substantially greater restraint in the use of surprise, often because of concern about taking advantage of a fellow lawyer (particularly one less experienced), as well as concern about fairness of trial methods from the point of view of the interests of the parties to the suit.

The reaction against trickery has contributed to severe criticism of surprise tactics and to a trend toward modification of rules of procedure to reduce possibilities for effective use of surprise. So long as we retain the adversary system of trial, however, no rules can be devised that will eliminate entirely the possibility of surprise. Furthermore, this characteristic is not merely a susceptibility of the system to abuse; it is also a reason for its effectiveness in achieving justice. The propriety of tactical

4. . . . [T]he Ethical Considerations and Disciplinary Rules associated with Canon 7 of the American Bar Association, Code of Professional Responsibility (1969), include forceful statements of the duty to the client — e.g., id., EC 7-1, 7-7 — but along with other statements qualifying the duty to the client in view of other interests. E.g., id., DR 7-101(B): "In his representation of a client, a lawyer may: (1) Where permissible, exercise his professional judgment to waive or fail to assert a right or position of his client."

See also id., EC 7-10, 7-20, 7-36 through 7-39. . . .

5. As to one particular use of surprise, however, see id. DR 7-106(C)(5), declaring that in appearing in his professional capacity before a tribunal a lawyer shall not: "Fail to comply with known local customs of courtesy or practice of the bar or a particular tribunal without giving to opposing counsel timely notice of his intent not to comply."

use of surprise in trials involves competing interests. Surprise may cause an unjust disposition of a controversy because of the want of preparation for an unexpected argument of fact or law, and want of time after it is made to discover and prepare available controverting matter. On the other hand, every exposure of a fabricated claim or defense comes about through some form of surprise tactics; no one would urge a false claim that he did not think he had fabricated so cleverly as to avoid discovery. Surprise often causes a just disposition of a controversy that otherwise would have been improperly decided because of failure of the fact-finder to realize the falsification. . . .

A lawyer sometimes holds the witness' statement in his hand as a means of frightening the witness (who does not exactly recall its contents) while questioning him, or as a method of conveying to the jury the impression that the statement contains certain comments as implied by the questions. This use of a statement, at least for the latter purpose and perhaps for the former, probably violates the Code of Professional Responsibility[7] and should be stopped by the trial judge if objection is made. The practice of holding the statement in view though not referring to it verbally is sometimes used when the lawyer does not want to introduce the statement itself, because of some risk of harm. . . . Even this use of a statement that you do not want in evidence involves a risk, however. For example, if you attempt to use a statement in this way, your opponent may call upon you to produce the statement; if you withhold it or object to its being placed in evidence by your opponent, the jury may draw an unfavorable inference from your conduct. It might be suggested that you could evade by the problem by refusing to produce the statement for your adversary to see in the absence of an agreement in advance that it can be received in evidence (with the expectation that your adversary will not so stipulate, for fear of thereby waiving objection to matters otherwise inadmissible). But that attitude is more likely to cause unfavorable reaction to your methods than to your adversary's

7. It would seem that deliberately conveying to the jury, by implication or innuendo, the impression that a document in your hands is a statement containing certain assertions, when in fact you know it does not contain them, would violate American Bar Association, Code of Professional Responsibility, Canon 7 (1969).

Id., DR 7-102(A)(4) and (5), declare that a lawyer shall not knowingly "use . . . false evidence" or knowingly "make a false statement of . . . fact."

Id., EC 7-25, declares that a "lawyer should not by subterfuge put before a jury matters which it cannot properly consider."

Consider also id., DR 7-106(C): "In appearing in his professional capacity before a tribunal, a lawyer shall not:

"(1) State or allude to any matter that he has no reasonable basis to believe is relevant to the case or that will not be supported by admissible evidence.

"(2) Ask any question that he has no reasonable basis to believe is relevant to the case and that is intended to degrade a witness or other person. . . .

"(7) Intentionally or habitually violate any established rule of procedure or of evidence." . . .

refusal to make the agreement with respect to some statement your adversary has never seen. . . .

§9.12   USING SUBTERFUGES

Should you use subterfuges in your investigation?

The Code of Professional Responsibility does not deal specifically with the use of subterfuge in investigation.[1] It is generally considered a permissible practice within reasonable limits, and it is often justified on the basis that it is a practical necessity in discovering falsification by the adverse party or his witnesses. It would be a violation of the Code, of course, for you to use subterfuge as a means of directly interviewing an adverse party who is represented by a lawyer.[2] Doubtless, the spirit of the Code may be violated by some uses of subterfuge in interviewing other witnesses, but the absence of an absolute prohibition leaves some area, not clearly defined, in which the use of subterfuge to interview persons other than the adverse party is proper. For example, if as defendant's lawyer in a personal injury case you suspect that the plaintiff is engaging in activities inconsistent with his claim, it is generally considered proper for you (or another person acting under your instructions) to interview under subterfuge (such as preparation of a credit report) persons with personal knowledge of those facts. The justification offered is the necessity for using subterfuge if the plaintiff's falsification is to be discovered without tipping him off. If you do not use subterfuge, he will undoubtedly learn of your interview and will then be warned to guard his activities more closely unless he has chosen the more commendable course of revising his claim (a course that is often more practical from the point of view of his realizing the most from the claim).

In addition to the ethical problem involved in using subterfuges in investigation, the danger of tactical disadvantages deserves your attention. If the fact of your using a subterfuge is disclosed during trial, it may cause an unfavorable reaction on the part of the jury. This danger is particularly apparent if your investigation by subterfuge fails to achieve the aim of revealing falsification by the adverse party. Subterfuges are often used for obtaining information that would otherwise be unavailable, even though it may not directly involve falsification by the adverse party or a witness; this danger of unfavorable reaction indicates, however, that you should be very cautious about using a subterfuge for a purpose other than one leading directly to disclosure of falsification. If you do succeed in exposing false testimony, the typical jury is willing

1. Probably the use of a subterfuge in investigation does not constitute "deceit" or "misrepresentation," proscribed by American Bar Association, Code of Professional Responsibility DR 1-102 (1969).
2. Id., DR 7-104(A)(1).

to forgive, as justified, methods to which they might otherwise have reacted adversely.

Another purpose for which investigation by subterfuge is sometimes used is checking the accuracy and truthfulness of statements of a witness the use of whose testimony you are considering as part of your own presentation. Usually it would be embarrassing at the least, and perhaps also damaging to your relationship with the witness, if he should discover that you are checking his story rather than taking his word for it. Even if the witness passes the test, he may resent the fact that you were not willing to accept him on his own word.

NOTE

Judge Keeton refers to "your legitimate interest in your own reputation and future effectiveness at the bar" as compelling moderation of what he regards as the "extreme view" of the lawyer's duty, p. 375. What do you think of a system that makes certain desirable strategies lawful but counsels the practitioner not to use them? What is the relationship between lawyers' choice of strategy and their view of their own reputation and future effectiveness? Should we limit the Keeton view to situations of borderline conduct?

A severe problem of professional responsibility was involved in the course of trial in In re Metzger, 31 Hawaii 929 (1931), where defense counsel (later United States District Judge) in a capital case was cross-examining an expert handwriting witness who had testified that the same hand (admittedly that of one of the defendants) that had written Exhibit E, a certain card, also had written a crucial letter. During a recess, counsel forged Exhibit E and then cross-examined the witness again, taking him carefully through the details of the writing contained in it. The expert failed to note the substitution; subsequently, the defendants were acquitted. Defense counsel was then charged with misconduct before the Supreme Court of Hawaii in an information by the attorney general. The court, in suspending counsel from practice for ten days, stated, in an opinion by Chief Justice Perry:

> . . . The plan had been carefully devised. His express purpose, as he admitted at the hearing in this court in answer to a question by a member of the court, was, in saying what he said and in doing what he did, to deceive the witness into thinking that he was handing him the genuine exhibit "E." The plan devised and followed was well calculated to accomplish that purpose; and succeeded. The respondent first deceived the clerk by failing to return to him, as was his duty, the precise paper (exhibit "E")

which he had received from him and for which he had given him a receipt and by the method pursued made the clerk an innocent and unwitting participant in the misrepresentation and deception, to the witness, which followed. When, after a lengthy examination and a lengthy cross-examination upon the handwriting of the letter, the envelope and the genuine card, the clerk, in answer to the cross-examining attorney's request, produced the letter and a card, the witness had a right to believe, and could only believe, that the card was the genuine exhibit "E." The presentation by the respondent to the witness of a card as exhibit "E" was a deliberate misrepresentation. If the representation had been made in words, e.g., "this is exhibit 'E,'" instead of by acts, it would have been a deliberate falsehood. So, also, forgery of the clerk's signature (by initials), for the purpose of conveying to the witness the clerk's apparent certification of the genuineness of the card, was in itself an offense which cannot be ignored.

There can be no doubt that it was the right and the duty of the respondent, who was entrusted with the defense of two men who were on trial for their lives, to expose if he could what he believed to be a lack of ability and a lack of credibility or accuracy on the part of the witness who had testified as an expert on handwriting; but there was a limitation upon that right and that duty and the limitation was that the test and the exposure must be accomplished by fair and lawful means, free from falsehood and misrepresentation. The so-called "necessities of the case," the keenness of the desire of the attorney to defend the accused to the best of his ability, cannot in our judgment justify falsehood or misrepresentation by the attorney to a witness or to the clerk of the court, whether that falsehood or misrepresentation be expressed in direct language or be conveyed by artful subterfuge. We are unwilling to certify to the younger attorneys who are beginning their experience at the bar of this court, or to any of the attorneys of this Territory, that it is lawful and proper for them to defend men, even though on trial for their lives, by the use of falsehood and misrepresentation, direct or indirect. The conduct of the respondent was unethical and unprofessional.

With reference to the action to be taken in consequence of this finding and this ruling, it is proper to consider the surrounding circumstances. The responsibility of an attorney who is defending men in a capital case is a serious one. Right and justice require that he should be zealous and active in securing all proper evidence in behalf of the accused and in cross-examining as effectively as may be the witnesses produced by the prosecution. The respondent testifies that when he devised and executed his plan he was not conscious of the fact that it might be deemed unethical or unprofessional. We accept his statement. The two attorneys whom he consulted as to the probable success of the plan did not utter any caution as to its possible impropriety. These are considerations tending towards leniency. As in the Trask case, 30 Haw. 736, 754, "a mere gesture of disapproval, however, such as a reprimand, would not suffice." In order to give emphasis to our disapproval of the respondent's conduct, we feel that it is our duty to suspend his license for a brief period of time.

Justice Banks, in dissent, commented as follows:

Metzger's right to impeach by every proper means Bailey's [the expert's] opinion that the letter, envelope and card were written by the same hand it seems to me must be conceded. Indeed it was not only his right to do this but his duty to do so — his duty to his clients, to the jury and to the court. Of course if he had known that the letter and the envelope were in the handwriting of one of his clients, as he knew that the writing on the card was, the situation would be quite different. Under such circumstances his effort would have been not to destroy what he believed to be false but to destroy what he knew to be true. I think a lawyer, even in his zeal to extricate his client from a serious position, may not ethically go so far. This, however, was not the case. At the hearing of the instant proceeding Metzger testified that having had considerable experience in chirography he believed that the writing on the card was not by the same person as the writing on the envelope and in the letter. There is no apparent reason for disbelieving him. His purpose therefore was not the evil one of misleading the jury as to a fact which he knew existed but the laudable one of exposing what he believed to be an erroneous opinion. This was in the interest of justice and not against it. Metzger also testified that he had been unable after a long cross-examination of Bailey to discredit his opinion and that there was no other handwriting expert available whom he could consult or to whose opinion he could submit the writings. His only alternative therefore was in some way to lead Bailey to disclose his own fallibility. The question that remains is whether the means he used to accomplish his purpose were unethical.

I do not think that his treatment of the witness was unfair. A cross-examiner is certainly under no professional obligation to warn an expert witness, whose opinion he wishes to test, of the pit which has been dug for him and into which he will fall unless he has sufficient technical learning to discover and avoid it. Nor do I think it a violation of legal ethics to withhold from such witness a fact which, if he knew it, would enable him to discover the pit independently of his technical knowledge. It is a principle peculiar to the cross-examination of expert witnesses that in order to evaluate their opinions things may be assumed as facts which are not facts. This is all that Metzger really did. He in effect assumed, in the presence of the witness, the court and the jury, that the fabricated card was the real exhibit about which the witness had already testified and proceeded to ascertain by cross-examination whether he was capable of discovering that the assumption was false. In doing this he was entirely fair to the witness. According to his testimony he required Bailey to subject the fabricated card to the same tests to which he had subjected the real exhibit and to compare it with the writing on the envelope and the letter just as he had compared the real exhibit. It was an acid test of the value of Bailey's opinion, but no more severe than that to which a handwriting expert may properly be put.

Under the evidence in this proceeding I likewise see no disregard of legal ethics on Metzger's part in delivering to the clerk the fabricated card instead of the original exhibit, without informing him of the substitution. I think the ethical quality of everything that Metzger did in carrying out the plan he devised for testing the accuracy of Bailey's opinion must be judged by the motive that actuated him to make the test, *unless what he did was otherwise inherently wrong.* His motive in making the test was to discredit an opinion that had been given by a putative expert, which opinion he believed to be erroneous. I see nothing *inherently wrong* in his temporarily withholding from the clerk the fact that the fabricated card which he delivered was not the original exhibit. That he only intended to temporarily withhold this fact from the clerk is shown by Metzger's testimony that when he handed the clerk the simulated card together with two of the exhibits he had withdrawn the clerk said to him, "I will destroy your receipt," and that he told the clerk not to do this because there would be further transactions with respect to these papers. He did in fact return the original exhibit to the clerk after he had concluded his cross-examination of Bailey. His purpose in withholding the fact from the clerk was to guard against the danger of having his plan for testing the value of Bailey's opinion frustrated by a premature exposure. This was not in my opinion a fraud on the clerk nor was it a fraud on the court nor was it intimical to the cause of justice. It was done not to defeat a fair trial but to promote it. If it had not been done the weakness of Bailey's opinion might not have been revealed and men whom the jury found to be innocent might have been found guilty and sent to the gallows.

NOTES

1. Is the only vice in Mr. Metzger's plan that he did not seek the trial judge's approval? If you were seeking such approval, would you invite the prosecutor to accompany you to see the trial judge? See DR 7-110(B)(3) and Model Rule 3.5(b).

2. If you had been the trial judge in State v. Poai and Spalding (the name of the case Mr. Metzger defended), and defense counsel had sought your permission to try the handwriting switch, would you have permitted it? Why?

3. Note that the dissenting judge makes the belief of the attorney in his client's innocence the crucial point. Do you agree? Presumably the dissenting judge would answer Professor Freedman's first question (p. 154) in the negative.

4. Meek v. Fleming, 3 All E.R. 148 (C.A. 1961), involved an action by a newspaper photographer against a police officer for assault and battery. The defendant was demoted from chief inspector to station sergeant while the case was pending because he had deceived a court in another matter. This was known to defendant's counsel who decided that the matter should not be revealed to the court. In pursuit of that decision, counsel had defendant appear at the trial in plain clothes, did not ask defendant his name and rank when he took the stand, and consistently referred to him as "Mr." In addition, neither he nor defendant corrected the judge or plaintiff's counsel when they referred to him as

"chief inspector," and on cross-examination defendant gave the answer, "Yes, that is true," to the question, "You are a chief inspector, and you have been in the force, you told us, since 1938." A jury verdict was given for defendant, but on appeal a new trial was granted because of the conduct of defendant and counsel when the true facts later became known. What conduct of counsel was improper? (1) Failure to inform plaintiff's counsel of the demotion as soon as it occurred? (2) Instructing defendant to appear in plain clothes and addressing him as "Mr."? (3) Failing to correct plaintiff's counsel and the judge when they addressed defendant as "chief inspector"? (4) Failing to have defendant correct in-accurate testimony on cross-examination or, if defendant would not do so, failing to correct the testimony himself?

How different is Meek v. Fleming from the case where the lawyer provides a client with shirt, tie, and a dark suit to wear at his trial for a particularly ugly murder? Where the prosecutor tells the victim witness in a rape case to wear less seductive clothing?

5. It is not only defense counsel who get involved in deceptive methods of seeking truth. In Nigrone v. Murtagh, 46 App. Div. 2d 343, 362 N.Y.S.2d 513 (2d Dept. 1974), aff'd. in part and appeal dismissed in part without reaching the issue of prosecutorial misconduct, 36 N.Y.2d 421, 369 N.Y.S.2d 75 (1975), the Appellate Division considered the conduct of Maurice Nadjari, a Special Prosecutor appointed by the governor to investigate corruption in New York City's criminal justice system. Acting on allegedly specific information about corruption in that system, Nad-jari caused a fake indictment to be returned by a grand jury against an undercover agent who then contacted Judge Rao of the United Customs Court and was put in touch with defendant lawyers, one of whom was Judge Rao's son. Subsequently, an Extraordinary Special Grand Jury, investigating whether defendants had conspired with a second judge to bribe a third judge in connection with the fake case, called defendants to testify. Based on discrepancies between their testimony and taped re-cordings of conversations between defendants and the undercover agent, defendants were indicted for perjury. They moved to have the indictments dismissed.

The Appellate Division was unanimous in condemning Mr. Nadjari's conduct in the strongest terms for numerous improprieties committed in the course of setting up a sham case, including deceiving various judges at the arraignment and setting of bail, the grand jury that re-turned the indictment, and the Assistant District Attorney who thought a real case was being presented. Nevertheless, the Appellate Division, on a 3-2 vote, denied the relief. The majority noted that the investigation in which the perjury was allegedly committed was before a different grand jury from the one that returned the fake indictment and refused to legitimate any reason to lie to a grand jury. It viewed an extension of the exclusionary rule to this "sui generis case" as an unwarranted interference into the investigation, and believed its condemnation of the conduct would be sufficient to prevent its repetition. 46 App. Div. 2d at 349, 362 N.Y.S.2d at 519.

The dissenters would have granted the motion on the ground that (1) the conduct occurred after the Second Circuit had condemned similar conduct of other prosecutors in United States v. Archer, 486 F.2d 670 (1973), a case in which Mr. Nadjari appeared as amicus curiae, and therefore condemnation was not an effective deterrent; (2) the events before the two grand juries cannot be separated because the second grand jury was investigating a case that was a sham and did not exist; and (3) most importantly, that outrageous governmental misuse of power and of the purposes of the criminal justice system corrupts the system and that the courts should announce that they will "not approve indictments resulting from an 'unprecedented' and illegal exercise of power by the Special Prosecutor." 46 App. Div. 2d at 358, 362 N.Y.S.2d at 527. On remand, however, Justice Murtagh of the Supreme Court on his own motion dismissed the indictments, on other evidential grounds. The Appellate Division, however, reversed this order and remanded the case for a hearing. 53 App. Div. 2d 904, 386 N.Y.S.2d 441 (2d Dept. 1976). On remand, Justice Sandler dismissed the indictment against Judge Rao but upheld the indictment against his son and another lawyer. Lawyer Rao was convicted but on appeal that conviction was reversed. The Appellate Division concluded that misconduct of the prosecutors constituted a denial of due process. The court's opinion supported its conclusion by reference to the original misconduct and further prosecutorial misconduct at the grand jury proceedings, including suppression of exculpatory evidence. 73 A.D.2d 88, 425 N.Y.S.2d 122 (2d Dept. 1980).

A modern example of aggressive litigation tactics that misfired is In re Beiny, 129 App. Div. 2d 126, 517 N.Y.S.2d 424, on motion for reargument or renewal and leave to appeal, 132 App. Div. 2d 190,. 522 N.Y.S.2d 511 (1st Dept. 1987). In connection with a trust accounting proceeding, the law firm for a beneficiary desired to obtain the files of a liquidated law firm that had represented the settlor of the trust. The factual situation was described in the opinion of the court on the motion for reargument:

> Petitioner's counsel, Sullivan & Cromwell, believing that the liquidator of the law firm of Greenbaum, Wolff & Ernst had factual information concerning the property at issue, served a subpoena duces tecum and notice of deposition directing the liquidator to appear for examination with all the papers concerning certain clients, including trustee Beiny. No notice was given by Sullivan & Cromwell to the other parties. The subpoena was knowingly aimed at privileged materials, and no court would have

sustained its broad demand. In order to give the subpoena a sharper edge, Sullivan & Cromwell enclosed it in a letter that deceptively represented to the liquidator that Sullivan & Cromwell's client, petitioner Wynyard, was the executor of the estate of a former client of the Greenbaum firm. Sullivan & Cromwell, having thereafter received from the liquidator the mass of papers to which no law but only its deceit entitled it, then canceled the day fixed for the liquidator's examination. Within weeks, the trustee, ignorant of the raid upon Greenbaum's papers, was examined in London by Sullivan & Cromwell who not only used those papers to surprise her but refused to disclose how the papers had been obtained. When the trustee's counsel learned how Sullivan & Cromwell had obtained the papers, they asked for their production, but Sullivan & Cromwell refused, unless the trustee made concessions in discovery. Only after the trustee was driven to obtain an order of the Surrogate in December 1985, granting the trustee access to the papers, did the trustee learn the extent of Sullivan & Cromwell's massive intrusion into the trustee's privileged papers; and not until July 1986 did the trustee have in hand an order of the Surrogate suppressing all but 7 of 114 documents as to which the trustee claimed privilege. . . .

The Surrogate suppressed most of the documents but refused to disqualify the law firm. The Appellate Division affirmed the suppression but also found that the abuse of the confidential information had been so great that disqualification was required not only to sanitize the proceeding but also to prevent the firm from deriving further benefit from its misconduct. On motion for reargument, the court focussed its entire attention on the conduct of the law firm.

In re BEINY

on motion for reargument or renewal and leave to appeal,
132 App. Div. 2d 190, 522 N.Y.S.2d 511 (1st Dept. 1987).

MURPHY, P. J.

We refer this proceeding to the Departmental Disciplinary Committee for investigation, including an inquiry by the Committee into the August 3, 1987 report of the Wall Street Journal that Donald Christ, a member of Sullivan & Cromwell, allegedly assaulted an attorney for trustee Beiny in the Surrogate's Court at a conference in this case. . . .

In ending this appeal, it might be useful to trace the lines of certain features of the case for they show how this court, faced each morning with matters involving profound issues of liberty and property, can be burdened by an appeal such as that at bar, an appeal that is before us solely because of the misconduct of lawyers in pursuit of a fee. We speak of the matter because it extends beyond the ownership and transfer of porcelains, and well beyond the interest of a law firm in its reputation. Our consideration of the case is enlarged by issues involving the ethical norms required of attorneys as advocates.

In consequence of Sullivan & Cromwell's conduct, this court has had placed before five of its Justices about 1,700 pages of record and briefs, to say nothing of paper footage given to motions that have since slid into the dark of appellate memory. Petitioner Wynyard's case, which may be one having substantial merit, has been delayed by about 2½ years given over to the legal debris that now lies before us. He has been left by Sullivan & Cromwell's conduct to search for other counsel who will probably bill him for the reading of the lengthy record generated by Sullivan & Cromwell's misconduct. Trustee Beiny has been driven down a legal gauntlet, arched by fees of expensive counsel and hedged by the anxiety to which Bench and Bar are often insensible. In short, upon facts that should have led Sullivan & Cromwell to a prompt, practical resolution, one that would have avoided delay, fees and the worrying of court and clients, Sullivan & Cromwell chose instead to drive the trustee toward the steps of the Surrogate's Court and, ultimately, both petitioner and the trustee to the steps of this court. Having arrived in this court, Sullivan & Cromwell, in protection of its reputation, then set about the making of arguments that, startlingly curious in design, required the time of this much pressed court to identify and answer. . . .

Sullivan & Cromwell argued on the appeal that its associate, Garrard Beeney, who had engineered the acquisition of the now suppressed documents, was procedurally correct in his obtaining of the papers without notice to the parties. The argument was notable if only because it might have caused an applicant's failure upon the Bar examination, to say nothing of its use against Sullivan & Cromwell by its adversaries in other actions. On reargument, petitioner's additional counsel, retained for the motions at bar, made for safer waters, conceding that Beeney was in error but that Beeney had acted innocently. In short, Beeney had known what he was doing but did not know that it was wrong. As far as our research has gone this is the first instance, at least in this court, in which a breach of the Civil Practice Law and Rules has been met with the defense raised in 1843 in *M'Naghten's Case* (8 Eng Rep 718), a fact that would have startled poor M'Naghten as he stood acquitted in the dock. The record shows that Beeney indeed knew what he was about when he palmed off petitioner as the executor of the estate of a decedent whose will was never probated, and when he canceled a deposition that he never intended to conduct. The record shows that even though Donald Christ, a senior partner at Sullivan & Cromwell, must have known at the very least of the way Beeney had acquired the privileged papers, still nothing was done to right what must have seemed to Mr. Christ to have been wrong. Instead, Sullivan & Cromwell in their prosecution of the case thereafter used the papers against the trustee. As for the argument that the liquidator was in substance a volunteer in need of a subpoena as a kind of receipt for his files, we give to it the same value that we have given to Beeney's singular belief that petitioner was the executor of an estate unknown to any probate court.

Petitioner's claim that the trustee and he had been jointly represented by the Greenbaum firm, a claim unproved before the Surrogate, can hardly be a foothold in justification of Sullivan & Cromwell's raid upon the Greenbaum files. Our cachet of approval upon such a primitive notion of discovery, to say nothing of the extension of such a principle throughout our law, would entice the invasive, disorderly mind in an area in which rights must be judicially or consensually fixed before parties proceed in the gathering of facts.

Last, it is disingenuous for petitioner's counsel to argue that we did not find that the suppressed documents were substantially related to the issues. We suppose that petitioner's counsel read our statement that "among the matters to which the documents refer are transactions involving the disposition of the very assets whose ownership is at issue in this proceeding" (129 A.D.2d 126, 142), or if they did not read our plain statement, they surely must have recalled their own repeated statements concerning the probative value of the suppressed documents. Nor do we think it an exercise in candor for petitioner's counsel to say on this motion that the suppressed documents are not substantially related to the issues before us when the record shows that, among other things, petitioner's counsel themselves characterized those documents as proof that the trustee unlawfully transferred the property at issue to entities in her control, defrauded the petitioner, violated her fiduciary duties to him, and is a perjurer.

In sum, this appeal is an example of the accidental subversion of the interests of a client by his own advocates who acted as if the law did not apply to them.

F.   NEGOTIATIONS AND PLEA BARGAINING

PROBLEM 51

During the course of settlement negotiations, D's lawyer makes a third and "final" offer to P's attorney who replies, "It's no better than any of the others. You are so low that I haven't even bothered my client with any of your other offers, and I'm not going to pass this one along either. I'll have my client consider an offer when you come into the ballpark." What course of conduct may D's lawyer pursue in order to have the offer considered by P? See DR 7-104(A)(1).

PROBLEM 52

(a) You are a prosecutor and there is a case in your office in which an indictment for aggravated assault has been returned by the grand jury. You are about to conclude a plea bargain with the defendant and his attorney when you learn that your main witness, without whose testimony there is only a weak case, has died. Do you reveal this information to counsel for the defendant?

NOTE

In Brady v. Maryland, 373 U.S. 83, 87 (1963), the Supreme Court held that "suppression by the prosecution of evidence favorable to an accused upon request violates due process where the evidence is material either to guilt or to punishment, irrespective of the good faith or bad faith of the prosecution." The awkwardness of the phrase limiting the holding to situations where the evidence is requested by defense counsel suggests that the limitation may have been inserted "upon request" of a member of the Court who might not otherwise have joined the opinion. In any event, the limitation does not appear in the Code's statement of the applicable disciplinary rule. See DR 7-103(B) and Model Rule 3.8(d). But do they or the *Brady* rule explicitly cover Problem 52(a)? See also Moore v. Illinois, 408 U.S. 786 (1972), reaffirming and elaborating the *Brady* rule, and United States v. Agurs, 427 U.S. 97 (1976), holding that constitutional error is to be found in nondisclosure even without a request for the information when the nondisclosed evidence creates a reasonable doubt that did not otherwise exist; and United States v. Bagley, 473 U.S. 667 (1985), holding that a conviction must be reversed for failure to comply with the *Brady* rule only if the nondisclosed evidence "is material in the sense that its suppression undermines confidence in the outcome of the trial."

PROBLEM 52

(b) Insurance company counsel (ICC) and plaintiffs' counsel (PC) are attempting to negotiate a settlement of an automobile accident case. ICC realizes from statements made by PC that one reason PC is willing to settle more reasonably than expected is that PC has misunderstood the facts of the relationship between the driver of the truck and its insured. PC appears to be concerned that a master-servant relationship might not exist when in fact ICC knows quite clearly that it does. Should ICC correct PC's factual misunderstanding? In summarizing her client's position, may ICC allude to the likelihood that PC will not be able to prove the existence of a master-servant relationship?

PC, on the other hand, has just learned that a main witness, without whose testimony there will be only a weak case, has just died. PC knows that this witness gave the insurance company adjuster a statement that is quite favorable to his client, but that ICC does not know of her death. Should PC reveal that fact to ICC?

PROBLEM 53

You represent a company that has just discovered that a trusted employee has embezzled $50,000. The company president wants to get as much of the money back as possible and is determined to get rid of the employee. On the other hand, having consulted the board, she believes that it would be very bad publicity for the company to have a criminal trial splashed all over the papers. She has therefore instructed you to threaten the employee's attorney that you will go to the prosecutor unless the employee immediately discloses to your satisfaction how every penny was spent, turns over as much cash as is unaccounted for and everything bought with the embezzled funds, plus whatever other assets that you can reasonably squeeze out of him. If you are in a Model Code jurisdiction, does DR 7-105(A) mean that you may not follow these instructions? What may you do in such a jurisdiction? If you are in a Model Rules jurisdiction, does the absence of a provision like DR 7-105(A) mean that you have no problem? See Livermore, Lawyer Extortion, 20 Ariz. L. Rev. 403 (1978) for a discussion of the relevance of extortion statutes to problems like this.

The following two excerpts present differing approaches to problems of professional responsibility that arise in the negotiation context. The first, by Judge Alvin Rubin of the Court of Appeals for the Fifth Circuit, should be compared with the views expressed by Marvin Frankel with respect to the lawyer's obligation to truth in our adversary system. See p. 160. The second, by Professor James J. White of the Michigan Law School, surveys the scene from the perspective of a very practical teacher of negotiation skills and theory.

RUBIN, A CAUSERIE ON LAWYERS'
ETHICS IN NEGOTIATION
35 La. L.Rev. 577, 578-593 (1975)

. . . Taken together, [the rules of the Model Code],* interpreted in the light of that old but ever useful candle, ejusdem generis, imply that a

---

*[and the Model Rules too. Ed.]

lawyer shall not himself engage in illegal conduct; since the meaning of assisting a client in fraudulent conduct is later indicated by the proscription of *other* illegal conduct. As we perceive, the lawyer is forbidden to make a false statement of law or fact *knowingly*. But nowhere is it ordained that the lawyer owes any general duty of candor or fairness to members of the bar or to laymen with whom he may deal as a negotiator, or of honesty or of good faith insofar as that term denotes generally scrupulous activity.

Is the lawyer-negotiator entitled, like Metternich, to depend on "cunning, precise calculation, and a willingness to employ whatever means justify the end of policy?" Few are so bold as to say so. Yet some whose personal integrity and reputation are scrupulous have instructed students in negotiating tactics that appear tacitly to countenance that kind of conduct. In fairness it must be added that they say they do not "endorse the *propriety*" of this kind of conduct, and indeed even indicate "grave reservations"[20] about such behavior; however, this sort of generalized disclaimer of sponsorship hardly appears forceful enough when the tactics suggested include:

— Use two negotiators who play different roles. (Illustrated by the "Mutt and Jeff" police technique; "Two lawyers for the same side feign an internal dispute. . . .")
— Be tough — especially against a patsy.
— Appear irrational when it seems helpful.
— Raise some of your demands as the negotiations progress.
— *Claim* that you do not have authority to compromise. (Emphasis supplied.)
— After agreement has been reached, have your client reject it and raise his demands.[21]

Another text used in training young lawyers commendably counsels sincerity, capability, preparation, courage and flexibility. But it also suggests "a sound set of tools or tactics and the know-how to use (or not to use) them."[22] One such tactic is, "Make false demands, bluffs, threats; even use irrationality."[23]

Let us consider the proper role for a lawyer engaged in negotiations when he knows that the opposing side, whether as a result of poor legal representation or otherwise, is assuming a state of affairs that is incor-

20. M. Meltsner & P. Schrag, Public Interest Advocacy; Materials for Clinical Legal Education 232 (1974) (emphasis in original).
21. Id. at 236-238. Regarding the tactic of having the client reject the agreement and raise his demand, the authors add, "This is the most ethically dubious of the tactics listed here, but there will be occasions where a lawyer will have to defend against it or even to employ it." Id. at 238.
22. H. Freeman & H. Weihofer, Clinical Law Training 122 (1972).
23. Id.

rect. Hypothesize: L, a lawyer, is negotiating the sale of his client's business to another businessman, who is likewise represented by counsel. Balance sheets and profit and loss statements prepared one month ago have been supplied. In the last month, sales have fallen dramatically. Counsel for the potential buyer has made no inquiry about current sales. Does L have a duty to disclose the change in sales volume?

Some lawyers say, "I would notify my client and advise him that *he* has a duty to disclose," not because of ethical considerations but because the client's failure to do so might render the transaction voidable if completed. If the client refused to sanction disclosure, some of these lawyers would withdraw from representing him *in this matter* on ethical grounds. As a practical matter, (i.e., to induce the client to accept their advice) they say, in consulting with the client, the lawyer is obliged to present the problem as one of possible fraud in the transaction rather than of lawyers' ethics.

In typical law school fashion, let us consider another hypothetical. L, the lawyer, is representing C, a client, in a suit for personal injuries. There have been active settlement negotiations with LD, the defendant's lawyer. The physician who has been treating C rendered a written report, containing a prognosis stating that it is unlikely that C can return to work at his former occupation. This has been furnished to LD. L learns from C that he has consulted another doctor, who has given him a new medication. C states that he is now feeling fine and thinks he can return to work, but he is reluctant to do so until the case is settled or tried. The next day, L and LD again discuss settlement. Does L have a duty either to guard his client's secret or to make a full disclosure? Does he satisfy or violate either duty if, instead of mentioning C's revelation he suggests that D require a new medical examination?

Some lawyers avoid this problem by saying that it is inconceivable that a competent LD would not ask again about C's health. But if the question as to whether L should be frank is persistently presented, few lawyers can assure that they would disclose the true facts.

Lawyers whose primary practice is corporate tend to distinguish the two hypotheticals, finding a duty to disclose the downturn in earnings but not the improvement in health. They may explain the difference by resorting to a discussion of the lower standards (expectations?) of the bar when engaged in personal injury litigation. "That's why I stay away from that kind of work," one lawyer said. The esteem of a lawyer for his own profession must be scant if he can rationalize the subclassifications this distinction implies. Yet this kind of gradation of professional ethics appears to permeate the bar.

Lawyers from Wall Street firms say that they and their counterparts observe scrupulous standards, but they attribute less morality to the personal injury lawyer, and he, in turn, will frequently point out the inferiority of the standards of those who spend much time in criminal litigation. The gradation of the ethics of the profession by the area of law becomes curiouser and curiouser the more it is examined, if one may purloin the words of another venturer in wonderland.

None would apparently deny that honesty and good faith in the sale of a house or a security implies telling the truth and not withholding information. But the Code does not exact that sort of integrity from lawyers who engage in negotiating the compromise of a law suit or other negotiations. Scant impetus to good faith is given by EC 7-9, which states, "When an action in the best interest of his client seems to him to be unjust, [the lawyer] may ask his client for permission to forego such action," for such a standard means that the client sets the ultimate ethical parameter for the lawyer's conduct. . . .

Do the lawyer's ethics protest more strongly against giving false information? DR 7-102(A)(5) . . . forbids the lawyer to "knowingly make" a false statement of law or fact. Most lawyers say it would be improper to prepare a false document to deceive an adversary or to make a factual statement known to be untrue with the intention of deceiving him. But almost every lawyer can recount repeated instances where an adversary of reasonable repute dealt with facts in such an imaginative or hyperbolic way as to make them appear to be different from what he knew they were.

Interesting answers are obtained if lawyers are asked whether it is proper to make false statements that concern negotiating strategy rather than the facts in litigation. Counsel for a plaintiff appears quite comfortable in stating, when representing a plaintiff, "My client won't take a penny less than $25,000," when in fact he knows that the client will happily settle for less; counsel for the defendant appears to have no qualms in representing that he has no authority to settle, or that a given figure exceeds his authority, when these are untrue statements. Many say that, as a matter of strategy, when they attend a pre-trial conference with a judge known to press settlements, they disclaim any settlement authority both to the judge and adversary although in fact they do have settlement instructions; estimable members of the bar support the thesis that a lawyer may not misrepresent a fact in controversy but may misrepresent matters that pertain to his authority or negotiating strategy because this is expected by the adversary.

To most practitioners it appears that anything sanctioned by the rules of the game is appropriate. From this point of view, negotiations are merely, as the social scientists have viewed it, a form of game; observance of the expected rules, not professional ethics, is the guiding precept. But gamesmanship is not ethics. . . .

The courts have seldom had occasion to consider these ethical problems, for disciplinary proceedings have rarely been invoked on any charge of misconduct in the area. But where settlements have in fact been made when one party acted on the basis of a factual error known to the other and this error induced the compromise, courts have set releases aside on the basis of mistake, or, in some cases, fraud.

A lawyer should not be restrained only by the legal inhibitions on his client. He enjoys a monopoly on the practice of law protected by sanctions against unauthorized practice. Through a subpart of the profession, lawyer-educators, the lawyer controls access to legal education. He licenses practitioners by exacting bar examinations. He controls access to the courts save in those limited instances when a litigant may appear pro se, and then he aptly characterizes this litigant as being his own lawyer, hence having a fool for his client.

The monopoly on the practice of law does not arise from the presumed advantages of an attorney's education or social status: it stems from the concept that, as professionals, lawyers serve society's interests by participating in the process of achieving the just termination of disputes. That an adversary system is the basic means to this end does not crown it with supreme value. It is means, not end.

If he is a professional and not merely a hired, albeit skilled hand, the lawyer is not free to do anything his client might do in the same circumstances. The corollary of that proposition does set a minimum standard: the lawyer must be at least as candid and honest as his client would be required to be. The agent of the client, that is, his attorney-at-law, must not perpetrate the kind of fraud or deception that would vitiate a bargain if practiced by his principal. Beyond that, the profession should embrace an affirmative ethical standard for attorneys' professional relationships with courts, other lawyers and the public: *The lawyer must act honestly and in good faith.* Another lawyer, or a layman, who deals with a lawyer should not need to exercise the same degree of caution that he would if trading for reputedly antique copper jugs in an oriental bazaar. It is inherent in the concept of an ethic, as a principle of good conduct, that it is morally binding on the conscience of the professional, and not merely a rule of the game adopted because other players observe (or fail to adopt) the same rule. Good conduct exacts more than mere convenience. It is not sufficient to call on personal self-interest; this is the standard created by the thesis that the same adversary met today may be faced again tomorrow, and one had best not prejudice that future engagement.

Patterson and Cheatham[52] correctly assert that the basic standard for the negotiator is honesty. "In terms of the standards of the profession, honesty is candor. . . ."[53] Candor is not inconsistent with striking a deal on terms favorable to the client, for it is known to all that, at least within limits, that is the purpose to be served. Substantive rules of law in some areas already exact of principals the duty to perform legal obligations honestly and in good faith. Equivalent standards should pervade the lawyer's professional environment. The distinction between honesty and

52. L. Patterson & E. Cheatham, The Profession of Law 121 (1971).
53. Id. at 123.

good faith need not be finely drawn here; all lawyers know that good faith requires conduct beyond simple honesty.

Since bona fides and truthfulness do not inevitably lead to fairness in negotiations, an entirely truthful lawyer might be able to make an unconscionable deal when negotiating with a government agency, or a layman or another attorney who is representing his own client. Few lawyers would presently deny themselves and their clients the privilege of driving a hard bargain against any of these adversaries though the opponent's ability to negotiate effectively in his own interest may not be equal to that of the lawyer in question. . . .

This raises the problem inevitable in an adversary profession if one opponent obeys a standard the other defies. As Countryman and Finman inquire,

> How is a lawyer who looks at himself as "an instrument for the furtherance of justice" likely to fare when pitted against an attorney willing to take whatever he can get and use any means he can get away with?[56]

While it might strain present concepts of the role of the lawyer in an adversary system, surely the professional standards must ultimately impose upon him a duty not to accept an unconscionable deal. While some difficulty in line-drawing is inevitable when such a distinction is sought to be made, there must be a point at which the lawyer cannot ethically accept an arrangement that is completely unfair to the other side, be that opponent a patsy or a tax collector. So I posit a second precept: *The lawyer may not accept a result that is unconscionably unfair to the other party.*

A settlement that is unconscionable may result from a variety of circumstances. There may be a vast difference in the bargaining power of the principals so that, regardless of the adequacy of representation by counsel, one party may simply not be able to withstand the expense and bear the delay and uncertainty inherent in a protracted suit. There may be a vast difference in the bargaining skill of counsel so that one is able to manipulate the other virtually at will despite the fact that their framed certificates of admission to the bar contain the same words.

The unconscionable result in these circumstances is in part created by the relative power, knowledge and skill of the principals and their negotiators. While it is the unconscionable result that is to be avoided, the question of whether the result is indeed intolerable depends in part on

---

56. V. Countryman & T. Finman, The Lawyer in Modern Society 281 (1966). See also Mathews, Negotiation: A Pedagogical Challenge, 6 J. Legal Ed. 93, 95 (1953), observing that in negotiation a lawyer "endowed with shrewdness and a sportive sense of outmaneuvering his opponent" has "an opportunity to indulge his proclivity almost devoid of risk of detection" provided he limits himself to "sharp practice" and does not step over into fraud, coercion or violations of law "or public policy." See Note, 112 U. Pa. L. Rev. 865 (1964).

examination of the relative status of the parties. The imposition of a duty to tell the truth and to bargain in good faith would reduce their relative inequality, and tend to produce negotiation results that are within relatively tolerable bounds. . . .

The lawyer should not be free to negotiate an unconscionable result, however pleasing to his client, merely because it is possible, any more than he is free to do other reprobated acts. He is not to commit perjury or pay a bribe or give advice about how to commit embezzlement. These examples refer to advice concerning illegal conduct, but we do already, in at least some instances, accept the principle that some acts are proscribed though not criminal; the lawyer is forbidden to testify as a witness in his client's cause,[61] or to assert a defense merely to harass his opponent;[62] he is enjoined to point out to his client "those factors that may lead to a decision that is morally just."[63] Whether a mode of conduct available to the lawyer is illegal or merely unconscionably unfair, the attorney must refuse to participate. This duty of fairness is one owed to the profession and to society; it must supersede any duty owed to the client. . . .

But, like other lawyers, judges hear not only of the low repute the public has for the bench but also of the even lower regard it has for the bar. We have been told so in innumerable speeches but, more important, our friends, neighbors and acquaintances tell us on every hand that they think little of the morality of our profession. They like us; indeed some of their best friends are lawyers. But they deplore the conduct of our colleagues. This is not merely an aftermath of Watergate: it is, in major part, because many members of the public, not without some support in the facts, view our profession as one that adopts ethics as cant, pays lip service to DR's and on behalf of clients stoops to almost any chicane that is not patently unlawful. We will not change that attitude by Law Days alone. It is to serve society's needs that professions are licensed and the unlicensed prohibited from performing professional functions. It is inherent in the concept of professionalism that the profession will regulate itself, adhering to an ethos that imposes standards higher than mere law observance. Client avarice and hostility neither control the lawyer's conscience nor measure his ethics. Surely if its practitioners are principled, a profession that dominates the legal process in our law-oriented society would not expect too much if it required its members to adhere to two simple principles when they negotiate as professionals: Negotiate honestly and in good faith; and do not take unfair advantage of another — regardless of his relative expertise or sophistication. This is inherent in

---

61. ABA Code of Professional Responsibility, DR 5-102(A). See also EC 5-9, DR 5-101(B).

62. ABA Code of Professional Responsibility, DR 7-102(A)(1).

63. ABA Code of Professional Responsibility, EC 7-8.

the oath the ABA recommends be taken by all who are admitted to the bar: "I will employ for the purpose of maintaining the causes confided to me such means only as are consistent with truth and honor."

NOTES

1. How would Judge Rubin's test answer his own hypotheticals on pp. 390-391? How would it answer Problems 52(a) and 52(b)? Does Problem 53 present an issue of professional responsibility at all? If a client would not have to make any disclosure under the common law of fraud, what would be the justification for putting a greater responsibility on the attorney?

2. There is a growing body of substantive law imposing obligations on lawyers to reveal certain kinds of factual information in negotiations. See Virzi v. Grand Trunk Warehouse and Cold Storage Co., 571 F. Supp. 507 (E.D. Mich. 1983) (death of a client); Kath v. Western Media, Inc., 684 P.2d 98 (Wyo. 1984) (perjury of a witness during depositions); and Nebraska State Bar Assn. v. Addison, 226 Neb. 585, 412 N.W.2d 855 (1987) (in negotiating with hospital for release of its lien against proceeds of settlement with insurance companies, plaintiff's lawyer had duty to disclose existence of unknown umbrella policy and to correct known misapprehension by hospital as to number of relevant insurance policies; lawyer suspended for failure to comply with this duty).

3. If his propositions are to be adopted only as ethical considerations, how does Judge Rubin resolve the problem he refers to on p. 393, that of one opponent obeying a standard the other defies?

4. How would Judge Rubin handle the negotiating strategy problem he poses on p. 391? Would he tell the opposing lawyer the bottom settlement figure for which he has authority to settle? Would he tell his client that he doesn't want to have that knowledge in a firm way because he would feel compelled to disclose it? Or does the authority given to settle at a particular figure have to be understood in a way that precludes disclosure of that figure?

5. Will adoption of Judge Rubin's proposed standards as ethical considerations get us from here to there? If not, what would you suggest if you agree with his general propositions?

6. Is the general negotiation framework as Judge Rubin envisages it preferable to the one currently in vogue in the profession, assuming the general accuracy of his description?

7. In order to reach a conclusion with respect to Note 6, one needs some background in the art of negotiation. A few sentences or even a few pages cannot supply it. It must be said, however, that at its best, negotiation represents a process in which lawyers for adverse parties test one another's positions in an effort to narrow differences and to perceive

the basis upon which agreement may be reached. The kind of openness advocated by Judge Rubin appears as each lawyer achieves better understanding of his or her own position and that of his or her adversary and, just as importantly, achieves confidence in one another. At its worst, however, negotiation involves lawyers one or both of whom are unskilled or too busy, or afraid, to contemplate going to trial. One wonders whether busyness, fear, and lack of skill are not in fact far greater obstacles to proper working of the negotiation process than lack of honesty.

The drafters of the Model Rules sought to meet the challenge posed by Judge Rubin and others. The first public draft, the Discussion Draft of Jan. 30, 1980, contained a provision primarily directed to the conduct of negotiations. Rule 4.2 of that draft provided:

4.2   *Fairness to Other Participants*
   (a) In conducting negotiations a lawyer shall be fair in dealing with other participants.
   (b) A lawyer shall not make a knowing misrepresentation of fact or law, or fail to disclose a material fact known to the lawyer, even if adverse, when disclosure is:
      (1) Required by law or the rules of professional conduct; or
      (2) Necessary to correct a manifest misapprehension of fact or law resulting from a previous representation made by the lawyer or known by the lawyer to have been made by the client, except that counsel for an accused in a criminal case is not required to make such a correction when it would require disclosing a misrepresentation made by the accused.
   (c) A lawyer shall not:
      (1) Engage in the pretense of negotiating with no substantial purpose other than to delay or burden another party;
      (2) Illegally obstruct another party's rightful access to information relevant to the matter in negotiation;
      (3) Communicate directly with another party who the lawyer knows is represented by other counsel, except with the consent of the party's counsel or as authorized by law.

The draft was attacked as impractical, ill-conceived, and destructive of the adversary system and in the end the attempt to require more truthtelling in negotiations failed. The current Model Rule 4.1 contains all that is left of the substance of the earlier proposed Rule and represents no advance over the provisions of the Model Code. The Comment indeed seeks to answer doubts raised about certain negotiating methods. The Comment to Model Rule 4.1 states, "Under generally accepted conventions in negotiation, certain types of statements ordinarily are not taken as statements of material fact. Estimates of price or value placed on the subject of a transaction and a party's intentions as to an acceptable settlement of a claim are in this category. . . ." Professor White's article on lawyers' standards of conduct in negotiation was written against the backdrop of the change in attitude proposed by draft Model Rule 4.2. While the draft was not adopted, Professor White's comments about general standards, specific cases, and the desirability of changes in current standards are still timely.

WHITE,* MACHIAVELLI AND THE BAR: ETHICAL LIMITS ON LYING IN NEGOTIATION
1980 Am. Bar Found. Res. J. 926

. . . The difficulty of proposing acceptable rules concerning truthfulness in negotiation is presented by several circumstances. First, negotiation is nonpublic behavior. If one negotiator lies to another, only by happenstance will the other discover the lie. If the settlement is concluded by negotiation, there will be no trial, no public testimony by conflicting witnesses, and thus no opportunity to examine the truthfulness of assertions made during the negotiation. Consequently, in negotiation, more than in other contexts, ethical norms can probably be violated with greater confidence that there will be no discovery and punishment. Whether one is likely to be caught for violating an ethical standard says nothing about the merit of the standard. However, if the low probability of punishment means that many lawyers will violate the standard, the standard becomes even more difficult for the honest lawyer to follow, for by doing so he may be forfeiting a significant advantage for his client to others who do not follow the rules.

The drafters appreciated, but perhaps not fully, a second difficulty in drafting ethical norms for negotiators. That is the almost galactic scope of disputes that are subject to resolution by negotiation. One who conceives of negotiation as an alternative to a lawsuit has only scratched the surface. Negotiation is also the process by which one deals with the opposing side in war, with terrorists, with labor or management in a labor agreement, with buyers and sellers of goods, services, and real estate, with lessors, with governmental agencies, and with one's clients, acquaintances, and family. By limiting his consideration to negotiations in which a lawyer is involved in his professional role, one eliminates some of the most difficult cases but is left with a rather large and irregular universe of disputes. Surely society would tolerate and indeed expect different forms of behavior on the one hand from one assigned to negotiate with terrorists and on the other from one who is negotiating with the citizens

*James J. White is Professor of Law, University of Michigan Law School, B.A., 1956, Amherst College; J.D., 1962, Michigan.

on behalf of a governmental agency.[3] The difference between those two cases illustrates the less drastic distinctions that may be called for by differences between other negotiating situations. Performance that is standard in one negotiating arena may be gauche, conceivably unethical, in another. More than almost any other form of lawyer behavior, the process of negotiation is varied; it differs from place to place and from subject matter to subject matter. It calls, therefore, either for quite different rules in different contexts or for rules stated only at a very high level of generality.

A final complication in drafting rules about truthfulness arises out of the paradoxical nature of the negotiator's responsibility. On the one hand the negotiator must be fair and truthful; on the other he must mislead his opponent. Like the poker player, a negotiator hopes that his opponent will overestimate the value of his hand. Like the poker player, in a variety of ways he must facilitate his opponent's inaccurate assessment. The critical difference between those who are successful negotiators and those who are not lies in this capacity both to mislead and not to be misled.

Some experienced negotiators will deny the accuracy of this assertion, but they will be wrong. I submit that a careful examination of the behavior of even the most forthright, honest, and trustworthy negotiators will show them actively engaged in misleading their opponents about their true positions. That is true of both the plaintiff and the defendant in a lawsuit. It is true of both labor and management in a collective bargaining agreement. It is true as well of both the buyer and the seller in a wide variety of sales transactions. To conceal one's true position, to mislead an opponent about one's true settling point, is the essence of negotiation.

Of course there are limits on acceptable deceptive behavior in negotiation, but there is the paradox. How can one be "fair" but also mislead? Can we ask the negotiator to mislead, but fairly, like the soldier who must kill, but humanely?

Truthtelling in General

The obligation to behave truthfully in negotiation is embodied in the requirement of Rule 4.2(a) that directs the lawyer to "be fair in dealing with other participants." Presumably the direction to be fair speaks to a

---

3. For a discussion of the circumstances that might justify a lie, even for one with an extraordinary commitment to truthfulness, see Sissela Bok, ch. 8, Lies in a Crisis in Lying: Moral Choice in Public and Private Life 107-122 (New York: Pantheon Books, 1978).

variety of acts in addition to truthfulness and also different from it. At a minimum it has something to say about the threats a negotiator may use, about the favors he may offer, and possibly about the extraneous factors other than threats and favors which can appropriately be used in negotiating. . . .

Pious and generalized assertions that the negotiator must be "honest" or that the lawyer must use "candor" are not helpful.[9] They are at too high a level of generality, and they fail to appreciate the fact that truth and truthful behavior at one time in one set of circumstances with one set of negotiators may be untruthful in another circumstance with other negotiators. There is no general principle waiting somewhere to be discovered as Judge Alvin B. Rubin seems to suggest in his article on lawyer's ethics. Rather, mostly we are doing what he says we are not doing, namely, hunting for the rules of the game as the game is played in that particular circumstance.

The definition of truth is in part a function of the substance of the negotiation. Because of the policies that lie behind the securities and exchange laws and the demands that Congress has made that information be provided to those who buy and sell, one suspects that lawyers engaged in SEC work have a higher standard of truthfulness than do those whose agreements and negotiations will not affect public buying and selling of assets. Conversely, where the thing to be bought and sold is in fact a lawsuit in which two professional traders conclude the deal, truth means something else. Here truth and candor call for a smaller amount of disclosure, permit greater distortion, and allow the other professional to suffer from his own ignorance and sloth in a way that would not be acceptable in the SEC case. In his article Rubin recognizes that there are such different perceptions among members of the bar engaged in different kinds of practice, and he suggests that there should not be such differences. Why not? Why is it so clear that one's responsibility for truth ought not be a function of the policy, the consequences, and the skill and expectations of the opponent?

Apart from the kinds of differences in truthfulness and candor which arise from the subject matter of the negotiation, one suspects that there are other differences attributable to regional and ethnic differences among negotiators. Although I have only anecdotal data to support this idea, it seems plausible that one's expectation concerning truth and candor might be different in a small, homogeneous community from what it would be in a large, heterogeneous community of lawyers. For one thing, all of the lawyers in the small and homogeneous community will share a common ethnic and environmental background. Each will have been subjected to the same kind of training about what kinds of lies are appropriate and what are not appropriate.

Moreover, the costs of conformity to ethical norms are less in a small community. Because the community is small, it will be easy to know those who do not conform to the standards and to protect oneself against that small number. Conversely, in the large and heterogeneous community, one will not have confidence either about the norms that have been learned by the opposing negotiator or about his conformance to those norms. . . .

If the Comments or the body of the Model Rules are to refer to truthfulness, they should be understood to mean not an absolute but a relative truth as it is defined in context. That context in turn should be determined by the subject matter of the negotiation and, to a lesser extent, by the region and the background of the negotiators. Of course, such a flexible standard does not resolve the difficulties that arise when negotiators of different experience meet one another. I despair of solving that problem by the promulgation of rules, for to do so would require the drafters of these rules to do something that they obviously could not wish to do. That is, unless they wish to rely on the norms in the various subcultures in the bar to flesh out the rules, they will have to draft an extensive and complex body of rules.

FIVE CASES

Although it is not necessary to draft such a set of rules, it is probably important to give more than the simple disclaimer about the impossibility of defining the appropriate limits of puffing that the drafters have given in the current Comments.[15] To test these limits, consider five cases. Easiest is the question that arises when one misrepresents his true opinion about the meaning of a case or a statute. Presumably such a misrepresentation is accepted lawyer behavior both in and out of court and is not intended to be precluded by the requirement that the lawyer be "truthful." In writing his briefs, arguing his case, and attempting to persuade the opposing party in negotiation, it is the lawyer's right and probably his responsibility to argue for plausible interpretations of cases and statutes which favor his client's interest, even in circumstances where privately he has advised his client that those are not his true interpretations of the cases and statutes.

A second form of distortion that the Comments plainly envision as permissible is distortion concerning the value of one's case or of the other subject matter involved in the negotiation. Thus the Comments make explicit reference to "puffery." Presumably they are attempting to draw the same line that one draws in commercial law between express warran-

---

15. "The precise contours of the legal duties concerning disclosure, representation, puffery, overreaching, and other aspects of honesty in negotiations cannot be concisely stated." Comment to Rule 4.2, Model Rules . . .

ties and "mere puffing" under section 2-313 of the Uniform Commercial Code.[17] . . .

A third case is related to puffing but different from it. This is the use of the so-called false demand. It is a standard negotiating technique in collective bargaining negotiation and in some other multiple-issue negotiations for one side to include a series of demands about which it cares little or not at all. The purpose of including these demands is to increase one's supply of negotiating currency. One hopes to convince the other party that one or more of these false demands is important and thus successfully to trade it for some significant concession. The assertion of and argument for a false demand involves the same kind of distortion that is involved in puffing or in arguing the merits of cases or statutes that are not really controlling. The proponent of a false demand implicitly or explicitly states his interest in the demand and his estimation of it. Such behavior is untruthful in the broadest sense; yet at least in collective bargaining negotiation its use is a standard part of the process and is not thought to be inappropriate by any experienced bargainer.

Two final examples may be more troublesome. The first involves the response of a lawyer to a question from the other side. Assume that the defendant has instructed his lawyer to accept any settlement offer under $100,000. Having received that instruction, how does the defendant's lawyer respond to the plaintiff's question, "I think $90,000 will settle this case. Will your client give $90,000?" Do you see the dilemma that question poses for the defense lawyer? It calls for information that would not have to be disclosed. A truthful answer to it concludes the negotiation and dashes any possibility of negotiating a lower settlement even in circumstances in which the plaintiff might be willing to accept half of $90,000. Even a moment's hesitation in response to the question may be a nonverbal communication to a clever plaintiff's lawyer that the defendant has given such authority. Yet a negative response is a lie.

It is no answer that a clever lawyer will answer all such questions about authority by refusing to answer them, nor is it an answer that some lawyers will be clever enough to tell their clients not to grant them authority to accept a given sum until the final stages in negotiation. Most of us are not that careful or that clever. Few will routinely refuse to answer such questions in cases in which the client has granted a much lower limit than that discussed by the other party, for in that case an honest answer about the absence of authority is a quick and effective method of chang-

17. Section 2-313(2) of the Uniform Commercial Code reads in part as follows: "It is not necessary to the creation of an express warranty that the seller use formal words . . . but an affirmation merely of the value of the goods or a statement purporting to be merely the seller's opinion or commendation . . . does not create a warranty." Put another way, puffing is permitted.

ing the opponent's settling point, and it is one that few of us will forego when our authority is far below that requested by the other party. Thus despite the fact that a clever negotiator can avoid having to lie or to reveal his settling point, many lawyers, perhaps most, will sometime be forced by such a question either to lie or to reveal that they have been granted such authority by saying so or by their silence in response to a direct question. Is it fair to lie in such a case?

Before one examines the possible justification for a lie in that circumstance, consider a final example recently suggested to me by a lawyer in practice. There the lawyer represented three persons who had been charged with shoplifting. Having satisfied himself that there was no significant conflict of interest, the defense lawyer told the prosecutor that two of the three would plead guilty only if the case was dismissed against the third. Previously those two had told the defense counsel that they would plead guilty irrespective of what the third did, and the third had said that he wished to go to trial unless the charges were dropped. Thus the defense lawyer lied to the prosecutor by stating that the two would plead only if the third were allowed to go free. Can the lie be justified in this case?[21]

How does one distinguish the cases where truthfulness is not required and those where it is required? Why do the first three cases seem easy? I suggest they are easy cases because the rules of the game are explicit and well developed in those areas. Everyone expects a lawyer to distort the value of his own case, of his own facts and arguments, and to deprecate those of his opponent. No one is surprised by that, and the system accepts and expects that behavior. To a lesser extent the same is true of the false demand procedure in labor-management negotiations where the ploy is sufficiently widely used to be explicitly identified in the literature. A layman might say that this behavior falls within the ambit of "exaggeration," a form of behavior that while not necessarily respected is not regarded as morally reprehensible in our society.

The last two cases are more difficult. In one the lawyer lies about his authority; in the other he lies about the intention of his clients. It would be more difficult to justify the lies in those cases by arguing that the rules of the game provide for such distortion, but I suspect that many lawyers would say that such lies are out of bounds and are not part of the rules of the game. Can the lie about authority be justified on the ground that the question itself was improper? Put another way, if I have a right to keep certain information to myself, and if any behavior but a lie will reveal that information to the other side, am I justified in lying? I think

---

21. Consider a variation on the last case. Assume that the defense lawyer did not say explicitly that the two would plead only if the third were allowed to go free but simply said, "If you drop the charges against one, the other two will plead guilty." In that case the lie is not explicit but surely the inference which the defense lawyer wishes the prosecutor to draw is the same. Should that change the outcome?

not. Particularly in the case in which there are other avenues open to the respondent, should we not ask him to take those avenues? That is, the careful negotiator here can turn aside all such questions and by doing so avoid any inference from his failure to answer such questions.

What makes the last case a close one? Conceivably it is the idea that one accused by the state is entitled to greater leeway in making his case. Possibly one can argue that there is no injury to the state when such a person, particularly an innocent person, goes free. Is it conceivable that the act can be justified on the ground that it is part of the game in this context, that prosecutors as well as defense lawyers routinely misstate what they, their witnesses, and their clients can and will do? None of these arguments seems persuasive. Justice is not served by freeing a guilty person. The system does not necessarily achieve better results by trading two guilty pleas for a dismissal. Perhaps its justification has its roots in the same idea that formerly held that a misrepresentation of one's state of mind was not actionable for it was not a misrepresentation of fact.

In a sense rules governing these cases may simply arise from a recognition by the law of its limited power to shape human behavior. By tolerating exaggeration and puffing in the sales transaction, by refusing to make misstatement of one's intention actionable, the law may simply have recognized the bounds of its control over human behavior. Having said that, one is still left with the question, Are the lies permissible in the last two cases? My general conclusion is that they are not, but I am not nearly as comfortable with that conclusion as I am with the conclusion about the first three cases.

Taken together, the five foregoing cases show me that we do not and cannot intend that a negotiator be "truthful" in the broadest sense of that term. At the minimum we allow him some deviation from truthfulness in asserting his true opinion about cases, statutes, or the value of the subject of the negotiation in other respects. In addition some of us are likely to allow him to lie in response to certain questions that are regarded as out of bounds, and possibly to lie in circumstances where his interest is great and the injury seems small. It would be unfortunate, therefore, for the rule that requires "fairness" to be interpreted to require that a negotiator be truthful in every respect and in all of his dealings. It should be read to allow at least those kinds of untruthfulness that are implicitly and explicitly recognized as acceptable in his forum, a forum defined both by the subject matter and by the participants. . . .

Conclusion

To draft effective legislation is difficult; to draft effective ethical rules is close to impossible. Such drafters must walk the narrow line between being too general and too specific. If their rules are too general, they will have no influence on any behavior and give little guidance even to those who wish to follow the rules. If they are too specific, they omit certain areas or conflict with appropriate rules for problems not foreseen but apparently covered.

There are other, more formidable obstacles. These drafters are essentially powerless. They draft the rules, but the American Bar Association must pass them, and the rules must then be adopted by various courts or other agencies in the states. Finally the enforcement of the rules is left to a hodgepodge of bar committees and grievance agencies of varied will and capacity. Thus the drafters are far removed from and have little control over those who ultimately will enact and enforce the rules. For that reason, even more than most legislators, drafters of ethical rules have limited power to influence behavior. This weakness presents a final dilemma and one they have not always faced as well as they should, namely, to make the appropriate trade-off between what is "right" and what can be done. To enact stern and righteous rules in Chicago will not fool the people in Keokuk. The public will not believe them, and the bar will not follow them. What level of violation of the rules can the bar accept without the rules as a whole becoming a mockery? I do not know and the drafters can only guess. Because of the danger presented if the norms are widely and routinely violated, the drafters should err on the conservative side and must sometimes reject better and more desirable rules for poorer ones simply because the violation of the higher standard would cast all the rules in doubt.

NOTES

1. There is a clear relation between Professor White's general views about the utility of general negotiation rules and the appropriateness of particular conduct on the one hand and, on the other, his answers to the specific hypotheticals he poses. In answering the third case, he appears to find it conclusive that the specific "untruthful" behavior "is not thought to be inappropriate by any experienced bargainer" (p. 401). If that factual assertion is accurate and conclusive, how do standards of conduct change? Much that was not thought inappropriate in the days when caveat emptor was supreme is no longer thought appropriate today. How did we get from there to here? Is it relevant that the "false demand" that takes the form of prosecutorial overcharging of defendants is under heavy attack today? Or should the different circumstances of the criminal justice system cause us to draw a sharp line between the false demand there and in civil negotiation?

2. Note that the drafters of the Comment to Rule 4.1 of the Model Rules have addressed Professor White's fourth case and imply that what Professor White calls "a lie" (p. 401) is actually not a statement of "material fact."

3. Does your reading of the way courts have interpreted the provisions of the Model Code and Model Rules lead you to agree with Professor White's view about the powerlessness of drafters? That is quite a different point from the one that he makes in conjunction with it — that the danger of wholesale disobedience to a particular rule ought to cause a drafting committee to be quite conservative in its attempt to alter "ethical" behavior. Does his observation account for or justify, say, the effort of the drafters of the Model Rules to provide a nearly absolute principle of confidentiality in Model Rule 1.6? Does his argument sufficiently take account of the nonlawyer interests that are not very well represented in the drafting process?

PROBLEM 54

A prosecutor in a capital offense case has offered to reduce the charge to one carrying a maximum six months' sentence on a plea of guilty. Although there is some evidence of guilt, the defendant maintains his innocence. Does the lawyer have an obligation to disclose the defendant's statement of innocence to the court when the plea is to be entered? How does the lawyer advise the client to respond to a trial judge's inquiry to tell how the crime occurred, when the lawyer knows that if the client states his innocence, the plea will not be accepted?

Former Chief Justice (then Judge) Warren Burger addressed the issue in Standards of Conduct for Prosecution and Defense Personnel, 5 Am. Crim. L.Q. 11, 15 (1966):

> . . . A judge may not properly accept a guilty plea from an accused who denies the very acts which constitute the crime. However, he may do so if the matter is in such dispute or doubt that a jury might find him guilty in spite of his denials. When an accused tells the court he committed the act charged to induce acceptance of the guilty plea, the lawyer to whom contrary statements have been made owes a duty to the court to disclose such contrary statements so that the court can explore and resolve the conflict. The key lies in the obligation to be candid with the court, and no plea of guilty should be accepted except upon a full disclosure which permits the court to make an informed and intelligent decision in acting on the plea. . . .

Professor Addison Bowman took a different view in Standards of Conduct . . . an Attorney's Viewpoint, 5 Am. Crim. L.Q. 28, 31 (1966):

> . . . counsel . . . should advise the defendant that the latter may attempt to enter a plea of guilty to assault and battery, and that the plea may be accepted if counsel points out to the court that the evidence against the defendant is sufficient to justify a jury verdict of guilty. However, counsel should also advise his client that the plea may not be accepted without an

> acknowledgement of guilt, whereupon the latter may suggest that he can tell the court he is guilty even though this is not true.

See North Carolina v. Alford, 400 U.S. 25 (1970), holding that it was not constitutional error for a judge to accept a guilty plea voluntarily and understandingly made, when the record contained strong evidence of guilt notwithstanding the defendant's protestation that he was innocent. The Court went on to state that it was not holding that a state had to afford a criminal defendant the right to have a guilty plea accepted. Id. at 38. Cf. Fed. R. Crim. Proc. 11(f), providing that a court should not enter a judgment upon a plea of guilty "without making such inquiry as shall satisfy it that there is a factual basis for the plea."

The ABA Standards Relating to the Defense Function originally provided in §5.3,

> If the accused discloses to the lawyer facts which negate guilt and the lawyer's investigation does not reveal a conflict with the facts disclosed but the accused persists in entering a plea of guilty, the lawyer may not properly participate in presenting a guilty plea, without disclosure to the court.

It is interesting to note the reasoning stated in the commentary to this section:

> In many, perhaps most, situations the accused is simply not capable of relating his conduct to the legal conclusion of guilt or innocence. The law does not permit his opinion on the ultimate and often complex question of his guilt as a matter of law to control the judgment of the court. That judgment can only be made in accordance with the processes of the law. . . . The essence of the principle . . . is that a court considering the acceptance of a plea of guilty should be fully informed and never misled and that both counsel have a duty in this respect.

The Standard's analysis of the problem seemed to ignore Canon 4's obligation not to reveal the confidences or secrets of the client. Which of the exceptions to DR 4-101 (C) justified Standard 5.3?

Standard 5.3 was eliminated in the 1979 revision of the Standards. The reason given is interesting for its lack of much reliance on the confidentiality obligation.

> If . . . a so-called *Alford* plea is either not accepted by the court or is not offered by the defendant, it does not follow that defense counsel should be required to reveal to the court that the defendant privately denies guilt to counsel. As long as the defendant openly acknowledges guilt to the court and a factual basis for the plea is present, this is deemed sufficient. If counsel were to tell the court that the defendant privately insists that he or she is innocent, the result is likely to be unsatisfactory. The defendant

will most likely insist to the court that he or she is, in fact, guilty because the defendant wants the plea to be accepted, and that any statements previously made to counsel were false. It is probable, moreover, that prior to entry of the guilty plea, defense counsel will have devoted considerable effort to convincing the defendant to do just what the defendant has finally done — to openly admit wrongdoing. When the defendant finally does plead guilty, and defense counsel then reports to the court that the defendant privately maintains innocence, the defendant is likely to find counsel's actions baffling. Meanwhile, acceptance of the guilty plea will be jeopardized, despite the presence of a factual basis and the defendant's public admission of guilt. The attorney-client relationship will also probably have been destroyed. As a matter of practice among defense counsel, it is believed that adherence to original standard 5.3 was virtually nonexistent. Under no circumstances, however, should a lawyer recommend to a defendant acceptance of a plea unless a full investigation and study of the case has been completed, including an analysis of controlling law and the evidence likely to be introduced at trial. See standards 4-4.1, 4-5.1(a), and 4-6.1(b).

If the defendant is placed under oath when the plea is offered, the problem for defense counsel seemingly becomes more difficult because the defendant's statements will be perjurious. This situation obviously is similar to that confronted when a defendant seeks to lie under oath at his or her trial. This chapter, however, does not address the so-called client perjury problem. See the editorial note to 4-7.7 [which is discussed at p. 173]. ABA Standards for Criminal Justice 4.69 n.* (2d ed. 1980).

Good discussion of the practical workings and professional responsibility problems of plea bargaining is contained in Alschuler, The Prosecutor's Role in Plea Bargaining, 36 U. Chi. L. Rev. 50 (1968), and Alschuler, The Defense Attorney's Role in Plea Bargaining, 84 Yale L.J. 1179 (1975). With respect to Problem 54 consider especially the latter, at 1278-1313. This particular problem disappears when a state adopts the radical course of formally "abolishing" plea bargaining between defendants and both prosecutors and judges, as Alaska has sought to do at the sentencing and at the charge stages. See Rubinstein and White, Alaska's Ban on Plea Bargaining 1-18 (Alaska Judicial Council 1978), reproduced in Zimring and Frase, The Criminal Justice System 674-684 (1980).

CHAPTER 7

SOME ADDITIONAL PROBLEMS OF LAWYERS' SPECIAL OBLIGATIONS TO THE COURT, THE PROFESSION, AND SOCIETY

A. THE OBLIGATION TO REPRESENT AN UNPOPULAR CLIENT

The profession has long recognized, at least as an ideal, the desirability of affording representation to all persons seeking it, and that obligation has in criminal matters been constitutionalized to a very large extent. Gideon v. Wainwright, 372 U.S. 335 (1963), and Argersinger v. Hamlin, 407 U.S. 25 (1972). Nevertheless, the profession in this country has been troubled by the tension between this objective and a recognition of the countervailing value in preserving some freedom for lawyers to select their own clients. See EC 2-26. The issue is an old one, and the most interesting debate took place over 100 years ago between David Dudley Field, perhaps the outstanding lawyer of his era, and his son, Dudley Field, on one side, and Samuel Bowles, one of the leading newspaper publishers of the nineteenth century, on the other.

THE LAWYER AND HIS CLIENTS —
CORRESPONDENCE OF MESSRS. DAVID DUDLEY
AND DUDLEY FIELD, OF THE NEW YORK BAR,
WITH MR. SAMUEL BOWLES, OF THE
SPRINGFIELD REPUBLICAN*

[privately printed 1871]

I. DAVID DUDLEY FIELD TO SAMUEL BOWLES

December 27, 1870.

Dear Sir:

I address you thus, taking it for granted that the scurrilous attack upon me in the form of a letter, published in a late number of the Springfield Republican, was inserted without your consent or knowledge. Allow me to call your attention to this attack, and ask you for a public disavowal of it. . . . Your relations with me make me believe, that you would not willingly lend its types to abuse me, and your relations with others make me also believe, that you would not knowingly consent to its degradation.

Yours very truly,
David Dudley Field.

[The "scurrilous attack" in question, was the following paragraph from a letter concerning the bar of New York in The Republican, and copied in this form in the New York Times:]

Correspondence of the Springfield Republican

David Dudley Field, though hardly old enough to be called a veteran, is one of the ablest lawyers in New York, and has, by far, the largest practice. His receipts as counsel for the Erie railroad company alone, are understood to have exceeded $200,000 in a single year, and his regular income is enormous. His connection with Fisk and Gould secures him the favor of Barnard and the other ring judges, though it has destroyed his reputation as a high-toned lawyer with the public, while the bar always disliked him for his avarice and meanness. David Dudley Field is a strong free-trade advocate, and often presides at the meetings of the reform club. He is an authority on international law, and was also the chief codifier of the present code of procedure of the state of New York. His reputation as a lawyer is based upon his knowledge of legal technicality, and once, during a legal controversy with the late James T. Brady,

---

*A more complete version was printed in the first and second editions of this work.

the latter dubbed him "the king of the pettifoggers," which title has stuck to Field ever since.

II. SAMUEL BOWLES TO DAVID DUDLEY FIELD

December 29, 1870.

My Dear Sir:

I did not see the letter about the New York lawyers, in which occurred the paragraph offensive to yourself, until after it was published in The Republican; nor did I read it, indeed, until since the receipt of your letter. I regret very much that it did not do fuller justice to the qualities that have won for you the position, which the letter assigned, of the leader of the active members of the New York bar. I am especially mortified and indignant that the line concerning your personal qualities, or rather the supposed opinion of your brother lawyers in regard to them, should have appeared in a paper under my control. Whether any or all of your associates think you "avaricious" or "mean," is a matter I know nothing about; but their judgment to that effect would not, knowingly by me, have found expression in The Republican.

But as to the general judgment concerning your professional associations with notorious parties, with generally conceded corrupt schemes, and the effect of them upon your professional standing, I should not have changed the character of the letter, though the wording of it is not exactly to my taste. Whether right or wrong, I think there is but one feeling among your old friends in Western Massachusetts on this subject; and that is one of mingled sorrow and indignation at your professional associations with Fisk and Gould and their desperate schemes.

The inclosed editorial paragraph in The Republican, a few days since, expressive, I think, of this common feeling or judgment, would have been rendered earlier, and I think made more condemnatory, but for the long-time pleasant personal relations between myself and your family. . . .

I am, sir, yours very truly,
Samuel Bowles.

[Editorial paragraph from The Republican inclosed in the above letter: —]

Now that a first-class British review, the Westminster, has broken ground in vigorous rebuke of that eminent lawyer, Mr. David Dudley Field, for his great share in prostituting the law and its instruments to the gross schemes of speculation, corruption and robbery, in which his distinguished client, James Fisk, Jr., has been engaged for the last few years, the New York journals begin to press home upon him his notorious sins in this respect. The Times, in particular, points out the impossibility of doing anything in the way of legal or judicial reform, so long as men of his high professional and social standing give their learning and their influence to break down all the safeguards of justice in behalf of notorious scoundrels, and sell their services to men like Fisk, Gould, Drew and Fremont, who are committing public robbery on Wall Street and Albany and before the courts of New York city and state. It is to be hoped these strictures may have some influence in arousing private consciences to their obligations, and in creating a public opinion that will make it impossible for these scandals to go on or be repeated by others.

III.   Dudley Field (Son) to Samuel Bowles

December 27, 1870.

Sir: . . .

Somebody connected with the New York Times has a spite against our firm, and almost every day some malicious and lying article appears about some of us. When this began some years ago, we attempted to answer, but they altered our reply, and each lie refuted enabled them to answer with a new one, so we have since paid no attention to them.

Not satisfied with attacking us in their editorial columns they take a malicious pleasure in digging out anything against us in other papers. Yesterday I was surprised to find in its columns what purports to be an extract from the correspondence of The Springfield Republican, as follows: —

[Extract published at bottom of Mr. David Dudley Field's first letter.]

Now the firm of Field & Shearman consists of three persons, myself, T. G. Shearman and J. W. Sterling, my father being counsel connected with us. He has had a large practice for many years, and since I have been with him, which is 18 years, we have probably had as much legal business in our office as any other office in New York, and we have been fairly rewarded for it. The Erie railway company has much litigation and many different lawyers. Some, a small proportion, of their suits are sent to us, and we are paid by it as by other clients. Neither my father nor the firm ever had $200,000 from the Erie railway company in one year, nor any sum in any manner approaching it. We are not bound to tell you or the public the exact sum that we receive, but we endeavor to get fees proportionate to the labor in each case, and if our clients do not complain, I do not perceive who else can. However, if when you are in New York, you will call at our office, I will give you a list of the services performed and the fees received by ourselves and other lawyers, who have been employed from time to time by Mr Fisk, Mr Gould or the Erie railway, and leave you to judge of the adequacy of the compensation of each.

As to my father's regular income, it is derived from professional services to many clients, from mortgage rents, and the investments of a lifetime. Last year and year before, his sworn returns to the internal revenue assessor were about $75,000. So much for the first statement. The second is that my father's connection "with Fisk & Gould secures him the favor of Barnard and the other ring judges." He has no "connection" with Fisk & Gould beyond being retained by them in lawsuits. Within the past three years, at various times, the following New York lawyers, among others, have also been retained by the same persons or by the Erie company: William M. Evarts, Edwin W. Stoughton, James T. Brady, Samuel J. Tilden, Aaron J. Vanderpoel, Dorman B. Eaton, William Fullerton, John C. Burrill, John K. Porter, Hamilton W. Robinson, Joseph S. Bosworth, F. J. Fithian and Clarence A. Seward; and any one of them has as much influence with any and every judge as we have. I defy anybody to point to a single instance where we have exercised any influence upon or received any favor or any order, which we had not a right to consider justified by the law and the facts, from any judge.

The communication further states that "the bar always disliked" my father "for his avarice and meanness." Now, my father is the principal author of the New York Code, which was, for a long time, very unpopular with the bar. He has been prominent as a lawyer, freesoiler and freetrader and public speaker, for many years, and naturally has many enemies; but if there is a single member of our bar, who has given away as much in public and private charity during his life, he is unknown to me. As but one example of this, I may take an institution near you, and well known to you, Williams College, to which he has given above $30,000. I could cite many other instances, and could bring many a poor family, as witness to the truth of my assertion; but my object is not to eulogize my father, but to defend him from aspersions.

Your article winds up with stating that "James T. Brady dubbed him the king of pettifoggers, which title has stuck to Field ever since." Mr Brady was a personal friend of mine, and during the latter part of his life, a friend, also, of my father. They at one time were engaged in a great legal contest, where both combatants used warm language, but Mr Brady never gave him any such title in my hearing, and I am sure I was present during the entire controversy.

I have exposed four untruths in an article of twenty-three lines, the whole of which is evidently dictated by malice. You can best judge whether one who knows personally of what he is talking, or a newspaper correspondent, who gives no authority, and can have no personal knowledge on the subject, is most worthy of credence. The attacks in the Times are curiosities in their way. One article asserts that our excuse for taking a retainer from Mr Fisk is, that we are legally bound to take all retainers. The Indianapolis Journal, an extract from which is published in the Times, just above the extract from your paper, refutes this supposed proposition of ours with great force and fury. The truth is, that we never did make any such proposition, or defend ourselves at all. The Times has another article, in which it says, the case would have been quite different if Mr Fisk had been a client of Mr Field, before he became so widely known, but that he retained Mr Field, after he became notorious, etc. And on this text it preaches a sermon of a column.

The truth is, that Mr Fisk became a client of mine years ago, when my father was in Europe, and has since continued to send more or less suits to our office. The Indianapolis Journal aforesaid, says: 1st, We "have accepted a general retainer from James Fisk." We have not. 2d, We "in other words have agreed in advance for a stipulated sum to advocate all of his schemes and defend all his villainies, etc." This is also untrue. In fact, if we [were] to copy all the false accusations, all inspired by the Times, or taken from its pages, and refute them one by one, we should have to make that our sole business. So I will go no further. . . .

I remain, sir, your obedient servant,
Dudley Field.

IV.   SAMUEL BOWLES TO DUDLEY FIELD (SON)

December 29, 1870.

Dear Sir: . . .

On the professional point . . . involved in the conspicuous relations of your father with Fisk and Gould, and their desperate measures, I believe the feeling expressed by the New York Times, and finding utterance in The Republican, is almost an universal one. . . .

The right or wrong of this feeling need not be discussed between you and me; it is a very large question; and I well understand that there is something to be said on the other side. But The Republican had long ago maintained, and applied to cases in Massachusetts, the doctrine that a lawyer was responsible, in a decided degree, for the character of his clients and the character of the suits which he undertook in their behalf; and I believe no professional conduct is more open to criticism, in this respect, than that of your father. If he is no more guilty than other prominent gentlemen of the New York bar, so much the worse for the New York bar. But whether correctly or not, the public have identified your father especially with the more desperate and notorious causes of your distinguished Erie clients, and are disposed, it would seem, to concentrate upon him a responsibility, which, perhaps, should be shared, in some degree, by others. . . .

Yours very truly and very gratefully,
Samuel Bowles.

V.   David Dudley Field to Samuel Bowles

December 30, 1870.

Dear Sir:

Your letter of the 29th, in answer to mine of the 27th, was received this morning. The disavowal of any knowledge of the offensive letter, till after its publication, and the expression of your regret for its omissions, and of your mortification and indignation for some of its expressions, are very well; and if you had stopped there, I should have had nothing more to say. But when you add, that "as to the general judgment concerning" my "professional association with notorious parties, with generally conceded corrupt schemes, and the effect of them upon" my "professional standing," you "should not have changed the character of the letter," and send me besides a most offensive editorial paragraph, previously published, saying of it that "the judgment would have been rendered earlier, and" you "think made more condemnatory but for the long-time pleasant personal relations" between yourself and my family; when you add these expressions to your disclaimer, I am amazed and indignant. . . .

You assail me for what you call my "professional association with notorious parties, with generally conceded corrupt schemes." Your meaning is cloudy, and I am not sure whether it be that I have a professional association with notorious parties who have "generally conceded corrupt schemes," or a "professional association with notorious parties" and also "with generally conceded corrupt schemes." You may take whichever meaning you please. If the latter, I must ask you to state what "generally conceded corrupt schemes," I have a professional association with. If the former, then the complaint is of my "professional association with notorious parties," having "generally conceded corrupt schemes," by which I suppose you mean, that I have a "professional association" with Messrs Gould & Fisk, and that they have "generally conceded corrupt schemes." Now I will not stop to argue with you whether they have "conceded" that they have corrupt schemes in view, or whether, without any concession on their part, it is true, in point of fact, that they have them. My place to discuss that question is in court, and not before you. But, assuming, for the sake of the argument, that they have, I must ask you what you mean by "professional association." Is it giving them legal opinions and arguing cases for them in court? Or is it something else? If it be something else, I must ask you what that something is, as I do not know. If it be only giving them legal opinions, and arguing cases for them, all that I need say is, that I have done not only what I had a right, but what I was bound to do. If, in giving an opinion, I have perverted or misunderstood the law, point out the instance, and I will admit myself wrong. If, in arguing a cause, I have suppressed evidence or misled the court, point out an instance of that also, and I will again admit myself wrong. I deny that I have done any of these things in any one instance. If you say I have, mention the instance, or admit yourself a false accuser.

You must remember that a lawyer, who is denied the shelter of his professional character, is necessarily put to great disadvantage. His communications with his client are confidential. He cannot in most cases say what advice he has given, because he cannot disclose the information which his client has given him. In that respect his lips are sealed. But if I cannot tell you now what advice I have given, I am, I suppose, at liberty to tell you what I have not been consulted about; and availing myself of this liberty, I say to you, that I have never been consulted, beforehand, about the management of the Erie railway, or the issue of any of its stocks or bonds, or the payment of any dividend to any stockholder or class of stockholders, or about what is known as the Erie classification bill, or about the gold operations of 1869, or any of the private transactions of Messrs Gould & Fisk, or either of them, or about any transaction whatever of this company or these gentlemen, to which, so far as I now recollect, any exception has been taken. If you think there is any defect in the comprehensiveness of this statement, you may question me to your heart's content. . . .

The storm of abuse, that is poured upon me, is really, however designed, an attack upon the independence of the bar. Such abuse of an advocate is not a new thing in the world. They who hate a client fancy, in their folly, that if they can frighten his advocate, they may destroy the client, not reflecting that they would thus weaken their own security. When Erskine, defending Thomas Paine, rose to address the jury, he said: "Every man, within hearing at this moment, nay, the whole people of England, have been witnesses to the calumnious clamor, that by every art has been raised against me. In every place, where business or pleasure collects the public together, day after day my name and character have been the topics of injurious reflection." "And for what?" he asked, and thereupon replied that it was due to the fact that he had not shrunk from the discharge of a duty "which no personal advantages recommended and which a thousand difficulties repelled." Then he boldly vindicated himself, saying, "I will forever, at all hazards, assert the dignity, independence and integrity of the English bar, without which impartial justice, the most valuable part of the English constitution, can have no existence." Do not mistake me by supposing that I am likening myself to Erskine, or my clients to Paine. I am stating a principle in better terms than I can state it myself.

I am not insensible to the respect of my fellow-men, and especially of my fellow-members of the bar, who are in the main a noble but much calumniated body of men; but I value still more my own self-respect, and if I were to be driven by clamor or by any means whatever short of absolute force to abandon my clients, I should lose my self-respect. That

I will not do, be the consequences what they may. I am resolved, that so far as I am able to effect it, my clients shall be judged according to the law of the land. I shall, whenever I speak for them in the courts of the country, stand between them and popular clamor, just as I would stand between them and power, if they were menaced by power of any kind, monarchical or republican. I have never cared for popularity. I have met many a scowl in my day; as when I defended the fugitive slave, or when I inveighed against arrests without legal warrant, under color of the war power, or when I denied the legality of test oaths, or argued against the constitutionality of the military governments in the South. . . .

Very truly yours,
David Dudley Field.

VI. SAMUEL BOWLES TO DAVID DUDLEY FIELD

January 3, 1871.

Dear Sir:

Of course I could not expect that my explanatory note of the 29th, would satisfy you. Had it been possible, to my own sense of truth and justice, to have stopped short at the point that you say would have satisfied you, the imperious tone of your first note would have forbidden it. But I did not suppose that you would be surprised at my opinions. I have found them so common among gentlemen of all professions, and especially among gentlemen of the bar in this state; they have been so often expressed in the independent press of the country, — that I had supposed you were familiar with their popularity, and had ceased to be surprised, if not annoyed, by their utterance. . . .

[Y]our . . . position . . . , certainly, is entitled to every possible respect; and I have neither the disposition nor the power to criticise it in detail. I have "walked backward with averted eyes" through much of the history of your professional association with those notorious clients that have dragged down your professional fame; — and I cannot measure the precise extent or character of the services you have rendered them. I can only say, my judgment has been formed from the general observation of your name in connection with their most desperate causes, and with some of the more extraordinary proceedings which have been had in their behalf in the New York courts, — as well as from the testimony of some of the local public journals, and of prominent members of your local bar; — as likewise, further, from gentlemen of your profession in this state, — all of whom would naturally watch the details with greater closeness and discrimination, than either my ability or inclination allowed. I am glad that you are able to satisfy yourself of the propriety of your conduct, — I hope you may be able to satisfy your friends, your profession and the public. But I must tell you, frankly, that if you are right, they are widely and deeply wrong, and you are one of the most misunderstood and best abused men in the country. . . .

The province of professional duty, to causes and to clients, is, I believe, an open question among lawyers themselves. Even the principles of it have never been stated to general acceptance; but it is much easier to agree upon a principle than to decide upon practice under it. Perhaps none would dispute the statements of Erskine. Certainly posterity honors him for the defense of a man, who was arraigned for opinions on abstract questions. But your clients, for whom you have incurred deep responsibilities and dared professional dishonor, are no martyrs to opinions, and are not arraigned for a bold adherence to, and publication of, unpopular principles. Their offenses are against the peace and integrity of business. They have achieved and hold possession of a railroad by means little short of robbery itself. They have sought, for mere purposes of personal aggrandizement, to corrupt the very head of the nation. And they have, with like purposes in view, brought temporary disorder into the financial condition of the country, and spread ruin, with a wanton hand, among its people. It is in assisting or defending these men in such plans and in such operations; in borrowing the forms and technicalities of law to sustain them in their positions, or to screen them from justice; it is in lending your great ability and your legal knowledge, either to the concoction or the defense of gross schemes of stock speculation or railroad and business aggrandizement, at the expense of innocent parties and the public; it is in interposing yourself and your professional services, between men, whom the nation supposes, rightly or wrongly, aye *believes*, with a faith that cannot be readily shaken, are men of public corruption and men of business dishonor, — between such men and their dispossession of their ill-gotten gains and power, and the relief of the business of the country from their paralyzing control and corrupting example; — it is for acts and influences like these, that you have been arraigned before the public, and that not only professional but popular opinion sits in judgment upon you. . . .

I am, sir, yours very truly,
Samuel Bowles.

VII. DAVID DUDLEY FIELD TO SAMUEL BOWLES

January 5, 1871.

Dear Sir:

Your letter of the 3d inst. received this morning, seems to have been written for publication, and is filled with as much general disparagement as could well be got into so many pages, without stating a single fact, from which lawyer or moralist could form an opinion, except the fact that the clients to whom you refer are, as you say, bad men. To give this as a reason for not defending them is equivalent to saying that the saints must have a monopoly of lawsuits. If a saint sues a sinner the sinner shall not be defended. If it should happen that a saint wrongs a sinner, the sinner cannot sue the saint. This is putting your case in a more palpable form than has occurred to you, perhaps, but I think it is essentially your position. Were you, however, to change it, and say, that you make no question of parties, but of causes, and that a lawyer should never engage in the wrong side of a cause, I must ask you what is to be taken beforehand as the test of wrong. If the lawyer were omniscient and the judge infallible, if all the facts on both sides and all the law could be known from the beginning, then, indeed, the lawyer would be justified in saying to a client, I will not assist you. But in the present condition of humanity facts are often misunderstood, the law often mistaken, and one court frequently pronounces right what another court has pronounced wrong.

In this state of things I know no better general rule than this: that the lawyer, being intrusted by government with the exclusive function of representing litigants before the courts, is bound to represent any person who has any rights to be asserted or defended. If a person has no rights, the lawyer is not bound to assist. If he has any rights, the lawyer is bound to see them respected if he can. Let me apply this rule to . . . my clients. . . . Suppose them . . . to be guilty of all the wrongs you charge them with, have they still no rights? If a ruffian beats one of them in the street, may he be sued for it? If he utter a falsehood concerning them, may he be prosecuted? Or suppose one, who has a spite against them, to buy a share or two of stock in the Erie railway company for the purpose of harassing them with a lawsuit, is it lawful to defend them against such a suit? Or suppose a speculator, who has sold stocks on time, to bring a suit, for the purpose of affecting the price, may such a suit be resisted? Or suppose an enemy, unwilling to take the responsibility himself, puts forward a third person, to bring suits against them, and keep them in continued litigation, for the gratification of revenge, are these suits to go on without resistance? Or suppose them to have enough of the stock of a corporation to give them the majority at an election, and the managers to manufacture secretly new stock to overcome their majority, using the property of the company to pay for it, and making away with the books to complete the secrecy, — must the wrong be acquiesced in and redress by the courts given up? Or suppose still further, that actions are brought against them for damages on alleged sales of gold, which they say they never bought, is it unprofessional to put in their answers and try the causes for them? These are not imaginary cases. They are mainly real cases for engaging in which I am assailed. . . .

Let us look at the question from another point of view. It is lawful to advocate what it is lawful to do. Would you have a judge decide against these men, because he thinks them of bad repute or of bad lives or of evil example? What would you think of him if, in pronouncing judgment, he were to say, I do not think the proof sustains the charges of this complaint, but the defendants are outraging decency and corrupting justice, and I shall decide against them? Nay, suppose you were a juror, trying one of the suits for damages on alleged gold contracts, would you violate your oath and find a verdict against them, contrary to the evidence, because they "have sought, for mere purposes of personal aggrandizement, to corrupt the very head of the nation," or because "they have, with like purposes in view, brought temporary disorder into the financial condition of the country, and spread ruin with a wanton hand among its people"? Of course you answer, that you are not a knave or a dog, that you should do this thing. But how in the name of all that is reconcilable, are you to be informed of the real case before you, if nobody may explain it to you; how is the evidence to be forthcoming, if they cannot have the aid of the law in obtaining it; how are they to get the facts fairly before you, if they are denied the privilege of counsel?

You should not answer me, like a sentimental school girl, by talking about walking "backward with averted eyes," or by uttering the politician's slang about my being "one of the most misunderstood and best abused men in the country," as if that had anything to do with the question between us; but you should have given me facts and reasons. Instead of doing so, you have dealt me a volume of vituperation. Let me tell you that you had better at once confess yourself wrong, and accept the theory that the lawyer is responsible, not for his clients, nor for their causes, but for the manner in which he conducts their causes. Here I admit the fullest responsibility. I do not assent to the theory of Brougham that the lawyer should know nobody but his client. I insist that he should defend his client per fas and not per nefas. By this rule, I am willing to be judged. That was the point of my letter, to which you have given no answer but the general one, just mentioned. You cannot escape in this way. You have ventured to arraign my professional conduct. I repel your charge, and challenge you to specify an instance. You fail to specify any; but say public opinion is against me. That may be so or it may not be so. I will not stop to discuss the question with you. You do not advance a step by declaring, never so confidently, that you think so or say so, because somebody else, or all men else; if you please, think so or say so. That will not do; you must go farther, or submit to be branded as a libeler. . . . I will not stop to comment upon your inconsistency. You applaud Erskine. Yet he defended a man who was believed by nearly the whole people of England to be undermining the foundations of all religion and all morality, aiming to subvert the throne and blot out the name of God. All that Messrs Gould & Fisk are charged with is as nothing, in quality or in consequence, compared with what he was charged with. His advocate was denounced, hunted, dismissed from office, for defending him. Now you say, "posterity honors him for the defense."

The prevalence or unanimity even of public opinion is quite foreign to our controversy. I should hope that you are mistaken; but whether reproached or not, I am confident that I have not deserved reproach. Perhaps my knowledge of professional opinion is as good as yours. I have certainly one test of it that you have not, and that is the experience of the Erie office. In answer to my inquiries made to-day, I am informed that within the last three years, the present managers of the company have employed many lawyers of the highest repute in New York, New Jersey, Pennsylvania, Ohio, Illinois, Missouri, and even Massachusetts, and that not in a single instance has a retainer been refused. I do not believe there is a lawyer in the United States who would to-day refuse it. In nearly every litigation, in which I have been concerned for them, I have been associated with the most respectable and eminent counsel. Indeed, in almost the only bona fide suit ever brought against the present managers (for most of the rest have been what I should call filibustering expeditions), the defense is conducted with the counsel and co-operation of the foremost lawyer, not only of Massachusetts, but of all New England.

In conclusion, I have to say that I have discussed these questions, on your own assumption that my clients are all that you charge them to be. It should seem scarcely necessary to add that the assumption is taken only for the sake of the argument. If they are justly chargeable with what is alleged against them, that will be made known when the cases are tried, and then, as at all times, I shall hope to act, as I think I have hitherto acted, according to the best lights I have, the part of an upright lawyer and honest citizen.

> Your obedient servant,
> *David Dudley Field.*

VIII.   SAMUEL BOWLES TO DAVID DUDLEY FIELD

January 10, 1871

My Dear Sir:

I have read with profound attention yours of the 5th, received yesterday, in the hope to find some reason for the modification of my judgment in the matter between us, even if not to "confess myself wrong." But I am utterly unable to do so. I am only impressed with the fact that you believe yourself right, and that you are acting sincerely, if not intelligently. But the grounds of your action, as of your defense, seem to me purely technical and altogether narrow. They do not reach the question, as it lies in my mind, and as it presents itself to the mind of the great public. It is not a question of law, nor even of abstract individual right, but of a broad public morality. You have sinned against no statute; I will not undertake to say, even, that you have violated any prescript of the code professional. Within those lines you are wiser than I, and I shall not follow you. But that you have offended the moral sense of the public, — that is what I insist upon; that is what, in my duty as a journalist, I have proclaimed to the public. If I am wrong, it is simply in reading wrongly the public judgment, — in transcribing incorrectly its verdict. Time and the developments of public testimony will judge between us here.

Thus I dismiss the most of your argument as purely technical, and not pertinent to my view of the subject. Still, let me say, that your assumption that your clients are not to suffer for their bad character, is neither good law nor good sense. Hardly a cause is tried, where the character of the parties for good or bad is not an element in the argument of the counsel, in the opinion of the judge, in the conclusion of the jury. It should, if it does not, go back to the assumption of the case by the counsel. A man *should* suffer for his bad character, as he should gain for his good character; and nothing more convinces me of the perverted views, which you take of your conduct and of the province of your professional duty, than your more than ignoring this consideration, — your denial of it. . . .

Do not deceive yourself, my dear sir; history may be relied upon to defend freedom of opinion, and to avenge its martyrs; but it will never put James Fisk, Jun., by the side of Thomas Paine, nor, for daring and losing for his cause, will it put David Dudley Field on a page parallel to that belonging to Erskine. . . .

> I am yours very truly,
> *Samuel Bowles.*

IX.   DUDLEY FIELD (SON) TO SAMUEL BOWLES

January 9, 1871.

Dear Sir: . . .

The rest of your letter amounts to this: . . .

Sixth — That "The Republican has long ago maintained, and applied to cases in Massachusetts, the doctrine that a lawyer was responsible in a decided degree for the character of his clients and the character of the suits which he undertook in their behalf." My letter was not to The Republican, but to you, and as you are its editor, I am justified in assuming your meaning to be that you maintain that doctrine. Put in that light, it has at least the merit of frankness, except as to the words "decided degree." These words are ambiguous, and as what is the extent of a "degree," and especially of a "decided degree," can hardly be determined, it is no more than fair to state the proposition thus: "A lawyer is responsible for the character of his clients." Shades of Webster, Choate and the numberless great Massachusetts advocates, that have passed away, defend us! Most of these men, whom Massachusetts delighted to honor, defended and prosecuted at divers times divers men accused of crime. When they represented the accused, and he was found guilty, did they share his guilt? When they represented the prosecution, and the accused was acquitted, did they share in the guilt of the wrongful prosecution? In almost all criminal prosecutions, there is a right and a wrong. In a large proportion of civil suits, there is also an absolute moral right and wrong. Where the right rests is determined by a jury, and upon your doctrine their verdict determines the moral character of the counsel for the defeated party. Now, as in almost all cases there are two lawyers, and as in all cases, where the jury do not disagree, there is a verdict one way or the other, and as every lawyer of any considerable practice loses and wins a number of cases each year, it follows that all lawyers must necessarily be wicked men. We have a traditional joke in our profession of a client who instantly discharged his lawyer because he saw him conversing with the lawyer on the other side. He hated his adversary, of course. He hated his adversary's lawyer because he was (in his mind) identified with his adversary, and the idea of friendly intercourse between *his* lawyer and *that* lawyer was too much for him to bear. I did not think to see the joke ever actually adopted as truth. It is true that there is a class of people who consider all lawyers thieves. The same people generally call physicians murderers, and clergymen imposters, and probably nine-tenths of them fully believe all that they read in the newspapers. I supposed few educated persons like yourself belonged to this class. Upon this monstrous doctrine a surgeon should refuse to set a broken limb, till he got a certificate of the good moral character of his patient, a clergyman should refuse to preach or minister to the low and debased, and a newspaper editor should restrict the sale of his paper to the most respectable families. If a lawyer on A.'s behalf brings an action against B. on a promissory note, and A. has been guilty of bigamy, the lawyer should go to the state prison, or, to put it in the most favorable terms for your theory, if on the trial B. proves that the note was procured by fraud, and defeats A., the lawyer is as guilty as A., because "he is responsible for the character of his client and for the character of the suits he undertakes in his behalf.". . .

> Your obedient servant,
> *Dudley Field.*

XII.   Samuel Bowles to Dudley Field (Son)

January 13, 1871.

Dear Sir: . . .

Here, again, is the old, oft-disputed and yet unsettled question of the responsibility of the counsel for his client or his cause. You contend, as I understand, not only for the right, but accept the duty, of every lawyer to assume, without discrimination and without responsibility, any cause or any client, that may come to him, and to give to such cause or client every advantage in the courts that your ability and ingenuity and the possibilities and opportunities of the law can be made to gain. I cannot accept this. I do not believe the profession, either in theory or practice, as a rule, accept it. A lawyer has his rights as a lawyer, and his duties also, as a lawyer. They may, and often do, justify him, and even require him to represent the criminal whom he believes guilty, or the civil cause which he believes wrong. It is due to that criminal or to that cause, that whatever mitigating circumstances there may be in the case, should be known and allowed; but, first, in accepting this position, and next, in discharging it, he takes a responsibility to the public, on which it may arraign, dispute and judge him. This much, I hope, on reflection, even you will be willing to admit. And if you admit it, you let in my whole case. The journalist has a right, as it is his duty, to discuss public measures and public men, — to do it boldly and fearlessly; but he has an equal responsibility to public opinion for the manner, the spirit, and the motive with which he does this, and to the law for any personal injury which he may cause, or for any malice which he may display, in doing it. You have a right, and you have exercised it freely, to arraign the manner in which I discharge my rights and duties as a journalist. I have a right, and it is my duty, as a journalist, to arraign and discuss the manner in which you and your father meet your rights and discharge your duties as lawyers. . . .

I presume this correspondence is now about at an end, and I take the occasion to renew to you the assurances of my personal good will, as well as my gratitude for the zeal of your services in my behalf on the night that your distinguished client clapped me in Ludlow street jail. I cannot but confess, indeed, to a fellow-feeling with you, in view of our relations, however different, to this distinguished personage; and I hope we may so live, that, whatever curious embalming process history has in store for him, we shall escape any, even the remotest, share of it.

I am yours truly,
Samuel Bowles.

[This letter was returned to the writer, unanswered.]

The Field-Bowles correspondence has been commented on by George Martin (see p. 2) in Causes and Conflicts — The Centennial History of the Association of the Bar of the City of New York, 1870-1970, at 55-56 (1970):

> . . . during the winter of 1871 the attention of many of the city's lawyers was diverted by another issue. Once again the question of David Dudley Field's actions in the Erie litigations had come to the fore, and in a most stimulating, noisy fashion. On December 7, 1870, The Springfield Republican, then a paper of national importance, had printed an unsigned letter about the New York City bar in which the writer, apparently a New York lawyer, had described Field in such terms as "[He] is one of the ablest lawyers in New York, and has by far the largest practice. . . . His connection with Fisk and Gould secures him the favor of Barnard and other Ring Judges, though it has destroyed his reputation as a high-toned lawyer with the public; while the Bar always disliked him for his avarice and meanness. . . . His reputation as a lawyer is based upon his knowledge of legal technicality, and once during a legal controversy with the late James T. Brady, the latter dubbed him 'the king of pettifoggers,' which title has stuck with Field ever since."
>
> The letter was a collection of obvious exaggerations, even falsehoods, and Field would not have seen it except that the Times printed an extract which his friends brought to his attention. Field was a man who loved controversy, and he rushed into this one. Professing not to care about the Times, "for it is the weak and wicked 'sound and fury signifying nothing,'" he started a correspondence with Samuel Bowles, the editor of the Republican. After Field and his son, Dudley, had exchanged several letters apiece with Bowles, Field had the lot printed as a pamphlet, which he first distributed privately and then gave to the World to publish.
>
> The letters debated the ancient question which, like the moon, is constantly renewed: Must a lawyer concern himself with the social and economic effects of his legal actions? Bowles argued in essence that Field had bad men as clients and that he helped them to rob the public; Field argued that he was not responsible for the character of his clients.
>
> Field won the exchange, at least in the opinion of most lawyers, if only because many of them had themselves been employed at one time by Fisk, Gould or the Erie Railroad. Among these were William M. Evarts, James T. Brady, Samuel J. Tilden, Aaron J. Vanderpoel, Dorman B. Eaton and Clarence Seward. On this particular issue, at least — the question of a lawyer's responsibility for the character of his client (which was taking Bowles's argument at its narrowest) — the bar as a whole, however, reluctantly, was with Field.*

---

*The problem is truly perennial. Several generations later, for example, writing of business and legal practice in the country after the Spanish-American War, Robert T. Swaine stated: "Holding companies, with inflated capitalizations top-heavy with debt, popped up like puffballs, controlling production and distribution in many industries, with little concern for the anti-trust laws. Those critics who ascribe to the corporate executives and bankers of the day and to their lawyers moral turpitude in these trans-

The obvious question to ask with regard to these materials is whether each of us prefers the Bowles view or the Field view of the duty of the individual lawyer. Or are there other positions that might be taken? Is there a difference between representation in the civil and in the criminal context? Between representation in connection with past events only and representation in connection with past events that have obvious future consequences, such as control of the Erie Railroad? If we assume that the machinations of Fisk and Gould were notorious, should that have imposed any additional duty of inquiry on Field? Does the nature of the inquiry as to duty change as the representations grow in number?

The Field-Bowles correspondence has also been dealt with in Michael Schudson, Public, Private and Professional Lives, 21 Am. J. Leg. Hist. 191 (1977). Schudson sees the exchange as representing an older pre-Civil War view of professional morality represented by Bowles's view of the public responsibility of the professional and Field's movement toward a more neutral amoral professional posture focusing on the private relationship between lawyer and client. More historical research is required to assess the accuracy of his view of the pre-Civil War stance of the legal profession and of the dominance of the "neutral" view in the period since the Civil War. Schudson's view of the modern stance of the profession's rules finds support in Bellow & Kettleson, The Mirror of Public Interest Ethics: Problems and Paradoxes in Professional Responsibility: A Guide for Attorneys 219, 258-265 (1978) and Schwartz, The Missing Rule of Professional Conduct, 52 L.A.B.J. 10, 11-12, 15 (1976). For a view that the modern professional rules still embody, albeit in somewhat obscured fashion, the tension between a professional devotion owed to client and a professional responsibility owed to society, see Andrew Kaufman, A Professional Agenda, 6 Hofstra L. Rev. 619, 621-623 (1978).

The articles referred to in the preceding paragraph were substantially based on the professional norms embodied in the Model Code. Obviously, a more complete study would require a careful look at other sources — court and ethics committee opinions, statutes, and most important and most difficult to ascertain, the actual practice of lawyers. But the disciplinary rules are important in forming a judgment about the professional stance on the role of lawyers because they represent the one effort to make a comprehensive professional statement. Thus the

---

actions are wrong, and unfairly so. Mistaken judgment there may have been — but not dishonesty or deliberate flouting of the law. As to lawyers, they did not regard the social and economic problems as theirs." Robert T. Swaine, The Cravath Firm and Its Predecessors, 1819-1947 (New York, Ad Press Ltd., 1946), Vol. 1, p. 667. But a large portion of the public would ask Swaine: Why not? Why don't lawyers regard the social and economic problems as theirs? Is a man truly divisible? Does membership in the legal profession bestow a right to loose vicious dogs on the public? And the suspicion remains that many lawyers think as they do on this point because it is convenient for their pocketbooks.

text, for convenience, discusses the provisions of the "Model Code" and the "Model Rules." It is, however, also important to understand that when we talk about the stance of the "profession," we need to remember that while there is certainly a common approach to many, if not most, problems throughout the country, there are many important differences among the various jurisdictions. These are reflected in the different rules they have adopted and different answers given by courts and advisory ethics committees on particular issues.

The tension between the professional devotion owed to clients and the professional responsibility to third parties, the profession, and society continues under the Model Rules. The materials in this book have commented rather heavily on aspects of the Rules where the primary focus is on duties to clients. But there are reminders of other responsibilities as well. See the Preamble to the Model Rules entitled "A Lawyer's Responsibilities," the discussion about objectives and means in Rule 1.2 and its Comment, and the requirement for, and purposes of, communication set forth in Rule 1.4. The lawyer's right to follow personal choices was specifically recognized in additions made to Rule 1.16, the section governing withdrawal, by the ABA House of Delegates at its February 1983 New Orleans meeting. That session has been criticized, and rightly so I believe, for upsetting the delicate balance between confidentiality and disclosure recommended by the Kutak Commission by restricting the number of situations in which disclosure was possible. See pp. 145, 211. At the same time, however, the delegates widened greatly the lawyer's ability to withdraw. They added two situations to that portion of Rule 1.16(b) permitting withdrawal without the condition of lack of material adverse effect on the client's interest: (1) where the client has used the lawyer's services to perpetrate a crime or fraud, and, more importantly for this discussion, (2) where the client "insists upon pursuing an objective that the lawyer considers repugnant or imprudent." Whatever one may think of allowing withdrawal where a client has simply been "imprudent," allowing it when a client's conduct has been "repugnant" certainly bespeaks concern for the lawyer's personal moral integrity.

Other materials on this general subject are contained in the topic immediately following.

B.   THE OBLIGATION TO GIVE "NONLEGAL" ADVICE

PROBLEM 55

Client is a utility with eminent domain power. It wishes to extend service to a proposed new development. The shortest, cheapest route is above ground through a wooded park, and there is a proposal before the board of directors to select that route and method and pursue the necessary legal steps to acquire that right of way. Alternative proposals to lay an underground cable or to skirt the park have been rejected in the report to the board. Your views as general counsel have been requested by the board. Do you confine yourself to the legal aspects of the various possibilities?

Assume that in addition to being general counsel to the utility, you are also very active in the local bird club, which has been trying to preserve the park because of its importance as a stopover point for migrating birds in the spring and fall. You believe that the utility's plans will be devastating to the birds' continuing use of the park. Will you speak to that issue to the board? If you do, how will you respond to the director who says that it is unfair of you, as trusted general counsel, to lay the burden of your strong personal feelings on the board? If you decide not to put your strong personal feelings before the board and not to resign as general counsel, what would you do in your capacity as member of the bird club? Would you at least urge its members to inform themselves and take a position on the issue?

PROBLEM 56

Your client bought supplies under a contract that obliged it to make 50% of the payment when half the material had been delivered pursuant to the periodic delivery schedule of the contract, and the final 50% when the rest of the material had finally been delivered one year later. The first half was delivered on time; deliveries have proceeded on schedule since then so that 90% has now been delivered, with the final 10% due in two months. Because of difficult economic conditions, which were entirely unforeseen, the supplier has asked Client if it would make another 25% installment payment. There is no reason to expect default and the 25% retained is more than enough to cover any damage that might be suffered if there were a default. The products supplied to date have been completely satisfactory, and Client has no cash problem. Client has asked you whether it has any legal obligation to make payment and you have responded that it does not. Should you say anything more about Client's course of action if you have a view about "nonlegal" reasons for complying with the request? Suppose you advise Client that fairness requires payment and Client rejects that advice. May you withdraw? If you may, would you? Compare DR 2-110(C)(1)(e) with EC 7-8. Are they consistent? Must one be able to find permission to withdraw within the provisions of DR 2-110(B) and (C) or else be in violation of the disciplinary rules if one withdraws? Do EC 7-5 (second sentence) and EC 7-8 (last sentence) suggest situations of permissible withdrawal that are not within the provisions of DR 2-110(B) and (C)? Model Rule 1.16(b), discussed at p. 427, is much clearer.

We have already seen the suggestion of former Commissioner Sommer, in a specialized context, that lawyers must keep a broader "public interest" in mind in the representation of their clients. See pp. 296-299. The Model Code addresses this matter to some extent in ECs 7-1 through 7-5, and 7-7 through 7-10, and the Model Rules deal with it explicitly in Rule 2.1. Some professional responsibility problems of lawyers who specialize in representing the "public interest" have been considered in Chapter 5, and additional problems will be considered in Chapter 9. Here we shall consider whether and to what extent the "public interest" should be a component of the thinking of all lawyers in the routine of their practice. The views expressed in the following article should be compared with those of Mr. Sommer. See also the excerpts from Patterson and Cheatham, The Profession of Law 133-149 (1971) reprinted at pp. 273-285 of the first edition of this book.

ABE KRASH, PROFESSIONAL RESPONSIBILITY TO CLIENTS AND THE PUBLIC INTEREST: IS THERE A CONFLICT?

55 Chicago Bar Record 31 (1974)

. . . My central thesis may strike some persons as a paradox. I insist upon the proposition that lawyers best serve the public interest when they faithfully and competently represent the private interests of their clients. That is not to say that lawyers — individually and as a group — do not have responsibilities to the social welfare. I most certainly believe the bar does have such obligations — especially to improve the administration of justice. But in an adversary system which proclaims the right of everyone to counsel, a lawyer's paramount responsibility is to his client. The title of my remarks could thus be restated as a question. Is there a conflict between a lawyer's duty of commitment and dedication to his client's interest and the public interest? . . .

The traditional point of view on the lawyer's obligations to his client is reflected in a recently published biography of John W. Davis. [Harbaugh, The Life of John W. Davis (1973).] As his biographer points out, Davis adhered "absolutely to the principle that the lawyer's duty was to represent his client's interests to the limit of the law, [and] not to moralize on the social and economic implications of the client's lawful action." Subject to certain qualifications, which I shall indicate, I too subscribe to that position.

During the past decade, however, that philosophy of legal practice has been sharply challenged by a number of parties. Ralph Nader has emerged as perhaps the foremost critic of the traditional approach. But he by no means stands alone. During the annual meeting of the American Bar Association in Washington last summer, there was a counter-convention devoted to the theme that lawyers have failed to discharge their responsibilities to the welfare of society. The indictment was lengthy, and the verdict was guilty. Lawyers, it was said, have devoted their talents to aiding corporations who degrade the environment, who advertise and distribute products hazardous to consumers, and who monopolize the economy. The theme of the counter-convention was sounded in the opening remark: "The problem with the legal profession today, contrary to the current fashion, is not Watergate lawyers, but lawyers."

A new and expanded view of lawyers' responsibilities to the public has appeared in some cases recently instituted by the Securities and Exchange Commission. The Commission maintains that private practitioners occupy a "peculiarly strategic" position in the investment process and that lawyers have obligations to the investing public which may override their professional obligations to their clients. The Commission takes the position that in certain circumstances lawyers have a duty under the securities laws to insist that their clients follow a particular course of action, and if the clients do not heed their advice, it is the Commission's view that counsel not only should cease representing their clients but they should also report their clients' conduct to the Commission. . . .

This issue of conflicting responsibilities is thus by no means an esoteric, academic matter. Profound questions have been raised as to the role and responsibilities of lawyers. The problems are intensely practical. After all, what is more practical than a decision whether to accept or reject a client, or to withdraw from a matter in which one has been engaged? I propose to comment on the problems from that perspective.

My first thesis is that the "public interest," unless it is defined more precisely, is a concept too nebulous — it is too ambiguous a standard — to serve as a basis for any practical action or judgment regarding a lawyer's professional conduct.

What is the "public interest" to which lawyers allegedly owe a duty? Who decides what the "public interest" is? What is the scope of these obligations to society's welfare? And what are the consequences if a lawyer does not discharge this responsibility?

Let me put a case before you as described in a recent book on the Wall Street bar [Hoffman, Lions In The Street 96-103 (1973).] which illustrates some of the extremely subtle and complex factors which are involved.

For many years, the outside General Counsel for The New York Times was an old and distinguished New York law firm. In 1971, the editors of The Times informed their General Counsel that they had obtained possession of secret documents involving America's involvement in Vietnam — the Pentagon papers — and the editors asked counsel for an opinion as to whether the materials could be published. Counsel reportedly advised The Times that if they published the documents before they were declassified there was a risk of criminal prosecution. The law firm reportedly advised the editors not to publish on the grounds, among others, that it would be contrary to the "public interest" to do so. The Times editors determined to publish notwithstanding this advice. When the Department of Justice notified The Times that it would seek a preliminary injunction to restrain further publication, the law firm informed The Times that the firm could not represent the newspaper. The Times was represented by other counsel in the litigation which followed. The rest, of course, is history.

My purpose in reciting these events is not to pass judgment on the advice or action taken by counsel for The Times — it would, of course, be presumptuous for me to do that — but rather to demonstrate how extraordinarily difficult it is in any given situation to know where the public interest lies.

This incident raises a number of important questions. Was counsel's personal view of the "public interest" a relevant factor in his advice? Or was it the responsibility of counsel to state only the legal consequences which would flow from publication, and to paraphrase John W. Davis, not to moralize about the implications of printing the secret documents? Let it be assumed that counsel's view had been that the public interest called for publication of the documents. Should that opinion have influenced his advice? Anyone who has ever given advice in a matter in which his personal feelings are deeply engaged knows how difficult it is to detach his private views from his professional advice. But that is the responsibility of a legal adviser. Lawyers are not precluded from expressing their personal views to their clients of what the public interest requires, but counsel do have the responsibility, candidly and meticulously, to segregate that aspect of their advice. It seems to me that they have the duty to state to their clients: "I will give you my personal view of the public interest if you are interested in knowing it, but it has nothing to do with the legality of your conduct." I may add that I distinguish such an expression of personal views from advice to a client concerning the probable public repercussions or reaction to particular conduct — obviously such advice may be of the utmost relevance and importance. . . .

The criticism of lawyers based on the theory that their clients are engaged in conduct which some people feel is pernicious to society's welfare seems to me both wrong and dangerous. Today, the criticism is leveled at lawyers who represent corporations. But no one who practiced in Washington in the early 1950s, as I did, will ever forget the dreadful problems in finding lawyers willing and able to help them faced by government employees who were driven from their jobs on loyalty and security charges. Many lawyers were unwilling to take on such cases because of fears that the public would attribute to them the views of their clients. Those who impute clients' views to counsel do a profound disservice to the position of an independent bar. . . .

My second thesis is that an individual lawyer, as a general rule, is privileged to accept or reject the representation of a particular client on the basis of counsel's personal predilections or his views of the public interest. However, once a lawyer has agreed to represent a party, he has a duty, to the best of his ability to advocate a position, if his client's interest so requires, which counsel may personally regard as contrary to the public interest.

There appear to be three stages at which the lawyer's view of the public interest could affect his representation in a particular matter.

First, a lawyer could decide at the outset to accept or reject a client on the basis of his views regarding the consistency of the client's conduct with the community's welfare.

Second, the arguments and the tactics pursued by counsel during the course of a particular matter could be influenced by counsel's views as to the requirements of the public interest.

Finally, a lawyer could conceivably withdraw from a case in midstream if he were to conclude that his client's activities were irreconcilable with the public interest.

I would like to say just a word about these alternatives.

To what extent should a lawyer refuse to take on a client because he does not approve of the client's conduct in terms of the public interest as the lawyer perceives it? There are two schools of thought on this issue. There are those who believe that lawyers should identify with their client's interests and not take on matters of which they personally disapprove. Some of our largest law firms have, in effect, adhered to this point of view by declining, for example, to represent a plaintiff in an antitrust case or a defendant in a criminal prosecution. On the other hand, there are those who believe that lawyers are like "common carriers" who should be available to any litigant, subject to the provisions in the Code of Professional Responsibility regarding conflicts of interest, professional competence to handle the matter, and the rules regarding furtherance of criminal behavior — and subject, of course, to the client's ability to pay the bills. Such persons believe that it is "the duty of the lawyer, just as it is the duty of the priest or the surgeon, to serve those who call on him."*

It is not difficult to posit extreme cases which would lead to exceptions by the adherents of each of these positions. Moreover, each of these positions has inspired criticism of the bar. The position that lawyers are privileged to refuse to handle matters personally distasteful to them is cited by those critics who contend that important interests are not represented by the bar as presently constituted. And the "common carrier" theory has been invoked to support the criticism that lawyers are only a "gun for hire" whose views do not merit respect.

I think it is fair to say that, given a choice, most of us would prefer to represent those parties whose causes are congenial to our social or political views. But the idea that a lawyer will represent, with all of his dedication, those persons with whose views he may profoundly disagree, seems to me basic to our system.

It has been suggested that a distinction should be made between acting as an advocate for a client with respect to past conduct and advising a client as to his future conduct. An advocate, it is said, is entitled in a courtroom to present every contention, regardless of its consistency with the public interest, whereas an adviser as to future conduct has a responsibility to take account of the public interest. This difference in a lawyer's responsibility has been particularly urged in connection with representation of clients seeking or opposing legislation.

In practice, it is extremely difficult to apply this distinction. Many firms represent clients as a General Counsel, defending their clients' past conduct and rendering advice as to future transactions. Moreover, as The New York Times case makes clear, it may be exceedingly difficult in a situation involving proposed conduct to assert with confidence that the public interest requires one thing but not another. To take another example: Assume that an opinion is requested of counsel concerning the legality of a proposed merger under the antitrust laws. If the client determines to proceed with the transaction notwithstanding counsel's opinion that the merger is likely to be adjudged illegal, the lawyer who rendered the opinion is certainly not disabled from representing the client in the event the merger is challenged. A competent adviser would, of course, point out to his client that not all that is legal is wise; and that short term profits may lead to long term difficulties. Moreover, I suspect that most lawyers feel freer than the lawyers of a generation ago to point out to a client the public policy implications of a proposed course of conduct. However, I remain of the view that the ultimate policy decision

---

*The quotation is from a letter by John W. Davis to Theodore Huntley, dated March 4, 1924, quoted in a letter to The New York Times by Judge Charles E. Wyzanski, Jr. (N.Y. Times Book Review, p. 26. Jan. 20, 1974).

must be made by the client. Further, I am of the view that the solution to this problem is not to impose on counsel the burden of representing interests other than those of his client, but rather to take appropriate steps to insure that all interests are effectively represented.

Turning to the question of whether, once representation has been accepted, arguments or tactics may be shaped by counsel's personal views as to the public interest, it seems to me that counsel's responsibility is clearcut once a matter has been undertaken — the client is entitled to counsel's wholehearted commitment, and counsel's views of the public interest are immaterial to his professional responsibility. Counsel does not have the right to compromise his client's position on the basis of his personal predilections. Similarly, if a lawyer agrees to take on a matter, he does not have the right to withdraw in mid-stream because the client's position seems to him incompatible with society's welfare. . . .

C.   LAWYERS AND THEIR OWN SPEECH AND CONDUCT

A theme in discussion of issues of professional responsibility is the extent to which lawyers lose the freedom of action or non-action that ordinary citizens have. The issue is framed in terms of "extent" rather than in terms of whether there is any difference at all because it is quite clear that lawyers do have some special obligations. For example, there is no doubt that as citizens we are free to reveal our friends' confidences without incurring any legal consequences, whereas as lawyers we are not free as a general rule to reveal our clients' confidences. And so the issue is "When and under what circumstances should professional requirements impose a special obligation to act or not to act where no such obligation is imposed on nonlawyers?" The question in each situation is whether the special privileges that are given to lawyers in connection with their "monopoly" of representation require or justify putting special obligations upon them to speak in a certain way or to remain silent.

In this section of materials, the relevant cases and text follow each Problem or group of Problems.

PROBLEM 57

(a) At a meeting with clients Lawyer is asked why they lost their case at trial. May he respond: "I think we'll have a much better chance on appeal because the trial judge is stupid, prejudiced against you and the minorities whose rights were involved in this case, and it wouldn't surprise me if he had been talked to by the powers that be in this town," if Lawyer honestly believes this to be the case? Suppose this statement is made to a newspaper reporter? Does Lawyer need "evidence" of some kind before he makes those charges? What kind of evidence? Does he need different "evidence" when talking to his clients from what he needs when talking to the reporter? If he has "evidence," is he precluded from talking to either the clients or the reporter until he has taken the matter up with the appropriate disciplinary body? Does it make any difference whether the case is civil or criminal? See DRs 7-106(C)(6), 7-107, and 8-102(B) of the Model Code and Rules 3.6, 8.2(a), and 8.3(b) of the Model Rules.

(b) Suppose that it is your observation (and that of others) that a lawyer is much more likely to receive favorable treatment, and probably even to win cases, before Judge X if he or she is part of the same political clique that was responsible for Judge X's elevation to the bench. Is it appropriate for you to tell this to your client when that judge is assigned to hear your client's case? Should you go further and suggest that your client associate a lawyer member of that clique with you at the trial? What other alternatives are open to you, assuming that you don't have sufficient evidence to prove corrupt conduct by the judge? See DR 9-101(C) and Model Rule 8.4(e). ABA Informal Opinion 1243 (Sept. 1, 1972) is relevant to this Problem. In a much less dramatic setting, it advises a lawyer that it is permissible to decline employment if the lawyer believes that a particular judge entertains a strong personal bias against him or her, but that it would be the lawyer's duty to explain the reason for so doing to the client.

In re SNYDER
472 U.S. 634 (1985)

Chief Justice BURGER delivered the opinion of the Court.

We granted certiorari to review the judgment of the Court of Appeals suspending petitioner from practice in all courts of the Eighth Circuit for six months.

I

In March 1983, petitioner Robert Snyder was appointed by the Federal District Court for the District of North Dakota to represent a defendant under the Criminal Justice Act. After petitioner completed the assignment, he submitted a claim for $1,898.55 for services and expenses. The claim was reduced by the District Court to $1,796.05.

Under the Criminal Justice Act, the Chief Judge of the Court of Appeals was required to review and approve expenditures for compensation in excess of $1,000. 18 U. S. C. §3006A(d)(3). Chief Judge Lay found the claim insufficiently documented, and he returned it with a request for additional information. Because of technical problems with his computer software, petitioner could not readily provide the information in the form requested by the Chief Judge. He did, however, file a supplemental application.

The secretary of the Chief Judge of the Circuit again returned the application, stating that the proffered documentation was unacceptable. Petitioner then discussed the matter with Helen Monteith, the District Court Judge's secretary, who suggested he write a letter expressing his view. Petitioner then wrote the letter that led to this case. The letter, addressed to Ms. Monteith, read in part:

> In the first place, I am appalled by the amount of money which the federal court pays for indigent criminal defense work. The reason that so few attorneys in Bismarck accept this work is for that exact reason. We have, up to this point, still accepted the indigent appointments, because of a duty to our profession, and the fact that nobody else will do it.
>
> Now, however, not only are we paid an amount of money which does not even cover our overhead, but we have to go through extreme gymnastics even to receive the puny amounts which the federal courts authorize for this work. We have sent you everything we have concerning our representation, and I am not sending you anything else. You can take it or leave it.
>
> Further, I am extremely disgusted by the treatment of us by the Eighth Circuit in this case, and you are instructed to remove my name from the list of attorneys who will accept criminal indigent defense work. I have simply had it.
>
> Thank you for your time and attention. . . .

The District Court Judge viewed this letter as one seeking changes in the process for providing fees, and discussed these concerns with petitioner. The District Court Judge then forwarded the letter to the Chief Judge of the Circuit. The Chief Judge in turn wrote to the District Judge, stating that he considered petitioner's letter "totally disrespectful to the federal courts and to the judicial system. It demonstrates a total lack of respect for the legal process and the courts." The Chief Judge expressed concern both about petitioner's failure to "follow the guidelines and [refusal] to cooperate with the court," and questioned whether, "in view of the letter" petitioner was "worthy of practicing law in the federal courts on any matter." He stated his intention to issue an order to show cause why petitioner should not be suspended from practicing in any federal court in the Circuit for a period of one year. Subsequently, the Chief Judge wrote to the District Court again, stating that if petitioner apologized the matter would be dropped. At this time, the Chief Judge approved a reduced fee for petitioner's work of $1,000 plus expenses of $23.25.

After talking with petitioner, the District Court Judge responded to the Chief Judge as follows:

> He [petitioner] sees his letter as an expression of an honest opinion, and an exercise of his right of freedom of speech. I, of course, see it as a youthful and exuberant expression of annoyance which has now risen to the level of a cause. . . .
>
> He has decided not to apologize, although he assured me he did not intend the letter as you interpreted it.

The Chief Judge then issued an order for petitioner to show cause why he should not be suspended for his "refusal to carry out his obligations as a practicing lawyer and officer of [the] court" because of his refusal to accept assignments under the Criminal Justice Act. Nowhere in the order was there any reference to any disrespect in petitioner's letter of October 6, 1983.

Petitioner requested a hearing on the show cause order. In his response to the order, petitioner focused exclusively on whether he was required to represent indigents under the Criminal Justice Act. He contended that the Act did not compel lawyers to represent indigents, and he noted that many of the lawyers in his District had declined to serve. He also informed the court that prior to his withdrawal from the Criminal Justice Act panel, he and his two partners had taken 15 percent of all the Criminal Justice Act cases in their district.

At the hearing, the Court of Appeals focused on whether petitioner's letter of October 6, 1983, was disrespectful, an issue not mentioned in the show cause order. At one point, Judge Arnold asked: "I am asking you, sir, if you are prepared to apologize to the court for the tone of your letter?" Petitioner answered: "That is not the basis that I am being brought forth before the court today." When the issue again arose, petitioner protested: "But, it seems to me we're getting far afield here. The question is, can I be suspended from this court for my request to be removed from the panel of attorneys."

Petitioner was again offered an opportunity to apologize for his letter, but he declined. At the conclusion of the hearing, the Chief Judge stated:

> I want to make it clear to Mr. Snyder what it is the court is allowing you ten days lapse here, a period for you to consider. One is, that, assuming there is a general requirement for all competent lawyers to do pro bono work that you stand willing and ready to perform such work and will comply with the guidelines of the statute. And secondly, to reconsider your position as Judge Arnold has requested, concerning the tone of your letter of October 6.

Following the hearing, petitioner wrote a letter to the court, agreeing to "enthusiastically obey [the] mandates" of any new plan for the implementation of the Criminal Justice Act in North Dakota, and to "make every good faith effort possible" to comply with the court's guidelines regarding compensation under the Act. Petitioner's letter, however, made no mention of the October 6, 1983, letter.

The Chief Judge then wrote to Snyder, stating among other things:

> The court expressed its opinion at the time of the oral hearing *that interrelated with our concern* and the issuance of the order to show cause *was the disrespect that you displayed* to the court by way of your letter addressed to Helen Montieth [*sic*], Judge Van Sickle's secretary, of October 6, 1983. The court expressly asked if you would be willing to apologize for the tone of the letter and the disrespect displayed. You serve as an officer of the court and, as such, the Canons of Ethics require every lawyer to maintain a respect for the court as an institution.
>
> Before circulating your letter of February 23, I would appreciate your response to Judge Arnold's specific request, and the court's request, for you to apologize for the letter that you wrote.
>
> Please let me hear from you by return mail. I am confident that if such a letter is forthcoming that the court will dissolve the order. (Emphasis added.)

Petitioner responded to the Chief Judge:

> I cannot, and will never, in justice to my conscience, apologize for what I consider to be telling the truth, albeit in harsh terms. . . .
>
> It is unfortunate that the respective positions in the proceeding have so hardened. However, I consider this to be a matter of principle, and if one stands on a principle, one must be willing to accept the consequences.

After receipt of this letter, petitioner was suspended from the practice of law in the federal courts in the Eighth Circuit for six months. 734 F. 2d 334 (1984). The opinion stated that petitioner "contumaciously refused to retract his previous remarks or apologize to the court." It continued:

> [Petitioner's] refusal to show continuing respect for the court *and his refusal to demonstrate a sincere retraction of his admittedly 'harsh' statements* are sufficient to demonstrate to this court *that he is not presently fit to practice law in the federal courts.* All courts depend on the highest level of integrity and respect not only from the judiciary but from the lawyers who serve in the court as well. Without public display of respect for the judicial branch of government as an institution by lawyers, the law cannot survive. . . . Without hesitation *we find Snyder's disrespectful statements* as to this court's administration of CJA *contumacious conduct.* We deem this unfortunate.
>
> We find that Robert Snyder shall be suspended from the practice of law in the federal courts of the Eighth Circuit for a period of six months; thereafter, Snyder should make application to both this court and the federal district court of North Dakota to be readmitted. (Emphasis added.)

The opinion specifically stated that petitioner's offer to serve in Criminal Justice Act cases in the future if the panel was equitably structured had "considerable merit."

Petitioner moved for rehearing en banc. In support of his motion, he presented an affidavit from the District Judge's secretary — the addressee of the October 6 letter — stating that she had encouraged him to send the letter. He also submitted an affidavit from the District Judge, which read in part:

> I did not view the letter as one of disrespect for the Court, but rather one of a somewhat frustrated lawyer hoping that his comments might be viewed as a basis for some changes in the process.
>
> . . . Mr. Snyder has appeared before me on a number of occasions and has always competently represented his client, and has shown the highest respect to the court system and to me. (Emphasis added.)

The petition for rehearing en banc was denied. An opinion for the en banc court stated:

> The gravamen of the situation is that Snyder in his letter [of October 6, 1983] became harsh and disrespectful to the Court. It is one thing for a lawyer to complain factually to the Court, it is another for counsel to be disrespectful in doing so. . . .
>
> . . . Snyder states that his letter is not disrespectful. We disagree. In our view, the letter speaks for itself. 734 F. 2d, at 343. (Emphasis added.)

The en banc court opinion stayed the order of suspension for 10 days, but provided that the stay would be lifted if petitioner failed to apologize. He did not apologize, and the order of suspension took effect. . . . [W]e consider first whether petitioner's conduct and expressions warranted his suspension from practice; . . .

Courts have long recognized an inherent authority to suspend or disbar lawyers. Ex parte Garland, 4 Wall. 333, 378-379 (1867); Ex parte Burr, 9 Wheat. 529, 531 (1824). This inherent power derives from the lawyer's role as an officer of the court which granted admission. Theard v. United States, 354 U.S. 278, 281 (1957). The standard for disciplining attorneys practicing before the courts of appeals is set forth in Federal Rule of Appellate Procedure 46:

> (b) Suspension or Disbarment. When it is shown to the court that any member of its bar has been suspended or disbarred from practice in any other court of record, or has been guilty of conduct unbecoming a member of the bar of the court, he will be subject to suspension or disbarment by the court. The members shall be afforded an opportunity to show good cause, within such time as the court shall prescribe, why he should not be suspended or disbarred. Upon his response to the rule to show cause, and after hearing, if requested, or upon

expiration of the time prescribed for a response if no response is made, the court shall enter an appropriate order. (Emphasis added.)

The phrase "conduct unbecoming a member of the bar" must be read in light of the "complex code of behavior" to which attorneys are subject. . . .

As an officer of the court, a member of the bar enjoys singular powers that others do not possess; by virtue of admission, members of the bar share a kind of monopoly granted only to lawyers. Admission creates a license not only to advise and counsel clients but also to appear in court and try cases; as an officer of the court, a lawyer can cause persons to drop their private affairs and be called as witnesses in court, and for depositions and other pretrial processes that, while subject to the ultimate control of the court, may be conducted outside courtrooms. The license granted by the court requires members of the bar to conduct themselves in a manner compatible with the role of courts in the administration of justice.

Read in light of the traditional duties imposed on an attorney, it is clear that "conduct unbecoming a member of the bar" is conduct contrary to professional standards that shows an unfitness to discharge continuing obligations to clients or the courts, or conduct inimical to the administration of justice. More specific guidance is provided by case law, applicable court rules, and "the lore of the profession," as embodied in codes of professional conduct.

B

Apparently relying on an attorney's obligation to avoid conduct that is "prejudicial to the administration of justice," the Court of Appeals held that the letter of October 6, 1983, and an unspecified "refusal to show continuing respect for the court" demonstrated that petitioner was "not presently fit to practice law in the federal courts." 734 F.2d, at 337. Its holding was predicated on a specific finding that petitioner's "disrespectful statements [in his letter of October 6, 1983] as to this court's administration of the CJA [constituted] contumacious conduct."

We must examine the record in light of Rule 46 to determine whether the Court of Appeals' action is supported by the evidence. In the letter, petitioner declined to submit further documentation in support of his fee request, refused to accept further assignments under the Criminal Justice Act, and criticized the administration of the Act. Petitioner's refusal to submit further documentation in support of his fee request could afford a basis for declining to award a fee; however, the submission of adequate documentation was only a prerequisite to the collection of his fee, not an affirmative obligation required by his duties to a client or the court. Nor, as the Court of Appeals ultimately concluded, was petitioner legally obligated under the terms of the local plan to accept Criminal Justice Act cases.

We do not consider a lawyer's criticism of the administration of the Act or criticism of inequities in assignments under the Act as cause for discipline or suspension. The letter was addressed to a court employee charged with administrative responsibilities, and concerned a practical matter in the administration of the Act. The Court of Appeals acknowledged that petitioner brought to light concerns about the administration of the plan that had "merit," 734 F.2d, at 339, and the court instituted a study of the administration of the Criminal Justice Act as a result of petitioner's complaint. Officers of the court may appropriately express criticism on such matters.

The record indicates the Court of Appeals was concerned about the tone of the letter; petitioner concedes that the tone of his letter was "harsh," and, indeed it can be read as ill-mannered. All persons involved in the judicial process — judges, litigants, witnesses, and court officers — owe a duty of courtesy to all other participants. The necessity for civility in the inherently contentious setting of the adversary process suggests that members of the bar cast criticisms of the system in a professional and civil tone. However, even assuming that the letter exhibited an unlawyerlike rudeness, a single incident of rudeness or lack of professional courtesy — in this context — does not support a finding of contemptuous or contumacious conduct, or a finding that a lawyer is "not presently fit to practice law in the federal courts." Nor does it rise to the level of "conduct unbecoming a member of the bar" warranting suspension from practice.

Accordingly, the judgment of the Court of Appeals is *Reversed.*

JUSTICE BLACKMUN took no part in the decision of this case.

NOTES

1. Compare Matter of Erdmann, 33 N.Y.2d 559, 301 N.E.2d 426 (1973), where a divided New York Court of Appeals in a brief per curiam opinion reversed a judgment of censure of a legal services attorney who referred to the judicial system of New York's First Department, in an interview given to Life magazine, in the following language (301 N.E.2d at 560):

> There are so few trial judges who just judge, who rule on questions of law, and leave guilt or innocence to the jury. And Appellate Division judges aren't any better. They're the whores who became madams.
> I would like to [be a judge] just to see if I could be the kind of judge I

think a judge should be. But the only way you can get it is to be in politics or buy it — and I don't even know the going price.

The Court of Appeals stated that while perhaps persistent or general courses of conduct that were "degrading to the law, the Bar, and the courts, and are irrelevant or grossly excessive would present a different issue," "isolated instances of disrespect for the law, Judges and courts expressed by vulgar and insulting words or other incivility, uttered, written, or committed outside the precincts of a court are not subject to professional discipline."

2. The issue of lawyers' free speech has been severely tested in a number of cases with strongly political overtones. In re Sawyer, 360 U.S. 622 (1959) is a major precedent. Defense counsel in a Smith Act prosecution in Hawaii made a speech while the trial was still going in which she referred, among other things, to the "shocking and horrible" things that were going on at the trial and the impossibility of getting a fair trial in a Smith Act case. After a close reading of the reported speech, a bare majority of the Court concluded that the record did not support the findings that the impartiality and character of the trial judge had been impugned. While the Court's opinion is phrased primarily in terms of the specific facts of the case, there are overtones, which bothered the dissenters and at least one of the majority, of a constitutional dimension to the right of a lawyer to make rather sharp attacks on the conduct of a pending trial.

3. After *Sawyer* and *Snyder*, the Oklahoma Supreme Court held that it would violate the First Amendment to apply the provisions of Model Code DR 1-102(A)(5) and (b) and DR8-102(B) to a lawyer who made out-of-court public charges to the media that a federal district judge who had just sentenced his client was racist. The court noted that, although the statements were in "extremely bad form," there was no evidence that they were "false" or "insincerely uttered by a speaker having no basis upon which to found them." Oklahoma ex rel. Oklahoma Bar Ass'n v. Porter, 1988 Okla LEXIS 122.

The conflict between free speech and fair trial was resolved by the Model Code in DR 7-107 and by the Model Rules in Rule 3.6, which should be read at this point. The issues are somewhat different when criminal and civil matters are involved. In the criminal field, a thorough canvas of the issues of In re Sawyer and of recent case law is contained in In re Hinds, 90 N.J. 604, 449 A.2d 483 (1982), involving a trial of a black woman "reputed to be a militant radical," for murder of a state trooper. A lawyer who had represented the defendant during some of the pretrial proceedings but not at the trial called a press conference during early stages of the trial and characterized the proceedings as "legalized lynching," and as leading to "the creation of a 'hangman's court' " and stated that unless the judge rescued himself, it would be a "kangaroo court."

Disciplinary proceedings, charging violation of DRs 1-102(A)(5) and 7-107(D), were begun against the lawyer by the County Ethics Committee after the trial was concluded. The attorney sought to enjoin the proceedings in federal court on the ground that those disciplinary rules were unconstitutional. The Supreme Court eventually concluded that the federal courts should abstain from interfering with the state disciplinary proceedings on the ground that they were judicial proceedings relating to the state's "extremely important interest" in professional regulation and that they afforded ample opportunity for raising federal constitutional issues. Middlesex Ethics Comm. v. Garden State Bar Assn., 457 U.S. 423 (1982).

Before the charges were heard by the Ethics Committee, the New Jersey Supreme Court considered the case on its own motion. It rejected constitutional attacks on DR 7-107(D) for overbreadth and vagueness. It also rejected defendant's argument that a "clear and present danger" test was required in order for DR 7-107(D) to survive constitutional attack. The court summarized its conclusion:

> We now affirm the constitutionality of the "reasonable likelihood" standard of DR 7-107(D) for restricting attorney extrajudicial speech in the specific setting of a criminal trial. We further hold that the determination of whether a particular statement is likely to interfere with a fair trial involves a careful balancing of factors, including consideration of the status of the attorney, the nature and timing of the statement, as well as the context in which it was uttered. [The court later added that the reasonable likelihood standard required "a showing by clear and convincing evidence that an attorney's extrajudicial speech truly jeopardized trial fairness. . . ." 90 N.J. at 626, 449 A.2d at 495.] In addition, we hold that DR 7-107(D) applies not only to an attorney of record in a criminal case but also to an attorney who cooperates with the defense on a regular and continuing basis, provides legal assistance in connection with the defense of a criminal charge, and holds himself out to be a member of the defense team. However, because this opinion represents the first time that we have interpreted the proper scope of DR 7-107(D) and the standard to be followed in applying this disciplinary rule to extrajudicial statements, we deem it appropriate to give our determination prospective effect only. Consequently, we dismiss these charges against Hinds, as well as related charges under DR 1-102(A)(5), which sanctions attorney conduct that is "prejudicial to the administration of justice." 90 N.J. at 707, 449 A.2d at 486.

The court further held that DR 1-102(A)(5) passed constitutional muster because its broad scope had been narrowed by frequent interpretation to "particularly egregious conduct." (See p. 667 infra for discussion of the constitutionality of disciplinary rules cast in general language.) The court went on to note, however, that since DR 1-102(A)(5) applies to attorneys in their capacity as ordinary citizens and not because of any special connection to a trial, the more stringent "clear and present danger test," or, to put it alternatively, a finding of "a serious and imminent threat to the fairness and integrity of the judicial system," 90 N.J. at 634, 449 A.2d at 499, should be required. A dissenter saw no need for that conclusion since the rule itself specifically required a showing that the attorney had engaged in conduct that was prejudicial to, i.e., did in fact obstruct, the administration of justice.

The following Problem and case illustrate the issues of free speech and fair trial in the civil context.

PROBLEM 58

For several years Lawyer has been engaged in conducting a class action suit against the state mental health department. There are many aspects to the suit, but its principal thrust attacks the inadequate treatment given to mental patients confined to state hospitals pursuant to court order. A judgment has been entered in favor of plaintiffs, finding inadequacy of treatment, but the case has dragged on with respect to implementation of the original judgment. A variety of unresolved matters is still pending with respect to the plans being proposed by the state regarding different classes of patients and different hospitals. Lawyer has been asked to address a society of medical and legal personnel interested in mental health matters about the situation as she views it in state mental hospitals. Obviously, the case will have to be discussed and, in addition, Lawyer would like to advocate that the audience urge certain specific reforms on the appropriate state agencies. May Lawyer make the speech she wants to make?

RUGGIERI v. JOHNS-MANVILLE
PRODUCTS CORP.
503 F. Supp. 1036 (D.R.I. 1980)

Pettine, Chief Judge.

The defendant, Raybestos-Manhattan, is asking this Court to disqualify Ronald L. Motley, an attorney for the plaintiff, from participating in this or any other "asbestos litigation" or prohibit him from making extrajudicial comments concerning such cases. Serious questions concerning the right of freedom of speech secured by the first and fourteenth amendments are involved.

This pending trial is only one of many highly publicized asbestos cases presently before the Court. On July 9, 1980, Mr. Motley appeared on a Columbia Broadcasting System network which nationally televised a show entitled "See You in Court." In part the broadcast dealt with nationwide asbestos litigation. Mr. Motley referred to the so-called Sumner Simpson papers — a series of letters allegedly locked in the safe of the president of an asbestos company; these letters produced through the discovery process purportedly show that the major asbestos companies were aware of the claimed danger of asbestos inhalation as early as 1935. Mr. Motley stated, "The tragedy of it is that this asbestos exposure occurred after 1935, when he chose to keep the lid on, and it — the exposure — occurred in the thirties, forties, fifties, and sixties, and now we're seeing thousands and thousands of people dying as a result of that exposure." The only other part of the show involving Mr. Motley is a scene wherein he is engaged in a conversation with a Mr. Roy Seckinger, an individual described as "an itinerant asbestos insulator." The exchange between them was as follows:

> *Motley*:   Did they ever tell you anything about this stuff making
>   you sick?
> *Seckinger*: No.
> *Motley*:   Nobody's ever told you anything but your doctor when
>   you got sick?
> *Seckinger*: Right.
> *Motley*:   Never told you anything?
> *Seckinger*: No.
> *Motley*:   Just — just didn't tell you anything.
> *Seckinger*: Just didn't tell me nothing.

The defendant argues that Mr. Motley violated the American Bar Association Disciplinary Rule 7-107(G) in that "[t]he statements were not a 'quotation from or reference to' public records" and, in light of the nature of the broadcast, Motley knew the statements would be "disseminated by means of public communication."

The defendant's reaction to these statements is quite understandable since they reflect adversely on the character of asbestos insulation manufacturers. Rule 39 of the Local Rules of this Court incorporates, except for certain minor changes, the entirety of Rule 7-107(G).

The right of an attorney to comment on pending litigation does not solely concern the first amendment right to free speech. There is necessarily involved the sixth and fourteenth amendments mandating a fair trial which is "the most fundamental of all freedoms [and] must be maintained at all costs." Estes v. Texas, 381 U.S. 532, 540 (1964). It is equally important that it be accommodated to first amendment rights so as not to improperly curtail access to information. Rigid restrictions upon the rights of attorneys to discuss pending litigation or disclose information concerning a case encroach upon his right to freedom of expression.

The accommodation lies in the degree of control the Court should exercise in curtailing the rights of attorneys who are officers of the Court but indeed private citizens as well. The Seventh Circuit has developed a "serious and imminent threat" test rejecting the "reasonable likelihood" test as adopted in the local rules of many district courts and by the American Bar Association in promulgating Rule 7-107. Chicago Council of Lawyers v. Bauer, 522 F.2d 242 (7th Cir. 1975) cert. denied, 427 U.S. 912 (1976).

The Fourth Circuit in Hirschkop v. Snead, 594 F.2d 356 (1979) reached a contrary result upholding the "reasonable likelihood" test. Though these circuits had their own unique reasoning as to the limitations to be imposed on attorneys in criminal cases, both held it unconstitutional to prohibit lawyers' comments during civil litigation.

Again some preliminary observations are necessary. In the context of these restrictions on attorneys' comment it is important to note particular distinctions between civil and criminal litigation. First, we should recognize that although we rightfully place a prime value on providing a system of impartial justice to settle civil disputes, we require even a greater insularity against the possibility of interference with fairness in criminal cases. Perhaps this is symbolically reflected in the Sixth Amendment's requirement of an "impartial jury" in criminal cases whereas the Seventh Amendment guarantees only "trial by jury" in civil cases. The point to be made is that the mere invocation of the phrase "fair trial" does not as readily justify a restriction on speech when we are referring to civil trials.

Another vital factor is the length of civil litigation. Normally, civil litigation will be more prolonged than criminal litigation. One reason is that priority is afforded criminal matters because of the constitutional right to a speedy trial. Also, our civil rules allow much more discovery than our criminal rules. A civil case may last for years just in the discovery stage. DR 7-107(G) is not geared to specific time frames. It provides for blanket coverage of the period of "investigation or litigation." We are not sure of the parameters of an "investigation" of a civil matter, but given rather lengthy statutes of limitations we assume that there might be a restriction on speech for many years before a complaint is even filed. And the use of the general term "litigation" implies that attorneys' comments are also proscribed while a case is on appeal. The criminal no-comment rules contain no restrictions on statements made after sentencing. It is clear that DR 7-107(G) cannot be deemed a prohibition on speech that applies only for a limited period. Restrictions for many years are quite possible. Therefore, the broad time span of this rule relating to civil matters is an influential factor weighing against its constitutionality.

Finally, there is the element of the nature of certain civil litigation. As plaintiffs indicate, in our present society many important social issues became entangled to some degree in civil litigation. Indeed, certain civil suits may be instigated for the very purpose of gaining information for the public. Often actions are brought on behalf of the public interest on a private attorney general theory. Civil litigation in general often exposes the need for governmental action or correction. Such revelations should not be kept from the public. Yet it is normally only the attorney who will have this knowledge or realize its significance. Sometimes a class of poor or powerless citizens challenges, by way of a civil suit, actions taken by our established private or semi-private institutions or governmental entities. Often non-lawyers can adequately comment publicly on behalf of these institutions or governmental entities. The lawyer representing the class plaintiffs may be the only articulate voice for that side of the case. Therefore, we should be extremely skeptical about any rule that silences that voice. *Chicago Council of Lawyers,* supra, p. 446; see *Hirschkop,* supra p. 446.

The Judicial Conference, at its September 1980 meeting, abandoned prohibiting attorney comment in civil litigation feeling that this area can best be handled by special orders when warranted.

As it pertains to civil cases, Rule 39 of this Court does not meet the standards set forth in the cases cited supra and shall not be controlling here. Counsel rightfully points to an inconsistency in this rule. The section on pending criminal litigation adopts a "serious and imminent threat" test while that portion concerning civil litigation is couched in the "reasonable likelihood" standard. This, of course, makes no sense. Counsel is correct in arguing that the standard in civil cases must necessarily be equal to or higher than that allowed for in criminal proceedings.

Whether we label a no-comment rule as a "prior restraint" carrying a "heavy presumption against its constitutional validity," Organization for a Better Austin v. Keefe, 402 U.S. 415, 419, or a rule outside such constitutional restrictions but nevertheless with certain inherent features of "prior restraints," *Chicago Council of Lawyers,* supra, it all distills itself to the ultimate conclusion that First Amendment expressions cannot be totally abridged. The fact is that the two constitutional rights involved in the judicial process must be protected; standards and definitions in other situations are not necessarily controlling; though precedent offers guidance, the aim is to fashion rules singularly applicable to insure a fair trial.

This is a civil case and what hereinafter follows pertains only to civil litigation. This is not to say, however, that much might not also apply to criminal cases.

Each civil case presents its own peculiar setting; no general rule can be established. However, it seems to me that when a court concludes there is a need in a case to formulate rules designed to protect the judicial process of that trial, the only comment that can be proscribed, when no other protective alternative exists, is that which in some meaningful way is targeted to the case to be tried and which poses a "serious and imminent threat" to that trial. I do not feel that this threat must be premised on a "prior restraint" rule. The competing interests of the two constitutional rights at stake justify their own unique standard. It must be one that maximizes, with minimum dilution, the safeguards of each. The "serious and imminent threat" test is best suited to accomplish this end. I do not believe that even this test is without its possible exceptions. Conceivably there may be cases where anticipated comment might present a serious and imminent threat to the trial if heard by a jury already impanelled but which in the best interest of the public should not be barred. In such cases the sequestration of the jury may well safeguard the competing rights of the First, Sixth and Seventh Amendments. It is inimical to a democratic society to curb the dissemination of such news and certainly unnecessary in light of the many procedures the court can employ, tailored to the unique circumstances at hand.

The impact of pretrial publicity can be evaluated through Rule 47(a) of the Federal Rules of Civil Procedure which gives the trial judge broad discretion in conducting the examination of prospective jurors. After many years on the bench, it is this Court's opinion that jurors who are properly instructed by the court as to the solemnity of their service rise to the occasion and express their biases candidly and honestly. It is a disservice to lose faith in these men and women, who in the main are being called upon for the first time in their lives to participate in the noble cause of justice. As they can be screened before trial so can they be controlled during the trial even to the point, as I have already stated, of sequestering them if the circumstances so demand. I know of no studies that disprove the conclusion that overwhelmingly they will follow instructions of the court not to read any news accounts of the case, discuss the evidence, or place themselves in any prejudicial ambience.

With all appreciation that a fair trial is the most fundamental of all freedoms, it cannot be gainsaid that its infinite capacity is best achieved when exposed in all its phases to an enlightened public. Overreaction by the courts to an occasional mistrial only jeopardizes one fundamental right against the other. Surely the Judicial Conference realized this in refusing to proscribe through preordained rules attorney comment in civil litigation.

In this case the defendant has submitted no evidence that the program in question was broadcast in this district; even assuming it was viewed in Rhode Island, there is no evidence as to the percentage of persons who viewed it. In short, there is no basis for any conclusion that Mr. Motley's statements impacted on any potential jurors. He was exer-

cising his First Amendment rights and it has not been shown that his
speech trespassed on the defendant's rights to a fair trial. It would be a
serious invasion of a treasured liberty to prohibit him from continuing
to discuss this very controversial issue of asbestos inhalation. When the
trial is reached, at some time in the future, the Court can then assess
what if anything need be done to assure a fair trial.

The defendant's motion is denied. So Ordered.

NOTE

Not all courts agree with the thrust of the principal case and the cases
cited therein. In Widoff v. Disciplinary Board, 54 Pa. Comm. 124, 420
A.2d 41, aff'd 491 Pa. 129, 430 A.2d 1151 (1980), cert. denied, 455 U.S.
914 (1982), the court rejected the argument of the state's consumer advocate that DR7-107(H) was unconstitutionally overbroad and vague.
The consumer advocate has brought an action for declaratory judgment
after the disciplinary board had warned him not to make "future public
statements that would be 'reasonably likely to interfere with a fair hearing.'" The warning was issued in connection with press releases issued
by the advocate and comments that were quoted in a newspaper article
in connection with a hearing in which the advocate was participating.
The board, however, dismissed the complaint in this particular proceeding because of the advocate's good faith effort to comply with the rule.

NOTE: The Integrated Bar and Lawyer Freedom

A very different issue with respect to lawyers' speech is presented by
the combination of two Supreme Court cases, Lathrop v. Donohue, 367
U.S. 820 (1961), and Abood v. Detroit Board of Education, 431 U.S. 209
(1977). In *Lathrop*, the Court rejected an attack on an order of the Wisconsin Supreme Court creating an "integrated" bar by requiring every
lawyer admitted to practice to join, and pay dues to, the State Bar. The
Court held that such compulsion did not violate any associational rights
of lawyers but there was no decision whether compelled dues could be
spent to advocate legislation and programs to which specific lawyers objected.

That issue was finally addressed in *Abood*, in the context of an agency
shop agreement between Detroit teachers and the Board of Education.
The Court held that notwithstanding ideological objections of specific
teachers to union activities as their exclusive representative, such interference was constitutionally justified so long as the union's activities related to "collective bargaining, contract administration, and grievance
adjustment purposes." The Court noted the difficulty of "drawing lines

between collective-bargaining activities, for which contributions may be compelled, and ideological activities unrelated to collective bargaining, for which such compulsion is prohibited." Id. at 236. It noted the complaint about union sponsorship of social activities, but, lacking specificity about the activities, it left that question to be resolved first by the state courts. It did, however, specifically forbid compulsion to contribute to support of political candidates and views.

The relevance of *Abood* to integrated bar activity is obvious, but it is not quite so easy to describe the central core of bar activity concern in a phrase such as "collective bargaining activity." Consider the following bar association activities: providing budgets for standing committees on substantive areas of law; supporting a change from election to appointment of judges; rating judges, both elected and appointed; sponsoring "Law Day" activities on television and in the schools; sponsoring pro-abortion or anti-abortion legislation; opposing legislation to regulate fees, or to bring lawyers under social security; sponsoring annual dinners and a golf tournament for lawyers, to which judges are invited as nonpaying guests.

Controversy about the appropriate role of integrated bars, which exist in a majority of jurisdictions in the United States, came to a head in the District of Columbia. Following a proposal for increasing lawyers' dues, opponents of programs initiated by the Bar sponsored a referendum of the members of the Bar to limit mandatory dues and assessments to "admission of attorneys; their continued registration; discipline of attorneys; and, client security fund." The referendum passed by a vote of 6,721 to 5,189. The District of Columbia Court of Appeals, under whose jurisdiction the District of Columbia Bar functions as an official arm of the court, stayed operation of the referendum to consider whether it conflicted with its Rules organizing the Bar and if so, whether those Rules should be amended. When the court divided four to four on whether it should override the referendum, Chief Judge Newman, who would have overridden it, nevertheless voted to vacate the stay because a majority of the court was not prepared to override. On Petition to Amend Rule 1, 431 A.2d 521 (1981).

The effect of the referendum on existing activities was characterized by one of the dissenters, Judge Ferren.

Almost precipitously, therefore, funding no longer is assured for virtually the entire program of professional and community activities overseen by the Board of Governors. These include continuing legal education (CLE) to help maintain lawyer competence; an array of 17 membership divisions and 11 standing committees (as well as special committees) to study and recommend improvements in the administration of justice; an Office of Public Service Activities to provide lawyer referral and information services, including help for the indigent; a major Bar publication, the District Lawyer, to report on local professional issues and on significant national trends; and a Citizens Advisory Committee to help assure lawyer accountability by putting hard questions from the client perspective. . . .

It is difficult to imagine, for example, an effective organized bar without membership divisions and study committees. Over the years, the courts, the profession, and the community have benefited enormously from the unified Bar's study of justice-related issues. For example, Division 2 (Antitrust, Trade Regulation and Consumer Affairs) issued a major report on consumer protection; Division 5 (Criminal Law and Individual Rights) scrutinized Superior Court appropriations; and Division 4 (Courts, Lawyers, Administration of Justice) has contributed a number of important evaluations on the unauthorized practice of law, six- and twelve-member juries, District Court rules, reciprocal admission to federal courts, fee arbitration, and lawyer competency requirements for the federal courts.

Bar committees have provided equally significant service. Recently, the Horsky Committee completed a comprehensive study of the local court system, released in ten volumes over a two-year period. In earlier years, committees have issued special reports on criminal defense services, complaints about ineffective assistance of counsel, the proposed transfer of prosecutive and judicial-appointive powers from the federal to the District of Columbia government, and the prospects for arbitration in conjunction with Superior Court proceedings. Important standing committees, such as the Committee on Legal Ethics, have made similar contributions.

The diversity of the Bar adds significant strength to the work of its divisions and committees. Recently, for example, this court received a comprehensive report on a matter of substantial professional and public concern from a Bar committee comprised of 19 lawyers engaged in a wide variety of fields. There were 4 lawyers from large firms, 3 from medium firms, 4 from small firms, 5 sole practitioners, 1 from a prepaid legal service plan, 1 law professor, and 1 federal administrative law judge. The makeup of this committee enhanced the quality and credibility of the report; such diversity reflects a special contribution that a unified bar assuredly can make.

There is another threatened program, the Office of Public Service Activities, which is of particular significance to the public. Through its Lawyer Referral and Information Service (LRIS) and related programs, this Office has been handling approximately 20,000 calls a year from persons in need of information or a lawyer's help. Last year, trained Bar staff, after carefully screening each matter, were able to assist 43% of the callers without need for referral. Of the others, the staff directed 18% to lawyers on a regular or reduced fee basis and referred the other 39% — unable to afford a fee — to legal aid organizations, pro bono lawyers, government agencies, community programs, and the courts. In addition, LRIS maintains a branch at the Landlord-Tenant Division of Superior Court, providing conciliation as well as referral service.

The Bar's ability to provide such comprehensive assistance has depended, in substantial measure, on full-time staff equipped not only to relay information about community resources, but also to recruit pro bono lawyers, to sponsor training for these lawyers in fields (such as Landlord-Tenant court) which do not easily generate paid CLE subscribers, and to match indigent clients with volunteer lawyers having particular interests and skills. These coordinated programs of the Office of Public Service Activities require money — $385,000 in 1980-81, of which $360,000 or $11.22 per lawyer are budgeted from Bar dues. In contrast with the outlook for certain other Bar programs, the prospect is dim for increased user charges to sustain this essentially pro bono service.

The four judges who voted to uphold the referendum concluded that it was essential to uphold the democratic procedures it had provided in the Rules promulgated to govern the Bar. While noting that a referendum may not infringe members' constitutional rights or amend the court's Rules governing the Bar without its permission, they found no such case since it read the Rules as not obligating the Bar to perform any of the functions whose funding out of mandatory dues was forbidden. They noted that on the contrary it had been argued that the funding of certain programs out of mandatory dues had violated members' constitutional rights but they did not discuss that argument any further. The four dissenters in separate opinions agreed that the court's Rules required the Bar to perform certain public and professional duties that were prohibited by the referendum. The major opinion was written by Judge Ferren, who would have continued the stay and created a task force to identify those Bar programs that are essential to the bar and public because they are "inherent Bar responsibilities." He viewed his court's original decision to create a unified bar as a decision to assure that the Bar would carry out certain public responsibilities and he was ready to have the court identify them. Indeed, he thought open-ended delegation of regulatory authority to lawyers themselves was improper. (See pp. 568-569 for discussion of the similar issues of mandatory pro bono service on an individual basis.)

A different type of attack on the integrated bar was mounted in Levine v. Supreme Court of Wisconsin, 679 F. Supp. 1478 (W.D. Wis. 1988). The court held that the mandatory membership requirement was an unconstitutional abridgment of the plaintiff lawyer's First Amendment rights. Although Lathrop v. Donohue, p. 449, upheld Wisconsin's integrated bar, the court noted two important changes since the Supreme Court's decision in that case. The first was that the Wisconsin Supreme Court had removed from the Bar the lawyer admission, discipline, and education functions that had given the Bar the "quasi-public" character referred to by the Supreme Court in *Lathrop*. Moreover, the Supreme Court's own analysis was perceived to have changed in the intervening years from a "balancing test" to one requiring the state to justify any significant infringement on First Amendment rights by showing a compelling interest achieved in the least restrictive manner. The court then found that a forced financial contribution constituted such an infringement, that the activities engaged in by the Bar did not constitute a compelling state interest, and that the Bar in any event had failed to demonstrate that compulsory membership was the least restrictive means of achieving its interests. *Levine* was reversed on appeal.

A more limited result was reached in Schneider v. Colegio de Abogados, 682 F. Supp. 674 (D.P.R. 1988), holding compelled membership in the Puerto Rico bar unconstitutional. The court viewed as crucial the inadequate protection given dissenters' rights when the bar engaged in a wide variety of ideological activities beyond the boundaries within which members' dues might permissibly be used over their objection. Permissible purposes were listed as those relating to control of the practice of law, the provision of legal services to the public, and the improvement of the functioning of the courts. The Court of Appeals for the Third Circuit, while remanding some issues for further hearing, was rather more favorable to the activities of the integrated Virgin Islands bar in Hollar v. Virgin Islands, 857 F.2d 163 (1988). It seems likely that these attacks represent the beginning of concerted attacks on the whole notion of the integrated bar, the form of bar organization in well over half of the states.

D. WHISTLEBLOWING ON OTHER LAWYERS

PROBLEM 59

Without asking you for any advice, a lawyer who has been your close friend for many years tells you that he has learned that his partner has paid, on request, a kickback to a judge who named her a guardian in an estate matter. The judge has recently been assigned to another county; the partner is enormously upset at having given in to the judge's hard luck story that led her to give him the money; and your friend tells you he has decided to do nothing. Must you report the conduct of the judge and lawyers to the local discipline committee?

Problem 59 invokes DR 1-103(A) of the Model Code and Model Rule 8.3(a), with their premise that the obligation of self-discipline that the profession has undertaken involves self-policing, which in turn requires reporting of unprofessional conduct by other lawyers. The requirement has been controversial, and there are very few cases in which violation of DR 1-103(A) has figured in discipline of a lawyer. But see In re Himmel, 1988 Ill. Lexis 121 (Ill. 1988) (lawyer suspended for one year for failure to report another lawyer's conversion of the funds of his client, who was also a lawyer). The arguments against the principle were set forth by retired Justice John Spalding of the Supreme Judicial Court of Massachusetts in his Report as special master to make recommendations to that court with respect to adoption of the provisions of the Model Code.

> The arguments against the rule are that it would create a profession of informants and would breed distrust among members of the Bar. . . . Professor [Livingston] Hall argues that disciplining lawyers for failure to report the misconduct of others, as would be required by Rule 1-103(A), is too harsh. It would be tantamount to reviving the common law crime of misprision of felony, a concept that has not gained favor in this country. He points out that most states have either rejected the offense completely, or have modified it. No court in the United States, he says, has held that a mere failure to disclose knowledge of a felony is itself punishable. . . . In this Commonwealth it is not certain that the crime exists but if it does, there must be proof of "an evil motive to prevent or delay administration of justice." Commonwealth v. Lopes, 313 Mass. 453, 459. In the Lopes case Lummus, J. quoted Chief Justice Marshall in Marbury v. Brooks, 7 Wheat. 556, 575, where in discussing misprision of felony he said, "It may be the duty of a citizen to accuse every offender, and to proclaim every offense which comes to his knowledge; but the law which would punish him in every case for not performing that duty is too harsh for man."
>
> That analogy of Rule 1-103A to the crime of misprision of felony, I submit, is close and the arguments against that offence are equally applicable against Rule 1-103A.
>
> The position of [the Boston Bar Association] appears to be that while it thinks that Rule 1-103A goes too far, it ought not to be eliminated in its entirety. . . . Boston proposes amending 1-103A as follows: "A lawyer possessing unprivileged knowledge of a violation of DR 1-102A (3) or (4) shall report this knowledge to a tribunal or other authority empowered to investigate or act upon such violation." (Proposed amendment is underscored.)
>
> Under this proposal a lawyer is subject to discipline only if he fails to report another lawyer who has "(3) [engaged] in illegal conduct involving moral turpitude" or "(4) [engaged] in conduct involving dishonesty, fraud, deceit, or misrepresentation.". . . The question is by no means free from difficulty. The amendment would subject an attorney to discipline for failure to inform against a fellow lawyer only in situations involving moral turpitude, dishonesty, fraud, deceit, or misrepresentation. While the rule, with the amendment, is an improvement and Boston's argument in favor of it is appealing, . . . I am inclined to agree with the position taken by Mass. Bar and Professor Hall. . . . I therefore recommend that Rule 1-103A be eliminated in its entirety.

Justice Spalding's recommendation was accepted by the Massachusetts Supreme Judicial Court when it adopted the Code. See Rule 3:22 of the Supreme Judicial Court, Massachusetts Rules of Court 271 (1975).

The ABA's Special Committee on Evaluation of Disciplinary Enforcement (called the Clark Committee after its chairman, former Supreme Court Justice Tom C. Clark) issued a report in 1970 on the status of disciplinary enforcement in this country. (See p. 669 where the topics considered in the report are reprinted.) One of the problems it discusses is the subject matter of DR 1-103(A). The attitude expressed therein is very different from that of Justice Spalding's opinion.

ABA COMMITTEE ON EVALUATION OF DISCIPLINARY ENFORCEMENT, PROBLEMS AND RECOMMENDATIONS IN DISCIPLINARY ENFORCEMENT

(1970)

PROBLEM 31

Reluctance on the part of lawyers and judges to report instances of professional misconduct.

DIMENSION

Although lawyers and judges have the necessary background to evaluate the conduct of attorneys and are far better equipped than laymen to recognize violations of professional standards, relatively few complaints are submitted to disciplinary agencies by members of the profession. This fact has been cited as a major problem by nearly every disciplinary agency in the United States surveyed by this Committee. The past president of a state bar testified:

> Lawyers are extremely reluctant to complain about their brethren. We have a false sense of fraternity that keeps us from complaining about other men when they do something wrong. Many lawyers have the attitude that you should not do anything to that man because what he can do if you disbar him or suspend his license. This tempering attitude can go so far as to result in dismissal or failure to find an attorney guilty.

The chairman of a local disciplinary agency reached the same conclusion:

The number of complaints we receive runs approximately 200 a year out of a group of some 2,500 to 3,000 active lawyers in the community. Of those 200 complaints, and I am speaking now of those in which the complainant thought enough of the matter to come in and sign an affidavit or make a written complaint, I would guess that slightly more than 1% come from lawyers.

Based on my contacts with my fellow attorneys in the community, I am sure that the reluctance of lawyers to come forward stems from a feeling that we are members of a brotherhood and so owe a sense of loyalty to one another so that we should not throw a stone.

RECOMMENDATION

Greater emphasis in law school and continuing legal education courses on the individual attorney's responsibility to assist the profession's efforts to police itself by reporting instances of professional misconduct to the appropriate disciplinary agency; sanctions, in appropriate circumstances, against attorneys and judges who fail to report attorney misconduct of which they are aware.

DISCUSSION

In an address at the 1965 annual meeting of the American Bar Association, then President Lewis F. Powell stated:

> Surely no one wants punitive action, but it must be remembered that the bar has the privilege of disciplining itself to a greater extent than any other profession or calling. This imposes upon the bar a higher responsibility, one which the bar must discharge with greater determination.

If individual attorneys and judges shirk that responsibility, permitting wrongdoers in their midst to escape disciplinary action unless the circumstances are reported by laymen, the public may conclude that "self-policing" is in reality "self-protection." The failure of attorneys and judges to report instances of misconduct, while undoubtedly the result of the almost universal reluctance to inform, hampers effective enforcement and does a disservice to the bench, the bar and the public.

The client who retains an unethical practitioner may form his opinion of the entire profession from a single experience. If other attorneys who have become aware of the misconduct take prompt action against the violator, the client's respect for the integrity of the bar may be restored. If, on the other hand, the other attorneys close their eyes and do nothing, the client may conclude that the bar is engaged in a conspiracy to protect its own. Moreover, the attorney who takes no action when he becomes aware of apparent misconduct on the part of another often subjects future clients of the unethical practitioner to serious harm. For example, disciplinary agencies occasionally receive complaints of conversion by an attorney and discover, on investigation, that the monies were converted in order to make restitution of monies previously converted from another client. Not infrequently, the second conversion will have occurred after a demand by a new attorney consulted by the first client that restitution be made so that a complaint to the appropriate disciplinary agency will be unnecessary. By not reporting the conversion of the first client's funds immediately, and agreeing not to do so if restitution is made, the new attorney not only permits the unethical practitioner to continue to practice but may encourage subsequent conversion of another client's funds.

The chairman of the inquiry division of a state bar association disciplinary agency outlined some of the situations he had experienced:

> A client who finds that he has been cheated by an attorney may go to another attorney. We find very often that the latter, instead of reporting the situation to the bar association and encouraging the client to do so, will end up representing that client and using the threat of a grievance complaint to exact restitution from the offending lawyer, and then drop it once restitution has been made. Or maybe there is no restitution at all, and this lawyer, out of some spirit of sympathy for his brother at the bar, will simply talk this client out of raising a fuss. And this happens in many instances.
>
> In my own town, I learned quite by accident in a restaurant about a week ago that about six weeks ago a lawyer was removed as executor of an estate because it had been found by the probate court that he had come up short and that he had misused funds, that he even compromised claims by the estate against other clients of his, at prices that were unfair to the estate. Various other allegations of wrongdoing were found to be warranted and on the basis of those findings he was removed. No report of this was made to the local grievance committee. No report was made to the state bar association, and none whatever had been made, although there were no less than six lawyers involved in that case who represented various heirs, at whose insistence this other lawyer was removed as executor. Nobody reported it. Why?
>
> The other example, another member of the disciplinary agency out in his area ran across a case just a couple of weeks ago where a lawyer had embezzled funds from no less than five different clients over a period of time, and one lawyer knew all about it but didn't say a word and sat on the information for a matter of years.
>
> Judges generally do not report instances of wrongdoing to us. I think I can count on one hand the number of complaints that we have received from judges throughout the state about lawyers in the eight years I have been connected with the grievance committee.
>
> Judges are not administering discipline on their own either. Don't get the impression that they are handling it in their own way. There are virtually no contempt of court proceedings against lawyers in this state. There may be a half a dozen here, but they would involve such things as

impertinence to the court. They ordinarily do not involve things that we consider breach of duty to a client.

The adverse effect on the reputation of the bar and the danger to the public stemming from this reluctance of attorneys and judges require that strong measures be taken. The individual attorney's responsibility to report instances of misconduct as a necessary element of the self-policing privilege should be stressed in law school so that it is impressed on the lawyer during his formative years. Bar associations should engage in extensive educational campaigns as part of their continuing legal education programs to call the attention of the profession to the harmful effects of its silence in the face of misconduct. . . .

Consideration should also be given to sanctions against attorneys and judges who fail to report misconduct to the proper disciplinary agency in appropriate cases. Such sanctions are fully justified in light of the obligation imposed by Disciplinary Rule 1-103(A) of the Code of Professional Responsibility ("A lawyer possessing unprivileged knowledge of a violation of DR 1-102 shall report such knowledge to a tribunal or other authority empowered to investigate or act upon such violation"); . . . and Canon 11 of the Canons of Judicial Ethics ("A judge should utilize his opportunities to criticize and correct unprofessional conduct of attorneys and counsellors, brought to his attention; and, if adverse comment is not a sufficient corrective, should send the matter at once to the proper investigating and disciplinary authorities"). . . .

A second aspect of the responsibility of lawyers for the conduct of other lawyers arises in the context of a law firm. Model Rules 5.1 and 5.2 address the responsibility of a supervising attorney for the conduct of a subordinate and the responsibility of the subordinate when ordered by a superior to perform an act that the subordinate views as ethically dubious. Note that Rule 5.2(a) expressly states the obligations of a subordinate to obey the Rules but Rule 5.2(b) then protects subordinates who obey a supervisory lawyer's reasonable resolution of an arguable question of professional duty.

PROBLEM 60

You are an associate in the law firm involved in the O.P.M. fraud, p. 193, Note 6, and you were present at the disclosure scene. When you are instructed to prepare the papers to close new loans, you are horrified because you do not believe the company officers who have assured the firm that its fraudulent practices have ceased. You state your beliefs to the partner in charge, who repeats his instructions, saying that on the basis of the disclosures and having pushed the company officers hard, he believes that these loans are genuine. You are not at all convinced. What do you do?

PROBLEM 61

You were an associate assigned to work on the plaintiff's case by your law firm in the *IBM* case, p. 42. You stated that it was clear that the firm was disqualified and that there was insufficient disclosure and consent to cure the disqualification. The partner in charge disagreed and instructed you to start work on the case. What do you do?

ABA INFORMAL OPINION 1203
(Feb. 9, 1972)

You have asked the Committee for an Opinion based on the following factual situation:

"In a law office a junior attorney forms a firm conviction that it is necessary in connection with a client matter pending before a tribunal to call some information to the attention of the tribunal — that it would be a fraud on the tribunal to maintain some part of the client's claim without revealing the information. In accordance with the customary practice of the office the junior operates under the general supervision of a senior attorney. The senior directs the junior not to reveal the information. The senior states that the withholding is not fraud or misrepresentation under then prevailing state of law and that the information is privileged. The junior, after thoughtful consideration and weighing the greater experience and learning of his elder colleague, disagrees. What is required of the junior under the Code of Professional Responsibility?"

You have correctly identified the relevant provisions of the Code of Professional Responsibility as DR 1-102(A)(4),(5); 1-103(A); 4-101(A),(B)(1), (C)(2), (D); 7-102(A),(B). However, we believe that the procedure to be followed under the circumstances given is governed by DR 2-110(C)(2). Whether or not the continued employment of the particular junior attorney will result in the violation of a Disciplinary Rule may be a matter of judgment, and great weight should be given to the senior attorney's judgment that it will not. But if the views of the two are irreconcilable, then the junior attorney should withdraw. To do more at this stage of the proceedings would be premature. Of course, if a violation of a disciplinary rule occurs of which the junior attorney has unprivileged knowledge, then the provisions of DR 1-103(A) should be followed.

[handwritten margin notes: lawyer should withdraw if continued emp't would violate rule.]

[handwritten note at bottom: → lawyer should tell on other lawyer.]

NOTES

1. Does the "unprivileged knowledge" spoken of in the Opinion refer to the relation between the firm and the client or to the relation between the junior and senior attorneys?

2. Why should a junior attorney always give "great weight" to a senior attorney's judgment in a matter like this? Does the greater experience of the senior attorney always make it so likely that no violation has taken place that this cautionary advice should be given to junior attorneys as a matter of course? A discussion of many of the problems that lawyers working with other lawyers may face is contained in Mary Twitchell, The Ethical Dilemma of Lawyers on Teams, 72 Minn. L. Rev. 697 (1988).

CHAPTER 8

SOME SPECIAL PROBLEMS OF ACCESS TO LEGAL SERVICES

This chapter deals with two areas of subject matter, fees and advertising-solicitation, that affect substantially the availability of legal services to the public. They are closely related to a third topic, specialization, that is discussed later. See pp. 639-644.

A. FEES

PROBLEM 62

You and Counsel were classmates in law school and assistant district attorneys for two years in the local district attorney's office. The two of you have recently opened your own law office. One of the first items on your agenda for discussion of partnership business is the matter of criteria for charging fees. Neither of you has any experience in private practice; between you, you have isolated the following questions to be answered:

(a) Is it proper to ascertain from other attorneys in town the customary range of fees they charge for certain kinds of business?

(b) Do certain kinds of services — for example, real estate title closings, uncontested divorce proceedings — have something that more or less approximates a market worth?

(c) Is it also proper to take into account, in setting a fee, the overhead of a particular office?

(d) Should an attorney establish a basic hourly rate for his or her time — to be used in matters where billing is done at least partly on that basis, and as a guideline in other matters? How does the lawyer go about establishing such a rate? Should such a rate be seen as an estimate of the lawyer's own intrinsic worth, using other lawyers' hourly rates as a starting point? What factors determine a lawyer's "intrinsic worth"? Or should a lawyer project yearly overhead, desired net income, and then establish an hourly rate on the basis of a reasonable estimate of billable hours — perhaps after some experience with actual figures for a year or two?

(e) Is it appropriate for a lawyer who does a large amount of pro bono work to charge somewhat higher fees to his or her nonpro bono clients? What kind of disclosure should be made to the client about this practice? When?

(f) What kind of explanation ought a lawyer to make to a client about fees, and especially about the basis on which charges are set?

PROBLEM 63

Lawyer sent a regular client to Specialist in connection with a personal injury action. Client, who was barely able to support his family, was injured at work by a defective machine. Client executed the usual 35% contingent fee arrangement with Specialist. In due course, the claim was settled for $30,000 and Specialist received her $10,500 fee. Shortly thereafter, Lawyer received a check in the mail for $3,500 with a note from Specialist stating that the check represented the usual forwarder's fee and thanking him for referring the matter to her. Lawyer did not request, and does not want, a forwarding fee. Should Lawyer return the check to Specialist or give it to Client? In either case, what, if anything, should he say to Client? To Specialist? Assume that Lawyer is in a jurisdiction where DR 2-107(A) or Model Rule 1.5(e) has been adopted. What should Lawyer do next time he refers a client to Specialist?

PROBLEM 64

You are a partner in a large firm that has a highly specialized corporate acquisition practice. Corporation X has offered the firm a large annual retainer. Although Corporation X does not expect to require any legal work from your firm, it wants to prevent any corporation attempting to take it over from utilizing your firm's services. If any legal work were actually done for Corporation X by your firm, however, it would be billed against the retainer.

At a partnership meeting to discuss whether or not to accept the retainer, what position will you take? Does it matter to you whether there are a large number of corporations offering such a retainer instead of just Corporation X?

PROBLEM 65

(a) Lawyers are representing a class of emotionally and mentally handicapped children who have been placed in the custody of state officials pursuant to state law. They are litigating a suit on behalf of the class alleging that state officials have violated the class's federal constitutional rights because of a variety of deficiencies in the educational and health services provided to the class. One week before trial, after three years of pretrial discovery and endless negotiations, the defendants have put forth a settlement plan offering virtually everything requested in the complaint. The condition to the offer, however, is that lawyers agree to waive any fee to which they might be entitled pursuant to the Civil Rights Attorney's Fee Award Act of 1976. What should the lawyers do? Is it relevant that fee awards under the statute are made to the client for the benefit of the lawyer?

(b) Next time the lawyers agree to handle an action in which the Civil Rights Attorney's Fee Award Act is relevant, may they at the outset of the action have the client agree, with court approval if necessary, that the client will not bargain away the lawyer's fee to get a better substantive result?

PROBLEM 66

George Brown, a sole practitioner, has died and his estate wants to sell his practice to another lawyer on the following basis. The lawyer would complete all pending matters and pay the estate that portion of fees collected that represented work done by Brown before his death and, in addition, a further payment of $25,000 representing a flat sum for the goodwill of Brown's practice. May that arrangement be made? See Model Code DR 3-102. Does it require client consent? If so, who should request it, the estate or the purchasing lawyer? Would the propriety of the arrangement be any different if it were made between Brown and the purchasing attorney in the lifetime of Brown? Does the answer to the question turn on whether Model Code 2-107 is in force in the jurisdiction? If Model Rule 1.5(e) were in effect, would that make a difference?

The subject of fees affects access to the legal system in two ways. The size of the lawyer's fee obviously affects such access. In addition, the availability of legal services is also affected by the basic premise of our system, in contrast to the British system, that each party in a private dispute should pay its own counsel. In certain situations, however, as a matter of equitable principle, a court may order payment of attorneys' fees out of a "common fund" involved in the litigation. See Dawson, Lawyers and Involuntary Clients, 87 Harv. L. Rev. 1597 (1974), 88 Harv. L. Rev. 849 (1975). In a variety of other situations a court may order payment of attorneys' fees by one party to another as a matter either of statutory interpretation or of equitable doctrine. The number of federal statutes under which fee awards may be made has expanded greatly. As of 1980, one commentator was able to find more than 90. Aronson, Attorney-Client Fee Arrangements: Regulation and Review 156 (The Federal Judicial Center 1980). This development has proceeded very far in recent years, so that some commentators had noted that our system was approaching the British system to a great extent. However, in Alyeska Pipeline Service Co. v. Wilderness Society, 421 U.S. 240 (1975), the Supreme Court cut back considerably on the ability of federal courts to order one party to pay the other's legal fees without statutory authority, except in a few well-defined situations. In those situations, however, the Court has still been sympathetic to the equitable notions underlying the common fund doctrine. See Boeing Co. v. Van Gemert, 444 U.S. 472 (1980). And after *Alyeska,* Congress enacted a very broad statute authorizing the award of a reasonable attorney's fee to the prevailing party in civil rights litigation, 42 U.S.C. §1988.

The standards governing payment of fees to a successful plaintiff, who is enforcing statutory policy against one who violated it, are quite different from those applied in favor of a successful defendant. In the former case, fees are awarded in all cases except where payment would be unjust, Newman v. Piggie Park Enterprises, 390 U.S. 400 (1968), although in determining the amount of the award, the extent of the success is crucial. Hensley v. Eckerhart, 461 U.S. 424 (1983); Ruckelshaus v. Sierra Club, 463 U.S. 680 (1983). Indeed, under that formulation, the Court has held that fees might be awarded against members of a state supreme court if they exercise enforcement as opposed to adjudicatory functions regarding discipline of lawyers, although it held that it was an abuse of discretion to award fees against them for acts or omissions in their legislative function of promulgating a code of professional responsibility. Supreme Court of Virginia v. Consumers Union, 446 U.S. 719 (1980), on remand, 688 F.2d 218 (4th Cir. 1982) (affirming district court fee award against Virginia Supreme Court Judges), cert. denied, 462 U.S. 1137 (1983). Where it is a successful defendant, however, who is seeking an award of legal fees, the Court has held that an award is to be made only when the action brought is "frivolous, unreasonable, or without foundation." Christianburg Garment Co. v. E.E.O.C., 434 U.S. 412, 421 (1978). The Supreme Court has held, however, that if a vexatious lawsuit is knowingly brought, such an abuse of judicial process justifies a fee award even against plaintiff's attorneys. Roadway Express Co. v. Piper, 447 U.S. 752 (1980).

The arguments concerning the locus of the burden of fees have been canvassed thoroughly in legal literature. One article discussing the British and American rules, and pro-plaintiff and pro-defendant models, from an economic standpoint is Shavell, Suit, Settlement, and Trial: A Theoretical Analysis Under Alternative Methods of Legal Costs, 11 J. Legal Stud. 55 (1982). Another piece discussing the conceptual underpinnings, or lack thereof, is Rowe, The Legal Theory of Attorney Fee Shifting: A Critical Overview, 1982 Duke L.J. 651. These are important issues and if one wishes to pursue them, those two articles are worth reading at this point.

Another large issue that has been the subject of considerable attention is the size of lawyers' fees. Newspapers, magazines, and even books have discussed the subject, sometimes in sensational terms that highlight the six — or even seven — figure fees that have been received by particular named large law firms from large corporations or as a result of victories in particular lawsuits. The size of fees, especially those of the largest law firms, has played an important role in the strengthening of inside corporate law departments. This aspect has been analyzed by Lawrence Perlman, former General Counsel and now President of Control Data Corporation, in The Impact of Changing Roles of Inside and Outside Counsel on the Control of Legal Costs (paper on file with the Program on the Legal Profession, Harvard Law School).

The conceptual underpinnings of the fee system and the payment of very large fees, however, raise issues that are quite different from the ordinary problems that lawyers' fees present to both lawyer and client. The problems of the client have received substantial public exposure — learning about what a matter will cost, assessing the fairness of the fee in relation to the job done, dealing with tendencies toward price-fixing, where it exists, and of course affording the fee. Lawyers' problems, however, exist too — setting a fair fee, educating a client to its fairness, and simply getting the fee paid. The large law firm receiving a big fee from a wealthy client appears to be having these problems more and more, but a more common situation involves a client who cannot pay the lawyer's charge easily, has difficulty appreciating the worth of the service performed, and is not overly happy about the necessity to pay for it. (Another kind of size of fee problem was dealt with by the Supreme Court in Walters v. National Association of Radiation Survivors, 473 U.S. 305 (1985), upholding a Civil War statute that limited the fee of a lawyer who appeared before the Veterans Association in a matter relating to a service-connected disability claim to $10.)

It is therefore understandable that one of the lawyer's most difficult tasks, perhaps the most difficult routine task, is the sending of a bill to a client. At that time, the lawyer must step out of the role of adviser-confidant and take what is essentially an adversary stand vis à vis the client. Moreover, the matter of the fee is typically a constant source of worry and irritation between attorney and client from the beginning to the very end of the relationship. Yet except in very standardized situations or in situations where a contingent fee is appropriate and agreed on, the uncertain nature of most legal services often makes it very difficult to give a client more than a very general notion of the possible range of the fee that will be involved. But see Model Rule 1.5(b).

Until recently, articles about fee charging had almost exclusively an office management flavor and were written from the lawyer's point of view, except perhaps for a few generalities about client rights. The main objective was to see that lawyers got paid for their efforts. More recently, an emphasis on worth of services from the point of view of the client and the public generally has crept into some of the literature and court decisions. DR 2-106(B)(1)-(7) of the Model Code sets out a series of factors to be kept in mind in fixing a fee. Subparagraphs (1)-(4) and (6) are based on provisions in Canon 12 of the former Canons of Ethics. Subparagraphs (5) and (7) were added, explicitly at least, by the Model Code. Recognizing the difficulty of setting fees, the Model Code obviously gives lawyers a great deal of discretion although, theoretically at least, it subjects the lawyer to disciplinary action for charging "in excess of a reasonable fee." DR 2-106(B). The same factors governing reasonableness are set forth in Model Rule 1.5.

The Model Code and Model Rules also address the subject of the contingent fee, which has, after great professional struggle, become accepted in civil litigation, except perhaps in divorce litigation. Compare EC 2-20 of the Model Code (where nothing is said about contingent fees in divorce litigation) with Model Rule 1.5(d)(1). While the contingent fee has been extolled for its role in achieving access to the courts for poor people, especially injured poor people, its exacerbation of the already present economic conflict that exists between lawyer and client continues to cause concern. Efforts to regulate it have been made in a number of states. See, for example, the limits on contingent fee charges imposed by the Appellate Division of the New York Supreme Court, except in special circumstances; these survived determined challenge in Gair v. Peck, 6 N.Y.2d 97, 160 N.E.2d 43 (1959), cert. denied, 361 U.S. 374 (1960); see also McCreary v. Joel, 186 So. 2d 4 (Fla. 1966), holding an agreement for a 66⅔% contingent fee to be unconscionable, and Roa v. Lodi Medical Group, 37 Cal. 3d 920, 695 P.2d 164 (1985), appeal dismissed, 474 U.S. 990 (1985), upholding California's statutory sliding scale limitation on contingent fees in medical malpractice cases against attack on due process, equal protection, and separation of powers grounds.

A proposal for reform containing a formula that would combine the hourly fee and contingency bases for fees in such a way as to lessen or remove the conflict is contained in Clermont and Currivan, Improving on the Contingent Fee, 63 Cornell L.Q. 529 (1978). With the rise of the class action, bringing more and more fees under direct court supervision, the attitude of courts is becoming crucial. Their potential impact exists not only in matters like probate, juvenile proceedings, and bankruptcy, where the court has direct supervision over fees, but also throughout the whole private practice of law because of the courts' power, albeit rarely invoked, to pass on the reasonableness of all legal charges.

The following opinion illustrates the kind of scrutiny being given fee awards, especially in class action cases, and also presents a particularly difficult professional responsibility problem that arises in connection with statutory fee awards.

PRANDINI v. NATIONAL TEA CO.
557 F.2d 1015 (3d Cir. 1977)

WEIS, Circuit Judge.

In certain types of litigation, a successful plaintiff may receive attorneys' fees in addition to the customary damages for his claim. Although the negotiation of a fee contemporaneously with the evaluation of damages may be conducted with diligence and honesty, the potential for impropriety gives rise to possible misunderstanding by the public. We agree with the district court's disapproval of the procedure, but remanded for further findings of fact necessary in calculation of reasonable fees.

As part of the settlement of a class action based upon sex discrimination in employment, counsel for the class requested court approval of statutorily authorized attorneys' fees. 42 U.S.C. §2000e-5(k). The proposed settlement petition provided for payment to the class of $97,000, later recalculated to $99,664, and recited the parties' agreement on counsel fees:

> 6. Within ninety days after final dismissal of Civil Action No. 72-870, Defendant National Tea Company shall pay Plaintiffs' attorney's fees in the following amounts:
> a. The sum of TWENTY-FOUR THOUSAND DOLLARS ($24,000) to Berger & Kapetan;
> b. The sum of SIXTEEN THOUSAND DOLLARS ($16,000) to Rosenberg & Lubow; and
> c. The sum of TEN THOUSAND DOLLARS ($10,000) to Sylvia Roberts, Esquire.

An affidavit attached to the petition stated that at normal billing rates the fees of the Berger & Kapetan (later restyled Berger, Kapetan & Malakoff) and Rosenberg & Lubow firms would be $42,910, and that Sylvia Roberts' fee was based on a contractual right to receive 20% of the total attorneys' fees awarded. The petition suggested that normal billing rates should be increased by 20% because of the contingent nature of the case and the quality of the work. The petition also requested payment of $3,000 for expenses incurred, including amounts paid to experts, paraprofessionals, court reporters, postage, copying and similar items. There was no request for counsel fees to be paid from the fund itself.

At the hearing for approval of the settlement, the district judge expressed concern about the request for counsel fees, particularly with the allocation to Ms. Roberts based on a percentage referral arrangement rather than on work performed. The award to the class was approved, but a separate proceeding was scheduled to address the issue of attorneys' fees. At the outset of that hearing, the court stated its dissatisfaction with settlement proposals that include both allowances for attorneys' fees and payment to the class because the combination may create a possible conflict of interest.

Ms. Roberts submitted a letter and affidavit in which she disclaimed any interest in a "referral fee" or a "broker's fee" and submitted an itemization of the time that she had spent on the case. She suggested that an hourly charge of $100 would be reasonable for the 22.75 hours that she had devoted to the matter.

The district court awarded fees as follows:

Berger, Kapetan & Malakoff	$21,000.00
Rosenberg & Lubow	14,000.00
	$35,000.00

No specific amount was awarded to Ms. Roberts, the court stating that she should be paid by counsel with whom she had consulted.

Beginning with the maximum of $50,000, to which defendants had agreed, the court began its calculations by first excluding the $10,000 "referral" fee as being forbidden by the Code of Professional Responsibility. The total was further reduced by $5,000 on the ground that Ms. Prandini, the named plaintiff, had received a $15,000 [damages] award but had borne no share of the attorneys' fees. The court stated that 33⅓% was a reasonable share of her recovery which should have been charged by the attorneys, despite counsel's contention that Prandini had worked as a key punch operator in preparing the case. Thus, the fee fund was reduced to $35,000. In the settlement petition, the two firms had agreed to accept $24,000 and $16,000 respectively, and the court allocated the remaining fee fund in the same proportions.

This appeal was taken by Berger, Kapetan & Malakoff, the other firm, Rosenberg & Lubow, not contesting the amount awarded to it. The defendant has advised us that, since the company had agreed to pay a sum up to $50,000 if approved by the court, it did not contest the fee award in the district court. In the interest of consistency, the company did not deem it appropriate to dispute plaintiffs' counsel's position in this court and, accordingly, has not participated in the appeal. We are presented, therefore, with an ex parte appeal by counsel whose fee was reduced from the $24,000 it had settled upon with the defendant to $21,000 as determined by the court.

The awarding of counsel fees is a matter of discretion with the trial court, but we have provided objective standards to guide and facilitate the sound exercise of that discretion. Lindy Bros. Builders, Inc. of Phila. v. American Radiator & Standard Sanitary Corp., 487 F.2d 161 (3d Cir. 1973) (*Lindy I*), and Lindy Bros. Builders, Inc. of Phila. v. American Radiator & Standard Sanitary Corp., 540 F.2d 102 (3d Cir. 1976), (*Lindy II*). The district court is required to employ the formula we devised and to articulate the values of its variable components. The total time expended and a reasonable hourly rate are the elements of the initial computation. That calculation in turn must be adjusted to reflect the quality of the work, benefit to the client, and contingency of the result in order to arrive at a reasonable value of the attorneys' services. . . .

[The court remanded awarding of counsel fees for calculation according to the formula.]

The trial court's opinion, however, raises several important issues that require comment. The district judge found that the agreement to pay a percentage of the fee to referring counsel, without regard to the work she had performed, violated established standards of professional conduct, particularly DR2-107 of the American Bar Association Code of Professional Responsibility, Pa. Stat. Ann. tit. 42. That rule reads:

> A lawyer shall not divide a fee for legal services with another lawyer who is not a partner in or associate of his law firm or law office, unless:
>
> (1) The client consents to employment of the other lawyer after a full disclosure that a division of fees will be made.
> (2) The division is made in proportion to the services performed and responsibility assumed by each.
> (3) The total fee of the lawyers does not clearly exceed reasonable compensation for all legal services they rendered the client.

A division of fees based on a percentage without regard to work performed or responsibility assumed is not in compliance with the standard. Consequently, when he was asked to approve a fee based only upon the percentage agreement, the trial judge properly refused to approve the arrangement. The appellants contend that the judge's attention should have been directed "at what amount it is ethical to receive, not at what share it is ethical to agree upon." Farmington Dowell Products Co. v.

Forster Mfg. Co., 436 F.2d 699 (1st Cir. 1970). But in disapproving the initial request for $10,000, the district judge was passing upon the amount to be received. To that extent we do not accept appellant's position.

After Ms. Roberts had submitted a claim for $2,275 based upon hourly charges, the court did not pass upon it but simply reduced the fee fund by $10,000. We agree with appellants that in this respect the court erred. Having been identified as a lawyer who represented the plaintiff and who had requested compensation. Ms. Roberts' fee should have been determined by the same standards applicable to the others and paid from the fee fund. The fund available should not have been reduced by the full $10,000.[4]

In appraising the fees requested by the Berger and Lubow firms, the district court was doubtful that hours expended is always a fair measurement of the value of legal services, stating at the hearing: ". . . I know many attorneys achieve results in two hours that takes another a week to get." We do not disagree, and observe that the "quality" factor requires the court to adjust a fee on the basis of results of the work performed. Quality in this sense includes efficiency. If the attorney achieves good results with a minimum time expenditure, the total award may be increased to reflect efficiency and benefit to the client. . . . Conversely, emphasis on the objective quantity of time spent should not shield wasteful or inefficient logging of hours from scrutiny, and the court should reduce the compensation when that practice occurs. Similarly, hours spent on purely clerical matters, easily delegable to non-professional assistants, should not be valued at legal service rates.[6] *Lindy* does not fetter a trial judge's ability to arrive at a reasonable fee but offers a principled means of achieving that result and, at the same time, provides an adequate record for appellate and public review. . . .

We are aware of the differences in rationale underlying the awards of fees from a fund produced for the benefit of a class and those provided by statute. In the former case, the court exercises its equitable jurisdiction over the relationship between an attorney and his amorphous client, and factors which would appropriately have influenced the fee arrangement made between private parties, such as the contingency of litigation, are relevant. In the latter case, the statutory fee is often a part of the defendant's penalty for violating the applicable law. Contingency may be

---

4. Similarly, we do not agree that the fee fund should have been reduced by the additional $5,000 attributable to a fee which might have been payable by Ms. Prandini. She had been awarded $15,000 by the court without any obligation to pay a fee from that amount. To suggest that counsel bill her thereafter is inconsistent with the court's approval of the damage aspect of the case.

6. See Smith, Standards for Judicial Approval of Attorneys' Fees in Class Action and Complex Litigation, 20 Howard L.J. 22, 62, 63 (1977).

of little significance in that situation if the result is to give a smaller fee to the plaintiff's lawyer who recovers from a defendant in flagrant violation than the attorney who succeeds in establishing liability in a very close case. The contingency factor would be less where the liability is easily proved than where it is questionable. Hence, the penalty fastened on the defendant would vary in inverse proportion to the strength of the case against him. . . .

The respective interests of lawyer and client may also vary, depending on whether the fee comes from a recovered fund or directly from the defendant in satisfaction of a separate obligation. In the common fund situation, the adverse interests are patent and the necessity for a court to recognize the equities of the absent and passive members of a class is obvious. When the statute provides that a fee is to be paid as a separate item, the conflict between client and attorney may not be as apparent, particularly in the event of settlement. It is often present nonetheless.

The district court concluded that it had been a mistake to approve the payment to the class separately because there was, in reality, only one fund for both the class and attorneys' fees. Reasoning that in cases of this nature a defendant is interested only in disposing of the total claim asserted against it, the court noted that the allocation between the class payment and the attorneys' fees is of little or no interest to the defense. As the court phrased it:

> The defendant is not faced with a group of claimants who are personally involved in the litigation, but only with one or a few representative parties whose award can be greatly increased over that of individual class members because of personal participation in the preparation of the case. In this case the sole representative plaintiff was awarded $15,000.00 for her initiation of the case and participation therein. The defendant deals with the representative party or parties and counsel who also represents the class. The impulse to treat opposing counsel and the representative party generously is an element that cannot be ignored.

The court went on to explain the unpleasant situation in which it found itself:

> Therefore, as devil's advocate, we must look at an agreement by defendants to pay counsel for the class a fee up to a certain maximum, as determined by the court, as having the potentiality of what is known in the labor field as a "sweetheart contract." This puts the judge who must determine its reasonableness and fairness in the posture of a "bad guy." None of the class members complained; counsel for the defendant does not complain; why should he interject himself into the arrangement?

We are placed in the similar unfortunate position of considering an appeal ex parte and are thus deprived of adversarial presentations.

The district judge's sentiments about the conflict of interest and "sweetheart contract" problems have been expressed in other cases. City of Detroit v. Grinnell Corp., 495 F.2d 448 (2d Cir. 1974); City of Philadelphia v. Chas. Pfizer & Co., 345 F. Supp. 454 (S.D.N.Y. 1972); Norman v. McKee, 290 F. Supp. 29 (N.D. Cal. 1968), aff'd, 431 F.2d 769 (9th Cir. 1970). The articulated difficulties are real and practical — present in all cases where the defendant pays the plaintiff's lawyers, and particularly so in class actions.[7] The court does have the duty to see to it that the administration of justice has the appearance of propriety as well as being so in fact. In this case the district court properly exercised its responsibility by requiring public disclosure of the basis for the fees, even though the defendant had agreed to the amount.

However, we recognize that with the increasingly heavy burden upon the courts, settlements of disputes must be encouraged, and in the absence of special circumstances, such as those mentioned by the district court in this case, we doubt the necessity to completely exclude statutorily authorized attorneys' fees from that policy. A reasonable solution, we suggest, is for trial courts to insist upon settlement of the damage aspect of the case separately from the award of statutorily authorized attorneys' fees. Only after court approval of the damage settlement should discussion and negotiation of appropriate compensation for the attorneys begin. This would eliminate the situation found in this case of having, in practical effect, one fund divided between the attorney and client.

This procedure may not be particularly appealing to the parties, but it preserves the benefits of the adversary system since the defendant continues to have an economic interest. Moreover, the merits of fee disputes become separated from those of damages, thus reducing the conflict between client and attorney. This procedure would make the court's task less burdensome and remove a source of uneasiness over the settle-

---

7. See Smith, supra n.6. Another commentator states: "It is obvious that in such a case it is the attorneys, not the class members, who are the true beneficiaries and the real parties in interest. This plain fact is even more apparent in large antitrust settlements where many millions of dollars in fees are at stake . . . it is the small purchasers, the supposed beneficiaries of class actions, who must pay these fees and other costs." Handler, The Shift From Substantive to Procedural Innovations in Antitrust Suits, 71 Colum. L. Rev. 1, 10 (1971). See also Attorneys' Fees in Individual and Class Action Antitrust Litigation, supra; 7A C. Wright & A. Miller, Federal Practice and Procedure §1803.

This sharp criticism has not gone unchallenged. "But 'private' fees between lawyers and corporate clients also have a very substantial public character even though they are subject to no public supervision. . . . It is unlikely that a class member in the unfamiliar position of recouping an overcharge on a commodity he purchased years before would begrudge the lawyer who brought it to him 15 or even 25 percent of his 'windfall;' despite loose assertions to the contrary. I am unaware of any major antitrust class action where fees and expenses have seriously diminished the class recovery." Springer, Fee Awards in Antitrust Litigation, 44 Antitrust L.J. 97, 120-121 (1975).

ment procedure without in any way impairing the power to set a proper fee.

The judgment of the district court will be vacated and the case will be remanded for further proceedings consistent with this opinion.

NOTES

1. Another aspect of the relationship between fees and class counsel has also spawned a per se rule in some jurisdictions that forbids attorneys from becoming class counsel if they have certain relationships with a class representative: "no member of the bar either maintaining an employment relationship, including a partnership or professional corporation, or sharing office or suite space with an attorney class representative during the preparation or pendency of a Rule 23(b)(3) class action may serve as counsel to the class if the action might result in the creation of a fund from which an attorneys' fee award would be appropriate." Kramer v. Scientific Control Corp., 534 F.2d 1085, 1093 (3d Cir.), cert. denied, 429 U.S. 830 (1976); accord, Zylstra v. Safeway Stores, Inc., 578 F.2d 102 (5th Cir. 1978). The fear is that attorneys' interest in the fee award might compromise their zeal for obtaining the most favorable settlement for the class, and in *Kramer,* the rule was applied even though the class representative stated that he would not share in any fee award.

2. The *Lindy* opinions, which are referred to in *Prandini,* are very important in the history of fee determination in class action cases. Prior to *Lindy,* class action fee awards were generally made on a percentage, contingency basis. *Lindy* established time worked and an hourly rate as the "lodestar" for awarding fees. It has been followed by almost all the courts of appeals. Recently, however, it has been attacked as inhibiting early settlements and as inducing wasteful expenditure of time, especially as settlement neared. See Solovy and Mendillo, Calculating Class Action Awards, 4 Nat'l L.J. 20 (May 2, 1983). See also Hensley v. Eckerhart, 461 U.S. 424 (1983). In Pennsylvania v. Delaware Valley Citizens' Council for Clean Air, 107 S. Ct. 3078 (1987), the Supreme Court held it was appropriate under the relevant statute to increase the "lodestar" to compensate for the risk of losing, although not in the circumstances of that case. See also Pierce v. Underwood, 108 S. Ct. 2541 (1988) where the Supreme Court found that the "special circumstances" exception to the $75 per hour cap on lawyers' fees in the Equal Access to Justice Act had not been met.

3. The court referred the so-called percentage referral arrangement that Ms. Robert later disclaimed. That is a reference to the thorny problem of "forwarding fees," where a lawyer who refers a matter to another lawyer receives a percentage of the fee, commonly without having per-

formed any services. The practice was generally understood to have been disapproved by the slightly ambiguous language of the old Canons of Ethics and of the Model Code. But it was also generally believed that the practice flourished. The argument was forcefully made that the forwarding fee served the beneficent purpose of encouraging lawyers who were not able to handle matters in a particular field to send their clients to specialists instead of trying to struggle through themselves.

Even before the promulgation of the Model Rules, a number of states had amended their disciplinary rules to permit the payment of forwarding fees not based on a division of work. Model Rule 1.5(e) also permits such payments although it requires not only notice and lack of objection (but not "consent") but also that the recipient of a forwarding fee accept joint responsibility. In other words, the recipient accepts malpractice liability in the event of malpractice by the lawyer to whom the matter is forwarded.

4. In a case where lawyers agreed to share the responsibility in a matter and the contingent fee equally, the court would not apportion the fee on a quantum meruit basis when it turned out that the work was not shared precisely equally, so long as there was no breach of contract. Stissi v. Interstate and Ocean Transport, 814 F.2d 848 (2d Cir. 1987).

5. Very much related to the issue of fee sharing is the ability of a lawyer, or the estate of a lawyer, to sell the good will of a practice to an attorney with whom the seller (or deceased attorney) never practiced. The Model Code specifically addresses a piece of the subject in DR 3-102(A)(2) when it permits payment to the estate of a deceased lawyer with respect to unfinished business only of an amount that represents compensation for services rendered by the decedent. See also Model Rule 5.4(a)(2). Sale of "good will" may be seen as putting a value on future fees to be derived from the legal practice and the sale could be governed by the rule pertaining to dividing legal fees with either lawyers or nonlawyers (viewing the estate of a deceased lawyer as a nonlawyer). Such sales may also be viewed, as was *Corti,* as efforts to transfer clients without their consent. In addition, the sale of a practice by a lawyer may very well create a conflict of interest between the desire to maximize price and the obligation to recommend the best possible lawyer for each individual client. Moreover, transfer of files without consent will create confidentiality problems. In any event, without much grounding in the specific language of the Disciplinary Rules, ethics committees have generally advised that sales of good will are unethical. ABA Formal Opinion 266 (1945), ABA Informal Opinion 550 (1962), Illinois Opinion 369 (1972), Los Angeles County Informal Opinion 79-1 (1979), Missouri Informal Opinion 4 (1978), New York State Bar Association Opinion 366 (1974), and Wisconsin Mem. Op. 3-78 (1978). For a report of a rejection by a Bar Association of such an interpretation of the Disciplinary Rules by its Ethics Committee, see 11 Mass. Lawyers Weekly 1041 (May 23,

1983). See also Dugan v. Dugan, 92 N.J. 423, 457 A.2d 1 (1983) (without passing on ethical question, court permitted equitable distribution of good will of a law practice in a divorce proceeding).

6. In Koehler v. Wales, 16 Wash. App. 304, 556 P.2d 233 (1976), plaintiff hired defendant to look after her practice while she was abroad for fourteen months. On her return she brought suit after discovering that he had taken all the new business received during her absence to his own practice. The court stated that whether the arrangement was characterized as an employment or a partnership agreement, it provided the ongoing relationship necessary for a lawful sharing of fees under DR 2-107. It therefore awarded plaintiff the agreed 15% of the fees earned on the disputed cases. It declined to make an award on any theory based on plaintiff's proprietary interest in her former clients who engaged defendant. That would in effect involve placing a price on the law business, which is against public policy.

7. For many years prior to 1975, local, county, and state bar associations published minimum fee schedules for a whole variety of standard legal services, from title closings and forming corporations to writing simple wills, to court appearances. While these schedules were justified as providing information and guidance to lawyers about common charges and reasonable fees, they also served at many times in many places as implicit and explicit efforts to set floors on charges so as to avoid price cutting. An attack on a minimum fee schedule that operated in such a fashion was mounted in Goldfarb v. Virginia State Bar, 421 U.S. 773 (1975). The Supreme Court held that price fixing was involved; that interstate commerce was sufficiently affected to bring the price fixing activities within section 1 of the Sherman Act; and that they were not exempt either because of a "learned profession" exclusion in that Act or because they constituted "state action" within the meaning of Parker v. Brown, 317 U.S. 341 (1943).

[handwritten margin note:] MIN. FEE SCHED = price fixing Goldfarb

The Supreme Court in *Goldfarb* was careful to say that it was not dealing with a purely advisory fee schedule but only with one that set a fixed, rigid price floor. Nevertheless, the Court's action, together with developments in advertising and the rise of legal clinics, has led to a virtual demise of the promulgation of minimum fee schedules. Of equal interest is what *Goldfarb* means for the future of professional regulation. The Court did specifically state that professional practices were not to be equated automatically with business practices, thus leaving open the possibility of greater immunity from Sherman Act regulation for the profession. Yet when dealing with the state agency exemption from anticompetitive practices that it created in Parker v. Brown, the Court adverted specifically to the fact that it intended "no diminution of the authority of the State to regulate its professions."

While these positions are not necessarily inconsistent, the issue being drawn in the general area of discipline (see Chapter 11 infra) between the profession's desire for self-regulation and growing interest in more state regulation may be affected by the Supreme Court's attitude. To the extent that the Court does not treat professional anticompetitive practices differently from similar business practices, then the profession may be forced, or the state may feel it wise, to seek greater state control over the profession. Thus the sequelae to *Goldfarb* may be very influential in helping determine the ultimate nature of control of the profession — whether it will involve some self-regulation by the profession or even more state regulation.

NOTE: *Conflict between Lawyer and Client with Respect to Fees*

As noted before, p. 466, it is apparent that there is a conflict of interest that is inherent in the setting of a price for lawyers' service. The court in *Prandini* noted that there is an additional difficulty when the lawyer is allowed a fee by the court out of a common fund created or preserved by the lawyer. It then observed that when a fee award is based on statutory authority, the conflict is less apparent because it is added to damages.

But the court goes on to point out that conflict may still exist. It may exist in two forms. One is the situation suggested by *Prandini*. The defendants made a $15,000 payment to the named plaintiff and offered what appears to have been a generous fee settlement to class counsel. This raises, as the court noted, the problem of a "sweetheart contract," and the possibility that the interests of the unnamed members of the class might not have been pursued sufficiently. Generous offers of this kind certainly create problems of conflict between named plaintiff and class counsel on the one hand and the remainder of the class on the other.

A second opportunity for conflict between counsel and client is presented when the defendants offer a satisfactory settlement to the class conditioned on waiver by class counsel of their statutory fee award. That is the issue presented by Problem 65 and by the principal case. In cases where the settlement is a monetary payment, such an offer forces counsel to seek its fee from the award. The resulting conflict created for counsel and class is just the problem that the statutory fee award was designed to avoid. In cases where the settlement consists not of a damage payment but of an agreement to undertake, or to desist from, certain conduct, the conditional offer is likely to mean that class counsel will get no fee at all if the offer is accepted. Needless to say, it is very difficult for class counsel to advise their clients in that situation.

The response of the *Prandini* court is an effort to effectuate the legislative policy embodied in the statutory fee award and to minimize the adversary relationship into which the fee problem puts plaintiff class and its lawyer. Efforts were made to incorporate the *Prandini* result into the Model Rules. They failed largely because of the perceived unfairness in forbidding defendants from making a settlement on the basis of its total liability for both damages and fees at the same time. The *Prandini* solution therefore continues to be problematic.

It is now time to note that the facts of Problem 65 are the facts of Evans v. Jeff D., 475 U.S. 717, reh'g. denied, 476 U.S. 1179 (1986). In the actual case, the lawyer for the class signed the stipulation accepting the settlement proposal, which contained a fee waiver. He then petitioned the district court to approve the settlement except for the fee waiver. The district court approved the settlement and denied the lawyer's motion to be permitted to present a request for a statutory fee. The Court of Appeals, however, citing *Prandini,* invalidated the fee waiver. The Supreme Court reversed, finding nothing in the language or policy of the Fee Act requiring that it be construed as embodying a general rule prohibiting settlements conditioned on fee waiver. The Court also did not regard the lawyer as having any "ethical dilemma"; no rule of ethics required the lawyer to seek a fee. Finally, the Court found no abuse of discretion in the approval by the district court of a settlement with a complete fee waiver. The Court suggested the possibility that approval might not be justified if the defendants had no realistic defense or if they had adopted a vindictive policy of forcing fee waiver to inhibit counsel from bringing such cases.

While the *Jeff D.* case settles the interpretation of the Fee Act, it does not remove the ethics problem for plaintiff counsel. While it is true that there is no ethical dilemma in the sense that counsel violate no ethical rule by waiving a fee, counsel who need to earn a living certainly have an ethical dilemma both in trying to decide whether they must accept the fee waiver if the settlement is good for the client class and in trying to decide what to do the next time they are asked to take on representation in a situation where the problem seems likely to arise. And so *Jeff D.* has not made the ethics issue that the *Prandini* court grappled with obsolete. It has simply added another dimension to the problem.

Watergate Fee Problems

Some interesting practical issues regarding payment of fees were raised in the Senate investigation of the Watergate incident. The first piece of testimony contains one version of the manner in which Mr. William Bittman, lawyer for Watergate defendant E. Howard Hunt, was paid. The testimony is that of Anthony Ulasewicz, former New York City policeman and employee of Herbert Kalmbach, personal counsel to President Nixon, telling how he carried out his instructions to arrange representation for the Watergate defendants by finding out the "cost of the script" [how much money was to be delivered to particular persons on account of representation of the defendants] and arranging to make secret payment of attorneys' fees.

TESTIMONY OF ANTHONY ULASEWICZ

6 Hearings before the Senate Select Committee on Presidential
Campaign Activities, 93d Cong., 1st Sess. 2225-2227 (1973)

Mr. Lenzner [*one of the Watergate Committee counsel and former director of OEO Legal Services*]: Did you get further instructions from Mr. Kalmbach?

Mr. Ulasewicz: Yes. I then was instructed to call Mr. Bittman in Washington, who I understood was an attorney. . . .

Mr. Lenzner: Did you call Mr. Bittman?

Mr. Ulasewicz: I did.

Mr. Lenzner: Did you speak to him?

Mr. Ulasewicz: I spoke to Mr. Bittman and I recall that in the first conversation, Mr. Bittman said, well, I understand. He was expecting a call. He said, well, this is very unusual. He said something like, I do not know if you are an attorney, but an attorney does not anticipate fees and costs in this manner.

I said, well, I am instructed not to negotiate in any manner. I understood that you would have a figure . . . I still wanted to get rid of all those cookies, $75,100.

And he brought in the situation that — he was not prepared at that time, something was not according to the way he liked. I so reported to Mr. Kalmbach, received my call back from Mr. Kalmbach. He told me again to call and contact Mr. Bittman.

Now, this is some period of time passes by. Mr. Bittman said, all right, his initial fee would be $25,000. . . .

Mr. Lenzner: And did you call Mr. Kalmbach and tell him Mr. Bittman had indicated he wanted an initial fee of $25,000?

Mr. Ulasewicz: I did.

Mr. Lenzner: What was Mr. Kalmbach's response?

Mr. Ulasewicz: He said to deliver it to Mr. Bittman in any manner I saw fit.

Mr. Lenzner: Did he give you any instructions about not being seen by Mr. Bittman?

Mr. Ulasewicz:	Oh, yes, that somehow conversations were arranged that I would not now be seen by anybody, to do the money without being observed, in a confidential manner.
Mr. Lenzner:	That was Mr. Kalmbach's instructions to you?
Mr. Ulasewicz:	Right. . . .
Mr. Lenzner:	Well, now, you arranged, as I understand it, Mr. Ulasewicz, to furnish Mr. Bittman with $25,000 for the script. Was that the end of the conversation?
Mr. Ulasewicz:	That is correct.
Mr. Lenzner:	And how did you arrange to deliver that money?
Mr. Ulasewicz:	I contacted Mr. Bittman right from the lobby of his office there. I spoke with him and I told him that I had the cash. Prior to that, I went out to a drugstore in the area, bought a couple of envelopes and some scotch tape, and I had to count out . . . $25,000 from the $75,100 original, which I did, and I put it into a plain Kraft brown envelope.

I called Mr. Bittman from the lobby of his building. There are two or three phone booths. On one side of the phone booth was a ledge with the phone books and I called Mr. Bittman. . . . |
| *Mr. Ulasewicz:* | I called from this telephone booth — (indicating) — to Mr. Bittman and told him that I had the delivery and that would he come right down and that it would be on the ledge at the telephone booth.

. . . There are two or three or four telephone books and there is a ledge above, a kind of space. I told him it would be a brown sack and that the money would be lying right there, would he come right down, if he walk [sic] right through and pick it up and go back to the elevator, I would be satisfied. |
Mr. Lenzner:	Now, thereafter, did an individual come down on the elevator?
Mr. Ulasewicz:	We had a description of clothing as I phoned, as I recall, that he would be wearing a brown suit or something at that time.
Mr. Lenzner:	Did somebody come down wearing those clothes?
Mr. Ulasewicz:	Yes.
Mr. Lenzner:	Where were you at that time?
Mr. Ulasewicz:	I was in a telephone booth. I had it half shut. There was another person in a booth. These booths on weekdays are very heavily used. There is a newsstand section in front. There is quite a bit of traffic on a weekday. This was taken on a Saturday afternoon.

> He came right out of this elevator, the first eleva-
> tor, and walked right over, picked it up, walked right
> back in, and went up. . . .

NOTES

1. No one will dispute the bizarre nature of the arrangements made
to deliver and receive the attorney's fee in this case. Assuming the accuracy of the testimony, did the lawyer's conduct violate any disciplinary
rule? Aside from any specific (or general) statement in the disciplinary
rules, should lawyers avoid taking fees in such manner? Why?

Is it that a lawyer should never take a fee in cash? A large fee? Is it
that a lawyer should never take a fee anonymously?

When the Watergate hearings resumed in September 1973, E. Howard Hunt testified that his lawyer received a total fee of some $156,000
for representation at the pretrial stages of the Watergate trial before Mr.
Hunt eventually pleaded guilty. 9 Hearings before the Senate Committee on Presidential Campaign Activities, 93d Cong., 1st Sess. 3750, 3755,
3798-3802 (1973). Mr. Hunt's lawyer was in fact a partner in a large
Washington law firm that apparently threw its large staff into Mr. Hunt's
representation. Assuming that the fee received represents the time
charge of this large staff, what does that tell us about a role for a large
firm on the criminal scene? Does the potential size of the fee have a
bearing on the questions in paragraphs one and two?

2. What about the common situation where the lawyer receives payment of client B's bill from A? Is that proper if there is a potential conflict of interest — as between employer and employee or parent and
child in particular types of matters? Would it be proper if B is a defendant charged with selling drugs and A is reputed to be high up in the
drug business. If B is a corporate employee charged with price fixing
and A is the corporation? Does it make any difference if the fee is agreed
upon in advance and paid over in escrow by A, with no right in A to
direct the conduct of the lawsuit?

3. These questions pose difficult issues for lawyers, not only with respect to their decision to undertake representation but also with respect
to subsequent conduct. The source of fee payments for representation
of particular defendants is often regarded as important in investigation
of "organized crime," and one way a prosecutor may attempt to ascertain
that information is to call the attorney before the grand jury. Whether
the attorney must testify is not always wholly clear. Compare In re Grand
Jury Proceedings, 680 F.2d 1026 (5th Cir. 1982) and In re Michaelson,
511 F.2d 882 (9th Cir.), cert. denied, 421 U.S. 978 (1975) with In re
Special Grand Jury No. 81-1, 676 F.2d 1005 (4th Cir. 1982) and In re
Grand Jury Proceedings, 517 F.2d 666 (5th Cir. 1975), pet. for rehearing
en banc denied, 521 F.2d 815 (1975).

4. Equally serious for lawyers is the use by the federal government of the Comprehensive Forfeiture Act to prohibit various assets owned by a criminal defendant from being used to pay the fees of defense counsel and, after conviction, to forfeit fees already paid unless counsel can establish that they were bona fide purchasers who had no reasonable cause to believe that the fees were subject to forfeiture when they were paid. 21 U.S.C. §§853(c) and 853(e)(1)(A). The initial decisions tended toward excluding attorneys' fees from coverage of the Act as a matter of statutory construction, United States v. Rogers, 602 F. Supp. 1332 (D. Colo. 1985), or holding that the Act, if construed to include attorneys' fees, would violate defendants' Sixth Amendment right to counsel. United States v. Harvey, 814 F.2d 905 (4th Cir. 1987). However, the Fourth Circuit upheld the statutes as applied to attorneys' fees in In re Caplin & Drysdale, 837 F.2d 637 (1988), overturning the panel decision in *Harvey*, and a panel of the Second Circuit agreed. United States v. Monsanto, 836 F.2d 74 (1987).

The Second Circuit then reheard *Monsanto* en banc and, 8-4, overturned the panel decision. Id., 852 F.2d 1400 (1988). It ordered that defendant be permitted to use the assets that had been restrained to pay legitimate attorneys' fees and further held that such payments were exempt from subsequent forfeiture. The majority was split three ways. One opinion was based on the insufficiency of the government's interest to overcome the defendants' Sixth Amendment right to counsel of their choice; a second construed the statute to confer discretion on the court and regarded it as an abuse of discretion, in the absence of countervailing government interest, to refuse to permit defendants to make ordinary lawful expenditures, including attorneys' fees, and to exempt such payments from subsequent forfeitures; and a third opinion was based on procedural due process grounds relating to lack of proper notice and hearing. The constitutional conclusion and especially the policy underlying the statute, as applied to lawyers, continue to be controversial because of the substantial effect on the ability of defendants to obtain counsel of their choice in certain kinds of cases when counsel know that their fees are at risk. The Supreme Court has granted certiorari in both *Monsanto* and *Caplin & Drysdale*. 57 U.S. L. Week 3333 (Nov. 8, 1988).

B. ADVERTISING AND SOLICITATION

PROBLEM 67

Law Firm wishes to advertise itself as "Best Lawyers in Town," or "Best lawyers, lowest fees in Town," or "Best lawyers, lowest fees, best results achieved in Town." May it do so under the Model Code or Model

Rules? Whatever the answer in a particular jurisdiction, should such advertising be forbidden?

PROBLEM 68

Law Firm, which does substantial advertising in the media of its personal injury practice, wishes to expand its business. It proposes to do the following: (1) have a partner offer free seminars to workers under the auspices of the local Council of Unions; (2) leave brochures describing its practice, expertness, and fees in the offices of doctors who do substantial personal injury work for display to patients; (3) mail those brochures to all the members of several local unions; and (4) subscribe to a newspaper clipping service, send the brochures to all persons identified as accident victims, and follow up with a telephone call or even a visit offering the firm's services. May it do so under the Model Code or Model Rules? Whatever the answer in a particular jurisdiction, should such practices be forbidden?

PROBLEM 69

For many years Lawyer has been a good friend of the Assistant Administrator of the Emergency Room of the local hospital. Her law business has fallen off recently, and she asks Administrator if he would keep her in mind if accident victims ever ask his advice about a lawyer. Is that request proper? Would it subject the lawyer to discipline? When Christmastime approaches, Lawyer realizes that she has had a good year financially. May she give Administrator a Christmas present?

PROBLEM 70

Consumers Union and the Virginia Citizens Consumer Council sought to produce a directory that would help the public to select lawyers by providing a variety of useful information. It chose Arlington County, Virginia, for a pilot program. The program contemplated sending a questionnaire to all lawyers practicing in the county and using the information gained thereby to produce a Lawyers' Directory. The Directory would contain the information reported by the lawyer, together with a Guide to its use. Excerpts from the Questionnaire and Guide follow. As you read it, consider whether you favor publication and public circulation of such a directory, in whole or in part, whether the bar should sponsor similar directories, whether it should require, if it can, all lawyers to cooperate in their publication and even to standardize such directories and forbid all advertising except the publication of information in the directory in the form in which it is published.

The Questionnaire first asks some descriptive questions, including questions about evening office hours, numbers and status of associated lawyers and support personnel, foreign language capability, education and honors, continuing legal education activities, books and articles published, outside law-related work and positions in profit or non-profit organizations. It then asks the following questions.

Excerpts from Questionnaire and Guide*

Description of Practice

15. Estimate the percentage of time you spend, and your firm spends, handling matters for the following types of clients:

	(You)	*(Firm)*
Individuals	___	___
Small Businesses	___	___
Large Businesses	___	___
Institutions (e.g., schools, unions)	___	___
Total	100%	100%

16. Estimate the percentage of time you spend, and your firm spends, handling matters in the following categories:

	(You)	*(Firm)*
Administrative Law	___	___
Admiralty Law	___	___
Consumer Law (e.g., credit, defective goods)	___	___
Criminal Law	___	___
Family Law	___	___
General Corporate	___	___
Labor Law — for management	___	___
Labor Law — for union (include all employee matters)	___	___
Landlord-Tenant — for landlord	___	___
Landlord-Tenant — for tenant	___	___
Military and Selective Service	___	___
Patent, Trademark or Copyright Law	___	___
Personal injury — for defendant	___	___
Personal injury — for plaintiff	___	___
Real estate — for developer	___	___
Real estate — for purchaser	___	___
Real estate — for seller	___	___

*The Questionnaire and Guide were prepared by Marsha N. Cohen and Peter H. Schuck, lawyers for Consumers Union, and are reprinted with permission.

Taxation _____ _____
Wills, Trusts, and estates/probate _____ _____
Workmen's compensation — for employee _____ _____
Workmen's compensation — for employer (or _____ _____
   insurance company)
Other (Specify) _____
                                   Total   100%   100%

17. Do you limit your practice to one or more of the above categories? _____ Yes _____ No If yes, specify _____ Does your firm limit its practice to one or more of the above categories? _____ Yes _____ No If yes, specify _____

Fees, Billing, and Client Relations

18. Is it your policy to discuss fees with the potential client at the initial interview? _____ Yes _____ No Do you present an estimate at the initial interview? _____ Yes _____ No If you do present an estimate, is it in writing? _____ Yes _____ No

19. a. Do you customarily charge a fee for an initial consultation when no further services are rendered to the client on the matter? _____ Yes _____ No If yes, how much? $_____

   b. What is the average time you allot for an interview with a client on a new matter? _____

20. Do you ever require a "retainer" from an individual client? _____ Yes _____ No If yes, specify the types of cases or the circumstances in which a retainer is required _____

21. a. What is the hourly billing charge for your service? $_____

   b. If you use law clerks or paralegal personnel on a case, what do you charge your clients per hour for their service? $_____

22. Do you itemize your bills? _____ Yes _____ No

23. How do you handle client complaints about billing? (Check all that are applicable.)

_____ Discuss with clients individually
_____ Refer to bookkeeper, office manager, or secretary
_____ Other (specify) _____

24. How do you handle other client complaints? (Check all that are applicable.)

_____ Discuss with clients individually
_____ Refer to bar association
_____ Other (specify) _____

25. How do you handle unpaid accounts? (Check all that are applicable.)

_____ Reminder notices
_____ Small claims court
_____ Collection agency
_____ Other (specify) _____

Average Fees for Common Legal Representations
Note the average fee you charge for representing a client in the following legal matters. If you do not handle certain classes of cases, omit fees. (If you charge a percentage rather than a flat rate for any of the legal matters listed, note the percentage.)
    26. *Adoption* (uncontested and without complications)
        a. With interlocutory order $_____
        b. Without interlocutory order $_____
    27. *Change of Name* $_____
    28. *Corporations.* Fee for preparing incorporation papers for a small business or organization $_____
    29. *Divorce*
        a. Representation of complainant, uncontested divorce $_____
        b. Representation of respondent, uncontested divorce $_____
    30. *Individual Bankruptcy* $_____
    31. *Personal Injury (Representation of Plaintiff).* Do you generally accept these cases on a contingent fee basis? _____ Yes _____ No If yes, what percentage of the award is the contingent fee in the following circumstances:
        a. When the case is settled before filing a complaint _____%
        b. When the case is settled after filing a complaint but before the selection of a jury _____%
        c. When the case goes to trial _____%
        d. When the case is appealed _____%
    32. *Real Estate.* Closing and settlement on single-family house, including title examination (60-years), certificate of title, and preparation of papers. $_____
    33. *Traffic Court.* Defense of charge involving potential loss of license, confinement, or both.
        Settled without trial $_____
        Full trial $_____
    34. *Wills and Probate.*
        a. Fee for will of basic type, not including future interests, trusts, or fiduciary powers (assuming minor children and ownership of a home and no other significant assets)
            For one person $_____
            For husband and wife $_____
        b. Fee for probating the type of will described above, assuming no estate or inheritance tax liability $_____

GUIDE TO LAWYERS' QUESTIONNAIRE . . .

DESCRIPTION OF PRACTICE

The profile of a firm's practice, including the type of client served and the type of legal matters handled, will often differ from that of an individual attorney in the firm. For example, a particular attorney may practice tax law almost exclusively, while the firm as a whole may also handle general corporate cases and labor law. For that reason, the responses of the firm as a whole to the questions in this section will appear under the firm listing as "firm profile." The responses of an individual attorney will appear under the name of the individual lawyer.

15. Most attorneys are general practitioners. But some firms represent primarily businesses; they may choose not to accept individual clients, except as a courtesy.

16. Attorneys are trained as generalists to analyze and deal with all types of legal problems. Virginia does not certify any attorney as a specialist (though certain attorneys may be licensed to practice only patent, trademark, copyright, and unfair competition cases under a narrow reciprocity agreement with the United States Patent Office).

An attorney who spends a great deal of time on legal matters similar to yours will bring experience to your problem. On the other hand, an attorney to whom your problem is relatively novel may handle it with extra interest and enthusiasm. Most attorneys are capable of handling most problems. If your case is extremely unique or complex, your attorney may refer you to a specialist in the field. . . .

FEES, BILLING, AND CLIENT RELATIONS

18. Fees should be discussed at the initial interview, and the client should ask for a written estimate. If the attorney does not bring up the subject, the client should be prepared to do so. Ask if there are alternative courses of legal action available, and the potential costs of pursuing each one.

19. Just as preventive medicine is important for continued good health, "preventive" legal consultation may be vital to your continued legal well-being. If you are faced, for example, with a major decision with possible legal ramifications, you would be wise to seek legal advice *before* a crisis arises, so that your rights will be protected. An "initial consultation" may be all that is necessary. At that session, the attorney will attempt to elicit the main facts about your problem and draw tentative conclusions about possible courses of action. This first interview is likely to last approximately as long as the attorney notes in this answer. The attorney may advise that legal action is premature or unnecessary, in which case you will be billed only the fee noted in this answer. (Some attorneys may not charge at all if no further action is taken.) If further

action is taken, you will be billed the attorney's regular fee for the type of legal work involved, or an hourly fee, which may include a charge for the initial visit. . . .

21. Law firms generally charge different hourly rates for different members of the firm. If you use a senior partner as your attorney, you will be billed at a higher rate than if you use a new associate. The sum quoted in the answer to this question is the fee for the named attorney services only.

Law clerks or paralegal personnel often assist an attorney on a case. Because they lack the background and experience of a practicing attorney, the hourly charge for their services should be lower.

22. Attorneys generally keep detailed records of the time they spend on each case doing research, writing, consulting with the client, making telephone calls, court work and so forth. You will be charged per hour of their time for those tasks. You will also be required to pay court costs (fees assessed for the filing of various legal documents, jury fees, costs of reporters and transcripts). In addition, you may have to reimburse your attorney for photocopying, printing charges, and telephone toll charges in connection with your case.

Because of all the considerations that go into making up your bill, an itemization of services will help you to understand it better, and to figure out if you are being unfairly charged.

AVERAGE FEES FOR COMMON LEGAL REPRESENTATIONS

Some attorneys may charge a flat rate for a certain type of legal work. The fees quoted in this section of the questionnaire are *average* figures charged for a specific type of representation. All the examples chosen are common legal problems of individuals, and all are for uncomplicated situations. Complications, which may or may not be foreseen by the attorney at the initial interview, can raise the fee considerably.

There is no simple way to determine whether Attorney X's $500 divorce will be more or less appropriate for a particular individual than Attorney Y's $200 divorce. The more expensive divorce may include more services, such as extensive financial planning aid. Or the difference in fees may result from the different experience levels of the two attorneys, or differences in overhead. Or Attorney Y's divorce may simply be a better buy. Because of those various possibilities, comparison shopping on the basis of price alone could be a serious mistake. Consumers should ask questions about fees to learn *why* one attorney's fees are higher than another. They will then be in a better position to make a choice. . . .

Think about the questionnaire, both from the point of view of the consumer of legal services and from the point of view of the lawyer answering it. How useful would the information be to someone looking for a lawyer? What kind of misuse of information is possible? Note that the Lawyers' Directory does not follow the typical Consumers Union format, which rates and compares the products it tests. Is that a wise or unwise decision? If you were asking a lawyer friend to recommend a lawyer for you, what information would you want? Is it feasible to find out and report that information to the public, assuming it is different from what is sought on the questionnaire?

As a lawyer answering this questionnaire, and assuming that there were no ethical inhibition against answering it, would you, could you, answer all the questions? What kinds of qualifications and explanations would be appropriate? Referring back to the earlier fee materials, if your fees varied for a variety of reasons depending upon the circumstances of each situation, how would you answer the questions about fees? Do you think that such an answer would make you "look bad"? What kinds of answers might lawyers give that would make them "look good"? Should there be some controls over the kinds of answers that a lawyer might properly give?

This Directory produced a lengthy lawsuit. Consumers Union contended that the Virginia State Bar had refused to authorize cooperation by lawyers with the Consumers Union endeavor, apparently because of verbal assurance from the ABA that it would not approve the Directory pursuant to DR 2-102(A)(6). Consumers Union sued the Virginia Supreme Court, the State Bar and various officers, and the ABA, contending that they had violated its First Amendment right to collect and disseminate information and consumers' First Amendment rights to receive it. After the *Bates* case, p. 492, a permanent injunction was entered against the enforcement of the advertising prohibitions then contained in DR 2-102(A)(6) against it. See Supreme Court of Virginia v. Consumers Union, 446 U.S. 719 (1980). (For the fee aspect of this case, see p. 498.)

NOTE: A Few Generalities

There are two aspects to the profession's rules governing advertising and solicitation. The first is the rules' efforts to control lawyers themselves and the methods by which they get business. The second is the rules' impact on the ability of the general populace to obtain legal services and to select a particular lawyer. This chapter does not purport to cover the myriad situations involving professional concern with advertising and solicitation by lawyers. It will make a few general observations and then consider some of the controversial aspects of the present rules.

The rules relating to advertising and solicitation used to be what many people thought about when the subject of ethics was mentioned. They were the stereotype of the perceived pettiness and self-protective nature of the profession's rules. And there was some truth to that view. Passing judgment on the size of business cards, the propriety of sending Christmas cards to clients, and the like was grist for the mills of many ethics committees. Sometimes, a novel problem surfaced and a committee decided whether a news story about a law firm and the unusual office building it has built, see State ex rel. Florida Bar v. Nichols, 151 So. 2d 257 (Fla. 1963), or the laudatory article in Life Magazine in which the law firm cooperated, In re Connelly, 18 App. Div. 2d 466, 240 N.Y.S.2d 126 (1st Dept. 1963), or a lawyer's endorsement of a brand of Scotch, Belli v. State Bar of California, 10 Cal. 3d 824, 519 P.2d 575 (1974), constituted a violation of the professional rules.

The triviality of some of the matters covered by the rules, however, should not obscure the serious professional concern that motivated them. They reflect in part a view of the practice of law as a profession, with no place for extravagant, misleading, deceptive, or outright false claims, and with no place for sensational methods of drawing attention to oneself.

The ideal was that business came to the lawyer and not vice versa. The rules prohibiting lawyers from engaging in activities that might draw attention to themselves have, however, never been absolute. Lawyers were never required to be hermits and to refrain from all activities that might draw attention to themselves. They traditionally engaged in all sorts of public and private community activities that were good for their business as well as for their community. But the policy considerations favoring involvement in this sort of activity so outweighed its mercenary aspects that rules against solicitation and advertising were not invoked against such activities, and lawyers were not required to forswear practical reasons for engaging in them. Thus in codifying the generally accepted prohibitions the drafters of the Model Code accepted the distinction between getting business through self-praise and through doing good works.

These rules, however, came under attack more and more from a variety of quarters. Justice Stewart of the Supreme Court made some remarks at the 1975 meeting of the ABA that instantly became quite controversial.* He first expressed the view that Goldfarb (p. 475, Note 7) "says that lawyers are primarily economic actors, men and women who perform a service, for profit. . . . And the members of the public, the consumers of lawyers, are best served if there is true competition among lawyers for their patronage." He then went on to make some more general remarks about the nature of a lawyer's professional responsibility:

---

*Stewart, Professional Ethics for the Business Lawyer: The Morals of the Market Place, 31 Bus. Law. 463, 466-467 (1975).

In this view of the legal profession, what is left for a code of professional responsibility for the business lawyer? Are professional ethics now to be no more elevated than the standards of a Better Business Bureau? Are we now to exalt the morals of the market place into a model of professional respectability? These are fundamental and difficult questions, but I submit that affirmative answers to them, rhetoric aside, may not be so calamitous as might be supposed.

It goes without saying, of course, that every lawyer has a duty to keep the confidences of his client, that every lawyer in whom is confided a trust must conduct himself as a trustee, that every lawyer should keep his word and deal honorably in all his associations. And it certainly is the duty of every lawyer, and of every association of lawyers, to denounce and to eliminate from our midst those who have betrayed our profession for their own ugly or dishonest purposes.

But beyond these and a few other self-evident precepts of decency and common sense, a good case can be made, I think, for the proposition that the ethics of the business lawyer are indeed, and perhaps should be, no more than the morals of the market place. The first rule for a business lawyer is to provide his total ability and effort to his client. But is this an ethical standard, or no more than a response to the economic forces of the market place? After all, the first rule in *any* occupation is to be competent. The business lawyer is in the business of providing legal advice for a businessman. If he performs that job with diligence, conscientiousness, and knowledgeable ability, his client will reap the benefits and will reward him accordingly. If not, . . . the lawyer will find his client less than eager to retain indefinitely a professional adviser who habitually directs him down the wrong path.

In short, it can fairly be argued that many aspects of what we call "ethics" are not really ethics at all, but are merely corollaries of the axiom of the better mousetrap, an axiom that is itself derived from enlightened self-interest.

While one may engage in endless argument about what Justice Stewart meant to say, his remarks appear to deemphasize the special ideals that have been associated with the most service-oriented concept of professionalism.

A second attack on the rules came from civil libertarians who focused on the effect of the restrictions on lawyers' speech and the public's access to information. They relied on the quartet of legal services cases discussed in the next chapter, (pp. 593-595) together with *Goldfarb* (p. 475, Note 7) and Bigelow v. Virginia, 421 U.S. 809 (1975) (holding unconstitutional a Virginia statute as applied to forbid advertising of a legal New York abortion referral service in a Virginia newspaper).

A third line of attack focused primarily on the effect of the rules on informed access by the public to legal services. It pointed to the Code of Professional Responsibility itself, which notes that changed conditions "have seriously restricted the traditional selection process" because of the disappearance of the former knowledge that potential clients had of the reputation of local lawyers for competence and integrity. (See EC 2-6, 2-7, and 2-8). But beyond noting that the selection is often the result of recommendation by third parties and that it should be disinterested and informed, the Model Code, and the Model Rules as well, offer very little in the way of new means for the client to acquire the information that it assumes was formerly available.

At a time when there was a great deal of ferment for change of the advertising and solicitation rules, the Supreme Court lifted the discussion to the level of constitutional law, deciding a whole series of cases that has put severe limits on the ability of the states to regulate advertising and, to a much lesser extent (for the time being), solicitation.

The first case was Bates & O'Steen v. State Bar of Arizona, 433 U.S. 350 (1977). It involved two lawyers who were disciplined for placing the newspaper advertisement shown in Figure 8-1 offering "legal services at very reasonable fees," listing fees for certain services.

The discipline was based on the admitted violation of a disciplinary rule that forbade newspaper or other media advertising by lawyers. The Supreme Court, 5-4, held that the First Amendment prohibited blanket suppression of advertising in general and this advertisement in particular. It rejected arguments in support of the rule that were based on an adverse effect on professionalism; the inherently misleading nature of lawyer advertising; the adverse effect on the administration of justice; the undesirable economic effects of advertising; and the adverse effect of advertising on the quality of services rendered. The court went on to note that it was dealing only with suppression of advertising; states were free to regulate, especially with respect to advertisements likely to mislead.

The dissenters disagreed very strongly with the Court's analysis, arguing that it had unnecessarily weakened the supervisory authority of the courts and the states over "officers of the court." It believed that most advertising of legal services was susceptible of being seriously misleading and that enforcement of rules based on deception was going to be very difficult.

The response of the ABA was to recommend two types of new advertising rules, Proposal A, called a "regulatory" approach, and Proposal B, called a "directive" approach. The regulatory approach tells lawyers what specific items may be advertised and prohibits advertising anything else. A lawyer wishing to advertise an unlisted item of information could apply to the appropriate agency for approval. The directive approach states that a lawyer may advertise in any way that is not "false, fraudulent, misleading or deceptive" and then goes on to specify what falls within those terms. The ABA recommended Proposal A to the states but transmitted both plans. Although one plan tells lawyers what they may do and the other tells them what they may not do, the plans tend to

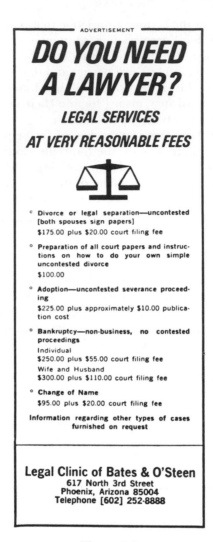

Figure 8-1

merge into one another because of their great specificity. The Ethical Considerations and Disciplinary Rules of Canon 2 as revised by Proposal A are now a portion of the "official" version of the Code of Professional Responsibility as recommended by the ABA. (Proposal B may be found in 46 U.S.L.W. 9 (Aug. 23, 1977).)

Many states refused to adopt either Proposal A or B. Some added additional provisions to Proposal A, and some subtracted permitted items from Proposal A. Several adopted a rule that permitted all advertising except that which was fraudulent, deceptive, or misleading. That was substantially the path taken in the various subdivisions of Model Rule 7.

The debate over these proposals has focused on two issues. First, what is the purpose of advertising legal services? Is it to safeguard the rights of lawyers and others to provide information about legal services and hence to safeguard consumers' rights to receive that information? That view is grounded both in "robust" first amendment and in "robust" competitive antitrust theories. Or is it to ensure that members of the public receive the most useful information to help them select lawyers? That view is grounded in a "functional" view of the First Amendment and of professional rules.

In In re R.M.J., 455 U.S. 191 (1982), the Supreme Court reversed disciplinary action based on Missouri's much less permissive version of Proposal A and on DR 2-102(A)(2)'s limitation of the classes of people to whom announcement cards may be mailed. Discipline was sought to be imposed because the lawyer had advertised membership in the bars of other states and the Supreme Court of the United States and because he had described fields in which he practiced by using different descriptions from those prescribed. The authority of the case is uncertain in view of the failure of the Missouri Supreme Court to justify its rules or explain the basis for its decision. Yet the Court did state that the lawyer's "speech" was neither misleading nor inherently misleading, nor did the state offer any other interest to justify its absolute prohibition.

Shortly after it decided the *Bates* case, the Supreme Court turned its attention to the constitutional aspects of the profession's solicitation rules in the following two opinions. "Solicitation" is that subdivision of advertising where the lawyer seeks business from specific persons on an individualized basis, either in person or by telephone or mail.

OHRALIK v. OHIO STATE BAR ASSOCIATION
436 U.S. 447 (1978)

Mr. Justice POWELL delivered the opinion of the Court. . . .

I

Appellant, a member of the Ohio Bar, lives in Montville, Ohio. Until recently he practiced law in Montville and Cleveland. On February 13, 1974, while picking up his mail at the Montville Post Office, appellant learned from the postmaster's brother about an automobile accident that had taken place on February 2 in which Carol McClintock, a young woman with whom appellant was casually acquainted, had been injured. Appellant made a telephone call to Ms. McClintock's parents, who informed him that their daughter was in the hospital. Appellant suggested that he might visit Carol in the hospital. Mrs. McClintock assented to the idea, but requested that appellant first stop by at her home.

During appellant's visit with the McClintocks, they explained that their daughter had been driving the family automobile on a local road when she was hit by an uninsured motorist. Both Carol and her passenger, Wanda Lou Holbert, were injured and hospitalized. In response to the McClintocks' expression of apprehension that they might be sued by Holbert, appellant explained that Ohio's guest statute would preclude such a suit. When appellant suggested to the McClintocks that they hire a lawyer, Mrs. McClintock retorted that such a decision would be up to Carol, who was 18 years old and would be the beneficiary of a successful claim.

Appellant proceeded to the hospital, where he found Carol lying in traction in her room. After a brief conversation about her condition,[1] appellant told Carol he would represent her and asked her to sign an agreement. Carol said she would have to discuss the matter with her parents. She did not sign the agreement, but asked appellant to have her parents come to see her.[2] Appellant also attempted to see Wanda Lou Holbert, but learned that she had just been released from the hospital. . . . He then departed for another visit with the McClintocks.

On his way appellant detoured to the scene of the accident, where he took a set of photographs. He also picked up a tape recorder, which he concealed under his raincoat before arriving at the McClintocks' residence. Once there, he re-examined their automobile insurance policy, discussed with them the law applicable to passengers, and explained the consequences of the fact that the driver who struck Carol's car was an uninsured motorist. Appellant discovered that the McClintocks' insurance policy would provide benefits of up to $12,500 each for Carol and Wanda Lou under an uninsured motorist clause. Mrs. McClintock acknowledged that both Carol and Wanda Lou could sue for their injuries, but recounted to appellant that "Wanda swore up and down she would not do it." The McClintocks also told appellant that Carol had phoned to say that appellant could "go ahead" with her representation. Two days later appellant returned to Carol's hospital room to have her sign a contract, which provided that he would receive one-third of her recovery.

In the meantime, appellant obtained Wanda Lou's name and address from the McClintocks after telling them he wanted to ask her some questions about the accident. He then visited Wanda Lou at her home, without having been invited. He again concealed his tape recorder and

---

1. Carol also mentioned that one of the hospital administrators was urging a lawyer upon her. According to his own testimony, appellant replied: "Yes, this certainly is a case that would entice a lawyer. That would interest him a great deal."

2. Despite the fact that appellant maintains that he did not secure an agreement to represent Carol while he was at the hospital, he waited for an opportunity when no visitors were present and then took photographs of Carol in traction.

recorded most of the conversation with Wanda Lou.[3] After a brief, unproductive inquiry about the facts of the accident, appellant told Wanda Lou that he was representing Carol and that he had a "little tip" for Wanda Lou: The McClintocks' insurance policy contained an uninsured motorist clause which might provide her with a recovery of up to $12,500. The young woman, who was 18 years of age and not a high school graduate at the time, replied to the appellant's query about whether she was going to file a claim by stating that she really did not understand what was going on. Appellant offered to represent her, also, for a contingent fee of one-third of any recovery, and Wanda Lou stated "O.K."[4]

Wanda's mother attempted to repudiate her daughter's oral assent the following day, when appellant called on the telephone to speak to Wanda. Mrs. Holbert informed appellant that she and her daughter did not want to sue anyone or to have appellant represent them, and that if they decided to sue they would consult their own lawyer. Appellant insisted that Wanda had entered into a binding agreement. A month later Wanda confirmed in writing that she wanted neither to sue nor to be represented by appellant. She requested that appellant notify the insurance company that he was not her lawyer, as the company would not release a check to her until he did so.[5] Carol also eventually discharged appellant. Although another lawyer represented her in concluding a settlement with the insurance company, she paid appellant one-third of her recovery[6] in settlement of his lawsuit against her for breach of contract.[7]

---

3. Appellant maintains that the tape is a complete reproduction of everything that was said at the Holbert home. Wanda Lou testified that the tape does not contain appellant's introductory remarks to her about his identity as a lawyer, his agreement to represent Carol McClintock, and his availability and willingness to represent Wanda Lou as well. Appellant disputed Wanda Lou's testimony but agreed that he did not activate the recorder until he had been admitted to the Holbert home and was seated in the living room with Wanda Lou.

4. Appellant told Wanda that she should indicate assent by stating, "Okay," which she did. Appellant later testified: "I would say that most of my clients have essentially that much of a communication. . . . I think most of my clients, that's the way I practice law."

In explaining the contingency fee arrangement, appellant told Wanda Lou that his representation would not "cost [her] anything" because she would receive two-thirds of the recovery if appellant were successful in representing her but would not "have to pay [him] anything" otherwise.

5. The insurance company was willing to pay Wanda Lou for her injuries but would not release the check while appellant claimed, and Wanda Lou denied, that he represented her. Before appellant would "disavow further interest and claim" in Wanda Lou's recovery, he insisted by letter that Wanda Lou first pay him the sum of $2,466.66, which represented one-third of his "conservative" estimate of the worth of her claim.

6. Carol recovered the full $12,500 and paid appellant $4,166.66. She testified that she paid the second lawyer $900 as compensation for his services.

7. Appellant represented to the Board of Commissioners at the disciplinary hearing that he would abandon his claim against Wanda Lou Holbert because "the rules say that if a contract has its origin in a controversy, that an ethical question can arise." Yet in fact appellant filed suit against Wanda for $2,466.66 after the disciplinary hearing.

Both Carol McClintock and Wanda Lou Holbert filed complaints against appellant with the Grievance Committee of the Geauga County Bar Association. The County Bar Association filed a formal complaint with the Board of Commissioners on Grievance and Discipline of the Supreme Court of Ohio.[8] After a hearing, the Board found that appellant had violated Disciplinary Rules (DR) 2-103(A) and 2-104(A) of the Ohio Code of Professional Responsibility. The Board rejected appellant's defense that his conduct was protected under the First and Fourteenth Amendments. The Supreme Court of Ohio adopted the findings of the Board,[10] reiterated that appellant's conduct was not constitutionally protected, and increased the sanction of a public reprimand recommended by the Board to indefinite suspension.

The decision in *Bates* was handed down after the conclusion of proceedings in the Ohio Supreme Court. We noted probable jurisdiction in this case to consider the scope of protection of a form of commercial speech, and an aspect of the State's authority to regulate and discipline members of the bar, not considered in *Bates*. 433 U.S. 350, 97 S. Ct. 2691, 53 L. Ed. 2d 810 (1977). We now affirm the judgment of the Supreme Court of Ohio.

II

The solicitation of business by a lawyer through direct, in-person communication with the prospective client has long been viewed as inconsistent with the profession's ideal of the attorney-client relationship and as posing a significant potential for harm to the prospective client. It has been proscribed by the organized Bar for many years. . . . The balance struck in *Bates* does not predetermine the outcome in this case. The entitlement of in-person solicitation of clients to the protection of the First Amendment differs from that of the kind of advertising approved in *Bates*, as does the strength of the State's countervailing interest in prohibition.

Albert Ohralik v. Wanda Lou Holbert, Case No. 76-CV-F-66, filed February 2, 1976, Chardon Municipal Court, Geauga County, Ohio. Appellant dismissed that suit with prejudice on January 27, 1977, after the decision of the Supreme Court of Ohio had been filed.

8. The Board of Commissioners is an agent of the Supreme Court of Ohio. Counsel for appellee stated at oral argument that the Board has "no connection with the Ohio State Bar Association whatsoever."

10. The Board found that Carol and Wanda Lou "were, if anything, casual acquaintances" of appellant; that appellant initiated the contact with Carol and obtained her consent to handle her claim; that he advised Wanda Lou that he represented Carol, had a "tip" for Wanda, and was prepared to represent her, too. The Board also found that appellant would not abide by Mrs. Holbert's request to leave Wanda alone, that both young women attempted to discharge appellant, and that appellant sued Carol McClintock.

A

Appellant contends that his solicitation of the two young women as clients is indistinguishable, for purposes of constitutional analysis, from the advertisement in *Bates*. Like that advertisement, his meetings with the prospective clients apprised them of their legal rights and of the availability of a lawyer to pursue their claims. According to appellant, such conduct is "presumptively an exercise of his free speech rights" which cannot be curtailed in the absence of proof that it actually caused a specific harm that the State has a compelling interest in preventing. But in-person solicitation of professional employment by a lawyer does not stand on a par with truthful advertising about the availability and terms of routine legal services, let alone with forms of speech more traditionally within the concern of the First Amendment.

Expression concerning purely commercial transactions has come within the ambit of the Amendment's protection only recently. In rejecting the notion that such speech "is wholly outside the protection of the First Amendment," Virginia Pharmacy, 425 U.S. [748], at 761, we were careful not to hold "that it is wholly undifferentiable from other forms" of speech. Id., at 771 n.24. We have not discarded the "common-sense" distinction between speech proposing a commercial transaction, which occurs in an area traditionally subject to government regulation, and other varieties of speech. Ibid. To require a parity of constitutional protection for commercial and noncommercial speech alike could invite dilution, simply by a leveling process, of the force of the Amendment's guarantee with respect to the latter kind of speech. Rather than subject the First Amendment to such a devitalization, we instead have afforded commercial speech a limited measure of protection, commensurate with its subordinate position in the scale of First Amendment values, while allowing modes of regulation that might be impermissible in the realm of noncommercial expression. . . .

In-person solicitation by a lawyer of remunerative employment is a business transaction in which speech is an essential but subordinate component. While this does not remove the speech from the protection of the First Amendment, as was held in *Bates* and *Virginia Pharmacy*, it lowers the level of appropriate judicial scrutiny.

As applied in this case, the disciplinary rules are said to have limited the communication of two kinds of information. First, appellant's solicitation imparted to Carol McClintock and Wanda Lou Holbert certain information about his availability and the terms of his proposed legal services. In this respect, in-person solicitation serves much the same function as the advertisement at issue in *Bates*. But there are significant differences as well. Unlike a public advertisement, which simply provides information and leaves the recipient free to act upon it or not, in-person solicitation may exert pressure and often demands an immediate response, without providing an opportunity for comparison or reflection.. The aim and effect of in-person solicitation may be to provide a one-sided presentation and to encourage speedy and perhaps uninformed decisionmaking; there is no opportunity for intervention or countereducation by agencies of the Bar, supervisory authorities, or persons close to the solicited individual. The admonition that "the fitting remedy for evil counsels is good ones" is of little value when the circumstances provide no opportunity for any remedy at all. In-person solicitation is as likely as not to discourage persons needing counsel from engaging in a critical comparison of the "availability, nature, and prices" of legal services, cf. *Bates,* supra, 433 U.S. at 364, 97 S. Ct. at 2699; it actually may disserve the individual and societal interest, identified in *Bates,* in facilitating "informed and reliable decisionmaking." Ibid.

It also is argued that in-person solicitation may provide the solicited individual with information about his or her legal rights and remedies. In this case, appellant gave Wanda Lou a "tip" about the prospect of recovery based on the uninsured motorist clause in the McClintocks' insurance policy, and he explained that clause and Ohio's guest statute to Carol McClintock's parents. But neither of the disciplinary rules here at issue prohibited appellant from communicating information to these young women about their legal rights and the prospects of obtaining a monetary recovery, or from recommending that they obtain counsel. DR 2-104(A) merely prohibited him from using the information as bait with which to obtain an agreement to represent them for a fee. The rule does not prohibit a lawyer from giving unsolicited legal advice; it proscribes the acceptance of employment resulting from such advice.

Appellant does not contend, and on the facts of this case could not contend, that his approaches to the two young women involved political expression or an exercise of associational freedom, "employ[ing] constitutionally privileged means of expression to secure constitutionally guaranteed civil rights." NAACP v. Button, 371 U.S. 415, 442 (1963); see In re Primus [p. 502]. Nor can he compare his solicitation to the mutual assistance in asserting legal rights that was at issue in United Transportation Union v. Michigan Bar, Mine Workers v. Illinois Bar Assn., and Railroad Trainmen v. Virginia Bar, [pp. 593-595]. A lawyer's procurement of remunerative employment is a subject only marginally affected with First Amendment concerns. It falls within the State's proper sphere of economic and professional regulation. . . . While entitled to some constitutional protection, appellant's conduct is subject to regulation in furtherance of important state interests.

B

The state interests implicated in this case are particularly strong. In addition to its general interest in protecting consumers and regulating commercial transactions, the State bears a special responsibility for maintaining standards among members of the licensed professions. . . . "The interest of the States in regulating lawyers is especially great since lawyers are essential to the primary governmental function of administering justice, and have historically been 'officers of the courts.'" Goldfarb v. Virginia State Bar, [p. 475, Note 7]. While lawyers act in part as "self-employed businessmen," they also act "as trusted agents of their clients, and as assistants to the court in search of a just solution to disputes." Cohen v. Hurley, 366 U.S. 117 (1961).

As is true with respect to advertising, . . . it appears that the ban on solicitation by lawyers originated as a rule of professional etiquette rather than as a strictly ethical rule. See H. Drinker, Legal Ethics 210-211, and n.3 (1953). . . . But the fact that the original motivation behind the ban on solicitation today might be considered an insufficient justification for its perpetuation does not detract from the force of the other interests the ban continues to serve. . . . While the Court in *Bates* determined that truthful, restrained advertising of the prices of "routine" legal services would not have an adverse effect on the professionalism of lawyers, this was only because it found "the postulated connection between advertising and the erosion of *true professionalism* to be severely strained." 433 U.S., at 368. The *Bates* Court did not question a State's interest in maintaining high standards among licensed professionals. Indeed, to the extent that the ethical standards of lawyers are linked to the service and protection of clients, they do further the goals of "true professionalism."

The substantive evils of solicitation have been stated over the years in sweeping terms: stirring up litigation, assertion of fraudulent claims, debasing the legal profession, and potential harm to the solicited client in the form of overreaching, overcharging, underrepresentation, and misrepresentation. The American Bar Association, as amicus curiae, defends the rule against solicitation primarily on three broad grounds: It is said that the prohibitions embodied in Disciplinary Rules 2-103(A) and 2-104(A) serve to reduce the likelihood of overreaching and the exertion of undue influence on lay persons; to protect the privacy of individuals; and to avoid situations where the lawyer's exercise of judgment on behalf of the client will be clouded by his own pecuniary self-interest.

We need not discuss or evaluate each of these interests in detail as appellant has conceded that the State has a legitimate and indeed "compelling" interest in preventing those aspects of solicitation that involve fraud, undue influence, intimidation, overreaching, and other forms of "vexatious conduct." We agree that protection of the public from these aspects of solicitation is a legitimate and important state interest.

III

Appellant's concession that strong state interests justify regulation to prevent the evils he enumerates would end this case but for his insistence that none of those evils was found to be present in his acts of solicitation.

He challenges what he characterizes as the "indiscriminate application" of the rules to him and thus attacks the validity of DR 2-103(A) and DR 2-104(A) not facially, but as applied to his acts of solicitation. And because no allegations or findings were made of the specific wrongs appellant concedes would justify disciplinary action, appellant terms his solicitation "pure," meaning "soliciting and obtaining agreements from Carol McClintock and Wanda Lou Holbert to represent each of them," without more. Appellant therefore argues that we must decide whether a State may discipline him for solicitation per se without offending the First and Fourteenth Amendments. . . .

[A]ppellant errs in assuming that the constitutional validity of the judgment below depends on proof that his conduct constituted actual overreaching or inflicted some specific injury on Wanda Holbert or Carol McClintock. His assumption flows from the premise that nothing less than actual proven harm to the solicited individual would be a sufficiently important state interest to justify disciplining the attorney who solicits employment in person for pecuniary gain.

Appellant's argument misconceives the nature of the State's interest. The rules prohibiting solicitation are prophylactic measures whose objective is the prevention of harm before it occurs. The rules were applied in this case to discipline a lawyer for soliciting employment for pecuniary gain under circumstances likely to result in the adverse consequences the State seeks to avert. In such a situation, which is inherently conducive to overreaching and other forms of misconduct, the State has a strong interest in adopting and enforcing rules of conduct designed to protect the public from harmful solicitation by lawyers whom it has licensed.

The State's perception of the potential for harm in circumstances such as those presented in this case is well-founded. The detrimental aspects of face-to-face selling even of ordinary consumer products have been recognized and addressed by the Federal Trade Commission, and it hardly need be said that the potential for overreaching is significantly greater when a lawyer, a professional trained in the art of persuasion, personally solicits an unsophisticated, injured, or distressed lay person. Such an individual may place his or her trust in a lawyer, regardless of the latter's qualifications or the individual's actual need for legal representation, simply in response to persuasion under circumstances conducive to uninformed acquiescence. Although it is argued that personal solicitation is valuable because it may apprise a victim of misfortune of his or her legal rights, the very plight of that person not only makes him or her more vulnerable to influence but also may make advice all the more intrusive. Thus, under these adverse conditions the overtures of an uninvited lawyer may distress the solicited individual simply because of their obtrusiveness and the invasion of the individual's privacy, even when no other harm materializes. Under such circumstances, it is not unreasonable for the State to presume that in-person solicitation by lawyers more often than not will be injurious to the person solicited.

The efficacy of the State's effort to prevent such harm to prospective clients would be substantially diminished if, having proved a solicitation in circumstances like those of this case, the State were required in addition to prove actual injury. Unlike the advertising in *Bates*, in-person solicitation is not visible or otherwise open to public scrutiny. Often there is no witness other than the lawyer and the lay person whom he has solicited, rendering it difficult or impossible to obtain reliable proof of what actually took place. This would be especially true if the lay person were so distressed at the time of the solicitation that he or she could not recall specific details at a later date. If appellant's view were sustained, in-person solicitation would be virtually immune to effective oversight and regulation by the State or by the legal profession, in contravention of the State's strong interest in regulating members of the Bar in an effective, objective, and self-enforcing manner. It therefore is not unreasonable, or violative of the Constitution, for a State to respond with what in effect is a prophylactic rule.

On the basis of the undisputed facts of record, we conclude that the disciplinary rules constitutionally could be applied to appellant. He approached two young accident victims at a time when they were especially incapable of making informed judgments or of assessing and protecting their own interests. He solicited Carol McClintock in a hospital room where she lay in traction and sought out Wanda Lou Holbert on the day she came home from the hospital, knowing from his prior inquiries that she had just been released. Appellant urged his services upon the young women and used the information he had obtained from the McClintocks, and the fact of his agreement with Carol, to induce Wanda to say "O.K." in response to his solicitation. He employed a concealed tape recorder, seemingly to insure that he would have evidence of Wanda's oral assent to the representation. He emphasized that his fee would come out of the recovery, thereby tempting the young women with what sounded like a cost-free and therefore irresistible offer. He refused to withdraw when Mrs. Holbert requested him to do so only a day after the initial meeting between appellant and Wanda Lou and continued to represent himself to the insurance company as Wanda Holbert's lawyer.

The court below did not hold that these or other facts were proof of actual harm to Wanda Holbert or Carol McClintock but rested on the conclusion that appellant had engaged in the general misconduct proscribed by the disciplinary rules. Under our view of the State's interest in averting harm by prohibiting solicitation in circumstances where it is likely to occur, the absence of explicit proof or findings of harm or injury is immaterial. The facts in this case present a striking example of the potential for overreaching that is inherent in a lawyer's in-person solicitation of professional employment. They also demonstrate the need for prophylactic regulation in furtherance of the State's interest in protecting the lay public. We hold that the application of Disciplinary

Rules 2-103(A) and 2-104(A) to appellant does not offend the Constitution.

Accordingly, the judgment of the Supreme Court of Ohio is Affirmed.

In re PRIMUS

436 U.S. 412 (1978)

Mr. Justice POWELL delivered the opinion of the Court.

We consider on this appeal whether a State may punish a member of its Bar who, seeking to further political and ideological goals through associational activity, including litigation, advises a lay person of her legal rights and discloses in a subsequent letter that free legal assistance is available from a nonprofit organization with which the lawyer and her associates are affiliated. Appellant, a member of the Bar of South Carolina, received a public reprimand for writing such a letter. The appeal is opposed by the State Attorney General, on behalf of the Board of Commissioners on Grievances and Discipline of the Supreme Court of South Carolina. . . .

I

Appellant, Edna Smith Primus, is a lawyer practicing in Columbia, S.C. During the period in question, she was associated with the "Carolina Community Law Firm,"[1] and an officer of and cooperating lawyer with the Columbia branch of the American Civil Liberties Union (ACLU).[2] She received no compensation for her work on behalf of the ACLU,[3] but was paid a retainer as a legal consultant for the South Carolina Council on Human Relations (Council), a nonprofit organization with offices in Columbia.

During the summer of 1973, local and national newspapers reported that pregnant mothers on public assistance in Aiken County, S.C. were

---

1. The court below determined that the Carolina Community Law Firm was "'an expense sharing arrangement with each attorney keeping his own fees.'" 268 S.C. 259, 261, 233 S.E.2d 301, 302 (1977). The firm later changed its name to Buhl, Smith & Bagby.

2. The ACLU was organized in 1920 by individuals who had worked in the defense of the rights of conscientious objectors during World War I and political dissidents during the postwar period. It views itself as a "national non-partisan organization defending our Bill of Rights for all without distinction or compromise." ACLU, Presenting the American Civil Liberties Union 2 (1948). The organization's activities range from litigation and lobbying to educational campaigns in support of its avowed goals. . . .

3. Although all three lawyers in the Carolina Community Law Firm maintained some association with the ACLU — appellant and Carlton Bagby as unsalaried cooperating lawyers, and Herbert Buhl as staff counsel — appellant testified that "the firm did not handle any litigation for [the] ACLU."

being sterilized or threatened with sterilization as a condition of the continued receipt of medical assistance under the "Medicaid" program. Concerned by this development, Gary Allen, an Aiken businessman and officer of a local organization serving indigents, called the Council requesting that one of its representatives come to Aiken to address some of the women who had been sterilized. At the Council's behest, appellant, who had not known Allen previously, called him and arranged a meeting in his office in July 1973. Among those attending was Mary Etta Williams, who had been sterilized by Dr. Clovis H. Pierce after the birth of her third child. Williams and her grandmother attended the meeting because Allen, an old family friend, had invited them and because Williams wanted "[t]o see what it was all about." . . . At the meeting, appellant advised those present, including Williams and the other women who had been sterilized by Dr. Pierce, of their legal rights and suggested the possibility of a lawsuit.

Early in August 1973 the ACLU informed appellant that it was willing to provide representation for Aiken mothers who had been sterilized. Appellant testified that after being advised by Allen that Williams wished to institute suit against Dr. Pierce, she decided to inform Williams of the ACLU's offer of free legal representation. Shortly after receiving appellant's letter dated August 30, 1973[6] — the centerpiece of this liti-

---

6. Written on the stationery of the Carolina Community Law Firm, the letter stated:

August 30, 1973

Mrs. Marietta Williams
347 Sumter Street
Aiken, South Carolina 29801

Dear Mrs. Williams:
   You will probabl[y] remember me from talking with you at Mr. Allen's office in July about the sterilization performed on you. The American Civil Liberties Union would like to file a lawsuit on your behalf for money against the doctor who performed the operation. We will be coming to Aiken in the near future and would like to explain what is involved so you can understand what is going on.
   Now I have a question to ask of you. Would you object to talking to a women's magazine about the situation in Aiken? The magazine is doing a feature story on the whole sterilization problem and wants to talk to you and others in South Carolina. If you don't mind doing this, call me *collect* at 254-8151 on Friday before 5:00, if you receive this letter in time. Or call me on Tuesday morning (after Labor Day) *collect*.
   I want to assure you that this interview is being done to show what is happening to women against their wishes, and is not being done to harm you in any way. But I want you to decide, so call me collect, and let me know of your decision. This practice must stop.
   About the lawsuit, if you are interested, let me know, and I'll let you know when we will come down to talk to you about it. We will be coming to talk to Mrs. Waters at the same time; she has already asked the American Civil Liberties Union to file a suit on her behalf.

Sincerely,
s/*Edna Smith*
Edna Smith
Attorney-at-law

gation — Williams visited Dr. Pierce to discuss the progress of her third child who was ill. At the doctor's office, she encountered his lawyer and at the latter's request signed a release of liability in the doctor's favor. Williams showed appellant's letter to the doctor and his lawyer, and they retained a copy. She then called appellant from the doctor's office and announced her intention not to sue. There was no further communication between appellant and Williams.

On October 9, 1974, the Secretary of the Board of Commissioners on Grievances and Discipline of the Supreme Court of South Carolina (Board) filed a formal complaint with the Board, charging that appellant had engaged in "solicitation in violation of the Canons of Ethics" by sending the August 30, 1973 letter to Williams. . . . Appellant denied any unethical solicitation and asserted, inter alia, that her conduct was protected by the First and Fourteenth Amendments and by Canon 2 of the Code of Professional Responsibility of the American Bar Association (ABA). The complaint was heard by a panel of the Board on March 20, 1975. The State's evidence consisted of the letter, the testimony of Williams,[7] and a copy of the summons and complaint in the action instituted against Dr. Pierce and various state officials, Doe v. Pierce, . . . aff'd in part and rev'd in part sub nom. Walker v. Pierce, 560 F.2d 609 (CA4 1977), cert. denied, 434 U.S. 1075 (1978).[8] Following denial of appellant's motion to dismiss, she testified in her own behalf and called Allen, a number of ACLU representatives, and several character witnesses.

The panel filed a report recommending that appellant be found guilty of soliciting a client on behalf of the ACLU, in violation of Disciplinary Rules (DR) 2-103(D)(5)(a) and (c) and 2-104(A)(5) of the Supreme Court of South Carolina, and that a private reprimand be issued. It noted that "[t]he evidence is inconclusive as to whether [appellant] solicited Mrs. Williams on her own behalf, but she did solicit Mrs. Williams on behalf of the ACLU, which would benefit financially in the

---

7. Williams testified that at the July meeting appellant advised her of her legal remedies, of the possibility of a lawsuit if her sterilization had been coerced, and of appellant's willingness to serve as her lawyer without compensation. Williams recounted she had told appellant that because her child was in critical condition, she "did not have time for" a lawsuit and "would contact [appellant] some more." She also denied that she had expressed to Allen an interest in suing her doctor. . . . On cross-examination, however, Williams confirmed an earlier statement she had made in an affidavit that appellant "did not attempt to persuade or pressure me to file [the] lawsuit." . . .

8. This class action was filed on April 15, 1974, by two Negro women alleging that Dr. Pierce, in conspiracy with state officials, had sterilized them, or was threatening to do so, solely on account of their race and number of children, while they received assistance under the Medicaid program. The complaint sought declaratory and injunctive relief, damages, and attorney's fees, and asserted violations of the Constitution and 42 U.S.C. §§1981, 1983, 1985(3) and 2000d.

Bagby, one of appellant's associates in the Carolina Community Law Firm and fellow cooperating lawyer with the ACLU, was one of several attorneys of record for the plaintiffs. Buhl, another of appellant's associates and a staff counsel for the ACLU in South Carolina, also may have represented one of the women.

event of successful prosecution of the suit for money damages." The panel determined that appellant violated DR 2-103(D)(5) "by attempting to solicit a client for a non-profit organization which, as its primary purpose, renders legal services, where respondent's associate is a staff counsel for the non-profit organization." Appellant also was found to have violated DR 2-104(A)(5) because she solicited Williams, after providing unsolicited legal advice, to join in a prospective class action for damages and other relief that was to be brought by the ACLU.

After hearing on January 9, 1976, the full Board approved the panel report and administered a private reprimand. On March 17, 1977, the Supreme Court of South Carolina entered an order which adopted verbatim the findings and conclusions of the panel report and increased the sanction, sua sponte, to a public reprimand. 268 S.C. 259, 233 S.E.2d 301. . . .

II

. . . Unlike the situation in *Ohralik*, . . . appellant's act of solicitation took the form of a letter to a woman with whom appellant had discussed the possibility of seeking redress for an allegedly unconstitutional sterilization. This was not in-person solicitation for pecuniary gain. Appellant was communicating an offer of free assistance by attorneys associated with the ACLU, not an offer predicated on entitlement to a share of any monetary recovery. And her actions were undertaken to express personal political beliefs and 'to advance the civil-liberties objectives of the ACLU, rather than to derive financial gain. The question presented in this case is whether, in light of the values protected by the First and Fourteenth Amendments, these differences materially affect the scope of state regulation of the conduct of lawyers. . . .

. . . The Supreme Court of South Carolina found appellant to have engaged in unethical conduct because she "'solicit[ed] a client for a non-profit organization, which, as its primary purpose, renders legal services, where respondent's associate is a staff counsel for the non-profit organization.'" 268 S.C., at 269, 233 S.E.2d, at 306[18] It rejected appellant's First Amendment defenses by distinguishing *Button* [p. 593] from the case before it. Whereas the NAACP in that case was primarily a "'political'" organization that used "'litigation as an adjunct to the overriding political aims of the organization,'" the ACLU "'has as one of its primary purposes, the rendition of legal services.'" Id., at 268, 269, 233 S.E.2d, at 305, 306. The court also intimated that the ACLU's policy of requesting an award of counsel fees indicated that the organization might "'ben-

---

18. In the discussion that follows, we do not treat separately the two disciplinary rules upon which appellant's violation was based. Since DR 2-103(D)(5) was held by the court below to proscribe in a narrower fashion the same conduct as DR 2-104(A)(5) . . . a determination of unconstitutionality as to the former would subsume the latter.

efit financially in the event of successful prosecution of the suit for money damages.'" Id., at 263, 233 S.E.2d, at 303.

Although the disciplinary panel did not permit full factual development of the aims and practices of the ACLU, . . . the record does not support the state court's effort to draw a meaningful distinction between the ACLU and the NAACP. From all that appears, the ACLU and its local chapters, much like the NAACP and its local affiliates in *Button*, "engage . . . in extensive educational and lobbying activities" and "also devote . . . much of [their] funds and energies to an extensive program of assisting certain kinds of litigation on behalf of [their] declared purposes." 371 U.S., at 419-420. . . . The court below acknowledged that "'the ACLU has only entered cases in which substantial civil liberties questions are involved . . .'" 268 S.C., at 263, 233 S.E.2d, at 303. . . .

It has engaged in the defense of unpopular causes and unpopular defendants and has represented individuals in litigation that has defined the scope of constitutional protection in areas such as political dissent, juvenile rights, prisoners' rights, military law, amnesty, and privacy. . . . For the ACLU, as for the NAACP, "litigation is not a technique of resolving private differences"; it is "a form of political expression" and "political association." 371 U.S., at 429, 431.[20]

We find equally unpersuasive any suggestion that the level of constitutional scrutiny in this case should be lowered because of a possible benefit to the ACLU. The discipline administered to appellant was premised solely on the possibility of financial benefit to the organization, rather than any possibility of pecuniary gain to herself, her associates, or the lawyers representing the plaintiffs in the Doe v. Pierce litigation.[21] It is conceded that appellant received no compensation for any of the activities in question. It is also undisputed that neither the ACLU nor any lawyer associated with it would have shared in any monetary recovery by the plaintiffs in Doe v. Pierce. If Williams had elected to bring suit, and had been represented by staff lawyers for the ACLU, the situation would have been similar to that in *Button*, where the lawyers for

20. There is nothing in the record to suggest that the ACLU or its South Carolina affiliate is an organization dedicated exclusively to the provision of legal services. See n.2, supra. Nor does the record support any inference that either the ACLU or its affiliate "is a mere sham to cover what is actually nothing more than an attempt," Eastern R. Conf. v. Noerr Motors, 365 U.S. 127, 144 (1961), by a group of attorneys to evade a valid state rule against solicitation for pecuniary gain. . . .

21. Appellee conjectures that appellant would have received increased support from private foundations if her reputation was enhanced as a result of her efforts in the cause of the ACLU. The decision below acknowledged, however, that the evidence did not support a finding that appellant solicited Williams on her own behalf. 268 S.C., at 263, 233 S.E.2d, at 303. Since the discipline in this case was premised solely on the possibility that appellant's solicitation might have conferred a financial benefit on the ACLU, ibid., and any award of counsel fees would have been received only for the organization's benefit, see n.24, infra, we also attach no significance to the fact that two of the attorneys in the Doe v. Pierce litigation were associated with appellant in an arrangement for sharing office expenses. . . .

the NAACP were "organized as a staff and paid by" that organization. 371 U.S., at 434. . . .

Contrary to appellee's suggestion, the ACLU's policy of requesting an award of counsel fees does not take this case outside the protection of *Button*. Although the Court in *Button* did not consider whether the NAACP seeks counsel fees, such requests are often made both by that organization, . . . and by the NAACP Legal Defense Fund, Inc. . . .

In any event, in a case of this kind there are differences between counsel fees awarded by a court and traditional fee-paying arrangements which militate against a presumption that ACLU sponsorship of litigation is motivated by considerations of pecuniary gain rather than by its widely recognized goal of vindicating civil liberties. Counsel fees are awarded in the discretion of the court; awards are not drawn from the plaintiff's recovery, and are usually premised on a successful outcome; and the amounts awarded often may not correspond to fees generally obtainable in private litigation. Moreover, under prevailing law during the events in question, an award of counsel fees in federal litigation was available only in limited circumstances. And even if there had been an award during the period in question, it would have gone to the central fund of the ACLU.[24] Although such benefit to the organization may increase with the maintenance of successful litigation, the same situation obtains with voluntary contributions and foundation support, which also may rise with ACLU victories in important areas of the law. That possibility, standing alone, offers no basis for equating the work of lawyers associated with the ACLU or the NAACP with that of a group that exists for the primary purpose of financial gain through the recovery of counsel fees. . . .

Appellant's letter of August 30, 1973 to Mrs. Williams thus comes within the generous zone of First Amendment protection reserved for associational freedoms. The ACLU engages in litigation as a vehicle for effective political expression and association, as well as a means of communicating useful information to the public. . . .

V

South Carolina's action in punishing appellant for soliciting a prospective litigant by mail, on behalf of the ACLU, must withstand the "exacting scrutiny applicable to limitations on core First Amendment rights. . . ." Buckley v. Valeo, 424 U.S. 1, 44-45 (1976). . . . Appellee con-

---

24. Appellant informs us that the ACLU policy then in effect provided that cooperating lawyers associated with the ACLU or with an affiliate could not receive an award of counsel fees for services rendered in an ACLU-sponsored litigation. . . . This policy was changed in 1977 to permit local experimentation with the sharing of court-awarded fees between state affiliates and cooperating attorneys. The South Carolina chapter has not exercised that option. . . . We express no opinion whether our analysis in this case would be different had the latter policy been in effect during the period in question.

tends that the disciplinary action taken in this case is part of a regulatory program aimed at the prevention of undue influence, overreaching, misrepresentation, invasion of privacy, conflict of interest, lay interference, and other evils that are thought to inhere generally in solicitation by lawyers of prospective clients, and to be present on the record before us. . . . We do not dispute the importance of these interests. . . .

A

The disciplinary rules in question sweep broadly. Under DR 2-103(D)(5), a lawyer employed by the ACLU or a similar organization may never give unsolicited advice to a lay person that he or she retain the organization's free services, and it would seem that one who merely assists or maintains a cooperative relationship with the organization also must suppress the giving of such advice if he or anyone associated with the organization will be involved in the ultimate litigation. . . .

Notwithstanding appellee's concession in this Court, it is far from clear that a lawyer may communicate the organization's offer of legal assistance at an informational gathering such as the July 1973 meeting in Aiken without breaching the literal terms of the rule. . . . Moreover, the disciplinary rules in question permit punishment for mere solicitation unaccompanied by proof of any of the substantive evils that appellee maintains were present in this case. In sum, the rules in their present form have a distinct potential for dampening the kind of "cooperative activity that would make advocacy of litigation meaningful," *Button*, 371 U.S., at 438, 83 S. Ct., at 340, as well as for permitting discretionary enforcement against unpopular causes.

B

Even if we ignore the breadth of the disciplinary rules, and the absence of findings in the decision below that support the justifications advanced by appellee in this Court, we think it clear from the record — which appellee does not suggest is inadequately developed — that findings compatible with the First Amendment could not have been made in this case.

Where political expression or association is at issue, this Court has not tolerated the degree of imprecision that often characterizes government regulation of the conduct of commercial affairs. The approach we adopt today in *Ohralik* . . . that the State may proscribe in-person solicitation for pecuniary gain under circumstances likely to result in adverse consequences, cannot be applied to appellant's activity on behalf of the ACLU. Although a showing of potential danger may suffice in the former context, appellant may not be disciplined unless her activity in fact involved the type of misconduct at which South Carolina's broad prohibition is said to be directed.

The record does not support appellee's contention that undue influence, overreaching, misrepresentation, or invasion of privacy actually occurred in this case. Appellant's letter of August 30, 1973, followed up the earlier meeting — one concededly protected by the First and Fourteenth Amendments — by notifying Williams that the ACLU would be interested in supporting possible litigation. The letter imparted additional information material to making an informed decision about whether to authorize litigation, and permitted Williams an opportunity, which she exercised, for arriving at a deliberate decision. The letter was not facially misleading; indeed, it offered "to explain what is involved so you can understand what is going on." The transmittal of this letter — as contrasted with in-person solicitation — involved no appreciable invasion of privacy; nor did it afford any significant opportunity for overreaching or coercion. Moreover, the fact that there was a written communication lessens substantially the difficulty of policing solicitation practices that do offend valid rules of professional conduct. . . . The manner of solicitation in this case certainly was no more likely to cause harmful consequences than the activity considered in *Button*. . . .

Nor does the record permit a finding of a serious likelihood of conflict of interest or injurious lay interference with the attorney-client relationship.

The State's interests in preventing the "stirring up" of frivolous or vexatious litigation and minimizing commercialization of the legal profession offer no further justification for the discipline administered in this case. The *Button* Court declined to accept the proffered analogy to the common-law offenses of maintenance, champerty, and barratry, where the record would not support a finding that the litigant was solicited for a malicious purpose or "for private gain, serving no public interest," 371 U.S., at 440. . . . The same result follows from the facts of this case. And considerations of undue commercialization of the legal profession are of marginal force where, as here, a nonprofit organization offers its services free of charge to individuals who may be in need of legal assistance and may lack the financial means and sophistication necessary to tap alternative sources of such aid.[31]

At bottom, the case against appellant rests on the proposition that a State may regulate in a prophylactic fashion all solicitation activities of lawyers because there may be some potential for overreaching, conflict

---

31. . . . In recognition of the overarching obligation of the lawyer to serve the community, see Canon 2 of the ABA Code of Professional Responsibility, the ethical rules of the legal profession traditionally have recognized an exception from any general ban on solicitation for offers of representation, without charge, extended to individuals who may be unable to obtain legal assistance on their own. See e.g., In re Ades, 6 F. Supp. 467, 475-476 (Md. 1934); Gunnels v. Atlanta Bar Assn., 191 Ga. 366, 12 S.E.2d 602 (1940); American Bar Association, Committee on Professional Ethics and Grievances, Formal Opinion 148, at 416-419 (1935).

of interest, or other substantive evils whenever a lawyer gives unsolicited advice and communicates an offer of representation to a layman. Under certain circumstances, that approach is appropriate in the case of speech that simply "propose[s] a commercial transaction," Pittsburgh Press Co. v. Human Relations Commn, 413 U.S. 376, 385 (1973). . . . In the context of political expression and association, however, a State must regulate with significantly greater precision.[32]

VI

The State is free to fashion reasonable restrictions with respect to the time, place, and manner of solicitation by members of its Bar. . . . The State's special interest in regulating members of a profession it licenses, and who serve as officers of its courts, amply justifies the application of narrowly drawn rules to proscribe solicitation that in fact is misleading, overbearing, or involves other features of deception or improper influence. A State also may forbid in-person solicitation for pecuniary gain under circumstances likely to result in these evils. . . . And a State may insist that lawyers not solicit on behalf of lay organizations that exert control over the actual conduct of any ensuing litigation. See *Button,* 371 U.S., at 447 (Mr. Justice White, concurring in part and dissenting in part). Accordingly, nothing in this opinion should be read to foreclose carefully tailored regulation that does not abridge unnecessarily the associational freedom of nonprofit organizations, or their members, having characteristics like those of the NAACP or the ACLU.

We conclude that South Carolina's application of its Disciplinary Rules 2-103(D)(5)(a) and (c) and 2-104(A)(5) to appellant's solicitation by letter on behalf of the ACLU violates the First and Fourteenth Amendments. The judgment of the Supreme Court of South Carolina is Reversed.

Mr. Justice MARSHALL, concurring in part and concurring in the judgments. . . .

---

32. Normally the purpose or motive of the speaker is not central to First Amendment protection, but it does bear on the distinction between conduct that is "an associational aspect of 'expression'", Emerson, Freedom of Association and Freedom of Expression, 74 Yale L.J. 1, 26 (1964), and other activity subject to plenary regulation by government. *Button* recognized that certain forms of "cooperative, organizational activity," 371 U.S., at 430, including litigation, are part of the "freedom to engage in association for the advancement of beliefs and ideas," NAACP v. Alabama, 357 U.S. 449, 460 (1958), and that this freedom is an implicit guarantee of the First Amendment. See Healy v. James, 408 U.S. 169, 181 (1972). As shown above, appellant's speech — as part of associational activity — was expression intended to advance "beliefs and ideas." In Ohralik v. Ohio State Bar Assn., . . . the lawyer was not engaged in associational activity for the advancement of beliefs and ideas: his purpose was the advancement of his own commercial interests. The line, based in part on the motive of the speaker and the character of the expressive activity, will not always be easy to draw, . . . but that is no reason for avoiding the undertaking.

What is objectionable about Ohralik's behavior here is not so much that he solicited business for himself, but rather the circumstances in which he performed that solicitation and the means by which he accomplished it. Appropriately, the Court's actual holding in *Ohralik,* 48 Ohio St. 2d 217, 357 N.E.2d 1097, is a limited one: that the solicitation of business, under circumstances — such as those found in this record — presenting substantial dangers of harm to society or the client independent of the solicitation itself, may constitutionally be prohibited by the State. In this much of the Court's opinion in *Ohralik,* I join fully.

II

The facts in *Primus,* 268 S.C. 259, 233 S.E.2d 301, by contrast, show a "solicitation" of employment in accordance with the highest standards of the legal profession. Appellant in this case was acting not for her own pecuniary benefit, but to promote what she perceived to be the legal rights of persons not likely to appreciate or to be able to vindicate their own rights. The obligation of all lawyers, whether or not members of an association committed to a particular point of view, to see that legal aid is available "where the litigant is in need of assistance, or where important issues are involved in the case," has long been established. In re Ades, 6 F. Supp. 467, 475 (Md. 1934). . . .

In light of this long tradition of public interest representation by lawyer volunteers, I share my Brother Blackmun's concern with respect to Part VI of the Court's opinion, and believe that the Court has engaged in unnecessary and unfortunate dicta therein. It would be most undesirable to discourage lawyers — so many of whom find time to work only for those clients who can pay their fees — from continuing to volunteer their services in appropriate cases. Moreover, it cannot be too strongly emphasized that, where "political expression and association" are involved, *Primus,* ante, . . . "a State may not, under the guise of prohibiting professional misconduct, ignore constitutional rights." NAACP v. Button, [p. 593]. For these reasons, I find particularly troubling the Court's dictum that "a State may insist that lawyers not solicit on behalf of lay organizations that exert control over the actual conduct of any ensuing litigation." . . . This proposition is by no means self-evident, has never been the actual holding of this Court, and is not put in issue by the facts presently before us. . . .

III

Our holdings today deal only with situations at opposite poles of the problem of attorney solicitation. In their aftermath, courts and professional associations may reasonably be expected to look to these opinions for guidance in redrafting the disciplinary rules that must apply across a spectrum of activities ranging from clearly protected speech to clearly proscribable conduct. A large number of situations falling between the poles represented by the instant facts will doubtless occur. In considering the wisdom and constitutionality of rules directed at such intermediate situations our fellow members of the Bench and Bar must be guided not only by today's decisions, but also by our decision last Term in Bates v. State Bar of Arizona. . . . In that context we rejected many of the general justifications for rules applicable to one intermediate situation not directly addressed by the Court today — the commercial but otherwise "benign" solicitation of clients by an attorney.[3] . . .

A

Like rules against advertising, rules against solicitation substantially impede the flow of important information to consumers from those most likely to provide it — the practicing members of the Bar. Many persons with legal problems fail to seek relief through the legal system because they are unaware that they have a legal problem, and, even if they "perceive a need," many "do not obtain counsel . . . because of an inability to locate a competent attorney." Bates v. State Bar of Arizona. . . . Notwithstanding the injurious aspects of Ohralik's conduct, even his case illustrates the potentially useful, information-providing aspects of attorney solicitation: Motivated by the desire for pecuniary gain, but informed with the special training and knowledge of an attorney, Ohralik advised both his clients (apparently correctly) that, although they had been injured by an uninsured motorist, they could nonetheless recover on the McClintocks' insurance policy. The provision of such information about legal rights and remedies is an important function, even where the rights and remedies are of a private and commercial nature involving no constitutional or political overtones. . . .

In view of the similar functions performed by advertising and solicitation by attorneys, I find somewhat disturbing the Court's suggestion in *Ohralik* that in-person solicitation of business, though entitled to some degree of constitutional protection as "commercial speech," is entitled to less protection under the First Amendment than is "the kind of advertising approved in *Bates.*" . . . The First Amendment informational interests served by solicitation, whether or not it occurs in a purely commercial context, are substantial, and they are entitled to as much protection as the interests we found to be protected in *Bates.*

The impact of the nonsolicitation rules, moreover, is discriminatory with respect to the suppliers as well as the consumers of legal services.

---

3. By "benign" commercial solicitation, I mean solicitation by advice and information that is truthful and that is presented in a noncoercive, nondeceitful and dignified manner to a potential client who is emotionally and physically capable of making a rational decision either to accept or reject the representation with respect to a legal claim or matter that is not frivolous.

Just as the persons who suffer most from lack of knowledge about lawyers' availability belong to the less privileged classes of society, . . . so the disciplinary rules against solicitation fall most heavily on those attorneys engaged in a single practitioner or small partnership form of practice[7] — attorneys who typically earn less than their fellow practitioners in larger, corporate-oriented firms. See Shuchman, Ethics and Legal Ehhics: The Propriety of the Canons as a Group Moral Code, [p. 30]. Indeed, some scholars have suggested that the rules against solicitation were developed by the professional bar to keep recently immigrated lawyers, who gravitated toward the smaller, personal injury practice, from effective entry into the profession. See J. Auerbach, Unequal Justice 42-62, 126-129 (1976). In light of this history, I am less inclined than the majority appears to be, . . . to weigh favorably in the balance of the State's interests here the longevity of the ban on attorney solicitation.

C

By discussing the origin and impact of the nonsolicitation rules, I do not mean to belittle those obviously substantial interests that the State has in regulating attorneys to protect the public from fraud, deceit, misrepresentation, overreaching, undue influence, and invasions of privacy. But where honest, unpressured "commercial" solicitation is involved — a situation not presented in either of these cases — I believe it is open to doubt whether the State's interests are sufficiently compelling to warrant the restriction on the free flow of information which results from a sweeping nonsolicitation rule and against which the First Amendment ordinarily protects. While the State's interest in regulating in-person solicitation may, for reasons explained in *Ohralik*, . . . be somewhat greater than its interest in regulating print advertisements, these concededly legitimate interests might well be served by more specific and less restrictive rules than a total ban on pecuniary solicitation. For example, the Justice Department has suggested that the disciplinary rules be reworded "so as to *permit* all solicitation and advertising except the kinds that are false, misleading, undignified or champertous."[8]

To the extent that in-person solicitation of business may constitutionally be subjected to more substantial state regulation as to time, place, and manner than printed advertising of legal services, it is not because such solicitation has "traditionally" been banned, nor because one form of commercial speech is of less value than another under the First

---

7. According to the American Bar Foundation, 72.7% of all lawyers were in private practice in 1970; of these, over half practiced as individual practitioners. The 1971 Lawyer Statistical Report 10 (1972).

8. Remarks of L. Bernstein, Chief, Special Litigation Section, Antitrust Division, Department of Justice, reprinted in 5 CCH Trade Reg. Rep. ¶50,197 (1974) (emphasis added). . . .

Amendment. Rather, any additional restrictions can be justified only to the degree that dangers which the State has a right to prevent are actually presented by conduct attendant to such speech, thus increasing the relative "strength of the State's countervailing interest in prohibition," *Ohralik,* ante. . . . As the majority notes, and I wholeheartedly agree, these dangers are amply present in the *Ohralik* case. . . .

Mr. Justice REHNQUIST, dissenting.

In this case and the companion case of Ohralik v. Ohio State Bar Assn., . . . the Court tells its own tale of two lawyers: One tale ends happily for the lawyer and one does not. If we were given the latitude of novelists in deciding between happy and unhappy endings for the heroes and villains of our tales, I might well join in the Court's disposition of both cases. But under our federal system it is for the States to decide which lawyers shall be admitted to the Bar and remain there; this Court may interfere only if the State's decision is rendered impermissible by the United States Constitution. We can of course develop a jurisprudence of epithets and slogans in this area, in which "ambulance-chasers" suffer one fate and "civil liberties lawyers" another. But I remain unpersuaded by the Court's opinions in these two cases that there is a principled basis for concluding that the First and Fourteenth Amendments forbid South Carolina from disciplining Primus here, but permit Ohio to discipline Ohralik in the companion case. I believe that both South Carolina and Ohio acted within the limits prescribed by those Amendments, and I would therefore affirm the judgment in each case. . . .

In distinguishing between Primus' protected solicitation and Ohralik's unprotected solicitation, the Court lamely declares, "We have not discarded the 'commonsense' distinction between speech proposing a commercial transaction, which occurs in an area traditionally subject to government regulation, and other varieties of speech." . . . Yet to the extent that this "commonsense" distinction focuses on the content of the speech, it is at least suspect under many of this Court's First Amendment cases, see, e.g. Police Dept. of Chicago v. Mosley, 408 U.S. 92, 96-98, (1972), and to the extent it focuses upon the motive of the speaker, it is subject to manipulation by clever practitioners. If Albert Ohralik, like Edna Primus, viewed litigation "'not [as] a technique of resolving private differences,'" but as "'a form of political expression' and 'political association,'" ante, for all that appears he would be restored to his right to practice. And we may be sure that the next lawyer in Ohralik's shoes who is disciplined for similar conduct will come here cloaked in the prescribed mantel of "political association" to assure that insurance companies do not take unfair advantage of policyholders. . . .

I do not believe that any State will be able to determine with confidence the area in which it may regulate prophylactically and the area in which it may regulate only upon a specific showing of harm. Despite the Court's assertion to the contrary, . . . the difficulty of drawing distinctions on the basis of the content of the speech or the motive of the speaker *is* a valid reason for avoiding the undertaking where a more objective standard is readily available. I believe that constitutional inquiry must focus on the character of the conduct which the State seeks to regulate, and not on the motives of the individual lawyers or the nature of the particular litigation involved. The State is empowered to discipline for conduct which it deems detrimental to the public interest unless foreclosed from doing so by our cases construing the First and Fourteenth Amendments. . . .

Here, South Carolina has not attempted to punish the ACLU or any laymen associated with it. Gary Allen, who was the instigator of the effort to sue Dr. Pierce, remains as free as before to solicit potential plaintiffs for future litigation. Likewise, Primus remains as free as before to address gatherings of the sort described in *Button* to advise potential plaintiffs of their legal rights. Primus' first contact with Williams took place at such a gathering, and South Carolina evidently in response to *Button*, has not attempted to discipline her for her part in that meeting. It has disciplined her for initiating further contact on an individual basis with Williams, who had not expressed any desire to become involved in the collective activity being organized by the ACLU. While *Button* appears to permit such individual solicitation for political purposes by lay members of the organization, id., at 422, it nowhere explicitly permits such activity on the part of lawyers.

As the Court understands the disciplinary rule enforced by South Carolina, "a lawyer employed by the ACLU or a similar organization may never give unsolicited advice to a lay person that he or she retain the organization's free services." . . . That prohibition seems to me entirely reasonable. A State may rightly fear that members of its Bar have powers of persuasion not possessed by laymen . . . and it may also fear that such persuasion may be as potent in writing as it is in person. Such persuasion may draw an unsophisticated layman into litigation contrary to his own best interests, . . . and it may force other citizens of South Carolina to defend against baseless litigation which would not otherwise have been brought. I cannot agree that a State must prove such harmful consequences in each case simply because an organization such as the ACLU or the NAACP is involved. I cannot share the Court's confidence that the danger of such consequences is minimized simply because a lawyer proceeds from political conviction rather than for pecuniary gain. A State may reasonably fear that a lawyer's desire to resolve "substantial civil liberties questions," 268 S.C. 259, 263, 233 S.E.2d 301, 303 (1976), may occasionally take precedence over his duty to advance the interests of his client. It is even more reasonable to fear that a lawyer in such circumstances will be inclined to pursue both culpable and blameless defendants to the last ditch in order to achieve his ideological goals. Although individual litigants, including the ACLU, may be free to use the courts for such purposes, South Carolina is likewise free to restrict the activities of the members of its Bar who attempt to persuade them to do so.

I can only conclude that the discipline imposed upon Primus does not violate the Constitution, and I would affirm the judgment of the Supreme Court of South Carolina.

[Justice Blackmun's concurring opinion is omitted.]

NOTE: The Aftermath of Bates, Ohralik, and Primus

While the decisions in *Ohralik* and *Primus* established constitutional rules at the ends of the spectrum of solicitation, it was immediately apparent that not only was there a great deal of room left in between but also, as indicated by the opinions of Justices Marshall and Rehnquist, that it remained to be seen whether the distinctions set forth in those cases could be maintained. Moreover, even the holding of *Bates* left many questions as to state regulatory power unanswered.

The Court has reconsidered the area in two major opinions, Zauderer v. Office of Disciplinary Counsel of Supreme Court of Ohio, 471 U.S. 626 (1985) and Shapero v. Kentucky Bar Association, 108 Ct. 1916 (1988). In *Zauderer,* the Supreme Court struck down a rule that prohibited an attorney from targeted and illustrated newspaper advertising, in this case an advertisement in a local newspaper that specifically sought employment from women injured by using the Dalkon Shield, a drawing of which was included in the advertisement. The Court, distinguishing in-person solicitation, refused to allow the state to apply a prophylactic rule to newspaper advertising that was not deceptive. The Court did, however, uphold certain disclosure requirements that the state had imposed on such advertising, specifically the obligation on clients to pay costs when they hire a lawyer on a contingent fee basis.

While *Zauderer* settled the issue of targeted newspaper advertising, a major solicitation issue was mail solicitation targeted to specific people or groups of people, especially those known to need legal services of the kind being offered. Model Rule 7.3, for example, prohibited the latter kind of solicitation. The Supreme Court addressed that issue in Shapero v. Kentucky Bar Association, 108 Ct. 1916 (1988), which reviewed the refusal, by Kentucky's Attorneys Advertising Commission, to approve a solicitation letter that a lawyer proposed to send to persons who had foreclosure suits filed against them. The Court held that nondeceptive, targeted mail solicitation was entitled to the same protection as targeted newspaper advertising had received in *Zauderer*. The Court found that the potential for overreaching and undue influence that had justified the prophylactic rule in the circumstances of in-person solicitation in *Ohralik* was not present in personalized mail solicitation where abuses could be reached by regulation less restrictive than a ban. The possibility of regulation by requiring filing of solicitation letters with a state agency was suggested.

Justice O'Connor, joined by Chief Justice Rehnquist and Justice Scalia in dissent, agreed that the result in *Shapero* was a logical extension of the decision in *Zauderer*. Nevertheless, she objected to the whole line of commercial speech cases relating to lawyer advertising that began with *Bates*. In particular, she believed that the Court had undervalued the state interests in regulation:

> Even if I agreed that this Court should take upon itself the task of deciding what forms of attorney advertising are in the public interest, I would not agree with what it has done. The best arguments in favor of rules permitting attorneys to advertise are founded in elementary economic principles. See, e.g., Hazard, Pearce, & Stempel, Why Lawyers Should Be Allowed to Advertise: A Market Analysis of Legal Services, 58 N.Y.U. L. Rev. 1084 (1983). Restrictions on truthful advertising, which artificially interfere with the ability of suppliers to transmit price information to consumers, presumably reduce the efficiency of the mechanisms of supply and demand. Other factors being equal, this should cause or enable suppliers (in this case attorneys) to maintain a price/quality ratio in some of their services that is higher than would otherwise prevail. Although one could probably not test this hypothesis empirically, it is inherently plausible. Nor is it implausible to imagine that one effect of restrictions on lawyer advertising, and perhaps sometimes an intended effect, is to enable attorneys to charge their clients more for some services (of a given quality) than they would be able to charge absent the restrictions.
>
> Assuming *arguendo* that the removal of advertising restrictions should lead in the short run to increased efficiency in the provision of legal services, I would not agree that we can safely assume the same effect in the long run. The economic argument against these restrictions ignores the delicate role they may play in preserving the norms of the legal profession. While it may be difficult to defend this role with precise economic logic, I believe there is a powerful argument in favor of restricting lawyer advertising and that this argument is at the very least not easily refuted by economic analysis.
>
> One distinguishing feature of any profession, unlike other occupations that may be equally respectable, is that membership entails an ethical obligation to temper one's selfish pursuit of economic success by adhering to standards of conduct that could not be enforced either by legal fiat or

through the discipline of the market. There are sound reasons to continue pursuing the goal that is implicit in the traditional view of professional life. Both the special privileges incident to membership in the profession and the advantages those privileges give in the necessary task of earning a living are means to a goal that transcends the accumulation of wealth. That goal is public service, which in the legal profession can take a variety of familiar forms. This view of the legal profession need not be rooted in romanticism or self-serving sanctimony, though of course it can be. Rather, special ethical standards for lawyers are properly understood as an appropriate means of restraining lawyers in the exercise of the unique power that they inevitably wield in a political system like ours.

It is worth recalling why lawyers are regulated at all, or to a greater degree than most other occupations, and why history is littered with failed attempts to extinguish lawyers as a special class. . . . Operating a legal system that is both reasonably efficient and tolerably fair cannot be accomplished, at least under modern social conditions, without a trained and specialized body of experts. This training is one element of what we mean when we refer to the law as a "learned profession." Such knowledge by its nature cannot be made generally available and it therefore confers the power and the temptation to manipulate the system of justice for one's own ends. Such manipulation can occur in at least two obvious ways. One results from overly zealous representation of the client's interests; abuse of the discovery process is one example whose causes and effects (if not its cure) is apparent. The second, and for present purposes the more relevant, problem is abuse of the client for the lawyer's benefit. Precisely because lawyers must be provided with expertise that is both esoteric and extremely powerful, it would be unrealistic to demand that clients bargain for their services in the same arms-length manner that may be appropriate when buying an automobile or choosing a dry cleaner. Like physicians, lawyers are subjected to heightened ethical demands on their conduct towards those they serve. These demands are needed because market forces, and the ordinary legal prohibitions against force and fraud, are simply insufficient to protect the consumers of their necessary services from the peculiar power of the specialized knowledge that these professionals possess.

Imbuing the legal profession with the necessary ethical standards is a task that involves a constant struggle with the relentless natural force of economic self-interest. It cannot be accomplished directly by legal rules, and it certainly will not succeed if sermonizing is the strongest tool that may be employed. Tradition and experiment have suggested a number of formal and informal mechanisms, none of which is adequate by itself and many of which may serve to reduce competition (in the narrow economic sense) among members of the profession. A few examples include the great efforts made during this century to improve the quality and breadth of the legal education that is required for admission to the bar; the concomitant attempt to cultivate a sub-class of genuine scholars within the profession; the development of bar associations that aspire to be more than trade groups; strict disciplinary rules about conflicts of interest and client abandonment; and promotion of the expectation that an attorney's history of voluntary public service is a relevant factor in selecting judicial candidates.

Restrictions on advertising and solicitation by lawyers properly and significantly serve the same goal. Such restrictions act as a concrete, day-to-day reminder to the practicing attorney of why it is improper for any member of this profession to regard it as a trade or occupation like any other. There is no guarantee, of course, that the restrictions will always have the desired effect, and they are surely not a sufficient means to their proper goal. Given their inevitable anticompetitive effects, moreover, they should not be thoughtlessly retained or insulated from skeptical criticism. Appropriate modifications have been made in the light of reason and experience, and other changes may be suggested in the future.

In my judgment, however, fairly severe constraints on attorney advertising can continue to play an important role in preserving the legal profession as a genuine profession. Whatever may be the exactly appropriate scope of these restrictions at a given time and place, this Court's recent decisions reflect a myopic belief that "consumers," and thus our nation, will benefit from a constitutional theory that refuses to recognize either the essence of professionalism or its fragile and necessary foundations. . . . In one way or another, time will uncover the folly of this approach. I can only hope that the Court will recognize the danger before it is too late to effect a worthwhile cure.

NOTES

1. After *Shapero,* the next major area of regulation that may come under scrutiny is in-person solicitation. Do you think that the Court was saying in *Ohralik* that substantial state interests justify a prophylactic rule banning all in-person solicitation? Or was it saying that the likelihood of overreaching was so substantial in the circumstances of that case that a prophylactic rule could be applied to Mr. Ohralik without the need to show actual injury?

If all it held was the latter, then the question remains whether all in-person solicitation may constitutionally be prohibited. For example, should the First Amendment be held to prohibit an absolute ban on lawyer solicitation of employment from persons and organizations engaged in business? If we put constitutional considerations aside, would you vote as a matter of public policy to permit such solicitation? See In re Amendment to S.J.C. Rule 3:07, DR 2-103 and DR 2-104, 398 Mass. 73 (1986), where the Massachusetts Supreme Judicial Court, by a vote of 4-3, refused to adopt a rule permitting such limited in-person solicitation.

2. One situation where solicitation rules are having an increasing, but uncertain, impact is when partners or associates leave a firm to join another or to start their own. Such an event does not just happen all at

once. The process of decision-making may take a long time. Indeed, an important consideration may be whether clients with whom the departing lawyer has a relationship will choose to stay with the departing lawyer or with the firm. The departing lawyer, however, may fear, and quite rightly, that to mention the possibility of departure will lead to immediate dismissal. Thus, the lawyer who is thinking about or planning a departure must worry about what it is permissible to say and do with respect to clients of the firm with whom he or she has a working relationship.

There is not a great deal of law, but there is some, with respect to this problem. Four associates of a law firm determined to leave and establish their own firm. They prepared letters to clients of the firm with open matters on which they had worked while employees of the firm. The letters informed Clients that they were leaving or had left the firm, and that Clients could choose to be represented by them, by Law Firm, or by any other attorney. Enclosed were a blank form discharging Law Firm and a contingent fee agreement. Some telephone calls and personal contacts were made with Law Firm clients to the same effect. A line of credit was obtained from a bank using as collateral Law Firm's cases on which they had worked and had not yet been turned over to them. The trial court enjoined the former associate from communicating with those persons who up to the date of their departure had active matters in which they were represented by Law Firm except that they could send out professional cards under DR 2-102. Clients of Law Firm were not precluded from discharging Law Firm and hiring the former associates. The injunction was reversed in the Superior Court and reinstated in the Pennsylvania Supreme Court. It found a clear violation of DR 2-103(A) and a clear interference with Law Firm's existing contractual relations with its clients. It found that the "contacts too easily could overreach and unduly influence . . . clients with active cases" and hence fell within the area of unprotected conduct outlined in *Ohralik*. Adler, Barish, Daniels, Levin, and Creskoff v. Epstein, 393 A. 2d 1175 (1978).

Another similar case that severely restricted a departing lawyer's ability to solicit employment from the clients of their former firm but allowed solicitation of clients on whose cases she was working at the time of her departure is Levine v. Morrison, 108 Wash. Daily L. Rep. 1133 (June 18, 1980) (D.C. Super. Ct.). See Hillman, Law Firms and Their Partners, 67 Tex. L. Rev. 1 (1988).

PROBLEM 71

Lawyer does a substantial amount of work as the negotiating agent for professional athletes. She wants to expand her activities by aggressive personal solicitation of the sort engaged in by her nonlawyer competitors. May she do so?

ABA FORMAL OPINION 336
June 3, 1974

The Committee has been asked from time to time whether the Code of Professional Responsibility is applicable to the conduct of a lawyer at a time when the lawyer is not engaged in the performance of his professional duties. The question has arisen since the "Watergate" episodes with some frequency in regard to DR 1-102(A)(3) and (4), which reads as follows:

(A) A lawyer shall not: . . . (3) Engage in illegal conduct involving moral turpitude. (4) Engage in conduct involving dishonesty, fraud, deceit, or misrepresentation.

The answer is that a lawyer must comply at all times with all applicable disciplinary rules of the Code of Professional Responsibility whether or not he is acting in his professional capacity.

Many, if not most, disciplinary rules by their nature relate only to conduct of a lawyer acting in his professional capacity. For example, DR 7-106, which regulates the trial conduct of a lawyer, obviously is concerned with the conduct of a lawyer in his professional capacity of a trial lawyer. However, other disciplinary rules are equally clearly designed to be applicable to a lawyer without regard to whether he is acting individually or as a lawyer. Examples include DR 8-102(A) and (B), proscribing false statements about judges and judicial candidates.

The provisions of DR 1-102(A)(3) and (4) are not limited to a lawyer's conduct while he is acting in his professional capacity as a lawyer. They are applicable to all conduct of the nature specified in those provisions without regard to the capacity in which the lawyer may be acting.[1]

In regulating a lawyer's nonprofessional as well as professional conduct, the Code of Professional Responsibility charted no new course. It is recognized generally that lawyers are subject to discipline for improper conduct in connection with business activities,[2] individual or personal activities,[3] and activities as a judicial, governmental or public official.[4] Furthermore, many states, by statute and independent of the code, discipline lawyers for certain illegal conduct.[5] And the grossly improper

---

1. Accord, In re Kirtz, 494 S.W.2d 324 (Mo. 1973).
2. See In re Wilson, 391 S.W.2d 914 (Mo. 1965); In re Gould, 164 N.Y.S.2d 48 (1957); In re Kirtz, 494 S.W.2d 324 (Mo. 1973); Murphy v. Erie County Bar Association, 328 N.Y.S.2d 949 (1972).
3. See Fellner v. Bar Association of Baltimore, 131 A.2d 729 (Md. 1957); Committee on Legal Ethics v. Scherr, 143 S.E.2d 141 (W.Va. 1965); Kentucky State Bar Association v. Martin, 490 S.W.2d 759 (Ky. 1973), and Anno., 36 A.L.R.3d 735 (1968).
4. See In re Wilson, 216 N.E.2d 555 (Ind. 1966); In re Chernoff, 26 A.2d 335 (Pa. 1942); Anno., 53 A.L.R.2d 305 (1957).
5. See In re Adams, 331 N.Y.S.2d 244 (1972); note, Disbarment: Non-Professional Conduct Demonstrating Unfitness to Practice, 43 CORNELL L.Q. 489 (1958).

conduct proscribed by DR 1-102(A)(3) and (4) is the kind of conduct that is sufficient to evidence lack of the requisite good moral character required of all members of the bar.

As stated in EC 1-2, the "public should be protected from those who are not qualified to be lawyers by reason of a deficiency in . . . moral standards." It would be utterly incongruous with the entire tenor of the code to find that its provisions regarding lawyers who engage in fraud, deceit, misrepresentation, or illegal conduct involving moral turpitude do not apply to them when they are acting as individuals or as public servants.

CHAPTER 9

ACCESS TO LEGAL SERVICES

A. PROGRAMS FOR NON-PAYING CLIENTS

At this point in our discussion of professional problems it seems appropriate to consider the manner in which the profession provides legal services to the public. One reason for doing this here is to take up some different issues of professional responsibility — issues that concern lawyers as a group instead of individually. A second reason is to reconsider a number of issues previously discussed in the context of legal assistance and group legal services offices. A third reason is to lay a foundation for subsequent topics in these materials, since much of the controversy concerning them has arisen in the context of the subject matter of this chapter.

This particular chapter may be approached in several different ways. Some may wish to focus more, or exclusively, on the profession's responsibility for the provision of services. Others may wish to spend a fair amount of time on problems that individual legal services and group legal services lawyers may face in the daily routine of their practice. The following problem relates to the materials in Subsections 1-3.

PROBLEM 72

You are charged with formulating policy recommendations for a group of legal assistance organizations with a central operating board but with a dozen operating branches. The following issues are on the agenda for discussion. Question one is whether and to what extent the individual branches should be allowed to make their own policy decisions. Question two is your preferred resolution of each of the following policy issues:

(a) Should each office take clients on a first-come, first-served basis, or should priority be given to class-action type suits or suits that may be labeled "law reform"? Such a choice must be made because it is anticipated that, like most other legal assistance organizations, these offices will not have sufficient resources to handle the caseload.

(b) If law reform is given priority, what criteria should be established for determining when a suit is "law reform"?

(c) Even if law reform issues are given priority, does the office have an obligation to try to handle as many cases as possible?

(d) What attitude should each office take toward the local bar? Should local bar leaders be involved in policy-making or advisory functions? Should general policy be established for all offices, or should an assessment be made of the local bar in each community before reaching a decision?

1. Legal Aid

As we consider the substantive issues of the direction that a legal services program should take, as presented by Problem 72, we should have in mind some of the history of the provision of legal services in this country.

The first systematic efforts to provide legal services to those who could not afford them began with the legal aid movement. The best known study is Emery Brownell, Legal Aid in the United States (1951 and Supp. 1961). A briefer, more critical assessment is contained in Chapter 1 of Justice and Reform (1974), by Earl Johnson, Jr., former director of the Legal Services Program of the Office of Economic Opportunity. See also Auerbach, Unequal Justice 53-62 (1976).

Throughout its history, as the Brownell and Johnson books demonstrate, the legal aid movement has encountered both conceptual and financial difficulties. To a large extent it tied itself to local bar associations for professional assistance and to private charity for financial assistance. A trend in the 1920s toward municipally funded legal assistance ended abruptly with the Depression. The tie to the local bar and private charity combined with a view that the great need was the provision of legal services to individuals who needed them. There was no focus on remedying the economic or social forces that produced the need. The result was that a group of underfinanced, overworked legal aid offices and lawyers handled an enormous number of cases for individual clients. As Johnson points out, at the beginning of the 1960s, "the equivalent of 400 full-time lawyers was available to serve almost 50 million Americans [who could not afford a lawyer] (a ratio of one lawyer for 120,000 persons) as compared with almost 250,000 full-time attorneys to take care of the remaining 140 million (a ratio of one lawyer for every 560 persons)."

Johnson, op. cit. supra, at 9. The concept of using a lawsuit as part of a general reform movement on behalf of the class of poor people — whom, as Abraham Lincoln put it, God must have loved because he made so many of them — became an issue in the provision of legal services only with the War on Poverty inaugurated under the auspices of President Johnson in the 1960s.

2. The OEO Legal Services Program and the Legal Services Corporation

ROGER C. CRAMTON,† CRISIS IN LEGAL SERVICES FOR THE POOR*

26 Villanova L. Rev. 521, 522 (1981)**

THE HISTORY OF CIVIL LEGAL ASSISTANCE

. . . Four eras in civil legal aid in the United States may be identified. Prior to 1875, legal aid was left to the unorganized and voluntary activities of individual lawyers. Although occasional representation was provided, the pro bono efforts of American lawyers were directed largely to the defense of indigents charged with crime, in itself no small task.

The rise of voluntary organizations — a typically American response to a tough social problem — characterizes the second era. The year 1875 marked the beginning of traditional legal aid through private organizations financed by charitable contributions, staffed by a small number of full-time lawyers, and assisted by the volunteered time of lawyers in private practice. Through the efforts of such pioneers as Reginald Heber Smith, and with the support of the organized bar, legal aid offices were established in most large metropolitan areas by 1962.

---

†Robert S. Stevens Professor of Law, Cornell University Law School; formerly, Chairman of the Board of Directors of the Legal Services Corporation, 1975-1978, and member of the Board, 1975-1979. I am indebted to various friends and colleagues for their helpful comments, especially Thomas Ehrlich, Steven Gold, Alan Houseman, and Richard Schmalbeck.

*This article was prepared from the fifth Donald A. Giannella Memorial Lecture of the Villanova University School of Law, April 9, 1981.

**The history recounted in this excerpt is updated in the Note by Kaufman and Singsen, pp. 547-550 infra.

It was a special honor for me to be invited to deliver this lecture because Don Giannella was a colleague in the work of the Administrative Conference of the United States in the early 1970's before his untimely death. He was a man of quiet force, tremendous integrity, and great dedication to teaching and scholarship. . . .

For the sake of convenience, material from the popular press will be cited by both author and title. Further, where citations do not include a specific page reference to the newspaper in which the source appears, a copy is on file at the Villanova Law Library.

Traditional legal aid was oriented toward individual client service, helping individuals with legal problems, such as landlord-tenant controversies, family quarrels, and consumer affairs. The implicit assumption was that justice was a civil right, not a commodity to be purchased.

A more controversial approach to legal aid characterized the third era, which began in 1965 with the legal services program of the now defunct Office of Economic Opportunity (OEO). The *Gideon* case had recognized a constitutional right to appointed counsel in criminal cases; a period of destructive urban riots had suggested the desirability of providing more peaceful methods of handling the grievances of the urban poor; and President Johnson, with large congressional support, had embarked on his War on Poverty.

The OEO legal services program did not reject the client-service objective of traditional legal aid, but it included an emphasis on two additional objectives: 1) social justice through law reform and income redistribution; and 2) political organization of the poor. It was assumed that legal rules and procedures would have a class bias against the poor. These rules could be reformed by impact litigation which would equalize the treatment of the poor and provide them with a larger share of the social pie. Similarly, the powerlessness of the poor — their lack of clout with elected officials — was attributed to their lack of organization. One major purpose of OEO legal services was to assist groups of poor people in organizing as groups. The formation of voting blocs would exert pressure on governmental institutions; poor people would acquire self-confidence and self-direction by participation in the power struggles of a pluralist society; and they would benefit from more favorable decisions by legislatures, administrative bodies, and the courts.

It is not surprising that a taxpayer-funded program with these objectives quickly became highly controversial. Many "poverty lawyers" funded by grants from OEO were viewed as left-wing agitators, engaged in a political agenda of their own and having little interest in the humdrum legal problems of the poor, with which traditional legal aid was almost exclusively concerned.

Political interference with the program began during the Johnson years and during the early '70s the program was fighting for its life. At one point President Nixon decided to dismantle the program and Howard Phillips, a young political lieutenant, was dispatched to the OEO to carry out the task. A series of bruising battles in Congress and the courts left the program in place but crippled in morale and funding. The American Bar Association, which had committed itself to publicly-funded legal assistance a few years earlier under the leadership of Lewis F. Powell, Jr., now Justice Powell, fought hard for the establishment of a permanent legal services program in a form that would remove it from the immediate supervision of the President and vicissitudes of politics. When President Nixon shifted ground and supported this approach, the

Legal Services Corporation Act was signed into law,[22] beginning the fourth era in civil legal aid. It was the last major piece of legislation signed by Nixon before his resignation in the summer of 1974. . . .

The Legal Services Corporation Act (Act) contained two features that were designed to cure most of the deficiencies of its OEO predecessor. The first was independence, both from political control by politicians and from political use by legal service attorneys; and the second was a strong focus on professionalism — delivering quality legal services in accordance with the best traditions of the profession. The creation of a new quasi-governmental body governed by an independent and non-partisan board of directors was designed to insulate legal services programs from the kind of political intervention that had troubled the OEO program. Statutory prohibitions prevented legal service grantees from using program funds or personnel for political purposes, organizational activities, or participation in strikes, picketing, and demonstrations.[27]

On the major issue of the nature and scope of representation to be provided to poor clients, the Act smothered quite different perspectives and objectives under a soothing new slogan: access to justice for all. This neutral principle clearly encompassed the individual-client service of traditional legal aid. It also included the law reform objective of the OEO program so long as the significant issues to be litigated arose out of client service in actual cases.

The governing principle was that a lawyer for the poor should do the best he can for his client, just as the lawyer for Exxon or anyone else does. If the zealous and complete representation required by the Code of Professional Responsibility leads the lawyer to believe that framing a test case, pursuing extensive discovery, or participating in adminstrative or legislative proceedings will best advance the interests of the client, then these activities should be undertaken.[29] The explicit statutory pro-

22. Legal Services Corporation Act, Pub. L. No. 93-355, 88 Stat. 378 (1974) (codified at 42 U.S.C. §2996 (1976 & Supp. 1979)). . . .

27. See 42 U.S.C. §2996a(7) (Supp. 1979) (forbidding legal assistance attorneys from participating in political activities such as voter registration and transportation); id. §2996(b)(5) (forbidding employees of recipients providing legal assistance from taking part in or encouraging public demonstrations, picketing, boycotts, or strikes); id. §2996f(a)(b) (forbidding staff attorneys from specified off-duty political activities). See also 45 C.F.R. §§1608, 1612 (1980) (implementing regulations). The constitutional issues raised by these and other restrictions are discussed in Note, Depoliticizing Legal Aid: A Constitutional Analysis of the Legal Services Corporation Act, 61 Cornell L. Rev. 734 (1976).

29. Congress, in defining the purposes of the Legal Services Corporation, declared that "attorneys providing legal assistance must have full freedom to protect the best interests of their clients in keeping with the Code of Professional Responsibility, the Canons of Ethics, and the high standards of the legal profession." 42 U.S.C. §2996(6) (1977). See also id. §2996e(b)(3) (Corporation must not interfere with any attorney carrying out his professional responsibilities).

viso was that the legal services attorney cannot dream up the law suit
and then solicit the client; the law suit must emerge out of routine client
service.[30] Nor could the legal services attorney organize a client group
so that he could litigate its rights.[31] But education of poor clients concerning their legal rights, including their right to organize, was not precluded.[32] These competing principles obviously require making a
number of fine distinctions.

Hence the present framework for legal services authorizes the full
armory of legal techniques and procedures to be brought to bear on
behalf of poor clients, as required in the particular case. Impact litigation and lobbying activities are included insofar as they arise out of client
representation.[33] But the more frankly political objectives of the OEO
program — to organize the poor or constituent segments as effective
pressure groups — are excluded by statute.[34] The Act substitutes more

---

30. The history of the "national back-up centers" created during the OEO years
provides the clearest illustration of this principle. These centers originally developed
in the mid-1960's and were designed to cure caseload and staffing problems of local
legal services projects by providing a national system of specialized legal services which
concentrated on cases involving issues affecting the entire class of the poor and by
providing expertise in poverty law that local service projects lacked. George [Develop-
ment of the Legal Services Corporation, 61 Cornell L. Rev. 681, 709-722 (1976)], at
709-722. After much success, these centers were attacked by conservative politicians as
an "intellectual brain trust which prepackages the lawsuits which go across the country."
119 Cong. Rec. 20,721 (1973) (remarks of Representative Conlan). The result was restrictive language in the Legal Services Corporation Act prohibiting the farming out of
research, training, and technical assistance by the Corporation. See 42 U.S.C.
§2996e(a)(3) (Supp. 1979). Restructured as "support centers," they now provide specialized litigation and lobbying services on behalf of *particular* clients and client groups
in such areas as education, health, housing, and welfare. See George, supra, at 709-722.
    31. The regulations of the Legal Services Corporation first prohibit staff attorneys
from participating in demonstrations, strikes, boycotts, and other such activities, but
then except "informing and advising a client about legal alternatives to litigation . . .
and [a]ttending a public demonstration . . . for the purpose of providing legal assistance
to a client. . . ." 45 C.F.R. §§1612.2, 1612.3 (1980). Similarly, legislative and administrative representation may be provided "on behalf of an eligible client . . . if the client may
be affected by a particular legislative or administrative measure but no employee shall
solicit a client in violation of professional responsibilities for the purpose of making
such representation possible. . . ." Id. §1612.4
    32. Id. §1612.3.
    33. See id. §1612.4(a)(2) ("An employee may engage in such activities [legislative
and administrative lobbying and representation] on behalf of an eligible client . . . if
the client may be affected by a particular legislative or administrative measure. . . .").
    34. See 42 U.S.C. §§2996e(d)(1)(4) (no use of corporation funds to advocate or op-
pose ballot measures, initiatives, or referenda); 2996f(a)(5)(A) (no use of corporation
funds to influence executive orders, administrative regulations, or legislation unless
necessary to representation of client); 2996f(b)(6) (no use of corporation funds to provide training programs to advocate or encourage public policies or political activities)
(Supp. 1979). See also 56 C.F.R. §1612.4(a)(2) (1980) ("no employee shall solicit a client
in violation of professional responsibilities for the purpose of making such representation [administrative or legislative] possible. . . .").

neutral rhetoric of "access to justice" for the more emotionally charged "law reform" and "social change" rhetoric of the OEO program.[35]

Description of the Current Program

Until the crisis precipitated by President Reagan's recent decision to eliminate the program, legal services prospered under the new structural arrangement. In 1975, when the Corporation came into being, the legal services program was clustered in major cities of the North and Far West; and the programs in these areas were starved and demoralized from five years of static funding and constant attack. In five short years, legal services has become a national program providing a minimum level of service to poor people in all parts of the country. Funding grew rapidly from $70 million in 1975 to $321 million in 1981.

The structure of the program is worth a brief explanation. The Corporation is not empowered to provide legal services to anyone.[39] It is a grant-making and regulatory organization that funds and supervises community-based organizations which hire attorneys to represent eligible poor persons.[40] The Corporation is governed by an eleven-member board of directors which selects a president, who in turn supervises an administrative staff.[41] The Corporation issues regulations governing the program (for example, defining the group eligible for service pursuant to general statutory guidelines),[42] makes grants to the local program for the delivery of legal services, audits and activities of these programs, and carries on general support activities such as training and research that assist the program as a whole.

Representation of poor clients is carried on by 323 local programs funded by the Corporation. They include a few specialized litigation organizations (referred to as support centers and having a national scope), a small number of specialized client programs for native Americans and migrants, and a large number of community-based programs scattered

---

35. 42 U.S.C. §§2996b, 2996e (Supp. III 1979). See Bellow, Turning Solutions into Problems: The Legal Aid Experience, 34 NLADA Briefcase 106, 107-108 (1977). Bellow describes the approach of the Legal Services Corporation as that of more of the same. Id. at 107. He describes the current technique of the Corporation as one to "expand existing programs, establish new ones in areas where services have not previously been available, dampen any excessively political rhetoric which might evoke images of the more controversial sixties, and eventually establish a 'national delivery system' of legal help to the poor." Id. at 107-108.

39. See 42 U.S.C. §2996e(a) (1976) (outlining the powers, duties and limitations of the Corporation); id. §2996f (outlining the requisites and limitations on recipient organizations and clients in making grants and contracts).

40. See id. §§2996b, 2996e.

41. Id. §2996c (dealing with the board of directors); id. §2996d (dealing with the appointment and powers of the president).

42. See 45 C.F.R. §1611 (1980).

throughout the country, each serving a particular geographic area. Each local program is a separate non-profit corporation, with its own board of directors and staff. Statutory provisions and Corporation regulations govern the composition and functions of the governing boards.[45]

The 323 independent programs funded by the Corporation are staffed by about 6,200 attorneys, 2,800 paralegals, and a large number of secretaries and clerks. They handle more than 1,000,000 poor clients a year through about 1,200 local offices. Although the independent programs receive support from other sources, over two-thirds of the total funding comes from the Corporation. Other federal funding sources provide about 22%, with private contributions and state and local government contributing the remaining 11%.

The staff lawyers employed by the local programs are generally relatively young and low paid; entering salaries average about $14,000 per year and average salaries for all lawyers are less than $17,000; both figures are well below compensation provided by private law firms or other government offices. Case loads are large, ranging up to 150-250 open cases per attorney. The new attorneys are generally liberal and idealistic, and there is a high turnover. About one-fourth of new attorneys leave the program in a year or less; more than 80% are gone after three years. Those who survive more than three years are likely to make a career of legal services; they become the leaders and supervisors of the more inexperienced attorneys who join the program, work with a burst of enthusiasm for a year or two, and leave "burned out" by the constant pressure of handling a large volume of generally routine cases.

An American Bar Foundation study of the legal needs of the public suggests that nearly one-fourth of poor people have a civil legal problem each year deserving of a lawyer's attention.[52] Under current eligibility standards, which permit an annual income no larger than $4,738 for a single person and $9,313 for a family of four, about 29 million Americans fall within the pool of eligible clients. Obviously, only a small fraction of them receive service each year. Although no precise information is available, it is estimated that the current program handles about one-eighth of the legal needs of eligible poor persons. An enormous but unlikely expansion in the program would be required to meet the needs of all.

Last year the legal services program handled about one and one-half million matters for over a million poor persons. The average cost of each matter handled is about $200. The program's clients are 51% white, 30% black, and 10% Hispanic. Only one-fifth of them are employed; most are living on welfare or Social Security.

45. 42 U.S.C. §2996f(c) (1976); 45 C.F.R. §1607 (1980).

52. B. Curran, The Legal Needs of the Public c. 4 (American Bar Foundation 1977).

The types of cases fall into expected categories. Thirty-four percent involve family matters; 17% involve landlord-tenant or other housing problems; 14% are concerned with income maintenance; and 12% involve consumer disputes. The rest involve an enormous variety of subjects.

CRITICISMS OF THE LEGAL SERVICES PROGRAM

Criticisms of the current legal services program fall into three categories: 1) the program is a political instrument of activist lawyers; 2) it is not a poor people's program but a lawyer's program; and 3) it is inefficient both in assisting poor people and in the costs it places on others. Each of these charges deserves examination.

A. POLITICAL ACTIVISM

The most common criticism of the legal services program is that it embodies or encourages activism by staff attorneys who seek to stir up litigation to force judicial resolution of matters that should be left to elected officials.[57] Even the statement of the criticism raises fundamental questions not limited to legal aid, concerning the appropriate role of courts, legislatures, and the executive in a democratic society, to say nothing of the difficulty of characterizing particular issues as "political" or "activist." The legal services program is attacked because it tempts judges to venture into areas in which critics believe they should not enter. . . .

The "political activism" critique, insofar as it does not overlap with more general concern about judicial activism, appears to involve two subthemes: the propriety of the government funding law suits against itself, and the relative emphasis in the legal services program of impact litigation as against individual client service.

Should the federal legal services program permit representation involving suits against governmental units or before legislative bodies, including administrative rulemaking? It is apparent that the program as we now know it would be crippled if these forms of representation were to be prohibited. Poor people would have effective recourse against merchants, landlords, and other private persons, but not against governmental agencies or officers. . . .

---

57. See Ostroff, Legal Aid Is Target of Conservatives Who See It As Subsidized Liberalism, Kansas City Times, Jan. 26, 1981, §A, at 1, col. 1. See also Schlafly, Lawyers for Poor Loaded with Fat, St. Louis Globe-Democrat, Mar. 13, 1981, col. 1. Ms. Schlafly argues that the "Legal Services Corp. . . . has turned into a monster which is fomenting radical and revolutionary programs at the taxpayers' expense. . . . Many activists financed by the Legal Services Corp. are committed to the goal of implementing a radical social and political agenda." Id.

Legal services lawyers sue governmental bodies to vindicate the legal rights of the poor. While it rankles some politicians to use government funds this way, there is every reason to make a large, bureaucratic, and fallible government accountable in its own courts. The legitimacy of the claims asserted, of course, is determined by the independent judiciary, not by the indigent clients or their lawyers. The counter argument appears to rest solely on a concern that such suits increase the cost of government because of the expense of defense and the fact that litigation sometimes requires increased expenditures such as payment of welfare benefits wrongly withheld. But such representation of the poor often reduces the work load of government agencies by putting the claims of poor people into a comprehensible form so that they may be handled easily and cheaply. Even if the increased costs more than offset the savings, the enhanced legitimacy of the government resulting from its compliance with the rule of law is itself of incalculable value.

The second subtheme concerns the relative emphasis of the legal services program on impact litigation rather than individual client service. The critics of the legal services program talk as if the only cases that a program should handle are those that are routine and unimportant, affecting the individual client and no one else. The normal rules of stare decisis and res judicata make that an impossible goal since a judicial precedent affects all persons similarly situated and res judicata may bind the same defendant when sued by other plaintiffs, now that issue preclusion has moved away from the former requirement of mutuality of estoppel.[61]

Moreover, whether the result in a law suit will turn out to be significant cannot be determined at its commencement. The importance of a decision results from the particular findings of fact and rulings of law that a court makes at the conclusion of a case. Many lawyers have been disappointed when their "landmark" cases were ultimately decided on trivial points, and major rulings have often emerged from routine cases. Nor can it be assumed that significant cases will all be decided in favor of the indigent client, since major cases can be lost as well as won.

It is true that the legal services movement has a shared ideology in which "law reform litigation" is highly valued.[62] Abandonment of any opportunity to engage in significant litigation or legislative activity would make the program uninteresting to many of the better lawyers who now find it a fulfilling career. Inability to raise and win significant victories for poor people — however "significance" is determined — would also make a mockery of our claim of equal justice under law. The lawyer for the poor client would be restricted to repetitive and insignificant problems, and presumably would have to abandon his client's in-

61. See Parklane Hosiery Co. v. Shore, 439 U.S. 322 (1979) (authorizing offensive use of issue preclusion in the federal courts).
62. See e.g., E. Johnson, [p. 532, supra] at 278-284; Bellow, supra note 35, at 106.

terests, in violation of professional ethics, when an issue of importance to others emerged.

Aside from these practical and philosophical difficulties with the concern about law reform, there is an efficiency concern. Repetitive litigation of the same problem in one-by-one litigation is wasteful of private and public resources. The disposition of significant issues in a manner that affects a large number of people provides a much more efficient use of taxpayer funds for legal services. Any other approach would be wasteful and duplicative, even if feasible.

The concern about impact litigation also rests on an inaccurate perception of the underlying facts. The critics of legal services have been mesmerized by the publicity given to a small number of highly visible controversies and by the ambitious rhetoric of an occasional legal services lawyer, who may talk enthusiastically and unrealistically about changing the world through test cases or class actions. The reality of day-by-day work in a legal services office, however, is far different.[63] . . .

Evaluations of individual programs and of the national effort almost invariably conclude that most programs are devoting a disproportionate amount of their time to routine matters and that federal dollars would be more effective if a larger portion were devoted to significant matters.[66] Data concerning the frequency of class actions point in the same direction. A survey of a random sample of legal services attorneys in 1978 revealed that only 29% of them had participated in at least one class action during the immediately prior period of more than three years.[67] These figures suggest that, whatever the occasional rhetoric may be at national meetings at which legal services attorneys exchange views, the individual programs find it impossible to resist the enormous pressure of the hurt, troubled people who fill their waiting rooms and request, with the most obvious need, routine legal services. . . .

B.   A LAWYERS' PROGRAM, NOT A POOR PEOPLES' PROGRAM

A more fundamental but less common critique of the legal services program is that, despite its noble pretense, its benefits go largely to lawyers instead of poor people. The argument has been most fully stated by Stephen Chapman.[69] Mr. Chapman raises provocative questions concerning the purposes and effects of the legal services program.

---

63. See Bellow, supra note 35, at 108-109 (stating that the recurrent features of legal services programs are routine processing of cases, low client autonomy, narrow definitions of client concerns, and inadequate outcomes).

66. See Bellow, supra note 35, at 121-122.

67. See Houseman, [Class Actions and Legal Services 11 (1980) (unpublished memorandum for the Legal Services Corporation)].

69. See Chapman, The Rich Get Rich, and the Poor Get Lawyers, The New Republic, Sept. 24, 1977, at 9, reprinted in 126 Cong. Rec. 14688 (1980) (remarks of Sen. Helms).

Who benefits from the program? asks Mr. Chapman. He answers that its principal benefits run to its lawyer supporters and proponents, not to the poor people who are its ostensible beneficiaries. The legal services program, according to Mr. Chapman, is a full employment bill for lawyers.[70] The ABA and other bar associations support the program because it provides employment for the current overflow of young lawyers from the law schools, who would otherwise be in competition with the existing private bar. Since legal services programs are prohibited from taking fee-generating cases, they do not compete with private lawyers. Even more important, every case handled by a legal services lawyer creates new business for other lawyers, since the opposing parties need the services of a lawyer. Thus the program has a tremendous multiplier effect; it not only relieves the competitive pressures of new lawyers entering the legal market, but also requires additional compensated lawyer time to defend the claims brought by legal services lawyers. . . .

The second wing of Mr. Chapman's argument characterizes the program as paternalistic and doubts the importance of the public provision of legal services in contrast to other possible benefits for the poor, especially money. Mr. Chapman argues that lawyers exaggerate the importance of legal counsel, regarding it, "like food, shelter, and medical care, as a basic right, the lack of which makes life practically intolerable."[71] Lawyers, like every other group, tend to "magnify the importance of what they do."[72] This is especially so when public provision of legal services serves lawyers' self interest and relieves them of the duty to provide pro bono services to those who can't afford to pay. . . .

The issues presented by these arguments are very broad, far beyond the scope of this discussion, but a brief response is required.

First, the opportunity to enforce legal rights and responsibilities involves more than just economics and efficiency. It is a question of the moral tone of a society and the legitimacy of its institutions. Although we must be self-critical of our tendency as lawyers to prefer the virtues of law over other things, many laymen share our view of the priority of the rule of law.

Second, the economic arguments in favor of distribution of money rather than legal services assume that substantial amounts of money would be available for distribution and that market imperfections do not prevent rational choices by poor people. Both assumptions are dubious. The current appropriation for the national legal services program amounts to only about ten dollars per eligible poor person. That amount

---

70. Id. at 10. Chapman argues that: "LSC-funded programs offer jobs that otherwise wouldn't exist, making the program something of a Humphrey-Hawkins bill of the legal community." Id.

71. Id.

72. Id.

of money will not purchase much in the way of legal services or anything else. And poor people, precisely because they are often uneducated and uninformed, may lack reliable information concerning their need for legal services and how to get them, as well as the ability to pay for them.[76] In using money made available by the state, they may not be able to make informed choices.

Finally, especially in situations in which poor people are affected, but each with respect to a small amount, there is a free-rider problem.[77] No one has an incentive to expend the amount necessary to litigate a $100 claim, but the pooling effect of legal services operates to confer a benefit on all members of the group by supporting litigation based on the aggregated value of the claims, which may be very large.

C. ECONOMIC EFFICIENCY

Arguments that the legal services program is paternalistic and lawyer-oriented are closely related to attacks on the program on grounds of economic efficiency. Professor Posner, for example, states some of the same points made by Chapman in language more familiar to economists.[78] Providing legal services to the poor at no price, he argues, "prevents many poor people from achieving their most efficient pattern of consumption."[79] A poor person will accept free legal services unless their value to him is outweighed by the lost time and other inconvenience of dealing with a lawyer. The demand for free legal services will invariably exceed the available supply, creating a serious rationing problem.[80] Since the value to some recipients will be less than its cost to the taxpayers, the distribution of free services is wasteful. It is better, in his view, to give poor persons $100 and let them decide how to spend it.[81]

Posner also argues that free legal services misallocate resources in other respects. Since legal services are usually employed in a dispute with another, the adverse party must increase its legal expenditures or abandon its stake in the dispute. These costs, if a market for services and products is involved, will inevitably be passed on as costs of production.

76. I am uncomfortable with the paternalism implicit in this argument. Moreover, even if there is a lack of information concerning legal needs and substantial options among poor people, a less intrusive approach for government would be to provide relevant information rather than the service itself.

77. "Free riders" are those who receive the benefits of successful litigation although they bear none of the costs. For discussion of the "free ride" problem in the administrative law field, see Cramton, The Why, Where, and How of Broadened Public Participation in the Administrative Process, 60 Geo. L.J. 525 (1972). For discussion of the alternative of aggregating numerous small claims through class action proceedings, see R. Posner, Economic Analysis of Law 449-450 (2d ed. 1977).

78. See R. Posner, supra note 77, at 355-359.

79. Id. at 355.

80. Id.

81. Id.

Thus, for example, enforcement of building codes against landlords will result in a substantial reduction in the supply of low-income housing, and a substantial rise in the price of the remaining supply.[82]

Litigation against governmental agencies has somewhat different effects, Posner argues, since the costs are borne by taxpayers rather than by those purchasing the product or service. In some situations such litigation may redistribute income to the poor who are beneficiaries of the social program under consideration, while in others it may merely redistribute the program's benefits among groups of beneficiaries.[83] In any event, if litigation results in increased taxes, legislative efforts may be made to reduce future eligibility or benefits.

The provision of free legal services also creates opportunities for abuse when particular opponents are singled out for extensive and repetitive litigation.[84] The typical litigant's hunger for justice is moderated by the relationship between what is at stake and the costs of getting it. The appetite for litigation will disappear as legal expenses approach the value of the expected outcome. Because a subsidized litigant does not operate under the same constraint, there is always the possibility that his willingness to devote an indefinite amount of legal resources to a case will extort unjust settlements.

A similar problem arises when the stakes of the parties in a legal controversy are widely disparate. If an injured plaintiff in a mass tort situation has only $1,000 at stake while the defendant is worried about the res judicata effect of an adverse decision on claims of a much larger amount, the willingness of the latter to litigate may force a settlement for an amount well below the value of the claim. Institutional litigants may thus often be able to bring great pressure upon individual litigants because they have more at stake.[85]

The ability to whipsaw opponents is present in some situations involving publicly funded legal services. As a factual matter, abuses do not appear to occur with great frequency, partly because legal services pro-

82. Id. at 356-359. The effects of the enforcement of housing codes is discussed in Ackerman, Regulating Slum Housing Markets on Behalf of the Poor: Of Housing Codes, Housing Subsidies and Income Redistribution Policy, 80 Yale L.J. 1093 (1971). See also Komesar, Return to Slumville: A Critique of the Ackerman Analysis of Housing Code Enforcement and the Poor, 82 Yale L.J. 1175 (1973).

83. See R. Posner, supra note 77, at 356.

84. See Bellow, supra note 35, at 122. Bellow writes: "[W]here such a 'focused case' strategy is followed, illegal and exploitative practices that affect poor people can be changed. This is so because they are often the product of cost calculations which are radically altered when (a) confronted with a substantial number of complainants; (b) with a real stake in the outcome; (c) who do not have to absorb the attorney and other costs which would ordinarily be involved in pursuing such grievances to completion. . . . [T]here is a great deal of potential for organization and leverage for low-income clients in systematically focusing intake and advocacy in individual cases in this way."

85. See Galanter, Why the 'Haves' Come Out Ahead: Speculations on the Limits of Legal Change, 9 Law & Soc. Rev. 95 (1974).

grams have such limited resources spread over so many potential cases.[86] An amendment to the statute now provides protection for those inconvenienced by frivolous suits.[87]

Arguments concerning the efficiency effects of the legal services programs fail to reflect the benefits provided to poor people as a class when small claims, uneconomic to be litigated individually by any claimant, are pursued systematically on behalf of such persons as consumers or tenants.[88] Moreover, one of the great advantages of the program is that substantial benefits accrue even to those who are not represented. To the extent that legal rules and procedures are modified in favor of welfare recipients, consumers, tenants, and other classes, everyone in the class, even those not eligible for free legal services, is benefitted. By assisting a small proportion of poor people, benefits are produced for a much larger group. Costs to the same class may also rise, but the choice of enforcing or not enforcing legal rights should be left to litigants rather than decided in the abstract by the social critic.

Supporters and critics of the legal services program do not question its effectiveness as an instrument for enforcing the legal rights of the poor.[89] Both agree that it produces substantial results. The criticisms, rather, are that the assertion of these claims tempts judges to do things they shouldn't do, benefits lawyers more than clients, or misallocates resources in the community.

Although the philosophical and economic objections of critics such as Chapman and Posner raise serious questions, the political opposition to the legal services program is based on its very success and the erroneous perspective that views its law reform aspects as more dominant than it

---

86. See Bellow, supra notes 35, at 108-109, 119-122. Bellow describes the actual practice of legal services programs as conforming to a "minimal help-maximum numbers" approach which provides routinized and limited service to as large a number of clients as possible. Id. at 110, 117. He severely criticizes this approach, urging a more focused law-reform strategy that would provide a much higher quality of service to a smaller group of clients. Id. at 121-122.

87. See 42 U.S.C. §2996d(f) (Supp. 1980). As amended, the statute provides that a defendant who prevails in an action brought by a legal services program is entitled to an award of reasonable costs and legal fees incurred in defense of the action if the court finds that the action was commenced or pursued for the sole purpose of harassment of the defendant or that the corporation or the plaintiff maliciously abused legal process.

88. See Brooke, Legal Services: Government at its Best, Wash. Star, Mar. 9, 1981, col. 3.

89. See Brill, Reagan Voters: Don't Read This, The American Lawyer, Oct. 1980. Brill describes the effectiveness of the legal services program in New Haven, Connecticut: "Morrison's work punctures these myths [that government poverty programs are ineffective] so clearly that Reagan should send a hit squad after him." Id., col. 1. See also Cockburn & Ridgeway, Poor Law: The Attack on Legal Services, Voice (Feb. 4, 1981), at 12, col. 1 ("Of all the liberal programs generated by the reforming spasm of the 1960s, [the legal services program has] been particularly successful, in terms of dollar value, effectiveness, and absence of corruption."). Similarly, critics of the program emphasize the effectiveness of the program in advancing what are perceived as ideological objectives. . . .

really is. Lawyers who do a good job representing poor people inevitably will collide with the interests of powerful business groups and government agencies; those who are on the receiving end of these not-so-tender ministrations of justice will usually not be pleased.

The claims brought by legal services programs on behalf of poor people are decided by judges, not by legal services lawyers. Approximately 85% of all matters are resolved favorably to the program's clients, a remarkably high success rate. The rub about the legal services program may be that it is successful, and its very success creates opposition among interests adversely affected. "Political activism" and similar slogans may be code words for another complaint: "their just claims have been upheld against us and we resent it."

THE CURRENT CRISIS

A.   TERMINATION

As previously indicated, President Reagan seeks to abolish the current program, leaving nothing in its place. Members of the private bar would once again assume collective responsibility for meeting the legal needs of the poor. Non-federal funds now available for legal services, estimated at about $48 million in a recent year, might continue to flow to legal services organizations;[95] and strenuous fundraising efforts at the state and local level might expand this total somewhat.

If termination of federal funding occurs, the legal services program will revert to the situation prevailing prior to 1965: traditional legal aid on the charity model. The American bar would then be faced with the tremendous challenge of meeting the most essential needs through volunteered services and financial contributions.

B.   TRANSFORMATION

Two major alternatives have been advanced that would transform the legal services program. One would abolish the Corporation as a governing body and funding conduit, and allow states to devote a portion of a federal block grant to legal services. Under this proposal, the administration of a large number of human-service programs would be transferred to the states under a block grant. No funds would be included in

---

95. See Legal Services Corporation, Delivery Systems Study: A Research Project on the Delivery of Legal Services to the Poor. This study reported that in 1976, 67% of total funds expended by legal services programs for civil legal assistance came from the Legal Services Corporation. Id. Almost two-thirds of the non-Corporation funding also came from federal sources. Funds from state and local governments and from private sources provided only about 9% of total funding.

the initial block grant for legal services, and all of the transferred programs would be reduced by 25%.[97] . . .

A second proposal for the transformation of the legal services program is also lurking in the wings. This is a substitution, in whole or part, of a judicare system for the current staff-attorney system.[99] Judicare, the legal analog to medicare, involves the provision of legal services to eligible clients by members of the private bar, who are then paid by the government for their services. A study by a Reagan transition team recommended a move to judicare, coupling it with a funding cut, the abolition of support centers, and legislation restricting both eligibility and representation. The study recommended that the portion of the Corporation budget devoted to judicare be increased from less than 1% now to 15% next year, 35% the following year, and 50% the year after.

The questions of organizational structure and relative efficiency raised by a judicare alternative are complex and controversial.[101] This is not the place for a full exploration of them. My view is that a complete legal services program would have staff attorney and judicare components, since each has some advantages. In some sparsely settled areas, reliance on private attorneys may be necessary, and for some routine problems such as divorces, bankruptcies, and the like, private attorneys may be able to perform the tasks at least as efficiently, leaving the staff attorneys to provide more specialized legal services for poor people. It is one thing, however, to add a judicare supplement to the existing programs, and quite another to dismember the existing staff attorney program, which is operating effectively, for an uncertain merger with judicare at lower funding levels.

The politics of judicare are troublesome because the organized bar, which is the most active lobbyist for legal services, is divided on the subject. Large firm lawyers tend to support the existing staff-attorney system, while solo practitioners and small firm lawyers, who feel increasingly threatened by the many changes affecting the legal profession, are very supportive of judicare. Under pressure from some state bars and its own general practice section, the ABA recently adopted a resolution urging Congress to amend the Act "to mandate the opportunity for substantial involvement of private lawyers in providing legal services for the poor."[102] This ambiguously worded resolution includes pro bono in-

97. See Ranii & Bourne, [Nat'l L.J., March 23, 1981] at 1, col. 2.

99. See Cockburn & Ridgeway, supra note 89, at 13, col. 2.

101. For the views of the Legal Services Corporation, see The Delivery Systems Study: A Policy Report to the Congress and the President of the United States (June 1980). For other views, see Brakel, Styles of Delivery of Legal Services to the Poor: A Review Article, 1977 Am. B. Foundation, Res. J. 219, criticizing Earl Johnson's views as expressed in the first part of M. Cappelletti, J. Gordley & E. Johnson, Toward Equal Justice: A Comparative Study of Legal Aid in Modern Societies 140-190 (1975).

102. 66 A.B.A.J. 1058 (Sept. 1980).

volvement of the private bar as well as compensated services, and in this form it is receiving the wholehearted support of the Legal Services Corporation. . . .

2. Crippling Restrictions

Another mode of attack on legal services is to cripple it with demeaning or inappropriate restrictions. Current hearings in the House of Representatives on the reauthorization are exploring a variety of restrictions on the persons eligible for service, the types of cases that may be undertaken, the scope of representation, and similar limitations. The harmful effect of such restrictions turns entirely on the content and effects of the particular restriction.

The Act has always contained restrictions on the availability and type of service. Questions of policy in the provision of publicly-funded services are appropriate for legislative resolution, especially when choices as to who enjoys a social benefit must inevitably be made. Examples of longstanding restrictions are those relating to criminal cases and fee-generating cases, which prevent the use of Corporation funds in situations in which representation is available from other sources.[104] More controversial are present restrictions on handling school desegregation cases, draft matters, abortion cases, and cases involving homosexual rights.[105] The ABA, the Corporation, and the legal services community have opposed such restrictions, but the existing restrictions have not been especially troublesome because their scope is so limited and most programs are inactive in the areas involved.

During the reauthorization hearings in 1980, however, and again in the current session, a number of restrictions were proposed which would have a more substantial effect on the program. Some of the major proposals are: exclusion of aliens or migrants from representation, prohibition of class suits, prohibition of administrative or legislative representation, and prohibition of suits against governmental units or officers. Any such restrictions on service would be highly unfortunate. Here again, however, there are substantial differences in relative effect. Exclusion of service to aliens, for example, especially if limited to illegal aliens, would not be disastrous and could be justified as expressing a legislative priority concerning the use of a scarce public resource.

Because of the political sensitivity concerning class actions, there has been a great deal of discussion of a broad prohibition of the use of this procedural device by legal services lawyers. Some opponents of the legal services program appear to suggest that withdrawal of this weapon

104. See 42 U.S.C. §2996f(b)(1) (1976) & 45 C.F.R. §1609 (1980) (fee-generating cases); 42 U.S.C. §2996f(b)(1) & 45 C.F.R. § 1615 (1980) (criminal cases).
105. See 42 U.S.C. §2996f(b)(8)-(10) (Supp. III 1979).

would eliminate impact litigation. They are uninformed or engaged in wishful thinking. Prohibiting class suits would have some adverse consequences on the program, but it would not eliminate law reform through impact litigation. This is so because individual cases against the same defendants would have much the same effect as class suits: the rules of stare decisis and res judicata would extend the benefits of one poor person's suit to others similarly situated.

The effects of a restriction of this kind would be more symbolic than practical. Concerning practical effects, discovery might be somewhat more limited in an action brought by an individual plaintiff than it would be in one brought on behalf of a class, and the contempt sanction for violation of a decree would not be as readily available. Each of these effects is relatively minor.

The real cost of a class action restriction is symbolic: the attorneys who represent the poor would not be able to employ the same armory of procedural devices that are available to other litigants. This pointed message would adversely affect the morale and self-image of legal services lawyers, who already feel besieged, and who are working for low salaries in unfavorable and often hostile environments. Statutory restrictions that prevent them from providing the complete and zealous representation that the Code of Professional Responsibility requires[113] — and that is available to other litigants — reinforces an image of second-class citizenship for themselves and their clients.

Of the possible restrictions listed above, the ones most damaging to the effective operation of the program and to any semblance of equal justice under the law are those which would prohibit suits against governmental units and all forms of legislative representation before legislatures and administrative bodies concerning statutes and rules affecting the poor. These restrictions would destroy the legal services program as we now know it. . . .

VI.   Why Legal Services for the Poor?

The legal services program is commonly viewed by its proponents, as well as its critics, as a mechanism for redistribution of social wealth to the poor. There are three difficulties with this view: 1) economic theory often denies that changing a legal rule will have the effect of redistributing income within the larger community; 2) the redistribution theory invites courts to decide issues that are more properly left to resolution by policy makers; and 3) it is inconsistent with the facts, both in respect to the bulk of the activities of legal service programs and in its overesti-

---

113. ABA Code of Professional Responsibility (August 1977): Canon 6: "A lawyer should represent a client competently." Canon 7: "A lawyer should represent a client zealously within the bounds of the law."

mation of the capacity of litigation to perform such dramatic changes in economic well-being.

These arguments have been touched upon at other points in this paper, so I offer only a brief recap at this point. Global changes such as large-scale redistribution of income within the community cannot be accomplished by lawsuit except in rare and limited situations.[120] The cooperation and action of legislative bodies is required for accomplishments of this character. . . .

So far, my justification for publicly-funded legal services has been negative in character, expressing doubts that broad claims of social justice are an achievable and appropriate goal of the national legal services program. But much of a positive nature needs to be said as to why publicly-funded legal assistance for the poor is an essential buttress of our enduring values. The arguments will be marshalled under three heads: 1) access to justice, 2) the bias of law against the unrepresented, and 3) helping individuals to help themselves.

A.   ACCESS TO JUSTICE

Provision of legal services for the poor is a conservative program in the sense that it helps preserve the enduring values of our republican form of government — access to justice on reasonably equal terms, and due process and equal justice for all. . . .

B.   THE BIAS OF THE LAW AGAINST THE UNREPRESENTED

The legal services program improves legal rules and procedures so that poor people get a fairer break. The thought behind this assertion is the reality that all of our institutions tend to respond to the interests that are present and represented. Just as regulatory agencies, if they are closeted with industry representatives for a period of years are frequently captured by them, so legislatures, courts, and administrative bodies re-

---

120. Marc Galanter sums up a large number of studies in the following sentences: "Legal professionals have tended to overestimate the benefits that could be delivered through obtaining rule-changes from eminent institutions, especially from courts. A vast literature has documented the constantly rediscovered and never-quite-believed truths that judicial . . . pronouncements do not change the world; that the benefits of such changes do not penetrate automatically and costlessly to their intended beneficiaries; that often they do not benefit the latter at all. We have some notion of why rule-changes produced by courts are particularly unlikely to be important sources of redistributive change. . . . Like everything else, favorable rules are resources and those who enjoy disproportionate shares of other resources tend also to reap the benefit of rules." Galanter, Delivering Legality: Some Proposals for the Direction of Research, 11 Law & Soc. Rev. 225, 228-229 (1976). See also Hazard, Law Reforming in the Anti-Poverty Effort, 37 U. Chi. L. Rev. 242 (1970).

spond to the viewpoints that are presented and the arguments that are made. . . .

Legal services for the poor offer an effective and efficient remedy. It is an efficient remedy because it is not essential that representation be provided to every tenant, consumer, borrower or the like in order for beneficient effects to be felt. Provision of legal services for some of the poor changes rules and procedures that benefit everyone in the affected class, even those who are not poor. . . .

C. HELPING THE HURT AND SUFFERING

Finally, in a society that values the dignity of the individual, the role of legal services in helping the poor to help themselves must remain the basic justification. The legal services program helps bring justice to individuals who are hurt, troubled, unfortunate, and dispossessed. What further justification is required other than: "Because they need it and they are important?". . .

NOTES

1. Note the explicit recognition by Professor Cramton that a major purpose of the OEO legal services program was not merely to achieve "social justice through law reform and income redistribution" but that it also envisaged and in many places undertook "political organization of the poor." (p. 526) It was this feature of the program, the actual organization and politicization of community groups through use of government money, that sparked a great deal of political opposition that when it came attacked not only the overt political activities but also the legal manifestation of those activities, especially the class action suits against governmental entities. See Agnew, What's Wrong With the Legal Services Program, 58 A.B.A.J. 930, 931 (1972): "What we may be on the way to creating is a federally funded system manned by ideological vigilantes, who owe their allegiance not to a client, not to the citizens of a particular state or locality and not to the elected representatives of the people, but only to a concept of social reform." For a response, see Klaus, Legal Services Program: Reply to Vice President Agnew, 58 A.B.A.J. 1178 (1972).

It was criticism of this sort that partly explains some of the restrictions on the activities of grantees of the Legal Services Corporation that are referred to by Professor Cramton and further elaborated in Notes 2, 3, and 4. They are also partly the product of the negotiations that led to support of the organized bar for the "depoliticized" Legal Services Corporation. The main casualty of the change in direction of legal services after establishment of the Legal Services Corporation was not the class action suit against government but rather the political organization of the local client community that had been the hallmark of many OEO legal services programs. Some see a potential for renewal of community political organization through the growing clinical education programs at law schools. That perception is fueled by a movement of legal services attorneys into such programs. It is ironic that it was the growing importance of the leadership of the organized bar, especially the American Bar Association, in legal services that helped dampen the political organization movement within legal services in the mid-1970s, for it is now the Section on Legal Education of the American Bar Association that is allied with the clinical teachers against at least some of the leadership of the Association of American Law Schools in a struggle to require law schools to change their criteria for tenure in order to create tenure positions for clinical faculty. See David Vernon, Status of Clinicians — Proposed Standard 405(e) in Association of American Law Schools, The President's Address 1 (January 1983).

2. Professor Cramton refers to some of the restrictions on use of funds that have been imposed by Congress on grantees from the Legal Services Corporation. They have been described in a summary form in a Note in the American Bar Association Journal, 60 A.B.A.J. 1045 (1974).

The act contains many restrictions, which for convenience may be classified as restrictions (1) on the corporation itself; (2) on the corporation and recipients; (3) on recipients and staff attorneys (a "staff attorney" being a lawyer who receives more than a half of his annual professional income from a recipient); (4) on employees of the corporation and recipients; (5) on attorneys employed full time; (6) on "all attorneys engaged in legal assistance activities supported in whole or in part" by L.S.C.; and (7) on the use of funds.

Restrictions on the corporation — The corporation may not participate in litigation on behalf of clients other than itself, and it may not undertake to influence legislation, except that personnel of L.S.C. may testify or make other "appropriate communication" when requested to do so by a legislative body or a member of one or in connection with legislation or appropriations affecting the corporation.

Restrictions on the corporation and recipients — Neither the L.S.C. nor a recipient may contribute or make available corporate funds or program personnel or equipment for political parties or candidates or to advocate or oppose "any ballot measures, initiatives, or referendums." The act adds at this point: "However, an attorney may provide legal advice and representation as an attorney to any eligible client with respect to such client's legal rights."

Restrictions on recipients and staff attorneys — Recipients and staff attorneys may not participate in a "class action suit, class action appeal, or amicus class action" without the express approval of a project director in accordance with policies established by the recipient. Staff attorneys also must refrain at any time during the period for which they receive compensation from providing transportation to voters to polls or engaging in voter registration activity or any activity of the type prohibited by 5 U.S.C. §1502(a).

Restrictions on employees of the corporation and of recipients — This broad category of persons is prohibited from intentionally identifying the corporation or a recipient with any "partisan or nonpartisan political activity associated with a political party or association, or the campaign of any candidate for public or private office." They also are enjoined, while carrying out legal assistance activities, not to engage in or encourage others to engage in public demonstrations, picketing, boycotts, strikes, riots, civil disturbances, violations of injunctions, or "any other illegal activity."

Restrictions on attorneys employed full time — Full-time lawyer employees must refrain from compensated outside practice and may engage in uncompensated outside practice only as authorized under L.S.C. policies.

Restrictions on "all attorneys" — All attorneys, while engaged in legal assistance activities, must refrain from "any political activity" and from providing voter transporation or engaging in voter registration activity. However, the phrase "(other than legal advice and representation)" is attached to the prohibitions relating to voter transporation and registration.

Restrictions on the use of funds — No funds made available by the corporation, either by grant or contract, may be used

(1) to provide legal assistance in a "fee-gathering" case, except in accordance with guidelines established by the corporation;

(2) for "any political activity";

(3) in criminal proceedings;

(4) in civil actions brought by a person convicted of a crime against court or law enforcement officials;

(5) to provide legal assistance to unemancipated persons under eighteen, except (a) on written request of parents or guardians, (b) on request of a court, or (c) in child abuse, persons-in-need-of-supervision, and institutionalization proceedings;

(6) to support or conduct training programs for the purpose of advocating particular public policies, or encouraging political, labor, or antilabor activities, or demonstrations, as distinguished from the dissemination of information;

(7) to organize or assist in the organization of any entity except one for the provision of legal assistance to eligible clients;

(8) in proceedings or litigation relating to the desegregation of elementary or secondary schools;

(9) in proceedings or litigation seeking to procure a nontherapeutic abortion or to compel an abortion when it is contrary to the "religious beliefs or moral convictions" of the individual or institution involved;

(10) in proceedings or litigation arising from a violation of the Military Selective Service Act or of desertion from the armed forces;

(11) to influence the issuance, amendment, or revocation of executive
orders or "similar promulgations" of any governmental agency; and

(12) to undertake to influence legislation, except in the representation
of a client or when requested to make representations by a legislative body
or governmental agency. . . .

3. Efforts were made to remove some of the restrictions on the Legal
Services Corporation, especially those relating to abortion and school
desegregation cases, at the time funding was renewed for three years in
December 1977. Those efforts failed although a number of changes
were made, including removal of restriction (5), supra, and addition of
a provision permitting use of funds for lobbying when necessary for representation of a client, so long as the client was not solicited in violation
of "professional responsibilities." In addition, attorneys were brought
under the Hatch Act, which does not prohibit seeking election to non-
partisan political office. 91 Stat. 1619 (Dec. 28, 1977). See 64 A.B.A.J.
189 (Feb. 1978).

4. In 1982, however, some additional restrictions were added in the
Joint Resolution of Congress providing continuing appropriations for a
number of government agencies for fiscal year 1983. The expenditure
of funds to provide legal assistance for most aliens unlawfully in the
United States was prohibited. The Legal Services Corporation was directed to enact regulations setting conditions on the use of funds to
bring class action suits against the federal government or any state or
local government. The ability of funded programs to lobby government
was also restricted. Finally, only private attorneys or nonprofit legal service organizations governed by a board of directors, a majority of whom
are attorneys appointed by bar associations representing a majority of
the attorneys practicing in the area served by the recipient, may receive
funds as a grantee of the Legal Services Corporation. These restrictions
were substantially continued in succeeding authorizations throughout
the 1980s.

5. A challenge to the constitutionality of the provision preventing staff
attorneys from seeking election to partisan or nonpartisan political offices failed in Smith v. Ehrlich, 430 F. Supp. 818 (D.D.C. 1976).

6. Is the Legal Services Corporation idea preferable to the OEO Legal
Services idea? Should the goals and policy of a legal services program be
set by governmental bodies, professionals, or clients? Does it depend
whether the issue is involvement in law reform and lobbying, or management of caseloads, or selection of clients and categories of legal problems?

7. Which of the listed restrictions are appropriate to a legal services
program funded with government funds?

8. Note that Problem 71 may be discussed in terms of the Legal Ser-

vices Corporation's policy-setting role for recipient organizations. How would you resolve those issues in this setting? The Act does not resolve the issue of the Corporation's role in "law reform," but it prohibits grants to public interest law firms. 42 U.S.C. §2996(f)(b)(5).

ANDREW L. KAUFMAN AND GERRY SINGSEN,*
LEGAL SERVICES IN THE 1980S

The two-term administration of President Reagan saw a struggle over the very existence of the Legal Services Corporation and the programs that it funds. As Professor Cramton indicated, p. 538, the President wanted to do away with the LSC entirely. He sought to achieve that end by eliminating its separate funding, although he would have allowed states to use for legal services a portion of the federal block grants for social services that he was proposing (albeit at substantially reduced levels from prior years). He also suggested that private lawyers contribute an increased amount of pro bono service. The first such proposal, at a time of massive cuts in many social programs, was defeated after extensive congressional debate, but LSC's appropriation was reduced from $321 million in 1981 to $241 million in 1982 and 1983. Thereafter, however, the friends of local legal services programs in Congress, with the strong support of the organized bar, restored much of those cuts. Appropriations were increased to $275 million for the fiscal year 1984 and to $305 million for fiscal 1985, where it remained through 1988, although Gramm-Rudman cut LSC's actual receipts to $292 million in fiscal 1986. Of course, with inflation, the real cuts in LSC's appropriations have been more than the numbers suggest.

Moreover, the President's proposals, together with the new directions taken by the management of the LSC, produced a great deal of stress within the staff of LSC and the programs funded by it. All of LSC's professional staff from 1981 and quite a few of the most experienced lawyers and administrators in local programs left during the Reagan era, and the morale of the staff in the field was greatly weakened. Although there were no personnel reports from LSC for several years, figures up to 1985 indicate that the number of lawyer positions in LSC-funded programs dropped from more than 6,000 at the start of 1981 to roughly 4,700 at the start of 1985. (Legal Services Corporation, Characteristics of Field Programs — A Fact Book — 1983, p. 13 (1983); Id. for 1986 (Final Draft 1987)).

* Director of the Program on the Legal Profession and Lecturer on Law, Harvard Law School; Vice-President, Legal Services Corporation, 1979-82.

While the appropriations for LSC dropped sharply after 1981 before recovering, it should also be noted that nonfederal resources devoted to civil legal services for the poor grew rapidly during the 1980s. State and local government grants and funds from private sources mushroomed from about $10 million in 1980 to nearly $100 million in 1988. In the same period, the number of lawyers contributing their services pro bono also expanded greatly, reaching perhaps 100,000 lawyers who provided some free service in 1988.

A major factor in the increase of non-federal funds was the adoption since 1979 in nearly all states of some kind of IOLTA (Interest on Lawyers' Trust Accounts) plan as a way of raising money to support legal services programs. The IOLTA programs permit or require lawyers to deposit trust funds that would otherwise not generate interest for clients (because they are too small or they are held for too short a time) into pooled interest-drawing trust accounts. The IOLTA programs follow three major patterns: mandatory, sometimes called "comprehensive," i.e., all lawyers must join; mandatory but with an opt-out provision; and voluntary. The mandatory programs have naturally raised the largest amounts of money and in some states the amount of money that has been raised is impressive. Through 1987 IOLTA programs have raised $121 million, $79 million of which the eight comprehensive programs have contributed, $49 million of that from California's mandatory program alone. States with voluntary plans average only 20%-30% participation of eligible lawyers. Report of the ABA Commission on Interest on Lawyers' Trust Accounts to the House of Delegates at the 1987-88 Midyear Meeting.

Even the backers of IOLTA, however, tell us that this is only a short-term aid for legal services, for more sophisticated technology is making it more and more administratively feasible for banks to pay interest to individual clients on short-term funds in relatively small amounts. Predictably, the IOLTA programs have come under constitutional attack for effecting an unconstitutional "taking," but thus far the attacks have all failed. E.g., Cone v. The Florida Bar, 819 F.2d 1002 (11th Cir.), cert. denied, 108 S. Ct. 268 (1987).

The growth in private pro bono services in the 1980s was preceded by increasing ABA activity and by an extensive LSC demonstration program on the efficient use of private lawyers in the delivery of legal services to the poor, including pro bono service, contracts with private law firms, and judicare. While the ABA's General Practice Section particularly supported use of delivery systems in which private attorneys would receive some compensation for their work, the ABA House of Delegates in 1980 voted a more general resolution encouraging all forms of private attorney involvement.

It was President Reagan's 1981 attack on LSC, however, that had the most dramatic effect on the relationship of private lawyers to local legal services programs. National, state, and local bar associations sent representatives to Washington to lobby against the Reagan proposals. The provisions relating to bar association control of local programs boards of directors, noted at p. 546, Note 4, partially derived from these efforts. In addition, Congress required LSC to insure private attorney involvement in delivery of services. LSC responded by requiring grantees to devote 10% of their grants to encouraging such involvement. Over the next seven years, more than 400 new pro bono and judicare programs were developed by legal services programs and state and local bar associations, usually working through cooperative agreements. These private attorney involvement programs, in turn, recruited tens of thousands of local lawyers to take on cases for poor clients.

Surviving President Reagan's funding proposals was only the beginning of the difficulties faced by legal services in the 1980s. During the Congress's Christmas recess in 1981, President Reagan appointed a new "recess" Board of Directors for LSC. In 1982, through chaotic internal struggles as well as proposals to eliminate class actions and legislative advocacy, this Board engendered so much suspicion in Congress about its qualifications to serve and its commitment to the purposes of the legal services program that none of its members were confirmed. Subsequent recess appointees ran the Corporation from 1983 to 1985. A challenge to this use of recess appointments to fill positions on the LSC Board was mounted but was unsuccessful. See McCalpin v. Dana, No. 85-542 (D.D.C. 1982), vacated as moot sub nom. McCalpin v. Durant, 766 F.2d 535 (D.C. Cir. 1985). Indeed, the Board's efforts to reshape the LSC-funded programs and its failure to comply with the provisions of the governing legislation led Congress on a number of occasions to impose limits on the Board's ability to withdraw funding from various already funded programs.

The activities of the Board continued to be controversial even after new Board members were finally confirmed in 1985. The chairman, Clark Durant, supported the cutting off of funding for a whole variety of programs, including various support and training centers and programs to help migrant workers. Moreover, he pushed a much larger agenda that would have eliminated the Legal Services Corporation entirely in favor of a new organization using a smaller appropriation to provide legal services to the poor through a combination of the efforts of the private bar and nonlawyers. As to the latter, he would simply have abolished the whole structure of unauthorized practice regulation in order to permit nonlawyers to provide services to poor people, among others.

In addition, the LSC in this period developed an extremely inquisitorial process for monitoring the behavior of grant recipients, exploring possible technical violations of regulations in great depth but rarely investing energy in questions about the quality or effectiveness of local advocacy for clients. Congressional reaction to the Durant board was, if anything, sharper than that given to its predecessors, and included riders to appropriation bills that forbade LSC from enforcing regulations with respect to legislative advocacy by local programs, local board composition, and even committee activity dealing with such minutiae as LSC's Audit Guide, computer purchases, and small experimental grants to law school clinics.

At the end of the hectic decade of the 1980s, then, with the LSC having survived a determined effort to put it out of existence, the issue, as we look forward to the 1990s, is to define the shape of the provision of legal services to the poor in the coming decades. The major questions are how the strife-torn system will respond to the continuing and expanding needs of the poor for service and whether any new idea or series of new ideas will arise to replace or to supplement the legal services model that has been in place since the late 1960s.

3.   Public Interest Law

PROBLEM 73

Community Law Firm, Inc., a public interest law firm, has been approached by two environmental groups that want to attack a decision of a state Forestry Department to open a piece of state forest to multiple use. One environmental group wishes the area to be kept forever wild. The other is willing to permit certain kinds of controlled camping, but opposes the Forestry Department's plans as too extensive. How does Community Law Firm, Inc. decide which client to represent?

PROBLEM 74

Community Law Firm represents a local action group that has been fighting the construction of a highway through a portion of city parkland. As the suit is about to come to trial, the Highway Department proposes an alternate route that would take the road through a relatively sparsely settled but poor neighborhood. The local action group wants to accept the proposal, but there is opposition from the people whose homes would be condemned and from the neighborhood generally. The members of Community Law Firm believe that acceptance of the alternate route is not in the public interest, but are unable to convince their client. What courses of action are open to Community Law Firm, and which one do you, as a member of the Firm, think it should follow?

PROBLEM 75

A number of civil rights organizations determine to begin a class action desegregation suit against School Board, alleging de jure segregation. A coordinator is appointed and, as a result of meetings of the local chapters of the organization, a variety of present parents and school children are selected and agree to become the named plaintiffs. The City has a lawyers' civil rights committee and after negotiations between the civil rights organizations and the committee, one law firm agrees to handle the litigation. Law Firm discusses the case with the named plaintiffs but its task essentially involves investigation and proof of acts of de jure segregation. At some point in the litigation, Law Firm becomes fairly confident that it is going to prevail on that issue and begins serious consideration of possible remedies. A major issue is whether it ought to urge the district judge to impose a metropolitan solution and, at the same time, devote the necessary resources to lay the factual predicate for such a remedy in accordance with the applicable Supreme Court decisions. Whom does the Law Firm consult and who instructs the Law Firm with respect to that decision? Cf. Problem 39 (p. 303). For excellent analyses of the issues presented by this problem, see Derrick Bell, Serving Two Masters: Integration Ideals and Client Interests in School Desegregation Litigation, 85 Yale L. J. 470 (1976), and Deborah Rhode, Class Conflicts in Class Actions, 34 Stan. L. Rev. 1183 (1982).

The newly focused interest in "public interest" aspects of the practice of law sparked by Ralph Nader and Edgar and Jean Cahn has already had an impact on discussion in earlier materials. See pp. 428 ff. The relationship between "public interest" law and access to legal services, however, is such that the subject deserves some attention on its own. The following two articles reflect two very different attitudes toward the phenomenon. One question to keep in mind in reading the remainder of Part A is its relation to the restrictions on legal services lawyers debated in Formal Opinion 334, and Informal Opinions 1232 and 1252 (see pp. 572-579) and the restrictions imposed in the legislation creating the National Legal Services Corporation (see pp. 544-546). Do the potentiality and the actuality of those and other restrictions suggest that effective representation of certain "public interests" is best conducted by private lawyers? Or are there disadvantages to the private practice of "public interest" law that make the existence of publicly-financed lawyers necessary or advisable for the conduct of "public interest" litigation?

CHARLES HALPERN* AND JOHN CUNNINGHAM,† REFLECTIONS ON THE NEW PUBLIC INTEREST LAW: THEORY AND PRACTICE AT THE CENTER FOR LAW AND SOCIAL POLICY

59 Geo. L.J. 1095 (1971)

As the influence of the corporations and the public bureaucracies has increased in recent decades, their accountability to the public has failed to increase; in the forums where their decisions are made, the concerns of the ordinary citizen are seldom accorded a hearing. In the sphere of federal agency decision-making, for example, important public policy matters such as the granting of licenses by the FCC, the regulation of the environment by the Departments of Agriculture and the Interior, and the supervision of auto safety by the Department of Transportation, are usually resolved with little or no participation by citizens with a stake in their outcome.

The problem is one which for years has concerned members of the legal profession; their concern is more than appropriate, since the powerlessness of citizens in the forums of the corporations and the public bureaucracies has been due in no small measure to the absence of lawyers willing to represent them. . . .

The role of lawyers. In the new movement of public interest activism, lawyers have a major role to play. First of all, the citizen public interest groups such as those described above need the services of lawyers as advocates in the specialized forums of the corporations and public bureaus. Secondly, lawyers are in a position to use their special knowledge and skill to help citizen groups formulate and clarify their objectives, and to suggest appropriate techniques by which to work for these objectives. . . .

AREAS OF PRACTICE

The practice of the Center is concentrated in the areas of environmental protection, consumer affairs, and health problems of the poor.

---

*B.A., 1961, Harvard College; LL.B., 1964, Yale University. Mr. Halpern . . . is co-founder and present director of the Center for Law and Social Policy. [He was later Dean of the innovative City University of New York Law School. — Ed.]

†B.A., 1964, Fordham University; M.A., 1965, J.D., 1971, University of Pennsylvania. Mr. Cunningham, formerly of the philosophy faculty of Georgetown University, participated for several months in the Center's research and litigation during the course of his legal studies. . . .

The authors wish to acknowledge their indebtedness to the staff and the students of the Center for their many contributions to the present article. Responsibility, however, for the interpretations presented in the article rests with the authors themselves.

This concentration of effort has led to the development of specialized skills and ongoing relationships with law and legal groups involved in these various areas. For example, in the area of environmental protection, Center attorneys have worked on a number of matters with the Wilderness Society, the Friends of the Earth, the Environmental Defense Fund, and the Sierra Club. In the area of automobile safety, the Center works with Ralph Nader and the Center for Auto Safety; in matters of corporate reform and shareholder rights, with the Project on Corporate Responsibility; and on mental health issues with the Washington, D.C. Public Defender Service.

. . . In selecting cases, the Center tries to identify points within the federal decisionmaking process at which key issues of public policy are being determined and to devise strategies to affect their resolution in a reasoned and competent manner. Thus, the Center's role is fundamentally conservative; it attempts through litigation to make the administrative process conform to its own statutory standards by compelling attention to the views of citizen and consumer representatives of the public interest.

The following guidelines are relied upon in the selection of cases:

(1) an important public interest is involved;
(2) the individuals and groups involved do not have the financial resources to retain and compensate competent counsel for the matter involved;
(3) no other legal institution is likely to provide effective representation;
(4) the area of the law has not been adequately explored;
(5) opportunities for innovation are present;
(6) the subject matter is one in which the staff of the Center has competence;
(7) the activity is one in which there is substantial room for participation by students at the Center; and
(8) the resources of the Center required are commensurate with the gains likely to be achieved.

It must be emphasized that the Center does not accept all matters presented to it. Unlike legal aid agencies and neighborhood legal service programs, the Center has limited its practice to matters of major importance.

PROBLEMS OF THE NEW PRACTICE

PRIORITIES

Institutions such as the Center for Law and Social Policy were established to fulfill a duty of public interest representation which traditional practice had neglected. But as the new practice has developed, it has had to confront a range of new problems peculiar to the practice of public interest law.

Perhaps the most searching challenge to the new practice comes from critics who assert that in pursuing its consumer and environmental cases and thus siphoning off resources from the service of minorities and the poor, the new practice itself causes neglect of the legal profession's primary duties. The issues of public interest practice, these critics argue, are essentially "middle class" issues, issues which can be solved by majoritarian politics; the urgent problems of the poor, by contrast, are not of concern to the majority, and hope for their solution lies largely in the courts and in dedicated legal advocacy.

Responses. A number of responses can be made to this criticism. First, it is misleading to imply that there is a single, all-embracing pool of legal resources and foundation funds from which various discrete portions are allotted to various social causes, and that most or all of the young lawyers and — perhaps more important — money now beginning to be devoted to the new practice would, in the absence of such a practice, be devoted to civil rights or to the range of problems peculiar to the poor. Indeed, the new practice rests on the idealism of many who were not formerly attracted to the cause of civil rights or poverty law, or who have come to regard conventional civil rights and poverty litigation as futile.

Secondly, it is misleading to say that environmental defense and consumer protection are middle class issues. If the nation's natural resources continue to be wasted and our earth, water, and sky poisoned, the poor as well as the middle class will suffer. As for consumer affairs, even now it is the poor, not the middle class, who are the worst victims of fallacious advertising, shoddy and unsafe merchandise, and corrupt credit practices. The issue dealt with by public interest lawyers provide an opportunity for the formation of new coalitions and the unification of disparate groups; through the growth of the consumer movement in the middle class, many grievances common to the poor and other disadvantaged groups in society now are being recognized as the concerns of all. Thirdly, it is by no means clear that majoritarian politics alone can achieve the goals of public interest law; at the very least, litigation in administrative forums and the courts will serve to expedite the process of legislative reform.

Finally, it is important to evaluate the new practice within its broad context and to understand that ultimately it is concerned not simply with environmental or consumer causes but with something much deeper. Its concern is with fundamental structural reform of the legal profession and of the way public bureaucracies dispose of public policy questions. The process of reforming corporate and bureaucratic power begins slowly with manageable issues, but its ultimate aim is far-reaching. Efforts in recent decades to attack directly the problems of the poor have experienced limited success. Perhaps the attack has not been fundamental enough and root causes have been neglected for symptoms. Efforts of public interest lawyers can provide a new and necessary complement to that attack.

Discretion of public interest lawyers. Even if the criticism of public interest practice as diversionary is not entirely fair or accurate, much can be learned from it. Public interest lawyers can choose between many possible clients and causes. They can defend little-known natural monuments lost in the wastelands of the West and threatened by the waters of new federal dams; or they can attack broadcasters for not providing as much classical music as certain members of the community would like. On the other hand, they can accept cases which, while focusing on issues of corporate or agency reform, also promise to improve the situation of the poor. Choosing cases from this second category represents a primary duty of the new practice — to handle public interest cases which serve at once the needs of the general public and the poor. The task may be demanding; but the obligation is clear.

DISCERNING THE PUBLIC INTEREST

The term "public interest lawyer" is in a sense an unfortunate one; it implies that public interest lawyers think they know where the public interest lies and are bent on imposing their own notions on society. . . . Needless to say, each lawyer in these firms has his own values and biases. But the underlying commitment of the new practice is not to specific social platforms, whether liberal or conservative; it is, rather, to the adversary system itself, and specifically, to the principle that everyone affected by corporate and bureaucratic decisions should have a voice in those decisions, even if he cannot obtain conventional legal representation. In the Alaska Pipeline case,[32] for example, the Center lawyers who decided in April 1970 to undertake the case could claim no privileged insight about the environmental implications of the pipeline. They did know, however, that the pipeline raised serious legal and scientific questions, and that in resolving them, the Department of the Interior must be compelled to listen not only to corporations and the state of Alaska but also to conservationists. . . .

ATTORNEY-CLIENT PROBLEMS

Representation. In public interest practice, an attorney is likely to have as his client an individual or group representing a public interest ex-

---

32. [Wilderness Socy. v. Hickel, Civil No. 928-70 (D.D.C. filed Mar. 26, 1970), 325 F. Supp. 422 (D.D.C. 1970), 479 F.2d 842 (D.C. Cir. 1973), cert. denied, 411 U.S. 917 (1973).]

tending well beyond the client's own immediate sphere of concern. If, having undertaken a given case, a public interest lawyer discovers that his client wants it handled in a fashion the attorney believes antithetical to the broad public interest involved, serious conflict may arise. For example, the lawyer may wish to press a case to a conclusion in order to establish an important precedent; the client may decide that what he wants is a quick out-of-court settlement. In most such cases the lawyer's duty to his client will clearly be paramount; in some instances, however — as where the client's wishes are capricious — the solution to such a conflict may lie in the lawyer's excusing himself from further service of his client in the case. But this course has obvious disadvantages, not merely for the lawyer himself but also for his client, who presumably retained him in the reasonable expectation that his service would be rendered throughout the duration of the suit. In the final analysis, perhaps the only way of coping with the problem is for the lawyer to be as candid as possible with his client from the outset of the case about his view of the meaning of the case and the strategies which should be employed. . . .

THE PROBLEM OF FUNDING

The basic problem for all public interest lawyers is funding. The gravity of the problem was reduced somewhat by the guidelines which the Internal Revenue Service issued on tax exemptions of public interest law firms. But the root of the funding problem remains. Several foundations have been generous in funding these firms. However, it seems unlikely the foundations can be expected to continue to do this indefinitely. Thus, even at this early stage of their history, public interest law firms are casting about for means of financing their efforts on a long-range basis. Traditional private fund-raising techniques, such as subscription campaigns for charitable contributions, may be one way of obtaining funds needed to support public interest litigation. Members of the bar, in particular, may be persuaded to support the creation of new institutions which will provide representation to unrepresented groups. If the citizen groups, which for the most part provide the new public interest practice with its clients, continue their present growth, they may begin to pay a significant part of the firm's expenses. Eventually, direct government subsidy ultimately may be a solution, although the threat that such funding will destroy the independence of the public interest firms is a serious one.

Finally, it is possible that consumer class actions for money damages and other forms of public interest litigation in which the victor wins lawyer's fees may provide significant income for the new practice. Some practitioners already are attempting to subsist on a traditional fee-taking basis while taking cases only in the field of public interest law. The likelihood of their success, like the solution of the whole funding problem, is presently uncertain. All that is clear at this point is that the ingenuity of public interest lawyers promises to be as powerfully tested by problems of funding as by those of litigation. . . .

KENNEY HEGLAND,* BEYOND ENTHUSIASM AND COMMITMENT
13 Ariz. L. Rev. 805 (1971)

The image: A large reception office, beige carpet, xerox machine, IBM electric typewriters, a tasteful peace poster on one wall, a bright Picasso on the other. Activity, noise, movement — phones ringing, the hum of the typewriters; a young man, sleeves up, collar loose, looking over a secretary's desk, dictating a hurried memo. In the inner offices, talking, writing, reading, stretching, the "Experts"; lawyers, sociologists, economists, political scientists, ecologists, planners. An efficient, organized and highly competent team. The goal: The "public interest."

The image excites — the sense of commitment, action, progress — but it also disturbs. While others in this symposium will focus on the excitement, here let us ask why the image is also disturbing.

The basic goal of the public interest law movement is to assure adequate representation of currently unrepresented or underrepresented interests and peoples. Democratic theory and the adversary system require that all be heard. All are not. Thus, the large "public interest" umbrella encompasses such diverse interests as racial equality, consumer protection, poverty and ecology.

While agreeing totally that a vast amount of legal talent must be shifted to the unrepresented, this article questions whether the public interest firm, as presently conceived, can accomplish this goal. First, the rhetoric of the movement, its seizure of the coveted mantle of "public interest," may in fact reduce the net pool of legal manpower available to the unrepresented. Such rhetoric alienates the private bar whose support and involvement is needed by the movement. Perhaps a greater danger with such rhetoric, however, is that it will be believed. When lawyers proclaim that they are the protectors of blacks, of the poor, and of the environment, the rest of the bar might conclude that these matters are no longer their concern. The result, therefore, would be a reduction of the number of lawyers involved in public interest work. Second, the public interest movement has generally failed to distinguish between unrepresented interests and peoples in terms of their relative need for legal

* Professor of Law, University of Arizona, A.B., 1963, Stanford University; L.L.B., 1966, University of California School of Law, Boalt Hall. Professor Hegland has been associated with a variety of legal aid and law reform projects in California.

manpower. It will be asserted that there is often adversity between those interests currently lumped together under the public interest label (racism, poverty, ecology) and that lawyers, because of the unique role of the law, should be concerned more with some than with others.

In addition to its rhetoric and its failure to focus — both of which are counterproductive to the goal of increased representation of the unrepresented — there are at least two other disturbing aspects of the public interest law movement. First, although the movement is in essence an attempt to make the adversary system more representative of all interests, its politicalization of the practice of law — the assertion that lawyers represent "interests" rather than people — may undermine the keystone of that system: the public's confidence, already shaky, that the law will protect the individual even if he is unpopular. Finally, and most fundamentally, there is the problem of the attorney-client relationship. Given the vast numbers of unrepresented interests and peoples, the public interest practitioner, to increase his effectiveness, attempts to assert generalized interests rather than specific interests; to view clients as representatives of large nebulous classes (blacks, the poor, consumers, ecologists) rather than as individuals. The attorney's role consequently shifts from that of advocate to that of planner. This is regrettable. First, there is the problem of the accountability of these new planners. Second, there is the notion that our major problems cannot be solved by planners and experts; that they can be solved only by returning decision making to the individual. That planning is the cure-all is an extremely dangerous trap for lawyers. Only lawyers are capable of protecting the rights of the individual against those who would plan for his happiness. . . .

The solution [to the problem of unrepresented interests] . . . advocated by the public interest movement, is to have more attorneys represent the poor and, similarly, blacks, consumers and ecologists. Given the vast numbers of unrepresented individuals and the magnitude of their interests (racial equality, consumer protection, poverty and ecology), the public interest movement simply cannot succeed by the infusion of small bands of dedicated attorneys.[3] What is needed is the active support and involvement of the private bar.[4]

Viewed from the perspective of allocation, what of the sign on the

3. Since their funding must come from the government, either by direct subsidy or by tax exemption, the support of the bar is needed to protect the small bands of public interest lawyers from political attack. This is shown by the experience of the O.E.O. Legal Services Program. When the government funded programs started suing governmental agencies on behalf of their clients, the response of many was predictable — rather than judging the legitimacy of the complaint, just eliminate the trouble-maker. The organized bar was instrumental in defeating these efforts. See Hannon, The Murphy Amendments and the Response of the Bar — An Accurate Test of Political Strength, 28 Leg. Aid Brief. 163 (1970).

4. As to the need of involving private practitioners in public interest law and the unique contribution they can make, see Cahn & Cahn, Power to the People or to the Profession? — The Public Interest in Public Interest Law, 79 Yale L.J. 1005, 1031-1037 (1970).

door, "Public Interest Law Firm"? It tends to reduce the net pool of legal help available. The assertion, represented both by the sign and much of the rhetoric of the movement, that there are two kinds of practitioners — public interest practitioners ("good guys") and other practitioners ("bad guys") — is bad politics. It undercuts the goal of representation of the unrepresented by alienating the "bad guys" so that they will not support, help or even possibly become "good guys." No one likes the black hat and this may explain much of the hostility that the private bar harbors for the public interest movement.[5] The assertion, however, has a greater danger: it may make the "bad guys" even worse by allowing them an easy way out of their professional responsibilities. One of the basic ideals of the legal profession is that of public service. While the very need for the public interest firm stems from the failure of the bar to conform to that ideal, the public interest firm may end in killing it. For example, the mere existence of legal aid has allowed many attorneys who previously did free work to now refer that work to legal aid and, with a clear conscience, focus on paying clients. A more basic example is that of prison reform. It must shame the private bar that public interest firms have been created to deal with the repugnant conditions of prisons. While knowing of the conditions, the bar itself did virtually nothing about them. It is ironic that many in the private bar condemn public interest firms by raising the ideal of the attorney-client relationship and by asserting that lawyers should represent people rather than causes. If this is to be the criteria, how does the bar fare? Has the private bar represented people? Clearly not in the area of criminal justice — there

---

Many private practitioners are anxious to involve themselves in public interest law. The major impediment to the solo practitioner's or small firm's participation is the lack of an effective mechanism that limits the attorney's commitment so to assure that he will not be flooded with free work. An attorney is not like a physician who can "give" a couple of hours a week in a free clinic, knowing that that will be the end of it. Each time an attorney sees a client, there is no way of predicting how much time his case will require. . . .

5. Those who oppose the public interest law movement should ask themselves just why they do so. Upon analysis, I believe, most objections disappear or are greatly weakened. Some may object that the goals sought by public interest firms are essentially political and hence not the proper subject of judicial redress. When one realizes that all judicial decisionmaking is ultimately based on political premises, this objection disappears. Public interest firms are simply asserting new political premises. See note 6 infra. Others may object to the active stance of public interest firms such as their greater willingness to seek cases, to attack traditional standing requirements and, generally, to force the courts into more active roles. This active stance is, however, inevitable in a society in which the rate of change is continually quickening and the time lag between problem and crisis is continually shortening. The job of lawyers and courts is to resolve conflict: they can no longer afford the luxury of passivity. . . . A third objection may stem from disagreement with the substantive claims asserted by public interest firms. If this is the objection, members of a profession committed to the right of all to be heard cannot oppose the mere existence of the public interest firm but could only oppose its substantive arguments in the court. Cf. note 3 supra. A final objection is that of the different nature of the attorney-client relationship in public interest law firms. As the text will indicate, I believe that this objection has merit.

the bar has presented only facets of the client's problems. The criminal defendant does not have a "bail problem" or a "plea problem"; he has the problem of surviving the criminal justice system. Yet lawyers routinely part company with their clients at the prison door — what happens inside is "someone else's" problem. Other examples could be given — the divorce lawyer who shrugs when told that the police cannot protect his client from physical assaults by her husband and the trial attorney who, while waiting for his case to be called, studiously examines his shoes while the magistrate runs rampant over the rights of an unrepresented defendant.

The danger with the assertion that there are two kinds of legal practice — public interest and private interest — is that the public interest law firm may become the institutionalized conscience of the bar. For the traditional practitioner, justice may become, even more than it is today, "someone else's" problem.

Further, the sign on the door, "Public Interest Law Firm," clouds the basic issues and hence prevents the movement from allocating help on a "greatest need" basis. Loggers, gleefully stripping the forest, are working for a public interest: cheaper operating costs means cheaper lumber, means cheaper houses. Under traditional economic theory (the public good being that which the public is willing to pay for) the loggers may have a stronger claim to the "public interest" than do the ecologists: people are clearly willing to pay for their product.

Quite simply, the public interest law movement is the assertion of special interests which are currently slighted or ignored by decision makers in defining the "public interest."[6] This elemental proposition is worth noting. Recognition that public interest law firms are really asserting

---

6. It will be objected that these other interests — interests in the quality of the environment, interests in . . . equality . . . — are essentially political and hence ones which the courts cannot properly handle. This can be best answered by the simple recognition that all judicial and legal decisions are based on political interests as broadly understood. Take, for example, the classic case of a man leaving his watch with a jeweler for repair. The jeweler sells it. Between the owner and the purchaser, who prevails? The decision will turn on the court's conception of which alternative before it will better aid commerce, protecting "title" or protecting "transactions." The goal is pure political theory: it is best to aid commerce because this will create more goods and the public good is served by the creation of more goods. "Public interest" or "other interest" is simply an assertion that other interests, interests in the past not generally asserted, must be taken into account. The traditional job of law is the balance of competing interests. This job will be made more difficult as qualitative, as well as quantitative, demands are made. The job must be done, however. It is the function of law. Of course, it will be a difficult task. The courts are currrently breaking down under the stress of traditional cases. For a multitude of reasons, such as the breakdown of such traditional dispute-resolving institutions as the church, we are turning more and more to courts. As the Cahn article suggests, supra note 4, lawyers, and especially the law schools, must work to relieve the pressure on the courts by developing alternative dispute-resolving institutions such as community land-lord-tenant courts, and by expanding the pool of legal manpower such as by the use of paraprofessionals.

special interests underscores the fact that there will be conflicts between public interest firms. The clearest example is the conflict between ecology firms and poverty firms. Insistence on strict conservation measures will raise the cost of low cost housing; curtailment of pollution causing power generation will mean that many poor families will go without heat.

As noted by Jean and Edgar Cahn,[7] there is a more subtle competition between various public interests. The basic thrust of the public interest movement is to represent people who currently do not have legal representatives. Given the fact that legal manpower is a scarce commodity, it should be allocated to those interests which have least chance of success without it. As the politically powerful — the upper and middle classes — cannot escape breathing smog and drinking impure water, the ecology movement can be expected to achieve its goal (if it is achievable at all) politically, without massive legal help. Indeed, the executive and legislative branches of government are expressly designed to respond to majority movements, which the ecology movement is fast becoming. Compare the "political muscle" of the black welfare recipient. Her goals cannot be achieved politically because the majority feels its interests are adverse to hers. Her problems, such as feeding, clothing and sheltering herself and her child . . . do not directly affect the majority. The governmental institution designed to protect the individual from the majority is the judiciary. Quite simply, the fight against poverty cannot be won without attorneys whereas the fight against pollution may be. Hence, under this analysis, the ecology movement, by drawing off legal talent, is adverse to the interests of the black welfare recipient. This should be remembered by law students planning their careers and by practitioners desiring to participate in "public interest" work.

Only one further comment on the sign, "Public Interest Law Firm." What does it tell the public? The traditional sign, "X & Y Law Firm" asserts that either X or Y will handle your case. The public interest firm label, however, adds a qualification — your case will be handled only if it is in the "public interest." The traditional ideal of the attorney is that he is a professional — one who will put aside personal belief in the practice of his skills. The ideal is currently under attack in the law schools where one repeatedly hears students assert that they will never work for a prosecutor or for a huge corporation. Further, it is debatable whether the public ever really believed the image of the lawyer as the nonpolitical technician. Finally, on the basis of the old saying that actions speak louder than words, it can be asserted that lawyers have always represented interests, since the majority has traditionally worked for primarily one interest — the rich and powerful.

7. See note 4 supra.

Upon analysis, the image proves more of a mirage. Does this mean we disregard it and simply put "Public Interest" or "X Interest" on the door? There is no doubt that the practice of public interest law in such areas as civil rights, poverty and consumer fraud has greatly enhanced the image of the lawyer as the defender of the downtrodden, as opposed to that of the mere spokesman for vested interests. But what of the sign or, more basically, the assertion that lawyers represent interests rather than individuals? There are dangers.

To lawyers, the practice of law may mean several things: money, excitement, power to bring social change, the ability to help others. In the current debate among lawyers as to what the practice of law should mean to them, it is easy to forget what it means to the public. To the individual in trouble, a lawyer is often his only hope. From such a person's standpoint, the role of the lawyer is simply to help him, even though the attorney does not agree with him or relate to him. For the members of the public, the bar should be striving to make the old ideal of the "professional" a reality, not casting it aside because it has often proven to be a sham. For practitioners and especially for law students, it must be affirmed that the role of the attorney is not to work out his own political philosophy or even to sleep well at night. It is to help others not as interests, but as individuals. It must be remembered that lawyers have a monopoly and that monopolies have a duty to serve all; to coin a phrase, it's in the "public interest."[9]

Having finally gotten beyond the door of the Public Interest Law Firm, let us continue our tour. Everything seems in order — conference room, library, coffee pot. But still, something seems to be missing. Suddenly, it hits us: "Where are the clients?"

Of course, there will be clients, but not traditional ones. By definition,

---

9. The problem of a lawyer as a "mere spokesman" versus a lawyer as an independent actor is an extremely difficult one. At the one extreme, few would defend the proposition that the lawyer must cease to be a moral being and assert any claim his client wishes. See ABA Code of Professional Responsibility, Canon 7 (1970).

The current reaction against the "mere spokesman" function stems from the belief that attorneys, in the past, have given up their morality to serve their clients. In many areas of law, I feel that the breakdown has occurred for the opposite reasons — the failure of lawyers to vigorously assert their clients' interests. This is clearly true in the area of criminal law where defense counsel have known for years the deplorable conditions of the prisons, but have done relatively nothing about them. What is needed is not a pronouncement that the lawyer should remain a moral being, but rather a pronouncement that lawyers represent people, not just cases. For example, the lawyer's responsibility extends beyond the guilt or innocence stage of a criminal proceeding to the human being whose sole interest is coming out of the criminal system whole.

There is a danger that the pendulum will swing too close to the other extreme, with lawyers, as moral beings, asserting only that with which they agree. It is good to alert practitioners that they cannot hide behind the adversary model. The danger lies in the assertion of this as a governing principle, the result of which will be that lawyers will become judges rather than advocates and the unpopular will find it even more difficult to obtain representaton.

the public interest law firm begins with a concept of the public interest and fashions its clients around that. This reverses the traditional process where attorneys begin with clients and then fashion a concept of the public interest to correspond to the interests of their clients. This is not to say, as is frequently alleged, that public interest law firms use their clients as pawns. There is enough "lawyer" in public interest practitioners to prevent them from sacrificing a client's interests on the altar of the higher good.[10] A more accurate view of public interest clients is that they are "tickets" — without which the firm could not play the law game.

So why should attorneys have clients — shouldn't they just be issued free passes allowing them to play? The question may sound flip, but raised is a fundamental question concerning the role of the courts. Traditionally, courts have existed to keep the peace. A did X to B. If the courts didn't do something about it, A and B might just fight it out in the street.

As the rate of social change increases, the time lag between problem and crisis decreases; to effectively cope with the problem, the courts simply must get involved at an earlier stage. So what's wrong with the "free pass" concept — groups of attorneys deciding, on their own motion, what suits should be filed and what suits vindicated? There are valid interests of society which should be considered in defining the "public good" — should they not be heard simply because they have not been verbalized by a traditional off-the-street client? Surely the magnitude of the conflicting interests in society means that the courts must become more active, must do away with technical standing requirements, case and controversy requirements, and bans against some forms of solicitation. But does this mean we should do away with clients?

Without clients, what are we doing? Without clients, we are setting up a law office that is indistinguishable from a good governmental bureaucracy. A governmental agency, whether concerned with housing, welfare or the environment, brings together diverse experts whose job is to define and implement the "public interest." Those advocating public interest law firms correctly argue that these governmental agencies have often failed. It is, however, ironic that they would adopt, as the means of solution, the governmental model. How are they to succeed where government has failed? Better experts? Bigger hearts?

---

10. There are problems, however. Even the most careful attorney, in presenting his client alternatives, will favor the one he thinks best. The attorney who begins with a concept of the public interest, as opposed to a commitment to his individual client, cannot help but let his preconception influence the kind of advice he gives the client. The attorney may not even be conscious of this. There is new substantial scientific support for the psychological view that one can subtly and even unconsciously transmit cues and suggestions to another during ordinary social intercourse. See, e.g., Rosenthal, Self-Fulfilling Prophecy, in Readings in Psychology Today 466 (CRM Books ed. 1969).

By viewing clients as tickets rather than as individuals, the lawyer becomes a planner rather than an advocate. The planner begins with a nebulous class, such as blacks, consumers, the poor, and then generalizes and distills the interests of that class, projects goals and finally adopts strategies. The advocate, on the other hand, begins with specific individuals or specific groups within the generalized class (Welfare Rights Association, C.O.R.E., the Black Panthers) and thereafter simply acts as their advocate, allowing them to define their interests, formulate their goals, and adopt methods of achieving them.[13]

The shift from advocacy to planning has been justified on the basis that it is the best way to allocate limited legal manpower; there are just too many blacks, too many poor people, too many consumers to treat them as individuals. To maximize the effectiveness of the limited number of attorneys involved, it is reasoned, they must focus on issues common to the generalized class rather than on problems of individuals or specific groups within the generalized class. This reasoning, for example, leads many legal services programs to reject service cases, such as divorce and bankruptcy, in favor of law reform — a focused attack on statutes which adversely affect the generalized class of poor persons.[14]

While the allocation analysis seems to demand the new role, there are dangers when lawyers become planners rather than advocates. Immediately, there arises the problem of accountability. How can one assume that these new planners truly represent the interests of blacks, con-

---

13. This does not mean, however, that the advocate representing specific individuals or groups within the generalized class (poor, blacks, consumers) will practice in the same manner as does the traditional practitioner. An attorney representing a group of poor persons, for example, will behave differently than the attorney representing a corporation: the client's interests, and hence the method of best serving those interests, differ. The attorney-client commitment, however, is the same. Thus, the poverty attorney helps organize groups and may engage in "direct action" such as picketing. For the details of such a practice, see Wexler, Practicing Law for Poor People, 79 Yale L.J. 1049 (1970).

14. At the other extreme from law reform there are those legal aid offices which, realizing that they do not have adequate legal manpower to serve all potential clients, attempt to stretch that manpower by offering the poor a watered down form of service. For example, many legal aid attorneys have open caseloads numbering in the hundreds; their clients cannot help but receive inadequate legal representation. This is grossly unjust to the client and to the attorney — a young attorney, given such a caseload, cannot help but develop habits which will likely prevent him from becoming truly competent. The argument for taking more cases than one can properly handle is powerful: "Look, I'm the only attorney who will help these people. They need help desperately. Something is better than nothing." Upon analysis, however, "something" proves worse than "nothing." That something means that all the clients receive less than they are entitled. Further, that something deludes the poor into believing that the "system" is protecting their legal rights. Obviously, the system is not . . . guaranteeing "equal justice under law." Those committed to the poor should not conceal this from them: glossing over injustice, even in the best of motives, perpetuates it. Legal aid attorneys must realize that it is not their fault that many go without legal assistance. They should not assume the responsibility and feel compelled to help everyone. It is unfair both to the attorney and the client and it is counter-productive to the proper solution of the ultimate problem.

sumers or the poor? Moreover, there is the basic problem of planning itself — to the degree that planners make decisions, the individual does not. This, in turn, contributes to the individual's sense that he has less and less control over his life. Perhaps the basic problem of our time, as well as the root cause of many others is precisely this: the individual's growing sense of loss of control, of lack of worth. Finally, there is the issue of the institutionalized role of law and of lawyers. The law is perhaps the only profession capable of protecting the individual in our ever increasingly planned society. While many can plan, only lawyers can protect the rights of the individual in the process.

Once the attorney breaks the moorings of a specific client's interests, how can he be held accountable? How can the attorney be sure of the correctness of his concept of the interests of a generalized class of people such as the poor? Take, for example, Shapiro v. Thompson,[15] the successful culmination of the attack on welfare residency laws. Does that decision further the interest of the poor? It undoubtedly helps many poor — those wishing to move to another state. It may, however, also harm others [who] if there is a great influx of recipients in those states may find their benefits reduced and their state taxes increased.

To cope with the accountability problem, many legal services programs and public interest law firms have created advisory bodies composed of representatives of the client community. Whether such bodies can achieve accountability is questionable. There is the danger that such lay bodies will be consciously or unconsciously manipulated by professional staff which has its own concept of its function: law reform versus service work. Further, there is the problem of just how representative the representatives are. Initial selection will tend to favor the more militant — those who have already taken on a "spokesman's" role. Even if selected in a manner to assure representativeness, they may quickly become an elite group, identifying more closely with the interests of the public interest firm than with those of their theoretical constituents.

It should be remembered that a major professed goal of public interest firms is to make government accountable to the individual. By adopting the governmental model of planning for generalized classes of individuals, however, the public interest firms may themselves become unaccountable to their "clients." If they do, all that has been accomplished is to subject the individual to the whims of yet another group of professionals. Nevertheless, even if a mechanism could be devised to assure that the attorney-planner was truly planning to achieve the best interests of the generalized group, the fundamental question remains whether the basic problem of our society has been inadequate planning or too much planning.

Our society has grown more complex; so too has our reliance on experts. When faced with a difficult problem, we turn to those who gave

15. 394 U.S. 618 (1969).

us penicillin and radar. Given our apparent inability to solve our critical problems — racism, pollution, poverty — it is tempting to conclude that there are simply not enough experts working on them or that those who are are on the wrong side. This appears to be the conclusion of the public interest law movement. Its thrust is to create groups of "counter-experts" who will be plugged into decision-making bodies. From heated yet scholarly debate (outsiders cannot be expected to understand their jargon), the true "public interest" will emerge — Joe's, yours, mine. In the pitched battle between urbanologist and ecologist, the insistence on clients seems rather picayunish — what, after all, do they know?

There is considerable support, however, for the proposition that our public interest machine (government) is not malfunctioning because of inadequate planning or biased experts, but rather the basic problem is inherent in the machine itself, in our reliance on experts. Quite simply, when experts decide, individuals don't. This demeans the individual as a person capable of governing his own life. . . . In the current rush to "solve" our pressing problems, we may overlook the most fundamental: the relationship of man, the decision maker, to the planned society. The implication of this to the attorney is clear. By viewing client as ticket, as representative of some generalized interest, the lawyer becomes a decision maker. While, arguably, his decisions may be "better" than that of the welfare worker or other bureaucratic decision makers, at bottom, they are the same: an expert deciding what the individual truly needs.

This tension between "expert" decision making and individual decision making is more acute for the lawyer attempting to define his proper role than it is for other professionals. The institution of law is probably the only one capable of protecting the individual in the planned society. There are simply enough experts and planners deciding the greatest good for the greatest number; once lawyers start playing that game, the individual suffers the hazard of escalating dehumanization.

The law has a unique role to play in society — the protection of the rights of the individual *against* the greatest good for the greatest number. Jerome Carlin provides an extremely helpful analysis.[21] There are, he believes, two models of justice, the adversary model and the welfare model. Under the adversary concept, individuals are deemed to have rights against each other and against the state. Not so under the welfare concept which recognizes no conflict between the interests of the individual and those of the state. Hence the state is free, even required, to control the individual for his own best interest. Typically, the welfare model is employed when dealing with the poor, as in the juvenile court where the judge does not act as referee between two competing interests, but rather adopts the role of parent to the child, looking to his needs rather than to his rights. Given the non-adversary framework, it is not

---

21. J. Carlin, J. Howard & S. Messinger, Civil Justice and the Poor 24-34 (1966).

surprising to find a loosening of procedural guarantees and the seed of total government control.

Public interest firms, viewing clients as tickets rather than as individuals, tend to adopt the welfare model. The question becomes "What are the needs of blacks?" rather than "What are the rights of this specific black man?" There are many experts asking the first question, lawyers are the only ones capable of asking the second. In a planned society, the law must not forget its fundamental mission: protecting the individual as the possessor of given rights, rights which he can assert even if not in the best interests of society; indeed, even if not in his own best interest.

NOTE

Since these two articles were written in the early 1970s public interest law has expanded dramatically and then fallen back somewhat. The reasons are several.

First, there has been little growth in funding. In 1975 private foundations contributed $14.5 million to tax-exempt public interest law firms; in 1980 that amount had increased to only $16.5 million, a decrease in real dollar terms.[1] Neither has the increase in statutory provisions for awards of attorneys' fees been as useful as its advocates had hoped. Fee awards have become mired in separate litigation resulting in delays that underfunded firms cannot afford. A comprehensive look at the problem of funding public interest work is contained in Council for Public Interest Law. Balancing the Scales of Justice (1976).

Public attitudes have become less favorable to public interest goals as the costs of delays, like those resulting from Alaska pipeline[2] and snail darter litigation[3] have been widely publicized. At the same time court rules on standing and class action procedures have tightened.

Finally, public interest law practice has fragmented into an increasing number of small specialized firms, sometimes in direct conflict with each other not only with respect to funding but also with respect to control of particular litigation.

PROBLEM 76

Law Firm has just about decided that it is going to become general counsel to a cigarette manufacturer when it discovers that on her own time, Associate (with firm knowledge) has been doing pro bono legal

---

1. White, From Sit-Ins in the South to Practice on Connecticut Avenue, 5 District Lawyer 42 (Mar/Apr '81).
2. See p. 555 n. 32.
3. Tennessee Valley Authority v. Hill, 437 U.S. 153 (1978).

work for the Citizens' Lobby Against Smoking and through that connection is assisting in a lawsuit brought by a lung cancer victim against the cigarette manufacturer. Must Law Firm decline the position of general counsel? If Associate ceases to work on the case, may the firm accept the representation? Suppose that instead of doing legal work for the Lobby, Associate had merely been President of the organization? Should the combination of DR 7-101(A)(3) and DR 5-105(D) of the Model Code and Rule 1.7(b) and Rule 1.10(a) of the Model Rules preclude Law Firm from accepting the position of general counsel?

The private bar has been seen by many as an important source of public interest support. Indeed, as we have seen, the Reagan administration saw the private bar as capable of replacing in substantial part the programs funded by the Legal Services Corporation. Starting in the middle of the 1970s, important parts of the organized bar have sought to make pro bono services by lawyers into a mandatory obligation.

There has been fairly general agreement that lawyers ought to feel a professional obligation on an individual basis to render pro bono service. The struggle has been over proposals that would require it. The arguments for mandatory service have stressed the effect of the inability of so many to use the justice system and the obligation of service owed by professionals with state-granted privileges. The arguments against mandatory service have centered on the undesirability of singling out lawyers for compulsory service and the difficulty and inefficiency in a time of growing specialization of forcing lawyers with no experience in poverty practice to engage in it on a very partial basis.

The House of Delegates of the American Bar Association in 1975 voted a resolution stating that "it is a basic professional responsibility of each lawyer to provide public interest services." The Resolution went on to define public interest services as falling into the areas of poverty law, civil rights law, public rights law, charitable organization representation, and activity improving the administration of justice. The report accompanying the resolution suggested the provision of 5%-10% of billable time but then modified the notion of individual responsibility by suggesting not only that a law firm might meet its obligation on a group basis but also that a financial substitute for service might also be considered.

Responding to that proposal, a Special Committee of the Association of the Bar of the City of New York on the Lawyer's Pro Bono Obligations recommended a general minimum contribution by lawyers on a mandatory basis, with some flexibility for individual exemptions, of 30 to 50 hours of service per year, with the potential for later increase to a 40 to 60 or 50 to 70 range. See that Committee's Report, p. 5. Shortly thereafter early drafts of the Kutak Commission's Model Rules of Professional Responsibility contained mandatory pro bono requirements in a series of differing proposals, one of which stated a 40-hour minimum, and others of which contained a financial alternative, reporting requirements, and a variety of definitions of pro bono service.

These proposals provoked enormous controversy and opposition. The result was that first the Executive Committee of the Association of the Bar of the City of New York rejected, in part, its Committee's proposal. It proposed an ethical obligation, backed not by disciplinary sanctions or reporting but by self-evaluations, that could be satisfied with a financial contribution. Subsequently, the Kutak Commission retreated to a position now set forth in Model Rule 6.1 that states the lawyer's responsibility in the aspirational sense of "should" rather than the disciplinary rule sense of "shall." A thorough analysis of the history of pro bono "requirements," and the constitutional, economic, and policy considerations related thereto is contained in Shapiro, The Enigma of the Lawyer's Duty to Serve, 55 N.Y.U. L. Rev. 735 (1980). He concludes that the position embodied in the Model Code and the Model Rules with respect to the general principle of pro bono service is about right.

A number of courts, however, including courts in El Paso, Texas, Westchester County, New York, and the federal district court in eight districts in Arkansas, Illinois, Iowa, and Texas have adopted mandatory programs requiring pro bono service in civil cases, and so has the California Supreme Court, on an ad hoc basis. See Payne v. Superior Court, 17 Cal. 3d 908, 553 P.2d 565 (1976). Bar associations in counties in Florida, Texas, Illinois, and Wisconsin have also imposed similar requirements on their members. At the same time, however, some courts have held that it is unconstitutional under both federal and state constitutions to order lawyers to represent indigents, even in criminal cases, without providing adequate compensation. E.g., State ex rel. Stephan v. Smith, 242 Kan. 336, 747 P.2d 816 (1987) (collecting numerous cases). The open issue for all lawyers is how much of a commitment to pro bono work they are willing and able to make, how they will define pro bono work, whether they favor imposing a mandatory pro bono requirement on all lawyers, and if so, on what terms. It is a major issue for the 1990s.

4. Some Specific Problems of Professional Responsibility in the Provision of Legal Services

PROBLEM 77*

County Legal Services, Inc. "is a nonprofit corporation whose direction is vested in a board of directors. Members of the board control the

---

* Adapted from an opinion of the New Jersey Advisory Committee on Professional Ethics, 94 N.J.L.J. 801 (1971).

general policy of the project, including determination of eligibility standards and determination of the type of services to be rendered. Members may, on occasion, determine the eligibility of specific clients by name and may determine the propriety of the project's furnishing specific types of service to named clients.

"No members of the board has access to any client's file. In determining the services to be rendered in general, or to particular clients, the board merely sets general policy guidelines. It may not control the actual handling of a case, dictate strategy or otherwise direct the attorney in the handling of a case. Questions of this nature are passed upon by the project administrator.

"The project operates on a countywide basis. It does a substantial amount of matrimonial, consumer and landlord and tenant litigation, which are also fields for specialization by the private bar. It is thus inevitable that from time to time attorneys employed by the project will be called upon to defend actions instituted either by board members, or by associates in firms in which board members are employed.

"1. May project attorneys defend an action instituted by a partner in a firm in which one of the board members is a partner or associate?

"2. Since membership on the board changes from time to time, how long after a board member resigns may project attorneys defend actions instituted by the board member or by the firm of which he is an associate or partner?"

3. Does it make a difference that the particular board member whose firm has brought the action is one of the three board members (out of 15) selected by the local bar association?

4. Does it make a difference that the law firm instituting the suit had reason to know that the defendant would seek representation by County Legal Services, Inc.?

PROBLEM 78*

Six months ago a legal assistance office opened in a neighborhood where there already was an active, outspoken community organization comprised almost exclusively of low income black residents. The immediate neighborhood where the office and organization are located is almost 100% black, but it is included within larger political and school districts that are approximately 60% white.

The purposes of the organization, which supports no political party as such, are (1) to awaken interest of the black citizenry in ward politics,

---

* This problem was developed by, and is used with the permission of, Judge John M. Ferren of the District of Columbia Court of Appeals, who used it in legal services courses and professional responsibility courses while teaching at Harvard Law School.

in order to promote "reform" candidates for city council and state representative who will represent the "people" instead of the "bosses"; (2) to inform the school board about incidents of arbitrary and discriminatory treatment of black schoolchildren by white teachers in the local school, which has a 40%-50% black enrollment, and to press for more black teachers and a greater voice in school affairs by the local community; (3) to expose incidents of police brutality against black teenagers and to achieve a more just handling of complaints against juveniles; (4) to establish a local credit union as an alternative to hard-sell, high-interest small loan companies; (5) to inform people about their legal rights under the welfare laws and as tenants; (6) to press the city for more frequent garbage collection and sewer inspections; (7) to pressure local chain stores and industrial plants into hiring more blacks.

From time to time the legal assistance office has assisted the organization with community education programs about the law. Usually these have been group discussions in the evening, but one lawyer in the office also has written a pamphlet entitled "Tenants' Rights"; its cover carries the names of both the legal assistance office and the organization. A neighborhood aide from the legal assistance office has been going around the community with officers of the organization looking for people who have legal problems. Last week the office agreed to draw up the papers for the organizations's proposed credit union.

Today, 15 minutes ago, the chief staff attorney of the office received a telephone call from the president of the organization, who said that he was on his way over to the office with 10 families, "each of which has a child who was summarily expelled today from high school for fighting with white students in the school cafeteria." In most cases both the child and at least one parent will be coming. Only two of the families are members of the organization, but the president said that he hopes his obtaining legal assistance for the other eight will inspire them to join the organization. He added that from the evidence he has gathered "this will be a great way for a lot of people to take a stand together against those high-handed school administrators and their discriminatory expulsion tactics."

The president has just arrived at the office with 25 people — fathers and/or mothers of all 10 who were expelled, and nine of the 10 students; at the last minute one student refused to come. Three staff attorneys, including the chief, are on hand. What should the chief do?

(a) Who is the client in this case? Would it make any difference if the credit union matter had already been completed, or if the office has never represented the organization before the school board?

(b) May the office represent both the children and the organization? If the office has several branches, may a different branch represent some of the children?

(c) May the office represent more than one child?

(d) How does the office obtain the facts to permit it to decide what to do?

(e) What happens in the event of a difference of opinion about a proposed course of action between a child and his or her parents?

(f) Suppose it looks as if this matter will consume a tremendous amount of the office's time and cause it to turn away other business. May it decide not to take the case? What factors ought it to consider before reaching such a decision?

(g) Should the office have taken on the organization as a client in the first place? What effect might that have on its ability to service the needs of individuals in the community?

(See In re Grand Jury Investigation, p. 80, Note 4)

PROBLEM 79

A legal service office instituted a class action suit to force a public Housing Authority to afford tenants their statutory right to safe, decent housing. The court, finding widespread and persistent violations of statute, appointed a receiver of the Housing Authority to run its public housing projects for a temporary period. Subsequently, an agreement was negotiated between class counsel and the receiver and embodied in a court order that permitted the receiver to use expedited eviction procedures whenever a tenant or member of the tenant's household committed or threatened to commit certain specified crimes of violence against other tenants in or near a housing authority project or carried or kept on the premises specified "controlled substances." Another attorney in the legal services office had for a long time represented an individual tenant on a variety of matters. That tenant sought advice from the attorney about the possibility that she was subject to eviction under the court order. The attorney, seeing the possibility of conflict between his client and the tenant class represented by his office with respect to both the validity of the original order and its current application, sent a memorandum to the Executive Director advising her that he was about to refer the client to a specified legal aid office. The Executive Director, who was heavily involved in supervising the class action, responded that she wanted to review the file to determine whether there was any conflict and that, if there was, she would make the referral. The attorney asks your legal advice about the propriety of turning over the file. What advice do you give? (The general problem is suggested by Spence v. Reeder, 382 Mass. 398, 416 N.E.2d 914 (1981).

The former Canons of Professional Ethics were not drafted to deal with specific problems faced by legal service attorneys, and courts and ethics committees occasionally had to adapt the Canons' provisions to the rather different circumstances of legal aid representation. The Model Code and Model Rules were drafted after the vast expansion in legal services to the poor in the 1960s and hence takes greater note of that phenomenon. The specific provisions of Model Rules 7.2(c) and 7.3 and of Model Code DRs 2-101(B), 2-103(C)(2), 2-103(D), and 2-104(A)(2) and (3) should be read carefully to note the efforts of the drafters to accommodate its provisions to legal services organizations.

Despite those efforts, a great deal of confusion and uncertainty remained. One of the major problems related to the problem of control of, and responsibility for, the policies of a legal services organization. The Committee on Ethics and Professional Responsibility of the American Bar Association promulgated one opinion, Formal Opinion 324 (August 9, 1970) in which it sought to provide some general guidelines, and followed with two controversial Informal Opinions, Nos. 1232 and 1252. Formal Opinion 324 and Informal Opinions 1232 and 1252 apparently provoked continuing discussion within the Committee, which took the unusual step of holding a public hearing on the subject matter of the opinions, then issuing a proposed opinion, and finally a new Formal Opinion 334, modifying and elaborating Formal Opinion 324 and the subsequent informal opinions. Because of the controversy and because of the public hearing and the comments the Committee solicited on its proposed opinion, Formal Opinion 334 has been quite influential in the internal arrangements of legal services offices.

Formal Opinion 334 explicitly sought to give guidance to legal service offices with respect to three categories of professional problems — (1) publicity, (2) independence of judgment (the issue of control), and (3) preservation of confidences and secrets.

ABA FORMAL OPINION 334
(August 10, 1974)[1]

The Standing Committee on Ethics and Professional Responsibility is limited in its opinions to interpretations of the Code of Professional Re-

---

1. The committee has heretofore issued a number of informal opinions upon various aspects of the above subject (Nos. 992, 1081, 1172, 1208, 1227, 1230, 1232, 1234, 1252 and 1287) and one formal opinion upon the subject generally (No. 324), some of which have been misunderstood in some quarters, and one of which (Informal Opinion 1232) declined a request to reconsider (Informal Opinion 1262). In view of the importance of the subject, the committee held a public hearing on October 25, 1973, in San Diego, California, on advance notice published in 59 A.B.A.J. 976 (1973). It was held during the annual meeting of the National Legal Aid and Defender Association. A large number of interested persons testified at the hearing. The committee published a proposed opinion in 60 A.B.A.J. 329 (1974). Numerous comments were received and considered by the committee. From all of this it is manifest to the committee that there is widespread interest in the subject which justifies the issuance of another formal opinion elaborating and clarifying Formal Opinion 324, issued more than three years ago, and relating the various informal opinions cited to it.

sponsibility. It is not the committee's function to determine the most effective means of achieving the goal of making adequate legal services available to the indigent. Nonetheless, this committee wishes to re-emphasize, at the outset of this opinion, the importance of all lawyers striving to make legal services available within the bounds of professional responsibility. [The opinion then quoted EC 2-25.] . . .

Most recently, the Legal Services Corporation Act of 1974 has provided funding to legal services offices through a public legal services corporation.

The general subject to which this opinion is addressed falls into three categories, each of which will be dealt with separately. They are publicity, independence of professional judgment, and preservation of confidences and secrets. The opinion does not involve ethical aspects of programs other than those of legal services offices; for example, it does not include prepaid legal service programs, which are concerned with making legal services available to all income groups rather than to the indigent. . . .

[The section of the opinion relating to permissible publicity has been omitted.]

2. INDEPENDENCE OF JUDGMENT.

Canon 5 requires a lawyer to exercise independent professional judgment on behalf of a client. To what extent may a governing board prescribe organizational rules and regulations or operational methods of a legal services office to limit or restrict the activities of lawyers acting on behalf of clients of the office without placing those lawyers in violation of the duty to exercise their independent judgment in legal matters? DR 5-107(B).

We hold that the activities on behalf of clients of the staff of lawyers of a legal services office may be limited or restricted only to the extent necessary to allocate fairly and reasonably the resources of the office and establish proper priorities in the interest of making maximum legal services available to the indigent, and then only to an extent and in a manner consistent with the requirements of the Code of Professional Responsibility.

A. *Broad Policy Matters.* [The opinion refers to Formal Opinion 324 and Informal Opinions 1232 and 1252.]

B. *Case-by-Case Supervision.* The committee further held in Formal Opinion 324 that there should be no interference with the lawyer-client relationship by the directors of a legal aid society after a case has been assigned to a staff lawyer and that the board should set broad guidelines respecting the categories or kinds of cases that may be undertaken rather than act on a case-by-case, client-by-client basis.

The above holdings still appear to the committee to be sound and fully supported by the sections of the Code of Professional Responsibility.

Although no one has really taken issue with the principles embodied in Formal Opinion 324, questions have arisen in connection with the committee's application of those principles to specific cases, particularly in Informal Opinions 1232 and 1252 cited above.

Informal Opinion 1232 involved class actions, and we turn first to problems concerning them as illustrative.

C. Class Actions. If a staff attorney has undertaken to represent a particular matter and the full representation of that client (aside from any collateral objective such as law reform) requires the filing of a class action in order to assert his rights effectively, then any limitation upon the right to do so would be unethical. Of course, in the case of any proposed class action it is the individual client who must make the decision to expand the suit into a class action after a full explanation of all of the foreseeable consequences. However, if the purpose of expanding the suit to a class action is not solely to protect the rights of the individual client, or a group of similarly situated clients, but primarily to obtain law reform, and law reform, as such, is not one of the authorized purposes of the legal services office, the case cannot be expanded to a class action unless the authorized purposes are changed to include law reform. This follows from our determination that it is a permissible function of the board in allocating resources to determine "the various services which the society will make available."

A governing board may legitimately exercise control by establishing priorities as to the categories or kinds of cases which the office will undertake. It is possible that, in order to achieve the goal of maximizing legal services, services to individuals may be limited in order to use the program's resources to accomplish law reform in connection with particular legal subject matter. The subject matter priorities must be based on a consideration of the needs of the client community and the resources available to the program. They may not be based on considerations such as the identity of the prospective adverse parties or the nature of the remedy ("class action") sought to be employed. E.C.-1.

D. Advisory Committees to Governing Boards. . . . It is difficult to see how the preservation of confidences and secrets of a client can be held inviolate prior to filing an action when the proposed action is described to those outside of the legal services office. It could be pointed out that the legal services office lawyers and the advisory committee may have equal access to "possible errors of judgment" or "exercise of poor judgment." However, if an advisory committee consisted entirely of lawyers, if it had no power to veto the bringing of a suit but was advisory only, and if the requirement of prior consultation did not in practice result in interference with the staff's ability to use its own independent professional judgment as to whether an action should be filed, there would appear to be no harm in requiring such consultation. But if such a requirement did in fact result in interference with the exercise of the staff's independent judgment, it would be improper.

The members of the advisory committee should not be given confidences or secrets of the client, for there is no lawyer-client relationship between the client and the advisory committee or any member of it. The requirement of prior consultation should recognize that the obligation of the staff lawyers to preserve the confidences and secrets of clients applies to statements to and information conveyed to the advisory committee or for that matter a state bar committee or any other person or body not privy to the lawyer-client relationship.

E. Supervision by Senior Staff Lawyer. This committee's response to . . . Opinion 1232 reiterated that it is improper to require prior approval on a case-by-case basis before a class action is filed, citing Formal Opinion 324. To the extent that this reponse indicated that the prior approval of a senior lawyer in a legal services office could not be required, it is hereby expressly overruled. It must be recognized that an indigent person who seeks assistance from a legal services office has a lawyer-client relationship with its staff of lawyers which is the same as any other client who retains a law firm to represent him. It is the firm, not the individual lawyer, who is retained. In fact, several different lawyers may work upon different aspects of one case, and certainly it is to be expected that the lawyers will consult with each other upon various questions where they may seek or be able to give assistance. Staff lawyers of a legal services office are subject to the direction of and control of senior lawyers, the chief lawyer, or the executive director (if a lawyer), as the case may be, just as associates of a law firm are subject to the direction and control of their seniors. Such internal communication and control is not only permissible but salutary. It is only control of the staff lawyer's judgment by an external source that is improper.

F. State Bar Committee. The final two inquiries in Informal Opinion 1232 raised a different question. . . .

The final inquiry . . . questioned the ethical propriety of assigning . . . a committee of the state bar the function of advising the Office of Economic Opportunity on a continuing basis whether the program of the legal services office was operated in a manner consistent with the applicable canons, guidelines, and legislation and within the terms of its grant. This the committee likewise held to be proper.

It is true that the inquiry dealt with the so-called "watchdog" function of the state bar committee, but that function was exercised over the operation of the legal services office itself and not over the staff lawyers. The same would be true of state advisory councils, such as those to be established pursuant to Section 1004(f) of the Legal Services Corporation Act of 1974. It therefore involved no question of legal ethics. . . .

There is no ethical reason why a lawyer could not serve upon such a watchdog committee or council so long as the provisions of the Code of Professional Responsibility were respected, but to the extent that such special scrutiny was motivated by hostility to legal services offices, or the effect of the state bar committee's activities was to impair the rendition of proper legal representation to the indigent, service upon such a committee by a lawyer would be contrary to the ethical considerations of Canon 2.

G. *Legislative Activity.* Informal Opinion 1252 said:

"In our view this proviso [former DR 2-103(D)(1)] does not bar the governing body of a legal aid society from broadly limiting the categories of legal services that its attorneys may undertake for a client — in this instance excluding political activity and lobbying in support of a bill, rule, regulation or ordinance drafted for a client. The proviso is directed against interference with the exercise of the attorney's independent professional judgment in those matters which they do undertake on behalf of a client."

The opinion certainly does not hold that a lawyer employed by a legal services office may not engage in law reform or seek to secure the passage of legislation. In fact, it says specifically that "any lawyer, whether he drafted legislation for a client or not, may of course as a citizen, gratuitously engage in activities of a political nature in support of it."

What the opinion does hold is that the governing body of a legal aid society may broadly limit the categories of legal services its lawyers may undertake for a client, and that in doing so it may, but need not, exclude such categories as political activity and lobbying. There are three important qualifications inherent in this statement. First, in the absence of such affirmative action by the board, no such limitation exists. Second, the action of the board must be a broad limitation upon the scope of services established prior to the acceptance by the staff lawyer of representation of any particular client, and preferably made known to its public and staff in advance like any other limitation on the scope of legal services offered. Once representation has been accepted, under DR 5-107(B) and DR 7-101 nothing can be permitted to interfere with that representation to the full extent permitted by law and the disciplinary rules, including, of course, legislative activity.

The phrase "independent professional judgment" is not specifically defined in the Code of Professional Responsibility and is not susceptible to easy interpretation, but a reading of EC 5-1 through 5-24 will establish the spirit with which the lawyer's duty should be carried out. Subordination of the lawyer's own interests is implicit, as is the correlative promotion of the client's legitimate objectives.

It has been suggested that even the limitations upon the activities of a legal services office permitted by Formal Opinion 324 are improper because, while a private law office may limit its activities in any way it pleases, as the services which it does not furnish will be available elsewhere, the indigents have nowhere else to turn and therefore any limitation upon the services available at a legal services office amounts to a deprivation of those services. The Code of Professional Responsibility does not ban such limitations. As a practical matter, the resources of a legal services office are always limited, and some allocation of them upon a basis of priorities must be made if they are to be effectively utilized. As long as this is done fairly and reasonably with the objective of making maximum legal services available, within the limits of available resources, it is not improper.

It has been urged that there are certain rights of indigent clients which can only be asserted through legislative means. There can be no limitation on the availability of the staff lawyer to give advice in connection with such legislative means. DR 5-107(B).

Finally, limitations upon the activities of a legal service office which stem from motives inconsistent with the basic tenet set out in EC 5-1 are always improper. As a general proposition it may be stated that the obligation of the bar to make legal services available to the indigent requires that no such limitations should be imposed upon a legal services office and no staff lawyer should subject himself to such limitations. Whether or not such reprehensible motives are present must necessarily be determined upon the facts of each individual case.

3.   PRESERVATION OF CONFIDENCES AND SECRETS

Canon 4 requires a lawyer to preserve the confidences and secrets of a client. To what extent may a legal services office allow its activities to be examined and administered without violating the rule requiring the preservation by lawyers of the confidences and secrets of a client?

Formal Opinion 324 held that, without causing a violation of DR 4-101(B)(1) or EC 4-2 and 4-3, the board of directors of a legal services office could require staff lawyers to disclose to the board such information about their clients and cases as was reasonably necessary to determine whether the board's policies were being carried out. Procedures to preserve the anonymity of the client approved in Informal Opinion 1081 and 1287 should be followed. It should be noted, however, that the information sought must be reasonably required by the immediate governing board for a legitimate purpose and not used to restrict the office's activities, and that in many contexts a request for such information by a board may be the practical equivalent of a requirement. Hence, a legal services lawyer may not disclose confidences or secrets of a client without the knowledgeable consent of the client. To the extent this is inconsistent with Formal Opinion 324, that opinion is overruled.

4. CONCLUSION

Much of the difficulty with the interpretation of Formal Opinion 324 and of the informal opinions discussed above lies in a general failure to distinguish between the disciplinary rules and the ethical considerations of the Code of Professional Responsibility. For the most part, the inquiries relate to what could be "required," and thus for the most part the answers were based upon the disciplinary rules. To say, as we have sometimes done, that a particular restriction upon the staff of a legal services office is not forbidden by the disciplinary rules is not to say that such a restriction is wise or is consistent with applicable ethical considerations. See EC 2-25, quoted above.

Viewing the problems discussed above on the aspirational level of the code's ethical considerations, we stress that all lawyers should use their best efforts to avoid the imposition of any unreasonable and unjustified restraints upon the rendition of legal services by legal services offices for the benefit of the indigent and should seek to remove such restraints where they exist. All lawyers should support all proper efforts to meet the public's need for legal services.

As modified and interpreted above, the committee's previous opinions are reaffirmed.

BOSTON BAR ASSOCIATION, COMMITTEE ON ETHICS, OPINION NO. 76-2

1976

FACTS:

On January 1, 1976, the Boston Legal Aid Society (BLAS) and the Boston Legal Assistance Project (BLAP) were consolidated into Greater Boston Legal Services (GBLS). Prior to the merger BLAS was a privately supported non-profit corporation which had been providing legal service to the indigent in the greater Boston area for over 70 years. It had functioned with its own staff of lawyers from a single office in the center of Boston. Before the merger, BLAP had been operating for almost nine years as an unincorporated legal services organization funded entirely with monies from the Federal Government. The governing board of BLAP consisted in part of lawyers who were members of the BLAS Board of Directors and the remainder of lawyers and laymen from the constituencies served by the agency. Under the terms of its grants, BLAP was limited to serving the poor of Boston proper and had operated offices in various locations in the city.

While they operated as independent agencies, BLAS and BLAP frequently represented opposing sides in legal matters. As a result of the merger, it is anticipated that some individuals may be deprived of legal representation of GBLS if denied the right to represent both sides.

GBLS has inquired under what, if any, circumstances the merged entity may represent both sides in legal controversies.

DISCUSSION:

In the traditional situation where two law firms merge, it is clear that the merged entity cannot continue to represent both sides. It may continue to represent one side, only after making full disclosure and obtaining client consent for continued representation. ABA Informal Opinion No. 1115 (1969). Code of Professional Responsibility, DR 5-105(C). In some situations, it is even advisable that the merged firm withdraw from representing either side. Ibid. See also ABA Informal Opinion No. C-437 (1961). The ABA's Code of Professional Responsibility is rigid in its restraints against conflicts of interest. See EC 5-14, DR 5-105(A) and 5-105(B). Further, "a lawyer should avoid the appearance of professional impropriety." ABA, Code of Professional Responsibility, Canon 9.

We are aware that in the matter before us, there is an apparent conflict of interest if GBLS is to undertake representation of both sides in legal matters, and we are sensitive to the fact that such dual representation may be open to suggestions of impropriety. On the other hand, we know that situations may arise where both parties are in need of legal assistance and one may go unrepresented if GBLS is barred by ethical considerations from representing that party. It is hoped that the private bar will come forward in such situations if requested and provide representation, but we must expect that this may not always be the case and the GBLS may, therefore, perceive an obligation to represent both sides. After thoughtfully weighing the matter, this committee has concluded that circumstances may exist from time to time where GBLS properly may undertake representation of both parties, if both clients are indigent and neither has feasible access to other counsel, but only provided strict procedures and standards are observed.

We feel there are sufficient differences between a private law firm and a publicly funded organization providing legal services to indigent clients to distinguish ABA Informal Opinions C-437 and 115 cited above. All lawyers working for GBLS may be considered quasi-public employees in that their salaries are largely funded [by] the National Legal Services Corporation and to a lesser extent by grants from United Way and other contributions from the private sector. GBLS is a non-profit organization whereas in a private law firm, lawyers are joined as partners and share in the profits.

GBLS has eight offices spread across the City of Boston with over 50 lawyers on its staff, each of which offices is largely self-administering. The geographical separation and semi-autonomy of local offices necessarily diminishes the close relationship which obtains in a proprietary law firm.

In ABA Informal Opinion 1233 (1969), it is stated that "the professional standards regarding representation of differing interests apply to legal aid offices the same as to other lawyers." We agree that the same standards should and do apply. We feel, however, that these same standards can be upheld in the limited number of instances where GBLS undertakes legal representation of both sides in a controversy if the following standards are adhered to:

(1) Diligent efforts are made to find an individual or group willing to undertake representation of one of the opposing parties.

(2) The Executive Director of GBLS or a majority of a committee composed of the Executive Director and two deputies, approves of GBLS's undertaking to represent both sides.

(3) Disclosure is made to both clients that GBLS is considering representing opposing sides and each party must signify his understanding of the arrangement and its implications by consenting in writing to the dual representation.

(4) Court approval must be obtained if the matter is in litigation.

(5) Attorneys assigned to the case must be located in separate offices of GBLS.

(6) Attorneys and those working with them who represent the two sides must be under the strictest rules of confidentiality.

NOTES

1. The Illinois Supreme Court has gone considerably beyond the reasoning of the Boston Bar Committee's Opinion. In People v. Banks, 121 Ill.2d 36, 520 N.E.2d 617 (1987), reh'g denied (1988), the Court held that an assistant public defender appointed to challenge the effectiveness of the assistance rendered by an assistant public defender from the same office was not automatically disqualified. Overruling earlier cases, the court stated that a case-by-case review was required to determine whether there were any peculiar circumstances to indicate the presence of an actual conflict of interest. A powerful dissent by Judge Simon collected cases coming out the other way and argued that the difficulty of arguing the incompetence of one's colleagues justified a per se rule of disqualification.

2. In Fiandaca v. Cunningham, 827 F.2d 825 (1st Cir. 1987), the court held that it was an abuse of discretion for a district court to have denied a motion to disqualify a legal services organization when its representation of a class of mentally retarded patients housed in a building at Laconia State School interfered with its ability to consider an offer of settlement by the state to a class of incarcerated female inmates. The inmates were also represented by the organization, and the state pro-

posed to relocate them to the same facility, displacing members of the
legal organization's patient class.

3. The application of the disciplinary rules to class actions, however,
presents special problems, as we have already seen. See Problem 75, p.
551. A good example of a flexible approach to application of the rules
is In re "Agent Orange" Product Liability Litigation, No. 84-6231 (2d
Cir. 1986), reported in vol. 2 1986 National Reporter on Legal Ethics
and Professional Responsibility 205. Although noting that there was an
apparent technical violation of the Model Code, the court refused to
order disqualification of two lawyers who, after being part of the team
that represented the entire class, broke ranks to oppose a negotiated
settlement on behalf of a group of dissenters. The court noted that there
were no allegations of receipt of confidences of the pro-settlement group
and no actual prejudice to that group. On the other hand, the disqualification of counsel intimately familiar with the intricacies of the litigation
would work great hardship on the anti-settlement group, which num-
bered 3,000 individuals.

Yet another effort by the American Bar Association to provide guidelines for practice is its Standards for Providers of Civil Legal Services to
the Poor. They were adopted in 1986 to provide guidance with respect
to issues that arise in the special context of that type of practice. They
are explicit in not altering ethical requirements of the Model Code or
Model Rules. Rather they attempt to spell out details of effective and
high-quality client representation, internal management procedures,
and governance of the legal services organization. They have already
been adopted by some bar associations and legal services programs and
seem likely to be quite influential in the legal services world.

NEW YORK STATE BAR ASSOCIATION, COMMITTEE ON PROFESSIONAL ETHICS, OPINION NO. 489 (July 31, 1978)

50 N.Y. St. B.J. 532 (Oct. 1978)

QUESTION

May a lawyer-member of a non-profit legal service organization's board
of directors, or one of his associates in private practice, agree to defend
a person sued by an indigent client of the organization?

OPINION

The question posed has not previously been addressed in this State. Ethics committees from other jurisdictions, however, have to some extent
considered the matter and generally appear to be divided.

Florida, for example, holds that a staff attorney for a federally funded legal service organization may defend an action brought by a party represented by one of the organization's board members provided that, after full disclosure, both parties give their consent and, further provided, that the board is completely removed from the relationship between the organization's staff attorney and its client. Fla. Op. 69-24 (1969), indexed at 6593, O. Maru, Digest of Bar Association Ethics Opinions (1970, Supp. 1975), hereinafter "Maru's Digest."

New Jersey, on the other hand, has held that under no circumstances may a legal service organization represent a party against whom an action has been instituted by a law firm with which one of the organization's directors is associated. N.J. Op. 218 (1971), indexed in Maru's Digest at 8820.

A third view of the subject is represented by an Idaho opinion which holds that, where both parties to an action are indigent, it is not improper for one side to be represented by a legal service organization staff member and the other to be represented by a member of the organization's board of directors. 18 Advocate 9 (Idaho State Bar Foundation, 1975), indexed in Maru's Digest at 8280. Contra, N.J. Op. 218, supra and N.C. Op. 805 (1972), indexed in Maru's Digest at 9556, which holds that "[a] legal aid society's board members may not represent indigents whom the society, because of conflict of interest, could not itself represent." On the facts presented, we need not consider this third alternative since it clearly appears that only one of the two parties to the lawsuit in question is indigent. Cf., N.Y. State 102 (1969).

We believe that the most appropriate rule is one which not only serves to promote the availability of legal services for the indigent, but secures for them their right to be represented by zealous counsel. Canon 7. The full and fair representation of indigent persons is essential to our system of justice. There should be but one standard bearing upon the manner in which a lawyer is expected to pursue the interests of his client, whether the client be indigent or otherwise. It is just as important for those who serve the poor to be free from divided loyalties as it is for those who serve the more affluent. Indeed, it should be obvious that the appearance of impropriety is only enhanced when conflicting interests are entertained at the expense of those who cannot pay for needed legal services.

The Code of Professional Responsibility states that "[a] lawyer should never represent in litigation multiple clients with differing interests." EC 5-15. Client consent to "multiple employment" is only effective "if it is obvious that [the lawyer] can adequately represent the interest of each [client]." DR 5-105(C). Taken together, these provisions of the Code have traditionally been understood to mean that clients can never confer upon counsel the right to represent adverse parties in litigation. See, e.g., N.Y. County 620 (1973).

Having noted the interaction between EC 5-15 and DR 5-105(C), we also note that the Code draws a distinction between the board of a legal service organization and counsel to its clientele for certain purposes. This distinction is particularly important in determining the board's right of access to confidential information or its ability to control the organization's legal staff. See, ABA Inf. 1137 (1970). Thus, for example, where non-lawyers serve on the board, the organization's staff attorneys are ethically forbidden to tolerate any interference by the board in the staff's handling of individual cases. See, Canon 5 and EC 5-24.

Nevertheless, in the context of the question posed, we believe that this distinction between the board and the organization's legal staff should have no application. Every lawyer-member of the board owes a duty to the organization which directly involves his professional training and status. The organization's staff, albeit possibly insulated from interference by the board in certain respects, is yet generally subordinate to its directors. Certainly, in the minds of the organization's indigent clientele, the staff could not reasonably be deemed free of compromising influences if the lawyer-members of its board were to accept retainers from relatively affluent adverse parties.

We therefore find it to be wholly inappropriate for a member of the board to accept a private retainer for the purpose of defending in litigation a person who has been sued by one of the organization's clients.

Since the lawyer-member of the board could not properly accept the proposed retainer, under the provisions of DR 5-105(D), "no partner or associate of his [could] accept or continue such employment." See, N.Y. State 426 (1976) and the opinions collected therein; see also, DR 5-105(A) and (B).

For the reasons stated, the question posed is answered in the negative.

NOTES

1. A number of cases have considered this problem as well. One of the most thoughtful opinions dealing with the Problem 77 situation is Estep v. Johnson, 383 F. Supp. 1323 (D. Conn. 1974). There Judge Newman found the only ethical stumbling block to a legal services organization and a board member being on opposite sides from one another to be the economic authority over salary and promotion wielded by the board member. Is there any practical way to overcome that obstacle?

2. Other ethics committees have rejected the approach of the New York Committee and sought to meet the serious issue raised by Judge Newman. See, e.g., Massachusetts Opinion No. 79-9, which advised that in many situations DR 5-105 should not even be regarded as applicable (I should disclose here that I was a member of the committee that produced this advisory opinion):

We conclude that in situations where the board of directors is effectively screened off from the professional relationship between staff and client and there is 1) no participation by the director in the particular case, 2) no infringement of the professional independence of the staff attorney, and 3) no disclosure of confidences either by or to the director with respect to the particular case, then the "clients" of the director ought not to be imputed to the legal service organization and the clients of the organization ought not to be imputed to the director. In that event, DR 5-105 is not applicable to this situation, because there is no representation of multiple clients.

We are influenced in this conclusion by public policy considerations similar to those that have influenced courts and other ethics committees interpreting DR 5-105, particularly in the context of an assertion that a former government attorney personally disqualified from representing a position adverse to the government disqualifies his or her whole law firm from such representation. These courts and ethics committees have interpreted DR 5-105 not to require such a result when the former government attorney is screened off, physically and financially, from any contact with the matter. (In addition, the government's consent is occasionally required.) In so doing, notice has been taken of the important public policy consideration of not discouraging lawyers from entering government service by adopting so severe a disqualification rule that would make it difficult for government lawyers to secure non-government employment. ABA Opinion 342 (1975); Association of the Bar of the City of New York, Opinion No. 889, Armstrong v. McAlpin, 461 F. Supp. 622 (S.D.N.Y. 1978); Kesselhaut v. United States, 555 F.2d 791 (Ct. Claims 1977). . . . We believe it is equally important to encourage lawyers to serve as directors of legal services and other pro bono organizations. We see no reason for us to strain to include the situation presented to us within the most stringent sections of the Disciplinary Rules included under Canon 5.

That conclusion, however, does not end the inquiry. Disciplinary Rule 5-101(A) states that, except with consent of the client after full disclosure, a lawyer shall not accept employment if his independent professional judgment will be affected by his own "financial, business, property or personal interests." Even though screened off from any contact with the particular case, the board member still has long term authority over the salary and promotion of the staff attorney. As the court in *Estep* noted, it is one thing to assure a client that no disclosures of confidences have occurred. "It is quite another to assure [a client] that the future course of her representation by a staff attorney might not in some subtle way be influenced by the board member status of her adversaries' lawyer." 383 F. Supp. at 1326. Likewise, in particular cases, there may be a whole network of relationships between a director and the staff of a legal services organization that would give some pause to the director's client that was on the other side of the case from the organization. Disciplinary Rule 5-101(A) deals with this problem. It permits the client to consent to the representation after full disclosure has been made of the nature of the influences that may potentially affect the lawyer's independent judgment. It is up to the lawyer, in situations such as this, to make certain that the disclosure is "full" and understood. Once that is accomplished, it is up to the client to choose.

ABA Opinion 345 (1979) reaches a similar result and also suggests ways for the lawyers involved to minimize the possibility of any effect on the ability of the legal service program to afford independent representation in such a situation. Rule 6.3 of the Model Rules of Professional Conduct follows the general thrust of these two opinions.

3. The problems of disqualification facing legal services lawyers and private law firms to which they move were discussed earlier, in Chapter 2, at pp. 133-134.

4. Other kinds of professional responsibility problems may also arise in group legal service programs. Conflict of interest problems, for example, may occur in rather unusual ways when a group legal service program is not carefully enough considered. One such situation occurred in Board of Education v. Nyquist, 590 F.2d 1241 (2d Cir. 1979). New York State United Teachers, an association of 180,000 school employees, provided legal representation free of charge to members in cases that were job-related and, in the judgment of the staff, meritorious. When the Board of Education of New York City was faced with opposite determinations from state and federal authorities about the use of separate seniority lists for male and female teachers, it brought a declaratory judgment action naming as defendants the various governmental parties and named male and female teachers as class representatives. The United Teachers took no position in the litigation but the male teachers sought and obtained representation under the group legal services program.

On motion of the female teachers, who objected to paying their opponents' legal expenses, the district judge ordered that either program counsel be disqualified or that the United Teachers should pay counsel for the female teachers. The Court of Appeals reversed. The court rejected the argument that first amendment associational rights recognized in the line of cases from NAACP v. Button (p. 593) through In re Primus (p. 502) protected either the lawyer's rights to make his views known or to represent a client in a particular matter in the circumstances of this case. In addition, the court believed that the ethical question "could be a very close one." Nevertheless, it thought disqualification was inappropriate. After referring to the delay caused by motions for disqualification, the court noted that there was no question that the program counsel's representation of the men would be vigorous or that he had access to any privileged information about the women. Except "in the rarest of cases," appearance of impropriety is "too slender a reed on which to rest a disqualification order."

The court noted briefly that part of the apparent unfairness of what occurred might be traced to the nature of the program, which left so much to its counsel's discretion. This is the sort of issue that ought to have been foreseen and provided for either substantively or procedurally — that is, either a rule should have been written into the program or a procedure should have been provided for resolution of disputes.

5. A thoughtful consideration of professional responsibility problems of lawyers for the poor that concludes by offering a model of a much less adversarial system is Bellow and Kettleson, From Ethics to Politics: Confronting Scarcity and Fairness in Public Interest Practice, 58 B.U.L. Rev. 337 (1978). A description of the shortcomings of practice in the federal legal services program, with prescriptions for reform, is contained in Bellow, Turning Solutions into Problems, 34 NLADA Briefcase 119 (1977).

PROBLEM 80

Legal aid offices and legal service programs have struggled for a long time with the conflicting aims of providing first-class legal service and of providing as much legal service as possible to the client community. One result has been an enormous caseload problem in some offices, with the whole variety of problems that come in its wake: inability to handle cases requiring the expenditure of a great deal of time, often cases that potentially present important issues of law reform involving a large segment of the "client community"; inability to spend sufficient time on cases actually in the office, with the result that lawyers come to feel they are providing insufficient representation; and various office management techniques that prevent continuity of representation of a client throughout a given matter.

Problems like this resulted in two strikes within a year in the Legal Aid Society of New York. The lawyers, who were unionized, also struck for higher wages. The Presiding Justices of the First and Second Departments of the Appellate Division were reported to have characterized the strike as "palpably unprofessional conduct." New York Times, September 27, 1974, p. 43, cols. 6-7.

Is that characterization appropriate? What other alternatives were available to the lawyers? Would it be unprofessional for the lawyers to file affidavits in connection with petitions seeking post-conviction relief, asserting inadequacy of their own representation or of the representation by other Legal Aid Society lawyers because of the caseload problem?

———————————

The New York County Lawyers Association has issued an opinion dealing with this strike in response to an inquiry (Question 645). The opinion follows (N.Y.L.J., June 5, 1975, p. 5, col. 1):

This Committee does not pass on issues of law, but for the purposes of this opinion it does not question the right of lawyer employees to belong to a labor union composed of lawyers or to engage in collective bargaining through such a union for the purpose of negotiating wages, hours and conditions of employment. It may also be true that the employees have the right, through their union (i) to negotiate with the employer with regard to the terms and conditions on which the society should deal with the municipality or the manner in which, as a matter of management, the society carries out its contractual obligations to supply legal services to indigent defendants, or (ii) to exert pressure on the municipality to supply more funds to the society to permit it to manage its affairs in the manner urged by the union. The latter activities may, however, be outside the scope of the employees' collective bargaining rights.

Also, the Committee does not question that lawyer employees have the legal right to strike. But, as in the case of all rights, the right to strike is not an absolute and wholly unrestricted right exercisable irrespective of rights possessed by others and irrespective of the duties and obligations assumed by the person who has the right. The public interest dictates that some rights and duties take precedence over others depending on the circumstances. Also, restraints may be imposed on the manner in which the right to strike is exercised. It cannot legally be exercised by violence or in any other manner that encroaches seriously on the fundamental rights of others.

When a lawyer elects to become a member of the bar he becomes an officer of the court and a part of the judicial system and he thereby assumes obligations, not imposed on other citizens, both to the court system and to the public. One of these is the duty not to "engage in conduct that is prejudicial to the administration of justice." DR 1-102(A)(5). This duty is also imposed in the same language in Section 90(2) of the Judiciary Law of the State of New York. Also, when a lawyer undertakes to represent a client he may "not withdraw from employment until he has taken reasonable steps to avoid foreseeable prejudice to the rights of his client, allowing time for employment of other counsel." DR 2-110(A)(2). In addition DR 6-101(A)(3) forbids a lawyer to "[n]eglect a legal matter entrusted to him."

In our opinion these duties, being obligations to the judicial system, to the public and to clients, take precedence over any right of lawyers to strike against their employer. Also, once a particular indigent client has been assigned to a staff lawyer by his employer he may not refuse to take whatever steps are reasonably necessary to protect the client from foreseeable prejudice.

But beyond these duties, it must be recognized that the society is a unique organization. By reason of its purpose to afford legal services to the poor of the municipality it owes an obligation, not alone to persons for whom it is already engaged on specific matters, but also to persons who are relying on it for professional services in the future. This obligation is shared by the individual members of the professional staff of the society. The staff lawyers also have a duty to the judicial system which makes them ethically obligated not to participate in action either individually or in concert with others which materially interferes with the operation of the courts.

Accordingly, staff lawyers of a legal aid society cannot ethically exercise their right to strike if doing so either disrupts the proper functioning of the courts and the judicial system or deprives indigent defendants of their right to proper representation and a speedy trial.

B.   PROGRAMS FOR PAYING CLIENTS

This section of materials is designed to present information and highlight current issues in attempts of group legal service programs to provide access to the legal system. Among the issues to keep in mind in reading the materials are the following:

(1) If cost, quality of service, and the ability to obtain information about lawyers are important to would-be clients, which of the described forms of group legal service programs seem more likely to be helpful in those regards?

(2) What are the major advantages and disadvantages of open-panel and closed-panel plans from the perspective of (a) the client, (b) the lawyer working in such a plan, and (c) the profession as a whole?

A Survey of the Scene

A great deal of attention has been paid since the mid-1960s to the needs of that large segment of the population who are not eligible for free legal services because they are above the "indigent" income level but who nevertheless cannot, or think they cannot, afford a lawyer and who, whether or not they can afford a lawyer, have great difficulty finding one who is ready, willing, and able to handle their problems competently. Since that time, and indeed, for a considerable time before it, a variety of lay organizations — unions, automobile clubs, civil rights organizations, and corporate law departments — sought to meet the public's need with a variety of formal and informal ways of providing group legal services. In addition, the bar provided lawyer referral programs as a method of assisting people to find lawyers. More recently, legal clinics and prepaid legal service plans have been added to the collection of alternate methods of affording access to the legal system. The following study of alternate legal delivery systems provides us with a brief description of three leading types of group legal service programs.

PROJECT, AN ASSESSMENT OF ALTERNATIVE
STRATEGIES FOR INCREASING ACCESS TO
LEGAL SERVICES

90 Yale L.J. 122, 128-131 (1980)

THREE ALTERNATIVE LEGAL DELIVERY SYSTEMS

During the past fifteen years, three alternative legal delivery systems — lawyer referral services (LRSs), prepaid legal service plans, and legal clinics — have grown in part as a response to increasing concern about unmet legal need.[39]

1.   LAWYER REFERRAL SERVICES

Lawyer referral services confer with those wishing to consult an attorney. ABA standards require the LRS person "screening" the request for an attorney to be an attorney but many LRS offices do not conform to the standards. In addition, not all LRSs provide for a screening interview. The capacity of an LRS to conduct an effective screening interview is limited by the number of staff lawyers employed by the LRS. After this initial interview, the LRS refers the caller to an attorney on its list of participating lawyers.[43] The potential client then makes an appointment to meet with the attorney at a nominal fee, usually between fifteen and twenty-five dollars. After the initial consultation, the lawyer and client are free to establish any fee arrangement that is mutually agreeable.[45] Lawyer referral services, generally sponsored by local bar associations, have constituted the organized bar's principal effort to increase access to lawyers during the last forty years.[46]

2.   PREPAID LEGAL SERVICES PLANS

Prepaid legal services plans, a more recent phenomenon,[47] seek to spread the risk of legal difficulty and the cost of legal services over a

39. Other alternatives have been suggested, including expanded use of lawyer lists and lawyer directories, see Christensen, Toward Improved Legal Services Delivery: A Look at Four Mechanisms, 1979 Am. B. Foundation Research J. 277, 285-289, and private referral services, see ABA Consortium on Legal Services and the Public, Legal Services for the Average Citizen 17-18 (1977) [hereinafter cited as Average Citizen]. These alternatives have yet to receive widespread attention or be implemented on a large scale, and therefore are not analyzed in this Project.

43. Some referral services give the client the names of three attorneys from which to choose. See Christensen, supra note 39, at 289. Others have panels of attorneys who specialize in a particular field of law. Licensed attorneys usually join an LRS list merely by volunteering, without undergoing extensive screening. See B. Christensen, supra note 23, at 178. But see Murphy, Lawyer Reference Plan — The Complete Delivery System for Legal Services, in Legal Delivery Systems: Available Alternatives 247, 255-257 (1977) (Chicago Bar Association uses extensive screening for LRS panel applicants).

45. Id. About one-half of all referrals do not go beyond the initial consultation stage. Haydock, Lawyer Referral in New York, in Legal Delivery Systems: Available Alternatives 279, 282 (1977).

46. See B. Christensen, [Lawyers for People of Moderate Means] 173, 176 (1970). In 1978, there were 294 referral services, and the 188 services that respond to a survey reported receiving 919,464 requests for assistance and making 610,928 referrals. Christensen, supra note 39, at 286 n.33.

47. The first prepaid legal services plan actually appeared as early as 1889. Delk, The Advent of Prepaid Legal Services in North Carolina, 13 Wake Forest L. Rev. 271, 274 (1977). The North Carolina and similar plans, however, did not succeed because of opposition from the organized bar. See L. Deitch & D. Weinstein, [Prepaid Legal Ser-

group of persons.[48] Prepaid plans, though appearing in many forms,[49] can be generally categorized as either open- or closed-panel arrangements.[50]

Open-panel prepaid legal insurance plans insure members for fixed amounts of legal services during specified time periods.[51] Open-panel plans have been sponsored primarily by bar associations but also by general third-party insurers and employers[53] or employee organizations.[54] With an open-panel plan, the insured selects his own attorney and the insurer pays the attorney directly for his services. The bar has consistently supported the open-panel concept rather than closed panels, in part, because of the importance of choice in selecting an attorney. However, the bar's opposition to closed panels may also have been motivated by considerations of self-interest.[56]

---

vices] 13-17 (1976); Delk, supra, at 274-275. More recently, under pressure from the Supreme Court, Congress, and trade unions, the ABA decided to liberalize its ethical restrictions on participation in prepaid plans. See L. Deitch & D. Weinstein, supra at 17-23.

48. See W. Pfennigstorf, Legal Expense Insurance 2 (1975). There are currently more than 2,000 prepaid plans operating nationally, see DeMent, Prepaid Legal Services: A Review of Theory and Practice, 30 Baylor L. Rev. 625, 635 (1978), covering more than five million families, (see Paying less for a lawyer, [44 Consumer Rep.] 526).

49. For discussions of the variety of prepaid legal services plans, see Broadman & Ohman, New Directions in Legal Services: Group and Prepaid Legal Services Plans in New York, in Legal Delivery Systems: Available Alternatives 107, 117-143 (1977); Ohman, An Overview of Five Legal Service Plans, 2 New Directions in Legal Services 5 (1977); Comment, Prepaid Legal Services: Obstacles Hampering Its Growth and Development, 47 Fordham L. Rev. 841, 843-857 (1979).

50. Some plans may combine elements of the open- and closed-panel arrangements. See Goodman, Development of Prepaid Legal Services Plans, in ABA, Legal Services for the Middle Class 15, 19 (1979).

51. Open-panel plans exhibit a variety of benefits and coverage. Some plans limit coverage to a percentage of fees charged for specified types of services. See e.g., Broadman & Ohman, supra note 49, at 136-137 (benefit schedule for New York County Legal Services Corporation Prepaid Legal Services Plan). Others state coverage in terms of a certain number of hours of legal work per year. See, e.g., Ellis, An Overview of Prepaid Legal Services — Open Panel, in Legal Delivery Systems: Available Alternatives 145, 153-154 (1977).

53. Open-panel plans often result from the joint efforts of employer and employee groups through collective bargaining agreements. More than 60 such arrangements existed in 1976. Usually, the employer contributes between 4 and 15 cents per worker hour to a joint fund for legal expenses while workers contribute between 3 and 10 cents per hour to the fund. Murphy, [Prepaid Taking Root, Trial, June 1976] 14-15. Employers appear not to have sponsored prepaid plans on their own. L. Deitch & D. Weinstein, supra note [47], at 36-37.

54. The Shreveport plan, begun in 1971 and considered by some the "first plan in the United States that offered substantial coverage of personal legal problems to the working man," was an open-panel plan covering union members. Murphy, supra note [53], at 14. See also F. Marks, The Shreveport Plan (1974).

56. See Hermann, Prepaid Legal Services Coming of Age, 48 N.Y. St. B.J. 438, 442-443 (1976). Bar discussion of prepaid plans has frequently involved a mix of public-interest and private-gain considerations. . . .

Closed-panel plans are sponsored by groups that retain a law firm or hire their own legal staffs to deal with many legal problems common to their covered members. Any group can sponsor a prepaid plan. Thus far plans have been sponsored by trade unions, teachers' associations, consumer cooperatives, and student organizations and schools. Reformers have preferred closed-panel plans over open-panel plans.[61] Closed-panel plans typically cover members only when they use the services of the retained staff or law firm. Although the member's freedom of choice is thus somewhat restricted, commentators have identified several advantages of closed panels, among them better quality control, lower cost, and greater lawyer contact.[62]

Both closed- and open-panel plans enable the insured to budget legal expenses and spread the risk of incurring major legal expenses across a large number of people. Another advantage common to both closed- and open-panel plans is the lower cost of fee collection. These savings can be passed on to consumers, decreasing the overall cost of providing legal services.

3.   LEGAL CLINICS

The third popular form of alternative legal services delivery, legal clinics,[65] are law firms designed to serve clients with routine legal problems. Routine legal problems are those that usually can be handled in the same way each time, such as uncontested divorces, simple wills, nonbusiness bankruptcies, and residential property transactions. Many clinics specialize only in routine services. Some, however, perform such nonroutine services as personal injury litigation.[68] Legal clinics, on average, charge lower fees than traditional law firms[69] and rely on extensive advertising to attract the large clientele such operations require.

Despite considerable criticism, lawyer reference services have shown substantial staying power and figures show increasing use of their facil-

61. See DeMent, supra note 48, at 633-634.

62. See L. Deitch & D. Weinstein, supra note [47], at 41; Ellis, supra note 51, at 148 (better cost and quality control). . . .

65. Barlow Christensen rekindled modern interest in the legal clinic concept first developed by Llewellyn. See B. Christensen, supra note 46, at 205. The first law firm to use the name legal clinic was The Legal Clinic of Jacoby & Meyers in Los Angeles, established in 1972. Maron, Legal Clinics: A Status Report, in Legal Delivery Systems: Available Alternatives 239, 241 (1977). Although there were only 12 clinics in 1977 prior to the decision in Bates v. State Bar of Ariz., 433 U.S. 350 (1977) (striking down flat ban on attorney advertising), there are now an estimated 700 clinics, including numerous branches of the same clinic, see Bodine, [Nat'l L.J., Dec. 31, 1979] 5.

68. See, e.g., Meyers, Legal Clinics: Their Theory and How They Work, 52 L.A.B.J. 106, 107 (1976) (Jacoby & Meyers' fee schedule for personal injury cases). But see Stark, Jacoby & Meyers Charges More Than Wall Street, Am. Law., Aug. 1979, at 1, col 1-2 (field study indicating that clinics may not deal effectively with nonroutine problems).

69. See D. Maron, Legal Clinics: Analysis and Survey 8 (2d ed. 1977). . . .

ities. Indeed, with the diminution of federal funds for legal services in the early 1980s and the institution of poverty programs by some referral services, the concept of the lawyer referral services has regained a certain vitality. Nevertheless, the concept of the referral program waiting passively for the public to come to it and the failure of most programs to provide sufficient information about the individual lawyers participating in the program have hurt their image as an effective force for providing legal services. See Christensen, p. 590 n. 39, for a description of the efforts of the District of Columbia to provide significant information about lawyer participants.

As far as group legal services are concerned, prior to widespread adoption of the Model Code and even for a time after, they operated on the other side of the tracks of professional respectability because the very conception was assumed to be condemned by the principles of the former Canons of Ethics. This assumption was based either on the existence of specific abuses or on the general prohibition in Canon 35 against interference by "lay intermediaries" with the professional judgment of the lawyer. The relationship between the lawyer and the sponsoring organization, often a union, was generally believed to involve, explicitly or implicitly, such interference. Nonetheless, a surprising number of what were essentially group legal service organizations continued to operate, often unknown to the profession at large. The awakening of professional conscience to the needs of that vast body of the populace that cannot afford legal services easily or at all has changed the professional attitude to a substantial extent. Group legal services have become respectable, albeit their respectability has been only grudgingly recognized by many. An important aspect of this growing recognition has been the prodding of the Supreme Court, which got into the field via the civil rights movement of the 1960s but has since taken substantial interest in constitutional aspects of the bar's attempts to restrict group legal services.

Until recently federal constitutional principles played almost no role in regulation of the practice of law. What little constitutional law there was developed with respect to efforts by states to restrict membership in the bar — usually because of a person's beliefs or membership in an organization (see the materials on admission to the bar, pp. 603-627), but sometimes on an even more discriminatory basis, e.g., Bradwell v. State, 16 Wall. 130 (1873)(sex). During the civil rights movement of the 1960s, however, efforts to restrict the activities of the NAACP legal staff resulted in a landmark opinion that led the Supreme Court to scrutinize other regulatory efforts of the state and of the profession, with state acquiescence.

NAACP v. Button, 371 U.S. 415 (1963), overturned Virginia's attempt to forbid the NAACP from seeking plaintiffs to institute civil rights suits and supplying lawyers for such suits when plaintiffs (whether members of the NAACP or not) were found.

The Supreme Court soon made it quite clear that *Button* was relevant to conventional attempts by unions to obtain the benefits of group legal services. Brotherhood of Railroad Trainmen v. Virginia State Bar, 377 U.S. 1, reh'g denied, 377 U.S. 960 (1964). The Brotherhood of Railroad Trainmen had been in the business of referring injured railroad employee union members to selected lawyers called Regional Counsel for years. The terms and conditions of these referral plans had been the subject of professional and judicial inquiry from 1932 on. See Norman Riedmueller, Group Legal Services and the Organized Bar, 10 Col. J.L. & Soc. Prob. 228, 232-245 (1974), for a description of the major cases. In *BRT,* Virginia enjoined the union "from holding out the lawyers selected by it as the only approved lawyers to aid . . . members . . . or in any other manner soliciting or encouraging such legal employment of the selected lawyers. . . ." 377 U.S. at 4.

The Court refused to distinguish *Button* on the basis that First Amendment principles controlled in that case only because of the important civil and political rights that were involved. The Court held that the desire of workers to counsel one another in the selection of a lawyer implicated First Amendment rights of speech, assembly, and petition. Relying also on the protective statutory policies embodied in the Federal Employers' Liability Act and the Federal Safety Appliance Act, and finding no substantial countervailing state policy involved, the Court reversed the Virginia decree. But cf. discussion in *Ohralik* and *Primus,* pp. 493-516.

The *BRT* case was extended in UMW v. Illinois State Bar Assn., 389 U.S. 217 (1967), to a plan in which the union employed a lawyer on a salaried basis to handle members' workers' compensation claims. Illinois had enjoined this practice as involving the unauthorized practice of law by the union, but the Court found that the same First Amendment principles that were controlling in *BRT* governed this case as well.

Some of the potentialities for abuse that exist in group legal service plans emerge from Justice Harlan's description of the plan in his dissent in the *UMW* case, 389 U.S. 225. Although the original letter of employment of the lawyer stated, "You will receive no further instructions or directions and have no interference from the District, nor from any officer, and your obligations and relations will be to and with only the several persons you represent," id. at 220, it also appeared that "[i]njured union members are furnished by the Union with a form which advises them to send the form to the Union's legal department. Upon receipt . . . the attorney assumes it to constitute a request that he file on behalf of the injured member a claim with the Industrial Commission, though no such explicit request is contained in the form. . . . In most instances, the attorney has neither seen nor talked with the union member at this stage. . . . Ordinarily the member and this attorney first meet at the time of the hearing before the Commission." Id. at 230.

Justice Harlan also stated: "Evidently, he [the attorney] negotiates with the employer's counsel about many claims at the same time," and he notes that the UMW attorney was "also an Illinois state senator." Id. at 231.

Assembly-line handling of cases, lack of contact with the client, and settlement of claims en masse are all problems that exist in the profession today. The apprehension even among many persons sympathetic to group legal service programs is that the likelihood of these events will be greater in group legal service programs. These fears also exist with respect to public defender programs in the criminal law sphere. The reasonableness of these fears was seen by Justice Harlan as sufficient to support the conclusion of the Illinois court. Although not mentioned by Justice Harlan, the problems of conflict that any lawyer-legislator must face in accommodating his or her duties to the public and to private clients are enhanced in a situation like the *UMW* case where the legislative interests of the union may exert pressures on the lawyer-legislator that might affect the handling of particular cases for individual union members.

The final Supreme Court decision in this field was United Transportation Union v. State Bar of Michigan, 401 U.S. 576 (1971), in which the court struck down portions of a Michigan decree which had been based on the injunction entered on remand after the Supreme Court opinion in the *BRT* case. The Court held that the decree interpreted prior Supreme Court cases too narrowly and emphasized that the "common thread" running through those decisions was that "collective activity undertaken to obtain meaningful access to the courts is a fundamental right within the protection of the First Amendment." Id. at 585.

The developing professional recognition of the importance of group legal services was given impetus by the quartet of Supreme Court decisions, and by pressure from various groups and lawyers interested in exploring the potential of group legal service programs.

In California, where hundreds of group legal services programs were operating, usually with very little public notice, see Progress Report of the Standing Committee on Group Legal Services of the State Bar of California, 39 Cal. State B.J. 639 (1964), the California Supreme Court finally responded to recommendations of the State Bar and adopted a rule validating participation by lawyers in group legal service plans so long as the group had been "formed principally for common purposes other than the rendering of legal services," whose furnishing must be "merely incidental." 1 Cal. 3d Rules 56 (1970).

The ABA was split in its views on the subject of group legal services when it approved the Code of Professional Responsibility, and it debated the relevant Code provisions throughout the 1970s. The struggle involved the Special Committee on Availability of Legal Services on the side of recognizing the need for group legal services, the Section on General Practice strongly opposed to them, and the Committee on Evaluation of Ethical Standards that proposed the Model Code in the middle. The original issue was recognition of the traditional type of group legal service program run by a union, and the Section on General Practice prevailed. DR 2-103(D)(5) permitted a lawyer to cooperate with such an organization "only in those instances and to the extent that controlling constitutional interpretation at the time of the rendition of the services requires the allowance of such legal service activities."

Subsequently, the *United Transporation Union* decision (p. 595) cast doubt on the continuing validity of the wording of DR 2-103. At the same time, many lawyers were becoming interested in the possibility of prepaid legal insurance plans as an alternative to group legal services programs. The debate during the 1974 revision of DR 2-103 focused on the issue of "open-panel" as against "closed-panel" plans. The ABA's House of Delegates in 1974 rejected the recommendation of the Committee on Ethics and Professional Responsibility that would have treated both types of plans alike. Instead it accepted the complicated and badly drafted recommendations of the Section on General Practice that reflected its strong preference for open panels by regulating the closed-panel plans much more strictly.

The ABA action did not settle the matter. A number of states had refused to adopt the restrictive version of DR 2-103 in the first place. In addition, the action of Congress in making legal services a mandatory subject of collective bargaining, Pub. L. 93-95, 87 Stat. 314 (1973), and setting federal standards for pension plans, including those providing legal services, Pub. L. 93-406, 88 Stat. 829 (1974), raised the specter of federal preemption. Senator Tunney's Subcommittee on Representation of Citizen Interests held hearings concerning the effect of the 1974 amendments, and lawyers in the Antitrust Division indicated their belief that there was possibly a violation of the antitrust laws. See Note, Justice Department and Other Views on Prepaid Legal Services Plans Get an Airing Before the Tunney Subcommittee, 60 A.B.A.J. 791 (1974). Thereafter the ABA created a special Ad Hoc Study Group, which advised a further revision of DR 2-103 and related provisions. Its suggestions, which eliminated the regulatory distinctions between open and closed panels, were adopted in the February 1975 ABA meeting and represent essentially the final version of this aspect of DR 2-103 of the Model Code before it was replaced by the Model Rules.

With this background it is now perhaps possible to read the Model Code's DR 2-103(D) with some understanding of the struggle that produced it. That Rule poses a number of complex problems of professional responsibility for lawyers who are involved in group legal services programs. For those interested in such matters, including the applicability of ERISA, the Employee Retirement Security Act, see pp. 660-669 of the second edition of this book and Lori Andrews, Regulation of Group Legal Services Under State Ethics Codes, 19 Am. Bar Found. Res. Rep. 1 (no. 19 Summer 1981). The provisions of Model Rules 7.2 and 7.3 were drafted to avoid most of the problems that plagued prepaid services under the Model Code. See Comment 7 to that Rule.

One final issue relating to group legal services remains to be discussed — viz., the relation between the premise of a large unmet need for legal services and different delivery systems for such services. The existence of "unmet legal needs" has itself been controversial. The American Bar Association and the American Bar Foundation collaborated all through the 1970s on a nationwide survey designed to determine the facts about the public's need for, and use of, lawyers and also about the public's attitude toward lawyers. The efforts produced several interim reports and a final report by Barbara Curran entitled The Legal Needs of the Public (1977); a Final Report of the ABA Special Committee to Survey Legal Needs; and Curran ed., The Lawyer Statistical Report (American Bar Foundation 1985); and a Supplement to that Report (American Bar Foundation 1986). Subsequently, an ambitious Project in the Yale Law Journal reanalyzed the Survey data to identify the major factors affecting the decision whether to use a lawyer's services and thereupon to discuss which forms of alternative delivery systems were most responsive to the findings. The article begins with a historical discussion of the concern with underutilization of legal services and then describes some major alternative delivery systems. It then discusses seven factors identified in the literature as significantly affecting a person's decision to use a lawyer: (1) the number of times a person has used a lawyer; (2) whether a person owns real property; (3) whether a person has personal contacts with a lawyer; (4) the person's income; (5) the person's estimate of the cost of legal services; (6) the positiveness of the person's attitude toward lawyers; and (7) the person's awareness of the legal implications involved in a particular situation.

The Project used various statistical techniques to study the Survey data and concluded that the last four listed explanations correlated weakly with lawyer use while the first three explanations correlated more strongly. The article then proceeded to discuss the implications of those conclusions.

PROJECT, AN ASSESSMENT OF ALTERNATIVE STRATEGIES FOR INCREASING ACCESS TO LEGAL SERVICES*

90 Yale L.J. 122, 146-154 (1980)

III. IMPLICATIONS FOR ALTERNATIVE LEGAL DELIVERY SYSTEMS

An examination of alternative legal delivery systems in light of the somewhat unexpected results of our analysis enables us to assess the systems'

* The authors wish to thank their advisor, Professor Stanton A. Wheeler, for his thoughtful comments, and Associate Dean Edward A. Dauer for his insights and support.

potential for increasing the public's use of lawyers.[132] Contrary to the
observations of some commentators, attitude, awareness, and income
have only a minor effect on lawyer use. The influence of price on lawyer
use is difficult to determine given the limits of the data. The potential
of alternative systems, therefore, must be evaluated in light of the three
strong explanations of lawyer use — experience, property ownership,
and lawyer contacts.

A.   THE LIMITS OF ALTERNATIVE DELIVERY SYSTEMS

The results of our empirical study imply a limited role in increasing
lawyer use for all alternative delivery systems. Our analysis indicates that
lawyer use is primarily a function of an individual's experience, which is
measured by the number of acute and nonacute problems he has encountered as well as his age. These experience factors, taken together,
account for twenty percent of the variation in lawyer use. Experience is
largely an external factor, unalterable by legal service delivery systems.

Alternative delivery systems, however, may modify the experience
component by altering the way in which a situation is perceived. An example is the concept of preventive legal services or an annual legal
checkup, which both prepaid plans and clinics have considered promoting. Such an approach, if successful, might greatly increase the number
of perceived legal problems.

Another strong determinant of lawyer use in our study is real property ownership, which accounts for eleven percent of the variation in
lawyer use alone and 1.8 percent when combined with experience and
lawyer contacts. Like experience, however, real property ownership is an
external factor that cannot be influenced by alternative delivery systems.
The remaining determinants of lawyer use that could be more readily
altered by alternative systems — price, attitude, awareness, and lawyer
contacts — correlate less strongly with lawyer use.

More particularly, the results of our analysis imply that two strategies
often recommended for increasing lawyer use — improving the image
of lawyers and raising the legal awareness of the public — may not sig-

---

132. Despite its large sample size, comprehensive questionnaire, and rigorous meth-
odology, certain limits of the ABA-ABF Survey mandate caution in attempting to draw
conclusions from any study that employs these data. A survey merely obtains responses
from a sample of respondents for one period of time. Such responses are subject to
change, and the attitude and price responses of the ABA-ABF Survey may be particularly prone to such temporal shifts because of changes in the market for legal services.
In particular, it should be emphasized that the current market for legal services differs
substantially from that of 1973 to 1974 as a result of Bates v. State Bar of Ariz., 433
U.S. 350 (1977), which overturned the profession's ban on advertising.

Finally, it must be emphasized that the conclusions of the Project are not derived
directly from the empirical data, but rather from inferences based on the model derived
from the data.

nificantly affect lawyer utilization. Many observers have argued that lawyers are under-used because the public generally holds the legal profession in low esteem. They have proposed, therefore, that the bar seek to improve its image as a means of increasing the use of lawyers. Frequently suggested is institutional advertising by state and local bar associations. Our analysis suggests, however, that a person's attitude toward the legal profession has little effect on whether he uses a lawyer. Attempts to improve the profession's public image and alter the public's attitude toward lawyers, therefore, are likely to achieve little success in increasing lawyer use.

Others have argued that increased public awareness of the legal dimensions of various problems will lead to increased lawyer use. Our analysis, however, shows that legal awareness has a relatively minor effect on lawyer use. Consequently, general educational campaigns and institutional advertising aimed at increasing public awareness of legal problems may also yield relatively minor increases in lawyer use.

B.   ENHANCING LAWYER CONTACTS THROUGH ALTERNATIVE
DELIVERY SYSTEMS

Although the individual experience and property ownership factors are virtually unalterable by legal services delivery systems, the three alternative systems may have some impact on the third important determinant of lawyer use — personal contacts with attorneys. Personal contacts serve as a general information source concerning the kinds and costs of services provided by lawyers. An attorney with whom one has personal contact can also serve as an intermediary, acquainting an individual with the legal system and particular local lawyers capable of resolving his problem. To the extent that an alternative delivery system can serve the same functions as a lawyer contact, it probably will succeed in increasing lawyer use.

1.   Lawyer Referral Service (LRS)

By enabling a client to consult with a lawyer at a nominal fee, the LRS provides potential for lawyer contact and access to information. Some information may be provided to the client at the initial screening interview, but the potential for providing information at this point is limited by the fact that so few LRSs have staff attorneys. Nevertheless, the client can use this opportunity to discover what, if anything, a lawyer can do to resolve his problem, and how much these services will cost. Although this may be useful, the potential client has similar opportunities with other alternative systems that he may be able to use at less cost. Unfortunately, the LRS provides information at a relatively high search cost, because the client must endure substantial inconvenience in order to arrange an initial screening. This cost limits the effectiveness of the LRS as a potential information source.

By actually making an appointment with an attorney for a prospective client, the LRS may be useful as a resource for lawyer selection. The service thus helps to overcome a potential client's initial hesitation in contacting an attorney. Unlike a lawyer contact who is a friend, relative or neighbor, however, the LRS lacks an ongoing relationship with the consumer. As a consequence, consumers may consider an LRS referral less reliable than a recommendation made by a lawyer friend or relative whom they know and trust. Consumer mistrust may be justified, as membership in LRS panels is not subject to careful screening; LRS panels represent only a cross-section of the bar.

2. Prepaid Plans: Open- and Closed-Panel

Open-panel plans may be effective information sources. Prior to enrollment in an open-panel plan an individual is usually informed about the legal services to which he will be entitled and their cost. Nevertheless, open panels may not provide full information on costs because benefits are sometimes listed in dollar amounts or hours of legal work. The consumer must still estimate how many hours or how many dollars a particular service will require in order to ascertain whether such expenses are fully covered by his policy.

More important, most open-panel plans offer members a limited number of free consultations and advise clients on what a lawyer can do to resolve a particular problem. Open-panel plans should increase lawyer use by offering this important information source as an integral part of the plan's operation.

Open-panel plans may also serve as either a formal or informal referral service. Most open-panel plans have this feature. In contrast to the LRS, however, these referrals come from an organization with which the consumer has an ongoing relationship. Consumers may therefore consider such open-panel referrals more reliable, and the likelihood that they will actually take advantage of the referral advice and consult a lawyer may be greater. Furthermore, open-panel plans have a financial incentive to provide referrals the consumer finds adequate. Poor referrals would threaten continued enrollment in the plan.

Closed-panel plans also provide specific cost information and the opportunity for free consultations. Information on cost may be more detailed than with open panels because some closed panels limit coverage to specific matters and not to specific dollar or hour amounts. Consultations under a closed-panel plan may involve lower search costs than consultations obtained under open-panel plans or through LRSs because closed-panel attorneys may be willing to take certain steps to ensure easy access to their services. As a further step, closed-panel plans often inform members about the benefits of consulting a lawyer through news-letters, meetings, and seminars.

To a greater extent than LRSs and open-panel plans, closed-panel arrangements reduce their members' search costs because the plan assumes total responsibility for selecting its members' attorneys. Many consumers may prefer to leave attorney selection in the hands of a trusted intermediary. The strong relationship between the member and sponsoring group can be expected to create more trust than found in LRSs and open-panel arrangements. This important combination of free consultation and general dissemination of information could enable closed-panel plans to provide their members with the greatest amount of information at the lowest search cost.

3. Legal Clinics

Legal clinics, by advertising, provide consumers with extensive information on the price of various legal services at relatively low search cost. Advertising may, however, convey only limited price information. Clinics can also provide information concerning the benefits of lawyer services both in their advertising and in free or low-fee consultations. Clinics have further sought to minimize the search costs involved in seeking out their services by using storefront locations and having flexible hours.

Clinics can serve a lawyer referral function by providing consumers with limited information about the clinic's lawyers in their advertising. As with the information provided by LRSs, however, this advertising is not offered by someone with whom the consumer has an ongoing relationship. The consumer will likely find such advertising information even less reliable than that from LRSs, because advertising is provided by someone who has an interest in supplying only positive information.

4. Conclusions

The foregoing assessment of the three alternative delivery systems yields suggestions for increasing lawyer use. For individuals who belong to a group that could readily employ a prepaid plan, closed panels offer the best source of information as to the costs and benefits of consulting a lawyer, and also the most direct form of lawyer selection. Closed-panel prepaids are thus most likely to fulfill the instrumental function of lawyer contact and thereby increase lawyer use. Legal clinics, rather than LRSs, are more likely to serve the function of lawyer contact through their advertising for those individuals who are not members of groups for which prepaid plans are marketable or feasible. . . .

NOTES

1. An issue not discussed in the Yale Project is whether there is any difference in the relative quality of services likely to be found in the various kinds of delivery systems. That is an issue that also arises in the controversy over provision of legal services to indigents among proponents and opponents of Judicare as an alternative to the more "traditional" legal aid or legal services office. See p. 539.

2. A good description of the operation of an early experimental prepaid legal insurance open-panel plan that also surveyed the users along the same lines as those used by the American Bar Association-American Bar Foundation Survey is Marks, Hallauer, & Clifton, The Shreveport Plan: An Experiment in the Delivery of Legal Services (1973).

3. Prepaid legal service plans, formerly heavily concentrated in unions, are now being marketed by a variety of financial service agencies, insurance companies, banks, and even large mail order houses that offer basic legal services such as wills, review of documents, and telephone consultation for a fixed fee per month or year. Fees vary, of course, with the services. A few operate on an open-plan basis but most do not. There are estimates that as many as 17 million individuals may be covered by some type of prepaid legal services plan. Wall Street Journal, Feb. 3, 1987. One problem with which such plans still struggle in many cases is whether they are "insurance" plans and as such subject to regulation of state insurance departments.

4. Legal clinics also expanded greatly in the 1980s. Two of the largest law firms in the country at the end of the 1980s were Hyatt Legal Services and Jacoby & Meyers, the former with nearly 200 offices, and the latter with 150. Hyatt operates not only as a legal clinic offering routine services for relatively low prices but also has its own prepaid legal insurance plan. See Wall Street Journal, May 6, 1987, p. 33, for a description of its operation and the management problems of such organizations.

CHAPTER 10

WHO MAY PRACTICE LAW

A. ADMISSION TO THE BAR

PROBLEM 81

You are general counsel to the Committee on Admissions of the Bar of your state. The President of the Committee has given you the job of preparing a questionnaire designed to be answered by every applicant for admission to the bar. The President's memorandum to you states:

"We are not interested in revising those portions of the questionnaire that ask the standard questions about residence, education, jobs, and the like. I have asked the Secretary of the Committee to look at those questions. What I am concerned about is fulfilling our statutory duty to satisfy ourselves that the applicant is of 'good moral character.'

"I have requested committee members to submit to me sample questions for our questionnaire. Here is the first group that I have received. With respect to each question, I would like you to tell me whether you think it should be on our questionnaire. If any question seems too general, please rephrase it to be more precise if you think it seeks information we should have. I am not asking for your opinion as a matter of constitutional law. I want you to forget constitutional law. I want your judgment about how far our Committee on Admissions ought to go in satisfying itself on an applicant's good moral character, at the same time respecting individual dignity and privacy.

"There is one thing we both should keep in mind. There is a big difference between asking for information and deciding what to do with information that is supplied. You should not assume that unfavorable responses to any of these questions will be used automatically to deny admission to the bar. Each case will be handled on an individual basis and, of course, your advice will be sought in each of the cases as it arises.

"Here are some of the questions I received:

(1) Have you ever been convicted of a crime, other than a minor traffic offense punishable by a fine of $500 or less? If so, please give details, date, and place for each such conviction.

(2) Have you ever been charged with, or arrested for, any of the crimes reportable under question 1? If so, please give details, date, and place for each such charge or arrest.

(3) To your knowledge, have you within the past three years violated any law, other than traffic and motor vehicle laws or laws carrying no possibility of imprisonment or fines greater than $500?

(4) Have you within the past five years received any traffic or parking summons to which you did not respond? If the answer is yes, please give details with respect to each summons, including approximate dates and places to the best of your memory.

(5) Were you the subject of any disciplinary charge, formal or informal, while in college or law school relating to any academic or nonacademic matter? What was the charge and what action was taken by the school? Please give details, date, and school.

(6) While you were at law school, did you ever fail to observe any rule or requirement set by the school or by an individual professor with respect to the taking of any examination? If the answer is yes, please give details including whether or not the matter came to the school's attention and action taken, if any.

(7) Have you ever sold any of the following drugs (listing every drug whose sale is illegal in the state)? If the answer is yes, please give details.

(8) To your knowledge, have you taken or used any of the drugs listed in question 7 within the past year? If the answer is yes, please give details.

(9) Have you consulted a psychologist or psychiatrist during the past three years? If the answer is yes, do not give details, but be prepared to discuss with the Committee in a general way any condition from which you were found to be suffering. In the alternative, please indicate whether you would permit the Committee to inquire of the psychologist or psychiatrist whether any condition he or she found would have a substantial effect on your conduct or ability as a lawyer. See In re Applicant, 443 So. 2d 71 (Fla. 1983).

(10) Have you read the disciplinary rules applicable to lawyers that are in force in this state? If the answer is yes, do you accept the principles and prohibitions set forth in the disciplinary rules as the guides to your professional conduct? If the answer to the latter question is no, please set forth which principles or prohibitions you do not accept and the reasons for your rejection.

"As you think about these questions, let me solicit your advice about how we should handle the following five cases pending before the Committee [Problems 82-86]."

PROBLEM 82

Case #1: We have received a letter from the law school professor who had supervisory responsibility for the legal aid program in which this student participated for the last two years of law school. The crucial sentence of the letter states: "I believe that I should tell you that despite constant warnings from me and from others, this student would continuously talk about his clients' affairs, including the revealing of confidential matters at cocktail parties and in informal conversations with other students who were not members of the legal aid office."

PROBLEM 83

Case #2: The question on our current form does not ask about minor traffic violations, but we received information, which we have verified indicating that while this student was at law school, he collected and ignored 25 parking tickets. We have spoken with the student about it and he offered as an explanation the fact that he was incensed at the police because they always came around to ticket right at the end of a morning class hour so as to catch students but never checked these meters at other hours of the days when townspeople occupied them.

PROBLEM 84

Case #3: This is another scofflaw parking ticket case in which the applicant offered no explanation except to say that she just never got around to paying them and finally decided "the heck with it" and left town. Yesterday our state Supreme Court handed down an opinion in In re X, which seems to have facts identical to Case #3, except that a practicing lawyer of twenty-five years' standing was involved. The court viewed the offense as very serious, suspended the lawyer for six months, and said that except for the lawyer's previous long unblemished record, the suspension would have been considerably longer.

PROBLEM 85

Case #4: We have a letter from the dean of the applicant's law school in response to our questionnaire. The dean reports that after a hearing the applicant admitted having lied about resources and expenses on two years' applications for financial aid in order to get larger awards. The student was suspended for two years but was then readmitted to the law school and has gotten the J.D. degree. The Dean writes that there were

no further incidents at law school, that he believes the student has
learned a valuable lesson, and that he therefore believes that the student
should not be denied admission to the bar.

PROBLEM 86

Case #5: We have an applicant who attended another law school who
was involved in a situation similar to case #4 except in one respect. The
student never admitted that her applications were deliberately falsified,
and advanced all sorts of explanations to justify the figures in her applications. Nevertheless, after a hearing, a law school faculty-student
committee found that the applications had been deliberately falsified.
The student was suspended for two years, but was later readmitted and
awarded her degree. In her application to us, she still asserts that she
did nothing wrong and told no falsehoods on her financial aid applications. Some members of our committee believe that it is important that
we reach a judgment as to whether the original financial aid applications
were falsified so as to be able to test her current sincerity. Others believe
that her current "moral character" is the crucial question, that a suspension from law school should not automatically prevent her admission
four years later, and that we should simply accept and not reexamine
the law school determination. What do you think we should do?

The materials in this section are concerned almost exclusively with the
issue of "moral character." Admission to the bar raises another crucial
question, that of competence. That issue is discussed in the following
chapter on discipline, and the materials of these two chapters should
therefore be considered together.

Over the years, admission to the bar has been almost totally a subject
for control by the apparatus established in each state. Educational pre-
requisites, residence and apprentice requirements, even the ability to
practice statewide, have been treated as matters of purely local concern,
and the practices have varied greatly. Most of the current issues relating
to bar admission, including the necessity for and the fairness of bar examination, their content and grading, are discussed in the very thoughtful Bar Admissions Study Committee, Report to the Supreme Court of
Oregon (1979).

Admission to federal practice in a particular state has tended to follow
the state practice, as has disbarment, although in recent years there has
been a little movement in the federal courts away from automatic following of state practice. See Spanos v. Skouras, 364 F.2d 161 (2d Cir. 1966),
cert. denied, 385 U.S. 987 (1966) (state may not constitutionally prohibit
citizen with a federal claim or defense from engaging an out-of-state

lawyer to collaborate with an in-state lawyer); Theard v. United States, 354 U.S. 278 (1957) (lawyer's disbarment by federal district court upon disbarment by state court reversed; federal court should give respect to state action but is not bound by it); but see In re Abrams, 521 F.2d 1094 (3d Cir. 1975), cert. denied with two dissents, 423 U.S. 1038 (1975) (reversing federal district court's disbarment of lawyer suspended for one year for same conduct by New Jersey Supreme Court; when district court relied on record in state court proceeding, it could not base its action in part on a charge that had been withdrawn in the state proceeding; nor could it rely on a state court precedent that had been distinguished by the state Supreme Court). In Leis v. Flynt, 439 U.S. 438 (1979), the Supreme Court, following the theory of procedural due process enunciated in Paul v. Davis, 424 U.S. 693 (1976), held that an out-of-state attorney has no property interest in appearing pro hac vice in a local court. The local court therefore need not accord the attorney any procedural due process before denying an application to appear.

For 165 years, however, federal interference with state control over the profession was almost nonexistent. There were only rare decisions like Cummings v. Missouri, 4 Wall. 277 (1866), holding unconstitutional Missouri's test oath for lawyers and other groups, requiring them to deny previous actions, words, or sympathies on behalf of those engaged in rebellion against the United States. In a series of decisions beginning in the mid-1950s, however, the Supreme Court has manifested greater concern with what the states were doing with their freedom to regulate the profession. The Court's increasing activity is in a sense reflective of its larger concerns in the past 35 years. It is also indicative perhaps of growing concern over the performance of the profession and the balance the profession has struck between the rights of individual lawyers and its own needs in the context of service to clients and society.

Most of the Supreme Court cases focused on the kinds of preliminary inquiries the state bar committees may make to test ultimate statements in one form or another of nonparticipation in revolutionary activity looking to violent overthrow of the government. Schware v. Board of Bar Examiners, 353 U.S. 232 (1957); Konigsberg v. State Bar, 353 U.S. 252 (1957) and 366 U.S. 36 (1961); Anastaplo v. Illinois, 366 U.S. 82 (1961); In re Stolar, 401 U.S. 23 (1971), and Baird v. State Bar, 401 U.S. 1 (1971). In all of the cases, however, the Court has recognized the general supervisory powers of the state over admission to the bar and, more particularly, its authority to set standards relating to character. See Law Students Civil Rights Research Council, Inc. v. Wadmond, 401 U.S. 154 (1971), upholding New York's requirement that applicants for admission to the bar must possess "the character and general fitness requisite for an attorney and counsellor-at-law."

A large number of recent cases have raised a different constitutional issue, the ability of states to impose residence or domicile requirements as a condition of taking a bar examination or of being admitted. The Supreme Court has consistently held that such requirements violate the Privileges and Immunities Clause of Article 4 of the Constitution because of the burden imposed and the failure of the restrictions to meet any substantial state interest. E.g., Supreme Court of New Hampshire v. Piper, 470 U.S. 274 (1985) and Supreme Court of Virginia v. Friedman, 108 S. Ct. 2260 (1988).

A whole variety of other constitutional issues have also been raised about admission requirements. See, e.g., Application of Hansen, 275 N.W.2d 790 (Minn. 1978), appeal dismissed for want of a substantial federal question, 441 U.S. 938 (1979) (denial of right to take bar examination because applicant did not attend ABA-accredited school upheld); Younger v. Colorado State Bd. of Bar Examiners, 625 F.2d 372 (10th Cir. 1980) (limitation on number of times bar examination may be taken upheld). Numerous other challenges have been made to grading practices on the bar examinations by minority groups and by others alleging antitrust violations because of limitations on numbers of attorneys admitted. See Hoover v. Ronwin, 466 U.S. 558, reh'g denied, 467 U.S. 1268 (1984). See also p. 617. The Court in that case held that members of the bar examination committee appointed by the Arizona Supreme Court who failed the applicant and whose recommendation that he be denied admission to the bar was accepted by the Arizona Supreme Court were immune from Sherman Act liability under the state action doctrine. See p. 636, Note 5. The Court noted that the Arizona Supreme Court had approved the Committee's grading formula, closely supervised its activities, and was the body that actually admitted or denied admission to the bar.

Another aspect of the admission process generally involves an assessment of the applicant's "moral character," a process that has become increasingly controversial. Excerpts from Supreme Court opinions discussing the requirement and a case applying it follow.

SCHWARE v. BOARD OF BAR EXAMINERS
353 U.S. 232, 247 (1957)

Justice FRANKFURTER, whom Justice CLARK and Justice HARLAN join, concurring.

Certainly since the time of Edward I, through all the vicissitudes of seven centuries of Anglo-American history, the legal profession has played a role all its own. The bar has not enjoyed prerogatives; it has been entrusted with anxious responsibilities. One does not have to inhale the self-adulatory bombast of after-dinner speeches to affirm that all interests of man that are comprised under the constitutional guarantees given to "life, liberty and property" are in the professional keeping of lawyers. It is a fair characterization of the lawyer's responsibility in our society that he stands "as a shield," to quote Devlin, J., in defense of right and to ward off wrong. From a profession charged with such responsibilities there must be exacted those qualities of truth-speaking, of a high sense of honor, of granite discretion, of the strictest observance of fiduciary responsibility, that have, throughout the centuries, been compendiously described as "moral character."

From the thirteenth century to this day, in England the profession itself has determined who should enter it. In the United States the courts exercise ultimate control. But while we have nothing comparable to the Inns of Court, with us too the profession itself, through appropriate committees, has long had a vital interest, as a sifting agency, in determining the fitness, and above all the moral fitness, of those who are certified to be entrusted with the fate of clients. With us too the requisite "moral character" has been the historic unquestioned prerequisite of fitness. . . .

KONIGSBERG v. STATE BAR
353 U.S. 252, 263 (1957)

BLACK, Justice. . . . A. *Good Moral Character.* — The term "good moral character" has long been used as a qualification for membership in the Bar and has served a useful purpose in this respect. However the term, by itself, is unusually ambiguous. It can be denied in an almost unlimited number of ways for any definition will necessarily reflect the attitudes, experiences, and prejudices of the definer.[18] Such a vague qualification, which is easily adapted to fit personal views and predilections, can be a dangerous instrument for arbitrary and discriminatory denial of the right to practice law.

While we do not have the benefit of a definition of "good moral character" by the California Supreme Court in this case, counsel for the State tells us that the definition of that term adopted in California "stresses elements of honesty, fairness and respect for the rights of others and for the laws of the state and nation." The decisions of California courts cited here do not support so broad a definition as claimed by counsel. These cases instead appear to define "good moral character" in terms of an absence of proven conduct or acts which have been historically considered as manifestations of "moral turpitude." To illustrate, California has held that an applicant did not have good character who had been con-

---

18. See Jordan v. De George, 341 U.S. 223, 232 (dissenting opinion); United States ex rel. Iorio v. Day, 34 F.2d 920, 921; Cahn, Authority and Responsibility, 51 Col. L. Rev. 838.

victed of forgery and had practiced law without a license,[19] or who had
obtained money by false representations and had committed fraud upon
a court,[20] or who had submitted false affidavits to the Committee along
with his application for admission.[21] It should be emphasized that neither the definition proposed by counsel nor those appearing in the California cases equates unorthodox political beliefs or membership in
lawful political parties with bad moral character. Assuming for purposes
of this case that counsel's broad definition of "good moral character" is
the one adopted in California, the question is whether on the whole record a reasonable man could fairly find that there were substantial
doubts about Konigsberg's "honesty, fairness and respect for the rights
of others and for the laws of the state and nation." . . .

APPLICATION OF GAHAN
279 N.W.2d 826 (Minn. 1979)

Todd, Justice.

William Gahan seeks admission to the bar of the State of Minnesota.
After his successful completion of the bar examination, he was requested
by the Board of Law Examiners to appear before them to review the
circumstances surrounding the discharge in bankruptcy of certain student loans obtained by Gahan to finance his education. After formal
hearing, the Board determined that Gahan did not meet the standards
required of applicants for admission to practice law in Minnesota. We
affirm.

The facts in this matter are not in dispute. Gahan received his law
degree from the University of San Francisco, California. He was admitted to practice law in California in 1976 and subsequently was admitted
to practice law in Wisconsin. Gahan is single, has never been married,
and has no dependents. During the time of his education, at both the
undergraduate and graduate level, Gahan required financial assistance
to obtain his law degree. To achieve this goal, he obtained a series of
student loans under a Federally funded guaranty program. At the time
of his graduation from law school, the total amount of these loans was
approximately $14,000. At the time he received the loans, Gahan agreed
to repay and understood that he would be expected to repay the loans
upon or shortly after graduation. Generally, student loans are amortized
over a 10-year period with interest at 7 percent, and the first payment
is to commence about 9 months after graduation. A monthly payment

19. In re Garland, 219 Cal. 661, 28 P.2d 354.
20. In re Wells, 174 Cal. 467, 163 P. 657.
21. Spears v. State Bar of California, 211 Cal. 183, 294 P. 697.

of approximately $175 would be required to repay the loans under such a repayment schedule.

In December 1976, Gahan was employed by an Oakland, California, law firm at an annual salary of $15,000. In the summer of 1977, his employer experienced financial difficulties and Gahan was not paid for 2 months, and, as a result, he terminated his employment on August 15, 1977. Shortly thereafter, he received all of his unpaid wages and expenses, except a small amount of out-of-pocket travel expenses. Gahan was unemployed until October 1977, a period of 2 months, when he obtained employment with another California law firm at an annual salary of $18,000.

Gahan claims he made some initial payments upon the loan. Subsequently, however, he defaulted. On September 27, 1977, during his period of unemployment, Gahan obtained legal counsel and filed a voluntary petition for bankruptcy in the United States District Court of the Northern District of California. Immediately prior to filing his petition for bankruptcy, Gahan mortgaged his 1959 Jaguar automobile to a friend for a loan of $2,500. He deposited $1,000 of the loan funds in an exempt account at a savings and loan institution and deposited the remaining $1,500 in an exempt account at a co-op credit union. Under California law, these deposits were the maximum amounts which could be claimed as exempt from creditors.

At the time of the filing of the bankruptcy petition, Gahan had a number of current obligations. He owed the balance on the student loans and $1,600 on a loan from the Hibernia Bank of San Francisco. These were the only debts scheduled in the bankruptcy petition. However, Gahan did disclose exempt items of $4,000, consisting of the $2,500 in the two bank deposits, the equity in the Jaguar automobile of $1,000, and $500 in household goods and wearing apparel. In addition, he disclosed the mortgage on the automobile in the amount of $2,500 and an $1,800 life insurance loan against a policy having a market value of $1,500. Gahan's bankruptcy petition showed total liabilities of $19,717.40 and $4,007 worth of assets, $4,000 of which was exempt.

After regaining employment and before his discharge in bankruptcy, Gahan reinstated his $1,600 obligation to Hibernia Bank and has paid this debt in full. He did so because he knew an officer at the bank and he believed he might need an additional loan from the bank some time in the future. Following his discharge in bankruptcy on February 7, 1978, Gahan used the balance of the $2,500 loan obtained from his friend and other funds to discharge the loan against his automobile which remained in his possession, free of encumbrances. As a result of these undertakings, the only debts actually discharged in the bankruptcy proceedings were the Federally insured student loans.

There is nothing connected with Gahan's bankruptcy to suggest that there was any fraud, deceit, or conduct which could be considered to involve moral turpitude. However, based on this evidence, the Board of Law examiners found in part:

XXIII

Procuring discharge of this indebtedness (and no other) with so little effort to repay or extend the same and with only temporary loss of employment, no exceptional financial or health problems and no major misfortunes, while neither illegal nor constituting action evincing moral turpitude, nonetheless is conduct which would cause a reasonable man to have substantial doubt concerning applicant's honesty, fairness, and respect for the rights of others and for the laws of this state and nation amounting thereby to a lack of good moral character having a rational connection with applicant's fitness or capacity to practice law.

XXIV

Applicant continues to have and maintain a lack of recognition and appreciation of the underlying moral obligation and social (as opposed to legal) responsibility which arose when he was entrusted with the student loan funds in question.

As a result of these findings, the Board found Gahan was not a person of good moral character within the contemplation of our Rules of Admission and recommended that he not be admitted to practice law in Minnesota. Gahan petitioned this court for review for this recommendation.

This issue on appeal is whether, in view of the facts of this case and the applicable Federal rights protecting those who elect to file voluntary bankruptcy, the applicant to the Minnesota bar was properly denied admission on the grounds of insufficient moral character.

I.   FEDERAL BANKRUPTCY RIGHTS

Initially, we observe that persons discharging their debts in bankruptcy are afforded certain rights under Federal law. The fact of filing bankruptcy or the refusal to reinstate obligations discharged in bankruptcy cannot be a basis for denial of admission to the bar of the State of Minnesota. Any refusal so grounded would violate the Supremacy Clause of the United States Constitution since applicable Federal law clearly prohibits such a result. The leading case on this issue is Perez v. Campbell, 402 U.S. 637 . . . (1971). In that case, the Supreme Court considered the constitutionality of a state statute which precluded a person from driving if he had an unsatisfied judgment arising out of an automobile accident. In effect, a person who had such a judgment discharged in bankruptcy could not drive unless he reaffirmed the discharged debt. The court held the statute violated the Supremacy Clause, and overruled Kesler v. Department of Public Safety, 369 U.S. 153, 82 S. Ct. 807, 7 L. Ed. 2d 641 (1962), and Reitz v. Mealey, 314 U.S. 33, 62 S. Ct. 24, 86 L. Ed. 21 (1941), by changing its focus from the *purpose* of the state statute to the *effect* of the state statute. The court reasoned that the effect of the statute was to coerce the person into paying a discharged debt, and that such coercion contravened the bankruptcy act's objective of giving debtors a "'new opportunity in life and a clear field for future effort, unhampered by the pressure and discouragement of pre-existing debt.'" 402 U.S. 648. . . .[1]

However, these constitutional limitations do not preclude a court from inquiring into the bar applicant's responsibility or moral character in financial matters. The inquiry is impermissible only when the fact of bankruptcy is labeled "immoral" or "irresponsible," and admission is denied for that reason. In other words, we cannot declare bankruptcy a wrong when Federal law has declared it a right.

Thus, in the present case, Gahan's conduct prior to bankruptcy surrounding his financial responsibility and his default on the student loans may be considered to judge his moral character. However, the fact of his bankruptcy may not be considered, nor may his present willingness or ability to pay the loans be considered because under Federal bankruptcy law, he now has a right to not pay the loans.

2. APPLICANT'S MORAL CHARACTER

Rule II of the Rules for Admission to the bar of the State of Minnesota states in part:

> No person shall be admitted to practice law who has not established to the satisfaction of the State Board of Law Examiners: . . .
> (2) That he is a person of good moral character; . . .
> Character traits that are relevant to a determination of good moral character must have a rational connection with the applicant's present fitness or capacity to practice law, and accordingly must relate to the State's legitimate interest in protecting prospective clients and the system of justice.

A requirement of good moral character has been recognized by the Supreme Court as a constitutionally permissible condition to bar admission, provided that the Constitution is not violated in the determination

---

1. For cases holding *Perez* not applicable to private institutions or actions, see Girardier v. Webster College, 563 F.2d 1267 (8 Cir. 1977), and McLellan v. Mississippi Power & Light Co., 545 F.2d 919, 930, n.57 (5 Cir. 1977).

of moral character. In re Stolar, 401 U.S. 23 (1971); Baird v. Arizona, 401 U.S. 1 (1971); Konigsberg v. State Bar, 353 U.S. 252 (1957); Schware v. Board of Bar Examiners, 353 U.S. 232 (1957).

The Board found that petitioner did not have good moral character because of conduct surrounding his failure to repay several student loans. No other discernible grounds for showing lack of good moral character — such as fraud or dishonesty — appear in the record. Consistent with the above discussion on constitutionally permissible factors, the specific question thus becomes whether petitioner showed a lack of good moral character prior to discharge in bankruptcy because he did not undertake or prepare for repayment of the student loans.

The conduct of a bar applicant in satisfying his financial obligations has been widely recognized as a relevant factor in assessing good moral character. See, In re Heller, 333 A.2d 401 (D.C. Ct. App.), cert. denied, 423 U.S. 840, 96 S. Ct. 70, 46 L. Ed. 2d 59 (1975); In re Cheek, 246 Or. 433, 425 P.2d 763 (1967). The failure of a person to honor his legal commitments adversely reflects on his ability to practice law, evincing a disregard for the rights of others. See, Matter of Connor, Ind., 358 N.E.2d 120 (1976). See, generally, Annotation, 64 A.L.R.2d 301.

The Florida court is apparently the only court to specifically consider whether a bar applicant's failure to repay his student loans demonstrates lack of good moral character so as to justify denial of admission. The Florida court has considered the issue twice, and the contrast in the cases is instructive. In the case of Florida Bd. of Bar examiners re G. W. L., 364 So. 2d 454 (Fla. 1978), the applicant, G. W. L., had approximately $10,000 in student loans upon graduation from law school. As of several months before graduation, he had not obtained law-related employment. Three days before graduation, he executed a voluntary petition for bankruptcy and released from his debts. At approximately the same time, the applicant obtained a job as law clerk at $70 per week. He applied for admission to the Florida bar, and the Board recommended that applicant not be admitted. The Florida Supreme Court agreed with the Board, stating (364 So. 2d 459):

> . . . We find that the Board had ample record evidence from which it could conclude that the principal motive of the petitioner in filing his petition for bankruptcy was to defeat creditors who had substantially funded seven years of educational training. Whether that motive was present as the debts were incurred or was formed toward the end of his law school training, the Board could fairly conclude from the petitioner's own testimony and prior behavior that he exercised his legal right to be freed of debt by bankruptcy well before the first installments on his debt became due, with absolutely no regard for his moral responsibility to his creditors. The petitioner's admittedly legal but unjustifiably precipitous action, initiated before he had obtained the results of the July bar examination, exhausted the job market, or given his creditors an opportunity to adjust

repayment schedules, indicates a lack of the moral values upon which we have a right to insist for members of the legal profession in Florida. The petitioner's course of conduct in these personal affairs raises serious questions concerning the propriety of his being a counselor to others in their legal affairs, and is rationally connected to his fitness to practice law. . . .

To foreclose any misconstruction of this decision we must emphasize that this ruling should not be interpreted to approve any general principle concerning bankruptcies nor to hold that the securing of a discharge in bankruptcy is an act inherently requiring the denial of admission to the bar. We further do not wish this decision to be construed to hold that any comparable exercise of a clear legal right will necessarily imperil bar admission.

Three justices dissented because, even though they did not condone the applicant's actions, the applicant had a Federal right to bankruptcy and therefore the court could not constitutionally deny admission on the basis of exercising that right. The majority did not address the constitutional issue or cite the *Perez* case.

In the second Florida case, Florida Bd. of Bar Examiners re Groot, 365 So. 2d 164 (Fla. 1978), the court held that an applicant who had discharged his student loans in bankruptcy should nevertheless be admitted because the circumstances surrounding his default were justified. In distinguishing the case from Florida Bd. of Bar Examiners re G. W. L., supra, the court said (365 So. 2d 168):

> Unlike G. W. L., Groot was the father and legal custodian of two children born of his recently-terminated marriage. His expenses included not only his own living costs and those of his dependents, but to some degree those of his former wife. When his personal resources became exhausted, he was forced to prevail upon family members to loan him the money, to meet current living expenses while he was without a job. Thus, unlike G. W. L., Groot had suffered unusual misfortune at the time he finally secured employment, and he had a valid present need to devote his entire employment income to his current, not past, financial responsibilities. His circumstances warranted his turning to the remedy provided by federal law for persons in just such situations, and we hold that Groot's conduct under these circumstances is not morally reprehensible or indicative of a present unfitness for admission to the bar.

In these two cases, the Florida court failed to squarely address the constitutional issue of denying employment licenses on the basis of bankruptcy. We have reservations as to whether it was constitutional for the Florida court to consider the morality of any motivations for filing bankruptcy when the Federal Government has declared the bankruptcy proceeding to be legal and presumably beneficial to the welfare of the individual and society.

Nevertheless, the Florida cases are instructive of the judicial concern over admitting to the bar those persons who disregard the rights of others and do not pay their debts even when they are reasonably able to do so. We hold that applicants who flagrantly disregard the rights of others and default on serious financial obligations, such as student loans, are lacking in good moral character if the default is neglectful, irresponsible, and cannot be excused by a compelling hardship that is reasonably beyond the control of the applicant. Such hardships might include an unusual misfortune, a catastrophe, an overriding financial obligation, or unavoidable unemployment.

We are, under the Minnesota Constitution, entrusted with the exclusive duty to assure the high moral standards of the Minnesota bar. We have no difficulty in concluding that Federal law does not preclude us from evaluating the responsibility of a bar applicant in satisfying his or her financial obligations. This is particularly true where, as here, the obligation has the significance of $14,000 in Federally insured student loans. A student loan is entrusted to a person, and is to be repaid to creditors upon graduation when and if financially able. Moreover, repayment provides stability to the student loan program and guarantees the continuance of the program for future student needs. A flagrant disregard of this repayment responsibility by the loan recipient indicates to us a lack of moral commitment to the rights of other students and particularly the rights of creditors. Such flagrant financial irresponsibility reflects adversely on an applicant's ability to manage financial matters and reflects adversely on his commitment to the rights of others, thereby reflecting adversely on his fitness for the practice of law. It is appropriate to prevent problems from such irresponsibility by denying admission, rather than seek to remedy the problem after it occurs and victimizes a client.

Applying the above principles to this case, we conclude that Gahan's failure to satisfy his obligations on the student loans cannot be excused for some compelling hardship reasonably beyond his control. During the period prior to bankruptcy, he was employed for most of the time at an annual salary of $15,000 and then $18,000. Monthly he grossed from $1,250 to $1,500, and he accounted for monthly expenses of approximately $500. The record indicates that his monthly payments on the loans would be approximately $175. He was healthy, single, and not subject to any unusual hardship. He was reasonably able to satisfy his legal and moral obligation to prepare for repayment and continue repayment of his student loans. His failure to do so demonstrates lack of good moral character and reflects adversely on his ability to perform the duties of a lawyer.

Consistent with Gahan's Federal bankruptcy rights, we expressly state that our decision is in no way influenced by any assessment of Gahan's motivation in seeking bankruptcy. Nor are we interested in whether Gahan has any present willingness or ability to reaffirm the debts. We have based our decision solely on the circumstances surrounding Gahan's default on the student loans and the resulting failure to satisfy this important obligation. Gahan's subsequent conduct of obtaining discharge in bankruptcy and release from the default is of no concern to us.

The decision of the Board of Law Examiners to deny membership to the bar of the State of Minnesota is affirmed.

NOTES

1. The Bankruptcy Code now provides that "a governmental unit may not deny . . . a license, permit, charter, franchise, or other similar grant to . . . a person that . . . has been . . . a bankrupt or debtor under the Bankruptcy Act . . . solely because such debtor or bankrupt . . . has not paid a debt . . . that was discharged under the Bankruptcy Act." (11 U.S.C. §525.) It also provides, however, that an educational loan is not dischargeable under the Code for five years from the date the loan first became due unless the court finds that excepting the debt from discharge imposes undue hardship on the debtor and the debtor's dependents (11 U.S.C. §523(a)). Assuming that the debtor in *Gahan* had commenced his case in bankruptcy five years and one day after his educational loan first became due but that the other facts in the case were the same, could the court still deny admission to Mr. Gahan? Suppose that a lawyer leaving her public interest firm in California after five years of practice there to join a very large firm in Minnesota at a high salary commences a case in bankruptcy to get rid of her student loans before starting her new job? What result when she applies for admission in Minnesota?

2. In In re Batali, 98 Wash. 2d 610, 657 P.2d 775 (1983), the Washington Supreme Court distinguished *Gahan* and ruled that the Supremacy Clause did not permit the imposition of a condition on readmission of a suspended lawyer that he pay federal income taxes that had been discharged in bankruptcy. However, in Brookman v. The State Bar, 46 Cal. 3d 1004, 760 P.2d 1023 (1988), the California Supreme Court held that imposition of a requirement that a disciplined lawyer repay $48,900 to the state's Client Security Fund as a condition of disciplinary probation did not contravene the purposes of §525(a) of the Bankruptcy Code. The purpose of the disciplinary requirement was not to penalize the lawyer but to protect the public and rehabilitate the lawyer.

MATTER OF RONWIN

136 Ariz. 566, 667 P.2d 1281, cert. denied 464 U.S. 977 (1983)

FELDMAN, Justice.

This application for admission to the Arizona Bar has a long, unhappy and complex history.

HISTORY OF PROCEEDINGS

Edward Ronwin (Ronwin) graduated from the College of Law at Arizona State University in January of 1974. He took both the Arizona and Iowa bar examinations during that year. He passed in Iowa, but failed the Arizona examination. He was admitted to practice by the Iowa Supreme Court in June 1974 and is still a member in good standing of that bar.

Ronwin petitioned the Committee on Examinations and Admissions for review of the grading of his examination papers. That petition was denied, as was a similar petition subsequently filed in this court. Certiorari was then denied by the United States Supreme Court. Ronwin v. Committee on Examinations and Admissions, 419 U.S. 967, 95 S. Ct. 231, 42 L. Ed.2d 183 (1974). Ronwin petitioned to retake the bar examination at the July 1974 sitting. Permission was denied because the Committee on Examinations and Admissions refused to certify that he was "mentally and physically able to engage in active and continuous practice of law" as required by Rule 28(c)(IV), Arizona Rules of the Supreme Court, 17A A.R.S. We then appointed a special committee to hold a formal evidentiary hearing regarding the allegations of mental unfitness. This hearing was conducted pursuant to Rule 28(c)(XII)(C). The special committee found that Ronwin suffered from a "personality disorder" which resulted in (a) unreasonable suspicions that persons who dealt with him and did not meet his desires were activated by bad motives and that he was, therefore, the "object of unfair persecution." As a result, the committee concluded that if admitted, Ronwin would "act upon such imagined wrongs" by: (b) making "irresponsible and highly derogatory untrue public accusations and charges against persons in responsible positions which he knows or reasonably should know are without any factual basis or support . . ."; and (c) bringing and pursuing "with great persistence groundless claims in court proceedings and otherwise", thereby subjecting others to needless expense and concern. The committee decided that in representing others Ronwin would subject his clients, adversaries, opposing counsel and the court to "groundless charges of misconduct and impropriety" if his views regarding the law were opposed and not sustained by the court. On these bases, the committee found Ronwin was not mentally fit for the practice of law and declined to recommend him for admission. Ronwin petitioned this court for review of that finding, seeking leave in the interim to take the Arizona bar examination. Permission to take the bar examination was denied.

After review of the record, we concluded that the committee had properly assessed Ronwin's personality problems, and that those problems would affect his ability to "reasonably deal with the type of social interaction" required in the practice of law. Application of Ronwin (Ronwin I), 113 Ariz. 357, 359, 555 P.2d 315, 317 (1976), cert. denied, 430

U.S. 907, 97 S. Ct. 1178, 51 L. Ed.2d 583 (1977). We concluded that finding (b) of the committee was sustained, and ordered that Ronwin not be admitted. We did not agree with the committee on ground (c) since we believed that Ronwin had a right to resort to the legal system to "express his grievances where, as in this case, there [was] credible evidence that the actions [filed by Ronwin] were brought with a good faith belief in their merit." Id. at 360, 555 P.2d at 318 (footnote omitted).

Ronwin applied for permission to take the bar examination in Arizona at various times between February 1977 and February 1980, and each application was denied. The current applications for admission, SB-52-8 and SB-52-9 were supplemented by Ronwin several times at the request of his court. In October of 1981, we ordered that Ronwin be permitted to take the February 1982 bar examination, and reserved the issue of his fitness. Ronwin failed a portion of the February 1982 bar examination, but passed the July 1982 examination.

For reasons which will become apparent later in this opinion, the current applications have not been referred again to the committee. The ultimate responsibility for admitting candidates for the practice of law is vested in this court. . . . We have determined to discharge that responsibility directly in this case.

We permitted Ronwin to support his applications by a written report from a psychiatrist who had examined him in Iowa. Ronwin also agreed to submit to examination by a psychiatrist and a clinical psychologist appointed by this court. . . .

As we stated in *Ronwin I,* supra, the practice of law is not a privilege; it is a right. While similar to the right to engage in other occupations, it is subject to regulation to ensure that those who engage in the practice of law have the necessary mental, physical and moral qualities required. Id., at 358, 555 P.2d at 316; see also Schware v. Board of Bar Examiners of State of New Mexico, 353 U.S. 232, 239, 77 S. Ct. 752, 756, 1 L. Ed.2d 796 (1957). Thus, the applicant for admission "has the burden of establishing . . . that he is 'mentally . . . able to engage in active and continuous practice of law.'" *Ronwin I,* supra. Each case must be judged on its own merits "and an ad hoc determination in each instance must be made by the court." . . .

INDEPENDENT REVIEW

THE ISSUE

In conducting our review, we find the expert medical opinions instructive. The psychiatrist from Iowa, Dr. Taylor, reported that he "found no indication that [Ronwin] now suffers . . . from any type of mental illness, mental disorder or mental defect." Acknowledging that applicant possessed personality traits "which might be termed unpleasant or abrasive by those adopting positions in opposition to those held by Ronwin," Dr. Taylor stated it was *"possible"* that such traits would not impair Ronwin's ability to competently practice law.

Both the psychiatrist and psychologist appointed by this court to make an independent examination found that Ronwin suffers from a "compulsive personality disorder" defined on Axis II of the DSM III of the American Psychiatric Association. The psychologist's opinion was that this disorder would *"not necessarily impair* [Ronwin's] capability to conform to the rules and ethical considerations of the American Bar Association." (Emphasis supplied.) The psychiatrist stated his opinion that Ronwin was *"capable of conforming* to the rules and ethics of the code of professional conduct." (Emphasis supplied.) Both doctors found that the compulsive personality disorder manifested itself in overzealousness in the pursuit of what Ronwin considered to be justice and was marked by paranoid attitudes, lack of flexibility, hypersensitivity, inability to compromise, perfectionism, obsessive preoccupation with details, suspiciousness and hostility.

We are aware that such traits are not exclusive to Ronwin and are found in the emotional makeup of many human beings. The question is whether these behavioral traits and the emotional problems which cause them are sufficient in magnitude and duration that they may be expected to affect the applicant's conduct as a lawyer and, to a significant degree, cause it to fall below acceptable standards. The issue thus is not merely capacity and capability, but also behavior. On the former issue, we must defer to the doctors and accept their findings that Ronwin is "capable." On the latter, we must examine the record to determine if it establishes that Ronwin's personality disorder impairs his conduct to such a degree that he is not mentally able to engage in the practice of law.

THE RECORD

Following the decision in *Ronwin I,* Ronwin commenced a series of legal actions against various members of the Arizona State Bar. The basis of these actions was Ronwin's belief that there was a conspiracy to prevent his admission to the Arizona Bar. In Ronwin v. Daughton, Ronwin brought a civil rights action (see 42 U.S.C. §1981 et seq.) against all members of the special committee appointed by this court to hold the evidentiary hearing regarding his mental ability to practice law. In addition, he included as defendants those attorneys who had represented the state bar in the proceedings before the committee, his own attorney, and several of the witnesses who testified, including the dean and assistant dean of the law school, both of whom had testified in his behalf. In Ronwin v. Segal, he brought a civil rights action against members of this court's Committee on Character and Fitness, formerly a part of the Committee on Examinations and Admissions. In Ronwin v. State Bar of Arizona, he brought an antitrust action against members of the Supreme Court Committee on Examinations and Admissions. In Ronwin v. Gage, applicant filed a third civil rights action against the members of an Arizona State Bar Administrative Committee, joining the members of this court. In Ronwin v. von Ammon *(von Ammon I)*, applicant brought a civil rights action against the attorneys who had represented the Arizona State Bar in several of the previous actions, joining in the process his former attorney, the members of this court and two judges of the United States District Court for the District of Arizona. In Ronwin v. von Ammon *(von Ammon II)*, applicant brought a fifth civil rights action against many of the same defendants previously sued. In addition, Ronwin named a third federal judge, the Clerk of the United States District Court and an Assistant United States Attorney as defendants. The members of this court were also joined as defendants. In Ronwin v. Shapiro, Ronwin commenced an action against a law student at the University of Arizona who had written a casenote on *Ronwin I*. In this action, one of the editors of the law review and the members of the Arizona Board of Regents were also named as defendants. This list does not exhaust the actions Ronwin has filed in response to the denial of his application for admission to the Arizona Bar.

We assume, arguendo, that much of this may have been precipitated by the religious harassment to which Ronwin alleges he was subjected during the years 1972-1974 at the hands of some students in the College of Law at Arizona State University. See *Ronwin I*, 113 Ariz. at 359, 555 P.2d at 317. Outrage over this certainly would be an appropriate reaction; given Ronwin's personality traits as described in the psychological reports, it is easy to understand why Ronwin's reaction exceeded outrage. Lawyers certainly have the right to become outraged and to resort to litigation when they have been wronged, but they do not have the right to file actions or commence proceedings which are vexatious or harassing in nature. See In re Martin-Trigona, 55 Ill.2d 301, 308-10, 302 N.E.2d 68, 72-73 (1973); see also Matter of Wetzel, 118 Ariz. 33, 35, 574 P.2d 826, 828 (1979). Nor do lawyers have the right to behave inappropriately while acting as lawyers, even if they are representing themselves. See In re Martin-Trigona, supra; In re Mezzacca, 67 N.J. 387, 389, 340 A.2d 658, 659 (1975).

These principles are not limited to case law. Arizona has adopted, with some modifications, the Model Code of Professional Responsibility. Rule 29(a). DR 7-106(C)(6) states that a lawyer shall not "[e]ngage in undignified or discourteous conduct which is degrading to a tribunal." DR 8-102(B) states that a "lawyer shall not knowingly make false accusations against a judge or other adjudicatory officer." Ariz. R. Civ. P. 11 also forbids inserting "scandalous or indecent" matters in pleadings and requires a belief in the existence of good grounds to support all allegations, with provision for disciplinary action where appropriate. Implicit in these rules is the requirement that lawyers exercise restraint in language and deed while acting as lawyers, particularly in relation to litigation. See Model Code of Professional Responsibility EC 7-36, 7-37, 7-38 (1980). The rules are explicit on the question of litigation. A lawyer "shall not" file actions, assert positions or take other action on behalf of clients when he or she knows "or *when it is obvious* that such action would serve merely to harass or maliciously injure another." DR 7-102(A)(1) (emphasis supplied). Nor should they file claims or actions unless the case is supported by law or tenable argument. Id. (A)(2). What lawyers cannot do for clients, they cannot do for themselves. Matter of Wetzel, supra. Violation of the foregoing requirements is grounds for denial of admission. . . .

From examination of the pleadings and affidavits prepared, signed and filed by Ronwin in our files and in the various federal court actions, it is apparent that applicant's personality disorder affects his conduct. With neither care nor caution, and restrained only by the outer limits of his intense anger, Ronwin has filled his pleadings with allegations of serious misconduct against the willing and unwilling participants in the proceedings which have led him to his present plight. These are not allegations of legal error, but, rather, accusations of knowing misconduct, plus misfeasance in office. In *von Ammon II*, Ronwin accuses the dean and assistant dean of the law school not only of tolerating anti-Semitic behavior, but also of knowingly participating in an "engineered fraud" to keep Ronwin out of the bar by sending Ronwin to a lawyer who would participate in "rigging" the hearing before the Special Committee. Ronwin alleges that a motion for security for costs filed by the defendants in one of the district court actions was granted because the judge was manipulated by the defendants' lawyers who were friends of the judge; for that reason, he alleges, the district court judge "knowingly tolerated criminal behavior" by those lawyers. He alleges further that this supposedly occurred because the Clerk of the United States District Court had joined the conspiracy against Ronwin and had intentionally altered procedures in the Clerk's office so that the case could be assigned to a district court judge who was friendly toward the lawyers representing the defendants. Ronwin alleges that an Assistant United States Attorney for the District of Arizona disregarded his duty by defending the federal judge instead of prosecuting him. In *von Ammon I*, we are told that a different federal judge knowingly tolerated illegal activity by attorneys; this allegedly occurred as a result of unlawful conduct by members of the Arizona State Bar who had influence over both the state and federal judiciary and engaged in a criminal and fraudulent process of manipulating court decisions. In Ronwin v. Gage, state bar counsel, committee chairmen and members of state bar committees are all accused of participating in an engineered sham and fraud. Lawyers in the various proceedings are accused of having committed perjury, of suborning witnesses, making fraudulent allegations and engaging in a conspiracy against Ronwin. Ronwin's counsel in a previous case is accused of having joined the conspiracy to violate Ronwin's rights. A list of these accusations could go on ad infinitum. . . .

Ronwin's pleadings in the United States District Court touch upon many if not most District Court Judges with whom he came in contact, including a visiting judge from the Southern District of California. The Clerk, Assistant Clerk and members of the Office of the United States Attorney are accused of involvement in the conspiracy. An Assistant United States Attorney was sued on the allegation of having joined the conspiracy by refusing Ronwin's request to prosecute a district judge who had allegedly acted illegally by knowingly tolerating the acts of applicant's attorney.

The record in our own court is similar. The decision in *Ronwin I* is alleged to have been "based on an engineered fraud and collusion by several members of the bar." In commenting on footnote 1 of *Ronwin I,* applicant states that it sets "an anti-semitic standard" which is that "if an applicant for admittance . . . becomes hypersensitive and aggressive against anti-semiticism that applicant becomes disqualified. . . ." In a complete manifestation of lack of perspective, Ronwin compares his situation to that of the European Jews whose fate in the holocaust was sealed by the world's diplomats in 1938 at the conference at Evian-les-Bains. The dean of the law school at Arizona State University is described as "that incompetent liar and fraud." The foregoing examples are taken from the first five pages of Ronwin's Motion to Rehear in *Ronwin I;* this was filed six years after the decision became final and is part of the file in SB-52-9. In other pleadings in the file, Ronwin accuses the clerk of this court of intentional and knowing destruction of part of the record in this case.

The examples cited suffice to establish that Ronwin's reaction to adversity manifests itself in behavior which is grossly improper for a lawyer and which cannot be tolerated. This conclusion does not evince a lack of toleration for Ronwin; it simply acknowledges that we can make no special rule for Ronwin. What is permitted Ronwin is necessarily permitted all other members of our bar. Habitual filing of actions against adjudicatory officers, witnesses and opposing counsel is both vexatious and harassing. Worse, it is a tactic calculated to intimidate. It cannot be tolerated unless we are willing to surrender reason to those whose conduct is uninhibited by reality and civility. Adjudication of facts and resolution of legal disputes cannot be properly accomplished in the absence of restraint and civilized behavior by lawyers. Care with words and respect for courts and one's adversaries is a necessity, not because lawyers and judges are without fault, but because trial by combat long ago proved unsatisfactory. . . .

The First Amendment

When questioned by members of this court in oral argument, Ronwin demonstrated a sincere belief in his right to behave in the manner described above. He contends that he has a first amendment right to speak and write as he wishes and to say anything which he believes to be true. This may be true, but we believe that any such absolute first amendment right must be exercised somewhere other than the courtroom.

We do not refuse admission because of an applicant's beliefs or an applicant's exercise of the right of free speech. We long ago crossed that bridge in Application of Levine, 97 Ariz. 88, 397 P.2d 205 (1964), reh'g den. (1965). In *Levine*, the committee recommended that admission be denied because it believed that the applicant did "not possess the sense of public responsibility which a lawyer should have" as evidenced by the fact that the applicant had publicly criticized the Federal Bureau of Investigation and its Director, J. Edgar Hoover. . . . We ordered that the applicant be admitted.

There is no inconsistency between our holding in *Levine* and the views expressed today. Levine's alleged transgressions, if criticism of a federal agency and its director can be considered as such, involved speaking his mind and writing his thoughts in a non-judicial forum. Public entities and their officers are subject to criticism, pleasant or unpleasant, whether based on fact or belief. In judicial proceedings, however, lawyers are required to show both accuracy and restraint; statements should not be made absent a basis in fact and law. We acknowledge, arguendo, that applicant believes he is the victim of a conspiracy which encompasses this court, most of the federal bench, the organized bar, the bar committees and the lawyers who have participated in the various cases. This is the recurring theme in the civil rights actions which Ronwin filed. We think, however, that Ronwin's sincere belief in this supposed, wide-ranging conspiracy against him is not all that is required for the practice of law. Belief unrelated to reason is a hallmark of fanaticism, zealotry or paranoia rather than reasoned advocacy. The practice of law requires the ability to discriminate between fact and faith, evidence and imagination, reality and hallucination. Further, epithets, verbal abuse, unfounded accusations and the like have no place in legal proceedings. While occasional lapses in decorum are usually overlooked, Ronwin's transgressions exceed occasional anger or loss of control. They form a pattern and a way of life which, on this record, appears to be applicant's normal reaction to personal or professional adversity. . . .

The profession's insistence that counsel show restraint, self-discipline and a sense of reality in dealing with courts, other counsel, witnesses and adversaries is more than insistence on good manners. It is based on the knowledge that civilized, rational behavior is essential if the judicial system is to perform its function. Absent this, any judicial proceeding is likely to degenerate into verbal free-for-all and some, no doubt, into physical combat. Thus, Ronwin's behavior does not present the question of free speech, but of habitual unreasonable reaction to adverse rulings. It is conduct of a type not to be permitted of a lawyer when acting as a lawyer. What cannot be permitted in lawyers, cannot be tolerated in those applying for admission as lawyers. . . .

EVIDENTIARY HEARING

Ronwin demands an evidentiary hearing at which he would present evidence in an attempt to establish his grounds to believe in the truth of each of the many allegations and charges which he has made against judges, lawyers, clerks, committee members, etc. If the truth or his belief in the truth of each of these allegations were of importance to this decision, due process would entitle Ronwin to such a hearing. We believe, however, that an evidentiary hearing is unnecessary and inappropriate for the following reasons: . . .

Second, we will not deny an applicant admission merely because he or she has filed legal actions accusing this court and the bar of violations of the applicant's civil rights or of the law. We will deny admission where, years after *Ronwin I* became final, applicant has refused to accept the decision and has continued to file vexatious actions, almost none of which was based on sound legal theory and most of which indicate that applicant's emotions have overcome his sense of proportion and his knowledge of the law. We reach this conclusion about the actions filed by Ronwin from the disposition of each case as shown in the files of the Clerk of the United States District Court for the District of Arizona. . . .

Third, even if Ronwin had grounds to sue some members of the bar and bench for misconduct, the accusations can and should be made without vilification and use of provocative language. It is, for example, required and possible to plead a cause of action for violation of civil rights without making the allegation that the defendant is an "incompetent liar and fraud." . . . It is possible to allege conspiracy to violate civil rights or antitrust law without supplying similar epithets.

Fourth, we do not believe that a lawyer has a right to use the legal process for the purpose of harassing those who act contrary to his wishes or offend him by failing to agree with his viewpoint. We find, for instance, the action which Ronwin brought against the author of the casenote in the Arizona Law Review, the editor and the board of regents to be harassing in nature and wholly without legal or procedural merit. This finding is based upon our reading of *Ronwin I*, the casenote and the decision in Ronwin v. Shapiro, 657 F.2d 1071, 1075-76 (9th Cir. 1981).

Fifth, we find Ronwin's use of language with regard to the federal bench and the clerk's office wholly inappropriate and demonstrative of a lack of respect for the judiciary.

Sixth, in our order of April 27, 1983, we allowed Ronwin to submit by affidavit or offer on proof any factual matter which he deemed relevant. Except for the additional medical reports, which we have not considered, he refused to submit such information.

Finally, the right to an evidentiary hearing must fall once the essential nature of the barrage of Ronwin's allegations is appreciated. Ronwin does not merely complain that a specific witness, lawyer, judge, clerk or officer acted improperly or illegally. The essence of his complaints, when viewed in their totality, is both implicitly and explicitly that judges, lawyers, court officers and others have engaged in a conspiracy to deprive him of his right to practice law. The essence of the factual question urged by Ronwin is not whether a particular judge or particular lawyer acted incorrectly — indeed much of this is foreclosed by the finality of *Ronwin I* — but, rather, that all these acts were part of a conspiracy against him. It is on this fundamental question that he demands a right to present evidence, and it is primarily on this fundamental question that we now deny him a factual hearing.

If applicant is entitled to an evidentiary hearing on the fundamental, ultimate proposition that bench and bar are involved in a conspiracy devoted to his destruction, it must be in a forum other than ours. We cannot, for instance, take evidence on our own integrity; we do not propose to hold a wide-ranging inquiry on the integrity and honesty of the Judges of the United States District Court for the District of Arizona, the attorneys in the United States Attorney's Office for the District of Arizona, the Clerk of this court, the Clerk of the United States District Court, their deputies, the Arizona Bar, the College of Law, etc., ad infinitum. . . .

NOTES

1. There is an obvious relation between the holding in *Ronwin* and the earlier material that considered the freedom of lawyers to speak their minds. See pp. 434-453. There is also a relation between *Ronwin* and the material of the next chapter relating to discipline. If the incidents described in the case had taken place after Ronwin's admission to the bar, should the standards for discipline be the same as those enunciated by the court in this case?

2. A very critical look at the operation of state admissions procedures is contained in Rhode, Moral Character as a Professional Credential, 94 Yale L.J. 491 (1984). Her conclusion is that the whole process of character assessment should be abandoned except perhaps for a few specific offenses and that the resources thus saved should be refocused on regulation of professional misconduct.

3. Issues of "moral character" also arise in connection with petitions

for readmission to practice after a lawyer has been disbarred or suspended indefinitely. One of the more famous cases was In re Alger Hiss, 368 Mass. 447, 333 N.E.2d 429 (1975), where Mr. Hiss was readmitted 22 years after having been disbarred upon conviction for perjury in his testimony to a congressional committee denying that he had turned over State Department documents to a Communist spy ring. Despite the fact that he refused to admit guilt and therefore to urge rehabilitation of character, the court found that he was presently of good moral character and that readmission would "not be detrimental to the integrity and standing of the bar, the administration of justice, or to the public interest." The court reached its conclusion despite the fact that it viewed the crime of which he was convicted as "a direct and reprehensible attack on the foundations of our judicial system," and "one that is further tainted by the breach of confidence and trust which underly his conviction." Compare In re Braverman, 271 Md. 196, 316 A.2d 246 (1974) (reinstating a lawyer disbarred after conviction of violation of the Smith Act, 18 U.S.C. §2385 (1940) on a finding of current good moral character and a further finding that there was insufficient evidence to have supported his conviction under the standard of proof subsequently required) with In re Braverman, 399 F. Supp. 801 (1975) (same lawyer not reinstated by divided United States District Court for the District of Maryland).

B. THE UNAUTHORIZED PRACTICE OF LAW

Closely related to problems of admission to the bar is the matter of what acts constitute the practice of law; in other words, which acts require a license? There has been a great deal of litigation in the field and many cases have gone quite far in prohibiting lay people, such as real estate brokers and title companies, from selecting and filling in the blanks on preprinted forms to consummate agreements among their customers. See Fischer and Lachman, Unauthorized Practice Handbook (1972). The issue has returned to prominence recently because unauthorized practice restrictions have been seen as raising serious antitrust problems, especially with respect to agreements between bar associations and organizations of banks, accountants, brokers, and the like defining the "practice of law," and they have also been seen as constituting barriers to access, especially inexpensive access, to legal rights of poor people. A comprehensive, critical study of unauthorized practice regulation is Deborah Rhode, Policing the Professional Monopoly: A Constitutional and Empirical Analysis of Unauthorized Practice Prohibitions, 34 Stan. L. Rev. 1 (1981).

FLORIDA BAR v. BRUMBAUGH
355 So. 2d 1186 (Fla. 1978)

PER CURIAM

The Florida Bar has filed a petition charging Marilyn Brumbaugh with engaging in the unauthorized practice of law, and seeking a permanent injunction prohibiting her from further engaging in these allegedly unlawful acts. We have jurisdiction under our constitutional authority to adopt rules for the practice and procedure in all the courts of this state. Article V, Section 2(a), Florida Constitution (1968). We now issue an injunction, delineating in this opinion those acts of respondent which we deem to constitute the unauthorized practice of law, and ordering her to stop such activities.

Respondent, Marilyn Brumbaugh, is not and has never been a member of the Florida Bar, and is, therefore, not licensed to practice law within this state. She has advertised in various local newspapers as "Marilyn's Secretarial Service" offering to perform typing services for "Do-It-Yourself" divorces, wills, resumes, and bankruptcies. The Florida Bar charges that she performed unauthorized legal services by preparing for her customers those legal documents necessary in an uncontested dissolution of marriage proceeding and by advising her customers as to the costs involved and the procedures which should be followed in order to obtain a dissolution of marriage. For this service, Ms. Brumbaugh charges a fee of $50.

Of course, we must determine whether the Florida Bar has presented sufficient evidence in the record before us to prove that respondent has engaged in the unauthorized practice of law. But, in cases such as this, the Florida Supreme Court is not confined to act solely in its judicial capacity. In addition, it acts in its administrative capacity as chief policy maker, regulating the administration of the court system and supervising all persons who are engaged in rendering legal advice to members of the general public. Such authority carries with it the responsibility to perform this task in a way responsive to the needs and desires of our citizens. . . .

The Florida Bar, as an agent of this Court, plays a large role in the enforcement of court policies and rules and has been active in regulating and disciplining unethical conduct by its members. Because of the natural tendency of all professions to act in their own self interest, however, this Court must closely scrutinize all regulations tending to limit competition in the delivery of legal services to the public, and determine whether or not such regulations are truly in the public interest. Indeed, the active role of state supreme courts in the regulation of the practice of law (when such regulation is subject to pointed reexamination by the state court as policy maker) is accorded great deference and exemption from federal interference under the Sherman Act. Bates v. State Bar of Arizona. [p. 636, Note 5].

The United States Supreme Court has recently decided issues which may drastically change the practice of law throughout the country, especially with regards to advertising and price competition among attorneys. Bates v. State Bar of Arizona, [p. 536]; Goldfarb, et al. v. Virginia State Bar, [p. 475, Note 7]. In addition, the Supreme Court has affirmed the fundamental constitutional right of all persons to represent themselves in court proceedings. Faretta v. California, 422 U.S. 806 (1975). In *Faretta,* the Supreme Court emphasized that an attorney is merely an assistant who helps a citizen protect his legal rights and present his case to the courts. A person should not be forced to have an attorney represent his legal interests if he does not consent to such representation. It is imperative for us to analyze these cases and determine how their holdings and the policies behind them affect our regulation of the legal profession in this state.

With regard to the charges made against Marilyn Brumbaugh, this Court appointed a referee to receive evidence and to make findings of fact, conclusions of law, and recommendations as to the disposition of the case. The referee found that respondent, under the guise of a "secretarial" or "typing" service prepares, for a fee, all papers deemed by her to be needed for the pleading, filing, and securing of a dissolution of marriage, as well as detailed instructions as to how the suit should be filed, notice served, hearings set, trial conducted, and the final decree secured. The referee also found that in one instance, respondent prepared a quit claim deed in reference to the marital property of the parties. The referee determined that respondent's contention that she merely operates a typing service is rebutted by numerous facts in evidence. Ms. Brumbaugh has no blank forms either to sell or to fill out. Rather, she types up the documents for her customers after they have asked her to prepare a petition or an entire set of dissolution of marriage papers. Prior to typing up the papers, respondent asks her customers whether custody, child support, or alimony is involved. Respondent has four sets of dissolution of marriage papers, and she chooses which set is appropriate for the particular customer. She then types out those papers, filling in the blank spaces with the appropriate information. Respondent instructs her customers how the papers are to be signed, where they are to be filed, and how the customer should arrange for a final hearing.

Marilyn Brumbaugh, who is representing herself in proceedings before this Court, has made various objections to the procedure and findings of fact of the referee. . . . Respondent argues that she has never held herself out as an attorney, and has never professed to have legal skills. She does not give advice, but acts merely as a secretary. She is a licensed counselor, and asserts the right to talk to people and to let her customers make decisions for themselves. Finally, respondent contends that her civil rights have been violated, and that she has been denied the right to make an honest living.

This case does not arise out of a complaint by any of Ms. Brumbaugh's customers as to improper advice or unethical conduct. It has been initiated by members of The Florida Bar who believe her to be practicing law without a license. The evidence introduced at the hearing below shows that none of respondent's customers believed that she was an attorney, or that she was acting in their behalf. Respondent's advertisements clearly addressed themselves to people who wish to do their own divorces. These customers knew that they had to have "some type of papers" to file in order to obtain their dissolution of marriage. Respondent never handled contested divorces. During the past two years respondent has assisted several hundred customers in obtaining their own divorces. The record shows that while some of her customers told respondent exactly what they wanted, generally respondent would ask her customers for the necessary information needed to fill out the divorce papers, such as the names and addresses of the parties, the place and duration of residency in this state, whether there was any property settlement to be resolved, or any determination as to custody and support of children. Finally, each petition contained the bare allegation that the marriage was irretrievably broken. Respondent would then inform the parties as to which documents needed to be signed, by whom, how many copies of each paper should be filed, where and when they should be filed, the costs involved, and what witness testimony is necessary at the court hearing. Apparently, Ms. Brumbaugh no longer informs the parties verbally as to the proper procedures for the filing of the papers, but offers to let them copy papers described as "suggested procedural education."

The Florida Bar argues that the above activities of respondent violate the rulings of this Court in The Florida Bar v. American Legal and Business Forms, Inc., 274 So. 2d 225 (Fla. 1973), and The Florida Bar v. Stupica, 300 So. 2d 683 (Fla. 1974). In those decisions we held that it is lawful to sell to the public printed legal forms, provided they do not carry with them what purports to be instructions on how to fill out such forms or how to use them. We stated that legal advice is inextricably involved in the filling out and advice as to how to use such legal forms, and therein lies the danger of injury or damage to the public if not properly performed in accordance with law. In *Stupica*, supra, this Court rejected the rationale of the New York courts in New York County Lawyer's Association v. Dacey, 28 A.D.2d 161, 283 N.Y.S.2d 984, reversed and dissenting opinion adopted 21 N.Y.2d 694, 234 N.E.2d 459 (N.Y. 1967), which held that the publication of forms and instructions on their use does not constitute the unauthorized practice of law if these instructions are addressed to the public in general rather than to a specific individual legal problem. The Court in *Dacey* stated that the possibility that the principles or rules set forth in the text may be accepted by a particular reader as solution to his problem, does not mean that the publisher is practicing law. Other states have adopted the principle of law set forth in *Dacey*, holding that the sale of legal forms with instructions for their use does not constitute unauthorized practice of law. See State Bar of Michigan v. Cramer, 399 Mich. 116, 249 N.W.2d 1 (1976); Oregon State Bar v. Gilchrist, 272 Or. 552, 538 P.2d 913 (1975). However, these courts have prohibited all personal contact between the service providing such forms and the customer, in the nature of consultation, explanation, recommendation, advice, or other assistance in selecting particular forms, in filling out any part of the forms, suggesting or advising how the forms should be used in solving the particular problems.

Although persons not licensed as attorneys are prohibited from practicing law within this state, it is somewhat difficult to define exactly what constitutes the practice of law in all instances. This Court has previously stated that: ". . . if the giving of such advice and performance of such services affect important rights of a person under the law, and if the reasonable protection of the rights and property of those advised and served requires that the persons giving such advice possess legal skill and a knowledge of the law greater than that possessed by the average citizen, then the giving of such advice and the performance of such services by one for another as a course of conduct constitute the practice of law." [State v. Sperry, 140 So. 2d 587, 591 (1962).] . . .

In determining whether a particular act constitutes the practice of law, our primary goal is the protection of the public. However, any limitations on the free practice of law by all persons necessarily affects important constitutional rights. Our decision here certainly affects the constitutional rights of Marilyn Brumbaugh to pursue a lawful occupation or business. . . . Our decision also affects respondent's First Amendment rights to speak and print what she chooses. In addition, her customers and potential customers have the constitutional right of self representation . . . and the right of privacy inherent in the marriage relationship. . . . All citizens in our state are also guaranteed access to our courts by Article I, Section 21, Florida Constitution (1968). Although it is not necessary for us to provide affirmative assistance in order to ensure meaningful access to the courts to our citizens, as it is necessary for us to do for those incarcerated in our state prison system . . . we should not place any unnecessary restrictions upon that right. We should not deny persons who wish to represent themselves access to any source of information which might be relevant in the preparation of their cases. There are numerous texts in our state law libraries which describe our substantive and procedural law, purport to give legal advice to the reader as to choices that should be made in various situations, and which also contain sample legal forms which a reader may use as an example. We generally do not restrict the access of the public to these law libraries, although many of the legal texts are not authored by attorneys licensed to practice in this state. These texts do not carry with them any guarantees of accuracy, and only some of them purport to update statements which have been modified by subsequently enacted statutes and recent case law.

The policy of this Court should continue to be one of encouraging persons who are unsure of their legal rights and remedies to seek legal assistance from persons licensed by us to practice law in this state. However, in order to make an intelligent decision as whether or not to engage the assistance of an attorney, a citizen must be allowed access to information which will help determine the complexity of the legal problem. Once a person has made the decision to represent himself, we should not enforce any unnecessary regulation which might tend to hinder the exercise of this constitutionally protected right. However, any restriction of constitutional rights must be "narrowly drawn to express only the legitimate state interests at stake." Roe v. Wade, [410 U.S. 113]. . . . "And if there are other reasonable ways to achieve those goals with a lesser burden on constitutionally protected activity, a state may not choose the way of greater interference. If it acts at all, it must choose less drastic means." Shelton v. Tucker, 364 U.S. 479, 488, 81 S. Ct. 247, 252, 5 L. Ed. 2d 231 (160).

It is also important for us to consider the legislative statute governing dissolution of marriage in resolving the question of what constitutes the practice of law in this area. Florida's "no fault" dissolution of marriage statute clearly has the remedial purpose of simplifying the dissolution of marriage whenever possible. Section 61.001, Florida Statutes (1975) states:

> (1) This chapter shall be liberally construed and applied to promote its purposes.
> (2) Its purposes are:
>   (a) To preserve the integrity of marriage and to safeguard meaningful family relationships;
>   (b) To promote the amicable settlement of disputes that have arisen between parties to a marriage;
>   (c) To mitigate the potential harm to the spouses and their children caused by the process of legal dissolution of marriage.

Families usually undergo tremendous financial hardship when they decide to dissolve their marital relationships. The Legislature simplified procedures so that parties would not need to bear the additional burden of expensive legal fees where they have agreed to the settlement of their property and the custody of their children. This Court should not place unreasonable burdens upon the obtaining of such divorces, especially where both parties consent to the dissolution.

Present dissolution procedures in uncontested situations involve a very simplified method of asserting certain facts required by statute, notice to the other parties affected, and a simple hearing where the trial court may hear proof and make inquiries as to the facts asserted in those pleadings.

The legal forms necessary to obtain such an uncontested dissolution of marriage are susceptible of standardization. This Court has allowed the sale of legal forms on this and other subjects, provided that they do not carry with them what purports to be instructions on how to fill out such forms or how they are to be used. . . . These decisions should be reevaluated in light of those recent decisions in other states which have held that the sale of forms necessary to obtain a divorce, together with any related textual instructions directed towards the general public, does not constitute the practice of law. The reasons for allowing the sale of such legal publications which contain sample forms to be used by individuals who wish to represent themselves are persuasive. State Bar of Michigan v. Cramer, supra, reasoned that such instructional material should be no more objectionable than any other publication placed into the stream of commerce which purports to offer general advice on common problems and does not purport to give a person advice on a specific problem particular to a designated or readily identified person. . . .

Although there is a danger that some published material might give false or misleading information, that is not a sufficient reason to justify its total ban. We must assume that our citizens will generally use such publications for what they are worth in the preparation of their cases, and further assume that most persons will not rely on these materials in the same way they would rely on the advice of an attorney or other persons holding themselves out as having expertise in the area. The tendency of persons seeking legal assistance to place their trust in the individual purporting to have expertise in the area necessitates this Court's regulation of such attorney-client relationships, so as to require that persons giving such advice have at least a minimal amount of legal training and experience. Although Marilyn Brumbaugh never held herself out as an attorney, it is clear that her clients placed some reliance upon her to properly prepare the necessary legal forms for their dissolution proceedings. To this extent we believe that Ms. Brumbaugh overstepped proper bounds and engaged in the unauthorized practice of law. We hold that Ms. Brumbaugh, and others in similar situations, may sell printed material purporting to explain legal practice and procedure to the public in general and she may sell sample legal forms. To this extent we limit our prior holdings in *Stupica* and *American Legal and Business Forms, Inc.* Further, we hold that it is not improper for Marilyn

Brumbaugh to engage in a secretarial service, typing such forms for her clients, provided that she only copy the information given to her in writing by her clients. In addition, Ms. Brumbaugh may advertise her business activities of providing secretarial and notary services and selling legal forms and general printed information. However, Marilyn Brumbaugh must not, in conjunction with her business, engage in advising clients as to the various remedies available to them, or otherwise assist them in preparing those forms necessary for a dissolution proceeding. More specifically, Marilyn Brumbaugh may not make inquiries nor answer questions from her clients as to the particular forms which might be necessary, how best to fill out such forms, where to properly file such forms, and how to present necessary evidence at the court hearings. Our specific holding with regard to the dissolution of marriage also applies to other unauthorized legal assistance such as the preparation of wills or real estate transaction documents. While Marilyn Brumbaugh may legally sell forms in these areas, and type up instruments which have been completed by clients, she must not engage in personal legal assistance in conjunction with her business activities, including the correction of errors and omissions.

Accordingly, having defined the limits within which Ms. Brumbaugh and those engaged in similar activities may conduct their business without engaging in the unauthorized practice of law, the rule to show cause is dissolved.

It is so ordered.

Judge KARL concurs specially.

There is a popular notion that every attempt to define the practice of law and restrict the activities within the definition to those who are authorized to practice law is nothing more than a method of providing economic protection for lawyers. I recognize that a small number of attorneys who advocate a broad definition of the practice coupled with severe penalties for those who encroach are motivated by economic self-interest. Indeed, regardless of motive, any law or rule that stakes out an area "for lawyers only" will result in some incidental benefit to those who are authorized to practice law — a form of serendipity for them.

What is often lost in the rush to condemn members of the legal profession for alleged selfishness is the existence of a genuine need to protect the public from those who are willing to give legal advice and render legal service, for their own profit, without being competent to do so and without being subject to restraint and punishment if they cause damage to some unsuspecting and uninformed persons in the process. Just as the public must be protected from physical harm inflicted by those who would prescribe drugs and perform surgery without proper training, so must we provide protection from financial and other damage inflicted by pseudo-lawyers.

We could develop a perfect set of disciplinary rules for attorneys and establish a procedure that quickly disbars and delicenses those who violate the rules, but if we should then permit nonmembers of the bar, including those who have been disbarred, to engage in the same activities as lawyers, we would have accomplished nothing. The members of the public would still be in serious jeopardy.

The problem, so well articulated in the majority opinion, is where to draw the lines between activities that constitute the practice of law and those that do not. There must be a balancing of constitutional rights with the recognized need to protect the public. The broader the definition, the more effective are the disciplinary rules and the greater is the public protection, but the need for protection must give way to rights guaranteed by the Constitution.

I concur with the majority because I am persuaded that the definition of the practice of law developed in The Florida Bar v. American Legal and Business Forms, Inc., 274 So. 2d 225 (Fla. 1973), and The Florida Bar v. Stupica, 300 So. 2d 683 (Fla. 1974), is too broad to withstand an attack based on the provisions of the First Amendment of the United States Constitution and must, therefore, be contracted. I reject as specious the argument that constitutionally permissible restrictions on activities defined as the practice of law are designed solely to produce high legal fees by discouraging competition and encouraging legal featherbedding.

NOTES

1. Following *Brumbaugh,* the Florida bar sought to enjoin Rosemary Furman, owner of a secretarial service that also helped people obtain uncontested divorces and a leading opponent of unauthorized practice rules, from practicing law. Ms. Furman attacked the *Brumbaugh* restrictions, arguing that because so many of her clients were uneducated, it was necessary to have some oral conversation with them. The prohibition against oral communication wastes judicial resources because papers are improperly filed, and is generally inhibiting to people who want to handle their own cases. She further argued that in many places a service like hers is the only place where poor people needing help can go. Legal aid doesn't exist or has put a limit on matrimonial matters because of the workload, and the Bar has provided no other help. In addition, Ms. Furman contended that the *Brumbaugh* rules violated the First Amendment and the Equal Protection Clause. They impinged on poor people's access to the courts by limiting their right to receive, and her right to disseminate, relevant information. Without even addressing the constitutional issues, the court found Ms. Furman guilty of unauthorized practice of law. The court also directed the Florida Bar to begin

a study and report to the court its findings regarding better ways to provide legal services to the poor, The Florida Bar v. Furman, 376 So.2d 378 (1979), appeal dismissed for want of a substantial federal question, 444 U.S. 1061 (1980), and in fact a simplified procedure for dissolution of marriages without need for participation by lawyers was put into effect by the Florida Supreme Court in June 1984. Subsequently, however, Ms. Furman was found in contempt on testimony of her customers that not only had she undertaken activity in violation of the court order but also that she had advised customers to falsify and conceal information in marriage dissolution documents on several occasions. Florida Bar v. Furman, 451 So.2d 808 (Fla. 1984), reh'g denied (1984), appeal dismissed for want of a substantial federal question, 469 U.S. 925 (1984). Governor Graham, however, commuted her jail sentence on the condition that she successfully complete the remaining two years of the court's injunction. 71 A.B.A. J. 19 (1985).

2. Should the answer to whether Ms. Furman was practicing law without a license have turned on the availability of affordable legal services? If that lack of availability is not conclusive, what should be? Is the line drawn in *Brumbaugh* about right? Does its justification lie in its definitional quality of the practice of law or in its prophylactic quality in stopping lay assistance at the point where policing becomes difficult? What is the difference between *Brumbaugh* and filling out someone's tax return? Or telling a sick friend to take some aspirin and go to bed? Is that practicing medicine?

3. Suppose the case involved a contest over custody and the lawyer for the other side called Ms. Brumbaugh to the stand and asked her to relate everything her "client" said. Would that be privileged?

4. One of Ms. Furman's lawyers in the Florida proceeding was Alan Morrison, director of the Public Citizen Litigation Group, members of which were popularly known at one time as Ralph Nader's lawyers. Mr. Morrison has taken a crack at answering some of the questions in Notes 2 and 3 in Defining the Unauthorized Practice of Law: Some New Ways of Looking at an Old Question, 4 Nova L.J. 363 (1980).

5. The earlier discussion of Bates and O'Steen v. State Bar of Arizona, p. 492, omitted consideration of an antitrust issue that is relevant here. The disciplined lawyers in that case attacked the application of DR 2-101(B) of the Code of Professional Responsibility to their activities as a violation of selection one and two of the Sherman Act. The Supreme Court rejected that attack, holding that the doctrine of Parker v. Brown, 317 U.S. 341 (1943) exempted certain state action from the coverage of that act. The Court viewed as crucial the fact that the Arizona Supreme Court had "adopted the rules, and it is the ultimate trier of fact and law in the enforcement process." 433 U.S. at 361. Since the state's policy was so clearly expressed and its supervision was so active, the Parker v. Brown exemption applied.

Remember that prior to the decision in *Bates,* the Supreme Court had already held that the Sherman Act did apply in an analogous situation when the state had not prescribed and supervised the activities of the bar alleged to be anticompetitive. See Goldfarb v. Virginia State Bar, p. 475, Note 7. The combination of *Goldfarb* and *Bates* made dubious the practice of many state bar associations of issuing advisory opinions relating to ethical practices, and especially unauthorized practice of the law, when coupled with a threat of disciplinary proceedings. After *Goldfarb* and before *Bates,* one court held that the Parker v. Brown exemption did not shield a state bar from the Sherman Act even though it was required to issue advisory opinions by the state supreme court. Advisory opinions relating to unauthorized practice were not seen as sufficiently related to the state's interests in granting lawyers a monopoly of the practice of law to justify their anticompetitive effects. Surety Title Ins. Agency v. Virginia State Bar, 431 F. Supp. 298 (E.D. Va. 1977). After *Bates,* the court of appeals vacated this decision in order that a companion state proceeding brought by the state attorney general charging the same title insurance companies with unauthorized practice could be decided first. 571 F.2d 205 (4th Cir. 1978). The Supreme Court denied certiorari, 436 U.S. 941 (1978). The Supreme Court of Virginia, on motion of the bar, then issued new rules with respect to issuance of advisory opinions that required all opinions finding that particular conduct constituted unauthorized practice eventually to be reviewed by that court. See Rule 10, Virginia State Bar, 219 Va. 367 (1979).

CHAPTER 11

COMPETENCE, MALPRACTICE, AND DISCIPLINE

A. COMPETENCE

Both the Model Code in DR 6 and the Model Rules in Rule 1.1 impose an "ethical" obligation on lawyers to practice competently. While the subject has arisen at various points throughout these materials, this chapter focuses on the issue of competence, and specifically, remedies for incompetence. Parts B and C, dealing with the action for malpractice and the discipline system are therefore sections whose subject matter is also "competence," although Part C deals with conduct issues in addition to competence. Part A, however, sets forth some of the profession's formal efforts to deal with problems of competence once lawyers have been admitted to the bar.

It is difficult to have a sense of the competence of the bar throughout the centuries. In this country in the last century, efforts to open the profession to children of the poor and of the immigrant have entangled the issues of greater competence and elitism into a hopeless snarl. See Jerold S. Auerbach, Unequal Justice: Lawyers and Social Change in Modern America 40-52 (1976), for a view focusing on the "elitist" elements of movements for higher standards. Indeed, there are some who see a danger that present movements for higher standards not only will be elitist but also will have the effect of stifling dissent. See statements of lawyers quoted in Levy, Is Specialization a Conspiracy?, 4 Juris Doctor 43, 44-45 (December 1974). Yet complaints about the poor lawyering of many lawyers are heard so often that it is difficult to believe that there is not a competence problem of major proportions. Perhaps research projects can be designed that would throw more light on this issue. For the moment, however, we are left to rely by and large on the instinctive judgments of experienced practitioners and students of the profession in whom we have confidence. They tell us that competence is an enormous problem in the profession.

If that is true, then that issue affects every other professional issue. It is one thing for us to define problems of professional responsibility when we assume a starting point of competent lawyers. It is quite another when we must assume that we are dealing with a large number of lawyers who are incompetent or who, perhaps because of the press of business, practice incompetently a large part of the time. The same is true when we focus on the availability of legal services. Just what quality of services is it that we are attempting to make available?

Thus the question of competence must be faced. This book simply cannot provide sufficient materials to study the whole problem of lawyers' education. See Reed, Training for the Public Profession of Law (1921); Packer & Ehrlich, New Directions in Legal Education (1972); and the Carrington Report on Training for the Public Professions of the Law (1971) (printed as an appendix to the Packer and Ehrlich book), for some exposition of the problem. Likewise, it did not seem advisable to deal with the bar examination as the profession's primary independent method of testing competence. For a thoughtful presentation of the question of competence as a matter of professional "self-regulation," see Steele and Nimmer, Lawyers, Clients and Professional Regulation, 1976 ABF Res. J. 919.

Two major developments in this field, one at the federal level and one at the state level, should be noted. Chief Justice Burger for a long time expressed his belief about the generally low level of competence displayed by trial lawyers in court. His remedy was a certification process. See Burger, The Special Skills of Advocacy, 42 Fordham L. Rev. 227 (1973). Although the underlying factual basis for his views were severely criticized, see Cramton and Jensen, The State of Trial Advocacy and Legal Education, 30 J. Leg. Educ. 253 (1979), the federal courts have proceeded slowly with planning for programs to attempt to improve the level of lawyers' performance in the federal courts.

The story is a progression from the 1977 recommendations of an advisory committee appointed in the Second Circuit (the Clare Committee) to the 1978 tentative and 1979 final recommendations of the Judicial Conference Committee appointed by Chief Justice Burger (the Devitt Committee), see 79 F.R.D. 187 (1978) and 83 F.R.D. 215 (1979), to the final implementation Committee Report of the King Committee in 1980. The major recommendations of the Devitt Committee were that a special admission examination in five federal practice subjects and professional responsibility, prior trial experience requirements, and a peer review procedure (to advise members whose trial performance is substandard) be established in several district courts on an experimental basis. These recommendations were approved by the Judicial Conference, the King Committee elaborated the details, and 14 district courts volunteered to participate in the experiment. The implementation has proceeded slowly and we will have to wait for assessments of the success of the proposals. Opposition has developed in many jurisdictions on the ground that the solutions are simplistic, burdensome, not likely to cure any problem of incompetence, prejudicial to young lawyers and those practicing alone or in small groups, and divisive insofar as they divide state and federal requirements.

More activity has taken place at the same level with respect to recognition of specialization. There were several decades of indecisive debate over the merits of official state recognition of categories of specialists who would be allowed to designate themselves as such. Those engaged in the discussion realized that the issue touched a whole variety of professional concerns and a great number of questions were raised and discussed. The following is a partial list.

Is the level of professional competence high enough to deal with the increasing complexity of law? If not, how shall it be raised? Is further "academic" training the answer, and if so, who shall administer it? Or is the answer "practical" training and experience? What is the relationship between the answers to these questions and the rules relating to advertising? What is the relation between specialization and cost of legal services? Will specialization and advertising of specialists tend to lead the public to lawyers who can do their work most efficiently and therefore most cheaply, or will it tend to lead the public to lawyers who will charge more for their expertness? Should a condition of certification of a specialist be the devotion of a certain amount of time to free legal "clinics" or some other kind of free representation? And finally, what will specialization do to the profession itself? Will it create, or increase, elitism? Will it mean greater fragmentation of the profession and the end of the general practitioner? Will it discriminate against young and minority members of the bar?

The profession asked itself questions like these for years, and for years it was so fearful about the answers and about guessing wrong that it preferred the status quo to experiment. It was uncertain both about the relevance of the medical model, which had existed for years, and about whether it liked the results of specialization in that profession. It also came to realize that limited experimentation was already taking place in the profession because there was an ever-increasing amount of specialization in fact among lawyers. Finally, perhaps spurred by the realization that temporizing was in fact a decision of sorts, but spurred even more by a growing feeling that there was a strong link between the issues involved in the specialization debate and the profession's duty to provide greater public access to legal services, the State Bar of California recommended, and the California Supreme Court approved, a pilot specialization program. The California plan adopted a model that provided for official certification of specialists by the state. The pilot program was limited initially to three fields: workers' compensation, taxation, and criminal law. Family law and immigration and nationality law were added thereafter.

As implemented by standards promulgated by the Board of Legal Specialization, see 23 West's Annotated Codes, Part 2, Civil and Criminal Rules 467-517 (1988 Supp.), the program sets forth detailed requirements for certification and recertification every five years that are somewhat different for all five fields. All contain substantial "task and experience" requirements involving participation in specified amounts of litigation and, in the case of tax specialists, preparation of written documents; completion of a specified number of units of educational programs; and either a written examination or completion of a prescribed alternate educational program. In addition, each applicant is required to produce references to attest to his or her level of competence, and the advisory commission that conducts an independent review of each applicant in each speciality field obtains further references on its own. There are also elaborate procedural provisions governing the initial decision and possible review of denial of certification or recertification.

Two other features of the California plan should be noted. The first is that the pilot plan originally adopted provided a limited time period in which lawyers could obtain certification by a so-called "grandfather" provision requiring lawyers with ten years of practice to show only "substantial involvement" in the particular fields. "Substantial involvement" was defined in different ways, but generally in terms of a percentage of time spent in practice in the particular field, or in numbers of court appearances, or both. When the pilot program was made permanent in 1985, no new "grandfathering" was provided. The second feature of the plan to note is this statement in Section 9 of the State Bar's program statement: "When a client is referred to a certified specialist by another attorney, the specialist shall not take advantage of his or her position to enlarge the scope of his or her representation. The specialist shall not represent the client in other matters without first notifying the client's lawyer who made the referral."

Some states, however, have experimented with a very different kind of approach, called a designation plan. Developed by New Mexico, it rejected the idea that expertness can be tested either by examination or in the field. Its proponents believed that a certain amount of misrepresentation is inherent in such certification and might result in harm to consumers and malpractice liability to practitioners. The New Mexico plan was basically an advertising plan, but examples of such plans today must be found elsewhere because New Mexico switched to a certification plan in 1987.

Iowa, however, has adopted a designation plan in DR 2-105 of its Code of Professional Responsibility. It permits lawyers who in fact limit their practice primarily to certain fields to indicate in any communication that their practice is "limited to," or that they are "practicing primarily in," not more than three of 34 listed areas. Prior to doing so, however, they must certify that they have devoted 200 hours or 20% of their practice time, whichever is greater, in each of the two most recent years to each indicated field and that they have completed ten hours of accredited Continuing Legal Education courses in each field within the most recent year.

While both the Iowa and the California plans come under the heading of "specialization" plans, they have very different objectives in mind. The Iowa plan focuses on the ability of the public to find lawyers who consider themselves de facto specialists by permitting those specialists to let the public know who they are. While it requires some verification of the de facto status and some educational training, it does not purport to measure or attest to competence, and lawyers are required in certain circumstances to disclaim certification as experts or specialists. The California Plan, on the other hand, focuses on competence and sets stringent standards for certification.

The American Bar Association has been active in the field of specialization since 1952 when it established a committee to study the issue. Committee recommendations to encourage or recognize the practice were consistently rejected by the House of Delegates through the 1950s and 1960s. In 1969, the Delegates approved a resolution stating that implementation of a nationwide plan was not desirable at that time and deferring action in favor of experimental state programs. However, the ABA Committee on Specialization did not want too much experimentation either, and its Committee Reports through the early 1970s consistently urged states to await evaluation of programs then in existence and the establishment of uniform standards.

After the decision of the Supreme Court in Bates v. State Bar, p. 492, the ABA Committee, spurred on by a perception of a close relation between regulation of specialization and truthful advertising of competence, renewed its interest in development of specialization programs and approved a Model Plan of Specialization that had been developed by its Specialization Committee. The Model Plan sought to steer a middle course between the quality and access focuses of the certification and designation proposals. Calling itself a "recognition program," it would mandate substantial involvement in the given field, continuing legal education, and peer review, but not necessarily examination. It would also provide flexibility in permitting standards to be met by equivalents. This last provision was the Committee's substitute for so-called "grandfather provisions." Many of the recent proposals being considered by various states would seem to have been influenced by the ABA Plan.

It is not easy to classify all the specialization programs that have been adopted in the various states. Programs that are basically certification programs have been adopted, at least on a pilot basis for some fields, in

Texas, Arizona, New Jersey, and South Carolina, and a plan was approved in principle in Arkansas in 1982, although it has been slow to be implemented. See 289 Ark. 597, 711 S.W.2d 446 (1986). Texas has even expanded its original program and made it permanent. Plans on the ABA Model have been approved in Utah and North Carolina.

Certification has, however, run into enormous opposition in California, especially from younger members of the bar and from minorities. Various proposals to strengthen or weaken the pilot program divided the bar for years until the Supreme Court finally made the program permanent in 1985. The designation programs have encountered difficulty too. A number of states have rejected designation proposals, at least partly on the ground that since the Supreme Court's decision in *Bates,* p. 492, designation does not seem to amount to much more than advertising by field, which enjoys constitutional protection in any event. Some states, like Florida and Iowa, have introduced continuing legal education requirements in their programs in order to add a quality component to the plans. Florida has also added a certification program for seven fields of practice. Georgia, on the other hand, terminated its designation program when only 12% of eligible lawyers took advantage of it. (The information contained in this discussion is taken from ABA Standing Committee on Specialization, Information Bulletins Nos. 8 and 9 (April 1982 and July 1983), Esau, Specialization and the Legal Profession, 9 Manitoba L.J. 255 (1979), Esau, Recent Developments in Specialization, 11 Manitoba L.J. 133 (1981), New Standards Set for Certification and Recertification, 50 Cal. St. Bar J. 309 (July/Aug. 1975), Morrison, The Debate Over Specialization Regulation, 3 Cal. Lawyer 49 (Feb. 1983), Mahan, Change Likely for California Specialization Program, 3 Cal. Lawyer 50 (Feb. 1983), Florida Bar J., p. 25 (Sept. 1987), ABA/BNA Lawyers' Manual on Professional Conduct, 21:4001 ff., and the relevant rules and regulations of the appropriate courts and boards in the jurisdictions discussed. There is a discussion of the various pros and cons of certification and designation plans at pp. 464-472 and 473-478 of the first edition of this book. An article questioning the whole development of specialization plans is Marvin W. Mindes, Proliferation, Specialization and Certification: The Splitting of the Bar, 11 U. Toledo L. Rev. 273 (1980).)

It should be added that while continuing legal education requirements are a component of specialization plans, they are also a growing feature in the states wholly apart from the debate over specialization. Starting in Minnesota in 1975, the idea has spread rapidly so that by 1988 approximately half of the states have imposed such requirements. Their constitutionality has been upheld against an argument that the requirement violated the 13th and 14th Amendments. Verner v. Colorado, 716 F.2d 1352 (10th Cir. 1983).

B. MALPRACTICE

<hr>

PROCANIK v. CILLO
206 N.J. Super. 270, 502 A.2d 94 (L. Div. 1985)

<hr>

BOYLE, J.S.C.

This case involves the pre-termination duties of an attorney who is a specialist in his field arising out of a legal malpractice claim within a medical malpractice suit. The primary issue is whether an attorney, a specialist in malpractice, has the duty, not only to advise his clients on the settled law, but whether he also has a duty to disclose to his clients, clearly and unmistakeably, an opinion held by him that the settled law is ripe for reconsideration. The subject matter, therefore, concerns what constitutes a complete, informed judgment. Additionally, there are contentions of a post-termination duty to advise clients of a decision subsequently reported in the advance sheets and whether these duties are mooted by a prospective application thereafter as to the applicable two-year statute of limitations. The issues arise out of a remand of the Supreme Court, Procanik By Procanik v. Cillo, 97 N.J. 339, 478 A.2d 755 (1984) (hereinafter cited as *Procanik*). Cross-motions for summary judgment have been made by all parties who agree that there are no genuine issues as to any material fact under R. 4:46-2. Therefore, a motion for summary judgment is appropriate for consideration. . . .

FACTUAL HISTORY

On June 8, 1976, co-plaintiff, Rosemarie Procanik (Procanik), placed herself under the medical care of the co-defendants, Dr. Joseph P. Cillo, Dr. Herbert Langer and Dr. Ernest P. Greenberg, who are board-certified obstetricians and gynecologists who apparently conduct a group practice. Thereafter, Procanik visited the offices of defendant-physicians from time to time. On June 9, 1977, she reported to defendant, Dr. Cillo, that her last menstrual period had been May 4, 1977. She further advised him that she had recently been diagnosed by family-physician as having measles but did not know if it was rubella (German measles). He examined Procanik and ordered "tests for German measles, known as Rubella Titer Test", at Rahway Hospital. The results "were 'indicative of past infection of Rubella.'" Instead of ordering further tests, it is alleged that Dr. Cillo negligently interpreted the results and told Procanik that she "had nothing to worry about because she had become immune to German measles as a child." In fact, the "past infection" disclosed by the tests was the German measles that had prompted Procanik to consult the defendant-physicians. Ignorant of what an accurate diagnosis would have disclosed, Procanik allowed her pregnancy to continue and delivered a son, the infant and incompetent, Peter Procanik; he having been born December 26, 1977. On January 16, 1978, the child was diagnosed as suffering from congenital rubella Down's syndrome.

As a result of the doctors' alleged negligence, Procanik was deprived of the choice of terminating the pregnancy, and Peter was "born with multiple birth defects," including eye lesions, heart disease, and auditory defects.

On April 26, 1978, the co-plaintiffs, Rosemarie Procanik and Michael Procanik, her husband, consulted with defendant-attorney, Harold Sherman (Sherman), regarding a possible claim for personal injuries as a result of the alleged medical malpractice of defendant-physicians. As a result of the consultation, Sherman determined that an opinion was necessary from a specialist in medical malpractice. Plaintiffs concede Sherman is a general practitioner in law. On November 6, 1978, Sherman consulted with Lee S. Goldsmith (Goldsmith), who was "of counsel" to the firm of Greenstone, Greenstone & Naishuler (Greenstone), a professional corporation specializing in medical malpractice claims. Goldsmith and Greenstone are also defendant-attorneys in this action. Goldsmith, in addition to being an attorney is a medical doctor. Answers to interrogatories disclosed that he had handled 300 cases involving medical malpractice. He specializes in medical malpractice cases. It was also conceded that Goldsmith, being "of counsel" (although not an employee of the Greenstone firm) acted as its agent.

Sherman collected plaintiffs' records and any other information regarding this matter and passed them along to defendants, Greenstone and Goldsmith. It was understood that Goldsmith would review the matter and render an opinion to Sherman.

Subsequently, Goldsmith referred the file to Dr. Leslie Iffy, professor of obstetrics and gynecology and director, division of maternal-fetal medicine at the New Jersey University of Medicine and Dentistry, for an expert medical opinion. Discovery revealed various correspondence between Goldsmith, Greenstone and Sherman. Of significance is a letter dated January 29, 1979 from Goldsmith to Greenstone.[1] It is clear from

---

1.

January 29, 1979

Herbert E. Greenstone, Esq. & Allen Naishuler, Esq.
Greenstone, Greenstone & Naishuler, Esq.
744 Broad Street
Newark, New Jersey 07102

Gentlemen:

We have, in the office, a Procanik file. This is a case in which a woman had a last menstrual period in May, measles at the end of May, then went to a gynecologist at the beginning of June; rubella test done, showed that she did have antibodies to it and

that letter that Goldsmith was aware of Gleitman v. Cosgrove, 49 N.J. 22, 227 A.2d 689 (1967), which precluded wrongful birth actions. Goldsmith indicated that in his opinion the Procanik case was an appropriate one to reverse *Gleitman*. The letter stated "I think the time is right, and I think we have a good shot at reversal." On February 7, 1979, Goldsmith and Greenstone received Dr. Iffy's medical report. In March 1979, Goldsmith delivered the entire file to Greenstone for his review. In a letter to Sherman dated April 26, 1979, Goldsmith and Greenstone decided not to accept the case.[2] They concluded that: (1) Gleitman "pro-

---

apparently never informed of this so as to get an abortion. Gave birth to a deformed child in the following year.

This case would fall into the area of Gleitman v. Cosgrove, 227 Atlantic 2d 689. The decision in this case was in 1967, at a time when abortions were still illegal. The decision was 4 to 3, and was, in part, based on the fact that abortions were illegal.

Recently in New York, (and a copy of this decision is enclosed) there were two cases decided, Becker v. Schwartz and Park v. Jessen [*Chessin,* 46 *N.Y.*2d 401, 413 *N.Y.S.*2d 895, 386 *N.E.*2d 807], which in effect reverses Gleitman v. Cosgrove, and the New York case, Stuart v. Long Island Hospital. I think that now, at this time, it is an appropriate time to determine clearly whether or not we wish to take on Gleitman v. Cosgrove, going up to the Supreme Court. I think the time is right, and I think we have a good shot at reversal. The reason for the memo, then, is please read Becker v. Schwartz which is enclosed as well as *Gleitman,* so that we can discuss it and discuss our options. The damages are heavy.

> Cordially,
> /s/ *Lee*
> Lee S. Goldsmith

2.

April 26, 1979

Harold A. Sherman, Esq.
Mandel, Wysoker, Sherman, Glassner & Weingartner, P.A.
313 State Street
Perth Amboy, New Jersey 08861

   Re: Rose Marie Procanik

Dear Harold:

We have finally come to a decision as to what to do with the Procanik case, after a great deal of discussion here in the office because of the problems presented by the case. Let me outline those problems to you as this forms the basis of our turning down this case.

The Procanik case basically falls into the area of a woman who had measles which was not definitively diagnosed, and, at approximately the same time was diagnosed as being pregnant. No steps were taken at that time. We are aware that Mrs. Procanik indicated that had she known of the potential problem, she would have undergone an abortion. We sent out the questions in the form of a possible malpractice case to an obstetrician/gynecologist, who felt that it was an extremely difficult position to put an obstetrician/gynecologist in. We did, however, decide not to leave it there and went ahead and reviewed the following:

   1) (Gleitman v. Cosgrove, 49 N.J. 22, 227 A.2d 689 (1967). As you are probably aware, this case prohibits the kind of action that would have to be brought herein. In other words, that type of action would be either a wrongful birth or an action

hibits the kind of action that would have to be brought herein"; (2) "It is possible that *Gleitman* could be reversed"; (3) "that it would have to be taken to the Supreme Court in order to obtain a reversal"; and (4) "The law is dead against us in the State and the reversal would be necessary."

As a result of this letter, Sherman determined to terminate the attorney-client relationship with Procanik. A meeting took place at his office with the Procaniks present. He discussed with them Goldsmith's letter of April 26, 1979, and reviewed a letter with them dated May 2, 1979[3] which constituted a termination of his services for the Procaniks. The letter indicated that Goldsmith was not interested in handling the case, and "his judgment is one on which I would certainly rely." It also advised the Procaniks "that you are free to consult another attorney, who after

---

for the purpose of trying to obtain damages for children who were born, and who would otherwise not have been born.

2) In January, 1979 two cases came down, reported as Nos. 559 and 560 of the Court of Appeals, New York entitled, Becker v. Schwartz and Park v. Chessin. These actions both are similar to Gleitman v. Cosgrove, and in effect, in New York, render a different opinion. It is possible that *Gleitman* could be reversed and it is further possible that the New Jersey courts could follow Becker v. Schwartz and Park v. Chessin. These cases do allow a person to sue under the circumstances of Procanik, and would allow the possibility of damages for life. It would mean, however, in Procanik, that the case would have to be started, face a dismissal at this level, and then obviously be appealed to the Supreme Court in the hopes of obtaining a reversal of Gleitman v. Cosgrove.

Considering the fact that the expert is somewhat weak on the case and considering the fact that it would have to be taken to the Supreme Court in order to obtain a reversal before a valid case could be brought, we have decided not to proceed. *The law is dead against us in the State and the reversal would be necessary.*

I am returning herewith all the hospital records that you were kind enough to send us. I will, if you like, send you a copy of the report of the expert. We have checked out every avenue and I think in all probability Mrs. Procanik did have measles, did become pregnant while she had the measles, and was not so informed. But because of the many and sundry other problems, we would not proceed.

Will you please be good enough to inform the Procaniks.

Cordially,
/s/ *Lee*
LEE S. GOLDSMITH

3.

May 2, 1979

Mr. & Mrs. Michael Procanik
17 Chase Avenue
Avenel, N.J. 07001

Re: Rose Marie Procanik
     Peter Procanik

Dear Mr. & Mrs. Procanik:

This will confirm that we have had a personal meeting to discuss the letter which I received from Mr. Lee Goldsmith, to whom I had referred the possible mal-practice claims, along with the materials and records collected up to this point.

all, might feel differently about the case." It also advised the Procaniks of the applicable statute of limitations both as to the parents' claims and that of the infant, Peter. It also suggested "that if you want to pursue this matter further, you contact another attorney immediately." After Sherman had been originally retained and before termination of that relationship, the Supreme Court granted certification on September 5, 1978 in Berman v. Allan, 80 N.J. 421, 404 A.2d 8 (1979), which was reported in the New Jersey Law Journal (Law Journal), 102 N.J.L.J. 576 (1978). Although all of the defendant-attorneys were readers of the Law Journal, none of them had read this certification in that publication. On February 26, 1978, Berman was argued before the Supreme Court. On July 5, 1979, shortly after the attorney-client relationship had been terminated and memorialized by letter of May 2, 1979, the Law Journal published the notification of the decision of Berman v. Allan, 104 N.J.L.J. 1 (1979), which was decided on June 26, 1979. On July 26, 1979, the full text of the opinion in *Berman* appeared in the Law Journal, 104 N.J.L.J. 73 (1979). The *Berman* decision was then published in the advance sheets on August 31, 1979. In Berman v. Allan, 80 N.J. 421, 404 A.2d 8 (1979), the Court recognized that parents may recover for emotional distress for the "wrongful birth" of a child born with birth defects. The defendant-attorneys had not read the certification in *Berman*, reported in the Law Journal prior to termination with the Procaniks, nor, as revealed by answers to interrogatories, could they recall with specific-

---

The sad truth is that while the probabilities are that the facts you relate are true, that under the law of New Jersey as it presently stands, the case would not survive a dismissal at the trial level. For your information, Mr. Goldsmith is not interested in handling the matter, and his judgment is one on which I would certainly rely.

Accordingly, I have returned the materials to you with the caution that you are free to consult another attorney, who after all, might feel differently about the case. You are also advised that, while the infant's claim survives until two years from attaining his 18th birthday, it is advisable to bring these cases within two years after the parents know or should have known that there was a possible mal-practice claim, because the parents' claims for loss of services and medical expenses may be barred within two years, even though the infant's claim for injury might survive, as previously stated. It is also true that witnesses become less available, including doctors, and the same applies to records and other necessary documents.

I would, therefore, suggest that if you want to pursue this further, you contact another attorney immediately. I will provide any such attorney with a copy of Mr. Goldsmith's letter, should this request be made.

You will recall that you advanced us $200.00 towards costs, which were as follows:

Rahway Hospital Records:	$ 54.00
Presbyterian Hospital Records:	48.00
Children's Hospital Records:	18.00
Total:	$120.00

Accordingly, enclosed find our check for $80.00

Very truly yours,
HAROLD A. SHERMAN

ity when, after termination, they had become aware of the reported decision. Consequently, defendant-attorneys never advised the Procaniks that they had a cause of action, and the two-year statute of limitations expired on their claims on January 16, 1980. However, after January 16, 1980, the Procaniks engaged new counsel and a complaint was filed on April 8, 1981, almost 15 months after the statute of limitations had expired and nearly 3½ years after the infant was diagnosed as suffering from congenital rubella Down's syndrome.

Specifically, plaintiffs' complaint alleges that defendant-physicians negligently failed to diagnose a rubella infection early in plaintiff-mother's pregnancy, as a result of which infant-plaintiff was born with multiple birth defects. This medical malpractice caused them to suffer emotional injury and to incur medical expenses. Plaintiffs also assert that their defendant-attorneys undertook to investigate plaintiffs' potential malpractice claims and, in the course of that undertaking, negligently discharged their professional responsibilities in several ways: (1) by failing to become aware of an appeal pending before the Supreme Court which implicated the areas of medical malpractice law; (2) by advising them that the then settled law in this State precluded their contemplated action without further advising them that "a decision [of the unrelated pending appeal in *Berman,* supra] could be expected shortly"; (3) if not, that a "precautionary suit" should be instituted; and (4) in failing to advise them, months after their professional relationship had terminated, of the publication of the Court's decision in *Berman* and its recognition of the actionability of their claim.

Defendant-attorneys, on the other hand, maintain that no duty existed and that the actions exercised by defendant-attorneys were within the standard of care of the legal profession. . . .

In order to find defendant-attorneys liable for negligence, a legal duty must be found to exist and there must have been a breach of that duty. . . .

The standard for determining legal malpractice is that an attorney is obligated to exercise that degree of reasonable knowledge and skill that lawyers of ordinary ability and skill possess. . . .

Our Supreme Court has adopted a North Carolina court's definition of the standard of care in legal malpractice actions . . . when it quoted Hodges v. Carter, 239 N.C. 517, 80 S.E.2d 144 (1954):

> Ordinarily when an attorney engaged in the practice of law and contracts to prosecute an action in behalf of his client, he impliedly represents that (1) he possesses the requisite degree of learning, skill and ability necessary to the practice of his profession and which others similarly situated ordinarily possess; (2) he will exert his best judgment in the prosecution of litigation entrusted to him; and (3) he will exercise reasonable and ordinary care and diligence in the use of his skill and in the application of his knowledge to his clients' cause. [239 N.C. at 519, 80 S.E.2d at 145]

PRE-TERMINATION DUTY

Plaintiffs contend that Goldsmith and Greenstone were negligent by not being aware of the *Berman* certification reported in the Law Journal which, by implication, requires a finding of a duty to read or be aware of the Law Journal. Plaintiffs also claim that upon the publication of the certification in the Law Journal the law on wrongful birth claims became unsettled.

Since there is no dispute factually that Goldsmith and Greenstone, at the time of the rendering of the opinion and before termination of the attorney-client relationship ended, had not read the *Berman* certification, this court must find whether a duty existed to nevertheless read the certification. This court finds that the specialists had no duty to read the Law Journal and the specific certification that implicated this area of medical malpractice law.

R. 2:12-1 states that the Supreme Court may, on its own motion, certify any action or class of actions for appeal. While it is apparent to this court: (1) That the issue in *Berman* presented a question of general public importance even though *Gleitman* had been previously settled by the Supreme Court as to wrongful birth claims; and (2) the decision under review was in potential conflict with the *Gleitman* doctrine and called for an exercise of the Supreme Court's supervision and other matters in the interest of justice, the certification did not render the law unsettled on wrongful birth claims. . . . Although the Law Journal publishes decisions of the courts, it is an unofficial publication in that regard. Reports of cases argued and determined in the courts are officially reported in the advance sheets and subsequently in the bound volumes of the New Jersey Reports and the New Jersey Superior Court Reports. A certification is a signal that the Supreme Court may be reconsidering settled law, not a final decision that the law, in fact, will change. . . .

This court holds, therefore, that *Gleitman* was the settled law at the time of the rendering of the opinion letter from Goldsmith to Greenstone dated April 26, 1979 as conveyed to the Procaniks May 2, 1979. This court also holds that the specialists had the right to decline the Procanik case. The closer question is whether the specialists' opinion reflected complete informed judgment. Their opinion certainly gave the settled law, but it did not convey to Sherman, for the benefit of Procanik, what the specialists knew, i.e., that *Gleitman* was ripe for reconsideration. An examination of the Goldsmith letter to Sherman of April 26, 1979 omits that vital piece of information. It is known that this opinion was held and conveyed by Goldsmith to Greenstone in his letter of January 29, 1979. This court holds that a lawyer has a duty to disclose to his client, clearly and unmistakably, a complete opinion giving his full informed judgment that the settled law is ripe for reconsideration, particularly when one is held out as a specialist in the complicated field of medical malpractice. . . . However, . . . the advice was not based upon the exercise of an informed judgment, limited to the facts in this case. In Boss-Harrison Hotel Company v. Barnard, 148 Ind. App. 406, 266 N.E.2d 810, 811 (1971), the court found that good appellate advocacy demands the regular reading of the advance sheets and that these advance sheets constitute central law since they are cases which have yet to be bound in their final volumes. . . . This court agrees that liability should attach in such a situation. Attorneys are absolutely responsible for case law decisions as well as all temporary supplemental office texts of the case law such as an advance sheet.

An examination of the letter of April 26, 1979 from Goldsmith to Sherman states: "It is possible that *Gleitman* could be reversed. . . ." In the last paragraph, the letter says: "The law is dead against us in the state and a reversal would be necessary." This court finds that although Goldsmith correctly and fully set forth the settled law in New Jersey, he failed to include in his letter to Sherman the clear opinion that he had given Greenstone, which stated: ". . . and I think we have a good shot at reversal." A fair reading of that phrase indicates an anticipation that the *Gleitman* doctrine is ripe for reconsideration. On the other hand, Goldsmith's letter to Sherman, while admittedly stating that *Gleitman* could possibly be reversed, is not in the same context. The former is affirmative; the latter is negative. Furthermore and more importantly, Goldsmith's letter to Sherman of April 26, 1979 is an incomplete informed judgment and opinion. While complete as to the settled law, it is incomplete with respect to the posture for change. Realistically, a client not informed of this additional and vital element of information that *Gleitman* is ripe for reversal could reasonably allow a jury to conclude that the Procaniks, based upon this advice and counsel of a specialist, would decide that their claim was almost hopeless, and would discourage them from seeking a second opinion.

An attorney's stock in trade is his counsel and advice. The duty involved here is to give the client all of the information in complete form. Here, we had those ingredients in which Greenstone and Goldsmith were perceptive as specialists. *Gleitman* was a doctrine of long standing. At the time of that holding, abortions were not legal. Subsequently, it was held that abortions were legal. *Roe v. Wade*, 410 U.S. 113 (1973). Goldsmith was aware of the then favorable New York decisions which caused him to be optimistic in this case. Both specialists knew this even without the benefit of the *Berman* certification.

The law is perpetually in regeneration. This duty does not include predicting with any certainty whether the change will, in fact, occur nor when. A specialist in his field has a duty to be alert, aware and sensitive to the fact that his counsel and advice will have substantial weight and influence on any subsequent decisions that a client might make in pursuing the engagement of another attorney for a second opinion. Historically, we know that the final decision as to *Berman* was officially reported only a few months after the termination of the attorney-client relationship and well within the two-year statute of limitations applied retrospectively.

A legal expert in medical malpractice, securely perched on the summit of his specialty, must give a complete, informed opinion to the referring attorney for conveyance to the client. He must do no less, nor is more demanded. A specialist has a multi-tier standard of duty. It not only includes the duty generally applicable to those attorneys in the general practice of law, but also a duty of counsel and advice in the specialty involved here — medical malpractice. . . .

This duty is not one to guaranty a change in the law, but rather to be aware that a realistic probability exists that the settled law is likely to be reconsidered.

It should be clear that this duty is not to be confused with hindsight or prescience. This duty does not require clairvoyance or the ability to predict as a prophet that the change in the law, in fact, will occur. It has been conceded by plaintiffs that if such a duty exists, it only applied to Greenstone and Goldsmith since they were specialists. Plaintiffs further conceded that Sherman, not being a specialist in medical malpractice, would not have a concurrent duty. Discovery and Sherman's termination letter of May 2, 1979 shows clearly that he, in fact, met the standard of reasonable care applicable to an admitted general practitioner as to this case. He discussed with the Procaniks Goldsmith's letter to him of April 26, 1979. He clearly relied on the judgment of Goldsmith. He advised his clients ". . . you are free to consult another attorney, who after all, might feel differently about the case." He advised them as to the statute of limitations. He also stated "I would, therefore, suggest that if you want to pursue this matter further, you contact another attorney immediately." Based on the foregoing, this court holds that Sherman exercised the knowledge, skill and ability ordinarily possessed and exercised by members of the legal profession similarly situated, and he exercised reasonable care and prudence in relying upon the advice of the specialists.

POST-TERMINATION DUTY

Plaintiffs contend that defendants, Greenstone and Goldsmith, were negligent in not calling back their clients (presumably via Sherman) after the Law Journal published the *Berman* decision on January 26, 1979. For the reasons previously expressed, this court holds that they had no duty to do so since the Law Journal is not an official publication on adjudicatory decisions by the Supreme Court. However, it raises the question as to whether said defendants were negligent in failing to contact their clients after the *Berman* decision was reported in the advance sheets and subsequently the bound volumes in the New Jersey Reports. *Boss-Har-*

rison Hotel Company, supra. *Berman* was published in the advance sheets on August 31, 1979, well within the remaining period of the statute of limitations. It is contended by the plaintiffs that the nature of the fiduciary relationship between Greenstone and Goldsmith and the Procaniks continued in force and did not terminate on May 2, 1979. They state that just as the obligation of confidentiality remains after termination, so does the duty of care remain as to relevant matters between the clients and the attorneys. Therefore, by not calling their clients to advise them of the *Berman* decision, said defendants were negligent.

"Generally, absent death or legal insanity of either party, the (attorney-client) relationship terminates only upon the accomplishment of the purpose for which the attorney was consulted, or upon mutual agreement of the parties." Tormo v. Yormark, supra, 398 F.Supp. at 1173. Therefore, the test regarding the termination of an attorney-client relationship asks (1) if there was a clear and unmistakeable termination by the attorney, or (2) whether the purpose for which the attorney has been retained has been fulfilled.

Here, the termination was clear and unmistakable. However, there is an additional ingredient: the attorney-specialists' opinion lacked full disclosure and was an incomplete conveyance of their opinion to their clients. Therefore, the second criterion in terminating an attorney-client relationship was not met in that they did not accomplish the purpose for which they were hired. Plaintiffs contend that Greenstone and Goldsmith had a post-termination duty. A jury could find that their relationship with the clients never terminated because the purpose of their retention was not fulfilled and, therefore, a pre-termination duty merely continued. Under the facts of this case, if the specialists are found to have breached a duty in the pretermination stage, they cannot utilize that wrong in evading responsibility subsequently.

The second criterion which this court imposes upon the specialists is not without precedent in the medical profession. In the case Tresemer v. Burke, 86 Cal. App. 3d 656, 150 Cal. Rptr. 384, 12 A.L.R. 4th 27 (1978), the court held that a physician had a duty to notify his client two years after the insertion of a dalcon shield that it could cause medical complications. The court stated that the patient had a cause of action by virtue of a confidential relationship between doctor and patient. The malpractice action was imposed from the continuing status of the physician-patient where the danger arose from that relationship. The situation in *Tresemer* is analogous to the case at bar. Although *Tresemer* involved a physician-patient relationship, the courts have continually held that similar rules of law and duties are applicable to physicians and attorneys. McCullough v. Sullivan, 102 N.J.L. 381, 384, 132 A. 102 (E. & A. 1925); Stewart v. Sbarro, 142 N.J. Super. 581, 590, 362 A.2d 581 (App. Div. 1976).

Accordingly, questions for the jury exist in that they might find: (1) a breach of the pre-termination duty involving an obligation to advise the clients that their case was ripe for reconsideration; (2) a breach of the post-termination duty involving an obligation to advise the clients of the favorable decision in *Berman* which would have prevented their medical malpractice claim from being time barred; and (3) that if there was a pre-termination duty that was breached by Greenstone and Goldsmith; the fiduciary relationship, limited to full disclosure, continued after the termination. . . .

For the reasons expressed herein, Sherman's motion for summary judgment is granted and all cross-claims against him are hereby dismissed. The summary judgment motion brought by Greenstone and Goldsmith is denied. An appropriate order consistent with this opinion shall be submitted.

PROCANIK v. CILLO

226 N. J. Super. 132, 543 A.2d 985 (App. Div. 1988)

The opinion of the court was delivered by PRESSLER, P.J.A.D.

. . . With respect to the trial judge's conclusion on the summary judgment motion that an attorney-client relationship existed between Goldsmith and plaintiffs, we point out first that that ruling was, insofar as we are able to determine, based on a fact which later turned out to be incorrect. The trial courts's factual recitation noted that Sherman had engaged Goldsmith to give his opinion and advice as to the Procaniks' prospective cause. By the time of trial it appeared that that characterization was not accurate. Sherman had not submitted the matter to Goldsmith for a specialist's opinion but had rather asked Goldsmith if he would be interested in accepting the representation. The relational posture was therefore not that of an undertaking to render advice by a "specialist" attorney but merely his declination to accept a proferred representation. It is clear that an attorney must affirmatively accept a professional undertaking before the attorney-client relationship can attach, whether his acceptance be by speech, writing, or inferred from conduct. . . . This case is about an affirmative refusal of a professional undertaking, not its acceptance. There was thus no attorney-client relationship.

We nevertheless do not intend to suggest that threshold communications between attorney and prospective client do not impose certain obligations upon the attorney. But it is only the nature of the attorney's obligation in that threshold context, an obligation we address hereafter, which we must consider, not the whole panoply of fiduciary responsibilities and duties which come into play when an attorney-client relationship is formed. Thus, the sole dispositive issue as we perceive it is whether, based on the undisputed facts and plaintiffs' proofs at trial, plaintiffs established a prima facie case of attorney negligence against Goldsmith in that context.

That issue is narrowly focused. First, plaintiff concedes that the Greenstone firm committed no act of independent or separate attorney negligence. Its liability is predicated exclusively on principles of agency and respondeat superior. Second, plaintiffs concede that Goldsmith was not guilty of any intentional conduct against them but only of negligent conduct. Third, plaintiffs concede that in declining to take the case, Goldsmith had no obligation to state any reason at all for his decision. What this case is consequently about is plaintiffs' theory, accepted by the trial judge both on the summary judgment motion and at trial, that if an attorney, and particularly a specialist, undertakes to give any reason at all for declining the case, he must give his full, complete and informed judgment. Plaintiffs assert that Goldsmith failed to do so.

The entire factual predicate on which plaintiffs construct their theory of Goldsmith's professional negligence is based on two alleged flaws in his letter of April 26, 1979 to Sherman which we have quoted in full. The first flaw was Goldsmith's failure to iterate in his letter to Sherman the statement made in his January 29, 1979 memorandum to Greenstone respecting Gleitman, namely, that "I think the time is right, and I think we have a good shot at reversal." Their point is that Goldsmith thereby misled them respecting the strength of their case on appeal. [The second alleged flaw is irrelevant to the issues under consideration in this chapter.] We reject both of these theses.

While we agree with the proposition that an attorney, in declining a representation, need give no reason at all, we disagree with the notion that if he gives any reason, it must fully explain his entire mental processes. In our view, if an attorney, including a specialist, voluntarily undertakes to give any reason for declining a case, whatever he does say must be professionally reasonable in the circumstances. We are also persuaded that there is not a scintilla of proof in this case that Goldsmith failed to comply with that standard.

We consider first the reason given by Goldsmith to Sherman respecting the state of the law on wrongful birth and wrongful life. Plaintiffs concede that Goldsmith's . . . letter to Sherman was entirely accurate. They acknowledge, moreover, that the letter not only correctly stated the then settled law in New Jersey, but also explained that the law was evolving elsewhere and hence that "it is possible that Gleitman could be reversed and it is further possible that the New Jersey courts could follow" the recent New York decision. And, they acknowledge, the letter correctly outlined the appellate procedure which would have to be prosecuted "in the hopes of obtaining a reversal of Gleitman v. Cosgrove." They complain only that Goldsmith did not say to Sherman, as he had to Greenstone, that the chances for reversal were good and the time was right for a change.

We regard the letter in this respect to be entirely reasonable and adequate as a matter of law. We wholly disagree with the trial judge's conclusion that Goldsmith was obligated to convey any private thoughts he might have had about the prospect of the success of an appeal seeking an overruling of the clearly stated decisional law. . . . [A] lawyer who correctly explains the existing decisional law of the jurisdiction, the recent disparate view of a sister jurisdiction, the consequent fact of potential change of decisional law on appeal, and the procedures for obtaining change has fulfilled any obligation he may have to explain his state-of-the-law reasons for declining the case. It is not a professional dereliction for him to withhold his gratuitous prediction of the prospect of success of an appeal which would be taken to obtain a change in the law. . . .

Our conclusion is based on what we believe to be established principle governing an attorney's communication respecting the state of the law whether to a client or a prospective client. First, where, as here, there is no attorney-client relationship, an attorney is free to decline the representation without stating any reason at all. He is not, however, without obligation with respect to a reason he does undertake to give. . . . [I]n In re Gavel, 22 N.J. 248, 265 (1956), Justice Vanderbilt . . . concluded that the attorney's fiduciary obligation extends to "persons who, although not strictly clients, he has or should have reason to believe rely on him." Ibid. . . . We have no doubt that when an attorney, and particularly one specializing in a specific area of the law, declines a representation because of the state of the law which he undertakes to express, he knows or should know that the prospective client will depend on the reliability of that expression. Nor is there any doubt there that Goldsmith knew that plaintiffs would so rely on his letter to Sherman. Indeed he asked Sherman to "please be good enough to inform the Procaniks."

We also regard as well settled the scope and nature of the duty of a lawyer who does undertake to state the law to a client or a prospective client. If the law is settled, he is expected to know what it is and to state it accurately. See generally Mallen and Levit, Legal Malpractice (2d ed. 1981) at pp. 282-284. If the law is unsettled, debatable or doubtful, he is not required to be correct, usually determinable only by hindsight, but only to exercise an informed judgment based on a reasoned professional evaluation. . . . Nor is an attorney obliged to anticipate a change in settled law. . . . And if, as here, the attorney has a degree of expertise in a complex and volatile area of the law which leads him to believe, because of developments elsewhere, that change in settled law is possible, it is surely enough for him to point that that is so and why — just as Goldsmith did here. That explanation need not and perhaps ought not be accompanied by a prediction of the likelihood that he can effect that change in the decisional law in that very case. Surely any experienced practitioner must understand the uncertainty of that prospect even if he believes that the time for seeking change is right and the chances reasonably good. And it is that very uncertainty which ultimately precludes imposition of liability based on his withholding of such a prediction. . . . Nor . . . can a lawyer be penalized when he not only accurately states the existing rule of law but also points out a reasoned basis supporting the possibility of its change. There was, in sum, nothing actionable in Goldsmith's legal explanation to Sherman.

NOTES

1. Note that the issues presented by the motions for summary judgment are related to one another. The first issue is whether the plaintiffs were "clients" of the specialists in the five-month period before the specialists turned down the case. The second issue, whether attorneys who turn down a case have an obligation to state their real reasons for so doing if they give any reasons at all, is affected by the reasonable beliefs of the client as to their relationship because of the length of time during which the specialists were considering the manner. In other words, the time lag is important on both issues.

2. At some point in the consideration of the difference in opinion between the trial court and the Appellate Division, the New Jersey Supreme Court, which has been asked to review the case, will present us with its views. The result will tell us how far that Court is willing to press the obligations of lawyers. Affirmance of the trial court's decision on the informing obligation of a specialist in the situation presented here would place an obligation on specialists that many thought they did not have.

3. It is also worth nothing that the plaintiffs alleged, and the trial court found, two kinds of incompetence. The first was incompetence of the specialists in failing to communicate their original views accurately and in failing to mention the new decision of the New Jersey Supreme Court. The second, however, is incompetence with respect to their expertness — the failure to keep up with the current decisions if in fact they did not become aware of the critical case in time. The trial court simply stated that good appellate advocacy required keeping up with the advance sheets. That whole issue apparently was never presented to the Appellate Division.

4. While the more common basis for a malpractice claim is in tort, the courts have also recognized a contract basis when an attorney fails to perform a task that a client has specifically instructed him or her to perform or when an attorney fails to keep a specific promise that was reasonably relied on by the client. E.g., Sherman Industries v. Goldhammer, 683 F. Supp. 502 (E.D. Pa. 1988).

5. In Russo v. Griffin, 147 Vt. 20, 510 A.2d 436 (1986), the court held that the geographical standard for measuring a lawyer's standard of care in a professional malpractice case was statewide and not limited to that

of the locality in which the lawyer practiced. The court noted that the standards for admission and the rules of practice were statewide and that a limitation of the standard of care to the locale of practice would make it harder to get expert witnesses and indeed could lead to a "conspiracy of silence."

The *Procanik* case dealt with the standard of care owed by a lawyer to a client, and indeed that is the setting in which claims about negligent practice are usually made. Occasionally, however, the claim of negligent practice is made by someone who is not a client, as in the following case.

ANGEL, COHEN & ROGOVIN v. OBERON INVESTMENT, N.V.

512 So.2d 192 (Fla. 1987)

PER CURIAM.

We review Oberon Investments v. Angel, Cohen and Rogovin, 492 So.2d 1113 (Fla. 3d DCA 1986), because of direct and express conflict with Amey, Inc. v. Henderson, Franklin, Starnes & Holt, P.A., 367 So.2d 633 (Fla. 2d DCA), cert. denied 376 So.2d 68 (Fla. 1979) and Drawdy v. Sapp, 365 So.2d 461 (Fla. 1st DCA 1978). Art. V, §3(b)(3), Fla. Const.

This case deals with the actions of petitioner in its representation of one Leonard Treister. Respondent brought suit against Treister alleging that, while acting as attorney and agent for respondent, Treister arranged a transaction whereby respondent sold its wholly-owned subsidiary to an undisclosed principal, actually Treister, for a certain sum while concurrently arranging a second transaction reselling the same property to a third-party buyer for a larger sum, thus defrauding respondent. In a separate count, respondent Oberon alleged that the petitioner law firm represented Treister in preparing the sale documents and should have foreseen the damage to Oberon; ergo the petitioner was negligent in preparing the documents or failing to inform respondent of the nature and extent of the transactions or in permitting Treister to use the documents for defrauding petitioner. There was no allegation that the petitioner engaged in fraudulent or conspiratorial conduct. The trial court granted summary judgment in favor of the petitioner. On appeal, the district court reversed, holding that a lack of privity did not bar recovery if petitioner knew that Treister was a fiduciary for respondent and knew of the potential conflict between the interests of Treister and respondent. The court reasoned that should the issues of fact be resolved in respondent's favor, petitioner had a duty to act in the best interest of respondent. Accordingly, because there were material facts in dispute relative to Treister's capacity and petitioner's knowledge, the summary judgment was reversed and the case remanded.

Assuming as we must in the posture of the case that the petitioner was aware that Treister was a fiduciary of respondent and was obligated to act in the best interests of respondent, the issue before this Court is whether such knowledge subjects the petitioner to an action in negligence brought by the third-party respondent.

Florida courts have uniformly limited attorneys' liability for negligence in the performance of their professional duties to clients with whom they share privity of contract. . . . The only instances in Florida where this rule of privity has been relaxed is where it was the apparent intent of the client to benefit a third party. The most obvious example of this is the area of will drafting. . . . Florida courts have refused to expand this exception to include incidental third-party beneficiaries. For the beneficiaries' action in negligence to fall within the exception to the privity requirement, testamentary intent as expressed in the will must be frustrated by the attorney's negligence and as a direct result of such negligence the beneficiaries' legacy is lost or diminished. We see no reason to expand this limited exception and specifically reject the invitation to adopt California's balancing of factors test. Biakanja v. Irving, 49 Cal. 2d 647, 320 P.2d 16 (1958).

In the instant case, respondent was not the client of the petitioner and thus lacked the requisite privity customarily required to maintain an action sounding in negligence against an attorney. Nor does the respondent, as an incidental third party beneficiary, fit within Florida's narrowly defined third-party beneficiary exception. Respondent's assertion that the petitioner knew or should have known of potential conflict between the interests of Treister and the respondent further undercuts his reliance on the third-party beneficiary exception. If, as respondent alleges, the petitioner knew of the conflict of interest between Treister and respondent, it was equally apparent that the professional services rendered Treister were not to benefit respondent. If, on the other hand, the petitioner did not know of the conflicting interest of Treister and respondent, petitioner's only duty was to its client, Treister. Accordingly, even should the material facts in dispute be resolved in the respondent's favor, they would not support its cause of action. The trial court correctly granted summary judgment. The district court's opinion is quashed and the case remanded for proceedings consistent with this opinion. . . .

NOTES

1. The court referred to California's balancing of facts test. The formulation in the *Biakanja* case, to which the court referred, was as follows:

The determination whether in a specific case the defendant will be held liable to a third person not in privity is a matter of policy and involves the balancing of various factors, among which are the extent to which the transaction was intended to affect the plaintiff, the foreseeability of harm to him, the degree of certainty that the plaintiff suffered injury, the closeness of the connection between the defendant's conduct and the injury suffered, the moral blame attached to the defendant's conduct, and the policy of preventing future harm.

2. While it is true that *Oberon* refused to relax the privity requirement to allow a third party to sue an attorney for negligent performance of his duty to a client, it should not be understood as meaning that a lawyer is not liable to a third party on the same basis that an ordinary citizen would be liable. See Riggs Nat'l Bank v. Freeman, 682 F. Supp. 519 (S.D. Fla. 1988) (attorney may be liable to third party for negligent misrepresentation).

3. Judge Posner discussed the doctrinal underpinnings of the causes of action against lawyers for professional malpractice and negligent misrepresentation in Greycas v. Proud, 826 F.2d 1560 (7th Cir. 1987) cert. denied, 108 S. Ct. 775 (1988). He related developments in those fields to general developments in torts, and his opinion is an interesting exposition of the approach of a judge whose former academic interest in the relation between economics and law has carried over into his judicial work.

NOTE: The Disciplinary Rules, Standards of Malpractice, and Rule 11

It is quite predictable that lawyers would attempt to use violation by lawyers of the disciplinary rules pertaining to their conduct as a basis for imposing liability on lawyers under both tort law and Rule 11. The reaction of the courts has been interesting and in some instances a little puzzling.

Both the Model Code and the Model Rules sought to prevent the standards of lawyer conduct promulgated therein from being used as the basis for civil liability. The Model Code states in its Preliminary Statement that it does not "undertake to define standards for civil liability of lawyers for professional conduct." The Model Rules are much more forceful. Their Scope note states: "Violation of a Rule should not give rise to a cause of action nor should it create any presumption that a legal duty has been breached. The Rules are designed to provide guidance to lawyers and to provide a structure for regulating conduct through disciplinary agencies. They are not designed to be a basis for civil liability. . . . [N]othing in the Rules should be deemed to augment any substantive legal duty of lawyers or the extra-disciplinary consequences of violating such a duty."

That language does not sit well alongside some of the idealistic language used to describe the purposes of these two codes of lawyers' conduct. The attempt to deny that there is anything in these codes of conduct that is relevant to the legal duty owed by a lawyer to a client is simply breathtaking. It is also quite wrong. To take just one obvious example, what of the duty of competent performance? It is no answer to say that that legal duty exists independently of these codes. A client is entitled to point to the statement of "independent" duty in the codes as evidence of its existence, just as, for example, the client should be entitled to point to the lawyer's duties with respect to confidentiality and conflicts of interest as they are set forth in the codes in an attempt to establish the nature of the duty owed by a lawyer in a civil action.

Once that point has been made, however, we should realize that it may not be enough for a client to point out that a breach of a disciplinary rule has occurred to establish a malpractice cause of action against his or her own lawyer. The plaintiff must still establish the requisite duty, breach, and causation necessary to make out a cause of action. Carlson v. Morton, 44 Mont. 1929, 745 P.2d 1133 (1987) is typical. A client alleged that a lawyer had negligently advised him in incorporating a business and guaranteeing a loan, encouraging him to hinder the lender's pursuit of collateral and then filing an affidavit against him. The plaintiff alleged that the rules stated the lawyer's duty of confidentiality, conflict of interest, competence, and honesty so clearly that no expert testimony was needed to establish the standard of care and breach thereof. The court disagreed, referring to the language quoted above from the Model Rules as instructive, even though Montana had not adopted the preamble and the conduct occurred before Montana adopted the Model Rules. The court went on to state that although the improprieties were seemingly straightforward, a nonlawyer jury might become confused and need expert testimony. But the court never said that the expert might not refer to the disciplinary rules in testifying about the relevant standard of care. Indeed, the court referred to the possibility that there might be cases where the negligence was so obvious that a trier of the fact might find it on the basis of common knowledge, and cases have so held. See Applegate v. Dobrovir, Oakes & Gebhardt, 628 F. Supp. 378 (D.D.C. 1985), aff'd 809 F.2d 930, cert. denied 107 S. Ct. 2181 (1987), quoting O'Neil v. Bergan, 452 A.2d 337 D.C. App. 1982).

It is not only in malpractice cases that violation of disciplinary rules may have some relevance. In the federal courts and those state courts that have followed them, Rule 11 mandates compliance with objective standards that have eliminated the former defense of good faith and imposes mandatory sanctions, including reasonable lawyers' fees and not permitting evidence to be used or issues to be litigated. Some courts have held that the violation of the disciplinary rules' injunctions with respect to citing contrary authority to the court, see DR 7-102(A)(2) of the Model Code and Model Rules 3.3(a)(3) and 3.1, constitutes a violation of Rule 11. E.g., Lyle v. Charlie Brown Flying Club, Inc., 112 F.R.D. 392 (N.D. Ga. 1986).

The issue bitterly divided the Court of Appeals for the Ninth Circuit in Golden Eagle Dist. Corp. v. Burroughs Corp., 801 F.2d 1531 (1986), five judges dissenting from denial of hearing en banc, 809 F.2d 590 (1987). District Judge Schwarzer, who has written extensively on Rule 11 (see his articles in 104 F.R.D. 181 (1985) and 101 Harv. L. Rev. 1013 (1988)), had imposed sanctions on a law firm (1) for contending that existing law supported a motion it was making when in fact a change or extension of law was required and (2) for failing to cite contrary authority. The panel opinion reversed, stating that the language of Rule 11 required only a certification that the motion was warranted by existing law or by a good faith argument for modification or reversal of existing law and that the motion was not interposed for an improper purpose. The fact that the motion itself was reasonably supportable in law and not frivolous met the terms of the Rule and the court was unwilling, given the mandatory nature of sanctions in Rule 11, to increase the burden on district courts by imposing on them the obligation "of evaluating under ethical standards the accuracy of all lawyers' arguments." 801 F.2d at 1542.

The dissenters on the denial of the en banc hearing, on the other hand, viewed Rule 11 as incorporating the citation requirements of the disciplinary rules. They argued that the law firm could not certify that the motion was supported by existing law on the court's "assumption" that the cases not cited were directly contrary to the firm's argument. Nor could the motion be a good faith argument for extension, modification, or reversal of existing doctrine when it did not argue for extension, modification, or reversal. The dissenters relied heavily on the standards of modern legal ethics embodied in the Model Code and the Model Rules to distinguish between vigorous advocacy and truthful advocacy and pointed to the Supreme Court's opinion in Nix v. Whiteside, p. 179, for support:

A client has as little right to the presentation of false arguments as he has to the presentation of false testimony. No conflict exists when a lawyer confines his advocacy by his duty to the court. The opinion is insensitive and unresponsive to the teaching of the Supreme Court that a restraint on the freedom of a lawyer to present falsity as truth does not create any true conflict. The lawyer has a duty to work within the boundaries of professional responsibility. He is not free to suborn testimony, to perjure himself, to offer perjured testimony, or to misrepresent facts or law. No conflict exists between his duty to work within these restraints and his duty to his client. The opinion suggests that there is the possibility of conflict over a duty to serve a client and a duty not to misrepresent the law. Fidelity to the relevant opinion of the Supreme Court and to the modern standards of the profession lead to a different conclusion.

Boritzer v. Blum, No. 80 CV 480 (E.D.N.Y. 1985) found a different route to impose costs on a law firm that failed to cite adverse controlling authority where the firm itself had been losing counsel in the relevant case. It used 28 U.S.C. §1927, which permits imposition of costs on counsel who unreasonably and vexatiously multiply proceedings. This case was reported in the advance sheets at 612 F. Supp. 522 but was not printed in the bound volume at the court's request. One can only speculate about the reason. Possibly it was related to the fact that in the original opinion, the judge stated that he would give the law firm an opportunity to explain its failure to cite relevant authority and that failing an adequate explanation, he would not only impose costs but would also forward the matter to the appropriate grievance committee. On reargument, the judge indicated that he was not satisfied with the explanation and remanded the matter to the Magistrate to fix the amount of costs, but he did not mention discipline. It is conceivable that the judge decided not to have the opinion published because of the reference to the possibility of discipline. See p. 739 for discussion of appropriate judicial behavior in that regard. See also Zick v. Verson Allsteel Press Co., 623 F. Supp. 927 (N.D. Ill. 1985), which imposed liability on counsel in a diversity case when Illinois law was clearly adverse even though there might have been a good faith argument for change of state law in a state court proceeding.

Another twist on the lawyer's obligation not to make frivolous arguments arose in connection with attempts by lawyers for indigents to withdraw when the only arguments to be made on behalf of a client's appeal would be frivolous. The Supreme Court, in Anders v. California, 386 U.S. 739 (1967), required that the motion to withdraw contain a brief that set forth everything that might arguably support the appeal. When Wisconsin also required that such a brief state why the lawyer believed the listed arguments lacked merit, the Supreme Court, 5-3, also upheld that requirement against an attack that such a requirement forced counsel to violate their duty to their client. McCoy v. Court of Appeals of Wisconsin, 108 S. Ct. 1895 (1988).

A reverse twist on the relation between the disciplinary rules and Rule 11 was presented in In re Kelly, 808 F.2d 549 (7th Cir. 1986) where the court held that a finding of violation of Rule 11 could provide the basis for imposition of discipline on an attorney. Judge Posner concluded:

Rule 46(c) of the appellate rules allows us to impose discipline on an attorney "for conduct unbecoming a member of the bar or for failure to comply with these rules or any rule of the court." Rule 11 is not one of "these rules" (i.e., the appellate rules) and is not incorporated by reference or otherwise in any rule of this court, but its requirements help to define conduct becoming a member of the bar. Compare Thornton v. Wahl, 787 F.2d 1151, 1153 (7th Cir. 1986), where we imposed a sanction for an appellate filing inconsistent with the standards of Rule 11.

The facts in that case bear mention. The attorney for the plaintiff, who was appealing a sex discrimination case against Marquette University, a Catholic university, moved, with his supporting affidavit, to disqualify Judge Coffey from sitting not only on the ground that he was a prominent Catholic alumnus of its College and Law School but also because Judge Coffey had "publicly and actively stated his opposition to abortion, an issue that has been injected into this case by the defendant." It turned out that the lawyer thought he remembered receiving many years before two brochures announcing Judge Coffey's participation in a St. Thomas More Society panel considering the abortion question. The attorney had made no effort to obtain the brochure or verify his memory when he filed his affidavit that made the flat assertion quoted above without disclosing the basis therefor. Judge Posner noted that although the amendments to Rule 11 were new, there was a "far older principle," that "requires that lawyers who make statements under oath concerning the conduct of fellow lawyers and judges and other participants in the administration of justice be scrupulous regarding the accuracy of those statements." *Id.* at 552. (On this point, compare the materials at pp. 434-444.)

C. DISCIPLINE

PROBLEM 87

Same factual situation as in Problem 83, except that the State Supreme Court, instead of having passed on a disciplinary case, has ruled in an admissions case that an applicant is not automatically disqualified from becoming a member of the bar by reason of having been found guilty of being a "scofflaw" two years previously in connection with 25 unpaid parking tickets. In a disciplinary hearing against a practicing lawyer "scofflaw" with 25 unpaid parking tickets, what effect should the admissions ruling have?

PROBLEM 88

Four lawyers have been convicted in separate cases of (a) embezzlement of a client's funds; (b) embezzlement of the funds of a company of which the lawyer is president; (c) willful failure to pay income taxes; and (d) an illegal campaign contribution. Each is appealing the conviction. You are counsel to the disciplinary committee with appropriate jurisdiction. You have been asked by the chairman whether the committee should institute proceedings looking toward at least temporary suspension pending the appeals, or whether the committee should await final disposition of the appeals, which will likely take at least two years.

PROBLEM 89

Client has made a complaint to the disciplinary committee of which you are chief counsel. The gist of the complaint is that he cannot get a proper accounting of funds that he claims Lawyer has been holding. The records that client gave you seem to indicate that he did not get the money to which he was entitled. You have communicated with Lawyer who has said that since the complaint in effect makes a criminal accusation, she is invoking her constitutional privilege against self-incrimination and, regretfully, will have nothing to say to the disciplinary committee. The committee has asked you whether the failure of Lawyer to respond to the accusation may be taken into account by it in determining what weight should be given to independent evidence that is produced to demonstrate a violation of the disciplinary rules.

PROBLEM 90

Counsel has been asked to write a letter of recommendation about Mr. Z, with whom she worked closely when he was in the legal department of one of her clients. Counsel believes that Z is a good lawyer but she knows that since Z left client's employment, he has been convicted of raping a guest at a party in a friend's house. The job Z seeks is a legal job with an insurance company. Does Counsel have any obligation to mention the conviction — i.e., should she be subject to discipline for failure to do so? Should the answer turn on whether the crime is related to professional competence? See The New York Times, Feb. 4, 1982, p. A17, col. 1, for the report of censure by the Massachusetts Medical Society of three doctors who failed to make such disclosure to a would-be employer in a similar case.

The issues with respect to discipline are very closely tied to those involved in admission. Indeed, in some places the same committee screens both applications for admission and disciplinary charges. Issues with respect to appropriate procedure or the substantive law of "bad moral character" or "unprofessional conduct" are obviously interrelated. Indeed, the same major tension can be perceived in both fields. At the same time that the profession is being attacked for laxness in self-policing and is being exhorted to screen lawyers more carefully and to be more responsive to the unprofessional conduct that exists, courts, including the Supreme Court, have been increasingly protective of the rights of individual applicants seeking admission and of practitioners against whom charges have been levied. The materials later in the chapter present examples of both these phenomena.

The problems set out on pages 665-666 raise a number of important issues in the discipline process. Some of the materials in the preceding chapter and in this chapter are specifically related to these issues. Some of the materials also address broader issues of discipline that must be faced by the profession and society: should the major focus of a disciplinary system be on lawyers' professional conduct or on lawyers' performance of their contractual obligations toward their clients? Should the discipline system be largely in professional control, through judicial supervision of boards staffed entirely or largely by lawyers? Or should the discipline system fall under more traditional legislative-executive control, with the legal staff under the control of nonlawyers? The materials in this chapter attempt to give a sense of the way various systems are operating and to offer controversial solutions to some of the shortcomings perceived by the authors. They are a starting point for discussion and are intended to be read critically.

NOTE: Disciplinary Rules — Problems of Generality

A particular difficulty to be considered in connection with the Disciplinary Rules of the Model Code, one that existed with the former Canons of Ethics as well, is that the drafters have given us two types of Disciplinary Rules. They are the hallmark of the statutory drafter who does not want to leave anything out. First we have the rather specific prohibition of certain types of conduct. This is followed by a very broad catchall. An example is contained in DR 1-102, entitled "Misconduct." Among other things that a lawyer shall not do, we find subsection (4), "Engage in conduct involving dishonesty, fraud, deceit, or misrepresentation," a rather specific prohibition; subsection (3), "Engage in illegal conduct involving moral turpitude," a more general prohibition that has usually been made specific by court opinions; subsection (5), "Engage in conduct that is prejudicial to the administration of justice"; and then subsection (6), "Engage in any other conduct that adversely reflects on his fitness to practice law." The Model Rules also contain the same combination of specific and general prohibitions because they replicate the exact wording of subsections (4) and (5), although there is no equivalent to subsections (3) and (6). See Model Rule 8.4(c) and (d).

What will happen if a very general disciplinary rule is used as the basis for imposition of discipline? In re Ruffalo, 390 U.S. 544 (1968), may provide some assistance. The Supreme Court reviewed a disbarment by a federal court of appeals that had been based on a prior state court disbarment. One ground for the state disbarment had been that the lawyer, who handled a lot of Federal Employer's Liability Act cases for plaintiffs, had hired an employee of the B. & O. Railroad as an investigator. He occasionally had the employee investigate suits against the B. & O. There was no evidence that the employee investigated cases in the yard where he worked, or that he used confidential information, or worked for the lawyer on company time.

The Ohio Supreme Court nevertheless concluded that "one who believes that it is proper to employ and pay another to work against the interest of his regular employer is not qualified to be a member of the Ohio Bar." Mahoning County Bar Assn. v. Ruffalo, 176 Ohio St. 263, 269, 199 N.E.2d 396, 401 (1964). The federal district court found no misconduct, but the lawyer was disbarred by the Court of Appeals for the Sixth Circuit. The Supreme Court reversed the Court of Appeals because its decision was infected by procedural defects amounting to a denial of due process in the state court proceeding. Justices White and Marshall disagreed with the procedural basis for the majority's decision but concurred on the merits. In considering general standards for disbarment, Justice White stated (390 U.S. at 555):

> . . . members of a bar can be assumed to know that certain kinds of conduct, generally condemned by responsible men, will be grounds for disbarment. This class of conduct certainly includes the criminal offenses traditionally known as malum in se. It also includes conduct which all responsible attorneys would recognize as improper for a member of the profession.

He then noted that neither of those situations was present in *Ruffalo*, where reasonable people might, and in fact did, differ, and went on to say (390 U.S. at 556):

> I would hold that a federal court may not deprive any attorney of the opportunity to practice his profession on the basis of a determination after the fact that conduct is unethical if responsible attorneys would differ in appraising the propriety of that conduct.

This view is, I think, very helpful to an understanding of those Disciplinary Rules of the Model Code that contain very general language. It indicates that there are some categories of conduct for which there can be disciplinary action even though there is only a general prohibitory rule in the Model Code, or no rule at all, but that when one gets into a doubtful area there must be specificity — and *Ruffalo* is such a case.

In making these comments about those Disciplinary Rules that are exceedingly broad, such as the ones relating to misconduct just quoted, I do not mean to imply that that such provisions ought to have been omitted. What is needed is that those charged with interpretation and enforcement build up the common law relating to these rules both as a guide to the profession and as a necessary predicate for enforcement. The necessity that these bodies be disinterested, responsible, and enjoy the confidence of the profession and the public is a subject all its own, and it was beyond the scope of the drafters' charge. But evidence that a problem exists with respect to disciplinary bodies in this country is everywhere.* (See especially the materials that follow this Note.)

The most thorough study of the status of disciplinary enforcement, with carefully considered recommendations for improvement, is that of the American Bar Association's Special Committee on Evaluation of Disciplinary Enforcement under the chairmanship of former Justice Clark of the Supreme Court. The Clark Committee presented its recommendations through a series of 36 problems whose mere listing gives a good insight into its conclusions. In the actual report there is discussion and a recommendation with respect to each problem. Only the summary listing is presented here.

ABA SPECIAL COMMITTEE ON EVALUATION OF DISCIPLINARY ENFORCEMENT, PROBLEMS AND RECOMMENDATIONS IN DISCIPLINARY ENFORCEMENT

(1970)

[Summary of Table of Contents]

---

*In *Ruffalo* itself the Supreme Court noted pointedly, although it did not pass on the issue, that the initial investigation was made by the Association of American Railroads, which referred charges to the president of the local county Bar Association, who happened to be local counsel to the B. & O. R.R., and that the County Bar Association then instituted charges against Mr. Ruffalo with regard to his employment of a B. & O. employee in connection with suits against the B. & O. 390 U.S. at 549.

Problem 25 Inadequate provisions concerning public disclosure of pending disciplinary proceedings

Problem 26 Failure to publish the achievements of disciplinary agencies

Problem 27 No provision for protecting clients when an attorney is disciplined, or when he disappears or dies while under investigation

Problem 28 Disbarred attorneys too readily reinstated by the courts

Part C — Interagency Relations

Problem 29 No procedure for notifying disciplinary agencies when attorneys admitted to practice in their jurisdiction are disciplined elsewhere

Problem 30 No consultation and exchange of information among disciplinary agencies about their mutual problems in disciplinary enforcement

Part D — Ancillary Problems

Problem 31 Reluctance on the part of lawyers and judges to report instances of professional misconduct

Problem 32 No requirement that attorneys keep accurate records of client funds in their possession and have records audited

Problem 33 No training courses on ethical standards and disciplinary enforcement for judges responsible for lawyer discipline

Problem 34 Attorneys accused of crime given preferential treatment by law enforcement authorities and the courts

Problem 35 No state-wide registration of attorneys (applicable to non-integrated jurisdictions only)

Problem 36 Limited ancillary bar association services to complement the work of disciplinary agencies

While the Clark Committee's Report is dated 1970 and while more attention has been paid to the disciplinary system in recent years, the problems noted by that committee still remain and in some places may even have worsened. A series of scathing reports about the operation of the disciplinary system in the nation's largest bar, California, was issued in the 1980s by Robert Fellmeth, law professor at San Diego Law School and director of the Center for Public Interest Law, who was appointed by the California legislature to monitor the state's disciplinary system. He highlighted especially the huge backlog, delay in complex cases, and failure to impose adequate discipline. One highly controversial response of the Board of Governors of the State Bar, which under California's unified bar operates the disciplinary system, was to propose raising dues to the highest level of any bar in the U.S. to help improve the disciplinary system.

Thus the conclusions of Messrs. Steele and Nimmer in the study of disciplinary machinery referred to earlier, p. 640, although undertaken in the 1970s, are still valid today. After examining a wealth of data relating to enforcement, defects in the current systems, and policy options for reform, they reported as follows:

A variety of tentative and experimental approaches are emerging in the field of professional regulation where the sole apparent concern has long been serious attorney deviance. They include specialization programs, mandatory post-licensing education, client security funds, fee arbitration, and client relations committees. This diversification of regulatory social control strategies is instructive in light of the basic characteristics of disciplinary process and caseload and, more broadly, the scope of the profession's underlying regulatory obligations.

The contemporary policy debate concerning the legal profession's regulation of the behavior of individual lawyers has, in large part, failed to address underlying issues as to the scope and focus of the regulatory function itself. The question whether the legal profession is doing an adequate job of controlling lawyer conduct has been hotly debated by diverse factions with repetitious polemic. Most participants in the debate have, however, accepted without discussion a severely restricted conception of the underlying function of regulation. The deviance control model has predominated.

Public debate has centered on whether ethical norms are routinely obeyed or ignored and whether the organized bar is zealous, indifferent, or corrupt in dealing with known instances of lawyer misconduct. The deviance perspective is important, but it cannot be viewed as the only important issue to be addressed in conceptualizing and implementing a regulatory system for the control of lawyers. In addition, it is important to note that deviance control cannot be effectively pursued in isolation from other regulatory objectives or divorced from an understanding of the contexts in which problematic attorney behavior occurs, whether or not such misconduct is retrospectively labeled as deviance.

The issues commonly addressed in the public debate are oversimplified. The deviance perspective cannot be maintained as the exclusive focus in the face of the real world environment of lawyer conduct and client and public grievances. Different jurisdictions at different times and in different situations have functioned well or poorly in the task of investigating, prosecuting, and imposing sanctions on instances of serious lawyer deviance. Whether this task is performed well or poorly, the necessary focus on deviance is not, in itself, responsive to the persistent, concrete problems that arise in attorney-client relationships. The deviance perspective expresses laudable indignation about serious lawyer misconduct and leads to a necessary focus on deviance control. The all-but-exclusive focus on deviance control, however, imposes artificial standards for determining what problematic lawyer conduct will be dealt with at all. The actual, though unintended, consequence of an overemphasis on deviance control is to preclude active response to most expressed grievances by the creation of an excessively high threshold for official intervention of any sort. At a minimum, client complaints to disciplinary agencies indicate important areas of public dissatisfaction with the conduct of attorneys. Can the regulatory system continue to ignore most of these grievances, at best dealing with them in informal and only marginally effective ways? It is our contention that the present regulation of lawyers overemphasizes the control of serious lawyer misconduct at the expense of a more balanced regulatory focus.

There has been a perceptible shift in the mix of regulatory control strategies. While no unified policy of regulation of lawyers has emerged, an institutional drift has begun away from total reliance on the deviance control model toward broader policies that include administrative and dispute management models. If this evolutionary change is to result in effective and responsive institutions and not disorganization and empty rhetoric, the level of discussion must be raised from the current politicized debate about ethically defective lawyers and corrupt or inactive disciplinary agencies to a broader conceptualization of the policy issues and alternatives available to the task of regulating lawyers. We have analyzed the functioning of current regulatory systems and have suggested a conceptual framework for the constructive consideration of policy options. The mix of intervention strategies as well as the total amount of intervention into the behavior of individual lawyers must be addressed as an integrated set of policy issues and options if the regulation of lawyers is to be effective.

"Self-regulation" by the profession has become a major focus of critical examination of the profession. Many attacks on the profession focusing on this feature, however, reveal a good deal of misunderstanding about the term. Very often the term is used to indicate a belief that the entire structure of professional regulation — admission and discipline — is conducted by the legal profession freed from governmental control or restraint. That view is misleading for often it fails to take account of the role that lawyers play in the normal regulatory process when the legal profession is not involved. The crucial question is whether lawyers are involved in the regulatory process merely as representatives of the profession or whether they are involved as government officials in a meaningful way — that is, are they functioning pursuant to relatively specific directions and are they subject to official supervision? The English Inns of Court, which manage the whole system for English barristers, are the paradigm case of self-regulation. A state agency, appointed by the governor pursuant to a detailed legislative mandate, that used lawyers only as subordinate staff to handle its normal legal work, would be the paradigm example of absence of self-regulation.

All jurisdictions in the United States fall somewhere in between and there is a good deal of diversity. In recent years, however, there has been noticeable movement toward lessening the self-regulation features. While lawyers predominate as the operative personnel even at policy-making levels, the bodies making disciplinary recommendations to the courts are tending more and more to be separated from the local bar associations through appointment by the state courts; their counsel, the "bar counsel," also often hold similar official appointments. Indeed, bar counsel have formed their own association, the National Organization of Bar Counsel, and, as governmental officials charged with policing the profession, they are beginning to express their own different perspective on professional issues. Thus, while it seems accurate to state, as Steele and Nimmer do in an unexcerpted portion of their article, that state supreme courts are generally passive in supervising the profession, we should not infer from the fact that the task of supervision is always being exercised by lawyers acting solely in their private capacity. The role of lawyers acting in an official governmental capacity is rising and the long-term prospect is for even greater official regulation of the profession.

A second issue is the desirability of including lay personnel in the regulatory process. The Clark Committee did not regard its mandate as including consideration of the issue whether there should be lay participation in the discipline process. It limited its investigation to suggestions for improvement of the present system. (Report, Preface at xvii.) In various places in the Clark Report, however, a preference for self-policing is disclosed. See, e.g., pp. 61-66 of the Report.

This premise of the Report is challenged, both implicitly and explicitly, by Messrs. Steele and Nimmer. It is true, as the Clark Report notes, that "the trier of facts should be familiar with the practices peculiar to the profession." (Report, p. 137.) On the other hand, the Report itself notes the reluctance of lawyers and judges "to report instances of professional misconduct" (Report, Problem 31, p. 671 supra, and Problem 59 of these materials, p. 453), and suggests reluctance and even hostility toward dealing with reported misconduct. Moreover, while the Report is undoubtedly correct that lay persons may have difficulty comprehending difficult and complicated professional issues, that is a problem that the profession "tolerates" or even cherishes with respect to jury trial of complicated cases. And it is interesting to note the example given in the Report of a situation where lay personnel might be too easy on lawyer misconduct. "For example, a jury of laymen unfamiliar with the abuses that necessitate the prohibition against improper solicitation may exhibit their hostility to a standard they do not understand by exonerating the accused attorney." (Report, p. 137.) Solicitation and advertising are areas where increasingly not only lay persons but also the Supreme Court have been stimulating rethinking about the bar's standards. See pp. 481-522. Lay personnel on a discipline committee might well ask the questions that would force the lawyers, in articulating a response, to rethink standards that formerly were automatically accepted. This line of thinking has led several states to reorganize their disciplinary procedures to include lay members on their statewide disciplinary committee. Their experience will be worth examining over the coming years to see whether this change in membership makes an appreciable difference in the resolution of disciplinary matters. Another possibility is a more traditional state agency. In many, if not most, jurisdictions that solution would present a substantial constitutional problem of violation of separation of powers, as illustrated by the following case.

WAJERT v. STATE ETHICS COMMN.
491 Pa. 255, 420 A.2d 439 (1980)

EAGEN, Chief Justice.

On March 12, 1979, the Honorable John M. Wajert, Judge of the Court of Common Pleas of Chester County, acting pursuant to Sections 7(9)(i) and (ii) of the State Ethics Act,[1] requested an opinion from the State Ethics Commission. The issue presented to the Commission was: "May a Judge of a Court of Common Pleas, upon retirement or resignation, represent a client before that Court within the first year after such resignation?"

On May 11, 1979, the Commission responded to the request as follows: "It is the Commission's Opinion that a Common Pleas Judge is barred by Sections 3(e) of the Act from representing any person before the Court with which he was associated for a period of one year following resignation or retirement." *Wajert*, Opinion 1978-5.

On May 29, 1979, Judge Wajert filed a Petition for Declaratory Judgment in Commonwealth Court seeking, inter alia, a declaration [that] the Act, 65 P.S. §401 et seq., in its application to judges and justices of the courts of the Commonwealth of Pennsylvania was unconstitutional and of no force and effect. On October 30, 1979, the Commonwealth Court, 407 A.2d 125, dismissed preliminary objections to the petition filed by the Ethics Commission. On November 27, 1979, the Commission consented to the entry of a final judgment in favor of the petitioner but specifically reserved its right to appeal from the judgment. On November 28, the Commonwealth Court entered a final judgment ruling Section 3(e) of the State Ethics Act, 65 P.S. §403 (e), to be of no force and effect to judges of the Courts of Common Pleas in the Commonwealth of Pennsylvania. The Commission then filed this appeal.

Section 3(e) of the Ethics Act, 65 P.S. §403(e), provides: "No former official or public employee shall represent a person, with or without compensation, on any matter before the governmental body with which he has been associated for one year after he leaves that body." Section 2 of the Act, 65 P.S. §402, defines the term "public official" to include any

---

1. Act of October 4, 1978, P.L. 883, No. 170 §1 et seq., 65 P.S. §401 et seq. (Supp. 1980-81) [hereinafter: 65 P.S. § —].

elected or appointed official in the judicial branch of the State or any political subdivision thereof and the term "governmental body" as: "Any department, authority, commission, committee, council, board, bureau, division, service, office, officer, administration, legislative body, or other establishment in the Executive, Legislative or Judicial Branch of the State or a political subdivision thereof."

In its opinion filed in support of the judgment, the Commonwealth Court reasoned that a judge who retired or resigned from his judicial office was clearly a "public official"; that the proscription of 65 P.S. §403(e) would apply to such an individual if a court of law was a "governmental body"; but, that a court of law was not within the definitional purview of "governmental body." The court explained that a court of law was not explicitly included within the definition of "governmental body"; that, since such a court was not explicitly included, the legislature could have intended it to be within the definitional purview of the term only if it was an "establishment in the . . . Judicial Branch of the State"; that whether a court was intended to be such an "establishment" was unclear because no similar nomenclature so referring to a court could be found; that, given this uncertainty, the legislative intent had to be determined by considering, inter alia, see 1 Pa. C.S.A. §1921(c), the purpose of the statute and the presumption that the legislature did not intend to violate the constitution, see 1 Pa. C.S.A. §1922(3); that the primary purpose of the statute was to expose and prevent real and potential conflicts of interests; that, given the fact that the Code of Judicial Conduct and the Code of Professional Responsibility address themselves to "the same mischief," the statute was not intended to proscribe the activities of judges and former judges of the Courts of Common Pleas; and, that a contrary construction of the statute would render it unconstitutional because it would result in the state being a "direct restriction upon the practice of law" and, hence, an improper usurpation of the exclusive power of the Supreme Court of Pennsylvania to regulate the practice of law.

While we consider the Commonwealth Court's effort to interpret this statute in such a way as to avoid declaring it unconstitutional when applied to a former judge laudable in light of the presumption that the legislature does not intend to violate the constitution, we are constrained to disagree with that court's interpretation of the statute. We are persuaded the statute was intended to apply to former judges, but, when so interpreted, it is unconstitutional. . . .

Moreover, since we agree with the Commonwealth Court's interpretation that the term former "public official" includes a judge who has retired or resigned, in our view, 65 P.S. §403(e) clearly applies to judges of the Courts of Common Pleas who have resigned or retired.

Having determined the statute is applicable, we are constrained to hold it unconstitutional insofar as it is applicable to a former judge.[5] In essence, we agree with the Commonwealth Court's reasoning that application of this statute to a former judge constitutes an infringement on the Supreme Court's inherent and exclusive power to govern the conduct of those privileged to practice law in this Commonwealth. Long before the Ethics Act was enacted, this Court adopted the Code of Professional Responsibility enunciating the standards governing the professional conduct of those engaged in the practice of law in this Commonwealth. In the rules enforcing that Code, this Court had made it abundantly clear that supervising the conduct of an attorney, including that of a former judge, before the courts of this Commonwealth was a matter exclusively for this Court. Pa. R.D.E. 103 states:

> The Supreme Court declares that it has inherent and *exclusive* power to supervise the conduct of attorneys who are its officers (which power is reasserted in Section 10(c) of Article V of the Constitution of Pennsylvania) and in furtherance thereof promulgates these rules which shall supersede all other court rules and statutes pertaining to disciplinary enforcement heretofore promulgated. [Emphasis added.]

There can be no doubt that the statute has infringed on this Court's *exclusive* power to govern the conduct of an attorney, and is, hence, unconstitutional. Moreover, that power has been specifically exercised to deal with the mischief the statute attempts to address. DR 9-101(A) of the Code of Professional Responsibility prohibits a lawyer from accepting private employment in a matter upon the merits of which he acted in a judicial capacity. See also DR 9-101(B) and (C).

Order affirmed.

NOTES

1. Note the strong hint in footnote 5 that the logic of *Wajert* covers not just court supervision of former judges but also attorneys generally. While most courts have regarded regulation of attorneys as falling with-

---

5. We are not unmindful that the reasons set forth infra for our ruling strongly suggest the statute is also unconstitutional in application to attorneys who seek to practice in Pennsylvania's courts. We need not now so rule and explicitly refrain from doing so, but feel compelled to point out our conscious consideration of the possible breadth of our ruling. Such consideration is essential, since, given our interpretation of the statute and its application to courts of law and its possible application to law clerks, see 65 P.S. §402, the courts of this Commonwealth might be effectively precluded from employing law school graduates as law clerks because persons would fear such employment would prohibit them from practicing before the court by which they were employed for one year after the termination of their employment.

in the "inherent" power of the judiciary, not all have been so inflexible as the Pennsylvania court. See Sadler v. Oregon State Bar, 275 Or. 279, 550 P.2d 1218 (1976) and Opinion of the Justices, 375 Mass. 795, 376 N.E.2d 810 (1978) for opinions upholding legislation similar to that of *Wajert* on the theory that it complemented and did not conflict with ultimate judicial power.

2. Consideration of the appropriate forum for attorney discipline involves not only issues of separation of powers among branches of government but also division of powers between the federal and state governments. Pieces of this issue have already been presented in Chapters 5 and 6, see pp. 288-300 and 360, in the context of the power of federal administrative agencies to regulate the conduct of attorneys who appear before them and the power of state courts to regulate the conduct of federal prosecutors practicing in those states. As we have seen, these matters involve not only procedural questions of the appropriate disciplinary body but substantive questions of the appropriate body to set standards of conduct.

One state Supreme Court has gone very far in asserting its jurisdiction to discipline federal prosecutors for activities in the federal courts. In Waters v. Barr, 747 P.2d 900 (1987), the Nevada Supreme Court asserted such authority with respect to federal prosecutors admitted and even those not admitted to practice in Nevada. In the latter situation, it defined its power as existing at least with respect to misbehavior that occurred in Nevada and that affected other Nevada lawyers or the integrity of the Nevada bar. Accord, In re Kolibash, — F. Supp. — (S.D. W. Va. 1988) (dealing only with members of the West Virginia bar).

An important problem with which every disciplinary committee must deal is the meaning of the major Supreme Court decision dealing with the rights of lawyers subjected to disciplinary proceedings. Spevack v. Klein, which follows, was a 5-4 decision that forbade disciplinary committees from imposing discipline for a certain type of non-cooperation by lawyers, and that also left an enormous area of uncertainty because of the generality of the language in the opinions making up the majority.

SPEVACK v. KLEIN
385 U.S. 511 (1967)

Justice DOUGLAS announced the judgment of the Court and delivered an opinion in which The Chief Justice, Justice BLACK and Justice BRENNAN concur.

This is a proceeding to discipline petitioner, a member of the New York Bar, for professional misconduct. Of the various charges made, only one survived, viz., the refusal of petitioner to honor a subpoena duces tecum served on him in that he refused to produce the demanded financial records and refused to testify at the judicial inquiry. Petitioner's sole defense was that the production of the records and his testimony would tend to incriminate him. The Appellate Division of the New York Supreme Court ordered petitioner disbarred, holding that the constitutional privilege against self-incrimination was not available to him in light of our decision in Cohen v. Hurley, 366 U.S. 117. See 24 App. Div. 2d 653. The Court of Appeals affirmed, 16 N.Y.2d 1048, 213 N.E.2d 457, 17 N.Y.2d 490, 214 N.E.2d 373. . . .

Cohen v. Hurley was a five-to-four decision rendered in 1961. It is practically on all fours with the present case. . . .

In 1964 the Court in another five-to-four decision held that the Self-Incrimination Clause of the Fifth Amendment was applicable to the States by reason of the Fourteenth. Malloy v. Hogan, 378 U.S. 1. . . .

And so the question emerges whether the principle of Malloy v. Hogan is inapplicable because petitioner is a member of the Bar. We conclude that Cohen v. Hurley should be overruled, that the Self-Incrimination Clause of the Fifth Amendment has been absorbed in the Fourteenth, that it extends its protection to lawyers as well as to other individuals, and that it should not be watered down by imposing the dishonor of disbarment and the deprivation of a livelihood as a price for asserting it. These views, expounded in the dissents in Cohen v. Hurley, need not be elaborated again.

We said in Malloy v. Hogan: "The Fourteenth Amendment secures against state invasion the same privilege that the Fifth Amendment guarantees against federal infringement — the right of a person to remain silent unless he chooses to speak in the unfettered exercise of his own will, and to suffer no penalty . . . for such silence." 378 U.S., at 8.

In this context "penalty" is not restricted to fine or imprisonment. It means, as we said in Griffin v. California, 380 U.S. 609, the imposition of any sanction which makes assertion of the Fifth Amendment privilege "costly." Id., at 614. . . . What we said in Malloy and Griffin is in the tradition of the broad protection given the privilege at least since Boyd v. United States, 116 U.S. 616, 634–635, where compulsory production of books and papers of the owner of goods sought to be forfeited was held to be compelling him to be a witness against himself. . . .

The threat of disbarment and the loss of professional standing, professional reputation, and of livelihood are powerful forms of compulsion to make a lawyer relinquish the privilege. That threat is indeed as powerful an instrument of compulsion as "the use of legal process to force from the lips of the accused individual the evidence necessary to convict him. . . ." United States v. White, 322 U.S. 694, 698.

Lawyers are not excepted from the words "No person . . . shall be compelled in any criminal case to be a witness against himself"; and we can imply no exception. Like the school teacher in Slochower v. Board of Education, 350 U.S. 551, and the policemen in Garrity v. New Jersey, . . . lawyers also enjoy first-class citizenship.

The Court of Appeals alternately affirmed the judgment disbarring petitioner on the ground that under Shapiro v. United States, 335 U.S. 1, and the required records doctrine he was under a duty to produce the withheld records. The Court of Appeals did not elaborate on the point; nor did the Appellate Division advert to it. . . .

The *Shapiro* case dealt with a federal price control regulation requiring merchants to keep sales records. The Court called them records with "public aspects," as distinguished from private papers (335 U.S., at 34); and concluded by a divided vote that their compelled production did not violate the Fifth Amendment. We are asked to overrule *Shapiro*. But we find it unnecessary to reach it. . . .

The Court of Appeals was the first to suggest that the privilege against self-incrimination was not applicable *to the records*. Petitioner, however, had been disbarred on the theory that the privilege was applicable *to the records*, but that the invocation of the privilege could lead to disbarment. His disbarment cannot be affirmed on the ground that the privilege was not applicable in the first place. Cole v. Arkansas, 333 U.S. 196, 201. For that procedure would deny him all opportunity at the trial to show that the Rule, fairly construed and understood, should not be given a broad sweep and to make a record that the documents demanded by the subpoena had no "public aspects" within the required records rule but were private papers.

Reversed.

Justice Fortas, concurring in the judgment. I agree that Cohen v. Hurley, 366 U.S. 117 (1961), should be overruled. But I would distinguish between a lawyer's right to remain silent and that of a public employee who is asked questions specifically, directly, and narrowly relating to the performance of his official duties as distinguished from his beliefs or other matters that are not within the scope of the specific duties which he undertook faithfully to perform as part of his employment by the State. This Court has never held, for example, that a policeman may not be discharged for refusal in disciplinary proceedings to testify as to his conduct as a police officer. It is quite a different matter if the State seeks to use the testimony given under this lash in a subsequent criminal proceeding. Garrity v. New Jersey, [385 U.S., at] 493.

But a lawyer is not an employee of the State. He does not have the responsibility of an employee to account to the State for his actions because he does not perform them as agent of the State. His responsibility to the State is to obey its laws and the rules of conduct that it has generally laid down as part of its licensing procedures. The special responsibilities that he assumes as licensee of the State and officer of the court do not carry with them a diminution, however limited, of his Fifth Amendment rights. Accordingly, I agree that Spevack could not be disbarred for asserting his privilege against self-incrimination.

If this case presented the question whether a lawyer might be disbarred for refusal to keep or to produce, upon properly authorized and particularized demand, records which the lawyer was lawfully and properly required to keep by the State as a proper part of its functions in relation to him as licensor of his high calling, I should feel compelled to vote to affirm, although I would be prepared in an appropriate case to re-examine the scope of the principle announced in Shapiro v. United States, 335 U.S. 1 (1948). I am not prepared to indicate doubt as to the essential validity of *Shapiro*. However, I agree that the required records issue is not appropriately presented here, for the reasons stated by my Brother Douglas. On this basis I join in the judgment of the Court.

Justice HARLAN, whom Justice CLARK and Justice STEWART join, dissenting. This decision, made in the name of the Constitution, permits a lawyer suspected of professional misconduct to thwart direct official inquiry of him without fear of disciplinary action. What is done today will be disheartening and frustrating to courts and bar associations throughout the country in their efforts to maintain high standards at the bar.

It exposes this Court itself to the possible indignity that it may one day have to admit to its own bar such a lawyer unless it can somehow get at the truth of suspicions, the investigation of which the applicant has previously succeeded in blocking. For I can perceive no distinction between "admission" and "disbarment" in the rationale of what is now held. The decision might even lend some color of support for justifying the appointment to the bench of a lawyer who, like petitioner, prevents full inquiry into his professional behavior. And, still more pervasively, this decision can hardly fail to encourage oncoming generations of lawyers to think of their calling as imposing on them no higher standards of behavior than might be acceptable in the general marketplace. The soundness of a constitutional doctrine carrying such denigrating import for our profession is surely suspect on its face. . . .

It should first be emphasized that the issue here is plainly not whether lawyers may "enjoy first-class citizenship." Nor is the issue whether lawyers may be deprived of their federal privilege against self-incrimination, whether or not criminal prosecution is undertaken against them. These diversionary questions have of course not been presented or even remotely suggested by this case either here or in the courts of New York. The plurality opinion's vivid rhetoric thus serves only to obscure the issues with which we are actually confronted, and to hinder their serious consideration. The true question here is instead the proper scope and effect of the privilege against self-incrimination under the Fourteenth Amendment in state disciplinary proceedings against attorneys. In particular, we are required to determine whether petitioner's disbarment for his failure to provide information relevant to charges of misconduct in carrying on his law practice impermissibly vitiated the protection afforded by the privilege. This important question warrants more complete and discriminating analysis than that given to it by the plurality opinion.

This Court reiterated only last Term that the constitutional privilege against self-incrimination "has never been given the full scope which the values it helps to protect suggest." Schmerber v. California, 384 U.S. 757, 762. The Constitution contains no formulae with which we can calculate the areas within this "full scope" to which the privilege should extend, and the Court has therefore been obliged to fashion for itself standards for the application of the privilege. In federal cases stemming from Fifth Amendment claims, the Court has chiefly derived its standards from consideration of two factors: the history and purposes of the privilege, and the character and urgency of the other public interests involved. See, e.g., Orloff v. Willoughby, 345 U.S. 83; Davis v. United States, 328 U.S. 582; Shapiro v. United States, 335 U.S. 1. . . .

It cannot be claimed that the purposes served by the New York rules at issue here, compendiously aimed at "ambulance chasing" and its attendant evils, are unimportant or unrelated to the protection of legitimate state interests. This Court has often held that the States have broad authority to devise both requirements for admission and standards of practice for those who wish to enter the professions. E.g., Hawker v. New York, 170 U.S. 189; Dent v. West Virginia, 129 U.S. 114; Barsky v. Board of Regents, 347 U.S. 442. The States may demand any qualifications which have "a rational connection with the applicant's fitness or capacity," Schware v. Board of Bar Examiners, 353 U.S. 232, 239, and may exclude any applicant who fails to satisfy them. In particular, a State may require evidence of good character, and may place the onus of its production upon the applicant. Konigsberg v. State Bar of California, 366 U.S. 36. Finally, a State may without constitutional objection require in the same fashion continuing evidence of professional and moral fitness as a condition of the retention of the right to practice. Cohen v. Hurley, 366 U.S. 117. All this is in no way questioned by today's decision.

As one prerequisite of continued practice in New York, the Appellate Division, Second Department, of the Supreme Court of New York has determined that attorneys must actively assist the courts and the appropriate professional groups in the prevention and detection of unethical legal activities. The Second Department demands that attorneys maintain various records, file statements of retainer in certain kinds of cases, and upon request provide information, all relevant to the use by the attorneys of contingent fee arrangements in such cases. These rules are intended to protect the public from the abuses revealed by a lengthy series of investigations of malpractices in the geographical area represented by the Second Department. It cannot be said that these conditions are arbitrary or unreasonable, or that they are unrelated to an attorney's continued fitness to practice. English courts since Edward I have endeavored to regulate the qualification and practice of lawyers, always in hope that this might better assure the integrity and evenhandedness of the administration of justice. Very similar efforts have been made in the United States since the 17th century. These efforts have protected the systems of justice in both countries from abuse, and have directly contributed to public confidence in those systems. Such efforts give appropriate recognition to the principle accepted both here and in England that lawyers are officers of the court who perform a fundamental role in the administration of justice. The rules at issue here are in form and spirit a continuation of these efforts, and accordingly are reasonably calculated to serve the most enduring interests of the citizens of New York.

Without denying the urgency or significance of the public purposes served by these rules, the plurality opinion has seemingly concluded that they may not be enforced because any consequence of a claim of the privilege against self-incrimination which renders that claim "costly" is an "instrument of compulsion" which impermissibly infringes on the protection offered by the privilege. Apart from brief obiter dicta in recent opinions of this Court, this broad proposition is entirely without support in the construction hitherto given to the privilege, and is directly inconsistent with a series of cases in which this Court has indicated the principles which are properly applicable here. The Court has not before held that the Federal Government and the States are forbidden to permit any consequences to result from a claim of the privilege; it has instead recognized that such consequences may vary widely in kind and intensity, and that these differences warrant individual examination both of the hazard, if any, offered to the essential purposes of the privilege, and of the public interests protected by the consequence. This process is far better calculated than the broad prohibition embraced by the plurality to serve both the purposes of the privilege and the other important public values which are often at stake in such cases. It would assure the integrity of the privilege, and yet guarantee the most generous opportunities for the pursuit of other public values, by selecting the rule or standard most appropriate for the hazards and characteristics of each consequence.

One such rule has already been plainly approved by this Court. It seems clear to me that this rule is applicable to the situation now before us. The Court has repeatedly recognized that it is permissible to deny a status or authority to a claimant of the privilege against self-incrimination if his claim has prevented full assessment of his qualifications for the status or authority. Under this rule, the applicant may not both decline to disclose information necessary to demonstrate his fitness, and yet demand that he receive the benefits of the status. He may not by his interjection of the privilege either diminish his obligation to establish his qualifications, or escape the consequences exacted by the State for a failure to satisfy that obligation.

This rule was established by this Court in Orloff v. Willoughby, 345 U.S. 83. The Court there held that a doctor who refused, under a claim of the privilege against self-incrimination, to divulge whether he was a Communist was not entitled by right to receive a commission as an Army officer, although he had apparently satisfied every other prerequisite for a commission. The Court expressly noted that "[n]o one believes he can be punished" for asserting the privilege, but said that it had "no hesitation" in holding that the petitioner nonetheless could not both rely on the privilege to deny relevant information to the commissioning authorities and demand that he be appointed to a position of "honor and trust." 345 U.S., at 91. The Court concluded that "we cannot doubt that the President of the United States, before certifying his confidence in an officer and appointing him to a commissioned rank, has the right to learn whatever facts the President thinks may affect his fitness." Ibid. . . .

[Prior] cases [citations omitted] . . . make plain that so long as state authorities do not derive any imputation of guilt from a claim of the privilege, they may in the course of a bona fide assessment of an employee's fitness for public employment require that the employee disclose information reasonably related to his fitness, and may order his discharge if he declines. Identical principles have been applied by this Court to applicants for admission to the bar who have refused to produce information pertinent to their professional and moral qualifications. Konigsberg v. State Bar of California, 366 U.S. 36; In re Anastaplo, 366 U.S. 82. In sum, all these cases adopted principles under the Fourteenth Amendment which are plainly congruent with those applied in Orloff v. Willoughby, supra, and other federal cases to Fifth Amendment claims. . . .

Justice WHITE, dissenting. In . . . Garrity v. New Jersey, [385 U.S. 493 (1967)], the Court apparently holds that in every imaginable circumstance the threat of discharge issued by one public officer to another will be impermissible compulsion sufficient to render subsequent answers to questions inadmissible in a criminal proceeding. . . . [W]ith *Garrity* on the books, the Court compounds its error in Spevack v. Klein. . . .

The petitioner . . . refused to testify and to produce any of his records. He incriminated himself in no way whatsoever. The Court nevertheless holds that he may not be disbarred for his refusal to do so. Such a rule would seem justifiable only on the ground that it is an essential measure to protect against self-incrimination — to prevent what may well be a successful attempt to elicit incriminating admissions. But Garrity excludes such statements, and their fruits, from a criminal proceeding and therefore frustrates in advance any effort to compel admissions which could be used to obtain a criminal conviction. I therefore see little legal or practical basis, in terms of the privilege against self-incrimination protected by the Fifth Amendment, for preventing the discharge of a public employee or the disbarment of a lawyer who refuses to talk about the performance of his public duty.* . . .

NOTES

1. Justice Fortas's concurrence clearly implies that a public employee may be discharged for invoking the privilege against self-incrimination with respect to "questions specifically, directly, and narrowly relating to the performance of his official duties." He distinguishes the situation of a lawyer who is not a state employee and whose only responsibility to the State "is to obey its laws and the rules of conduct that it has generally laid down as part of its licensing procedures." (p. 680.) Unless Justice Fortas meant to include the rules that the profession has imposed on itself — not only rules of behavior but also of responsibility — within the "licensing procedures" of the State, his conception of what it means to become a lawyer is unfortunately narrow. Is it unfair to link Justice Fortas's apparent failure in *Spevack* to acknowledge the responsibilities of lawyers to the public with an insensitivity that later resulted in his own forced resignation from the Court? See MacKenzie, The Appearance of Justice 72-76 (1974) and Murphy, Fortas: The Rise and Ruin of a Supreme Court Justice (1988), for a discussion of those events. In any event, the relationship between the state and the profession is considerably more intricate than his opinion recognizes. In a thoughtful discussion of *Spevack*, Russell Niles and Judith Kaye made the following comments about the Fortas concurrence (Niles & Kaye, Spevack v. Klein: Milestone or Millstone in Bar Discipline?, 53 A.B.A.J. 1121, 1122 (1967)):

> The practice of law is now, more than ever, a public profession involving a public trust.[10] The Supreme Court has recently gone farther than ever before in insisting on the right to counsel — in calling on lawyers to be the protectors of the accused, the indigent and, most recently, certain juveniles. Merely by reason of license, attorneys are entrusted with the defense of the life and liberty of others. No other citizens have such power.
>
> Other extraordinary powers of lawyers are commonplace in a commercial practice. Only a lawyer can represent in court the interests of other

---

*The opinion of my Brother Douglas professes not to resolve whether policemen may be discharged for refusing to cooperate with an investigation into alleged misconduct. However, the reasoning used to reach his result in the case of lawyers would seemingly apply with equal persuasiveness in the case of public employees.

10. See Mayer, The Lawyers, Chapter 1 (1967); Cole, Bar Discipline and Spevack v. Klein, 53 A.B.A.J. 819 (1967).

persons and corporations; he can enter into stipulations and settlements and receive money in his client's behalf. In New York a lawyer on his signature alone may issue subpoenas,[11] requiring personal attendance and production of documents; he can cause expense, mental anguish, degradation and even the loss of liberty for anyone who chooses to ignore his subpoena. On his signature alone, he can require the sheriff to seize personal property[12] and he can place an encumbrance on real property.[13] There are many important ex parte orders available to him where without contest or adversary, the court must rely on the attorney's word.[14]

In the interests of the public, these powers presuppose that the attorney is an individual of utmost honesty and good character, that he continues to meet high professional standards. . . .

Once one reaches an opinion about the proper scope of the public responsibilities of a lawyer, however, one is still left to decide the proper scope of *Spevack*, for the former does not automatically decide the latter.

2. The distinction between lawyers and public officials, urged by Justice Fortas in *Spevack*, was adopted, at least in dicta, by the Court in Gardner v. Broderick, 392 U.S. 273 (1968), in an opinion by Justice Fortas.

3. Cohen v. Hurley (p. 679, supra) and Spevack v. Klein both involved situations where the New York courts disbarred lawyers solely on the basis of their assertion of the privilege against self-incrimination. Is the situation in Problem 89 sufficiently different that a different result might obtain?

4. Another issue left open by *Spevack* is the effect of the grant of immunity from criminal prosecution given by the state to a lawyer in connection, say, with an investigation of the conduct of a public official. May a disciplinary committee later disbar the attorney solely on the basis of that compelled testimony? A number of cases have held that it may, on the ground that a disciplinary proceeding is not criminal. See, e.g., In re Unger, 27 App. Div. 2d 925, 282 N.Y.S.2d 158 (1st Dept.), motion for leave to appeal denied, 20 N.Y.2d 642 229 N.E.2d 236, cert. denied, 389 U.S. 1007 (1967); Anonymous Attorneys v. Bar Assn., 41 N.Y. 2d 506, 362 N.E.2d 592 (1977).

5. Some courts have also concluded that *Spevack* does not answer conclusively the question of the scope of the immunity that must be given an attorney to compel testimony against another person in a criminal proceeding. The Florida Supreme Court, after first ruling that the

---

11. New York Civil Practice Laws and Rules [CPLR] §2302(a). In the federal courts the subpoena is technically issued by the clerk, but as a practical matter it is the work of the attorney.

12. CPLR §7102.

13. CPLR §6501.

14. Examples are an order of arrest (CPLR §6111) and an order of attachment (CPLR §6211).

immunity must include immunity against disciplinary proceedings, changed its mind on rehearing and held that it need not because disciplinary proceedings were remedial, not criminal. The dissenters thought that *Spevack* had answered that question for this case as well. DeBock v. State, 512 So.2d 164 (1987), cert. denied, 108 S. Ct. 748 (1988).

6. The final issue remaining unresolved after *Spevack* relates to the required records doctrine of Shapiro v. United States, 335 U.S. 1 (1947). In that case the Supreme Court held, 5-4, that sales records that sellers of fruits and vegetables were required to keep under the Emergency Price Control Act were "public" documents, at least to the extent that no privilege against self-incrimination attached when sellers were subpoenaed to produce the records, and that the statutorily granted immunity did not follow, and was not constitutionally required to follow, from their production. The *Spevack* court left open the question whether in an appropriate case the "required records doctrine" could be applied to any lawyers' records. Many states have a variety of requirements with respect to record keeping, not only with respect to certain kinds of fee arrangements, but also with respect to client funds held by the lawyer. See Niles and Kaye, supra, Note 1, at 1125. Should the privilege against self-incrimination cover such items? If so, how does the disciplinary committee prove its case?

7. The impact of Supreme Court decisions regarding the privilege against self-incrimination on lawyer discipline in the years after *Spevack* is reviewed in Hazard and Beard, A Lawyer's Privilege Against Self-Incrimination in Disciplinary Proceedings, 96 Yale L.J. 1060 (1987).

CHAPTER 12

PROFESSIONAL RESPONSIBILITY AND THE JUDICIAL SYSTEM

PROBLEM 91*

The following questions have been put to (1) a nominee for the federal judiciary by a member of the Senate Judiciary Committee, and (2) a candidate for state judicial office by a newspaper reporter.

(a) To what extent and under what circumstances do you believe that courts should attempt to bring about social, political, or economic changes in society?

(b) What is your opinion of the extent of congressional power under the Fourteenth Amendment to determine which state practices deny equal protection of the laws and to legislate with respect to them?

(c) What are your views regarding the current drug laws, and would your sentencing practices be affected by those views?

(d) Would you evaluate the constitutionality of the provisions in the Legal Services Corporation Act that prohibit funding for lawsuits brought to procure abortions or desegregation?

(e) Whom would you endorse as your party's next Presidential candidate?

May the nominee or the candidate respond to any of those questions?

* This problem is used with the permission of Peter Kirby, Esquire. It is derived from a hypothetical that he created in a paper entitled Judicial Candidates and the First Amendment: The Validity of the New Code of Judicial Conduct. The paper is on file in The Harvard Law School library.

PROBLEM 92

The governor, who has judicial appointing power in your jurisdiction, is not a lawyer; he has put you in charge of recommending judicial appointments. The principal instruction he has given is that when you consider "quality," he wants you to consider quality of result more than so-called quality of mind. He wants judges more interested in doing justice than in following precedent. He asks for your reaction to his views. Respond.

PROBLEM 93

The governor, who has judicial appointing power in your jurisdiction, is dissatisfied with the decisions of the state supreme court, which have wrecked her legislative program. Since her party controls both branches of the state legislature, she has asked you, her attorney general, to draft legislation to add five new members to that court so that her appointees will then form a majority. What do you say to her?

She is also toying with the idea of recommending that all state judges, or perhaps all state appellate judges, be elected. She wants your views on that too. What is your response?

PROBLEM 94

Judge is a member of a state supreme court. The legislature has before it a proposal to alter substantially its "no fault" auto insurance.

(a) May the judge testify before the appropriate legislative committee about the impact of the proposed changes on the business of the judicial system — the effect on caseload, need for juries, costs, and the like?

(b) May the judge express her strongly felt views about the substantive merits of the proposed changes?

(c) Judge teaches a torts course at the local law school. May she discuss the merits of the proposed changes in her class? May she express her strongly held views that the changes are highly undesirable?

(d) May Judge deliver a public speech or write an article attacking the proposed changes?

(e) If Judge does any of the activities set forth in (a) through (d), should she disqualify herself if the proposed changes are enacted and a suit challenging their constitutionality comes before her court?

PROBLEM 95

If the statute described in Problem 91 passes and its constitutionality is upheld in an opinion by Judge, may she in her reelection campaign use a poster stating, truthfully, that "I wrote the opinion in the no fault case that has already saved consumers millions in premiums"?

PROBLEM 96

Judge is a member of the court that is reviewing an order of the regulatory commission that has just allowed an increase in the rates of the local electric company.

(a) Judge's wife owns $500 in stock in the local electric company. It was given to her by her parents as a gift when she was a child. For sentimental reasons, she does not wish to sell it even though it pays only $10 a year in dividends. Must Judge disqualify himself? Does it make any difference whether Judge is a federal or state court judge? Compare Canon 3(C)(1)(c) of the Code of Judicial Conduct with 28 U.S.C. §455(a), p. 709.

(b) Suppose that the Judge's parents own a number of rental properties whose electric bills will rise substantially. Should Judge disqualify himself? If he does, should he withdraw, or should he follow the procedure outlined in Canon 3D of the Code of Judicial Conduct?

PROBLEM 97

Federal District Judge has a case that raises, as a subsidiary issue, a difficult question of professional responsibility, a subject that she has not followed closely. She would like to try out her ideas on one or more of the following friends:

(a) Professor A, her former legal profession teacher;

(b) Judge B, a federal district judge in her district;

(c) Mr. C, Judge B's law clerk;

(d) Judge D, a federal district judge in a neighboring state;

(e) Judge E, a Court of Appeals judge in her circuit;

(f) Judge F, a Court of Appeals judge in another circuit; and

(g) Judge G, a member of the state trial court of general jurisdiction in the state in which she sits.

May she talk to any or all of them about the matter and on what basis?

PROBLEM 98

In In re Beiny, p. 383, the court clearly believed that a lawyer had obtained confidential information of an adverse party improperly. Should the court have referred the matter to disciplinary authorities? See Canon 3(B)(3) of the Code of Judicial Conduct. How certain does a judge have to be that there has been a disciplinary violation in deciding when that Canon requires action? When the judge decided to refer the matter to disciplinary authorities, should he have mentioned the reference publicly in his opinion?

The subject of the Canons of Judicial Ethics could be a course in itself. A book focusing on issues of professional responsibility of lawyers can do no more than give a glimpse into the kinds of problems that confront judges. I have chosen to suggest a few problems of judicial professional responsibility in areas that have substantial professional impact on lawyers generally. Anyone interested in a survey of problems of judicial responsibility should read Robert Mathews's thoughtful piece, Adjudicative Responsibility: Its Place in the Curriculum, 1972 Utah L. Rev. 421.

Three books published in the last 15 years deal with specific problems. John P. MacKenzie, The Appearance of Justice (1974), discusses a number of recent incidents. An accusation of a particular judicial impropriety is discussed in Preble Stolz, Judging Judges: The Investigation of Rose Bird and the California Supreme Court (1981). In 1978, the California Supreme Court issued a controversial decision just after Chief Justice Bird had won the election to confirm her in office. The book both explores the charge that the court had reached a decision prior to the election, but had delayed it in order to assist Bird's confirmation by the electorate, and discusses the formal proceedings that investigated the court's conduct. Thereafter, however, a recall election removed Chief Justice Bird and Associate Justices Reynoso and Grondin from office. See Wold and Culver, The Defeat of the California Justices: the Campaign, the Electorate, and the Issue of Judicial Accountability, 70 Judicature 348 (No. 6 April-May 1987) and the excerpted panel discussion, After California, What's Next for Judicial Elections, Id., at 356.

Another controversial issue of judicial ethics is presented in a book detailing the extrajudicial activities undertaken by Justice Brandeis during his Supreme Court career both on his own and through the substantial annual financial support he provided for the activities of the then Professor Felix Frankfurter. A great deal of the book is concerned with Brandeis's efforts with respect to legislation that came, or might have come, before the Court. Murphy, The Brandeis/Frankfurter Connection

(1982); for a somewhat different position by the same author, see Levy and Murphy, Preserving the Progressive Spirit in a Conservative Time: The Joint Reform Efforts of Justice Brandeis and Professor Frankfurter, 1916-1933, 78 Mich. L. Rev. 1252 (1980). Critical assessments of Murphy's conclusions are contained in Cover, The Framing of Justice Brandeis, The New Republic, p. 17 (May 5, 1982) and John Frank's book review in 32 J. Leg. Educ. 432 (1982). See p. 64, Note 6 supra for a citation to Mr. Frank's views on various problems of professional responsibility in Justice Brandeis's career as a practicing lawyer.

The major document to be consulted is another project sponsored by the American Bar Association, its Code of Judicial Conduct. The ABA Special Committee on Judicial Standards, under the chairmanship of Chief Justice Traynor of California, was appointed in 1969 following adoption of the Code of Professional Responsibility. The final draft was adopted by the ABA's House of Delegates in 1972 and has since been widely adopted throughout the United States. As of 1988, the District of Columbia and every state except Montana, Rhode Island, and Wisconsin had adopted the Code of Judicial Conduct, albeit with some modifications. Also in 1988, the ABA appointed a committee to revise the Code of Judicial Conduct. We should test their various proposals as they are circulated against the problems discussed in this chapter.

The Judicial Conference of the United States, which had adopted a variety of regulations of its own during the 1960s, (see Ainsworth, Impact of the Code of Judicial Conduct on Federal Judges, 1972 Utah L. Rev. 369), subsequently adopted the ABA-sponsored Code and made it applicable to all federal judges, full-time bankruptcy judges and full time magistrates, with some modifications. 1973 Report of the Judicial Conference of the United States 9-11, 52; 1974 Report of the Judicial Conference of the United States 17. The Judicial Conference has created an Advisory Committee to respond to inquiries from federal judges with respect to matters of their own judicial conduct. It has been issuing Advisory Opinions since 1970 and in 1988 made them public.

A description of the Code and some general observations on its content are contained in the following articles. Some changes were subsequently made in the draft then under consideration, but they are not material to this discussion. The author of the first article, Professor E. Wayne Thode, was Reporter to the ABA Committee that produced the Code. Professor Grossman, author of the second article, is described in the first note to his article and is also author of several pieces on judges and decision making.

THODE, THE DEVELOPMENT OF THE CODE OF JUDICIAL CONDUCT
9 San Diego L. Rev. 793 (1972)

HIGHLIGHTS

. . . Some persons have criticized [Canon 1] and its text as hortatory and useless and have suggested that it be eliminated. There has been some sentiment on the Committee to do just that. My own view is that it sets a proper tone for the rest of the Code, and that placing an obligation on judges to participate in establishing and maintaining proper standards of conduct is essential to a complete judicial code.

Canon 2 provides general conduct standards taken largely from the old canons. Although these general conduct standards are broad and almost hortatory, at least in part, the Committee nevertheless viewed them as essential to the Code. The last sentence, "He should not voluntarily testify as a character witness," raises the most difficult issue under this Canon. The Committee received numerous reports of attempts to use the prestige of a judge, called as a character witness, to bolster a defendant's standing with a jury. Is this a matter that should be dealt with in a code of judicial conduct? If so, has the Committee adopted the right solution?

Canon 3 establishes the standards for a judge in performing the duties of his office. This canon applies to all of his duties of office, not just adjudicative duties. Many of the principles of Canon 2 have their origin in the old canons, but some of the significant changes and additions are as follows: (1) Under the new Code competence in law and in judicial administration is a facet of proper judicial conduct. (2) A method is established whereby a judge may consult with a disinterested person on issues of law, but he must give notice of the name of the person consulted and the substance of the advice received. (3) Broadcasting and televising from the courtroom are authorized for purposes of judicial administration, and a limited educational use of media reporting from the courtroom is sanctioned. (4) Extra-judicial statements about pending cases are prohibited. (5) A judge's responsibility for the conduct of his staff and court officials subject to his control is established. (6) Many bases for disqualification are specified, with a hard line being taken with regard to financial interests of a judge and members of his family residing in his household — any economic interest will require the judge's disqualification. (7) A waiver procedure is made available if the lawyers *and parties* believe a judge's interest to be insubstantial or his relationship to a party or lawyer to be immaterial. (8) Investments in mutual funds, savings associations, and government securities are excluded from the financial interest definition unless the litigation will substantially affect their value, thereby giving a judge a few investment possibilities without great danger of disqualification.

The technique of incorporation of a procedural device into a standard of conduct was used twice in Canon 3, with regard to communications from disinterested persons and with regard to waiver of the disqualification of a judge. . . .

I should point out that the provision of the Canons of Judicial Ethics that "ours is a government of law and not of men" is not to be found in this Code. I hope that no one feels aggrieved by its absence.

Canon 4 pertains to a judge's quasi-judicial activities. These are not mandatory activities, but the text makes clear that they are proper and are encouraged to the extent that they do not interfere with judicial duties or cast doubt on a judge's impartiality. You may be interested to learn that approximately 200 judges regularly teach or lecture part-time in law schools. Many lawyers and judges recommended to the Committee that this area of conduct be very substantially curtailed, but the Committee took the opposite position.

In addition to the general limitations in Canon 4, two specific limitations have been added. A judge may consult with the executive or a legislative body only on matters of judicial administration. He may not be a general political or economic advisor to the executive. The other limitation is that a judge may not participate in public fund raising activities on behalf of "legal" organizations — that is organizations devoted to the improvement of the law, the legal system, or the administration of justice — although he may assist in fund raising for such organizations.

The fund raising issue is a difficult one. In Canon 5 a judge is precluded from soliciting funds for an educational, religious, charitable, fraternal, or civic organization, although in Canon 4 he is authorized to assist in fund raising for a "legal" organization provided he does not personally participate in public fund raising activities. Can this distinction be justified? I think so.

Some "legal" organizations have only judges as members. If judges can't assist in fund raising, then those organizations are effectively precluded from being involved in projects that require substantial financial backing. Indeed, the Committee felt that the projects of all "legal" organizations that require outside financing would probably be in jeopardy if judges in the membership could not even voice their approval of the project — hence the "assist in fund raising" authorization. The Committee did not view the role of a judge to be nearly as significant with regard to fund raising by Canon 5 organizations, and the prohibition was made absolute.

I look upon the solution to the fund raising issue as another example of an attempt to upgrade the ethical standard. The minimum standard was adhered to in Canon 4, but the Committee was able to upgrade the minimum in Canon 5. The Committee has put a great deal of time and thought into this fund raising issue — possibly more than it has put into any other single issue in the Code, and these sections on fund raising have drawn more suggestions and criticisms than has any other section. Taking the long view of standards of judicial conduct, I think this issue may be minor, but it certainly engenders a great deal of response, whatever the solution suggested.

Canon 5 sets the minimum standards for a judge's extra-judicial activities. The types of potential activities vary widely. Some are a matter of choice, such as avocational or civil and charitable activities. Others, such as financial activities, must be engaged in, whatever the size of a judge's income.

The standards adopted for avocational and civil and charitable activities hopefully avoid discouraging these activities. On the other hand, the standards for financial activities are much stricter than those of the old Canons of Judicial Ethics. To sum it up succinctly, a judge should not engage in business. This, however, is the upgraded standard, and a jurisdiction that does not pay its full time judges an adequate salary may adopt the minimum standard that allows the judge to engage in business if such activity does not: (1) reflect adversely on his impartiality, (2) interfere with the proper performance of his judicial duties, (3) exploit his judicial position, or (4) involve him in frequent transactions with lawyers or persons likely to come before the court on which he serves. As you can see, even the minimum standard rather severely limits the full time judge's business potentialities.

The attempt to place rational limits on gifts, loans, bequests, and favors to a judge and his family has also taken a great deal of the Committee's time and thought. . . . Basically the position is that neither a judge nor a member of his family residing in his household should accept a gift, loan, bequest, or favor from a lawyer, a party, or a potential litigant, but there must be some exceptions to this hard line. Must a judge go out of town to obtain financing for the purchase of a house or car because the local financial institutions are, or may be, litigants in his court? This is only one of the many problems encountered in this area.

Fiduciary activities of a judge are severely curtailed under the new Code. He may act as a fiduciary only for a member of his family. However, a judge may not be a desirable fiduciary in any event because he must apply the same standards to his financial activities as a fiduciary that he is required to apply in handling his own financial affairs.

The practice of law by a full time judge, as well as his acting as an arbitrator or mediator, is forbidden. Extra-judicial appointments of judges to commissions and committees are also precluded unless the matter at issue involves the improvement of the law, the legal system, or the administration of justice — the same standard applied in Canon 4 to the judge's quasi-judicial activities. Although extra-judicial appointments of Supreme Court Justices in times past immediately come to mind, the same problem also exists on the state level. The Committee squarely faced and answered this issue. . . .

Canon 6 authorizes payment of compensation and reimbursement of expenses for quasi-judicial and extra-judicial activities permitted by the Code. There are limitations on the amount and the source, and the compensation received for these activities must be publicly *reported*. The Committee has not receded from its original position that the public is entitled to know to whom and for how much a full time judge "sells" his extra time.

The reporting provision of Canon 6 has engendered more reaction *from judges* than has any other provision of this proposed code. The responses indicate that most state judges oppose this requirement, but that most federal judges do not (probably because they are presently operating under an even broader reporting requirement). On the other hand, lawyers and others who have responded have in general either approved of Canon 6 or have opted for a broader reporting requirement. If this code runs into trouble when it is presented to the various states for adoption, the public reporting provision is likely to be the issue causing the trouble.

Canon 7, the political activity canon, has much in common with old Canons 28 and 30, but the Committee has attempted to be much more specific and concrete in the Code. One major change is that of requiring a candidate for judicial office, even if he is not a judge, to comply with this Canon. Some criticism has been received on the basis that the Canon cannot be enforced against a candidate who is not a judge. I think the criticism is not well taken. Public opinion is often the most important enforcement weapon in a political campaign. The very threat of a public statement that a candidate for judicial office is violating Canon 7 may induce the candidate to comply.

As pointed out earlier, Canon 7 is filled with compromises with the ethical ideal that a judge be impartial and appear to be impartial. The clash between that important judicial policy and the policy of Jacksonian democracy that a judge regularly and frequently be subject to the will of the electorate is obvious. Can a judge ever "appear to be impartial" to the lawyers and potential litigants who publicly opposed his election? . . .

Canon 7 does attempt to place a buffer between the candidate and those being solicited for funds or publicly stated support. Also, it places responsibility on a judge to prohibit court personnel subject to his control from doing for him what he is prohibited from doing for himself during a campaign — a much needed improvement, in my opinion. . . .

JOEL B. GROSSMAN,* A POLITICAL VIEW OF JUDICIAL ETHICS

9 San Diego L. Rev. 803 (1972)

Law and legal institutions in the United States today are faced with a crisis of public confidence that may be unequalled in American history and is at least the worst such crisis since 1937. The law and legal institutions have always been under attack from one or another side of the political spectrum. The role they play in allocating values and resources for the society and in regulating processes of change is much too important and complex to expect a continuing pattern of general acquiescence and support. What makes the present crisis of special concern, therefore, is not that the courts and the law are under fire but that they appear to be under attack from all sides of the political arena. Except possibly in the abstract, who speaks for the courts today? Given the heterogeneous makeup of our population and the essential pluralism of our political system, it is unlikely that everyone and all positions can be kept satisfied. The courts, and particularly the Supreme Court, can operate reasonably well, if not entirely effectively, without majority support. But to survive they will need — and have in the past had — the support of at least one major — if not majority — faction which actively gives its support and a second segment which if it does not extend specific support for what the Court is doing at least supports it symbolically as an institution. Public support at this level may be the necessary foundation for effective judicial functioning in a democratic society.

To some extent the present lack of confidence in legal institutions is part of a more widespread withdrawal of support from the political system. But for many, especially young people, it also reflects a recognition of the inadequacy of courts and the law to achieve their social objectives and/or a feeling that the legal system is hopelessly biased against the values to which they subscribe. . . .

There has always been and always will be a gap between law and justice. It is inherent in the nature of the two concepts. And it seems equally the case that resort to the law as a primary means of accomplishing social change will almost always prove to be a disappointment in the long run. The law, and particularly the courts, plays a significant role in the processes of change in the United States, perhaps more significant than in other countries. Since, as a mediating institution, the law is also concerned with order and peaceful resolution of conflicts, total goal realization by any one group is unlikely. Thus, to the extent that one chooses to invoke the law in the pursuit of social goals there is an expectable

---

* Professor of Political Science and Director of the Center for Law and Behavioral Science, University of Wisconsin, Madison.

tariff of reduced achievement. Perhaps a tension between achievement and aspiration is a necessary ingredient of societal stability and progress.

But where the judicial process is seen not only as inadequate to the realization of certain goals, but positively dysfunctional to their achievement, lack of confidence could indeed reach serious proportions. If an increasingly large radical segment of the society believes, as Robert Lefcourt has argued, that "the judicial process appears to worsen pressing problems rather than solve them," then the costs to the society of a loss of legitimacy in the courts are readily apparent.[3] When "Legalism"[4] becomes an epithet instead of a tribute to the rationality of the legal system the seeds of crisis have begun to sprout.

All of this, a necessarily abbreviated discussion of an important subject in itself, is by way of preface to my comments on the proposed new Code of Judicial Conduct. I have begun this way to underscore (and perhaps exaggerate) what I believe to be the disparity between crisis conditions and the response which the Code makes to that crisis. I am aware, of course, that it is not within the scope or purview of a document like the Code to respond fully to this crisis. The behavior of judges is not our only problem; perhaps it is not even the most pressing problem of the legal system. Nor am I oblivious to the limitations inherent in the efforts of a quasi-public professional group, such as the American Bar Association, to provide solutions to problems and conditions which represent a far-reaching indictment of our entire social, economic and political system. Nonetheless it does not seem wholly unfair to subject this Code, representing some of the best thinking in the legal profession today, to the critical test of relevance. How accurately and effectively does the Code conceptualize and state the problems that exist? And how well does it provide solutions to these problems?

This is the first major revision of the Canons of Judicial Ethics. It reflects a consensus that a modernized and updated document was needed, but also some lesser consensus as to *how* that document should be changed, what subjects should be covered and which items ignored. The Canons combined an effort to regulate economic conflicts of interest in which a judge might find himself with some extensive sermonizing about the nature of the judicial function, the evils of dissent on appellate courts and related proscriptions then of concern to some members of the bar. Quite naturally they reflected the prevailing opinion of 45 years ago about the "ideally" mechanical nature of the judicial process. The Canons were hardly even touched by the influence of judicial realism. By comparison the proposed new Code is a refreshing change. Sermons and biblical injunctions are kept to a minimum, if not virtually eliminat-

---

3. R. Lefcourt, Law Against the People 21 (1971).
4. J. Skhlar, Legalism (1964).

ed, and the useless but deceptive admonition, "ours is a government of laws and not of men" is omitted. Dissent is no longer condemned and some of the least defensible mechanical conceptions of the judge's function have been excised. But, primarily, the focus still is on the avoidance of individual economic bias, with additional admonitions about courtroom demeanor and behavior in electoral contests. . . .

What is the function of a Code of Judicial Conduct? Primarily, I gather, it is to contribute to the maintenance for a quasi-public profession of a relatively autonomous system of self-regulation, particularly where most judges are elected and thus perceived as subject to a variety of undesirable political pressures. A second, and derivative, purpose of such a code is public relations, in the best sense of that term. While the Code itself is likely to be invisible to the general public, the norms of behavior which it endorses may contribute to public education about the judicial process and the proper judicial role, as well as to some reassurance about the integrity of the courts. Of course, for those on the fringes of the system the code may be just another "put on" by the establishment.

The American Bar Association cannot regulate the behavior of either judges or lawyers, but it can influence judicial conduct by promulgation of norms which may also receive the force of law if incorporated into law or the disciplinary machinery of state bar groups. The first requirement of any code of conduct is that it must be reasonably clear about what is or is not prohibited behavior. The second is that standards must be acceptable to most groups within a relatively diverse profession, and must at least be within sight of actual practices. The code cannot be successful if it appeals only to an abstract sense of right or wrong. It must contain some recognition of the realities of the professional roles which it seeks to regulate. . . .

Do the standards set down in the Code flow from an accurate and realistic conception of the judicial process and of how the public is likely to view that process? On the whole it does not assume or try to prescribe a cloistered judicial role; indeed, to the extent that it encourages a judge to engage in a variety of activities and not recede into monastic contemplation it recognizes that the business of judging is more than the mere application of precedents and requires more than merely being "learned" in the law. It does not appear to set impossible standards for urban criminal court judges. Its fault in this regard, if any, is simply to ignore the special problems of such courts and judges.

To strictly prohibit judges from all extra-judicial activity, as many have suggested, would be counterproductive; the small possible net gain in diminished conflicts of interest would be outweighed by the resulting losses in judicial vision and independence of thought. Judicial independence is a value worth supporting if it implies and creates the conditions under which judges can offer a fresh, enriched, and informed view of solutions to society's problems. It is not worth supporting if it means only that judges are to be artificially and excessively isolated. . . . The babies of ignorance and parochialism seem to me, on the whole, more difficult to combat than economic partiality.

On the other hand, the new Code tends to support perpetuation of the image of judges as nonpolitical actors, with allowances made only for that minimum political involvement necessary to secure election to judicial office. And flowing from this it forbids judges or judicial candidates from engaging in certain proscribed behavior without adequate allowance for the political cultures or machinery within which they must operate.

Because the official position of the Bar is in opposition to judicial elections, the old Canons as well as the revised Code severely limit the freedom of judicial candidates to mobilize voters, to discuss relevant issues, and thereby to educate citizens about the operation of the courts. Most judges in the United States are elected, so this is no minor point.[12] Not surprisingly voter turnout at judicial elections is poor, especially where these are held separately from the general election. One reason for poor public response — perhaps the main reason — is that the voters don't understand the issues or perceive much salience in the outcome. Since judicial candidates rarely attempt an intelligent discussion of issues, the voters are asked to make an impossible choice, to perform a relatively meaningless act, and it is little wonder that they decline to do so in wholesale numbers.

All Americans are now well aware that Supreme Court justices are chosen because they espouse judicial and political philosophies compatible with those of the appointing President. What reason is there to deny citizen voters in judicial elections the information they need to make a similar choice? In Wisconsin, and I assume in other states with contested judicial elections, some of this information is transmitted surreptitiously. The candidates openly say very little, but their general policy views and political backgrounds and affiliations are openly described by their supporters and the media. This is done usually without any intimation of how a prospective or incumbent judge would decide any particular case; it could be done even more effectively by the candidate himself. The result is that the Canons are not effectively enforceable while at the same time [they] prevent realization of the full benefits of judicial elections. The worst of both worlds is effectively realized. And the chief losers are the voters who remain apathetic because they have not been attracted by the candidates or informed as to what difference it makes who is chosen as a judge.

12. It should be noted that most judges in election states first reach the bench by gubernatorial appointment.

I do not believe that judicial candidates, or the judiciary as a whole, will be demeaned by a clear but careful rendition of issues and policy choices. On the contrary, public confidence in the judiciary might positively increase if the workings of the process and the values of the aspirants are exposed to public view. In a democracy, after all, elections are a primary if not exclusive means of legitimation. If voters are able to perceive that they have a stake in the outcome they are more likely to participate and, at least arguably, choose better judges. There are countless studies by social scientists which do more than merely suggest that the outcomes of the judicial process depend in part on who the judges are, that judges with different backgrounds follow different decisional patterns. Trial lawyers have always known this to be a fact, and litigants are likely to arrive at the same conclusions. And there is evidence that citizens want this information. For the Bar to maintain to the contrary *and enforce these norms* becomes increasingly difficult, especially when the Bar's campaign to influence judicial selection constitutes at least an implicit recognition of this fact.

For many years the American Bar Association has advocated what has become known as the Missouri Plan [*] for selection of judges. It has supported this plan "to take the selection of judges out of politics." But recent studies have shown that the Plan doesn't materially result in the selection of different judges, and that far from removing the selection process from politics it merely substitutes a more elitist version of the same political game.[18] Cleavages within the Bar roughly approximate popular political divisions and indeed, at least in Missouri, the two lawyers factions have even taken over some "party" functions such as nomination for candidates and campaigning. Upper status lawyers tend to favor continuation, lower status lawyers are less favorable. Even within Bar politics there is a strong ideological component and many of the interests and values that might concern interested publics are apparently effectively raised in the Missouri Plan context.

While the final verdict on the operations and consequences of the Missouri Plan is not yet in, there is as yet little evidence to support the Bar's continued and *exclusive* preference for this method of judicial selection. If one were to take into account the question of public confidence, raised earlier, then perhaps other options ought to be explored. Election of judges — especially nonpartisan elections — might lead to greater minority and ethnic representation, would give the public more information about how courts operate, and might well serve to reinforce rather than destroy support for the judiciary. We know that lawyers are not held in particularly high esteem by their fellow citizens, and it is thus even more difficult to sustain the elitist argument, often voiced by Mis-

[*] See p. 707. — Ed.
18. R. Watson and R. Dowing, The Politics of the Bench and the Bar (1969).

souri Plan advocates, that lawyers have special qualities which entitle them to a *monopoly* in the selection process, and that giving them this monopoly will result both in better judges and more general support for the judiciary.[19]

I am not arguing, perhaps knowing it would be futile, that the Bar should endorse judicial elections. Nor am I proposing that lawyers play no role in the selection process. What I am saying is that in times of change some of the old premises should be re-examined. After all I suspect that few lawyers today would share the ideological opposition to economic reform which was so central to the evolution of the ABA's position against popular judicial election.

Since I am talking about public confidence, and that is almost certainly related to legitimacy, I must concede that there are some arguments, not entirely unpersuasive, that judicial elections are likely to be destructive of public confidence in the courts. It is said that the "declaratory" theory of judicial decision-making, under which a judge impersonally performs a mechanical function and exercises no individual choice, supports a myth which is necessary in securing respect for, and obedience to, judicial decisions. Belief in the ideal of a "government of laws and not of men" is said to be essential to public support for the judiciary. I am opposed to this view and agree with those who argue that the solution is to educate people to the reality rather than perpetuate the myth. . . .

One way to increase support for judicial institutions may well be to reinforce the myth-holding propensities of American citizens. But many would argue that the social costs of this endeavor are too high. Increased myth-holding is likely to result in more rather than less elite control of policy-making and a diminished role for citizens' views. And it also seems a distinct possibility that changing public attitudes about political realism and toward the disclosure of the government's business will require more rather than less openness about judges and the judicial process. If the Code of Judicial Conduct is to present the judiciary in its best public light then it should seek not the "best" image of the courts but the most accurate portrayal. And, reflecting the temper of the times, it will, or ought to, encourage the increase rather than contribute to a decrease in the contacts between judges and citizens.

Any attempt to set norms for judicial behavior must recognize the changing role of the courts. To a greater extent than ever before the courts have, in the last 30 years, functioned as positive social change

19. What produces "better" judges is, in one sense, a non-question. Better in what respect? better educated? more compassionate? more common sense? smarter? There is certainly no evidence that a particular recruitment system produces better judges. See Jacob, The Effect of Institutional Differences in the Recruitment Process: The Case of State Judges, 13 J. Public Law 104 (1964); J. Hurst, The Growth of American Law; . . .

policymakers. They have been called upon to decide issues previously considered unsuitable for judicial action, requiring, in many cases, considerations of data and theory beyond the scope of traditional legal knowledge and legal education. Courts have always played a representative role in the American political system. But in the past generation they have emerged as the best representatives of the black and the poor and the politically unpopular and others trying to overcome the effects of past exclusion from the political system. It is true that it has been nonelective courts which have taken the lead in advancing the "idea of progress."[23] But there is no reason to assume that it was the way these judges were selected which made them more responsive or progressive.

In American history the courts were traditionally the voice of achievement. Now some have become, and are being asked to become even more, perhaps even too much, the voice of aspiration. In so doing they have occasionally had to leave the protective umbrella of middle-class consensus, precedent and authority. In a very real sense the courts have developed a new constituency. The new constituency is not nearly as stable in values or membership as the old. Consensus about societal goals is not only lacking but replaced by polarization. And this new constituency lacks the weapons to protect the courts effectively in time of crisis. But, in the process they have also acquired many new problems. . . . The result is that, as [Professor] Miller has so cogently argued, the legal system presently operates under almost unbearable tension.[24] And the courts have as yet not found the way out from under. For the courts now to reject further aspirations to justice and equality would be, from the point of view of the continued need for stable change, suicidal. The increased attention which the courts have paid to the rights of the poor and the black has only highlighted the extent to which those and other groups are *still* treated unjustly. The initial recognition of injustice has only led to increased emphasis and heightened demands to remove the considerable maltreatment which still remains. For the courts to reject out of hand the invitation to rejoin old friends would be damaging to the courts and incomparably more damaging to the political system as a whole.

The Code of Judicial Conduct cannot solve this dilemma. But it might help to reduce the destructive tensions by giving at least symbolic support to this new and evolving judicial role. I do not think that widely shared maxims of judicial self-restraint should be rejected. But the code might at least suggest the primacy of certain substantive values such as, but not limited to, justice and equality. Except for a brief mention in

23. A. Bickel, The Supreme Court and the Idea of Progress (1970).
24. Miller, Public Confidence in the Judiciary: Some Notes and Reflections, 25 Law and Contemp. Probs. 69 (1970).

Canon 1, one looks in vain for any admonition to judges along these lines.

In light of the foregoing comments I would propose consideration of the following thoughts as additions or amendments to the proposed Code of Judicial Conduct: . . .

(1) To make it eminently clear what the courts should stand for, I would insert in Canon 3A, possibly at the end of A(1): "His primary duty is to achieve justice in each individual case, applying the law so that a fair and equitable result is achieved." I am aware, of course, that many believe that the consistency of the law is more important than the achievement of individual equitable results. Without denying that there is some merit in the notion of consistency, I would argue that there are already strong inducements toward stare decisis and consistency but insufficient reaffirmation of the primary need to achieve justice or, at least, to make citizens believe that justice is being done. There would be no way of enforcing this command, but there are many other statements in the Code which are equally unenforceable.

[(2)] I would substitute the following for [Canon 7B(1)(c)]: "A candidate for judicial office should (a) endeavor to inform the electorate as fairly and honestly as he can about his general views on important and controversial social and political issues without announcing or promising how he would decide any particular case that might come before him, or, if he is an incumbent judge, which is presently before him for decision. He should make no pledges or promises of conduct in office other than the faithful, impartial, and compassionate performance of his duties; he should not misrepresent his identity, qualification, present position or other fact; . . ." While following this policy would help solve the problem of the ignorant or apathetic elector, it would also invite the pronouncement of popular views on questions unrelated to judicial performance. And it would countenance the proclamation of views that we dislike ("segregation now and forever") as well as encourage those that we favor. But this is not a serious problem since we know that in some jurisdictions a candidate's views of race relations or law and order or even Vietnam will not be in doubt, whatever else he may articulate as his campaign platform.

SUMMARY OF THE REPLY BY E. WAYNE THODE
TO SUGGESTIONS OF PROFESSOR GROSSMAN
9 San Diego L. Rev. 816 (1972)

Professor Grossman's paper is a valuable contribution. . . . The views of an expert in a discipline other than law have special relevance with regard to the proposed new Code.

I now wish to give my reaction to . . . the . . . suggestions Professor Grossman makes at the end of his paper:

1. Duty to achieve justice.   Everyone is, or should be, in favor of justice and fair and equitable application of the law. The issue is: "Should such a standard be a part of a code of conduct for judges?" My answer is "No." Professor Grossman states that such a command in the Code could not be enforced but that there are many other statements in the Code which are equally unenforceable. He doesn't point them out, and I do not know to which provisions he is referring. All standards in mandatory language in the Code are intended to be enforceable, so I am opposed to the statement of a standard in the mandatory language he suggests unless there is the expectation that it will be enforced.

I believe, as stated above, that the requirement that a judge should apply the law so that "a fair and equitable result is achieved" is misplaced as a standard in a general code of judicial conduct. The effect would be to transform every claim of injustice or inequity in a decision on the merits into a basis for challenging the judge for a violation of the ethical standard prescribed for him. The loser at trial level in many cases reversed on the merits by a higher court would have a prima facie claim of a violation of the Code against the trial judge rendering the decision. Errors by a judge in a decision on the merits, unless there is a history of them that raises the competency issue, should not be dealt with as a matter of claimed breach of a standard of judicial conduct. . . .

[2.] *Campaigning for an elective judicial office.*   Professor Grossman is in agreement with President Andrew Jackson's philosophy that a close check should be kept on the judiciary through the popular election process. Professor Grossman proposes that each candidate for judicial office enter into political combat on the vital issues of the day. If the issues are of the type that cannot be settled in the judicial arena, the election to judicial office will obviously be determined on the basis of factors having nothing to do with competence in judicial office. If the issues can be settled within the judicial arena, Professor Grossman is willing to sacrifice the policies of impartiality and the appearance of impartiality on the altar of "full information" for the voter. The Committee and Professor Grossman are at opposite philosophical poles on the issue of the kind of campaigning that should be engaged in by candidates for elective judicial office.

One interesting anomaly in Professor Grossman's position is found in the following statements by him:

But in the past generation they [the courts] have emerged as the best representatives of the black and the poor and the politically unpopular and others trying to overcome the effects of past exclusion from the political system. It is true that it has been non-elective courts which have taken the lead in advancing the "idea of progress."

Professor Grossman, with what I believe is a great deal of naivete, then states:

> But there is no reason to assume that it was the way these judges were selected which made them more responsive or progressive.

I suggest that the processes by which the judges were selected — in most instances either appointment or a merit system type of election — played a very substantial part in the developments in the areas Professor Grossman mentions. . . .

The Problems that have been chosen for inclusion in this chapter relate to the selection process, the independence of the judicial system, and the conduct of individual judges.

The major issue with respect to selection of judges is the manner of selection. For federal judges, the Constitution provides the answer of appointment by the President "by and with the Advice and Consent of the Senate." Art. 2, §2. The states have experimented with a variety of different solutions. In the beginning, the predominant method was appointive judges; starting with the Jacksonian period and continuing for a large part of the nineteenth century, the trend was to more and more elective judges; since that time there has been some movement away from elective to appointive or hybrid systems, although most states still elect most of their judges. The best known of the hybrid systems is the Missouri Plan, which its proponents have named the "merit" plan of selection. The governor appoints judges from a list of nominees submitted by a nominating commission composed of one judge ex officio, two or three lawyers elected by the bar, and two or three citizens (always a minority of the commission) appointed by the governor. At the end of the term, the electorate votes on the question whether Judge X should "be retained in office." The materials urging one plan or another are voluminous. An interesting collection, somewhat weighted toward the Missouri Plan but describing numerous other systems, is contained in Winters ed., Judicial Selection and Tenure (rev. ed. 1973), which also contains a lengthy bibliography on the subject. The negative views of Professor Grossman concerning the Missouri Plan are contained at p. 702. An interesting catalogue of the problems of judicial campaign financing, complete with illustrative statistics showing the amounts of money being raised and the roles played by lawyers who practice in the courts to which judges are being elected, is contained in Schotland, Elective Judges' Campaign Financing, 2 J. L. & Pol. 57-167 (1985). He also has what he calls modest but feasible proposals for reform that do not do away with elections.

Assuming, however, the existence of one system or another, what may a nominee say to aid his or her appointment or election? If the state has opted for an elective system, does that necessarily imply that the electorate is entitled to be informed of the issues in the same manner as in any other election? The Code of Judicial Conduct answers that question with a clear negative. Canon 7B(1)(C), among other prohibitions, forbids a candidate to "announce his views on disputed legal or political issues." Does that prohibit the candidate for election in Problem 91 (p. 689) from answering any of the questions put by the reporter? See remarks of Professor Grossman, pp. 701 ff.

What of the nominee for the federal bench? Canon 7B(1)(C) does not cover the nominee in an appointive situation at all. The omission is deliberate. The 1972 Proposed Final Draft referred, in what was then Canon 7D but is now Canon 7B, to a "candidate for judicial office." That was capable of being read as either including or excluding nominees for appointive office. The Association of American Law School's Special Committee to review the tentative Draft of the Code of Judicial Ethics (I should disclose that I was a member of that Committee) reviewed the Tentative Draft of the Canons. It noted the First Amendment problems with Canon 7, but suggested that if the prohibition remained, it "should apply as well to a candidate appearing before a Senate Committee in order to seek confirmation." Report contained in letter of Professor A. Leo Levin, Chairman, to Professor E. Wayne Thode, Oct. 6, 1971; see also Weckstein, Introductory Observations on the Code of Judicial Conduct, 9 San Diego L. Rev. 785, 791 (1972). The response of the drafters to this suggestion was to make it quite clear that candidates for appointive office were excluded from the prohibitions of Canon 7B. Neither the commentary to the Code nor the Reporter's Notes to Code of Judicial Conduct, which have been published by Professor Thode, give us any clue to the precise reasons that led the drafters to allow more latitude in the one case and not the other. It does remain the case, however, that a person nominated for judicial office ought to be careful lest he or she do something that may subsequently require disqualification under Canon 3. (For a view that Canon 7B(1)(C) is unconstitutional under the First Amendment as overbroad, see Kirby, op. cit., p. 689 n. *. This discussion became quite relevant in the 1987 Senate confirmation hearings when Judge Robert Bork was nominated to the Supreme Court. He was the first nominee to have responded so fully to questions about his judicial philosophy across a wide spectrum of issues. Those hearings emphasized the tension that exists between the desire of Senators to obtain the information they think necessary to exercise their constitutional power of advising and consenting to judicial appointments and the contending desire of judicial nominees to preserve the necessary degree of judicial independence and impartiality. Whether those hearings have created a new balance or were an aberration remains to be seen.

Problems 91-93, relating to the independence of the judicial system, draw on our knowledge of history and government, our general view of the purposes of judging, and the appropriate relation between the judiciary and other branches of government. A brief bibliography on President Roosevelt's court-packing plan of 1937 is contained in Gunther, Constitutional Law 152 n.* (10th ed. 1980). Problems 94-97 involve the conduct of judges in individual cases. The *Parrish* case, which follows, is most relevant to Problems 94 and 96.

Disqualification of federal judges is dealt with by statute in 28 U.S.C. §§144 and 455. They are set forth below. As the following case indicates, their interpretation has caused enormous difficulty for the courts.

§144

Whenever a party to any proceeding in a district court makes and files a timely and sufficient affidavit that the judge before whom the matter is pending has a personal bias or prejudice either against him or in favor of any adverse party, such judge shall proceed no further therein, but another judge shall be assigned to hear such proceeding.

The affidavit shall state the facts and the reasons for the belief that bias or prejudice exists, and shall be filed not less than ten days before the beginning of the term at which the proceeding is to be heard, or good cause shall be shown for failure to file it within such time. A party may file only one such affidavit in any case. It shall be accompanied by a certificate of counsel of record stating that it is made in good faith.

§455

(a) Any justice, judge, or magistrate of the United States shall disqualify himself in any proceeding in which his impartiality might reasonably be questioned.

(b) He shall also disqualify himself in the following circumstances:

(1) Where he has a personal bias or prejudice concerning a party, or personal knowledge of disputed evidentiary facts concerning the proceeding;

(2) Where in private practice he served as lawyer in the matter in controversy, or a lawyer with whom he previously practiced law served during such association as a lawyer concerning the matter, or the judge or such lawyer has been a material witness concerning it;

(3) Where he has served in governmental employment and in such capacity participated as counsel, adviser or material witness concerning the proceeding or expressed an opinion concerning the merits of the particular case in controversy;

(4) He knows that he, individually or as a fiduciary, or his spouse or minor child residing in his household, has a financial interest in the subject matter in controversy or in a party to the proceeding, or any other interest that could be substantially affected by the outcome of the proceeding;

(5) He or his spouse, or a person within the third degree of relationship to either of them, or the spouse of such a person:

(i) Is a party to the proceeding, or an officer, director, or trustee of a party;

(ii) Is acting as a lawyer in the proceeding;

(iii) Is known by the judge to have an interest that could be substantially affected by the outcome of the proceeding;

(iv) Is to the judge's knowledge likely to be a material witness in the proceeding.

(c) A judge should inform himself about his personal and fiduciary financial interests, and make a reasonable effort to inform himself about the personal financial interests of his spouse and minor children residing in his household.

(d) For the purposes of this section the following words or phrases shall have the meaning indicated:

(1) "proceeding" includes pretrial, trial, appellate review, or other stages of litigation;

(2) the degree of relationship is calculated according to the civil law system;

(3) "fiduciary" includes such relationships as executor, administrator, trustee, and guardian;

(4) "financial interest" means ownership of a legal or equitable interest, however small, or a relationship as director, adviser, or other active participant in the affairs of a party, except that:

(i) Ownership in a mutual or common investment fund that holds securities is not a "financial interest" in such securities unless the judge participates in the management of the fund;

(ii) An office in an educational, religious, charitable, fraternal, or civic organization is not a "financial interest" in securities held by the organization;

(iii) The proprietary interest of a policyholder in a mutual insurance company, of a depositor in a mutual savings association, or a similar proprietary interest, is a "financial interest" in the organization only if the outcome of the proceeding could substantially affect the value of the interest;

(iv) Ownership of government securities is a "financial interest" in the issuer only if the outcome of the proceeding could substantially affect the value of the securities.

(e) No justice, judge, or magistrate shall accept from the parties to the proceeding a waiver of any ground for disqualification enumerated in subsection (b). Where the ground for disqualification arises only under subsection (a), waiver may be accepted provided it is preceded by a full disclosure on the record of the basis for disqualification.

PARRISH v. BOARD OF COMMISSIONERS

524 F.2d 98 (5th Cir. 1975) (en banc), cert. denied, 425 U.S. 944
(1976)

BELL, Circuit Judge:

This appeal involves one assignment of error directed to the denial of a motion, filed pursuant to 28 U.S.C.A. §144, to disqualify the district judge who decided the matter. . . .

I

The threshold requirement under the §144 disqualification procedure is that a party file an affidavit demonstrating personal bias or prejudice on the part of the district judge against that party or in favor of an adverse party. Once the affidavit is filed, further activity of the judge against whom it is filed is circumscribed except as allowed by the statute. In terms of the statute, there are three issues to be determined: (1) was the affidavit timely filed; (2) was it accompanied by the necessary certificate of counsel of record; and (3) is the affidavit sufficient in statutory terms?

We are concerned only with the third issue. As we said in Davis v. Board of School Commissioners of Mobile County, 5th Cir., 517 F.2d 1044 (1975): "Once the motion is filed under §144, the judge must pass on the legal sufficiency of the affidavit, but may not pass on the truth of the matters alleged." See Berger v. United States, 1921, 255 U.S. 22, . . . 517 F.2d at 1051.

Legal sufficiency is determined as a question of law on the basis whether the affidavit sets out facts and reasons for the party's belief that the judge has a personal bias and prejudice against the party or in favor of the adverse party. The facts and reasons set out in the affidavit "must give fair support to the charge of a bent of mind that may prevent or impede impartiality of judgment." Berger v. United States, supra, 255 U.S. at 33, . . . 65 L. Ed. at 485.

The legal question presented is determined by applying the reasonable man standard to the facts and reasons stated in the affidavit. See United States v. Thompson, 483 F.2d 527 (3d Cir. 1973), which states the standard as requiring that the facts be such, their truth being assumed, as would "convince a reasonable man that a bias exists," 483 F.2d at 528. The tripartite test of the Third Circuit is as follows:

> In an affidavit of bias, the affiant has the burden of making a three-fold showing:
> 1. The facts must be material and stated with particularity;

2. The facts must be such that, if true they would convince a reasonable man that a bias exists.

3. The facts must show the bias is personal, as opposed to judicial in nature.

483 F.2d at 528.

The pertinent part of the affidavit filed against Judge Varner is set out in the margin.[5] We consider it in light of the transcript developed in an examination of the district judge some weeks before the affidavit was filed. See the discussion of the content of the transcript in the panel opinion, 5th Cir., 505 F.2d 12.

The factual bases in the affidavit of disqualification are also summarized in the panel opinion as follows:

(1) that while Judge Varner was President of the Montgomery County Bar Association two years ago, the Association had a clause in its bylaws barring black members and that the judge never made any effort to invite black lawyers whom he knew to join;

(2) that Judge Varner was acquainted with several defendants in the suit and all of defendants' counsel, and that he said he did not believe that

5. 2. Plaintiff believes and avers that the judge before whom this action is pending, the Honorable Robert E. Varner, has a personal bias and prejudice against him, the other named plaintiffs, and the class represented by plaintiffs in this action.

3. The facts and reasons for the belief that such personal bias and prejudice exist are as follows:

a. The instant action complains, inter alia, that the defendants maintain a policy of excluding blacks from the practice of law in the State of Alabama. The Honorable Robert E. Varner is presently a member of the Montgomery County (Alabama) Bar Association; and when he served as President of that association two years ago, black lawyers were excluded from membership in the said association under the terms of its by-laws. The Honorable Judge Varner was then acquainted with the five or six black lawyers who then practiced in Montgomery; but never made an effort to invite them to join the association. It was only after the aforesaid judge became interested in a federal judgeship that he, as president of the Montgomery County Bar Association, appointed a committee to revise the said by-laws; and the record is unclear as to whether the "white only" membership clause of the Montgomery County Bar Association was removed during his tenure as president of the aforesaid association.

b. None of the plaintiffs in this case are personally acquainted with the Honorable Robert E. Varner. The said judge considers the defendant Commissioner Hill as a personal friend; he is a friend of Reginald Hamner, one of the chief defendants in the case; he is a friend of John Scott, defendant Hamner's predecessor in office and proposed to be called by the plaintiffs as an adverse witness; he is also a friend of counsel for all of the defendants. Further the said judge is personally acquainted with many of the other defendants in this cause. Although the testimony of the witness at the trial of this cause is expected to be conflicting in nature, the aforesaid Judge Varner has indicated that he does not believe that any of the defendants with whom he is acquainted would intentionally misrepresent any of the matters related to this lawsuit. Thus, plaintiffs sincerely believe that where the judge is called upon to make credibility choices throughout the trial, as he will be, he will attach undue weight to the testimony of his friends and acquaintances, all to the detriment of the plaintiffs and the class they represent.

any of the defendants whom he knew would intentionally misrepresent any of the matters related to the lawsuit.

505 F.2d at 17.

II

With these facts and the recited legal principles in mind we proceed to a consideration of the sufficiency of the affidavit. Personal bias or prejudice is required under §144. Neither of the factual bases alleged for recusal here raises an inference of personal bias or prejudice.

The first ground asserted, Judge Varner's past activities in the Montgomery Bar Association, is essentially an allegation based on the judge's background and states no specific facts that would suggest he would be anything but impartial in deciding the case before him. The claim of bias is general or impersonal at best. . . .

The second ground, regarding Judge Varner's acquaintance with some of the defendants and counsel, has been rejected as a basis for requiring the disqualification of a trial judge. [citing cases] The argument is that Judge Varner would be biased when it came to making credibility choices among witnesses. His statements made when being examined by counsel as to his possible disqualification were no more than an acknowledgement of friendship or acquaintanceship, and a refusal to condemn these persons as unworthy of belief in advance of whatever their testimony might prove to be. A statement by Judge Varner that he would believe, without question, any testimony of such persons would require a different result. Here, however, Judge Varner's answers did not reflect a lack of impartiality. The additional ground of the friendship between the judge and counsel for appellees, without more, is so lacking in merit as to warrant no discussion.

In short, the affidavit, including the facts on which it was based, was legally insufficient under §144 to require disqualification. Judge Varner did not err in so ruling.

III

We next consider . . . §455, . . . amended effective December 5, 1974. . . .[8]

8. . . . We described the relationship between §144 and §455 in *Davis* as follows: "The office of the procedure under §144 is to disqualify a judge prior to trial on motion of a party. Section 455 is the statutory standard for disqualification of a judge. It is self-enforcing on the part of the judge. It may also be asserted by a party by motion in the trial court, Rapp v. Van Dusen, 350 F.2d 806, 809 (3d Cir. 1965); through assignment of error on appeal United States v. Seiffert, 501 F.2d 974 (5th Cir. 1974); Shadid v. Oklahoma City, 494 F.2d 1267, 1268 (10th Cir. 1974), by interlocutory appeal, as here, or by mandamus, Texaco, Inc. v. Chandler, 354 F.2d 655 (10th Cir. 1965)." 517 F.2d at 1051-1052.

There are now several standards in §455. Some go to specific conduct, but one, set out in §455(a), is general and does not rest on the personal bias and prejudice stricture of §§144 and 455(b)(1). As we noted in *Davis,* supra, 517 F.2d at 1052, the language of §455(a) was intended to displace the subjective "in the opinion of the judge" test for recusal under the old statute, and the so-called "duty to sit decisions." We also noted that §455(a) was intended to substitute a "reasonable factual basis — reasonable man test" in determining whether the judge should disqualify himself. See 13 Wright, Miller & Cooper, Federal Practice and Procedure §3542 (1975). See also, Frank, Commentary on Disqualification of Judges-Canon 3c, 1972, Utah L. Rev. 377, 379. Note, Disqualification of Judges and Justices in the Federal Courts, 86 Harv. L. Rev. 736, 745-750 (1973).

Considering first the §455(a) claim, and the relevant facts and circumstances, we are of the view that a reasonable man would not infer that Judge Varner's "impartiality might reasonably be questioned." The facts have been stated in our discussion of the §144 issue.

Judge Varner was president of a local bar association in which black lawyers were denied membership. This policy was changed during or shortly after his administration as president. As the affidavit makes clear, see Note 5, supra, he, at the least, set the change in policy in motion by appointing a committee to revise the by-laws. He is faulted for not making an effort to obtain membership for black lawyers through inviting them to join, yet he, in effect, did just this in having the by-law changed. Appellants' logic would catch saint and sinner alike. There is hardly any judge in this circuit who was not a member of a segregated bar association at one time, and many have held a high office in the bar associations. The way of life which included segregated bar associations has been eliminated but only a new generation of judges will be free from such a charge. In any event, this circumstance will not support a claim of lack of impartiality. Such a claim must be supported by facts which would raise a reasonable inference of a lack of impartiality on the part of a judge in the context of the issues presented in a particular law suit. There are no such facts here. The stated conduct of Judge Varner does not support such an inference.

The allegation of lack of impartiality stemming from Judge Varner's acquaintanceship or friendship with witnesses and defense counsel is likewise tenuous. It does not exceed what might be expected as background or associational activities with respect to the usual district judge. As a factual basis, the allegations fall short of supporting an inference of lack of impartiality under §455(a).

The factual basis also falls short under §455(b)(1), in that there is no particularized allegation that Judge Varner had "personal knowledge of disputed evidentiary facts concerning the proceeding." Credibility choices are not disputed facts.

There are two additional claims of disqualification under amended

§455. They are based on the membership of Judge Varner in the Alabama State Bar, an organization in which membership has long been compulsory under the integrated bar concept. Title 46, §§30, 42, Code of Alabama. Each claim is attenuated in the extreme.

First, it is suggested that Judge Varner has a substantial interest in the success of defendants in the suit because of his identification with the bar association. Appellants rely on §455(b)(4) for this proposition. No interest exceeding mere membership is asserted. This is not a ground for disqualification.

The second ground based on the judge's bar association membership is that he has a financial interest in the outcome of this case because the bar association may be compelled to pay attorneys' fees should plaintiffs succeed. Although the amended §455 states that any "financial interest" in the subject matter in controversy or any party to the proceeding requires recusal, the spectre of the potential obligation of the Board of Commissioners, a judicial organ of the state, Title 46, §21 et seq., Code of Alabama, for attorneys' fees does not fall within the statutory definition of "financial interest." Section 455(d)(4). . . .

We affirm as to the denial of the motion to disqualify. Except as to that issue, the appeal is remanded to the original panel for disposition.

GEE, Circuit Judge (specially concurring):

The proper interpretation of Section 144 is a vexed matter with which I have long struggled. The belief of the parties that they are receiving even-handed justice, the apparency of justice to those not parties, the importance of both perceptions in maintaining the legitimacy of the judicial institution, the difficult decisions faced by a judge called upon to stand recused, and the practical implications of §144 for the continued efficient functioning of the district courts in our circuit are some of the competing considerations. They are not easily harmonized, and, indeed, there may be no entirely satisfactory manner of implementing Section 144. And though I concur fully in the opinion of the court on the assumption that United States v. Berger, 255 U.S. 22 remains good law, I feel obliged to express my doubt that it does or should. For, in my respectful view, *Berger* represents an outdated rule which has been made tolerable in present circumstances only by engraftment of dubious exceptions.

The majority opinion reaffirms *Berger's* antique rule that whatever "facts" the recusal affidavit may assert cannot be questioned but must be accepted as gospel.[1] Such an approach gives free play to the unscrupu-

---

1. And though it also reaffirms the settled rule that judicial actions cannot be made the basis of an accusation of bias, it should not be difficult for an inventive affiant to assert extra-judicial bases that disguise an aversion actually grounded in judicial philosophy and approach.

lous or reckless affiant, willing to run his chance of a ponderous and unlikely prosecution for perjury — and perhaps in little danger, since *Berger* seems to say that "affidavit" assertions made on mere information and belief will suffice for §144 purposes. Perjury charges have traditionally been based on falsely stated physical facts, and are rarely extended to representation of opinions. Suffice to say, establishing beyond reasonable doubt bad faith in assertion of a belief purportedly held at the time of an affidavit's filing is no light task.[3] For similar reasons, counsel will not likely fear disciplinary proceedings initiated by the local bar. I am reluctant to join in mandating a procedure which envisions, for example, that a judge must take as true an affidavit asserting, perhaps on "information and belief," that he has recently engaged in an acrimonious personal dispute with a defendant — complete with particulars — and is therefore disqualified to sit in his case, when the judge well knows that the affidavit has misidentified him and is mistaken. We go far enough when we read §144 as withdrawing from the judge decision of the final fact, his own actual bias. We should not require him to conduct such a curious and hypothetical proceeding as deciding whether an apprehension or bias is reasonably supported by whatever suppositious state of facts a daring and unscrupulous, or perhaps merely misadvised and agitated, party may be willing to swear to.

Factual matters necessary to decision of preliminary questions, of which recusal is a prickly example, are routinely resolved by weighing and evaluating affidavits. See, e.g., Wright & Miller, Federal Practice and Procedure §1373, at 714. Only three workable modes of deciding this particular question occur: (1) peremptory disqualification upon the mere filing of an affidavit; (2) decision of the issue by another magistrate than the one accused; or (3) decision either of actual bias or the reasonable appearance of it by the magistrate sought to be disqualified.

There are indications in the legislative history that peremptory disqualification was the legislative intent;[4] but this construction has never been adopted by any court. Reference to another magistrate is utterly foreign to the statutory scheme and raises its own problems of administrative inconvenience and delay. The statute's language gives fair support to the construction that the judge is not to determine bias-in-fact, and common sense supports the view that few if any humans can fairly decide whether they themselves are or are not biased in any given matter. But it is not too much to ask that a conscientious magistrate determine whether a given affidavit contains enough truth to fairly support

---

3. The author of Note, 79 Harv. L. Rev. 1435 (1966), found no cases in which a perjury charge stemming from a §144 affidavit had ever been prosecuted during the (then) forty-five years since *Berger*. Id. at 1442. Indeed, I have found none to date.

4. The chief sponsor of the bill, asked if the judge retained any discretion after the filing of the recusal affidavit, replied: "No, it provides the judge shall proceed no further with the case." 46 Cong. Rec. 2627 (1911).

a reasonable apprehension that he may be biased, or that an appellate court review that decision effectively. There is, therefore, no need to discern in §144 a rule by which a party who really wants to do so and has the nerve can at pleasure disqualify any federal judge in a given proceeding by presenting to him a spurious set of ex parte "facts" which he cannot question — and by which his opponent can disqualify his first replacement by the same means.[5]

I freely admit that *Berger* appears on its face to foreclose my reading of §144. The *Berger* decision, however, has not gone unscathed — even by its authors — in the many years since 1921. It is notorious that, faced with its quixotism, courts on the firing line have, addressing other issues, limited its scope in ways perhaps dubious. As is duly observed, for example, in Comment, 57 Minn. L. Rev. 749, 755 (1973), the lower federal courts have effectively rejected a liberal reading of *Berger* by such anomalous and desperate devices as requiring that the affidavit establish *bias-in-fact*, United States v. Gilboy, 162 F. Supp. 384, 393 (M.D. Pa. 1958), by restricting the *types* of facts which may constitute a sufficient affidavit, Chessman v. Teets, 239 F.2d 205, 215 (9th Cir. 1956), rev'd on other grounds, 354 U.S. 156, (1957), and by requiring that the bias be directed to the party *personally*, Cole v. Lowe's Inc., 76 F. Supp. 872, 876 (S.C. Cal. 1948), rev'd on other grounds, 185 F.2d 641 (9th Cir. 1950), cert. denied, 340 U.S. 954 . . . (1951). The Supreme Court has directly approved one such inroad in United States v. Grinnell Corp., 384 U.S. 563 . . . (1966), holding that the alleged bias "must stem from an extra-judicial source and result in an opinion on the merits on some basis other than what the judge learned from his participation in the case." Although the *Grinnell* Court cited *Berger,* the proposition stated can be construed far more broadly than anything mentioned there. Also, *Berger* to the contrary notwithstanding, it is far from clear that the Supreme Court in *Grinnell* felt itself bound to accept as given fact the allegations made by the affiants: in its opinion the Court quotes from what can only be the transcript of pretrial proceedings, a type of matter which the *Berger* Court went out of its way to declare irrelevant. In other instances the Court has denied certiorari and left standing inroads on and narrow interpretations of *Berger*. [citing cases]. I am all but convinced that if faced with the facts of *Berger* today the Supreme Court would decide it otherwise. Being so persuaded, I would not lightly expose our circuit to such risks of wholesale disruption as an untimely resurrection of *Berger* in its pristine and literal form threatens, to be endured until the Supreme Court — grappling with the mighty concerns which face it — is able to reconsider these questions.

Finally, I realize that the approach to §144 I advance is likely foreclosed even by previous panel decisions in our own circuit. [citing cases].

5. Section 144 limits a *party* to ". . . one such affidavit in any case."

But I do not think such a position wise or practical, and the court en banc is free to adopt a different one. I would grasp the nettle now.

TUTTLE, Circuit Judge, with whom GOLDBERG, Circuit Judge, joins, dissenting.

With deference I disagree with the opinion of the Court as to the standard that is to be used by the Court in determining whether an affidavit for bias filed under §144 is "sufficient." I agree with the statement quoted in the opinion from Davis v. Board of School Commissioners of Mobile County, 517 F.2d 1044 (5th Cir. 1975): "Once the motion is filed under §144, the judge must pass on the legal sufficiency of the affidavit, but may not pass the truth of the matters alleged. . . . I cannot agree, however, that the standard of determining the "legal sufficiency of the affidavit" is one that requires that the facts be such, their truth being assumed, as would "convince a reasonable man that a bias exists." As stated in the panel opinion of the Court, subsequently withdrawn, 505 F.2d 12, 5th Cir., I am of the view that the standard is one that merely requires that the facts be such, their truth being assumed, as would convince a reasonable man that the affiant reasonably *believed* that bias exists.

Of course, this Court, sitting en banc, is writing on a clean slate, and in doing so the Court, very properly, I think, considers that the standard to be applied to the decision of this issue is one that must meet the requirements of §455. It is my opinion that the *Berger* case, construing the predecessor of §144 and the new amended §455, outlined and discussed in the majority opinion, both require that the judge against whom an affidavit for bias is lodged must determine only whether the allegations are such as would cause a reasonable person standing in the same relationship as does the affiant to *believe* that the challenged judge has a "bent of mind that may prevent or impede impartiality of judgment." Berger v. United States, 255 U.S. 22, 33, 41 S. Ct. 230, 233, 65 L. Ed. 481.

If what is called the "objective" standard, that is whether a reasonable man would conclude that bias actually exists had been the standard intended by the Supreme Court in *Berger* the Court would not have said that the affidavit "must give fair support to the charge of a bent of mind that may prevent or impede impartiality of judgment." It would have said rather that the affidavit "must give fair support to the existence or fact of a bent of mind, etc." In discussing the standard in *Berger*, the Court referred to the language that the "affidavit shall state the facts and the reasons for the belief" of the existence of the bias or prejudice. The Court said: "Of course the reasons and facts for the belief the litigant entertains are an essential part of the affidavit, and must give fair support to the *charge* of a bent of mind. . . ." [Emphasis added.] It seems clear to me that this statement means that the affidavit must reasonably support the *belief* of the affiant and not that it must reasonably support the actual existence of bias. . . .

I would conclude that a trial court cannot be free from "any hint or appearance of bias" unless a party's sworn *belief* of the existence of bias, supported by substantial facts, and tested by a standard of reasonableness, is of primary concern.

The view which I hold as to the proper interpretation of §144 is fortified by the recent enactment by Congress of amendments to §455. This section of the Code provides as follows: "(a) Any justice, judge, magistrate, or referee in bankruptcy of the United States shall disqualify himself in any proceeding in which his impartiality might reasonably be questioned."

The House Report on this bill which adopted major portions of the Senate Report, No. 93-419 to accompany the Senate Bill commented expressly on the relation between this amendment and the newly adopted Code of Judicial Conduct for United States Judges. The Report contains the following language:

> Thus, the present situation is one where the Judicial Conference has made applicable to all federal judges the new Code of Judicial Conduct, including Canon 3C relating to disqualification of judges. The present language of §455 of title 28 is less restrictive than the new Canon on disqualification. The bill (S. 1064) under consideration would amend section 455 by making it conform, with two exceptions, to the requirements of the canon on disqualification.

1974 U.S. Code Congressional & Administrative News, p. 6353.

Only one of the "exceptions" referred to in the foregoing language is relevant to our discussion. This exception is the change made in the third word of the Code of Judicial Conduct. Congress saw fit to change the words "a judge *should* disqualify himself in a proceeding in which his impartiality might reasonably be questioned" to "a judge *shall* disqualify himself in a proceeding in which his impartiality might reasonably be questioned," thus indicating more clearly the intent of Congress that the standards be tightened up to the extent that less discretion was to be left to the particular judge.

Furthermore, the changing of the word from "should" to "shall" is explained by comments in the House Committee Report:

> The language also has the effect of removing the so-called "duty to sit" which has become a gloss on the existing statute. See Edwards v. United States, 334 F.2d 360 (5th Cir. 1964). Under the interpretation set forth in the *Edwards* case, a judge, faced with a close question on disqualification, was urged to resolve the issue in favor of a "duty to sit." Such a concept

has been criticized by legal writers and witnesses at the hearings were unanimously of the opinion that elimination of this "duty to sit" would enhance public confidence in the impartiality of the judicial system.

More importantly, however, it seems to me to be clear that both the Code and the new §455, which now speak in the same terms, have set up a standard involving the reasonableness of the belief or fear of the litigant rather than the reasonable likelihood of the existence of actual lack of impartiality. It will be noted that the language speaks in terms of the judge's impartiality being reasonably "questioned." It does not speak in terms of his partiality being reasonably likely to exist. Moreover, in the Committee Report the following language makes clear, it seems to me, that we are dealing with the reasonableness of the litigant's belief or fear of the existence of bias rather than the reasonableness of the claim that bias actually exists: "Nothing in this proposed legislation should be read to warrant the transformation of a litigant's fear that a judge may decide a question against him into a 'reasonable fear' that the judge will not be impartial." By clearest implication, it seems to me that this language says that the standard must be whether the litigant has a "reasonable fear" that the judge will not be impartial.

The use of the terms "objective" and "subjective" are somewhat confusing in this context. I agree that there must be an objective determination as to whether the facts and circumstances fairly support the litigant's belief or fear that there is a lack of impartiality. To this extent it is an objective test.

Under this test, therefore, I would have no doubt but that the affidavit in this case, considered in connection with the transcript of the hearing, which is proper in that it was attached as an exhibit to the affidavit, meets the test. We must bear in mind when we consider the facts alleged that what the whole case is about was the allegations that the defendants had intentionally discriminated in the conducting of bar examinations, the only means by which black applicants could become members of the Alabama Bar. Thus, the significance of each of the several facts, and the effect of their accumulation is what we should bear in mind.

Here, we have a challenge to the judge assigned to try this case alleging discrimination on account of race in the grading of bar examinations on the basis of the following factual setting: the lawyer for the plaintiffs and counsel for the defendants had held conversations off the record in the judge's chambers, apparently discussing the doubts that were in the minds of plaintiffs. At this time no affidavit under §144 had been filed. In effect, plaintiffs were undertaking to develop a basis for determining whether to file such an affidavit. The hearing conducted was in the form of questions and answers put to the judge by Mr. Clemon, counsel for the plaintiffs. This hearing developed the fact that the judge had been president of the Montgomery Bar Association shortly prior to being appointed to the bench and that at the time the rules of the Association forbade admission of black lawyers. When comment had been made in the public press about this fact and of Judge Varner's being considered for appointment to the United States Court, he appointed a commission to review the bar association by-laws, but gave no direction or recommendation that the racial restrictions be changed. They were subsequently changed, at a time which the judge thought was during his term of office; but as to this he was not certain.

We are not considering here merely former membership by the judge in a club or other social organization having restricted membership. We are concerned with a challenge to a judge who shortly before his appointment had been president of the bar association of the state's capital city, 50 years after the State Bar of Alabama had become, by law, the organized state bar. See Alabama Code Recompiled, Title 46, §21 et seq. It is not difficult to perceive the likelihood of a non-lawyer's confusing the status of the Montgomery Bar Association and its relationship with the State Bar of Alabama.

The additional grounds asserted in the affidavit as to the judge's relationship to the defendants cannot, it seems to me, be lightly overlooked because of prior decisions of this Court that an allegation that a judge was on a friendly basis with one of the witnesses expected to testify was not sufficient. Such was the case of Simmons v. United States, 89 F.2d 591 (5th Cir. 1937). Here, Judge Varner was acquainted with ten of the thirteen defendants who were members of the Board of Bar Examiners, three only slightly and several on a basis of what he considered friendship. Three of them he did not know at all. When asked as to the effect of his acquaintance or friendship with defendants in the event of a possible conflict in testimony in the anticipated hearings, Judge Varner, indicated a strong feeling of confidence in the veracity and trustworthiness of his friends. When asked expressly with respect to Mr. Scott, who had previously been secretary of the commission, and thus the one person who had custody of all of the documents, he expressed similar confidence in his likely credibility, noting that "if [Scott] appeared to evade I think I could detect it."[3]

The opinion of the Court proceeds on the theory that Judge Varner should not be faulted for answering honestly that he had a strong feeling of confidence in the veracity and trustworthiness of his friends. Of course, no one can take exception to the judge's answers to the inquiry. The point is that if a trial judge already has sufficient contacts with liti-

---

3. It is of significance that none of these persons appeared to testify personally. The motion for summary judgment was based solely upon their affidavits. There, of course, were no opportunities to make any credibility choices by use of the normal standards available to a trial judge.

gants who are to testify before him that he is compelled to answer truthfully that he already has a belief that they will be likely to tell the truth, the solution of the problem is not for him to refuse to answer or to hedge in answering a question but to recuse himself on the ground that one of the ingredients in the making of the final judgment will be matters dehors the record, that is, those qualities of friendship which have resulted in the judge having understandably a feeling of confidence in the veracity of the witnesses who are his friends. Of course, the judge answered the question in the only way he could. The problem arises from the fact to which he testified in making his answer; that is, that the affiants entered the litigation with at least a predilection in the judge's mind of favoring the veracity of opposing parties.

In sum, it appears to me that the combination of the facts alleged in the affidavit satisfied the requirements of §144. Whether either one of the allegations standing alone would have been sufficient it is not necessary for me to decide. In addition to concluding, as I do, that the allegations in the affidavit were sufficient, it is more than clear that, even though the trial court should have adopted what the court now states to be the proper standard he did not even do that. He failed in two respects. In the first place, his statement quoted above clearly shows that he followed the theory of a "duty to sit," which clearly has been now eliminated under §455. In the second place, he merely decided the question of bias vel non rather than attempting to determine whether the affidavit was or was not sufficient by any standard.

Especially in light of the recent enactment of the amendments to §455 it seems peculiarly inappropriate for an appellate court to take away from the trial court the opportunity to determine whether under the provisions of this newly enacted statute he should recuse himself because of his consciousness that "his impartiality might reasonably be questioned." This is an inquiry which, it seems to me, Congress clearly meant to have the trial judge make for himself. He is best able, under standards which are entirely new since the matter was before the trial court, to weigh the allegations of fact in the affidavit in connection with the particular lawsuit then pending before him and make a determination as contemplated under §455. It seems to me that it is not our place to substitute our judgment for that of the trial court in the making of this initial determination.

I think this is peculiarly required in this case, since the trial judge clearly indicated an inclination to recuse himself but for his idea of a "duty to sit."[4]

Thus, even under the standard of inquiry announced by the Court it seems inappropriate to me for the Court to decide for the trial judge

---

4. . . . . "Heretofore, I had felt that a judge should recuse himself very quickly *because it made the court appear more fair.*" [Emphasis added.]

whether the affidavit was "sufficient" within the contemplation of §144, with the gloss which is placed upon it by the amended §455.

I would reverse the determination by the trial court overruling the affidavit and send the case back either under a determination that the affidavit was sufficient or to permit the trial court himself to determine under the standards now announced for the first time by this Court whether the affidavit met the requirements of the statute.

[Concurring opinions by Judges Brown, Godbold and Roney and dissenting opinion by Judge Wisdom omitted.]

NOTES

1. Leitch, Judicial Disqualification in the Federal Courts, 67 Iowa L. Rev. 525 (1982) contains a useful discussion of the cases adopting the various positions taken by the judges in *Parrish.* He concludes:

> The better view of the relationship of the three substantive provisions to allegations of bias, or the appearance of bias, is as follows: (1) section 144 requires legally sufficient allegations of bias-in-fact but no proof on the veracity of the allegations, (2) section 455(b)(1) requires allegations of bias-in-fact that are subject to a test of veracity, (3) section 455(a) requires allegations of the appearance of bias that are subject to a test of veracity, but only to substantiate an appearance of bias rather than to substantiate actual bias. This view of the three sections seems to best give effect to the natural meaning of the language in each section. Furthermore, this view is most widely followed in the circuits. Id. at 538.

2. Other provisions of §455 cause difficulty. In In re Cement and Concrete Antitrust Litigation, 515 F. Supp. 1076 (D. Ariz. 1981), mandamus denied, 688 F.2d 1297 (9th Cir. 1982), judgment aff'd for lack of a quorum, 102 S. Ct. 1173 (1983), the per se rule of §455(b)(4) required a judge who had been handling the case for five years to disqualify himself when he realized that his wife held some stock in corporations that were part of one class although the litigation could not have benefited her by more than $30.

3. The tough standards of the federal statutes and the Code of Judicial Conduct have created a problem with respect to en banc hearings in the federal courts of appeals. A number of the circuits have rules that require a fixed number of judges to vote for rehearing en banc and do not alter that number when judges are recused. There have therefore been a number of cases in which rehearing en banc has been denied despite a majority vote of sitting judges for rehearing. This is particularly a problem if the subject matter of a case requires recusal of a number of judges in the circuit, because the problem may then occur in a great number of cases. See Harper, The Breakdown in Federal appeals, 70 A.B.A.J. 56 (1984).

The most recent exposition of the reach of §455(a) by the Supreme Court arose in the context of the rather unusual situation where a judge, who was clearly disqualified, sat and decided the case because, as the trial court found, he had forgotten about the disqualifying circumstances.

LILJEBERG v. HEALTH SERVICES ACQUISITION CORP.

108 S. Ct. 2194 (1988)

Justice STEVENS delivered the opinion of the Court.

. . . In November 1981, respondent Health Services Acquisition Corp. brought an action against petitioner John Liljeberg, Jr., seeking a declaration of ownership of a corporation known as St. Jude Hospital of Kenner, Louisiana (St. Jude). The case was tried by Judge Robert Collins, sitting without a jury. Judge Collins found for Liljeberg and, over a strong dissent, the Court of Appeals affirmed. Approximately 10 months later, respondent learned that Judge Collins had been a member of the Board of Trustees of Loyola University while Liljeberg was negotiating with Loyola to purchase a parcel of land on which to construct a hospital. The success and benefit to Loyola of these negotiations turned, in large part, on Liljeberg prevailing in the litigation before Judge Collins.

Based on this information, respondent moved pursuant to Federal Rule of Civil Procedure 60(b)(6) to vacate the judgment on the ground that Judge Collins was disqualified under §455 at the time he heard the action and entered judgment in favor of Liljeberg. Judge Collins denied the motion and respondent appealed. The Court of Appeals determined that resolution of the motion required factual findings concerning the extent and timing of Judge Collins' knowledge of Loyola's interest in the declaratory relief litigation. Accordingly, the panel reversed and remanded the matter to a different judge for such findings. On remand, the District Court found that based on his attendance at Board meetings Judge Collins had actual knowledge of Loyola's interest in St. Jude in 1980 and 1981. The court further concluded, however, that Judge Collins had forgotten about Loyola's interest by the time the declaratory judgment suit came to trial in January 1982. On March 24, 1982, Judge Collins reviewed materials sent to him by the Board to prepare for an upcoming meeting. At that time — just a few days after he had filed his opinion finding for Liljeberg and still within the 10-day period allowed for filing a motion for a new trial — Judge Collins once again obtained actual knowledge of Loyola's interest in St. Jude. Finally, the District Court found that although Judge Collins thus lacked actual knowledge during trial and prior to the filing of his opinion, the evidence nonetheless gave rise to an appearance of impropriety. However, reading the Court of Appeals' mandate as limited to the issue of actual knowledge, the District Court concluded that it was compelled to deny respondent's Rule 60(b) motion.

The Court of Appeals again reversed. The court first noted that Judge Collins should have immediately disqualified himself when his actual knowledge of Loyola's interest was renewed. The court also found that regardless of Judge Collins' actual knowledge, "a reasonable observer would expect that Judge Collins would remember that Loyola had some dealings with Liljeberg and St. Jude and seek to ascertain the nature of these dealings." 796 F. 2d 796, 803 (1986). Such an appearance of impropriety, in the view of the Court of Appeals, was sufficient ground for disqualification under §455(a). Although recognizing that caution is required in determining whether a judgment should be vacated after becoming final, the court concluded that since the appearance of partiality was convincingly established and since the motion to vacate was filed as promptly as possible, the appropriate remedy was to vacate the declaratory relief judgment. . . .

In considering whether the Court of Appeals properly vacated the declaratory relief judgment, we are required to address two questions. We must first determine whether §455(a) can be violated based on an appearance of partiality, even though the judge was not conscious of the circumstances creating the appearance of impropriety, and second, whether relief is available under Rule 60(b) when such a violation is not discovered until after the judgment has become final.

Title 28 U.S.C. §455 provides in relevant part:

> (a) Any justice, judge, or magistrate of the United States shall disqualify himself in any proceeding in which his impartiality might reasonably be questioned.
>
> (b) He shall also disqualify himself in the following circumstances: . . .
>
> (4) He knows that he, individually or as a fiduciary, or his spouse or minor child residing in his household, has a financial interest in the subject matter in controversy or in a party to the proceeding, or any other interest that could be substantially affected by the outcome of the proceeding. . . .
>
> (c) A judge should inform himself about his personal and fiduciary financial interests, and make a reasonable effort to inform himself about the personal financial interests of his spouse and minor children residing in his household.

Scienter is not an element of a violation of §455(a). The judge's lack of knowledge of a disqualifying circumstance may bear on the question of remedy, but it does not eliminate the risk that "his impartiality might reasonably be questioned" by other persons. To read §455(a) to provide that the judge must know of the disqualifying facts, requires not simply ignoring the language of the provision — which makes no mention of knowledge — but further requires concluding that the language in subsection (b)(4) — which expressly provides that the judge must *know* of his or her interest — is extraneous. A careful reading of the respective subsections makes clear that Congress intended to require knowledge under subsection (b)(4) and not to require knowledge under subsection (a). Moreover, advancement of the purpose of the provision — to promote public confidence in the integrity of the judicial process, see S. Rep. No. 93-419, p. 5 (1973); H. R. Rep. No. 93-1453, p. 5 (1974) — does not depend upon whether or not the judge actually knew of facts creating an appearance of impropriety, so long as the public might reasonably believe that he or she knew. As Chief Judge Clark of the Court of Appeals explained:

> The goal of section 455(a) is to avoid even the appearance of partiality. If it would appear to a reasonable person that a judge has knowledge of facts that would give him an interest in the litigation then an appearance of partiality is created even though no actual partiality exists because the judge does not recall the facts, because the judge actually has no interest in the case or because the judge is pure in heart and incorruptible. The judge's forgetfulness, however, is not the sort of objectively ascertainable fact that can avoid the appearance of partiality. Hall v. Small Business Administration, 695 F. 2d 175, 179 (5th Cir. 1983). Under section 455(a), therefore, recusal is required even when a judge lacks actual knowledge of the facts indicating his interest or bias in the case if a reasonable person, knowing all the circumstances, would expect that the judge would have actual knowledge. 796 F.2d, at 802.

Contrary to petitioner's contentions, this reading of the statute does not call upon judges to perform the impossible — to disqualify themselves based on facts they do not know. If, as petitioner argues, §455(a) should only be applied prospectively, then requiring disqualification based on facts the judge does not know would of course be absurd; a judge could never be expected to disqualify himself based on some fact he does not know, even though the fact is one that perhaps he should know or one that people might reasonably suspect that he does know. But to the extent the provision can also, in proper cases, be applied retroactively, the judge is not called upon to perform an impossible feat. Rather, he is called upon to rectify an oversight and to take the steps necessary to maintain public confidence in the impartiality of the judiciary. If he concludes that "his impartiality might reasonably be questioned," then he should also find that the statute has been violated. This is certainly not an impossible task. No one questions that Judge Collins could have disqualified himself and vacated his judgment when he finally realized that Loyola had an interest in the litigation. The initial appeal was taken from his failure to disqualify himself and vacate the judgment *after* he became aware of the appearance of impropriety, not from his failure to disqualify himself when he first became involved in the litigation and lacked the requisite knowledge.

In this case both the District Court and the Court of Appeals found an ample basis in the record for concluding that an objective observer would have questioned Judge Collins' impartiality. Accordingly, even though his failure to disqualify himself was the product of a temporary lapse of memory, it was nevertheless a plain violation of the terms of the statute.

A conclusion that a statutory vision occurred does not, however, end our inquiry. As in other areas of the law, there is surely room for harmless error committed by busy judges who inadvertently overlook a disqualifying circumstance. There need not be a draconian remedy for every violation of §455(a). It would be equally wrong, however, to adopt an absolute prohibition against any relief in cases involving forgetful judges.

Although §455 defines the circumstances that mandate disqualification of federal judges, it neither prescribes nor prohibits any particular remedy for a violation of that duty. Congress has wisely delegated to the judiciary the task of fashioning the remedies that will best serve the purpose of the legislation. In considering whether a remedy is appropriate, we do well to bear in mind that in many cases — and this is such an example — the Court of Appeals is in a better position to evaluate the significance of a violation than is this Court. Its judgment as to the proper remedy should thus be afforded our due consideration. A review of the facts demonstrates that the Court of Appeals' determination that a new trial is in order is well supported.

Section 455 does not, on its own, authorize the reopening of closed litigation. However, as respondent and the Court of Appeals recognized, Federal Rule of Civil Procedure 60(b) provides a procedure whereby, in appropriate cases, a party may be relieved of a final judgment. In particular, Rule 60(b)(6), upon which respondent relies, grants federal courts broad authority to relieve a party from a final judgment "upon such terms as are just," provided that the motion is made within a reasonable time and is not premised on one of the grounds for relief enumerated in clauses (b)(1) through (b)(5). The rule does not particularize the factors that justify relief, but we have previously noted that it provides courts with authority "adequate to enable them to vacate judgments whenever such action is appropriate to accomplish justice," Klapprott v. United States, 335 U.S. 601, 614-615 (1949), while also cautioning that it should only be applied in "extraordinary circumstances," Ackermann v. United States, 340 U.S. 193 (1950). Rule 60(b)(6) relief is accordingly neither categorically available nor categorically unavailable for all §455 violations. We conclude that in determining whether a judgment should be vacated for a violation of §455, it is appropriate to consider the risk of injustice to the parties in the particular case, the risk that the denial of relief will produce injustice in other cases, and the risk of undermining the public's confidence in the judicial process. . . .

Like the Court of Appeals, we accept the District Court's finding that while the case was actually being tried Judge Collins did not have actual knowledge of Loyola's interest in the dispute over the ownership of St. Jude and its precious certificate of need. When a busy federal judge concentrates his or her full attention on a pending case, personal concerns are easily forgotten. The problem, however, is that people who have not served on the bench are often all too willing to indulge suspicions and doubts concerning the integrity of judges. The very purpose of §455(a) is to promote confidence in the judiciary by avoiding even the appearance of impropriety whenever possible. See S. Rep. No. 93-419, at 5; H. R. Rep. No. 93-1453, at 5. Thus, it is critically important in a case of this kind to identify the facts that might reasonably cause an objective observer to question Judge Collins' impartiality. [The Court then noted that it was remarkable that the judge who had regularly attended meetings that discussed the University's interest in St. Jude's Hospital should have forgotten about it; that it was unfortunate that although before he entered judgment he had received minutes of a meeting that he did not attend at which the subject was discussed, he did not open the envelope in time; that it was remarkable and inexcusable that when he did have actual knowledge, within 10 days after entering judgment, he did not recuse himself and said nothing; and finally that when he denied the motion to vacate the judgment, he did not mention that he had known of the University's interest both shortly before and shortly after the trial.]

These facts create precisely the kind of appearance of impropriety that §455(a) was intended to prevent. The violation is neither insubstantial nor excusable. Although Judge Collins did not know of his fiduciary interest in the litigation, he certainly should have known. In fact, his failure to stay informed of this fiduciary interest, may well constitute a separate violation of §455. See §455(c). Moreover, providing relief in cases such as this will not produce injustice in other cases; to the contrary, the Court of Appeals' willingness to enforce §455 may prevent a substantive injustice in some future case by encouraging a judge or litigant to more carefully examine possible grounds for disqualification and to promptly disclose them when discovered. It is therefore appropriate to vacate the judgment unless it can be said that respondent did not make a timely request for relief, or that it would otherwise be unfair to deprive the prevailing party of its judgment.

If we focus on fairness to the particular litigants, a careful study of [dissenting] Judge Rubin's analysis of the merits of the underlying litigation suggests that there is a greater risk of unfairness in upholding the judgment in favor of Liljeberg than there is in allowing a new judge to take a fresh look at the issues. Moreover, neither Liljeberg nor Loyola University has made a showing of special hardship by reason of their reliance on the original judgment. Finally, although a delay of 10 months after the affirmance by the Court of Appeals would normally foreclose relief based on a violation of §455(a), in this case the entire delay is attributable to Judge Collins' inexcusable failure to disqualify himself on March 24, 1982; had he recused himself on March 24, or even disclosed Loyola's interest in the case at that time, the motion could have been made less than 10 days after the entry of judgment. "The guiding consideration is that the administration of justice should reasonably appear to be disinterested as well as be so in fact." Public Utilities Comm'n v. Pollak, 343 U.S. 451, 466-467 (1952) (Frankfurter, J., in chambers). In sum, we conclude that Chief Judge Clark's opinion of the Court of Appeals reflects an eminently sound and wise disposition of this case.

The judgment of the Court of Appeals is accordingly Affirmed.

Chief Justice REHNQUIST, with whom Justice WHITE and Justice SCALIA join, dissenting.

The Court's decision in this case is long on ethics in the abstract, but short on workable rules of law. The Court first finds that 28 U.S.C. §455(a) can be used to disqualify a judge on the basis of facts not known to the judge himself. It then broadens the standard for overturning final judgments under Federal Rule of Civil Procedure 60(b). Because these results are at odds with the intended scope of §455 and Rule 60(b), and are likely to cause considerable mischief when courts attempt to apply them, I dissent.

As detailed in the Court's opinion, §455(a) provides that "[a]ny justice, judge, or magistrate of the United States shall disqualify himself in any proceeding in which his impartiality might reasonably be questioned." Section 455 was substantially revised by Congress in 1974 to conform with the recently adopted Canon 3C of the American Bar Association's Code of Judicial Conduct (1974). Previously, a federal judge was required to recuse himself when he had a substantial interest in the proceedings, or when "in his opinion" it was improper for him to hear the case. Subsection (a) was drafted to replace the subjective standard of the old disqualification statute with an objective test. Congress hoped that this objective standard would promote public confidence in the impartiality of the judicial process by instructing a judge, when confronted with circumstances in which his impartiality could reasonably be doubted, to disqualify himself and allow another judge to preside over the case. The amended statute also had the effect of removing the so-called "duty to sit," which had become an accepted gloss on the existing statute.

Subsection (b) of §455 sets forth more particularized situations in which a judge must disqualify himself. Congress intended the provisions of §455(b) to remove any doubt about recusal in cases where a judge's interest is too closely connected with the litigation to allow his participation. Subsection (b)(4), for example, disqualifies a jurist if he knows that he, his spouse, or his minor children have a financial interest in the subject matter in controversy. Unlike the more open-ended provision adopted in subsection (a), the language of subsection (b) requires recusal only in specific circumstances, and is phrased in such a way as to suggest a requirement of actual knowledge of the disqualifying circumstances.

The purpose of §455 is obviously to inform judges of what matters they must consider in deciding whether to recuse themselves in a given case. The Court here holds, as did the Court of Appeals below, that a judge must recuse himself under §455(a) if he *should have known* of the circumstances requiring disqualification, even though in fact he did not know of them. I do not believe this is a tenable construction of subsection (a). A judge considering whether or not to recuse himself is necessarily limited to those facts bearing on the question of which he has knowledge. To hold that disqualification is required by reason of facts which the judge does *not* know, even though he should have known of them, is to posit a conundrum which is not decipherable by ordinary mortals. While the concept of "constructive knowledge" is useful in other areas of the law, I do not think it should be imported into §455(a).

At the direction of the Court of Appeals, Judge Schwartz of the District Court for the Eastern District of Louisiana made factual findings concerning the extent and timing of Judge Collins' knowledge of Loyola's interest in the underlying lawsuit. Judge Schwartz determined that Judge Collins had no actual knowledge of Loyola's involvement when he tried the case. Not until March 24, 1982, when he reviewed materials in preparation for a Board meeting, did Judge Collins obtain actual knowledge of the negotiations between petitioners and Loyola.

Despite this factual determination, reached after a public hearing on the subject, the Court nevertheless concludes that "public confidence in the impartiality of the judiciary" compels retroactive disqualification of Judge Collins under §455(a). This conclusion interprets §455(a) in a manner which Congress never intended. As the Court of Appeals noted, in drafting §455(a) Congress was concerned with the "appearance" of impropriety, and to that end changed the previous subjective standard for disqualification to an objective one; no longer was disqualification to be decided on the basis of the opinion of the judge in question, but by the standard of what a reasonable person would think. But the facts and circumstances which this reasonable person would consider must be the facts and circumstances *known* to the judge at the time. In short, as is unquestionably the case with subsection (b), I would adhere to a standard of actual knowledge in §455(a), and not slide off into the very speculative ground of "constructive" knowledge.

The Court then compounds its error by allowing Federal Rule of Civil Procedure 60(b)(6) to be used to set aside a final judgment in this case.

Rule 60(b) authorizes a district court, on motion and upon such terms as are just, to relieve a party from a final judgment, order, or proceeding for any "reason justifying relief from the operation of the judgment." However, we have repeatedly instructed that only truly "extraordinary circumstances" will permit a party successfully to invoke the "any other reason" clause of §60(b). See Klapprott v. United States, 335 U.S. 601, 613 (1949); see also Ackermann v. United States, 340 U.S. 193, 199 (1950). This very strict interpretation of Rule 60(b) is essential if the finality of judgments is to be preserved.

For even if one accepts the Court's proposition that §455(a) permits disqualification on the basis of a judge's constructive knowledge, Rule 60(b)(6) should not be used in this case to apply §455(a) retroactively to Judge Collins' participation in the lawsuit. In the first place, it is beyond cavil that Judge Collins stood to receive no *personal* financial gain from the transactions involving petitioner, respondent, and Loyola. Judge Collins' only prior tie to the dealings was as a member of Loyola's rather large Board of Trustees and, although Judge Collins was a member of at least two of the Board's subcommittees, he had no connection with the Real Estate subcommittee, the entity responsible for negotiating the sale of the Monroe Tract. In addition, the motion to set aside the judgment was made by respondent almost 10 months after judgment was entered in March 1982; although relief under Rule 60(b)(6) is subject to no absolute time limitation, there can be no serious argument that the time elapsed since the entry of judgment must weigh heavily in considering the motion. Finally, and most important, Judge Schwartz determined that Judge Collins did not have actual knowledge of his conflict of interest during trial and that he made no rulings after he acquired actual knowledge. I thus think it very unlikely that respondent was subjected to substantial injustice by Judge Collins' failure to recuse himself, and believe that the majority's use of Rule 60(b)(6) retroactively to set aside the underlying judgment is therefore unwarranted.

Justice O'CONNOR, dissenting.

For the reasons given by Chief Justice Rehnquist, *ante,* at [p. 729 of this book], I agree that "constructive knowledge" cannot be the basis for a violation of 28 U.S.C. §455(a). The question then remains whether respondent is entitled to a new trial because there are other "extraordinary circumstances," apart from the §455(a) violation found by the Fifth Circuit, that justify "relief from operation of the judgment." See Fed. Rule Civ. Proc. 60(b)(6); Ackermann v. United States, 340 U.S. 193, 199 (1950); Klapprott v. United States, 335 U.S. 601, 613 (1949). Although the Court collects an impressive array of arguments that might support the granting of such relief, I believe the issue should be addressed in the first instance by the courts below. I would therefore remand this case with appropriate instructions.

NOTES

1. In considering the strength of the point made by the dissent that the judge's disqualification depends on what the judge knew, not what he should have known, note that the focus of §455(a) is not on either of those facts but rather on the appearance to third parties. Looked at that way, the majority's point ought to be that the parties or the public would have questioned the judge's impartiality if they had known all the circumstances, and the dissent's point ought to be that it would not be reasonable to question the impartiality of the judge when the judge does not have the disqualifying factors in mind during the trial. That is where Judge Stevens' recitation of the facts becomes quite relevant. The parties and the public might well question the impartiality of a judge who knew about the disqualifying factors just before and just after the trial even if he did not "know" of them during the trial. Those factors might well be feared to be operating in the judge's unconscious.

Which of course brings us to the other possible interpretation of Judge Stevens' remarks — that they are a signal that although the Court was not prepared to reverse the finding about the trial judge's lack of knowledge, it was sufficiently doubtful about it that it was willing to give §455(a) something of a retroactive reading so that it could be applied to a case whose facts were perceived as giving rise to reasonable fear of partiality.

2. There are some lessons in this case for judges and lawyers. The first is that their judicial obligations require them to pay very close attention to the details of their extrajudicial activities. The second is that when their extrajudicial activities have widespread ramifications throughout the community in which they live, they ought at least to consider whether those ramifications are consistent with their judicial duties — that is, their obligation not to put themselves in situations that will require their disqualification. One may also wonder why the lawyers were not aware of the judge's position on the board of trustees of the University.

3. Another kind of recusal problem arose in Matter of Ronwin, which was discussed at pp. 617-626. The Arizona Supreme Court was faced with deciding an admissions to the bar problem in the context of a situation in which the applicant had already sued the members of the Court in connection with those problems. The Court responded as follows:

Recusal Problems

Yet another problem arises. One member of this court recused himself after oral argument because he felt too personally involved in the case to participate in the decision. That leaves four members of this court. Each has been made a defendant by Ronwin in various actions. If we are to recuse ourselves simply because we have been sued by the applicant, then who is left to decide this case? As the Ninth Circuit stated: "'[A] judge is not disqualified merely because a litigant sues or threatens to sue him.' Such an easy method for obtaining disqualification should not be encouraged or allowed." Ronwin v. State Bar of Arizona, 686 F.2d at 701, quoting United States v. Grismore, 564 F.2d 929, 933 (10th Cir. 1977); . . . We agree; the mere fact that a judge has been sued by reason of his rulings in a case does not require recusal. Nor can the fact that all judges in the court have been sued require recusal. To honor such a technique would be to put the weapon of disqualification in the hands of the most unscrupulous. . . . 136 Ariz. 566, 575-576, 667 P.2d 1281, 1290-1291 (1983).

4. Chief Justice Rehnquist's view on the subject of disqualification may well be tempered by his own controversial refusal to disqualify himself in Laird v. Tatum and his opinion justifying that refusal. 409 U.S. 824 (1972). The issue was the relation between testimony that he gave on behalf of the Justice Department before a Senate Committee on the general subject of the executive constitutional powers to gather information and the subject matter of the actual case in which he sat. His opinion is excerpted and criticized at pp. 785-795 of the second edition of this book.

Earlier materials in this book cover the effect of lawyers' rules of conduct on lawyers' freedom of speech. See pp. 434-453. There are similar problems with respect to the effect of judges' rules of conduct on their freedom of speech.

In re MANDEVILLE
481 A.2d 1048 (Vt. 1984)

Before Billings, C.J., and Hill, Underwood, Peck and Gibson, J.J. Per Curiam.

This is a disciplinary procedure brought against a judicial officer pursuant to the Rules of Supreme Court for Disciplinary Control of Judges, 12 V.S.A. App. I, Part IV. The defendant is a district judge, Brandon-Waterbury Circuit, for the State of Vermont. A complaint was lodged against the defendant charging that he had violated Canon 2 A of the Code of Judicial Conduct, in that he failed to conduct himself, at all times, in a manner that promotes public confidence in the integrity and impartiality of the judiciary.

Judge Mandeville granted an interview to a reporter for the Rutland Herald, a newspaper of general circulation in Vermont. In the subsequent article published in the Herald, the judge was quoted as having said, "A plea of guilty shows that the defendant has some kind of repentance for what he did that would not hold true in a trial. In that case he would not be dealt with as leniently." The issue before us is whether the judge's statements violated the judicial canon requiring public confidence in the integrity and impartiality of the judiciary. We hold that they do.

We have held that the burdens imposed by the Canons of Judicial Conduct upon those who accept judicial office are extremely high. "The Canons of Judicial Conduct are standards measuring fitness for judicial office and therefore embrace tests of behavior relating to integrity and propriety that condemn actions in which the average citizen can freely indulge without consequence." In re Douglas, 135 Vt. 585, 592, 382 A.2d 215, 219 (1977).

The Sixth Amendment to the United States Constitution and Chapter I, Article 10 of the Vermont Constitution provide that in all criminal prosecutions a person has the right to a trial before an impartial jury. We have taken these constitutional guarantees seriously, holding that since due process is involved in the right to trial by an impartial jury, the law is sensitive to any infringement or impairment. State v. Ovitt, 126 Vt. 320, 324, 229 A.2d 237, 240 (1967).

Any pronouncement relative to the right to trial by jury as made by this judge may have a chilling effect on that constitutionally protected right. Such effect is an impairment of that right. Such impairment results in conduct of a manner that fails to promote public confidence in the integrity and impartiality of the judiciary in contravention of Canon 2 A.

We find the defendant guilty of the charge, and a disciplinary order is required.

Under the authority of 4 V.S.A. §3, and 12 V.S.A. App. I, Part IV, Rule 11, the Court finds a violation of Canon 2 A of the Code of Judicial Conduct, 12 V.S.A.App. VIII, A.O. 10, on the part of the appellant, Theodore S. Mandeville, Jr., and orders that the appellant be publicly reprimanded.

<hr>

In re GRIDLEY

417 So.2d 950 (Fla. 1982)

ALDERMAN, Justice.

The Florida Judicial Qualifications Commission has filed its recommendations with this Court that Judge William C. Gridley, Circuit Judge for the Ninth Judicial Circuit, be reprimanded for violating Florida Bar Code of Judicial Conduct, Canons 2 A, 2 B, and 5 A. These recommendations are premised on its findings that Judge Gridley is guilty as charged in counts 1 and 2 of the formal charges filed against him by the

Commission. [Count 1 dealt with charges that Judge Gridley had inject-ed himself as an advocate into a particular matter.]

Count 2 of the formal charges is predicated on two letters to the edi-tor written by Judge Gridley and published in the *Orlando Sentinel Star* and an article written by Judge Gridley and published in an Episcopal church newsletter. One of the letters expressed his views on Christian forgiveness, and the other expressed his view against capital punish-ment. His article in the newsletter discussed his views against capital punishment but made clear that he would do his duty as a judge and follow the law as written.

The Commission recommends that we find that this conduct violates Canon 2 A, requiring him to act in a manner that promotes public con-fidence in the integrity and impartiality of the judiciary, and Canon 5 A, permitting a judge to write, lecture, teach, and speak on nonlegal sub-jects, if these activities do not detract from the dignity of his office or interfere with the performance of his duties.

Judge Gridley argues that to penalize him for these utterings violates his first amendment right to free speech and alternatively argues that his particular conduct does not offend the Code of Judicial Conduct. We agree with this latter contention and therefore do not reach his free speech argument.

Although finding no violation of the canons in this case, we caution judges against indiscriminately voicing their objection to the law lest they be misunderstood by the public as being unwilling to enforce the law as written, thereby undermining public confidence in the integrity and im-partiality of the judiciary. In In re Kelly, 238 So.2d 565 (Fla. 1970), cert. denied, 401 U.S. 962, 91 S. Ct. 970, 28 L. Ed.2d 246 (1971), we discussed responsible methods that could be utilized by a judge in expressing his views on law reform. We said:

> There are many authorized methods of protest, dissent and criticism within the framework of the judiciary, such as the preparation of dissent-ing opinions, petitions to the Supreme Court for changes in the rules of procedure, submission of suggested changes to various committees of The Florida Bar, participating in the various legal seminars conducted by the Committee on Legal Education, or taking an active part in the state and local conferences of judges.

238 So.2d at 569. In our subsequent decision of In Re Inquiry Concern-ing a Judge, 357 So.2d 172 (Fla. 1978), we stated that differences of opinion and variations in philosophy among judicial officers are toler-ated, and strong minority views expressed by members of the judiciary are not grounds for disciplinary action. But we stressed that there are limits that judicial officers must observe. We said: "Judges are required to follow the law and apply it fairly and objectively to all who appear

before them. *No judge is permitted to substitute his concept of what the law ought to be for what the law actually is.*" 357 So.2d at 179 (emphasis supplied).

There is no doubt that a judge in an appropriate forum may express his protest, dissent, and criticism of the present state of the law as long as he does not appear to substitute his concept of what the law ought to be for what the law actually is, and as long as he expresses himself in a manner that promotes public confidence in his integrity and impartiality as a judge. The manner in which Judge Gridley expressed his criticism of the death penalty is close to the dividing line between what is appropriate and what is not. Most judges, we believe, would not have expressed their dissent in the same manner as Judge Gridley because, even if this conduct did not violate the Code of Judicial Conduct, they would have considered it to be in poor taste and subject to possible misinterpretation by the public. With the benefit of hindsight, it appears that today even Judge Gridley would consider more appropriate forums in which to express his dissent. Considering all of the circumstances of this case, however, we conclude that Judge Gridley did not violate the Code of Judicial Conduct in writing his two letters to the editor and publishing an article in an Episcopal church newsletter. The record in this case does not establish that his letters and article caused any disrespect for the law or his judicial office, interfered with the performance of his official duties, or resulted in a loss of public confidence in the integrity and impartiality of the judicial system. Judge Gridley made it clear that he was duty bound to follow the law and that he would do so although he did advocate law reform in the area of capital punishment. . . .

SUNDBERG, Chief Justice, concurring specially.

Although I concur in the Court's opinion in this proceeding, I must voice my reservation about one aspect of the opinion. The majority concludes that Judge Gridley's speaking out on the subject of the death penalty in the fashion which he did constituted no violation of the Code of Judicial Conduct. I agree. I also agree that judges should be circumspect in their public statements because of the special role of impartial arbiter which they play in our society. The judge must always guard against making public statements which compromise his impartiality or appearance of impartiality.

Nevertheless, I do not subscribe to the notion that the judge's forum is limited to those means of expression categorized in In re Kelly, 238 So.2d. 565 (Fla. 1970), cert. denied, 401 U.S. 962, 91 S. Ct. 970, 28 L. Ed.2d 246 (1971), as suggested by the majority. The methods therein enumerated are limited to the judicial and legal communities. I believe judges, on occasion, may be obliged to speak out to a much larger community through other mediums. The efforts of members of this Court in support of the revision of Article V of our Constitution in 1972 and again in 1980 prove this assertion. There are times and issues which will compel judges to speak out in forums quite afield of those suggested in In re Kelly. I would not discourage fulfillment of that responsibility on their part.

ADKINS and EHRLICH, J.J., concur.

OVERTON, Justice, concurring in part, dissenting in part.

I fully concur in the majority's decision that Judge Gridley's course of conduct in the Farmer matter was a clear violation of the Code of Judicial Conduct, Canon 2. I strongly dissent, however, from the finding that the judge's course of conduct in publicly advocating the elimination of the death penalty did not interfere with the impartial performance of his duties and was not prohibited by the Code of Judicial Conduct. The fact that the comments of the judge deal directly with an issue which may come before him, in addition to the importance of the circuit judge's role in the death sentence process, gives me considerable concern about the impact of the majority's decision on our present Code of Judicial Conduct.

The instant conduct which I find improper took the form of two letters to the editor of the *Orlando Sentinel Star* and an article published in an Episcopalian church newsletter. I find that these publications have essentially destroyed Judge Gridley's image of impartiality in death penalty cases, a very sensitive area of his jurisdiction.

A circuit judge has an extremely critical position in our death sentence procedure, which is illustrated by the fact that, irrespective of the jury's recommendation or the desires of an appellate court, only a circuit judge can impose the death sentence. If the judge chooses not to do so, the state may not appeal that decision.

In my opinion, no reasonable person could read Judge Gridley's letters or article and still realistically believe that the judge would actually impose a death sentence, even if it was in accordance with a jury's recommendation. Even less realistic would be that the judge would override a jury recommendation of life and impose a death sentence in an appropriate circumstance as allowed by law. Assuming that Judge Gridley would, in accordance with his concluding remarks in the article, impose a death sentence where appropriate, his conduct in publishing the letters and article could adversely affect the death penalty process. For example, in Smith v. State, 197 So.2d 497 (Fla. 1967), defense counsel advised the defendant that the circuit judge before whom he was to appear had publicly spoken in opposition to the death penalty. Defendant and his counsel believed that the judge, because of those comments, would impose a life sentence, a defendant accordingly entered a plea of nolo contendere. After the judge imposed the death sentence, defendant on appeal argued before this Court that the judge's public expression of his views on the death penalty had convinced him that he would receive only a life sentence. This Court rejected that claim, although it reversed no other grounds and allowed defendant to withdraw his plea.

Judge Gridley contends that his first amendment right to free speech protected his conduct, that the Code of Judicial Conduct affirmatively allows this type of conduct through which judges may advocate the improvement of the administration of justice, and that other circuit judges have expressed themselves concerning the death penalty, their statements being distinguished only in that they were in favor of rather than opposed to the death penalty. Judge Gridley points out that those judges have not been disciplined.

As to the first point, the judicial canons clearly state that judges may *not* advocate a position on matters which may come before them for decision. The reason is simple. In each adversary proceeding, at least two sides must have the opportunity to be heard. No party wishes to appear before a judge who is predisposed as to an issue unless of course, he is predisposed in that party's favor. In my view, the first amendment rights of a judge are properly restricted by the judicial canons when those rights concern areas of the law in which the judge must reach a judicial decision. This is necessary to assure impartiality in the decision-making process. It is in fact a balancing test between the judge's constitutional right to free speech and the constitutional right of the litigants to due process and a fair trial. Under the circumstances of this case, given the sensitive and emotional nature of the proceeding and the critical position of the circuit judge, I find that the canons, as I construe them, do not improperly limit or infringe upon the judge's first amendment rights.

As to the second point, while the canons clearly and affirmatively suggest that judges should actively seek changes which improve the administration of justice, they do not grant a judicial officer a license to publicly project a strong impression of how he will rule in a particular matter. I find that Judge Gridley's actions travel beyond the scope of acceptable speech for the improvement of justice because they destroy his image of impartiality.

Finally, Judge Gridley claims that other judges who have participated in similar conduct favoring the death penalty have suffered no discipline. The inference is that Judge Gridley was prosecuted before the Judicial Qualifications Commission because he opposed the death penalty. I find both types of conduct improper, whether opposing or advocating the death penalty, and would expect equal administration of judicial discipline.

Our judicial system requires public support and confidence for its existence. Public support in turn depends upon judicial credibility, established in my view only by a clear appearance of judicial integrity and impartiality. The Code of Judicial Conduct was promulgated to furnish judges guidelines which, if followed, would assure that judges' conduct conformed to these standards.

I find that Judge Gridley clearly breached the letter and intent of the Code of Judicial conduct. I would emphatically approve all the recommendations of the Judicial Qualifications Commission and publicly reprimand Judge Gridley accordingly.

NOTE

In a talk given to federal judges in 1988, I made the following comments about the ability of federal judges to speak out on legal matters:

As a formal matter, the Code of Conduct tries to walk a fine line between, on the one hand, respecting the needs of judges to exercise their own freedom of speech and, not to put too fine a point on it, to earn additional money, and on the other hand, to forbid judges from engaging in the kind of speech that may lead to fears of partiality in matters that come before them or ultimately to disqualification. Thus Canon 4 of the Code of Conduct reflects that tension when it tells judges that so long as they do not cast doubt on their capacity to decide any issue impartially, judge may write and teach about the law, may appear at public hearings before legislative or executive bodies on matters concerning the law or the administration of justice, may consult with such bodies on the latter topic, and may also serve on organizations devoted to the improvement of the legal system.

I should interject here that I have been surprised, to use a mild word, at the increasing numbers of articles and speeches by judges, especially Supreme Court Justices, in the past 20 years in which they discuss all sorts of issues that seem likely to come before them and discuss also the views and foibles of their colleagues. There is a line between exhibiting greater willingness to discuss the business of courts by way of educating the public and engaging in public argument for positions they hold dear. I believe that there is a relation between the perceived power of judges and public scrutiny of the propriety of their activities. I think that there is also a relation between the willingness of judges to enter into the public fray and the increasing tendency of some academics and some media figures to equate judges with legislators.

The Judicial Conference's Advisory Committee on Judicial Activities has addressed the general permission given by Canon 4 to appear before legislative and executive hearings on matters concerning the law by reading that permission narrowly to include only situations where the matter deserves the comment of a judge in his or her professional capacity. (Advisory Opinion No. 50.) The reason given is that legislation involving important political and social issues may well spawn litigation likely to come before the judge. The connection between that reason and the language of the Canon is the reasonableness of the perception that a judge who had urged the legislature or executive to follow a particular course of action with respect to a particular issue had cast doubt on his or her ability to decide impartially a case involving such an issue. If that is the case, however, why does the same problem not exist when a judge makes a speech on the same subject matter although not in a legislative or judicial forum?

Of course we are on two slippery slopes here, each beginning at different ends of the spectrum. Many judges when they are appointed have taken positions either in their capacity as advocates or as citizens, on the general subject matter that will come before them. But those positions were taken without the institutional responsibility that comes with being a judge. Moreover, the judiciary could not function if that were a basis for disqualification. Likewise, many judges who have sat on the bench long enough have well established positions on certain issues. When a similar issue arises, a party might reasonably believe such a judge will not approach the issue with the perfect disinterestedness of one considering the issue de novo. But we do not expect that kind of disinterestedness in our judges. Indeed, we expect them to develop positions as a result of their judicial service. On the other hand, Canon 4 would seem clearly to prohibit judges from publicly announcing their views about cases pending before them.

Canon 4 therefore requires the exercise of a prudential judgement in interpreting its injunction against engaging in such outside activities that might cause a litigant or the public reasonably to question their judge's impartiality. It certainly isn't the development of views on matters that might come before judges that we fear. We want our judges to read, to think, to educate themselves about law in the largest sense. But there is a difference between a private thought and a public speech or published article. Going public requires much more care and responsibility and may also indicate a desire to persuade others that brings it within the range of Canon 4's prohibition of speech that casts doubt on the impartiality of the judge.

An early opinion of the Advisory Committee (no. 3) resolved the tension inherent in the language and policies of Canon 4 by stating that a judge should "circumscribe his comments so as to avoid a positive commitment on any legal issue which is likely to arise before him." More recently, however, the Committee has quoted with approval the statement in the Reporter's Notes to the ABA's Code of Judicial Conduct that a "judge may write or lecture on a legal issue, analyzing the present law or propose legal reform without compromising his capacity to decide impartially the very issue on which he has spoken or written." (Advisory Opinion no. 55).

I think that that advice ought not be given without the caveat about not making a positive commitment that appeared in the earlier advisory opinion and indeed still appears in Canon 4 of the Code of Conduct. If a judge ought not appear before a legislature to urge repeal of capital punishment, for example, then it ought not be permissible for a judge to write an article or to give a public talk on the deficiencies of our law with respect to capital punishment that urges an end to capital punishment. The reasonable public fear regarding the judge's impartiality in reviewing a capital sentence seems equivalent in those two situations because both the testimony before the committee and the article bespeak a significant commitment to oppose capital punishment.

The failure of the Advisory Committee to repeat the Canon's caveat in its most recent opinion may be due to a fear that an expansive rendering of the prohibition would make it difficult for judges to engage in law school teaching, a practice sanctioned by long history and a virtual necessity for some judges if they are to remain on the bench. But one quality teaching may have is that it is exploratory, tentative, informal, and impermanent. Such teaching is different from the typical public speech or article. On the other hand teaching may be just as authoritative as a speech or article. Such teaching carries the same danger of compromising the appearance of impartiality. If I had to engage in prudential line drawing, I would interpret the Canon as permitting the former, but not the latter style of teaching. While that may be "too nice" a distinction, the language of Canon 4 seems to contemplate just that kind of fine distinction.

Thus, if I had to choose between the phrasing of Advisory Opinion No. 3 and that of Advisory Opinion No. 55, I would choose the former, more restrictive statement. One reason for that choice is that, except for egregious conduct, judges enjoy what lawyers often say they themselves enjoy but which lawyers really have less and less these days — a self-regulating profession. The critical thing about such a status is that it is regarded quite jealously by those that do not enjoy it. If judges are perceived as abusing that status, it will come under fire and they may lose it.

The second reason for my restrictive attitude toward public speech by judges is that notwithstanding the policy-making function of the judiciary, there is still a big difference between judges and legislators. One difference is that traditionally, most judges, most of the time, have waited for cases to present issues to them before speaking out. I would hope that today's judges will not narrow that difference, for if we eliminate the differences between judges and legislators one by one, we may find that we have eroded one of the more distinctive features of our form of government, the separation of powers between our legislative and judicial branches that has left each a very powerful feature of our society.

NOTE: Public Exposure of Disciplinary Reference by Judges

A good example of the situation presented by Problem 98 is United States v. Ofshe, 817 F.2d 1508 (11th Cir. 1987), cert. denied, 108 S. Ct. 451 (1988). A defendant in a federal trial in Florida claimed denial of due process by reason of prosecutorial misconduct. The author, Scott Turow, (One L and Presumed Innocent) was then an Assistant United States Attorney in Illinois. While he was investigating the defendant's lawyer in connection with "Operation Greylord," a federal investigation of corruption in the Cook County courts, the lawyer offered to provide information in relation to the drug trade. The result was that without informing the prosecutors in Florida or the court, Mr. Turow arranged to "wire up" the lawyer to record conversations with the defendant and instructed the lawyer not to violate the attorney-client privilege. At that precise moment, the indictment against the defendant had been dismissed, but criminal proceedings were reinstituted shortly thereafter. No notice of the monitoring was given to defendant and indeed the attorney did not move to withdraw until ten months later, and even then the withdrawal was sealed so that defendant did not discover the reason for nearly a year.

After conviction, the court refused to order dismissal of the indictment because it found that the defendant had not demonstrated any prejudice. It added a footnote that although the conduct of Mr. Turow and of defendant's counsel was not "sufficiently outrageous" to require reversal of the conviction, it was "reprehensible." It therefore assumed that the district judge would "refer this matter to the Illinois Attorney Registration and Discipline Commission, 203 N. Wabash, Suite 1900, Chicago, Illinois 60601, for appropriate action." Id. at 1516 n. 6. It did not state why it was not, in view of this conclusion, imposing any discipline itself. Perhaps it thought that procedural fairness necessary to support the imposition of discipline required notice and an evidentiary hearing whose focus was the lawyer's conduct. Perhaps it thought that a trial that occurred in Florida and was reviewed in the Eleventh Circuit ought not to be the occasion for discipline of a government lawyer who worked in Illinois and had taken no part in the Florida trial, although defendant's counsel, whose conduct was also criticized as reprehensible, had participated in the trial.

After the opinion was filed, Mr. Turow moved to have the footnote removed from the opinion. The court responded in a 13-page opinion, still unpublished, that rejected the motion. It concluded that since the defendant had argued that his conviction should be reversed because the lawyers' conduct had violated his due process, the review process necessarily had focused on the lawyer's conduct. Going beyond its earlier footnote, the court then concluded that criminal conduct on the part of the government attorney might be involved, and therefore ordered the clerk to forward its order to the United States Attorney for the Southern District of Florida. Subsequently, the Department of Justice announced that there was no basis for criminal prosecution because Mr. Turow's behavior had been proper.

The court was quite correct in taking so seriously its duty to initiate disciplinary investigations of lawyers' conduct. The issue is whether it should have done so publicly. The issue is a subcategory of the larger question of the stage at which disciplinary authorities should make public the fact that disciplinary proceedings are pending against lawyers or judges. The difference here is that the notice is from the court itself, a body that might at least in some cases be taking further action after the disciplinary authorities have acted.

In *Ofshe*, the notice given by the court had the beneficial effect of sending an educational message to lawyers concerning the court's view of appropriate lawyer conduct. It also had the beneficial effect of assuring the public that the court was doing its duty with respect to required reporting. Those are important considerations. On the other hand, it clearly did serious injury to a lawyer's reputation in a proceeding in which he never appeared as a party.

It is true that the court was required to focus on the lawyer's conduct in connection with the defendant's appeal and it is also probably true that the major damage to the lawyer's reputation came from the description of his conduct rather than the reference to the disciplinary authorities. It is nevertheless one thing to reach a judgment about the lawyer's conduct for the purpose of dealing with defendant's rights and quite another to link the lawyer so publicly with charges of disciplinary violation when the court was unwilling to undertake the task of disciplinary assessment itself.

The court could certainly have sent a sufficient message to lawyers without the specific reference to possible discipline of this lawyer. The further message regarding discipline would come later if the disciplinary authorities found that the lawyer had engaged in disciplinable conduct. If, however, the state disciplinary authorities find no violation, it is possible that there will be no public notice of that at all. The only item of the record in such a situation would be the court's negative comment and not any exoneration. Thus it seems to me that a court that has the power but is unwilling to undertake the discipline process itself, either directly or through a master or other body appointed by it, ought to be very cautious about the specific comments it makes about discipline. Compare Beiny v. Wynyard, 132 App. Div. 190, 522 N.Y.S.2d 511 (1987) where the court gave public notice of the referral to disciplinary authorities not only of the law firm's conduct in improperly obtaining confidential information but also of the allegation in a newspaper report that a member of the law firm had assaulted another attorney in the Surrogate's Court at a conference in the proceeding. See p. 384.

CHAPTER 13

SOME FINAL THOUGHTS

This concluding chapter contains excerpts from articles by Deborah Rhode and M.B.E. Smith and two final Notes from me, one on the rules of professional responsibility and one on more general themes. Professor Rhode's article considers the same issue discussed by Professor Charles Frankel in the opening chapter of this book from the very different perspective of a law teacher and social scientist examining the legal profession's proposed new rules for what they reveal about the sociology of the profession. The 1981 draft examined by Professor Rhode differs in a number of respects from the final version adopted by the ABA but the changes would not appear to alter her conclusions in any substantial way.

RHODE,[*] WHY THE ABA BOTHERS: A FUNCTIONAL PERSPECTIVE ON PROFESSIONAL CODES

59 Tex. L. Rev. 689 (1981)

I. Introduction

In January 1980, just ten years after the American Bar Association adopted the Model Code of Professional Responsibility, a special ABA commission chaired by Robert Kutak recommended "comprehensive re-

[*] Professor of Law, Stanford University, B.A. 1974, J.D. 1977, Yale University.

The comments of Professors Paul Brest, Lawrence Friedman, John Kaplan, Michael Moore, and William Simon on an earlier draft are gratefully acknowledged.

Financial support was provided in part by the Stanford Legal Research Fund, made possible by a bequest from the Estate of Ira S. Lillick and by gifts from Roderick E. and Carla A. Hills and other friends of the Stanford Law School.

formulation" of that document.[2] The Kutak Commission's suggested replacement, the Model Rules of Professional Conduct, has generated considerable controversy within the profession, culminating in a large volume of comment and two counterproposals.[3] So heated a debate invites the question suggested by the titles of this and Professor Abel's articles.[4] Of course, at one level of generality, the answer seems self-evident. As both the history and content of ABA codifications make plain, the bar bothers because its interests so dictate. Like any other occupational group, the ABA formulates and fulminates for its health, collectively speaking. What is less obvious, and what this Article will explore, is the range of concerns at stake in the codification enterprise and the wisdom of placing that endeavor under bar control.

From the profession's standpoint, codes of ethics are a primary instrument for attaining what Talcott Parsons posited as the dominant goals for any occupation: objective achievement and recognition.[5] Codified standards can generate monetary and psychic benefits by enhancing occupational status and self-image; constraining competition; preserving autonomy; and reconciling client, colleague, and institutional interests. From a societal perspective, however, professional codes are desirable only insofar as they serve common goals to a greater extent than other forms of control, namely market forces or government regulation. For the legal profession, such goals presumably would include promoting the impartial and efficient administration of justice and ensuring competent legal assistance at the lowest possible price.[6]

As the Kutak Commission acknowledges, the regulatory interests of the public and the profession are now always coextensive. Rather, "difficult ethical problems arise from conflict between a lawyer's responsi-

2. ABA Model Rules of Professional Conduct, Introduction, at i (Proposed Final Draft May 1981) [hereinafter cited as Model Rules Final Draft]. The Final Draft followed several earlier drafts, the most recent of which was released in January 1980. See ABA Model Rules of Professional Conduct (Discussion Draft Jan. 1980) [hereinafter cited as Model Rules Discussion Draft].

3. The counterproposals are Roscoe Pound — American Trial Lawyers Foundation, The American Lawyer's Code of Conduct (Discussion Draft June 1980) [hereinafter cited as American Lawyer's Code], and National Organization of Bar Counsel, Report and Recommendations on Study of the Model Rules of Professional Conduct (Aug. 1980).

4. Abel, Why Does the ABA Promulgate Ethical Rules?, 59 Texas L. Rev. 639 (1981).

5. Parsons, A Sociologist Looks at the Legal Profession, in Essays on Sociological Theory 38, 44-45 (1957). See generally B. Bledstein, The Culture of Professionalism 99 (1976); Parsons, The Professions and Social Structure, 17 Soc. Forces 457 (1939).

6. See, e.g., Remarks of President Carter before the Los Angeles Bar Association (May 4, 1978), reprinted in 64 A.B.A.J. 840 (1978), and rejoinders to the President's address; Gillers, How Wrong Can You Be?: Carter and the Lawyers, Nation, July 22, 1978, at 74; The Trouble with Lawyers, New Republic, May 20, 1978, at 5.

For further variations on the same theme, see Subcomm. on Representation of Citizen Interests of the Senate Comm. on the Judiciary, 93rd Cong., 2d Sess., Reducing the Costs of Legal Services (Comm. Print 1974); Pound, The Causes of Popular Dissatisfaction With the Administration of Justice, 29 A.B.A. Rep. 395 (1906).

bilities to clients, to the legal system and to the lawyer's own interest in remaining an upright person while earning a satisfactory living."[7] Given this concession, it is striking that so little effort is made to justify the bar's arrogation of exclusive authority to resolve such conflicts. In marked contrast to the recently appointed British Royal Commission on Legal Services, which has a majority of laymen, only one of the Kutak Commission's thirteen members is not an attorney.[8] This imbalance between professional and public representation in the drafting phase is exacerbated by a ratification process in which only the views of professionals are systematically solicited, and in which they alone cast the decisive vote. . . .

Neither the Code nor the Model Rules indicate why the bar should proceed as if it were exempt from the natural human tendency to prefer private over public ends. Confronted with conflict between their self-interest and their perception of societal interests, many individuals will attempt to discount or reconstrue the less immediate concern so as to reduce internal tension. Simply through normal processes of dissonance — reduction and acculturation — professionals may lose sensitivity to interests at odds with their own. Nothing in the bar's extended history of self-governance suggests it to be an exception. As has been convincingly demonstrated elsewhere, both the Code of Professional Responsibility and the Canons of Ethics it replaced consistently resolved conflicts between professional and societal objectives in favor of those doing the resolving.[15] So too, given the political constraints under which the Kutak Commission is operating, one would expect the Model Rules to serve first and foremost the interests of the bar.

Of course, this observation, without more, is neither startling nor especially damning. By choice or inertia, we often delegate responsibility for monitoring professional conduct to private organizations or member-dominated licensing boards. Whether such delegations are prudent depends in large measure on the degree to which public and professional objectives converge. Thus, this Article attempts, through a functional overview of the bar's objectives, to lodge them in the context of broader social concerns.

---

7. Model Rules Final Draft Preamble, at 2.

8. Nine of the Royal Commission's fifteen members, including the chairman were nonattorneys, and two other members were "critics from within the profession." M. Zander, Legal Services for the Community 256 & nn. 62-64 (1978).

There were no lay members on the twelve-person committee charged with drafting the ABA Code of Professional Responsibility. See Code at v.

15. Among the most comprehensive expositions are J. Auerbach, Unequal Justice: Lawyers and Social Change in Modern America 40-48, 286-288 (1976); Morgan, The Evolving Concept of Professional Responsibility, 90 Harv. L. Rev. 702 (1977); Schuchman, Ethics and Legal Ethics: The Propriety of the Canons as a Group Moral Code, 37 Geo. Wash. L. Rev. 244 (1968); Frankel, Book Review, 43 U. Chi. L. Rev. 874 (1976) (reviewing the Code of Professional Ethics).

Concededly, such a conceptual framework shares the limitations of any functionalist approach that analyzes heterogeneous occupational groups as discrete entities. Like other such groups, the bar is not a monolithic organization whose members share a single view on regulatory issues. Rather, the legal profession is a stratified body with crosscutting interests and allegiances.[17] Even so, the very concept of a professional code presupposes a common core of functions and concerns. Only by exploring those concerns can we understand why the ABA codifies and, more importantly, whether it should enjoy that prerogative.

II.   Enhancing Status and Self-Image

A principal function of all professional organizations is to protect their members' economic and psychological stake in public esteem. Codes of ethics are useful insofar as they define a satisfactory self-image and help persuade the general public that practitioners are especially deserving of confidence, respect, and substantial remuneration. Never the best beloved of professionals, lawyers have been particularly preoccupied with enhancing their status.[20] Attorneys responding to a 1977 survey ranked "low public regard of the profession" as the most urgent issue facing the bar.[21] Indeed, comparable sentiments were largely responsible for lawyers' initial efforts at codification.

For over two centuries, the American bar functioned without any formal rules of conduct. Not until the early 1900s, when an influx of new practitioners threatened to "debase [the profession's] high calling in the eyes of the public,"[22] did ABA leaders become interested in written canons of ethics. Their avowed objective was to establish attorneys as "high

---

17. See, e.g., Heinz & Laumann, The Legal Profession: Client Interests, Professional Roles, and Social Hierarchies, 76 Mich. L. Rev. 1111 (1978).

20. Lawyers' poor public standing is a familiar refrain among commentators. See, e.g., M. Frankel, Partisan Justice 3-4, 60-67 (1978); G. Hazard, Ethics in the Practice of Law xiii (1978); Barzun, The Professions Under Siege, Harper's Oct. 1978, at 61; Kasnoff, Book Review, 89 Yale L.J. 1438, 1442 (1980), Popular opinion polls confirm these impressions. In a 1978 Harris survey of institutions in which Americans have confidence, law firms won only 12% approval, lagging behind sanitation departments, Congress, and the police. Those Lawyers, Time, Apr. 10, 1978, at 56. Similarly, in a 1978 Gallup poll only 26% of respondents had a "very high" or "high" view of lawyers' honesty or ethics, a rating that again placed them below policemen or congressmen. Bodine, People of Wisconsin Trust Lawyers, Bar Survey Finds, Nat'l L.J., Jan. 28, 1980, at 6.
This mistrust is by no means a recent phenomenon. For accounts of the hostility directed toward lawyers at various stages of American history, see generally L. Friedman, A History of American Law 81-88, 265-275 (1973); E. Griswold, Law and Lawyers in the United States 12-25 (1964); C. Warren, A History of the American Bar 212-233 (1911).

21. Project 1977 Results: Incompetence Rising, Juris Dr., July-Aug. 1977, at 23.

22. Committee on Code of Professional Ethics Report, 29 A.B.A. Rep. 600, 602 (1906).

priests of justice . . . robed in priestly garments of truth, honor, integrity," and, most of all, decorum.[23] To that end, the Canons of Ethics concentrated on preserving proprieties in the acquisition of clients. Judge Sharswood, from whose lectures the Canons liberally drew, was of the opinion that business should seek the young attorney, rather than the converse.[24] That same anticommercial philosophy colors the Code of Professional Responsibility, which was adopted a half century later. Although the caption to Canon 2 of the Code submits that "A Lawyer Should Assist the Legal Profession in Fulfilling Its Duty to Make Legal Counsel Available," the Code's disciplinary rules speak primarily to the manifold ways in which a lawyer should refrain from so doing. Advertising and solicitation were particularly disfavored until recent Supreme Court holdings forced some accommodation to the realities of a complex urban economic order.

The bar's response to this judicial intervention has been less than enthusiastic. One survey, conducted after the Supreme Court's decision upholding attorney advertising in Bates v. State Bar,[26] revealed that only three percent of the bar had taken advantage of the opportunity.[27] Many lawyers oppose advertising in any form, and a substantial majority wants it strictly curtailed.[28] Part of that opposition undoubtedly stems from the anticompetitive concerns discussed below, but many attorneys also contend that commercialization will diminish "public respect" for the profession.[29]

As the Kutak draft candidly acknowledges, such prohibitions rest largely on "subjective judgment as to taste."[36] Yet the Commission does not advance the one recommendation most likely to yield significant improvement: that supervision over lawyer advertising vest in a group less ill-disposed to the concept. A more detached regulatory body, such as a state consumer protection agency, presumably would be less preoccu-

23. Id. at 601-602.

24. See G. Sharswood, An Essay on Professional Ethics 131-132 (5th ed. 1884), reprinted in 32 A.B.A. Rep. 131-132 (1907).

26. 433 U.S. 350 (1977) (first amendment protects right of lawyers to advertise, subject to reasonable state regulation).

27. Slavin, It's Legal, but Few Lawyers Are Prepared to Advertise, N.Y. Times, Apr. 23, 1979, §A, at 12, col. 4. See also Law Poll: Advertising Still Laying an Egg, 65 A.B.A. J. 1014 (1979).

28. In a survey of Arizona attorneys shortly after the *Bates* decision, 50% of the respondents indicated that they opposed any form of advertising, and 69% believed it would lower public esteem. Of the 50% who favored advertising, 35% wanted it strictly limited. Meyer & Smith, Attorney Advertising: *Bates* and a Beginning, 20 Ariz. L. Rev. 427, 470, 476 (1978).

29. Id. See also S. Tisher, L. Bernabei & M. Green, Bringing the Bar to Justice 54-55 (1977) (reporting comments of ABA delegates voicing concern over "creeping commercialism"); Rueschemeyer, supra note 16, at 18 (noting that "restriction of advertising serves to emphasize symbolically the subcultural distinction between the professions and business world").

36. Model Rules Final Draft 7.2, Comment.

pied with the profession's image and more attentive to the public's need for information and to the economies of scale realizable through mass marketing.[37] . . .

The profession's preoccupation with status is not confined to rules of etiquette for acquiring clients. It also figures prominently in a variety of other Code prescriptions, such as those governing courtroom decorum, commingling of funds, conflicts of interest, and public service. In general, the Kutak draft either replicates unobjectionable provisions of its antecedents or effects significant improvements. There are, however, two exceptions worth noting.

The first is the Commission's treatment of a problem frequently discussed in the literature on public interest representation: A nominal client's interests may not fully coincide with his attorney's ideological aspirations. Few would contest the Model Rules' general admonition that a lawyer should not accept employment if his personal concerns or responsibilities to third parties might "adversely affect the best interest of the client." Yet this maxim presupposes a monolithic client, whose "best interest" can be readily ascertained and made controlling throughout the course of representation. Such a paradigm is out of step with much public interest advocacy, in which the client is a diffuse class with shifting or divergent preferences that the lawyer must intuit or impute rather than systematically solicit. The reality of test case litigation is that "the client" often enables the attorney to express his views, not the converse. Having failed to confront this fact of life, the Rules may prove unilluminating to those most in need of guidance.

Equally dissatisfying is the Commission's attempt to come to terms with lawyers' pro bono responsibilities. No code of ethics would, of course, be complete without some recognition of its disciples' commitment to good works. Although few members of the public are likely to be aware of, let alone impressed by, such testimonials, code rhetoric nonetheless serves a significant expressive function. By codifying their role in "advancement of the public good," professionals reinforce their sense of self-importance and entitlement to special status. An ostensibly altruistic involvement in pro bono activity is one of the traditional "signs and symbols" used to distinguish professionals from the laity. Yet it is not necessarily in any individual practitioner's interest that the public service obligation have teeth, particularly if an impression of commitment can be engineered without financial sacrifice. It is to that end that both the Code and the Model Rules evidently aspire.

The current Code offers much admonition but no disciplinary rule regarding pro bono work; Canon 2 contains the relevant void. Initially,

37. For a detailed analysis of the benefits to consumers from legal advertising, see Muris & McChesney, Advertising and the Price and Quality of Legal Services: The Case for Legal Clinics, 1979 Am. B. Found. Research J. 179.

the Kutak Commission proposed to replace this reticence with a mandatory requirement. . . . Nonetheless, vehement protest quickly convinced the Commission to delete the mandatory minimum and to substitute an annual reporting requirement. When this compromise proved unacceptable, the Commission retreated to a purely hortatory formulation similar to that presently in effect.

Thus, nowhere is the disparity between rhetoric and reality more apparent than in the assertion of both the Model Rules and the Code that "the basic responsibility for providing legal services for those unable to pay rests upon the individual lawyer." If the nation had relied exclusively upon the private bar to assume that responsibility, the legal services movement undoubtedly would still be in an incipient stage. The most comprehensive survey of lawyers' pro bono activity revealed that about three-fifths of respondents devoted less than five percent of billable hours to such work, and that half of this group spent no time at all.[60] The average investment for the bar as a whole was 6.2 percent of billable hours.[61] Moreover, the vast bulk of these contributions did not redound to the advantage of chronically underrepresented interests. One third of individual pro bono clients were relatives and friends.[62] Of the organizations receiving assistance, eighty-two percent were churches, hospitals, and middle class-oriented community groups, such as Boy Scouts, Jaycees, Masons, and garden clubs.[63] Only five percent were legal aid and public defender organizations.[64] Considering the extent to which most attorneys now manifest their "responsibility to those unable to pay," the Commission's rhetorical posturing is at best rank hypocrisy. At worst, it is counterproductive, insofar as it deflects attention from more fundamental questions about the distribution of legal talent.

What is ultimately most discomfiting about the Kutak draft's treatment of professional *noblesse oblige* is not what the Rules exhort, but what they elide. A strong argument can be made that it is neither equitable nor efficient to saddle the private bar with a minimum pro bono requirement. Asking corporate attorneys to dabble in poverty law issues is hardly a cost-effective approach to delivering legal assistance. Yet a more efficient alternative, substituting dollar contributions for in-kind service,

---

60. Handler, Hollingsworth, Erlanger & Ladinsky, The Public Interest Activities of Private Practice Lawyers, 61 A.B.A.J. 1388, 1389 (1975); cf. J. Handler, F. Hollingsworth & H. Erlanger, Lawyers and the Pursuit of Legal Rights 19 (1978) (In 1964, before substantial infusions of federal support, the collective budget of all poverty law programs was $4 million, of which bar associations and lawyers provided 17%.). See also note 56 supra. But see Christensen, The Lawyer's Pro Bono Publico Responsibility, 1981 Am. B. Found. Research J. 1 (suggesting that the Handler, Hollingsworth, Erlanger & Ladinsky data may underrepresent private bar contributions).

61. Handler, Hollingsworth, Erlanger & Ladinsky, supra note 60, at 1389.

62. Id.

63. Id.

64. Id.

raises troubling issues of fairness. Why should a tithe be levied only on attorneys, when "society at large is the ultimate beneficiary?"[66]

Moreover, as a practical matter, no pro bono requirement on the order of forty hours a year would make a substantial dent in the nation's unmet legal needs, however narrowly defined. An ABA study has estimated that "lawyers are consulted for slightly less than a third of all the problems encountered that reasonably could be called legal problems."[67] Similarly, the Legal Services Corporation projected that persons below the official poverty line would encounter between 6 and 132 million legal problems in 1980, while Corporation-funded offices could handle at most 2 million matters.[68] . . .

. . . But even granting the problems of qualifying such a highly contextual concept as "legal needs," millions plainly exist, at least in the eyes of the beholders. And if history is any guide, no codified directive to the private bar to go forth and do good for forty hours a year would materially affect a problem of such dimensions.

Except as a vehicle for airing the profession's narcissistic concerns, the debate over mandatory public service contributions has been mostly sound and fury. An entity concerned more with substance than self-image would have invested its energy in proposals with greater potential for enhancing access to justice, such as alternative forms of dispute resolution or relaxation of the professional monopoly.

Finally, codes of ethics enhance status in two additional ways that deserve at least passing reference. As will be discussed more fully below, specifying minimum standards permits the bar to oust individuals whose conduct jeopardizes the standing of the profession as a whole. And, in a more subtle but equally significant sense, codification fosters self-esteem by rationalizing a convenient definition of the professional's moral role. On the whole, the Kutak draft perpetuates a vision of attorneys as technicians, whose assistance "does not constitute an endorsement of the client's political, economic, social or moral views or activities."[72] This codification of "role-differentiated morality" affords an expedient escape from contexts of ethical complexity.[73] For the attorney unsettled by involvement in activities of dubious social value, the Model Rules offer

---

66. Bazelon, And Justice for All, 35 Nat'l Legal Aid & Defender Ass'n Briefcase 172, 176 (1978) (arguing that "the moral claim of equal justice applies no less to each member of society than to members of the legal profession").

67. B. Curran, The Legal Needs of the Public 261 (1977).

68. The Legal Services Corporation and the Activities of its Grantees: A Fact Book 5-18 (1979), reprinted in Legal Services Corp.: General Oversight Hearings Before the Subcomm. on Courts, Civil Liberties, and the Administration of Justice of the House Comm. on the Judiciary, 96th Cong., 1st Sess. 69-82 (1979).

72. Model Rules . . . Rule 1.2(b).

73. Wasserstrom, Lawyers as Professionals: Some Moral Issues, 5 Human Rights 1 (1975); cf. E. Durkheim, Professional Ethics and Civil Morals 3-13 (1957) (discussing "moral particularism" that arises from divergent role definitions).

reassurance; legal representation should not be denied to those whose "cause is controversial or the subject of popular disapproval."[74]

Yet, lest this disclaimer of responsibility either grate unduly on those practitioners who do exercise moral choice, or contribute to the lawyer's already tarnished image, the Kutak draft temporizes somewhat. If a client "insists upon pursuing an objective that the lawyer considers repugnant or imprudent, the lawyer may withdraw if doing so can be accomplished without material adverse effect on the interests of the client. . . ."[75] Of course, it may well be that such equivocation also serves a useful social function by reinforcing individuals willing to defend social pariahs, as well as those desiring some congruence between their own and their clients' objectives. Still, from the profession's point of view, a more congenial compromise is difficult to envision. In general, a lawyer asked to espouse a morally distasteful cause is neither damned if he does, nor damned if he doesn't.

III. Constraining Competition

A principal force animating any occupation's efforts at self-regulation is a desire to minimize competition from both internal and outside sources. As to internal rivalry, Roscoe Pound captured the ABA's traditional posture in his tart observation that a "member of a profession does not regard himself as in competition with his professional brethren."[79] Although the last decade has witnessed some infusion of a capitalist ethos into bar policies on advertising, solicitation, minimum fees, and group legal services, the profession's response has been generally grudging. Neither the Commission nor local bar associations have supported innovations that would significantly facilitate comparison shopping by consumers, such as directories with standardized information concerning attorney's fees, qualifications, and previous client complaints.

To be sure, the Model Rules . . . are less rabidly protectionist than their precursors. Not only has the Commission loosened restrictions on advertising and solicitation, it has dropped entirely the limitations on group legal services. However, ABA members responsible for these revisions disproportionately represent the elite of the profession, which is least threatened by the rivalry that such reforms could encourage. And, as previously noted, the Rules can be amended by individual states, and will be construed by local enforcement committees, many of whose members have displayed little support for Commission proposals. It strains credulity to believe that these committees, with all the features of trade associations, will behave otherwise when confronted with issues

74. Model Rules . . . Rule 1.2, Comment.
75. Id. Rule 1.2(c). [See changed wording in final version of Rule 1.16(b)(3).]
79. R. Pound, [The Lawyer from Antiquity to Modern Times 10 (1953)].

involving competition. Thus, the Commission's unwillingness to address the structural defects of a regulatory system controlled by the regulated makes significant liberalization unlikely. So long as the bar's self-governance structure remains unchanged, the best one can reasonably expect is a policy somewhat tempered by the fear of outside intrusion if protectionist sentiment becomes too overt.

Similar structural issues are presented by the bar's hardly disinterested role in restricting outside competition. Any organized occupation has an obvious economic stake in protecting its members' monopoly over whatever activity colorably requires their special skills. A professional Code can secure such protection in several ways. Most obviously it may erect barriers to entry by restricting admissions or unauthorized practice by nonprofessionals. Of equal significance are provisions that indirectly validate the professional monopoly. For example, strictures on competence, conflicts of interest, and confidentiality can be invoked to rationalize excluding those not subject to the code from encroachment on professional turf. Accordingly, the bar defends its exclusive domain over even ministerial form-preparation activities on the ground that lay competitors need not conform to Code standards and cannot promise the confidentiality that attaches to an attorney-client relationship. Since, by its terms, the Code governs only members of the profession, it can aid their struggle to establish a "monopoly of credibility" with the public. Thus, codification may deflect attention from the possibility that laymen could be held to the same standards as professionals, and be granted the same privileges for client confidences.[91]

The Model Rules are far less forthcoming than the Code on issues of lay competition. An entire canon of the Code is devoted to enlisting lawyers' efforts in "protect[ing] . . . members of the public" from the predations of lay practitioners.[92] Curiously enough, what constitutes legal practice is something that draftsmen found "neither necessary nor desirable" to define with any specificity.[93] They did, however, venture a tentative formulation notable for its circularity: the "practice of law" constitutes "services for others that call for the professional judgment of a lawyer."[94] By contrast, the Kutak Commission seems intent on evading

---

91. Already many courts and administrative agencies hold lay practitioners and attorneys to the same standards of competence and integrity. See, e.g., Latson v. Eaton, 341 P.2d 247 (Okla. 1959); Biakanja v. Irving, 49 Cal. 2d 647, 320 P.2d 16 (1958); Alaska Ad. Code §48.080 (1980); Ohio Admin. Code §4121-2-01 (1978); Wash. Ad. Code §263-12-020 (1979). See also Savings Bank v. Ward, 100 U.S. 195 (1879).

Laymen could also be required to disclose their lack of professional qualifications. See, e.g., Hunter & Klonoff, A Dialogue on the Unauthorized Practice of Law, 25 Vill. L. Rev. 6, 27 (1979); Weckstein, Limitations on the Right to Counsel: The Unauthorized Practice of Law, 1978 Utah L. Rev. 649, 676-679.

92. Code EC 3-4; see id. Canon 3 ("A Lawyer Should Assist in Preventing the Unauthorized Practice of Law.").

93. Id. EC 3-5.

94. Id.

the issue altogether. Discussion is relegated to a subsection of the catch-all rule on misconduct, which simply enjoins lawyers from "assist[ing] a person who is not a member of the bar in the performance of activity that constitutes the practice of law."[95] Displaying greater prudence than its predecessors, the Commission makes no attempt to specify what exactly is proscribed. The reader learns only that the definition of legal practice "varies from one jurisdiction to another," and that "[w]hatever the definition, limiting the practice of law to members of the bar protects the public against rendition of legal services by unqualified persons."[96] To the logical next questions, such as "How well?" or "At what cost?," the Model Rules never speak.

Moreover, the Commission appears to have overlooked a possibility suggested not only by jurisdictional variations in unauthorized practice doctrine, but also by the history of bar enforcement efforts. The scope of state prohibitions seems to be as much a function of the power and persistence of local bar associations as of any identifiable threat to the public. Contrary to the Model Rules' implication, it is by no means apparent that "whatever" the prevailing definition of legal practice, it is designed to prevent "unqualified" assistance. Such a rationale seems somewhat contrived in the face of doctrine that allows criminal defense lawyers but not accountants to give tax advice, or personal injury specialists but not real estate brokers to consummate title and closing arrangements.

If the welfare of consumers were in fact the bar's animating concern, one would expect consumers to play a significant role in the regulatory enterprise. Yet only five of the forty-four states with active unauthorized practice enforcement committees include any lay members on those committees.[100] On those rare occasions when its views have been solicited, the public has evinced considerable skepticism about its need for extensive protection from lay practitioners. Thus, in the ABA's own 1974 survey of public needs and perceptions regarding legal services, over three-quarters of respondents agreed that "[t]here are many things that lawyers handle — for example, tax matters or estate planning — that can be done as well and less expensively by nonlawyers — like tax accountants, trust officers of banks, and insurance agents."[101] Given this apparent consensus, the Kutak Commission should have faced rather than finessed the issue of whether attorneys should continue to police the boundaries of their own monopoly. As with its treatment of adver-

---

95. Model Rules . . . Rule [5.5(b)].
96. Id. Rule 8.4, Comment.
100. Rhode, Policing the Professional Monopoly, 34 Stan. L. Rev., 58-60 (1981).
101. B. Curran, supra note 67, at 231. Arizona voters voiced similar sentiments a decade earlier by strongly endorsing a state constitutional amendment to permit form preparation by real estate brokers. Marks, The Lawyers and the Realtors: Arizona's Experience, 49 A.B.A.J. 139 (1963).

tising and solicitation, what the draft fails to acknowledge, let alone justify, is the potential for protectionism under a regulatory structure dominated by professionals. Lawyers who volunteer for service on unauthorized practice enforcement committees may have a vested psychological as well as economic interest in viewing even ministerial legal tasks as beyond the competence of laymen. Concern over the antitrust dimensions of these committees' policies might make the Model Rules' low profile politic. But on any other grounds, that posture is difficult to defend. . . .

[Omitted here are discussions of the manner in which the Model Rules reconcile client, colleague, and institutional interests and maintain the profession's autonomy.]

VI.   CONCLUSION

In a celebrated history of the profession prepared under ABA auspices, Roscoe Pound reassured his sponsor that it was not, after all, "the same sort of thing as a retail grocers' association."[178] If he was right, it was almost certainly for the wrong reasons.[179] Lawyers no less than grocers are animated by parochial concerns. What distinguishes professionals is their relative success in packaging occupational interests as societal imperatives. In that regard, codes of ethics have proved highly useful. Seldom, of course, are such documents baldly self-serving; it is not to a profession's long-term advantage that it appear insensitive to the common good. But neither are any profession's own encyclicals likely to incorporate public policies that might significantly compromise members' status, monopoly, working relationships, or autonomy.

In part, the problem is one of tunnel vision. Without doubt, most lawyers — including those on the Kutak Commission — are committed to improving the legal system in which they work. What *is* open to doubt is whether a body of rules drafted, approved, and administered solely by attorneys is the most effective way of realizing that commitment. No matter how well-intentioned and well-informed, lawyers regulating lawyers cannot escape the economic, psychological, and political constraints of their position. If, as one Commission member readily acknowledges, the bar's past regulatory endeavors have foundered on self-interest and

---

178. Pound, supra note 6, at 7.
179. In Pound's view, the purpose of a bar association was to "promote and maintain the practice of law as a profession, that is, as a learned art, practiced in the spirit of a public service." Id. at 14. A review of the organized bar's activities over the last century affords little empirical support for Pound's vision. See, e.g., Green, The ABA as Trade Association, in Verdicts on Lawyers (R. Nader & M. Green eds. 1976); [and the arguments in this article].

self-deception,[180] what justifies attorneys' continued resistance to any external oversight? By abjuring outside interference, professionals can readily become victims of their own insularity, losing perspective on the points at which fraternal and societal objectives diverge. No ethical code formulated under such hermetic constraints can be expected to make an enduring social contribution. The Model Rules are no exception.

To effect significant improvements in the quality, cost, and delivery of legal services, the bar must accept fundamental changes in its regulatory structure. Anointing a few laymen to serve on drafting commissions or disciplinary committees will not suffice. As experience with token representation in other contexts makes clear, such cosmetic gestures serve more to legitimate than to affect the decisions of professionally controlled regulatory systems. Rather, structural deficiencies in the bar's present governance system mandate reforms offering nonprofessionals more than a supporting role. Lacking a constituency intent on such reforms, the Kutak Commission has proposed none. This is not, of course, to suggest that the recodification enterprise was meaningless from the profession's point of view. Quite the contrary, it is obvious why the ABA bothers. What remains is to convince the public to do likewise.

NOTES

1. If in fact it could be demonstrated that the rules of professional responsibility did not favor "the profession's self-interest," such a determination would not mean that Professor Rhode's view that there should be significant lay participation in, and control of, the rule-making and rule-application process was invalid. That view is supported by the arguments for greater diversity of perspective and by theories about ultimate "civilian" control of what is essentially governmental rule-making. Can you think of any arguments, practical or theoretical, against such control by nonprofessionals? How persuasive do you find them? What is the relevance to this discussion of the pervasive presence of lawyers in the legislative process?

2. Having considered so many professional problems and the rules applicable to their solution, do you have a view about whether the rules overly reflect "professional self-interest"? If you think of specific examples of rules subject to that criticism, would your alternative formulations be subject to the same criticism?

3. Note Professor Rhode's discussion of "unmet legal needs." That is

---

180. Frankel, Why Does Professor Abel Work at a Useless Task?, 59 Texas L. Rev. 723 (1981).

a staple of discussion not only with respect to the programs funded by the Legal Services Corporation but generally with respect to the responsibilities of the profession to that large segment of society that does not qualify for such programs but has great difficulty affording and finding legal services. The phrase "unmet legal needs" often appears with numbers purporting to quantify it, but the concept is very slippery, for the numbers can be virtually limitless. In a sense, whenever there is a very serious disagreement between spouses, or parents and children, or two parties to a contract, or whenever a person may theoretically qualify for some governmental benefit or may be threatened with some governmental burden, say, the receipt of a questioning letter from the Internal Revenue Service, and does not obtain the help of a lawyer, there is an "unmet legal need." And so it is very important in entering into discussion with anyone who uses that term to know exactly the sense in which the term is being used.

I have excerpted at several points in this book the views of philosophers who have reflected upon the role of lawyers and moral problems that they face. Indeed, the opening piece in the book is that of Richard Wasserstrom, a philosopher who had been a lawyer. It is perhaps fitting then that the last excerpt in the book should be that of a philosopher who has become a lawyer.

M. B. E. SMITH,* SHOULD LAWYERS LISTEN TO PHILOSOPHERS ABOUT LEGAL ETHICS?

publication forthcoming

[Smith takes his text from David Hume, recalling that Hume's "'suspicion with regard to the decisions of philosophers on all subjects'" was most profound with respect to their "'reasonings concerning human life and the methods of attaining happiness.'"[21] Smith then makes the point that philosophic argument tends to be long on abstract reasoning and short on empirical investigation.]

. . . I . . . suggest that this habit of disregard for ordinary empirical fact tends to distort philosophers' judgment about questions of practical morality in the way that Hume described. It encourages them to believe that collection of relevant fact is easy, that, e.g., by browsing through a few books and law review articles on legal ethics, philosophers can learn all they need to know about the practical situation of practicing lawyers,

---

* M. B. E. Smith is Professor of Philosophy, Smith College, and a practicing lawyer in Northampton, Mass.

21. [David Hume, the Sceptic, Hume's Moral and Political Philosophy 338 (H. Aiken ed. 1970).]

in order to make informed moral judgments about their obligations. Moreover, it encourages them to select those factual assertions therein recounted which support their already-formed judgments as to the worth of lawyers' lives. . . .

[Using David Luban's essay in The Good Lawyer (Luban ed. 1984), p. 247, n.7, as an example, Smith then argues that philosophers over-emphasize the hyperadversary aspects of the practice of law and official approval thereof.]

However, the primary factual shortcoming of philosophers who write on legal ethics is not that they overemphasize the combative element in most lawyers' lives, but that they wholly ignore clients, except as persons who have wicked desires which lawyers can help to satisfy or who have legal rights which morally ought not be secured.[38] One might suppose from reading philosophers' accounts that clients' ends are always well formed before they seek legal advice, and that the lawyer's task is merely to find an effective means towards their fulfillment. And perhaps in some practices such clients predominate. But in general practice they're rare, at least among clients who are actually embroiled in a dispute. The typical divorce client, for example, is under extreme stress, feels much bitterness and resentment, and has scant knowledge of his legal rights. Hence, before the lawyer can seek to achieve the client's ends, she must help him to determine what ends he has, in view of the various practical possibilities. In this phase of representation, she will be both a legal and a moral counselor to him, for she will exert strong pressure upon him to be reasonable, to be attentive not merely to his rights, but also to his obligations (e.g., to support his children both economically and emotion-ally). She will do so not because she is legally bound to aim directly at his moral improvement, but (if for no other reason) because it is in her interest. Courts tend to favor proposals which are fair and reasonable. If she can persuade him to adopt a position that is morally sound, she will be much more likely to obtain a result with which he can rest fairly content.

The typical scenario just sketched also exemplifies the (to lawyers) banal fact that they have enormous influence over the attitudes and ac-tions of their clients. Most persons who face being party to a lawsuit, even the most highly educated, are under substantial stress and are con-fused about their legal rights. They are helpless, needy and dependent upon their lawyer's good judgment and will. Every lawyer knows that he

---

38. This criticism does not hold good of R. Wasserstrom, Lawyers as Professionals, [p. 2], which was the first philosophical scrutiny of lawyerly behavior and which largely has inspired the rest. Wasserstrom is there acutely aware of client helplessness, and he warns lawyers equally against moral risk from unjust injury to opposing parties and from bad behavior towards their clients. Philosophers have taken up the first criticism, and have largely ignored the second. He does not return to it in his subsequent article in Luban, ed., The Good Lawyer, p. 15 n.2.

is potentially a much greater risk to his client than he is to any third person with whom the client may have a dispute or grievance. It is easy to neglect a client's interests, but often hard to promote them against skillful and determined opposition. And the complexity of law, especially that of procedure, is such that a layman has little effective means of checking whether his lawyer is doing a good job. Moreover, the lawyer's role as a confidential and trusted advisor offers obvious scope for abuse and fraud. It is surely for these and similar reasons that the Model Code and the Model Rules are primarily concerned to advise against, and to recommend for professional discipline, behavior which places clients' interests in jeopardy, rather than to place primary proscription against behavior which threatens third persons.

Philosophers tend to believe that this is mistaken, that the public good (justice, or whatever other moral value may be thought advanced) would be better served were lawyers under stronger duties to third parties. And perhaps this is true. But it might equally be true that such change would interfere generally with effective representation of clients, particularly if these duties were very stringent, so that the public which consumes legal services would not be made better off. What the precise effects of change would be is matter of empirical fact, albeit contrafactual fact which is extraordinarily difficult to ascertain with any certainty. We have neither the data nor a conceptual research model which we could use to measure even roughly what the present situation is, and how it will or might change. Such facts must inevitably be matters of conjecture, informed by experience.[41]

But then, why should philosophers' conjectures be credited at all, informed as they are by no relevant experience? Most philosophers are academics. . . . Their "clients" are either graduate or undergraduate students. And it is my conjecture, based upon the experience of some twenty years of teaching undergraduates and occasional graduate students and upon that of three years in half-time general practice, that there are scant similarities between the student-teacher relationship and that of lawyer-client. There are a great many differences, but perhaps the most crucial is that students are virtually never terribly vulnerable to their teachers, whereas vulnerability to their lawyers is typical of clients in general practice.

Unfortunately, paucity of relevant experience has not deterred philosophers from making very detailed empirical claims as to what commonly occurs in legal practice and what practitioners can reasonably expect to achieve. For example, most lawyers in criminal practice believe

---

41. Luban suggests that such conjectures are "nonempirical, a mix of a priori theories and armchair psychology." "The Adversary System Excuse," [p. 247, n.7], at 94. Strangely, he accords no weight to lawyers' practical experience in assessing whether their conjectures might be worthy of belief, nor does he note that philosophers have no basis upon which to offer rival ones.

that, unless clients know that lawyers are bound not to reveal their confidences, they will be deterred in significant numbers, both the innocent and the guilty, from revealing information which is relevant and helpful to their defense. But Alan Donagan, who is a very highly regarded philosopher, pooh-poohs this belief, calling a law professor "reckless" for having so said, and styling it a "dogma cherished by the National Association of Criminal Defense Lawyers."[42] He expresses doubt that what is feared "will generally be the case," and that "It seems more probable that a lawyer of ordinary competence would be able to discern the nature of the fears that might prompt a client to lie or to conceal the truth, and that it would be enough to explain what the law in fact is."[43] Donagan's argument is curiously abstract — as though pure reason alone can discern the characteristic psychological states of innocent persons charged with crime, and what ordinary competent lawyers may reasonably be expected to accomplish with respect of persons in those states. Of course, he doesn't really believe this — no competent philosopher would. But on what else is his confidence based? And why does he call "mere dogma" the opinion of ordinary competent lawyers on this question of empirical fact, which undoubtedly lacks scientific support (as does his), but which is at least based upon their experiences with clients and with what they have been able to do with them? More to our present point, why should lawyers pay any attention whatsoever to Donagan's conjectures, or indeed to those of anyone else who has never had a client?

. . . The burden of the scolding philosophers' complaint against lawyers does not really turn on any detailed knowledge of their professional activities or typical traits of character. Rather it turns on the general proposition that, since clients fairly often have untoward goals which they wish vindicated by law and since legal rights are not identical with moral rights, lawyers must fairly often work on the wrong side of cases, and must therefore sometimes work zealously towards unjust results.

Many lawyers will contest the application of this proposition to their particular practices, particularly those who work in areas of the law which are not normally adversarial, e.g., conveyancing, estate administration or planning, etc. It's rare in such practice that there are two "sides;" the lawyer's task is usually only that of realizing the lawful desires of her client. Moreover, even in adversarial situations, fairly frequently neither side will advance an unjust claim, e.g., as in bankruptcy, when two equally innocent creditors dispute as to whose claim has priority to the assets in the bankrupt estate. Nonetheless, litigators and lawyers in general practice will not fairly be able to deny that they must (at

---

42. A. Donagan, Justifying Legal Practice in the Adversary System, in Luban ed. [p. 247 n.7], at 145, 146. His criticism directed against Monroe Freedman. The philosophers in Luban [*ibid.*,] generally treat Freedman very roughly.

43. Id. at 145.

least unwittingly) spend a portion of their professional lives working towards legal outcomes which are unjust. One may have a policy of turning down causes which one finds morally distasteful, but that cannot wholly eliminate the moral risk (if indeed that is what the situation poses). For there is the practical difficulty that it is often very hard to know whether a cause is just: the facts, e.g., of a contested divorce and custody case, are often obscure even at its end; and of course the facts make all the difference to objective justice. So it appears that at least many lawyers must admit that inevitably they will sometimes work conscientiously towards morally untoward results. What moral conclusion follows from this general proposition? . . .

[Smith then reads Wasserstrom's latest essay in Luban, The Good Lawyer, p. 15, Note 2, as adopting a "considerably more cheerful" attitude about the moral prospects for lawyers. He believes that Wasserstrom now finds a reasonably satisfactory justification for role-differentiation although Wasserstrom still expresses "certain nagging dissatisfactions with efforts of this sort to put these worries to rest."]

Lawyers will find Wasserstrom's latest conclusion to be one which they can accept with equanimity. . . . Morality apparently does not require that [lawyers] give up their usual practice of looking to the demands and ideals of the lawyers' role as governing their conduct in their professional lives; instead, they need only endeavor conscientiously to follow these in practice, and to reflect from time to time on how these normative standards might be improved. Nonetheless, lawyers may yet have reservations. Firstly, they may reasonably point out that a busy practice leaves a lawyer little time for abstract speculation about her professional role. Hence, she will not be inclined to worry over conundrums in legal ethics until she finds herself in one; and she will then seek the advice of her peers. . . . How an existing social role can be improved is a question which must again turn upon difficult propositions of contrafactual fact, which concern alternative sets of consequences that would result from the legal profession's adopting various proposals for change. . . . Hence, it will only seldom be possible to know with certainty whether a proposed change will cause improvement. Moreover, imposing deliberate change into a social role very often has costs: role-holders must learn new ways, and their "clients" of whatever kind must acquire new expectations. Lawyers therefore may reasonably argue that they should be reluctant to change their role, unless there is a demonstrated need that is apparent to some authoritative body of practitioners, judges and law professors. . . . Lawyers' moral universe is not overtly immoral, because (as Wasserstrom now acknowledges) lawyers are in general morally justified in acting within the traditional confines of their role. Nor is it a simple moral universe which they inhabit. To speak of my own, the Disciplinary Rules of the Model Code (with some changes) have been incorporated into Massachusetts law, and its Ethical Considerations are expressly recognized as a body of principles which govern interpretation of the DRs. If it be supposed that Massachusetts lawyers are subject to some special prima facie moral obligation to comply with this body of law, sorting out what this requires in the concrete circumstance of practice poses for us not merely a problem in legal analysis, but also an exercise in determining what we ought morally to do. Now, it is a commonplace of contemporary jurisprudence that hard cases often arise in every area of law, i.e., those about which superb lawyers may sincerely hold strong divergent opinions as to what the law requires. Hence, fairly frequently, lawyers may find it difficult to know exactly what professional obligation requires them to do — although they will all pray that they never face so hard a case as the Lake Pleasant bodies case! [See page 221.] Moreover, supposing that the role obligation is clear, further difficulty may arise if, in some concrete situation, a lawyer has some other sort of strong prima facie obligation which conflicts with her role obligation. The lawyer's moral universe is evidently exceedingly complex, if this supposition be correct about the moral weight of professional obligation.

But do lawyers have such a moral obligation? Luban appears to deny this. After a lengthy discussion of possible "justifications" for the adversary system, he concludes that the best to be said for it is that no other system is clearly superior, so that there is no good reason to replace it.[58] One might suppose this to be high praise, for it implies that there is no practicable alternative that is more just. But Luban is grudging, calling this but a "weak" and "pragmatic" justification. And from the proposition that no stronger justification of the adversary system is possible, he concludes that "since [its] force is more inertial than moral, [it] creates insufficient counterweight to resolve dilemmas in favor of the role obligation."[59] And again, "This implies . . . that when professional and moral obligation conflict, moral obligation takes precedence. When they don't conflict, professional obligations rule the day. . . . When moral obligation conflicts with professional obligation, the lawyer must become a civil disobedient."[60]

Luban does not offer lawyers any concrete guidance as to when exactly they must be disobedient nor does he speculate as to how often such situations are likely to occur. However, his position seems to imply that these will be frequent. He appears to hold that lawyers' role requirements have no moral weight at all, that they are always outweighed by any conflicting moral reason. And this implies, e.g., that if asked by a landlord to represent her in a summary eviction proceeding, and if he

58. Id. at 116-118.
59. Id. at 118. To accord it such little moral force, Luban apparently must believe that the establishment and maintenance of a reasonably just adjudicative system is an insignificant moral achievement. I suggest to the contrary that this requires the constant diligent effort of morally serious women and men.
60. Id.

holds some background political conviction that tenants have a moral right to never be evicted solely because they have insufficient funds to pay rent, an advocate is absolutely obligated to try to frustrate his client's attempt to regain possession. Now, perhaps Luban really does believe that something like this is true; but every lawyer will find the supposition outrageous, and I am confident most laypeople would believe such an advocate to be guilty of grave moral error. My conjecture — again I know of no reliable relevant empirical evidence — is that most laypeople would agree that the weight of lawyers' role obligations is quite substantial. Since Luban offers neither clarification nor supporting argument for his contrary position, it is hard to see why lawyers may not ignore it, following both common moral opinion and their own inclination.

Moreover, there are persuasive arguments towards this conclusion, that rely upon some of the classic philosophical arguments which purport to show that citizens of reasonably just societies have (at least) a prima facie obligation to obey the law. These latter arguments have recently drawn much fire: many contemporary philosophers, including myself, deny that citizens generally are under any such obligation. The nerve of much of this criticism is that, even in just societies, most citizens fail to satisfy the factual conditions which trigger the principles of obligation on which the traditional arguments rest. No one denies, e.g., that consenting or promising to obey the laws of Massachusetts would establish a prima facie obligation to obey its laws; rather it is denied that most citizens of Massachusetts have performed any act which clearly constitutes consent or a promise always to obey. But unlike most citizens, all lawyers have taken an oath of office, which is plausibly interpreted as containing a promise to obey the law, at least that part which governs their actions as lawyers. Hence, their oath may reasonably be thought to ground a prima facie obligation to fulfil their legal obligations which they incur in practice. Another promising argument, which fails with respect of citizens generally, but which appears applicable to lawyers, is Rawls' argument from fair play.[64] Yet another which converges to much the same conclusion is that, in accepting remuneration, lawyers impliedly promise to clients that they will furnish beneficial services, which surely includes inter alia an undertaking to safeguard their interests no less than the law requires. Much work needs to be done in spelling out these

---

64. Rawls holds that ". . . a person is under an obligation to do his part as specified by the rules of an institution whenever he has voluntarily accepted the benefits of the scheme or has taken advantage of the opportunities it offers to advance his interests, provided that this institution is just or fair. . . ." A Theory of Justice 343 (1971). Lawyers clearly satisfy these conditions. And I assume that the sundry legal institutions in the United States are reasonably just, including their requirements for lawyerly behavior. Indeed, [in "The Adversary System Excuse," in Luban ed., The Good Lawyer 113-118 (1984)] Luban seems to concede as much in allowing a "pragmatic" justification for the adversary system: surely any system of adjudication would be worth replacing were it not reasonably just.

arguments, and in assessing how to weigh the prima facie obligations which they yield. Still, even before this is fairly begun, it is reasonable to believe that there are a variety of persuasive arguments to the conclusion that lawyers' professional obligations are strong prima facie moral obligations, which must ordinarily carry the day, except when a lawyer is confronted with the gravest of moral reason to the contrary. . . .

[Smith then argues against compelling lawyers to educate themselves in the texts and principles of moral philosophy, partly on the basis that such study would be likely to have the unfortunate effect of causing many lawyers to adopt a stance of moral scepticism.]

The profession of law is therefore not rationally compelled to adopt any official posture of moral scepticism. But we have also seen that the profession has reason to be fearful of lawyers being disturbed from their inchoate moral objectivism, and that mandatory courses in philosophical ethics will probably have such an effect upon an indeterminate number. And we failed to find any probable benefit in lawyers being required to take such courses, either by way of character improvement or of providing them with a set of moral principles which they ought to adopt. Therefore, if it be important to raise the moral sensibilities of practicing lawyers — if raising, rather than maintaining, be what really is required —, the legal profession is undoubtedly best advised to rely yet even more intensively upon its own considerable resources of moral exhortation and education. It should perhaps ignore philosophical ethics altogether — except, as individuals, for whatever inspiration or intellectual diversion the study can afford to them.

A Final Note on Codes and Rules

A great danger in teaching professional responsibility is to present only one view whereas there are many with respect to every topic in these materials. I have therefore attempted to present a diversity of different approaches in the selections I have made, and to suggest problems with each through the questions I have asked. In this chapter I would like to make some general observations on issues that cut across the specific topics previously discussed. It is clear that a course in professional responsibility is not just a course in teaching the Model Code or Model Rules. It could not be, even if one wanted it to be, because there are so many places where the disciplinary rules are unclear, or give discretion, or are silent. Nevertheless, they are the public expression of principles of professional responsibility that the profession gives to lawyers to guide their conduct. As such, they should be examined by anyone seeking guidance on a question of professional responsibility. Indeed, a practicing lawyer ignores them at his or her peril.

One question that may fairly be asked is by what right does the American Bar Association, a voluntary association of some lawyers, draft a Model Code or Model Rules for all lawyers in the entire country. In fact, each jurisdiction makes its own decision about adoption of its rules of professional responsibility and many jurisdictions made changes when adopting the Model Code or Model Rules. Nevertheless, the impetus for each set of professional rules has come from the ABA. It has done the drafting and submitted the final product to the various state and federal jurisdictions for adoption. It functioned, as it were, as an independent Commission on Uniform State Laws. And while the state and local units of the bar have had their own committees on professional ethics, for a long time it was the ABA's Committee on Ethics and Professional Responsibility whose Opinions were most influential, although that preeminence now has lessened.

Almost by historical accident, the ABA became the dominant national professional organization before most local bar associations were well established. Although it is a private organization, it has acquired substantial power to influence, and sometimes virtually to exercise, governmental power on a national scale in matters affecting the profession. It is beyond the scope of these materials to assess or even to describe in any detail the power and achievements of the ABA. They must, however, be taken account of in any assessment of the Model Code or Model Rules, the ideals they espouse, and the guidance they give in applying those ideals to concrete situations.

Calculated Imprecision in the Professional Rules.   A constant refrain in these materials is the extent to which the Model Code and Model Rules are unclear, ambiguous, silent. Focusing on their problems does distort one's view, and it is apparent to anyone who reads those documents that many things are stated quite clearly. But that is not true with respect to some of the most important matters that they cover — the question of confidentiality for example. The Model Code left the "continuing crime" and perjury issues unresolved and created a tension between its own DR 4-101 and DR 7-102(B)(1) that brought the profession into conflict with the Securities and Exchange Commission over a whole range of matters. The attempt to resolve the conflict by amending DR 7-102(B)(1) made matters worse. The amendment was itself ambiguous and was adopted only in a minority of jurisdictions. The Model Code's ambiguity contributed to what I would call public misunderstanding of the profession but for the fact that there was no professional position to misunderstand.

The conflict that lay just below the surface when the Model Code was drafted surfaced in the numerous attempts to apply its provisions during the 1970s and then again in the drafting of the Model Rules. The angry debates indicated the depths of the divisions. The Kutak Commission struggled to achieve both precision and an acceptable consensus and, except for its failure to deal with the "continuing crime or fraud problem," succeeded in its first objective. It failed, at least in the ABA House of Delegates, in its second objective and as the materials of Chapter 3 suggest, the solution incorporated by that body into the Model Rules reintroduced dangerous ambiguity into the product. The imprecision may not have been "calculated," but the problem that the language of, and Comment to, Rule 1.6 created ought to have been "calculated." Likewise, the most common amendments to Rule 1.6 in Model Rule states have left unresolved the problems that exist in "continuing" crime situations.

The Extent of Discretion Given to Lawyers.   Related to the problems of ambiguity and incompleteness in the disciplinary rules are the problems raised by the extent to which they appear quite deliberately to leave a good deal to the discretion of individual lawyers. I say "extent to which," because in many cases it is uncertain how much discretion is indeed left. For example, do Model Rule 1.7 and DR 5-105 leave it to the individual lawyer to decide whether he or she may represent buyer and seller in the ordinary residential sale of a house? While the Model Rules have removed some of the semantic problems that exist in the Model Code with respect to multiple representation, they operate at the same level of generality. That necessarily leaves a substantial area in which lawyers must make individual assessments with respect to the application of the general principles to particular fact situations — but always looking over their shoulders in the realization that someone else may be applying the test of the "reasonable person" after the fact in the event something goes wrong. Moreover, the drafters of the Model Rules did not tell us whether the new formulation of the conflict of interest rules was simply to deal with the awkward language of the Model Code or was also meant to alter in any substantial way the body of law that grew up under DR 5-105.

Another example where the grant of discretion has caused a problem is the material in Chapter 3, which discusses the Model Code's explicit discretion given to lawyers to reveal confidences in certain situations. The Code ignores the situation of "continuing crimes," where revelation may not only prevent harm from future crime but may also disclose the commission of past crimes. To the extent that Model Rule jurisdictions have amended their Rule 1.6 to increase the number of situations in which a lawyer has discretion to reveal confidences, the same problems exist.

Whenever lawyers have discretion to reveal confidences, they also have to deal with the further consequence of that discretion: the built-in inhibition of a free exercise of discretion, and the proper standards for the exercise of discretion.

Inhibiting the Exercise of Discretion.   The disciplinary rules of the Model Code and Model Rules gives lawyers, either by design or because of ambiguity of drafting, a great deal of discretion. In all these situations where a lawyer might wish as a matter of professional sense or personal morality to refrain from taking a certain action that would be advantageous to a client, the unfairness to the client because of the chance choice of counsel is a powerful inhibiting factor. On the contrary, the pressure is to choose the course of action that is favorable to one's client, either because one's adversary might be following similar allowable, but less desirable tactics, or because another lawyer to whom the client might have gone would have followed the allowable course of action. A lawyer must have a strong and confident sense of his or her self and his or her professional role to exercise discretion in a way that disfavors the client in a situation like Problem 29 (turning in the fugitive, p. 214), or in the Bodies Case (p. 221), or in Dean Freedman's question 3 (advising the client, p. 203).

Standards to Guide the Exercise of Discretion.   The second issue is closely related. Once the disciplinary rules give the lawyer discretion in difficult matters, where is the lawyer to turn for guidance? Shall the lawyer continue to view the matter wholly in a professional context, resolving apparently conflicting principles on his or her own? Or are there principles outside professional ones that become relevant?

The issue may be different in different contexts. Take, for example, any of the problems of conflict of interest discussed in Chapter 2. When the disciplinary rules are not clear, a lawyer can resolve the matter by making a decision whether the duties to make counsel available and to represent a client zealously are outweighed in a particular case by the duties to preserve confidences and secrets of another client, or by the threat that multiple employment poses to the exercise of an independent professional judgment on a client's behalf. Issues of personal morality will probably not loom large in most of these conflict of interest cases, although the possibility that a potential client may go unrepresented or that a long-time client with close personal ties may have to be turned away does raise that dimension.

The dimension of a lawyer's personal morality and its conflict with the urge to choose the path most favorable to a client is raised much more urgently in confidentiality problems. The Bodies Case presents the issue quite forcefully, and so does the fugitive case if one fears that the fugitive will commit crimes, especially crimes of violence, while at large. It is precisely in this area that the drafters of the disciplinary rules have failed us — perhaps even more in failing to define the area where no fixed guides exist than in failing to give us definite solutions. Obviously, what is involved in a case like the Bodies Case or the the fugitive case is a clash between the two major themes of those rules — the lawyer's obligation to represent a client zealously, and the lawyer's obligations to the profession and society. What the drafters have done, however, is to cover over the situations in which these obligations clash, either by ignoring them, or by using ambiguous language, or by giving the lawyer discretion. The result is that we are not only puzzled by particular problems, but we are also not able to be certain of the dimensions of the area of uncertainty. In addition, we do not know how far we are or should be free to resolve these issues by letting our own personal morality, or political and social ideals, sway our professional decision.

The Profession and Personal Morality.   Previous paragraphs have criticized the disciplinary rules for leaving unclear the areas in which lawyers are free to make their own decisions, and the standards that they are supposed to use in making such decisions. I do not, however, mean to suggest that there is a clear answer to the question whether the profession should be so tightly regulated that there is little room for the exercise of discretion in matters of professional responsibility. But this question must be faced by the profession and those who set its rules. Do we want a code that takes a stand on these issues, sets the most precise standards in its rules that it possibly can, provides machinery for answering doubtful cases definitively, and then enforces those standards rigorously? Or do we want a code that sets forth rather more general standards and leaves it to lawyers to resolve questions in the overlapping grey areas largely on their own, except in those sporadic instances, usually after the fact, when courts may lay down rules of law? Resolution of this problem requires us to have some views on many issues, including those raised by many of the authors whose writings are excerpted in this book. How amenable is a particular problem to specific rules? How much do we trust lawyers to take into account the "right" factors and reach the "right" balance in particular cases? What are the costs of "wrong" decisions? Can we identify a weighty self-interest that threatens decision-making by lawyers in particular cases?

This issue of how much discretion, whether in client selection, conflict of interest, confidentiality, withdrawal from representation, or other problems is a part of the larger issue of what we mean by saying that law is a profession. There is also a sociological aspect to the discussion. It may well be that the need for rule-making is considerably less in a small homogeneous, tightly-knit bar where the force of custom is greater than in a bar comprised of a great many diverse elements from different backgrounds and cultures. Not only do rules serve a socializing function in such a setting; they also represent an effort to assure that all are working under the same rules, thus protecting clients against their own lawyers and against the perceived "unfair" actions of the other side's lawyer.

Aside from the matters already discussed, we should note one additional substantial problem with tight regulation. It may produce more

situations in which the profession requires conduct that the lawyer regards as contrary to his or her own sense of personal morality. This issue
is not peculiar to the legal profession, but that does not mean that it
should be overlooked in setting standards that apply solely to the legal
profession.

The imposition of particular standards has already caused problems
in criminal practice. The state must prove its case beyond a reasonable
doubt; the defendant cannot be forced to testify and is entitled to have
a court exclude evidence obtained in violation of a variety of constitutional and nonconstitutional standards. The combination of these substantive notions with the constitutional right to counsel and the
profession's tenet that a lawyer's belief in a defendant's guilt is not a
reason for declining employment (EC 2-29; but see Model Rule 6.2(c))
produces a major problem of personal morality in the criminal field, that
of "getting the guilty defendant off." This is especially troublesome if
that defendant is a likely repeater of serious criminal activity.

It may well be true that more lawyers would be better able to live with
helping set a guilty person free if they were better educated to the admittedly somewhat speculative benefits to the system of particular rules,
especially constitutional rules, establishing important individual rights.
It may also be true that lawyers should avoid passing judgment in any
circumstances on the guilt of their clients. Perhaps lawyers should hard-
en themselves even more to the role in representation that the profession
has set for them. But those who make the rules should also be aware that
there are some, perhaps many, lawyers who are so troubled by some of
the consequences of this role that they shun criminal practice. Once
aware of this phenomenon the rule makers might well take feelings of
personal morality into some account when establishing other rules of
professional conduct that have less of a constitutional basis in our tradition.

The rules relating to confidentiality are a good example. Although a
constitutional basis for those rules might be asserted in the right to counsel in criminal cases, the discussion has not generally been carried on in
those terms. Professional, evidential, and statutory requirements have
been the battleground in the two major areas of conflict. Discussion of
the content of professional rules has focused largely on the need of the
criminal defendant to have freedom of communication with his or her
lawyer versus the harm that may ensue in certain situations when a lawyer does not disclose particular items of information. More recent debate
has added the dimension of the SEC's view of the wider clientele of the
corporate lawyer, with a correspondingly greater obligation to disclose
information.

Little attention, however, has been paid to the effect of the choice
of a particular solution on lawyers, especially in the crucial matter of
whether lawyers in this situation are being asked to take action that

offends their own sense of what is right. Of course that should be an ingredient in every obligation the profession considers putting on a lawyer; but the issue seems especially difficult in dealing with some aspects of the reach of the obligation of confidentiality, especially disclosure of the intention to commit a crime, or disclosure of fraud, or of the whole range of matters in which the SEC is interested. (A far-reaching argument for the proposition that lawyers should engage in much more ethical decision-making than they do in deciding whom they should represent and, more radically, how they should represent clients, is discussed in Simon, Ethical Discretion in Lawyering, 101 Harv L. Rev. 1083, (1988).)

It should be noted that the problem of personal morality is caused by the decision to require greater confidentiality, or by factors that inhibit revelation of information where the lawyer has discretion to reveal. To the extent that the profession requires disclosure of certain kinds of information to prevent harm to others, or to the extent it gives discretion and the lawyer overcomes any inhibition, the problem is largely avoided, at least if the profession or the lawyer gives the client sufficient notice. I say "largely avoided," because some might regard a system that did not provide a client with that kind of freedom to communicate with a lawyer as "immoral." However, I regard that characterization as being on a different plane of morality — dealing with the substantive rules of the system — from that invoked by an individual lawyer who would like to prevent a specific harm in a given situation, but cannot.

(For purposes of completeness I should add that I am aware that the preceding materials raise a further question of professional responsibility, namely, when is one justified in deliberately violating professional rules of conduct. There is simply not room in these materials to present the problem of civil disobedience in the appropriate philosophic context it requires. The question may be more difficult for a lawyer, but the issues are essentially the same as for any citizen faced with such a decision.)

Another substantial issue of personal morality was presented by DR 1-103(A) of the Model Code. In contrast to the issues just discussed, this problem is caused by the obligation to make disclosure of information, if not of confidences or secrets. For some lawyers, being forced to "tell on" other lawyers involves a breach of personal honor. For other lawyers, the failure of DR 1-103(A) to discriminate between serious and minor violations or to give any discretion to lawyers comparable to DR 4-101's "may" language is what creates the difficulty. Quite clearly, the policy of policing the profession was viewed as outweighing any uncomfortable feelings on the part of its members. On the other hand, there are many signs that DR 1-103(A) is not being complied with. The drafters of the Model Rules compromised this obligation a bit in an attempt to make it more realistic. Model Rule 8.3(a) continues the lawyer's reporting obligation but limits it to serious offenses. It remains to be seen whether the profession will take it seriously in those jurisdictions where it may be adopted.

The point being made in this discussion is not that the personal morality of individual lawyers should be determinative in deciding any of these matters, but that it is a factor that should not be ignored or treated too lightly. It must be considered and assessed in each particular situation, for in building a professional code of ethics the rule makers ought not override the personal ethical morality of the members of the profession, or at least of substantial numbers of them, without strong policy reasons clearly expressed.

The Role of the Profession and the Lawyer.   One final matter needs to be superimposed on this discussion. There has been an enormous amount of writing on the appropriate role of a judge — usually under the somewhat misleading title of judicial activism. The question is asked: "When is it appropriate for judges to take a leading role in reshaping common law, in interpreting statutes creatively, or in adapting constitutional principles to changes in society?" There is a spectrum of opinion ranging from those who, at least in certain fields and at certain times, urge the ultimate in creativity on judges, to those who see the legislatures and the executive as the primary expounders of political, social, and economic policy, with judges in a more subordinate position.

Just as there is an issue with respect to the role of the judiciary in our legal system, so too are there issues with respect to the role of the legal profession and of the individual lawyer. The context is different, but the issues are similar. Both in the broader sphere of substantive legislation and in the narrower field of professional regulation, the bar can play a submissive or an active role. It has more and more chosen activity. In matters of substantive legislation, its power has been exercised largely through lobbying for or against proposals made by others, and it is usually just one of myriad interest groups clamoring for attention. In matters of professional regulation, however, the bar has carved out an area of policy-making for itself in competition, or in collaboration, with the three branches of government, especially the judiciary.

This Note began with a reference to the role of the ABA in the drafting of each set of rules of professional responsibility. That is one example of an area of policy-making where the profession has taken a leading role. There are numerous others. Admission to the bar, prevention of the "practice of law" by nonlawyers, specialization, control of advertising, approval of prepaid insurance and group legal service plans, discipline, and passing on the qualifications of judges all have implications for the kinds of legal service that will be rendered to the public, and by whom.

The profession's record in these areas of policy-making, especially with respect to its regulation of the conduct and performance of its members, and its apparent lack of success in making legal services widely enough available, has led to a reaction against this exercise of power. The reaction has so far been ill-defined; it has not yet resulted in a full-fledged attack on the policy-making powers of the profession. Rather the attack has come in the form of pressures with respect to specific problems—pressures against restrictions on group legal services, against minimum fee schedules, for lay participation on disciplinary bodies, and the like. But the combination of these individualized pressures does raise the larger issue, which will increasingly have to be faced, of the extent to which the profession should be regulated by government.

Side by side with this issue is a similar one involving the relationship of power between the individual lawyer and the profession. That issue also permeates these materials. It is present in every situation where an effort is made to state either a substantive rule of law, as in the matters involved in Chapter 7, or a rule of professional conduct telling lawyers what they must or must not do. To the extent that the issues of discretion or the areas of ambiguity are resolved in the direction of greater specificity, the profession is exerting greater power in matters of professional responsibility. To the extent that these issues are resolved by leaving the ambiguity or a large area of discretion, power to define what is professionally responsible is flowing toward individual lawyers. The same result obtains where the specificity is present but the standards are not enforced.

A similar issue is involved in the stance that a lawyer takes toward his or her client. To the extent that the profession tells lawyers, or lawyers decide for themselves, that the appropriate role is one that takes a concept of "public interest" into account, lawyers are engaging in a policy-making role that might be performed by other bodies (or perhaps might not be performed at all). For example, while the lawyer who persuades a corporate client not to engage in a transaction because it is on the periphery of an antitrust violation is effecting a regulation of the client at the margin of antitrust law coverage, the lawyer who persuades a corporate client not to engage in a particular transaction because it is simply not in the "public interest" is engaging in regulation of a much more pervasive character. An argument not to install air polluting machinery or to buy property in an area of run-down housing, evict some inhabitants, and build a noisy factory is of that sort. The debate over the propriety or desirability of lawyers engaging in such persuasion is a debate over professional "activism."

Students struggling with the difficult issues dealt with in this Note should recognize that they are reflections of similar problems in society at large. Moreover, among the considerations affecting problems of professional responsibility is a variety of political, social, and economic factors outside the profession with which this book has not dealt. We should also be aware of the historical dimension: the profession today is a product of an evolution that is still imperfectly understood. Greater understanding will be required to aid our assessment of the profession and our efforts to find our place in it.

A Final Note on the Lawyer's Role

Earlier in these materials I quoted extensively from the views of a philosopher, Professor Alan Goldman, about the justification for a "heavily differentiated role" for lawyers. His main focus was on the confidentiality obligation in our adversary system. At this point, at the end of the book, it may be appropriate to set forth a portion of my reaction to his thesis.* For another attempt, see pp. 274-278, responding to Professor Pepper. The reader should first return to pages 278-282 and read the materials summarizing Professor Goldman's views.

My review first took issue with the descriptive portion of Goldman's book and his characterization of the lawyer's role as "full advocacy," arguing that while the role is differentiated, there is a fair range both of possible characterizations and of possible courses of action for individual lawyers to choose. The review then continued:

"I have, up to this point, simply disagreed somewhat with Professor Goldman's view of what the profession's rules currently provide. That is a relatively minor point. More important is his attack on the principle of 'full' (or, as I would prefer to describe it, 'nearly full') advocacy.

"He demonstrates that a principle of full advocacy is undesirable because the ensuing harms to third persons sometimes outweigh the principles urged on behalf of 'full' (or 'nearly full') advocacy. Nevertheless, as we examine his refutation of the claims of full advocacy, it is appropriate to point out that demonstration of the failure of grounds urged to justify a thoroughgoing principle of full advocacy does not necessarily prove that those grounds do not justify considerable role-differentiated behavior in particular instances.

"Professor Goldman considers and rejects the major justifications that have been advanced for the model of full advocacy: advancement of the truth-seeking function of the adversary system (pp. 106-107), the autonomy of clients (pp. 107-109), the duty of confidentiality (pp. 110-111), and the preservation of democratic values by not permitting lawyers to control exercise of legal choice through refusal to urge legal interests of clients (pp. 108, 111-112).

---

* As presented in Book Review of Alan H. Goldman, The Moral Foundations of Professional Ethics (Rowman & Littlefield 1980), 94 Harv. L. Rev. 1504, 1507-1517 (1981). This Review is adapted from a paper presented before the Society for the Study of Professional Ethics at the meeting of the American Philosophical Association in December 1980.

"He first considers the argument that full advocacy in the context of an adversary system advances the truth-seeking function of the process. In brief compass he demonstrates what will be familiar to all lawyers, that full advocacy frequently results in distortion and delay in a truth-seeking process.

"Professor Goldman realizes, however, that the major argument in favor of full advocacy rests on principles of autonomy and confidentiality. First dealing with the autonomy notion in the criminal context, he urges that all the tactics of full advocacy are not justified in the case of known guilt. 'Although lack of full zeal might be a betrayal of client trust and due process in all such cases, *these wrongs are not absolute,* but must be weighed against the harm that will be caused to others by the proposed tactics' (p. 119, emphasis in original). His example (which also involves confidentiality problems) is the aggressive cross-examination of the mentally fragile and vulnerable rape victim, designed to destroy the credibility of testimony that is known by the lawyer to be truthful. Professor Goldman believes that principles of client autonomy do not justify such conduct.[16] We may all agree that such conduct is a moral wrong to the victim, but this is not such an easy case. What is involved here if the lawyer does not cross-examine is not simply the failure of the lawyer to use tactics that might gain an acquittal for a guilty client. The lawyer's very failure to cross-examine the crucial witness will probably be understood by judge or jury to indicate that the victim is telling the truth and hence that the client is guilty.

"Such cross-examination is a harsh example of what happens in every case in which the client has told the lawyer that he is guilty. The state must prove its case beyond a reasonable doubt. In the face of such important constitutional guarantees as the privilege against self-incrimination and right to counsel, do we really want defense counsel to sit by silently as the state presents its case, when they believe that searching cross-examination may be harmful to a prosecution witness? Or to take another example, consider the implications of Professor Goldman's argument that full advocacy may be justified in the defense of a guilty client where the crime committed was not serious and the client's procedural rights have been violated by the police (pp. 119-120). That formulation suggests that if a guilty defendant has committed a serious crime, her lawyer should not raise a question of unlawful search and seizure on her behalf. I believe that his arguments seriously undervalue the constitutional guarantees and their moral underpinning. The moral

16. The ABA Committee that proposes the Standards for the Defense Function once agreed with Professor Goldman, but now says that a lawyer *may* question a witness known to be truthful with the intention of undermining credibility. Compare ABA Standards Relating to the Administration of Criminal Justice, The Defense Function §7.6(b) (1974), with 1 ABA Standards for Criminal Justice Standard 4-7.6(b) (2d ed. 1980). See also Fed. R. Evid. 611(a)(3) (court "shall exercise reasonable control over the mode and order of interrogating witnesses . . . so as to . . . protect witnesses from harassment or undue embarrassment").

rights of each of us to freedom and privacy are at stake in all these claims of violations of the fourth, fifth, and sixth amendments. That is the rationale the courts have enunciated in setting convicted persons free because of violations of constitutional rights. It therefore appears inadvisable to give lawyers discretion to exercise individualized moral judgments as to whether they will urge a procedural constitutional violation or force the government to prove its case to the fullest when their clients are known to be guilty.

"Perhaps more interesting is Professor Goldman's apparent concession that a substantial amount of strongly role-differentiated conduct is justified when the client is not known to be guilty. If I am right in so understanding his argument, then in a practical sense virtually the whole criminal field is reserved for 'nearly full' advocacy, for once a defendant is informed that his lawyer is following the Goldman Model, he will make certain that she does not come to believe that he is guilty. The one area that would still require a decision about role-differentiated conduct is one that is very controversial among lawyers but is not analyzed in this book — the problem for the lawyer who learns during the trial that the client-defendant proposes to commit perjury or has just committed perjury.

"Professor Goldman argues, and I agree with the general statement, that justifications of 'full' advocacy built on the autonomy principle have considerably less force in the civil context. His model is the rich corporate client with powerful legal representation arrayed against interests that are less well represented or unrepresented (pp. 120-122). In a society with maldistribution of legal resources he sees much to be gained by way of restoring moral responsibility in forcing clients to justify their objectives to their lawyers. The model he chooses is the most dramatic, but I agree that, especially in the civil context, it is highly desirable that lawyers be forced to think through the moral implications of the legal work that they are being asked to handle.[17] As the later discussion will indicate, however, I think that there is scope for role-differentiated conduct even in the civil context.

"Professor Goldman next responds to the argument that, under a government of laws, lawyers should not deny clients freedom to perform actions that government has not condemned as illegal (pp. 128-129). His first response is that lawyers are being told only to exercise their own moral autonomy, because they do not have authority to make clients' decisions for them. Unlike judges, lawyers do not usually act collectively with regard to their clients.[18] The client can always seek another lawyer;

17. A similar, thoughtful argument from a somewhat different perspective is contained in Postema, Moral Responsibility in Professional Ethics, 55 N.Y.U.L. Rev. 63 (1980).

18. Professor Goldman devotes a whole chapter in the book to defense of a strongly differentiated role for judges.

and if a client is refused by all lawyers on account of immoral objectives, 'his purpose would have to be blatantly immoral on normal criteria' (p. 130). To forestall criticism on grounds that his views fail to take account of the needs of unpopular defendants for counsel, he draws a sharp distinction between representing unpopular clients, which he favors, and representing the immoral objectives of unpopular clients, which he does not.

"Insofar as the lawyer claims the right to engage in full advocacy to defend a client against an opponent who is feared to be doing likewise, Professor Goldman simply dismisses that argument as 'morally perverse' (p. 132). Here it would be helpful to have some examples of what Professor Goldman is talking about. Perhaps he is referring to the difficult problem of nondisclosure of facts to the other side in litigation or negotiation situations when it is feared that disclosure would not be reciprocated. Part of that problem is covered by the requirement that lawyers not be dishonest and part is covered by the common law of fraud, which makes some nondisclosure tortious.[19] One can pose extreme cases in which the other side does not know a crucial fact and injustice results. Lawyers are quick to perceive, however, that almost any piece of relevant information may turn out to be crucial either by itself or in its cumulative impact. If everything of that sort must be revealed to the other side, the whole nature of the attorney-client relationship will be very different. In that sense the actions of individual lawyers will have a collective impact, with respect both to autonomy and to confidentiality notions. No one yet has been able to propose a satisfactory resolution of this serious problem that does not also seem to create more serious problems.

"Finally, Professor Goldman turns to the argument that confidentiality justifies a principle of full advocacy. He addresses two wrongs claimed if a full advocacy principle is not followed: frustration of a client's expectation of full advocacy and use to the client's detriment of information gained under an assumption of confidentiality (pp. 133-137). Professor Goldman first treats the argument on its substantive merits, concluding that the moral wrong proposed to be done to third parties must be weighed against the wrong of breaking a confidence (p. 134). Furthermore, an expectation of assistance in an immoral purpose carries less weight (pp. 134-135). Only after making these points does Goldman fall back on the notion that the lawyer can remove the expectations by an appropriate disclaimer at the outset of the relationship. He does consider the argument that adequate representation requires that a client be willing to tell the lawyer everything. In the criminal context, however, he concludes that we need only trouble ourselves about the innocent. Lawyers should be able to convince the innocent that the lawyer needs to know all the facts, including harmful facts, in order to be

---

19. ABA Code of Professional Responsibility DR 1-102(A)(4), 7-102(A)(5), (7) (1980). See also Rubin, A Causerie on Lawyers' Ethics in Negotiation, p. 388.

able to defend. To accomplish that result, lawyers should assure clients that they 'will assume innocence in the absence of indubitable knowledge of guilt' (p. 136).

"The reality of practice, unfortunately, is not so simple. The matter of innocence or guilt is not always clear to a defendant, especially in white-collar crime. Even as to the 'known guilty,' as indicated before, a 'moral' lawyer should properly be concerned that failure to argue a defense will be taken as an indication of guilt by judge or jury, and Professor Goldman's assurance to clients would often be understood as meaning that the client should never confess guilt to the lawyer. That would make Professor Goldman's principle rather high sounding but ineffective in criminal practice.

"In the noncriminal context, Professor Goldman argues that clients may reveal proposed undesirable activity even when warned about the uncertainty of confidentiality, and that in any event 'a promise of complicity is too high a price to pay for knowledge of wrongdoing' (p. 137). Under all views, however, lawyers are forbidden to become parties to wrongdoing. If the proposed conduct is legal but viewed as immoral, complicity is also not usually required unless one adopts the full advocacy principle. Moreover, an ongoing relationship between a lawyer and a client is a relatively complicated affair. It can develop into one of trust, in which the lawyer's advice has substantial impact on the client's actions. It can develop into a more ordinary arm's-length relationship where the lawyer is expected to fulfill a rather narrow function and nothing more. It is hard to prove, but I am prepared to assert with some assurance, that lawyers who have their clients' trust are often able to dissuade them from taking 'immoral' actions, and that the confidentiality principle is important in obtaining that trust. As I have previously stated, however, I do not believe that the reasons supporting the confidentiality principle justify a principle of full or nearly full advocacy.[20] The task for those who believe that the confidentiality principle is important in the proper long-range operation of the legal system is to balance that purpose against particular harms to which it may lead in the short run. . . .

"This synopsis gives the main outlines (although it does not do justice to the nuances) of Professor Goldman's argument. After considering all the arguments on behalf of the principle of full advocacy, he concludes that they 'fail to show that the moral ends of the legal system require that lawyers willingly violate moral rights or ignore otherwise morally relevant considerations in pursuit of their clients' interests' (p. 137). I

---

20. While it is true that the codes of professional responsibility and the common law already recognize, in different measure in different states, breaches in the confidentiality principle, see, e.g., ABA Code of Professional Responsibility DR 4-101(C), 7-102(B) (1) (1980), those breaches are still relatively confined and still relatively easy to explain.

think that he has demonstrated only that there are instances in which lawyers should not do so.

"Professor Goldman then turns to consider three alternatives to the principle of full advocacy:

> First, the lawyer could be required to advance his client's cause only through means compatible with settlement of the conflict on the legal merits. He would then forego those tactics that are not strictly illegal, but that function in the circumstances to delay, impose prohibitive expenses on adversaries, or force settlement based upon ignorance of law or fact. . . .
>
> A second possible principle would require a lawyer to aid his clients in achieving all and only that to which they have moral rights. This would call upon lawyers to exercise independent judgment in refusing to violate moral rights of others even in the pursuit of that to which clients might be legally entitled. It also might call upon them to exceed legal bounds in order to realize moral rights of their clients.
>
> A third principle, one that grants lawyers yet more moral authority, would have them aid clients only in doing what is moral to do. (Pp. 137-138).[21]

Professor Goldman recommends adoption of the second alternative as the one most morally appropriate for lawyers.

"He considers these alternatives in the context of three hypothetical cases, but two seem to me to be most important: (1) A childless couple that wants to fabricate evidence for an amicable divorce in a jurisdiction that does not grant divorces by mutual consent; and (2) A welfare mother who has failed to report income to the welfare bureau and wants the lawyer to ignore this in filing required reports in a divorce proceeding, lest she lose her benefits and face a possible jail term. Professor Goldman finds his chosen alternative preferable in case (1) because it would permit (why not require?) the lawyer to advise them so as to achieve their aim. 'Faced with such an archaic and objectionable law, it seems to me that only a fanatic on the subject of obedience to law would find either the lawyer's or the couple's action objectionable if they pursued their moral right' (p. 139). Likewise in case (2), 'the strict application of law would again have an unjust result, a jail sentence for the struggling mother and failure to provide for the basic needs of her children' (pp. 139-140). Therefore, while a lawyer who did not want to risk his career might be excused, the 'morally praiseworthy act' is to submit the false documents to the court.

"The justification for these decisions is that 'moral rights form too fine a grid to be captured by general rules' and that law, as a 'blunt social instrument,' cannot be 'a substitute for good moral sense of citizens, law-

---

21. Under the third principle, the lawyer would refuse to help a client exercise a moral right if it were "morally wrong" to exercise the right in a particular way.

yers included' (p. 140). The realization of a client's moral autonomy depends upon the lawyer's 'overlooking the precise bounds of law,' although of course 'he would have to risk the penalty for doing so' (pp. 141, 146).

"At the risk of confessing to being a 'fanatic,' I would argue that Professor Goldman's solutions are not preferable. Of course there will be cases in which people will believe it moral to violate the law and in which lawyers will believe it moral to help them. Some of those cases will even involve secret help. Where Professor Goldman and I part company is that I believe such instances should involve extreme situations and that lawyers should not be told that they are to become involved in deceitful smoothing out of the rough edges of legislation. Being just on the wrong side of the entitlement line does not seem to me to give the welfare mother any moral claim to a lawyer's services to help her conceal her thefts from society. Obsolete divorce laws present a difficult case, especially if there are no alternative jurisdictions where the matter can be resolved. But earlier I noted Professor Goldman's point that if all lawyers reject a client because his objectives are immoral, then 'his purpose would have to be blatantly immoral on normal criteria' (p. 130). Is it unfair to argue that the claim of moral right cannot be so strong if not recognized by any jurisdiction? In any event, except in extreme cases, I am dubious about placing moral responsibility on lawyers to make judgments concerning whether a particular divorce law is more immoral than the deceit they are being paid to practice. Lawyers have a license and a monopoly to practice (not violate) law (not morality). Lawyers often have the power, and are constantly tempted, to behave illegally within the system. I fear the argument that gives them a license to do so, and on very subjective grounds at that.

"This brings me to the other side of the coin of Professor Goldman's alternative: refusing, on moral grounds, to aid the client to achieve a legal objective. I have earlier noted my agreement with his argument that in the civil context lawyers should — indeed, must — think through the moral implications of work they are asked to do. Professor Goldman's discussion is written in terms of lawyers refusing to aid in immoral objectives or to use immoral tactics. But objectives and tactics do not come with labels, even one's own subjective labels. For most people, except in obvious situations, moral judgments come hard, especially when one is not a casual observer, but an actor with responsibility. It is easiest for lawyers to make judgments when they have no existing ties to the proposed client. At the outset of a relationship lawyers, except those committed in principle to taking on all clients who want their services, have considerable freedom to reject a client when they have moral qualms, without even the necessity of reaching firm conclusions.

"With a longtime client or after representation has been commenced, the matter is quite different. Clients often invest a great deal in educating lawyers in their affairs and often come to rely enormously on them. Those factors justify lawyers in being considerably more careful about concluding that what is proposed is immoral than they would be in ordinary circumstances (at least for purposes of withdrawing as opposed to giving advice).

"Let us use one of Professor Goldman's own examples as illustrative. A wine shipper uses a preservative that is 'about to be banned' as carcinogenic by the Food and Drug Administration. (Presumably he is referring to an initial determination without prior hearing.) The lawyer knows that experts can be found to question the evidence and make a 'good faith' case but believes from 'preliminary study' that the substance will ultimately be banned. The client, in financial difficulties, wants delay so that a big shipment can be made (p. 102). Professor Goldman concludes that 'if the substance in the wine presents a serious health risk as determined by adequate impartial testing, then the producer has no right to inflict this risk on unsuspecting consumers, and the principle of moral right would prohibit a lawyer who perceived the situation in this way from aiding the client in marketing the wine' (p. 146).

"As consumers, most of us will have a surge of sympathy for Professor Goldman's conclusion that the lawyer should not assist the client. The example is so designed. Yet it illustrates the difficulties that face lawyers in cases like this. Indeed, to resolve the problem, Professor Goldman in his conclusion is forced to change his own statement of facts. He adds the adequate impartial testing, subtracts the expert testimony, assumes that the FDA has no way of warning 'unsuspecting consumers,' and assumes that the lawyer perceives risk and ultimate resolution the same way (without mentioning whether this is still on 'preliminary study') (p. 146). Of course there will be situations in which health risks to third parties will cause lawyers to decline to help clients. This might even be one such case. But what of the lawyer who says:

> Our whole modern society is built on a technology that produces food and goods in a variety of ways. These remove many of the risks to health and ease the enormous physical strains on human existence of former years, but in the process have created other risks. While there are moral issues involved, they cannot be answered simply by focusing on one particular substance as if it were the only one that involved a cancer hazard. Indeed, why doesn't Professor Goldman use as his illustrative example the automobile and its pollutants? They may be infinitely more harmful than this wine shipment. Because one is more morally necessary than the other? If my client wants delay solely for delay, I don't oblige him, but if my client wants to defend his product and has a good faith case, I will present it. After all, we are not acting in secret. The FDA knows all about the product; if it wants to seek a preliminary injunction, it will be up to the court to decide the matter of risk pursuant to law.

"Whether we agree with the lawyer's conclusion or not, are we so sure of ourselves that we want to force the lawyer to make a moral judgment on pain of moral condemnation? In other situations, such as the car or saccharine, will we be willing to hear our lawyer talk also about the millions of citizens whose livings are tied up with the suspect product? Do we want to hear him talk about the rights of citizens to make up their own minds as to the risks they are willing to take with their own lives? Obviously what I am suggesting in all of this is that in many cases the morality of proposed client conduct will be at issue, but lawyers will be morally justified in declining to make moral judgments that they might reach as ordinary citizens. But I do agree that sometimes the issues and harm will be so clear to the lawyer that the justification will not exist. Those decisions are among the most difficult a lawyer must make.

"Perhaps a recapitulation is now in order.

"1. The 'full advocacy' notion that some lawyers urge is not, even in its strongest statement and application, as strong as Professor Goldman states.

"2. There is, however, a 'nearly full' advocacy standard that is, in Professor Goldman's terms, quite role differentiated.

"3. There is also a spectrum of other views about the appropriate professional advocacy standard that would make it somewhat less role differentiated, although not 'weakly' role differentiated.

"4. Most who reject the 'full' or 'nearly full' advocacy standards, including the reviewer, believe that it is necessary to examine each type of situation and particular situations within each type in a very ad hoc manner to determine whether a strongly role-differentiated answer is required or advisable. The product of my own examination indicates a substantial number of situations calling for strong role differentiation, making it fair to conclude that the total professional role is at least moderately role differentiated.

"5. The infusion of personal moral judgments into lawyers' professional responsibility decision-making presents lawyers with some difficult problems. It should be remembered that the codes of professional responsibility already impose special moral obligations on lawyers as legal obligations. For example, there is no general obligation on citizens not to lie, but the codes impose such an obligation on lawyers in their professional roles. There is also no general obligation on citizens to turn in violators of society's rules, but the codes of most states impose such a requirement on lawyers with respect to other lawyers' violations of the disciplinary rules. Moreover, although there are many situations in which lawyers may have freedom to take action based on ordinary moral considerations, nevertheless the special nature of the lawyer-client relationship justifies caution in some situations. It does not, however, justify lawyers in closing their eyes and ears to the problems raised by Professor Goldman. All lawyers should ponder these issues and reach morally satisfying — sometimes they will be the least morally dissatisfying — conclusions about their decisions each time an issue presents itself. . . ."

In thinking over what I wrote a few years ago, I came to wish that I had written a few more words exploring my unease with Professor Goldman's view of law. This final Note gives me that opportunity.

Philosophers who write about law approach the field from their own perspective, which involves thinking about systems of, or individual approaches to, right and wrong. The lawyer's theoretical concern, justice, may be different from"right and wrong" because of the law's concern with procedural matters. Even more important, the perspective of practicing lawyers is shaped by the daily necessity of speaking and acting for others. That difference in perspective may make it difficult for one not a lawyer to appreciate fully all the conflicts that face practicing lawyers. It is often (but not always) difficult for a lawyer to pass moral judgment on a client's proposed actions when the lawyer sees only a slice of the context and can only be privy to a portion of the inner motivation that goes into the client's decisions. But having said that, I do not mean to suggest that that difficulty necessarily clinches the argument for more "role differentiation." That answer lies in an assessment whether the one role or the other suits our individual perspective of the kind of lawyer we want to be — to the extent that we are permitted to make an individual choice. To the extent that we are not, then the issue for us is to decide whether in today's political, social, and economic context, the choice for the profession of one role or the other is likely to be more helpful in promoting our vision of social good. I realize that that formulation "ups the ante" so to speak at the very end of these materials. But it is apparent that one must have a vision of social good, of the kind of fair and just society that seems realizable in a world of imperfect human beings, to which to connect one's view of the legal profession. An important question to ask, if one concludes that great changes are needed in the profession, is whether that conclusion is related to a more utopian view of the possibilities for improving the whole society. If one does not believe that great changes are needed in the profession, if one is a tinkerer, it is useful to ask whether that conclusion is connected to a less utopian view of the possibilities for improving our society.

Much of the discussion in this final Note is cast in terms of "more" or "less." That is the way I tend to look at the clash between the moral absolutists and the moral relativists (and the regulators and the deregulators), at least in this field. The difficult decisions that we have been considering involve accommodation of conflicting principles (professional principles with moral elements or moral principles with professional elements). They rarely lend themselves to choice of one over the other along the whole spectrum of possible situations. It is usually a question of drawing a line that is not at either end of the spectrum. Although argumentation lends itself to absolute statements of principle, that realization ought to temper the edges of conflict over these issues.

Moreover, in addition to connecting one's view of "role differentiated" individual behavior to one's larger world vision, one must also connect that view to issues of professionalism that relate to lawyers as a group — how much monopoly, how much regulation and, conversely, how much deregulation, the nature of any regulation, who should regulate, and what special obligations should be imposed on lawyers as a group. Collectively, the answers will tell us whether and to what extent lawyers will remain professionals.

TABLE OF CASES

INDEX